Great Issues in Western Civilization

Since 1500
From Renaissance Civilization
through the Cold War

Great Issues in Western Civilization

Since 1500
From Renaissance Civilization through the Cold War

Brian Tierney
Cornell University

Donald Kagan
Yale University

L. Pearce Williams
Cornell University

SECOND EDITION

McGraw-Hill, Inc.
New York St. Louis San Francisco Auckland Bogotá
Caracas Lisbon London Madrid Mexico City Milan
Montreal New Delhi San Juan Singapore
Sydney Tokyo Toronto

1. V.I. Lenin
2. Charles Darwin
3. William Jennings Byron
4. Winston Churchill
5. Adolpf Hitler
6. William Gladstone
7. Benjamin Disraeli
8. Karl Marx
9. Galileo
10. John Stuart Mill
11. Jean Jacques Rousseau
12. Voltaire
13. Adam Smith
14. Isaac Newton
15. David Hume
16. Jeremy Bentham
17. Thomas R. Malthus
18. Mary Wollstonecraft
19. Rene Descartes
20. John Locke
21. Niccolo Machiavelli
22. Baron De Montesquieu
23. Edmund Burke
24. Francis Bacon
25. Denis Diderot
26. Louis XIV
27. Frederick the Great

GREAT ISSUES IN WESTERN CIVILIZATION
Since 1500: From Renaissance Civilization through the Cold War

Acknowledgments appear on pages 931–938, and on this page by reference.

    3 4 5 6 7 8 9 0 DOC DOC 9 0 9 8 7 6 5

ISBN 0-07-064596-5

This book was set in Palatino by The Clarinda Company.
The editors were David C. Follmer and Bernadette Boylan;
the production supervisor was Louise Karam.
The cover was designed by Carla Bauer;
cover illustration by Daniel Sachs.
R. R. Donnelley & Sons Company was printer and binder.

Library of Congress Cataloging-in-Publication Data

Great issues in Western Civilization: since 1500.
    Includes bibliographical references and indexes.
    Contents: v. 1. From ancient Egypt through
Louis XIV — v. 2. From Louis XIV through the Cold War —
From Renaissance civilization through the Cold War.
    1. Civilization, Western.   I. Tierney, Brian.
II. Kagan, Donald.   III. Williams, L. Pearce (Leslie Pearce), (date).
CB245.G68   1992   909'.09812   91-30207
ISBN 0-07-064576-0 (v. 1)
ISBN 0-07-064577-9 (v. 2)
ISBN 0-07-064596-5

This book is printed on acid-free paper.

To Frederick G. Marcham
Teacher—Scholar—Colleague—Friend

Contents

The Absolutism of Louis XIV—The End of Anarchy
or the Beginning of Tyranny?

The Enlightenment—The Age of Reason?

The Origins of the French Revolution—Popular Misery,
Social Ambitions, or Philosophical Ideas?

The Industrial Revolution in England—Blessing or Curse
to the Working Man?

The Marxists—Revolutionaries or Reformers?

Preface

A major purpose of this work is to convince students in Western civilization courses that the essential task of a historian is not to collect dead facts but to confront live issues. The issues are alive because they arise out of the tensions that people have to face in every generation—tensions between freedom and authority, between reason and faith, between human free will and all the impersonal circumstances that help to shape our lives.

In order to achieve any sophisticated understanding of such matters, students need to read the views of great modern historians as they are set out in their own words. Students need to develop a measure of critical historical insight by comparing these often conflicting views with the source material on which they are based. They need above all to concern themselves with the great issues that have shaped the course of Western civilization and not with historical "problems" that are mere artificially contrived conundrums.

This volume is divided into fifteen sections. Each of them presents both original source material and a variety of modern interpretations; and each deals with a truly great issue in Western history.

We believe that there are three major themes whose development and interplay have shaped the distinctive characteristics that set Western civilization apart from the other great historic cultures. They are the growth of a tradition of rational scientific inquiry, the persistence of a tension between Judaeo-Christian religious ideals and social realities, the emergence of constitutional forms of government. These three themes are introduced in the first sections. The reader will find them recurring in new forms and changing contexts throughout the rest of the work. We hope that in studying them readers will come to a richer understanding of the heritage of Western civilization—and of the historian's approach to it.

Brian Tierney
Donald Kagan
L. Pearce Williams

Note on the Second Edition

This new edition of *Great Issues Since 1500* presents a substantial revision of the original text, with several new chapters and many new readings from historical sources and from modern scholars.

The Preface to the first edition defined three great themes that have characterized Western civilization throughout its history—"a tradition of rational scientific inquiry, the persistence of a tension between Judaeo-Christian ideals and social realities, and the emergence of constitutional forms of government." In this edition a new chapter on the Renaissance is included to introduce readers to the world of 1500. Then the following chapters introduce the themes of religion, absolutism versus constitutionalism, and scientific progress. The chapter on the Scientific Revolution has been broadened in scope to include a discussion of Enlightenment culture. A new chapter on Social Darwinism relates a nineteenth-century movement of scientific thought to the ideologies of racism and imperialism. The new readings on English liberalism present a nineteenth-century alternative to newly emerging forms of authoritarian government. The former chapter on the Fall of the Russian Monarchy has been reorganized with a new selection of readings to focus on communist ideology and tactics.

We hope that, in this new form, *Great Issues Since 1500* will continue to stimulate and interest many students of the Western heritage.

Great Issues in Western Civilization
Since 1500
From Renaissance Civilization
through the Cold War

Renaissance Civilization— Medieval or Modern?

CONTENTS

QUESTIONS FOR STUDY

1 What characteristics of the Renaissance have been regarded as distinctively "modern"? Do you agree that these characteristics are in fact typical of the modern world?

2 How did political conditions in Renaissance Italy encourage the growth of individualism according to Burckhardt? Are his arguments convincing?

3 What do Petrarch, della Mirandola, Vasari, and Cellini tell us about Renaissance attitudes toward nature and art?

4 Do you think that the qualities Castiglione praises in a Renaissance courtier would fit a man well to serve in the entourage of a modern head of state—as a White House aide, for instance?

5 Burckhardt held that the spirit of Italian humanism was "irreligious and pagan." What evidence can you find for and against this view?

6 Was the culture of the Renaissance essentially different from that of the Middle Ages? If so, in what ways?

In its simplest literal meaning the term "Renaissance" refers to a "rebirth" of classical art and letters in Italy during the fourteenth, fifteenth, and sixteenth centuries. Many works of the ancient world had been known all through the Middle Ages, of course, but the Renaissance humanists studied them in a fresh spirit, with a new enthusiasm for the felicities of Latin style and the poetic values of Greek literature. Moreover, the revived classical studies inspired—or were inspired by—a changing attitude toward nature and toward man that expressed itself in a brilliant outburst of art and literature and also in new forms of political experimentation. Many historians have seen in this period a decisive break with the medieval tradition and the beginnings of a distinctively modern civilization. Others have reacted against this interpretation. The argument is still continuing.

Much of the modern writing on the Renaissance centers on the theses advanced by Jacob Burckhardt in his Civilisation of the Renaissance in Italy, first published in 1860 (pp. 7–11). Burckhardt very strongly emphasized the novelty and modernity of the Renaissance, arguing that Renaissance Italy produced the first fully self-aware, modern individual personalities. These first modern men deliberately created the modern state and embarked on new ways of exploring nature through science and art. Burckhardt attributed their emergence partly to a revival of "the influence of the ancient world" but mainly to "the genius of the Italian people."

Certainly Burckhardt was not wholly mistaken in his assertions. Many of the characteristics that he attributed to Renaissance Italy can be amply illustrated from the sources of that period—for example, the revival of classical studies (pp. 13–15), the existence of highly self-conscious individuals and of theorizing about the dignity of human nature (pp. 23–24). and the growth of secular ideas of the state (pp. 33–40). The criticism of Burckhardt's work is directed not so much against his delineation of such aspects of Renaissance life as against his whole periodization of Western history. Burckhardt seems to have regarded the medieval period as simply an irrelevant interruption in the development of modern society. For him, the Middle Ages were an era of "faith, illusion and childish prepossession." The modern world could grow into existence only when Renaissance men recovered the heritage of classical antiquity and turned their backs on the gloomy half-life of the medieval world.

Views like these still color some general histories of Western civilization, but many modern scholars find them quite unacceptable. Medievalists have pointed out with some warmth that the Middle Ages also produced passionate, fully self-aware individuals (pp. 43–45), coherent theories of the state (pp. 45–47), and great naturalistic art (pp. 48–51). They also argue that many features of the modern, twentieth-century world in which we live have their origins in the Middle Ages, not in classical antiquity or in the Renaissance period—for example, parliamentary government, university education, and the Anglo-American legal tradition. In the works of the most enthusiastic medievalists this argument is sometimes carried so far as to imply that no really significant changes occurred *at all in the age of the Renaissance. But this is obviously an oversimplification, to say the least. A Renaissance church is very different from a Gothic cathedral; Machiavelli's political philosophy is very different from that of Aquinas.*

It seems, then, that a new historical synthesis is required. In his article "Reinterpretation of the Renaissance" (pp. 53–55), W. K. Ferguson argues that early medieval culture was basically ecclesiastical, feudal, and rural. From the early twelfth century onward influences making for change were at work; but by 1300 they had not succeeded in changing the essential nature of medieval society. In the following two centuries their cumulative impact did have this effect. Ferguson discusses only economic history, but similar arguments might be advanced concerning the history of art, science, and politics. If this kind of interpretation proves acceptable, historians will be able to insist on the reality of decisive change during the age of the Renaissance without having to invent the fiction of a sudden break in the continuity of Western history at that time.

1

Burckhardt's Renaissance

The most brilliant of the nineteenth-century works on the Renaissance was that of Jacob Burckhardt. In his view the Renaissance saw the beginning of both the modern state and modern man.

FROM The Civilization of the Renaissance in Italy
by Jacob Burckhardt

THE STRUGGLE BETWEEN the Popes and the Hohenstaufen left Italy in a political condition which differed essentially from that of other countries of the West. While in France, Spain and England the feudal system was so organized that, at the close of its existence, it was naturally transformed into a unified monarchy, and while in Germany it helped to maintain, at least outwardly, the unity of the empire, Italy had shaken it off almost entirely. The Emperors of the fourteenth century, even in the most favourable case, were no longer received and respected as feudal lords, but as possible leaders and supporters of powers already in existence; while the Papacy, with its creatures and allies, was strong enough to hinder national unity in the future, not strong enough itself to bring about that unity. Between the two lay a multitude of political units—republics and despots—in part of long standing, in part of recent origin, whose existence was founded simply on their power to maintain it. In them for the first time we detect the modern political spirit of Europe, surrendered freely to its own instincts, often displaying the worst features of an unbridled egotism, outraging every right, and killing every germ of a healthier culture. But, wherever this vicious tendency is overcome or in any way compensated, a new fact appears in history—the State as the outcome of reflection and calculation, the State as a work of art. . . .

* * *

Jacob Burckhardtk, *The Civilization of the Renaissance in Italy* (1860), trans. by S. G. C. Middlemore, pp. 4, 100–104, 128–129. Reprinted by permission of Random House Inc.

In the character of these States, whether republics or despotisms, lies, not the only, but the chief reason for the early development of the Italian. To this it is due that he was the first-born among the sons of modern Europe.

In the Middle Ages both sides of human consciousness—that which was turned within as that which was turned without—lay dreaming or half awake beneath a common veil. The veil was woven of faith, illusion, and childish pre-possession, through which the world and history were seen clad in strange hues. Man was conscious of himself only as a member of a race, people, party, family, or corporation—only through some general category. In Italy this veil first melted into air; an *objective* treatment and consideration of the State and of all the things of this world became possible. The *subjective* side at the same time asserted itself with corresponding emphasis; man became a spiritual *indi-vidual,* and recognized himself as such. In the same way the Greek had once distinguished himself from the barbarian, and the Arab had felt himself an indi-vidual at a time when other Asiatics knew themselves only as members of a race. It will not be difficult to show that this result was owing above all to the political circumstances of Italy.

In far earlier times we can here and there detect a development of free personality which in Northern Europe either did not occur at all, or could not display itself in the same manner. The band of audacious wrongdoers in the tenth century described to us by Liudprand, some of the contemporaries of Gregory VII (for example, Benzo of Alba), and a few of the opponents of the first Hohenstaufen, show us characters of this kind. But at the close of the thir-teenth century Italy began to swarm with individuality; the ban laid upon human personality was dissolved; and a thousand figures meet us each in its own special shape and dress. Dante's great poem would have been impossible in any other country of Europe, if only for the reason that they all still lay under the spell of race. For Italy the august poet, through the wealth of individuality which he set forth, was the most national herald of his time. But this unfolding of the treasures of human nature in literature and art—this many-sided repre-sentation and criticism—will be discussed in separate chapters; here we have to deal only with the psychological fact itself. This fact appears in the most deci-sive and unmistakable form. The Italians of the fourteenth century knew little of false modesty or of hypocrisy in any shape; not one of them was afraid of sin-gularity, of being and seeming unlike his neighbours.

Despotism, as we have already seen, fostered in the highest degree the individuality not only of the tyrant or Condottiere himself, but also of the men whom he protected or used as his tools—the secretary, minister, poet, and com-panion. These people were forced to know all the inward resources of their own nature, passing or permanent; and their enjoyment of life was enhanced and concentrated by the desire to obtain the greatest satisfaction from a possi-bly very brief period of power and influence.

But even the subjects whom they ruled over were not free from the same impulse. Leaving out of account those who wasted their lives in secret opposition and conspiracies, we speak of the majority who were content with a strictly private station, like most of the urban population of the Byzantine empire and the Mohammedan States. No doubt it was often hard for the subjects of a Visconti to maintain the dignity of their persons and families, and multitudes must have lost in moral character through the servitude they lived under. But this was not the case with regard to individuality; for political impotence does not hinder the different tendencies and manifestations of private life from thriving in the fullest vigour and variety. Wealth and culture, so far as display and rivalry were not forbidden to them, a municipal freedom which did not cease to be considerable, and a Church which, unlike that of the Byzantine or of the Mohammedan world, was not identical with the State—all these conditions undoubtedly favoured the growth of individual thought, for which the necessary leisure was furnished by the cessation of party conflicts. The private man, indifferent to politics, and busied partly with serious pursuits, partly with the interests of a *dilettante,* seems to have been first fully formed in these despotisms of the fourteenth century. Documentary evidence cannot, of course, be required on such a point. The novelists, from whom we might expect information, describe to us oddities in plenty, but only from one point of view and in so far as the needs of the story demand. Their scene, too, lies chiefly in the republican cities.

In the latter, circumstances were also, but in another way, favourable to the growth of individual character. The more frequently the governing party was changed, the more the individual was led to make the utmost of the exercise and enjoyment of power. The statesmen and popular leaders, especially in Florentine history, acquired so marked a personal character, that we can scarcely find, even exceptionally, a parallel to them in contemporary history, hardly even in Jacob van Artevelde.

The members of the defeated parties, on the other hand, often came into a position like that of the subjects of the despotic States, with the difference that the freedom or power already enjoyed, and in some cases the hope of recovering them, gave a higher energy to their individuality. Among these men of involuntary leisure we find, for instance, an Agnolo Pandolfini (d. 1446), whose work on domestic economy is the first complete programme of a developed private life. His estimate of the duties of the individual as against the dangers and thanklessness of public life is in its way a true monument of the age.

Banishment, too, has this effect above all, that it either wears the exile out or develops whatever is greatest in him. "In all our more populous cities," says Gioviano Pontano, "we see a crowd of people who have left their homes of their own free will; but a man takes his virtues with him wherever he goes." And, in fact, they were by no means only men who had been actually exiled, but thousands left their native place voluntarily, because they found its political or economical condition intolerable. The Florentine emigrants at Ferrara and the Lucchese in Venice formed whole colonies by themselves.

The cosmopolitanism which grew up in the most gifted circles is in itself a high stage of individualism. Dante, as we have already said, finds a new home in the language and culture of Italy, but goes beyond even this in the words, "My country is the whole world." And when his recall to Florence was offered him on unworthy conditions, he wrote back: "Can I not everywhere behold the light of the sun and the stars; everywhere mediate on the noblest truths, without appearing ingloriously and shamefully before the city and the people. Even my bread will not fail me." The artists exult no less defiantly in their freedom from the constraints of fixed residence. "Only he who has learned everything," says Ghiberti, "is nowhere a stranger; robbed of his fortune and without friends, he is yet the citizen of every country, and can fearlessly despise the changes of fortune." In the same strain an exiled humanist writes: "Wherever a learned man fixes his seat, there is home."

An acute and practised eye might be able to trace, step by step, the increase in the number of complete men during the fifteenth century. Whether they had before them as a conscious object the harmonious development of their spiritual and material existence, is hard to say; but several of them attained it, so far as is consistent with the imperfection of all that is earthly. It may be better to renounce the attempt at an estimate of the share which fortune, character, and talent had in the life of Lorenzo il Magnifico. But look at a personality like that of Ariosto, especially as shown in his satires. In what harmony are there expressed the pride of the man and the poet, the irony with which he treats his own enjoyments, the most delicate satire, and the deepest goodwill!

*   *   *

Now that this point in our historical view of Italian civilization has been reached, it is time to speak of the influence of antiquity, the "new birth" of which has been one-sidedly chosen as the name to sum up the whole period. The conditions which have been hitherto described would have sufficed, apart from antiquity, to upturn and to mature the national mind; and most of the intellectual tendencies which yet remain to be noticed would be conceivable without it. But both what has gone before and what we have still to discuss are coloured in a thousand ways by the influence of the ancient world; and though the essence of the phenomena might still have been the same without the classical revival, it is only with and through this revival that they are actually manifested to us. The Renaissance would not have been the process of world-wide significance which it is, if its elements could be so easily separated from one another. We must insist upon it, as one of the chief propositions of this book, that it was not the revival of antiquity alone, but its union with the genius of the Italian people, which achieved the conquest of the western world. The amount of independence which the national spirit maintained in this union varied according to circumstances. In the modern Latin literature of the period, it is very small, while in plastic art, as well as in other spheres, it is remarkably great; and hence the alliance between two distant epochs in the civilization of the same people, because concluded on equal terms, proved justifiable and fruitful. The rest of Europe was free either to repel or else partly or wholly to accept the mighty impulse which came forth from Italy. Where the latter was the case we may as well be spared the complaints over the early decay of mediaeval faith and civilization. Had these been strong enough to hold their ground, they would be alive to this day. If those elegiac natures which long to see them return could pass but one hour in the midst of them, they would gasp to be back in modern air. That in a great historical process of this kind flowers of exquisite beauty may perish, without being made immortal in poetry or tradition, is undoubtedly true; nevertheless, we cannot wish the process undone. The general result of it consists in this—that by the side of the Church which had hitherto held the countries of the West together (though it was unable to do so much longer) there arose a new spiritual influence which, spreading itself abroad from Italy, became the breath of life for all the more instructed minds in Europe.

2

The Cult of the Classics

Petrarch (1304–1374) was the first of the great Italian humanists. The following letter illustrates his devotion to Latin literature.

FROM Petrarch's Letters

YOUR CICERO HAS BEEN in my possession four years and more. There is a good reason, though, for so long a delay; namely, the great scarcity of copyists who understand such work. It is a state of affairs that has resulted in an incredible loss to scholarship. Books that by their nature are a little hard to understand are no longer multiplied, and have ceased to be generally intelligible, and so have sunk into utter neglect, and in the end have perished. This age of ours consequently has let fall, bit by bit, some of the richest and sweetest fruits that the tree of knowledge has yielded; has thrown away the results of the vigils and labours of the most illustrious men of genius, things of more value, I am almost tempted to say, than anything else in the whole world. . . .

But I must return to your Cicero. I could not do without it, and the incompetence of the copyists would not let me possess it. What was left for me but to rely upon my own resources, and press these weary fingers and this worn and ragged pen into the service? The plan that I followed was this. I want you to know it, in case you should ever have to grapple with a similar task. Not a single word did I read except as I wrote. But how is that, I hear someone say; did you write without knowing what it was that you were writing? Ah! but from the very first it was enough for me to know that it was a work of Tullius, and an extremely rare one too. And then as soon as I was fairly started I found at every step so much sweetness and charm, and felt so strong a desire to advance, that the only difficulty which I experienced in reading and writing at the same time came from the fact that my pen could not cover the ground so rapidly as I wanted it to, whereas my expectation had been rather that it would outstrip my

"Petrarch's Letters," (Epistolae) from *Petrarch, The First Modern Scholar and Man of Letters*, trans. by J. Robinson and H. Rolfe (1899), pp. 275–278/pp. 307–317. Reprinted by permission.

eyes, and that my ardour for writing would be chilled by the slowness of my reading. So the pen held back the eye, and the eye drove on the pen, and I covered page after page, delighting in my task, and committing many and many a passage to memory as I wrote. For just in proportion as the writing is slower than the reading does the passage make a deep impression and cling to the mind.

And yet I must confess that I did finally reach a point in my copying where I was overcome by weariness; not mental, for how unlikely that would be where Cicero was concerned, but the sort of fatigue that springs from excessive manual labour. I began to feel doubtful about this plan that I was following, and to regret having undertaken a task for which I had not been trained; when suddenly I came across a place where Cicero tells how he himself copied the orations of—someone or other; just who it was I do not know, but certainly no Tullius, for there is but one such man, one such voice, one such mind. These are his words: "You say that you have been in the habit of reading the orations of Cassius in your idle moments. But I," he jestingly adds, with his customary disregard of his adversary's feelings, "have made a practice of *copying* them, so that I might *have* no idle moments." As I read this passage I grew hot with shame, like a modest young soldier who hears the voice of his beloved leader rebuking him. I said to myself, "So Cicero copied orations that another wrote, and you are not ready to copy his? What ardour! what scholarly devotion! what reverence for a man of godlike genius!" These thoughts were a spur to me, and I pushed on, with all my doubts dispelled. If ever from my darkness there shall come a single ray that can enhance the splendour of the reputation which his heavenly eloquence has won for him, it will proceed in no slight measure from the fact that I was so captivated by his ineffable sweetness that I did a thing in itself most irksome with such delight and eagerness that I scarcely knew I was doing it at all.

So then at last your Cicero has the happiness of returning to you, bearing you my thanks. And yet he also stays, very willingly, with me; a dear friend, to whom I give the credit of being almost the only man of letters for whose sake I would go to the length of spending my time, when the difficulties of life are pressing on me so sharply and inexorably and the cares pertaining to my literary labours make the longest life seem far too short, in transcribing compositions not my own. I may have done such things in former days, when I thought myself rich in time, and had not learned how stealthily it slips away: but I now know that this is of all our riches the most uncertain and fleeting; the years are closing in upon me now, and there is no longer any room for deviation from the beaten path. I am forced to practice strict economy; I only hope that I have not begun too late. But Cicero! he assuredly is worthy of a part of even the little that I still have left. Farewell.

Petrarch admired Greek literature too, but he had to read it in translation, as the next letter indicates. A century later any scholar of comparable eminence would have been trained in both Greek and Latin.

FROM *Petrarch's Letters*

YOU ASK ME FINALLY to lend you the copy of Homer that was on sale at Padua, if, as you suppose, I have purchased it; since, you say, I have for a long time possessed another copy; so that our friend Leo may translate it from Greek into Latin for your benefit and for the benefit of our other studious compatriots. I saw this book, but neglected the opportunity of acquiring it, because it seemed inferior to my own. It can easily be had with the aid of the person to whom I owe my friendship with Leo; a letter from that source would be all-powerful in the matter, and I will myself write him.

If by chance the book escape us, which seems to me very unlikely, I will let you have mine. I have been always fond of this particular translation and of Greek literature in general, and if fortune had not frowned upon my beginnings, in the sad death of my excellent master, I should be perhaps today something more than a Greek still at his alphabet. I approve with all my heart and strength your enterprise, for I regret and am indignant that an ancient translation, presumably the work of Cicero, the commencement of which Horace inserted in his *Ars Poetica,* should have been lost to the Latin world, together with many other works. It angers me to see so much solicitude for the bad and so much neglect of the good. . . .

As for me, I wish the work to be done, whether well or ill. I am so famished for literature that just as he who is ravenously hungry is not inclined to quarrel with the cook's art, so I await with lively impatience whatever dishes are to be set before my soul. And in truth, the morsel in which the same Leo, translating into Latin prose the beginning of Homer, has given me a foretaste of the whole work, although it confirms the sentiment of St. Jerome, does not displease me. It possesses, in fact, a secret charm, as certain viands, which have failed to take a moulded shape, although they are lacking in form, nevertheless preserve their taste and odor. May he continue with the aid of Heaven, and may he give us Homer, who has been lost to us!

In asking of me the volume of Plato which I have with me, and which escaped the fire at my trans-Alpine country house, you give me proof of your ardor, and I shall hold this book at your disposal, whenever the time shall come. I wish to aid with all my power such noble enterprises. But beware lest it should be unbecoming to unite in one bundle these two great princes of Greece, lest the weight of these two spirits should overwhelm mortal shoulders. Let your messenger undertake, with God's aid, one of the two, and first him who has written many centuries before the other. Farewell.

The mixture of introspection and sensitivity to natural beauty in the following passage has sometimes been taken as reflecting the "medieval" and "modern" elements in Petrarch's personality. The whole passage can be read as an allegory of "the ascent of the soul to God."

FROM *Petrarch's Letters*

To-DAY I MADE THE ASCENT of the highest mountain in this region, which is not improperly called Ventosum [*i.e., windy—Ed.*] My only motive was the wish to see what so great an elevation had to offer. I have had the expedition in mind for many years; for, as you know, I have lived in this region from infancy, having been cast here by that fate which determines the affairs of men. Consequently the mountain, which is visible from a great distance, was ever before my eyes, and I conceived the plan of some time doing what I have at last accomplished to-day. The idea took hold upon me with especial force when, in re-reading Livy's *History of Rome,* yesterday, I happened upon the place where Philip of Macedon, the same who waged war against the Romans, ascended Mount Haemus in Thessaly, from whose summit he was able, it is said, to see two seas, the Adriatic and the Euxine. Whether this be true or false I have not been able to determine, for the mountain is too far away, and writers disagree. Pomponius Mela, the cosmographer—not to mention others who have spoken of this occurrence—admits its truth without hesitation; Titus Livius, on the other hand, considers it false. I, assuredly, should not have left the question long in doubt, had that mountain been as easy to explore as this one. Let us leave this matter to one side, however, and return to my mountain here,—it seems to me that a young man in private life may well be excused for attempting what an aged king could undertake without arousing criticism.

* * *

At the time fixed we left the house, and by evening reached Malaucàene, which lies at the foot of the mountain, to the north. Having rested there a day, we finally made the ascent this morning, with no companions except two servants; and a most difficult task it was. The mountain is a very steep and almost inaccessible mass of stony soil. But, as the poet has well said, "Remorseless toil conquers all." It was a long day, the air fine. We enjoyed the advantages of vigour of mind and strength and agility of body, and everything else essential to those engaged in such an undertaking, and so had no other difficulties to face than those of the region itself. We found an old shepherd in one of the mountain dales, who tried, at great length, to dissuade us from the ascent, saying that some fifty years before he had, in the same ardour of youth, reached the summit, but had gotten for his pains nothing except fatigue and regret, and clothes

"Petrarch's Letters," (Epistolae) from *A Literary Source Book of the Renaissance*, trans. by M. Whitcomb (1900), pp. 13–15. Reprinted by permission.

and body torn by the rocks and briars. No one, so far as he or his companions knew, had ever tried the ascent before or after him. But his counsels increased rather than diminished our desire to proceed, since youth is suspicious of warnings. So the old man, finding that his efforts were in vain, went a little way with us, and pointed out a rough path among the rocks, uttering many admonitions, which he continued to send after us even after we had left him behind. Surrendering to him all such garments or other possessions as might prove burdensome to us, we made ready for the ascent, and started off at a good pace. But, as usually happens, fatigue quickly followed upon our excessive exertion, and we soon came to a halt at the top of a certain cliff. Upon starting on again we went more slowly, and I especially advanced along the rocky way with a more deliberate step. While my brother chose a direct path straight up the ridge, I weakly took an easier one which really descended. When I was called back, and the right road was shown me, I replied that I hoped to find a better way round on the other side, and that I did not mind going farther if the path were only less steep. This was just an excuse for my laziness; and when the others had already reached a considerable height I was still wandering in the valleys.

After being frequently misled in this way, I finally sat down in a valley and transferred my winged thoughts from things corporeal to the immaterial, addressing myself as follows:—"What thou has repeatedly experienced to-day in the ascent of this mountain, happens to thee, as to many, in the journey toward the blessed life. But this is not so readily perceived by men, since the motions of the body are obvious and external while those of the soul are invisible and hidden. Yes, the life which we call blessed is to be sought for on a high eminence, and strait is the way that leads to it. Many, also, are the hills that lie between, and we must ascend, by a glorious stairway, from strength to strength. At the top is at once the end of our struggles and the goal for which we are bound. All wish to reach this goal, but, as Ovid says, 'To wish is little; we must long with the utmost eagerness to gain our end.' Thou certainly dost ardently desire, as well as simply wish, unless thou deceivest thyself in this matter, as in so many others. What, then, doth hold thee back? Nothing, assuredly, except that thou wouldst take a path which seems, at first thought, more easy, leading through low and worldly pleasures. But nevertheless in the end, after long wanderings, thou must perforce either climb the steeper path, under the burden of tasks foolishly deferred, to its blessed culmination, or lie down in the valley of thy sins, and (I shudder to think of it!), if the shadow of death overtake thee, spend an eternal night amid constant torments." These thoughts stimulated both body and mind in a wonderful degree for facing the difficulties which yet remained. . . .

One peak of the mountain, the highest of all, the country people call "Sonny," why, I do not know, unless by antiphrasis, as I have sometimes suspected in other instances; for the peak in question would seem to be the father of all the surrounding ones. On its top is a little level place, and here we could at last rest our tired bodies.

Now, my father, since you have followed the thoughts that spurred me on in my ascent, listen to the rest of the story, and devote one hour, I pray you, to reviewing the experiences of my entire day. At first, owing to the unaccustomed quality of the air and the effect of the great sweep of view spread out before me, I stood like one dazed. I beheld the clouds under our feet, and what I had read of Athos and Olympus seemed less incredible as I myself witnessed the same things from a mountain of less fame. I turned my eyes toward Italy, whither my heart most inclined. The Alps, rugged and snowcapped, seemed to rise close by, although they were really at a great distance; the very same Alps through which that fierce enemy of the Roman name once made his way, bursting the rocks, if we may believe the report, by the application of vinegar. I sighed, I must confess, for the skies of Italy, which I beheld rather with my mind than with my eyes.

* * *

The sinking sun and the lengthening shadows of the mountain were already warning us that the time was near at hand when we must go. As if suddenly wakened from sleep, I turned about and gazed toward the west. I was unable to discern the summits of the Pyrenees, which form the barrier between France and Spain; not because of any intervening obstacle that I know of but owing simply to the insufficiency of our mortal vision. But I could see with the utmost clearness, off to the right, the mountains of the region about Lyons, and to the left the bay of Marseilles and the waters that lash the shores of Aigues Mortes, altho' all these places were so distant that it would require a journey of several days to reach them. Under our very eyes flowed the Rhone.

While I was thus dividing my thoughts, now turning my attention to some terrestrial object that lay before me, now raising my soul, as I had done my body, to higher planes, it occurred to me to look into my copy of St. Augustine's *Confessions,* a gift that I owe to your love, and that I always have about me, in memory of both the author and the giver. I opened the compact little volume, small indeed in size, but of infinite charm, with the intention of reading whatever came to hand, for I could happen upon nothing that would be otherwise than edifying and devout. Now it chanced that the tenth book presented itself. My brother, waiting to hear something of St. Augustine's from my lips, stood attentively by. I call him, and God too, to witness that where I first fixed my eyes it was written: "And men go about to wonder at the heights of the mountains, and the mighty waves of the sea, and the wide sweep of rivers, and the circuit of the ocean, and the revolution of the stars, but themselves they consider not." I was abashed, and, asking my brother (who was anxious to hear more) not to annoy me, I closed the book, angry with myself that I should still be admiring earthly things who might long ago have learned from even the pagan philosophers that nothing is wonderful but the soul, which, when great itself, finds nothing great outside itself. Then, in truth, I was satisfied that I had seen enough of the mountain; I turned my inward eye upon myself, and from that time not a syllable fell from my lips until we reached the bottom again.

Many Renaissance men expressed a sense of affinity with classical civilization and of alienation from medieval culture. This attitude is apparent in the following comments by the sixteenth-century painter and art historian Giorgio Vasari. First published in Italian in 1550.

FROM *Lives of the Most Eminent Painters, Sculptors and Architects*

BY *Giorgio Vasari*

IT IS WITHOUT DOUBT a fixed opinion, common to almost all writers, that the arts of sculpture and painting were first discovered by the nations of Egypt, although there are some who attribute the first rude attempts in marble, and the first statues and relievi, to the Chaldeans, while they accord the invention of the pencil, and of colouring, to the Greeks. But I am myself convinced, that design, which is the foundation of both these arts, nay, rather the very soul of each, comprising and nourishing within itself all the essential parts of both, existed in its highest perfection from the first moment of creation, when the Most High having formed the great body of the world, and adorned the heavens with their resplendent lights, descended by his spirit, through the limpidity of the air, and penetrating the solid mass of earth, created man; and thus unveiled, with the beauties of creation, the first form of sculpture and of painting. For from this man, as from a true model, were copied by slow degrees (we may not venture to affirm the contrary), statues and sculptures: the difficulties of varied attitude,—the flowing lines of contour—and in the first paintings, whatever these may have been, the softness, harmony, and that concord in discord, whence result light and shade. The first model, therefore, from which the first image of man arose, was a mass of earth; and not without significance, since the Divine Architect of time and nature, Himself all-perfect, designed to instruct us by the imperfection of the material, in the true method of attaining perfection, by repeatedly diminishing and adding to; as the best sculptors and painters are wont to do, for by perpetually taking from or adding to their models they conduct their work, from its first imperfect sketch, to that finish of perfection which they desire to attain. The Creator further adorned his model with the most vivid colours, and these same colours, being afterwards drawn by the painter from the mines of earth, enable him to imitate whatsoever object he may require for his picture. . . .

We find, then, that the art of sculpture was zealously cultivated by the Greeks, among whom many excellent artists appeared; those great masters, the Athenian Phidia, with Praxiteles and Plycletus, were of the number, while Lysippus and Pyrgoteles, worked successfully in intaglio, and Pygmalion produced admirable reliefs in ivory—nay, of him it was affirmed, that his prayers

Giorgio Vasari, *Lives of the Most Eminent Painters, Sculptors, and Architects* trans. by Mrs. J. Foster (1855), pp. 9–10, 12–13, 15–1`6, 20–22, 30–31. Reprinted by permission.

obtained life and soul for the statue of a virgin which he had formed. Painting was in like manner honoured, and those who practised it successfully were rewarded among the ancient Greeks and Romans; this is proved by their according the rights of citizenship, and the most exalted dignities, to such as attained high distinction in these arts, both of which flourished so greatly in Rome, that Fabius bequeathed fame to his posterity by subscribing his name to the pictures so admirably painted by him in the Temple of *Salus,* and calling himself Fabius Pictor. It was forbidden, by public decree, that slaves should exercise this art within the cities, and so much homage was paid by the nations to art and artists, that works of rare merit were sent to Rome and exhibited as something wonderful, among other trophies in the triumphal processions, while artists of extraordinary merit, if slaves, received their freedom, together with honours and rewards from the republics. . . .

I suggested above that the origin of these arts was Nature herself—the first image or model, the most beautiful fabric of the world—and the master, that divine light infused into us by special grace, and which has made us not only superior to all other animals, but has exalted us, if it be permitted so to speak, to the similitude of God Himself. This is my belief, and I think that every man who shall maturely consider the question, will be of my opinion. And if it has been seen in our times—as I hope to demonstrate presently by various examples—that simple children, rudely reared in the woods, have begun to practise the arts of design with no other model than those beautiful pictures and sculptures furnished by Nature, and no other teaching than their own genius—how much more easily may we believe that the first of mankind, in whom nature and intellect were all the more perfect in proportion as they were less removed from their first origin and divine parentage,—that these men, I say, having Nature for their guide, and the unsullied purity of their fresh intelligence for their master, with the beautiful model of the world for an exemplar, should have given birth to these most noble arts, and from a small beginning, ameliorating them by slow degrees, should have conducted them finally to perfection? . . .

But as fortune, when she has raised either persons or things to the summit of her wheel, very frequently casts them to the lowest point, whether in repentance or for her sport, so it chanced that, after these things, the barbarous nations of the world arose, in divers places, in rebellion against the Romans; whence there ensued, in no long time, not only the decline of that great empire, but the utter ruin of the whole and more especially of Rome herself, when all the best artists, sculptors, painters, and architects, were in like manner totally ruined, being submerged and buried, together with the arts themselves, beneath the miserable slaughters and ruins of that much renowned city. . . .

But infinitely more ruinous than all other enemies to the arts above named, was the fervent zeal of the new Christian religion, which, after long and sanguinary combats, had finally overcome and annihilated the ancient creeds of the pagan world, by the frequency of miracles exhibited, and by the earnest sincerity of the means adopted; and ardently devoted, with all diligence, to the extirpation of error, nay, to the removal of even the slightest temptation to heresy, it not only destroyed all the wondrous statues, paintings, sculptures, mosaics, and other ornaments of the false pagan deities, but at the same time extinguished the very memory, in casting down the honours, of numberless excellent ancients, to whom statues and other monuments had been erected, in public places, for their virtues, by the most virtuous times of antiquity. Nay, more than this, to build the churches of the Christian faith, this zeal not only destroyed the most renowned temples of the heathens, but, for the richer ornament of St. Peter's, and in addition to the many spoils previously bestowed on that building, the tomb of Adrian, now called the castle of St. Angelo, was deprived of its marble columns, to employ them for this church, many other buildings being in like manner despoiled, and which we now see wholly devastated. And although the Christian religion did not effect this from hatred to these works of art, but solely for the purpose of abasing and bringing into contempt the gods of the Gentiles, yet the result of this too ardent zeal did not fail to bring such total ruin over the noble arts, that their very form and existence was lost. . . .

In like manner, the best works in painting and sculpture, remaining buried under the ruins of Italy, were concealed during the same period, and continued wholly unknown to the rude men reared amidst the more modern usages of art, and by whom no other sculptures or pictures were produced, than such as were expected by the remnant of old Greek artists. They formed images of earth and stone, or painted monstrous figures, of which they traced the rude outline only in colour. These artists—the best as being the only ones—were conducted into Italy, whither they carried sculpture and painting, as well as mosaic, in such manner as they were themselves acquainted with them: these they taught, in their own coarse and rude style, to the Italians, who practised them, after such fashion, as I have said, and will further relate, down to a certain period. The men of those times, unaccustomed to works of greater perfection than those thus set before their eyes, admired them accordingly, and, barbarous as they were, yet imitated them as the most excellent models. It was only by slow degrees that those who came after, being aided in some places by the subtlety of the air around them, could begin to raise themselves from these depths; when, towards 1250, Heaven, moved to pity by the noble spirits which the Tuscan soil was producing every day, restored them to their primitive condition. It is true that those who lived in the times succeeding the ruin of Rome, had seen remnants of arches, colossi, statues, pillars, storied columns, and other works of art, not wholly destroyed by the fires and other devastations; yet they had not known how to avail themselves of this aid, nor had they derived any benefit from it, until the time specified above. When the minds then awakened, becoming capable of distinguishing the good from the worthless, and abandoning old methods, return to the imitation of the antique, with all the force of their genius, and all the power of their industry.

3

Renaissance Men and Women

One characteristic of Renaissance humanism was a buoyant confidence in the dignity and capabilities of human nature itself. Pico della Mirandola (1463–1494) gave eloquent expression to this sentiment.

FROM *Oration on the Dignity of Man*
BY *Pico della Mirandola*

I HAVE READ IN THE RECORDS of the Arabians, reverend fathers, that Abdala the Saracen, when questioned as to what on this stage of the world, as it were, could be seen most worthy of wonder, replied: "There is nothing to be seen more wonderful than man." In agreement with this opinion is the saying of Hermes Trismegistus: "A great miracle, Asclepius, is man." But when I weighed the reason for these maxims, the many grounds for the excellence of human nature reported by many men failed to satisfy me—that man is the intermediary between creatures, the intimate of the gods, the king of the lower beings; by the acuteness of his senses, by the discernment of his reason, and by the light of his intelligence the interpreter of nature; the interval between fixed eternity and fleeting time, and (as the Persians say) the bond, nay, rather, the marriage song of the world, on David's testimony but little lower than the angels. Admittedly great though these reasons be, they are not the principal grounds, that is, those which may rightfully claim for themselves the privilege of the highest admiration. For why should we not admire more the angels themselves and the blessed choirs of heaven? At last it seems to me I have come to understand why man is the most fortunate of creatures and consequently worthy of all admiration and what precisely is that rank which is his lot in the universal chain of Being—a rank to be envied not only by brutes but even by the stars and by minds beyond this world. It is a matter past faith and a wondrous one.

Pico della Mirandola, "Oration on the Diginity of Man," from *The Renaissance of Man* Ernst Cassier, Paul Oskar Kristeller, and John Herman Randall, Jr., eds. (1948), pp. 223–225. Copyright 1948 by The University of Chicago. Reprinted by permission of the University of Chicago Press.

Why should it not be? For it is on this very account that man is rightly called and judged a great miracle and a wonderful creature indeed. But hear, Fathers, exactly what this rank is and, as friendly auditors, conformably to your kindness, do me this favor. God the Father, the supreme Architect, had already built this cosmic home we behold, the most sacred temple of His godhead, by the laws of His mysterious wisdom. The region above the heavens He had adorned with Intelligences, the heavenly spheres He had quickened with eternal souls, and the excrementary and filthy parts of the lower world He had filled with a multitude of animals of every kind. But, when the work was finished, the Craftsman kept wishing that there were someone to ponder the plan of so great a work, to love its beauty, and to wonder at its vastness. Therefore, when everything was done (as Moses and Timaeus bear witness), He finally took thought concerning the creation of man. But there was not among His archetypes that from which He could fashion a new offspring, nor was there in His treasurehouses anything which He might bestow on His new son as an inheritance, nor was there in the seats of all the world a place where the latter might sit to contemplate the universe. All was now complete; all things had been assigned to the highest, the middle, and the lowest orders. But in its final creation it was not the part of the Father's power to fail as though exhausted. It was not the part of His wisdom to waver in a needful matter through poverty of counsel. It was not the part of His kindly love that he who was to praise God's divine generosity in regard to others should be compelled to condemn it in regard to himself. At last the best of artisans ordained that the creature to whom He had been able to give nothing proper to himself should have joint possession of whatever had been peculiar to each of the different kinds of being. He therefore took man as a creature of indeterminate nature and, assigning him a place in the middle of the world, addressed him thus: "Neither a fixed abode nor a form that is thine alone nor any function peculiar to thyself have we given thee, Adam, to the end that according to thy longing and according to thy judgment thou mayest have and possess what abode, what form, and what functions thou thyself shalt desire. The nature of all other beings is limited and constrained within the bounds of laws prescribed by Us. Thou, constrained by no limits, in accordance with thine own free will, in whose hand We have placed thee, shalt ordain for thyself the limits of thy nature. We have set thee at the world's center that thou mayest from thence more easily observe whatever is in the world. We have made thee neither of heaven nor of earth, neither mortal nor immortal, so that with freedom of choice and with honor, as though the maker and molder of thyself, thou mayest fashion thyself in whatever shape thou shalt prefer. Thou shalt have the power to degenerate into the lower forms of life, which are brutish. Thou shalt have the power, out of thy soul's judgment, to be reborn into the higher forms, which are divine." O supreme generosity of God the Father, O highest and most marvelous felicity of man! To him it is granted to have whatever he chooses, to be whatever he wills.

Baldassare Castiglione (1478–1529) described the qualities of an ideal Renaissance courtier. First published in Italian in 1518.

FROM *The Book of the Courtier*

BY *Baldassare Castiglione*

I WISH, THEN, THAT THIS Courtier of ours should be nobly born and of gentle race; because it is far less unseemly for one of ignoble birth to fail in worthy deeds, than for one of noble birth, who, if he strays from the path of his predecessors, stains his family name, and not only fails to achieve but loses what has been achieved already; for noble birth is like a bright lamp that manifests and makes visible good and evil deeds, and kindles and stimulates to virtue both by fear of shame and by hope of praise. . . .

But to come to some details, I am of opinion that the principal and true profession of the Courtier ought to be that of arms; which I would have him follow actively above all else, and be known among others as bold and strong, and loyal to whomsoever he serves. And he will win a reputation for these good qualities by exercising them at all times and in all places, since one may never fail in this without severest censure. And just as among women, their fair fame once sullied never recovers its first lustre, so the reputation of a gentleman who bears arms, if once it be in the least tarnished with cowardice or other disgrace, remains forever infamous before the world and full of ignominy. Therefore the more our Courtier excels in this art, the more he will be worthy of praise; and yet I do not deem essential in him that perfect knowledge of things and those other qualities that befit a commander; since this would be too wide a sea, let us be content, as we have said, with perfect loyalty and unconquered courage, and that he be always seen to possess them. . . .

Not that we would have him look so fierce, or go about blustering, or say that he has taken his cuirass to wife, or threaten with those grim scowls that we have often seen in Berto, because to such men as this, one might justly say that which a brave lady jestingly said in gentle company to one whom I will not name at present; who, being invited by her out of compliment to dance, refused not only that, but to listen to the music, and many other entertainments proposed to him,—saying always that such silly trifles were not his business; so that at last the lady said, "What is your business, then?" He replied with a sour look, "To fight." Then the lady at once said, "Now that you are in no war and out of fighting trim, I should think it were a good thing to have yourself well oiled, and to stow yourself with all your battle harness in a closet until you be

Baldassare Castiglione, *The Book of the Courtier,* trans, by Opdycke (1903), pp. 22, 25–31, 62–63, 65–66, 93–95. Reprinted by permission.

needed, lest you grow more rusty than you are"; and so, amid much laughter from the bystanders, she left the discomfited fellow to his silly presumption.

Therefore let the man we are seeking, be very bold, stern, and always among the first, where the enemy are to be seen; and in every other place, gentle, modest, reserved, above all things avoiding ostentation and that impudent self-praise by which men ever excite hatred and disgust in all who hear them. . . .

I say, however, that he, who in praising himself runs into no errour and incurs no annoyance or envy at the hands of those that hear him, is a very discreet man indeed and merits praise from others in addition to that which he bestows upon himself; because it is a very difficult matter. . . .

I would have our Courtier's aspect; not so soft and effeminate as is sought by many, who not only curl their hair and pluck their brows, but gloss their faces with all those arts employed by the most wanton and unchaste women in the world; and in their walk, posture and every act, they seem so limp and languid that their limbs are like to fall apart; and they pronounce their words so mournfully that they appear about to expire upon the spot: and the more they find themselves with men of rank, the more they affect such tricks. Since nature has not made them women, as they seem to wish to appear and be, they should be treated not as good women but as public harlots, and driven not merely from the courts of great lords but from the society of honest men.

Then coming to the bodily frame, I say it is enough if this be neither extremely short nor tall, for both of these conditions excite a certain contemptuous surprise, and men of either sort are gazed upon in much the same way that we gaze on monsters. Yet if we must offend in one of the two extremes, it is preferable to fall a little short of the just measure of height than to exceed it, for besides often being dull of intellect, men thus huge of body are also unfit for every exercise of agility, which thing I should much wish in the Courtier. And so I would have him well built and shapely of limb, and would have him show strength and lightness and suppleness, and know all bodily exercises that befit a man of war: whereof I think the first should be to handle every sort of weapon well on foot and on horse, to understand the advantages of each, and especially to be familiar with those weapons that are ordinarily used among gentlemen; for besides the use of them in war, where such subtlety in contrivance is perhaps not needful, there frequently arise differences between one gentleman and another, which afterwards result in duels often fought with such weapons as happen at the moment to be within reach: thus knowledge of this kind is a very safe thing.

* * *

There are also many other exercises, which although not immediately dependent upon arms, yet are closely connected therewith, and greatly foster manly sturdiness; and one of the chief among these seems to me to be the chase, because it bears a certain likeness to war: and truly it is an amusement for great lords and befitting a man at court, and furthermore it is seen to have been much cultivated among the ancients. It is fitting also to know how to swim, to leap, to run, to throw stones, for besides the use that may be made of this in war, a man often has occasion to show what he can do in such matters; whence good esteem is to be won, especially with the multitude, who must be taken into account withal. Another admirable exercise, and one very befitting a man at court, is the game of tennis, in which are well shown the disposition of the body, the quickness and suppleness of every member, and all those qualities that are seen in nearly every other exercise. Nor less highly do I esteem vaulting on horse, which although it be fatiguing and difficult, makes a man very light and dexterous more than any other thing; and besides its utility, if this lightness is accompanied by grace, it is to my thinking a finer show than any of the others.

*　*　*

I think that the conversation which the Courtier ought most to try in every way to make acceptable, is that which he holds with his prince; and although this word "conversation" implies a certain equality that seems impossible between a lord and his inferior, yet we will call it so for the present. Therefore, besides daily showing everyone that he possesses the worth we have already described, I would have the Courtier strive, with all the thoughts and forces of his mind, to love and almost to adore the prince whom he serves, above every other thing, and mould his wishes, habits and all his ways to his prince's liking. . . .

Moreover it is possible without flattery to obey and further the wishes of him we serve, for I am speaking of those wishes that are reasonable and right, or of those that in themselves are neither good nor evil, such as would be a liking for play or a devotion to one kind of exercise above another. And I would have the Courtier bend himself to this even if he be by nature alien to it, so that on seeing him his lord shall always feel that he will have something agreeable to say; which will come about if he has the good judgment to perceive what his prince likes, and the wit and prudence to bend himself thereto, and a deliberate purpose to like that which perhaps he by nature dislikes. . . . He will not be an idle or untruthful tattler, nor a boaster nor pointless flatterer, but modest and reserved, always and especially in public showing that reverence and respect which befit the servant towards the master. . . .

He will very rarely or almost never ask anything of his lord for himself, lest his lord, being reluctant to deny it to him directly, may sometimes grant it with an ill grace, which is much worse. Even in asking for others he will choose his time discreetly and ask proper and reasonable things; and he will so frame his request, by omitting what he knows may displease and by skilfully doing away with difficulties, that his lord shall always grant it, or shall not think him offended by refusal even if it be denied; for when lords have denied a favour to an importunate suitor, they often reflect that he who asked it with such eagerness, must have desired it greatly, and so having failed to obtain it, must feel ill will towards him who denied it; and believing this, they begin to hate the man and can never more look upon him with favour.

The autobiography of the artist Benvenuto Cellini (1500–1571) provides many vignettes of life in Renaissance Italy. Written in Italian between 1558 and 1562.

FROM *Autobiography*

BY *Benvenuto Cellini*

[*Cellini has shown Pope Clement VII a model of a jeweled ornament—Ed.*]

WHILE WE WERE WAITING for the money, the Pope turned once more to gaze at leisure on the dexterous device I had employed for combining the diamond with the figure of God the Father. I had put the diamond exactly in the centre of the piece; and above it God the Father was shown seated, leaning nobly in a sideways attitude, which made a perfect composition, and did not interfere with the stone's effect. Lifting his right hand, he was in the act of giving the benediction. Below the diamond I had placed three children, who, with their arms upraised, were supporting the jewel. One of them, in the middle, was in full relief, the other two in half-relief. All round I set a crowd of cherubs, in divers attitudes, adapted to the other gems. A mantle undulated to the wind around the figure of the Father, from the folds of which cherubs peeped out; and there were other ornaments besides which made a very beautiful effect. The work was executed in white stucco on a black stone. When the money came, the Pope gave it me with his own hand, and begged me in the most winning terms to let him have it finished in his own days, adding that this should be to my advantage.

* * *

[*Cellini's brother was murdered at this time—Ed.*]

I went on applying myself with the utmost diligence upon the goldwork for Pope Clement's button. He was very eager to have it, and used to send for me two or three times a week, in order to inspect it; and his delight in the work always increased. Often would he rebuke and scold me, as it were, for the great grief in which my brother's loss had plunged me; and one day, observing me more downcast and out of trim than was proper, he cried aloud: "Benvenuto, oh! I did not know that you were mad. Have you only just learned that there is no remedy against death? One would think that you were trying to run after him." When I left the presence, I continued working at the jewel and the dies for the Mint; but I also took to watching the arquebusier who shot my brother, as though he had been a girl I was in love with. The man had formerly been in

Benvenuto Celline, *Autobiography*, from *The Life of Benvenuto Celini*, trans. by J. Symonds (1893), pp. 102, 114, 116. Reprinted by permission.

the light cavalry, but afterwards had joined the arquebusiers as one of the Bargello's corporals; and what increased my rage was that he had used these boastful words: "If it had not been for me, who killed that brave young man, the least trifle of delay would have resulted in his putting us all to flight with great disaster." When I saw that the fever caused by always seeing him about was depriving me of sleep and appetite, and was bringing me by degrees to sorry plight, I overcame my repugnance to so low and not quite praiseworthy an enterprise, and made my mind up one evening to rid myself of the torment. The fellow lived in a house near a place called Torre Sanguigua, next door to the lodging of one of the most fashionable courtesans in Rome, named Signora Antea. It had just struck twenty-four, and he was standing at the house-door, with his sword in hand, having risen from supper. With great address I stole up to him, holding a large Pistojan dagger, and dealt him a back-handed stroke, with which I meant to cut his head clean off; but as he turned round very suddenly, the blow fell upon the point of his left shoulder and broke the bone. He sprang up, dropped his sword, half-stunned with the great pain, and took to flight. I followed after, and in four steps caught him up, when I lifted my dagger above his head, which he was holding very low, and hit him in the back exactly at the junction of the nape-bone and the neck. The poniard entered this point so deep into the bone, that, though I used all my strength to pull it out, I was not able. For just at that moment four soldiers with drawn swords sprang out from Antea's lodging, and obliged me to set hand to my own sword to defend my life. Leaving the poniard then, I made off, and fearing I might be recognised, took refuge in the palace of Duke Alessandro, which was between Piazza Navona and the Rotunda. On my arrival, I asked to see the Duke, who told me that, if I was alone, I need only keep quiet and have no further anxiety, but go on working at the jewel which the Pope had set his heart on, and stay eight days indoors. . . .

More than eight days elapsed, and the Pope did not send for me according to his custom. Afterwards he summoned me through his chamberlain, the Bolognese nobleman I have already mentioned, who let me, in his own modest manner, understand that his Holiness knew all, but was very well inclined toward me, and that I had only to mind my work and keep quiet. When we reached the presence, the Pope cast so menacing a glance towards me that the mere look of his eyes made me tremble. Afterwards, upon examining my work, his countenance cleared, and he began to praise me beyond measure, saying that I had done a vast amount in a short time. Then, looking me straight in the face, he added: "Now that you are cured, Benvenuto, take heed how you live." I, who understood his meaning, promised that I would. Immediately upon this, I opened a very fine shop in the Banchi, opposite Raffaello, and there I finished the jewel after the lapse of a few months.

People in Renaissance Florence were not interested only in cultivating their individual personalities. Another major concern was the advancement of family fortunes. Leo Battista Alberti (1404–1472), a distinguished artist as well as a writer on Florentine affairs, gave the following advice.

FROM *The Books on the Family*

BY *Leon Battista Alberti*

Since a child comes into the world as a tender and delicate creature, he needs someone to whose care and devotion he comes as a cherished trust. This person must nourish him with diligence and love and must defend him from harm. Too much cold or too much sun, rain, and the wild blowing of a storm are harmful to children. Woman, therefore, did first find a roof under which to nourish and protect herself and her offspring. There she remained, busy in the shadow, nourishing and caring for her children. And since woman was busy guarding and taking care of the heir, she was not in a position to go out and find what she and her children required for the maintenance of their life. Man, however, was by nature more energetic and industrious, and he went out to find things and bring what seemed to him necessary.

Nature showed, further, that this relationship could not be permitted with more than one wife at a time, since man was by no means able to provide and bring home more than was needed for himself and one wife and children. . . . To satisfy nature, then, a man need only choose a woman with whom he can dwell in tranquility under one roof all his life.

Young people, however, very often do not cherish the good of the family enough to do this. Marriage, perhaps, seems to them to take away their present liberty and freedom. It may be, as the comic poets like to tell us, that they are held back and dissuaded by some mistress. Sometimes, too, young men find it hard enough to manage one life, and fear as an excessive and undesirable burden the task of supporting a wife and children besides. They may doubt their capacity to maintain in honorable estate a family which grows in needs from day to day. Viewing the conjugal bed as a troublesome responsibility, they then avoid the legitimate and honorable path to the increase of a family.

If a family is not to fall for these reasons into what we have described as the most unfortunate condition of decline, but is to grow, instead, in fame and in the prosperous multitude of its youth, we must persuade our young men to take wives. We must use every argument for this purpose, offer incentive, promise reward, employ all our wit, persistence, and cunning. A most appropriate reason for taking a wife may be found in what we were saying before, about the evil of sensual indulgence, for the condemnation of such things may lead young men to desire honorable satisfactions. As other incentives, we may also speak to them of the delights of this primary and natural companionship of marriage.

Leon Batista Albert: I Libri della Famiglia, trans. by Renée N. Watkins in *The Family in Renaissance Florenc* (1969), pp. 111–116, reprinted by permission of the University of South Carolina Press.

Children act as pledges and securities of marital love and kindness. At the same time they offer a focus for all a man's hopes and desires. Sad, indeed, is the man who has labored to get wealth and power and lands, and then has no true heir and perpetuator of his memory. No one can be more suited than a man's true and legitimate sons to gain advantages by virtue of his character, position, and authority, and to enjoy the fruits and rewards of his labor. If a man leaves such heirs, furthermore, he need not consider himself wholly dead and gone. His children keep his own position and his true image in the family. . . .

When, by the urging and counsel of their elders and of the whole family, young men have arrived at the point of marriage, their mothers and other female relatives and friends, who have known the virgins of the neighborhood from earliest childhood and know the way their upbringing has formed them, should select all the well-born and well-brought-up girls and present that list to the new groom-to-be. He can then choose the one who suits him best. The elders of the house and all of the family shall reject no daughter-in-law unless she is tainted with the breath of scandal or bad reputation. Aside from that, let the man who will have to satisfy her satisfy himself. He should act as do wise heads of families before they acquire some property—they like to look it over several times before they actually sign a contract. . . . The man who has decided to marry must be still more cautious. I recommend that he examine and anticipate in every way, and consider for many days, what sort of person it is he is to live with for all his years as husband and companion. Let him be minded to marry for two purposes: first to perpetuate himself in his children, and second to have a steady and constant companion all his life. A woman is needed, therefore, who is likely to bear children and who is desirable as a perpetual mate. . . .

In her body he must seek not only loveliness, grace, and charm but must also choose a woman who is well made for bearing children, with the kind of constitution that promises to make them strong and big. There's an old proverb, "When you pick your wife, you choose your children." All her virtues will in fact shine brighter still in beautiful children. It is a well-known saying among poets: "Beautiful character dwells in a beautiful body." The natural philosophers require that a woman be neither thin nor very fat. Those laden with fat are subject to coldness and constipation and slow to conceive. They say that a woman should have a joyful nature, fresh and lively in her blood and her whole being. They have no objections to a dark girl. They do reject girls with a frowning black visage, however. They have no liking for either the undersized or the overlarge and lean. They find that a woman is most suited to bear children if she is fairly big and has limbs of ample length. They always have a preference for youth, based on a number of arguments which I need not expound here, but particularly on the point that a young girl has a more adaptable mind. Young girls are pure by virtue of their age and have not developed any spitefulness. They are by nature modest and free of vice. They quickly learn to accept affectionately and unresistingly the habits and wishes of their husbands.

4

The Renaissance State

In the transitional period at the end of the Middle Ages, Marsilius of Padua produced a thoroughly secular theory of politics. He argued that all political authority was derived from the community and that only the state—not the church—could lawfully exercise coercive power.

FROM *The Defender of the Peace*

BY *Marsilius of Padua*

THE STATE, ACCORDING TO Aristotle in the *Politics,* Book I, Chapter 1, is "the perfect community having the full limit of self-sufficiency, which came into existence for the sake of living, but exists for the sake of living well." This phrase of Aristotle—"came into existence for the sake of living, but exists for the sake of living well"—signifies the perfect final cause of the state, since those who live a civil life not only live, which beasts or slaves do too, but live well, having leisure for those liberal functions in which are exercised the virtues of both the practical and the theoretic soul.

* * *

But the living and living well which are appropriate to men fall into two kinds, of which one is temporal or earthly, while the other is usually called eternal or heavenly. However, this latter kind of living, the eternal, the whole body of philosophers were unable to prove by demonstration, nor was it self-evident, and therefore they did not concern themselves with the means thereto. But as to the first kind of living and living well or good life, that is, the earthly, and its necessary means, this the glorious philosophers comprehended almost completely through demonstration. Hence, for its attainment they concluded the necessity of the civil community, without which this sufficient life cannot be obtained. Thus the foremost of the philosophers, Aristotle, said in his *Politics,*

Marsilius of Padua, *The Defender of the Peace,* trans. by A. Gerwith (1956) Vol. 2, pp. 12–13, 44–45, 61, 100, 174–175. Reprinted by permission of Columbia University Press.

Book I, Chapter 1: "All men are driven toward such an association by a natural impulse." Although sense experience teaches this, we wish to bring out more distinctly that cause of it which we have indicated, as follows: Man is born composed of contrary elements, because of whose contrary actions and passions some of his substance is continually being destroyed; moreover, he is born "bare and unprotected" from excess of the surrounding air and other elements, capable of suffering and of destruction, as has been said in the science of nature. As a consequence, he needed arts of diverse genera and species to avoid the afore-mentioned harms. But since these arts can be exercised only by a large number of men, and can be had only through their association with one another, men had to assemble together in order to attain what was beneficial through these arts and to avoid what was harmful.

But since among men thus assembled there arise disputes and quarrels which, if not regulated by a norm of justice, would cause men to fight and separate and thus finally would bring about the destruction of the state, there had to be established in this association a standard of justice and a guardian or maker thereof. . . .

But it must be remembered that the true knowledge or discovery of the just and the beneficial, and of their opposites, is not law taken in its last and most proper sense, whereby it is the measure of human civil acts, unless there is given a coercive command as to its observance, or it is made by way of such a command, by someone through whose authority its transgressors must and can be punished. Hence, we must now say to whom belongs the authority to make such a command and to punish its transgressors. This, indeed, is to inquire into the legislator or the maker of the law.

Let us say, then, in accordance with the truth and the counsel of Aristotle in the *Politics,* Book III, Chapter 6, that the legislator, or the primary and proper efficient cause of the law, is the people or the whole body of citizens, or the weightier part thereof, through its election or will expressed by words in the general assembly of the citizens, commanding or determining that something be done or omitted with regard to human civil acts, under a temporal pain or punishment. By the "weightier part" I mean to take into consideration the quantity and the quality of the persons in that community over which the law is made. The aforesaid whole body of citizens or the weightier part thereof is the legislator regardless of whether it makes the law directly by itself or entrusts the making of it to some person or persons, who are not and cannot be the legislator in the absolute sense, but only in a relative sense and for a particular time and in accordance with the authority of the primary legislator. . . .

It now remains to show the efficient cause of the ruler, that is, the cause by which there is given to one or more persons the authority of rulership which is established through election. For it is by this authority that a person becomes a ruler in actuality, and not by his knowledge of the laws, his prudence, or moral virtue, although these are qualities of the perfect ruler. For it happens that many men have these qualities, but nevertheless, lacking this authority, they are not rulers, unless perhaps in proximate potentiality.

Taking up the question, then, let us say, in accordance with the truth and the doctrine of Aristotle in the *Politics,* Book III, Chapter 6, that the efficient power to establish or elect the ruler belongs to the legislator or the whole body of the citizens, just as does the power to make the laws, as we said in Chapter XII. And to the legislator similarly belongs the power to make any correction of the ruler and even to depose him, if this be expedient for the common benefit. . . . The Roman bishop called pope, or any other priest or bishop, or spiritual minister, collectively or individually, as such, has and ought to have no coercive jurisdiction over the property or person of any priest or bishop, or deacon, or group of them, and still less over any secular ruler or government, community, group, or individual, of whatever condition they may be; unless, indeed, such jurisdiction shall have been granted to a priest or bishop or group of them by the human legislator of the province. . . . Since, then, the heretic, the schismatic, or any other infidel is a transgressor of divine law, if he persists in this crime he will be punished by that judge to whom it pertains to correct transgressors of divine law as such, when he will exercise his judicial authority. But this judge is Christ, who will judge the living, the dead, and the dying, but in the future world, not in this one. For he has mercifully allowed sinners to have the opportunity of becoming deserving and penitent up to the very time when they finally pass from this world at death. But the other judge, namely, the pastor, bishop or priest, must teach and exhort man in the present life, must censure and rebuke the sinner and frighten him by a judgment or prediction of future glory or eternal damnation; but he must not coerce, as is plain from the previous chapter.

Now if human law were to prohibit heretics or other infidels from dwelling in the region, and yet such a person were found there, he must be corrected in this world as a transgressor of human law, and the penalty fixed by that law for such transgression must be inflicted on him by the judge who is the guardian of human law by the authority of the legislator, as we demonstrated in Chapter XV of Discourse I. But if human law did not prohibit the heretic or other infidel from dwelling among the faithful in the same province, as heretics and Jews are now permitted to do by human laws even in these times of Christian peoples, rulers, and pontiffs, then I say that no one is allowed to judge or coerce a heretic or other infidel by any penalty in property or in person for the status of the present life. And the general reason for this is as follows: no one is punished in this world for sinning against theoretic or practical disciplines precisely as such, however much he may sin against them, but only for sinning against a command of human law.

*The Florentine diplomat Niccoláo Machiavelli (1469–1527) startled his
contemporaries by writing a book on politics that did not aim at instructing rulers
in the moral virtues, but rather gave them pragmatic advice on how to win and
hold power. This work was first published in Italian, in 1532.*

FROM *The Prince*

BY *Niccolò Machiavelli*

IT NOW REMAINS FOR US to consider what ought to be the conduct and bearing of
a Prince in relation to his subjects and friends. And since I know that many
have written on this subject, I fear it may be thought presumptuous in me to
write of it also: the more so, because in my treatment of it I depart from the
views that others have taken.

But since it is my object to write what shall be useful to whosoever understands it, it seems to me better to follow the real truth of things than an imaginary view of them. For many Republics and Princedoms have been imagined
that were never seen or known to exist in reality. And the manner in which we
live, and that in which we ought to live, are things so wide asunder, that he
who quits the one to betake himself to the other is more likely to destroy than
to save himself; since any one who would act up to a perfect standard of goodness in everything, must be ruined among so many who are not good. It is
essential, therefore, for a Prince who desires to maintain his position, to have
learned how to be other than good, and to use or not to use his goodness as
necessity requires.

* * *

Beginning, then, with the first of the qualities above noticed, I say that it may
be a good thing to be reputed liberal, but, nevertheless, that liberality without
the reputation of it is hurtful; because, though it be worthily and rightly used,
still if it be not known, you escape not the reproach of its opposite vice. Hence,
to have credit for liberality with the world at large, you must neglect no circumstance of sumptuous display; the result being, that a Prince of a liberal disposition will consume his whole substance in things of this sort, and, after all, be
obliged, if he would maintain his reputation for liberality, to burden his subjects
with extraordinary taxes, and to resort to confiscations and all the other shifts
whereby money is raised. But in this way he becomes hateful to his subjects,
and growing impoverished is held in little esteem by any. So that in the end,
having by his liberality offended many and obliged few, he is worse off than
when he began, and is exposed to all his original dangers. Recognizing this, and
endeavouring to retrace his steps, he at once incurs the infamy of miserliness.

Niccolo Machiavelli, *The Prince*, trans. by N. Thompson (1897), pp. 109–110, 113–115, 118–119, 125–130.
Reprinted by permission of the Oxford University Press Oxford.

A Prince, therefore, since he cannot without injury to himself practise the virtue of liberality so that it may be known, will not, if he be wise, greatly concern himself though he be called miserly. Because in time he will come to be regarded as more and more liberal, when it is seen that through his parsimony his revenues are sufficient; that he is able to defend himself against any who make war on him; that he is able to defend himself against any who make war on him; that he can engage in enterprises against others without burdening his subjects; and thus exercise liberality towards all from whom he does not take, whose number is infinite, while he is miserly in respect of those only to whom he does not give, whose number is few.

* * *

Passing to the other qualities above referred to, I say that every Prince should desire to be accounted merciful and not cruel. Nevertheless, he should be on his guard against the abuse of this quality of mercy. Cesare Borgia was reputed cruel, yet his cruelty restored Romagna, united it, and brought it to order and obedience; so that if we look at things in their true light, it will be seen that he was in reality far more merciful than the people of Florence, who, to avoid the imputation of cruelty, suffered Pistoja to be torn to pieces by factions.

A Prince should therefore disregard the reproach of being thought cruel where it enables him to keep his subjects united and obedient. For he who quells disorder by a very few signal examples will in the end be more merciful than he who from too great leniency permits things to take their course and so to result in rapine and bloodshed; for these hurt the whole State, whereas the severities of the Prince injure individuals only.

* * *

A Prince should, therefore, understand how to use well both the man and the beast. And this lesson has been covertly taught by the ancient writers, who relate how Achilles and many others of these old Princes were given over to be brought up and trained by Chiron the Centaur; since the only meaning of their having for instructor one who was half man and half beast is, that it is necessary for a Prince to know how to use both natures, and that the one without the other has no stability.

But since a Prince should know how to use the beast's nature wisely, he ought of beasts to choose both the lion and the fox; for the lion cannot guard himself from the toils, nor the fox from wolves. He must therefore be a fox to discern toils, and a lion to drive off wolves.

To rely wholly on the lion is unwise; and for this reason a prudent Prince neither can nor ought to keep his word when to keep it is hurtful to him and the causes which led him to pledge it are removed. If all men were good, this would not be good advice, but since they are dishonest and do not keep faith with you, you, in return, need not keep faith with them; and no Prince was ever at a loss for plausible reasons to cloak a breach of faith. Of this numberless recent instances could be given, and it might be shown how many solemn treaties and engagements have been rendered inoperative and idle through want of faith in Princes, and that he who has best known to play the fox has had the best success.

It is necessary, indeed, to put a good colour on this nature, and to be skilful in simulating and dissembling. But men are so simple, and governed so absolutely by their present needs, that he who wishes to deceive will never fail in finding willing dupes. One recent example I will not omit. Pope Alexander VI had no care or thought but how to deceive, and always found material to work on. No man ever had a more effective manner of asseverating, or made promises with more solemn protestations, or observed them less. And yet, because he understood this side of human nature, his frauds always succeeded.

It is not essential, then, that a Prince should have all the good qualities which I have enumerated above, but it is most essential that he should seem to have them; I will even venture to affirm that if he has and invariably practises them all, they are hurtful, whereas the appearance of having them is useful. Thus, it is well to seem merciful, faithful, humane, religious, and upright, and also to be so; but the mind should remain so balanced that were it needful not to be so, you should be able and know how to change to the contrary.

And you are to understand that a Prince, and most of all a new Prince, cannot observe all those rules of conduct in respect whereof men are accounted good, being often forced, in order to preserve his Princedom, to act in opposition to good faith, charity, humanity, and religion. He must therefore keep his mind ready to shift as the winds and tides of Fortune turn, and, as I have already said, he ought not to quit good courses if he can help it, but should know how to follow evil courses if he must.

A Prince should therefore be very careful that nothing ever escapes his lips which is not replete with the five qualities above named, so that to see and hear him, one would think him the embodiment of mercy, good faith, integrity, humanity, and religion. And there is no virtue which it is more necessary for him to seem to possess than this last; because men in general judge rather by the eye than by the hand, for every one can see but few can touch. Every one sees what you seem, but few know what you are, and these few dare not oppose themselves to the opinion of the many who have the majesty of the State to back them up.

Moreover, in the actions of all men, and most of all of Princes, where there is no tribunal to which we can appeal, we look to results. Wherefore if a prince succeeds in establishing and maintaining his authority, the means will always be judged honourable and be approved by every one. For the vulgar are always taken by appearances and by results, and the world is made up of the vulgar, the few only finding room when the many have no longer ground to stand on.

*In The Prince Machiavelli seemed content to give practical advice to absolute rulers.
But in his other major work, The Discourses, he praised popular government and
the rule of law.*

FROM *The Discourses*

BY *Niccolò Machiavelli*

When I see antiquity held in such reverence, that, to omit other instances, the
mere fragment of some ancient statue is often bought at a great price, in order
that the purchaser may keep it by him to adorn his house, or to have it copied
by those who take delight in this art; and how these, again, strive with all their
skill to imitate it in their various works; and when, on the other hand, I find
those noble labours which history shows to have been wrought on behalf of
the monarchies and republics of old times, by kings, captains, citizens, law-
givers, and others who have toiled for the good of their country, rather admired
than followed, nay, so absolutely renounced by every one that not a trace of
that antique worth is now left among us, I cannot but at once marvel and grieve
at this inconsistency. . . . Desiring to rescue men from this error, I have
thought fit to note down with respect to all those books of Titus Livius which
have escaped the malignity of Time, whatever seems to me essential to a right
understanding of ancient and modern affairs; so that any who shall read these
remarks of mine, may reap from them that profit for the sake of which a knowledge of History is to be sought. . . .

*   *   *

I maintain, therefore, contrary to the common opinion which avers that a people when they have the management of affairs are changeable, fickle, and
ungrateful, that these faults exist not in them otherwise than as they exist in
individual princes; so that were any to accuse both princes and peoples, the
charge might be true, but that to make exception in favour of princes is a mistake; for a people in command, if it be duly restrained, will have the same prudence and the same gratitude as a prince has, or even more, however wise he
may be reckoned; and a prince on the other hand, if freed from the control of
the laws, will be more ungrateful, fickle, and short-sighted than a people. And
further, I say that any difference in their methods of acting results not from any
difference in their nature, that being the same in both, or, if there be advantage
on either side, the advantage resting with the people, but from their having
more or less respect for the laws under which each lives. And whosoever attentively considers the history of the Roman people, may see that for four hundred

Niccolo Machiarelli, *Discourese on the First Decade of Titus Livius,* trans. by N. H. Thomson (1883), pp. 4–5,
177–179. Reprinted by permission.

years they never relaxed in their hatred of the regal name, and were constantly devoted to the glory and welfare of their country, and will find numberless proofs given by them of their consistency in both particulars. And should any allege against me the ingratitude they showed to Scipio, I reply by what has already been said at length on that head, where I proved that peoples are less ungrateful than princes. But as for prudence and stability of purpose, I affirm that a people is more prudent, more stable, and of better judgment than a prince. Nor is it without reason that the voice of the people has been likened to the voice of God; for we see that wide-spread beliefs fulfil themselves, and bring about marvellous results, so as to have the appearance of presaging by some occult quality either weal or woe. Again, as to the justice of their opinions on public affairs, we seldom find that after hearing two speakers of equal ability urging them in opposite directions, they do not adopt the sounder view, or are unable to decide on the truth of what they hear. And if, as I have said, a people errs in adopting courses which appear to it bold and advantageous, princes will likewise err when their passions are touched, as is far oftener the case with them than with a people.

We see, too, that in the choice of magistrates a people will choose far more honestly than a prince; so that while you shall never persuade a people that it is advantageous to confer dignities on the infamous and profligate, a prince may readily, and in a thousand ways, be drawn to do so. Again, it may be seen that a people, when once they have come to hold a thing in abhorrence, remain for many ages of the same mind; which we do not find happen with princes. For the truth of both of which assertions the Roman people are my sufficient witness, who, in the course of so many hundred years, and in so many elections of consuls and tribunes, never made four appointments of which they had reason to repent; and, as I have said, so detested the name of king, that no obligation they might be under to any citizen who affected that name, could shield him from the appointed penalty.

Further, we find that those cities wherein the government is in the hands of the people, in a very short space of time, make marvellous progress, far exceeding that made by cities which have been always ruled by princes; as Rome grew after the expulsion of her kings, and Athens after she freed herself from Pisistratus; and this we can ascribe to no other cause than that the rule of a people is better than the rule of a prince.

In modern discussions concerning Machiavelli the problem always arises of reconciling the views of The Prince *with those of* The Discourses. *Machiavelli has been called, among other names, a cynic, a satirist, a realist, and a patriot. Perhaps the most satisfying explanations see him as reasserting a whole pagan classical world view—within which both princely and republican forms of government could be defended—against the prevailing Christian world view inherited from the medieval past.*

FROM *The Originality of Machiavelli*

BY *Isaiah Berlin*

It is commonly said, especially by those who follow Croce, that Machiavelli divided politics from morals—that he recommended as politically necessary courses which common opinion morally condemns: e.g. treading over corpses for the benefit of the state. Leaving aside the question of what was his conception of the state, and whether he in fact possessed one, it seems to me that this is a false antithesis. For Machiavelli the ends which he advocates are those to which he thinks wise human beings, who understand reality, will dedicate their lives. Ultimate ends in this sense, whether or not they are those of the Judaeo-Christian tradition, are what is usually meant by moral values.

What Machiavelli distinguishes is not specifically moral from specifically political values; what he achieves is not the emancipation of politics from ethics or religion, which Croce and many other commentators regard as his crowning achievement; what he institutes is something that cuts deeper still—a differentiation between two incompatible ideals of life, and therefore two moralities. One is the morality of the pagan world: its values are courage, vigour, fortitude in adversity, public achievement, order, discipline, happiness, strength, justice, above all assertion of one's proper claims and the knowledge and power needed to secure their satisfaction; that which for a Renaissance reader Pericles had seen embodied in his ideal Athens, Livy had found in the old Roman Republic, that of which Tacitus and Juvenal lamented the decay and death in their own time. These seem to Machiavelli the best hours of mankind and, Renaissance humanist that he is, he wishes to restore them.

Against this moral universe (moral or ethical no less in Croce's than in the traditional sense, that is, embodying ultimate human ends however these are conceived) stands in the first and foremost place, Christian morality. The ideals of Christianity are charity, mercy, sacrifice, love of God, forgiveness of enemies, contempt for the goods of this world, faith in the life hereafter, belief in the salvation of the individual soul as being of incomparable value—higher than, indeed wholly incommensurable with, any social or political or other terrestrial goal, any economic or military or aesthetic consideration. Machiavelli lays it down that out of men who believe in such ideals, and practise them, no satisfactory human community, in his Roman sense, can in principle be constructed. It is not simply a question of the unattainability of an ideal because of human imperfection, original sin, or bad luck, or ignorance, or insufficiency of material means. It is not, in other words, the inability in practice on the part of ordinary human beings to rise to a sufficiently high level of Christian virtue (which may, indeed, be the inescapable lot of sinful men on earth) that makes it, for him, impracticable to establish, even to seek after, the good Christian state. It is the

"The Originality of Machiavelli," Isaiah Brlin, *Against the Current* (1950), pp. 44–47. Reprinted by permission of The Viking Press.

very opposite: Machiavelli is convinced that what are commonly thought of as the central Christian virtues, whatever their intrinsic value, are insuperable obstacles to the building of the kind of society that he wishes to see; a society which, moreover, he assumes that it is natural for all normal men to want—the kind of community that, in his view, satisfies men's permanent desires and interests. . . .

He does not say or imply (as various radical philosophical reformers have done) that humility, kindness, unworldliness, faith in God, sanctity, Christian love, unwavering truthfulness, compassion, are bad or unimportant attributes; or that cruelty, bad faith, power politics, sacrifice of innocent men to social needs, and so on, are good ones.

But if history, and the insights of wise statesmen, especially in the ancient world, verified as they have been in practice, are to guide us, it will be seen that it is in fact impossible to combine Christian virtues, for example meekness or the search for spiritual salvation, with a satisfactory, stable, vigorous, strong society on earth. Consequently a man must choose. To choose to lead a Christian life is to condemn oneself to political impotence: to being used and crushed by powerful, ambitious, clever, unscrupulous men; if one wishes to build a glorious community like those of Athens or Rome at their best, then one must abandon Christian education and substitute one better suited to the purpose.

5

The Revolt of the Medievalists

W. K. Ferguson has described one modern trend in Renaissance historiography as a "revolt of the medievalists." The following extract will serve to illustrate the meaning of this phrase.

FROM *Héloïse and Abélard*

BY *Etienne Gilson*

THERE IS NOTHING QUITE COMPARABLE to the passion of the historians of the Renaissance for its individualism, its independence of mind, its rebellion against the principle of authority, unless perchance it is the docility with which those same historians copy one another in dogmatizing about the Middle Ages of which they know so little. We should not attach much importance to this attitude, save that those who speak thus of things they understand so poorly pretend to act in defense of reason and of personal observation. Their charge that all those who hold a different opinion are yielding to prejudice would, indeed, be sad, were it not so comic. Indifference to facts, distrust of direct observation and personal knowledge, the tendency to prune their data to suit their hypotheses, the naïve and dogmatic tendency to charge that those who would refute their position with self-evident facts lack a critical sense—these are the substance of their charge against the Middle Ages. Certainly, the Middle Ages had its fair share of these limitations. But at the same time these same limitations provide a perfect picture of the attitude of these historians of the Renaissance. They themselves possess the weaknesses of which they accuse the Middle Ages.

For Jacob Burckhardt, who only echoes the Preface to Volume VII of Michelet's *History of France,* the Renaissance is characterized by the discovery of the world and by the discovery of man. . . . What he wishes to prove before everything else is that such strong individuals could only have appeared first in the tiny Italian tyrannies of the fourteenth century where men led so intense a

Etienne Gilson, *Heloise and Abelard,* trans. by L Shook (1951), pp. 124–128. Reprinted by permission of Henry Regnery Company.

personal life that they had to talk about it. And so we read that "Even autobiography (and not merely history) takes here and there in Italy a bold and vigorous flight, and puts before us, together with the most varied incidents of external life, striking revelations of the inner man. Among other nations, even in Germany, at the time of the Reformation, it deals only with outward experiences, and leaves us to guess at the spirit within. It seems as though Dante's *La Vita nuova,* with the inexorable truthfulness that runs through it, had shown his people the way." We can, moreover, find a reason for this absence of individuality among medieval folk. Need we speak it? It is to be found in the subjugation and standardization which Christianity forced upon them. "Once mistress, the Church does not tolerate the development of the individual. All must be resigned to becoming simple links in her long chain and to obeying the laws of her institutions."

A man lacking individuality, incapable of analyzing himself, without the taste for describing others in biography or himself in autobiography, such is the man Christianity produces. Let us cite, as an example, St. Augustine! But to confine ourselves to the twelfth century, and without asking from what unique mould we could fashion at the same time a Bernard of Clairvaux and a Pierre Abélard, let us make a simple comparison between the Renaissance of the professors and the facts which become manifest in the correspondence of Héloäise and Abélard.

If all we need for a Renaissance is to find individuals developed to the highest point, does not this pair suffice? To be sure, Abélard and Héloïse are not Italians. They were not born in some tiny Tuscan "tyranny" of the fourteenth century. They satisfy, in brief, none of the conditions which the theory demands except that they were just what they ought not to have been if the theory were true. One insists, however, upon persons capable of "freely describing the moral man," even as the great Italians could do it. Perhaps even here Abélard and Héloäise labored with some success! No one would be so foolish as to compare their correspondence with the *Vita nuova* as literature. But if it is just a matter of stating in which of the two works one finds the moral man more simply and more directly described, the tables are turned. It is the *Vita nuova* that can no longer bear the comparison. Historians still wonder whether Beatrice was a little Florentine or a symbol. But there is nothing symbolic about Héloäise, nor was her love for Abélard but the unfolding of allegorical remarks. This story of flesh and blood, carried along by a passion at once brutal and ardent to its celebrated conclusion, we know from within as, indeed, we know few others. Its heroes observe themselves, analyze themselves as only Christian consciences fallen prey to passions can do it. Nor do they merely analyze themselves, but they talk about themselves. What Renaissance autobiographies can be compared with the correspondence of Abélard and Héloïse? Perchance Benvenuto Cellini's? But even Burckhardt recognizes that this does not claim to be "founded on introspection." Moreover, the reader "often detects him bragging or lying." On the contrary, it is absolutely certain that it is their

inmost selves about which Abélard and Héloïse instruct us; and if they sometimes lie to themselves, they never lie to us.

Before such disagreement between facts and theory, we might reasonably
expect the theory to yield a little. But not a bit of it! . . . No fact, whatever it
may be, no facts, however numerous they may be, can ever persuade those
who hold this theory that it is false, because it is of its very essence and by
definition that the Renaissance is the negation of the Middle Ages.

*Gaines Post argued that the origins of the modern state are to be found in the
twelfth and thirteenth centuries rather than in the age of the Renaissance.*

FROM *Studies in Medieval Legal Thought*

BY *Gaines Post*

ALMOST FORTY YEARS AGO Charles Homer Haskins applied the word renaissance to
the twelfth century. Whether or not it was a renaissance, the twelfth century
was in fact a period of great creative activity. The revival of political, economic,
and social life, along with the appearance of new learning, new schools and
new literatures and styles of art and architecture, signified the beginnings, in the
West, of modern European civilization. In the thirteenth century what had
begun in the twelfth arrived at such maturity that it is safe to say that early
modern Europe was coming into being.

Among the institutions and fields of knowledge created by medieval men,
the university and the State and the legal science that aided in the creation of
both were, as much as the rise of an active economy and the organization of
towns, important manifestations of the new age. While accepting and respecting
tradition and believing in the unchanging higher law of nature that came from
God, kings, statesmen, and men of learning confidently applied reason and skill
to the work of introducing order into society and societies, into feudal kingdoms, Italian communes, and lesser communities of the clergy and laity. Long
before the recovery of Aristotle's *Politics,* the naturalness of living in politically
and legally organized communities of corporate guilds, chapters, towns, and
States was recognized both in practice and in legal thought. Nature itself sanctioned the use of human reason and art to create new laws for the social and
political life on earth—provided always, of course, that the new did not violate
the will of God.

At the very time when merchants, artisans, townsmen, and schoolmen
were forming their associations for mutual aid and protection, the study of the
Roman and Canon law at Bologna introduced lawyers, jurists, and secular and
ecclesiastical authorities to the legal thought of Rome on corporations. When

kings were trying to overcome the anarchy of feudalism, the new legal science furnished those principles of public law that helped them convert their realms into States. . . .

The objection is often raised, however, that medieval kingdoms were not States because (1) they accepted the spiritual authority of the pope and the universal Church, (2) king and realm were under God and the law of nature, and (3) the royal government was poorly centralized. As for the first argument, it might be raised against the use of the term "State" for Eire and Spain today. Yet we assume that these two countries are States even though they are essentially Catholic and in some fashion recognize the spiritual authority of the Roman Church. With respect to other ideals of universalism, the United States and Italy, not to mention other nations, are sovereign States while belonging to the United Nations. As for the second argument, on subjection to God and a moral law, it must be replied that the official motto of the United States is "In God We Trust," and Americans take an oath of loyalty to "one nation indivisible under God." Furthermore, the sovereignty of the American people and their State is surely limited in fact by a moral law that belongs to the Judaeo-Christian tradition: it is not likely that the representatives of the people in Congress will ever think of making laws that violate the Ten Commandments, nor that the Supreme Court will approve them. It is therefore not absurd to call medieval kingdoms States despite limitations within which derived from the ideal of law and justice, and despite limitations from without (also within) from the universalism of Christianity and the Church. Papal arbitration of "international" disputes in the thirteenth century interfered with the sovereign right of kings to go to war (always the "just war" in defense of the *patria* and the *status regni*) no more and no less than international organizations do in the twentieth century. And "world opinion" was respected as much or as little.

In reply to the third argument, regarding the amount of centralization, one must ask, what degree of centralization is necessary for a State to exist? If the central government must be absolute in power, then the United States might not qualify, since a great many powers remain in the fifty states within. And did France become a State only with the more thorough centralization that resulted from the Revolution? Logically we might conclude that only a totalitarian State is a true State.

*   *   *

[During the Middle Ages—Ed.], in the emergency of a danger that threatened the safety of all, the ruler had a superior right to take such action as would ensure the public welfare or safety, that is, maintain the *status* or state of the realm. This emergency was a case of necessity—usually, as I have had occasion to say above, a just war of defense. Now the case of necessity, Meinecke has shown, was asserted by Machiavelli as a part of his theory of the State: the State is above all; and the prince, to assure the noble end of the State, has the right to use any means to meet the necessity and preserve the State. Necessity is

Guicciardini's reason of State. But it had its medieval background—Meinecke finding the earliest statement in the maxim, "Necessity knows no law," in the late fourteenth century—in Gerson: Helene Wieruszowski finding it stated, along with public utility, in the time of Frederick II.

Actually it goes back farther—if not to the Greeks, at any rate to Mark 2, 25–26; and above all to the *Corpus Iuris Canonici* and the *Corpus Iuris Civilis*. A pseudo-Isidorian canon in Gratian (De cons., Dist. 1, c. 11) uses the very expression, "quoniam necessitas non habet legem"; decretists and decretalists from the late twelfth century on state the maxim and in their glosses explain its meaning in connection with the equitable interpretation of the law. For example, the necessity of hunger, says one, excuses theft; poverty, says another, knows no law; and the law ends, says a glossator, when necessity begins. Azo in his *Brocardica* discusses the rule and gives many citations *pro* and *con* to *Code* and *Digest*. To *D.* 9, 2, 4, where we find that it is lawful to kill a thief in the night (the correspondence to *Exod.* 22, 2–3, had been noted by St. Augustine and was discussed by the canonists) because "natural reason" permits one to defend oneself against danger, Accursius gives complete approval.

Here, "Necessity knows no law" was a principle of private law. But because of the theory of the just war, that is, the right of the kingdom to defend itself against the aggressor (St. Augustine stated it, as did the scholastic philosophers), the case of necessity became a principle of public laws in the thirteenth century; the equivalent of "just cause," "evident utility," and the common welfare, it was perforce connected with the preservation of the *status regni*. From the twelfth century on, the kings of France and England appealed to necessity as the justification for demanding extraordinary taxes. As we have seen, the Church had already recognized the validity of necessity in the lay taxation of the clergy. No wonder, then, that in the late thirteenth century French lawyers, not only Beaumanoir and Pierre Dubois, but royal councillors like Pierre Flot and William of Nogaret, were asserting that in a case of necessity the defense of the kingdom and all its members was a superior right of the *status regni;* and that if "what touched all must be approved of all," the king had the right to compel all, even the clergy, to consent to measures taken to meet the danger.

At the same time, the situation of "international wars," necessity, public welfare, and the rise of powerful monarchies broke down the corporate hierarchy of communities within the Empire. Each great kingdom, like England or France, by the middle of the thirteenth century was independent of the Empire in theory and practice alike. And at the end of the century each was independent of the Church—and even above the Church, except in purely spiritual matters.

* * *

On the foundation of the two laws and of the rise of feudal monarchies, the theory, and some practice, of public law and the State thus arose in the twelfth and thirteenth centuries. Private rights and privileges remained powerful and enjoyed a recrudescence in localism and privileged orders in the fourteenth century and later. At times, in periods of war and civil dissension, they weakened the public authority of kings and threatened the very survival of the State.[1] But the ideas and ideal of the State and public order, of a public and constitutional law, were constantly at hand to remind statesmen of their right to reconstitute the State.

Lynn Thorndike criticized Burckhardt's interpretation of the Renaissance from the standpoint of a historian of science.

FROM *Renaissance or Prenaissance?*

BY *Lynn Thorndike*

MICHELET CALLED THE RENAISSANCE "the discovery of the world and of man," and was followed in this lead by the very influential book of Burckhardt, in which, on what seem too often to be dogmatic or imaginary grounds without sufficient presentation of facts as evidence, the Renaissance was no longer regarded as primarily a rebirth of classical learning and culture but rather as a prebirth or precursor of present society and of modern civilization—"a period," to quote the *Boston Transcript* (February 27, 1926) concerning Elizabethan England, "that witnessed the birth pangs of most that is worth while in modern civilization and government."

This made a well-calculated appeal to the average reader who is little interested to be told that Erasmus was a great Greek scholar or that Leonardo da Vinci copied from Albert of Saxony, but whose ego is titillated to be told that Leonardo was an individual like himself or that Erasmus's chief claim to fame is that he was the first modern man—the first one like you and me. All this was quite soothing and flattering and did much to compensate for one's inability to read Horace or to quote Euripides.

---

[1]Naturally I cannot attempt to outline the history of the failures of the public order of the State and of the public authority of the king in the fourteenth and fifteenth centuries. At times, in France for example, king and realm meant little except in the continuity of the ideas and ideal of the public law symbolized by the crown. As late as the eighteenth century, local and individual privileges and local resistance to the commands of the central government made the State weak. On this see in general the excellent book by R. R. Palmer, *The Age of the Democratic Revolution.* To return to the fourteenth century, in France, after the time of Philip IV, particularly in the period of the disasters of the Hundred Years' War and the Black Death, there was far less of a State than in the thirteenth century. *Plena potestas, quod omnes tangit,* and *status regni* apparently no longer manifested the power as well as the theoretical right of the king to obtain more than haphazard and sporadic consent, chiefly in local assemblies, to extraordinary taxes. In England the situation was different, but even there the legal thought I have investigated needs study in relation to the political events. For the situation in France see, besides C. H. Taylor in Strayer and Taylor, *Studies,* Fredric Cheyette, "Procurations by Large-Scale Communities in Fourteenth-Century France," *Speculum,* xxxvii (1962), 18–31.

Lynn Thorndike, "Renaissance of Prenaissance?" from *Journal of the History of Ideas*, Vol. 4 (1943), pp. 69–74. Reprinted by permission.

* * *

Was the individual freed and personality enhanced by the Renaissance or Prenaissance? Burckhardt affirmed that with it "man became a spiritual individual and recognized himself as such," whereas "in the middle ages both sides of human consciousness—that which was turned within as that which was turned without—lay dreaming or half awake beneath a common veil." It might be remarked that individualism may be a mark of decline rather than progress. The self-centered sage of the Stoics and Epicureans rang the knell of the Greek city-state. Basil, on the verge of the barbarian invasions, complained that men "for the greater part prefer individual and private life to the union of common life." Carl Nemann held that "true modern individualism has its roots in the strength of the barbarians, in the realism of the barbarians, and in the Christian middle ages." Cunningham believed that the Roman Empire "left little scope for individual aims and tended to check the energy of capitalists and laborers alike," whereas Christianity taught the supreme dignity of man and encouraged the individual and personal responsibility. Moreover, in the thirteenth century there were "fewer barriers to social intercourse than now." According to Schäafer, "So far as public life in the broadest sense, in church and state, city and country, law and society, is concerned, the middle ages are the time of most distinctive individuality and independent personality in volition and action." We may no longer think of the Gothic architects as anonymous, and de Mely discovered hundreds of signatures of miniaturists hidden in the initials and illuminations of medieval manuscripts. No period in the history of philosophy has discussed individuality and its problems more often or more subtly than did the medieval schoolmen. Vittorino da Feltre and other humanist educators may have suited their teaching to the individual pupil; at the medieval university the individual scholar suited himself. The humanists were imitative in their writing, not original. Vitruvius was the Bible of Renaissance architects who came to follow authority far more than their creative Gothic predecessors. For the middle ages loved variety; the Renaissance, uniformity.

Not only has it been demonstrated that the thirteenth and fourteenth centuries were more active and penetrating in natural science than was the quattrocento, but the notion that "appreciation of natural beauty" was "introduced into modern Europe by the Italian Renaissance" must also be abandoned. Burckhardt admitted that medieval literature displayed sympathy with nature, but nevertheless regarded Petrarch's ascent of Mount Ventoux (which is only 6260 feet high) in 1336 as epoch-making. Petrarch represented an old herdsman who had tried in vain to climb it fifty years before as beseeching him to turn back on the ground that he had received only torn clothes and broken bones for his pains and that no one had attempted the ascent since. As a matter of fact, Jean Buridan, the Parisian schoolman, had visited it between 1316 and 1334, had given details as to its altitude, and had waxed enthusiastic as to the Cevennes. So that all Petrarch's account proves is his capacity for story-telling and sentimental ability to make a mountain out of a molehill. Miss Stockmayer, in a book on feeling for nature in Germany in the tenth and eleventh centuries, has noted various ascents and descriptions of mountains from that period. In the closing years of his life archbishop Anno of Cologne climbed his beloved mountain oftener than usual.

As for the feeling for nature in medieval art, let me repeat what I have written elsewhere anent the interest displayed by the students of Albertus Magnus in particular herbs and trees.

This healthy interest in nature and commendable curiosity concerning real things was not confined to Albert's students nor to "rustic intelligences." One has only to examine the sculpture of the great thirteenth-century cathedrals to see that the craftsmen of the towns were close observers of the world of nature, and that every artist was a naturalist too. In the foliage that twines about the capitals of the columns in the French cathedrals it is easy to recognize, says M. Mâle, a large number of plants: "the plantain, arum, ranunculus, fern, clover, coladine, hepatica, columbine, cress, parsley, strawberry-plant, ivy, snapdragon, the flower of the broom, and the leaf of the oak, a typically French collection of flowers loved from childhood." *Mutatis mutandis,* the same statement could be made concerning the carved vegetation that runs riot in Lincoln cathedral. "The thirteenth-century sculptors sang their *chant de mai.* All the spring delights of the Middle Ages live again in their work—the exhilaration of Palm Sunday, the garlands of flowers, the bouquets fastened on the doors, the strewing of fresh herbs in the chapels, the magical flowers of the feast of Saint John—all the fleeting charm of those old-time springs and summers. The Middle Ages, so often said to have little love for nature, in point of fact gazed at every blade of grass with reverence."

It is not merely love of nature but scientific interest and accuracy that we see revealed in the sculptures of the cathedrals and in the note-books of the thirteenth-century architect, Villard de Honnecourt, with its sketches of insect as well as animal life, of a lobster, two parroquets on a perch, the spirals of a snail's shell, a fly, a dragonfly, and a grasshopper, as well as a bear and a lion from life, and more familiar animals such as the cat and the swan. The sculptors of gargoyles and chimeras were not content to reproduce existing animals but showed their command of animal anatomy by creating strange compound and hybrid monsters—one might almost say, evolving new species—which nevertheless have all the verisimilitude of copies from living forms. It was these breeders in stone, these Burbanks of the pencil, these Darwins with the chisel, who knew nature and had studied botany and zoology in a way superior to the scholar who simply pored over the works of Aristotle and Pliny. No wonder that Albert's students were curious about particular things.

* * *

The concept of the Italian Renaissance or Prenaissance has in my opinion done a great deal of harm in the past and may continue to do harm in the future. It is too suggestive of a sensational, miraculous, extraordinary, magical, human and intellectual development, like unto the phoenix rising from its ashes after five hundred years. It is contrary to the fact that human nature tends to remain much the same in all times. It has led to a chorus of rhapsodists as to freedom, breadth, soaring ideas, horizons, perspectives, out of fetters and swaddling clothes, and so on. It long discouraged the study of centuries of human development that preceded it, and blinded the French *philosophes* and revolutionists to the value of medieval political and economic institutions. It has kept men in general from recognizing that our life and thought is based more nearly and actually on the middle ages than on distant Greece and Rome, from whom our heritage is more indirect, bookish and sentimental, less institutional, social, religious, even less economic and experimental.

But what is the use of questioning the Renaissance? No one has ever proved its existence; no one has really tried to. So often as one phase of it or conception of it is disproved, or is shown to be equally characteristic of the preceding period, its defenders take up a new position and are just as happy, just as enthusiastic, just as complacent as ever.

6

A Suggested Synthesis

W. K. Ferguson has defended the older interpretation of the Renaissance as an age of brilliant innovation, while taking note of the criticisms of the medievalists.

FROM *The Reinterpretation of the Renaissance*

BY *Wallace K. Ferguson*

IT SHOULD BE UNDERSTOOD, of course, that recognition of the Renaissance as a period in history does not imply that it was completely different from what preceded and what followed it. Even in a dynamic view of history, periodization may prove a very useful instrument if properly handled. The gradual changes brought about by a continuous historical development may be in large part changes in degree, but when they have progressed far enough they become for all practical purposes changes in kind. To follow a good humanist precedent and argue from the analogy of the human body, the gradual growth of man from childhood to maturity is an unbroken process, yet there is a recognizable difference between the man and the child he has been. Perhaps the analogy, as applied to the Middle Ages and the Renaissance, is unfortunate in that it suggests a value judgment that might be regarded as invidious. However that may be, it is my contention that by about the beginning of the fourteenth century in Italy and somewhat later in the North those elements in society which had set the tone of medieval culture had perceptibly lost their dominant position and thereafter gradually gave way to more recently developed forces. These, while active in the earlier period, had not been the determining factors in the creation of medieval culture but were to be the most influential in shaping the culture of the Renaissance.

That somewhat involved statement brings me to the hazardous question of what were the fundamental differences between medieval and Renaissance civilization, and to the approach to the problem which I have found most generally satisfactory. It is an approach suggested by the work of the recent economic

Wallace K. Ferguson, "The Reinterpretation of the Renaissance," W. H. Werkmeister ed., pp. 13–17. Reprinted from *Facets of the Renaissance* (1959) by permission of the University of Southern California Press. Copyright © by the University of Southern California, 1959.

historians who have called attention to the dynamic influence of the revival of trade, urban life, and money economy in the midst of the agrarian feudal society of the high Middle Ages. Unfortunately, economic historians have seldom spared much thought for the development of intellectual and aesthetic culture, having been content to leave that to the specialists, while, on the other hand, the historians whose special interest was religion, philosophy, literature, science, or art have all too frequently striven to explain the developments in these fields without correlating them with changes in the economic, social, and political structure of society. In the past few years, however, historians have become increasingly aware of the necessity of including all forms of human activity in any general synthesis, an awareness illustrated by Myron Gilmore's recent volume on *The World of Humanism*. Further, there has been a growing tendency to find the original motive forces of historical development in basic alterations of the economic, political, and social system, which in time exert a limiting and directing influence upon intellectual interests, religious attitudes, and cultural forms. As applied to the Renaissance, this tendency has been evident in the work of several historians, notably, Edward P. Cheyney, Ferdinand Schevill, Eugenio Garin, Hans Baron, and some of the contributors to the *Propyläen Weltgeschichte*.

To state my point as briefly as possible, and therefore more dogmatically than I could wish: let us begin with the axiomatic premise that the two essential elements in medieval civilization were the feudal system and the universal church. The latter represented an older tradition than feudalism, but in its external structure and in many of its ideals and ways of thought it had been forced to adapt itself to the conditions of feudal society. And feudalism in turn was shaped by the necessity of adapting all forms of social and political life to the limitations of an agrarian and relatively moneyless economy. Into this agrarian feudal society the revival of commerce and industry, accompanied by the growth of towns and money economy, introduced a new and alien element. The first effect of this was to stimulate the existing medieval civilization, freeing it from the economic, social, and cultural restrictions that an almost exclusive dependence upon agriculture had imposed upon it, and making possible a rapid development in every branch of social and cultural activity. That the twelfth and thirteenth centuries were marked by the growth of a very vigorous culture no longer needs to be asserted. They witnessed the recovery of much ancient learning, the creation of scholastic philosophy, the rise of vernacular literatures and of Gothic art, perhaps on the whole a greater advance than was achieved in the two following centuries. Nevertheless, it seems to me that, despite new elements and despite rapid development, the civilization of these two centuries remained in form and spirit predominantly feudal and ecclesiastical.

But medieval civilization, founded as it was upon a basis of land tenure and agriculture, could not continue indefinitely to absorb an expanding urban society and money economy without losing its essential character, without gradually changing into something recognizably different. The changes were most obvious in the political sphere, as feudalism gave way before the rise of city states or centralized territorial states under princes who were learning to utilize the power of money. The effect upon the church was almost equally great. Its universal authority was shaken by the growing power of the national states, while its internal organization was transformed by the evolution of a monetary fiscal system which had, for a time, disastrous effects upon its moral character and prestige. Meanwhile, within the cities the growth of capital was bringing significant changes in the whole character of urban economic and social organizations, of which not the least significant was the appearance of a growing class of urban laymen who had the leisure and means to secure a liberal education and to take an active part in every form of intellectual and aesthetic culture.

Taking all these factors together, the result was an essential change in the character of European civilization. The feudal and ecclesiastical elements, though still strong, no longer dominated, and they were themselves more or less transformed by the changing conditions. The culture of the period we call the Renaissance was predominantly and increasingly the product of the cities, created in major part by urban laymen whose social environment, personal habits, and professional interests were different from those of the feudal and clerical aristocracy who had largely dominated the culture of the Middle Ages. These urban laymen, and with them the churchmen who were recruited from their midst as the medieval clergy had been recruited from the landed classes, did not break suddenly or completely with their inherited traditions, but they introduced new materials and restated the old in ways that reflected a different manner of life. The Renaissance, it seems to me, was essentially an age of transition, containing much that was still medieval, much that was recognizably modern, and, also, much that, because of the mixture of medieval and modern elements, was peculiar to itself and was responsible for its contradictions and contrasts and its amazing vitality.

This interpretation of the Renaissance leaves many of the old controversial points unanswered, though a partial answer to most of them is implied in it. It may be as well not to attempt to answer all questions with a single formula. There was certainly enough variety in the changing culture of western Europe during both the Middle Ages and the Renaissance to provide historians with material to keep them happily engaged in controversy for some time to come. All that can be claimed for the approach I have suggested is that it seems to offer the broadest basis for periodization, that it points to the most fundamental differences between the civilization of the Renaissance and the Middle Ages, while recognizing the dynamic character of both. At the same time, by suggesting a broad theory of causation in the gradual transformation of the economic and social structure of western Europe, it tends to reduce the controversial questions regarding the primary influence of the classical revival, of the Italian genius, Germanic blood, medieval French culture, or Franciscan mysticism to a secondary, if not irrelevant, status. Finally, such an approach to the problem might make it possible to take what was genuinely illuminating in Burckhardt, without the exaggerations of the classical-rational-Hegelian tradition, and also without the necessity of attacking the Renaissance *per se* in attacking Burckhardtian orthodoxy.

Martin Luther—Reformer or Revolutionary?

CONTENTS

QUESTIONS FOR STUDY

1 What was Luther's position on the relation of God to man?

2 To what extent was Luther heretical before the indulgence controversy?

3 What, according to Luther, was the true liberty of a Christian?

4 How could Luther reconcile his position with that of the Apostle James?

5 What role in the making of the Reformation do the various historians cited assign to Luther?

6 Would there have been a Reformation if Luther had never lived?

The advent of the Protestant Reformation is generally taken to mark the end of the Middle Ages in northern Europe and the beginnings of the modern world. The unity of Western Christendom was destroyed and one of the most important medieval ideals—that of the unified, Christian, Catholic empire—was dealt a death blow. In its place emerged the idea of the nation-state in which, ultimately, the religion of the state became a question of national policy. The sixteenth-century formula cujus regio, ejus religio *("the religion of the ruler shall be the religion of the ruled") explicitly acknowledged the breakdown of the monopoly of religious truth and practice exercised by the Catholic Church for more than a millennium. From this breakdown was to emerge the emphasis upon individual conscience, religious tolerance, and awareness of cultural and national differences that marks the modern world.*

The Reformation was a revolution of considerable magnitude. Moreover, all the aforementioned modern elements, except tolerance, were present in the "pre-revolutionary" times. Martin Luther's individual conscience was what drove him into religious orders and ultimately into religious rebellion. Luther was intensely German in his outlook and was quite aware of the cultural gulf between Germany and Latin Christendom. The national question was also present in the Germany of the early sixteenth century. German gold flowed to Rome, and the Germans resented it. The policies and politics of Rome influenced the German scene, and some of the German princes resented this too. Finally, the ideal of Christian unity, which was to appeal so strongly to Charles V, elected Holy Roman Emperor in 1519, was a threat to the independence of these princes, and it has been argued that they protected Luther and embraced Protestantism less because of sincere religious belief than because of political expediency. All of this has led some historians to see the Protestant Reformation as both inevitable and impersonal. The Reformation, they argue, was the inevitable result of the economic, social, and political development of Germany in the fifteenth century. If it had not been initiated by Luther, it would have been started by someone else. Luther just happened to be the one who threw down the challenge to the church.

It is, of course, impossible to answer the question "Would the Reformation have occurred if Luther had never lived?" since Luther did live and there is no way to alter that. We can, however, question the answer given by those who would make Luther a mere cipher in the coming of the Reformation. After all, the church had been corrupt in previous ages and had been successfully reformed. Other times had witnessed resentment of Rome and princes jealous of their powers without also undergoing irreparable schism. Might not the difference between these times and the early sixteenth century be precisely the presence of one man, Luther? This is not to say that Luther, single-handedly, made the Reformation. But it is to suggest that there were essential ingredients in the Reformation that owed their existence to his personal and unique experiences. Not the least of these ingredients was Luther's determination to purify the faith. We can legitimately ask a number of questions about this aspect of the Reformation, and we may also expect to find historical evidence to permit us to draw some rather firm conclu-

sions from it. For example, did Luther's initial hostility to Rome derive from any of the aforementioned social, economic, and political "sources" of the Reformation, or were they much more personal? Did the selling of indulgences trigger Luther's attack on corruption in Rome, or was this merely the occasion for Luther to launch a much more fundamental attack against theoretical theology rather than corrupt practice? Finally, did Luther really believe that he could reform *the church? Certainly all the public issues were negotiable. What was not was Luther's private conviction that he had found the way to salvation and that this way, to put it mildly, appeared to conflict with the traditional way of the Catholic Church. It was this private conviction that sustained Luther in the years of battle that were to ensue. As historians we may legitimately ask its source from the historical evidence, and if we discover it, we may then attempt to understand how such a private conviction could receive such widespread public support.*

The problem posed by the documents that follow is central to all historical investigation. It involves the question of the role of the individual in historical crises and, as a subsidiary issue, the question of whether an individual actually known what he is doing. For even if we accept the thesis that Luther, the man, was essential to the Reformation, we must still ask to what extent Luther was merely the vehicle for the expression of more general social or psychological forces. The reader should be aware of the fact that no answer can be proved but that some answer must be given. The answer the reader decides on will affect his or her interpretation of the past as well as his or her actions in the present.

1

The Road to Reformation

In May 1515 Jacob Wimpheling wrote a "response" to a famous letter on Germany written by Enea Silvio Piccolomini (later Pius II) in 1457 in which he detailed the grievances of the Germans against papal misrule. This is what the church looked like to a devout member just two years before Luther posted his famous theses.

FROM *Response*

BY *Jacob Wimpheling*

RIGHTLY DOES ENEA SILVIO PRAISE Germany as the source of his elevation[to cardinal]. Because he is an Italian, however, and loves the land of his birth, he would not enjoy seeing the flow of money from our country to his own slowed to a trickle. He therefore flatters us with stories of the translation of the *imperium* from the Greeks to the Germans, though we all know that our ancestors had to win this imperium with their courage and their life's blood. He goes on to laud the ample treasures to be found in our churches and homes. But even if Germany really did possess so abundant a store of hard-earned and frugally managed wealth, how much of it would remain to us after we had taken care of our daily needs, had seen to the maintenance of our churches, cities, streets, and public institutions, assured our country's protection from its enemies, provided for orphans, widows, and the victims of plague, pox, and French disease, and comforted beggars, as Christian piety demands?

Enea makes much of the fact that we Germans received our Christian faith from his compatriots. "Rome," he writes, "preached Christ to you; it was faith in Christ, received from Rome, that extinguished barbarism in you." We concede, of course, that missionaries from Rome brought the saving message of Christ to our land. But by the same token Rome herself was, like Germany, converted to the Christian faith, and Rome should therefore show no less gratitude than Germany for the reception of her faith. For was it not Peter, a Jew from

Jacob Whimpheling, "Response," from Gerald Strauss *Manifestations of Dicscontent in Germay on the Eve of the Reformation* (1971), pp. 41–45. Reprinted by permission of Indiana University Press.

Palestine, who preached the Gospel of Christ in Rome? If Enea's argument were
applied to the Romans themselves, they would now be obliged to send annual
tributes of gold and silver to Syria. . . .

It is not that we deny our debt to Rome. But we ask: Is Rome not also
indebted to us? Have not two of our compatriots, clever and skillful men hailing
from Strassburg and Mainz, invented the noble art of printing, which makes it
possible to propagate the correct doctrines of faith and morals throughout the
world and in all languages? . . . Do we, who have been true and industrious in
our service to religion and to the Holy Roman Church, who are steadfast in our
faith and even—as Enea admits—prepared to shed our blood for it, who willingly obey orders, buy indulgences, travel to Rome, and send money—do we
who perform all these duties deserve to be called barbarians? . . . Despite this
slanderous label, Enea speaks with lavish praise of our fatherland, of our cities
and buildings. For what purpose? For one only: to make our ears more receptive to the demands coming from Rome dressed in Christian garb but serving
Italian interests; in other words, to put us in the mood for wasting our fortunes
on foreigners. . . . As it is, our compatriots crowd the road to Rome. They pay
for papal reservations and dispensations. They appear before papal courts—and
not always because they have appealed a case to Rome, but rather because
their cases have been arbitrarily transferred there. Is there a nation more patient
and willing to receive indulgences, though we well know that the income from
them is divided between the Holy See and its officialdom? Have we not paid
dearly for the confirmation of every bishop and abbot? . . .

Thus we are done out of fortune, and for no purpose other than to support the innumerable retainers and hangers-on that populate the papal court.
Enea himself gives us a list of these papal lackeys, the number of which
increases daily. True, if the pope must furnish court rooms for all the legal business in Christendom, he requires a huge staff. But there is no need for this.
Apart from imperial courts, there exist in our German cities learned and honorable judges to whom appeals from lower episcopal courts could be directed. It
is in the highest degree objectionable that Rome bypasses courts of higher
resort—often on trivial pretexts or out of pique—and compels our compatriots,
laymen included, to appear in Rome. No one will deny that intricate and
weighty matters should be appealed to Rome as the seat of highest power and
of greatest wisdom and justice. But the rights of imperial and episcopal jurisdiction must not be infringed. If these rights had remained intact, the Apostolic See
would not today stagger under an unmanageable weight of legal and administrative business. . . .

The Council of Basel pointed out that our sacred church fathers had written their canons for the purpose of assuring the Church of good government,
and that honor, discipline, faith, piety, love, and peace reigned in the Church as
long as these regulations were observed. Later, however, vanity and greed
began to prevail; the laws of the fathers were neglected, and the Church sank
into immorality and depravity, debasement, degradation and abuse of office.

This is principally due to papal reservations of prelacies and other ecclesiastical benefices, also to the prolific award of expectancies to future benefices, and to innumerable concessions and other burdens placed upon churches and clergy. To wit:

Church incomes and benefices are given to unworthy men and Italians.
High offices and lucrative posts are awarded to persons of unproven merit and character.
Few holders of benefices reside in their churches, for as they hold several posts simultaneously they cannot reside in all of them at once. Most do not even recognize the faces of their parishioners. They neglect the care of souls and seek only temporal rewards.
The divine service is curtailed.
Hospitality is diminished.
Church laws lose their force.
Ecclesiastical buildings fall into ruin.
The conduct of clerics is an open scandal.
Able, learned, and virtuous priests who might raise the moral and professional level of the clergy abandon their studies because they see no prospect of advancement.
The ranks of the clergy are riven by rivalry and animosity; hatred, envy, and even the wish for the death of others are aroused.
Striving after pluralities of benefices is encouraged.
Poor clerics are maltreated, impoverished, and forced from their posts.
Crooked lawsuits are employed to gather benefices.
Some benefices are procured through simony.
Other benefices remain vacant.
Able young men are left to lead idle and vagrant lives.
Prelates are deprived of jurisdiction and authority.
The hierarchical order of the Church is destroyed.

In this manner, a vast number of violations of divine and human law is committed and condoned. . . . "It is the pope's special mission," writes Enea, "to protect Christ's sheep. He should accomplish this task in such a way as to lead all men to the path of salvation. He must see that the pure Gospel is preached to all, that false doctrines, blasphemies, and unchristian teachings are eradicated, and that enemies of the faith are driven from the lands of Christendom. He must heal schisms and end wars, abolish robbery, murder, arson, adultery, drunkenness and gluttony, spite, hatred and strife. He must promote peace and order, so that concord might reign among men, and honor and praise be given to God."

So Enea. My question is: Does a court of ephebes and muleteers and flatterers help the pope prevent schism and abolish blasphemy, wars, robbery, and the other crimes mentioned by Enea? Would he not be better served by men learned in canon law and Scripture, by men who know how to preach and can help the faithful ease their conscience in the confessional? The Council of Basel was surely inspired when it decreed that a third of all benefices should go to men versed in the Bible. . . . If I am not mistaken, the conciliar fathers wished to see the true Gospel of Christ preached everywhere. They wished honor and glory given to God. We ourselves want nothing else. We would rejoice if many men were to praise God, if every priest in his sufficiently endowed benefice were to serve God and celebrate the Eucharist, if popes and emperors, if the whole Church were to draw rich benefit from this holy work, the most efficacious office of them all. . . .

The English historian Gordon Rupp puts Luther and the problems facing him at the very outset of the Reformation in historical perspective.

FROM *The Righteousness of God*

BY *Gordon Rupp*

IT WAS A CRITICAL MOMENT during the Leipzig Disputation (1519) when Martin Luther, out-manoeuvred by his opponent, Dr. Eck, was goaded into declaring that "among the articles of John Huss . . . which were condemned, are many which are truly Christian." The audience was horrified, and perhaps Luther himself was a little shocked. For he had grown to accept the judgment of contemporary opinion against the heretic of a former generation. "I used to abhor the very name of Huss. So zealous was I for the Pope that I would have helped to bring iron and fire to kill Huss, if not in very deed, at least with a consenting mind." In this verdict faith and party loyalty combined, for the Erfurt Augustinians were proud that a member of their own order, John Zachariae, had earned the title "Scourge of Huss" and his tomb bore in effigy the Golden Rose bestowed upon him by a grateful Pope. It was not until Luther himself entered a similar context of Papal condemnation that he turned to examine the writings of Huss, and to criticize this unexamined assumption. Then indeed he could cry to Spalatin, "We are all Hussites, without knowing it . . . even Paul and Augustine!"

*   *   *

Luther prided himself on the fact that while others had attacked the manners and the morals of particular popes, or the abuses and corruptions of the Curia, he had begun with doctrine. We know that in its essentials Luther's theology existed before the opening of the Church struggle in 1517, and that it was not an improvization devised in the course of that conflict. Nevertheless, it was as the conflict developed out of the Indulgence controversy that he began to ques-

Gordon Rupp. *The Righteousness of God: Luther Studies* (1953). pp. 3–15. Reprinted by permission of Hodder & Stoughton Ltd., London.

tion the basis of the Papal power, and turned to the issues raised in a preceding generation by the theologians of the Conciliar movement, the question whether the Papacy were of divine or of human institution. Early in 1519 he could still write, "If unfortunately there are such things in Rome as might be improved, there neither is, nor can be, any reason that one should tear oneself away from the Church in schism. Rather, the worse things become, the more a man should help, and cling to her, for by schism and contempt nothing can be mended." In fateful weeks before the Leipzig Disputation, Luther studied church history and the Papal decretals. On 13th March 1519 he wrote to his friend Spalatin, "I do not know whether the Pope is Anti-Christ himself, or only his apostle, so grievously is Christ, i.e. Truth, manhandled and crucified by him in these decretals."

The Leipzig Disputation forced Luther to face the implications of his revolt, and made him realize that he could not come so far, without going further in repudiation of papal authority. Then, early in 1520, he read Hutten's edition of Valla's exposure of the "Donation of Constantine," and he wrote in disgust, "I have hardly any doubt left that the Pope is the very Anti-Christ himself, whom the common report expects, so well do all the things he lives, does, speaks, ordains, fit the picture."

In June 1520 he wrote solemn, final words, in a writing of exceptional vehemence. "Farewell, unhappy, hopeless, blasphemous Rome! The wrath of God is come upon thee, as thou deservest. . . . We have cared for Babylon, and she is not healed: let us leave her then, that she may be the habitation of dragons, spectres and witches, and true to her name of Babel, an everlasting confusion, a new pantheon of wickedness."

There are battles of the mind which most men cannot go on fighting again and again. We make up our minds, as we say, and the account is settled. Thereafter we reopen that particular issue only with great reluctance. No doubt this is a weakness of our spirit, though to be able to keep an open mind requires detachment from the hurly-burly of decision, and is more easily achieved in academic groves than in the battlefield or marketplace or temple. Luther's words here perhaps show us the point at which he hardened his mind with terrible finality against the Papacy, as later on he reached a point at which Zwingli and Erasmus were to him as heathen men and publicans. He had become convinced that the Papacy had become the tool of the Devil, that it was blasphemous . . . "possessed and oppressed by Satan, the damned seat of Anti-Christ."

The papacy which Luther attacked was not the Post-Tridentine papacy. On the other hand, he meant something more when he called it "Anti-Christ" than we mean by the adjective "Anti-Christian." Like many great Christians from St. Cyprian to Lord Shaftesbury, Luther believed himself to be living in the last age of the world, on the very edge of time. He believed that the papacy was toppling to its doom, and that this fate was a merited judgment upon a perversion of spiritual power to which there could be no parallel in the temporal realm, and for which only one category would serve, the Biblical category of Anti-Christ.

There are striking words in his "Of Good Works" (1520) which go to the root of this conviction. "There is not such great danger in the temporal power as in the spiritual, when it does wrong. For the temporal power can do no harm, since it has nothing to do with preaching and faith, and the first three commandments. But the spiritual power does harm not only when it does wrong, but also when it neglects its duty and busies itself with other things, even if they were better than the very best works of the temporal power." For Luther the blessed thing for men and institutions is that they should be where God intends them, doing what God has called them to do, and the cursed thing for men and institutions is when they run amok in God's ordered creation, going where God has not sent them, and occupied with other things than their divine vocation.

The papacy had become entangled in diplomatic, juridical, political, finan-cial pressure. Its crime was not that these things were necessarily bad in them-selves, but that for their sake the awful, supreme, God-given task of the pastoral care and the cure of souls had been neglected and forsaken. Two consequences had followed. In the first place, it had become a tyranny, like any other institu-tion which succumbs before the temptation of power. In that exposition of the Magnificat, which was interrupted by the famous journey to Worms in 1521, Luther had profoundly diagnosed this corrupting effect of power upon institu-tions. The tract embodies Luther's reflections upon the fate of great Empires in the Bible and in secular history. It is not empire, but the abuse of it which is wrong. "For while the earth remains authority, rule, power . . . must needs remain. But God will not suffer men to abuse them. He puts down one king-dom, and exalts another: increases one people and destroys another: as he did with Assyria, Babylon, Persia, Greece and Rome, though they thought they should sit in their seats forever."

But when empire is abused, then power becomes an incentive to arro-gance, and a terrible inflation begins. These institutions or individuals swell and stretch their authority with a curious bubble-like, balloon-like quality. Outwardly they seem omnipotent, and those who take them at their face value can be paralysed and brought into bondage to them. But in fact they are hollow shams, corroded from within, so that doom comes upon them, that swift col-lapse so often the fate of tyrants and empires. "When their bubble is full blown, and everyone supposes them to have won and overcome, and they feel them-selves safe and secure, then God pricks the bubble . . . and it is all over . . . therefore their prosperity has its day, disappears like a bubble, and is as if it had never been." It is interesting that Shakespeare turns to the same metaphor when he describes the fall of Wolsey:

I have ventured,
Like little wanton boys that swim on bladders,

This many summers in a sea of glory,
But far beyond my depth: my high-blown pride
At length broke under me.

Luther is fond of punning on the double meaning of the Latin word "Bulla," which means bubble, but also the papal bull.

It may well be that Luther's meditation on this quality of tyranny derives from his own experiences, 1517–20. The initial threat of excommunication, and the final promulgation of the papal bull had a deep significance for him. These were the challenge which focused all his doubts and fears, and evoked his courage at a time when he had no reason to anticipate anything but the dire fate prophesied for him by friends and foes. But, in fact, these papal sanctions led to the revelation of the weakness of the papal authority, a revelation of immense significance, from which all over Christendom (not forgetting the England of Henry VIII) men could draw their own conclusions. It was not that a man could defy the papacy and get away with it. After all, Wyclif had died in his bed, and throughout most of the Middle Ages there were parts of Europe where heresy flourished openly. But there was a new background which echoed and reverberated Luther's defiance, and a concentration of public attention on it which rallied great historical forces.

For centuries the papal sanctions had been as thunder and lightning, and there had been times and places when princes and peoples had cowered before them. Even now the sonorous phrases, the hallowed ritual, did not lack of menacing effect and struck deep into Luther's mind, always hypersensitive to words. The extraordinary agitation of his sermon, "On the Power of Excommunication" (1518), an utterance so outspoken that it was perhaps more effectual than the Ninety-five Theses in securing his impeachment, reveals the tension in his mind. It is noticeable that in the printed elaboration of this sermon he turns to the "bladder" motif. "They say . . . our Ban must be feared, right or wrong. With this saying they insolently comfort themselves, swell their chests, and puff themselves up like adders, and almost dare to defy heaven, and to threaten the whole world: with this bugaboo they have made a deep and mighty impression, imagining that there is more in these words than there really is. Therefore we would explain them more fully, and prick this bladder which with its three peas makes such a frightful noise." The publication of the Bull in 1520 evoked the same tension, and in his writings against it he affirms, "The Truth is asserting itself and will burst all the bladders of the Papists."

Only gradually did Luther and his friends realize how the world had changed since the days of Huss, that the Diet of Worms would not be as the Council of Constance, though the devout Charles V might be as anxious to dispose of heretics as any Emperor Sigismund. Now the accumulated weight of the past intervened, with paralysing effect. An enormous moral prestige had been frittered away, and the papal authority was revealed as a weak thing in comparison with the deep moving tide of anti-clericalism, nationalism and the fierce energies of a changing society.

But the papacy is for Luther not simply a tyranny, which can be described, as a liberal historian might describe it, in terms of the corrupting influence of power. Its tyranny is of a unique kind, for which there can only be one category, the demonic, Biblical category of Anti-Christ. By its entanglement with law and politics, the papacy has brought the souls of men and women into bondage, has confused disastrously the Law and Gospel, has become the antithesis of the Word of God which comes to free and liberate men's souls. Thus he cannot regard the papacy simply as a corrupt institution, as did the mediaeval moralists and the heretics. In Luther's later writings the papacy is included along with the Law, Sin and Death among the tyrants who beset the Christians, and is part of a view of salvation which demands an apocalyptic interpretation of history.

Two sets of Luther's writings are of special virulence: those against the Jews, the apostates of the Old Israel, and those against the Pope, the apostate of the New. Against what he considered the capital sin of blasphemy Luther turned all his invective. It is noticeable that like Ezekiel, he turned to an imagery of physical repulsion. Blasphemy and apostasy are not simply evil: they are filthy things, which must be described in language coarse enough and repulsive enough to nauseate the reader. That is not in any sense to excuse Luther's language, or to justify his reading of the papacy. But those sadly over-simplify who see in these tracts the vapourings of a dirty mind.

Luther's epitaph was premature. He had indeed plagued the papacy. He could say, "While I slept or drank Wittenberg beer with my Philip and my Amsdorf, the Word so greatly weakened the Papacy that never Prince or Emperor inflicted such damage on it." He did not kill the papacy, but in strange partnership with Ignatius Loyola, the Popes of the Counter-Reformation, the Society of Jesus, not to mention the Anabaptists, he had provoked a new historical pattern which made an end, for good and all, of the peculiar perversions of the later Middle Ages. But I think we can understand how it seemed to him that the papacy was doomed and dying, how it seemed to him the engine of Satin, the embodiment of Anti-Christ in what he believed to be the closing act of the human drama.

2

Luther Before the Controversy Over Indulgences

The Reuchlin case, to which Luther alludes in this letter, is one of considerable complexity, involving the place of Hebraic studies in Christian theology. This issue need not concern us here; what is important is Luther's attitude toward both Reuchlin's approach—which he was to imitate when he proposed the Ninety-five Theses for debate in 1517—and the importance of Scripture.

Martin Luther's Letter to George Spenlein

Wittenberg (January or February, 1514).

PEACE BE WITH YOU, Reverend Spenlein! Brother John Lang has just asked me what I think of the innocent and learned John Reuchlin and his prosecutors at Cologne, and whether he is in danger of heresy. You know that I greatly esteem and like the man, and perchance my judgment will be suspected, because, as I say, I am not free and neutral; nevertheless as you wish it I will give my opinion, namely that in all his writings there appears to be absolutely nothing dangerous.

I much wonder at the men of Cologne ferreting out such an obscure perplexity, worse tangled than the Gordian knot as they say, in a case as plain as day. Reuchlin himself has often protested his innocence, and solemnly asserts he is only proposing questions for debate, not laying down articles of faith, which alone, in my opinion, absolves him, so that had he the dregs of all known heresies in his memorial, I should believe him sound and pure of faith. For if such protests and expressions of opinion are not free from danger, we must needs fear that these inquisitors, who strain at gnats though they swallow

"Martin Luther's to George Spenlein," from *Luther's Correspondence and Other Contemporary Letters*, trans. by P. Smith (1913), Vol. I, pp. 28–29. Reprinted by permission of Fortress Press.

camels, should at their own pleasure pronounce the orthodox heretics, no matter how much the accused protested their innocence.

What shall I say? that they are trying to cast out Beelzebub but not by the finger of God. I often regret and deplore that we Christians have begun to be wise abroad and fools at home. A hundred times worse blasphemies than this exist in the very streets of Jerusalem, and the high places are filled with spiritual idols. We ought to show our excessive zeal in removing these offences which are our real, intestine enemies. Instead of which we abandon all that is really urgent and turn to foreign and external affairs, under the inspiration of the devil who intends that we should neglect our own business without helping that of others.

Pray can anything be imagined more foolish and imprudent than such zeal? Has unhappy Cologne no waste places nor turbulence in her own church, to which she could devote her knowledge, zeal and charity, that she must needs search out such cases as this in remote parts?

But what am I doing? My heart is fuller of these thoughts than my tongue can tell. I have come to the conclusion that the Jews will always curse and blaspheme God and his King Christ, as all the prophets have predicted. He who neither reads nor understands this, as yet knows no theology, in my opinion. And so I presume the men of Cologne cannot understand the Scripture, because it is necessary that such things take place to fulfill prophecy. If they are trying to stop the Jews blaspheming, they are working to prove the Bible and God liars.

But trust God to be true, even if a million men of Cologne sweat to make him false. Conversion of the Jews will be the work of God alone operating from within, and not of man working—or rather playing—from without. If these offences be taken away, worse will follow. For they are thus given over by the wrath of God to reprobation, that they may become incorrigible, as Ecclesiastes says, for every one who is incorrigible is rendered worse rather than better by correction.

Farewell in the Lord; pardon my words, and pray the Lord for my sinning soul.

Your brother,
MARTIN LUTHER

Spenlein was a fellow Augustinian brother to whom Luther could reveal his most intimate thoughts on theology and the relation of man to God. The date (April 8, 1516) is significant, a year and a half before Luther posted his Ninety-five Theses.

Martin Luther's Letter to George Spenlein

Wittenberg, April 8, 1516.

GRACE AND PEACE to you from God the Father and the Lord Jesus Christ.

Dear Brother George:

Now I would like to know whether your soul, tired of her own righteousness, would learn to breathe and confide in the righteousness of Christ. For in our age the temptation to presumption besets many, especially those who try to be just and good before all men, not knowing the righteousness of God, which is most bountifully and freely given us in Christ. Thus they long seek to do right by themselves, that they may have courage to stand before God as though fortified with their own virtues and merits, which is impossible. You yourself were of this opinion, or rather error, and so was I, who still fight against the error and have not yet conquered it.

Therefore, my sweet brother, learn Christ and him crucified; learn to pray to him despairing of yourself, saying: Thou, Lord Jesus, art my righteousness, but I am thy sin; thou has taken on thyself what thou wast not, and hast given to me what I was not. Beware of aspiring to such purity that you will not wish to seem to yourself, or to be, a sinner. For Christ only dwells in sinners. For that reason he descended from heaven, where he dwelt among the righteous, that he might dwell among sinners. Consider that kindness of his, and you will see his sweetest consolation. . . .

If you firmly believe this (and he is accursed who does not believe it) then take up your untaught and erring brothers, patiently uphold them, make their sins yours, and, if you have any goodness, let it be theirs. Thus the apostle teaches: Receive one another even as Christ received you, for the glory of God, and again: Have this mind in you which was also in Christ Jesus, who, when he was in the form of God, humbled himself, &c. Thus do you, if you seem pretty good to yourself, not count it as booty, as though it were yours alone, but humble yourself, forget what you are, and be as one of them that you may carry them. . . . Do this, my brother, and the Lord be with you. Farewell in the Lord.

Your brother,
MARTIN LUTHER, AUGUSTINIAN

"Martin Luther's Letter to George Spenlein," from *Luther's Correspondence and Other Contemporary Letters*, trans. by P. Smith (1913), Vol. I pp. 33–35, 98. Reprinted by permission of Fortress Press.

Luther, as a professor of theology, had been thoroughly grounded in the Scholastic philosophy of the Middle Ages. Of the three pillars upon which Scholastic theology rested—Scripture, the writings of the church fathers, and the philosophy of Aristotle—Scripture had become increasingly de-emphasized by Luther's time. It was to remind people that the central point of the scriptural message was not the achievement of philosophical distinctions but the salvation of man's soul that Luther composed his disputation against Scholastic theology in 1517.

Disputation Against Scholastic Theology
BY *Martin Luther*

IT IS THEREFORE TRUE THAT MAN, being a bad tree, can only will and do evil. [Cf. Matt. 7:17–18.]

It is false to state that man's inclination is free to choose between either of two opposites. Indeed, the inclination is not free, but captive. This is said in opposition to common opinion.

It is false to state that the will can by nature conform to correct precept. . . .

As a matter of fact, without the grace of God the will produces an act that is perverse and evil.

It does not, however, follow that the will is by nature evil, that is, essentially evil; as the Manichaeans maintain.

It is nevertheless innately and inevitably evil and corrupt.

* * *

No act is done according to nature that is not an act of concupiscence against God.

Every act of concupiscence against God is evil and a fornication of the spirit.

* * *

The best and infallible preparation for grace and the sole means of obtaining grace is the eternal election and predestination of God.

On the part of man, however, nothing precedes grace except ill will and even rebellion against grace.

* * *

In brief, man by nature has neither correct precept nor good will.

It is not true that an invincible ignorance excuses one completely (all scholastics notwithstanding);

Martin Luther, "Desputation Aganist Scholastic Theology," from *Luther's Works*, Helmut T. Lehman and Jaroslav Pelikan, eds., (1957), Vol. 31, pp. 9–12. Reprinted by permission of Fortress Press.

For ignorance of God and oneself and good works is by nature always invincible.

Nature, moreover, inwardly and necessarily glories and takes pride in every work which is apparently and outwardly good.

There is no moral virtue without either pride or sorrow, that is, without sin.

We are never lords of our actions, but servants. This in opposition to the philosophers.

We do not become righteous by doing righteous deeds but, having been made righteous, we do righteous deeds. This in opposition to the philosophers.

Virtually the entire *Ethics* of Aristotle is the worst enemy of grace. This in opposition to the scholastics.

It is an error to maintain that Aristotle's statement concerning happiness does not contradict Catholic doctrine. This in opposition to the doctrine on morals.

It is an error to say that no man can become a theologian without Aristotle. This in opposition to common opinion.

Indeed, no one can become a theologian unless he becomes one without Aristotle.

To state that a theologian who is not a logician is a monstrous heretic— this is a monstrous and heretical statement. This in opposition to common opinion.

In vain does one fashion a logic of faith, a substitution brought about without regard for limit and measure. This in opposition to the new dialecticians.

No syllogistic form is valid when aplied to divine terms. . .

Nevertheless it does not for that reason follow that the truth of the doctrine of the Trinity contradicts syllogistic forms. . . . .

If a syllogistic form of reasoning holds in divine matters, then the doctrine of the Trinity is demonstrable and not the object of faith.

Briefly, the whole Aristotle is to theology as darkness is to light. This in opposition to the scholastics.

3

Luther and the Break with Rome

The doctrine of indulgences had a long history before Luther posted his opposition to it on October 31, 1517. It was based on Matthew 16:18–19: "Thou art Peter, and upon this rock I will build my church; and the gates of hell shall not prevail against it. And I will give unto thee the keys of the kingdom of heaven: and whatsoever thou shalt bind on earth shall be bound in heaven: and whatsoever thou shalt loose on earth shall be loosed in heaven."

Thus Christ granted to St. Peter (and to his successors, the popes) the power to remit the penalties for sins. This power was eagerly exploited by the Renaissance popes, who found themselves in almost constant financial difficulties.

Luther's challenge to debate the doctrine of indulgences, however, was not restricted to a narrow issue. It ranged over many fundamental points of church doctrine. Did Luther really believe that such basic things could be reformed? Or, without really facing up to it, must he not have known that he was proposing nothing less than a revolution?

Ninety-five Theses

BY *Martin Luther*

OUT OF LOVE AND ZEAL for truth and the desire to bring it to light, the following theses will be publicly discussed at Wittenberg under the chairmanship of the reverend father Martin Luther, Master of Arts and Sacred Theology and regularly appointed Lecturer on these subjects at that place. He requests that those who cannot be present to debate orally with us will do so by letter.

In the Name of Our Lord Jesus Christ. Amen.

When our Lord and Master Jesus Christ said, "Repent" [Matt. 4:17], he willed the entire life of believers to be one of repentance.

This word cannot be understood as referring to the sacrament of penance, that is, confession and satisfaction, as administered by the clergy.

Yet it does not mean solely inner repentance; such inner repentance is worthless unless it produces various outward mortifications of the flesh.

Martin Luther, "Ninety-Five Theses," from *Luther's Works*, Vol. 31, pp. 25–29. Reprinted by permission.

The penalty of sin remains as long as the hatred of self, that is, true inner repentance, until our entrance into the kingdom of heaven.

The pope neither desires nor is able to remit any penalties except those imposed by his own authority or that of the canons.

The pope cannot remit any guilt, except by declaring and showing that it has been remitted by God; or, to be sure, by remitting guilt in cases reserved to his judgment. If his right to grant remission in these cases were disregarded, the guilt would certainly remain unforgiven.

* * *

The dying are freed by death from all penalties, are already dead as far as the canon laws are concerned, and have a right to be released from them.

Imperfect piety or love on the part of the dying person necessarily brings with it great fear; and the smaller the love, the greater the fear.

This fear or horror is sufficient in itself, to say nothing of other things, to constitute the penalty of purgatory, since it is very near the horror of despair.

Hell, purgatory, and heaven seem to differ the same as despair, fear, and assurance of salvation.

* * *

If remission of all penalties whatsoever could be granted to anyone at all, certainly it would be granted only to the most perfect, that is, to very few.

For this reason most people are necessarily deceived by that indiscriminate and high-sounding promise of release from penalty.

* * *

The pope does very well when he grants remission to souls in purgatory, not by the power of the keys, which he does not have, but by way of intercession for them.

They preach only human doctrines who say that as soon as the money clinks into the money chest, the soul flies out of purgatory.

It is certain that when money clinks in the money chest, greed and avarice can be increased; but when the church intercedes, the result is in the hands of God alone.

* * *

Any truly repentant Christian has a right to full remission of penalty and guilt, even without indulgence letters.

Any true Christian, whether living or dead, participates in all the blessings of Christ and the church; and this is granted him by God, even without indulgence letters.

* * *

If, therefore, indulgences were preached according to the spirit and intention of the pope, all these doubts would be readily resolved. Indeed, they would not exist.

Away then with all those prophets who say to the people of Christ, "Peace, peace," and there is no peace! [Jer. 6:14.]

Blessed be all those prophets who say to the people of Christ, "Cross, cross," and there is no cross!

Christians should be exhorted to be diligent in following Christ, their head, through penalties, death, and hell;

And thus be confident of entering into heaven through many tribulations rather than through the false security of peace [Acts 14:22].

The letter by the Apostle James discusses one of the fundamental issues raised by Luther, namely the role of good works in salvation. This also involved the doctrine of indulgences for an the money paid for an indulgence was a good work to be devoted to charity by the church.

The General Epistle of James
CHAPTER 1

The Sources of Temptation and Wisdom
JAMES, a servant of God and of the Lord Je'sus Christ, to the twelve tribes which are scattered abroad, greeting.

2 My brethren, count it all joy when ye fall into divers temptations.

3 Knowing *this,* that the trying of your faith worketh patience.

4 But let patience have *her* perfect work, that ye may be perfect and entire, wanting nothing.

5 If any of you lack wisdom, let him ask of God, that giveth to all *men* liberally, and upbraideth not; and it shall be given him.

6 But let him ask in faith, nothing wavering. For he that wavereth is like a wave of the sea driven with the wind and tossed.

7 For let not that man think that he shall receive any thing of the Lord.

8 A double minded man *is* unstable in all his ways.

9 Let the brother of low degree rejoice in that he is exalted:

10 But the rich, in that he is made low: because as the flower of the grass he shall pass away.

11 For the sun is no sooner risen with a burning heat, but it withereth the grass, and the flower thereof falleth, and the grace of the fashion of it perisheth: so also shall the rich man fade away in his ways.

The Holy Bible (King James Version), The World Publishing Co., Cleveland, Ohio & New York City, n. d., The New Testament, pp. 216–21.

12 Blessed *is* the man that endureth temptation: for when he is tired, he shall receive the crown of life, which the Lord hath promised to them that love him.

13 Let no man say when he is tempted, I am tempted of God: for God cannot be tempted with evil, neither tempteth he any man:

14 But every man is tempted, when he is drawn away of his own lust, and enticed.

15 Then when lust hath conceived, it bringeth forth sin: and sin, when it is finished, bringeth forth death.

16 Do not err, my beloved brethren.

17 Every good gift and every perfect gift is from above, and cometh down from the Father of lights, with whom is no variableness, neither shadow of turning.

18 Of his own will begat he us with the word of truth, that we should be a kind of firstfruits of his creatures.

19 Wherefore, my beloved brethren, let every man be swift to hear, slow to speak, slow to wrath:

20 For the wrath of man worketh not the righteousness of God.

21 Wherefore lay apart all filthiness and superfluity of naughtiness, and receive with meekness the engrafted word, which is able to save your souls.

22 But be ye doers of the word, and not hearers only, deceiving your own selves.

23 For if any be a hearer of the word, and not a doer, he is like unto a man beholding his natural face in a glass:

24 For he beholdeth himself, and goeth his way, and straightway forgetteth what manner of man he was.

25 But whoso looketh into the perfect law of liberty, and continueth *therein,* he being not a forgetful hearer, but a doer of the work, this man shall be blessed in his deed.

26 If any man among you seem to be religious, and bridleth not his tongue, but deceiveth his own heart, this man's religion *is* vain.

27 Pure religion and undefiled before God and the Father is this, To visit the fatherless and widows in their affliction, *and* to keep himself unspotted from the world.

CHAPTER 2

Solidarity of the Law, and the Barren Faith.
My brethren, have not the faith of our Lord Jē′sus Christ, *the Lord* of glory, with respect of persons.

2 For if there come unto your assembly a man with a gold ring, in goodly apparel, and there come in also a poor man in vile raiment;

3 And ye have respect to him that weareth the gay clothing, and say unto him, Sit thou here in a good place; and say to the poor, Stand thou there, or sit here under my footstool:

4 Are ye not then partial in yourselves, and are become judges of evil thoughts?

5 Hearken, my beloved brethren, Hath not God chosen the poor of this world rich in faith, and heirs of the kingdom which he hath promised to them that love him?

6 But ye have despised the poor. Do not rich men oppress you, and draw you before the judgment seats?

7 Do not they blaspheme that worthy name by the which ye are called?

8 If ye fulfil the royal law according to the scripture, Thou shalt love thy neighbour as thyself, ye do well:

9 But if ye have respect to persons, ye commit sin, and are convinced of the law as transgressors.

10 For whosoever shall keep the whole law, and yet offend in one *point,* he is guilty of all.

11 For he that said, Do not commit adultery, said also, Do not kill. Now if thou commit no adultery, yet if thou kill, thou art become a transgressor of the law.

12 So speak ye, and so do, as they that shall be judged by the law of liberty.

13 For he shall have judgment without mercy, that hath shewed no mercy; and mercy rejoiceth against judgment.

14 What *doth it* profit, my brethren, though a man say he hath faith, and have not works? can faith save him?

15 If a brother or sister be naked, and destitute of daily food,

16 And one of you say unto them, Depart in peace, be *ye* warmed and filled; notwithstanding ye give them not those things which are needful to the body; what *doth it* profit?

17 Even so faith, if it hath not works, is dead, being alone.

18 Yea, a man may say, Thou hast faith, and I have works: shew me thy faith without thy works, and I will shew thee my faith by my works.

19 Thou believest that there is one God; thou doest well: the devils also believe, and tremble.

20 But wilt thou know, O vain man, that faith without works is dead?

21 Was not Ā′bră-hăm our father justified by works, when he had offered Ī′saac his son upon the altar?

22 Seest thou how faith wrought with his works, and by works was faith made perfect?

23 And the scripture was fulfilled which saith, Ā′brăhăm believed God, and it was imputed unto him for righteousness: and he was called the Friend of God.

24 Ye see then how that by works a man is justified, and not by faith only.

25 Likewise also was not Rā′hăb the harlot justified by works, when she had received the messengers, and had sent *them* out another way?

26 For as the body without the spirit is dead, so faith without works is dead also.

That Luther's position as stated in the Ninety-five Theses involved more than technical and abstruse questions of theology can be seen in the reaction of the Holy Roman Emperor to Luther's proposed debate.

Maximilian's Letter to Leo X

Augsburg, August 5, 1518.

MOST BLESSED FATHER and most revered Lord! We have recently heard that a certain Augustinian Friar, Martin Luther by name, has published certain theses on indulgences to be discussed in the scholastic way, and that in these theses he has taught much on this subject and concerning the power of papal excommunication, part of which appears injurious and heretical, as has been noted by the Master of your sacred palace. This has displeased us the more because, as we are informed, the said friar obstinately adheres to his doctrine, and is said to have found several defenders of his errors among the great.

And as suspicious assertions and dangerous dogmas can be judged by no one better, more rightly and more truly than by your Holiness, who alone is able and ought to silence the authors of vain questions, sophisms and wordy quarrels, than which nothing more pestilent can happen to Christianity, for these men consider only how to magnify what they have taught, so your Holiness can maintain the sincere and solid doctrine approved by the consensus of the more learned opinion of the present age and of those who formerly died piously in Christ.

There is an ancient decree of the Pontifical College on the licensing of teachers, in which there is no provision whatever against sophistry, save in case the decretals are called in question, and whether it is right to teach that, the study of which has been disapproved by many and great authors.

Since, therefore, the authority of the Popes is disregarded, and doubtful, or rather erroneous opinions are alone received, it is bound to occur that those little fanciful and blind teachers should be led astray. And it is due to them that not only are many of the more solid doctors of the Church not only neglected, but even corrupted and mutilated.

We do not mention that these authors hatch many more heresies than were ever condemned. We do not mention that both Reuchlin's trial and the present most dangerous dispute about indulgences and papal censures have been brought forth by these pernicious authors. If the authority of your Holiness and of the most reverend fathers does not put an end to such doc-

"Maxmillion's Letter to Leo X.," from *Luther's Correspondence and Other Contemporary Letters,* Vol. I, p. 98. Reprinted by permission of Frotress Press.

trines, soon their authors will not only impose on the unlearned multitude, but will win the favor of princes, to their mutual destruction. If we shut our eyes and leave them the field open and free, it will happen, as they chiefly desire, that the whole world will be forced to look on their follies instead of on the best and most holy doctors.

Of our singular reverence for the Apostolic See, we have signified this to your Holiness, so that simple Christianity may not be injured and scandalized by these rash disputes and captious arguments. Whatever may be righteously decided upon in this our Empire, we will make all our subjects obey for the praise and honor of God Almighty and the salvation of Christians.

The reaction that followed the publication of his Ninety-five Theses forced Luther to define and defend his position in some detail. This he did in 1520 in the two treatises from which the following selections are taken. After their publication a reconciliation with Rome appeared doubtful.

FROM *Address to the Christian Nobility of the German Nation*

BY *Martin Luther*

GRACE AND POWER FROM God, Most Illustrious Majesty, and most gracious and dear Lords.

It is not out of sheer forwardness or rashness that I, a single, poor man, have undertaken to address your worships. The distress and oppression which weigh down all the Estates of Christendom, especially of Germany, and which move not me alone, but everyone to cry out time and again, and to pray for help, have forced me even now to cry aloud that God may inspire some one with His Spirit to lend this suffering nation a helping hand. Ofttimes the councils have made some pretense at reformation, but their attempts have been cleverly hindered by the guile of certain men and things have gone from bad to worse. I now intend, by the help of God, to throw some light upon the wiles and wickedness of these men, to the end that when they are known, they may not henceforth be so hurtful and so great a hindrance. God has given us a noble youth to be our head and thereby has awakened great hopes of good in many hearts, wherefore it is meet that we should do our part and profitably use this time of grace.

In this whole matter the first and most important thing is that we take earnest heed not to enter on it trusting in great might or in human reason, even though all power in the world were ours; for God cannot and will not suffer a good work to be begun with trust in our own power or reason. Such works He

Martin Luther, "Address to the Christian Nobility of the German Nation" from *Three Treatises* (1947), pp. 10–16, 20–25,. Reprinted by permission of Fortress Press.

crushes ruthlessly to earth, as it is written in the Thirty-third Psalm, "There is no king saved by the multitude of an host; a mighty man is not delivered by much strength." On this account, I fear, it came to pass of old that the good Emperors Frederick I and II and many other German emperors were shamefully oppressed and trodden under foot by the popes, although all the world feared them. It may be that they relied on their own might more than on God, and therefore they had to fall. In our own times, too, what was it that raised the bloodthirsty Julius II to such heights? Nothing else, I fear, except that France, the Germans and Venice relied upon themselves. The children of Benjamin slew 42,000 Israelites because the latter relied on their own strength.

That it may not so fare with us and our noble young Emperor Charles, we must be sure that in this matter we are dealing not with men, but with the princes of hell, who can fill the world with war and bloodshed, but whom war and bloodshed do not overcome. We must go at this work despairing of physical force and humbly trusting God; we must seek God's help with earnest prayer, and fix our minds on nothing else than the misery and distress of suffering Christendom, without regard to the deserts of evil men. Otherwise we may start the game with great prospect of success, but when we get well into it the evil spirits will stir up such confusion that the whole world will swim in blood, and yet nothing will come of it. Let us act wisely, therefore, and in the fear of God. The more force we use, the greater our disaster if we do not act humbly and in God's fear. The popes and the Romans have hitherto been able, by the devil's help, to set kings at odds with one another, and they may well be able to do it again, if we proceed by our own might and cunning, without God's help.

THE THREE WALLS OF THE ROMANISTS

The Romanists, with great adroitness, have built three walls about them, behind which they have hitherto defended themselves in such wise that no one has been able to reform them and this has been the cause of terrible corruption throughout all Christendom.

First, when pressed by the temporal power, they have made decrees and said that the temporal power has no jurisdiction over them, but, on the other hand, that the spiritual is above the temporal power. Second, when the attempt is made to reprove them out of the Scriptures, they raise the objection that the interpretation of the Scriptures belongs to no one except the pope. Third, if threatened with a council, they answer with the fable that no one can call a council but the pope.

In this wise they have slyly stolen from us our three rods, that they may go unpunished, and have ensconced themselves within the safe stronghold of these three walls, that they may practice all the knavery and wickedness which we now see. Even when they have been compelled to hold a council they have weakened its power in advance by previously binding the princes with an oath to let them remain as they are. Moreover, they have given the pope full authority over all the decisions of the council, so that it is all one whether there are many councils or no councils-except that they deceive us with puppet-shows and sham battles. So terribly do they fear for their skin in a really free council! And they have intimidated kings and princes by making them believe it would be an offense against God not to obey them in all these knavish, crafty deceptions.

Now God help us, and give us one of the trumpets with which the walls of Jericho were overthrown, that we may blow down these walls of straw and paper, and may set free the Christian rods of the punishment of sin, bringing to light the craft and deceit of the devil, to the end that through punishment we may reform ourselves, and once more attain God's favor.

Against the *first wall* we will direct our first attack.

It is pure invention that pope, bishops, priests and monks are to be called the "spiritual estate"; princes, lords, artisans and farmers the "temporal estate." That is indeed a fine bit of lying and hypocrisy. Yet no one should be frightened by it and for this reason—viz., that all Christians are truly of the "spiritual estate," and there is among them no difference at all but that of office, as Paul says in I Corinthians 12. We are all one body, yet every member has its own work, whereby it serves every other, all because we have one baptism, one Gospel, one faith, and are all alike Christians; for baptism, Gospel, and faith alone make us "spiritual" and a Christian people.

But that a pope or a bishop anoints, confers tonsures, ordains, consecrates, or prescribes dress unlike that of the laity—this may make hypocrites and graven images, but it never makes a Christian or "spiritual" man. Through baptism all of us are consecrated to the priesthood, as St. Peter says in I Peter 2, "Ye are a royal priesthood, a priestly kingdom," and the book of Revelation says, "Thou hast made us by thy blood to be priests and kings." For if we had no higher consecration than pope or bishop gives, the consecration by pope or bishop would never make a priest, nor might anyone either say mass or preach a sermon or give absolution. Therefore when the bishop consecrates it is the same thing as if he, in the place and stead of the whole congregation, all of whom have like power, were to take one out of their number and charge him to use this power for the others; just as though ten brothers, all king's sons and equal heirs, were to choose one of themselves to rule the inheritance for them all—they would all be kings and equal in power, though one of them would be charged with the duty of ruling.

To make it still clearer. If a little group of pious Christian laymen were taken captive and set down in a wilderness, and had among them no priest consecrated by a bishop, and if there in the wilderness they were to agree in choosing one of themselves, married or unmarried, and were to charge him with the office of baptizing, saying mass, absolving and preaching, such a man would be as truly a priest as though all bishops and popes had consecrated him. That is why in cases of necessity anyone can baptize and give absolution, which would be impossible unless we were all priests. This great grace and power of baptism and of the Christian Estate they have well-nigh destroyed and caused us to forget through the canon law. It was in the manner aforesaid that Christians in olden days chose from their number bishops and priests, who were afterwards confirmed by other bishops, without all the show which now obtains. It was thus that Sts. Augustine, Ambrose, and Cyprian became bishops.

Since, then, the temporal authorities are baptized with the same baptism and have the same faith and Gospel as we, we must grant that they are priests and bishops, and count their office one which has a proper and a useful place in the Christian community. For whoever comes out of the water of baptism can boast that he is already consecrated priest, bishop, and pope, though it is not seemly that everyone should exercise the office. Nay, just because we are all in like manner priests, no one must put himself forward and undertake, without our consent and election, to do what is in the power of all of us. For what is common to all, no one dare take upon himself without the will and the command of the community; and should it happen that one chosen for such an office were deposed for malfeasance, he would then be just what he was before he held office. Therefore a priest in Christendom is nothing else than an office-holder. While he is in office, he has precedence; when deposed, he is a peasant or a townsman like the rest. Beyond all doubt, then, a priest is no longer a priest when he is deposed. But now they have invented *characters indelebiles,* and prate that a deposed priest is nevertheless something different from a mere layman. They even dream that a priest can never become a layman, or be anything else than a priest. All this is mere talk and man-made law.

From all this it follows that there is really no difference between laymen and priests, princes and bishops, "spirituals" and "temporals," as they call them, except that of office and work, but not of "estate"; for they are all of the same estate—true priests, bishops and popes—though they are not all engaged in the same work, just as all priests and monks have not the same work.

*   *   *

The *second wall* is still more flimsy and worthless. They wish to be the only Masters of the Holy Scriptures even though in all their lives they learn nothing from them. They assume for themselves sole authority, and with insolent juggling of words they would persuade us that the pope, whether he be a bad man or a good man, cannot err in matters of faith, and yet they cannot prove a single letter of it. Hence it comes that so many heretical and unchristian, nay, even unnatural ordinances have a place in the canon law, of which, however, there is no present need to speak. For since they think that the Holy Spirit never leaves them, be they never so unlearned and wicked, they make bold to decree whatever they will. And if it were true, where would be the need or use of the Holy Scriptures? Let us burn them, and be satisfied with the unlearned lords at Rome, who are possessed of the Holy Spirit—although He can possess only pious hearts! Unless I had read it myself, I could not have believed that the devil would make such clumsy pretensions at Rome, and find a following.

But not to fight them with mere words, we will quote the Scriptures. St. Paul says in I Corinthians 14: "If to anyone something better is revealed, though he be sitting and listening to another in God's Word, then the first, who is speaking, shall hold his peace and give place." What would be the use of this commandment, if we were only to believe him who does the talking or who has the highest seat? Christ also says in John 6 that all Christians shall be taught of God. Thus it may well happen that the pope and his followers are wicked men, and no true Christians, not taught of God, not having true understanding. On the other hand, an ordinary man may have true understanding; why then should we not follow him? Has not the pope erred many times? Who would help Christendom when the pope errs, if we were not to believe another, who had the Scriptures on his side, more than the pope?

Therefore it is a wickedly invented fable, and they cannot produce a letter in defense of it, that the interpretation of Scripture or the confirmation of its interpretation belongs to the pope alone. They have themselves usurped this power; and although they allege that this power was given to Peter when the keys were given to him, it is plain enough that the keys were not given to Peter alone, but to the whole community. Moreover, the keys were not ordained for doctrine or government, but only for the binding and loosing of sin, and whatever further power of the key they arrogate to themselves is mere invention. But Christ's word to Peter, "I have prayed for thee that they faith fail not," cannot be applied to the pope, since the majority of the popes have been without faith, as they must themselves confess. Besides, it is not only for Peter that Christ prayed, but also for all Apostles and Christians, as he says in John 17: "Father, I pray for those whom thou hast given me, and not for these only, but for all who believe on me through their word." It not this clear enough?

Only think of it yourself! They must confess that there are pious Christians among us, who have the true faith, Spirit, understanding, word, and mind of Christ. Why, then, should we reject their word and understanding and follow the pope, who has neither faith nor Spirit? That would be to deny the whole faith and the Christian Church. Moreover, it is not the pope alone who is always in the right, if the article of the Creed is correct: "I believe in one holy Christian Church"; otherwise the prayer must run: "I believe in the pope at Rome," and so reduce the Christian Church to one man—which would be nothing else than a devilish and hellish error.

Besides, if we were all priests, as was said above, and all have one faith, one Gospel, one sacrament, why should we not also have the power to test and judge what is correct or incorrect in matters of faith? What becomes of the words of Paul in I Corinthians 2: "He that is spiritual judgeth all things, yet he himself is judged of no man," and II Corinthians 4: "We have all the same Spirit of faith"? Why, then, should not we perceive what squares with faith and what does not, as well as does an unbelieving pope?

All these and many other texts should make us bold and free, and we should not allow the Spirit of liberty, as Paul calls Him, to be frightened off by the fabrications of the popes, but we ought to go boldly forward to test all that they do or leave undone, according to our interpretation of the Scriptures, which rests on faith, and compel them to follow not their own interpretation, but the one that is better. In the olden days Abraham had to listen to his Sarah, although she was in more complete subjection to him than we are to anyone on earth. Balaam's ass, also, was wiser than the prophet himself. If God then spoke by an ass against a prophet, why should He not be able even now to speak by a righteous man against the pope? In like manner St. Paul rebukes St. Peter as a man in error. Therefore it behooves every Christian to espouse the cause of the faith, to understand and defend it, and to rebuke all errors.

The *third wall* falls of itself when the first two are down. For when the pope acts contrary to the Scriptures, it is our duty to stand by the Scriptures, to reprove him, and to constrain him, according to the word of Christ in Matthew 18: "If thy brother sin against thee, go and tell it him between thee and him alone; if he hear thee not, then take with thee one or two more; if he hear them not, tell it to the Church; if he hear not the Church, consider him a heathen." Here every member is commanded to care for every other. How much rather should we do this when the member that does evil is a ruling member, and by his evil-doing is the cause of much harm and offense to the rest! But if I am to accuse him before the Church, I must bring the Church together.

They have no basis in Scripture for their contention that it belongs to the pope alone to call a council or confirm its actions; for this is based merely upon their own laws, which are valid only in so far as they are not injurious to Christendom or contrary to the laws of God. When the pope deserves punishment, such laws go out of force, since it is injurious to Christendom not to punish him by means of a council.

Thus we read in Acts 15 that it was not St. Peter who called the Apostolic Council, but the Apostles and the elders. If, then, that right had belonged to St. Peter alone, the council would not have been a Christian council, but a heretical *conciliabulum*. Even the Council of Nicaea—the most famous of all—was neither called nor confirmed by the Bishop of Rome, but by the Emperor Constantine, and many other emperors after him did the like, yet these councils were the most Christian of all. But if the pope alone had the right to call councils, then all these councils must have been heretical. Moreover, if I consider the councils which the pope has created, I find that they have done nothing of special importance.

Therefore, when necessity demands, and the pope is an offense to Christendom, the first man who is able should, as a faithful member of the whole body, do what he can to bring about a truly free council. No one can do this so well as the temporal authorities, especially since now they also are fellow-Christians, fellow-priests, "fellow-spirituals," fellow-lords over all things, and whenever it is needful or profitable, they should give free course to the office and work in which God has put them above every man. Would it not be an unnatural thing, if a fire broke out in a city, and everybody were to stand by and let it burn on and on and consume everything that could burn, for the sole reason that nobody had the authority of the burgomaster, or because, perhaps, the fire broke out in the burgomaster's house? In such case is it not the duty of every citizen to arouse and call the rest? How much more should this be done in the spiritual city of Christ, if a fire of offense breaks out, whether in the papal government, or anywhere else? In the same way, if the enemy attacks a city, he who first rouses the others deserves honor and thanks; why then should he not deserve honor who makes known the presence of the enemy from hell, and awakens the Christians, and calls them together?

But all their boasts of an authority which dare not be opposed amount to nothing after all. No one in Christendom has authority to do injury, save for edification. Therefore, if the pope were to use his authority to prevent the calling of a free council, his bans thunderbolts, we should despise his conduct as that of a madman, and relying on God, hurl back the ban on him, and coerce him as best we could. For this presumptuous authority of his is nothing; he has no such authority, and he is quickly overthrown by a text of Scripture; for Paul says to the Corinthians, "God has given us authority not for the destruction, but for the edification of Christendom." Who is ready to overlap this text? It is only the power of the devil and of Antichrist which resists the things that serve for the edification of Christendom; it is, therefore, in no wise to be obeyed, but is to be opposed with life and goods and all our strength.

FROM *A Treatise on Christian Liberty*

BY *Martin Luther*

MANY HAVE THOUGHT CHRISTIAN faith to be an easy thing, and not a few have given it a place among the virtues. This they do because they have had no experience of it, and have never tasted what virtue there is in faith. For it is impossible that anyone should write well of it or well understand what is correctly written of it, unless he has at some time tasted the courage faith gives a man when trials oppress him. But he who has had even a faint taste of it can never write, speak, meditate, or hear enough concerning it. For it is a living fountain springing up into life everlasting, as Christ calls it in John 4. For my part, although I have no wealth of faith to boast of and know how scant my story is, yet I hope that, driven about by great and various temptations, I have attained to a little faith, and that I can speak of it, if not more elegantly, certainly more to the point, than those literalists and all too subtle disputants have hitherto done, who have not even understood what they have written.

Martin Luther, "A Treatise in Christian Liberty," form *Three Treatises*, pp. 251–255. Reprinted by permission of Fortress Press.

That I may make the way easier for the unlearned—for only such do I serve—I set down first these two propositions concerning the liberty and the bondage of the spirit:

A Christian man is a perfectly free lore of all, subject to none.
A Christian man is a perfectly dutiful servant of all, subject to all.

Although these two theses seem to contradict each other, yet, if they should be found to fit together they would serve our purpose beautifully. For they are both Paul's own, who says, in I Corinthians 9, "Whereas I was free, I made myself the servant of all," and Romans 8, "Owe no man anything, but to love one another." Now love by its very nature is ready to serve and to be subject to him who is loved. So Christ, although Lord of all, was made of a woman, made under the law, and hence was at the same time free and a servant, at the same time in the form of God and in the form of a servant.

Let us start, however, with something more remote from our subject, but more obvious. Man has a twofold nature, a spiritual and a bodily. According to the spiritual nature, which men call the soul, he is called a spiritual, or inner, or new man; according to the bodily nature, which men call the flesh, he is called a carnal, or outward, or old man, of whom the Apostle writes, in 2 Corinthians 4, "Though our outward man is corrupted, yet the inward man is renewed day by day." Because of this diversity of nature the Scriptures assert contradictory things of the same man, since these two men in the same man contradict each other, since the flesh lusteth against the spirit and the spirit against the flesh (Galatians 5).

First, let us contemplate the inward man, to see how a righteous, free, and truly Christian man, that is, a new spiritual, inward man, comes into being. It is evident that no external thing, whatsoever it be, has any influence whatever in producing Christian righteousness or liberty, nor in producing unrighteousness or bondage. A simple argument will furnish the proof. What can it profit the soul if the body fare well, be free and active, eat, drink, and do as it pleases? For in these things even the most godless slaves of all the vices fare well. On the other hand, how will ill health or imprisonment or hunger or thirst or any other external misfortune hurt the soul? With these things even the most godly men are afflicted, and those who because of a clear conscience are most free. None of these things touch either the liberty or the bondage of the soul. The soul receives no benefit if the body is adorned with the sacred robes of the priesthood, or dwells in sacred places, or is occupied with sacred duties, or prays, fasts, abstains from certain kinds of food, or does any work whatsoever that can be done by the body and in the body. The righteousness and the freedom of the soul demand something far different, since the things which have been mentioned could be done by any wicked man, and such works produce nothing but hypocrites. On the other hand, it will not hurt the soul if the body is clothed in secular dress, dwells in unconsecrated places, eats and drinks as others do, does not pray aloud, and neglects to do all the things mentioned above, which hypocrites can do.

Further, to put aside all manner of works, even contemplation, meditation, and all that the soul can do, avail nothing. One thing and one only is necessary for Christian life, righteousness, and liberty. That one thing is the most holy Word of God, the Gospel of Christ, as he says, John 11, "I am the resurrection and the life: he that believeth in me shall not die forever"; and John 8, "If the Son shall make you free, you shall be free indeed"; and Matthew 4, "Not in bread alone doth man live; but in every word that proceedeth from the mouth of God." Let us then consider it certain and conclusively established that the soul can do without all things except the Word of God, and that where this is not there is no help for the soul in anything else whatever. But if it has the Word it is rich and lacks nothing, since this Word is the Word of life, of truth, of light, of peace, of righteousness, of salvation, of joy, of liberty, of wisdom, of power, of grace, of glory, and of every blessing beyond our power to estimate. This is why the prophet in the entire One Hundred and Nineteenth Psalm, and in many other places of Scripture, with so many sighs yearns after the Word of God and applies so many names to it. On the other hand, there is no more terrible plague with which the wrath of God can smite men than a famine of the hearing of His Word, as He says in Amos, just as there is no greater mercy than when He sends forth His Word, as we read in Psalm 107, "He sent His word and healed them, and delivered them from their destructions." Nor was Christ sent into the world for any other ministry but that of the Word, and the whole spiritual estate, apostles, bishops and all the priests, has been called and instituted only for the ministry of the Word.

You ask, "What then is this Word of God, and how shall it be used, since there are so many words of God?" I answer, the Apostle explains that in Romans 1. The Word is the Gospel of God concerning His Son, who was made flesh, suffered, rose from the dead, and was glorified through the Spirit who sanctifies. For to preach Christ means to feed the soul, to make it righteous, to set it free, and to save it, if it believe the preaching. For faith alone is the saving and efficacious use of the Word of God, Romans 10, "If thou confess with thy mouth that Jesus is Lord, and believe with thy heart that God hath raised Him up from the dead, thou shalt be saved"; and again, "The end of the law is Christ, unto righteousness to everyone that believeth"; and, in Romans 1, "The just shall live by his faith." The Word of God cannot be received and cherished by any works whatever, but only by faith. Hence it is clear that, as the soul needs only the Word for its life and righteousness, so it is justified by faith alone and not by any works; for if it could be justified by anything else, it would not need the Word, and therefore it would not need faith. But this faith cannot at all exist in connection with works, that is to say, if you at the same time claim to be justified by works, whatever their character; for that would be to halt between two sides, to worship Baal and to kiss the hand, which, as Job says, is a very great iniquity. Therefore the moment you begin to believe, you learn that all things in you are altogether blameworthy, sinful, and damnable, as Romans 3 says, "For all have sinned and lack the glory of God"; and again,

"There is none just, there is none that doeth good, all have turned out of the way: they are become unprofitable together." When you have learned this, you will know that you need Christ, who suffered and rose again for you, that, believing in Him, you may through this faith become a new man, in that all your sins are forgiven, and you are justified by the merits of another, namely, of Christ alone.

Since, therefore, this faith can rule only in the inward man, as Romans 10 says, "With the heart we believe unto righteousness"; and since faith alone justifies, it is clear that the inward man cannot be justified, made free, and be saved by any outward work or dealing whatsoever, and that works, whatever their character, have nothing to do with this inward man. On the other hand, only ungodliness and unbelief of heart, and no outward work, make him guilty and a damnable servant of sin. Wherefore it ought to be the first concern of every Christian to lay aside all trust in works, and more and more to strengthen faith alone, and through faith to grow in the knowledge, not of works, but of Christ Jesus, who suffered and rose for him, as Peter teaches, in the last chapter of his first Epistle; since no other work makes a Christian. Thus when the Jews asked Christ, John 6, what they should do that they might work the works of God, He brushed aside the multitude of works in which He saw that they abounded, and enjoined upon them a single work, saying, "This is the work of God, that you believe in Him whom He hath sent. For him hath God the Father sealed."

Luther's declaration of theological independence was made at Worms in 1521. He had been summoned there to appear before the emperor and appropriate members of the church hierarchy to defend himself against the charge of heresy. The break with Rome now became irrevocable.

Speech Before Emperor Charles
BY *Martin Luther*

"MOST SERENE EMPEROR , most illustrious princes, most clement lords, obedient to the time set for me yesterday evening, I appear before you, beseeching you, by the mercy of God, that your most serene majesty and your most illustrious lordships may deign to listen graciously to this my cause—which is, as I hope, a cause of justice and of truth. If through my inexperience I have either not given the proper titles to some, or have offended in some manner against court customs and etiquette, I beseech you to kindly pardon me, as a man accustomed not to courts but to the cells of monks. I can bear no other witness about myself but that I have taught and written up to this time with simplicity of heart,

Martin Luther, "Speech Before Emperor Charles, from *Luther's Works*, Vol. 32, pp. 109–112. Reprinted by permission of Fortress Press.

as I had in view only the glory of God and the sound instruction of Christ's faithful.

"Most serene emperor, most illustrious princes, concerning those questions proposed to me yesterday on behalf of your serene majesty, whether I acknowledged as mine the books enumerated and published in my name and whether I wished to persevere in their defense or to retract them, I have given to the first question in my full and complete answer, in which I still persist and shall persist forever. These books are mine and they have been published in my name by me, unless in the meantime, either through the craft or the mistaken wisdom of my emulators, something in them has been changed or wrongly cut out. For plainly I cannot acknowledge anything except what is mine alone and what has been written by me alone, to the exclusion of all interpretations of anyone at all.

"In replying to the second question, I ask that your most serene majesty and your lordships may deign to note that my books are not all of the same kind.

"For there are some in which I have discussed religious faith and morals simply and evangelically, so that even my enemies themselves are compelled to admit that these are useful, harmless, and clearly worthy to be read by Christians. Even the bull, although harsh and cruel, admits that some of my books are inoffensive, and yet allows these also to be condemned with a judgment which is utterly monstrous. Thus, if I should begin to disavow them, I ask you, what would I be doing? Would not I, alone of all men, be condemning the very truth upon which friends and enemies equally agree, striving alone against the harmonious confession of all?

"Another group of my books attacks the papacy and the affairs of the papist as those who both by their doctrines and very wicked examples have laid waste the Christian world with evil that affects the spirit and the body. For no one can deny or conceal this fact, when the experience of all and the complaints of everyone witness that through the decrees of the pope and the doctrines of men the consciences of the faithful have been most miserably entangled, tortured, and torn to pieces. Also, property and possessions, especially in this illustrious nation of Germany, have been devoured by an unbelievable tyranny and are being devoured to this time without letup and by unworthy means. [Yet the papists] by their own decrees (as in dist. 9 and 25; ques. 1 and 2) warn that the papal laws and doctrines which are contrary to the gospel or the opinions of the fathers are to be regarded as erroneous and reprehensible. If, therefore, I should have retracted these writings, I should have done nothing other than to have added strength to this [papal] tyranny and I should have opened not only windows but doors to such great godlessness. It would rage farther and more freely than ever it has dared up to this time. Yes, from the proof of such a revocation on my part, their wholly lawless and unrestrained kingdom of wickedness would become still more intolerable for the already wretched people; and their rule would be further strengthened and established, especially if it should be reported that this evil deed had been done by me by virtue of the authority of your most serene majesty and of the whole Roman Empire. Good God! What a cover for wickedness and tyranny I should have then become.

"I have written a third sort of book against some private and (as they say) distinguished individuals—those, namely, who strive to preserve the Roman tyranny and to destroy the godliness taught by me. Against these I confess I have been more violent than my religion or profession demands. But then, I do not set myself up as a saint; neither am I disputing about my life, but about the teaching of Christ. It is not proper for me to retract these words, because by this retraction it would again happen that tyranny and godlessness would, with my patronage, rule and rage among the people of God more violently than ever before.

"However, because I am a man and not God, I am not able to shield my books with any other protection than that which my Lord Jesus Christ himself offered for his teaching. When questioned before Annas about his teaching and struck by a servant, he said: `If I have spoken wrongly, bear witness to the wrong' [John 18:19–23]. If the Lord himself, who knew that he could not err, did not refuse to hear testimony against his teaching, even from the lowliest servant, how much more ought I, who am the lowest scum and able to do nothing except err, desire and expect that somebody should want to offer testimony against my teaching! Therefore, I ask by the mercy of God, may your most serene majesty, most illustrious lordships, or anyone at all who is able, either high or low, bear witness, expose my errors, overthrowing them by the writings of the prophets and the evangelists. Once I have been taught I shall be quite ready to renounce every error, and I shall be the first to cast my books into the fire.

"From these remarks I think it is clear that I have sufficiently considered and weighted the hazards and dangers, as well as the excitement and dissensions aroused in the world as a result of any teachings, things about which I was gravely and forcefully warned yesterday. To see excitement and dissension arise because of the Word of God is to me clearly the most joyful aspect of all in these matters. For this is the way, the opportunity, and the result of the Word of God, just as He [Christ] said, `I have not come to bring peace, but a sword. For I have come to set a man against his father, etc.' [Matt. 10:34–35]. Therefore, we ought to think how marvelous and terrible is our God in his counsels, lest by chance what is attempted for settling strife grows rather into an intolerable deluge of evils, if we begin by condemning the Word of God. And concern must be shown lest the reign of this most noble youth, Prince Charles (in whom after God is our great hope), become unhappy and inauspicious. I could illustrate this with abundant examples from Scripture—like Pharaoh, the king of Babylon, and the kings of Israel who, when they endeavored to pacify and strengthen their kingdoms by the wisest counsels, most surely destroyed themselves. For it is He who takes the wise in their own craftiness [Job 5:13] and overturns mountains before they know it [Job 9:5]. Therefore we must fear God. I do not say these things because there is a need of either my teachings or my warnings for such leaders as you, but because I must not withhold the allegiance which I owe my Germany. With these words I commend myself to your most serene majesty and to your lordships, humbly asking that I not be allowed through the agitation of my enemies, without cause, to be made hateful to you. I have finished."

When I had finished, the speaker for the emperor said, as if in reproach, that I had not answered the question, that I ought not call into question those things which had been condemned and defined in councils; therefore what was sought from me was not a horned response, but a simple one, whether or not I wished to retract.

Here I answered:

"Since then your serene majesty and your lordships seek a simple answer, I will give it in this manner, neither horned nor toothed: Unless I am convinced by the testimony of the Scriptures or by clear reason (for I do not trust either in the pope or in councils alone, since it is well known that they have often erred and contradicted themselves), I am bound by the Scriptures I have quoted and my conscience is captive to the Word of God. I cannot and I will not retract anything, since it is neither safe nor right to go against conscience.

"I cannot do otherwise, here I stand, may God help me, Amen."

4

The Problem of Martin Luther

Gordon Rupp's discussion of the critical psychological period in Luther's life provides a historical counterweight to Erikson's reading of Luther's psychology.

FROM *The Righteousness of God*

BY *Gordon Rupp*

WE DO NOT KNOW WHEN Luther began to study the Bible, though he must have begun his novitiate by learning portions of scripture which he would recite in the divine offices. It is certain that it became for him an all-important and absorbing study, until his mind was impregnated with the words and themes of the Bible, and he could handle the Biblical material with a facility which was the envy of his enemies, and with a frequent penetration into the exactness of Biblical vocabulary which modern Biblical scholarship has confirmed. But if the Bible was soon to become paramount with him, beyond Augustine and the Fathers, it was initially the meeting-place of all his problems, concentrated in one word. Here is his testimony, in the autobiographical preface which he wrote, at the end of his life (1545), before the Wittenberg edition of his Latin works. After rehearsing his career down to the year 1519, he pauses, and there follows this statement:

"Meanwhile then, in that year (1519), I turned once more to interpret the Psalms, relying on the fact that I was the more expert after I had handled in the schools the letters of St. Paul to the Romans and the Galatians, and that which is to the Hebrews. Certainly I had been seized with a greater ardour to understand Paul in the Epistle to the Romans (captus fueram cognoscendi), but as Virgil says, it was not 'coldness of the blood' which held me up until now, but one word (unicum vocabulum), that is, chapter 1. 'The Justice of God is revealed in it' (Justitia Dei). For I hated this word (vocabulum istud) 'Justitia Dei' which by the use and consent of all doctors I was taught (usu et consuetu-

Gordon Rupp, *The Righteousness of God: Luther Studies* (1953), pp. 121–127. Reprinted by permission of Hodder & Stoughton Ltd., London.

dine omnium doctorum doctus eram) to understand philosophically of that formal or active justice (as they call it) with which God is just, and punishes unjust sinners.

"For, however irreproachably I lived as a monk, I felt myself in the presence of God (coram Deo) to be a sinner with a most unquiet conscience nor could I trust that I had pleased him with my satisfaction. I did not love, nay, rather I hated this just God who punished sinners and if not with 'open blasphemy' certainly with huge murmuring I was angry with God, saying: 'As though it really were not enough that miserable sinners should be eternally damned with original sin, and have all kinds of calamities laid upon them by the law of the ten commandments, God must go and add sorrow upon sorrow and even though the Gospel itself bring his Justice and his Wrath to bear!' I raged in this way with a fierce and disturbed conscience, and yet I knocked importunately at Paul in this place, thirsting most ardently to know what St. Paul meant.

"At last, God being merciful, as I meditated day and night on the connection of the words, namely, 'the Justice of God is revealed in it, as it is written, "the Just shall live by Faith," ' there I began to understand the Justice of God as that by which the just lives by the gift of God, namely by faith, and this sentence, 'the Justice of God is revealed in the gospel,' to be that passive justice, with which the merciful God justifies us, by faith, as it is written 'The just lives by faith.'

"This straightway made me feel as though reborn, and as though I had entered through open gates into paradise itself. From then on, the whole face of scripture appeared different. I ran through the scriptures then, as memory served, and found the same analogy in other words, as the Work of God (opus) that which God works in us, Power of God (virtus Dei) with which he makes us strong, wisdom of God (sapientia Dei) with which he makes us wise, fortitude of God, salvation of God, glory of God.

"And now, as much as I had hated this word 'Justice of God' before, so much the more sweetly I extolled this word to myself now, so that this place in Paul was to me as a real gate of paradise. Afterwards, I read Augustine, 'On the Spirit and the Letter,' where beyond hope I found that he also similarly interpreted the Justice of God: that with which God endues us, when he justifies us. And although this were said imperfectly, and he does not clearly explain about 'imputation,' yet it pleased me that he should teach a Justice of God with which we are justified.

"Armed with these cogitations I began to interpret the Psalms again."

The narrative is in the main straightforward, and most of it can be checked against quotations already cited in these pages. But there are certain problems which must be faced. In the first place, to what period of his career does Luther refer when he speaks of his discovery about "justitia Dei"? A superficial reading might suggest that he refers to the year (1519), when "armed with these cogitations" he began the second course of lectures on the Psalms.

But it can be demonstrated that Luther had developed his teaching on this subject in these terms, at least by the time of his lectures on Romans (1515–16).
The notion of a dislocation of the text, that refuge of desperate scholars, put
forward by A. V. Müller, has no documentary evidence to support it, and as
K. Holl pointed out, would make Luther commit grammatical solecisms. The
suggestion that Luther in his old age made a slip of memory and confused his
first and second lectures on the Psalms is hardly more convincing. Stracke has
made a careful examination of the whole of this autobiographical fragment,
and Luther emerges surprisingly well from the test. After thirty years, he is not
unnaturally a month or two out here and there, gets a detail misplaced now and
again, but when we remember that famous edition of the letters of Erasmus,
which had more than half the dates wrong, and some of them years out, we
can count this preface yet another disproof of the legend of Luther's anecdo-
tage.

In fact, as Stracke pointed out, Luther's use of the phrase "captus fueram"
makes perfectly tenable the interpretation that Luther has gone back in his
reflection to an earlier period. Before attempting to identify this date more precisely, we must discuss the authenticity of the statement as a whole.

To impugn this was intended as a crowning demonstration of Denifle's
"Luther and Luthertum." Denifle brought forward, in an appendix, a catena of
360 pages, giving the exposition of Rom. 1:17 by sixty doctors of the Western
Church, which, he said, demonstrated beyond a doubt "not a single writer from
the time of Ambrosiaster to the time of Luther understood this passage (Rom.
1:17) in the sense of the justice of God which punishes, of an angry God. All,
on the contrary, have understood it of the God who justifies, the justice
obtained by faith." Here, then, is the dilemma. Either Luther was a fool, or he
was a liar. Either he was a bragging incompetent, boasting in his senility, or he
was adding the last untruth to a long series of lying inventions. For Denifle, the
two conclusions were not mutually exclusive.

Denifle included in the demonstration passages from the recently rediscovered lectures of Luther on Romans. This was intended as proof that Luther
himself had used the supposed newly discovered meaning at a time anterior to
1515.

That part of his argument falls to the ground if we suppose Luther in fact
to have spoken of a period before 1515. We may, therefore, re-sharpen
Denifle's usefulness as an advocatus diaboli at this point, and present polemic
with an argument here which, as far as we know, has been little noticed. In the
Sentences of Peter Lombard, on which Luther lectured in 1509, and in the
famous Dist. XVII of Book 1, to which, as we have seen, Luther paid special
attention, there is imbedded a quotation from St. Augustine's "Spirit and Letter"
which gives the so-called "passive" interpretation of "Justitia Dei":

"The love of God is said to be shed abroad in our hearts, not because he
loves us, but because he makes us his lovers: just as the justice of God (Justitia
Dei) is that by which we are made just by his gift (justi ejus munere efficimur):

and 'salvation of the Lord' by which he saves us: and 'faith of Jesus Christ' that which makes us believers (fideles)."

The words are glossed by the Master of the Sentences, "And this is called the Justice of God, not with which he is just, but because with it he makes us just." At any rate, it seems clear that although in 1509 Luther had not read Augustine's "Spirit and the Letter," he had read an extract concerning this interpretation of the "Justitia Dei" during his study of Peter Lombard.

Denifle's *tour de force* was impressive, and like most polemics of this kind, got a good start of its pursuers. Among many replies the most notable were the essays by Karl Holl and Emmanuel Hirsch.

In the first place, it was pointed out that Luther in speaking of the "use and consent of all doctors" was referring not to Rom. 1:17, but to the "unicum vocabulum" of "Justitia Dei." The distinction is important, for, if granted, it means that the doctors in question were not the exegetes but the systematic theologians, and their views are to be found, not in the commentaries on the Epistles of St. Paul, but in those passages which concerned the conception of divine justice in Commentaries on the Sentences, and the like. Denifle's enormous collection of documents attested a wrong indictment.

Denifle, it is true, could appeal to a passage in Luther's lectures on Genesis, in which he referred to "hunc locum," i.e., Rom. 1:17, as the centre of his difficulties. But these lectures were not published until after Luther's death, and then only in the form in which they were reported. If there is glossing to be done, the 1545 fragment is primary, and Denifle, in his argument, showed some embarrassment at this point. As Holl was not slow to point out, nobody could say how many of Denifle's sixty doctors of the West could have been known, at first-or second-hand, to Luther, or whether he had studied the exegesis concerning Rom. 1:17. Holl proceeded thoroughly to analyse Denifle's authorities and disentangled two main streams of mediaeval exegesis, going back to Ambrosiaster and to Augustine. He showed that Ambrosiaster keeps in mind the problem of the Divine integrity, how the just God can receive sinners, and that while stressing the merciful promises of God, he keeps also the conception of retributive justice. Augustine is less concerned with justice as a divine property than with that bestowed righteousness, the work of grace infused within the human soul, on the ground of which sinners are made just in the presence of God. But Holl pointed out that neither of these expositions, nor all the permutations and combinations of them made thereafter, really met Luther's problem. "That from the time of St. Augustine the Western Church spoke of justifying grace, and that the later schoolmen strengthened this conception by their teaching about an 'habitus' is something known to all, and it is quite certain that Luther was not unaware of it." Emmanuel Hirsch dealt with a notable and fundamental omission from Denifle's authorities, namely, the Nominalist doctors whom Luther knew, and whom he had in mind when he said, "I was taught." He showed that Gabriel Biel, though admitting, even stressing the need for grace, and for the divine "Misericordia," normally preferred to reserve "Justitia" for the retributive justice of God which punishes sinners. This interpretation, which Hirsch based on Biel's commentary on the Sentences, seems confirmed by an examination of some scores of sermons by Biel upon the feasts of the Christian year.

Even more important than these arguments is the abundant testimony of Luther's good faith in this matter which is yielded by writings of other years, many of which, since they had never been published, might well have been completely forgotten by Luther. It is quite certain that, whatever the truth about his statement, it was no later invention, made up at the end of his life. Thus, in 1515:

"Wherefore, if I may speak personally, the word 'Justitia' so nauseated me to hear, that I would hardly have been sorry if somebody had made away with me."

In 1531 (published 1538):

"For thus the Holy Fathers who wrote about the Psalms were wont to expound the 'justus deus' as that in which he vindicates and punishes, not as that which justifies. So it happened to me as a young man, and even today I am as though terrified when I hear God called 'the just.'

"Justice, i.e. grace. This word I learned with much sweat. They used to expound justice as the truth of God which punishes the damned, mercy as that which saves believers. A dangerous opinion which arouses a secret hatred of the heart against God, so that it is terrified when he is so much as named. Justice is that which the Father does when he favours us, with which he justifies, or the gift with which he takes away our sin."

There are three passages in the Table Talk which must embody some core of truth. These suggest that Luther met his difficulty, before he came to the Epistle to the Romans, and in the interpretation of Psalm 31:1. "In justitia tua libera me." But the difficulty, "Justitia Dei" understood as retributive justice, is the same.

Two facts seem clear. First, that in his early career Luther found the conception of the "Justitia Dei" a stumbling block. Second, that this rock of offence did become for him the very corner-stone of his theology. The doctrine of Justification by Faith came to hold, in consequence, for him and for subsequent Protestant theology an altogether more important place than in the Catholic and mediaeval framework. In the sixteenth century men like Sir Thomas More and Stephen Gardiner found it hard to understand what all the Protestant fuss was about, and some striking parallels might be cited among modern Anglican scholars. Thus, even if we had not Luther's explicit testimony in the fragment under consideration, it would be necessary to invent something very like it to account for the remarkable and fundamental transformation in his thought. Denifle's demonstration may be held to have failed in so far as he attempted to show that Luther had wittingly perverted mediaeval teaching, and to have failed, too, in the more fundamental charge that Luther had in fact made no theological discoveries at all.

Thus in his narrative Luther explains simply and clearly why Rom. 1:17 was the climax of his difficulties. Luther already knew and believed that God condemned sinners through the Law. Now, in Rom. 1:17, he found that through the Gospel also was revealed the "Justitia Dei," which he took to mean the strict, retributive justice of God.

If the reader, having absorbed the academic roughage of this critical discussion, will turn back to the autobiographical fragment, he will find it tolerably plain. We can understand how, in the presence of a God who weighted everything against the sinner, Luther was filled with that "huge murmuring" which he elsewhere often and eloquently described, but which a man dared hardly admit to himself, so closely did it approximate to "open blasphemy." This inward ferment added to the outward practices of devotion and penitence an element of strain and unreality, and enforced hypocrisy which in turn aggravated the spiritual conflict. This was not merely an academic affair, though we need not shrink from admitting the theological enquiry of a theological professor into such a category. What he learned and taught about the Justice of God became for him a "carnifex theologistria," however, by reason of the unquiet conscience within. It was this fifth column, within the citadel of the soul, which betrayed him. Miegge's judgment is valid: "In the case of Luther, the religious crisis and the theological crisis are not to be separated."

Henri Daniel-Rops is a member of the French Academy and has written a number of popular works on the history of the church. The following selection gives a view of Luther's evolution toward heresy from a Catholic vantage point.

FROM *The Protestant Reformation*
BY *Henri Daniel-Rops*

THE AFFAIR OF THE INDULGENCES

IT WAS 31ST OCTOBER 1517. In the little town of Wittenberg, a part of the Elector of Saxony's possessions, the crush and animation were at their height. Every year the Feast of All Saints attracted countless pious folk, who came to see the precious relics which His Highness the Elector, Frederick the Wise, had collected at great expense, and which were brought out for the occasion from the storerooms of the Schlosskirche. There were plenty of them—several thousand—and they were of the most varied kind: they included not only the complete corpses of various saints, nails from the Passion and rods from the Flagellation, but part of the Child Jesus' swaddling-clothes and some wood from

Henri Daniel-Rops, *The Protestant Reformation,* trans. by Audrey Butler, pp. 9–26. Translation copyrighty 1961 by E. P. Dutton & Co., Inc., and reprinted by permission.

His crib, and even a few drops of His Blessed Mother's milk! Large numbers of most valuable indulgences were attached to the veneration of these distinguished treasures.

That same morning a manifesto, written in scholastic Latin and consisting of ninety-five theses, was found nailed to the door of the castle's chapel. Its author was an Augustinian monk who was extremely well known in the town, and he declared his intention of defending its contents against any opponent prepared to stand up and argue with him. In fact, the document concerned those very indulgences which honest folk were even then showing such eagerness to obtain by praying before the relics and slipping their guilders into the offertory boxes. The pilgrims assembled outside the church heard the more knowledgeable among them translate its words: "Those preaching in favour of indulgences err when they say such indulgences can deliver man and grant him salvation. The man who gives to the poor performs a better action than the one who buys indulgences." There were three hundred yet more bitter lines in this strain. And the worthy pilgrims wondered what could be the purpose of this monk in thus shaking one of the pillars of the Church.

For this was what indulgences seemed to have become: a pillar of the faith. Palz, Master of Erfurt, actually taught that they were "the modern way of preaching the Gospel." Was there anything intrinsically reprehensible about them? A rereading of the treatise which the learned Johann Pfeffer had devoted to the subject a quarter of a century earlier, in that same town of Wittenberg, or a glance at the sermons of the celebrated Johann Geiler of Kayserberg, makes the real meaning of indulgences clear beyond any shadow of a doubt. What the Church understood by *indulgence* was the total or partial remission of the penalties of sin—to which everyone was liable, either on earth or in Purgatory—after the Sacrament of Penance had afforded him absolution from his fault and remission of eternal punishment. But the state of grace was indispensable for the obtaining of such temporal remission; good works, in the shape of prayers, fasting, pilgrimages, visits to churches and almsgiving, were only an incidental, or, to put it another way, a contributory factor. Where there was no firm resolve or inward glow there was no remission. In strict doctrine an indulgence was certainly not an automatic means of gaining a cheap discharge from penalties that were justly deserved. In 1476 a bull of Sixtus IV had recognized that indulgences could be applied to the souls of the departed, whose sufferings in the next world would be alleviated thereby; and the declaration of this principle had contributed to the success of the jubilee of 1500.

It was not of recent origin. As early as the eleventh century crusaders had reaped the benefits of the plenary indulgence. Since then it had been awarded more generally and bestowed on less heroic occasions. It had had a number of happy results, and countless works of religious or social utility had been financed by the money collected in this way; churches too, hospitals, pawnshops, even dikes and bridges. Thanks to indulgences the Church in France had been materially restored on the morrow of the Hundred Years War. Nor had the spiritual results been insignificant: when proclaimed by special preachers the grant of an indulgence provided a spiritual jolt rather like the "missions" of modern times, and was the means of bringing numerous penitents to the confessional.

But it was not these excellent reasons alone which caused the institution to become so widespread, particularly from the fourteenth century onwards. For close on two centuries years of indulgence had been granted with unrestrained liberality in return for the briefest visit to a church, or the least meritorious of pilgrimages. In a period of twelve months the pious Elector Frederick the Wise laid up no fewer than 127,799 years, sufficient to empty a whole province of Purgatory and ensure himself more than one heaven. It is not difficult to imagine the kind of excesses which found their way into this practice, and they had already been condemned in 1312 by the decretal *Abusionibus.* Simony discovered some splendid material here and it is open to doubt whether preachers of indulgences, with their attendant collectors stationed at the foot of the pulpit, were primarily interested in saving souls or in collecting ducats. All too often the grant of an indulgence was part and parcel of some shady deal, and sometimes the right to collect for it was actually sold at auction. Pope Leo X himself once empowered the Fuggers, a celebrated firm of bankers at Augsburg, to preach an indulgence by way of security for a loan. The climate of the age was only too favourable to this type of proceedings. In 1514 when the Hohenzollern Albert of Brandenberg secured his election as Archbishop of Mainz, the heavy chancellery dues of 14,000 ducats, plus a "voluntary settlement" of a further 10,000 intended to ease the scruples of the Curia, were financed by the Fuggers, who were guaranteed in return one-third of the revenues from the great papal indulgence.

Misconduct such as this was not the only menace to the institution; the doctrine itself was affected by something even worse. Far too many preachers taught that an indulgence possessed a kind of magical quality, and that by spending money to obtain it men were taking out a mortgage on Heaven. One popular jingle ran:

Sobald das Geld im Kasten klingt
Die Seele aus dem Fegfeuer springt!

[As soon as the money in the collection box rings
The soul from out of hellfire springs—Ed.]

Moreover Germany was not the only country where such rubbish was taught. In 1482 the Sorbonne had condemned one preacher who recited it from the pulpit; at Besançon, in 1486, a certain Franciscan swore that provided a man wore the habit of his Order, St. Francis would come in person to collect him from Purgatory. Naturally enough there were lively reactions to these specious claims. As early as 1484 a priest named Lallier had publicly rejected the view that the Pope had the power to remit the pains of another world by means of indulgence, and despite objections from the theological faculty, the Bishop of Paris had absolved him. In 1498 the Franciscan Vitrier had been hauled before the Sorbonne for having declared that "money must not be given in order to obtain forgiveness." His disciple Erasmus had lately written: "Any trader, mercenary soldier or judge has but to put down his money, however nefariously acquired, and he imagines that he has purged the whole Lemean Marsh of his life." Views of this sort were taught in the University of Wittenberg, which considered itself the rival of Leipzig and Erfurt; and trenchancy of tone helped to further the renown of that centre, where, during 1516, statements such as the following had been heard: "It is an absurdity to preach that the souls in Purgatory are ransomed by indulgences."

In 1517 the most important indulgence preached in Germany was that which the popes had twice accorded to generous Christians donating money for the new basilica of St. Peter's: Julius II in 1506, in order that building might begin, and Leo X in 1514, to enable it to continue. It was the fruits of this indulgence which had been the object of that extraordinary share-out which we have already noticed on the occasion of the Mainz election. The archbishop had entrusted the task of preaching the indulgence to the Dominicans, and this had provoked a fraternal but somewhat bitter jealousy among the Augustinians.

At the head of these preachers was a certain Brother Tetzel, a burly, voluble fellow, who pleaded his case with extreme enthusiasm. He was a well-intentioned man, whose own moral conduct was perfectly honourable, and he did not deserve the calumnies with which his opponents were to befoul him; but his theology was highly questionable. His method of procedure merely increased the public belief that an indulgence was a mere financial transaction. He visited the whole area dependent on Mainz, and would arrive with a vast retinue, preceded by the bull which was carried on a velvet cushion embroidered with gold. The people who come out in procession to meet him, accompanied by the ringing of bells and waving of banners; and Tetzel would then mount the pulpit, or stand in the town square, offering "passports to cross the sea of wrath and go direct to Paradise." This was indeed a splendid opportunity to make certain of escaping the seven years of suffering—which, as all agreed, any forgiven sin still required in the Beyond—by obtaining the plenary indulgence accorded by a confessor of Tetzel's choice. Besides, here also was an opportunity to snatch some friend or loved one from the fires of Purgatory. Nor was the price extortionate. The penitent must go to confession, visit seven churches, recite five *Paters* and five *Aves,* and place an offering in the indulgence box. The offering demanded was a modest one, scaled to the resources of each individual believer: for the poorest a quarter of a florin was sufficient.

It was against such practices and such teaching that the manifesto nailed to the door of the Schlosskirche protested so strongly. Tetzel had not preached in Wittenberg, which was Saxon territory, but all recognized the target of this attack. It was all very well for the author to maintain discretion by advising his readers to receive "the Apostolic Commissioners with respect"; his theses rejected not only the Dominican's interpretation of the indulgence, but protested against the institution itself. He denounced its financial side. "The indulgences so extolled by preachers have only one merit, that of bringing in money." Or again: "Nowadays the Pope's money-bag is fatter than those of the richest capitalists; why does he not build this basilica with his own resources rather than with the offerings of the poor?" These somewhat clumsy arguments made a deep impression among the common people. He also criticized the theological basis of the institution, suggesting that the indulgences caused men to lose their sense of penitence. "True contrition gladly accepts the penalties and seeks them out; indulgence remits them and inspires us with aversion for them. When a Christian is truly penitent he has the right to plenary remission, even without an ecclesiastical indulgence. The grace of Jesus Christ remits the penalties of sin, not the Pope. Man can hope to receive this grace by experiencing a hatred of self and of his sin, and not by the accomplishment of a few acts or the sacrifice of a little money." Although, in so far as they contain authentic Catholic doctrine, these theses are acceptable in many respects, they deviate from orthodoxy to the extent that they deny the Pope's power to remit penalties and refer implicitly to a theory of grace according to which man's merits are almost worthless.

What motive had impelled the author of this document to defy the official teaching of the Church? Indignation against traffickers in sacred things? Undoubtedly. Hatred of the Pope and contempt for the simoniacal Roman Curia? No. There was something deeper, more decisive, and it is revealed in the very last sentence of his ninety-five theses. Tetzel was trying to persuade the faithful that salvation was easily effected through works; he was concealing from his hapless listeners that it is necessary "to enter Heaven by way of many tribulations," as the Acts of the Apostles makes quite clear; he was encouraging them to "rest in false security." Here was the crux of the matter. It was against "this appalling error" that the professor of Wittenberg entered the lists; and he entered them with all the violence of a man for whom this theological dispute represented a drama played out in his own life, and whom false security had brought very close indeed to a total despair and unbelief. His name was *Martin Luther*.

A BRILLIANT YOUNG MONK

At this date Luther was a tall, bony man with powerful expressive hands. They were never still: they were forever pointing at an enemy or punctuating an argument. Everything about him indicated a passion, unease and a latent violence that was always on the verge of erupting to produce total destruction. The eyes in the rough-hewn face, with its high cheekbones, square chin and lined cheeks, often sparkled with anger or intelligence, but no less frequently they allowed a glimpse of uncontrollable anguish. It is difficult to escape the fascination which this monk in his simple Augustinian robe exerted on everyone who saw him. In 1517 he was thirty-four years old.

What had Luther's life been like up to this time? What events and reasoning had led him to quarrel openly with official conformity and make the gesture which, by setting him in the forefront of world affairs, was to turn him into the living symbol of contradiction? The *Rückblick,* that rapid and superficial glance which he threw back to his youth in 1545, a year before his death, is hardly an adequate answer to these questions; when old people evoke their memories they very often amend both truth and falsehood.

As for the traditional account, still widely believed, it seems best to retain here only the bare outline of the facts and not their substance. The explanation of Martin Luther's attitude must not be sought in his allegedly unhappy childhood and adolescence, nor, as the psychoanalysts would have it, in the crisis of a monk beset by temptations of the flesh, nor even in the scandalized indignation he is supposed to have felt during a brief visit to Rome. It is to be found rather in an inner conflict, something like those experienced by St Paul, St Augustine and Pascal—a conflict through which Luther lived in keen spiritual agony and uncertainty, and from which he unhappily emerged along a path which was no longer that approved by Mother Church.

Martin Luther was born on 10th November 1483, at Eisleben in Saxony, the second of eight children. He was brought up at Mansfeld, where Hans, his father, had settled six months after the boy's birth. His early years were no more and no less happy than that of many sons of ordinary folk. The harsh realities of life brutalized this class of persons, and in a large family there was no time for emotional refinement. Hans was a devout, stern man whose morals were irreproachable but who was easily roused to anger. He was striving with all his might to rise from artisan to foreman, and finally to become a small foundry owner on his own account, and his sole desire was that his entire household should behave with absolute propriety. Hans Luther's hard-working wife, Margaret, *née* Ziegler, was a stolid Franconian. She did not find it difficult to share her husband's ideas and she directed her family with a firm hand which her children occasionally found too heavy.

Martin's parents sent him to school at Mansfeld when he was six years old. There he received the customary education of the age, consisting of the old *trivium* and the catechism, instilled by the pedagogic methods which were then in current use and in which the cane played a large part. When it became apparent that he was an exceptionally gifted boy, his father decided that he should continue his studies with a view to the law. He spent a year in the Cathedral School at Magdeburg, which was excellently conducted by the Brethren of the Common Life, and there he acquired an unhappily all too brief experience of genuine spirituality: it was most probably here that he made his first real contact with the Bible. Then, because his great-uncle was sacristan of St Nicholas's, Luther was drawn back to Eisenach, and there he developed his innate talents for music. Finally, at the age of eighteen, he entered Erfurt University—his father, who was now more comfortably off, was henceforth able to pay him an allowance—where he obtained an outstanding degree and greatly improved his powers of self-expression and reasoning. His teachers, Fathers Usingen and Palz, trained him in their methods, which were those of Ockhamist scholasticism. His fellow students regarded him as an honourable, devout, but merry companion. So far everything about Luther's life had been utterly normal and ordinary. Then, just as he had begun his legal studies, an unforeseen event completely altered his destiny.

On 2nd July 1505, while he was returning alone from Mansfeld to Erfurt, a thunderstorm of unusual violence suddenly broke upon him. The lightning flashed so close that he believed himself lost. In the midst of this danger he invoked St Anne according to custom, and promised: "If you come to my aid I will become a monk." This was perhaps a rash vow, but it was certainly not spontaneous. Various other incidents had preceded this spiritual decision. Legend has embroidered upon them so much that their detail has become obscured, but their meaning is abundantly plain. A serious illness during adolescence, the sudden death of a friend, a sword wound acquired in a student's duel and which had bled for a long time—all these had brought Luther face to face with the one great fact that youth tends to ignore—the fact of death. The episode of the thunderstorm set the seal on this revelation. Luther's impressionable nature and naturally vivid sensibility responded urgently to that mortal fear which the thunderclap had inspired in his soul. He remembered the good Brethren of the Common Life, the Anhalt ruler in the Franciscan habit whom he had known at Magdeburg, and dedicated young Carthusians he often saw at Erfurt. He thought of all the people he knew who seemed to have found peace of heart, and the answer to the most dreadful of all questions beneath the homespun of the monastic robe. This vow of his was undoubtedly forced from his soul by terror, but the terror was not caused by the thunderstorm alone. Neither his family nor his friends could prevent him from remaining faithful to his promise. Fifteen days after the incident on the Erfurt road he set off to knock on the door of the Augustinian monastery there.

In 1517 then, when he nailed his theses on the door of the Schlosskirche in Wittenberg, he was a monk—and a monk of some importance in his Order—and he was moreover a monk who had not the slightest desire to renounce his vows. "I have been a pious monk for twenty years," he was to say; "I have said a Mass every day; I have worn myself out in prayer and fasting." Witnesses have described him as a good monk, "certainly not without sin, but above serious reproach." In 1507 he was ordained priest. Luther mounted the altar steps for the first time with an ardour mingled with fear, as befitted one who was about to hold the living God in his own hands. Theology had made him increasingly fervent; Duns Scotus and St Thomas, Pierre d'Ailly and Gerson, William of Ockham and others in the same tradition, notable Gabriel Biel, had been the object of his voracious reading, together with the Bible, and St

Augustine, and all the mystics from St Bernard to Master Eckhart. In 1508, by order of Staupitz, the wise Vicar-General for Germany, who was much interested in this brilliant young man, Luther was transferred to Wittenberg, there to teach philosophy and acquire the title of Bachelor of Arts. He enjoyed a high reputation in his Order.

This was made very clear when, during the winter of 1510–11, he was chosen to go to Rome to submit the dispute between the Augustinians of the strict and conventual observances to the superiors of the Order. Legend has it that what he saw in the Eternal City so upset the young monk that he resolved to undertake the reform of the Church. This is a convenient story, but all the evidence is against it. Luther stayed in Rome for four short weeks, behaving like any other pious pilgrim. He was most anxious to see as many churches as possible, to win the indulgences attached to these visits and to climb the "scala sancta" on his knees; in short, as he himself recalled, he was filled with "holy madness." All he saw of the Papal Court were the usual glimpses that any humble visiting German cleric might expect to obtain. He obviously heard a good deal of gossip, but this did not have much immediate effect upon him. It was not until much later on, when he had been condemned by the Catholic Church, that he sought to justify his own attitude by reviving his memories of Rome. So great was men's ignorance in the capital of Christendom, he recalled, that he had been unable to find a confessor there; in St Sebastian's he had seen seven priests hurry through the Mass within the hour at a single altar; and he himself had witnessed the shameless behaviour of women in church. Perhaps; but he did not pronounce these strictures until twenty-five years after the incidents concerned—very much *a posteriori*.

On his return to Germany Luther was assigned to the Augustinian house in Wittenberg; in the following year, having been made doctor of theology, he was awarded the chair of Holy Scripture at the university. His lectures were outstandingly successful: he spoke on the Psalms and the Pauline Epistles; he was also a celebrated preacher, highly regarded by his congregations. Staupitz, his immediate superior, had a very exalted opinion of him; he made him "district vicar," in other words, provincial, with jurisdiction over eleven of the Order's houses; and he even went so far as to tell Luther: "God speaks through your mouth." Thus Luther's importance and prestige added considerable weight to his stand against the preachers of indulgences on All Saints' Eve 1517.

THE DRAMA OF A SOUL

In order to understand Luther's reasons for acting as he did we must penetrate his soul and reach into those dark and dangerous recesses of the mind wherein each man worthy of the name seeks, amid suffering and contradiction, to give a meaning to his own destiny. Because the light which he himself sheds upon the

drama of his youth was given long after the period concerned, a number of critics have treated it all as legend. The aged Luther, they allege, invented the
background of a Pascalian debate in order to provide his rebellion with fundamentally lofty and mystical origins. But an impartial study of the documents
covering the decisive years—for example, his commentary on the Epistle to
the Romans—is sufficient to convince the reader that their author could have
adopted certain attitudes at the end of a secret and painful effort to find the
answer to the gravest of man's problems. Anyone who refuses to believe that
Luther was fundamentally one of those individuals for whom life and belief are
serious matters is guilty of traducing historical and psychological truth. He was
essentially a protagonist in great spiritual battles. The Augustinian monk who
seemed to be making for himself such a brilliant career was inwardly tormented
by that peculiarly religious anxiety which it is easier to feel than to define.

Luther had entered the monastery hoping to discover peace of mind, but
he had not found it. He was very much a son of his age and of his native
land—of Germany, where man's struggle against the powers of darkness was
translated into a multitude of terrible or sublime legends; of Christianity at the
crossroads, where morbid sermons and dances of death caused the faithful to
be haunted with thoughts of their ultimate destiny. He had not been able to get
rid of these phantoms merely by donning the monastic robe. "I know a man,"
he wrote in 1518, "who declared he has experienced such mortal terror that no
words can describe it; he who has not suffered the like would never believe
him. But it is a fact that if anyone were obliged to endure for long, for half an
hour or even the tenth part of an hour, he would perish utterly, and his very
bones would be reduced to ashes." Luther was in the grip of terrible anguish,
and his friend Melanchthon relates that during the whole of his monastic life he
was never able to throw it off. "My heart bled when I said the Canon of the
Mass," Luther confesses, in reference to his years as a young priest. These are
words that no one can read without emotion.

Whence came this anguish? Certain authors have suggested that it was
caused by hereditary neurosis, but there is no real proof of this. It is perfectly
clear to anyone reading many of his own confessions that Luther was not so
much a sick man as one burdened with the tragic sense of sin in all its intensity.
But of what sin? It is futile to pretend to find an answer in the stirrings of his
flesh. Some have seen Luther as a monk in the grip of secret lusts, a familiar of
the *delectatio morosa*, unable to quell the beast within him and revolting against
the discipline of the Church in order to satisfy his craving. Yet if this were a
true picture, if he had acted on the strength of such contemptible motives, his
influence would scarcely have been so far-reaching, and would scarcely have
inflicted so much suffering upon the Church. Besides, Luther himself frequently
emphasized that the worst temptations were not carnal: "evil thoughts, hatred of
God, blasphemy, despair and unbelief—these are the main temptations." The
concupiscence which he had to conquer was not primarily that which draws
male to female, but an irresistible craving of both body and soul that urges man

to embrace all that is terrestrial and manifest—in a word, human—deflecting him from the invisible and divine.

In the monastery he had hoped to be delivered from these monsters. He was a mystical personality in many ways, and he dreamed of a warm, consoling presence which would shield him from evil and from himself, but he had discovered nothing in the monastic routine to provide such comfort. Was this because he lacked true humility, or because he had not the spirit of prayer? Only God, who has already judged the soul of Martin Luther, can supply an answer. One obstacle, however, certainly prevented him from running like the Prodigal Son to the arms of his Father, for whenever the least flicker of impurity, violence or doubt crossed his mind he believed himself damned. He tried prayer, asceticism, and even daily confession, but none of them could rid him of this ever-present obsession with hell, which continually threatened to overwhelm him. "I did penance," Luther says, "but despair did not leave me."

The obstacle which barred Luther's way to the path of peace and love was his concept of God. He insists that this was the picture shown him in religious life. "We paled at the mere mention of Christ's Name, for He was always depicted as a stern judge who was angry with us." Was it necessary to work oneself to death in prayer, fasting and mortifications from fear of a Master wielding the rod of chastisement, a Divine Executioner? What was the good of it all, since one could not even be sure of melting His wrath? "When will you do enough to obtain God's mercy?" he asked himself in anguish. In that age of misery the message of Christ's love seemed sterile; there remained only the atrocious doctrine of inevitable punishment meted out by an inexorable judge.

It has not been difficult for Catholic critics to show that this doctrine has never been that of Holy Church. In a book of no fewer than 378 pages, Father Denifle has conclusively demonstrated that the "justice of God" mentioned in a famous passage of the Epistle to the Romans (1:17), and which Luther took to be the supreme spiritual reality, was intended to signify something far more than *justitia puniens,* divine wrath punishing the sins of men; the words were used rather of sanctifying grace, of the omnipotent mercy lavished by God on all who believe in Him and submit to His ordinances. Luther's interpretation of the phrase reveals a surprising failure to understand the philosophy of such writers as St Augustine and St Bernard, with whose works he was undoubtedly well acquainted. To explain the spiritual drama of the young Augustinian monk, however, it is sufficient to acknowledge that he himself regarded this erroneous doctrine as valid, and as that which his own professors had taught him.

The fact may have been due to the imperfect theological training offered by the representations of decadent scholasticism who filled all the university chairs. Moreover the teaching then in fashion contained one feature calculated to impel a restless soul along the downward slope. To such a man as Luther, obsessed with the desire to appease his terrible God, and deriving not the slightest comfort from his prayers and mortifications, one system in particular provided a kind of answer: Ockhamist Nominalism, in which, as we have seen, he had been brought up. Luther had discovered from the writings of this school not only that man could overcome sin by will alone, but also that no human action became meritorious unless God acknowledged it and willed it to be so. But if man's will failed it had no means of recovery, for reason was unavailing and grace was not conceived as a supernatural principle raising man's spiritual forces to the level of Divine Justice. Thus nothing was left save a capricious God, granting or withholding His grace and forgiveness for motives that defied all the rules of logic. Before Him stood a defenceless man, inert and passive in relation to the work of salvation. Destiny appeared to be regulated by the cold mechanics of a despot in whose eyes nothing had any merit. Luther strove hard to find confirmation of these theories in certain passages of St Paul and St Augustine, for they corresponded all too well with his fundamental and powerful belief in the futility of all human effort. In several respects he remained an Ockhamist all his life; but he rejected the voluntarism taught by Ockham's disciples, he denied the human liberty which they recognized, and he gave it a ring of predestinationism which was absent from the master's philosophy. None of this did anything to grant him peace of mind.

But a number of more peaceful influences were at work. Luther had read all the mystics, especially the German writers of the late Middle Ages, notably Tauler. Here too he had found elements that tended to deny the importance of external works, to discard free will and to exalt the part played by faith in Christ the Redeemer. Man must lay himself open to God's action, submit to it and do nothing to resist it. This was one of the fundamental ideas of the *Theologica Germanica*. Furthermore Staupitz, anxious to heal this ravaged soul, had gone a long way in the same direction by showing Luther the gentleness of God's love and the need for supreme surrender to Providence. Neither the subtleties of the schools more ritual practices would give him the divine life to which he aspired, but only the impulse of a believing soul, and the piety which sprang from the most secret recesses of the heart. "True repentance begins with love of justice and of God." Once the young monk felt that part of his burden had been lifted, that he was on the way to a new enlightenment; and it seemed that ideas, arguments and biblical references poured in from all sides to confirm this doctrine "and dance a jig around it."

It was now that there happened the "discovery of mercy," a wholly spiritual event to which Luther's disciples afterwards traced the origins of the Reformation. The date and place of this occurrence are the subject of some dispute. He may have had his first glimpse of it in Rome, while making the pious pilgrimage on his knees up the "Scala sancta." It may, on the other hand, be necessary to advance the date to 1518 or 1519; if so he can have had only a kind of presentiment of his doctrine on the day when he nailed his theses to the chapel door. Its main features, however, are already apparent in the university lectures which he gave between 1514 and 1517. The most probable truth is that the "discovery" took place in his mind by gradual stages, before imposing itself on his soul with such force that all arguments and reservations became as nothing in the blinding clarity of what seemed to him to be incontrovertible evidence.

In the preface to the 1545 edition of his *Works* Luther describes in detail this "sudden illumination of the Holy Spirit." He was pondering once again the terrible seventeenth verse in the first chapter of the Epistle to the Romans when the true meaning—that is to say, the meaning he henceforth considered to be true—was revealed to him. "While I pursued my meditations day and night, examining the import of these words, 'The justice of God is revealed in the Gospel, as it is written, the just live by faith,' I began to understand that the justice of God signifies that justice whereby the just live through the gift of God, namely, through faith. Therefore the meaning of the sentence is as follows: "the Gospel shows us the justice of God, but it is a passive justice, through which, by means of faith, the God of mercy justifies us." To the young monk, tortured by fear and anguish, this was indeed a prodigious discovery! The hangman God, armed with His whip, faded away, yielding place to Him towards whom the soul could turn with perfect trust and confidence. . . .

At this juncture, as always happens where great minds are concerned, all kinds of reflections and arguments crystallized around this one apparently quite straightforward idea. It became the basis of a system. "System" is perhaps the wrong word here; for Luther there was no question of dry doctrine or paper thesis, but of a vital experience, the answer to all his own terrible problems. But he saw the answer so clearly that he was able to express it in the form of categorical principles. Man is a sinner, incapable of making himself just (i.e. righteous) and condemned to impotence by the enemy he bears within himself. Even though he conforms outwardly to the law, he remains in a state of sin. Even though he tries to behave righteously and hopes to acquire merit, he is unable to do so, for at the root of his very being there is a deadly germ. There must therefore be, and indeed there is, a justice exterior to man, which alone will save him. Through the grace of Jesus Christ all the soul's blemishes are, as it were, covered by a cloak of light. Thus the one means and only hope of salvation is to entrust oneself to Christ, as it were, to cling to Him. "The faith that justifies is that which seizes Jesus Christ." Compared with this saving reality all man's miserable efforts toward repentance and self-improvement were ridiculous and worthless. "The just live by faith."

It must be admitted that this view was perfectly adapted to set an anguished soul at rest. Where did it deviate from the orthodox? The Church teaches that God is "just" in the simplest sense of the term, that is to say, He distributes His graces to us all in an equitable manner, and not by virtue of a kind of incomprehensible caprice. She teaches that salvation and eternal bliss are earned in the world through positive effort and good works. She affirms the importance of sin, but she refuses to admit that man can do nothing to combat it. She does indeed proclaim the indispensability of the love of God and union with Christ, but she asserts that they demand from man a positive effort to acquire a supernatural resemblance. Faith is but the beginning of justification. It is completed by reception of the sacrament, in the act of contribution or the act of charity. Salvation demands much more than mere belief.

Luther, however, was so intoxicated by his discovery, so exalted by the joy of escaping at last from the vice which had held him in its grip, that he would consider no argument advanced against his theory. "I felt suddenly born anew," he said, "and it seemed that the doors of Paradise itself were flung wide open to me, and I entered in." He was saved! He knew he was a sinner, but Christ had taken upon His shoulders the sins of the whole world. It was distasteful to realize that all the pious exercises and all the theological reasoning to which he had recourse were of no effect, but in the blinding light of the Redemption all human things were nothing but dry dust. The dialectic of sin and grace contained the answer to everything. The exultant professor of Wittenberg announced his discovery at all his lectures even before his own philosophy had been fully defined, before it had been crowned with the maxim (not formulated until after 1518) that in order to be saved all that one needed was the inner certainty of one's own salvation. He set out his thesis at Easter 1517, at the beginning of a series of lectures on the Epistle to the Hebrews. "Man is incapable of obtaining relief from any sin by his own efforts alone. In the sight of God all human virtues are sin." He also directed one of his pupils, Bernhardi, to take "Grace and Free Will" as the subject of his thesis for the doctorate; it was to conform in all respects with the principles of Luther, who later admitted that at this period he felt "divinely possessed."

The preaching of indulgences offered Luther a splendid opportunity to make the truth blindingly clear to everyone. He was disgusted most of all by this computation of so-called merits shamefully acquired, in order to escape the just pains of the after-life. He himself enjoyed true security in that prodigious wager upon Christ which he intended to maintain from now onwards. The false, pitiable thing which these wretched folk believed that they acquired, by kneeling in front of some relics and throwing their money into a box provided by someone like Tetzel, was no true security. As for the authority of the Pope, who guaranteed the value of such practices, the Ockhamist in Luther recalled what the leaders of that school had to say, their reservations on papal infallibility and indeed on the function of the Papacy in general. He remembered Gabriel Biel's declaration that every Catholic was competent to reform the Church. He had, of course, not the slightest idea that in adopting positions of this kind he was going to set in motion the gravest crisis which Christianity had ever experienced. He was, in his own words, "a blind wretch who set off without knowing where he was going." Spiritual argument did not really interest him. He was fundamentally interested only in making the world hear and understand Heaven's response to his *De Profundis;* but "the voice of Germany, restless and secretly trembling with unrestrained passion," was not slow to answer his cry, and the drama of one soul unleashed a revolution.

The English Civil War— Religious Conflict? Class Struggle? Constitutional Dispute?

CONTENTS

QUESTIONS FOR STUDY

1   How do Haller, Hill, and Stone differ in their approaches to the causes of the civil war?
2   What evidence can you find in the documents of (a) economic, (b) religious, and (c) constitutional grievances against the crown?
3   How do the views on fundamental law expressed by James I, Coke, Pym, Rainborow, and Ireton resemble and differ from one another?
4   Why did civil war break out in 1642? Which side would you have fought on? (Consider the views of Macaulay and Wingfield-Stratford.)
5   How did Oliver Cromwell defend his actions? Do you find the defense convincing?
6   On the scaffold Charles I said he was "the martyr of the people." Was he?
7   All the legislation signed by Charles before the outbreak of war remained in force after the Restoration. How would this affect future relationships between king and Parliament?

At a time when nearly all the states of Europe were adopting absolutist forms of government, England embarked on a new experiment in parliamentary constitutionalism.

When Queen Elizabeth died in 1603, she was succeeded by her nephew James (1603–1625), who was already king of Scotland. Elizabeth had had a long and glorious reign, but she left many problems for her successor. James succeeded only in exacerbating them all. In the first place, there was a constitutional problem. Everyone agreed that the king had the right to direct affairs of state. But, during the sixteenth century, Parliament had grown into a powerful representative assembly whose members expected to be consulted on major issues of policy. There was no written constitution to define where the authority of the king ended and the rights of Parliament began. In King James's native Scotland no such parliamentary institution had grown up, and he never learned to understand the English Parliament or its traditions. Hence all through his reign the members of the House of Commons felt obliged to adopt an attitude of prickly self-assertiveness in upholding their rights and privileges (pp. 131–133).

Second, James inherited a serious religious problem. During Elizabeth's reign, most Englishmen had come to accept the Church of England as the true church for them and the queen as its legitimate head. There were some dissident Puritans and some Roman Catholics who refused to join the established church, but they formed only small and unpopular minorities. The real problem for James was the fact that within the Church of England itself a substantial faction of reformers wanted to modify the rites and doctrines of the church in a generally Puritan, Calvinistic way. They were opposed by a High Church party called "Arminians."[1] Puritans emphasized preaching and Bible reading in the conduct of worship; Arminians emphasized ritual and sacraments. Puritans emphasized the Calvinist doctrine of predestination; Arminians emphasized human free will. The more extreme Puritans favored a Presbyterian system of church government, and all tended to minimize the authority of bishops; Arminians regarded episcopacy as essential to a rightly ordered church. In general, Puritans regarded Arminian attitudes as dangerous survivals of Roman Catholicism; Arminians regarded Puritan attitudes as dangerous novelties that departed from the early tradition of the church. King James had no sympathy with Puritan ideas. But the Puritans became increasingly influential in the House of Commons during his reign. This contributed to the continuing ill feeling between king and Parliament.

Finally, Elizabeth bequeathed a major financial problem to her successor. The basic trouble here was inflation. Most of the king's rents and traditional revenues had remained fixed while the costs of government had been constantly rising. Here again James made things worse by maintaining an ostentatiously extravagant court. By this time it was plainly established that the king could not levy direct taxation without consent of Parliament. But the situation was not so

[1] From the name of a Dutch theologian, Arminius.

clear as regards indirect taxes, especially customs duties. Major disputes arose in 1610 and 1628 concerning the duties known as "impositions" and "tonnage and poundage" (pp. 132–133, 135).

Under James's son Charles I (1625–1649), events moved to a crisis. Charles was a devout Anglican by conviction, but his enemies denounced his "Arminianism" as a mere mask for popery (p. 136). From the beginning of Charles's reign the king's opponents, who were now able to command a majority in the House of Commons, deliberately tried to destroy the king's power to pursue his own chosen policies in religion and foreign affairs by withholding taxation. Their opposition culminated in 1629 in a scene of unprecedent turmoil in the House of Commons (pp. 137). After this Charles ruled for eleven years without summoning a Parliament. His financial expedients during this period led his adversaries to formulate explicitly the doctrine that taxes could be levied only through Parliament, even in times of national emergency (pp. 138–140).

In 1640 a rebellion in Scotland (once again a consequence of the king's Arminian religious policies) made it impossible for Charles to carry on his government without new parliamentary grants of taxation. The Parliament that he summoned quickly took advantage of the king's weakness by enacting a series of measures designed to curtail the powers of the crown for the future (pp. 142–144). Early in 1641 the House of Commons supported these measures by overwhelming majorities. But then a split developed between the moderates, who were content with the reforms they had enacted, and the radicals, who wanted to make the king a mere figurehead and seize real power for themselves. The subsequent deterioration of the situation, which ultimately led to open civil war, can be attributed either to Charles's clumsiness in handling his opponents (pp. 147–148) or to the implacability of the king's enemies (pp. 148–149). In the course of the war the parliamentary leaders quarreled with the army that they had created to fight the king, and the army established a military dictatorship under Oliver Cromwell (pp. 163–164). The eventual outcome of the whole conflict was the restoration of monarchy—but of a monarchy limited by the important constitutional legislation that had been enacted in 1641.

A peculiar feature of the twenty-year-long "crisis of the constitution" was that, even as the situation degenerated into a naked struggle for power, all parties in the conflict claimed to be defending lawful government and the ancient rights of Englishmen. Partly for this reason, perhaps, the English people succeeded in carrying through a constitutional revolution in the seventeenth century without abandoning any of their medieval institutions of government. King, Parliament, and courts of common law entered into new relationships with one another, and all survived into the modern world.

1

Backgrounds—Religious and Economic

William Haller saw the English revolution as essentially a struggle for religious liberty that broadened into a political conflict.

FROM *Tracts on Liberty in the Puritan Revolution*
BY *William Haller*

The pamphlets of the Puritan Revolution have seemed to later generations like relics of a universe

where eldest Night
And Chaos, ancestors of Nature, hold
Eternal anarchy, amidst the noise
Of endless wars,

and yet those "embryon atoms" there engaged in elemental strife were the seeds of the modern world. Controversy in that great crisis revolved in ever-widening circles about religious questions which came to be not solved, so much as dismissed, or, it would be better to say, transformed beyond recognition. To attempt reform of the English Church in the seventeenth century was to attempt the reorganization of society. Dissenting religious minorities, one after another, seized the occasion to demand toleration for themselves, but the argument for toleration supplied ideas, terms and images with which men of any or of no religion might also contend for freedom of thought, of expression, of government and of trade. The religious doctrine of a supernatural law, and of a divine right vested in established institutions, evoked the rational or quasi-rational doctrine of natural law and of natural rights vested in the individual. Thus emerged the modern doctrine of liberty. But the religious and theological terms

William Haller, *Traces on Liberty in the Puritan Revolution*, Vol. I (1934), pp. 1, 3–4. Reprinted by permission of Columbia University Press.

and images in which that doctrine took form did much to obscure the source from which it sprang. . . .

The reader of Puritan revolutionary literature must, of course, be prepared to cope with modes of thought and discussion which in such connection are now obsolete, even when they are not repellent. Broadly speaking, the men of the seventeenth century thought of organized society as a religious body or church, with which the state was intimately and peculiarly related. The advancement of printing and the spread of literacy made the Bible above all the book, and theology the science, of the people. Consequently, discontent first expressed itself in religious terms. Liberty was conceived first as religious, and as appertaining especially to the church, and the doctrine of liberty was expressed in Biblical images and theological formulas. Thus Lilburne stands up as a soldier of Christ, converted to the true faith. Lord Brooke and Milton present the theory of liberty in terms of a theory of church government. Parker derives the social contract from the fall of Adam. John Goodwin lays hold of the Protestant doctrine of conscience as the justification for rebellion, Walwyn upon that of universal grace as the basis for democratic equality. But as the Revolution moved on, both the objects of revolutionary effort and the terms of revolutionary thought and expression, became less peculiarly religious and theological. . . . Thus the argument that began as a plea for religious liberty and reform of church government rapidly extended itself to include civil liberty and political revolution, and the terms of the argument, so largely scriptural and theological to begin with, became increasingly rationalistic, naturalistic and secular.

Marxist theory holds that an era of feudalism must be followed by a "bourgeois revolution." Christopher Hill applied this conceptual model to seventeenth-century England. In his opinion, religious rhetoric cloaked economic impulses.

FROM *The English Revolution*
BY *Christopher Hill*

THE object of this essay is to suggest an interpretation of the events of the seventeenth century different from that which most of us were taught at school. To summarise it briefly, this interpretation is that the English Revolution of 1640–60 was a great social movement like the French Revolution of 1789. An old order that was essentially feudal was destroyed by violence, a new and capitalist social order created in its place. The Civil War was a class war, in which the despotism of Charles I was defended by the reactionary forces of the established Church and feudal landlords. Parliament beat the King because it could appeal to the enthusiastic support of the trading and industrial classes in town

Christopher Hill, *The English Revolution* (1949), pp. 9–17. Reprinted by permission of Lawrence and Wishart Ltd., London.

and countryside, to the yeomen and progressive gentry, and to wider masses of the population whenever they were able by free discussion to understand what the struggle was really about. The rest of this essay will try to prove and illustrate these generalisations.

The orthodox attitude to the seventeenth-century revolution is misleading because it does not try to penetrate below the surface, because it takes the actors in the revolution at their face value, and assumes that the best way to find out what people were fighting about is to consider what the reasons readers said they were fighting about. Thus we all know that during the seventeenth century England underwent a profound political revolution. Everyone has heard of Oliver Cromwell and his Roundheads, King Charles and his Cavaliers, and we all know that a King of England had his head cut off. But why did this happen? What was it all about? Has it any significance for us at the present day? . . .

The most usual explanation of the seventeenth-century revolution is one that was put forward by the leaders of the Parliament of 1640 themselves in their propaganda statements and appeals to the people. It has been repeated with additional detail and adornments by Whig and Liberal historians ever since. This explanation says that the Parliamentary armies were fighting for the liberty of the individual and his rights in law against a tyrannical Government. . . . All that is true. And although Parliament in the seventeenth century was even less genuinely representative of ordinary people than it is at the present day, still its victory was important as establishing a certain amount of self-government for the richer classes in society. But further questions are still unanswered. Why did the King become tyrannical? Why did the landed and commercial classes represented in Parliament have to fight for their liberties? . . .

Another school of historians—which we may call "Tory," as opposed to the Whigs—holds that the royal policy was not tyrannical at all, that Charles I, as he told the Court which sentenced him to death, spoke "not for my own right alone, as I am your King, but for the true liberty of all my subjects." . . . Their idea is that Charles I and his advisers were really trying to protect ordinary people from economic exploitation by a small class of capitalists on the make; and that the opposition which faced Charles was organised and worked up to serve their own purposes by those business men who identified their interests with the House of Commons in politics and Puritanism in religion.

Now, it is true that the English Revolution of 1640, like the French Revolution of 1789, was a struggle for political, economic and religious power, waged by the middle class, the bourgeoisie, which grew in wealth and strength as capitalism developed. But it is not true that as against them the royal Government stood for the interests of the common people. . . . It represented the bankrupt landowning nobles, and its policy was influenced by a Court clique of aristocratic commercial racketeers and their hangers-on, sucking the life-blood from the whole people by methods of economic exploitation which we shall be considering later on. The middle-class struggle to shake off the control of this group was not merely selfish; it fulfilled a progressive historical function. . . . It was necessary for the further development of capitalism that this choking parasitism should be ended by the smashing of the feudal state. And free capitalist development was of much more benefit to the masses of the population than the maintenance of an out-moded, unproductive and parasitic feudalism.

The new economic facts of the sixteenth and seventeenth centuries made the feudal economic and social system unworkable, and those of its defenders who looked regretfully back to the stability and relative security of the peasantry in the Middle Ages were quite unrealistic and in effect reactionary. . . .

A third and more familiar theory is emphasised by both sides: that the conflict was to decide which of two religions, Puritanism or Anglicanism, was to be dominant in England. Here, again, the effect of this explanation is to make us pity and misunderstand the men of the seventeenth century, and congratulate ourselves on being so much more sensible to-day; however much Anglicans and Nonconformists may dislike one another personally, we say, they no longer fight in the village street. But this is to miss the point. Certainly religious squabbles fill many pages of the pamphlet literature of the seventeenth century: both sides justified their attitude ultimately in religious terms, believed they were fighting God's battles. But "religion" covered something much wider than it does to-day. . . .

The Church, then, defended the existing order, and it was important for the Government to maintain its control over this publicity and propaganda agency. For the same reason, those who wanted to overthrow the feudal state had to attack and seize control of the Church. That is why political theories tended to get wrapped up in religious language. . . . But the fact that men spoke and wrote in religious language should not prevent us realising that there is a social content behind what are apparently purely theological ideas. Each class created and sought to impose the religious outlook best suited to its own needs and interests. But the real clash is between these class interests: behind the parson stood the squire.

A major difficulty in Marxist interpretations of the English civil war is that the leaders of parliamentary opposition to the king were landowning country gentry—themselves members of the "feudal" class. Most modern accounts seek to explain what motives—religious, economic, or political—led this class to divide into royalist and anti-royalist factions.

In the following readings Lawrence Stone criticizes Hill's views and then suggests some alternative approaches.

FROM *The Past and the Present*

BY *Lawrence Stone*

According to Dr Hill the core of the Puritan movement was "the industrious sort of people," namely the small merchants, the self-employed shopkeepers and manufacturers, and the artisans . . . The political theories of the Puritans demanded the transfer of power from nobles and priests to a wider oligarchy of properties householders, though certainly not to women, children, servants or the poor. Religious toleration was "the natural concomitant of the emerging economic order of free industrial production and internal free trade."

It is impossible to deny the force of this massively documented and powerfully argued thesis. One may seriously question, however, whether the picture it presents both of Puritanism and of the seventeenth century scene is more than one aspect of a more complex and ambiguous reality. In the first place, the Puritans are throughout assumed to consist of small merchants, manufacturers and artisans. But a crucial element in the Puritan movement was the landed nobility and gentry who provided the patronage, the protection, and the political weight. Second, it is assumed that in the seventeenth century English society ceased to be rural, agricultural, and feudal, and became urban, industrial, and capitalist. Now a good test of modernization is the degree of urbanization. But, even allowing for the explosion of London, the proportion of the population living in towns in 1650 was probably not so very much greater than in 1550; the major shift had to wait till the late eighteenth century. . . . Third, even if we admit, as we have to, that a middle-class culture and a middle-class ethic developed in the course of the seventeenth century, there is a lot of evidence to suggest that the dominant political and social interest and the dominant value-system remained that of the landed classes well into the nineteenth century. And fourth, this cool, rational analysis of Puritanism as a sensible preparation for the new capitalist environment fails to go to the heart of the matter. Where is the blind fanaticism that tormented witches and tore down maypoles, where the stunning pedantry of Bibliolatry, where the searing introspection?

Lawrence Stone, T*he Past and the Present* (1981), pp. 150–151, 186–188. Reprinted by permission of Routledge and Kegan Paul Ltd.

Some modern accounts of the origins of the civil war emphasize a long-standing tension between "Court" and "Country," that is, between a centralizing royal government and a class of independent-minded country gentry who were accustomed to controlling their own localities.

Lawrence Stone points out that more specific and concrete grievances were needed to cause an actual breakdown of government and that there was perhaps an element of "historical accident" in the way the different grievances coalesced into an opposition movement.

The Court/Country polarity in politics is, therefore, little more than a version of the normal state of tension that exists in all organized societies between the centralizing and the decentralizing forces: between Hamilton and Jefferson, for example. Since the polarity continued to play an important political role in England at least for another 75 years after 1640, it cannot be regarded as the exclusive cause for a breakdown of government. This is especially so, since when the crisis came, the lines of division did not run with mathematical precision between the country gentry and the courtiers. Many gentry saw the virtues of strong monarchical rule, and not a few courtiers fell off the bandwagon when it began to totter.

In order to provide a convincing interpretation of the collapse of the central government in 1640, the other forces have therefore to be brought into play. The collapse was caused not only by the undeniable ineptitude of Charles and his advisors, but also by certain specific historical trends. Unfortunately for the crown, the ideals, interests and programs of the Country found powerful allies in two other ideologies and three other interest groups: Puritanism and the Puritans, the Common Law and the common lawyers, and the new West Indies and American trade and the merchants engaged in it. The objectives of none of these groups were the same as those of the Country, but they became linked to them by a process of convergence which owes more to historical accident than inexorable necessity.

As for the Puritans, had Elizabeth, and later the Stuarts, continued to keep their options open, to admit aristocratic and bureaucratic Puritan sympathizers to the privy council and the court, to go easy on the persecution of Puritan dissidents, and to keep the official doctrinal policies and religious ceremonies on the fairly Low Church lines of early Elizabethan Anglicanism, the intimate association of Puritanism with the Country might not have taken place. There was a long prehistory of elective affinity between the two, but there is now little doubt that it was the policy of Archbishop Laud and his associates which finally drove them together in the 1630s. And even so, the gentry still remained solidly Erasmian and had no sympathy for the theocratic pretensions of the Puritan clergy.

As for the lawyers, they had their own grievances against the crown and the prerogative courts, notably their hostility to the interference of the church courts in common law business. They also strongly resented the competition to the common law courts by the overlapping jurisdictions of the two regional pre-rogative courts and the several courts at Westminster dealing with particular types of clients, like Admiralty or Exchequer or Wards, or certain types of offenses, like the Star Chamber. This intra-mural dispute between lawyers would not have taken on political overtones had the crown not come too readi-ly to the help of the embattled prerogative courts and of Chancery, and if its search for extra revenue had not led it to stretch its own prerogative powers too far. The result was the growth of a `Magna Carta' ideology among some lawyers about the nature of the constitutional balance, and an alliance of these common lawyers with the gentry and the Puritans. But once again the basic objectives of the lawyers were not those of the Country; the two were merely tactical allies in a joint battle for control over the central direction of the state.

The third group of allies of the country gentry in their political battle were drawn from the merchant community. They were men who lacked an ideology, but possessed a program. Most merchants stayed on the sidelines, part of the vast silent majority which stood idly by as the tides of war and revolution lapped over closer around their feet. Others were tied to the royal side by dependence on trade monopoly favors, or on support for the oligarchic control of their own communities in the face of rising pressure from below. But other important merchant elements can now be identified, men interested especially in the American trades, in New England colonization, and in breaking the monopoly of the East India and Levant Companies. They were new men in new fields of entrepreneurial endeavor who chafed at the political and economic stranglehold of the older established monopolistic oligarchies. They were usual-ly Puritan in their religious opinions, they wanted to reorient English foreign policy and commercial policy to a more aggressive and dynamic thrust toward the Americas, and they wanted to open up the Mediterranean and Indian trade to newcomers. These men were important members of the group of radicals who seized control of London at a critical moment in 1641, and so swung the power and influence of the City decisively on the side of parliament. The City was an ally without whom the Country would not have dared to launch a war on its own; indeed parliament would have been defeated in a matter of weeks without the support of London. On the other hand, these merchants had little except a leavening of Puritanism, an interest in North American colonization, and a common enemy to bind them to the grandees of the Country.

2

Law, Religion, and Taxation, 1604–1640

In the early years of the seventeenth century, although there were some complaints about royal policies, no one dreamed that they could lead on to a civil war. There was broad agreement about the general principles of government. The following reading describes some constitutional ideas that were generally accepted in England at the accession of James I (1603).

FROM *The Crisis of the Constitution*

BY *Margaret A. Judson*

[THE KING.] made the important appointments to the council, the law courts, other departments of government, and to the church. As head of the state he summoned and dismissed parliament at his pleasure. Prerogatives of this sort were seldom mentioned in the law courts and, when they were, never denied. They came to be discussed and eventually questioned and challenged in parliament, but they were not directly attacked there until 1641 and 1642. When at that time some members of parliament worked to take away these particular prerogatives from the king and transfer them to parliament, the civil war soon broke out.

In the years leading up to that war, men agreed also that the king as head of the state was peculiarly competent and solely responsible in certain realms they called government. Here he was most particularly the head of the state, practicing the art of governing, a craft possessed only by kings. Within these realms his authority was accepted as absolute. It must be, they believed, or else he would be unable to carry on his craft as a true artist. These realms of government within which his authority was accepted as absolute included foreign

Margaret A. Judson, *The Crisis of the Constitution* (1964), pp. 24–25, 34, 35, 44–46. Reprinted by permission of the author.

policy, questions of war and peace, the coinage, and the control of industries and supplies necessary for the defense of the realm.

*   *   *

As kings possessed prerogatives, so subjects possessed rights; and those rights, like the king's prerogative, were part of the law and basic in the constitution. Only when the nature and extent of the subjects' rights are understood is it possible to present some aspects of the prerogative and some controversies concerning it which have not been discussed up to this point.

The most important of these rights were property rights. To protect them was the principal concern of the common law. It was also the main concern of great English subjects in the sixteenth and early seventeenth centuries. . . . Among the many reasons why the growing absolutism of the Tudors did not become complete absolutism under the Stuarts is the fact that the medieval concept of the inviolability of a man's property did not disappear or become weaker in the sixteenth or early seventeenth centuries. Tudor and Stuart noblemen, gentry, and merchants who were acquiring property did not forget that although "government belonged to kings, property belonged to subjects."

*   *   *

Englishmen entered into the constitutional controversies of the seventeenth century with a profound belief in the importance of law. To them law was not primarily a decree enacted by a sovereign legislature to deal with a particular problem of the moment. Law was normally regarded as more than human, as the reflection of eternal principles of justice. When men considered it in relation to their own England, they looked upon it as a binding, cohesive force in their polity without which there would be no commonwealth, no government, no rights, and no justice.

They believed that the law was impartial—serving well both the king and the subject, enabling the king to fulfill his divine mission of governing with justice and protecting the subject in his God-given rights. To the seventeenth-century mind, rule by the king and rule by law were harmonious and not competing concepts. As the king's authority gave sanction to the law, so the law gave strength to the king's rule. To Yelverton, a faithful servant of Queen Elizabeth, "to live without government is hellish and to governe without lawes is brutish." James himself remarked that both king and parliament have a "union of interest" "in the lawes of the Kingdome, without which as the Prerogative cannot subsist, soe without that the Lawe cannot be maynteyned." . . .

It is well known that the parliamentarians based much of their case against the king on the law, but it is sometimes forgotten that the royalists also looked to the law to sanction the great authority they claimed for the monarch. In the long period of controversy between 1603 and 1642, both royalists and parliamentarians turned to the law to justify their actions, and both believed that the law was on their side. Even after the civil war broke out with its appeal to force, both groups strove to prove the legality of their actions, and only a few men admitted that the law had failed them.

James I, as king of Scotland, had propounded a theory of absolute monarchy before he inherited the crown of England. The following extract is from his True Law of Free Monarchies, *published in 1598.*

FROM *True Law of Free Monarchies*

BY *James I*

THE KINGS THEREAFTER in Scotland were before any estates or ranks of men within the same, before any Parliaments were holden or laws made; and by them was the land distributed (which at the first was wholly theirs), states erected and decerned [*decreed—Ed.*], and forms of government devised and established. And it follows of necessity that the Kings were the authors and makers of the laws and not the laws of the Kings. . . . And according to these fundamental laws already alleged, we daily see that in the Parliament (which is nothing else but the head court of the King and his vassals) the laws are but craved by his subjects, and only made by him at their rogation and with their advice. For albeit the King made daily statutes and ordinances, enjoining such pains thereto as he thinks meet, without any advice of Parliament or Estates, yet it lies in the power of no Parliament to make any kind of law or statute without his sceptre be to it for giving it the force of a law. . . . And as ye see it manifest that the King is overlord of the whole land, so is he master over every person that inhabiteth the same, having power over the life and death of every one of them. For although a just prince will not take the life of any of his subjects without a clear law, yet the same laws whereby he taketh them are made by himself or his predecessors, and so the power flows always from himself; as by daily experience we see good and just princes will from time to time make new laws and statutes, adjoining the penalties to the breakers thereof, which before the law was made had been no crime to the subject to have committed. Not that I deny the old definition of a King and of a law which makes the King to be a speaking law and the law a dumb King; for certainly a King that governs not by his law can neither be countable to God for his administration nor have a happy and established reign. For albeit it be true, that I have at length proved, that the King is above the law as both the author and giver of strength thereto, yet a good King will not only delight to rule his subjects by the law, but even will conform himself in his own actions thereunto; always keeping that ground, that the health of the commonwealth be his chief law.

James I, "True Law of Free Monarch," from J. R. Tanner, *Constitutional Documents of the Reign of James I. 1602–1625* (1930), pp. 9–10. Reprinted by permission of Cambridge University Press.

Edward Coke, chief justice of the Court of Common Pleas, opposed these views of James I with a doctrine of the supremacy of law. He informed James that a king of England could administer justice only through the anciently established courts.

Edward Coke on the Supremacy of Law

THEN THE KING SAID that he thought the law was founded upon reason, and that he and others had reason as well as the Judges. To which it was answered by me, that true it was that God had endowed his Majesty with excellent science and great endowments of nature, but his Majesty was not learned in the laws of his realm of England; and causes which concern the life or inheritance or goods or fortunes of his subjects are not to be decided by natural reason but by the artificial reason and judgment of law, which law is an act which requires long study and experience before that a man can attain to the cognizance of it; and that the law was the golden metwand and measure to try the causes of the subjects, and which protected his Majesty in safety and peace. With which the King was greatly offended, and said that then he should be under the law, which was treason to affirm, as he said; to which I said that Bracton saith, *quod Rex non debet esse sub homine sed sub Deo et lege [that the King ought not to be under man but under God and under the law—Ed.].*

In January 1604 James held a conference of clergy at Hampton Court to discuss the state of the Church of England. His attitude is conveyed in the following account.

FROM *The Sum and Substance of the Conference of Hampton Court*

BY *William Barlow*

SO ADMIRABLY, BOTH for understanding, speech, and judgment, did his Majesty handle all those points, sending us away not with contentment only but astonishment, and, which is pitiful you will say, with shame to us all that a King brought up among Puritans, not the learnedest men in the world, and schooled by them; swaying a kingdom full of business and troubles; naturally given to much exercise and repast; should in points of Divinity shew himself as expedite and perfect as the greatest scholars and most industrious students there present might not outstrip him. But this one thing I might not omit, that his Majesty should profess, howsoever he lived among Puritans and was kept for the most

"Edward Coke on the Supremacy of Law," from J. R. Tanner, *Constitutional Documents of the Reign of James I,* 1602–1625, p. 187. Reprinted by permission of Cambridge University Press.
William Barlow, The Sum and Substance of the Conference of Hampton Court (London:1625). Reprinted by permission.

part as a ward under them [*in Scotland*], yet since he was of the age of his son, ten years old, he ever disliked their opinions. As the Saviour of the world said, Though he lived among them he was not of them. . . .

Already by June 1604 the members of the House of Commons thought it necessary to explain to the new king that he had been "misinformed" about their rights and to warn him not to make laws concerning religion without the consent of Parliament.

The Rights of the House of Commons, 1604

[W]ITH ALL HUMBLE and due respect to your Majesty our Sovereign Lord and Head, against those misinformations we must truly avouch,

First, That our privileges and liberties are our right and due inheritance, no less than our very lands and goods.

Secondly, That they cannot be withheld from us, denied, or impaired, but with apparent wrong to the whole state of the realm. . . .

The rights of the liberties of the Commons of England consisteth chiefly in these three things:

First, That the shires, cities, and boroughs of England, by representation to be present, have free choice of such persons as they shall put in trust to represent them.

Secondly, That the persons chosen, during the time of the Parliament as also of their access and recess, be free from restraint, arrest, and imprisonment.

Thirdly, That in Parliament they may speak freely their consciences without check and controlment, doing the same with due reverence to the Sovereign Court of Parliament, that is, to your Majesty and both the Houses, who all in this case make but one politic body whereof your Highness is the Head. . . .

For matter of religion, it will appear by examination of truth and right that your Majesty should be misinformed if any man should deliver that the Kings of England have any absolute power in themselves either to alter Religion (which God defend should be in the power of any mortal man whatsoever), or to make any laws concerning the same otherwise than, as in temporal causes, by consent of Parliament. We have and shall at all times by our oaths acknowledge that your Majesty is Sovereign Lord and Supreme Governor in both. . . .

There remaineth, dread Sovereign, yet one part of our duty at this present which faithfulness of heart, not presumption, doth press. We stand not in place to speak or do things pleasing; our care is and must be to confirm the love and tie the hearts of your subjects the commons most firmly to your Majesty. Herein lieth the means of our well deserving of both. There was never prince entered

"The Rights of the House of Commons, 1604," from J. R. Tanner, *Constitutional Documents of the Reign of James, I, 1602–1625*, pp. 220–226, 230. Reprinted by permission Cambridge Univ. Press.

with greater love, with greater joy and applause of all his people. This love, this joy, let it flourish in their hears for ever. Let no suspicion have access to their fearful thoughts that their privileges, which they think by your Majesty should be protected, should now by sinister informations or counsel be violated or impaired, or that those which with dutiful respects to your Majesty speak freely for the right and good of their country shall be oppressed or disgraced. Let your Majesty be pleased to receive public information from our Commons in Parliament as to the civil estate and government, for private informations pass often by practice: the voice of the people, in the things of their knowledge, is said to be as the voice of God. And if your Majesty shall vouchsafe, at your best pleasure and leisure, to enter into your gracious consideration of our petition for the ease of these burdens under which your whole people have of long time mourned, hoping for relief by your Majesty, then may you be assured to be possessed of their hearts, and if of their hearts, of all they can do or have.

And so we Your Majesty's most humble and loyal subjects, whose ancestors have with great loyalty, readiness, and joyfulness served your famous progenitors, Kings and Queens of this Realm, shall with like loyalty and joy, both we and our posterity, serve your Majesty and your most royal issue for ever, with our lives, lands, and goods, and all other our abilities, and by all means endeavour to protect your Majesty honour, with all plenty, tranquillity, content, joy and felicity.

In 1610 the Commons complained about new customs duties (impositions) levied by the king.

Parliament and Taxation, 1610

THE POLICY AND CONSTITUTION of this your kingdom appropriates unto the Kings of this realm, with the assent of the Parliament, as well the sovereign power of making laws as that of taxing or imposing upon the subjects' goods or merchandises, wherein they have justly such a propriety as may not without their consent be altered or changed. This is the cause that the people of this kingdom, as they ever shewed themselves faithful and loving to their Kings and ready to aid them in all their just occasions with voluntary contributions, so have they been ever careful to preserve their own liberties and rights when anything hath been done to prejudice or impeach the same. . . . We therefore, your Majesty's most humble Commons assembled in Parliament, following the example of this worthy care of our ancestors and out of a duty to those for whom we serve, finding that your Majesty, without advice or consent of Parliament, hath lately in time of peace set both greater impositions and far

"Parliament and Taxation," from J. R. Tanner, Constitutional Documents of the Reign of James I, 1602–1625, p. 150. Reprinted by permission of Cambridge Univ. Press.

more in number than any your noble ancestors did ever in time of war, have with all humility presumed to present this most just and necessary petition unto your Majesty, That all impositions set without the assent of Parliament may be quite abolished and taken away.

A "protestation" of 1621 declared that any important matter of state was a fit subject for debate in Parliament.

Commons Protestation, 1621

THE COMMONS NOW ASSEMBLED in Parliament, being justly occasioned thereunto concerning sundry liberties, franchises, and privileges of Parliament, amongst others here mentioned, do make this Protestation following, That the liberties, franchises, privileges, and jurisdictions of Parliament are the ancient and undoubted birthright and inheritance of the subjects of England; and that the arduous and urgent affairs concerning the King, State, and defence of the realm and of the Church of England, and the maintenance and making of laws, and redress of mischiefs and grievances which daily happen within this realm, are proper subjects and matter of counsel and debate in Parliament; and that in the handling and proceeding of those businesses every member of the House of Parliament hath, and of right ought to have, freedom of speech to propound, treat, reason, and bring to conclusion the same.

The accession of Charles I did not improve matters. Charles was, by conviction, a High Church Anglican. Moreover, he had married a papist wife (Henrietta Maria of France) and was inclined to tolerate Catholicism. The leaders of the House of Commons were deeply suspicious of his religious policy, and they hated his chief minister, Buckingham. Accordingly, they withheld grants of taxation. Charles resorted to forced loans, which led to another constitutional protest, the Petition of Right of 1628.

Petition of Right, 1628

HUMBLY SHOW UNTO OUR Sovereign Lord the King, the Lords Spiritual and Temporal, and Commons in Parliament assembled, that whereas it is declared and enacted by a statute made in the time of the reign of King Edward the First, commonly called *Statutum de Tallagio non concedendo,* that no tallage or aid shall be laid or levied by the King or his heirs in this realm, without the good-

"Commons Protestation, 1621," from J. R. Tanner, *Constitutional Documents of the Reign of James I.,* 1602–1625, pp. 288–289. Reprinted by permission of Cambridge University Press.
"Petition of Right, 1628," from S. R. Gardiner ed., *The Constitutional Documents of Puritan Revolution,* 2d ed. (1899), pp. 66–69. Reprinted by permission of Oxford University Press, Oxford.

will and assent of the Archbishops, Bishops, Earls, Barons, Knights, Burgesses, and other the freemen of the commonalty of this realm: and by authority of Parliament holden in the five and twentieth year of the reign of King Edward the Third, it is declared and enacted, that from thenceforth no person shall be compelled to make any loans to the King against his will, because such loans were against reason and the franchise of the land; and by other laws of this realm it is provided, that none should be charged by any charge or imposition, called a Benevolence, or by such like charge, by which the statutes before-mentioned, and other the good laws and statutes of this realm, your subjects have inherited this freedom, that they should not be compelled to contribute to any tax, tallage, aid, or other like charge, not set by common consent in Parliament.

Yet nevertheless, of late divers commissions directed to sundry Commissioners in several counties with instructions have issued, by means whereof your people have been in divers places assembled, and required to lend certain sums of money unto your Majesty, and many of them upon their refusal so to do, have had an oath administered unto them, not warrantable by the laws or statutes of this realm, and have been constrained to become bound to make appearance and give attendance before your Privy Council, and in other places, and others of them have been therefore imprisoned, confined, and sundry other ways molested and disquieted. . . .

And where also by the statute called, "The Great Charter of the Liberties of England," it is declared and enacted, that no freeman may be taken or imprisoned or be disseised of his freeholds or liberties, or his free customs, or be outlawed or exiled; or in any manner destroyed, but by the lawful judgment of his peers, or by the law of the land.

They do therefore humbly pray your Most Excellent Majesty, that no man hereafter be compelled to make or yield any gift, loan, benevolence, tax, or such like charge, without common consent by Act of Parliament; and that none be called to make answer, or take such oath, or to give attendance, or be confined, or otherwise molested or disquieted concerning the same, or for refusal thereof; and that no freeman, in any such manner as is before-mentioned, be imprisoned or detained. . . .

Charles accepted the Petition of Right. But a new dispute broke out at once over a tax called "tonnage and poundage," not specifically mentioned in the petition. Charles protested that he had never intended to deprive himself of this source of revenue.

FROM *Charles I's Speech at the Prorogation of Parliament, 1628*

NOW SINCE I AM TRULY INFORMED , that a second Remonstrance is preparing for me to take away the profit of my Tonnage and Poundage, one of the chiefest maintenances of my Crown, by alleging I have given away my right thereto by my answer to your Petition.

This is so prejudicial unto me, that I am forced to end this Session some few hours before I meant, being not willing to receive any more Remonstrances, to which I must give a harsh answer. And since I see that even the House of Commons begins already to make false constructions of what I granted in your Petition, lest it be worse interpreted in the country, I will now make a declaration concerning the true intent thereof.

The profession of both Houses in the time of hammering this Petition, was no ways to trench upon my Prerogative, saying they had neither intention or power to hurt it. Therefore it must needs be conceived that I have granted no new, but only confirmed the ancient liberties of my subjects; yet to show the clearness of my intentions, that I neither repent, nor mean to recede from anything I have promised you, I do here declare myself, that those things which have been done, whereby many have had some cause to expect the liberties of the subjects to be trenched upon—which indeed was the first and true ground of the Petition—shall not hereafter be drawn into example for your prejudice, and from time to time; in the word of a king, ye shall not have the like cause to complain; but as for Tonnage and Poundage, it is a thing I cannot want, and was never intended by you to ask, nor meant by me—I am sure—to grant.

To conclude, I command you all that are here to take notice of what I have spoken at this time, to be the true intent and meaning of what I granted you in your Petition; but especially, you my Lords the Judges, for to you only under me belongs the interpretation of laws, for none of the Houses of Parliament, either joint or separate (what new doctrine soever may be raised), have any power either to make or declare a law without my consent.

P:564 "Charles I's Speech at the Protogation of Parliament, 1628," from S. R. Gardinet, ed., The Constitutional Documents of the Puritan Revolution, pp. 73–74. Reprinted by permission.

The Parliament of 1629 continued to attack the fiscal and religious policies of Charles's government. It ended in the unprecedented scene described next.

FROM *A True Relation of . . . Proceedings in Parliament*

THIS DAY, BEING THE LAST DAY of the Assembly, as soon as prayers were ended the Speaker went into the Chair, and delivered" the Kings command for the adjournment of the House until Tuesday sevennight following.

The House returned him answer, that it was not the office of the Speaker to deliver any such command unto them, but for the adjournment of the House it did properly belong unto themselves; and after they had settled some things they thought fit and convenient to be spoken of they would satisfy the King.

The Speaker told them that he had an express command from the King as soon as he had delivered his message to rise; and upon that he left the Chair, but was by force drawn to it again by Mr. Denzil Holles, son of the Earl of Clare, Mr. Valentine, and others. And Mr. Holles, notwithstanding the endeavour of Sir Thomas Edmondes, Sir Humphrey May, and other Privy Councellors to free the Speaker from the Chair, swore, Gods wounds, he should sit still until they pleased to rise. . . .

*   *   *

Sir John Eliot. God knows I now speak with all duty to the King. It is true the misfortunes we suffer are many, we know what discoveries have been made; how Arminianism creeps in and undermines us, and how Popery comes in upon us; they mask not in strange disguises, but expose themselves to the view of the world. In search whereof we have fixed our eyes not simply on the actors (the Jesuits and priests), but on their masters, they that are in authority, hence it comes we suffer. The fear of them makes these interruptions. You have seen prelates that are their abettors. That great Bishop of Winchester, we know what he hath done to favour them; this fear extends to some others that contract a fear of being discovered, and they draw from hence this jealousy. This is the Lord Treasurer, in whose person all evil is contracted. I find him acting and building on those grounds laid by his Master, the late great Duke of Buckingham, and his spirit is moving for these interruptions. And from this fear they break Parliaments lest Parliaments should break them. I find him the head of all that great party the Papists, and all Jesuits and priests derive from him their shelter and protection.

"A True Relation of . . . Proceedings on Parliament," from Wallace Notestein and Frances H. Relf, eds., *Commons Debates for 1629* (1921), pp. 101–106. Reprinted by permission.

In this great question of Tonnage and Poundage, the instruments moved at his command and pleasure; he dismays our merchants, and invites strangers to come in to drive our trade, and to serve their own ends.

The Remonstrance was put to the question, but the Speaker refused to do it; and said he was otherwise commanded from the King.

Whereupon Mr. Selden spake as followeth:

"You, Mr. Speaker, say you dare not put the question which we command you; if you will not put it we must sit still, and thus we shall never be able to do any thing; they that come after you may say they have the Kings command not to do it. We sit here by commandment of the King, under the great Seal of England; and for you, you are by his Majesty (sitting in his royal chair before both Houses) appointed our Speaker, and yet now you refuse to do us the office and service of a Speaker."

Then they required Mr. Holles to read certain Articles as the Protestations of the House, which were jointly, as they were read, allowed with a loud *Yea* by the House. The effect of which Articles are as followeth:

First, Whosoever shall bring in innovation in Religion, or by favour or countenance, seek to extend or introduce Popery or Arminianism or other opinions disagreeing from the true and orthodox Church, shall be reputed a capital enemy to this Kingdom and Commonwealth.

Secondly, Whosoever shall counsel or advise the taking and levying of the Subsidies of Tonnage and Poundage, not being granted by Parliament, or shall be an actor or instrument therein, shall be likewise reputed an innovator in the government, and a capital enemy to this Kingdom and Commonwealth.

Thirdly, If any merchant or person whatsoever shall voluntarily yield or pay the said subsidies of Tonnage and Poundage, not being granted by Parliament, he shall likewise be reputed a betrayer of the liberties of England and an enemy to the same.

These being read and allowed of, the House rose up after they had sitten down two hours.

The King hearing that the House continued to sit (notwithstanding his command for the adjourning thereof) sent a messenger for the serjeant with the mace, which being taken from the table there can be no further proceeding; but the serjeant was by the House stayed, and the key of the door taken from him, and given to a gentleman of the House to keep.

After this the King sent Maxwell [*the usher—Ed.*] with the black rod for the dissolution of Parliament, but being informed that neither he nor his message would be received by the House, the King grew into much rage and passion, and sent for the Captain of the Pensioners and Guard to force the door, but the rising of the House prevented the bloodshed that might have been spilt.

Notwithstanding the Parliament was but as yet adjourned until that day sevennight, being the tenth of March, yet were the principal gentlemen attached by pursuivants, some the next morning; and on Wednesday by order from the Council-board sent to sundry prisons.

After this incident Charles ruled for eleven years without Parliament. He obtained revenue by reviving ancient rights of the crown that had fallen into disuse. When such procedures were challenged in the courts, the judges upheld their legality. The following extracts deal with the "Case of Ship Money" (1637).

Case of Ship Money, 1637

AN ENQUIRY OF CHARLES TO THE JUDGES

WHEN THE GOOD AND SAFETY of the kingdom in general is concerned; and the whole kingdom in danger, whether may not the King, by writ under the Great Seal of England, command all the subjects of our kingdom at their charge to provide and furnish such a number of ships, with men, victuals, and munition, and for such time as we shall think fit for the defence and safeguard of the kingdom from such danger and peril, and by law compel the doing thereof, in case of refusal or refractoriness; and whether in such a case is not the King the sole judge both of the danger, and when and how the same is to be prevented and avoided?

REPLY OF THE JUDGES

May it please your Most Excellent Majesty:

We have, according to your Majesty's command, every man by himself, and all of us together, taken into serious consideration the case and question signed by your Majesty, and inclosed in your royal letter; and we are of opinion, that when the good and safety of the kingdom in general is concerned, and the kingdom in danger, your Majesty may, by writ under the Great Seal of England, command all your subjects of this your kingdom, at their charge to provide and furnish such a number of ships, with men, victuals, and munition, and for such time as your Majesty shall think fit for the defence and safeguard of this kingdom from such danger and peril: and that by law your Majesty may compel the doing thereof in case of refusal, or refractoriness: and we are also of opinion, that in such case your Majesty is the sole judge both of the danger, and when and how the same is to be prevented and avoided.

"Case of Ship Money, 1637," from S. R. Gardinet, ed., *The Constitutional Documents of the Puritan Revolution*, pp. 108–114. Reprinted by permission of Oxford University Press.

SPEECH OF OLIVER ST. JOHN AGAINST SHIP MONEY

My Lords, not to burn daylight longer, it must needs be granted that in this business of defence the *suprema potestas [supreme power—Ed.]* is inherent in His Majesty, as part of his crown and kingly dignity.

So that as the care and provision of the law of England extends in the first place to foreign defence, and secondly lays the burden upon all, and for ought I have to say against it, it maketh the quantity of each man's estate the rule whereby this burden is to be equally apportioned upon each person; so likewise hath it in the third place made His Majesty the sole judge of dangers from foreigners, and when and how the same are to be prevented, and to come nearer, hath given him power by writ under the Great Seal of England, to command the inhabitants of each county to provide shipping for the defence of the kingdom, and may by law compel the doing thereof.

So that, my Lords, as I still conceive the question will not be *de persona,* in whom the *suprema potestas* of giving the authorities or powers to the sheriff, which are mentioned in this writ, doth lie, for that it is in the King; but the question is only *de modo,* by what medium or method this supreme power, which is in His Majesty, doth infuse and let out itself into this particular. . . .

And as without the assistance of his Judges, who are his settled counsel at law, His Majesty applies not the law and justice in many cases until his subjects . . . neither can he out of Parliament alter the old laws, nor make new, or make any naturalizations or legitimations, nor do some other things; and yet is the Parliament His Majesty's Court too, as well as other his Courts of Justice.

That amongst the *ardua Regni negotia,* for which Parliaments are called, this of the defence is not only one of them, but even the chief, is cleared by this, that of all the rest none is named particularly in the summons, but only this; for all the summons to Parliament show the cause of the calling of them to be *pro quibusdam arduis negotiis nos et defensionem Regni nostri Angliae et Ecclesiae Anglicanae concernentibus [for certain arduous affairs concerning us and the defense of our realm of England and of the English church—Ed.].*

My Lords, the Parliament, as it is best qualified and fitted to make this supply for some of each rank, and that through all the parts of the kingdom being there met, His Majesty having declared the danger, they best knowing the estates of all men within the realm, are fittest, by comparing the danger and men's estates together, to proportion the aid accordingly.

And secondly, as they are fittest for the preservation of that fundamental propriety which the subject hath in his lands and goods, because each subject's vote is included in whatsoever is there done; so that it cannot be done otherwise, I shall endeavour to prove to your Lordships both by reason and authority.

My first reason is this, that the Parliament by the law is appointed as the ordinary means for supply upon extraordinary occasions, when the ordinary supplies will not do it. . . .

My second reason is taken from the actions of former Kings in this of the defence.

The aids demanded by them, and granted in Parliament, even for this purpose of the defence, and that in times of imminent danger, are so frequent, that I will spare the citing of any of them; it is rare in a subject, and more in a prince, to ask and take that of gift, which he may and ought to have of right, and that without so much as a *salvo,* or declaration of his right.

3

The Limitation of Royal Power, 1640–1641

In 1640 Charles was compelled by a rebellion in Scotland (touched off by religious grievances) to summon Parliament once more. The Parliament promptly passed a series of acts curtailing royal power for the future. Charles was obliged to consent to these measures because of the threat of an invasion from Scotland. The first act decreed that henceforth Parliament was to meet at least every three years.

Triennial Act

AN ACT FOR THE PREVENTING OF INCONVENIENCES HAPPENING BY THE LONG INTERMISSION OF PARLIAMENTS

I. WHEREAS BY THE LAWS AND STATUTES of this realm the Parliament ought to be holden at least once every year for the redress of grievances, but the appointment of the time and place for the holding thereof hath always belonged, as it ought, to His Majesty and his royal progenitors; and whereas it is by experience found that the not holding of Parliaments accordingly hath produced sundry and great mischiefs and inconveniences to the King's Majesty, the Church and Commonwealth; for the prevention of the like mischiefs and inconveniences in time to come.

II. Be it enacted by the King's Most Excellent Majesty, with the consent of the Lords spiritual and temporal, and the Commons in this present Parliament assembled, that the said laws and statutes be from henceforth duly kept and observed; . . . and be it enacted accordingly, by the authority of this present Parliament, that in case there be not a Parliament summoned by writ under the Great Seal of England, and assembled and held before the 10th of September, which shall be in the third year next after the last day of the last meeting and

"Triennial Act," from S. R. Gardiner, ed., *The Constitutional Documents of the Puritan Revolution*, pp. 144–145. Reprinted by permission of Oxford Uneversity Press.

sitting in this present Parliament, . . . and in all times hereafter, if there shall not be a Parliament assembled and held before the 10th day of September, which shall be in the third year next after the last day of the last meeting and sitting in Parliament . . . that then in every such case as aforesaid, the Parliament shall assemble and be held in the usual place at Westminster. *[The act required the Lord Chancellor to issue writs for a new Parliament whether the king commanded it or not—Ed.]*

The earl of Strafford, one of the king's leading ministers, was declared guilty of high treason by act of attainder and executed. The chief prosecutor, John Pym, was now emerging as the leader of the radical opposition to Charles in the House of Commons. Since Strafford's only real offense was that he had been an exceptionally loyal and energetic servant of the king, Pym found it necessary to propound a new theory of treason as an offense against fundamental law.

Attainder of Strafford

MY LORDS, MANY DAYS have been spent, in maintenance of the impeachment of the earl of Strafford, by the House of Commons, whereby he stands charged with high treason; and your lordships have heard his defence with patience and with as much favour as justice would allow. We have passed through our evidence, and the result of all this is, that it remains clearly proved, that the earl of Strafford hath endeavoured by his words, actions, and counsels, to subvert the fundamental laws of England and Ireland, and to introduce an arbitrary and tyrannical government. . . .

The law is that which puts a difference betwixt good and evil, betwixt just and unjust; if you take away the law, all things will fall into a confusion, every man will become a law to himself, which in the depraved condition of human nature, must needs produce many great enormities. Lust will become a law, and envy will become a law, covetousness and ambition will become laws; and what dictates, what decisions such laws will produce, may easily be discovered in the late government of Ireland. . . .

The law is the boundary, the measure, betwixt the King's prerogative and the people's liberty; whilst these move in their own orbs, they are a support and a security to one another; the prerogative a cover and defence to the liberty of the people, and the people by their liberty are enabled to be a foundation to the prerogative; but if these bounds be so removed, that they enter into contestation and conflict, one of these mischiefs must ensue: if the prerogative of the King overwhelm the liberty of the people, it will be turned to tyranny; if liberty undermine the prerogative, it will grow into anarchy.

"Attainder of Stafford," from S. Reed Brett, *John Pym* (1940), pp. 171–172. Reprinted by permission of John Murray (Publishers) Ltd.

Parliament also decreed that it could not be dissolved without its own consent.

Act Against Dissolving the Long Parliament Without Its Own Consent

WHEREAS GREAT SUMS OF MONEY must of necessity be speedily advanced and provided for the relief of His Majesty's army and people in the northern parts of this realm, and for preventing the imminent danger it is in, and for supply of other His Majesty's present and urgent occasions, which cannot be so timely effected as is requisite without credit for raising the said monies; which credit cannot be obtained until such obstacles be first removed as are occasioned by fears, jealousies and apprehensions of divers His Majesty's loyal subjects, that this present Parliament may be adjourned, prorogued, or dissolved, before justice shall be duly executed upon delinquents, public grievances redressed, a firm peace between the two nations of England and Scotland concluded, and before sufficient provision be made for the repayment of the said monies so to be raised; all which the Commons in this present Parliament assembled, having duly considered, do therefore most humbly beseech your Majesty that it may be declared and enacted.

And be it declared and enacted by the King, our Sovereign Lord, with the assent of the Lords and Commons in this present Parliament assembled, and by the authority of the same, that this present Parliament now assembled shall not be dissolved unless it be by Act of Parliament to be passed for that purpose.

Act Abolishing Star Chamber

WHEREAS BY THE GREAT CHARTER many times confirmed in Parliament, it is enacted that no freeman shall be taken or imprisoned, or disseized of his freehold or liberties or free customs, or be outlawed or exiled or otherwise destroyed, and that the King will not pass upon him or condemn him but by lawful judgment of his Peers or by the law of the land; and by another statute made in the fifth year of the reign of King Edward the Third, it is enacted that no man shall be attached by any accusation nor forejudged of life or limb, nor his lands, tenements, goods nor chattels seized into the King's hands against the form of the Great Charter and the law of the land . . . ; and forasmuch as all matters examinable or determinable before the Court commonly called the Star Chamber, may have their proper remedy and redress, and their due punishment

"Act Against Dissolving the Long Parliament Without Its Own Consent," from S. R. Gardiner, *The Constitutional Documents of the Puritan Revolution*, pp. 158–159. Reprinted by permission of Oxford University Press.
"Act Abolishing Star Chamber," from S. R. Gardiner, *The Constitutional Documents of the Puritan Revolution*, pp. 179–182 Reprinted by permission of Oxford University Press.

and correction by the common law of the land . . . be it ordained and enacted by the authority of this present Parliament, that the said Court commonly called the Star Chamber, and all jurisdiction, power and authority belonging unto or exercised in the same Court, or by any of the Judges, Officers or Ministers thereof be, from the first day of August in the year of our Lord God one thousand six hundred forty and one, clearly and absolutely dissolved, taken away, and determined.

The collection of ship money was declared illegal. Other acts of Parliament abolished all the other nonparliamentary procedures that Charles had used to raise taxes during the preceding ten years. It is important to note that all these acts of 1641 were signed by the king and so became valid statutes.

Act Abolishing Ship Money

[B]E IT THEREFORE DECLARED AND ENACTED by the king's most excellent majesty and the lords and the commons in this present parliament assembled, and by the authority of the same, that the said charge imposed upon the subject for the providing and furnishing of ships commonly called ship money . . . , and the said writs . . . and the said judgment given against the said John Hampden, were and are contrary to and against the laws and statutes of this realm, the right of property, the liberty of the subjects, former resolutions in parliament, and the Petition of Right made in the third year of the reign of his majesty that now is.

"Act Abolishing Ship Money," from *Sources of English Constitutional History,* translated and edited by Carl Stephenson and Frederick G. Marcham (1937), p. 482. Reprinted by permission of Harper & Row, Publishers, Inc.

4

The Outbreak of War

The acts of 1640 and 1641 that limited royal authority were passed by large majorities. But, toward the end of 1641, a division between the more moderate and the more radical members of the House of Commons became apparent in debates over the Grand Remonstrance. This document was a diffuse statement of all the grievances of the preceding twenty years. The petition accompanying the Grand Remonstrance, which follows, sets out its main points.

Petition Accompanying the Grand Remonstrance

MOST GRACIOUS SOVEREIGN,

Your Majesty's most humble and faithful subjects the Commons in this present Parliament assembled, do with much thankfulness and joy acknowledge the great mercy and favour of God, in giving your Majesty a safe and peaceable return out of Scotland into your kingdom of England, where the pressing dangers and distempers of the State have caused us with much earnestness to desire the comfort of your gracious presence, and likewise the unity and justice of your royal authority, to give more life and power to the dutiful and loyal counsels and endeavours of your Parliament, for the prevention of that eminent ruin and destruction wherein your kingdoms of England and Scotland are threatened. The duty which we owe to your Majesty and our country, cannot but make us very sensible and apprehensive, that the multiplicity, sharpness and malignity of those evils under which we have now many years suffered, are fomented and cherished by a corrupt and ill-affected party, who amongst other their mischievous devices for the alteration of religion and government, have sought by many false scandals and imputations, cunningly insinuated and dispersed amongst the people, to blemish and disgrace our proceedings in this Parliament. . . .

"Petition Accompanying the Grand Remonstrance," from S. R. Gardiner, ed., *The Constitutional Documents of the Puritan Revolution*, pp. 202–205. Reprinted by permission of Oxford University Press.

* * *

And because we have reason to believe that those malignant parties, whose proceedings evidently appear to be mainly for the advantage and increase of Popery, is composed, set up, and acted by the subtile practice of the Jesuits and other engineers and factors for Rome, and to the great danger of this kingdom, and most grievous affliction of your loyal subjects, have so far prevailed as to corrupt divers of your Bishops and others in prime places of the Church, and also to bring divers of these instruments to be of your Privy Council, and other employments of trust and nearness about your Majesty, the Prince, and the rest of your royal children.

And by this means have had such an operation in your counsel and the most important affairs and proceedings of your government, that a most dangerous division and chargeable preparation for war betwixt your kingdoms of England and Scotland, the increase of jealousies betwixt your Majesty and your most obedient subjects, the violent distraction and interruption of this Parliament, the insurrection of the Papists in your kingdom of Ireland, and bloody massacre of your people, have been not only endeavoured and attempted, but in a great measure compassed and effected.

* * *

We, your most humble and obedient subjects, do with all faithfulness and humility beseech your Majesty:

1. That you will be graciously pleased to concur with the humble desires of your people in a parliamentary way, for the preserving the peace and safety of the kingdom from the malicious designs of the Popish party:

For depriving the Bishops of their votes in Parliament, and abridging their immoderate power usurped over the Clergy, and other your good subjects, which they have perniciously abused to the hazard of religion, and great prejudice and oppression to the laws of the kingdom, and just liberty of your people:

For the taking away such oppressions in religion, Church government and discipline, as have been brought in and fomented by them:

For uniting all such your loyal subjects together as join in the same fundamental truths against the Papists, by removing some oppressions and unnecessary ceremonies by which divers weak consciences have been scrupled, and seem to be divided from the rest, and for the due execution of those good laws which have been made for securing the liberty of your subjects.

2. That your Majesty will likewise be pleased to remove from your council all such as persist to favour and promote any of those pressures and corruptions wherewith your people have been grieved, and that for the future your Majesty will vouchsafe to employ such persons in your great and public affairs, and to take such to be near you in places of trust, as your Parliament may have cause to confide in; that in your princely goodness to your people you will

reject and refuse all mediation and solicitation to the contrary, how powerful and near soever.

The last part of the preceding petition was, in effect, a demand by Parliament to take over the king's government, and Charles refused to assent to it. But the petition was approved by a majority of only 159 to 148. Nearly half the members of the House did not vote. It is by no means clear that a real majority of Commons wanted to limit the king's powers still more. At this point, however, Charles made a tactical blunder. Perhaps provoked by rumors that his queen was to be impeached, he denounced his enemies in Parliament as traitors and tried to arrest them.

Case of the Five Members

AND AS HIS MAJESTY CAME THROUGH Westminster Hall, the Commanders, etc., that attended him made a lane on both sides the Hall (through which his Majesty passed and came up the stairs to the House of Commons) and stood before the guard of Pensioners and Halbedeers (who also attended the king's person) and, the door of the House of Commons being thrown open, his Majesty entered the House, and as he passed up towards the Chair he cast his eye on the right hand near the Bar of the House, where Mr. Pym used to sit; but his Majesty not seeing him there (knowing him well) went up to the Chair, and said, "By your leave, Mr. Speaker, I must borrow your chair a little." Whereupon the Speaker came out of the Chair and his Majesty stepped up into it; after he had stood in the Chair a while, casting his eye upon the members as they stood up uncovered, but could not discern any of the five members to be there, nor indeed were they easy to be discerned (had they been there) among so many bare faces all standing up together. Then his Majesty made this speech.

"Gentlemen, I am sorry for this occasion of coming unto you. Yesterday I sent a Serjeant at Arms upon a very important occasion, to apprehend some that by my command were accused of high treason; whereunto I did expect obedience and not a message. And I must declare unto you here that, albeit no king that ever was in England shall be more careful of your privileges, to maintain them to the uttermost of his power, than I shall be; yet you must know that in cases of treason no person hath a privilege. And therefore I am come to know if any of these persons that were accused are here. For I must tell you, Gentlemen, that so long as these persons that I have accused (for no light crime, but for treason) are here, I cannot expect that this House will be in the right way that I do heartily wish it. Therefore I am come to tell you that I must have them wheresoever I find them. Well, since I see all the birds are flown, I do expect from you that you shall send them unto me as soon as they return hither. But I

"Case of the Five Members," from John Rushworth, *Historical Collections* (1721), Vol. 4, pp. 477–7478. Reprinted by permission.

assure you, on the word of a king, I never did intend any force, but shall proceed against them in a legal and fair way, for I never did intend any other.

"And now, since I cannot do what I came for, I think this no unfit occasion to repeat what I have said formerly, that whatsoever I have done in favor and to the good of my subjects, I do mean to maintain it.

"I will trouble you no more, but tell you I do expect as soon as they come to the House you will send them to me; otherwise I must take my own course to find them."

When the king was looking about the House, the Speaker standing below by the Chair, his Majesty asked him whether any of these persons were in the House. Whether he saw any of them? And where they were? To which the Speaker, falling on his knee, thus answered, "May it please your Majesty, I have neither eyes to see, nor tongue to speak in this place but as the House is pleased to direct me, whose servant I am here; and humbly beg your Majesty's pardon, that I cannot give any other answer than this to what your Majesty is pleased to demand of me."

The king, having concluded his speech, went out of the House again, which was in great disorder, and many members cried out aloud, so as he might hear them, "Privilege! Privilege" and forthwith adjourned till the next day at one of the clock.

After this abortive attempt Charles withdrew from London. The decisive breach came when the houses of Parliament, without royal consent, raised an army on their own authority. (An army was urgently needed to suppress a rebellion in Ireland.)

Militia Ordinance

AN ORDINANCE OF THE LORDS AND COMMONS IN PARLIAMENT, FOR THE SAFETY AND DEFENCE OF THE KINGDOM OF ENGLAND AND DOMINION OR WALES

WHEREAS THERE HATH BEEN OF LATE a most dangerous and desperate design upon the House of Commons, which we have just cause to believe to be an effect of the bloody counsels of Papists and other ill-affected persons, who have already raised a rebellion in the kingdom of Ireland; and by reason of many discoveries we cannot but fear they will proceed not only to stir up the like rebellion and insurrections in this kingdom of England, but also to back them with forces from abroad.

"Militia Ordinance," from S. R. Gardiner, ed., The Constitutioal Documents of the Puritan Revolution, pp. 245–246. Reprinted by permission of Oxford University Press.

For the safety therefore of His Majesty's person, the Parliament and kingdom in this time of imminent danger.

It is ordained by the Lords and Commons now in Parliament assembled, that Henry Earl of Holland shall be Lieutenant of the County of Berks, Oliver Earl of Bolingbroke shall be Lieutenant of the County of Bedford, &c.

* * *

And shall severally and respectively have power to assemble and call together all and singular His Majesty's subjects, within the said several and respective counties and places, as well within liberties as without, that are meet and fit for the wars, and them to train and exercise and put in readiness, and them after their abilities and faculties well and sufficiently from time to time to cause to be arrayed and weaponed, and to take the muster of them in places most fit for that purpose.

The king, in reply, insisted on his ancient right to command the armed forces of the realm.

Charles I's Proclamation Condemning the Militia Ordinance

WHEREAS, BY THE STATUTE MADE in the seventh year of King Edward the First, the Prelates, Earls, Barons and Commonalty of the realm affirmed in Parliament, that to the King it belongeth, and his part it is by his royal seigniory straightly to defend wearing of armour and all other force against the peace, at all times when it shall please him, and to punish them which do the contrary according to the laws and usages of the realm; and hereunto all subjects are bound to aid the King as their sovereign lord, at all seasons when need shall be; and whereas we understand that, expressly contrary to the said statute and other good laws of this our kingdom, under colour and pretence of an Ordinance of Parliament, without our consent, or any commission or wartions, to prevent that some malignant persons in this our kingdom do not by degrees seduce our good subjects from their due obedience to us and the laws of this our kingdom . . . do therefore, by this our Proclamation, expressly charge and command all our sheriffs, and all colonels, lieutenant-colonels, sergeant-majors, captains, officers and soldiers, belonging to the trained bands of this our kingdom, and likewise all high and petty constables, and other our officers and subjects whatsoever, upon their allegiance, and as they tender the peace of this our kingdom, not to muster, levy, raise or march, or to summon or warn, upon any warrant, order or ordinance from one or both of our Houses of Parliament.

"Charles I's Proclamation Condemning the Millitia Ordinance," from S. R. Gardiner," *The Constitutional Documents of the Puritan Revolution*, pp. 248–249. Reprinted by permission.

A Whig Interpretation

BY *Thomas Babington Macaulay*

Now [*1629*] COMMENCED a new era. Many English Kings had occasionally committed unconstitutional acts: but none had ever systematically attempted to make himself a despot, and to reduce the Parliament to a nullity. Such was the end which Charles distinctly proposed to himself. From March 1629 to April 1640, the Houses were not convoked. Never in our history had there been an interval of eleven years between Parliament and Parliament. Only once had there been an interval of even half that length. This fact alone is sufficient to refute those who represent Charles as having merely trodden in the footsteps of the Plantagenets and Tudors.

It is proved, by the testimony of the King's most strenuous supporters, that, during this part of his reign, the provisions of the Petition of Right were violated by him, not occasionally, but constantly, and on system; that a large part of the revenue was raised without any legal authority; and that persons obnoxious to the government languished for years in prison, without being ever called upon to plead before any tribunal.

For these things history must hold the King himself chiefly responsible. From the time of his third Parliament he was his own prime minister. Several persons, however, whose temper and talents were suited to his purposes, were at the head of different departments of the administration.

Thomas Wentworth, successively created Lord Wentworth and Earl of Strafford, a man of great abilities, eloquence, and courage, but of a cruel and imperious nature, was the counsellor most trusted in political and military affairs. . . . His object was to do in England all, and more than all, that Richelieu was doing in France; to make Charles a monarch as absolute as any on the Continent; to put the estates and the personal liberty of the whole people at the disposal of the crown; to deprive the courts of law of all independent authority, even in ordinary questions of civil rights between man and man; and to punish with merciless rigour all who murmured at the acts of the government, or who applied, even in the most decent and regular manner, to any tribunal for relief against those acts.

This was his end; and he distinctly saw in what manner alone this end could be attained. There was, in truth, about all his notions a clearness, coherence, and precision which, if he had not been pursuing an object pernicious to his country and to his kind, would have justly entitled him to high admiration. He saw that there was one instrument, and only one, by which his vast and daring projects could be carried into execution. That instrument was a standing army. To the forming of such an army, therefore, he directed all the energy of his strong mind. In Ireland, where he was viceroy, he actually succeeded in

Thomas Babington Macaulay, "A Whig Interptetation," form *The History of England*, 9th ed. (1853), Vol. I, pp. 85–88, 96–99, 102–109. Reprinted by permission.

establishing a military despotism, not only over the aboriginal population, but also over the English colonists, and was able to boast that, in that island, the King was as absolute as any prince in the whole world could be.

The ecclesiastical administration was, in the meantime, principally directed by William Laud, Archbishop of Canterbury. Of all the prelates of the Anglican Church, Laud had departed farthest from the principles of the Reformation, and had drawn nearest to Rome. . . . Under his direction every corner of the realm was subjected to a constant and minute inspection. Every little congregation of separatists was tracked out and broken up. Even the devotion of private families could not escape the vigilance of his spies. Such fear did his rigour inspire that the deadly hatred of the Church, which festered in innumerable bosoms, was generally disguised under an outward show of conformity. On the very eve of troubles, fatal to himself and to his order, the Bishops of several extensive dioceses were able to report to him that not a single dissenter was to be found within their jurisdiction.

*   *   *

In November 1640 met that renowned Parliament which, in spite of many errors and disasters, is justly entitled to the reverence and gratitude of all who, in any part of the world, enjoy the blessings of constitutional government.

During the year which followed, no very important division of opinion appeared in the Houses. The civil and ecclesiastical administration had, through a period of near twelve years, been so oppressive and so unconstitutional that even those classes of which the inclinations are generally on the side of order and authority were eager to promote popular reforms, and to bring the instruments of tyranny to justice. It was enacted that no interval of more than three years should ever elapse between Parliament and Parliament, and that, if writs under the Great Seal were not issued at the proper time, the returning officers should, without such writs, call the constituent bodies together for the choice of representatives. The Star Chamber, the High Commission, the Council of York, were swept away. Men who, after suffering cruel mutilations, had been confined in remote dungeons, regained their liberty. On the chief ministers of the crown the vengeance of the nation was unsparingly wreaked. The Lord Keeper, the Primate, the Lord Lieutenant were impeached. Finch saved himself by flight. Laud was flung into the Tower. Strafford was impeached, and at length put to death by act of attainder. On the same day on which this act passed, the King gave his assent to a law by which he bound himself not to adjourn, prorogue, or dissolve the existing Parliament without its own consent.

*   *   *

At a later period the Royalists found it convenient to antedate the separation between themselves and their opponents, and to attribute the Act which restrained the King from dissolving or proroguing the Parliament, the Triennial Act, the impeachment of the ministers, and the attainder of Strafford, to the faction which afterwards made war on the King. But no artifice could be more disingenuous. Every one of those strong measures was actively promoted by the men who were afterwards foremost among the Calaliers. . . .

But under this apparent concord a great schism was latent; and when, in October 1641, the Parliament reassembled after a short recess, two hostile parties, essentially the same with those which, under different names, have ever since contended, and are still contending, for the direction of public affairs, appeared confronting each other. During some years they were designated as Cavaliers and Roundheads. They were subsequently called Tories and Whigs; nor does it seem that these appellations are likely soon to become obsolete.

* * *

Neither party wanted strong arguments for the measures which it was disposed to take. The reasonings of the most enlightened Royalists may be summed up thus:—"It is true that great abuses have existed; but they have been redressed. It is true that precious rights have been invaded; but they have been vindicated and surrounded with new securities. The sittings of the Estates of the realm have been, in defiance of all precedent and of the spirit of the constitution, intermitted during eleven years; but it has now been provided that henceforth three years shall never elapse without a Parliament. The Star Chamber, the High Commission, the Council of York, oppressed and plundered us; but those hateful courts have now ceased to exist. . . . Henceforth it will be our wisdom to look with jealousy on schemes of innovation, and to guard from encroachment all the prerogatives with which the law has, for the public good, armed the sovereign."

Such were the views of those men of whom the excellent Falkland may be regarded as the leader. It was contended on the other side with not less force, by men of not less ability and virtue, that the safety which the liberties of the English people enjoyed was rather apparent than real, and that the arbitrary projects of the court would be resumed as soon as the vigilance of the Commons was relaxed. True it was,—such was the reasoning of Pym, of Hollis, and of Hampden,—that many good laws had been passed: but, if good laws had been sufficient to restrain the King, his subjects would have had little reason ever to complain of his administration. The recent statutes were surely not of more authority than the Great Charter or the Petition of Right. Yet neither the Great Charter, hallowed by the veneration of four centuries, nor the Petition of Right, sanctioned, after mature reflection, and for valuable consideration, by Charles himself, had been found effectual for the protection of the people. If once the check of fear were withdrawn, if once the spirit of opposition were suffered to slumber, all the securities for English freedom resolved themselves into a single one, the royal word; and it had been proved by a long and severe experience that the royal word could not be trusted.

The two parties were still regarding each other with cautious hostility, and had not yet measured their strength, when news arrived which inflamed the passions and confirmed the opinions of both. The great chieftains of Ulster, who, at the time of the accession of James, had, after a long struggle, submitted to the royal authority, had not long brooked the humiliation of dependence. They had conspired against the English government, and had been attainted of treason. Their immense domains had been forfeited to the crown, and had soon been peopled by thousands of English and Scotch emigrants. The new settlers were, in civilisation and intelligence, far superior to the native population, and sometimes abused their superiority. The animosity produced by difference of race was increased by difference of religion. Under the iron rule of Wentworth, scarcely a murmur was heard: but, when that strong pressure was withdrawn, when Scotland had set the example of successful resistance, when England was distracted by internal quarrels, the smothered rage of the Irish broke forth into acts of fearful violence. . . To raise a great army had always been the King's first object. A great army must now be raised. It was to be feared that, unless some new securities were devised, the forces levied for the reduction of Ireland would be employed against the liberties of England. Nor was this all. A horrible suspicion, unjust indeed, but not altogether unnatural, had arisen in many minds. The Queen was an avowed Roman Catholic: the King was not regarded by the Puritans, whom he had mercilessly persecuted, as a sincere Protestant; and so notorious was his deplicity, that there was no treachery of which his subjects might not, with some show of reason, believe him capable. It was soon whispered that the rebellion of the Roman Catholics of Ulster was part of a vast work of darkness which had been planned at Whitehall.

After some weeks of prelude, the first great parliamentary conflict between the parties which have ever since contended, and are still contending, for the government of the nation, took place on the twenty-second of November 1641. It was moved by the opposition, that the House of Commons should present to the King a remonstrance, enumerating the faults of his administration from the time of his accession, and expressing the distrust with which his policy was still regarded by his people. That assembly, which a few months before had been unanimous in calling for the reform of abuses, was now divided into two fierce and eager factions of nearly equal strength. After a hot debate of many hours, the remonstrance was carried by only eleven votes.

The result of this struggle was highly favourable to the conservative party. It could not be doubted that only some great indiscretion could prevent them from shortly obtaining the predominance in the Lower House. The Upper House was already their own. Nothing was wanting to insure their success, but that the King should, in all his conduct, show respect for the laws and scrupulous good faith towards his subjects.

His first measures promised well. He had, it seemed, at last discovered that an entire change of system was necessary, and had wisely made up his mind to what could no longer be avoided. He declared his determination to govern in harmony with the Commons, and, for that end, to call to his councils men in whose talents and character the Commons might place confidence. Nor was the selection ill made. Falkland, Hyde, and Colepepper, all three distinguished by the part which they had taken in reforming abuses and in punishing evil ministers, were invited to become the confidential advisers of the crown, and were solemnly assured by Charles that he would take no step in any way affecting the Lower House of Parliament without their privity.

Had he kept this promise, it cannot be doubted that the reaction which was already in progress would very soon have become quite as strong as the most respectable Royalists would have desired. Already the violent members of the opposition had begun to despair of the fortunes of their party, to tremble for their own safety, and to talk of selling their estates and emigrating to America. That the fair prospects which had begun to open before the King were suddenly overcast, that his life was darkened by adversity, and at length shortened by violence, is to be attributed to his own faithlessness and contempt of law.

The truth seems to be that he detested both the parties into which the House of Commons was divided: nor is this strange; for in both those parties the love of liberty and the love of order were mingled, though in different proportions. The advisers whom necessity had compelled him to call round him were by no means men after his own heart. They had joined in condemning his tyranny, in abridging his power, and in punishing his instruments. They were now indeed prepared to defend by strictly legal means his strictly legal prerogatives; but they would have recoiled with horror from the thought of reviving Wentworth's projects of Thorough. They were, therefore, in the King's opinion, traitors, who differed only in the degree of their seditious malignity from Pym and Hampden.

He accordingly, a few days after he had promised the chiefs of the constitutional Royalists that no step of importance should be taken without their knowledge, formed a resolution the most momentous of his whole life, carefully concealed that resolution from them, and executed it in a manner which overwhelmed them with shame and dismay. He sent the Attorney General to impeach Pym, Hollis, Hampden, and other members of the House of Common of high treason at the bar of the House of Lords. Not content with this flagrant violation of the Great Charter and of the uninterrupted practice of centuries, he went in person, accompanied by armed men, to seize the leaders of the opposition within the walls of Parliament.

The attempt failed. The accused members had left the House a short time before Charles entered it. A sudden and violent revulsion of feeling, both in the Parliament and in the country, followed. The most favourable view that has ever been taken of the King's conduct on this occasion by his most partial advocates is that he had weakly suffered himself to be hurried into a gross indiscretion by the evil counsels of his wife and of his courtiers. But the general voice loudly charged him with far deeper guilt. At the very moment at which his subjects, after a long estrangement produced by his maladministration, were returning to him with feelings of confidence and affection, he had aimed a deadly blow at all their dearest rights, at the privileges of Parliament, at the very principle of trial by jury. . . . Had Charles remained much longer in his stormy capital, it is probable that the Commons would have found a plea for making him, under outward forms of respect, a state prisoner.

He quitted London, never to return till the day of a terrible and memorable reckoning had arrived. A negotiation began which occupied many months. Accusations and recriminations passed backward and forward between the contending parties. All accommodation had become impossible. The sure punishment which waits on habitual perfidy had at length overtaken the King.

5

Democracy or Oligarchy?

As the civil war proceeded, many radical groups emerged with social ideas that were much more revolutionary and egalitarian than those of the respectable leaders of Parliament. Often their protests were couched in fiery religious language as in the following example.

FROM *A Fiery Flying Roll*

BY *Abiezer Coppe*

THUS SAITH THE LORD: Be wise now therefore, O ye Rulers, &c. Be instructed, &c. . . . Yea, kisse Beggers, Prisoners, warme them, feed them, cloathe them, money them, relieve them, release them, take them into your houses, don't serve them as dogs without doore, &c.

Owne them, they are flesh of your flesh, your owne brethren, your owne Sisters, every whit as good (and if I should stand in competition with you) in some degrees better than your selves.

Once more, I say, owne them; they are your self, make them one with you, or else go howling into hell; howle for the miseries that are coming upon you, howle.

The very shadow of levelling, sword-levelling, man-levelling, frightened you, (and who, like your selves, can blame you, because it shook your Kingdome?) but now the substantiality of levelling is coming.

The Eternall God, the mighty Leveller is comming, yea come, even at the door; and what will you do in that day. . . .

Mine eares are filled brim full with cryes of poore prisoners, Newgate, Ludgate cryes (of late) are seldome out of mine eares. Those dolefull cryes, Bread, bread, bread for the Lords sake, pierce mine eares, and heart, I can no longer forebeare.

Werefore high you apace to all prisons in the Kingdome.

Abiezer Coppe, *A Fiery Roll* (London, 1649).

Bow before those poore, nasty, lousie, ragged wretches, say to them, your humble servants, Sir, (without a complement) we let you go free, and serve you, &c.

Do this or (as I live saith the Lord) thine eyes (at least) shall be boared out, and thou carried captive into a strange Land. . . .

Loose the bands of wickednesse, undo the heavy burdens, let the oppressed go free, and breake every yoake. Deale thy bread to the hungry, and bring the poore that are cast out (both of houses and Synagogues) to thy house. Cover the naked: Hide not thy self from thine owne flesh, from a creeple, a rogue, a begger, he's thine owne flesh. From a Whoremonger, a thief, &c. he's flesh of thy flesh, and his theft, and whoredome is flesh of thy flesh also, thine owne flesh. Thou maist have ten times more of each within thee, then he that acts outwardly in either, Remember, turn not away thine eyes from thine *OWN FLESH*.

The group called "Levellers" wanted a more democratic system of representative government. Their arguments were based on appeals to the Bible and to the natural rights of man.

FROM *The Free-man's Freedom Vindicated*

BY *John Lilburne*

ADAM . . . AND . . . EVE . . . are the earthly original fountain of all and every particular and individual man and woman in the world since, who are, and were, by nature all equal and alike in power, dignity, authority, and majesty, none of them having by nature, dominion or magisterial power one over or above another; neither have they, or can they exercise any, but merely by institution or donation, or assumed by mutual consent and agreement. . . . And unnatural, irrational, sinful, wicked, unjust, devilish, and tyrannical, it is for any man whatsoever, spiritual or temporal, clergyman or layman, to appropriate and assume unto himself a power, authority, and jurisdiction to rule, govern or reign over any sort of man in the world without their free consent, and whosoever doth it . . . do thereby, as much as in them lies, endeavour to appropriate and assume unto themselves the office and sovereignty of God (who alone doth, and is to, rule by his will and pleasure) and to be like the Creator, which was the sin of the devils, not being content with their first station, would be like God, for which sin they were thrown down into Hell. . . .

John Lilburne, *The Free-man's Freedom Vindicated* (London,1646).

The idea of instituting a democratic system was put forward in the course of a debate held among the army leaders in 1647 concerning the future form of government. The views expressed by Colonel Rainborough in the following exchange, however, proved totally unacceptable to the monarchists, the parliamentary leaders, and the generals. There was never any serious possibility of their being put into practice.

FROM *The Army Debates*

RAINBOROUGH: . . . [R]eally I think that the poorest he that is in England hath a life to live, as the greatest he; and therefore truly, sir, I think it's clear, that every man that is to live under a government ought first by his own consent to put himself under that government; and I do think that the poorest man in England is not at all bound in a strict sense to that government that he hath not had a voice to put himself under; and I am confident that, when I have heard the reasons against it, something will be said to answer those reasons, insomuch that I should doubt whether he was an Englishman or no, that should doubt of these things.

IRETON: . . . Give me leave to tell you, that if you make this the rule I think you must fly for refuge to an absolute natural right, and you must deny all civil right; and I am sure it will come to that in the consequence. . . . For my part, I think it is no right at all. I think that no person hath a right to an interest or share in the disposing of the affairs of the kingdom, and in determining or choosing those that shall determine what laws we shall be ruled by here—no person hath a right to this, that hath not a permanent fixed interest in this kingdom, and those persons together are properly the represented of this kingdom, and consequently are[also] * to make up the representers of this kingdom, who taken together do comprehend whatsoever is of real or permanent interest in the kingdom. . . . We talk of birthright. Truly [by] birthright there is thus much claim. Men may justly have by birthright, by their very being born in England, that we should not seclude them out of England, that we should not refuse to give them air and place and ground, and the freedom of the highways and other things, to live amongst us. . . . That I think is due to a man by birth. But that by a man's being born here he shall have a share in that power that shall dispose of the lands here, and of all things here, I do not think it a sufficient ground. I am sure if we look upon that which is the utmost (within [any] man's view) of what was originally the constitution of this kingdom, upon that which is most radical and fundamental, and which if you take away, there is no man hath any land, any goods, [or] any civil interest, that is this: that those that choose the representers for the making of laws by which this state and kingdom are to be governed, are the persons who, taken together, do comprehend the local interest of this kingdom; that is, the persons in whom all land lies, and those in corporations in whom all trading lies. This is the most fundamental constitution of this kingdom and [that] which if you do not allow, you allow none at all. This constitution hath limited and determined it that only those shall have voices in elections.

RAINBOROUGH: Truly, sir, I am of the same opinion I was, and am resolved to keep it till I know reason why I should not. . . . I do hear nothing at all that can convince me, why any man that is born in England ought not to have his voice in election of burgesses. It is said that if a man have not a permanent interest, he can have no claim; and [that] we must be no freer than the laws will let us be, and that there is no [law in any] chronicle will let us be freer than that we [now] enjoy. Something was said to this yesterday. I do think that the main cause why Almighty God gave men reason, it was that they should make use of that reason, and that they should improve it for that end and purpose that God gave it them. . . . I think there is nothing that God hath given a man that any [one] else can take from him. And therefore I say, that either it must be the Law of God or the law of man that must prohibit the meanest man in the kingdom to have this benefit as well as the greatest. I do not find anything in the Law of God, that a lord shall choose twenty burgesses, and a gentleman but two, or a poor man shall choose none: I find no such thing in the Law of Nature, nor in the Law of Nations. But I do find that all Englishmen must be subject to English laws, and I do verily believe that there is no man but will say that the foundation of all law lies in the people. . . .

IRETON: . . . All the main thing that I speak for, is because I would have an eye to property. I hope we do not come to contend for victory—but let every man consider with himself that he do not go that way to take away all property. For here is the case of the most fundamental part of the constitution of the kingdom. . . . Now I wish we may all consider of what right you will challenge that all the people should have right to elections. Is it by the right of nature? If you will hold forth that as your ground, then I think you must deny all property too, and this is my reason. For thus: by that same right of nature (whatever it be) that you pretend, by which you can say, one man hath an equal right with another to the choosing of him that shall govern him—by the same right of nature, he hath the same [equal] right in any goods he sees—meat, drink, clothes—to take and use them for his sustenance. He hath a freedom to the land, [to take] the ground, to exercise it, till it; he hath the [same] freedom to anything that any one doth account himself to have any propriety in. Why now I say then, if you, against the most fundamental part of [the] civil constitution (which I have now declared), will plead the Law of Nature, that a man should (paramount [to] this, and contrary to this) have a power of choosing those men that shall determine what shall be law in this state, though he himself have no permanent interest in the state, [but] whatever interest he hath he may carry about with him—if this be allowed, [because by the right of nature] we are free, we are equal, one man must have as much voice as another, then show me what step or difference [there is], why [I may not] by the same right [take your property] . . .

RAINBOROUGH: . . . For my part, as I think, *you* forgot something that was in *my* speech, and you do not only yourselves believe that [some] men are inclining to anarchy, but you would make all men believe that. And, sir, to say because a man pleads that every man hath a voice [by right of nature], that therefore it destroys [by] the same [argument all property—this is to forget the Law of God]. That there's a property, the Law of God says it; else why [hath] God made that law, *Thou shalt not steal?* I am a poor man, therefore I must be[op] pressed: if I have no interest in the kingdom, I must suffer by all their laws be they right or wrong. . . . And therefore I think that to that it is fully answered: God hath set down that thing as to propriety with this law of his, *Thou shalt not steal.* And for my part I am against any such thought, and, as for yourselves, I wish you would not make the world believe that we are for anarchy.

CROMWELL: I know nothing but this, that they that are the most yielding have the greatest wisdom; but really, sir, this is not right as it should be. No man says that you have a mind to anarchy, but [that] the consequence of this rule tends to anarchy, must end in anarchy; for where is there any bound or limit set if you take away this[limit] , that men that have no interest but the interest of breathing [shall have no voice in elections]? Therefore I am confident on 't, we should not be so hot one with another.

6

From Monarchy to Commonwealth

By the autumn of 1648 the parliamentary armies had defeated both the Cavaliers and the Scots—with whom Charles had formed an alliance in 1647. But at this point a quarrel broke out between the leaders of Parliament and the generals. Parliament wanted to continue negotiating with the king; the army was determined to kill him. Parliament wanted to impose a rigid Presbyterian discipline on the English church; the army sought toleration for the various extremist Protestant sects included in its ranks. Oliver Cromwell justified a takeover of power by the army in the following letter (November 25, 1648).

Oliver Cromwell's Letter to Colonel Hammond

DEAR ROBIN, THOU AND I were never worthy to be door-keepers in this service. If thou wilt seek, seek to know the mind of God in all that chain of Providence, whereby God brought thee thither, and that person to thee; how, before and since, God has ordered him, and affairs concerning him: and then tell me, whether there be not some glorious and high meaning in all this, above what thou hast yet attained? And, laying aside thy fleshly reason, seek of the Lord to teach thee what that is; and He will do it. . . .

You say: "God hath appointed authorities among the nations, to which active or passive obedience is to be yielded. This resides in England in the Parliament. Therefore active or passive *[obedience should be yielded to Parliament"—Ed.]*.

Authorities and powers are the ordinance of God. This or that species is of human institution, and limited, some with larger, others with stricter bands, each one according to its constitution. "But" I do not therefore think the authorities may do anything, and yet such obedience "be" due, but all agree there are cases in which it is lawful to resist. If so, your ground fails, and so likewise the

"Oliver Cromwell's Letter to Colonel Hammond," from Thomas Carlyle, *The Letters and Speeches of Oliver Cromwell*, S. C. Lomas ed., (1904), pp. 394–397. Reprintd by permission of Methuen and Co. Ltd.

inference. Indeed, dear Robin, not to multiply words, the query is, Whether ours be such a case? This ingenuously is the true question.

To this I shall say nothing, though I could say very much; but only desire thee to see what thou findest in thy own heart as to two or three plain considerations. First, whether *Salus Populi* be a sound position? *[Cromwell referred to the maxim "The safety of the people is the supreme law"—Ed.]* Secondly, whether in the way in hand, really and before the Lord, before whom conscience must stand, this be provided for, or the whole fruit of the war like to be frustrated, and all most like to turn to what it was, and worse? And this, contrary to engagements, declarations, implicit covenants with those who ventured their lives upon these covenants and engagements, without whom perhaps, in equity, relaxation ought not to be? Thirdly, Whether this Army be not a lawful power, called by God to oppose and fight against the King upon some stated grounds; and being in power to such ends, may not oppose one name of authority, for those ends, as well as another, the outward authority that called them, not by their power making the quarrel lawful, but it being so in itself? If so it may be acting will be justified *in foro humano.*—But truly these kinds of reasonings may be but fleshly, either with or against: only it is good to try what truth may be in them. And the Lord teach us.

My dear friend, let us look into providences; surely they mean somewhat. They hang so together; have been so constant, so clear and unclouded. Malice, swoln malice against God's people, now called Saints, to root out their name; and yet they, "these poor Saints," by providence, having arms and therein blessed with defence and more. . . .

What think you of Providence disposing the hearts of so many of God's people this way, especially in this poor Army, wherein the great God has vouchsafed to appear. I know not one officer among us but is on the increasing hand. And let me say it is here in the North, after much patience, we trust the same Lord who hath framed our minds in our actings, is with us in this also. And this contrary to a natural tendency, and to those comforts our hearts could wish to enjoy with others. And the difficulties probably to be encountered with, and the enemies, not few, even all that is glorious in this world, with appearance of united names, titles and authorities, and yet not terrified, only desiring to fear our great God, that we do nothing against His will. Truly this is our condition.

And to conclude. We in this Northern Army were in a waiting posture, desiring to see what the Lord would lead us to.

On December 6, 1648, a Colonel Pride, acting for the army leaders, "purged"
Parliament of all the members opposed to the army's policies. The surviving
remnant then enacted the following decree.

Declaration of the Supremacy of Parliament

(RESOLVED) That the commons of England, in parliament assembled, do declare that the people are, under God, the original of all just power. And do also declare, that the commons of England, in parliament assembled, being chosen by and representing the people have the supreme power in this nation. And do also declare, that whatsoever is enacted, or declared for law, by the commons in parliament assembled, hath the force of a law; and all the people of this nation are concluded thereby, although the consent of king, or house of peers, be not had thereunto.

This decree was followed by an act creating a high court of justice to try the king.
The act was passed by the Commons but not by the Lords.

Act Erecting a High Court of Justice for the King's Trial

WHEREAS IT IS NOTORIOUS that Charles Stuart, the now King of England, not content with the many encroachments which his predecessors had made upon the people in their rights and freedom, hath had a wicked design totally to subvert the ancient and fundamental laws and liberties of this nation, and in their place to introduce an arbitrary and tyrannical government, and that besides all other evil ways and means to bring his design to pass, he hath prosecuted it with fire and sword, levied and maintained a civil war in the land, against the Parliament and kingdom; whereby this country hath been miserably wasted, the public treasure exhausted, trade decayed, thousands of people murdered, and infinite other mischiefs committed; for all which high and treasonable offences the said Charles Stuart might long since have justly been brought to exemplary and condign punishment: whereas also the Parliament, well hoping that the restraint and imprisonment of his person, after it had pleased God to deliver him into their hands, would have quieted the distempers of the kingdom, did forbear to proceed judicially against him, but found, by sad experience, that such their remissness served only to encourage him and his accomplices in the continuance of their evil practices, and in raising new commotions, rebellions and invasions: for prevention therefore of the like or greater inconveniences, and to the

"Declaration the Supremacy of Parliament," from W. Cobbett, *Parliamentary History of England* (1808), Vol. 3, col. 1257. Reprinted by permission.
"Act Erecting a High Court of Justice for the King's Trial," from S. R. Gardiner, The Constitutional Documents of the Puritan Revolution, pp. 357–358. Reprinted by permission of Oxford University Press.

end no Chief Officer or Magistrate whatsoever may hereafter presume, traitorously and maliciously, to imagine or contrive the enslaving or destroying of the English nation, and to expect impunity for so doing; be it enacted and ordained by the [Lords] and Commons in Parliament assembled, and it is hereby enacted and ordained by the authority thereof, that the Earls of Kent, Nottingham, Pembroke, Denbigh and Mulgrave, the Lord Grey of Wark, Lord Chief Justice Rolle of the King's Bench, Lord Chief Justice St. John of the Common Pleas, and Lord Chief Baron Wylde, the Lord Fairfax, Lieutenant-General Cromwell, &c. [in all about 150], shall be and are hereby appointed and required to be Commissioners and Judges for the hearing, trying and judging of the said Charles Stuart.

Charles was not permitted to speak at his trial. He said at that time: "I am not suffered to speak. Expect what justice other people will have." On the scaffold he gave a last defense of his reign.

Charles I's Defense of His Reign

I THINK IT IS MY DUTY , to God first, and to my country, for to clear myself both as an honest man, a good king, and a good Christian.

I shall begin first with my innocence. In truth I think it not very needful for me to insist long upon this, for all the world knows that I never did begin a war with the two Houses of Parliament; and I call God to witness, to whom I must shortly make an account, that I never did intend to incroach upon their privileges. They began upon me. It was the Militia they began upon. They confessed that the Militia was mine but they thought it fit to have it from me. . . . So that the guilt of these enormous crimes that are laid against me, I hope in God that God will clear me of it. I will not (I am in charity) God forbid that I should lay it upon the two Houses of Parliament. There is no necessity of either. I hope that they are free of this guilt, for I do believe that all instruments between them and me have been the chief cause of all this bloodshed. . . . will only say this, that an unjust sentence that I suffered to take effect *[i.e., the execution of Strafford—Ed.]* is punished now by an unjust sentence upon me. That is, so far as I have said, to show you that I am an innocent man.

Now for to show you that I am a good Christian. I hope there is a good man that will bear me witness that I have forgiven all the world, and even those in particular that have been the chief causes of my death. Who they are God knows. I do not desire to know. I pray God forgive them. But this is not all. My charity must go further. I wish that they may repent, for indeed they have committed a great sin in that particular. I pray God, with St. Stephen, that this be not laid to their charge; nay, not only so, but that they may take the right way

"Charles I's Defense of Reign," from *England's Black Tribunal,* 5th ed. (1720), pp. 43–46. Reprinted by permission.

to the peace of the kingdom, for my charity commands me, not only to forgive particular men, but my charity commands me to endeavor to the last gasp the peace of the kingdom. . . .

[As] for the people—truly I desire their liberty and freedom as much as anybody whosoever. But I must tell you that their liberty and freedom consists in having of government those laws by which their lives and goods may be most their own. It is not for having share in government. That is nothing pertaining to them. A subject and a sovereign are clean different things, and therefore, until they do that—I mean that you do put the people in that liberty as I say—certainly they will never enjoy themselves.

Sirs, it was for this now that I am come here. If I would have given way to an arbitrary way, for to have all laws changed according to the power of the sword, I needed not to have come here. And therefore I tell you (and I pray God it be not laid to your charge) that I am the martyr of the people.

Act Declaring England to Be a Commonwealth, 1649

BE IT DECLARED AND ENACTED by this present Parliament, and by the authority of the same, that the people of England, and of all the dominions and territories thereunto belonging, are and shall be, and are hereby constituted, made, established, and confirmed, to be a Commonwealth and Free State, and shall from henceforth be governed as a Commonwealth and Free State by the supreme authority of this nation, the representatives of the people in Parliament, and by such as they shall appoint and constitute as officers and ministers under them for the good of the people, and that without any King or House of Lords.

Cromwell finally dismissed the surviving "rump" of Parliament in 1653 in the following fashion.

Oliver Cromwell's Dismissal of the Rump Parliament

CALLING TO Major-General Harrison, who was on the other side of the House, to come to him, he told him, that he judged the Parliament ripe for a dissolution, and this to be the time of doing it. The Major-General answered, as he since told me, "Sir, the work is very great and dangerous, therefore I desire you seriously to consider of it before you engage in it." "You say well," replied the General, and thereupon sat still for about a quarter of an hour; and then the question for passing the Bill being to be put, he said again to Major-General

"Act Declaring England to Be A Commonwealth, 1649," from S. R. Gardiner, *The Constitutional Document of the Puritan Revolution*, p. 388. Reprinted by permission of Oxford University Press.
"Oliver Cromwell's Dismissal of the Rump Parliament," from C. H. Firth ed., *The Memoirs of Edmund Ludlow* (1894), Vol. 1, pp. 352–354 Reprinted by permission.

Harrison, "this is the time I must do it"; and suddenly standing up, made a speech, wherein he loaded the Parliament with the vilest reproaches, charging them not to have a heart to do any thing for the publick good, to have espoused the corrupt interest of Presbytery and the lawyers, who were the supporters of tyranny and oppression, accusing them of an intention to perpetuate themselves in power, had they not been forced to the passing of this Act, which he affirmed they designed never to observe, and thereupon told them, that the Lord had done with them, and had chosen other instruments for the carrying on his work that were more worthy. This he spoke with so much passion and discomposure of mind, as if he had been distracted. Sir Peter Wentworth stood up to answer him, and said, that this was the first time that ever he had heard such unbecoming language given to the Parliament, and that it was the more horrid in that it came from their servant, and their servant whom they had so highly trusted and obliged: but as he was going on, the General stept into the midst of the House, where continuing his distracted language, he said, "Come, come, I will put an end to your prating"; then walking up and down the House like a mad-man, and kicking the ground with his feet, he cried out, "You are no Parliament, I say you are no Parliament; I will put an end to your sitting; call them in, call them in": whereupon the serjeant attending the Parliament opened the doors, and Lieutenant-Colonel Worsley with two files of musqueteers entered the House; which Sir Henry Vane observing from his place, said aloud, "This is not honest, yea it is against morality and common honesty." Then Cromwell fell a railing at him, crying out with a loud voice, "O Sir Henry Vane, Sir Henry Vane, the lord deliver me from Sir Henry Vane." Then looking upon one of the members, he said, "There sits a drunkard"; and giving much reviling language to others, he commanded the mace to be taken away, saying, "What shall we do with this bauble? here, take it away." Having brought all into this disorder, Major-General Harrison went to the Speaker as he sat in the chair, and told him, that seeing things were reduced to this pass, it would not be convenient for him to remain there. The Speaker answered, that he would not come down unless he were forced. "Sir," said Harrison, "I will lend you my hand"; and thereupon putting his hand within his, the Speaker came down. Then Cromwell applied himself to the members of the House, who were in number between 80 and 100, and said to them, "It's you that have forced me to this, for I have sought the Lord night and day, that he would rather slay me than put me upon the doing of this work."

Cromwell subsequently tried to legitimize his de facto power by summoning several elected assemblies. In the end he ruled as a military dictator. The following account refers to the case of a man who refused to pay a tax levied by Cromwell without parliamentary authorization. Clarendon began writing his history in 1646. It was first published in 1702.

FROM *Clarendon's History of the Rebellion*

MAYNARD, WHO WAS OF COUNSEL with the prisoner, demanded his liberty with great confidence, both upon the illegality of the commitment, and the illegality of the imposition, as being laid without any lawful authority. The judges could not maintain or defend either, but enough declared what their sentence would be; and therefore the Protector's Attorney required a farther day to answer what had been urged. Before that day, Maynard was committed to the Tower, for presuming to question or make doubt of his authority; and the judges were sent for, and severely reprehended for suffering that license; and when they with all humility mentioned the law and *Magna Charta,* Cromwell told them, their *magna farta* should not control his actions, which he knew were for the safety of the commonwealth. He asked them who made them judges; [whether] they had any authority to sit there but what he gave them; and that if his authority were at an end, they knew well enough what would become of themselves; and therefore advised them to be more tender of that which could only pre-serve them; and so dismissed them with caution, that they should not suffer the lawyers to prate what it would not become them to hear.

Six years of army rule made most Englishmen long for a restoration of monarchy. Charles II smoothed the way for his return to the throne by issuing the following declaration.

Declaration of Breda

WE DO MAKE IT OUR daily suit to the Divine Providence, that He will, in compas-sion to us and our subjects, after so long misery and sufferings, remit and put us into a quiet and peaceful possession of that our right, with as little blood and damage to our people as is possible; nor do we desire more to enjoy what is ours, than that all our subjects may enjoy what by law is theirs, by a full and entire administration of justice throughout the land, and by extending our mercy where it is wanted and deserved.

Clarencon, The History of the Rebellion and Civil Wars in England (Oxford, 1888), Vol. 6, p. 93.
"Declaration of Breda." from S. R. Gardiner, *The Constitutional Documents of the Puritan Revolution*, pp. 465–466. Reprinted by permission of Oxford University Press.

And to the end that the fear of punishment may not engage any, conscious to themselves of what is past, to a perseverance in guilt for the future, by opposing the quiet and happiness of their country, in the restoration of King, Peers and people to their just, ancient and fundamental rights, we do, by these presents, declare, that we do grant a free and general pardon, which we are ready, upon demand, to pass under our Great Seal of England, to all our subjects, of what degree or quality soever, who, within forty days after the publishing hereof, shall lay upon this our grace and favour, and shall, by any public act, declare their doing so, and that they return to the loyalty and obedience of good subjects; excepting only such persons as shall hereafter be excepted by Parliament, those only to be excepted. . . .

And because the passion and uncharitableness of the times have produced several opinions in religion, by which men are engaged in parties and animosities against each other (which, when they shall hereafter unite in a freedom of conversation, will be composed or better understood), we do declare a liberty to tender consciences, and that no man shall be disquieted or called in question for differences of opinion in matter of religion, which do not disturb the peace of the kingdom; and that we shall be ready to consent to such an Act of Parliament, as, upon mature deliberation, shall be offered to us, for the full granting that indulgence.

And because, in the continued distractions of so many years, and so many and great revolutions, many grants and purchases of estates have been made to and by many officers, soldiers and others, who are now possessed of the same, and who may be liable to actions at law upon several titles, we are likewise willing that all such differences, and all things relating to such grants, sales and purchases, shall be determined in Parliament, which can best provide for the just satisfaction of all men who are concerned.

And we do further declare, that we will be ready to consent to any Act or Acts of Parliament to the purposes aforesaid, and for the full satisfaction of all arrears due to the officers and soldiers of the army under the command of General Monk; and that they shall be received into our service upon as good pay and conditions as they now enjoy.

A Case for the King

BY *Esmé Wingfield-Stratford*

It was now [*1629—Ed.*] just upon four years since King Charles had come to the throne, years of continued difficulty and frustration, that had brought him to a pass unprecedented in the history of English monarchy. For now one tremendous fact stared him in the face: Parliamentary government had broken down;

Esmé Wingfield-Stratford, "A Case for the King," from *Charles, King of England*, 1600–1637 (1949), pp. 241, 245–246, 318. Also from Esmé Wingfield-Stratford, *King Charles and King Pym*, 1637–1643 (1949), pp. 260–264, 267–270. Reprinted by permission of Hollis & Carter, London.

had become, for the time being, impossible, from the standpoint of a monarch who aspired to govern as well as to reign.

That riot in the House had been enough to prove that under such leadership as Eliot's, there were no lengths to which the Commons could not be driven along the path to revolution. Not content with openly defying the King's authority, they were capable of inciting his subjects in general to set it at naught—nay more, of actually intimidating them into doing so. They were determined to take all before giving him anything; to destroy everyone on whom he leaned, or on whose loyalty he could count, in Church or State; to strip him of the barest minimum of necessary revenue; and to leave him as abject a puppet as Richard II had been in the days of the Merciless Parliament, or Henry III when he was the crowned captive of Simon de Montfort.

It is therefore misleading to talk as if, after that memorable scene which closed the career of his third Parliament, Charles had formed some novel and sinister design of governing without Parliament. Humanly speaking, he had no choice in the matter. He had to do so if he was to govern at all and the only question was—how to do it?

* * *

It is odd that even so prejudiced an historian as John Richard Green should have chosen to describe this period in a section of his famous *Short History* entitled *The Tyranny*. The idea of setting up a despotism on the Continental model had never entered Charles's mind. It was Parliament and not he that had been trying to upset the balance of the Constitution. There was nothing in the law or practice of that Constitution to compel him to summon Parliament before he needed its help. If he could carry on without it—so much the better for the Taxpayer!

Meanwhile the law, stiffened up as it had recently been against the Crown, remained supreme, and the King had not the power, even if he had the will, to set it at defiance. For unlike the real tyrants overseas, he had practically no armed force to back him. The handful of royal guards would not have been equal to defending his royal person against a really determined mob. Thus the King was compelled to govern with at least the passive acquiescence of a people, who certainly would not have endured any flagrant assertion of arbitrary power.

* * *

Let us remember that the object of King Charles's government was to tide over a situation in which it was only too plain that to summon a Parliament would be to open the flood gates of revolution. The policy of which Wentworth and Laud were to become the two leading exponents, was to observe the strictest bounds of constitutional propriety, narrowed as these were by the Petition of Right; to scrape along on the peace-time income of the Crown without resort to taxation; to withdraw from any attempt to interfere in the politics of the

Continent; and to devote all the energy and resources available to building up such a Utopia of ordered prosperity as would in time cause the revolutionary fires to die from lack of fuel, and enable the normal course of Parliamentary government to be resumed in an atmosphere of loyal cooperation between King, Church, Parliament, and people.

* * *

[On December 23, 1641, Charles rejected the demands of the Grand Remonstrance (above, p. 145-148)—Ed.]

When the bells of the London steeples were heard ringing in the year 1642, the same thought must surely have come to the mind of every hearer. Long before the end of the year England would again, as in that unforgotten time of troubles when White Rose had contended with Red, be a house divided against itself—a self-created shambles. It was the horror of all others that had been most deeply seared into the English soul. Even Pym, in his lodging at Westminster, must have regarded the prospect with apprehension. Nature had not made him a man of war, nor even a man of blood; he would no doubt have far preferred to arrive at his goal in what he himself would have described as a Parliamentary way. But having once set his face towards it, neither remorse nor scruple would turn him aside. Though the steeples themselves should be silenced, he at least would see this year out with his head on.

Meanwhile in Whitehall, with its improvised guard house and its informal garrison, King Charles must have been listening to the same sounds with an even keener anxiety, in proportion as he lacked his rival's unimaginative tough-ness of fibre. To him, with his almost feminine horror of violence, the prospect of civil war must have been more bitter than that of death itself, of which he was never to show the least fear. But in these last months he had come to real-ize that for him too the die was cast. Nothing of all that he had conceded, noth-ing that he ever could concede short of the trust that he held for his people, could satisfy these few who were banded together to make their will law for the rest of the community.

* * *

[On January 2, 1642, Charles appointed three moderate leaders of Parliament to his government. It seemed then that opinion in and out of Parliament might swing to the support of the royal administration—Ed.]

Some days must needs elapse before the . . . new ministers, who were quite without administrative experience, would be ready to take over their departments, and by that time the whole face of the situation was destined to be transformed. For on Monday, the third day of the year, the Attorney General, Sir Edward Herbert, appeared before the Lords, to present, in the King's name, articles of impeachment for treason against Pym, Hampden, and three others of the extremist stalwarts in the commons, Haslerigg, Denzil Holles, and Strode, as well as one of the Peers, Lord Kimbolton. . . . It was an amazing and, to those not in the secret, must have seemed and unaccountable move. It is certain that the King's new advisers had had no part in it, and they can hardly have failed to regard it with consternation, since they must have realized to what an extent it was calculated to frustrate all their efforts, and to give the game, in which their Constitutional party had built up for itself a position of winning advantage, into the hands of Pym and his extremists. But the fact that none of the trio, not even Falkland, did what might have seemed the obvious thing, and retired from the service of a master who had to all appearance let them down so hopelessly, suggests that they may have had a more discerning insight into his motives than that of the conventional version on which he figures as a crowned villain plotting to establish his abosolute power by eliminating the noblest champions of his peoples' liberties. The truth was not so crudely melodramatic.

Not improbably the person who was least surprised at the news, was Pym himself, who must have felt all the satisfaction of a chess player who has forced his opponent to make a fatal move. Paradoxical as it may seem to characterize him as the prime mover in getting himself arraigned by the highest legal authority in the land on the most heinous charge known to the law, we have only to regard the matter from what must have been his standpoint, to realize that this offered him his only way of escape from otherwise practically certain ruin. He had committed himself to destroying the King, and the King had entrenched himself in a constitutional postition form which, so long as he sat quiet, there appeared to be no means of dislodging him, before the not distant date when the forces gathering to his support had renderd him strong enough to turn the tables on his assailants.

It had come to this. The only person who could defeat the King now was the King himself. Once let him quit his secure defensive to launch out with some premature counter-stroke, and the revolutionary forces in the field, with public opinion rallied to their supprt, would have him at a fatal disadvantage. It is true that the King had hitherto not shown the faintest disposition to oblige his enemies in this way, and that with Hyde at his elbow, he would be even less likely to do so now. But what if his hand could be forced? What if means could be found of compelling him at the last moment to throw patience to the winds, and to rush , with suicidal precipitation, into the trap prepared for him?

Anyone who had followed Pym's strategy up to this point would have seen the such a design was its necessary culmination. For it had been his invariable principle to repeat every once successful manoeuvre as nearly as possible to pattern when the next opportunity occurred. The former great royal surrender he had forced by bringing all his pressure to bear on the King's most vulnerable point, which was constituted by his love for the Queen. In the even more difficult and delicate operation he had now to perform Pym could not fail to exploit the same weakness. He would confront his opponent with the choice between attacking him, and sacrificing her. Or what was equally to the purpose, bluff him into thinking so.

* * *

If Charles had been playing political chess with the same cold calculation as his opponent, it might have occurred to him that just because the threat to the Queen was being made with such ostentation, it was his game to ignore it. But this was more a matter of the heart than of the head with him. And that, I think, accounts for the fact that he went ahead without pausing to take the advice of his new counsellors, who, just because of their loyalty, would have taken a more detached view than his own. Perhaps he may have divined, in his innermost soul, the sort of advice he would have received from Hyde:

"Have no fear, Sir. Pym is desperate, and you can safely dare him to do his worst. It is to the last degree unlikely that he will go to the length of moving an impeachment against Her Majesty. That he could get a majority for it in the Commons is at least doubtful; that he could ever get the Lords to condemn her is unthinkable. Pym is no fool. Even if he could get her as far as the Tower, he knows that she would be safer in the care of Sir John Byron than she would at Whitehall. And the spectacle of its Queen in distress would rally nine tenths of the nation, in its present mood, to your support. Be advised, Sir! Hold your hand for a very little longer and all will be well. But give Pym the opportunity he is seeking, to transfer the issue to one of Parliamentary privilege, and you give him the one chance he has left of turning the tide against you."

That would, I believe, have been not only a just appreciation, but one that Charles, if he had felt himself free to do so, would have been the first to endorse. A masterly restraint had been the keynote of his policy during all these months, and now that he was just about to harvest its fruits, why should he wish to jettison it unless it was that policy had to give way to honour? Rather than run the slightest risk of harm to the Queen, he was ready to forgo any advantage to himself. And the bitter repentance, that haunted him to the scaffold, for his surrender of Strafford, had planted in him a resolve, from which he never wavered, that his loyalty even to the humblest of his followers—and how much more to the wife he adored—should be unconditional, and unswayed by prudential considerations.

And if this had not been enough to spur him to action, there was the indignation that he must have felt against these men who were striking down right and left his ministers, judges, and bishops, and were now preparing to strike down his Consort, on charges of treason so impudently unsubstantiated that an impeachment had come to signify, in effect, a proscription for loyalty. Whereas they themselves. . . .

But let us examine the charges one by one on which he had directed Sir Edward Herbert to proceed against them.

1. *That they have traitorously endeavoured to subvert the fundamental laws and government of this Kingdom; and deprive the King of his regal power;*

and place his subjects under an arbitrary and tyrannical power.

A more modestly worded, or historically correct, description of the aims unswervingly held by Pym and his associates, from the days of the Providence Island Company and their Broughton Castle caballing to those of the plot against the Queen, it would be hard, even now, to frame.

2. *That they have endeavoured, by many foul aspersions upon his Majesty, and his government, to alienate the affections of his people and to make His Majesty odious to them.*

Not only endeavoured, but largely succeeded, owing to Pym's consummate mastery of the arts of propaganda.

3. *That they have endeavoured to draw His Majesty's late army to disobedience to His Majesty's command and to side with them in their traitorous design.*

To what other purpose had been their endeavours to place it under the command of their own stooges, to prevent it taking the least step to oppose the invasion or interfere with the occupation of English soil, their relentless proscription of all officers suspected of disloyalty to their faction, and now their open conspiracy to wrest the control of it out of the King's hands altogether and lodge it in their own?

4. *That they have traitorously endeavoured and encouraged a foreign power to invade His Majesty's Kingdom of England.*

Their most ardent supporters have not denied the substantial truth of this.

5. *That they have traitorously endeavoured to subvert the very rights and being of Parliament.*

What milder description could be applied to their Perpetual Parliament Act and the means whereby it had been jockeyed through Parliament and forced on the Crown?

6. *That . . . they have endeavoured . . . by force and terror to compel the Parliament to join with them in their traitorous designs, and to that end have actually raised and countenanced tumults against King and Parliament.*

Notoriously and consistently, and Pym had recently gone out of his way openly to applaud and justify such tumults.

7. *That they have traitorously conspired to levy and actually have levied, war against the King.*

By foreign invasion, by terror of the mob, and now—though it had not yet got beyond the stage of conspiracy—by civil war.

I have set down the terms of this brief indictment in order to show that every item of it is as indisputable a statement of historical fact as that England was conquered in 1066, or that Queen Anne died in 1714. Nor are they, in point of fact, any more disputed, the invariable line of justification being that even if these things were done, provided they were done by men like John Hampden against a King like Charles Stuart, they *must* be justified, and that to count them as treason is one of those things that are not done. But even so, it seems a little hard on the King to blame him for being too biased to have anticipated this convenient standpoint.

The Absolutism of Louis XIV— The End of Anarchy or The Beginning of Tyranny?

CONTENTS

QUESTIONS FOR STUDY

1   In what ways does Bossuet's king differ from the medieval king?
2   How does Bossuet define absolutism?
3   How successful did Louis XIV think his absolute rule had been?
4   How well did absolutism work?
5   What did absolutism in France accomplish?
6   In your opinion, was absolutism as practiced by Louis XIV a good thing for France?

The reign of Louis XIV, which extended from 1643 until 1715, was both the longest and most "glorious" in French history. During this period France established its supremacy over every rival for power on the Continent and at the same time made French culture dominant in the Western world. French replaced Latin as the universal language of the cultivated class and the royal palace at Versailles served as the model for petty princelings all over Europe. All this, seemingly, was the result of the new system of government created by Louis XIV and his ministers. The Sun King's government was based upon the principle that the king was absolute. No other power existed or should exist in the state but his. This power was given to him by God and he was responsible to God alone for its proper use. The king was literally the father of his people and, like the old Roman paterfamilias, had the power of life and death over his "children."

Surprisingly enough, absolutism seems to have been perfectly acceptable to the French people, at least in the early stages of Louis' reign. Our surprise at this vanishes when we examine the alternatives. For almost two generations France had been wracked by civil and religious wars of a particularly bitter and brutal kind. The French protestants—the Huguenots—had been able to force the royal power to grant them certain privileges, which in some parts of the country were used to create semi-independent Protestant enclaves. Cardinal Richelieu, Louis XIII's great minister, had managed to curtail the independence of the Huguenots, but they still existed apart from the main body of the French state when Louis XIV, at age twenty-two, picked up the effective reins of power in 1661. The wars that had established the political privileges of the Huguenots had not been fought solely over religious matters. The great noble families whose ancestors had shared the royal power in the Middle Ages were increasingly jealous of the increased power of the king brought about by military innovations such as gunpowder and by the financial support of the middle class, or bourgeoisie. In Louis XIV's childhood this jealousy erupted into another civil war, this time nakedly exposed as noble ambitions directed against the king. The Fronde, or War of the Chamber Pots, as it was called, was a comic-opera war in which the total inability of the nobles to govern was starkly revealed. Also evident was the ability of the nobles to disrupt the orderly processes of government, and it was undoubtedly this aspect that struck the great mass of the French people. A strong king could guarantee internal peace, order, and tranquillity. If it took absolute power to do this, then so be it.

The threat of the nobility was perfectly clear to Louis. He remembered all his life the intrusion of hostile men into his bedroom in his childhood during the Fronde and took a vow never to permit such lèse majesté again. He set out to restore royal authority, and this meant that all competing authority throughout France had to be either eliminated or brought under royal control. To do this, he had first to tame the nobility. To this end the great palace at Versailles was built, where Louis could house all the important nobles and literally keep an eye on them. It is a mark of Louis' political genius that he was able, in fact, to lure the great nobles to Versailles and keep them obedient throughout his reign. To govern

*the provinces Louis and his great minister Colbert created a bureaucracy respon-
sible to the crown alone. From this bureaucratic network information flowed to
Colbert and Louis, and on the basis of this information Louis exercised his absolute control of the French state.*

*There are two problems that immediately come to mind after contemplating
the French state in the seventeenth century. The first is: Just how absolute was
Louis in reality? It is one thing to give orders at Versailles, where one can immediately see to their execution. It is another thing to give orders that must pass
down a chain of command and that are to be carried out far from the royal
presence. Was Louis as absolute as he thought he was? If not, who were the men
who diluted his authority? How did they do it? And did they get away with it?
These questions should be asked of the documents that make up the problem.*

*The second and perhaps more important problem is that of the uses to
which absolute power was put. No doubt, the French people as a whole felt that
absolutism was a good thing in 1660. Did they still feel so in 1715? Had Louis
really been a "father" to his people, or was the proper word "tyrant"? The reign of
Louis XIV was to raise some fundamental questions in political theory, not the
least of which was whether anyone—even a competent, hardworking king like
Louis XIV—could be trusted to exercise absolute power wisely.*

1

The Theory of Absolutism

Jacques Bénigne Bossuet (1627–1704) was a bishop, popular preacher, and tutor to the Dauphin under Louis XIV. His political writings provided the most eloquent justification of the divine right of kings. (Citations from the Bible are taken directly from the King James Version.) The selection below was first published in 1709.

FROM *Politics Drawn from the Very Words of Holy Scripture*

BY *J. B. Bossuet*

TO HIS LORDSHIP THE DAUPHIN, God is the king of kings: it is his place to instruct them and to regulate them as his ministers. Hence listen well, Your Lordship, to the lessons that he gives to them in his Scripture, and learn from him the rules and the examples on which they should base their conduct.

BOOK I

Proposition 1

In order to form nations and unite peoples, it was necessary to establish a government.

It is not enough that men live in the same country or speak the same language, because becoming unsociable by the violence of their passions, and incompatible by their different humors, they cannot act as one unless they submit themselves altogether to a single government which rules over all.

Without that, even Abraham and Lot could not get along together and were forced to separate. . . .

If Abraham and Lot, two just men who were moreover closely related, could not get along with one another because of their servants, what kind of disorder must be expected among those who are bad! . . .

J. B. Bossuet, *Politique tirée des propress paroles de l'Écriture Sainte*, I (1870), pp. 229, 305, 306, 308, 313, 322, 325, 326, 333, 335, translated by L. Pearce Williams.

Justice has no other support than authority and the subordination of powers.

It is this order which restrains license. When everyone does what he wishes and has only his own desires to regulate him, everything ends up in confusion.

* * *

Proposition 3

It is only by the authority of the government that union is established amongst men.

The effect of this legitimate commandment is marked by these words often repeated in Scripture: to the command of Saul and of legitimate power, "all Israel obeyed as one man. They were forty thousand men, and all this multitude was as one." This is what is meant by the unity of a people, when each man renouncing his own will takes it and joins it to that of the prince and the magistrate. Otherwise there is no union; the people wander as vagabonds like a dispersed flock. . . .

* * *

Proposition 5

By means of government each individual becomes stronger.

The reason is that each is helped. All the forces of the nation concur in one and the sovereign magistrate has the right to reunite them. . . .

Thus the sovereign magistrate has in his hand all the forces of the nation which submits itself to obedience to him. . . .

Thus, an individual is not troubled by oppression and violence because he has an invincible defender in the person of the prince and is stronger by far than all those who attempt to oppress him.

The sovereign magistrate's own interest is to preserve by force all the individuals of a nation because if any other force than his own prevails among the people his authority and his life is in peril. . . .

Proposition 6

The law is sacred and inviolable.

In order to understand perfectly the nature of the law it is necessary to note that all those who have spoken well on it have regarded it in its origin as a pact and a solemn treaty by which men agree together under the authority of princes to that which is necessary to form their society.

This is not to say that the authority of the laws depends on the consent and acquiescence of the people; but only that the prince who, moreover by his very station has no other interest than that of the public good, is helped by the sagest heads in the nation and leans upon the experience of centuries gone by.

BOOK II

Proposition 7

A monarchy is the most common, the oldest, and the most natural form of government.

The people of Israel themselves formed a monarchy as being the universally received government. "Make us a king to judge us like all the nations."

If God was annoyed it was because up to then he had governed why he said to Samuel: "They have not rejected thee but they have this people by himself and that he had been their true king. This is rejected me, that I should not reign over them."

For the rest, his government was so clearly the most natural, that it is to be found at the beginning in all peoples.

We have seen it in sacred history: but here a short look at profane histories will show us that even those who lived in republics had begun first of all under kings.

Rome started that way and finally came back to it as to its natural state.

It was only later and little by little that the Greek cities formed their republics. The old opinion of Greece was that expressed by Homer in this famous sentence in the *Iliad:* "Many princes is not a good thing: let there be only one prince and one king."

At the present time there is no republic which was not at one time subject to a monarch. The Swiss were the subjects of the princes of the house of Austria. The United Provinces have only just escaped the domination of Spain and that of the house of Burgundy. The free cities of Germany have their individual lords other than the emperor who was the common head of the entire Germanic body. The cities of Italy which turned themselves into republics at the time of the emperor Rudolf bought their liberty from him. Venice even, which so boasts of having been a republic since its founding, was yet subject to the emperors, under the reign of Charlemagne and even long after: since then she has become a popular state from which she has now only recently become the state which we see.

Everybody thus begins with a monarchy and almost everybody has retained it as being the most natural state.

We have also seen that it has its foundation and its model in the rule of the father, that is to say in nature itself.

All men are born subjects: and paternal authority which accustoms them to obey, accustoms them at the same time to have only one chief.

Proposition 8

Monarchical government is the best.

   If it is the most natural, it is consequently the most durable and from that it follows also the strongest.

   It is also the most opposed to divisiveness, which is the worst evil of states, and the most certain cause of their ruin. . . . "Every kingdom divided against itself is brought to desolation; and every city or house divided against itself shall not stand."

   We have seen that Our Lord in this sentence has followed the natural progress of government and seems to have wished to show to realms and to cities the same means of uniting themselves that nature has established in families.

   Thus, it is natural that when families wish to unite to form a body of State, they will almost automatically coalesce into the government that is proper to them.

   When states are formed there is the impulse to union and there is never more union than under a single leader. Also there is never greater strength because everything works in harmony. . . .

BOOK III

Where we begin to explain the nature and properties of royal authority.

Article I

There are four characters or qualities essential to royal authority: First, royal authority is sacred; second, it is paternal; third, it is absolute; fourth, it is ruled by reason. . . .

Article II

Royal authority is sacred.

Proposition 1

God established kings as his ministers and rules peoples by them.

   We have already seen that all power comes from God. "The prince," St. Paul adds, "is the minister of God to thee for good. But if thou do that which is evil, be afraid; for he beareth not the sword in vain; for he is the minister of God, a revenger to execute wrath upon him that doeth evil."

   Thus princes act as ministers of God, and as his lieutenants on earth. It is by them that he exercises his rule.

Thus we have seen that the royal throne is not the throne of a man but the throne of God himself. . . .

He thus governs all peoples and gives to them all their kings; even though he governs Israel in a more particular and more explicit way. . . .

Proposition 2

The person of kings is sacred.

It thus appears that the person of kings is sacred and that to make an attempt on their lives is a sacrilege.

God has had them anointed by his prophets with a sacred unction as he has his pontiffs and his alters anointed.

But without the external application of this unction, they are sacred by their office, as being the representatives of the divine majesty, deputized by his providence to the execution of his designs. . . .

The title of Christ is given to kings; and they are everywhere called christs, or the anointed of the lord.

Article III

Royal authority is paternal and its proper character is goodness.

After what has been said, this truth has no need of proof.

We have seen that kings take the place of God, who is the true father of the human species. We have also seen that the first idea of power which exists among men is that of the paternal power; and that kings are modeled on fathers.

Everybody is also in accord, that the obedience which is owed to the public power can be found in the ten commandments only in the precept which obliges him to honor his parents.

Thus it follows from this that the name of king is a name for father and that goodness is the most natural character of kings. . . .

Proposition 3

The prince must provide for the needs of the people.

It is a royal right to provide for the needs of the people. He who undertakes it at the expense of the prince undertakes royalty: this is why it has been established. The obligation to care for the people is the foundation of all the rights that sovereigns have over their subjects.

This is why, in time of great need, the people have the right to have recourse to its prince. . . .

BOOK IV

Article I

The royal authority is absolute.

In order to make this term odious and insupportable, many wish to confuse absolute government and arbitrary government. But there is nothing more distinct than these two as we shall see when we speak of justice.

Proposition 1

The prince owes no account to anyone on what he orders.

"I counsel thee to keep the king's commandments, and that in regard to the oath of God. Be not hasty to go out of his sight, stand not in an evil thing; for he doeth whatsoever pleaseth him. Where the word of a king is, there is power: and who may say unto him what doest thou? Who so keepeth the commandment shall feel no evil thing."

Without this absolute authority, he cannot do good nor can he repress evil: it is necessary that his power be such that no one can hope to escape him; and finally the only defense of individuals against the public power ought to be their innocence. . . .

. . . The prince is by his office the father of his people; he is placed by his grandeur above all petty interests; even more: all his grandeur and his natural interests are that the people shall be conserved, for once the people fail him he is no longer prince. There is thus nothing better than to give all the power of the state to him who has the greatest interest in the conservation and greatness of the state itself. . . .

*   *   *

Proposition 4

Kings are not by this above the laws.

"Thou shalt in any wise set him king over thee . . . but he shall not multiply horses to himself. . . . Neither shall he multiply wives to himself that his heart turn not away: neither shall he greatly multiply to himself silver and gold. And it shall be, when he sitteth upon the throne of his kingdom, that he shall write him a copy of this law in a book out of that which is before the priest the Levite: and it shall be with him and he shall read therein all the days of his life: that he may learn to fear the Lord his god, to keep all the words of this law and these statutes to do them: that his heart be not lifted up above his brethren and that he turn not aside from the commandment to the right hand, or to the left: to the end that he may prolong his days in his kingdom, he, and his children."

It should be noticed that this law does not include only religion, but the law of the realm as well to which the prince was subject as much as any other, or even more than others by the justness of his will.

It is this that princes find difficult to understand. . . .

Kings therefore are subject like any others to the equity of the laws both because they must be just and because they owe to the people the example of protecting justice; but they are not subject to the penalties of the laws: or, as theology puts it, they are subject to the laws, not in terms of its coactive power but in terms of its directive power.

Louis XIV was in the habit of keeping a journal in which he noted the course of his reign. He was also concerned to pass on to his heirs the lessons he had learned over the years. The selection that follows reveals his thoughts from the age of twenty-one —when he first assumed full control of the state—to the end of his reign, when he took stock of what he had accomplished.

FROM *Louis XIV's Letters to His Heirs*

MANY REASONS, ALL VERY important, my son, have decided me, at some labour to myself, but one which I regard as forming one of my greatest concerns, to leave you these Memoirs of my reign and of my principal actions. I have never considered that kings, feeling in themselves, as they do, all paternal affection, are dispensed from the obligation common to fathers of instructing their children by example and by precept. On the contrary, it has seemed to me that in the high rank in which we are placed, you and I, a public duty is added to private, and that in the midst of all the respect which is given us, all the abundance and brilliancy with which we are surrounded—which are nothing more than the reward accorded by Heaven itself in return for the care of the peoples and States confided to our charge—this solicitude would not be very lofty if it did not extend beyond ourselves by making us communicate all our enlightenment to the one who is to reign after us.

I have even hoped that in this purpose I might be able to be more helpful to you, and consequently to my subjects, than any one else in the world; for there cannot be men who have reigned of more talents and greater experience than I, nor who have reigned in France; and I do not fear to tell you that the higher the position the greater are the number of things which cannot be viewed or understood save by one who is occupying that position.

I have considered, too, what I have so often experienced myself—the throng who will press round you, each for his own ends, the trouble you will have in finding disinterested advice, and the entire confidence you will be able to feel in that of a father who has no other interest but your own, no ardent wish but for your greatness.

* * *

Louis XIV *Letters to His Heirs,* in Jean Longnon, *A King's Lessons in Statecraft: Louis XIV* (1925), pp. 39-45, 47-53, 58, 66-70, 129-131, 149-151, 177-178, translated by Herbert Wilson. Reprinted by permission of Albert & Charles Boni, Inc., and Routledge & Kegan Paul Ltd., London.

I have given, therefore, some consideration to the condition of Kings—hard and rigorous in this respect—who owe, as it were, a public account of their actions to the whole world and to all succeeding centuries, and who, nevertheless, are unable to do so to all and sundry at the time without injury to their greatest interests, and without divulging the secret reasons of their conduct. And, not doubting that the somewhat important and considerable affairs in which I have taken part, both within and without my kingdom, will one day exercise diversely the genius and passions of writers, I should not be sorry for you to possess in these Memoirs the means of setting history aright if it should err or not rightly interpret, through not having faithfully reported or well divined my plans and their motives. I will explain them to you without disguise, even where my good intentions have not been happily conceived, being persuaded that only a small mind and one usually at fault could expect never to make a mistake, and that those who have sufficient merit to succeed the more often, discover some magnanimity in recognising their faults.

* * *

I made a beginning by casting my eyes over all the different parties in the State, not indifferently, but with the glance of experience, sensibly touched at seeing nothing which did not invite and urge me to take it in hand, but carefully watching what the occasion and the state of affairs would permit. Everywhere was disorder. My Court as a whole was still very far removed from the sentiments in which I trust you will find it. Men of quality and officials, accustomed to continual intrigue with a minister who showed no aversion to it, and to whom it had been necessary, arrogated to themselves an imaginary right to everything that suited them. There was no governor of a city who was not difficult to govern; no request was preferred without some complaint of the past, or some hint of discontent for the future, which I was allowed to expect and to fear. The favours demanded, and extorted, rather than awaited, by this one and that, and always considerable, no longer were binding on any one, and were only regarded as useful in order to maltreat thenceforth those to whom they wished me to refuse them.

The finances, which give movement and action to the great organisation of the monarchy, were entirely exhausted, so much so that we could hardly find the ways and means. Much of the most necessary and most privileged expenses of my house and of my own privy purse were in arrears beyond all that was fitting, or maintained only on credit, to be a further subsequent burden. At the same time a prodigality showed itself among public men, masking on the one hand their malversations by every kind of artifice, and revealing them on the other in insolent and daring luxury, as though they feared I might take no notice of them.

The Church, apart from its usual troubles, after lengthy disputes on matters of the schools, a knowledge of which they allowed was unnecessary to salvation for any one, with points of disagreement augmenting day by day through the heat and obstinacy of their minds, and ceaselessly involving fresh human interests, was finally threatened with open schism by men who were all the more dangerous because they were capable of being very serviceable and greatly deserving, had they themselves been less opinionated. It was not a question only of a few private and obscure professors, but of Bishops established in their Sees and able to draw away the multitude after them, men of high repute, and of piety worthy of being held in reverence had it been accompanied by submission to the sentiments of the Church, by gentleness, moderation, and charity. Cardinal de Retz, Archbishop of Paris, whom for well-known reasons of State I could not permit to remain in the kingdom, encouraged all this rising sect from inclination or interest, and was held in favour by them.

The least of the ills affecting the order of Nobility was the fact of its being shared by an infinite number of usurpers possessing no right to it, or one acquired by money without any claim from service rendered. The tyranny exercised by the nobles over their vassals and neighbours in some of my provinces could no longer be suffered or suppressed save by making severe and rigorous examples. The rage for duelling—somewhat modified by the exact observance of the latest regulations, over which I was always inflexible—was only noticeable in a now well advanced recovery from so inveterate an ill, so that there was no reason to despair of the remedy.

The administration of Justice itself, whose duty it is to reform others, appeared to me the most difficult to reform. An infinity of things contributed to this state of affairs: the appointments filled haphazard or by money rather than by selection and merit; scant experience and less knowledge on the part of some of the judges; the regulations referring to age and service almost everywhere eluded; chicanery firmly established through many centuries, and fertile in inventing means of evading the most salutary laws. And what especially conduced to this was the fact that these insatiable gentry loved litigation and fostered it as their own peculiar property, applying themselves only to prolong and to add to it. Even my Council, instead of supervising the other jurisdictions, too often only introduced disorder by issuing a strange number of contrary regulations, all in my name and as though by my command, which rendered the confusion far more disgraceful.

All this collection of evils, their consequences and effects, fell principally upon the people, who, in addition, were loaded with impositions, some crushed down by poverty, others suffering want from their own laziness since the peace, and needing above all to be alleviated and occupied.

Amid so many difficulties, some of which appeared to be insurmountable, three considerations gave me courage. The first was that in these matters it is not in the power of Kings—inasmuch as they are men and have to deal with men—to reach all the perfection they set before themselves, which is too far removed from our feebleness; but that this impossibility of attainment is a poor reason for not doing all we can, and this difficulty for not always making progress. This, moreover, is not without its uses, nor without glory. The second was that in all just and legitimate enterprises, time, the fact of doing them even, and the aid of Heaven, open out as a rule a thousand channels and discover a thousand facilities which we had not looked for. And the last was one which of itself seemed to me to hold out visibly that help, by disposing everything to the same end with which it inspired me.

In fact, all was calm everywhere. There was no movement, nor fear or seeming of any movement in my kingdom which might interrupt or oppose my designs. Peace was established with my neighbours, and to all seeming for as long as I myself wished it, owing to the conditions of affairs then prevailing.

It would assuredly have been to make a bad use of conditions of such perfect tranquillity, such as might only be met with very rarely in several centuries, not to turn them to the only account capable of making me appreciate them, at a time when my youth and the pleasure of being at the head of my armies would have caused me to wish to have more matters to deal with abroad. But inasmuch as my chief hope in these reforms was based on my will, their foundation at the outstart rested on making absolute my will by conduct which should impose submission and respect; by rendering scrupulous justice to all to whom I owed it; but in the bestowing of favours, giving them freely and without constraint to whomsoever I would, and when it should please me, provided that my subsequent action should let others know that while giving reasons to no one for my conduct I ruled myself none the less by reason, and that in my view the remembrance of services rendered, the favouring and promoting of merit—in a word, doing the right thing—should not only be the greatest concern but the greatest pleasure of a prince.

Two things without doubt were absolutely necessary: very hard work on my part, and a wise choice of persons capable of seconding it.

As for work, it may be, my son, that you will begin to read these Memoirs at an age when one is far more in the habit of dreading than loving it, only too happy to have escaped subjection to tutors and to have your hours regulated no longer nor lengthy and prescribed study laid down for you.

On this heading I will not warn you solely that it is none the less toil *by which* one reigns, and *for which* one reigns, and that the conditions of royalty, which may seem to you sometimes hard and vexatious in so lofty a position, would appear pleasant and easy if there was any doubt of your reaching it.

There is something more, my son, and I hope that your own experience will never teach it to you: nothing could be more laborious to you than a great amount of idleness if you were to have the misfortune to fall into it through beginning by being disgusted with public affairs, then with pleasure, then with idleness itself, seeking everywhere fruitlessly for what can never be found, that is to say, the sweetness of repose and leisure without having the preceding fatigue and occupation.

I laid a rule on myself to work regularly twice every day, and for two or three hours each time with different persons, without counting the hours which I passed privately and alone, nor the time which I was able to give on particular occasions to any special affairs that might arise. There was no moment when I did not permit people to talk to me about them, provided that they were urgent; with the exception of foreign ministers who sometimes find too favourable moments in the familiarity allowed to them, either to obtain or to discover something, and whom one should not hear without being previously prepared.

I cannot tell you what fruit I gathered immediately I had taken this resolution. I felt myself, as it were, uplifted in thought and courage; I found myself quite another man, and with joy reproached myself for having been too long unaware of it. This first timidity, which a little self-judgment always produces and which at the beginning gave me pain, especially on occasions when I had to speak in public, disappeared in less than no time. The only thing I felt then was that I was King, and born to be one. I experienced next a delicious feeling, hard to express, and which you will not know yourself except by tasting it as I have done. For you must not imagine, my son, that the affairs of State are like some obscure and thorny path of learning which may possibly have already wearied you, wherein the mind strives to raise itself with effort above its purview, more often to arrive at no conclusion, and whose utility or apparent utility is repugnant to us as much as its difficulty. The function of Kings consists principally in allowing good sense to act, which always acts naturally and without effort. What we apply ourselves to is sometimes less difficult than what we do only for our amusement. Its usefulness always follows. A King, however skilful and enlightened be his ministers, cannot put his own hand to the work without its effect being seen. Success, which is agreeable in everything, even in the smallest matters, gratifies us in these as well as in the greatest, and there is no satisfaction to equal that of noting every day some progress in glorious and lofty enterprises, and in the happiness of the people which has been planned and thought out by oneself. All that is most necessary to this work is at the same time agreeable; for, in a word, my son, it is to have one's eyes open to the whole earth; to learn each hour the news concerning every province and every nation, the secrets of every court, the mood and the weaknesses of each Prince and of every foreign minister; to be well-informed on an infinite number of matters about which we are supposed to know nothing; to elicit from our subjects what they hide from us with the greatest care; to discover the most remote opinions of our own courtiers and the most hidden interests of those who come to us with quite contrary professions. I do not know of any other pleasure we would not renounce for that, even if curiosity alone gave us the opportunity.

I have dwelt on this important subject longer than I had intended, and far more for your sake than for my own; for while I am disclosing to you these methods and these alleviations attending the greatest cares of royalty I am not unaware that I am likewise depreciating almost the sole merit which I can hope for in the eyes of the world. But in this matter, my son, your honour is dearer to me than my own; and if it should happen that God call you to govern before you have yet taken to this spirit of application and to public affairs of which I am speaking, the least deference you can pay to the advice of a father, to whom I make bold to say you owe much in every kind of way, is to begin to do and to continue to do for some time, even under constraint and dislike, for love of me who beg it of you, what you will do all your life from love of yourself, if once you have made a beginning.

I gave orders to the four Secretaries of State no longer to sign anything whatsoever without speaking to me; likewise to the Controller, and that he should authorise nothing as regards finance without its being registered in a book which must remain with me, and being noted down in a very abridged abstract form in which at any moment, and at a glance, I could see the state of the funds, and past and future expenditure.

The Chancellor received a like order, that is to say, to sign nothing with the seal except by my command, with the exception only of letters of justice, so called because it would be an injustice to refuse them, a procedure required more as a matter of form than of principle; and I allowed to remain the administering and remissions of cases manifestly pardonable, although I have since changed my opinion on this subject, as I will tell you in its proper place. I let it be understood that whatever the nature of the matter might be, direct application must be made to me when it was not a question that depended only on my favour; and to all my subjects without distinction I gave liberty to present their case to me at all hours, either verbally or by petitions.

At first petitions came in very great numbers, which nevertheless did not discourage me. The disorder in which my affairs had been placed was productive of many; the novelty and expectation, whether vain or unjust, attracted not less. A large number were presented connected with law-suits, which I could not and ought not to take out of the ordinary tribunals in order to have them adjudicated before me. But even in these things, apparently so unprofitable, I found great usefulness. By this means I informed myself in detail as to the state of my people; they saw that I was mindful of them, and nothing won their heart so much. Oppression on the part of the ordinary tribunals might be represented to me in such a way as to make me feel it desirable to gain further information in order to take special measures when they were required. One or two examples of this kind prevented a thousand similar ills; the complaints, even when they were false and unjust, hindered my officers from giving a hearing to those which were more genuine and reasonable.

Regarding the persons whose duty it was to second my labours, I resolved at all costs to have no prime minister; and if you will believe me, my son, and all your successors after you, the name shall be banished for ever from France, for there is nothing more undignified than to see all the administration on one side, and on the other, the mere title of King.

To effect this, it was necessary to divide my confidence and the execution of my orders without giving it entirely to one single person, applying these different people to different spheres according to their diverse talents, which is perhaps the first and greatest gift that Princes can possess.

I also made a resolution on a further matter. With a view the better to unite in myself alone all the authority of a master, although there must be in all affairs a certain amount of detail to which our occupations and also our dignity do not permit us to descend as a rule, I conceived the plan, after I should have made choice of my ministers, of entering sometimes into matters with each one of them, and when they least expected it, in order that they might understand that I could do the same upon other subjects and at any moment. Besides, a knowledge of some small detail acquired only occasionally, and for amusement rather than as a regular rule, is instructive little by little and without fatigue, on a thousand things which are not without their use in general resolutions, and which we ought to know and do ourselves were it possible that a single man could know and do everything.

*   *   *

Time has shown what to believe, and I have now been pursuing for ten years fairly consistently, as it seems to me, the same course, without relaxing my application; kept well-informed of everything; listening to the least of my subjects; at any hour knowing the number and quality of my troops, and the state of my fortified towns, unremitting in issuing my orders for all their requirements; dealing at once with foreign ministers; receiving and reading dispatches; doing myself a portion of the replies and giving to my secretaries the substance of the others; regulating the State receipts and expenditure; requiring those whom I placed in important posts to account directly to me; keeping my affairs to myself as much as any one before me had ever done; distributing my favours as I myself chose; and retaining, if I mistake not, those who served me in a modest position which was far removed from the elevation and power of prime ministers, although loading them with benefits for themselves and their belongings.

The observation by others of all these things doubtless gave rise to some opinion of me in the world; and this opinion has in no small measure contributed to the success of what I have since undertaken, inasmuch as nothing could have produced such great results in so short a time as the reputation of the Prince.

*   *   *

After having thus fully informed myself in private discussions with them I entered more boldly into practical action. There was nothing that appeared more pressing to me than to alleviate the condition of my people, to which the poverty of the provinces and the compassion I felt for them strongly urged me. The state of my finances, as I have shown you, seemed to oppose this, and in any case counselled delay; but we must always be in haste to do well. The reforms I took in hand, though beneficial to the public, were bound to be irksome to a large number of private people. It was appropriate to make a beginning with something that could only be agreeable, and besides, there was no other way of maintaining any longer even the name of peace without its being followed by some sort of sop of this kind as a promise of greater hopes for the future. I therefore put aside any other considerations and, as a pledge of further alleviation, I first remitted three millions of the taxes for the following year which had already been prescribed and were awaiting collection.

At the same time, but with the intention of having them better observed than heretofore, I renewed the regulations against wearing gold and silver on clothes, and a thousand other foreign superfluities which were a kind of charge and contribution, outwardly voluntary but really obligatory, which my subjects, especially those most qualified and the persons at my Court, paid daily to neighbouring nations, or, to be more correct, to luxury and vanity.

For a thousand reasons, and also to pave the way for the reform of the administration of justice so greatly needed, it was necessary to diminish the authority of the chief jurisdictions which, under the pretext that their judgments were without appeal, and, as we say, sovereign and of final resort, regarded themselves as separate and independent sovereignties. I let it be known that I would no longer tolerate their assumptions. The *Cour des Aides* in Paris having been the first to exceed its duties and in some degree its jurisdiction, I exiled a few of its most offending officers, believing that if this remedy were thoroughly employed at the outset, it would relieve me of the necessity of its frequent application afterwards; and my action has been successful.

Immediately afterwards I gave them to understand my intentions still better in a solemn decree by my Supreme Council. For it is quite true that these jurisdictions have no cause to regulate each other in their different capacities, which are defined by laws and edicts. In former times these sufficed to make them live in peace with each other, or in the event of certain differences arising between them, especially in matters regarding private individuals, these were so rare and so little difficult of adjustment, that the Kings themselves decided them with a word, more often than not during a walk, on the report of the Magistrates, who then consisted of a very small number, until, owing to the growth in the kingdom of these matters and still more of chicanery, this duty was entrusted principally to the Chancellor of France and to the Administrative Council of which I have spoken already to you. Now these officials of necessity should be fully authorised to regulate the competence of the other jurisdictions (and also all other matters of which from time to time we deem it suitable for reasons of public utility, or of our own proper service, to give them cognisance exceptionally) by taking it over from them inasmuch as they derive their power only from us. Notwithstanding, owing to this spirit of self-sufficiency and the disorder of the times, they only yielded in so far as seemed good to them, and outstepped their powers daily and in all manner of cases in spite of their proper limitations, often enough going so far as to say that they recognised the King's will in no other form than that contained in the Ordinances and the authorised Edicts.

By this decree I forbade them all in general to give any judgments contrary to those of my Council under any pretext whatsoever, whether in their own jurisdiction or in their private capacity, and I commanded them, when one or the other felt they had suffered hurt to make their complaint to me and have recourse to my authority, inasmuch as I had only entrusted to them to exercise justice towards my subjects and not to create their own justice of themselves, which thing constitutes a part of sovereignty so clearly united to the Crown and so much the prerogative of the King alone that it cannot be communicated to any other.

In the same year, but a little later, for I shall not observe too closely the order of dates, in a certain matter connected with the finances of all the record offices in general, and one which they had never dared carry through in connection with those of the Parliament in Paris, because the property belonged to the officers of that body and sometimes to the chambers as a whole, I made it be seen that these officers must submit to the common law, and that there was nothing to prevent my absolving them from it when it pleased me to give this reward for their services.

About the same time, I did a thing which seemed even too bold, so greatly had the gentlemen of the law profited by it up till then, and so full were their minds of the importance they had acquired in the recent troubles through the abuse of their power. From three quarters I reduced to two all the fresh mortgages which were charged upon my revenue, which had been effected at a very extortionate rate during the war, and which were eating up the best of my farms of which the officials of the corporations had acquired the greater part. And this made them regard it as a fine thing to treat them as harshly as possible in their most vital interests. But at bottom this action of mine was perfectly just, for two quarters was still a great deal in return for what they had advanced. The reform was necessary. My affairs were not in such a state that I had nothing to fear from their resentment. It was more to the purpose to show them that I feared nothing they could do and that the times were changed. And those who from different interests had wished that these corporations might win the day learnt on the contrary from their submission what was due to me.

*   *   *

I also made a change in my household at that time, in which all the nobility of the realm had an interest. This had to do with my chief stables in which I increased the number of pages by more than half, and took pains both that the selection was made with more care and that they were better instructed than they had been up till then.

I was aware that what had prevented people of quality from aspiring to these kinds of positions was either the ease with which all conditions of folk had been recommended and admitted to them, or the scant opportunity afforded to them as a rule of approaching my person, or the neglect to perfect them in their duties which had insensibly arisen. To remedy all this I determined to take care to appoint all the pages myself, to make them share with those of my private stables all the domestic services which the latter rendered me, and to choose the best instructors in my realm to train them.

As regards the public, the results I hoped to obtain were to provide an excellent education for a large number of gentlemen, and for my own private benefit to have always a supply of people coming from this school more capable, and better disposed than the general run of my subjects, to enter my service.

I had yet another object for my personal attention which concerned principally people of substance, but the effect of which was afterwards spread over my kingdom generally. I knew what immense sums were spent by private individuals and were perpetually being withdrawn from the State by the trade in lace of foreign manufacture. I saw that the French were wanting neither in industry nor in the material for undertaking this work themselves, and I had no doubt that if they did this on the spot they could provide it far more cheaply than what they imported from such a distance. From these considerations I determined to establish works here, the effect of which would be that the great would moderate their expenditure, the people would derive the entire benefit of what the rich spent, and the large sums leaving the State would insensibly produce additional abundance and wealth by being retained in it, and beyond this would provide occupation for many of my subjects who up till then had been forced either to become slack through want of work or to go in search of it among our neighbours.

However, inasmuch as the most laudable plans are never carried out without opposition, I foresaw well that the lace merchants would oppose this with all their power, because I had no doubt that they found it paid them better to sell their wares which came from a distance, whereof the proper value could not be known, than those which were manufactured here within sight of everybody.

But I was determined to cut short by my authority all the trickery they might use, and so I gave them sufficient time to sell the foreign lace which they had before my edict was published, and when this time had expired I caused all that they still had to be seized as having come in since my prohibition, while, on the other hand, I caused shops filled with new manufactures to be opened, at which I obliged private individuals to make their purchases.

The example of this in a short while set up the manufacture of many other things in my State, such as sheets, glass, mirrors, silk stockings, and similar wares.

I took special plans to find out how to augment and assure to my subjects their maritime trade by making the ports I possessed safer, and seeking places to construct new ones. But while doing this I took in hand another enterprise of no lesser utility, which was to link by a canal the Ocean with the Mediterranean, in such wise that it would be no longer necessary to go round Spain to pass from one sea to the other. It was a great and difficult undertaking.

But it was infinitely advantageous to my realm, which thus became the centre, and as it were the arbiter of the trade of the whole of Europe. And it was no less glorious for me who in the accomplishing of this object raised myself above the greatest men of past centuries who had undertaken it without result.

* * *

I have never failed, when an occasion has presented itself, to impress upon you the great respect we should have for religion, and the deference we should show to its ministers in matters specially connected with their mission, that is to say, with the celebration of the Sacred Mysteries and the preaching of the doctrine of the Gospels. But because people connected with the Church are liable to presume a little too much on the advantages attaching to their profession, and are willing sometimes to make use of them in order to whittle down their most rightful duties, I feel obliged to explain to you certain points on this question which may be of importance.

The first is that Kings are absolute *seigneurs,* and from their nature have full and free disposal of all property both secular and ecclesiastical, to use it as wise dispensers, that is to say, in accordance with the requirements of their State.

The second is that those mysterious names, the Franchises and Liberties of the Church, with which perhaps people will endeavour to dazzle you, have equal reference to all the faithful whether they be laymen or tonsured, who are all equally sons of this common Mother; but that they exempt neither the one nor the other subjection to Sovereigns, to whom the Gospel itself precisely enjoins that they should submit themselves.

The third is that all that people say in regard to any particular destination of the property of the Church, and to the intention of founders, is a mere scruple without foundation, because it is certain that, inasmuch as the founders of benefices when transmitting their succession were not able to free them either from the quit-rental or the other dues which they paid to particular *seigneurs,* so for a far stronger reason they could not release them from the first due of all which is payable to the Prince as *Seigneur* over all, for the general welfare of the whole realm.

The fourth is that if up till now permission has been given to ecclesiastics to deliberate in their assemblies on the amount which it is their duty to provide, they should not attribute this custom to any special privilege, because the same liberty is still left to the people of several provinces as a former mark of the probity existing in the first centuries, when justice was sufficient to animate each individual to do what he should according to his ability and, notwithstanding, this never prevented either laymen or ecclesiastics when they refused to fulfil their obligations of their own free will, from being compelled to do so.

And the fifth and last is that if there are dwellers in our Empire more bound than others to be of service to us as regards their property as a whole, these should be the beneficiaries who only hold all they have at our option.

The claims attaching to them have been established as long as those of their benefices, and we have titles to them which have been preserved from the first period of the monarchy. Even Popes who have striven to despoil us of this right have made it more clear and more incontestable by the precise retractation of their ambitious pretensions which they have been obliged to make.

But we might say that in this matter there is no need of either titles or examples, because natural equity alone is sufficient to illustrate this point. Would it be just that the Nobility should give its services and its blood in the defence of the realm and so often consume its resources in the maintenance of the offices with which it is charged, and that the people (with so little substance and so many mouths to fill) should bear in addition the sole weight of all the expenses of the State, while ecclesiastics, exempt by their profession from the dangers of war, from the profusion of luxury and the burden of families, should enjoy in abundance all the advantages of the general public without ever contributing anything to its necessities?

* * *

I have sustained this war with the high hand and pride which becomes this realm; through the valour of my Nobility and the zeal of my subjects I have been successful in the undertakings I have accomplished for the good of the State; I have given my whole concern and application to reach a successful issue; I have also put in motion the measures I thought necessary in fulfilling my duties, and in making known the love and tenderness I have for my people, by procuring by my labours a peace which will bring them rest for the remainder of my reign so that I need have no other care than for their welfare. After having extended the boundaries of this Empire, and protected my frontiers with the important strongholds I have taken, I have given ear to the proposals of peace which have been made to me, and I have exceeded perhaps on this occasion the limits of prudence in order to accomplish so great a work. I may say that I stepped out of my own character and did extreme violence to myself in order promptly to secure repose for my subjects at the expense of my reputation, or at least of my own particular satisfaction, and perhaps of my renown, which I willingly risked for the advantage of those who have enabled me to acquire it. I felt that I owed them this mark of gratitude. But seeing at this hour that my most vehement enemies have only wished to play with me and that they have employed all the artifices they could to deceive me as well as their allies by forcing them to contribute to the immense expenditure which their disordered ambition demanded, I do not see any other course to take than that of considering how to protect ourselves securely, making them understand that a France thoroughly united is stronger than all the powers they have got together at so great pains, by force and artifice, to overwhelm her. Up to now I have made use of the extraordinary measures which on similar occasions I have put into practice in order to provide sums proportionate to the expenditure indispensable to uphold the glory and safety of the State. Now that all sources are *quasi*-exhausted I come to you at this juncture to ask your counsel and your assistance, whence a safe issue will arise. Our enemies will learn from the efforts we shall put forth together that we are not in the condition they would have people believe, and by means of the help which I am asking of you and which I believe to be indispensable, we shall be able to force them to make a peace which shall be honourable to ourselves, lasting for our tranquillity, and agreeable to all the Princes of Europe. This is what I shall look to up to the moment of its conclusion, even in the greatest stress of the war, as well as to the welfare and happiness of my people which have always been, and will continue to be to the last moment of my life, my greatest and most serious concern.

2

Absolutism in Practice

One of the ways in which Louis XIV tamed the nobility of France was to create a totally artificial society at Versailles in which only the nobles knew how to behave. He thus granted status to the aristocracy without having to yield any political power to them. This society may be appreciated from this brief glimpse of the social mores of the time.

FROM *The Splendid Century*
BY *W. H. Lewis*

COURT ETIQUETTE WAS A life study. Who for instance could guess that at Versailles it was the height of bad manners to knock at a door? You must scratch it with the little finger of the left hand, growing the finger nail long for that purpose. Or could know that you must not *tutoyer* an intimate friend in any place where the King was present? That if the lackey of a social superior brought you a message, you had to receive him standing, and bareheaded? You have mastered the fact that you must not knock on a door, so when you go to make your first round of calls in the great houses in the town, you scratch: wrong again, you should have knocked. Next time you rattle the knocker, and a passing exquisite asks you contemptuously if you are so ignorant as not to know that you give one blow of the knocker on the door of a lady of quality? Who could guess that if you encounter the royal dinner on its way from the kitchens to the table, you must bow as to the King himself, sweep the ground with the plume of your hat, and say in a low, reverent, but distinct voice, *La viande du Roi?* Many times must the apprentice courtier have echoed the psalmist's lament, "Who can tell how oft he offendeth?" And it behoved you not to offend, for the King had an eye like a hawk, or shall we say, like a school prefect, for any breach of etiquette, and not even the most exalted were safe from his reproof. One night at supper his chatterbox of a brother put his hand in a dish before Louis had helped himself: "I perceive," said the King icily, "that you are no better able to control your hands than your tongue." Once at Marly, Mme. de Torcy, wife of a

W. H. Lewis, *The Splendid Century*, pp. 39-40, 45-47. Adapted by permission of Octopus Publishing Group.

minister, took a seat above a duchess at supper. Louis, to her extreme discomfort, regarded her steadfastly throughout the meal, and when he reached Mme. de Maintenon's room, the storm broke; he had, he said, witnessed a piece of insolence so intolerable that the sight of it had prevented him from eating: a piece of presumption which would have been unendurable in a woman of quality. It took the combined efforts of Mme. de Maintenon and the Duchess of Burgundy the rest of the evening to pacify him. Decidedly not a king with whom to take liberties, or even make mistakes. . . .

* * *

It was perhaps as well that the courtier had no inducement to linger abed of a morning, for it behoved him to make an early start if he was to be at his post in the ante-room when the King was awakened at eight o'clock. (We are inclined at this time of the day to envy the ladies, who are still in bed, and will not be making a move until nine.) The courtier had had his own toilet to make, which, even if it did not include washing, meant an elaborate powdering and prinking, before attending his patron's *lever* and following him to that of the King.

In the King's room the day began at about a quarter to eight, when the First Valet de Chambre, who had slept in the room, would dismantle and put away his folding bed; if it was winter, the two *porte-buchon du roi,* the royal faggot bearers, would next make their appearance to light the King's fire, followed a minute or two later by the King's watchmaker to wind up the royal watch. From a side door would enter the royal wigmaker, coming from the room in which the King's wigs reposed, each on its pedestal, in glass-fronted wardrobes—hunting wigs, council wigs, evening wigs, walking wigs, an endless array of wigs. But at the moment the wigmaker carries two only, the short wig which the King wears whilst dressing, and the first wig of the day.

All this time Louis would be in bed asleep, or pretending to be so, with the bedclothes turned down to his hips, as is his uncomfortable custom, winter and summer. On the first stroke of eight his valet would wake him, and the exciting news that His Majesty was awake would pass into the closely packed ante-room to set the courtiers rustling like a field of ripe corn in a summer breeze. At the same moment the First Physician and the First Surgeon entered the room, together with the King's old nurse, who went up to the bed, kissed him, and asked how he had slept, whilst the two medical men rubbed the King down and changed his shirt. At a quarter-past eight the Grand Chamberlain was admitted, together with those courtiers who had the coveted *grandes entrées,* and Louis was presented with Holy Water. Now was the time to ask the King a favour, we are told, which suggests that in this, as in so many other respects, his psychology differed considerably from that of ordinary mortals.

Had I been Louis, with Louis' day in prospect, it would certainly have been no propitious moment to approach me. The *Grande Entrée* now withdrew, while the King recited the Office of the Holy Ghost, after which they were re-admitted for the treat of seeing him put on his dressing gown and wig;

and a few minutes later the common herd of the nobility swarmed in and packed the room to watch Louis dress. We are grateful to one of them for having recorded the fact that they found him putting on his breeches, "which he did very cleverly and gracefully." When the moment came for him to put on his shirt, that garment would be handed to the senior person present by the First Valet and the man so favoured would then hand it to the King. So far, we notice that there has been no mention of washing, much less of taking a bath, in spite of the fact that so long ago as 1640 the well-bred person is recommended to wash his hands every day "and his face nearly as often." Not of course in water, which was considered a dangerous proceeding, but by rubbing the face with cotton soaked in diluted and scented alcohol. Perhaps Louis confined his washing to those occasions on which he was shaved, that is every other day. After that operation, during which the valet held a mirror in front of him, he washed in water mixed with spirits of wine, and then dried his own face without any assistance from his entourage. The barber, we may note in passing, was one of the King's five hundred attendants who had free board and lodging at Court. Perhaps it was in the evening that Louis had his bath, for we know that he sometimes took one; and that it was a rare event may perhaps be inferred from the fact that when he did so, an official of the Fifth Section of the First Kitchen stood by with perfume burning on a red-hot shovel to keep the air sweet. This section of the kitchen department, some forty-five strong, also included the two *porte-chaise d'affaires,* gentlemen in black velvet and swords, who had the exclusive privilege of emptying the royal *chaise percée,* at what stage in the *lever* is not stated. By this time the first awe of the King's presence had worn off a trifle, and some conversation was got up, more often than not about hunting.

The Duke of Saint-Simon (1675–1755) came from one of the oldest noble families in France. He was typical of the feudal nobility that Louis XIV wished to bring under the authority of the monarchy. His memoirs describe court life and give insight into the ways in which Louis XIV tried to control the aristocracy. His reports on politics in the provinces were clearly influenced by his own position at court. His memoirs were written in 1739–51 and were first published in French in 1788.

FROM *The Memoirs of the Duke of Saint-Simon*

LOUIS XIV WAS MADE for a brilliant Court. In the midst of other men, his figure, his courage, his grace, his beauty, his grand mien, even the tone of his voice and the majestic and natural charm of all his person, distinguished him till his death as the King Bee, and showed that if he had only been born a simple private gentleman, he would equally have excelled in fêtes, pleasures, and gal-

The Memoirs of the Duke of Saint-Simon on the Reign of Louis XIV and the Regency, I (1857), pp 315-319; II (1857), pp. 3-6, 64-66, 95-98, 214-219, 354-357; III (1857), 225-228, 232-233, translated by Bayle St. John.

lantry, and would have had the greatest success in love. The intrigues and adventures which early in life he had been engaged in—when the Comtesse de Soissons lodged at the Tuileries as superintendent of the Queen's household, and was the centre figure of the Court group—had exercised an unfortunate influence upon him: he received those impressions with which he could never after successfully struggle. From this time, intellect, education, nobility of sentiment, and high principle in others, became objects of suspicion to him, and soon of hatred. The more he advanced in years the more this sentiment was confirmed in him. He wished to reign by himself. His jealousy on this point unceasingly, became weakness. He reigned, indeed, in little things; the great he could never reach: even in the former, too, he was often governed. The superior ability of his early ministers and his early generals soon wearied him. He liked nobody to be in any way superior to him. Thus he chose his ministers, not for their knowledge, but for their ignorance; not for their capacity, but for their want of it. He liked to form them, as he said; liked to teach them even the most trifling things. It was the same with his generals. He took credit to himself for instructing them; wished it to be thought that from his cabinet he commanded and directed all his armies. Naturally fond of trifles, he unceasingly occupied himself with the most petty details of his troops, his household, his mansions; would even instruct his cooks, who received, like novices, lessons they had known by heart for years. This vanity, this unmeasured and unreasonable love of admiration, was his ruin. His ministers, his generals, his mistresses, his courtiers, soon perceived his weakness. They praised him with emulation and spoiled him. Praises, or to say truth, flattery, pleased him to such an extent, that the coarsest was well received, the vilest even better relished. It was the sole means by which you could approach him. Those whom he liked owed his affection for them to their untiring flatteries. This is what gave his ministers so much authority, and the opportunities they had for adulating him, of attributing everything to him, and of pretending to learn everything from him. Suppleness, meanness, an admiring, dependent, cringing manner—above all, an air of nothingness—were the sole means of pleasing him.

This poison spread. It spread, too, to an incredible extent, in a prince who, although of intellect beneath mediocrity, was not utterly without sense, and who had had some experience. Without voice or musical knowledge, he used to sing, in private, the passages of the opera prologues that were fullest of his praises! He was drowned in vanity; and so deeply, that at his public suppers—all the Court present, musicians also—he would hum these selfsame praises between his teeth, when the music they were set to was played!

And yet, it must be admitted, he might have done better. Though his intellect, as I have said, was beneath mediocrity, it was capable of being formed. He loved glory, was fond of order and regularity; was by disposition prudent, moderate, discreet, master of his movements and his tongue. Will it be believed? He was also by disposition good and just! God had sufficiently gifted him to enable him to be a good King; perhaps even *a tolerably great King!* All the evil came to him from elsewhere. His early education was so neglected that nobody dared approach his apartment. He has often been heard to speak of those times with bitterness, and even to relate that, one evening he was found in the basin of the Palais Royale garden fountain, into which he had fallen! He was scarcely taught how to read or write, and remained so ignorant, that the most familiar historical and other facts were utterly unknown to him! He fell, accordingly, and sometimes even in public, into the grossest absurdities.

It was his vanity, his desire for glory, that led him, soon after the death of the King of Spain, to make that event the pretext for war; in spite of the renunciations so recently made, so carefully stipulated, in the marriage contract. He marched into Flanders; his conquests there were rapid; the passage of the Rhine was admirable; the triple alliance of England, Sweden, and Holland only animated him. In the midst of winter he took Franche Comté, by restoring which at the peace of Aix la-Chapelle, he preserved his conquests in Flanders. All was flourishing then in the state. Riches everywhere. Colbert had placed the finances, the navy, commerce, manufactures, letters even, upon the highest point; and this age, like that of Augustus, produced in abundance illustrious men of all kinds,—even those illustrious only in pleasures.

*   *   *

Thus, we see this monarch grand, rich, conquering, the arbiter of Europe; feared and admired as long as the ministers and captains existed who really deserved the name. When they were no more, the machine kept moving some time by impulsion, and from their influence. But soon afterwards we saw beneath the surface; faults and errors were multiplied, and decay came on with giant strides; without, however, opening the eyes of that despotic master, so anxious to do everything and direct everything himself, and who seemed to indemnify himself for disdain abroad by increasing fear and trembling at home.

*   *   *

A short time after the death of Mademoiselle de l'Enclos, a terrible adventure happened to Courtenvaux, eldest son of M. de Louvois. Courtenvaux was commander of the Cent-Suisses, fond of obscure debauches; with a ridiculous voice, miserly, quarrelsome, though modest and respectful; and in fine a very stupid fellow. The King, more eager to know all that was passing than most people believed, although they gave him credit for not a little curiosity in this respect, had authorised Bontemps to engage a number of Swiss in addition to those posted at the doors, and in the parks and gardens. These attendants had orders to stroll morning, noon, and night, along the corridors, the passages, the staircases, even into the private places, and, when it was fine, in the court-yards and gardens; and in secret to watch people, to follow them, to notice where they went, to notice who was there, to listen to all the conversation they could hear, and to make reports of their discoveries. This was assiduously done at

Versailles, at Marly, at Trianon, at Fontainebleau, and in all the places where the King was. These new attendants vexed Courtenvaux considerably, for over such new-comers he had no sort of authority. This season, at Fontainebleau, a room, which had formerly been occupied by a party of the Cent-Suisses and of the body-guard, was given up entirely to the new corps. The room was in a public passage of communication indispensable to all in the château, and in consequence, excellently well adapted for watching those who passed through it. Courtenvaux more than ever vexed by this new arrangement, regarded it as a fresh encroachment upon his authority, and flew into a violent rage with the new-comers, and railed at them in good set terms. They allowed him to fume as he would; they had their orders; and were too wise to be disturbed by his rage. The King, who heard of all this, sent at once for Courtenvaux. As soon as he appeared in the cabinet, the King called to him from the other end of the room, without giving him time to approach, and in a rage so terrible, and for him so novel, that not only Courtenvaux, but Princes, Princesses, and everybody in the chamber, trembled. Menaces that his post should be taken away from him, terms the most severe and the most unusual, rained upon Courtenvaux, who, fainting with fright, and ready to sink under the ground, had neither the time nor the means to prefer a word. The reprimand finished by the King saying, "Get out." He had scarcely the strength to obey.

The cause of this strange scene was that Courtenvaux, by the fuss he had made, had drawn the attention of the whole Court to the change effected by the King, and that, when once seen, its object was clear to all eyes The King, who hid his spy system with the greatest care, had counted upon this change passing unperceived, and was beside himself with anger when he found it made apparent to everybody by Courtenvaux's noise. He never regained the King's favour during the rest of his life; and but for his family he would certainly have been driven away, and his office taken from him. . . .

* * *

The death of the Abbé de Vatteville occurred at the commencement of this year, and made some noise, on account of the prodigies of the Abbé's life. This Vatteville was the younger son of a Franche Comté family; early in life he joined the Order of the Chartreux monks, and was ordained priest. He had much intellect, but was of an impetuous spirit, and soon began to chafe under the yoke of a religious life. He determined, therefore, to set himself free from it, and procured some secular habits, pistols, and a horse. Just as he was about to escape over the walls of the monastery by means of a ladder, the prior entered his cell. Vatteville made no to-do, but at once drew a pistol, shot the prior dead, and effected his escape.

Two or three days afterwards, travelling over the country and avoiding as much as possible the frequented places, he arrived at a wretched road-side inn, and asked what there was in the house. The landlord replied—"A leg of mutton and a capon." "Good!" replied our unfrocked monk; "put them down to roast."

The landlord replied that they were too much for a single person, and that he had nothing else for the whole house. The monk upon this flew in a passion, and declared that the least the landlord could do was to give him what he would pay for; and that he had sufficient appetite to eat both leg of mutton and capon. They were accordingly put down to the fire, the landlord not daring to say another word. While they were cooking, a traveller on horseback arrived at the inn, and learning that they were for one person, was much astonished. He offered to pay his share to be allowed to dine off them with the stranger who had ordered this dinner; but the landlord told him he was afraid the gentleman would not consent to the arrangement. Thereupon the traveller went up stairs and civilly asked Vatteville if he might dine with him on paying half of the expense. Vatteville would not consent, and a dispute soon arose between the two; to be brief, the monk served this traveller as he had served the prior, killed him with a pistol shot. After this he went down stairs tranquilly, and in the midst of the fright of the landlord and of the whole house, had the leg of mutton and capon served up to him, picked both to the very bone, paid his score, remounted his horse, and went his way.

Not knowing what course to take, he went to Turkey, and in order to succeed there, had himself circumcised, put on the turban, and entered into the militia. His blasphemy advanced him, his talents and his colour distinguished him; he became *Bacha,* and the confidential man in the Morea, where the Turks were making war against the Venetians. He determined to make use of this position in order to advance his own interests, and entering into communication with the generalissimo of the Republic, promised to betray into his hands several secret places belonging to the Turks, but on certain conditions. These were, absolution from the Pope for all crimes of his life, his murders and his apostasy included; security against the Chartreux and against being placed in any other Order; full restitution of his civil rights, and liberty to exercise his profession of priest with the right of possessing all benefices of every kind. The Venetians thought the bargain too good to be refused, and the Pope, in the interest of the Church, accorded all the demands of the Bacha. When Vatteville was quite assured that his conditions would be complied with, he took his measures so well that he executed perfectly all he had undertaken. Immediately after he threw himself into the Venetian army, and passed into Italy. He was well received at Rome by the Pope, and returned to his family in Franche Comté, and amused himself by braving the Chartreux.

At the first conquest of the Franche Comté, he intrigued so well with the Queen-mother and the ministry, that he was promised the Archbishopric of Besançon; but the Pope cried out against this on account of his murders, circumcision, and apostasy. The King sided with the Pope, and Vatteville was obliged to be contented with the abbey of Baume, another good abbey in Picardy, and divers other advantages.

Except when he came to the Court, where he was always received with great distinction, he remained at his abbey of Baume, living there like a grand seigneur, keeping a fine pack of hounds, a good table, entertaining jovial company, keeping mistresses very freely; tyrannising over his tenants and his neighbours in the most absolute manner. The intendants gave way to him, and by express orders of the Court allowed him to act much as he pleased, even with the taxes, which he regulated at his will, and in his conduct was oftentimes very violent. With these manners and this bearing, which caused him to be both feared and respected, he would often amuse himself by going to see the Chartreux, in order to plume himself on having quitted their frock. He played much at *hombre*, and frequently gained *codille* (a term of the game), so that the name of the Abbé Codille was given to him. He lived in this manner, always with the same licence and in the same consideration, until nearly ninety years of age. . . .

*   *   *

Such was our military history of the year 1706—a history of losses and dishonour. It may be imagined in what condition was the exchequer with so many demands upon its treasures. For the last two or three years the King had been obliged, on account of the expenses of the war, and the losses we had sustained, to cut down the presents that he made at the commencement of the year. Thirty-five thousand louis in gold was the sum he ordinarily spent in this manner. This year, 1707, he diminished it by ten thousand louis. It was upon Madame de Montespan that the blow fell. Since she had quitted the Court the King gave her twelve thousand louis of gold each year. This year he sent word to her that he could only give her eight. Madame de Montespan testified not the least surprise. She replied, that she was only sorry for the poor, to whom indeed she gave with profusion. A short time after the King had made this reduction—that is, on the 8th of January,—Madame La Duchesse de Bourgogne gave birth to a son. The joy was great, but the King prohibited all those expenses which had been made at the birth of the first-born of Madame de Bourgogne, and which had amounted to a large sum. The want of money indeed made itself felt so much at this time, that the King was obliged to seek for resources as a private person might have done. A mining speculator, named Rodes, having pretended that he had discovered many veins of gold in the Pyrenees, assistance was given him in order that he might bring these treasures to light. He declared that with eighteen hundred workmen he would furnish a million (francs' worth of gold) each week. Fifty-two millions a year would have been a fine increase of revenue. However, after waiting some little time, no gold was forthcoming, and the money that had been spent to assist this enterprise was found to be pure loss.

    The difficulty of finding money to carry on the affairs of the nation continued to grow so irksome that Chamillart, who had both the finance and the war departments under control, was unable to stand against the increased trouble and vexation which this state of things brought him. More than once he had represented that this double work was too much for him. But the King had in former times expressed so much annoyance from the troubles that arose between the finance and war departments, that he would not separate them, after having once joined them together. At last, Chamillart could bear up against his heavy load no longer. The vapours seized him: he had attacks of giddiness in the head; his digestion was obstructed; he grew thin as a lath. He wrote again to the King, begging to be released from his duties, and frankly stated that, in the state he was, if some relief was not afforded him, everything would go wrong and perish. He always left a large margin to his letters, and upon this the King generally wrote his reply. Chamillart showed me this letter when it came back to him, and I saw upon it with great surprise, in the handwriting of the King, this short note: "Well! let us perish together."

The necessity for money had now become so great, that all sorts of means were adopted to obtain it. Amongst other things, a tax was established upon baptisms and marriages. This tax was extremely onerous and odious. The result of it was a strong confusion. Poor people, and many of humble means, baptised their children themselves, without carrying them to the church, and were married at home by reciprocal consent and before witnesses, when they could find no priest who would marry them without formality. In consequence of this there were no longer any baptismal extracts; no longer any certainty as to baptisms or births; and the children of the marriages solemnised in the way I have stated above were illegitimate in the eyes of the law. Researches and rigours in respect to abuses so prejudicial were redoubled therefore; that is to say, they were redoubled for the purpose of collecting the tax.

From public cries and murmurs the people in some places passed to sedition. Matters went so far at Cahors, that two battalions which were there had great difficulty in holding the town against the armed peasants; and troops intended for Spain were obliged to be sent there. It was found necessary to suspend the operation of the tax, but it was with great trouble that the movement of Quercy was put down, and the peasants, who had armed and collected together, induced to retire into their villages. In Perigord they rose, pillaged the bureaux, and rendered themselves masters of a little town and some castles, and forced some gentlemen to put themselves at their head. They declared publicly that they would pay the old taxes to King, curate, and lord, but that they would pay no more, or hear a word of any other taxes or vexation. In the end it was found necessary to drop this tax upon baptism and marriages, to the great regret of the tax-gatherers, who, by all manner of vexations and rogueries, had enriched themselves cruelly.

It was one thing to claim that the royal will was absolute; it was another thing to enforce it throughout France. To do this, Louis XIV and his great minister Jean Baptiste Colbert (1619–1683) set out to create a bureaucracy that would extend into the farthest reaches of the realm. Through this bureaucracy, information would flow to Versailles and orders could be carried out in the localities. The effectiveness of absolutism was determined by the efficiency of both operations.

Memoires of Nicolas-Joseph Foucault (1850), pp. 417 ff., translated by L. Pearce Williams.

FROM *Memoirs of Nicolas-Joseph Foucault*

COLBERT TO THE COMMISSIONERS IN THE FIELD, April 28, 1679

You know that I have written yo3u by order of the King every year before this in order to stimulate you to make your visit to all the elections [an administrative unit] of the generality of . . . with great care and also in order to let you know what you should occupy yourself with principally in this visit. Since this is a way of procuring the easing of the people's lot, almost equal to that which the King has given them by the great decrease that he has made in the taxes, His Majesty has ordered me to tell you that he wishes that this year you will make a more complete visit of all the elections and parishes of the above generality that you have not yet made, and that you should start this immediately and without any hesitation; and to this effect I will give you, in a few words, the principal points that you should examine.

The first and the most important is the imposition of the *tailles* [*a property tax from which the nobility and clergy were exempt—Ed.*], on which, although I am persuaded that the application that you already have shown prevents many abuses, nevertheless, since it is certain that, either in the drawing up of the tax rolls, or in the levying and collection of the *tailles,* or in the actual reception that the receivers make of the collectors, or in the pressures that one exercises and the expenses that the taxable people are forced to pay, there is still a good deal of disorder of which you are not aware since those who are guilty and who profit from it take care to hide it from you—this being the case the King wants you to enter into detail on all these points, in order that there is nothing on which you are not exactly informed and to which you will not be able to apply whatever remedies may be necessary.

His Majesty also wishes that you should examine the state of commerce and manufactures in the same generality, together with the food supply and the number of domestic animals, and that you should consider these three points as the fertile sources from which the people draw their money, not only for their own subsistence, but also for paying all their taxes; so that His Majesty desires that you should look into with care the means not only of maintaining them but even of augmenting them and of re-establishing commerce and manufactures which had disappeared because of not having received any help. . . .

You know well enough the intentions of the king regarding the garrisoning of troops. . . . This is why I shall rest content merely to add that His Majesty has been informed that in the greatest number of cities and places where the inhabitants have furnished the housing of troops for the last ten or twelve years, the mayors and aldermen have kept and distributed amongst themselves the money which was given to them by the general receivers of finances for the reimbursement of the said inhabitants; and since there is no theft more obvious than this, and none which merits more to be punished,

Mémoires of Nicolas-Joseph Foucault (1850), pp. 417ff., translated by L. Pearce Williams.

since the people are in the hands of their magistrates and since this theft can consequently begin every day, His Majesty wishes that in the visit that you are going to make, you will examine carefully if the inhabitants of the cities and places of your generality which have furnished housing for troops make the same complaints against the mayors and aldermen, and in case you find some-one who has been in charge for five or six years and who has applied for his own profit a large enough sum, let me know about it so that I can render an account to His Majesty and he will be able to send you orders so that you can give an exemplary punishment of this crime. . . .

FROM *Administrative Correspondence Under the Reign of Louis XIV*

THE BISHOP OF MARSEILLES TO COLBERT, LAMBESC, November 20, 1668

No matter with what care I tried, I was unable to get the deputies to this assembly to go beyond the sum of 400,000 [*French pounds—Ed.*] without certain conditions. The main ones are compensation for the expense that the troops have caused this year, the revocation of the edict on soap, and the revocation of the edict on genealogical experts.

They defend themselves in terms of the sum of money by pointing to the exhaustion of money in the province which is, in truth, very great, and which proceeds from the taxes on the businessmen, from the inquest on false nobility, which has drawn out enormous amounts of money by rather extraordinary avenues, the considerable expenses which have fallen on the communities with the arrangement of the [*royal—Ed.*] domain, from which apparently the money does not come back into the treasury, and the circulation of counterfeit five-sous pieces which has used up a great deal of good money and which will destroy commerce if there is not a true remedy forthcoming. In truth, if the province was only assessed for what the King wishes to draw from it and which he demands as his free gift there would be no trouble in arranging that and in persuading the deputies.

The province by law has a right to compensation [*for garrisoning—Ed.*], and this year it has cost almost one hundred thousand livres, and since the King, no doubt, will not wish to subtract this amount from his gift this will mean it will cost the province five hundred thousand pounds and there is some justice to the position that the province should be assured of this compensation for the future in order to dismiss the apprehension under which these people labor that in giving to H. M. a considerable gift they will at the same time be asked, in the province, to pay for the lodging of troops or any other expense that may be demanded.

G. B. Depping, ed., *Correspondence administrative sous le règne de Louis XIV*, I (1850), pp. 381-382, 384-385, 389, 399, translated by L. Pearce Williams.

As for the affair of the soap, it is certain that not everything is being done to carry out the ordinance of H. M. as the price of soap has gone up. Since the old manufactories no longer work and since new ones are being established in neighboring provinces, there is the fear that this manufacture, which is one of the largest in the realm and which gives so much profit in this province, will be destroyed in the end if something is not done about it. You will do, Monsieur, what you will consider just.

As for the edict on the genealogical experts, if this is carried out it will mean the establishment of more than 800 officers at the same time that the King is working so well to abolish those who are useless and a burden on the people; moreover, paying them will force the disbursement of immense sums.

I also feel it necessary, Monsieur, to inform you that the nobility of this province, having the desire to sell their wheat at an excessive price, would like to restrain the public liberty (the right to import wheat by sea) on a foodstuff so necessary to life. They have worked, by all kinds of means, to force this assembly to join with them; but the deputies know the famine that would affect all the poor people of the province, and on this affair I have no doubt that they will oppose themselves to this unjust proposition, which is so harmful to the public. . . . Since the assembly has been meeting for almost three months without accomplishing much, and as it cannot disband until the return of the courier that has been sent to you, you would be doing a great favor to send him back soon, and you will find complete acquiescence to all that H. M. may order.

COLBERT TO PRESIDENT D'OPPÈDE, Saint-Germain, March 6, 1671

I have given an account to the King of the request that you have made to the assembly of the communities of Provence, in conformity to the order of H. M. He orders me to tell you that it is necessary to terminate this affair promptly considering how long it has been going on. . . .

I have already received several complaints that the aldermen of the city of Marseilles are not carrying out the execution of the edicts for the liberation (of the port) and particularly for the payment of the 20 per cent, and the confiscation of merchandise which would enter without paying. . . .

March 13 . . . I will not even answer the offer that the province has made of giving 200,000 pounds as the free gift, since you know that the King wishes the amount that is mentioned in your instructions and is waiting for you to get it done.

COLBERT TO THE COUNT DE GRIGNAN, Saint-Germain, March 20, 1671

I have reported to the King what you have been pleased to write me on the offer that the assembly of the communities of Provence have made for his free gift and the difficulty that you are encountering in raising it to the sum that H. M. desires; but he has told me at the same time to let you know that he will not rest content with less than what he has asked for and thus has no doubt that you will employ all the means that you consider necessary to oblige the said assembly to give him this satisfaction.

COLBERT TO THE COUNT DE GRIGNAN, Saint-Germain, October 16, 1671

I can assure you that H. M. wanted 500,000 pounds from the province last year, as this, and it was only the pleading of your letters and those of Monsieur d'Oppède, that led H. M. to reduce it to 450,000 pounds for particular reasons that I cannot remember at present; but this year H. M. wants 500,000 pounds. . . .

COLBERT TO PRESIDENT D'OPPÈDE, Saint-Germain, October 23, 1671

The King was somewhat surprised to hear that the deputies of the communities have returned to their homes under the pretext of holidays and that after a negotiation of three weeks you have only obtained from them the sum of 300,000 pounds. I ought to tell you that I really fear that the King may take the resolution to dismiss this assembly without taking anything from it since H. M. is not accustomed, by the conduct of other estates, to all these long negotiations for such a modest sum as that which he demands from Provence. . . .

COLBERT TO THE COUNT DE GRIGNAN, Paris, December 25, 1671

I have reported to the King on the bad conduct of the assembly of the communities of Provence and, since H. M. is not disposed to suffer it any longer, he has given the necessary orders to dismiss it and at the same time has sent *lettres de cachet* intended to exile the ten deputies who caused the most trouble to Grandville, Cherbourg, Saint-Malo, Morlaix, and Concarneau. The said letters and orders will be sent to you by the first ordinary post, and I do not think it necessary to recommend that you be punctual and exact in executing them, knowing with how much warmth and zeal you act in everything that concerns the service of the King.

COLBERT TO THE BISHOP OF MARSEILLES, Versailles, December 31st, 1671

The King accepts the 450,000 pounds that the assembly of the communities of Provence offered for the free gift, but H. M. is so indignant at the conduct of the deputies in making their deliberation that he has sent orders to exile ten of the worst troublemakers to the provinces of Normandy and Brittany, which orders have been addressed to Monsieur the Count de Grignan. Provence should easily know how disadvantageous it has been to it to have chosen deputies so little attached to its true interest, but I do not know if these complaints may not be useless since it looks as though H. M. will not permit another such assembly of the communities in Provence.

3

The Evaluation of the Reign

Absolutism depended upon the efficiency of the bureaucracy created to make it effective. This machinery of government is the subject studied by James E. King, who sees its development as the result of the new science of the seventeenth century. Just as the new science emphasized facts over theories, so the government of Louis XIV was an attempt to apply reason to actual situations. To do so channels of information and chains of command had to be created.

FROM *Science and Rationalism in the Government of Louis XIV*

BY *James E. King*

SUCH WAS THE CENTRAL government of France in the period 1661 to 1683. It is necessary to remind oneself that most of its actual work was performed in committees, subcommittees of the councils, and in the bureaus functioning under the various ministers and secretaries of state. In the provinces the will of this organization was exercised, in the main, through four distinct structures: that of justice, finances, the military, and the church. The last of these we can omit from our considerations as it has no direct bearing on our story.

The justice of the King was carried to the kingdom by the "sovereign" parlements. These were, for all but extraordinary cases, the supreme courts of the realm. To them came appeals from all the lower courts, as the *présidiaux, bailliages,* or *sénéchaussées,* in their particular jurisdictions. The chief of these parlements in prestige and real authority was that at Paris. This might be called the King's parlement. Other parlements were situated at Toulouse, Rouen, Grenoble, Bordeaux, Dijon, Aix, Rennes, Pau, Metz, and Besançon, and several sovereign courts functioned elsewhere. The natural head, excluding the King, of all these courts was the chancellor of France, and it was through his department that appointments to them were made. The *conseil du Roi,* as represented in any of its four divisions, might override the decisions or opinions of the parlements.

James E. King, *Science and Rationalism in the Government of Louis XIV, 1661-1683* (1950), pp. 124-130, 136-137. Copyright Johns Hopkins Press. Reprinted by permission of The Johns Hopkins Press.

The financial administration of the kingdom, and this must be extended to include economic as well as tax administration, was carried on, primarily, by the intendants with their subordinates. In our period, France was divided into twenty-six large tax districts, for administrative purposes, called generalities. These were headed by twenty-five intendants. The generalities, in turn, were subdivided into smaller districts called elections and the elections into parishes. A regular hierarchy of officials, within these areas, supervised the levying and collection of taxes, judged cases involving taxation, performed accounting, kept tax rolls, and allocated sums for local costs of government. Under the intendants operated a separate group of officials, with undefined power, who supervised or interfered in these functions.

The so-called military government of the King was exercised by royal governors in thirty-seven governments. These men were ordinarily the peers of the realm or princes of the blood. Many of the ancient prerogatives of these gentlemen, as governors, had been drained off by the agents of the secretary of state for war and the intendants, but their prestige was still very considerable and if the governor was a man of capacity, cooperated with the intendants, was friendly to and trusted by the King and ministers, he could still wield considerable influence. Below the governor were usually four or five lieutenant-generals and, beneath them, governors of local places, cities or royal chateaux. Lieutenant-generals and these local governors were often almost independent of the provincial governor and were also usually chosen from the higher nobility. The primary duties of the governors were to maintain order and obedience to the crown in the provinces and to give armed support, if necessary, to the executions and functions of the other administrations.

*   *   *

The administrative prerogatives of the intendant as supervisor of the royal services of justice, police, and finances in the provinces had been rather clearly defined by the time that Colbert assumed his full role in the government. During the personal reign of Louis XIV, these powers were even more definitely organized and solidified and the monarchy assumed the form which it was to retain almost to the end of the *ancien régime*. At the center of this monarchy was the officer called the *contrôleur général*, and, intimately allied to his functions and carrying his authority throughout the realm, were the intendants of the provinces. This close relationship, or interdependence, was largely the creation of Colbert. The expression of it was the development of the practice of regular correspondence between the intendants and the *contrôleur général*. From the very beginning of his administration, Colbert maintained a prodigious correspondence with his subordinates and, particularly, with the intendants. The reciprocal necessity of submitting reports, surveys and memoirs to the *contrôleur général* became a regular duty of these officials. This was the most striking innovation of the minister in the government. As Usher writes in his *History of the Grain Trade in France,* "The development of the informing function of the intendants was thus one of the most direct results of the personal influence of Colbert. Nor was any function of the new administration more important or more literally unique."

Under the regime of Colbert and Louis XIV, the intendant assumed the part of delegate administrator in the most obscure sections that the royal power penetrated. . . . A literal reading of the instructions and circular letters sent to the intendants or *commissaires départis* into the generalities and *pays d'élections* from 1663 through 1683 would probably leave the researcher at a loss to imagine any possible field of government which was not committed to their inspection. But every inspection required the return of a report or written survey to the King, the secretaries of state, or the *contrôleur général,* and it was on such reports that *ordonnances* were formed, policies decreed, and projects drawn up by the ministry for presentation to the councils and the King.

It was the desire of the King, according to his Minister, that the intendants should come to know "perfectly all abuses" in the area of their responsibility, and to know them appears to have been considered as equal to remedying them. The insistence on thorough penetration into the most obscure corners of provincial affairs was the theme dominating instructions. The King recognized the physical limitations of his own personal desire to learn of the details of his realm "piece by piece," details which he would acquire himself if it were possible; therefore, trusted emissaries must perform the vicarious functions of a protean crown.

*   *   *

The intendants were, then, the legal eyes of the Monarchy. Colbert wrote his intendants and ordered them carefully, and personally, to investigate the levying of all taxes in all the elections of their generality "in a way that nothing escapes you." He spurred them on to greater thoroughness by representing these requests as being relayed from "His Majesty" who urged them to make "a serious reflection on all that which happens in the area of the Generality in which you serve . . . that you enter into the detail of the conduct of all those who are employed thereto." He acknowledged the difficulty of knowing all the various matters to "the depth," but this difficulty only emphasized the need of more continuous application to the task, in order that he might give to "His Majesty all your advice on all that which can apply in the future to the end which he sets for himself."

*   *   *

The multifarious functions of the intendants and the essentially informative character of these functions are progressively evident in early correspondence of Colbert with them. Usher asserts that technical and statistical information was less frequently required of the intendant than a statement of the general impression of conditions in his generality; however, as time passed the Minister became ever more exacting in his demands and increasingly discriminating in the segregation of fact from rumor. His persistency in insisting on adequate and valid information had the end result of developing an administrative standard of expectation and compliance which accounts for the fullness of the reports of the intendants after Colbert's death. The requirement of continuous reporting, the necessity for presenting, to the ministry, digested summary statements of the most diverse facts in his generality, placed the intendant, perforce, as another writer has observed, in the midst of numbers. By the very nature of his functions, he became a statistical agent of the central government.

The general pattern of government by inquiry was precisely laid down in the *Instruction pour les maîtres des requêtes, commissaires départis dans les provinces* of September 1663. This circular letter significantly and, in a sense, officially underlined the henceforth consistent policy of Colbert and Louis XIV in regard to the duties of the intendants. It initiated a vast inquest into the state of the realm with the intendants as the royal investigators; an inquest which was never completed in the life of its originator. The correspondence of Colbert reveals that most of the information requested at this time was still being sought by him twenty years later. Twenty years after that the Duke of Beauvillier made almost the same inquiries when forming his famous memoirs for the instruction of Louis XIV's grandson, the Duke of Burgundy. However imperfectly the designs of the inquest might be carried out, the instruction of 1663 was an unqualified endorsement by Louis XIV and his Minister of the ideal of administration based on the accumulation of political and social statistics.

* * *

Among the memoirs resulting from the inquest of 1663 those of Charles Colbert de Croissy, a brother of the Minister, are singled out by Clement as of superior quality, displaying, besides a diversity of information, an unusual frankness. His reports on Poitou, Touraine, Anjou, Alsace and the three bishoprics of Metz, Toul and Verdun were notably detailed and revealed the sad plight of their peoples. Other such memoirs have been discovered on Brittany, Rouen, Champagne, Burgundy, Bourges, Berry, and Moulins dating from the early years of Colbert's administration.

The utility of a summary account of the personal qualities of the members of the parlements, and other superior courts, probably seemed particularly pointed to Louis XIV and Colbert, both of whom always kept the lessons of the Fronde carefully nurtured in their memories. We have seen the attention given to this detail in the third section of the memoir. All the intendants of the provinces were requested to submit careful notes on the morals, capacities, influence, property, connections, and functions of the personnel of these courts. The resulting reports were in many cases partial and in most cases must have appeared inadequate. But this might be expected at a time when the intendants were but beginning to assume the new role assigned to them by an exacting Minister. At any rate, the *"Notes sécrètes"* sent to Colbert in response to this request form an extensive and entertaining part of the administrative correspondence edited by Depping.

M. Lamoignon of the Parlement of Paris was a pompous person with an "affectation of great probity and of a great integrity hiding a great ambition." M. Bailleul had a "gentle and easy disposition, acquiring through his civility many friends in the Palais [of the Parlement] and at the court." One de Nesmond "married to the sister of Mr the first president, is governed by her." M. Menardeau-Sampré was "very capable, firm, obstinate . . . governed by a damlle of the rue Saint-Martin." As for M. Fayet, he was "less than nothing." In the *Chambre des Enquestes,* M. Faure was "stupid, ignorant, brutal, fearing extraordinarily M. Hervé; he is a man of letters, but loves extraordinarily his own interests." But this was a report on all the major courts of the kingdom; in the Parlement of Brittany, the sieur De Brequingy had good intention "but he is weak and of a very mediocre mind." Jacquelot, sieur de la Motte, was "without capacity, and addicted to debauches with women and wine," but M. Montigny had "many of all kinds of good qualities and no bad ones." The reporter on the councillors of the *cours des Aydes* at Rouen contented himself almost entirely with variations on the two words: *"probité"* and *"capacité."* If his subject was very commendable he had both *"probité"* and *"capacité."*

However deficient some of the first reports of the intendants might be, it would appear that, with practice, the technique could be too well mastered. In July 1676, Colbert wrote in perplexity to M. Le Blanc at Rouen, "I have received the account of the provender which has been consumed in your generality during the winter quarter; but you fail to explain for what reason you send it to me, and I cannot supply it."

François-Marie Arouet (1694–1778), or Voltaire, was one of the most prominent and prolific writers of the Enlightenment in France. The age of Louis XIV was, to him, the golden age of French culture, and he attributed much of this excellence to the regime of absolutism instituted by the Su-King. The selection below was first published in French in 1751.

FROM *The Age of Louis XIV*

BY *Voltaire*

WE OWE IT TO PUBLIC MEN who have benefited their age to look at the point from which they started in order better to appreciate the changes they have brought about in their country. Posterity owes them an eternal debt of gratitude for the examples they have given, even when their achievements have been surpassed, and this well-deserved glory is their only reward. It was certainly the love of this sort of glory that inspired Louis XIV when, as soon as he began to govern for himself, he set out to reform his kingdom, embellish his court and perfect the arts.

Not only did he impose upon himself the duty of working regularly with each one of his ministers, but any man of repute could obtain a private audience with him, and every citizen was free to present him with petitions and projects. The petitions were received, first of all, by a master of requests, who noted his comments in the margin and sent them on to the offices of the ministers. The projects were examined in Council when they deserved it and their authors were more than once admitted to discuss their proposals with the ministers in the King's presence. In this way, despite Louis's absolute power, the nation could still communicate with the monarch.

Louis XIV trained and accustomed himself to work, and this work was all the more difficult because it was new to him and because he could easily be distracted by the lures of pleasure. The first dispatches he sent to his ambassadors he wrote himself, and he later often minuted the most important letters in his own hand. None were written in his name without his having them read to him.

After the fall of Fouquet, Colbert had scarcely re-established order in the finances when the King canceled all the arrears due on taxes from 1647 to 1656 and, above all, three millions of the taille. Five hundred thousand crowns' worth of onerous duties were abolished. So the Abbé de Choisi seems to be either very misinformed or very unjust when he says that the receipts were not decreased. It is clear that they were decreased by these remissions, though they were later increased as a result of better administration.

The efforts of the First President of Bellièvre, helped by the generosity of the Duchess of Aiguillon and several other citizens, had already established the general hospital in Paris. The King enlarged it and had others built in all the principal towns of the kingdom.

The highways, which up till then had been impassable, were no longer neglected and gradually became what they are today under Louis XV—the admiration of all foreigners. Whatever direction one goes from Paris, one can now travel for nearly two hundred miles, except for a few places, on well-surfaced roads lined with trees. The roads built by the ancient Romans were more lasting, but not as spacious or as beautiful.

Colbert directed his genius principally toward commerce, which was still largely undeveloped and whose basic principles were still unknown. The English, and still more the Dutch, carried almost all French trade in their ships. The Dutch in particular loaded their ships with our goods in our ports and distributed them throughout Europe. In 1662 the King began to exempt his subjects from a duty called the freight tax, which all foreign vessels had to pay, and he gave French merchants every facility for transporting their goods themselves more cheaply. It was then that our maritime trade began to develop. The council of commerce, which still exists today, was established, and the King presided over it every fortnight.

The ports of Dunkirk and Marseilles were declared free, and very soon this advantage attracted the trade of the Levant to Marseilles and that of the North to Dunkirk.

* * *

The West India company was encouraged no less than the others; the King supplied a tenth of all its funds. He gave thirty francs a ton on exports and forty on imports. All those who had ships built in French ports received five francs for each ton their vessel could carry.

* * *

Paris in those days was very far from being what it is now. There was neither lighting, police protection nor cleanliness. Provision had to be made for the continual cleaning of the streets and for lighting them every night with five thousand lamps; the whole town had to be paved; two new gates had to be built and the old ones restored; a permanent guard, both mounted and on foot, was needed for the security of citizens. All this the King took upon himself, allotting the funds for these necessary expenses. In 1667 he appointed a magistrate whose sole duty was to supervise the police. Most of the large cities of Europe only initiated these examples many years later; none has equaled them. There is no city paved like Paris, and even Rome has no street lighting.

Everything was beginning to improve so noticeably that the second holder of the office of lieutenant of police in Paris acquired a reputation which placed him among the distinguished men of his age; and indeed he was a man of great ability. He was afterward in the Ministry and he would have made a fine general. The post of lieutenant of police was below his birth and merit, and yet it gained him a much greater reputation than did the uneasy and transient ministerial office which he obtained toward the end of his life.

It is worth noting here that M. d'Argenson was not the only member of the old nobility to hold the office of magistrate. Far from it; France is almost the only country in which the old nobility has often worn magisterial robes. Almost all other states, from motives which are a remnant of Gothic barbarity, fail to realize that there is greatness in this profession.

From 1661 onward, the King was continually occupied in building the Louvre, Saint-Germain and Versailles. Private individuals, following his example, built hundreds of superb, spacious buildings in Paris. Their number increased to such an extent that there sprang up around the Palais-Royal and Saint-Sulpice two new towns vastly superior to the old one. This same time saw the invention of that splendid convenience, the coach, ornamented with mirrors and suspended on springs; thus a citizen of Paris could travel about this great city in far greater luxury than that in which the ancient Romans rode in triumph to the Capitol. This custom, which began in Paris, soon spread to the rest of Europe and has became so common that it is no longer a luxury.

Louis XIV had a taste for architecture, gardens and sculpture, and his taste was characterized by a liking for grandeur and impressiveness. In 1664, Controller General Colbert assumed the office of director of buildings (which is really the Ministry of the Arts), and no sooner had he done so than he set about furthering his master's schemes. The first task was to complete the Louvre. François Mansart, one of the greatest architects France has ever had, was chosen to construct the vast buildings that were planned. He was unwilling to undertake this commission unless he had freedom to reconstruct any parts of the edifice which seemed to him defective when he had completed them, and this mistrust of himself, which might have involved too great an expenditure, led to his exclusion. The chevalier Bernini was then sent for from Rome, a man whose name was famous by virtue of the colonnade surrounding St. Peter's Square, the equestrian statue of Constantine and the Navonna fountain. Carriages were provided for his journey. He was brought to Paris like a man who came to honor France. Apart from five louis a day during the eight months he stayed, he also received a present of fifty thousand crowns, together with a pension of two thousand, and one of five hundred for his son. Louis XIV's generosity to Bernini was even greater than that of Francis I to Raphael. By way of acknowledgment, Bernini later made, in Rome, the equestrian statue of the King which is now to be seen at Versailles. But when he arrived in Paris with so much circumstance, he was amazed to see the plan of the façade of the Louvre which faces Saint-Germain l'Auxerrois, and which soon after, when executed, became one of the most august monuments of architecture in the world. Claude Perrault had made this plan, and it was put into execution by Louis Levau and Dorbay. Perrault invented the machines by which were transported the stones, fifty-two feet long, that formed the pediment of this majestic edifice. Sometimes people go a long way to find what they already have at home. No palace in Rome has an entrance comparable to that of the Louvre, for which we are indebted to the Perrault whom Boileau dared to ridicule. Travelers admit that the famous Italian villas are inferior to the château of Maisons, which was built at such a small cost by François Mansart. Bernini was magnificently rewarded and did not deserve his rewards; he merely furnished plans which were never put into execution.

While building the Louvre, the completion of which is so greatly to be desired, while creating a town at Versailles near the Château which has cost so many millions, while building the Trianon and Marly and embellishing many other edifices, the King also built the Observatory, which was begun in 1666, at the same time as he founded the Academy of Sciences. But his most glorious monument, by its usefulness and its greatness as much as by the difficulties of its construction, was the canal which joins the two seas and which finds an outlet at the port of Sète, built especially for the purpose. All this work was begun in 1664 and continued without interruption until 1681. The foundation of the Invalides, with its chapel, the finest in Paris, and the establishment of Saint-Cyr, the last of many works built by the King—these by themselves would suffice to make his memory revered. Four thousand soldiers and a large number of officers find consolation in their old age and relief for their wounds and wants in the first of these great institutions; two hundred and fifty daughters of noblemen receive an education worthy of them in the other; together they are like so many voices praising Louis XIV. The establishment of Saint-Cyr will be surpassed by the one which Louis XV has just created for the education of five hundred noblemen; but so far from causing Saint-Cyr to be forgotten, it serves to remind one of it; the art of doing good has been brought to perfection.

At the same time, Louis XIV wanted to achieve something even greater and more generally useful, though more difficult; he wanted to reform the laws. For this task he employed the Chancellor Seguier, Lamoignon, Talon, Bignon, and above all, the councilor of state, Pussort. Sometimes he attended their meetings himself. The year 1667 was marked both by his first laws and by his first conquests. The civil ordinance appeared first and was followed by the code for the rivers and forests, and then by statutes concerning all the industries, by a criminal code, one for commerce and one for the marine. These followed one another in an almost annual succession. New laws were even established in favor of the Negroes of our colonies, a race of men who had hitherto not enjoyed the common rights of humanity.

One cannot expect a sovereign to possess a profound knowledge of jurisprudence, but the King was well informed about the principal laws: he was imbued with their spirit and knew how to enforce or mitigate them as the occasion demanded. He often judged his subjects' cases, not only in the Council of the Secretaries of State, but also in the so-called Council of Parties. There are two celebrated judgments of his in which he decided against his own interest.

In the first, in 1680, the issue was one between himself and some private citizens of Paris who had built on his land. He decided that they should keep the houses, together with the land which belonged to him and which he ceded to them.

The other case concerned a Persian called Roupli, whose goods had been seized by his revenue commissioners in 1687. His decision was that all should be returned to him, and the King added a present of three thousand crowns. Roupli returned to his country full of admiration and gratitude. When we later met Mehemet Rizabeg, the Persian ambassador to Paris, we found that he had known about this incident for a long time, for it had become famous.

* * *

[*The King—Ed.*] was the legislator of his armies as well as of his people as a whole. It is surprising that, before his time, there was no uniform dress among the troops. It was he who, in the first year of his administration, ordered that each regiment should be distinguished by the color of its dress or by different badges; this regulation was soon adopted by all other nations. It was he who instituted brigadiers and who put the household troops on their present footing. He turned Cardinal Mazarin's guards into a company of musketeers and fixed the number of men in the companies at five hundred; moreover, he gave them the uniform which they still wear today.

Under him there were no longer constables, and after the death of the Duke of Epernon, no more colonel generals of infantry; they had become too powerful, and he quite rightly wanted to be sole master. Marshal Grammont, who was only colonel of horse of the French Guards under the Duke of Epernon and who took his orders from this colonel general, now took them only from the King, and was the first to be given the title of Colonel of the Guards. The King himself installed his colonels at the head of the regiments, giving them with his own hand a gilt gorget with a pike, and afterward, when the use of pikes was abolished, a spontoon, or kind of half-pike. In the King's Regiment, which he created himself, he instituted grenadiers, on the scale of four to a company in the first place; then he formed a company of grenadiers in each regiment of infantry. He gave two to the French Guards. Nowadays there is one for each battalion throughout the whole infantry. He greatly enlarged the Corps of Dragoons, and gave them a colonel general. The establishment of studs for breeding horses, in 1667, must not be forgotten, for they had been completely abandoned beforehand and they were of great value in providing mounts for the cavalry, an important resource which has since been too much neglected.

It was he who instituted the use of the bayonet affixed to the end of the musket. Before his time, it was used occasionally, but only a few companies fought with this weapon. There was no uniform practice and no drill; everything was left to the general's discretion. Pikes were then thought of as the most redoubtable weapon. The first regiment to have bayonets and to be trained to use them was that of the Fusiliers, established in 1671.

The manner in which artillery is used today is due entirely to him. He founded artillery schools, first at Douai, then at Metz and Strasbourg; and the Regiment of Artillery was finally staffed with officers who were almost all capable of successfully conducting a siege. All the magazines in the kingdom were well stocked, and they were supplied annually with eight hundred thousand pounds of powder. He created a regiment of bombardiers and one of hussars; before this only his enemies had had hussars.

In 1688 he established thirty regiments of militia, which were provided and equipped by the communes. These militia trained for war but without abandoning the cultivation of their fields.

Companies of cadets were maintained in the majority of frontier towns; there they learned mathematics, drawing and all the drills, and carried out the duties of soldiers. This institution lasted for ten years, but the government finally tired of trying to discipline these difficult young people. The Corps of Engineers, on the other hand, which the King created and to which he gave its present regulations, is an institution which will last forever. During his reign the art of fortifying strongholds was brought to perfection by Marshal Vauban and his pupils, who surpassed Count Pagan. He built or repaired a hundred and fifty fortresses.

To maintain military discipline, the King created inspectors general and later directors, who reported on the state of the troops; from their reports it could be seen whether the war commissioners had carried out their duties.

He instituted the Order of Saint-Louis, an honorable distinction which was often more sought after than wealth. The Hôtel des Invalides put the seal on his efforts to merit loyal service.

It was owing to measures such as these that he had, by 1672, a hundred and eighty thousand regular troops, and that, increasing his forces as the number and strength of his enemies increased, he finished with four hundred and fifty thousand men under arms, including the troops of the navy.

Before his time such powerful armies were unknown. His enemies could scarcely muster comparable forces, and to do so they had to be united. He showed what France, on her own, was capable of, and he always had either great successes or great resources to fall back on.

*   *   *

This short account is enough to illustrate the changes which Louis XIV brought about in the state; and that they were useful changes is shown by the fact that they still exist. His ministers vied with each other in furthering his plans. They were responsible for all the details and for the actual execution, but the over-all plan was his. Of one thing one can be certain: the magistrates would not have reformed the laws; order would not have been restored in the finances; discipline would not have been introduced into the armies and into the general policing of the kingdom; there would have been no fleets; the arts would not have been encouraged; and all this would not have been achieved in such an organized and determined fashion at one single time (though under different ministers) if there had not been at the head of affairs a master who conceived in general terms all these great aims, and had the will power to accomplish them.

He never separated his own glory from the well-being of France, and he never looked on his kingdom in the same light as a lord looks on the lands from which he extracts all he can in order to live a life of luxury. Every king who loves glory loves the public welfare; Colbert and Louvois were no longer there when, in 1698, he ordered each intendant to produce a detailed description of his province for the instruction of the Duke of Burgundy. In this way it was possible to have an exact account of his kingdom and an accurate census of his peoples. This was a most useful achievement, although not every intendant had the capacity or the attention to detail of M. de Lamoignon de Bâville. If the King's intentions had been carried out as thoroughly in every other province as they were by this magistrate in his census of Languedoc, this collection of reports would have been one of the finest monuments of the age. Several others were well done; but a general plan was lacking, insofar as the intendants did not all receive the same instructions. What would have been most desirable was for each intendant to give, in columns, an account of the number of inhabitants of each district—nobles, citizens, farm workers, artisans and workmen—together with livestock of all kinds, lands of various degrees of fertility, the whole of the regular and secular clergy, their revenues, those of the towns and those of the communes.

In most of the reports returned, these aims are confused; some subjects are dealt with superficially and inaccurately, and it is often quite difficult to find the information one is looking for and which should be immediately available to a minister wanting to discover, at a glance, the forces, needs and resources of the community. The plan was an excellent one, and it would be most useful if someday it is executed in a uniform manner.

This, then, in general terms, is what Louis XIV did or tried to do to make his country more flourishing. It seems to me hardly possible to consider all this work and all these efforts without a feeling of gratitude and without being filled with the concern for the welfare of the people which inspired them. Consider what the country was like at the time of the *Fronde* and what it is like today. Louis XIV did more for his people than twenty of his predecessors put together; and even then he did not do everything he might have done. The war which ended with the Peace of Rijswijk began the ruin of the flourishing commerce established by his minister Colbert, and the War of Spanish Succession completed it.

He spent immense sums on the aqueducts and works of Maintenon and on conveying water to Versailles, and both these projects were abandoned and thereby rendered useless. If he had spent this money, or a fifth part of what it cost to force nature at Versailles, on embellishing his capital, Paris today would be, throughout its whole extent, as beautiful as is the area around the Tuileries and the Pont-Royal, and would have become the most magnificent city in the universe.

It is a great achievement to have reformed the laws, but legal chicanery could not be abolished by legislation. The government tried to make justice uniform, and it has become so in criminal matters and in those of commerce and procedure; it could become so in the laws regulating the fortunes of individual citizens. It is most inconvenient that the same tribunal often has to give judgment on the basis of a hundred different customs. Certain land rights, which are either equivocal, onerous or harmful to society, still exist like remnants of a feudal government which no longer survives; they are the rubbish from a ruined Gothic building.

We are not claiming that the different orders in the state should all be subjected to the same laws. It will be realized that the customs of the nobility, the clergy, the magistracy and the peasantry must be different. But there is no doubt that it is desirable that each order should have its own law, which should be uniform throughout the kingdom, and that what is just or true in Champagne should not be considered false or unjust in Normandy. In every branch of administration, uniformity is a virtue; but the difficulties of achieving it have deterred people from the attempt.

Louis XIV could much more easily have done without the dangerous assistance of tax-farmers, to whom he was forced to have recourse because he almost always anticipated on his revenues. . . .

If he had not believed that his will was sufficient to make a million men change their religion, France would not have lost so many citizens. Yet despite these upsets and losses, the country is still one of the most prosperous in the world, because all the good which Louis did remains and the evil which it was difficult to avoid doing in those stormy times has been repaired. In the final analysis it is posterity which judges kings and of whose judgment they must always be mindful; and when it comes to weigh up the virtues and weaknesses of Louis XIV, posterity will admit that, although he received too much praise during his lifetime, he deserves the praise of all future ages and was worthy of the statue which was erected to him at Montpellier, with a Latin inscription the sense of which is "To Louis the Great after his death." Don Ustariz, a statesman who has written on the finances and commerce of Spain, calls Louis XIV "an astounding man."

All these changes in government and in all the orders of society, which we have just examined, necessarily produced a vast change in our manners. The spirit of faction, intemperance and rebellion which had possessed the citizens of France ever since the time of Francis II gave place to a desire to excel in serving the King. The lords of large estates no longer remained quartered at home; the governors of provinces no longer had important posts to bestow; and as a result, the sovereign's favors were the only ones people strove to deserve; in this way, the state acquired a sort of geometrical unity, with each line leading to the center.

Charles Guignebert was for many years professor of history at the University of Paris. Educated under the Third Republic, he saw the age of Louis XIV from a perspective somewhat different from Voltaire's.

FROM *A Short History of the French People*
BY *Charles Guignebert*

THE DESPOTISM OF LOUIS XIV

IT WAS A GREAT MISFORTUNE for France and the monarchy that every means of resisting royal absolutism and every desire to do so should have disappeared towards 1661. The evolution of royalty, which might have proceeded in closer and closer adaptation to the needs of the country, was cut short and crystallised into a practical *deification of the king*. And since, in fact, the *uncontrolled*

Charles Guignebert, *A Short History of the French People,* (1930) pp. 86-105, translated by F. G. Richmond.

authority of the prince cannot possibly do all that is needed, it gives less than it takes away, and any government which it provides has inevitably many short-comings; further, by supplanting every other principle on which public action can be based, *it rapidly vitiates its own administration and transforms it into a mere exploitation of the subjects for the benefit of the monarch.*

The character and the political theories of Louis XIV largely contributed to this disastrous result; but this character assumed its visible shape under the influence of a definite environment. These theories did not spring spontane-ously to birth in the spirit of the young king; they are the result of impressions made on him by his surroundings. When Bossuet, preaching before him in the Lent of 1662, said, *"Il se remue pour votre Majesté quelque chose d'illustre et de grand et qui passe la destinée des rois vos prédécesseurs" (There broods over your Majesty something illustrious and great, foreshadowing a destiny above that of the kings your predecessors),* he expressed a prevalent opinion. It was with the complicity of his own subjects that Louis XIV developed his despotic egotism. Neither they nor he understood from the start the danger they were running.

*   *   *

At the death of Mazarin the king was twenty-two, and was commonly consid-ered the handsomest man in his kingdom. It was said at court that only the poet Racine could compare with him. In other words, he fulfilled the ideal of royal beauty, formed by his contemporaries. Though he was but of moderate stature, he had a perfect nobility and majesty of deportment, so natural as never to seem in the least affected. Easy and gracious, with the most courteous manners in the world, he exercised an extraordinary attraction when he cared to trouble himself so far. Saint-Simon, who had no affection for him, nevertheless praises his fine manners and his perfect politeness. His subjects had a genuine admira-tion for him. *"The respect aroused by his presence, no matter where or when,"* writes Saint-Simon, *"imposed silence and almost terror on all."* Even in old age and depression he never lost his grand air.

His mind without being *"below mediocrity,"* as the redoubtable memorial-ist alleges, was ordinary and above all *passive,* but *"capable of forming itself,"* being well able both to attend and to reflect. It was, in other respects, ill-served by a most inadequate education, conducted without order or method during the Fronde, which Mazarin made no effort to remedy effectively, in so far as essen-tially political knowledge was concerned, until the last of his life. Louis XIV in compensation for these insufficiencies had indeed the precious gift of *knowing how to be silent, and how to listen,* and another, even rarer among absolute monarchs: he could tolerate ability in those about him and turn it to his own use and profit.

His character was headstrong and his temper in all probability violent, but he could keep it under control; a perfect self-mastery seemed to him essential to his dignity, and Saint-Simon assures us that he did not lose his self-control *"more than ten times in the whole of his life";* that is to say, he did not allow himself to be visibly angered more than ten times. He was endowed with a certain instinct for right, justice and equality which he did not always follow, but never completely lost. His politeness, too, tempered and controlled his keen susceptibilities, but it unfortunately fostered a tendency to dissimulation, a fault to which he was by nature only too prone, and this dissimulation was accompanied by a tendency to be vindictive which led him at times to ill-feeling and ill-dealing. His *pride* was unbounded, such that *"but for the fear of the devil which God never took from him, however disturbed he might be, he would have caused himself to be worshipped."* His pride never pardoned an offense, and to offend him was easy.

It is possible that his good will, his diligence, certain qualities of prudence and moderation, his basic benevolence, if not real generosity—an assortment, in fact, of inconspicuous but by no means negligible virtues—might, after some years of experience of life, if each reinforced the other, have made him a type of much that a king should be, had not all been ruined by flattery. Unfortunately Louis XIV was the prey *"of flattery so egregious as to deify him in the very heart of Christianity."* During his whole life he drank deep of this deadly poison. It gave him extreme pleasure and cost him his sense of reality. Thus he came to believe himself of a different kind and of a different clay from other men, to find it both natural and necessary that all men and everything should be sacrificed to him. His egotism developed into a kind of unconscious ferocity and his *Ego,* his *"Moi,"* became a monstrosity. The interested and ingenious servility of courtiers, the crowd of adulators constantly pressing about him, were more responsible than himself for this disastrous distortion of his judgment.

He was extremely devout, or at least he became so when his early youthful fires had waned. He believed himself in all respects a good Christian. In reality he neither professed nor comprehended any but a religion of outward show, compounded of habit, ceremony, superstition and *"fear of the devil."* It was impotent either to make him moral or repress his inordinate sensuality. His private life was a scandal up to the threshold of middle age and he paraded his irregularities before the world with a sedate absence of all shame, apparently in the belief that he was privileged by Heaven and need not concern himself with the code that must rule the rest of the world. Not only did he live openly in adultery, but he had the assurance to give his bastards the rank of princes of the blood. It is probable that the eminent preachers whose office it was, every Lent, to remind him of the Christian virtues and of repentance for sin, sometimes found themselves in an embarrassing position. The warnings and the stern rebukes, to which he had to listen from some among them, fell on deaf ears till he had grown old, or at least was aging after 1681.

He owed the dignity of the latter part of his life, in all probability, to Madame de Maintenon. It was she who brought him and the queen again together in 1681, and after the death of the latter, in 1683, she was secretly married to the king, probably in January, 1684. Thenceforward he was a faithful husband and grew steadily more absorbed in religious devotion. On his death-bed he asked pardon from the bystanders for the scandals occasioned by his transgressions.

His political theories, which he took the trouble to embody by his own hand in writing for the instruction of his son, were in keeping with the education which had persuaded him that for him there was no law but his own will, and no control but that of God. One of his childish copybook headings, which has been preserved, is in these words, *"Homage is due to kings, they do everything that pleases them."* His youth was spent in hearing this reiterated by all about him, and the Fronde itself helped to convince him that all hung attendant on the king's will.

That kings were *"instituted by God,"* held their sceptre from Him alone, need render no account of their acts but to Him alone, was the complete conviction of his contemporaries as of himself and the few bold spirits who still recalled the political doctrines of the jurists of the Renaissance and their chimeras concerning *Organised Monarchy*—that is to say, monarchy controlled and limited—were careful after the end of the troubles to raise no voice in France. The work of Bossuet *Politique tirée des propres paroles de l'Ecriture sainte* has been commonly considered as the classical presentation of the doctrine in precise propositions and in a style of great magnificence. Fundamentally it added nothing essential to what had been said again and again for forty or fifty years by every political theorist of royalty. Is it not curious to hear on the lips of Parliamentarians formulas which no servility could surpass, taken as a matter of course as the expression of received opinion?—the king is *"a visible divinity"* or *"a divine image of the divinity . . . , an august law-giver, who with one hand has access to the laws in the breast of God himself, and with the other communicates the gathered treasure through us to his people."*

Louis XIV was thus naturally led to believe himself as a *"station above that of other men."* He saw himself as *"standing in the place of God"* and as *"sharing in his knowledge as well as in his authority."* He persuaded himself that for a man of his rank to be under *"the necessity of receiving the law from his people"* was the *"greatest calamity"* into which he could fall, that every man who was his *"born subject"* must *"blindly obey,"* and that *"however bad"* a prince might be, revolt against him was *"always infinitely criminal,"* because a prince could be judged only by God. These convictions were held by him to be clearly established both by direct evidence and by the sovereign strength of revelation.

However, he did not, for a moment, imagine that divine favour had raised him to the throne merely to indulge himself with a life of ease and material satisfaction. He believed thoroughly that the *interest of the State must come first* and that his own duty was clear: he must never *"reproach himself in any important matter with having done less than his best."* It was borne in upon him that the *"trade"* he practised was one which exacted abnegation and forgetfulness of self. *"The trade of king,"* he wrote, *"is great, noble and delightful when the workman can feel that he has acquitted himself worthily in all his undertakings, but it does not exempt him from pain, fatigue and anxiety."* Above all, it exacts continual labour: *"it is by this he reigns, for this he reigns, and it were ingratitude and insolence towards God, injustice and tyranny towards men to desire the one without the other."*

Louis XIV was indeed a life-long labourer; that is to say, he devoted several hours a day to audiences with his ministers and councils, he made decisions, he really believed that he himself transacted all the chief business of the State, though in this he was not free from illusions; neither in quantity nor in quality was his work all that he believed it to be. Nevertheless he did his best according to the measure of his ability and was persuaded that he was the inspirer of his ministers.

There is certainly some grandeur in this conception which shows the sovereign, rising superior to human frailty, to all individual interests and to his own inclinations, bending his mind and will to the sole service of his State. Unfortunately Louis XIV thought that *"when one has the State in view one works for oneself"* and he held that *the nation* had no embodiment in France, save as it might express itself solely *"in the person of the king."* Thus *it was easy for him to confuse the State with his person, and the public service with worship of himself.*

A strange phenomenon indeed is the feeling displayed at this time towards the monarch, professed as it is by men in whom a genuine revival of faith has engendered an energetic Catholicism and amounting as it does to a kind of *idolatry*. Louis XIV had merely to make a gesture to inaugurate a cult. Did not, in 1686, the Marshal of La Feuillade go so far as to have lighted lanterns placed at night about the prince's statue on the Place des Victoires at Paris? Other acts of like servility are met with; we feel that more than one of those courtiers to whom the king's countenance was *"felicity complete,"* as La Bruyère puts it, tended to accept as truth the ejaculation of Bossuet, *"O kings, ye are gods!"* And this devotional sentiment and this religious respect undoubtedly are a better explanation than the universal lassitude which followed the Fronde, of the abasement of character and the abdication of all will in face of the king.

* * *

Louis XIV always claimed to govern by himself; the examples of his father dominated by Richelieu, and of his mother led by Mazarin, the memories of his youth, which were certainly not unmixed so far as his associations and personal relations with the late cardinal were concerned, had taught him a salutary lesson. He was determined that another should never be *"king in function"* while he was but King in name. Thus he decided to do without a prime minister and entrusted the preparation and the execution of business only to *commis* (clerks). Nor did he ever make of any man a favourite, or at any rate he allowed no one with whom he formed a friendship to exercise any influence whatever in State affairs any more than he allowed his mistresses to do so.

Saint-Simon alleges that in reality he was led by his ministers, even the least able among them, and that he was master only in his own imagination.

There is undoubtedly some truth in this view, but it should not be unreservedly accepted. The Fronde had taught him suspicion of men; he knew that they might deceive him and he was always on his guard. Those of his *commis* who really influenced him successfully were those who, as students of human nature, had the address to persuade him that the ideas and the resolutions which he owed to their suggestion were originated by himself. Le Tellier, father of Louvois, relates that of twenty agenda submitted by himself to a Council meeting there was always one which the king returned for examination after refusing the proposed solution, but it was impossible to know beforehand which one it would be. Louis XIV said *No* to show that he was master and in a position to do so, not because he had come to any opinion of his own upon the case in question. As he could not possibly know or examine everything for himself, it may be considered as certain that his ministers sometimes duped him, that they wielded more power than he wished, but this was only achieved surreptitiously and by running a risk from the authority which hung over them, always ready to strike. The perfidious and tenacious rancour which the king displayed towards Fouquet, his superintendent of finance, after his disgrace and arrest, helps us to realise to what lengths he could go when he felt certain that he had been deceived.

He was not a man to think of great innovations in matters of government or even to realise that they might be necessary. On the other hand, he showed himself capable of approving improvements, more or less considerable, on the tradition which he received from the hands of Mazarin, provided that they seemed likely to advance his power or add lustre to his name.

During his reign the organisation of central government on the lines laid down by Francis I was completed. His ministers were six: *the Chancellor,* for justice; *the Controller-General of Finance*—the title of *superintendent* was thus altered, as being unacceptable to the king—*the four Secretaries of State:* of the *King's Household,* of *Foreign Affairs,* of *War* and of the *Navy.* But it must not be assumed that the apparent precision of their titles implied a clear and invariable ascription of duties among these four last functionaries. The limits of their respective jurisdictions are always giving rise to doubt, dispute and transpositions between them. The confusion is still further increased by the fact that each retains the general administration of one of the four sections into which the kingdom is still divided; each minister has a numerous staff, assigned to different *bureaux.* In these, current business is considered and carried on by the officials who form their staff, and are soon to become an important factor in the State. *The reign of the bureaucracy is beginning.*

The traditional practice of the French monarchy was to surround itself with competent advisers. These came to form what were practically government Councils. Under Louis XIV the tendency to specialisation, already frequently mentioned, has reached a definite result; we see four regular and largely specialised *Councils* now at work. The *Council* "par excellence," called also the *High Council,* examines all great questions of policy and government, as does our Council of Ministers today. Its numbers do not exceed four or five persons, including the king. They are entitled *Ministers of State*. The *Council of Despatches* has cognisance of all business affecting the interior administrative life of the kingdom. It conducts, with the four Secretaries of State as intermediaries, correspondence with the intendants. It consists of not more than a dozen or so members and is presided over by the king: it includes the dauphin, the Ministers of State, the Chancellor, the Controller-General of Finance and the Secretaries of State. The *Council of Finance* dealt with the assessment and distribution of direct taxes, conducted negotiations with the financiers and examined all that the financial administration thought fit to submit to it. The king sat as its president twice a week.

The *Privy Council* or *Council of Parties* was essentially, like our present Council of State, a *superior* court; that is to say, all the administrative difficulties, conflicts as to jurisdiction, besides a number of purely judicial affairs that the king consigned to it, came within its province which was both extremely vague and extensive. It consisted of thirty members assisted by eighty-eight *Masters of Requests,* who examined and reported upon cases. These masters paid high prices for their posts, since their work prepared them for that of higher administration and the king chose his provincial *Intendants* from among them. The Privy Council was presided over by the Chancellor, the king rarely attending, though its business was conducted in his name as though he himself were present.

This organisation of the central government of Louis XIV is undoubtedly still far from perfection. It still fails in the distinct differentiation between functions which we know to be necessary to the smooth working of a political machine. It is nevertheless a great advance on its predecessor though it runs on similar lines. The *Duke of Beauvilliers,* who was head of the Council of Finance and afterwards Minister of State, was almost the only exception to the rule that no authentic noble had part or portion in this central government; no prince of the blood except the dauphin had even the right to membership on any of the four Councils. This despotism meant, as Saint-Simon said, *"the reign of the long robe"* in all things. The titles of nobility borne by many among these confidential men or ministers of the king should not mislead us as to their origin; they are bourgeois or they come from the ranks of the *officers* of the robe. Ennoblement was the reward for their services.

The provincial government likewise becomes better defined; the provinces are now fixed areas, each has its governor, a noble and a swordsman, well paid and much looked up to, but in reality now no more than a figurehead, indeed so much so that except on special ceremonial occasions the majority of these great personages dispense with residence in their "government." The real authority is in the hands of the *Intendant*. As the experiment attempted by Richelieu proved successful, it was continued by Mazarin and completed by Louis XIV. In his reign the kingdom was divided into financial districts, known as *Généralités* or *Intendances,* of which there were thirty-one in 1700. Their limits did not coincide with those of the provinces in which they were established.

The *Intendant,* his appointment being decided by the Council of the Parties, was chosen by the king, under whose control he remained. He started his career in an intendantship of small importance and his advancement depended on his zeal and success in the *"execution of the orders of his Majesty."* His powers may be described as extending over the whole provincial administration and his work as comprising all duties such as now fall to the heads of the various services in a modern department. Taxes, police, public works, commerce, industry, religious matters, recruiting, supervision and control of the courts of justice and of the administrators of all ranks, the judgment of many contentious or even criminal cases and the selection of those chosen for submission to the king; his work and his authority both covered an immense field.

Louis XIV would naturally wish to abolish such *Provincial States* as still survived, many of which did, in fact, disappear during his reign, for instance, those of Auvergne, Normandy, Quercy and others. If he left some as they were (Brittany, Flanders, Artois, Burgundy, Provence, Languedoc) this would be because they gave him no trouble and because he had probably no intention of abolishing wholesale all the institutions of the past still extant in the provinces. He allowed various anomalies in local administrative usage to continue, and left uncorrected defects of organisation, highly detrimental to those who came under them. They could be justified by established custom and the king seems to have been little concerned with them, being, as he always was, supremely preoccupied with securing two things from his people: *passive obedience and money.*

The government is one which settles all questions in secret. It is absolutely uncontrolled. The *nobility* are no longer a separate body, and politically they count for nothing; to the prince they are *"mere people,"* says Saint-Simon. The *Assembly of the Clergy,* held at regular intervals, deals only with its own affairs, except that it is attempting to secure the abolition of the Edict of Nantes. All ecclesiastical appointments are in the hands of the king. The *States-General* are now altogether out of the field. Their name alone was sufficient to set Louis XIV beside himself. There was now not even an Assembly of Notables. The *Parliament,* deprived of all right of remonstrance, could now do no more than register the edicts of the king without comment. As to the *subjects,* they had merely to take their orders. Discussion is considered as revolt and as a kind of sacrilege. It will be only towards the end of the reign that *opposition,* born from the misery of the country and from the failures of the king, will venture to find a home in men's minds and occasionally an outward expression. Not even a genius could have succeeded in realising the immeasurable pretensions of this appalling despotism; and Louis XIV was no genius.

*   *   *

The administration of the kingdom is entirely directed for the service and benefit of the king, against which no consideration whatever can prevail. The care, which it outwardly devotes to the public interest, is no more than a way of promoting the king's. If the subjects are well off and contented they will be able to pay better and more. Although men of all ranks are merely "people" before the king, equally subjected to his will, in practice the administration takes account of the *social inequalities* that the founders of the French monarchy had never attempted to abolish, which were so unfortunately confirmed by the States-General of 1614 and which were now maintained by Louis XIV. It seems probable that no idea that they were unjust or detrimental to the State ever entered his head; all prescription was in their favour. His absolutism, in fact, heavy as it was upon all men, was particularly severe upon the *small folk,* on whose shoulders it laid the greater portion of public expenditure.

In principle, they are the sole bearers of the direct impost (*la taille,* a tax on real property), besides most of those which are indirect, the chief of which are *aids,* diverse taxes upon merchandise of prime necessity and common consumption, and *gabelle,* a tax upon salt. These imposts are raised in a way which makes them particularly difficult to bear. The State farms them out to private companies which can appeal to public force for support; they greatly abuse the power thus given them to bring pressure upon the defenceless taxpayers. In those times it was no honour to a man to say that he was in the *Farms* or *Parties;* this last word designating the tenders made to the State by financiers in relation to the adjudication of taxes. From this deplorable system the peasants were the sufferers in chief.

After the death of Colbert (1683), who had done his best to restrain the insane extravagance of the king, the impoverishment of the country proceeded apace, assisted by the exigencies of an expensive foreign policy. The returns from the ordinary taxes then diminished as the need of the royal treasury for money grew greater. The government had recourse to various expedients, not altogether honourable, which furthermore were far from fulfilling expectation. The verses of Boileau are well known (*Satire* III).

D'où vous vient aujourd'hui cet air sombre et sévère,
Et ce visage enfin plus pâle qu'un rentier
A l'aspect d'un édit qui supprime un quartier?

Why do you look so sombre and severe today,
With a face indeed paler than a rentier's
At the appearance of an edict which abrogates a quarter?

A *quartier* of the *rentes* covers a *trimestre,* period of three months; to abrogate it was a method of raising a special tax on the creditors of the State. The creation of useless and sometimes ridiculous posts is an indirect method of establishing new taxes, as the newly created officials will not fail to reimburse themselves from the pockets of the public; thus we find controllers appointed for faggots, fresh butter, oysters and the like, without mentioning *conseillers semestres* (semestrial councillors) who, sitting in their courts for six months only, enable the State to double the number of those functionaries.

The fiscal necessities became so great that even a restriction in the number of the *privileged* had to be accepted. The poll-tax, established in 1695, was to be paid by all Frenchmen without distinction in proportion to their income; only the poorest were exempted. As a matter of fact the privileged, by diverse expedients, for instance, by paying a composition by which they escaped on good terms—as was done by the Assembly of the Clergy—or by obtaining the appointment of special receivers, materially decreased their obligations. This was similarly the case with another tax upon income, the *tenth,* superimposed in 1710, upon all contributions and upon all subjects.

The government was not unaware of the defects in its fiscal system and could easily realise the disastrous results to which they must lead, but it seems to have been only concerned to fill the treasury by no matter what means, and to have considered inevitable, if not natural, evils for which it had neither leisure nor will to devise adequate remedies. Those which were suggested to it from without, for instance by *Vauban* beginning in 1695 and by *Boisguillebert* starting from 1699, left it indifferent or brought more or less disagreeable consequences upon the heads of their authors.

Justice remained in the hands of the old local jurisdictions, over which were the *Présidiaux,* which went back to Henry II (over them again were the *Parliaments,* then about twelve in number), but its orderly working is disturbed by the privileges of the clergy, who have their own tribunals, and of the nobles, who still often enjoy the abusive right to be judged only by the Parliament of Paris; above all, it is impaired by the *right of evocation* retained by the king. He, being theoretically supreme judge and the fountainhead of all justice, is able, when he thinks fit, to transfer any case from its regular judges and bring it before the *Council of Parties.* These exceptions and privileges are detrimental to the proper working of one of the essential functions of the State.

The diversity of laws and customs had similar effects. It is impossible to find a way through their inextricable confusion. A methodical synopsis would have been indispensable. Colbert thought of having one made and of drafting a kind of civil code, but his plans came to nothing.

The criminal procedure remains barbarous and the penalties are harsh in the extreme. When the king wants oarsmen for his galleys, conviction for any petty crime is enough to send a man to the benches. Generally speaking, the law takes no thought for the moral improvement of delinquents; its one aim is to induce terror by extreme severity. Here as elsewhere the government follows its most immediate interest, regardless of equity, of the needs of its subjects, or of the progress of manners, which are much milder than those of the Middle Ages though its spirit still survives in the practice of torture.

The administration of Louis XIV is in close correspondence with the principles and intentions of the government for which it acts. Rigorous, exacting, and generally exact, it confounds the service of the king with the good of the State, and for the good of the State it deliberately sacrifices individual interests, even those which most call for respect. It is, in fact, an instrument of despotism and not in the least an organism established and set to work for the good of the nation.

In a general work on the sixteenth and seventeenth centuries the modern French historian Roland Mousnier, a professor at the University of Strasbourg, defined the dimensions of Louis XIV's absolutism and its effect.

FROM *The XVIth and XVIIth Centuries*
BY *Roland Mousnier*

THE ABSOLUTE MONARCHY

ABSOLUTISM WAS THE WISH of the crowds who saw their salvation in the concentration of powers in the hands of one man—the incarnation of the realm, the living symbol of order and of the desired unity. Everyone wished to see in the king the image of God: "You are God on earth. . . ." To this conception was added, with many, the old humanist dream: the king ought to be a hero, lover of glory as in antiquity, protector of Letters like Augustus, protector of the Church like Constantine, a legislator like Justinian, but with a "predilection for arms," because "the role of conqueror is esteemed to be the most noble and the highest of titles," by all contemporaries.

As lieutenant of God, the king is sovereign. "The sovereign Prince makes the law, consequently he is absolved of the law." He acts according to his own good pleasure. Thus it results that kings "naturally have the full and free disposition of all properties, secular as well as ecclesiastic, to make wise use of like good stewards, that is to say according to the needs of their states." Public good is above the right of property. Thus it follows that the Church is subject to the sovereign and owes him rental on its possessions which have been given to it "for the general welfare of the entire realm. . . ." (The comparison with the sun arose by itself, and Louis XIV, Nec Pluribus Impar [None His Equal], did no more than insist on an old monarchical symbol.)

But, as an image of God, the king ought to be a providence on earth. He should make justice reign, "precious trust that God has put in the hand of kings as a participation in his wisdom and his power." He ought to bring to perfection each of the professions of which society is constituted, because "each of them has its functions, which the others may do without only with great difficulty. . . . This is why, far from disdaining any of these conditions, or of raising one at the expense of others, we should take care to bring them all, if

Roland Mousnier, *Les XVIè et XVIIè Siècles. Les progrès de la Civilisation Européenne et le déclin de l'Orient* (1492-1715). *Tome IV, Histoire Generale des Civilisations* (1954), pp. 229-236. Translated by L. Pearce Williams by permission of Presses Universitaires de Frances, Paris.

it can be done, to the perfection of which they are capable," [realizing] the ideal of a society where social work is directed and the professions form a hierarchy according to the needs of man. Finally, the king should be the protector of the weak; he ought "to give to the people who are subject to us the same marks of paternal goodness that we receive from God every day," to have "nothing more at heart than to guarantee the most feeble from the oppression of the most powerful and to find some ease for the neediest in their misery."

The king mistrusted his ministers and his secretaries of state. He reverted to a division of labor, and tried to divide up the affairs which were interconnected in such a way that no specialist would be able to block his will. He opposed his officials to one another, provoked them, divided them, stimulated their mutual jealousies, saw in the opposition of Colbert and of Le Tellier a guarantee of his power.

. . . The problem for the king is not only to make his subjects obey, but also to subject to his will his own officers who had become independent thanks to the venality of office, and to exercise the fullness of the legislative judiciary police or administrative powers.

For this purpose the king used *lettres de cachet* by which he made known his will directly to individuals or to bodies. By *lettres de cachet,* the king arrested, imprisoned, exiled; at the request of families, he punished the bad conduct of a son or of a spouse; he weakened resistance, arbitrarily punished seditions and plots with the enemy. When the king himself had spoken, there was nothing else to do but to bow before his authority, the legal source of justice.

More and more, the king utilized commissioners named by him and removable at his will. The Counselors of State of the administrative councils were only commissioners. . . .

The king used the intendants of the army and the intendants of justice, police, and finance. They were above all inspectors, charged with the surveillance of the officers and subjects of the king, and were required to give an account to the council. The council could then either deal with the question itself by a decree or give the necessary powers to the intendant to decide, judge, or regulate the problem by means of an ordinance. The intendant could thus meet with the council of the governor and give his advice; he could preside over courts of justice, reform justice by means of ordinances, make sure that the officers carried out their functions and suspend them if they did not, listen to the complaints of the king's subjects and make sure justice was given them by the judges. The intendant presided over the assemblies of the cities, . . . elections, checked the debts of communities, and oversaw the carrying out of orders and regulations. . . . The intendant supervised the raising of taxes, presided over the bureau of finances, and guaranteed the observance of ordinances and regulations. Only in two cases did he have a general and discretionary power and a sovereign judgment: malpractices and falsification of accounts by financial officers, and illicit assemblies, seditions, riots, and raising of armed men.

The intendant was a very supple instrument. In time of war or of internal crisis, the council could extend his powers indefinitely, to the point that the intendant could perform all the functions of the officers and leave them only their hollow title. At these times, with their assistants the intendants formed an administration of commissioners in competition with the administration of the regular officers. But the royal government, Richelieu, and Colbert considered such times as exceptional and as an unhappy necessity. In time of peace, the king strove to keep the intendant, who always wanted to extend his powers, in his role of inspector. He forbade him to substitute himself for the royal officers—he was instructed only to supervise them, and, if they were not working well, to let the council know and to wait for the necessary powers to remedy the situation.

The king used a political police. It was run by the intendants, by spies and agents to be found everywhere—at Paris by the governor of the Bastille, the chief criminal officer, and, since 1667, the lieutenant general of police, La Reynie. One misinterpretation and, duke or lackey, one was in the Bastille. On such feeble suspicions, the intendants or the council constructed accusations of *lèse majesté;* judgment was given on mere suspicion because Richelieu, Louis XIII, and Louis XIV all believed that when conspiracy was concerned it was almost impossible to have mathematical proofs, and one should not wait for the event itself by which everything would be lost. Most often than for mere trials, the king had recourse to preventive imprisonment of indefinite length by means of the *lettres de cachet.* . . .

In all important offices, like that of ministers, secretaries of state, controller general, and so on, Louis XIV desired only "devoted servants" who joined to their public functions domestic services and, like Colbert, carried the notes from the monarch to his favorites or received the adulterine children of the king at the childbirth of the royal mistresses. He used the sentiments of vassalage but he wished to be the sole object of them. He wished to achieve absolutism by tying all Frenchmen directly to the king by means of a personal connection, just as vassals were tied to their suzerain. He wished to be the unique and universal suzerain or at least the universal patron. . . . All ties of sentiment and of interest converged on the king, who thus incarnated the wishes and the hopes of all his subjects, and in this way, not less than by the personal exercise of power, concentrated the State in himself; achieved in himself the unity of the State and thus prepared his subjects, by means of very old sentiments, to pass to the concept of the abstract State. Through the intermediary of medieval survivals, Louis XIV prepared the foundations of the modern State.

The king prepared them by opposing class to class and by making the bourgeois rise in a social scale. His ministers, his counselors, and his intendants were drawn more and more in the course of the century from among the bourgeois officers. These were his men, "rising from pure and perfect commonness," but "exalted above all grandeur." The king ennobled the Le Tellier and the Colbert families, made marquises of them, lords were known by the name of their estates, Louvois, Barbeziux, Croissy, Torcy. He created dynasties of ministers, bourgeois family groups and dynasties whose strength he used in face of the dynasties and noble family groups. . . .

The gentlemen grumbled. They despised these "bourgeois." "It was the reign of the vile bourgeoisie," complained Saint-Simon. They suffered by the leveling accomplished by a state which broke all resistance. The prisons were filled with eminent prisoners: the Count of Cramaing, the Marshal of Bassompierre, Barabas—one of the favorites of Louis XIII. The kings also sought, however, to procure honors and a means of existence for the nobility. The place of governor was reserved for them, and they filled most of the grades in the army. To their younger sons went the greater part of the ecclesiastical functions; they [the Kings] used them in their service, inculcating in them the spirit of subordination and little by little turning them into functionaries. Louis XIV succeeded in organizing the court. Around him he grouped, at Saint Germain, at Fontainebleau, at Versailles, all who counted among the nobility. He ruined them by alternating between the onerous life of military camps and the ostentatious life of the Court. He had no hesitation in waging war to find them employment and the opportunity for glory and reputation. He rendered them servile by pensions, dowries, and properties of the church. . . . He even provided a psychological alibi to this nobility. In a series of marvelous fairy-like festivals, the king appeared costumed as a god from Olympus, the courtiers appearing as secondary divinities or as heroes. Thus they could transpose their false dreams of power and grandeur to this copy of the life of the immortals, raised above common humanity and, if it had to obey, at least obeyed the "Lord Jupiter," the king god. Etiquette habituated them to see in the king a superhuman being. Men uncovered themselves before the king's bed, women curtsied to it as in church before the high altar. The princes of the blood disputed the honor of handing him the sleeve of his shirt at his rising. A whole ceremonial filled with reverences was present at his rising in the morning, at his retiring, at his meals, and for his whole life. . . .

Thus the king, by dividing governmental functions between two classes but reserving the most important to the lower one—the bourgeoisie—and by systematically raising this one and opposing the other—the strongest—brought the class struggle to an equilibrium which assured his personal power and— both in the government and in the state—unity, order, and hierarchy. But also, perhaps forced by crises and war, and without wishing to change the social structure of the realm, the king leveled and equalized more and more in the service due to the state. When Louis XIV had achieved total submission and limitless obedience his power became autocratic and revolutionary.

The Enlightenment—
The Age of Reason?

CONTENTS

QUESTIONS FOR STUDY

1 What is the difference between induction and deduction as illustrated by Bacon and Descartes?
2 Is Newton a Baconian?
3 What are the basic principles upon which the new physics depended?
4 How would philosophers of the Age of Reason define science?
5 What relationship is there between nature and morality in the Age of Reason?
6 How would an enlightened citizen argue for the existence of natural rights?
7 Are liberty and reason compatible?

In 1687 Isaac Newton published his great scientific work Philosophiae naturalis principia mathematica (The Mathematical Principles of Natural Philosophy) *in London. In 1789 the Estates General of France met at Versailles to inaugurate a reform of the French state that rapidly grew into the French Revolution. Between those two dates lay the Age of Reason, or the Enlightenment. Like most major intellectual movements, it cannot be defined simply, for it involved a whole host of issues and methods. Certain aspects of the Age of Reason, however, stand out from the very terms used to describe the period. "Age of Reason" is simple enough. It makes explicit the desire of the men and women of the eighteenth century to submit all important questions to the test of reason. Tradition, custom, history, interest—all earlier justifications for actions and institutions—were declared no longer valid. In theory, at least, reason was to be the judge of all values.*

The sudden upsurge of confidence in reason was the direct result of what modern historians have called the Scientific Revolution of the seventeenth century. Newton's Principia *is the ultimate result of this revolution. What his work involved was the solution of the problem of the motions of the heavenly bodies (and of all other material bodies). The Greeks had first tried to make sense out of stellar and planetary motion without notable success. The problem had worried philosophers ever since, but no significant advances had been made until Nicholas Copernicus published his work* On the Revolutions of the Heavenly Orbs *in 1543. By suggesting that the earth was simply another planet and that all planets went around the sun, Copernicus greatly simplified the picture of the cosmos by eliminating a fairly large number of mathematical circles necessary for the accurate computation of planetary positions. To gain this simplicity, however, Copernicus had to introduce a major difficulty: What made the earth go around the sun? If one throws a shovelful of dirt into the air, it does not move in circles, yet Copernicus was prepared to argue that the earth, as a whole, moved in a circle around the sun. Both Galileo Galilei (1564–1642) and René Descartes (1596–1650) wrestled unsuccessfully with this problem. Newton solved it with apparent ease. With his three laws of motion and the principle of universal gravitation, everything fell into place (see p. 262). The paths of the planets and the earth could be calculated accurately for the first time in human history.*

This point is worth underscoring. European intellectuals had suffered from a massive inferiority complex since the time of the fall of Rome. The major intellectual task for centuries had been to recapture the heritage of Greece and Rome. The whole educational system, the arts, and the sciences had all been devised to emulate or appreciate antiquity. Now, for the first time, a "modern" had surpassed anything that the ancients had done. Isaac Newton, with the instrument of the new experimental and mathematical science, had solved a major scientific problem that had baffled the brightest of the Hellenes. Almost overnight, the intellectual atmosphere in Europe changed. Henceforth, only antiquarians and academics looked backward; progressive intellectuals could dream of a world of the future surpassing anything that had gone before. The idea of progress became central to the Enlightenment, as a direct result of the scientific triumphs of rea-

son. *If reason could decipher and explain nature, surely it could do the same for political and social problems. Through reason, utopia could be attained.*

It was this vision of material, social, and political progress that inspired the men and women of the Enlightenment to seek to broaden their audience. It was not enough that truth be discovered; it also had to be made available. The Biblical quotation "Ye shall know the Truth and the truth shall make you free" took on new meaning in the eighteenth century. To make truth available, it was necessary to create new media for its dissemination. The old, heavy Latin tome with learned citations was intended for the scholarly few. Only real specialists actually read Newton's Principia, *but when Voltaire digested it and reported on it with his inimitable wit and style, everyone could understand its main points. Wit and style became central to the spread of truth, and this subtly altered the messages that could be transmitted. One's reader had to be entertained and seduced into comprehension of philosophical conclusions. Hence, it was impossible to qualify and specify every little detail, as one would do in a learned treatise. Instead, the broad generalization and the easily digested concept became the current coin. Philosophes (as the great French publicists of the eighteenth century liked to style themselves) were not philosophers, but dealers in philosophical ideas packaged for a wide audience that sought entertainment as well as enlightenment. The danger in packaging ideas for this market was that they tended to become oversimplified and even banal. How simple and beautiful the world looked when viewed through the eyes of reason, as exemplified by Voltaire (p. 291) or Diderot (p. 288) or David Hume (p. 276). And how grim and crusted with outworn traditions did the actual political and social world look when compared to the simplicities of nature. What could be more natural than to assume that the same simplicity that obtained in the physical world must exist in the social world of men, if only men would use their reason. In spite of the many different systems that emerged and in spite of the disagreements over details, that search for simplicity and order in the social and political world was what the Enlightenment was all about.*

1

The Sources of the Enlightenment

The Scientific Revolution is usually dated from 1543, when Copernicus suggested moving the sun to the center of the cosmos. This was a revolutionary idea, but it had been derived from very conservative methods. Far more radical was the philosophy of Sir Francis Bacon, who argued that the laws of nature could be discovered only by questioning nature herself and not by arguing about the meaning of words or by finding elegant mathematical solutions to scientific problems. Bacon wished to use induction rather than deduction to arrive at broad principles, for he correctly mistrusted the desire of the human mind to seize upon apparent generalizations prematurely. Go to nature, he argued, and torture her by experiment until all aspects of a phenomenon are revealed. Only then will it be possible to rise to a general law of its occurrence and causes. With a series of short and pithy aphorisms, Bacon described this method in his work Novum Organum, or New Instrument, *first published in 1620. He felt that these aphorisms would aid in the search for truth.*

In the selection that follows, Bacon deals first with sources of error, then takes up the reasons why science had not flourished earlier, and finally offers his method.

FROM *Novum Organum*

BY *Francis Bacon*

APHORISM XL

THE RAISING OF NOTIONS AND AXIOMS by *legitimate Induction*, is doubtless the proper Remedy for removing and driving out the Idols of the Mind; yet the *Indication of Idols* is a thing of great Use: the Doctrine of them being to the *Interpretation of Nature*, what the Doctrine of the Confutation of *Sophisms* is to the common *Logic*.

Francis Bacon, *Novum Organum*.

APHORISM XLI

Idols of the Tribe have their Foundation in human Nature, and the whole Tribe or Race of Mankind: for it is a false Assertion, that the Human Sense is the Measure of Things; since all Perceptions, both of the Sense and Mind, are with relation to Man, and not with relation to the Universe. But the human Understanding is like an unequal Mirror to the Rays of Things; which, mixing its own Nature with the Natures of Things, distorts and perverts them.

APHORISM XLII

Idols of the Den, are the Idols of every Man in particular; for, besides the general Aberrations of human Nature, we every one of us have our peculiar *Den* or *Cavern;* which refracts and corrupts the Light of Nature: either because every Man has his respective Temper, Education, Acquaintance, Course of Reading, and Authorities: or because of the Differences of Impressions, as they happen in a Mind prejudiced or prepossessed; or in one that is calm and equal, &c. So that the human Spirit, according to its Disposition in Individuals, is an uncertain, very disorderly, and almost accidental thing. . . .

APHORISM XLIII

There are also *Idols* that have their Rise, as it were, from Compact, and the Association of Mankind; which, on Account of the Commerce and Dealings that Men have with one another, we call *Idols of the Market.* For Men associate by Discourse; but Words are imposed according to the Capacity of the Vulgar: whence a false and improper Imposition of Words strangely possesses the Understanding. Nor do the Definitions and Explanations, wherewith Men of Learning, in some Cases, defend and vindicate themselves, any way repair the Injury: for Words absolutely force the Understanding, put all Things in Confusion, and lead Men away to idle Controversies and Subtleties, without Number.

APHORISM XLIV

Lastly, there are *Idols* which have got into the human Mind, from the different Tenets of Philosophers; and the perverted Laws of Demonstration. And these we denominate *Idols of the Theatre;* because all the Philosophies that have been hitherto invented or received, are but as so many Stage-Plays, written or acted;

as having shewn nothing but fictitious and theatrical Worlds. Nor is this said only of the ancient or present Sects and Philosophies; for numberless other Fables, of the like Kind, may be still invented and dress'd up; since quite different Errors will proceed from almost the same common Causes. Nor, again, do we mean it only of general Philosophies; but likewise of numerous *Principles* and *Axioms* of the Sciences, which have prevailed thro' Tradition, Belief, and Neglect. But these several Kinds of *Idols* must be more fully and distinctly shewn, that the Mind may be upon its Guard against them.

APHORISM XLV

The Mind has this Property, that it readily supposes a greater Order and Conformity in Things, than it finds: and tho' many Things in Nature are singular, and extremely dissimilar; yet the Mind is still imagining Parallels, Correspondencies, and Relations between them; which have no Existence. Hence the Fiction, that all the celestial Bodies moved in perfect Circles; hence the fictitious Element of Fire, with its Orb, was added to the three sensible Elements, to make them four; and such kind of Dreams. Nor does this Folly prevail only in Tenets, but also in simple Notions.

* * *

APHORISM L

But much the greatest Impediment and Deviation of the Understanding, proceeds from the Dullness, Incompetency, and Fallacies of the Senses; whence the Things that strike the Sense, unjustly over-balance those that do not strike it immediately: So that Contemplation usually ends with Sight; and little or no Observation is made of Things invisible. And hence all the Operations of the Spirits, included in tangible Bodies, all subtile Organizations, and the Motions of the Parts, are unknown to Mankind: and yet, unless these are discover'd and brought to Light, nothing very considerable can be done in Nature, with regard to Works. Nay, the Properties of the common Air, and numerous Bodies of greater Subtlety than that, remain almost unknown: For Sense, of itself, is a weak and erroneous Thing. Nor can Instruments, for improving and sharpening the Senses, be here of any great Service: all true *Interpretations* of Nature being made by proper and apposite *Instances* and *Experiments;* wherein Sense judges of the Experiment only; and the Experiment judges of Nature, and the Fact.

* * *

APHORISM LXXXI

Another great Reason of the slow Progress of the *Sciences,* is this; that 'tis impossible to proceed well in a Course, where the End is not rightly fix'd and defined. Now the true and genuine End of the Sciences, is no other, than to enrich human Life with new Inventions, and new Powers; but much the greater Number of the *Sciences* produce nothing in this Kind; being mere Hirelings, and professorial: unless sometimes, by Accident, an ingenious Artificer, thro' Desire of Glory, endeavours after some new Invention; which he generally pursues to his own Loss; whilst the Bulk of Mankind are so far from proposing to enlarge the Mass of Arts and Sciences, that they only take from the present Collection, or covet so much as they can convert to the Use of their Profession; their own Advantage, Reputation, or some such narrow and inferior Purpose.

*　　*　　*

APHORISM CII

Again; the Number, or, as it were, the Army of Particulars, being so large, scatter'd, and confused, as to distract and confound the Mind; little Good can be expected from the Skirmishes and Sallies of the Understanding; unless it be fitted, and brought close to them, by means of proper, well-disposed, and actuating *Tables of Invention,* containing such Things as belong to the Subject of every Enquiry: and unless the Mind be applied to receive the prepared and digested Assistance they afford.

APHORISM CIII

And even when a Stock of Particulars is exactly and orderly placed before us; we must not immediately pass on to the Enquiry, and Discovery, of new Particulars, or Works: at least, if this be done, we must not dwell upon it. We deny not, that, after all the Experiments of every Art shall be collected, digested, and brought to the Knowledge and Judgment of a single Person; many new Discoveries may be made, for the Use and Advantage of Life, thro' the Translation of the Experiments of one Art into another; by means of what we call *Learned Experience:* yet less Hope is to be conceived hereof; and a much greater of a *new Light of Axioms,* drawn regularly, and in a certain manner, from those Particulars; so that such *Axioms* may again point out, and lead to new Particulars. For the Way lies not thro' a Plain; but thro' Mountains and Valleys: first ascending to *Axioms,* and then descending to *Works.*

APHORISM CIV

But the Understanding must not be allowed to leap, or fly from Particulars, to remote, or the most general kind, of *Axioms,* at once; (such as are called the *Principles* of Arts and Things;) and so prove, and draw out, middle *Axioms,* according to the established Truth of the former; as has hitherto been done by a natural Sally of the Understanding: which is naturally inclined this Way; and has been long trained and accustomed to it, by the Use of those Demonstrations, which proceed upon *Syllogism.* But we may conceive good Hopes of the Sciences, when, by continued Steps, like *real Stairs, uninterrupted or broken,* Men shall ascend from Particulars to lesser *Axioms;* and so on to middle ones; from these again to higher; and lastly, to the most general of all. For the lowest *Axioms* differ not much from bare Experience; and the highest, and most general ones, as they are now esteem'd, prove only notional, theoretical, and of no Solidity; whilst the *middle Axioms,* are the real, the solid, and animated Kind, wherein the Affairs and Fortunes of Men are placed: and above these, come such as are truly the most general; yet not metaphysical; but justly limited by these intermediate ones.

And, therefore, the Understanding does not want Sail, so much as Ballast; to keep it from skipping and bounding: but as this is hitherto a *Desideratum;* when it shall be supplied, we may have better Hopes of the *Sciences.*

APHORISM CV

Again; a different Form of *Induction,* from what has hitherto been used, must be invented, for the raising of *Axioms:* and that not only for the discovering and proving of *Principles,* as they are call'd; but likewise for ascertaining the lesser, middle, and, in short, all kinds of *Axioms.* For that *Induction* which proceeds by simple Enumeration, is a childish Thing; concludes with Uncertainty; stands exposed to Danger from *contradictory Instances;* and generally pronounces upon scanty *Data;* and such only as are ready at hand: but the *Induction* useful in the Discovery and Demonstration of *Arts* and *Sciences,* ought to sift Nature, by proper *Rejections* and *Exclusions;* and then conclude upon *Affirmatives,* after the due Number of Negatives are thrown out: a Thing never yet done, nor attempted; unless by *Plato,* who made some little Use of this Form of *Induction,* in the sifting of Definitions and Ideas. But for the just and regular forming of this *Induction,* or *Demonstration,* numerous Particulars are required, which have been hitherto thought of by no Mortal; so that greater Pains must be bestowed upon it, than has been bestowed upon *Syllogisms.* And the Assistance of this *Induction* must be used, not only for the discovering of *Axioms;* but also for the defining of *Notions.* And in this Business of *Induction* is lodged the greatest Hope of improving the Sciences.

*René Descartes (1596–1650) was one of the foremost "revolutionaries" in the
Scientific Revolution. He not only contributed such fundamental instruments to the
advance of science as analytical geometry but also laid down what he considered to
be the only proper method for the pursuit of scientific truth. His* Discourse on
Method, *first published in French in 1637, was intended to lay out the future course
of the Scientific Revolution.*

FROM *A Discourse on Method*

BY *René Descartes*

AMONG THE BRANCHES OF PHILOSOPHY, I had, at an earlier period, given some attention to Logic, and among those of the Mathematics of Geometrical Analysis and
Algebra,—three Arts or Sciences which ought, as I conceived, to contribute
something to my design. But, on examination, I found that, as for Logic, its syllogisms and the majority of its other precepts are of avail rather in the communication of what we already know, or even as the Art of Lully, in speaking without judgment of things of which we are ignorant, than in the investigation of
the unknown; and although this Science contains indeed a number of correct
and very excellent precepts, there are, nevertheless, so many others, and these
either injurious or superfluous, mingled with the former, that it is almost quite
as difficult to effect a severance of the true from the false as it is to extract a
Diana or a Minerva from a rough block of marble. Then as to the Analysis of
the ancients and the Algebra of the moderns, besides that they embrace only
matters highly abstract, and, to appearance, of no use, the former is so exclusively restricted to the consideration of figures, that it can exercise the
Understanding only on condition of greatly fatiguing the Imagination; and, in
the latter, there is so complete a subjection to certain rules and formulas, that
there results an art full of confusion and obscurity calculated to embarrass, instead of a science fitted to cultivate the mind. By these considerations
I was induced to seek some other Method which would comprise the advantages of the three and be exempt from their defects. And as a multitude
of laws often only hampers justice, so that a state is best governed when,
with few laws, these are rigidly administered; in like manner, instead of the
great number of precepts of which Logic is composed, I believed that the four
following would prove perfectly sufficient for me, provided I took the firm and
unwavering resolution never in a single instance to fail in observing them.

The *first* was never to accept anything for true which I did not clearly
know to be such; that is to say, carefully to avoid precipitancy and prejudice,
and to comprise nothing more in my judgment than what was presented to my
mind so clearly and distinctly as to exclude all ground of doubt.

René Descartes, "A Discourse on the Method of Rightly Conducting the Reason," in *The Philosophy of Descartes*
(1901), pp. 60-64, 74-76, 102-106, translated by Jong Veitch. Reprinted by permission of Leon Amiel Pub.

The *second,* to divide each of the difficulties under examination into as many parts as possible, and as might be necessary for its adequate solution.

The *third,* to conduct my thoughts in such order that, by commencing with objects the simplest and easiest to know, I might ascend by little and little, and, as it were, step by step, to the knowledge of the more complex; assigning in thought a certain order even to those objects which in their own nature do not stand in a relation of antecedence and sequence.

And the *last,* in every case to make enumerations so complete, and reviews so general, that I might be assured that nothing was omitted.

The long chains of simple and easy reasonings by means of which geometers are accustomed to reach the conclusions of their most difficult demonstrations, had led me to imagine that all things, to the knowledge of which man is competent, are mutually connected in the same way, and that there is nothing so far removed from us as to be beyond our reach, or so hidden that we cannot discover it, provided only we abstain from accepting the false for the true, and always preserve in our thoughts the order necessary for the deduction of one truth from another.

* * *

I am in doubt as to the propriety of making my first meditations in the place above mentioned matter of discourse; for these are so metaphysical, and so uncommon, as not, perhaps, to be acceptable to every one. And yet, that it may be determined whether the foundations that I have laid are sufficiently secure, I find myself in a measure constrained to advert to them. I had long before remarked that, in relation to practice, it is sometimes necessary to adopt, as if above doubt, opinions which we discern to be highly uncertain, as has been already said; but as I then desired to give my attention solely to the search after truth, I thought that a procedure exactly the opposite was called for, and that I ought to reject as absolutely false all opinions in regard to which I could suppose the least ground for doubt, in order to ascertain whether after that there remained aught in my belief that was wholly indubitable. Accordingly, seeing that our senses sometimes deceive us, I was willing to suppose that there existed nothing really such as they presented to us; and because some men err in reasoning, and fall into paralogisms, even on the simplest matters of Geometry, I, convinced that I was as open to error as any other, rejected as false all the reasonings I had hitherto taken for demonstrations; and finally, when I considered that the very same thoughts (presentations) which we experience when awake may also be experienced when we are asleep, while there is at that time not one of them true, I supposed that all the objects (presentations) that had ever entered into my mind when awake, had in them no more truth than the illusions of my dreams. But immediately upon this I observed that, whilst I thus wished to think that all was false, it was absolutely necessary that I, who thus thought, should be somewhat; and as I observed that this truth, *I think, hence I am,* was so certain and of such evidence, that no ground of doubt, however extravagant, could be alleged by the Sceptics capable of shaking it, I concluded that I might, without scruple, accept it as the first principle of the Philosophy of which I was in search.

In the next place, I attentively examined what I was, and as I observed that I could suppose that I had no body, and that there was no world nor any place in which I might be; but that I could not therefore suppose that I was not; and that, on the contrary, from the very circumstance that I thought to doubt of the truth of other things, it most clearly and certainly followed that I was; while, on the other hand, if I had only ceased to think, although all the other objects which I had ever imagined had been in reality existent, I would have had no reason to believe that I existed; I thence concluded that I was a substance whose whole essence or nature consists only in thinking, and which, that it may exist, has need of no place, nor is dependent on any material thing; so that "I," that is to say, the mind by which I am what I am, is wholly distinct from the body, and is even more easily known than the latter, and is such, that although the latter were not, it would still continue to be all that it is.

After this I inquired in general into what is essential to the truth and certainty of a proposition; for since I had discovered one which I knew to be true, I thought that I must likewise be able to discover the ground of this certitude. And as I observed that in the words *I think, hence I am,* there is nothing at all which gives me assurance of their truth beyond this, that I see very clearly that in order to think it is necessary to exist, I concluded that I might take, as a general rule, the principle, that all the things which we very clearly and distinctly conceive are true, only observing, however, that there is some difficulty in rightly determining the objects which we distinctly conceive.

* * *

I have never made much account of what has proceeded from my own mind; and so long as I gathered no other advantage from the Method I employ beyond satisfying myself on some difficulties belonging to the speculative sciences, or endeavouring to regulate my actions according to the principles it taught me, I never thought myself bound to publish anything respecting it. For in what regards manners, every one is so full of his own wisdom, that there might be found as many reformers as heads, if any were allowed to take upon themselves the task of mending them, except those whom God has constituted the supreme rulers of his people, or to whom he has given sufficient grace and zeal to be prophets; and although my speculations greatly pleased myself, I believed that others had theirs, which perhaps pleased them still more. But as soon as I had acquired some general notions respecting Physics, and beginning to make trial of them in various particular difficulties, had observed how far they can carry us, and how much they differ from the principles that have been employed up to the present time, I believed that I could not keep them concealed without sinning grievously against the law by which we are bound to promote, as far as in us lies, the general good of mankind. For by them I perceived it to be possible to arrive at knowledge highly useful in life; and in room of the Speculative Philosophy usually taught in the Schools, to discover a Practical, by means of which, knowing the force and action of fire, water, air, the stars, the heavens, and all the other bodies that surround us, as distinctly as we know the various crafts of our artizans, we might also apply them in the same way to all the uses to which they are adapted, and thus render ourselves the lords and possessors of nature. And this is a result to be desired, not only in order to the invention of an infinity of arts, by which we might be enabled to enjoy without any trouble the fruits of the earth, and all its comforts, but also and especially for the preservation of health, which is without doubt, of all the blessings of this life, the first and fundamental one; for the mind is so intimately dependent upon the condition and relation of the organs of the body, that if any means can ever be found to render men wiser and more ingenious than hitherto, I believe that it is in Medicine they must be sought for. . . .

I remarked, moreover, with respect to experiments, that they become always more necessary the more one is advanced in knowledge; for, at the commencement, it is better to make use only of what is spontaneously presented to our senses, and of which we cannot remain ignorant, provided we bestow on it any reflection, however slight, than to concern ourselves about more uncommon and recondite phaenomena: the reason of which is, that the more uncommon often only mislead us so long as the causes of the more ordinary are still unknown; and the circumstances upon which they depend are almost always so special and minute as to be highly difficult to detect. But in this I have adopted the following order: first, I have essayed to find in general the principles, or first causes of all that is or can be in the world, without taking into consideration for this end anything but God himself who has created it, and without educing them from any other source than from certain germs of truths naturally existing in our minds. In the second place, I examined what were the first and most ordinary effects that could be deduced from these causes; and it appears to me that, in this way, I have found heavens, stars, and earth, and even on the earth, water, air, fire, minerals, and some other things of this kind, which of all others are the most common and simple, and hence the easiest to know. Afterwards, when I wished to descend to the more particular, so many diverse objects presented themselves to me, that I believe it to be impossible for the human mind to distinguish the forms or species of bodies that are upon the earth, from an infinity of others which might have been, if it had pleased God to place them there, or consequently to apply them to our use, unless we rise to causes through their effects, and avail ourselves of many particular experiments. Thereupon, turning over in my mind all the objects that had ever been presented to my senses, I freely venture to state that I have never observed any which I could not satisfactorily explain by the principles I had discovered. But it is necessary also to confess that the power of nature is so ample and vast, and these principles so simple and general, that I have hardly observed a single particular effect which I cannot at once recognise as capable of being deduced in many different modes from the principles, and that my greatest difficulty usually is to discover in which of these modes the effect is dependent upon them; for out of this difficulty I cannot otherwise extricate myself than by again seeking certain experiments, which may be such that their result is not the same, if it is in the one of these modes that we must explain it, as it would be if it were to be explained in the other. As to what remains, I am now in a position to discern, as I think, with sufficient clearness what course must be taken to make the majority of those experiments which may conduce to this end: but I perceive likewise that they are such and so numerous, that neither my hands nor my income, though it were a thousand times larger than it is, would be sufficient for them all; so that, according as henceforward I shall have the means of making more or fewer experiments, I shall in the same proportion make greater or less progress in the knowledge of nature.

In his Principia, *which appeared in 1687, Newton triumphantly presented the solution to the problem of motion. In his* Rules of Reasoning, *he indicated the proper methodological road to follow when investigating nature. Rule III is particularly important, for in it Newton indicated how experiments could be used to draw valid inferences about the properties of those insensible atoms which he thought the world was composed of.*

Rules of Reasoning in Philosophy
BY *Isaac Newton*

RULE I

We are to admit no more causes of natural things than such as are both true and sufficient to explain their appearances.
TO THIS PURPOSE THE PHILOSOPHERS say that Nature does nothing in vain, and more is in vain when less will serve; for Nature is pleased with simplicity, and affects not the pomp of superfluous causes.

RULE II

Therefore to the same natural effects we must, as far as possible, assign the same causes.

As to respiration in a man and in a beast; the descent of stones in *Europe* and in *America;* the light of our culinary fire and of the sun; the reflection of light in the earth, and in the planets.

RULE III

The qualities of bodies, which admit neither intensification nor remission of degrees, and which are found to belong to all bodies within the reach of our experiments, are to be esteemed the universal qualities of all bodies whatsoever.

For since the qualities of bodies are only known to us by experiments, we are to hold for universal all such as universally agree with experiments; and such as are not liable to diminution can never be quite taken away. We are certainly not to relinquish the evidence of experiments for the sake of dreams and vain fictions of our own devising; nor are we to recede from the analogy of Nature, which is wont to be simple, and always consonant to itself. We no other way know the extension of bodies than by our senses, nor do these reach it in all bodies; but because we perceive extension in all that are sensible, therefore we ascribe it universally to all others also. That abundance of bodies are hard, we learn by experience; and because the hardness of the whole arises from the hardness of the parts, we therefore justly infer the hardness of the undivided particles not only of the bodies we feel but of all others. That all bodies are impenetrable, we gather not from reason, but from sensation. The bodies which we handle we find impenetrable, and thence conclude impenetrability to be an universal property of all bodies whatsoever. That all bodies are movable, and endowed with certain powers (which we call the inertia) of persevering in their motion, or in their rest, we only infer from the like properties observed in the bodies which we have seen. The extension, hardness, impenetrability, mobility, and inertia of the whole, result from the extension, hardness, impenetrability, mobility, and inertia of the parts; and hence we conclude the least particles of all bodies to be also all extended, and hard and impenetrable, and movable, and endowed with their proper inertia. And this is the foundation of all philosophy. Moreover, that the divided but contiguous particles of bodies may be separated from one another, is matter of observation; and, in the particles that remain undivided, our minds are able to distinguish yet lesser parts, as is mathematically demonstrated. But whether the parts so distinguished, and not yet divided, may, by the powers of Nature, be actually divided and separated from one another, we cannot certainly determine. Yet, had we the proof of but one experiment that any undivided particle, in breaking a hard and solid body, suffered a division, we might by virtue of this rule conclude that the undivided as well as the divided particles may be divided and actually separated to infinity.

Lastly, if it universally appears, by experiments and astronomical observations, that all bodies about the earth gravitate towards the earth, and that in proportion to the quantity of matter which they severally contain; that the moon likewise, according to the quantity of its matter, gravitates towards the earth; that, on the other hand, our sea gravitates towards the moon; and all the planets one towards another; and the comets in like manner towards the sun; we must, in consequence of this rule, universally allow that all bodies whatsoever are endowed with a principle of mutual gravitation. For the argument from the appearances concludes with more force for the universal gravitation of all bodies than for their impenetrability; of which, among those in the celestial regions, we have no experiments, nor any manner of observation. Not that I affirm gravity to be essential to bodies: by their *vis insita* I mean nothing but their inertia. This is immutable. Their gravity is diminished as they recede from the earth.

RULE IV

In experimental philosophy we are to look upon propositions inferred by general induction from phenomena as accurately or very nearly true, notwithstanding any contrary hypotheses that may be imagined, till such time as other phenomena occur, by which they may either be made more accurate, or liable to exceptions.

This rule we must follow, that the argument of induction may not be evaded by hypotheses.

The physical world that the Greeks had described was the world that the senses revealed in all its richness and variety. Sights, smells, colors, and textures were the real properties of bodies, and Greek science had wrestled with the problem of introducing some kind of intellectual order into this welter of qualities. All this was to change with the Scientific Revolution. Qualities were mere appearances produced by the deeper reality of bodies. The distinction between these primary qualities, resulting from the essential nature of bodies, and the secondary qualities, produced by our sensory organs, was graphically described by the Italian physicist and astronomer Galileo Galilei (1564–1642). This work was first published in Italian in 1623.

FROM *Discoveries and Opinions of Galileo*

IT NOW REMAINS FOR ME to tell Your Excellency, as I promised, some thoughts of mine about the proposition "motion is the cause of heat," and to show in what sense this may be true. But first I must consider what it is that we call heat, as I suspect that people in general have a concept of this which is very remote from the truth. For they believe that heat is a real phenomenon, or property, or quality, which actually resides in the material by which we feel ourselves warmed. Now I say that whenever I conceive any material or corporeal substance, I immediately feel the need to think of it as bounded, and as having this or that shape; as being large or small in relation to other things, and in some specific place at any given time; as being in motion or at rest; as touching or not touching some other body; and as being one in number, or few, or many. From these conditions I cannot separate such a substance by any stretch of my imagination. But that it must be white or red, bitter or sweet, noisy or silent, and of sweet

Discoveries and Opinions of Galileo, pp. 273–278, translated by Stillman Drake. Copyright 1957 by Stillman Drake. Reprinted by permission of Doubleday & Co., Inc.

or foul odor, my mind does not feel compelled to bring in as necessary accompaniments. Without the senses as our guides, reason or imagination unaided would probably never arrive at qualities like these. Hence I think that tastes, odors, colors, and so on are no more than mere names so far as the object in which we place them is concerned, and that they reside only in the consciousness. Hence if the living creature were removed, all these qualities would be wiped away and annihilated. But since we have imposed upon them special names, distinct from those of the other and real qualities mentioned previously, we wish to believe that they really exist as actually different from those.

I may be able to make my notion clearer by means of some examples. I move my hand first over a marble statue and then over a living man. As to the effect flowing from my hand, this is the same with regard to both objects and my hand; it consists of the primary phenomena of motion and touch, for which we have no further names. But the live body which receives these operations feels different sensations according to the various places touched. When touched upon the soles of the feet, for example, or under the knee or armpit, it feels in addition to the common sensation of touch a sensation on which we have imposed a special name, "tickling." This sensation belongs to us and not to the hand. Anyone would make a serious error if he said that the hand, in addition to the properties of moving and touching, possessed another faculty of "tickling," as if tickling were a phenomenon that resided in the hand that tickled. A piece of paper or a feather drawn lightly over any part of our bodies performs intrinsically the same operations of moving and touching, but by touching the eye, the nose, or the upper lip it excites in us an almost intolerable titillation, even though elsewhere it is scarcely felt. This titillation belongs entirely to us and not to the feather; if the live and sensitive body were removed it would remain no more than a mere word. I believe that no more solid an existence belongs to many qualities which we have come to attribute to physical bodies—tastes, odors, colors, and many more.

A body which is solid and, so to speak, quite material, when moved in contact with any part of my person produces in me the sensation we call touch. This, though it exists over my entire body, seems to reside principally in the palms of the hands and in the finger tips, by whose means we sense the most minute differences in texture that are not easily distinguished by other parts of our bodies. Some of these sensations are more pleasant to us than others. . . . The sense of touch is more material than the other sense; and, as it arises from the solidity of matter, it seems to be related to the earthly element.

Perhaps the origin of two other senses lies in the fact that there are bodies which constantly dissolve into minute particles, some of which are heavier than air and descend, while others are lighter and rise up. The former may strike upon a certain part of our bodies that is much more sensitive than the skin, which does not feel the invasion of such subtle matter. This is the upper surface of the tongue; here the tiny particles are received, and mixing with and penetrating its moisture, they give rise to tastes, which are sweet or unsavory according to the various shapes, numbers, and speeds of the particles. And those minute particles which rise up may enter by our nostrils and strike upon some small protuberances which are the instrument of smelling; here likewise their touch and passage is received to our like or dislike according as they have this or that shape, are fast or slow, and are numerous or few. The tongue and nasal passages are providently arranged for these things, as the one extends from below to receive descending particles, and the other is adapted to those which ascend. Perhaps the excitation of tastes may be given a certain analogy to fluids, which descend through air, and odors to fires, which ascend.

Then there remains the air itself, an element available for sounds, which come to us indifferently from below, above, and all sides—for we reside in the air and its movements displace it equally in all directions. The location of the ear is most fittingly accommodated to all positions in space. Sounds are made and heard by us when the air—without any special property of "sonority" or "transonority"—is ruffled by a rapid tremor into very minute waves and moves certain cartilages of a tympanum in our ear. External means capable of thus ruffling the air are very numerous, but for the most part they may be reduced to the trembling of some body which pushes the air and disturbs it. Waves are propagated very rapidly in this way, and high tones are produced by frequent waves and low tones by sparse ones.

To excite in us tastes, odors, and sounds I believe that nothing is required in external bodies except shapes, numbers, and slow or rapid movements. I think that if ears, tongues, and noses were removed, shapes and numbers and motions would remain, but not odors or tastes or sounds. The latter, I believe, are nothing more than names when separated from living beings, just as tickling and titillation are nothing but names in the absence of such things as noses and armpits. And as these four senses are related to the four elements, so I believe that vision, the sense eminent above all others in the proportion of the finite to the infinite, the temporal to the instantaneous, the quantitative to the indivisible, the illuminated to the obscure—that vision, I say, is related to light itself. But of this sensation and the things pertaining to it I pretend to understand but little; and since even a long time would not suffice to explain that trifle, or even to hint at an explanation, I pass this over in silence.

Having shown that many sensations which are supposed to be qualities residing in external objects have no real existence save in us, and outside ourselves are mere names, I now say that I am inclined to believe heat to be of this character. Those materials which produce heat in us and make us feel warmth, which are known by the general name of "fire," would then be a multitude of minute particles having certain shapes and moving with certain velocities. Meeting with our bodies, they penetrate by means of their extreme subtlety, and their touch as felt by us when they pass through our substance is the sensation we call "heat." This is pleasant or unpleasant according to the greater or smaller speed of these particles as they go pricking and penetrating; pleasant when this assists our necessary transpiration, and obnoxious when it causes too great a separation and dissolution of our substance. The operation of fire by means of its particles is merely that in moving it penetrates all bodies, causing their speedy or slow dissolution in proportion to the number and velocity of the fire-corpuscles and the density or tenuity of the bodies. Many materials are such that in their decomposition the greater part of them passes over into additional tiny corpuscles, and this dissolution continues so long as these continue to meet with further matter capable of being so resolved. I do not believe that in addition to shape, number, motion, penetration, and touch there is any other quality in fire corresponding to "heat"; this belongs so intimately to us that when the live body is taken away, heat becomes no more than a simple name. . . .

Since the presence of fire-corpuscles alone does not suffice to excite heat, but their motion is needed also, it seems to me that one may very reasonably say that motion is the cause of heat. . . . But I hold it to be silly to accept that proposition in the ordinary way, as if a stone or piece of iron or a stick must heat up when moved. The rubbing together and friction of two hard bodies, either by resolving their parts into very subtle flying particles or by opening an exit for the tiny fire-corpuscles within, ultimately sets these in motion; and when they meet our bodies and penetrate them, our conscious mind feels those pleasant or unpleasant sensations which we have named heat, burning, and scalding. And perhaps when such attrition stops at or is confined to the smallest quanta, their motion is temporal and their action calorific only; but when their ultimate and highest resolution into truly indivisible atoms is arrived at, light is created. This may have an instantaneous motion, or rather an instantaneous expansion and diffusion, rendering it capable of occupying immense spaces by its—I know not whether to say its subtlety, its rarity, its immateriality, or some other property which differs from all these and is nameless.

In Principia *(1687) Newton defined laws of motion that applied to all material bodies. They are exemplary for their brevity, clarity, and simplicity. In order to complete his system, he needed only to assume a principle of universal attraction by which the particles of matter were drawn to one another according to the now well-known law of force,*

$$F = \frac{km_1 m_2}{r^2}$$

where m_1 and m_2 are the two masses; r is the distance between their centers; and k is a constant.

Axioms or Laws of Motion

BY *Isaac Newton*

LAW I

Every body perseveres in its state of rest, or of uniform motion in a right [straight] line, unless it is compelled to change that state by forces impressed thereon.

Projectiles persevere in their motions, so far as they are not retarded by the resistance of the air, or impelled downwards by the force of gravity. A top, whose parts by their cohesion are perpetually drawn aside from rectilinear motions, does not cease its rotation, otherwise than as it is retarded by the air. The greater bodies of the planets and comets, meeting with less resistance in more free spaces, preserve their motions both progressive and circular for a much longer time.

LAW II

The alteration of motion is ever proportional to the motive force impressed; and is made in the direction of the right line in which that force is impressed.

If any force generates a motion, a double force will generate double the motion, a triple force triple the motion, whether that force be impressed altogether and at once, or gradually and successively. And this motion (being always directed the same way with the generating force), if the body moved before, is added to or subducted [subtracted] from the former motion, according as they directly conspire with or are directly contrary to each other; or obliquely joined, when they are oblique, so as to produce a new motion compounded from the determination of both.

LAW III

To every action there is always opposed an equal reaction: or the mutual actions of two bodies upon each other are always equal, and directed to contrary parts.

Whatever draws or presses another is as much drawn or pressed by that other. If you press a stone with your finger, the finger is also pressed by the stone. If a horse draws a stone tied to a rope, the horse (if I may so say) will be equally drawn back towards the stone: for the distended rope, by the same endeavour to relax or unbend itself, will draw the horse as much towards the stone, as it does the stone towards the horse, and will obstruct the progress of the one as much as it advances that of the other. If a body impinge upon another, and by its force change the motion of the other, that body also

Isaac Newton, *Philosophiae naturalis principia mathematica*, Book I, translated by Andrew Motte (1729). Reprinted by permission.

(because of the equality of the mutual pressure) will undergo an equal change, in its own motion, towards the contrary part. The changes made by these actions are equal, not in the velocities, but in the motions of bodies; that is to say, if the bodies are not hindered by any other impediments. For, because the motions are equally changed, the changes of the velocities made towards contrary parts are reciprocally proportional to the bodies. This law takes place also in attractions.

In his work on optics, first published in Latin in 1704, Newton speculated on the ultimate nature of physical reality. He illustrated how he used his rules of reasoning to arrive at certain physical principles. He also tried to differentiate between physical laws and divine causes. Newton felt strongly that God had created both matter and the universe and that His intervention was periodically required to restore the harmony of the cosmos. Newton's "active principles" appear to be very much like the old medieval angels who kept the world going properly.

FROM *Opticks*

BY *Isaac Newton*

ALL BODIES SEEM TO BE composed of hard Particles: For otherwise Fluids would not congeal; as Water, Oils, Vinegar, and Spirit or Oil of Vitriol do by freezing; Mercury by Fumes of Lead; Spirit of Nitre and Mercury, by dissolving the Mercury and evaporating the Flegm; Spirit of Wine and Spirit of Urine, by deflegming and mixing them; and Spirit of Urine and Spirit of Salt, by subliming them together to make Sal-armoniac. Even the Rays of Light seem to be hard Bodies; for otherwise they would not retain different Properties in their different Sides. And therefore Hardness may be reckon'd the Property of all uncompounded Matter. At least, this seems to be as evident as the universal Impenetrability of Matter. For all Bodies, so far as Experience reaches, are either hard, or may be harden'd; and we have no other Evidence of universal Impenetrability, besides a large Experience without an experimental Exception. Now if compound Bodies are so very hard as we find some of them to be, and yet are very porous, and consist of Parts which are only laid together; the simple Particles which are void of Pores, and were never yet divided, must be much harder. For such hard Particles being heaped up together, can scarce touch one another in more than a few Points, and therfore must be separable by much less Force than is requisite to break a solid Particle, whose Parts touch in all the Space between them, without any Pores or Interstices to weaken their Cohesion. And how such very hard Particles which are only laid together and touch only in a few Points, can stick together, and that so firmly as they do, without the assistance of something which causes them to be attracted or press'd towards one another, is very difficult to conceive.

Isaac Newton, *Opticks*, the selection comes from Queries 30 and 31 from the fourth English edition of 1730.

All these things being consider'd, it seems probable to me, that God in the Beginning form'd Matter in solid, massy, hard, impenetrable, moveable Particles, of such Sizes and Figures, and with such other Properties, and in such Proportion to Space, as most conduced to the End for which he form'd them; and that these primitive Particles being Solids, are incomparably harder than any porous Bodies compounded of them; even so very hard, as never to wear or break in pieces; no ordinary Power being able to divide what God himself made one in the first Creation. While the Particles continue entire, they may compose Bodies of one and the same Nature and Texture in all Ages: But should they wear away, or break in pieces, the Nature of Things depending on them, would be changed. Water and Earth, composed of old worn Particles and Fragments of Particles, would not be of the same Nature and Texture now, with Water and Earth composed of entire Particles in the Beginning. And therefore, that Nature may be lasting, the Changes of corporeal Things are to be placed only in the various Separations and new Associations and Motions of these permanent Particles; compound Bodies being apt to break, not in the midst of solid Particles, but where those Particles are laid together, and only touch in a few Points.

It seems to me farther, that these Particles have not only a *Vis inertiae,* accompanied with such passive Laws of Motion as naturally result from that Force, but also that they are moved by certain active Principles, such as is that of Gravity, and that which causes Fermentation, and the Cohesion of Bodies. These Principles I consider, not as occult Qualities, supposed to result from the specifick Forms of Things, but as general Laws of Nature, by which the Things themselves are form'd; their Truth appearing to us by Phaenomena, though their Causes be not yet discover'd. For these are manifest Qualities, and their Causes only are occult. And the *Aristotelians* gave the Name of occult Qualities, not to manifest Qualities, but to such Qualities only as they supposed to lie hid in Bodies, and to be the unknown Causes of manifest Effects: Such as would be the Causes of Gravity, and of magnetick and electrick Attractions, and of Fermentations, if we should suppose that these Forces or Actions arose from Qualities unknown to us, and uncapable of being discovered and made manifest. Such occult Qualities put a stop to the Improvement of natural Philosophy, and therefore of late Years have been rejected. To tell us that every Species of Things is endow'd with an occult specifick Quality by which it acts and produces manifest Effects, is to tell us nothing: But to derive two or three general Principles of Motion from Phaenomena, and afterwards to tell us how the Properties and Actions of all corporeal Things follow from those manifest Principles, would be a very great step in Philosophy, though the Causes of those Principles were not yet discover'd: And therefore I scruple not to propose the Principles of Motion above-mention'd, they being of very general Extent, and leave their Causes to be found out.

Now by the help of these Principles, all material Things seem to have been composed of the hard and solid Particles above-mention'd, variously associated in the first Creation by the Counsel of an intelligent Agent. For it became him who created them to set them in order. And if he did so, it's unphilosophical to seek for any other Origin of the World, or to pretend that it might arise out of a Chaos by the mere Laws of Nature; though being once form'd, it may continue by those Laws for many Ages. For while Comets move in very excentrick Orbs in all manner of Positions, blind Fate could never make all the Planets move one and the same way in Orbs concentrick, some inconsiderable Irregularities excepted, which may have risen from the mutual Actions of Comets and Planets upon one another, and which will be apt to increase, till this System wants a Reformation. Such a wonderful Uniformity in the Planetary System must be allowed the Effect of Choice. And so must the Uniformity in the Bodies of Animals, they having generally a right and a left side shaped alike, and on either side of their Bodies two Legs behind, and either two Arms, or two Legs, or two Wings before upon their Shoulders, and between their Shoulders a Neck running down into a Back-bone, and a Head upon it; and in the Head two Ears, two Eyes, a Nose, a Mouth, and a Tongue, alike situated. Also the first Contrivance of those very artificial Parts of Animals, the Eyes, Ears, Brain, Muscles, Heart, Lungs, Midriff, Glands, Larynx, Hands, Wings, swimming Bladders, natural Spectacles, and other Organs of Sense and Motion; and the Instinct of Brutes and Insects, can be the effect of nothing else than the Wisdom and Skill of a powerful ever-living Agent, who being in all Places, is more able by his Will to move the Bodies within his boundless uniform Sensorium, and thereby to form and reform the Parts of the Universe, than we are by our Will to move the Parts of our own Bodies. And yet we are not to consider the World as the Body of God, or the several Parts thereof, as the Parts of God. He is an uniform Being, void of Organs, Members or Parts, and they are his Creatures subordinate to him, and subservient to his Will; and he is no more the Soul of them, than the Soul of Man is the Soul of the Species of Things carried through the Organs of Sense into the place of its Sensation, where it perceives them by means of its immediate Presence, without the Intervention of any third thing. The Organs of Sense are not for enabling the Soul to perceive the Species of Things in its Sensorium, but only for conveying them thither; and God has no need of such Organs, he being every where present to the Things themselves.

2

The Application of the New Science to the Age of Reason

What was it, precisely, that the thinkers and publicists of the Age of Reason wanted to discover and conclude? The new science provided them with both a model and a method, but the men and women of the Enlightenment were less interested in the world of nature than they were in the world of man. One major aspect of the Enlightenment, then, is the attempt made by writers to apply what they had learned from the new science to the human condition. This involved a major change in philosophy, which is described in the following selection by Professor Ira O. Wade, one of the leading modern authorities on the Age of Reason.

FROM *The Intellectual Origins of the French Enlightenment*

BY *Ira O. Wade*

THE ENLIGHTENMENT . . . started with the realm of nature and that of mind, understanding its task to be the penetration of nature's reality by an intellectual awareness of that reality. What the age wanted to do was to collect the largest body of impressions in nature from which to deduce the greatest number of principles which would contribute to maximum human activity and happiness.

Nature, to the thinkers of the Enlightenment, is a closed system of causes and effects, of reasons and implications; there is nothing accidental or arbitrary therein. Everything is subjected to universal laws which can be known by conceptual analysis rather than by experience or observation. The method practiced was to reduce the natural event to mathematical statement. The principle, once established in natural phenomena, was introduced likewise in the area of social and historical fact. The being of man can be explained by the same universal laws which govern the being of nature, since no distinction can be made between nature and human nature. Man's world being no longer separate from nature's world, he has no exceptional place in the scheme of things.

The Enlightenment was concerned not only with the penetration of nature, that is total organic nature, by reason, it wanted also to devise an absolute identity between the natural and the reasonable. Natural law is right reason working in the field of human and natural relationships. Natural religion is the working of right reason in the field of religion. Finally, natural morality is right reason working in the field of ethics. The just, the true, and the good are both reasonable and natural. They transcend both time and space, and they have a universal validity because they stand at the origin of positive laws, religions, and moralities. The Enlightenment was fascinated with those laws which are not of "yesterday," and the thinkers inquired diligently into the origin of things as a means of comprehending their meaning for man.

The Enlightenment did not attempt to develop a new body of teachings, though, nor did it seek a new dogma. Anxious to discover new facts, it insisted upon their dissemination among the widest number of people. It was by nature encyclopedic and propagandistic. Convinced that in the corps of facts lay an infinite number of inner formative forces, it conceived as its task to seek out the structures which, treated properly, could transform a world of contradiction and chaos into an organic unity. It recommended an effort to sift, clarify, arrange, and organize the ideas which it already possessed. It was confident, too, that the inner formative forces which derived from its corps of facts could create a whole new spirit. This conviction, indeed, led to a totally new kind of philosophical thought, based upon systematic analysis. Cassirer explains that "instead of tying philosophy to definite, immutable axioms and deductions from them, the Enlightenment wants it to move freely and in this immanent activity to discover the fundamental form of reality." No longer a special field of knowledge, philosophy is rather the all-comprehensive medium in which the principles of all knowledge are free to develop. No longer mere thought, it wants to enter into the activity of the spirit. Its task is not to reflect but to shape life. Hence, the Enlightenment's inquiry concerned first the competence of thought. The problem was naturally derived from Locke's *Essay,* but the solution differed from Locke's conception in that it involved both the limits of thought and its capabilities as a dynamic force. Thought became the center of all activity, regarded not only as the unifying element, but also as the immutable factor in all life. In addition to being a collection of knowledge, of truths, and of principles, it was conceived as a dynamic process, an energy, which can be grasped only in its activity. It is a *manner of thinking,* devoted to constant analysis, to separation into component parts, to the reconstruction of those parts into a whole, and to the expression of this whole in terms of laws. It functions in every enterprise in which the human being is engaged, and by its *manner of thinking,* it aims to change the *common way of thinking and doing.* Thus Enlightenment thought carries within itself powers of destruction as well as powers of construction. Finally, knowledge of the world does not stop with knowledge of external objects; it is the means whereby one sees reflected the possibilities of his inner reality. Since the cosmos is limitless both in time and space, knowledge tends to become a never-ending series of relationships between the self and the phenomena of life, in which the correlation between the universe and the self guarantees the validity of thought and the legality of the external world. Knowledge thus involves both thinking and feeling, sensibility and thought, experience and rational awareness. Being and knowing are consequently two poles of the same ontological phenomenon, present both in nature and in all the creations of human nature: history, morality, the state, religion, and aesthetics.

Thus the eighteenth century gave a priority to nature, in which were incorporated all the phenomena of man. The real achievement of natural science did not lie in the all-embracing content, but rather in the possibility which this content offered to the human mind for self-realization. The limitless expansion of natural science increased the mind's awareness of a new force within itself. It is not in its infinity, however, that nature informs man of his real intensity. His deepest meaning lies in the mind's maintaining itself against the infinite universe. Thus there is a double tendency seen in nature: toward the particular, the concrete, the factual, and contrariwise to the absolutely universal. It is this duality which shifts the importance of nature from the realm of the created to that of the creative process. Nature participates in the divine essence, and eventually identifies herself with God. Contained within herself is the whole plan of the cosmos waiting for the human mind to recognize and express it, and when this occurs, the operation carries with it both identity and autonomy. With one stroke, is brought out the self-sufficiency of nature and mind, the one perfectly accessible to the other.

The Enlightenment accepted, though, that certain changes must be effected. The sciences must be organized in a unified way; and the bond between theology and physics must be severed. Nature must incorporate within herself all the intellectual sciences, even laws, society, politics, and poetry; she can be grasped only by that method which begins with facts and attempts to reach to principles. In theory, however, one should never expect to venture beyond description of natural phenomena, since there is no way whereby we can explain the mechanism of the universe or see into the essence of things. We possess no knowledge of first principles, and consequently no final criterion of the truth of phenomena, only a "moral certainty," which is not logical, but rather biological. Indeed, there is a definite shift, recorded by Diderot in the *Pensées sur l'interprétation de la nature,* from mathematics and mathematical physics to biology and physiology, exhibiting a strong tendency to materialism.

For the Enlightenment the basic science became psychology, despite the fact that the word itself became current only late in the century. Thought cannot turn to the objects of external nature without at the same time reverting to itself. The truth which it perceives in nature becomes in a way the truth in itself. Hence the two questions which are constantly propounded in the eighteenth century concern the reality of the objects of nature and the capacity of the mind to penetrate that reality. Involved in those two problems are two larger issues:

the limits of the understanding and the nature of the things understood. The question constantly posed is: what kind of object is commensurate with, and determinable by, our knowledge? No legitimate answer, however, can be given to this question until an exact insight into the specific character of the human understanding is achieved by examining the extent of its activity and the course of its development. Thus psychology became the foundation of epistemology. The capacities of knowledge are known only by tracing the processes of thought: the critical analysis of the instrument discloses the extent of its possibilities.

Fundamentally, what the Enlightenment wanted to ascertain was how one can know, and the connection between knowledge and action. It was faced with the necessity of seeking the agreement between concepts and objects, expressed by the simple question: What is the relationship between knowledge and reality? The Enlightenment's answer to this question was that every idea in our minds is based on a previous impression. This belief resulted in the reassertion of the Stoic statement that "nihil est in intellectu quod non antea fuerit in sensu." But there was no proof of this statement.

There were in fact three explanations for ideas in the Enlightenment. Locke stuck to the senses as their source, but he retained in his explanation of the operations of the understanding such innate factors as comparing, reflection, judging, and willing. Leibniz for his part thought ideas took their origin in the active energy of the mind. Condillac saw the senses as the source, but he eliminated all such innate notions as reflection, comparing, etc.

In these explanations there was some ground for agreement: the insistence upon the dominance of the passions, the stress laid upon the concept of effort, the drive toward the active energy. In fact, though only Leibniz stated so categorically, the century tended to insist that the mind is not a composite of faculties, mechanically organized, but a composite of formative forces. The task of philosophy henceforth is to elucidate those forces in their structure and to understand their reciprocal relations. In this way there was opened up a new approach to the spontaneity of the ego, and new paths for progress in epistemology, aesthetics, and morality.

Since the initial shift of the Enlightenment was from a system dominated by a religious order to one in which the individual accepted responsibility for making his world, it was inevitable that the institution of religion should be put in question. Usually this attitude was interpreted as an attack which the writers and thinkers of the Enlightenment made against established religion. A thoroughgoing review of the proofs of the divinity of Christianity—miracles, prophecies, the continuity of Christian history from the old to the new dispensation, its morality, and its martyrs—was made. Many works investigating these proofs circulated in France and England. Many analyzed the *Bible* in an effort to point out the inaccuracies of a historical, scientific, moral, even of a computational, order. The conclusion drawn was that a work so filled with errors could not be accorded universal religious significance. Practically all these works affirmed the validity of natural religion, natural morality, and natural law, basing them upon a divinely inspired reason, and stressing that this reason was the source of love of God, justice toward one's fellowmen, and social and political morality.

These ideas were propagated by the deists who in a negative way denied the need for dogma, rites and ceremonies, religious organization and a priesthood, but who in a positive way reasserted their belief in the existence of God and in the necessity for a reasonable, natural morality. As a religious movement, deism was very widespread in the eighteenth century. It drew its strength from its pretense to universality, having been the religion of all the wise men of the past. But it was also the religion of all men everywhere, since it was the voice of God-given reason in the hearts of all men. It had its weaknesses, however, the foremost being its instability. Deists found it difficult to explain how every man with God-given reason acted so terribly unreasonably at times, more difficult still to explain how the divine sense of justice seldom led to just acts. The whole realm of evil—natural evil; positive, moral evil; metaphysical evil— became an inexplicable phenomenon in a universe filled with wonders which declared the glory of God, while pain, suffering, and sin declared at least that something had gone awry. It was not consoling to realize that everything lived in this world at the expense of everything else. Since the deist affirmed the wisdom, the goodness, and the all-powerfulness of the Deity, evil could not be explained by reason without putting into question at least one of these qualities. And any rejection of these qualities reduced the concept of the Deity to Nature, and left the way open to atheism, naturalism, determinism, materialism. Pascal had long before seen the deist dilemma and had reaffirmed the doctrine of original sin and the necessity for the Atonement. He experienced difficulty in making salvation universal, however, but the Enlightenment did succeed in making it universal, though not without involving the all-powerfulness of the Deity, and even His mode of existence.

Cassirer explains that this impossible situation merely indicates that the period was not ripe for the creation of a theodicy, and consequently, the Enlightenment sought replacements for the deficiency, one of which was the doctrine of tolerance. Since there is no metaphysical imperative in any formal religion, there is no absolute validity in any religious sect. Therefore the only reasonable way of approaching a sect is respect for its beliefs and the elimination of all forms of persecution. The Enlightenment was prepared to proclaim that even heresy was the natural state of man and was entitled to the respect of everybody. Indeed, in accordance with the formula expressed by Spinoza in the *Tractatus,* the century maintained that every man was entitled to the freedom of his beliefs, which the State should protect. The doctrine of tolerance, accordingly, became grounded upon the brotherhood of man and the right to err. In a way this was a social theodicy which justified the ways of God to man, but it was strictly limited to this world and to this life. It led straight to the suggestion of two other replacements for the old theodicy: with Shaftesbury and down to

Diderot, the highest form of spiritual expression was not theological but aesthetic; with Rousseau, its highest form was moral and above all political. For the Enlightenment as a whole, however, all of these replacements merely put great emphasis upon the moral category and attributed a preponderant importance to the inner energy of man and his right to express that energy in any manifestation of human creation.

As Wade has made clear, John Locke was the first philosopher to pick up the Newtonian methods and concepts and apply them to humanity. He was second only to Newton in his influence on the Enlightenment. In An Essay Concerning Human Understanding, *first published in 1690, he analyzed man's moral instincts and indicated how they flowed reasonably from man's basic physiology. He also indicated how certain fundamental political urges also arose from man's nature.*

FROM *An Essay Concerning Human Understanding*
BY *John Locke*

OF MODES OF PLEASURE AND PAIN

1. AMONGST THE SIMPLE IDEAS, which we receive both from sensation and reflection, pain and pleasure are two very considerable ones. For as in the body there is sensation barely in itself, or accompanied with pain or pleasure: so the thought or perception of the mind is simply so, or else accompanied also with pleasure or pain, delight or trouble, call it how you please. These, like other simple ideas, cannot be described, nor their names defined; the way of knowing them is, as of the simple ideas of the senses, only by experience. For to define them by the presence of good or evil, is no otherwise to make them known to us, than by making us reflect on what we feel in ourselves, upon the several and various operations of good and evil upon our minds, as they are differently applied to or considered by us.

2. Things then are good or evil, only in reference to pleasure or pain. That we call good, which is apt to cause or increase pleasure, or diminish pain in us; or else to procure or preserve us the possession of any other good, or absence of any evil. And on the contrary, we name that evil, which is apt to produce or increase any pain, or diminish any pleasure in us; or else to procure us any evil, or deprive us of any good. By pleasure and pain, I must be understood to mean of body or mind, as they are commonly distinguished; though in truth they be only different constitutions of the mind, sometimes occasioned by disorder in the body, sometimes by thoughts of the mind.

John Locke, *An Essay Concerning Human Understanding*. Chapters XX and XXI of Book 2.

3. Pleasure and pain, and that which causes them, good and evil, are the hinges on which our passions turn: and if we reflect on ourselves, and observe how these, under various considerations, operate in us; what modifications or tempers of mind, what internal sensations (if I may so call them) they produce in us, we may thence form to ourselves the ideas of our passions.

4. Thus any one reflecting upon the thought he has of the delight, which any present or absent thing is apt to produce in him, has the idea we call love. For when a man declares in autumn, when he is eating them, or in spring, when there are none, that he loves grapes, it is no more but that the taste of grapes delights him; let an alteration of health or constitution destroy the delight of their taste, and he then can be said to love grapes no longer.

5. On the contrary, the thought of the pain, which any thing present or absent is apt to produce in us, is what we call hatred. Were it my business here to inquire any farther than into the bare ideas of our passions, as they depend on different modifications of pleasure and pain, I should remark, that our love and hatred of inanimate insensible beings, is commonly founded on that pleasure and pain which we receive from their use and application any way to our senses, though with their destruction: but hatred or love, to beings capable of happiness or misery, is often the uneasiness or delight, which we find in ourselves arising from a consideration of their very being or happiness. Thus the being and welfare of a man's children or friends, producing constant delight in him, he is said constantly to love them. But it suffices to note, that our ideas of love and hatred are but the dispositions of the mind, in respect of pleasure and pain in general, however caused in us.

6. The uneasiness a man finds in himself upon the absence of any thing, whose present enjoyment carries the idea of delight with it, is what we call desire; which is greater or less, as that uneasiness is more or less vehement. Where, by the by, it may perhaps be of some use to remark, that the chief, if not only spur to human industry and action, is uneasiness. For whatsoever good is proposed, if its absence carries no displeasure or pain with it, if a man be easy and content without it, there is no desire of it, nor endeavour after it; there is no more but a bare velleity, the term used to signify the lowest degree of desire, and that which is next to none at all, when there is so little uneasiness in the absence of any thing, that it carries a man no farther than some faint wishes for it, without any more effectual or vigorous use of the means to attain it. Desire also is stopped or abated by the opinion of the impossibility or unattainableness of the good proposed, as far as the uneasiness is cured or allayed by that consideration. This might carry our thoughts farther, were it seasonable in this place.

7. Joy is a delight of the mind, from the consideration of the present or assured approaching possession of a good: and we are then possessed of any good when we have it so in our power, that we can use it when we please. Thus a man almost starved has joy at the arrival of relief, even before he has the pleasure of using it: and a father, in whom the very well-being of his chil-

dren causes delight, is always, as long as his children are in such a state, in the possession of that good; for he needs but to reflect on it, to have that pleasure.

8. Sorrow is uneasiness in the mind, upon the thought of a good lost, which might have been enjoyed longer; or the sense of a present evil.

9. Hope is that pleasure in the mind, which every one finds in himself, upon the thought of a profitable future enjoyment of a thing, which is apt to delight him.

10. Fear is an uneasiness of the mind, upon the thought of future evil likely to befal us.

11. Despair is the thought of the unattainableness of any good, which works differently in men's minds, sometimes producing uneasiness or pain, sometimes rest and indolency.

12. Anger is uneasiness or discomposure of the mind, upon the receipt of any injury, with a present purpose of revenge.

13. Envy is an uneasiness of the mind, caused by the consideration of a good we desire, obtained by one we think should not have had it before us.

14. These two last, envy and anger, not being caused by pain and pleasure, simply in themselves, but having in them some mixed considerations of ourselves and others, are not therefore to be found in all men, because those other parts of valuing their merits, or intending revenge, is wanting in them; but all the rest terminating purely in pain and pleasure, are, I think, to be found in all men. For we love, desire, rejoice, and hope, only in respect of pleasure; we hate, fear, and grieve, only in respect of pain ultimately: in fine, all these passions are moved by things, only as they appear to be the causes of pleasure and pain, or to have pleasure or pain some way or other annexed to them. Thus we extend our hatred usually to the subject (at least if a sensible or voluntary agent) which has produced pain in us, because the fear it leaves is a constant pain: but we do not so constantly love what has done us good; because pleasure operates not so strongly on us as pain, and because we are not so ready to have hope it will do so again. But this by the by.

15. By pleasure and pain, delight and uneasiness, I must all along be understood (as I have above intimated) to mean not only bodily pain and pleasure, but whatsoever delight or uneasiness is felt by us, whether arising from any grateful or unacceptable sensation or reflection.

16. It is farther to be considered, that in reference to the passions, the removal or lessening of a pain is considered, and operates as a pleasure: and the loss or diminishing of a pleasure, as a pain.

17. The passions too have most of them in most persons operations on the body, and cause various changes in it; which not being always sensible, do not make a necessary part of the idea of each passion. For shame, which is an uneasiness of the mind upon the thought of having done something which is indecent, or will lessen the valued esteem which others have for us, has not always blushing accompanying it.

18. I would not be mistaken here, as if I meant this as a discourse of the passions; they are many more than those I have here named: and those I have taken notice of would each of them require a much larger, and more accurate discourse. I have only mentioned these here as so many instances of modes of pleasure and pain resulting in our minds from various considerations of good and evil. I might perhaps have instanced in other modes of pleasure and pain more simple than these, as the pain of hunger and thirst, and the pleasure of eating and drinking to remove them: the pain of tender eyes, and the pleasure of musick; pain from captious uninstructive wrangling, and the pleasure of rational conversation with a friend, or of well-directed study in the search and discovery of truth. But the passions being of much more concernment to us, I rather made choice to instance in them, and show how the ideas we have of them are derived from sensation and reflection. . . .

*   *   *

56. These things duly weighed, will give us, as I think, a clear view into the state of human liberty. Liberty, it is plain, consists in a power to do, or not to do; to do, or forbear doing, as we will. This cannot be denied. But this seeming to comprehend only the actions of a man consecutive to volition, it is farther inquired, "whether he be at liberty to will, or no." And to this it has been answered, that in most cases a man is not at liberty to forbear the act of volition: he must exert an act of his will, whereby the action proposed is made to exist, or not to exist. But yet there is a case wherein a man is at liberty in respect of willing, and that is, the choosing of a remote good, as an end to be pursued. Here a man may suspect the act of his choice from being determined for or against the thing proposed, till he has examined whether it be really of a nature in itself and consequences to make him happy, or no. For when he has once chosen it, and thereby it is become a part of his happiness, it raises desire, and that proportionably gives him uneasiness, which determines his will, and sets him at work in pursuit of his choice on all occasions that offer. And here we may see how it comes to pass, that a man may justly incur punishment, though it be certain that in all the particular actions that he wills, he does, and necessarily does will that which he then judges to be good. For, though his will be always determined by that which is judged good by his understanding, yet it excuses him not: because, by a too hasty choice of his own making, he has imposed on himself wrong measures of good and evil; which, however false and fallacious, have the same influence on all his future conduct, as if they were true and right. He has vitiated his own palate, and must be answerable to himself for the sickness and death that follows from it. The eternal law and nature of things must not be altered, to comply with his ill-ordered choice. If the neglect, or abuse, of the liberty he had to examine what would really and truly make for his happiness, misleads him, the miscarriages that follow on it must be imputed to his own election. He had a power to suspend his determination: it was given him, that he might examine, and take care of his own hap-

piness, and look that he were not deceived. And he could never judge, that it was better to be deceived than not, in a matter of so great and near concernment.

What has been said may also discover to us the reason why men in this world prefer different things, and pursue happiness by contrary courses. But yet, since men are always constant, and in earnest, in matters of happiness and misery, the question still remains, How men come often to prefer the worse to the better; and to choose that, which by their own confession, has made them miserable?

David Hume (1711–1776) was England's most powerful philosophical mind in the eighteenth century. His powers of reason were directed at all systems of metaphysics and thought that went beyond the senses to suggest supersensory realities. In this work, which appeared in 1751, he illustrates the almost unconscious assumption of the Age of Reason that morality must be capable of rational study and analysis. He simply ignores those who would claim that morality is human action in accordance with the will of God, as presented in Holy Scripture.

FROM *An Inquiry Concerning the Principles of Morals*
BY *David Hume*

THERE HAS BEEN A CONTROVERSY started of late, much better worth examination, concerning the general foundation of MORALS; whether they be derived from REASON or from SENTIMENT; whether we attain the knowledge of them by a chain of argument and induction, or by an immediate feeling and finer internal sense; whether, like all sound judgment of truth and falsehood, they should be the same to every rational intelligent being; or whether, like the perception of beauty and deformity, they be founded entirely on the particular fabric and constitution of the human species. . . .

It must be acknowledged, that both sides of the question are susceptible of specious arguments. Moral distinctions, it may be said, are discernible by pure *reason:* Else, whence the many disputes that reign in common life, as well as in philosophy, with regard to this subject; the long chain of proofs often produced on both sides, the example cited, the authorities appealed to, the analogies employed, the fallacies detected, the inferences drawn, and the several conclusions adjusted to their proper principles? Truth is disputable; not taste: What exists in the nature of things is the standard of our judgment: what each man feels within himself is the standard of sentiment. Propositions in geometry may be proved, systems in physics may be controverted; but the harmony of verse, the tenderness of passion, the brilliancy of wit, must give immediate pleasure. No man reasons concerning another's beauty; but frequently concerning the justice or injustice of his actions. In every criminal trial, the first object of

David Hume, *An Inquiry Concerning the Principles of Morals.* Section I the prisoner is to disprove the facts alleged, and deny the actions imputed to him: The second, to prove that, even if these actions were real, they might be justified as innocent and lawful. It is confessedly by deductions of the understanding, that the first point is ascertained: How can we suppose that a different faculty of the mind is employed in fixing the other?

On the other hand, those who would resolve all moral determinations into *sentiment,* may endeavour to show, that it is impossible for reason ever to draw conclusions of this nature. To virtue, say they, it belongs to be *amiable,* and vice *odious.* This forms their very nature or essence. But can reason or argumentation distribute these different epithets to any subjects, and pronounce beforehand, that this must produce love, and that hatred? Or what other reason can we ever assign for these affections, but the original fabric and formation of the human mind, which is naturally adapted to receive them?

The end of all moral speculations is to teach us our duty; and, by proper representations of the deformity of vice and beauty of virtue, beget correspondent habits, and engage us to avoid the one, and embrace the other. But is this ever to be expected from inferences and conclusions of the understanding, which of themselves have no hold of the affections, or set in motion the active powers of men? They discover truths: But where the truths which they discover are indifferent, and beget no desire or aversion, they can have no influence on conduct and behaviour. What is honourable, what is fair, what is becoming, what is noble, what is generous, takes possession of the heart, and animates us to embrace and maintain it. What is intelligible, what is evident, what is probable, what is true, procures only the cool assent of the understanding; and gratifying a speculative curiosity, puts an end to our researches.

Extinguish all the warm feeling and prepossessions in favour of virtue, and all disgust or aversion to vice; render men totally indifferent towards these distinctions; and morality is no longer a practical study, nor has any tendency to regulate our lives and actions.

These arguments on each side (and many more might be produced) are so plausible, that I am apt to suspect they may, the one as well as the other, be solid and satisfactory, and that *reason* and *sentiment* concur in almost all moral determinations and conclusions. The final sentence, it is probable, which pronounces characters and actions amiable, or odious, praiseworthy or blameable; that which stamps on them the mark of honour or infamy, approbation or censure; that which renders morality an active principle, and constitutes virtue our happiness, and vice our misery: It is probable, I say, that this final sentence depends on some internal sense or feeling, which nature has made universal in the whole species. For what else can have an influence of this nature? But in order to pave the way for such a sentiment, and give a proper discernment of its object, it is often necessary, we find, that much reasoning should precede, that nice distinctions be made, just conclusions drawn, distant comparisons formed, complicated relations examined, and general facts fixed and ascertained. Some species of beauty, especially the natural kinds, on their first appearance, command our affection and approbation; and where they fail of this effect, it is impossible for any reasoning to redress their influence, or adapt them better to our taste and sentiment. But in many orders of beauty, particularly those of the finer arts, it is requisite to employ much reasoning, in order to feel the proper sentiment; and a false relish may frequently be corrected by argument and reflection. There are just grounds to conclude that moral beauty partakes much of this latter species, and demands the assistance of our intellectual faculties, in order to give it a suitable influence on the human mind.

But though this question, concerning the general principles of morals, be curious and important, it is needless for us, at present, to employ farther care in our researches concerning it. For if we can be so happy, in the course of this inquiry, as to discover the true origin of morals, it will then easily appear how far either sentiment or reason enters into all determinations of this nature. In order to attain this purpose, we shall endeavour to follow a very simple method: We shall analyze that complication of mental qualities, which form what, in common life, we call PERSONAL MERIT: We shall consider every attribute of the mind, which renders a man an object either of esteem and affection, or of hatred and contempt; every habit or sentiment or faculty, which, if ascribed to any person, implies either praise or blame, and may enter into any panegyric or satire of his character and manners. The quick sensibility which, on this head, is so universal among mankind, gives a philosopher sufficient assurance, that he can never be considerably mistaken in framing the catalogue, or incur any danger of misplacing the objects of his contemplation: He needs only enter into his own breast for a moment, and consider whether or not he should desire to have this or that quality ascribed to him, and whether such or such an imputation would proceed from a friend or an enemy. The very nature of language guides us almost infallibly in forming a judgment of this nature; and as every tongue possesses one set of words which are taken in a good sense, and another in the opposite, the least acquaintance with the idiom suffices, without any reasoning, to direct us in collecting and arranging the estimable or blameable qualities of men. The only object of reasoning is to discover the circumstances on both sides, which are common to these qualities; to observe that particular in which the estimable qualities agree on the one hand, and the blameable on the other; and thence to reach the foundation of ethics, and find those universal principles, from which all censure or approbation is ultimately derived. As this is a question of fact, not of abstract science, we can only expect success by following the experimental method, and deducing general maxims from a comparison of particular instances. The other scientifical method, where a general abstract principle is first established, and is afterwards branched out into a variety of inferences and conclusions, may be more perfect in itself, but suits less the imperfection of human nature, and is a common source of illusion and mistake, in this as well as in other subjects. Men are now cured of their passion for hypotheses and systems in natural philosophy, and will hearken to no arguments but those which are derived from experience. It is full time they should attempt a like reformation in all moral disquisitions; and reject every system of ethics, however subtle or ingenious, which is not founded on fact and observation.

Hume, like Locke, was concerned with the nature of politics. Unlike Locke, however, he wished to draw his political science from the study of history and of human institutions, rather than from the study of the human psyche. Nevertheless, he felt that politics could be turned into a political science. We may note, with some amusement, that most eighteenth-century Englishmen who set out to discover the scientific principles of the perfect state tended, like Hume, to find them brilliantly visible in the England of their day. This work was first published in 1742.

FROM *That Politics May Be Reduced to a Science*

BY *David Hume*

IT IS A QUESTION WITH SEVERAL, whether there be any essential difference between one form of government and another? and, whether every form may not become good or bad, according as it is well or ill administered? Were it once admitted, that all governments are alike, and that the only difference consists in the character and conduct of the governors, most political disputes would be at an end, and all *Zeal* for one constitution above another must be esteemed mere bigotry and folly. But, though a friend to moderation, I cannot forbear condemning this sentiment, and should be sorry to think, that human affairs admit of no greater stability, than what they receive from the casual humours and characters of particular men.

*   *   *

So great is the force of laws, and of particular forms of government, and so little dependence have they on the humours and tempers of men, that consequences almost as general and certain may sometimes be deduced from them, as any which the mathematical sciences afford us.

The constitution of the Roman republic gave the whole legislative power to the people, without allowing a negative voice either to the nobility or consuls. This unbounded power they possessed in a collective, not in a representative body. The consequences were: When the people, by success and conquest, had become very numerous, and had spread themselves to a great distance from the capital, the city tribes, though the most contemptible, carried almost every vote: They were, therefore, most cajoled by every one that affected popularity: They were supported in idleness by the general distribution of corn, and by particular bribes, which they received from almost every candidate: By this means, they became every day more licentious, and the Campus Martius was a perpetual scene of tumult and sedition: Armed slaves were introduced

David Hume, "That Politics May Be Reduced to a Science" in *Essays, Moral, Political, and Literary.*

among these rascally citizens; so that the whole government fell into anarchy; and the greatest happiness, which the Romans could look for, was the despotic power of the Caesars. Such are the effects of democracy without a representative.

A Nobility may possess the whole, or any part of the legislative power of a state, in two different ways. Either every nobleman shares the power as a part of the whole body, or the whole body enjoys the power as composed of parts, which have each a distinct power and authority. The Venetian aristocracy is an instance of the first kind of government; the Polish, of the second. In the Venetian government the whole body of nobility possesses the whole power, and no nobleman has any authority which he receives not from the whole. In the Polish government every nobleman, by means of his fiefs, has a distinct hereditary authority over his vassals, and the whole body has no authority but what it receives from the concurrence of its parts. The different operations and tendencies of these two species of government might be made apparent even *a priori*. A Venetian nobility is preferable to a Polish, let the humours and education of men be ever so much varied. A nobility, who possess their power in common, will preserve peace and order, both among themselves, and their subjects; and no member can have authority enough to control the laws for a moment. The nobles will preserve their authority over the people, but without any grievous tyranny, or any breach of private property; because such a tyrannical government promotes not the interests of the whole body, however it may that of some individuals. There will be a distinction of rank between the nobility and people, but this will be the only distinction in the state. The whole nobility will form one body, and the whole people another, without any of those private feuds and animosities, which spread ruin and desolation every where. It is easy to see the disadvantages of a Polish nobility in every one of these particulars.

It is possible so to constitute a free government, as that a single person, call him a doge, prince, or king, shall possess a large share of power, and shall form a proper balance or counterpoise to the other parts of the legislature. This chief magistrate may be either *elective* or *hereditary;* and though the former institution may, to a superficial view, appear the most advantageous; yet a more accurate inspection will discover in it greater inconveniences than in the latter, and such as are founded on causes and principles eternal and immutable. The filling of the throne, in such a government, is a point of too great and too general interest, not to divide the whole people into factions: Whence a civil war, the greatest of ills, may be apprehended, almost with certainty, upon every vacancy. The prince elected must be either a *Foreigner* or a *Native:* The former will be ignorant of the people whom he is to govern; suspicious of his new subjects, and suspected by them; giving his confidence entirely to strangers, who will have no other care but of enriching themselves in the quickest manner while their master's favour and authority are able to support them. A native will carry into the throne all his private animosities and friendships, and will never be viewed in his elevation without exciting the sentiment of envy in those who formerly considered him as their equal. Not to mention that a crown is too high a reward ever to be given to merit alone, and will always induce the candidates to employ force, or money, or intrigue, to procure the votes of the electors: So that such an election will give no better chance for superior merit in the prince, than if the state had trusted to birth alone for determining the sovereign.

It may therefore be pronounced as an universal axiom in politics, *That an hereditary prince, a nobility without vassals, and a people voting by their representatives, form the best* MONARCHY, ARISTOCRACY, *and* DEMOCRACY. But in order to prove more fully, that politics admit of general truths, which are invariable by the humour or education either of subject or sovereign, it may not be amiss to observe some other principles of this science, which may seem to deserve that character.

It may easily be observed, that, though free governments have been commonly the most happy for those who partake of their freedom; yet are they the most ruinous and oppressive to their provinces: And this observation may, I believe, be fixed as a maxim of the kind we are here speaking of. When a monarch extends his dominions by conquest, he soon learns to consider his old and his new subjects as on the same footing; because, in reality, all his subjects are to him the same, except the few friends and favourites with whom he is personally acquainted. He does not, therefore, make any distinction between them in his *general* laws; and, at the same time, is careful to prevent all *particular* acts of oppression on the one as well as on the other. But a free state necessarily makes a great distinction, and must always do so, till men learn to love their neighbours as well as themselves. The conquerors, in such a government, are all legislators, and will be sure to contrive matters, by restrictions on trade, and by taxes, so as to draw some private, as well as public advantage from their conquests. Provincial governors have also a better chance, in a republic, to escape with their plunder, by means of bribery or intrigue; and their fellow-citizens, who find their own state to be enriched by the spoils of the subject provinces, will be the more inclined to tolerate such abuses. Not to mention, that it is a necessary precaution in a free state to change the governors frequently; which obliges these temporary tyrants to be more expeditious and rapacious, that they may accumulate sufficient wealth before they give place to their successors.

Philosophers had been concerned about economics since antiquity, but the "scientific" study of commerce, industry, money, and banking is generally acknowledged to be an eighteenth-century innovation. Among the founders of the new science was Adam Smith, whose An Inquiry into the Nature and Causes of the Wealth of Nations, *first published in 1776, was the* Principia *of classical economics. In this selection, Smith deals with commerce as an almost astronomical balance of*

*forces of attraction and repulsion. Note the "invisible hand" which greatly resembles
Newton's use of God to put the world back into harmony after perturbations have
disturbed it.*

FROM *An Inquiry into the Nature and Causes of the Wealth of Nations*

BY *Adam Smith*

EVERY INDIVIDUAL IS CONTINUALLY EXERTING HIMSELF to find out the most advantageous employment for whatever capital he can command. It is his own advantage, indeed, and not that of the society, which he has in view. But the study of his own advantage naturally, or rather necessarily, leads him to prefer that employment which is most advantageous to the society.

First, every individual endeavours to employ his capital as near home as he can, and consequently as much as he can in the support of domestic industry; provided always that he can thereby obtain the ordinary, or not a great deal less than the ordinary profits of stock.

Thus, upon equal or nearly equal profits, every wholesale merchant naturally prefers the home trade to the foreign trade of consumption, and the foreign trade of consumption to the carrying trade. In the home trade his capital is never so long out of his sight as it frequently is in the foreign trade of consumption. He can know better the character and situation of the persons whom he trusts, and if he should happen to be deceived, he knows better the laws of the country from which he must seek redress. In the carrying trade, the capital of the merchant is, as it were, divided between two foreign countries, and no part of it is ever necessarily brought home, or placed under his own immediate view and command. The capital which an Amsterdam merchant employs in carrying corn from Konnigsberg to Lisbon, and fruit and wine from Lisbon to Konnigsberg, must generally be the one-half of it at Konnigsberg and the other half at Lisbon. No part of it need ever come to Amsterdam. The natural residence of such a merchant should either be at Konnigsberg or Lisbon, and it can only be some very particular circumstances which can make him prefer the residence of Amsterdam. The uneasiness, however, which he feels at being separated so far from his capital generally determines him to bring part both of the Konnigsberg goods which he destines for the market of Lisbon, and of the Lisbon goods which he destines for that of Konnigsberg, to Amsterdam: and though this necessarily subjects him to a double charge of loading and unloading, as well as to the payment of some duties and customs, yet for the sake of having some part of his capital always under his own view and command, he willingly submits to this extraordinary charge; and it is in this manner that every country which has any considerable share of the carrying trade becomes always

Adam Smith, *An Inquiry into the Nature and Causes of the Wealth of Nations.* Book IV, Chapter II.

the emporium, or general market, for the goods of all the different countries whose trade it carries on. The merchant, in order to save a second loading and unloading, endeavours always to sell in the home market as much of the goods of all those different countries as he can, and thus, so far as he can, to convert his carrying trade into a foreign trade of consumption. A merchant, in the same manner, who is engaged in the foreign trade of consumption, when he collects goods for foreign markets, will always be glad, upon equal or nearly equal profits, to sell as great a part of them at home as he can. He saves himself the risk and trouble of exportation, when, so far as he can, he thus converts his foreign trade of consumption into a home trade. Home is in this manner the centre, if I may say so, round which the capitals of the inhabitants of every country are continually circulating, and towards which they are always tending, though by particular causes they may sometimes be driven off and repelled from it towards more distant employments. But a capital employed in the home trade, it has already been shown, necessarily puts into motion a greater quantity of domestic industry, and gives revenue and employment to a greater number of the inhabitants of the country, than an equal capital employed in the foreign trade of consumption: and one employed in the foreign trade of consumption has the same advantage over an equal capital employed in the carrying trade. Upon equal, or only nearly equal profits, therefore, every individual naturally inclines to employ his capital in the manner in which it is likely to afford the greatest support to domestic industry, and to give revenue and employment to the greatest number of people of his own country.

Secondly, every individual who employs his capital in the support of domestic industry, necessarily endeavours so to direct that industry that its produce may be of the greatest possible value.

The produce of industry is what it adds to the subject or materials upon which it is employed. In proportion as the value of this produce is great or small, so will likewise be the profits of the employer. But it is only for the sake of profit that any man employs a capital in the support of industry; and he will always, therefore, endeavour to employ it in the support of that industry of which the produce is likely to be of the greatest value, or to exchange for the greatest quantity either of money or of other goods.

But the annual revenue of every society is always precisely equal to the exchangeable value of the whole annual produce of its industry, or rather is precisely the same thing with that exchangeable value. As every individual, therefore, endeavours as much as he can both to employ his capital in the support of domestic industry, and so to direct that industry that its produce may be of the greatest value; every individual necessarily labours to render the annual revenue of the society as great as he can. He generally, indeed, neither intends to promote the public interest, nor knows how much he is promoting it. By preferring the support of domestic to that of foreign industry, he intends only his own security; and by directing that industry in such a manner as its produce may be of the greatest value, he intends only his own gain, and he is in this, as in many other cases, led by an invisible hand to promote an end which was no part of his intention. Nor is it always the worse for the society that it was no part of it. By pursuing his own interest he frequently promotes that of the society more effectually than when he really intends to promote it. I have never known much good done by those who affectated to trade for the public good. It is an affectation, indeed, not very common among merchants, and very few words need be employed in dissuading them from it.

*   *   *

What is the species of domestic industry which his capital can employ, and of which the produce is likely to be of the greatest value, every individual, it is evident, can, in his local situation, judge much better than any statesman or lawgiver can do for him. The statesman who should attempt to direct private people in what manner they ought to employ their capitals would not only load himself with a most unnecessary attention, but assume an authority which could safely be trusted, not only to no single person, but to no council or senate whatever, and which would nowhere be so dangerous as in the hands of a man who had folly and presumption enough to fancy himself fit to exercise it.

3

The Medium and the Message

The Enlightenment did not take place in a vacuum. In the selection that follows, J. H. Brumfitt, professor of French at St. Andrews University, Scotland, briefly sketches the social milieu in which enlightened ideas circulated and had their effects. The audience for these new ideas wanted to be entertained as well as enlightened. Hence, ideas had to be presented in novel guise. The old philosophical treatise was out; the new, slightly risqué novel, short story, or dialogue was in. This had an inevitable effect on the profundity of the concepts that could be conveyed. The philosophes, almost necessarily when they chose these media, had to be superficial.

FROM *The French Enlightenment*
BY *J. H. Brumfitt*

. . . IT IS NOT ENOUGH to define the Enlightenment . . . in terms of the development of its critical philosophical method. It is equally important to see it in terms of the society from which it sprang and which it sought to alter. It would never have preached its ideals with such propagandist fervour if it had not sensed the existence of an audience willing to receive them and potentially numerous enough to put them into practice. Often, indeed, it would have been quite unable to do so. The greatest collective enterprise of enlightenment thought—the *Encyclopédie* of Diderot and d'Alembert—was also a major commercial enterprise which the publishers would never have promoted had they not been sure that even so expensive and voluminous a work would find a ready market. The Enlightenment reflected its age.

The age was a stable and a prosperous one. If wars continued to be fought, they were less devastating than those of the previous century and, in Western Europe at least, were mainly confined to frontier areas. If famine could still occur (as in France in 1709) and the plague could still strike (as in Provence a decade later), neither scourge produced the calamitous results

J. H. Brumfitt, *The French Enlightenment*, pp. 18–20, 22–24. London, 1972. Reprinted by permission of Macmillan London and Basingstoke.

known in earlier centuries. Civil strife had not ceased, but major religious civil wars were a thing of the past, and the Revolution of 1688—from which one may conveniently, if somewhat arbitrarily, date the beginning of the Enlightenment in England—had been (in England itself) almost bloodless. Agricultural production, static, or even declining, in the seventeenth century, was to revive again in the eighteenth, and population was to begin to increase. Above all, the nations of Western Europe witnessed an unprecedented growth in their commercial prosperity. All these developments provided grounds for considering the possibility of social progress in a far more optimistic light than ever before.

Those who had contributed most to this advance, and who had benefited most from it, were the middle classes. In England, as a result of the Great Rebellion and the Revolution of 1688, they had gained a share of political power. Similar developments had taken place in Holland. In France, under the authoritarian rule of Louis XIV, they had at least supplanted the aristocracy as the principal agents of royal government. To describe the Enlightenment as essentially bourgeois has its dangers. The nineteenth-century concept of class struggle was foreign to eighteenth-century thought; in some countries, political and social reforms were to be undertaken primarily by enlightened despots; in France, the aristocracy was to make an important contribution to the ferment of ideas which characterised the Regency and the period immediately preceding it. Yet it was in the countries where the middle classes were most numerous and most powerful—England, Holland, France and parts of Germany—that the Enlightenment first took root; it was, on balance, the bourgeois who contributed most to it (though in the case of France, this could be disputed); it was certainly, for the most part, middle-class ideals that it preached. Technological progress was dear to its heart. If the *Encyclopédie* is now mainly consulted for its "subversive" views on religion and politics, it was primarily intended, as its sub-title made clear, to be a dictionary of sciences, arts and crafts. The English Royal Society, in its promotion of the study of astronomy and geographical exploration, never lost sight of the interests of the maritime trader. The most positive achievement of the reforming ministers of Charles III of Spain was the promotion of local societies dedicated to agricultural and economic reform.

*   *   *

. . . The *philosophe* saw himself, like the Chinese hero of Goldsmith's novel, as a "citizen of the world." *"Homo sum; humani nil a me alienum puto"* ran one of his favourite Latin tags. He enthused over the wisdom of the Chinese, the simple nobility of the North American Indians, the sexual freedom of the Tahitians. Except for the Pyrenees (for nothing good could possibly come out of the lands of the Inquisition) there were no frontiers which his sympathies could not cross. It is true that he often took more with him in these spiritual journeyings than he brought back, for he was a "Newtonian" cosmopolitan who believed that nature remained constant, and he tended to find evidence of eighteenth-century "rational" principles in the most remote and unlikely places. When he travelled into the distant past, he could become even more confused; Voltaire, for example, spent a great deal of time denouncing Herodotus' account of ritual prostitution in ancient Babylon because he could not conceive of Parisian duchesses behaving in the same way. However, such blind spots, regrettable though they may have been, only served to intensify the *philosophe*'s belief in the universality of his own values.

In the narrower European context, moreover, material circumstances aided the spread of cosmopolitanism. To begin with, especially around the turn of the century, the intellectual life of the continent had, as its focal point, the most "open" of all European nations. Holland offered a refuge to persecuted thinkers from many lands: Descartes, Locke and Bayle are merely the most famous of the many who profited from it. The Dutch publishing trade was the freest and most flourishing in the world, and without it many of the outstanding works of the Enlightenment would probably never have seen the light of day. Dutch journals, particularly those published in French by Protestant exiles such as Bayle, Le Clerc or Basnage, became the market-places and melting-pots of all that was new in European thought long before either England or France had anything to rival them. If we seldom speak of a Dutch Enlightenment, this is partly because Holland (after the death of Spinoza in 1677) did not itself produce any thinkers of the first magnitude, but it is still more because the innumerable lesser men it did produce (who contributed more than anyone to the diffusion of the thought of Descartes, Newton, Locke and many others) seemed European rather than Dutch figures.

This was partly because they thought and wrote in "European"—or rather in one or both of the two languages which served as international media of communication: Latin and French. Latin had long been the universal language of scholarship, and still remained so, to some extent, in the early eighteenth century. It was, however, being rapidly replaced by French. At the same time, moreover, French was in process of becoming the language of diplomacy, the language of many European courts, in short, *the* language of civilised living. The linguistic nationalisms of the nineteenth century were still in their infancy, and Frederick the Great, and thousands like him, regarded French as infinitely superior to their native tongues. This gave cultured Europe a linguistic unity which later, despite improved means of communication, it was to lose.

The men of the Enlightenment made full use of these advantages for they were, in the main, great travellers. This was the age of the grand tour, an age when even war only partially restricted the comings and goings of those who wished to see the world for themselves. Many of the French *philosophes*—Montesquieu, Voltaire, Diderot, d'Holbach, for example—travelled extensively. Visitors to France were just as numerous—Englishmen like Bolingbroke or Gibbon, Scots like Hume or Adam Smith, Italians like Algarotti or Beccaria,

Spaniards like Aranda or Olavide. The *salons* of Paris, and learned bodies such as the Royal Society, or the many academies which mushroomed throughout Europe, facilitated personal contacts. How extensive this intercourse was can be judged from the endless stream of visitors from every country in Europe who made their pilgrimage to Ferney to visit the aged Voltaire.

The great encyclopedia that was edited by Denis Diderot and, initially Jean Le Rond d'Alembert, was one of the great vehicles for the conveyance of the ideas of the Enlightenment to a wide audience. The first volume appeared in 1751; others followed over the next 15 years. Many of the articles were orthodox and dull, but some were delightfully subversive, and part of the fun of being a subscriber to the Encyclopédie *was to discover which articles were subversive. The really good articles are too long to publish here, but the faithful way in which the* Encyclopédie *reflected the leading ideas of the Enlightenment can be seen in this extract on natural law.*

FROM *Denis Diderot's Encyclopédie*

IN ITS BROADEST SENSE the term [natural law] is taken to designate certain principles which nature alone inspires and which all animals as well as all men have in common. On this law are based the union of male and female, the begetting of children as well as their education, love of liberty, self-preservation, concern for self-defense.

It is improper to call the behavior of animals natural law, for, not being endowed with reason, they can know neither law nor justice.

More commonly we understand by natural law certain laws of justice and equity which only natural reason has established among men, or better, which God has engraved in our hearts.

The fundamental principles of law and all justice are: to live honestly, not to give offense to anyone, and to render unto each whatever is his. From these general principles derive a great many particular rules which nature alone, that is, reason and equity, suggest to mankind.

Since this natural law is based on such fundamental principles, it is perpetual and unchangeable: no agreement can debase it, no law can alter it or exempt anyone from the obligation it imposes. In this it differs from positive law, meaning those rules which only exist because they have been established by precise laws. This positive law is subject to change by right of the same authority that established it, and individuals can deviate from it if it is not too strict. Certain people improperly mistake natural law for the law of nations. This latter also consists in part of rules which true reason has established among all men; but it also contains conventions established by men against the natural order, such as wars or servitude, whereas natural law admits only what conforms to true reason and equity.

The principles of natural law, therefore, form part of the law of nations, particularly the primitive law of nations; they also form part of public and of private law: for the principles of natural law, which we have stated, are the purest source of the foundation of most of private and public law. . . . From these general ideas on natural law it becomes clear that this law is nothing other than what the science of manners and customs calls morality. . . .

*   *   *

It would not be proper for men to live without rules; rules presuppose a final goal; that of man is to aspire to happiness; this is the system of Providence; it is the essential desire of man, inseparable from reason which is man's basic guide. Since true happiness cannot be incompatible with the nature and condition of man, rules of conduct consist in a distinction between good and evil, in a comparison of past and present, in not seeking a good that may give rise to greater evil, in accepting a small evil if it is followed by a great good, in giving preference to the greatest good, in certain cases in being persuaded only by probability or verisimilitude and finally in acquiring the inclination toward the truly good.

In order really to know natural law, one has to understand what is meant by obligation in general. Law taken as power produces obligations; rights and obligations are several: some are natural, others are acquired; some are such that they cannot be rigidly fulfilled, others cannot be renounced. These obligations are also distinguished by their object. For instance, there is the right we have over ourselves, which is called liberty; the right of property or estate over things that belong to us; the right one has over the person or actions of another, which is called sovereignty or authority; finally the right one can have over things belonging to someone else, which is also of several kinds.

Man, by nature a dependent being, must take law as the rule of his action, for law is nothing other than a rule set down by the sovereign. The true foundations of sovereignty are power, wisdom, and goodness combined. The goal of laws is not to impede liberty but to direct properly all man's actions.

*   *   *

Natural law is the systematization, the collection, or the body of these same laws. Natural jurisprudence is the art of arriving at the knowledge of the laws of nature, of developing them, and of applying them to man's actions.

We cannot doubt realities of natural law since everything contributes to proving the existence of God. He has the right to prescribe laws to men and it is a consequence of His power, wisdom, and goodness to give men rules of conduct.

The ways by which one can distinguish what is just and unjust or what is dictated by natural law are:

1. Instinct or a certain inner feeling that makes us lean toward certain actions or away from them.
2. Reason, which confirms instinct; it develops principles and deduces consequences.
3. God's will, made known to man—and so becoming the supreme rule.

Man cannot arrive at a knowledge of natural laws except by examining his nature, his make-up, and his condition. All natural laws are concerned with three objects: God, the self, and others.

Religion is the principle of the laws which concern God.

Self-love is the principle of natural laws relating to ourselves.

*   *   *

The authority of natural laws stems from the fact that they owe their existence to God. Men submit to them because to observe them leads to the happiness of men and society. This is a truth demonstrated by reason. It is equally true that virtue by itself is a principle of inner satisfaction whereas vice is a principle of unrest and trouble. It is equally certain that virtue produces great external advantage, while vice produces great ills.

Yet virtue does not always have for those who practice it as happy outward effects as it should have. One can frequently observe the good and evil of nature and of fortune distributed unequally and not according to the merits of each individual. Evils resulting from injustice fall upon the innocent as well as upon the guilty and often virtue itself is subject to persecution.

All man's prudence is not sufficient to relieve such disorders. Still another consideration is necessary to force men to observe the natural laws, namely, the immortality of the soul and the belief in the future, where what might be missing in the sanction of natural laws will be carried out if divine wisdom deems it necessary.

The Encyclopédie *was a very expensive set of books, not available to everyone. At best, the ideas in it could affect only the top layer of society. If one wished to make a point to more than this elite few, the best way was through popular literature. Voltaire (1694–1778) was a master of this genre of literature, and* Candide *is one of his masterpieces. Voltaire was a reformer who found the philosophy of the German metaphysician Gottfried Wilhelm von Leibniz utterly intolerable. Leibniz "proved" in learned pieces that since God is both good and omnipotent, this must be the best of all the possible worlds God could have made—in spite of plagues, earthquakes, and man's inhumanity to man. Instead of writing another learned tome to attack Leibniz, Voltaire held him up to ridicule. He kept his reader's interest by weaving his philosophical message around an erotic adventure tale first published in French in 1759.*

The first chapter, which appears below, illustrates his technique.

FROM *Candide*

BY *Voltaire*

HOW CANDIDE WAS BROUGHT UP IN A MAGNIFICENT CASTLE AND HOW HE WAS DRIVEN THENCE

IN THE COUNTRY OF WESTPHALIA, in the castle of the most noble baron of Thunder-ten-tronckh, lived a youth whom nature had endowed with a most sweet disposition. His face was the true index of his mind. He had a solid judgment joined to the most unaffected simplicity; and hence, I presume, he had his name of Candide. The old servants of the house suspected him to have been the son of the baron's sister, by a very good sort of a gentleman of the neighborhood, whom that young lady refused to marry, because he could produce no more than threescore and eleven quarterings in his arms; the rest of the genealogical tree belonging to the family having been lost through the injuries of time.

The baron was one of the most powerful lords in Westphalia; for his castle had not only a gate, but even windows; and his great hall was hung with tapestry. He used to hunt with his mastiffs and spaniels instead of greyhounds; his groom served him for huntsman; and the parson of the parish officiated as his grand almoner. He was called My Lord by all his people, and he never told a story but every one laughed at it.

My lady baroness weighed three hundred and fifty pounds, consequently was a person of no small consideration; and then she did the honors of the house with a dignity that commanded universal respect. Her daughter was about seventeen years of age, fresh colored, comely, plump, and desirable. The baron's son seemed to be a youth in every respect worthy of the father he sprung from. Pangloss, the preceptor, was the oracle of the family, and little Candide listened to his instructions with all the simplicity natural to his age and disposition.

Master Pangloss taught the metaphysico-theologo-cosmolo-nigology. He could prove to admiration that there is no effect without a cause; and, that in this best of all possible worlds, the baron's castle was the most magnificent of all castles, and my lady the best of all possible baronesses.

It is demonstrable, said he, that things cannot be otherwise than as they are; for as all things have been created for some end, they must necessarily be created for the best end. Observe, for instance, the nose is formed for spectacles, therefore we wear spectacles. The legs are visibly designed for stockings, accordingly we wear stockings. Stones were made to be hewn, and to construct castles, therefore My Lord has a magnificent castle; for the greatest baron in the province ought to be the best lodged. Swine were intended to be eaten, there-

Voltaire, *Candide.* This selection is from Chapter I.

fore we eat pork all the year round: and they, who assert that everything is *right,* do not express themselves correctly; they should say that everything is *best.*

Candide listened attentively, and believed implicitly; for he thought Miss Cunegund excessively handsome, though he never had the courage to tell her so. He concluded that next to the happiness of being baron of Thunder-ten-tronckh, the next was that of being Miss Cunegund, the next that of seeing her every day, and the last that of hearing the doctrine of Master Pangloss, the greatest philosopher of the whole province, and consequently of the whole world.

One day when Miss Cunegund went to take a walk in a little neighboring wood which was called a park, she saw, through the bushes, the sage Doctor Pangloss giving a lecture in experimental philosophy to her mother's chambermaid, a little brown wench, very pretty, and very tractable. As Miss Cunegund had a great disposition for the sciences, she observed with the utmost attention the experiments, which were repeated before her eyes; she perfectly well understood the force of the doctor's reasoning upon causes and effects. She retired greatly flurried, quite pensive and filled with the desire of knowledge, imagining that she might be a *sufficing reason* for young Candide, and he for her.

On her way back she happened to meet the young man; she blushed, he blushed also; she wished him a good morning in a flattering tone, he returned the salute, without knowing what he said. The next day, as they were rising from dinner, Cunegund and Candide slipped behind the screen. The miss dropped her handkerchief, the young man picked it up. She innocently took hold of his hand, and he as innocently kissed hers with a warmth, a sensibility, a grace—all very particular; their lips met; their eyes sparkled; their knees trembled; their hands strayed. The baron chanced to come by; he beheld the cause and effect, and, without hesitation, saluted Candide with some notable kicks on the breech, and drove him out of doors. The lovely Miss Cunegund fainted away, and, as soon as she came to herself, the baroness boxed her ears. Thus a general consternation was spread over this most magnificent and most agreeable of all possible castles.

Newtonian science was not the only science to affect the Enlightenment. The eighteenth century witnessed great strides in the study of living matter as well. Denis Diderot, editor of the Encyclopédie, *was struck with the results of biology and used them to establish his own outlook. In D'Alembert's Dream, written in 1769 and privately circulated in 1784, he presents his daring philosophical ideas within the framework of a slightly pornographic imaginary dialogue, involving Diderot; d'Alembert; d'Alembert's mistress, Julie de l'Espinasse; and his doctor, Dr. Bordeu.*

FROM *D'Alembert's Dream*

BY *Denis Diderot*

The preliminary to d'Alembert's dream in this

CONVERSATION BETWEEN D'ALEMBERT AND DIDEROT

D'ALEMBERT: I grant you that a Being who exists somewhere but corresponds to no one point in space, a Being with no dimensions yet occupying space, who is complete in himself at every point in this space, who differs in essence from matter but is one with matter, who is moved by matter and moves matter but never moves himself, who acts upon matter yet undergoes all its changes, a Being of whom I have no conception whatever, so contradictory is he by nature, is difficult to accept. But other difficulties lie in wait for anyone who rejects him, for after all, if this sensitivity that you substitute for him is a general and essential property of nature, then stone must feel.

DIDEROT: Why not?

D'ALEMBERT: That takes a bit of swallowing.

DIDEROT: Yes, for the person who cuts it, carves it, crushes it yet doesn't hear it crying out.

D'ALEMBERT: I wish you would tell me what difference you think there is between a man and a statue, between marble and flesh.

DIDEROT: Not very much. You can make marble out of flesh and flesh out of marble.

D'ALEMBERT: But still the one is not the other.

DIDEROT: Just as what you call actual energy is not potential energy.

D'ALEMBERT: I don't follow you.

DIDEROT: Let me explain. When a thing is moved from one place to another that is not motion, but only its effect. Motion is inherent in the thing itself, whether it is moved or remains stationary.

D'ALEMBERT: That is a novel way of looking at it.

DIDEROT: But none the less true. Take away the obstacle resisting that particular movement of the motionless body and it will move. If by a sudden rarefaction you take away the air surrounding the trunk of that huge oak, the water it contains will suddenly expand and blow it into a hundred thousand splinters. And I say the same thing about your own body.

D'ALEMBERT: All right. But what relationship is there between motion and sensitivity? Could it possibly be that you take cognizance of active and latent sensitivity as of actual and potential energy? Actual energy manifests itself by

Denis Diderot, *D'Alembert's Dream*, translated by L. W. Tancock, pp. 149–152, 158–159, 172–175, 179–180, 207, 209, 217–219. Reprinted by permission of Penguin Books Ltd.

motion and potential energy by pressure. In the same way there is an active sensitivity which is characterized by certain reactions observable in animals and perhaps plants, and a latent sensitivity, the existence of which can only be verified when it changes into active sensitivity.

DIDEROT: That's exactly it. You have hit the nail on the head.

D'ALEMBERT: Thus the statue has only latent sensitivity while man, the animal world and perhaps even plants, are vouchsafed active sensitivity.

DIDEROT: There is of course this difference between the block of marble and the living tissue of flesh, but you realize, don't you, that it is not the only one?

D'ALEMBERT: Yes, of course. Whatever resemblance there may be between the external forms of the man and the statue, there is no relationship between their internal organizations. The chisel of the most skilful sculptor can't even make an epiderm. But whereas there is a very simple method for making potential energy turn into actual energy (it is an experiment being repeated before our eyes a hundred times a day), I don't quite see how you can make a body pass from a state of latent sensitivity into one of active sensitivity.

DIDEROT: That's because you don't want to see. It is an equally common phenomenon.

D'ALEMBERT: And what is this equally common phenomenon, may I ask?

DIDEROT: I'm about to tell you, since you don't mind having to be told. It happens every time you eat.

D'ALEMBERT: Every time I eat!

DIDEROT: Yes, for what do you do when you eat? You remove the obstacles which were resisting the active sensitivity of the food. You assimilate the food with yourself, you turn it into flesh, you animalize it, make it capable of feeling. What you do to that food I will do to marble, and whenever I like.

D'ALEMBERT: How?

DIDEROT: How? By making it eatable.

D'ALEMBERT: Make marble eatable . . . doesn't sound very easy to me.

DIDEROT: It's my business to show you how it is done. I take this statue you can see, put it into a mortar, and with some hard bangs with a pestle. . . .

* * *

D'ALEMBERT: All right, pulverize away, then.

DIDEROT: When the marble block is reduced to the finest powder I mix this powder with humus or compost, work them well together, water the mixture, let it rot for a year, two years, a century, for I am not concerned with time. When the whole has turned into a more or less homogeneous substance—into humus—do you know what I do?

D'ALEMBERT: I am sure you don't eat it.

DIDEROT: No, but there is a way of uniting that humus with myself, of appropriating it, a *latus,* as the chemists would call it.

D'ALEMBERT: And this *latus* is plant life?

DIDEROT: Precisely. I sow peas, beans, cabbages and other leguminous plants. The plants feed on the earth and I feed on the plants.

D'ALEMBERT: It may be true or it may not, but I like this transition from marble to humus, from humus to vegetable matter and from vegetable matter to animal, to flesh.

DIDEROT: So I can make flesh, or souls as my daughter calls it, that is to say an actively sensitive substance. And if I don't solve the problem you have put to me, at least I get quite near to the solution, for you will admit that it is much more of a far cry from a piece of marble to a being who can feel than from a sentient being to a thinking one. . . .

                              *   *   *

DIDEROT: Look at this egg: with it you can overthrow all the schools of theology and all the churches in the world. What is this egg? An insensitive mass before the germ is put into it, and after the germ is in it what is it then? Still an insensitive mass, for the germ itself is merely inert and thick fluid. How does this mass evolve into a new organization, into sensitivity, into life? Through heat. What will generate heat in it? Motion. What will the successive effects of motion be? Instead of answering me, sit down and let us follow out these effects with our eyes from one moment to the next. First there is a speck which moves about, a thread growing and taking colour, flesh being formed, a beak, wing-tips, eyes, feet coming into view, a yellowish substance which unwinds and turns into intestines—and you have a living creature. This creature stirs, moves about, makes a noise—I can hear it cheeping through the shell—it takes on a downy covering, it can see. The weight of its wagging head keeps on banging the beak against the inner wall of its prison. Now the wall is breached and the bird emerges, walks, flies, feels pain, runs away, comes back again, complains, suffers, loves, desires, enjoys, it experiences all your affections and does all the things you do. And will you maintain, with Descartes, that it is an imitating machine pure and simple? Why, even little children will laugh at you, and philosophers will answer that if it is a machine you are one too! If, however, you admit that the only difference between you and an animal is one of organization, you will be showing sense and reason and be acting in good faith; but then it will be concluded, contrary to what you had said, that from an inert substance arranged in a certain way and impregnated by another inert substance, subjected to heat and motion, you will get sensitivity, life, memory, consciousness, passions, thought. Only one of these two lines of argument is left: either to suppose that within the inert mass of that egg there was a hidden element waiting for the egg's development before revealing its presence, or to assume that this imperceptible element had found its way through the shell at some particular moment in the process. But what was this element? Did it occupy any space or not? How did it get in or out without moving? Where was it? What was it doing there or elsewhere? Was it only created when the need for it arose? Or did it exist already, waiting for somewhere to go? Was it of the same nature as this "somewhere" or not? If of the same nature it must have been matter, if not it is impossible to understand its inertia before the hatching or its energy in the fully developed bird. Just listen to your own arguments and you will feel how pitiful they are. You will come to feel that by refusing to entertain a simple hypothesis that explains everything—sensitivity as a property common to all matter or as a result of the organization of matter—you are flying in the face of common sense and plunging into a chasm of mysteries, contradictions and absurdities.

* * *

MADEMOISELLE DE L'ESPINASSE: He went on: "Well, Mr Philosopher, so you think there are polyps of all kinds, even human ones? But we don't find any in nature."

BORDEU: He obviously hadn't heard of the two girls who were connected by the head, shoulders, back, buttocks and thighs, and lived in that condition, stuck together, up to the age of twenty-two, and then died within a few minutes of each other. What did he say next?

MADEMOISELLE DE L'ESPINASSE: The sort of nonsense you only hear in the madhouse. He said: "That is past or to come. And besides, who knows the state of affairs on other planets?"

BORDEU: There's probably no need to go so far afield.

MADEMOISELLE DE L'ESPINASSE: "Human polyps in Jupiter or Saturn! Males splitting up into males and females into females—that's a funny idea. . . . (At that he went off into bellows of laughter which frightened me.) Man splitting up into myriads of men the size of atoms which could be kept between sheets of paper like insect-eggs, which spin their own cocoons, stay for some time in the chrysalis stage, then cut through their cocoons and emerge like butterflies, in fact a ready-made human society, a whole province populated by the fragments of one individual, that's fascinating to think about. . . . (More bursts of laughter.) If there is a place where man can divide himself up into myriads of microscopic men, people there should be less reluctant to die, for the loss of one man can so easily be made up that it must give rise to little regret."

BORDEU: This extravaganza is almost the true history of all existing and future animal species. Man may not divide up into myriads of men, but at any rate he does break up into myriads of minute creatures whose metamorphoses and future and final state are impossible to foresee. Who knows whether this is not the breeding-ground of another generation of beings separated from this one by an inconceivable interval of successive centuries and modifications?

MADEMOISELLE DE L'ESPINASSE: What are you muttering about now, doctor?

BORDEU: Nothing, nothing. I was having my dream, too. Go on with your reading, Mademoiselle.

MADEMOISELLE DE L'ESPINASSE: "All things considered, however, I prefer our present method of renewing the population," he went on. "Mr Philosopher, you know what is going on here or elsewhere, so tell me this: doesn't the splitting up of different parts of a man produce men of as many different kinds? The brain, the heart, chest, feet, hands, testicles. . . . Oh how this simplifies morality! A man born a . . . A woman who had come from . . . (Doctor, will you let me skip this bit?) . . . a warm room, lined with little phials, each one bearing a label: warriors, magistrates, philosophers, poets—bottle for courtiers, bottle for prostitutes, bottle for kings."

BORDEU: All very amusing and idiotic. This is only a dream, yet it is a vision that reminds me of some rather curious phenomena.

MADEMOISELLE DE L'ESPINASSE: Then he began mumbling something or other about seeds, bits of flesh pounded up in water, different races of animals he saw coming into being and perishing one after the other. He was holding his right hand to make it look like the tube of a microscope, and his left, I think, represented the mouth of some receptacle. He looked down the tube into the receptacle and said: "That Voltaire can joke as much as he likes, but the Eelmonger is right; I believe my own eyes, and I can see them, and what a lot of them there are darting to and fro and wriggling about!" He compared the receptacle, in which he could see so many instantaneous births, to the universe, and in a drop of water he could see the history of the world. This idea struck him as sublime, and he thought it quite consistent with good scientific method, which finds out about large bodies by studying small ones. Then he went on: "In Needham's drop of water everything begins and ends in the twinkling of an eye. In the real world the same phenomenon lasts somewhat longer, but what is the duration of our time compared with eternity? Less than the drop I have taken up on a needle-point compared with the limitless space surrounding me. Just as there is an infinite succession of animalculae in one fermenting speck of matter, so there is the same infinite succession of animalculae in the speck called Earth. Who knows what animal species preceded us? Who knows what will follow our present ones? Everything changes and passes away, only the whole remains unchanged. The world is ceaselessly beginning and ending; at every moment it is at its beginning and its end. There has never been any other world, and never will be.

"In this vast ocean of matter not a single molecule resembles any other, not a single molecule remains for a moment just like itself: *Rerum novus nascitur ordo,* that is its unvarying device. . . ." Then he added with a sigh: "Oh, vanity of human thought! oh, poverty of all our glory and labours! oh, how pitiful, oh, how limited is our vision! There is nothing real except eating, drinking, living, making love and sleeping. . . . Mademoiselle de L'Espinasse, where are you?" "Here." Then his face became flushed. I wanted to feel his pulse, but he had hidden his hand somewhere. He seemed to be going through some kind of convulsion. His mouth was gaping, his breath gasping, he fetched a deep sigh, then a gentler one and still gentler, turned his head over on the pillow and fell asleep. I was watching him very attentively, and felt deeply moved without knowing why; my heart was beating fast, but not with fear. A few moments later I saw a little smile flicker round his lips, and he whispered: "On a planet where men reproduced like fish, where a man's spawn was simply spread over that of a woman . . . I should have fewer regrets. . . . Nothing must be lost if it might be useful. Mademoiselle, if that stuff could be collected into a phial and sent first thing in the morning to Needham. . . ." Doctor, don't you call this sheer raving?

BORDEU: In your presence, I suppose so.

MADEMOISELLE DE L'ESPINASSE: In my presence or not, it's all the same, and you don't know what you are talking about. I had hoped that the rest of the night would be undisturbed.

BORDEU: It usually does work out like that.

* * *

BORDEU: Listen.

D'ALEMBERT: Why am I what I am? Because I had to be as I am. Yes, in this particular place, no doubt, but elsewhere? At the Pole? On the Equator? Or on Saturn? If a distance of a few thousand leagues can change me into another species, what about a distance of several thousand times the earth's diameter? And if everything is in a state of flux, as the spectacle of the universe shows everywhere, what might not be the result here and elsewhere of several million years of changes? Who can tell what a thinking and sentient being on Saturn is like? But do thought and feeling exist on Saturn? Why not? Has the thinking and sentient being on Saturn more senses than I have? If that is the case how unhappy that Saturnian must be! Without senses there would be no more needs.

BORDEU: He is right; the organs produce the needs, and conversely the needs produce the organs.

MADEMOISELLE DE L'ESPINASSE: Doctor, are you seeing visions as well?

BORDEU: Why not? I have seen two stumps finish by turning into two arms.

MADEMOISELLE DE L'ESPINASSE: That is not true.

BORDEU: I know it isn't, but when the arms were missing I have seen two shoulder-blades grow longer, develop into pincers and become a pair of stumps.

MADEMOISELLE DE L'ESPINASSE: How ridiculous!

BORDEU: It's a fact. Let us assume a long succession of armless generations, and at the same time unremitting efforts, and you would see the two members of these pincers get longer and longer, cross each other at the back and come round to the front again, possibly develop fingers at the extremities and so make new arms and hands. The original shape of a creature degenerates or perfects itself through necessity and habitual functioning. We walk so little, work so little, but think so much that I wouldn't rule out that man might end by being nothing but a head.

MADEMOISELLE DE L'ESPINASSE: Nothing but a head! a head! that's not much use.

For my part I was hoping that with unlimited love-making . . . What awful ideas you are putting into my head!

*   *   *

MADEMOISELLE DE L'ESPINASSE: . . . let us come to your conclusions.

BORDEU: It would be an endless job.

MADEMOISELLE DE L'ESPINASSE: All the better. Fire away then.

BORDEU: I daren't.

MADEMOISELLE DE L'ESPINASSE: Why not?

BORDEU: Because at the rate we are going one can only skim the surface of everything and not go into anything properly.

*   *   *

MADEMOISELLE DE L'ESPINASSE: Doctor, you are dodging my questions instead of answering them.

BORDEU: No, I'm not dodging anything. I'm telling you what I know, and I would be able to tell you more about it if I knew as much about the organization of the centre of the network as I do about the threads, and if I had found it as easy to observe. But if I am not very strong on specific details I am good on general manifestations.

MADEMOISELLE DE L'ESPINASSE: And what might these be?

BORDEU: Reason, judgement, imagination, madness, imbecility, ferocity, instinct.

MADEMOISELLE DE L'ESPINASSE: Yes; all these things are only products of the original or habitually acquired relationship between the centre of the network and its ramifications.

BORDEU: Precisely. If the nerve-centre or trunk is too vigorous in relation to the branches we find poets, artists, people of imagination, cowards, fanatics, madmen. If it is too weak we get what we call louts or wild beasts. If the whole system is flaccid, soft, devoid of energy, then idiots. On the other hand, if it is energetic, well balanced and in good order the outcome is the great thinkers, philosophers, sages.

MADEMOISELLE DE L'ESPINASSE: And according to which branch dominates the rest we see various specialized instincts in animals and special aptitudes in men: a sense of smell in the dog, of hearing in fish, of sight in the eagle. D'Alembert is a mathematician, Vaucanson a mechanical genius, Grétry a musician, Voltaire a poet—all diverse effects of some one thread of the bundle being more vigorous in them than any other and than the corresponding one in other people of their kind.

BORDEU: And then there is force of habit which can get the better of people, such as the old man who still runs after women, or Voltaire still turning out tragedies.

*   *   *

MADEMOISELLE DE L'ESPINASSE: . . . But what about vice and virtue, doctor? Virtue, that most holy word in all languages, most sacred idea in all nations!

* * *

BORDEU: We must transform it into the words doing good and its opposite, doing harm. One is born fortunate or unfortunate, and each of us is imperceptibly carried along by the general current which leads one to glory and another to ignominy.

MADEMOISELLE DE L'ESPINASSE: What about self-respect, a sense of shame, remorse?

BORDEU: Childish notions founded on the ignorance and vanity of a person who takes upon himself the credit or blame for a quite unavoidable moment of evolution.

MADEMOISELLE DE L'ESPINASSE: And rewards and punishments?

BORDEU: Methods of correcting the modifiable person we call evil and encouraging the one we call good.

MADEMOISELLE DE L'ESPINASSE: Isn't there something dangerous in all this?

BORDEU: Is it true or is it false?

MADEMOISELLE DE L'ESPINASSE: True, I think.

BORDEU: That is to say you think falsehood has its advantages and truth its drawbacks?

MADEMOISELLE DE L'ESPINASSE: It seems so to me.

BORDEU: And to me, but the advantages of the lie are only for the moment, while those of truth are eternal; the unpleasant consequences of truth, if any, soon pass, but those of the lie can only end with the lie itself. Consider the effects of lying upon a man's mind and upon his behaviour: in his mind either the lie is more or less mixed up with the truth and he is incapable of clear thought, or else it all fits in beautifully and he is wrongheaded. Now what sort of behaviour can you expect from a mind either thoroughly illogical in its reasoning or logical in its errors?

MADEMOISELLE DE L'ESPINASSE: The second of these two vices, though less despicable, is perhaps more to be feared than the first.

D'ALEMBERT: Right, and that brings everything back to sensitivity, memory and organic functions. That suits me. But what about imagination or abstract thought?

BORDEU: Imagination—

MADEMOISELLE DE L'ESPINASSE: Just a minute, doctor, let us recapitulate. According to your principles it seems to me that with a series of purely mechanical operations I could reduce the greatest genius in the world to a mass of unorganized flesh; and given that this formless mass retained nothing but sensitivity to things of the moment it could be brought back from the most utterly stupid state imaginable to that of a man of genius. The first of these operations would consist of depriving the original bundle of some of its threads and shuffling up the rest, and the second and opposite operation of replacing the detached threads in the bundle and allowing the whole organism to develop properly. Example: take away from Newton the two auditory threads, and he loses all sense of sound; the olfactory ones, and he has no sense of smell; the optic ones and he has no notion of colours; the taste threads and he cannot distinguish flavours. The others I destroy or jumble up, and so much for the organization of the man's brain, memory, judgement, desires, aversions, passions, willpower, consciousness of self; there is nothing left but a hulk retaining only life and sensitivity.

BORDEU: Which are almost identical qualities. Life is the whole and sensitivity a part.

MADEMOISELLE DE L'ESPINASSE: Well then, I take this hulk and return its olfactory threads, and it starts to sniff, its auditory threads and it listens, optic threads and it can see, taste threads and it can taste. By sorting out the rest of the skein and allowing the other threads to develop normally I see the revival of memory, ability to make comparisons, judgement, reason, desires, aversions, passions, natural aptitudes, talent, and lo! my man of genius again. And all that without the intervention of any unintelligible outside agency.

BORDEU: Yes, perfect. Leave it at that, for the rest is all mumbo-jumbo. But what about abstract thought and imagination?

4

The Ideals of the Enlightenment

The Enlightenment, as we have already remarked, was more than the education of Europe in the new science. It was, as well, a call to action. The vision of reason as supreme led to calls for reform or new justifications of old institutions in rational terms.

The institution of the monarchy was one that had its origin in the mists of past time. Could it survive in an Age of Reason? Frederick the Great of Prussia thought so, but in defending monarchy, he admitted certain bases of the state that could, ultimately, be destructive of the institution he wished to buttress. This essay was first published in French in 1777.

FROM *An Essay on Forms of Government*
BY *Frederick the Great*

WE ARE ASTONISHED at imagining the human race so long existing in a brutal state, and without forming itself into societies. Reasons are accordingly suggested, such as might induce people like these to unite in bodies. It must have been the violence and pillage which existed, among neighboring hordes, that could have first inspired such savage families with the wish of uniting, that they might secure their possessions by mutual defense. Hence laws took birth, which taught those societies to prefer the general to individual good. From that time, no person durst seize on the effects of another, because of the dread of chastisement. The life, the wife, and the wealth of a neighbor were sacred; and, if the whole society were attacked, it was the duty of the whole to assemble for its defense. The grand truth—"That we should do unto others as they should do unto us"—became the principle of laws, and of the social compact. Hence originated the love of our country, which was regarded as the asylum of happiness.

But, as these laws could neither be maintained nor executed, unless some one should incessantly watch for their preservation, magistrates arose, out of

Frederick the Great *An Essay on Forms of Government*. Selection is from the English translation of Thomas Holcroft (1789).

this necessity, whom the people elected, and to whom they subjected themselves. Let it be carefully remembered that the preservation of the laws was the sole reason which induced men to allow of, and to elect, a superior; because this is the true origin of sovereign power. The magistrate, thus appointed, was the first servant of the state. When rising states had anything to fear from their neighbors, the magistrate armed the people, and flew to the defense of the citizens.

*   *   *

With respect to the true monarchical government, it is the best or the worst of all others, accordingly as it is administered.

We have remarked that men granted pre-eminence to one of their equals, in expectation that he should do them certain services. These services consisted in the maintenance of the laws; a strict execution of justice; an employment of his whole powers to prevent any corruption of manners; and defending the state against its enemies. It is the duty of this magistrate to pay attention to agriculture; it should be his care that provisions for the nation should be in abundance, and that commerce and industry should be encouraged. He is a perpetual sentinel, who must watch the acts and the conduct of the enemies of the state. His foresight and prudence should form timely alliances, which should be made with those who might most conduce to the interest of the association.

Paradoxical as it may seem, some of the very ideas that Frederick the Great used to justify benevolent despotism could be turned against it. When George III of England appeared to have lost whatever benevolence he may have had, the American colonists reacted ideologically. Their justification for the actions they proposed to take drew heavily on the thought of the Enlightenment.

FROM *The Declaration of Independence*

WHEN IN THE COURSE of human events, it becomes necessary for one people to dissolve the political bands which have connected them with another, and to assume among the powers of the earth, the separate and equal station to which the laws of nature and of nature's God entitle them, a decent respect to the opinions of mankind requires that they should declare the causes which impel them to the separation.—We hold these truths to be self-evident, that all men are created equal, that they are endowed by their Creator with certain unalienable rights, that among these are life, liberty, and the pursuit of happiness— That to secure these rights, governments are instituted among men, deriving their just powers from the consent of the governed,—That whenever any form of government becomes destructive of these ends, it is the right of the people

---

Quotation from the American Declaration of Independence.

to alter or to abolish it, and to institute new government, laying its foundation on such principles and organizing its powers in such form, as to them shall seem most likely to effect their safety and happiness. Prudence, indeed, will dictate that governments long established should not be changed for light and transient causes; and accordingly all experience hath shewn, that mankind are more disposed to suffer, while evils are sufferable, than to right themselves by abolishing the forms to which they are accustomed. But when a long train of abuses and usurpations, pursuing invariably the same object evinces a design to reduce them under absolute despotism, it is their right, it is their duty, to throw off such government, and to provide new guards for their future security.—Such has been the patient sufferance of these colonies; and such is now the necessity which constrains them to alter their former systems of government. The history of the present king of Great Britain is a history of repeated injuries and usurpations, all having in direct object the establishment of an absolute tyranny over these states. To prove this, let facts be submitted to a candid world.

If reason was to be the sole arbiter, and if men claimed natural rights because of their reason, how could the same rights be denied to women? It was this question that Mary Wollstonecraft, a pioneer in the fight for women's rights, raised in 1791 in her A Vindication of the Rights of Women.

FROM *A Vindication of the Rights of Women*

BY *Mary Wollstonecraft*

CONSIDER—I ADDRESS YOU as a legislator—whether, when men contend for their freedom, and to be allowed to judge for themselves respecting their own happiness, it be not inconsistent and unjust to subjugate women, even though you firmly believe that you are acting in the manner best calculated to promote their happiness? Who made man the exclusive judge, if woman partake with him the gift of reason.

In this style, argue tyrants of every denomination, from the weak king to the weak father of a family; they are all eager to crush reason; yet always assert that they usurp its throne only to be useful. Do you not act a similar part, when you *force* all women, by denying them civil and political rights, to remain immured in their families groping in the dark? for surely, sir, you will not assert that a duty can be binding which is not founded on reason? If, indeed, this be their destination, arguments may be drawn from reason; and thus augustly supported, the more understanding women acquire, the more they will be attached to their duty—comprehending it—for unless they comprehend it, unless their morals be fixed on the same immutable principle as those of man, no authority

---

Mary Wollstonecraft, *A Vindication of the Rights of Women*. Dedicatory Letter to Talleyrand of France.

can make them discharge it in a virtuous manner. They may be convenient slaves, but slavery will have its constant effect, degrading the master and the abject dependent.

But, if women are to be excluded, without having a voice, from a participation of the natural rights of mankind, prove first, to ward off the charge of injustice and inconsistency, that they want reason—else this flaw in your NEW CONSTITUTION will ever show that man must, in some shape, act like a tyrant; and tyranny, in whatever part of society it rears its brazen front, will ever undermine morality.

I have repeatedly asserted, and produced what appeared to me irrefragable arguments drawn from matters of fact, to prove my assertion, that women cannot, by force, be confined to domestic concerns; for they will, however ignorant, intermeddle with more weighty affairs, neglecting private duties only to disturb, by cunning tricks, the orderly plans of reason which rise above their comprehension.

Besides, whilst they are only made to acquire personal accomplishments, men will seek for pleasure in variety, and faithless husbands will make faithless wives; such ignorant beings, indeed, will be very excusable when, not taught to respect public good, nor allowed any civil rights, they attempt to do themselves justice by retaliation.

The box of mischief thus opened in society, what is to preserve private virtue, the only security of public freedom and universal happiness?

Let there be, then, no coercion *established* in society, and the common law of gravity prevailing, the sexes will fall into their proper places. And, now that more equitable laws are forming your citizens, marriage may become more sacred; your young men may choose wives from motives of affection, and your maidens allow love to root out vanity.

The father of a family will not then weaken his constitution and debase his sentiments by visiting the harlot, nor forget, in obeying the call of appetite, the purpose for which it was implanted. And the mother will not neglect her children to practice the arts of coquetry, when sense and modesty secure her the friendship of her husband.

But, till men become attentive to the duty of a father, it is vain to expect women to spend that time in their nursery which they, "wise in their generation," choose to spend at their glass; for this exertion of cunning is only an instinct of nature to enable them to obtain indirectly a little of that power of which they are unjustly denied a share; for, if women are not permitted to enjoy legitimate rights, they will render both men and themselves vicious, to obtain illicit privileges.

5

Was Enlightenment Good for Western Man's Condition? Some Evaluations

In 1750 a short treatise won the prize offered by the Academy Dijon for the best essay on the subject: If the reestablishment of the sciences and the arts has contributed to the purification of morals. It was written by Jean Jacques Rousseau, a citizen of Geneva, whose main literary efforts hitherto had involved music and musical notation. Rousseau looked at the Age of Reason with a somewhat jaundiced eye and, contrary to the other philosophes of the time, was willing to entertain the notion that, in fact, science and art lowered man rather than raised him.

FROM *Discourse on the Sciences and Arts*

BY *Jean Jacques Rousseau*

HAS THE RESTORATION of the sciences and arts tended to purify or corrupt morals? That is the subject to be examined. Which side should I take in this question? The one, gentlemen, that suits an honorable man who knows nothing and yet does not think any the less of himself.

* * *

The mind has its needs as does the body. The needs of the body are the foundations of society, those of the mind make it pleasant. While government and laws provide for the safety and well-being of assembled men, the sciences, letters, and arts, less despotic and perhaps more powerful, spread garlands of flowers over the iron chains with which men are burdened, stifle in them the sense of that original liberty for which they seemed to have been born, make them love their slavery, and turn them into what is called civilized peoples. Need raised thrones; the sciences and arts have strengthened them. Earthly

Jean Jacques Rousseau, *Discourse on the Sciences and Arts,* edited by Roger D. Masters, translated by R. D. Masters and J. R. Masters, pp. 34, 36–39, 49–50. St. Martin's Press, Inc. Reprinted by permission.

powers, love talents and protect those who cultivate them. Civilized peoples, cultivate talents: happy slaves, you owe to them that delicate and refined taste on which you pride yourselves; that softness of character and urbanity of customs which make relations among you so amiable and easy; in a word, the semblance of all the virtues without the possession of any. . . .

* * *

How pleasant it would be to live among us if exterior appearance were always a reflection of the heart's disposition; if decency were virtue; if our maxims served as our rules; if true philosophy were inseparable from the title of philosopher! But so many qualities are too rarely combined, and virtue seldom walks in such great pomp. Richness of attire may announce a wealthy man, and elegance a man of taste; the healthy, robust man is known by other signs. It is in the rustic clothes of a farmer and not beneath the gilt of a courtier that strength and vigor of the body will be found. Ornamentation is no less foreign to virtue, which is the strength and vigor of the soul. The good man is an athlete who likes to compete in the nude. He disdains all those vile ornaments which would hamper the use of his strength, most of which were invented only to hide some deformity.

Before art had moulded our manners and taught our passions to speak an affected language, our customs were rustic but natural, and differences of conduct announced at first glance those of character. Human nature, basically, was no better, but men found their security in the ease of seeing through each other, and that advantage, which we no longer appreciate, spared them many vices.

Today, when subtler researches and a more refined taste have reduced the art of pleasing to set rules, a base and deceptive uniformity prevails in our customs, and all minds seem to have been cast in the same mould. Incessantly politeness requires, propriety demands; incessantly usage is followed, never one's own inclinations. One no longer dares to appear as he is; and in this perpetual constraint, the men who form this herd called society, placed in the same circumstances, will all do the same things unless stronger motives deter them. Therefore one will never know well those with whom he deals, for to know one's friend thoroughly, it would be necessary to wait for emergencies—that is, to wait until it is too late, as it is for these very emergencies that it would have been essential to know him.

What a procession of vices must accompany this uncertainty! No more sincere friendships; no more real esteem; no more well-based confidence. Suspicions, offenses, fears, coldness, reserve, hate, betrayal will hide constantly under that uniform and false veil of politeness, under that much vaunted urbanity which we owe to the enlightenment of our century. The name of the Master of the Universe will no longer be profaned by swearing, but it will be insulted by blasphemies without offending our scrupulous ears. Men will not boast of their own merit, but they will disparage that of others. An enemy will not be grossly insulted, but he will be cleverly slandered. National hatreds will die out, but so will love of country. For scorned ignorance, a dangerous Pyrrhonism will be substituted. There will be some forbidden excesses, some dishonored vices, but others will be dignified with the name of virtues; one must either have them or affect them. Whoever wants to praise the sobriety of the wise men of our day may do so; as for me, I see in it only a refinement of intemperance as unworthy of my praise as their cunning simplicity.

Such is the purity our morals have acquired. Thus have we become respectable men. It is for literature, the sciences, and the arts to claim their share of such a wholesome piece of work. I will add only one thought: an inhabitant of some faraway lands who wanted to form a notion of European morals on the basis of the state of the sciences among us, the perfection of our arts, the decency of our entertainments, the politeness of our manners, the affability of our speech, our perpetual demonstrations of goodwill, and that tumultuous competition of men of all ages and conditions who seem anxious to oblige one another from dawn to dark; that foreigner, I say, would guess our morals to be exactly the opposite of what they are.

When there is no effect, there is no cause to seek. But here the effect is certain, the depravity real, and our souls have been corrupted in proportion to the advancement of our sciences and arts toward perfection. Can it be said that this is a misfortune particular to our age? No, gentlemen; the evils caused by our vain curiosity are as old as the world. The daily ebb and flow of the ocean's waters have not been more steadily subject to the course of the star which gives us light during the night than has the fate of morals and integrity been subject to the advancement of the sciences and arts. Virtue has fled as their light dawned on our horizon, and the same phenomenon has been observed in all times and in all places.

*   *   *

What dangers there are! What false paths when investigating the sciences! How many errors, a thousand times more dangerous than the truth is useful, must be surmounted in order to reach the truth? The disadvantage is evident, for falsity is susceptible of infinite combinations, whereas truth has only one form. Besides, who seeks it sincerely? Even with the best intentions, by what signs is one certain to recognize it? In this multitude of different opinions, what will be our *criterium* in order to judge it properly? And hardest of all, if by luck we finally find it, who among us will know how to make good use of the truth?

If our sciences are vain in the objects they have in view, they are even more dangerous in the effects they produce. Born in idleness, they nourish it in turn; and irreparable loss of time is the first injury they necessarily cause society. . . . Answer me then, illustrious philosophers—you who taught us in what proportions bodies attract each other in a vacuum; what are, in the orbits of planets, the ratios of areas covered in equal time intervals; what curves have conjugate points, points of inflexion, and cusps; how man sees everything in

God; how soul and body could be in harmony, like two clocks, without communicating; which stars could be inhabited; what insects breed in an extraordinary manner—answer me, I say, you from whom we have received so much sublime knowledge: had you taught us none of these things, would we consequently be fewer in number, less well governed, less formidable, less flourishing or more perverse? Reconsider, then, the importance of your products; and if the works of the most enlightened of our learned men and our best citizens provide us with so little that is useful, tell us what we must think of that crowd of obscure writers and idle men of letters who uselessly consume the substance of the State.

Did I say idle? Would God they really were! Morals would be healthier and society more peaceful. But these vain and futile declaimers go everywhere armed with their deadly paradoxes, undermining the foundations of faith, and annihilating virtue. They smile disdainfully at the old-fashioned words of fatherland and religion, and devote their talents and philosophy to destroying and debasing all that is sacred among men. Not that at bottom they hate either virtue or our dogmas; they are enemies of public opinion, and to bring them to the foot of altars it would suffice to send them among atheists. O passion to gain distinction, of what are you not capable?

J. L. Talmon, an Israeli scholar, would locate the origins of what he calls totalitarian democracy in the Age of Reason. Such a development, he feels, flowed naturally from the attack launched by the philosophes on traditional institutions.

FROM *The Origins of Totalitarian Democracy*
BY *J. L. Talmon*

FROM THE POINT of view of this study the most important change that occurred in the eighteenth century was the peculiar state of mind which achieved dominance in the second part of the century. Men were gripped by the idea that the conditions, a product of faith, time and custom, in which they and their forefathers had been living, were unnatural and had all to be replaced by deliberately planned uniform patterns, which would be natural and rational.

This was the result of the decline of the traditional order in Europe: religion lost its intellectual as well as its emotional hold; hierarchical feudalism disintegrated under the impact of social and economic factors; and the older conception of society based on status came to be replaced by the idea of the abstract, individual man.

The rationalist idea substituted social utility for tradition as the main criterion of social institutions and values. It also suggested a form of social determinism, to which men are irresistibly driven, and which they are bound to accept one day. It thus postulated a single valid system, which would come into

J. L. Talmon, *The Origins of Totalitarian Democracy*, pp. 3–5, 21–22, 34–37, published in 1960 by Praeger Publishers, Inc., New York. Reprinted by permission of Octopus Publishing Group.

existence when everything not accounted for by reason and utility had been removed. This idea was, of course, bound to clash with the inveterate irrationality of man's ways, his likings and attachments.

The decline of religious authority implied the liberation of man's conscience, but it also implied something else. Religious ethics had to be speedily replaced by secular, social morality. With the rejection of the Church, and of transcendental justice, the State remained the sole source and sanction of morality. This was a matter of great importance, at a time when politics were considered indistinguishable from ethics.

The decline of the idea of status consequent on the rise of individualism spelt the doom of privilege, but also contained totalitarian potentialities. If, as will be argued in this essay, empiricism is the ally of freedom, and the doctrinaire spirit is the friend of totalitarianism, the idea of man as an abstraction, independent of the historic groups to which he belongs, is likely to become a powerful vehicle of totalitarianism.

These three currents merged into the idea of a homogeneous society, in which men live upon one exclusive plane of existence. There were no longer to be different levels of social life, such as the temporal and the transcendental, or membership of a class and citizenship. The only recognized standard of judgment was to be social utility, as expressed in the idea of the general good, which was spoken of as if it were a visible and tangible objective. The whole of virtue was summed up as conformity to the rationalist, natural pattern. In the past it was possible for the State to regard many things as matters for God and the Church alone. The new State could recognize no such limitations. Formerly, men lived in groups. A man had to belong to some group, and could belong to several at the same time. Now there was to be only one framework for all activity: the nation. The eighteenth century never distinguished clearly between the sphere of personal self-expression and that of social action. The privacy of creative experience and feeling, which is the salt of freedom, was in due course to be swamped by the pressure of the permanently assembled people, vibrating with one collective emotion. The fact that eighteenth-century thinkers were ardent prophets of liberty and the rights of man is so much taken for granted that it scarcely needs to be mentioned. But what must be emphasized is the intense preoccupation of the eighteenth century with the idea of virtue, which was nothing if not conformity to the hoped-for pattern of social harmony. They refused to envisage the conflict between liberty and virtue as inevitable. On the contrary, the inevitable equation of liberty with virtue and reason was the most cherished article of their faith. When the eighteenth-century secular religion came face to face with this conflict, the result was the great schism. Liberal democracy flinched from the spectre of force, and fell back upon the trial-and-error philosophy. Totalitarian Messianism hardened into an exclusive doctrine represented by a vanguard of the enlightened, who justified themselves in the use of coercion against those who refused to be free and virtuous.

*   *   *

THE SECULAR RELIGION

Eighteenth-century *philosophes* were never in doubt that they were preaching a new religion. They faced a mighty challenge. The Church claimed to offer an absolute point of reference to man and society. It also claimed to embody an ultimate and all-embracing unity of human existence across the various levels of human and social life. The Church accused secular philosophy of destroying these two most essential conditions of private and public morality, and thereby undermining the very basis of ethics, and indeed society itself. If there is no God, and no transcendental sanction, why should men act virtuously? Eighteenth-century philosophy not only accepted the challenge, but turned the accusation against the Church itself. The *philosophes* felt the challenge so keenly that, as Diderot put it, they regarded it their sacred duty to show not only that their morality was just as good as religious ethics, but much better. Holbach was at pains to prove that the materialistic principle was a much stronger basis for ethics than the principle of the "spirituality of the soul" could ever claim to be. A great deal of eighteenth-century thought would assume a different complexion, if it was constantly remembered that though a philosophy of protest, revolt and spontaneity, eighteenth-century philosophy, as already hinted, was intensely aware of the challenge to redefine the guarantees of social cohesion and morality. The *philosophes* were most anxious to show that not they, but their opponents, were the anarchists from the point of view of the natural order.

The philosophical line of attack on the Church was that apart from the historic untruth of the revealed religion, it also stood condemned as a sociological force. It introduced "imaginary" and heterogeneous criteria into the life of man and society. The commandments of the Church were incompatible with the requirements of society. The contradiction was harmful to both, and altogether demoralizing. One preached ascetic unworldliness, the other looked for social virtues and vigour. Man was being taught to work for the salvation of his soul, but his nature kept him earthbound. Religion taught him one thing, science another. Religious ethics were quite ineffective, where they were not a source of evil. The promise of eternal reward and the threat of everlasting punishment were too remote to have any real influence on actual human conduct. This sanction at best engendered hypocrisy. Where the teachings of religion were successful, they resulted in human waste, like monasticism and asceticism, or in cruel intolerance and wars of religion. Moreover, the "imaginary" teachings and standards of the Church offered support and justification to tyrannical vested interests harmful to society as a whole. Rousseau, Morelly, Helvetius, Holbach, Diderot, Condorcet, not to mention of course Voltaire, were unanimous in their insistence on the homogeneous nature of morality. Some, the Voltairians and atheists, speak in terms of a deliberate plot against society, when attacking the claims of religious ethics. Others, like Rousseau, lay all the emphasis on matters of principle, above all the principle of social unity. You cannot be a citizen and Christian at the same time, for the loyalties clash.

* * *

THE NATURAL ORDER, THE LEGISLATOR, AND THE INDIVIDUAL

These ideas on self-interest and the power of education have strong political and social implications. As justice only has meaning in reference to social utility, it is clear that a just action is one that is useful to the greater number. It could thus be said that morality consists in the interest of the greater number. The greater number embodies justice. "It is evident," says Helvetius, "that justice is in its own nature always armed with a power sufficient to suppress vice, and place men under necessity of being virtuous." Why have the few, representing a minority and therefore an immoral interest, for so long dominated the greater number? Because of ignorance and misleading influences. The existing powers are interested in maintaining ignorance and in preventing the growth of genius and virtue. It is therefore clear that a reform of education could not take place without a change of political constitution. The art of forming man, in other words education, depends ultimately on the form of government.

Self-love as applied to the political sphere means the love of power. Political wisdom consists not in thwarting this natural instinct, but in giving it an outlet. The satisfaction of this urge like the satisfaction of man's legitimate self-interest is conducive to virtue. From this point of view democracy appears as the best system, as it satisfies the love of power of all or of most.

The totalitarian potentialities of this philosophy are not quite obvious at first sight. But they are nevertheless grave. The very idea of a self-contained system from which all evil and unhappiness have been exorcised is totalitarian. The assumption that such a scheme of things is feasible and indeed inevitable is an invitation to a régime to proclaim that it embodies this perfection, to exact from its citizens recognition and submission and to brand opposition as vice or perversion.

The greatest danger is in the fact that far from denying freedom and rights to man, far from demanding sacrifice and surrender, this system solemnly re-affirms liberty, man's self-interest and rights. It claims to have no other aims than their realization. Such a system is likely to become the more totalitarian, precisely because it grants everything in advance, because it accepts all liberal premises *a priori*. For it claims to be able by definition to satisfy them by a positive enactment as it were, not by leaving them alone and watching over them from the distance. When a régime is by definition regarded as realizing rights and freedoms, the citizen becomes deprived of any right to complain that he is being deprived of his rights and liberties. The earliest practical demonstration of this was given by Jacobinism.

Thus in the case of Rousseau his sovereign can demand from the citizen the total alienation of all his rights, goods, powers, person and life, and yet claim that there is no real surrender. In the very idea of retaining certain rights and staking out a claim against the sovereign there is, according to Rousseau, an implication of being at variance with the general will. The proviso that the general will could not require or exact a greater surrender than is inherent in the relationship between it and the subject does not alter the case, since it is left to the sovereign to decide what must be surrendered and what must not. Rousseau's sovereign, like the natural order, can by definition do nothing except secure man's freedom. It can have no reason or cause to hurt the citizen. For it to do so would be as impossible as it would be for something in the world of things to happen without a cause.

There is no need to insist that neither Helvetius, Holbach nor any one of their school envisaged brute force and undisguised coercion as instruments for the realization of the natural system. Nothing could have been further from their minds. Locke's three liberties figure prominently in all their social catechisms. They could not conceive any clash between the natural social pattern and the liberties, the real liberties, of man. The greater the freedom, the nearer, they believed, was the realization of the natural order. In the natural system there would simply be no need to restrict free expression. Opposition to the natural order would be unthinkable, except from fools or perverted individuals. The Physiocrats, for instance, were second to none in their insistence on a natural order of society "simple, constant, invariable and susceptible of being demonstrated by evidence." Mercier de la Rivière preached "despotism of evidence" in human affairs. The absolute monarch was the embodiment of the "force naturelle et irrésistible de l'évidence," which rules out any arbitrary action on the part of the administration. The Physiocrats insisted at the same time on the freedom of the press and the "full enjoyment" of natural rights by the individual. A government conducted on the basis of scientific evidence could only encourage a free press and individual freedom!

Eighteenth-century believers in a natural system failed to perceive that once a positive pattern is laid down, the liberties which are supposed to be attached to this pattern become restricted within its framework, and lose their validity and meaning outside it. The area outside the framework becomes mere chaos, to which the idea of liberty simply does not apply, and so it is possible to go on re-affirming liberty while denying it. Robespierre was only the first of the European revolutionaries who, having been an extreme defender of the freedom of the press under the old dispensation, turned into the bitterest persecutor of the opposition press once he came into power. For, to quote the famous sophism launched during the later period of the Revolution against the freedom of the press, the very demand for a free press when the Revolution is triumphant is counter-revolutionary. It implies freedom to fight the Revolution, for in order to support the Revolution there is no need for special permission. And there can be no freedom to fight the Revolution.

On closer examination the idea of the natural order reaches the antithesis of its original individualism. Although *prima facie* the individual is the beginning and the end of everything, in fact the Legislator is decisive. He is called upon to shape man in accordance to a definite image. The aim is not to enable men as they are to express themselves as freely and as fully as possible, to assert their uniqueness. It is to create the right objective conditions and to educate men so that they would fit into the pattern of the virtuous society.

The foremost proponent of the idea that the Enlightenment was a beneficent movement of fundamental importance for the development of modern liberal humanitarianism is Peter Gay of Yale University. According to him the Age of Reason did introduce logic into hitherto barbaric areas and did serve to advance the cause of humanity.

FROM *The Unity of the French Enlightenment*
BY *Peter Gay*

THE PHILOSOPHES WERE men of letters. This is more than a phrase. It defines their vantage point, and eliminates the stale debate over their status as philosophers. As men of letters who took their craft seriously, they devoted to their writing an incessant care which is one of the secrets of their style. Their output was enormous, and they sent less to the printer than they threw away. They knew the pleasure of self-criticism, and the sweeter pleasure of criticizing others. Grimm corrected Diderot, Diderot corrected Voltaire, and Voltaire corrected everybody. Rousseau, far from tossing off his masterpieces in a fit of feverish inspiration, struggled with them for years; Voltaire rewrote untiringly, and treated first editions as drafts to be recast in the next printing; Diderot poured early versions of articles into his letters to Sophie Volland. While there is no single Enlightenment style, all *philosophes* had style.

* * *

The *philosophes,* then, much as they wished to change it, were at home in their world. To divide the century into two sharply defined forces—the subversive *philosophes* against the orthodox—may be convenient and dramatic, but it is also much too simple. There were moments of crisis when two parties crystallized and Catholics squared off against unbelievers, but subtler and more pervasive than hostility were the ties that bound the *philosophes* to their society. They edited respectable magazines, flattered royal mistresses, wrote unexceptional entertainments, and held responsible posts.

Nor was their attachment to the existing order based solely on calculation: they shared with literate Christians a religious education, a love for the classics of Roman and French literature, and an affection for the pleasures of cultivated leisure. Seeking to distinguish themselves, they did not wish to abolish all distinctions. When they participated in politics, they often supported one orthodox party against another: Montesquieu, the *parlements* against the king; Voltaire,

Peter Gay, "The Unity of the French Enlightenment," in *The Party of Humanity*, pp. 117-121, 124-130. New York, 1964. Cited with permission of Alfred A Knopf.

the king against the *parlements*. While they helped to prepare the way for the Jacobins, they were not Jacobins themselves.

Yet this did not prevent them from being at war with it at the same time. The *philosophes* never developed a coherent political program or even a consistent line of political tactics, but their polemics called for a France profoundly different from the country in which they lived—France after, not before, 1791. The regime could make concessions: boredom, a lost sense of purpose, could make many a bourgeois, priest, or aristocrat receptive to subversive propaganda. But aggressive deism or materialism, doctrines of the rule of law, complete toleration, and subordination of church to state—these tenets could not be assimilated by the old order. To neglect either side of their dual situation is to make the *philosophes* more revolutionary or more conservative than in fact they were.

This tension, which is yet not alienation, places not only the *philosophes* in their century, it places the century itself. To say that the eighteenth century was an age of contradictions, is to say nothing: all ages have this characteristic in common. We must be specific: eighteenth-century France was a Christian culture that was rapidly losing its Christian vocation without being fully aware of it.

"One day," writes Paul Hazard, "the French people, almost to a man, were thinking like Bossuet. The day after, they were thinking like Voltaire." This is doubly wrong. The *philosophes* had much opposition among the educated and the powerful. While the writings of Montesquieu, Voltaire, and Diderot have survived, those of their adversaries have not, but survival is an unreliable guide to the intellectual map of the past: in the age of Louis XV Christianity had many a persuasive and intelligent defender. Moreover, we cannot properly speak of a "French people" in the eighteenth century. Most Frenchmen were wholly untouched by the Enlightenment and lived, as it were, in an earlier century. They believed in witches, applied spells, used home remedies long condemned by physicians, displayed a trust in authority long discarded by the educated, lived and died happily ignorant of the battles between Cartesians and Newtonians.

Yet for men sensitive or educated enough to be aware of intellectual currents, the eighteenth century was a time of turmoil. A whole complex of ideas and experiences, usually lumped together in the slippery word "secularization," came together in the reign of Louis XV to haunt thinking men. The literature of travel offered the spectacle of happy and civilized non-Christian cultures; the demands of international politics forged secular rather than sectarian alliances; the growth of the European economy stimulated the desire for worldly goods; the great discoveries of science suggested the appalling possibility of a universe without God.

Secularization did not mean the death of religion. Eight Frenchmen out of ten—perhaps nine—were uncontaminated by skepticism. Even the businessman or artisan, who greatly benefited from advances in technology, rarely allowed them to affect his faith. Still, what Troeltsch has called the "Church-directed civilization" was crumbling. Christians lived by the image of hierarchy: as God, his angels, and his creatures were arranged in an order of rank, so by analogy the skies, the family, law, society, the Church, were naturally hierarchical. Now, as natural scientists demonstrated that the hierarchies of terrestrial and celestial motion, or the spheres of the heavens, were absurd, other revolutionaries were exposing the absurdity of other hierarchies.

* * *

. . . The *philosophes* had two enemies: the institutions of Christianity and the idea of hierarchy. And they had two problems: God and the masses. Both the enemies and the problems were related and woven into the single task of rethinking their world. The old questions that Christianity had answered so fully for so many men and so many centuries had to be asked anew: What—as Kant put it—what can I know? What ought I to do? What may I hope?

Science itself did not answer these questions. It only suggested—ever more insistently as the century went on—that the old answers were wrong. Now, the *philosophes* were products of Christian homes and Christian schools. If they became enemies of Christianity, they did so not from indifference or ignorance: they knew their Bible, their catechism, their Church Fathers, their apologetics. And they knew, because it had been drummed into them early, the fate that awaits heretics or atheists in the world to come. Their anticlerical humor therefore has the bitter intimacy of the family joke; to embrace materialism was an act of rejection.

The struggle of the *philosophes* was a struggle for freedom. They did not fully understand it, but to the extent that they did understand it, they knew their situation to be filled with terror and delight. They felt the anxiety and exhilaration of the explorer who stands before the unknown.

Diderot, the most ebullient of *philosophes,* the freest and most inventive of spirits, was driven from position to position and haunted by doubts. Born into a family richly endowed with priests, of pious parents and with a fanatical brother, long toying with entering the priesthood, Diderot moved from Catholicism to theism, from theism to deism, from deism to skepticism, and from skepticism to atheism. But atheism, with its cold determination, repelled him even though he accepted it as true; while Catholicism, with its colorful ceremony, moved him even though he rejected it as false. Writing to his mistress, Sophie Volland, he cursed the philosophy—his own—that reduced their love to a blind encounter of atoms. "I am furious at being entangled in a confounded philosophy which my mind cannot refrain from approving and my heart from denying."

The materialists of course claimed to be defiantly happy at being cosmic orphans. But the question—If God is dead, what is permitted?—was not a question calculated to make men sleep easy.

I am not simply arguing that the *philosophes* were less cheerful than they appeared in their social roles—most of us are. Nor that they suffered personal crises—philosophers, especially young philosophers, often do. I am arguing that the *philosophes'* anguish was related to the crisis in their Christian civilization; that (to use different language) whatever childhood experiences made them psychologically vulnerable in adult life, their obsessions, their self-questionings, their anxieties, were poured into their religious, moral, and political speculation.

* * *

But the *philosophes'* crisis was not only a crisis felt, it was also a crisis conquered. And this brings me back to the idea of work, and to the philosophy of energy.

* * *

But work as consolation is only the most primitive level of the philosophy of energy. Its most familiar expression, which pervaded the *philosophes'* writings through the century, was the drive to assert man's power over his environment. Even the materialists, for all their determinism, taught the virtue of rational activity and the possibility of modifying nature.

Power over nature was more than a cliché: the *philosophes* knew precisely what they meant by it. They had learned it, partly from Bacon, partly (although rather less) from Descartes, and above all from the needs and possibilities of their time. Medieval man had not abjectly resigned himself to misery or pathetic dependence on divine intervention in his behalf. Yet even sympathetic historians have conceded that the Middle Ages were an age of precarious and violent existence. Men aged young and died young; those fortunate enough to survive infancy, epidemics, or famines, were likely victims of bandits, pirates, sudden war, or brutal migrations. "Beneath all social life," Marc Bloch writes, "there was a soil of primitivism, of submission to ungovernable powers."

To remedy this—to prolong life, clear the roads of assassins, keep men from starving, and give them hope of enjoying the fruits of their labors—required more than a stable political organization. It required a spiritual revolution, and the culmination of that revolution was the philosophy of the *philosophes*.

* * *

The *philosophes'* task cannot . . . be contained in the word *humanitarianism*. It was greater than that: the campaign to abolish torture cannot be divorced from the campaign to abolish Jesuits or to spread technological knowledge—all are part of the struggle to impose man's rational will on the environment. Nor was it simply the acquisition of knowledge. As good Baconians, the *philosophes* preached that knowledge is power, but few of them were naïve enough to believe that knowledge automatically creates virtue: their writings are filled with warnings against the misuse of intelligence or the brutalizing of learning. They did argue that since knowledge is power, ignorance is impotence. It followed that the men who wanted to keep others in ignorance were enemies of humanity. What does one do with monsters who want to castrate mankind? All—or almost all—methods are fair against them.

The philosophers of energy face to face with their enemies: this confrontation leads us back to the beginning, for it helps to solve the puzzling contradictions that beset the interpreter of the Enlightenment. The French Enlightenment had its own history, and that history mirrors, and helped to shape, the history of the century. Something happened in Europe in the 1760's. It was the beginning of industrial society; the beginning of modern politics and the great democratic revolt against aristocratic regimes. It was a time of turmoil within the Christian world itself: witness the suppression of the Jesuits, and the outbursts of hysterical prosecutions of Huguenots and blasphemers.

In this time of trouble, the *philosophes* added to their sense of power over the environment a sense of mission. The moderate anticlericalism of a Montesquieu gave way to the belligerent cry, *Écrasez l'infâme;* democratic political ideas found a favorable hearing even from the skeptic Voltaire. The *philosophes* grew more radical, more combative, more convinced than ever that they were the prophets of a new age that would rise on the ruins of the old.

As they became more violently partisan, the contradictions in their views became more obvious. As a historian, Voltaire delighted in the past for its own sake; as an aesthetician, Diderot delighted in the play of light and shade on canvas. But as prophets, both found it necessary to import moral lessons into their writings. If the old civilization must give way to the new, if men must learn to dare and to rely on themselves, if even the uneducated are to find their place in this revolution, then *philosophes* must teach, and teach again, and teach everywhere. Cultivated men possessed by a sense of mission temper their cultivation for the sake of their mission. This will lead to inconsistencies. But these inconsistencies do not destroy, they merely dramatize, the richness and the unity of the French Enlightenment.

The Origins of the French Revolution—Popular Misery, Social Ambitions, or Philosophical Ideas?

CONTENTS

QUESTIONS FOR STUDY

1   In what ways do Montesquieu and Rousseau criticize the foundations of the French
state in the eighteenth century?
2   How desperate was the plight of the peasantry in France in 1789?
3   How does the Declaration of the Rights of Man reflect the influence of ideas on the
makers of the Revolution? In what ways does it deal with very practical concerns?
4   Who were the makers of the French Revolution? In what ways could their motives be
affected by misery, social ambitions, and ideas?
5   What do you feel to be sufficient motives for revolutionary action?

The reign of Louis XIV in France revealed some of the problems associated with the exercise of absolute power by the king. Although Louis created a brilliant society and stimulated the development of the arts and sciences—so much so that the age of Louis XIV was later regarded as a golden age—he also bled France white with his interminable wars and search for "glory." The wars and the Revocation of the Edict of Nantes in 1685 struck heavy blows at French commercial development, and this, along with the sheer expense of continuous fighting, brought France to the brink of bankruptcy in 1715. Throughout the eighteenth century France was to remain tottering on the verge of financial collapse, and it should not be forgotten that it was this collapse that led directly to the convocation of the Estates-General in 1789. In the financial sense the origins of the French Revolution go back to Louis XIV.

Finances, however, were not the whole story. Had the French state been sound in 1789, the financial system might simply have been reformed and the monarchy restored to strength. The crisis in France went much deeper. The whole constitution of the state was in question. Several important flaws of absolutism had become apparent under Louis XIV, primary of which was that of the misuse of power. Except for his megalomania and pursuit of la gloire, *however, Louis was a competent and hardworking executive. His successors Louis XV and Louis XVI, were not. Louis XV was a poorly educated, rather dull fellow who ultimately found his goal in life to be the care and feeding of a series of royal mistresses. One of them, Madame de Pompadour, had the intelligence and political ambition that Louis lacked and took advantage of her position to exercise both. For some twenty years she was the most important politician in France. Her successor, Madame du Barry, inherited Madame de Pompadour's power without the latter's intellectual attributes. Madame du Barry had received only a rudimentary education, having plied the trade of prostitute in Paris before her elevation to royal mistress, and she was incompetent to succeed Madame de Pompadour, at least politically.*

Louis XVI was virtuous but uninterested in governing. His twin passions were hunting and the mechanisms of locks. The entry in his diary for July 14, 1789, when the Bastille fell, was "rien" (nothing), referring to the fact that his hunting had been unsuccessful.

The reigns of Louis XV and Louis XVI could not help but raise some political questions. They might be no more general than whether France could afford such royal incompetents at a critical time in its history—a position taken by the Duke of Orleans, for example, who had royal ambitions. This was not to question the monarchy, only the monarchs. Others went further in their criticism. Did not the experience of Louis XIV, XV, and XVI indicate that no monarch could be trusted with absolute power? And if this were the case, with whom should power be shared? In 1788 there were a number of candidates for political participation in the French state. The nobles, of course, could and did argue that they had traditionally shared power with the king and had in ages past prevented the abuses of absolutism from appearing. By 1788, however, another group was eager for political action. The bourgeoisie had grown in wealth and numbers in the eighteenth century. Its members were educated, competent, and ambitious. They had read the philosophes, whose abstract theories they felt competent to translate into concrete realities. As men of affairs, who were better suited to steer the French ship of state through the financial shoals than they?

Nobility and bourgeoisie made up but a small fraction of the French people. The majority were peasants and artisans. What of them? Did they read Voltaire, Montesquieu, and Rousseau? Did they dream of political power? What were their grievances and what did they expect from the government? Fortunately, we have sources that permit us to evaluate the aspirations of this great mass of the French people on the eve of the French Revolution. By royal decree, every parish and corporate group in France was to compose a cahier des doléances *(notebook of grievances) in which the people could spell out the evils that afflicted them (see p. 342).*

There is no doubt that the woes of France in 1789 were many and grievous. Nor can there be any doubt that reform was necessary. What is puzzling is the reasons for the transformation of cries for reform into cries for revolution. For many, if not most, Frenchmen the old regime became intolerable, and it is the historian's task to try to discover who found it so, for what reasons, and how this discontent was channeled into politically effective action. Could the Revolution have succeeded without the energies produced by the frustrated masses demanding bread? Could it have succeeded without the ambitions of the middle class, who saw the road to power open before it? Finally, could the Revolution have been successful without the theories of the philosophes, which provided the only chart for those who wished to embark upon the uncertain seas of rebellion? And in any case, were these frustrations, ambitions, and theories sufficient to cause the Revolution? We are left with the fundamental question: Why do men revolt against their legal government when they know that the price of failure is their very lives?

1

Man and the State in the Age of Reason

Charles de Secondat, Baron de Montesquieu (1689–1755), was one of the keenest political analysts of the eighteenth century. His most influential work was The Spirit of the Laws *first published in French in 1748*

FROM *The Spirit of the Laws*
BY *Baron de Montesquieu*

OF THE LAWS WHICH ESTABLISH POLITICAL LIBERTY, WITH REGARD TO THE CONSTITUTION

A General Idea

I MAKE A DISTINCTION BETWEEN the laws that establish political liberty, as it relates to the constitution, and those by which it is established, as it relates to the citizen. . . .

Different Significations of The Word, Liberty

There is no word that admits of more various significations, and has made more different impressions on the human mind, than that of *liberty*. Some have taken it for a facility of deposing a person on whom they had conferred a tyrannical authority: others, for the power of choosing a superior whom they are obliged to obey: others, for the right of bearing arms, and of being thereby enabled to use violence: others, in fine, for the privilege of being governed by a native of their own country, or by their own laws. A certain nation, for a long time, thought liberty consisted in the privilege of wearing a long beard. Some have

The Complete Works of M. de Montesquieu, translated from the French in Four Volumes, I (1778), pp. 195–212. Reprinted by permission.

annexed this name to one form of government exclusive of others: those who had a republican taste applied it to this species of polity: those who liked a monarchical state gave it to monarchy. Thus they have all applied the name of *liberty* to the government most suitable to their own customs and inclinations; and as, in republics, the people have not so constant and so present a view of the causes of their misery, and as the magistrates seem to act only in conformity to the laws, hence liberty is generally said to reside in republics, and to be banished from monarchies. In fine, as in democracies the people seem to act almost as they please, this sort of government has been deemed the most free, and the power of the people has been confounded with their liberty.

In What Liberty Consists

It is true that, in democracies, the people seem to act as they please; but political liberty does not consist in an unlimited freedom. In governments, that is, in societies directed by laws, liberty can consist only in the power of doing what we ought to will, and in not being constrained to do what we ought not to will.

We must have continually present to our minds the difference between independence and liberty. Liberty is a right of doing whatever the laws permit; and, if a citizen could do what they forbid, he would be no longer possessed of liberty, because all his fellow-citizens would have the same power.

The Same Subject Continued

Democratic and aristocratic states are not in their own nature free. Political liberty is to be found only in moderate governments; and even in these it is not always found. It is there only when there is no abuse of power: but constant experience shews us that every man invested with power is apt to abuse it, and to carry his authority as far as it will go. Is it not strange, though true, to say, that virtue itself has need of limits.

To prevent this abuse, it is necessary, from the very nature of things, power should be a check to power. A government may be so constituted, as, no man shall be compelled to do things to which the law does not oblige him, nor forced to abstain from things which the law permits.

Of The End or View Of Different Governments

Though all governments have the same general end, which is that of preservation, yet each has another particular object. Increase of dominion was the object of Rome; war, that of Sparta; religion, that of the Jewish laws; commerce, that of Marseilles; public tranquility, that of the laws of China; navigation, that of the laws of Rhodes; natural liberty, that of the policy of the savages; in general, the pleasure of the prince, that of despotic states; that of monarchies, the prince's and the kingdom's glory: the independence of individuals is the end aimed at by the laws of Poland; from thence results the oppression of the whole.

One nation there is also in the world, that has, for the direct end of its constitution, political liberty. We shall presently examine the principles on which this liberty is founded: if they are sound, liberty will appear in its highest perfection.

To discover political liberty in a constitution, no great labour is requisite. If we are capable of seeing it where it exists, it is soon found, and we need not go far in search of it.

Of The Constitution of England

In every government there are three sorts of power; the legislative; the executive in respect to things dependent on the law of nations; and the executive in regard to matters that depend on the civil law.

By virtue of the first, the prince or magistrate enacts temporary or perpetual laws, and amends or abrogates those that have been already enacted. By the second, he makes peace or war, sends or receives embassies, establishes the public security, and provides against invasions. By the third, he punishes criminals, or determines the disputes that arise between individuals. The latter we shall call the judiciary power, and the other, simply, the executive power of the state.

The political liberty of the subject is a tranquility of mind arising from the opinion each person has of his safety. In order to have this liberty, it is requisite the government be so constituted as one man need not be afraid of another.

When the legislative and executive powers are united in the same person, or in the same body of magistrates, there can be no liberty; because apprehensions may arise, lest the same monarch or senate should enact tyrannical laws, to execute them in a tyrannical manner.

Again, there is no liberty if the judiciary power be not separated from the legislative and executive. Were it joined with the legislative, the life and liberty of the subject would be exposed to arbitrary controul; for the judge would be then the legislator. Were it joined to the executive power, the judge might behave with violence and oppression.

There would be an end of every thing, were the same man, or the same body, whether of the nobles or of the people, to exercise those three powers, that of enacting laws, that of executing the public resolutions, and of trying the causes of individuals.

Most kingdoms in Europe enjoy a moderate government, because the prince, who is invested with the two first powers, leaves the third to his subjects.

In Turkey, where these three powers are united in the sultan's person, the subjects groan under the most dreadful oppression.

In the republics of Italy, where these three powers are united, there is less liberty than in our monarchies. Hence their government is obliged to have recourse to as violent methods, for its support, as even that of the Turks; witness the state-inquisitors, and the lion's mouth into which every informer may at all hours throw his written accusation.

In what a situation must the poor subject be, under those republics! The same body of magistrates are possessed, as executors of the laws, of the whole power they have given themselves in quality of legislators. They may plunder the state by their general determinations; and, as they have likewise the judiciary power in their hands, every private citizen may be ruined by their particular decisions.

The whole power is here united in one body; and, though there is no external pomp that indicates a despotic sway, yet the people feel the effects of it every moment.

Hence it is that many of the princes of Europe, whose aim has been levelled at arbitrary power, have constantly set out with uniting, in their own persons, all the branches of magistracy, and all the great offices of state.

I allow, indeed, that the mere hereditary aristocracy of the Italian republics does not exactly answer to the despotic power of the Eastern princes. The number of magistrates sometimes moderates the power of the magistracy; the whole body of the nobles do not always concur in the same design; and different tribunals are erected, that temper each other. Thus, at Venice, the legislative power is in the *council,* the executive in the *pregadi,* and the judiciary in the *quarantia.* But the mischief is, that these different tribunals are composed of magistrates all belonging to the same body; which constitutes almost one and the same power.

The judiciary power ought not to be given to a standing senate; it should be exercised by persons taken from the body of the people, at certain times of the year, and consistently with a form and manner prescribed by law, in order to erect a tribunal that should last only so long as necessity requires.

By this method, the judicial power, so terrible to mankind, not being annexed to any particular state or profession, becomes, as it were, invisible. People have not then the judges continually present to their view; they fear the office, but not the magistrate.

In accusations of a deep and criminal nature, it is proper the person accused should have the privilege of choosing, in some measure, his judges, in concurrence with the law; or, at least, he should have a right to except against so great a number, that the remaining part may be deemed his own choice.

The other two powers may be given rather to magistrates or permanent bodies, because they are not exercised on any private subject; one being no more than the general will of the state, and the other the execution of that general will.

But, though the tribunals ought not to be fixt, the judgements ought; and to such a degree, as to be ever conformable to the letter of the law. Were they to be the private opinion of the judge, people would then live in society without exactly knowing the nature of their obligations.

The judges ought likewise to be of the same rank as the accused, or, in other words, his peers; to the end, that he may not imagine he is fallen into the hands of persons inclined to treat him with rigour.

If the legislature leaves the executive power in possession of a right to imprison those subjects who can give security for their good behaviour, there is an end of liberty; unless they are taken up in order to answer, without delay, to a capital crime; in which case they are really free, being subject only to the power of the law.

But, should the legislature think itself in danger, by some secret conspiracy against the state, or by a correspondence with a foreign enemy, it might authorize the executive power, for a short and limited time, to imprison suspected persons, who, in that case, would lose their liberty only for a while, to preserve it for ever.

And this is the only reasonable method that can be substituted to the tyrannical magistracy of the *Ephori,* and to the *state inquisitors of* Venice, who are also despotical.

As, in a country of liberty, every man who is supposed a free agent ought to be his own governor, the legislative power should reside in the whole body of the people. But, since this is impossible in large states, and in small ones is subject to many inconveniences, it is fit the people should transact by their representatives what they cannot transact by themselves.

The inhabitants of a particular town are much better acquainted with its wants and interests than with those of other places; and are better judges of the capacity of their neighbours than of that of the rest of their countrymen. The members, therefore, of the legislature should not be chosen from the general body of the nation; but it is proper, that, in every considerable place, a representative should be elected by the inhabitants.

The great advantage of representatives is their capacity of discussing public affairs. For this, the people collectively are extremely unfit, which is one of the chief inconveniences of a democracy.

* * *

When the deputies, as Mr. Sidney well observes, represent a body of people, as in Holland, they ought to be accountable to their constituents; but it is a different thing in England, where they are deputed by boroughs.

All the inhabitants of the several districts ought to have a right of voting at the election of a representative, except such as are in so mean a situation as to be deemed to have no will of their own.

* * *

Neither ought the representative body to be chosen for the executive part of government, for which it is not so fit; but for the enacting of laws, or to see whether the laws in being are duly executed; a thing suited to their abilities, and which none indeed but themselves can properly perform.

In such a state, there are always persons distinguished by their birth, riches, or honours: but, were they to be confounded with the common people, and to have only the weight of a single vote, like the rest, the common liberty would be their slavery, and they would have no interest in supporting it, as most of the popular resolutions would be against them. The share they have, therefore, in the legislature ought to be proportioned to their other advantages in the state; which happens only when they form a body that has a right to check the licentiousness of the people, as the people have a right to oppose any encroachment of theirs.

The legislative power is, therefore, committed to the body of the nobles, and to that which represents the people; each having their assemblies and deliberations apart, each their separate views and interests.

Of the three powers abovementioned, the judiciary is, in some measure, next to nothing: there remain, therefore, only two: and, as these have need of a regulating power to moderate them, the part of the legislative body composed of the nobility is extremely proper for this purpose.

The body of the nobility ought to be hereditary. In the first place, it is so in its own nature; and, in the next, there must be a considerable interest to preserve its privileges; privileges that, in themselves, are obnoxious to popular envy, and of course, in a free state, are always in danger.

But, as an hereditary power might be tempted to pursue its own particular interests, and forget those of the people, it is proper, that, where a singular advantage may be gained by corrupting the nobility, as in the laws relating to the supplies, they should have no other share in the legislation than the power of rejecting, and not that of resolving.

By the *power of resolving* I mean the right of ordaining by their own authority, or of amending what has been ordained by others. By the *power of rejecting,* I would be understood to mean the right of annulling a resolution taken by another, which was the power of the tribunes at Rome. And, though the person possessed of the privilege of rejecting may likewise have the right of approving, yet this approbation passes for no more than a declaration that he intends to make no use of his privilege of rejecting, and is derived from that very privilege.

The executive power ought to be in the hands of a monarch, because this branch of government, having need of dispatch, is better administered by one than by many: on the other hand, whatever depends on the legislative power, is oftentimes better regulated by many than by a single person.

But, if there were no monarch, and the executive power should be committed to a certain number of persons, selected from the legislative body, there would be an end of liberty, by reason the two powers would be united; as the same persons would sometimes possess, and would be always able to possess, a share in both.

Were the legislative body to be a considerable time without meeting, this would likewise put an end to liberty. For, of two things, one would naturally follow: either that there would be no longer any legislative resolutions, and then the state would fall into anarchy; or that these resolutions would be taken by the executive power, which would render it absolute.

* * *

The legislative body should not meet of itself. For a body is supposed to have no will but when it is met: and besides, were it not to meet unanimously, it would be impossible to determine which was really the legislative body, the part assembled, or the other. And if it had a right to prorogue itself, it might happen never to be prorogued; which would be extremely dangerous, in case it should ever attempt to encroach on the executive power. Besides, there are seasons (some more proper than others) for assembling the legislative body: it is fit, therefore, that the executive power should regulate the time of meeting, as well as the duration, of those assemblies, according to the circumstances and exigences of a state, known to itself.

Were the executive power not to have a right of restraining the encroachments of the legislative body, the latter would become despotic: for, as it might arrogate to itself what authority it pleased, it would soon destroy all the other powers.

But it is not proper, on the other hand, that the legislative power should have a right to stay the executive. For, as the executive has its natural limits, it is useless to confine it: besides, the executive power is generally employed in momentary operations.

* * *

Here, then, is the fundamental constitution of the government we are treating of. The legislative body being composed of two parts, they check one another by the mutual privilege of rejecting. They are both restrained by the executive power, as the executive is by the legislative.

These three powers should naturally form a state of repose or inaction: but, as there is a necessity for movement in the course of human affairs, they are forced to move, but still in concert.

As the executive power has no other part in the legislative than the privilege of rejecting, it can have no share in the public debates. It is not even necessary that it should propose; because, as it may always disapprove of the resolutions that shall be taken, it may likewise reject the decisions on those proposals which were made against its will.

* * *

Were the executive power to determine the raising of public money otherwise than by giving its consent, liberty would be at an end; because it would become legislative in the most important point of legislation.

If the legislative power were to settle the subsidies, not from year to year, but for ever, it would run the risk of losing its liberty, because the executive power would be no longer dependent; and, when once it was possessed of such a perpetual right, it would be a matter of indifference whether it held it of itself or of another. The same may be said if it should come to a resolution of intrusting, not an annual, but a perpetual, command of the fleets and armies to the executive power.

To prevent the executive power from being able to oppress, it is requisite that the armies with which it is intrusted should consist of the people, and have the same spirit as the people, as was the case at Rome till the time of *Marius*. To obtain this end, there are only two ways; either that the persons employed in the army should have sufficient property to answer for their conduct to their fellow-subjects, and be enlisted only for a year, as was customary at Rome; or, if there should be a standing-army composed chiefly of the most despicable part of the nation, the legislative power should have a right to disband them as soon as it pleased; the soldiers should live in common with the rest of the people; and no separate camp, barracks, or fortress should be suffered.

Of The Monarchies We Are Acquainted With

The monarchies we are acquainted with have not, like that we have been speaking of, liberty for their direct view: the only aim is the glory of the subject, of the state, and of the sovereign. But from hence there results a spirit of liberty, which, in those states, is capable of achieving as great things, and of contributing as much, perhaps, to happiness, as liberty itself.

Here the three powers are not distributed and founded on the model of the constitution abovementioned: they have each a particular distribution, according to which they border more or less on political liberty; and, if they did not border upon it, monarchy would degenerate into despotic government.

As the French Revolution developed, increasing attention was given to the ideas of Jean Jacques Rousseau (1712–1778). It soon became possible to claim Rousseau as the most important philosophical instigator of the Revolution. Robespierre himself was proud to be known as a disciple. Some of Rousseau's most important ideas are to be found in this essay first published in French in 1762.

FROM *An Inquiry into the Nature of the Social Contract*
BY *Jean Jacques Rousseau*

OF THE SOCIAL COMPACT

WE WILL SUPPOSE THAT men in a state of nature are arrived at that crisis, when the strength of each individual is insufficient to defend him from the attacks he is subject to. This primitive state can therefore subsist no longer; and the human race must perish, unless they change their manner of life.

An Inquiry into the Nature of the Social Contract, or Principles of Political Right, translated from the French of John James Rousseau (1771), pp. 33–49. Reprinted by permission.

As men cannot create for themselves new forces, but merely unite and direct those which already exist, the only means they can employ for their preservation is to form by aggregation an assemblage of forces that may be able to resist all assaults, be put in motion as one body, and act in concert upon all occasions.

This assemblage of forces must be produced by the concurrence of many: and as the force and the liberty of a man are the chief instruments of his preservation, how can he engage them without danger, and without neglecting the care which is due to himself? This doubt, which leads directly to my subject, may be expressed in these words:

"Where shall we find a form of association which will defend and protect with the whole aggregate force the person and the property of each individual; and by which every person, while united with ALL, shall obey only HIMSELF, and remain as free as before the union?" Such is the fundamental problem, of which the Social Contract gives the solution.

The articles of this contract are so unalterably fixed by the nature of the act, that the least modification renders them vain and of no effect. They are the same everywhere, and are everywhere understood and admitted, even though they may never have been formally announced: so that, when once the social part is violated in any instance, all the obligations it created cease; and each individual is restored to his original rights, and resumes his native liberty, as the consequence of losing that conventional liberty for which he exchanged them.

All the articles of the social contract will, when clearly understood, be found reducible to this single point—THE TOTAL ALIENATION OF EACH ASSOCIATE, AND ALL HIS RIGHTS, TO THE WHOLE COMMUNITY. For every individual gives himself up entirely—the condition of every person is alike; and being so, it would not be the interest of anyone to render himself offensive to others.

Nay, more than this—the alienation is made without any reserve; the union is as complete as it can be, and no associate has a claim to anything: for if any individual was to retain rights not enjoyed in general by all, as there would be no common superior to decide between him and the public, each person being in some points his own proper judge, would soon pretend to be so in everything; and thus would the state of nature be revived, and the association become tyrannical or be annihilated.

In fine, each person gives himself to ALL, but not to any INDIVIDUAL: and as there is no one associate over whom the same right is not acquired which is ceded to him by others, each gains an equivalent for what he loses, and finds his force increased for preserving that which he possesses.

If, therefore, we exclude from the social compact all that is not essentially necessary, we shall find it reduced to the following terms:

"We each of us place, in common, his person, and all his power, under the supreme direction of the general will; and we receive into the body each member as an indivisible part of the whole."

From that moment, instead of so many separate persons as there are contractors, this act of association produces a moral collective body, composed of as many members as there are voices in the assembly; which from this act receives its unity, its common self, its life, and its will. This public person, which is thus formed by the union of all the private persons, took formerly the name of *city,* and now takes that of *republic* or *body politic.* It is called by its members *state* when it is passive, and *sovereign* when in activity: and whenever it is spoken of with other bodies of a similar kind, it is denominated *power.* The associates take collectively the name of *people,* and separately that of *citizens,* as participating in the sovereign authority: they are also styled *subjects,* because they are subjected to the laws. But these terms are frequently confounded, and used one for the other; and a man must understand them well to distinguish when they are properly employed.

OF THE SOVEREIGN POWER

It appears from this form that the act of association contains a reciprocal engagement between the public and individuals; and that each individual contracting as it were with himself, is engaged under a double character; that is, as a part of the *sovereign power* engaging with individuals, and as a member of the *state* entering into a compact with the *sovereign power.* But we cannot apply here the maxim of civil right, that no person is bound by any engagement which he makes with himself; for there is a material difference between an obligation contracted towards *one's self* individually, and towards a collective body of which *one's self* constitutes a part.

It is necessary to observe here that the will of the public, expressed by a majority of votes—which can enforce obedience from the subjects to the sovereign power in consequence of the double character under which the members of that body appear—cannot bind the sovereign power to itself; and that it is against the nature of the body politic for the sovereign power to impose any one law which it cannot alter. Were they to consider themselves as acting under one character only, they would be in the situation of individuals forming each a contract with himself: but this is not the case; and therefore there can be no fundamental obligatory law established for the body of the people, not even the social contract. But this is of little moment, as that body could not very well engage itself to others in any manner which would not derogate from the contract. With respect to foreigners, it becomes a single being, an individual only.

But the body politic, or sovereign power, which derives its existence from the sacredness of the contract, can never bind itself, even towards others, in any thing that would derogate from the original act; such as alienating any portion of itself, or submitting to another sovereign: for by violating the contract its own existence would be at once annihilated; and by nothing nothing can be performed.

As soon as the multitude is thus united in one body, you cannot offend one of its members without attacking the whole; much less can you offend the whole without incurring the resentment of all the members. Thus duty and interest equally oblige the two contracting parties to lend their mutual aid to each other; and the same men must endeavour to unite under this double character all the advantages which attend it.

The sovereign power being formed only of the individuals which compose it, neither has, or can have, any interest contrary to theirs; consequently the sovereign power requires no guarantee towards its subjects, because it is impossible that the body should seek to injure all its members: and we shall see presently that it can do no injury to any individual. The sovereign power by its nature must, while it exists, be everything it ought to be: but it is not so with subjects towards the sovereign power; to which, notwithstanding the common interest subsisting between them, there is nothing to answer for the performance of their engagements, if some means is not found of ensuring their fidelity.

In fact, each individual may, as a man, have a private will, dissimilar or contrary to the general will which he has as a citizen. His own particular interest may dictate to him very differently from the common interest; his mind, naturally and absolutely independent, may regard what he owes to the common cause as a gratuitous contribution, the omission of which would be less injurious to others than the payment would be burthensome to himself; and considering the moral person which constitutes the state as a creature of the imagination, because it is not a man, he may wish to enjoy the rights of a citizen, without being disposed to fulfil the duties of a subject: an injustice which would in its progress cause the ruin of the body politic.

In order therefore to prevent the social compact from becoming a vain form, it tacitly comprehends this engagement, which alone can give effect to the others—That whoever refuses to obey the general will, shall be compelled to it by the whole body, which is in fact only forcing him to be free; for this is the condition which guarantees his absolute personal independence to every citizen of the country: a condition which gives motion and effect to the political machine; which alone renders all civil engagements legal; and without which they would be absurd, tyrannical, and subject to the most enormous abuses.

OF THE CIVIL STATE

The passing from a state of nature to a civil state, produces in man a very remarkable change, by substituting justice for instinct, and giving to his actions a moral character which they wanted before.

It is at the moment of that transition that the voice of duty succeeds to physical impulse; and a sense of what is right, to the incitements of appetite. The man who had till then regarded none but himself, perceives that he must act on other principles, and learns to consult his reason before he listens to his propensities.

2

Conditions of Life on the Eve of the Revolution

Arthur Young (1741–1820) was a wealthy English farmer whose passion was the study of agriculture. In 1787 he set out to see how France conducted farming operations. His descriptions of parts of France, published in 1792–1794, provide a vivid picture of the peasant's standard of living in the years immediately preceding the Revolution.

FROM *Travels in France During the Years 1787, 1788, 1789*

BY *Arthur Young*

POVERTY AND POOR CROPS to Amiens; women are now ploughing with a pair of horses to sow barley. The difference of the customs of the two nations is in nothing more striking than in the labours of the sex; in England, it is very little that they will do in the fields except to glean and make hay; the first is a party of pilfering, and the second of pleasure: in France, they plough and fill the dung cart. . . .

* * *

To La Ferté Lowendahl, a dead flat of hungry sandy gravel, with much heath. The poor people, who cultivate the soil here, are *métayers,* that is, men who hire the land without ability to stock it; the proprietor is forced to provide cattle and seed, and he and his tenant divide the produce; a miserable system, that perpetuates poverty and excludes instruction. . . .

* * *

The same wretched country continues to La Loge; the fields are scenes of pitiable management, as the houses are of misery. Yet all this country is highly improveable, if they knew what to do with it: the property, perhaps, of some

Arthur Young, *Travels in France During the Years 1787, 1788, 1789,* (1889), pp. 8-9, 19, 27, 61, 123, 125, 189, 201. Reprinted by permission.

of those glittering beings, who figured in the procession the other day at Versailles. Heaven grant me patience while I see a country thus neglected—and forgive me the oaths I swear at the absence and ignorance of the possessors. . . .

Pass Payrac, and meet many beggars, which we had not done before. All the country, girls and women, are without shoes or stockings; and the ploughmen at their work have neither sabots nor feet to their stockings. This is a poverty, that strikes at the root of national prosperity; a large consumption among the poor being of more consequence than among the rich; the wealth of a nation lies in its circulation and consumption; and the case of poor people abstaining from the use of manufacturers of leather and wool ought to be considered as an evil of the first magnitude. It reminded me of the misery of Ireland.

* * *

Take the road to Moneng, and come presently to a scene which was so new to me in France, that I could hardly believe my own eyes. A succession of many well built, tight, and COMFORTABLE farming cottages, built of stone, and covered with tiles; each having its little garden, inclosed by clipt thorn hedges, with plenty of peach and other fruit-trees, some fine oaks scattered in the hedges, and young trees nursed up with so much care, that nothing but the fostering attention of the owner could effect any thing like it. To every house belongs a farm, perfectly well inclosed, with grass borders mown and neatly kept around the corn fields, with gates to pass from one inclosure to another. The men are all dressed with red caps, like the highlanders of Scotland. There are some parts of England (where small yeomen still remain) that resemble this country of Bearne; but we have very little that is equal to what I have seen in this ride of twelve miles from Pau to Moneng. It is all in the hands of little proprietors, without the farms being so small as to occasion a vicious and miserable population. An air of neatness, warmth, and comfort breathes over the whole. It is visible in their new built houses and stables; in their little gardens; in their hedges; in the courts before their doors; even in the coops for their poultry, and the sties for their hogs. A peasant does not think of rendering his pig comfortable, if his own happiness hangs by the thread of a nine years lease. We are now in Bearne, within a few miles of the cradle of Henry IV. Do they inherit these blessings from that good prince? The benignant genius of that good monarch, seems to reign still over the country; each peasant has *the fowl in the pot*.

* * *

September 1st. To Combourg, the country has a savage aspect; husbandry not much further advanced, at least in skill, than among the Hurons, which appears incredible amidst inclosures; the people almost as wild as their country, and their town of Combourg one of the most brutal filthy places that can be seen; mud houses, no windows, and a pavement so broken, as to impede all passengers, but ease none—yet here is a château, and inhabited; who is this Mons. de Chateaubriant, the owner that has nerves strung for a residence amidst such filth and poverty? Below this hideous heap of wretchedness is a fine lake, surrounded by well wooded inclosures. . . .

*   *   *

1788

To Montauban. The poor people seem poor indeed; the children terribly ragged, if possible worse clad than if with no cloaths at all; as to shoes and stockings they are luxuries. A beautiful girl of six or seven years playing with a stick, and smiling under such a bundle of rags as made my heart ache to see her: they did not beg and when I gave them any thing seemed more surprized than obliged. One third of what I have seen of this province seems uncultivated, and nearly all of it in misery. What have kings, and ministers, and parliaments, and states, to answer for their prejudices, seeing millions of hands that would be industrious, idle and starving, through the execrable maxims of despotism, or the equally detestable prejudices of a feudal nobility. . . .

*   *   *

1789

The 12th. Walking up a long hill, to ease my mare, I was joined by a poor woman, who complained of the times, and that it was a sad country; demanding her reasons, she said her husband had but a morsel of land, one cow, and a poor little horse, yet they had a *franchar* (42 lb.) of wheat, and three chickens, to pay as a quit-rent to one Seigneur; and four *franchar* of oats, one chicken and 1 £. to pay to another, besides very heavy tailles and other taxes. She had seven children, and the cow's milk helped to make the soup. But why, instead of a horse, do not you keep another cow? Oh, her husband could not carry his produce so well without a horse; and asses are little used in the country. It was said, at present, that *something was to be done by some great folks for such poor ones, but she did not know who nor how,* but God send us better, [*car les tailles & les droits nous écrasent.*]*—This woman, at no great distance, might have been taken for sixty or seventy, her figure was so bent, and her face so furrowed and hardened by labour,—but she said she was only twenty-eight. An Englishman who has not travelled cannot imagine the figure made by infinitely the greater part of the country women in France; it speaks, at the first sight,

---

*"because the taxes and imports are crushing us."[Ed.]

hard and severe labour: I am inclined to think, that they work harder than the men, and this, united with the more miserable labour of bringing a new race of slaves into the world, destroys absolutely all symmetry of person and every feminine appearance. To what are we to attribute this difference in the manners of the lower people in the two kingdoms? To GOVERNMENT. . . .

*   *   *

Nangis is near enough to Paris for *the people* to be politicians; the perruquier that dressed me this morning tells me, that every body is determined to pay no taxes, should the National Assembly so ordain. But the soldiers will have something to say. No, Sir, never:—be assured as we are, that the French soldiers will never fire on the people: but, if they should, it is better to be shot than starved. He gave me a frightful account of the misery of the people; whole families in the utmost distress; those that work have a pay insufficient to feed them—and many that find it difficult to get work at all. I enquired of Mons. de Guerchy concerning this, and found it true. By order of the magistrates no person is allowed to buy more than two bushels of wheat at a market, to prevent monopolizing. It is clear to common sense, that all such regulations have a direct tendency to increase the evil, but it is in vain to reason with people whose ideas are immovably fixed. Being here on a market-day, I attended, and saw the wheat sold out under this regulation, with a party of dragoons drawn up before the market-cross to prevent violence. The people quarrel with the bakers, asserting the prices they demand for bread are beyond the proportion of wheat, and proceeding from words to scuffling, raise a riot, and then run away with bread and wheat for nothing: this has happened at Nangis, and many other markets; the consequence was, that neither farmers nor bakers would supply them till they were in danger of starving, and, when they did come, prices under such circumstances must necessarily rise enormously, which aggravated the mischief, till troops became really necessary to give security to those who supplied the markets. . . .

*   *   *

Letters from Paris! all confusion! the ministry removed: Mons. Necker ordered to quit the kingdom without noise. The effect on the people of Nancy was considerable.—I was with Mons. Willemet when his letters arrived, and for some time his house was full of enquires; all agreed, that it was fatal news, and that it would occasion great commotions. *What will be the result of Nancy?* The answer was in effect the same from all I put this question to: *We are a provincial town, we must wait to see what is done at Paris; but every thing is to be feared from the people, because bread is so dear, they are half starved, and are consequently ready for commotion.*—This is the general feeling; they are as nearly concerned as Paris; but they dare not stir; they dare not even have an opinion of their own till they know what Paris thinks; so that if a starving populace were not in question, no one would dream of moving. This confirms what I have often heard remarked, that the *deficit* would not have produced the revolution but in concurrence with the price of bread. Does not this shew the infinite consequence of great cities to the liberty of mankind? Without Paris, I question whether the present revolution, which is fast working in France, could possibly have had an origin.

The peasant was not always as miserable as he seemed. This selection was first published in French in 1782.

FROM *The Confessions of Jean Jacques Rousseau*

ONE DAY, AMONGST OTHERS, having purposely turned out of my way to get a nearer view of a spot which appeared worthy of admiration, I was so delighted with it, and went round it so often that, at last, I completely lost myself. After several hours of useless walking, tired, and dying of hunger and thirst, I entered a peasant's hut, not much to look at, but the only dwelling I saw in the neighbourhood. I expected to find it the same as in Geneva, or Switzerland, where all the well-to-do inhabitants are in a position to show hospitality. I begged him to give me dinner, and offered to pay for it. He offered me some skimmed milk and coarse barley bread, saying that that was all he had. I drank the milk with delight, and ate the bread, husks and all; but it was not very invigorating fare for a man exhausted by fatigue. The peasant, who examined me closely, estimated the truth of my story by my appetite, and immediately afterwards declared that he could see that I was a good and honourable young man, who had not come there to betray him for money. He opened a little trapdoor near the kitchen, went down, and came up a minute afterwards with a nice brown wheaten loaf, a very tempting-looking ham, although considerably cut down, and a bottle of wine, the sight of which rejoiced my heart more than all the rest; to this he added a substantial omelette, and I made a dinner such as none but a pedestrian ever enjoyed. When it came to the question of payment, his uneasiness and alarm returned; he would take none of my money, and refused it with singular anxiety; and the amusing thing was that I could not imagine what he was afraid of. At last, with a shudder, he uttered the terrible words, "Revenue officers and excisemen." He gave me to understand that he hid his wine on account of the excise, that he hid his bread on account of the tax, and that he was a lost man, if anyone had a suspicion that he was not starving. All that he said to me on this subject, of which I had not the least idea, made an impression upon me which will never be forgotten. It was the germ of the inextinguishable hatred which subsequently grew up in my heart against the oppression to which these unhappy people are subject, and against their oppressors. This man, although in good circumstances, did not dare to eat the bread which he had obtained by the sweat of his brow, and could only escape utter ruin by

The Confessions of Jean Jacques Rousseau (Modern Library ed., n. d.), pp. 169-170. Reprinted by permission.

displaying the same poverty as prevailed around him. I left his house, equally indignant and touched, lamenting the lot of these beautiful countries, upon which Nature has only lavished her gifts to make them the prey of barbarous farmers of taxes.

The French Revolution is unique among revolutions in that there was an extensive sampling of public opinion immediately preceding the Revolution itself. Once the decision was made to call the Estates-General, the king was prevailed upon to order the compilation of notebooks of grievances (cahiers des doléances) *to be drawn up by the three estates (Clergy, Nobility, Third). It was the first attempt to sample "grassroots" opinion, for literally every French subject was forced to think of the ills that afflicted France and was given the opportunity to make his views known.*

The number of cahiers that have survived is immense. The one that follows is typical of those submitted by the Third Estate.

FROM *The Notebook of Grievances of the Third Estate of the Parish of Saint-Vaast*

TODAY, SUNDAY, THE TWENTY-NINTH day of March 1789, following vespers, at the sound of the church bell, in the customary way, the inhabitants of the parish of Saint-Vaast, Bailiwick of Auge, citizens of the Third-Estate, assembled according to the terms of the letters of convocation given by His Majesty at Versailles, the 24th of January 1789, for the convocation and holding of the Estates-general of the realm, and according to the ordinance of the Lieutenant General of the Bailiwick of Auge at Pont-l'Evêque, dated the 16th of this month and announced in the pulpit of this parish on Sunday the 22nd of this month, and affixed to the main door of the Church on the same day, to the effect that they should confer among themselves and proceed to the writing of their notebook of grievances, complaints and remonstrances, means and advice that they wish to propose to the general assembly of the nation:

Begin, by assuring the King that they are ready to sacrifice their fortunes and their very persons for him and for the State;

And vote unanimously that the representatives of this province, in the Assembly of the Estates-general, before consenting to any new taxes to pay the debts of the government, shall employ their efforts and their zeal to the end that there shall be drawn up a *Declaration of the Rights of the French Nation* as a charter between the King, head of the nation and sole executor of the laws, and the nation, which will include the following:

M. J. Mavidal and M. E. Laurent, *Archives parlementaires de 1787 à 1860, Premiére Serie*, v (1879), pp. 609–612, translated by L. Pearce Williams. Reprinted by permission.

NATIONAL CONSTITUTION

1. That the King consents to a law of *habeas corpus* which will guarantee every citizen, no matter how low his condition, from ever being subjected to the abuse of *lettres de cachet* or letters of exile, as well as from the actions and the arbitrary power of ministers, of governors and of intendants of provinces exercised through sealed letters.

2. That only the nation has the right to tax itself, that is to say, to accede or to refuse taxes, to regulate their size, their use, their assessment and their scope; the nation can also ask for an account and must be consulted before loans are made. Any other means of taxation or of borrowing are declared unconstitutional, illegal and of no force.

3. That the periodical and regular reconvening of the Estates-general be set for every four years, at a specific time of the year, so that the nation can there consider the state of the realm, the use of taxes granted in the previous session in order to decide whether to continue or suppress them, and to propose, besides, reforms and other helps for all branches of the political economy.

4. That in the case (unhappily too frequent) where, by the intrigues of an ambitious minister intent upon administering everything according to his caprice, the lines of communication between the nation and its king are broken so that the convocation of the Estates-general does not take place as provided for in the *national charter,* the particular Estates of this province (of which more later) shall be authorized to oppose the levy of all taxes, and the parlements shall be authorized to publish their opposition by an ordinance which shall be sent to all lesser tribunals in their circuit and which will permit the public authorities to prosecute those who continue to collect them for malfeasance of office.

5. That all taxes on real and personal property shall be levied equally on all the goods of ecclesiastics, nobles and commoners, on perpetual rents and those of recent creation, and that all privileges which are really subsidies shall be wiped out.

6. That the Third-Estate, greatly superior in number to the two other orders, in order that it may be judged at least in part by its peers, as it was in the old exchequer court, will have, in the parlement of this undivided and indivisible province, forty magistrates drawn from this Estate; reason and experience have shown that the laws which guarantee the property, the liberty and the rights of the Third-Estate from the attacks and pretensions of the clergy and the nobility are illusory, useless and poorly obeyed so long as the maintenance and execution of justice rest in the hands of the two first orders to the exclusion of the third.

These representatives of the Third-Estate, presented to the King by the province and armed by the King with their powers, will be chosen among those of his subjects who have shown proof of their capacity by their study of the law and in the exercise of their talents at the bar, during ten years, either before the parlement or before other, lesser, courts. But, they shall cease to be the representatives of the Third-Estate, and their mandate shall become null and void if and when they are ennobled, no matter by what means. . . .

* * *

The small income of a commoner should be no reason for exclusion from the parlement. The magistrate should not be based on the brilliance coming from opulence but on the brilliance of knowledge; this is especially true of a sense of justice which nothing can tarnish. How worthy of respect is the man who is always just!

The undersigned also vote that the representatives of this province to the Estates-general will insist that His Majesty grant, before they consent to any new taxes:

PROVINCIAL ESTATES

1. The re-establishment of the particular Estates of this province, which shall meet at Caen, center of Normandy, or elsewhere, each year, composed of a number of members of the Third-Estate equal to those of the two orders of the clergy and of the nobility together. . . .
2. *The unlimited liberty of the press,* with the requirement that the printer or the author place his name at the bottom of the printed matter so that he may be held responsible for whatever is contrary to dominant religious sentients, or to the respect of the sovereign, public decency and the honor of citizens.
3. The destruction of all particular commissions of attribution or evocation, for whatever cause, so that no citizen can ever be transferred from out his own jurisdiction. . . .
4. Great modifications in the ordinance of 1669, called the *Hunting Code,* most of which turns free commoners into true serfs. It is contrary to human rights that a cultivator who owns his land cannot lift a finger to destroy the wild animals which devastate his harvest, which is even more destroyed by those who chase these animals with great noise and numbers. The too abundant nature of the wild game (hitherto given greater privileges than the cultivator) leads to the real destruction of property; it also is contrary to reason as well as to the principle of liberty that a peaceful inhabitant of the country, merely because he is a commoner, can be seized from the center of his family and sent to prison by order of the governor of the province, simply because he has a gun to assure his own safety and is, therefore, suspect of having killed a Lord's rabbit.

In order to reconcile the interests of the possessors of fiefs with those of the commoner vassal (who is, after all, a man), it is necessary that the representatives of the Third-Estate solicit and obtain from the sovereign a hunting law such that:

No game warden can be believed on his own word unless he produce two witnesses who will swear to the day and the hour of the crime and to the person of the criminal. . . .

* * *

That game wardens who have killed commoners who were armed or caught hunting, or without authorization in the woods, shall no longer be immune from punishment, as has been the case recently in this province, among others in four recent cases of killing by the wardens of Madame A. . . ., of Madame N. . . ., of a prelate and of a Marshal of France, and others, all residents of this province.

That the cultivator be authorized to shoot, but not to carry away, the pigeons which devastate his harvest, from July 15 to August 20, as well as during the sowing season. This is the only way to force the Lords to close their dovecotes during this short time, since the laws passed on this point are not enforced since their enforcement is in the hands of those who have an interest in perpetuating the abuse.

Madame Roland was the wife of a moderate revolutionary who served for a time as Minister of the Interior before his execution in the Terror. Madame Roland followed him to the scaffold. Her memoirs were written as she awaited execution; in them she recalls her own feelings as a young girl confronted with the pretensions of the nobility. The memoirs were published in French in 1820.

FROM *The Private Memoirs of Madame Roland*

MY GRANDMOTHER ONE DAY took it into her head to pay a visit to Madame de Boismorel, either for the pleasure of seeing her, or of displaying her little daughter. Great preparations in consequence; long toilet in the morning: at length behold us setting off with Aunt Angélique for the *rue Saint-Louis, au Marais,* where we arrived about noon. On entering the house every one, beginning with the *portier,* salutes Madame Phlipon with an air of respect and affection, emulous who shall treat her with the greatest civility. She repays their attention with courtesy, tinged at the same time with dignity. So far very well; but her granddaughter is perceived; and, not satisfied with pointing her out to one another, they proceed to pay her a number of compliments. . . . We go on; a tall lackey announces us, and we enter the *salon,* and find the lady seated, with her lap-dog beside her, upon what we called then, not an *ottomane,* but a *canapé,* gravely embroidering tapestry. Madame de Boismorel was about the age, the height, and the figure of my grandmother; but her dress betokened

The Private Memoirs of Madame Roland (1900), pp.121–125, 136–137, 200–205, edited, with an Introduction by Edward Gilpin Johnson. Reprinted by permission.

the pride of wealth, rather than taste; and her countenance, far from expressing any plebeian desire to please, plainly demanded that all attention should
be bestowed upon herself, and manifested her consciousness of deserving it.
. . . The rouge, spread one layer over another, lent to eyes naturally dull a
much greater air of fierceness than was sufficient to make me fix mine upon the
ground.

    "Ah, Mademoiselle Rotisset, good morning to you," cried, in a loud and
cold tone, Madame de Boismorel, as she rose to meet us. ("*Mademoiselle!*" So
my grandmother is mademoiselle in this house.) "Upon my honor I am very
glad to see you. And this pretty child is your granddaughter? She will make a
fine woman. Come here, my dear, sit down by my side. . . . Did you never
venture in the lottery?"

    "Never, madame; I am not fond of gaming."

    "So, so! very likely indeed! At your age children are apt to think their
game is sure. . . . She is so grave too: I suppose you have a devotional turn?"

    "I know my duty to God, and I endeavor to fulfil it."

    "That is a good girl! You wish to take the veil: is it not so?"

    "I do not know my future destination, and I do not seek to pry into it." . . .

    The conversation next turned upon the family and friends of the mistress
of the house, . . . for example of Madame Roudé, who, notwithstanding her
great age, was still absurd enough to pretend to a fine bosom, and accordingly
greatly exposed this part of her person, except when she got in and out of her
carriage, for which occasion she had always an immense handkerchief ready in
her pocket, because, as she observed, it is not decent to make such an exhibi-
tion to the footmen. . . . I did not at this age ask myself, why my grandmother
did not sit upon the *canapé,* or for what reason in particular Madame de
Boismorel always called her *"Mademoiselle"* Rotisset; but I had the feeling that
led to this reflection, and I saw the end of the visit with joy, as if I were just liberated from some hard confinement.

                                          *   *   *

Mademoiselle d'Hannache, at that time at law for the inheritance of her uncle,
"the captain," was accommodated in the house of my mother, and resided with
us nearly a year and a half. During this interval I was her secretary; I wrote her
letters, copied her precious genealogy, drew up the petitions she presented to
the president and the attorney-general of the Parliament of Paris, the administrators of some annuities bequeathed by a M. de Saint-Vallier to females to rank in
reduced circumstances, and accompanied her sometimes in her solicitations to
various persons, which her affairs made necessary. I observed upon these occasions that, notwithstanding her ignorance, her illiterate language, her starched
manners, her old-fashioned dress, and her other absurdities, she was treated
with respect on account of her pedigree. They listened with attention to the
names of her ancestors, which she never failed to enumerate, and were ready
to side with her in her claims to the disputed inheritance. I could not but con-

trast this honorable treatment with the reception I had met with at Madame de Boismorel's, which had left a deep impression on my mind. It was impossible to conceal from myself my superiority to Mademoiselle d'Hannache, who, with all her genealogy and her forty years to boot, could not write a letter that was either legible, or dignified with a word of common sense; and I thought mankind extremely unjust, and the institutions of society extravagantly absurd.

*   *   *

The old Haudry, creator of the vast fortune of the family, was deceased, and had left a large estate to his son, who, born and educated in opulence, was fashioned to dissipate it. This son, who had already lost a charming wife, lived extravagantly, and, according to the custom of the rich, spent a part of the year at his château of Soucy, whither he transplanted the manners and mode of life of the town, instead of adopting those of the country. He had several neighboring estates, of which that nearest to Soucy (Fontenay), had an old mansion belonging to it that he loved to have occupied; and he had prevailed on M. and Madame Besnard to accept apartments there, in which they passed a part of the summer. This at once contributed to keep up the place, and to give that air of magnificence to his establishments, of which he was ambitious. M. and Madame Besnard were well accommodated, and enjoyed the use of the park, the wildness of which made an agreeable contrast with that of Soucy, and delighted me more than the artificial luxury, which distinguished the abode of the *fermier-général.* Soon after our arrival, Madame Besnard requested us to make a visit with her to Soucy, where the sister-in-law and stepmother of Haudry resided with him and did the honors of his house. This visit was modestly paid before dinner; and I entered, without the least feeling of pleasure, into the *salon,* where Madame Pénault and her daughter received us, with great politeness, it is true, but a politeness that savored a little of superiority. The propriety of my mother's behavior, and something too that appeared in me, in spite of that air of timidity which is produced by a feeling of our value and a doubt whether it will be appreciated by others, scarcely allowed them to exercise it. . . .

The ladies did not fail, a few days after, to return our visit. Three or four persons accompanied them, who happened to be at the château, their paying their respects to us serving merely for the termination of their walk. Upon this occasion I was more agreeable, and succeeded in infusing into my part of the reception the proportion of modest and decent politeness which re-established the equilibrium. Madame Pénault invited us to dinner; but I was never more astonished than on learning that it was not to her own table, but to that of the servants. I was sensible, however, that, as M. Besnard had formerly been in that station, I ought not, out of respect to him, to appear averse to accompanying them; but I felt that Madame Pénault ought to have arranged things otherwise, or spared us this contemptuous civility. My aunt saw it in the same light; but, to avoid any little scene, we accepted the invitation. These inferior household deities were a new spectacle to me, for I had formed no conception of ladies'-

maids personating grandeur. They were prepared to receive us; and, indeed, aped their superiors admirably well. Toilet, gesture, affectation, graces, nothing was forgotten. The cast-off dresses of their mistresses gave to the female part of the household a richness of appearance that honest tradespeople would think out of character to themselves. The caricature of *bon ton* added to their garb a sort of elegance, not less foreign to *bourgeois* simplicity than odious in the eye of an artist. In spite of all this, however, the fluency of their prate and the multiplicity of their grimaces would no doubt have inspired awe into rustics. It was still worse with the men. The sword of "M. *le maître,*" the attentions of "M. *le chef,*" the graces and fine clothes of the valets, could not cloak their *gaucheries* or the jargon they affected when they wished to seem distinguished, or their native vulgarity of speech when for a moment they forgot their assumed gentility. The conversation glittered with marquises, counts, financiers, whose titles, fortunes, and alliances shed a second-hand splendor on those who so glibly discoursed of them. The superfluities of the first table were transferred to the second with an order and despatch that made them appear as if then served for the first time, and with a profusion that sufficed to deck a third table, that of the servants—for it seems the domestics of the first grade called themselves *"officiers."* After dinner, cards were introduced: the stake was high; it was that for which these *"demoiselles"* were accustomed to play, and they played every day. I was introduced to a new world, in which were reflected the prejudices, the vices, and the follies of the great world, the value of which is not really superior, though the show be somewhat more dazzling. I had heard a thousand times of the beginnings of old Haudry, of his coming to Paris from his village, and rising by degrees to the accumulation of thousands at the expense of the public; of his marrying his daughter to Montule, his granddaughters to the Marquis du Chillau and Count Turpin, and leaving his son heir to immense treasures. I agreed with Montesquieu that financiers support the state, just as the cord supports the criminal. I judged that publicans who found means to enrich themselves to this degree, and to use their wealth as an engine by which to unite themselves with families of rank, which the policy of courts regards as essential to the glory and safety of a kingdom—I judged that characters like these could belong only to a detestable government and a depraved nation.

3

The Ideals of the Revolution

On August 27, 1789, the National Assembly decreed the Declaration of the Rights of Man as the preamble to the constitution of France yet to be written. It was, like the American Bill of Rights, to serve as the basic definition of the goals of the Revolution.

Declaration of the Rights of Man and of the Citizen
BY *J. H. Robinson*

THE REPRESENTATIVES OF THE FRENCH PEOPLE, organized as a national assembly, believing that the ignorance, neglect or contempt of the rights of man are the sole causes of public calamities and of the corruption of governments, have determined to set forth in a solemn declaration, the natural, inalienable and sacred rights of man, in order that this declaration, being constantly before all the members of the social body, shall remind them continually of their rights and duties; in order that the acts of the legislative power, as well as those of the executive power, may be compared at any moment with the ends of all political institutions and may thus be more respected; in order that the grievances of the citizens, based hereafter upon simple and incontestable principles, shall tend to the maintenance of the constitution and redound to the happiness of all. Hence the national assembly recognizes and proclaims in the presence and under the auspices of the Supreme Being the following rights of man and of the citizen:

Articles

1. Men are born and remain free and equal in rights. Social distinctions can only be founded upon the general good.
2. The aim of all political association is the preservation of the natural and imprescriptible rights of man. These rights are liberty, property, security, and resistance to oppression.

J. H. Robinson, ed., "The French Revolution, 1789–1791," in *Translations and Reprints from the Original Sources of European History*, I, No. 5 (1897), pp 6–8. Reprinted by permission.

3. The principle *(principe)* of all sovereignty resides essentially in the nation. No body nor individual may exercise any authority which does not proceed directly from the nation.

4. Liberty consists in being able to do everything which injures no one else; hence the exercise of the natural rights of each man has no limits except those which assure to the other members of the society the enjoyment of the same rights. These limits can only be determined by law.

5. Law can only prohibit such actions as are hurtful to society. Nothing may be prevented which is not forbidden by law, and no one may be forced to do anything not provided for by law.

6. Law is the expression of the general will. Every citizen has a right to participate personally or through his representative in its formation. It must be the same for all, whether it protects or punishes. All citizens being equal in the eyes of the law are equally eligible to all dignities and to all public positions and occupations according to their abilities and without distinction except that of their virtues and talents.

7. No person shall be accused, arrested or imprisoned except in the cases and according to the forms prescribed by law. Any one soliciting, transmitting, executing or causing to be executed any arbitrary order shall be punished. But any citizen summoned or arrested in virtue of the law shall submit without delay as resistance constitutes an offence.

8. The law shall provide for such punishments only as are strictly and obviously necessary, and no one shall suffer punishment except it be legally inflicted in virtue of a law passed and promulgated before the commission of the offence.

9. As all persons are held innocent until they shall have been declared guilty, if arrest shall be deemed indispensable all severity not essential to the securing of the prisoner's person shall be severely repressed by law.

10. No one shall be disquieted on account of his opinions, including his religious views, provided their manifestation does not disturb the public order established by law.

11. The free communication of ideas and opinions is one of the most precious of the rights of man. Every citizen may, accordingly, speak, write and print with freedom, being responsible, however, for such abuses of this freedom as shall be defined by law.

12. The security of the rights of man and of the citizen requires public military force. These forces are, therefore, established for the good of all and not for the personal advantage of those to whom they shall be entrusted.

13. A common contribution is essential for the maintenance of the public forces and for the cost of administration. This should be equitably distributed among all the citizens in proportion to their means.

14. All the citizens have a right to decide either personally or by their representatives as to the necessity of the public contribution, to grant this freely, to know to what uses it is put, and to fix the proportion, the mode of assessment, and of collection, and the duration of the taxes.

15. Society has the right to require of every public agent an account of his administration.
16. A society in which the observance of the law is not assured nor the separation of powers defined has no constitution at all.
17. Property being an inviolable and sacred right, no one shall be deprived thereof except where public necessity, legally determined, shall clearly demand it, and then only on condition that the owner shall have been previously and equitably indemnified.

The Declaration of the Rights of Man rather blatantly ignored half the population of France, namely, the women. Women played important roles in the French Revolution, and some of them were insistent that their rights be recognized as well. One of these was Olympe de Gouges, a butcher's daughter from Montauban, the author of a number of plays and of some pamphlets concerning the convening of the Estates-General in 1789. In 1791, she produced a Declaration of the Rights of Woman that reveals both the disabilities women suffered in eighteenth-century France and the aspirations of those who wished to put an end to them.

Declaration of the Rights of Woman
BY *Olympe de Gouges*

THE RIGHTS OF WOMEN

Man, are you capable of being just? It is a woman who poses the question; you will not deprive her of that right at least. Tell me, what gives you sovereign empire to oppress my sex? Your strength? Your talents? Observe the Creator in his wisdom; survey in all her grandeur that nature with whom you seem to want to be in harmony, and give me, if you dare, an example of this tyrannical empire. Go back to animals, consult the elements, study plants, finally glance at all the modifications of organic matter, and surrender to the evidence when I offer you the means; search, probe, and distinguish, if you can, the sexes in the administration of nature. Everywhere you will find them mingled; everywhere they cooperate in harmonious togetherness in this immortal masterpiece.

Man alone has raised his exceptional circumstances to a principle. Bizarre, blind, bloated with science and degenerated—in a century of enlightenment and wisdom—into the crassest ignorance, he wants to command as a despot a sex which is in full possession of its intellectual faculties; he pretends to enjoy the Revolution and to claim his rights to equality in order to say nothing more about it.

Olympe de Gouge, "Declaration of the Rights of Women," in *Women in Revolutionary Paris 1789–1795*, selected documents, translated with notes and commentary by Darline Gay Levy, Harriet Branson Applewhite, and Mary Durham Johnson, pp. 89–95. Reprinted by permission.

DECLARATION OF THE RIGHTS OF WOMAN AND THE FEMALE CITIZEN

For the National Assembly to decree in its last sessions, or in those of the next legislature:

PREAMBLE

Mothers, daughters, sisters [and] representatives of the nation demand to be constituted into a national assembly. Believing that ignorance, omission, or scorn for the rights of woman are the only causes of public misfortunes and of the corruption of governments, [the women] have resolved to set forth in a solemn declaration the natural, inalienable, and sacred rights of woman in order that this declaration, constantly exposed before all the members of the society, will ceaselessly remind them of their rights and duties; in order that the authoritative acts of women and the authoritative acts of men may be at any moment compared with and respectful of the purpose of all political institutions; and in order that citizens' demands, henceforth based on simple and incontestable principles, will always support the constitution, good morals, and the happiness of all.

Consequently, the sex that is as superior in beauty as it is in courage during the sufferings of maternity recognizes and declares in the presence and under the auspices of the Supreme Being, the following Rights of Woman and of Female Citizens.

ARTICLE I

Woman is born free and lives equal to man in her rights. Social distinctions can be based only on the common utility.

ARTICLE II

The purpose of any political association is the conservation of the natural and imprescriptible rights of woman and man; these rights are liberty, property, security, and especially resistance to oppression.

ARTICLE III

The principle of all sovereignty rests essentially with the nation, which is nothing but the union of woman and man; no body and no individual can exercise any authority which does not come expressly from it [the nation].

ARTICLE IV

Liberty and justice consist of restoring all that belongs to others; thus, the only limits on the exercise of the natural rights of woman are perpetual male tyranny; these limits are to be reformed by the laws of nature and reason.

ARTICLE V

Laws of nature and reason proscribe all acts harmful to society; everything which is not prohibited by these wise and divine laws cannot be prevented, and no one can be constrained to do what they do not command.

ARTICLE VI

The law must be the expression of the general will; all female and male citizens must contribute either personally or through their representatives to its formation; it must be the same for all: male and female citizens, being equal in the eyes of the law, must be equally admitted to all honors, positions, and public employment according to their capacity and without other distinctions besides those of their virtues and talents.

ARTICLE VII

No woman is an exception; she is accused, arrested, and detained in cases determined by law. Women, like men, obey this rigorous law.

ARTICLE VIII

The law must establish only those penalties that are strictly and obviously necessary, and no one can be punished except by virtue of a law established and promulgated prior to the crime and legally applicable to women.

ARTICLE IX

Once any woman is declared guilty, complete rigor is [to be] exercised by the law.

ARTICLE X

No one is to be disquieted for his very basic opinions; woman has the right to mount the scaffold; she must equally have the right to mount the rostrum, provided that her demonstrations do not disturb the legally established public order.

ARTICLE XI

The free communication of thoughts and opinions is one of the most precious rights of woman, since that liberty assures the recognition of children by their fathers. Any female citizen thus may say freely, I am the mother of a child which belongs to you, without being forced by a barbarous prejudice to hide the truth; [an exception may be made] to respond to the abuse of this liberty in cases determined by the law.

ARTICLE XII

For the support of the public force and the expenses of administration, the contributions of woman and man are equal; she shares all the duties [*corvées*] and all the painful tasks; therefore, she must have the same share in the distribution of positions, employment, offices, honors, and jobs [*industrie*].

ARTICLE XIII

Female and male citizens have the right to verify, either by themselves or through their representatives, the necessity of the public contribution. This can only apply to women if they are granted an equal share, not only of wealth, but also of public administration, and in the determination of the proportion, the base, the collection, and the duration of the tax.

ARTICLE XIV

The collectivity of women, joined for tax purposes to the aggregate of men, has the right to demand an accounting of his administration from any public agent.

ARTICLE XV

No society has a constitution without the guarantee of rights and the separation of powers; the constitution is null if the majority of individuals comprising the nation have not cooperated in drafting it.

ARTICLE XVI

Property belongs to both sexes whether united or separate; for each it is an inviolable and sacred right; no one can be deprived of it, since it is the true patrimony of nature, unless the legally determined public need obviously dictates it, and then only with a just and prior indemnity.

POSTSCRIPT

Woman, wake up; the tocsin of reason is being heard throughout the whole universe; discover your rights. The powerful empire of nature is no longer surrounded by prejudice, fanaticism, superstition, and lies. The flame of truth has dispersed all the clouds of folly and usurpation. Enslaved man has multiplied his strength and needs recourse to yours to break his chains. Having become free, he has become unjust to his companion. Oh, women, women! When will you cease to be blind? What advantage have you received from the Revolution? A more pronounced scorn, a more marked disdain. In the centuries of corruption you ruled only over the weakness of men. The reclamation of your patrimony, based on the wise decrees of nature—what have you to dread from such a fine undertaking? The *bon mot* of the legislator of the marriage of Cana? Do you fear that our French legislators, correctors of that morality, long ensnared by political practices now out of date, will only say again to you: women, what is there in common between you and us? Everything, you will have to answer. If they persist in their weakness in putting this non sequitur in contradiction to their principles, courageously oppose the force of reason to the empty pretentions of superiority; unite yourselves beneath the standards of philosophy; deploy all the energy of your character, and you will soon see these haughty men, not groveling at your feet as servile adorers, but proud to share with you the treasures of the Supreme Being. Regardless of what barriers confront you, it is in your power to free yourselves; you have only to want to. Let us pass now to the shocking tableau of what you have been in society; and since national education is in question at this moment, let us see whether our wise legislators will think judiciously about the education of women.

Women have done more harm than good. Constraint and dissimulation have been their lot. What force had robbed them of, ruse returned to them;

they had recourse to all the resources of their charms, and the most irreproach-able person did not resist them. Poison and the sword were both subject to them; they commanded in crime as in fortune. The French government, espe-cially, depended throughout the centuries on the nocturnal administration of women; the cabinet kept no secret from their indiscretion; ambassadorial post, command, ministry, presidency, pontificate, college of cardinals; finally, any-thing which characterizes the folly of men, profane and sacred, all have been subject to the cupidity and ambition of this sex, formerly contemptible and respected, and since the revolution, respectable and scorned.

In this sort of contradictory situation, what remarks could I not make! I have but a moment to make them, but this moment will fix the attention of the remotest posterity. Under the Old Regime, all was vicious, all was guilty; but could not the amelioration of conditions be perceived even in the substance of vices? A woman only had to be beautiful or amiable; when she possessed these two advantages, she saw a hundred fortunes at her feet. If she did not profit from them, she had a bizarre character or a rare philosophy which made her scorn wealth; then she was deemed to be like a crazy woman; the most inde-cent made herself respected with gold; commerce in women was a kind of industry in the first class [of society], which, henceforth, will have no more credit. If it still had it, the revolution would be lost, and under the new relation-ships we would always be corrupted; however, reason can always be deceived [into believing] that any other road to fortune is closed to the woman whom a man buys, like the slave on the African coasts. The difference is great; that is known. The slave is commanded by the master; but if the master gives her lib-erty without recompense, and at an age when the slave has lost all her charms, what will become of this unfortunate woman? The victim of scorn, even the doors of charity are closed to her; she is poor and old, they say; why did she not know how to make her fortune? Reason finds other examples that are even more touching. A young, inexperienced woman, seduced by a man whom she loves, will abandon her parents to follow him; the ingrate will leave her after a few years, and the older she has become with him, the more inhuman is his inconstancy; if she has children, he will likewise abandon them. If he is rich, he will consider himself excused from sharing his fortune with his noble victims. If some involvement binds him to his duties, he will deny them, trusting that the laws will support him. If he is married, any other obligation loses its rights. Then what laws remain to extirpate vice all the way to its root? The law of dividing wealth and public administration between men and women. It can eas-ily be seen that one who is born into a rich family gains very much from such equal sharing. But the one born into a poor family with merit and virtue—what is her lot? Poverty and opprobrium. If she does not precisely excel in music or painting, she cannot be admitted to any public function when she has all the capacity for it. I do not want to give only a sketch of things; I will go more deeply into this in the new edition of all my political writings, with notes, which I propose to give to the public in a few days.

I take up my text again on the subject of morals. Marriage is the tomb of trust and love. The married woman can with impunity give bastards to her husband, and also give them the wealth which does not belong to them. The woman who is unmarried has only one feeble right; ancient and inhuman laws refuse to her for her children the right to the name and the wealth of their father; no new laws have been made in this matter. If it is considered a paradox and an impossibility on my part to try to give my sex an honorable and just consistency, I leave it to men to attain glory for dealing with this matter; but while we wait, the way can be prepared through national education, the restoration of morals, and conjugal conventions.

FORM FOR A SOCIAL CONTRACT BETWEEN MAN AND WOMAN

We, _____ and _____, moved by our own will, unite ourselves for the duration of our lives, and for the duration of our mutual inclinations, under the following conditions: We intend and wish to make our wealth communal, meanwhile reserving to ourselves the right to divide it in favor of our children and of those toward whom we might have a particular inclination, mutually recognizing that our property belongs directly to our children, from whatever bed they come, and that all of them without distinction have the right to bear the name of the fathers and mothers who have acknowledged them, and we are charged to subscribe to the law which punishes the renunciation of one's own blood. We likewise obligate ourselves, in case of separation, to divide our wealth and to set aside in advance the portion the law indicates for our children, and in the event of a perfect union, the one who dies will divest himself of half his property in his children's favor, and if one dies childless, the survivor will inherit by right, unless the dying person has disposed of half the common property in favor of one whom he judged deserving.

The Declaration of the Rights of Man was followed almost within a month by the first ten amendments to the Constitution of the new United States of America. This was a Bill of Rights, insisted upon by the former colonies to guarantee their freedom from tyranny. A close comparison between this document and the French Declaration is instructive, for it will reveal two quite different concepts of government and the individual. Both, it should be remarked, owe much to the Enlightenment.

ARTICLE [I]†

Congress shall make no law respecting an establishment of religion, or prohibiting the free exercise thereof; or abridging the freedom of speech, or of the press; or the right of the people peaceably to assemble, and to petition the Government for a redress of grievances.

ARTICLE [II]

A well regulated Militia, being necessary to the security of a free State, the right of the people to keep and bear Arms, shall not be infringed.

ARTICLE [III]

No Soldier shall, in time of peace be quartered in any house, without the consent of the Owner, nor in time of war, but in a manner to be prescribed by law.

ARTICLE [IV]

The right of the people to be secure in their persons, houses, papers, and effects, against unreasonable searches and seizures, shall not be violated, and no Warrants shall issue, but upon probable cause, supported by Oath or affirmation, and particularly describing the place to be searched, and the persons or things to be seized.

ARTICLE [V]

No person shall be held to answer for a capital, or otherwise infamous crime, unless on a presentment or indictment of a Grand Jury, except in cases arising in the land or naval forces, or in the Militia, when in actual service in time of War or public danger; nor shall any person be subject for the same offence to be twice put in jeopardy of life or limb; nor shall be compelled in any criminal case to be a witness against himself, nor be deprived of life, liberty, or property, without due process of law; nor shall private property be taken for public use, without just compensation.

ARTICLE [VI]

In all criminal prosecutions, the accused shall enjoy the right to a speedy and public trial, by an impartial jury of the State and district wherein the crime shall have been committed, which district shall have been previously ascertained by law, and to be informed of the nature and cause of the accusation; to be confronted with the witnesses against him; to have compulsory process for obtaining witnesses in his favor, and to have the Assistance of Counsel for his defence.

ARTICLE [VII]

In Suits at common law, where the value in controversy shall exceed twenty dollars, the right of trial by jury shall be preserved, and no fact tried by a jury, shall be otherwise re-examined in any Court of the United States, than according to the rules of the common law.

ARTICLE [VIII]

Excessive bail shall not be required, nor excessive fines imposed, nor cruel and unusual punishments inflicted.

ARTICLE [IX]

The enumeration in the Constitution, of certain rights, shall not be construed to deny or disparage others retained by the people.

ARTICLE [X]

The powers not delegated to the United States by the Constitution, nor prohibited by it to the States, are reserved to the States respectively, or to the people.

4

The Origins of the Revolution

The most eloquent opponent of the French Revolution in Europe was Edmund Burke (1729–1797). He is the classic spokesman for conservatism, and he used the events of the French Revolution to illustrate his thesis that abstract reasoning is no substitute for a slow, careful, organic growth of the state.

FROM *Reflections on the Revolution in France*
BY *Edmund Burke*

DEAR SIR,

You are pleased to call again, and with some earnestness, for my thoughts on the late proceedings in France.

I flatter myself that I love a manly, moral, regulated liberty as well as any gentleman of that society, be he who he will; and perhaps I have given as good proofs of my attachment to that cause, in the whole course of my public conduct. I think I envy liberty as little as they do, to any other nation. But I cannot stand forward, and give praise or blame to any thing which relates to human actions, and human concerns, on a simple view of the object, as it stands stripped of every relation, in all the nakedness and solitude of metaphysical abstraction. Circumstances (which with some gentlemen pass for nothing) give in reality to every political principle its distinguishing colour, and discriminating effect. The circumstances are what render every civil and political scheme beneficial or noxious to mankind. Abstractedly speaking, government, as well as liberty, is good; yet could I, in common sense, ten years ago, have felicitated France on her enjoyment of a government (for she then had a government) without enquiry what the nature of that government was, or how it was administered? Can I now congratulate the same nation upon its freedom? Is it because liberty in the abstract may be classed amongst the blessings of mankind, that I am seriously to felicitate a madman, who has escaped from the protecting restraint and wholesome darkness of his cell, on his restoration to the enjoyment of light and liberty? Am I to congratulate an highwayman and murderer,

Edmund Burke, *Reflections on the Revolution in France an on the Processings in Certain Societies in London Relative to that Event* (1790), pp. 1, 7–9, 11, 35–36, 50–51, 74–75, 86–89, 90–92, 115. Reprinted by permission.

who has broke prison, upon the recovery of his natural rights? This would be to act over again the scene of the criminals condemned to the gallies, and their heroic deliverer, the metaphysic Knight of the Sorrowful Countenance.

The effect of liberty to individuals is, that they may do what they please: We ought to see what it will please them to do, before we risque congratulations, which may be soon turned into complaints. Prudence would dictate this in the case of separate insulated private men; but liberty, when men act in bodies, is *power*. Considerate people before they declare themselves will observe the use which is made of *power;* and particularly of so trying a thing as *new* power in *new* persons, of whose principles, tempers, and dispositions, they have little or no experience, and in situations where those who appear the most stirring in the scene may possibly not be the real movers.

It looks to me as if I were in a great crisis, not of the affairs of France alone, but of all Europe, perhaps of more than Europe. All circumstances taken together, the French revolution is the most astonishing that has hitherto happened in the world. The most wonderful things are brought about in many instances by means the most absurd and ridiculous; in the most ridiculous modes; and apparently, by the most contemptible instruments. Every thing seems out of nature in this strange chaos of levity and ferocity, and of all sorts of crimes jumbled together with all sorts of follies. In viewing this monstrous tragi-comic scene, the most opposite passions necessarily succeed, and sometimes mix with each other in the mind; alternate contempt and indignation; alternate laughter and tears; alternate scorn and horror.

A few years ago I should be ashamed to overload a matter, so capable of supporting itself, by the then unnecessary support of any argument; but this seditious, unconstitutional doctrine is now publicly taught, avowed, and printed. The dislike I feel to revolutions, the signals for which have so often been given from pulpits; the spirit of change that is gone abroad; the total contempt which prevails with you, and may come to prevail with us, of all ancient institutions, when set in opposition to a present sense of convenience, or to the bent of a present inclination: all these considerations make it not unadviseable, in my opinion, to call back our attention to the true principles of our own domestic laws; that you, my French friend, should begin to know, and that we should continue to cherish them. We ought not, on either side of the water, to suffer ourselves to be imposed upon by the counterfeit wares which some persons, by a double fraud, export to you in illicit bottoms, as raw commodities of British growth though wholly alien to our soil, in order afterwards to smuggle them back again into this country, manufactured after the newest Paris fashion of an improved liberty.

You might, if you pleased, have profited of our example, and have given to your recovered freedom a correspondent dignity. Your privileges, though discontinued, were not lost to memory. Your constitution, it is true, whilst you were out of possession, suffered waste and dilapidation; but you possessed in some parts the walls, and in all the foundations of a noble and venerable castle.

You might have repaired those walls; you might have built on those old foundations. Your constitution was suspended before it was perfected; but you had the elements of a constitution very nearly as good as could be wished. In your old states you possessed that variety of parts corresponding with the various descriptions of which your community was happily composed; you had all that combination, and all that opposition of interests, you had that action and counteraction which, in the natural and in the political world, from the reciprocal struggle of discordant powers, draws out the harmony of the universe. These opposed and conflicting interests, which you considered as so great a blemish in your old and in our present constitution, interpose a salutary check to all precipitate resolutions. They render deliberation a matter not of choice, but of necessity; they make all change a subject of *compromise*, which naturally begets moderation; they produce *temperaments*, preventing the sore evil of harsh, crude, unqualified reformations; and rendering all the headlong exertions of arbitrary power, in the few or in the many, for ever impracticable. Through that diversity of members and interests, general liberty had as many securities as there were separate views in the several orders; whilst by pressing down the whole by the weight of a real monarchy, the separate parts would have been prevented from warping and starting from their allotted places.

You had all these advantages in your antient states; but you chose to act as if you had never been moulded into civil society, and had everything to begin anew. You began ill, because you began by despising every thing that belonged to you. You set up your trade without a capital. If the last generations of your country appeared without much lustre in your eyes, you might have passed them by, and derived your claims from a more early race of ancestors. Under a pious predilection of those ancestors, your imaginations would have realized in them a standard of virtue and wisdom, beyond the vulgar practice of the hour; and you would have risen with the example to whose imitation you aspired. Respecting your forefathers, you would have been taught to respect yourselves. You would not have chosen to consider the French as a people of yesterday, as a nation of low-born servile wretches until the emancipating year of 1789.

* * *

Nothing is a due and adequate representation of a state, that does not represent its ability, as well as its property. But as ability is a vigorous and active principle, and as property is sluggish, inert, and timid, it never can be safe from the invasions of ability, unless it be, out of all proportion, predominant in the representation. It must be represented too in great masses of accumulation, or it not rightly protected. The characteristic essence of property, formed out of the combined principles of its acquisition and conservation, is to be *unequal*. The great masses therefore which excite envy, and tempt rapacity, must be put out of the possibility of danger. Then they form a natural rampart about the lesser properties in all their gradations. The same quantity of property, which is by the natural course of things divided among many, has not the same operation. Its defensive power is weakened as it is diffused. In this diffusion each man's portion is less than what, in the eagerness of his desires, he may flatter himself to obtain by dissipating the accumulations of others. The plunder of the few would indeed give but a share inconceivably small in the distribution to the many. But the many are not capable of making this calculation; and those who lead them to rapine, never intend this distribution.

*   *   *

Far am I from denying in theory; full as far is my heart from withholding in practice (if I were of power to give or to withhold) the *real* rights of men. In denying their false claims of right, I do not mean to injure those which are real, and are such as their pretended rights would totally destroy. If civil society be made for the advantage of man, all the advantages for which it is made become his right. It is an institution of beneficence; and law itself is only beneficence acting by a rule. Men have a right to live by that rule; they have a right to justice; as between their fellows, whether their fellows are in politic function or in ordinary occupation. They have a right to the fruits of their industry; and to the means of making their industry fruitful. They have a right to the acquisitions of their parents; to the nourishment and improvement of their offspring; to instruction in life, and to consolation in death. Whatever each man can separately do, without trespassing upon others, he has a right to do for himself; and he has a right to a fair portion of all which society, with all its combinations of skill and force, can do in his favour. In this partnership all men have equal rights; but not to equal things. He that has but five shillings in the partnership, has as good a right to it, as he that has five hundred pound has to his larger proportion. But he has not a right to an equal dividend in the product of the joint stock; and as to the share of power, authority, and direction which each individual ought to have in the management of the state, that I must deny to be amongst the direct original rights of man in civil society; for I have in my contemplation the civil social man, and no other. It is a thing to be settled by convention.

If civil society be the offspring of convention, that convention must be its law. That convention must limit and modify all the descriptions of constitution which are formed under it. Every sort of legislative, judicial, or executory power are its creatures. They can have no being in any other state of things; and how can any man claim, under the conventions of civil society, rights which do not so much as suppose its existence? Rights which are absolutely repugnant to it? One of the first motives to civil society, and which becomes one of its fundamental rules, is, *that no man should be judge in his own cause.* By this each person has at once divested himself of the first fundamental right of uncovenanted man, that is, to judge for himself, and to assert his own cause. He abdicates all right to be his own governor. He inclusively, in a great measure, abandons the right of self-defence, the first law of nature. Men cannot enjoy the rights of an uncivil and of a civil state together. That he may obtain justice he gives up his right of determining what it is in points the most essential to him. That he may secure some liberty, he makes a surrender in trust of the whole of it.

Government is not made in virtue of natural rights, which may and do exist in total independence of it; and exist in much greater clearness, and in a much greater degree of abstract perfection: but their abstract perfection is their practical defect. By having a right to every thing they want every thing. Government is a contrivance of human wisdom to provide for human *wants*. Men have a right that these wants should be provided for by this wisdom. Among these wants is to be reckoned the want, out of civil society, of a sufficient restraint upon their passions. Society requires not only that the passions of individuals should be subjected, but that even in the mass and body as well as in the individuals, the inclinations of men should frequently be thwarted, their will controlled and their passions brought into subjection. This can only be done *by a power out of themselves;* and not, in the exercise of its function, subject to that will and to those passions which it is its office to bridle and subdue. In this sense the restraints on men, as well as their liberties, are to be reckoned among their rights. But as the liberties and the restrictions vary with times and circumstances, and admit of infinite modifications, they cannot be settled upon any abstract rule; and nothing is so foolish as to discuss them upon that principle.

*   *   *

The science of constructing a commonwealth, or renovating it, or reforming it, is like every other experimental science, not to be taught *a priori.* Nor is it a short experience that can instruct us in that practical science; because the real effects of moral causes are not always immediate; but that which in the first instance is prejudicial may be excellent in its remoter operation; and its excellence may arise even from the ill effects it produces in the beginning. The reverse also happens; and very plausible schemes, with very pleasing commencements, have often shameful and lamentable conclusions. In states there are often some obscure and almost latent causes, things which appear at first view of little moment, on which a very great part of its prosperity or adversity may most essentially depend. The science of government being therefore so practical in itself, and intended for such practical purposes, a matter which requires experience, and even more experience than any person can gain in his whole life, however sagacious and observing he may be, it is with infinite caution that any man ought to venture upon pulling down an edifice which has answered in any tolerable degree for ages the common purposes of society, or on building it up again, without having models and patterns of approved utility before his eyes.

These metaphysic rights entering into common life, like rays of light which pierce into a dense medium, are, by the laws of nature, refracted from their straight line. Indeed in the gross and complicated mass of human passions and concerns, the primitive rights of men undergo such a variety of refractions and reflections, that it becomes absurd to talk of them as if they continued in the simplicity of their original direction. The nature of man is intricate; the objects of society are of the greatest possible complexity; and therefore no simple disposition or direction of power can be suitable either to man's nature, or to the quality of his affairs. When I hear the simplicity of contrivance aimed at and boasted of in any new political constitutions, I am at no loss to decide that the artificers are grossly ignorant of their trade, or totally negligent of their duty. The simple governments are fundamentally defective, to say no worse of them. If you were to contemplate society in but one point of view, all these simple modes of polity are infinitely captivating. In effect each would answer its single end much more perfectly than the more complex is able to attain all its complex purposes. But it is better that the whole should be imperfectly and anomalously answered, than that, while some parts are provided for with great exactness, others might be totally neglected, or perhaps materially injured, by the over-care of a favourite member.

The pretended rights of these theorists are all extremes; and in proportion as they are metaphysically true, they are morally and politically false. The rights of men are in a sort of *middle,* incapable of definition, but not impossible to be discerned. The rights of men in governments are their advantages; and these are often in balances between differences of good; in compromise sometimes between good and evil, and sometimes, between evil and evil. Political reason is a computing principle; adding, subtracting, multiplying, and dividing, morally and not metaphysically or mathematically, true moral denominations.

*　*　*

On the scheme of this barbarous philosophy, which is the offspring of cold hearts and muddy understandings, and which is as void of solid wisdom, as it is destitute of all taste and elegance, laws are to be supported only by their own terrors, and by the concern, which each individual may find in them, from his own private speculations, or can spare to them from his own private interests. In the groves of *their* academy, at the end of every vista, you see nothing but the gallows. Nothing is left which engages the affections on the part of the commonwealth. On the principles of this mechanic philosophy, our institutions can never be embodied, if I may use the expression, in persons; so as to create in us love, veneration, admiration, or attachment. But that sort of reason which banishes the affections is incapable of filling their place. These public affections, combined with manners, are required sometimes as supplements, sometimes as correctives, always as aids to law. . . . There ought to be a system of manners in every nation which a well-formed mind would be disposed to relish. To make us love our country, our country ought to be lovely.

But power, of some kind or other, will survive the shock in which manners and opinions perish, and it will find other and worse means for its support. The usurpation which, in order to subvert antient institutions, has destroyed antient principles, will hold power by arts similar to those by which it has acquired it. When the old feudal and chivalrous spirit of *Fealty,* which, by freeing kings from fear, freed both kings and subjects from the precautions of tyranny, shall be extinct in the minds of men, plots and assassinations will be anticipated by preventive murder and preventive confiscation, and that long roll of grim and bloody maxims, which form the political code of all power, not standing on its own honour, and the honour of those who are to obey it. Kings will be tyrants from policy when subjects are rebels from principle.

When antient opinions and rules of life are taken away, the loss cannot possibly be estimated. From that moment we have no compass to govern us; nor can we know distinctly to what port we steer. Europe undoubtedly, taken in a mass, was in a flourishing condition the day on which your Revolution was compleated. How much of that prosperous state was owing to the spirit of our old manners and opinions is not easy to say; but as such causes cannot be indifferent in their operation, we must presume, that, on the whole, their operation was beneficial.

Alphonse Aulard was a leading historian of the French Revolution and the foremost proponent of the primary role of the ideas of the eighteenth century in bringing about the French Revolution.

FROM *The French Revolution*

BY *A. Aulard*

ON AUGUST 10, 1972, THE Legislative Assembly, in establishing universal suffrage, constituted France a democratic State, and the Convention, in establishing the Republic on the following September 22nd, gave to this democracy the form of government which in the eyes of the Convention was logically expedient.

Can we say that by these two acts a preconceived system was brought into being? Many have thought so; many of our teachers and writers, with much eloquence, have advanced the theory that democracy and the Republic sprang, fully fledged, from the eighteenth-century philosophy, from the works of the Encyclopaedists, from the doctrine of the precursors of the Revolution. Let us see if the facts, and the written word, justify these assertions.

One prime and important fact is this: that in 1789, at the time of the convocation of the Estates-General, there was no Republican party in France.

Now the best testimony to be found as to contemporary French opinion is contained in the *cahiers* in which the people embodied their grievances and their desires. Of these we have many, different in origin and in kind, and in none is a republic demanded, nor even a change of dynasty; and I think my study of these justifies the assertion that in none is there found any criticism, even indirect, of the King's conduct. It would seem that none of the petitioners

A. Aulard, *The French Revolution,* pp. 79–81, 89–99, 125–126, 127–132, translated by Bernard Miall (1910). Reprinted by permission of Charles Scribner's Sons.

dream of attributing their stated grievances to the Monarchy, nor even to the King. In all these documents the French are seen imbued with an ardent royalism, a warm devotion to the person of Louis XVI. Above all, in documents of the more humble kind, petitions from parishes, and the like, there is a note of confidence, love, and gratitude. "Our good King! The King our father!"—so the peasants and the workers address him. The nobles and the clergy, less ingenuously enthusiastic, appear equally loyal.

* * *

If all Frenchmen were at one in wishing to maintain the Monarchy, they were not agreed as to the manner of regulating the royal authority, and we may go so far as to say that they did not all see the throne with the same eyes.

The masses of the people, in their unreasoned loyalty, did not, it would appear, discern the excesses of the royal prerogative. No doubt the commissaries were unpopular. But complaints of "ministerial despotism," as they preferred to call it, came from the nobles, the *bourgeoisie,* the rich and enlightened classes, rather than from the peasantry. The latter more especially lamented a "feudal despotism," because, in fact, they were the greatest sufferers from it.

Far from regarding the King as responsible for the conduct of his agents, the people would say that his agents deceived the King, that they annulled or hampered his power of doing good. The popular idea was to deliver the King from these unjust stewards in order that he might be enlightened, the better to direct his omnipotent power, to the profit of the nation, against the remnants of feudalism. The masses were beginning to have a certain idea of their rights, yet, so far were they from thinking to restrain his royal omnipotence, that it was precisely on that omnipotence that all their hopes were based. One petition said that, in order that all should go well, it was only necessary for the King to cry: *"To me, my people!"*

Enlightened Frenchmen, on the other hand, knowing well what manner of men Louis XIV and XV had been, feared the abuse of the royal power, and were not all reassured by the paternal character of Louis XVI's despotism. They wished to restrain, by means of political institutions, this fantastic and capricious power, so that it should no longer be dangerous to liberty, while leaving it sufficient force to destroy the aristocracy and what remained of the feudal system, thus making France a nation. To ensure that the King should govern according to the laws—this was what they called "organising the Monarchy."

The way to this organisation of the Monarchy was prepared by the writers of the eighteenth century.

They, with the logical spirit natural to the French, did not attempt merely to prevent abuses and to regulate the exercise of sovereign power; they discussed the very essence of this power, of the pretended right Divine; they sapped the Catholic faith by which the throne was propped, sought publicly for the origins of sovereignty and authority, in history, in the assent of subjects, and in the national will.

Thus, without desiring to establish a republic, and solely with a view to "organising" the Monarchy, they attacked the monarchical principle, and put in circulation republican ideas of such a nature that, although in 1789 no one wished for a republic, yet whoever thought at all was impregnated with these republican ideas; and this is why, in 1792, when circumstances made the Republic necessary, there was a sufficient number of thinking men prepared to accept, and to force on others, a form of government of which they had already adopted the principles.

A few examples will show the diffusion and elaboration of republican ideas before the Revolution.

*   *   *

Montesquieu, in 1748, in his *l'Esprit des Lois,* defined a republic: "The republican form of government," he says, "is that in which the people as a whole, or one party only of the people, exercises the sovereign power." This definition became classic. In 1765 it was reproduced in the article on "republics" in the *Encyclopédie* (vol. xiv), which consists entirely of quotations from Montesquieu.

Could not such a republic exist under a king? Montesquieu does not think so; but Mably does—when, for instance, he dreams of a "republican monarchy"; and the same idea is held by those whom we shall find, in 1789, speaking of a "monarchical democracy."

Montesquieu undoubtedly pronounces against a republic, and is of opinion that in a republic "the laws are evaded with greater danger than they can be violated by a prince, who, being always the chief citizen of the State, has the greatest interest in its conservation. None the less, we see how he elsewhere commends the republican form of government, as when he says that virtue is its very mainspring, while a monarchy is founded upon respect and honour; or when, in approval of the popular elections, he writes: "It is an admirable thing that the people should select those to whom they are bound to confide some part of their authority."

It was after reading Montesquieu that Frenchmen became accustomed to regard the republican form of government—which they did not desire to see in France—as a theoretically noble and interesting form.

This theorist of the Monarchy thus found that he had deprived monarchical government of some of its prestige; and, by his views upon the separation of the three forms of authority, he touched royalty itself to the quick—that royalty which pretended, by Divine right, to concentrate all authority in itself.

In this manner did Montesquieu, so admired, so widely read, contribute towards the development of republican ideas and the formation of the republican spirit.

*   *   *

Jean Jacques Rousseau, in his *Contrat social,* had written "that, in general, government by democracy was suited to small States, government by aristocracy to

those of medium size, and government by Monarchy to large States." He further
stated "that there is no form of government so liable to civil wars and
internecine tumult as the democratic or popular," and that "if there existed a
nation of gods, they would govern themselves by a democracy: so perfect a
government is unsuited to mankind." But he was preparing for the ruin of the
monarchical system when he said that "the two principal objects of every system of legislation should be liberty and equality." Prudent and reserved though
he was in theory, he preached revolt by his conduct, in his speeches, and in his
romantic writings—revolt, in the name of Nature, against the vicious and
artificial social system of his time; and, although fundamentally a Christian, he
replaced the mystical ideals of charity and humility by the republican ideal of
fraternity.

*   *   *

From the writings of these philosophers one idea stands out, an idea that
quickly became almost general: that the nation is above the King; and is not
this a republican idea? Although these writers wish to maintain the Monarchy,
they habitually speak of the republican system in honourable terms. A posthu-
mous work of d'Argenson's, *Considérations sur le Gouvernement,* published in
1765, recommends the fortification of the Monarchy by an "infusion" of republican institutions; and d'Argenson praises the government which he does not
desire for his own country in terms so sympathetic as to invite misconception,
so greatly does this work of royalist tendencies, which was much read at the
time, do honour to the republican idea.

*   *   *

The idea that the King should be only a citizen subject to the law, causing the
law to be executed, had gradually become popularised; of its popularity there is
endless proof. When Voltaire wrote, in his tragedy of *Don Pèdre* (1775):

A king is but a man with name august,
First subject of the laws: and, by law, just,

he knew well that he would win applause. And if it be objected that this
tragedy was not presented, that these lines were not actually heard by the the-
atre-going public, I will cite the line borrowed by Favart from a poem by Louis
Racine, published in 1744, which drew applause in the *Trois Sultanes,* at the
Théâtre des Italiens, on April 9, 1761:

Each citizen a king, under a citizen king.

That such maxims were applauded in the theatre, nearly thirty years before the
Revolution, that the Government was obliged to tolerate them: does not this
prove that public opinion had already, so to say, despoiled the King and his
kingship of the mystical principle of sovereignty? And is not this idea of the "cit-

izen king," so unanimously applauded, one of the most startling signs of the republicanisation of the general mind?

*   *   *

To sum up: no one on the eve of the Revolution had ever dreamed of the establishment of a republic in France: it was a form of government that seemed impossible in a great State in course of unification. It was through the King that men sought to establish a free government. Men wished to organise the Monarchy, not to destroy it. No one dreamed of calling the ignorant mass of the people to political life; the necessary revolution was to be brought about by the better class of the nation, the educated, property-owning class. It was believed that the people, blind and inconstant as they were thought, could only prove an instrument of reaction in the hands of the privileged. However, the future date of democracy was announced in the proclamation of the principle of the sovereignty of the people: and the republic, the logic form of democracy, was prepared by the diffusion of republican idea—for example, from America; by the sight of an impotent monarch and by the continual proclamation of the necessity of a violent revolution, which, undertaken in order to reform the monarchy, was to expose its very existence to the dangers of a general upheaval. The ruling classes of society were steeped in republicanism. Such a state of mind was so prevalent that if the King, in whom men saw the historical indispensable guide to a new France, were to fail in his mission, or discard, for example, his authority as hereditary defender of French independence, a republic would be accepted without dislike and without enthusiasm, first by the better class, and then by the mass of the nation.

*   *   *

We have seen that in 1789 there appeared to be two Frances; the enlightened France and the ignorant France, a rich France and a poor France. As for the political rights which the publicists of the day were demanding, it was only for the well-to-do and the educated that these rights were claimed. Owners of property were to be "active citizens" they alone having the right to vote. Those without property were to be "passive citizens." In short, "the nation is the *bourgeoisie*."

Between the *bourgeoisie* and the people there is a gulf. The richer classes exaggerate the stupidity and obliviousness of the people—above all, of the rural masses. There is ill-feeling and misunderstanding between the two classes. To clear up this misunderstanding will require a conference, a general meeting and mingling of the middle classes with the people as a whole.

Such a result will follow the convocation of the Estates-General.

At the Parish Assemblies the Third Estate is admitted almost without exception, under a slight property restriction, to fulfil the condition of being "included in the roll of taxpayers." This is very nearly universal suffrage.

Had royalty established this suffrage, so contrary to the ideas of the century, for the very reasons that induced the philosophers and the writers in favour of reform to reject it? Did the King hope, in the poor and ignorant masses, to find an element of resistance against the new and revolutionary ideas of the middle class? I have not found any documentary evidence which will allow me to answer this question precisely, but to me it does not seem impossible that the King did have some confused idea of appealing to universal suffrage against the opposition of the middle class, to darkness against light.

If such a calculation did really exist, it was disproved by the event.

To be sure, the *cahiers* are more timid than the books and pamphlets of the time; but as a general thing they demand a Constitution and a Constitution is the end of absolutism—it is, to some extent the Revolution.

Moreover, there are *cahiers* which are bold in the extreme.

However, neither the hopes of royalty nor the fears of the *bourgeoisie* were realised—supposing that such hopes and fears existed.

In any case, we must note how the misunderstanding between the *bourgeoisie* and the people was dissipated or diminished on the occasion of convocation and the drawing up of the *cahiers*.

Collaboration took place between the *bourgeoisie* and the people in the drafting of the *cahiers* of the first degree, or the parish *cahiers;* and in general we must not, in the case of rural communities, regard these *cahiers* as the personal work of peasants. It was usually a man of the middle classes who held the pen, and in most localities, even in the most rustic, there were a few educated men. The majority of the parish *cahiers* that we possess testify to a considerable amount of culture—a culture higher than that of the provincial middle classes of today.

If the *cahier* is not dictated by peasants, it is at least read to and approved by them. There is an assembly at which peasants and middle classes mingle together, chat with one another, and publicly discuss and debate. It is the first time such a colloquy has taken place; the occasion is a fraternal one, and the classes are quickly in agreement. The middle-class man sees that the peasant is more intelligent or less imbecile than he had supposed; that—by what obscure channels who knows?—the spirit of the times has touched him. The peasants, once they have met together, soon rise to the idea of a common interest; they have the sense that they are many and powerful, and they obtain, from the middle classes, a perception of their rights. For them this Parish Assembly is a civic apprenticeship.

We must not picture the whole peasantry rising at once to the revolutionary idea of the mother-country. But they take the Convocation seriously; they feel that it will bring about an event which will be beneficial to themselves, and they conceive an image of the King, an image which is a reflection of the idea of country. To them, it appears in deadly earnest that the King is going to concern himself with the cure of the ills which afflict them; it is in earnest that they recount these ills, or, rather, accept the account of them that the gentlemen of the village write for them; and when they sign with a cross at the bottom of the document, they have no fear that this cross will subject them to surcharges of taxation and the nuisance of collectors. By no means; their signature is an act of confidence and hope.

We have here no longer the vile populace, slighted and feared by Mably, Rousseau, and Condorcet. But it is not as yet the sovereign people. They are men who at last are counting on being treated as men; almost candidates for the dignity of citizen; and who, tomorrow, by an electric impulse issuing, at the fall of the Bastille, from Paris, will feel themselves animated by an impetus of union and agglomeration from which will issue the new nation, the new France.

Let us repeat that the middle classes also have found somewhat to learn at these assemblies—namely, to be less scornful of the poor and the ignorant. It is true that men will still declaim against the populace, and the middle class will even establish itself as a caste politically privileged. But enlightened Frenchmen will no longer, after this royal experiment in universal suffrage, be unanimous in declaring the unlettered to be incapable of exercising political rights. A democratic party is about to declare itself, and will soon be fully formed. The method of convening the Third Estate at the Estates-General allows us almost to foretell the advent of universal suffrage, and, as a consequence, the establishment of the Republic, the national form of Democracy.

Georges Lefebvre devoted his whole scholarly life to the study of the French Revolution. In 1939 his unmatched knowledge of the origins of the Revolution was distilled into the little book from which the following selection is drawn.

FROM *The Coming of the French Revolution*
BY *Georges Lefebvre*

THE PEASANTRY

THERE WAS SCARCELY ANY question of the peasants before July 14. Yet they formed at least three quarters of the population of the kingdom, and we realize today that without their adherence the Revolution could with difficulty have succeeded. Their grievances had been disregarded in the drafting of the bailiwick petitions, or had at best received little emphasis. Their complaints were by no means uppermost among the interests of the National Assembly, in which there were no peasant members. Then suddenly they too revolted, taking their cause into their own hands and delivering a death blow to what was left of the feudal and manorial system. The peasant uprising is one of the most distinctive features of the Revolution in France.

The Peasant and the Land

In 1789 the great majority of the French peasants had been free for many generations, i.e., they could move about and work as they wished, possess property and bring suit in the law courts. Some "serfs" could still be found, principally in Franche-Comté and the Nivernais, but they were no longer really attached to the soil, and in 1779 the king had even abolished the right of pursuit, which had allowed the lord to make good his claims over the serf wherever the latter might go. The main characteristic of serfdom in France was lack of freedom in disposing of goods. The serf was a *mainmortable* or man under a mortmain; if, at his death, he did not have at least one living child residing with him, all his possessions reverted to the lord. In France the serf was far better off than in central and eastern Europe, where the peasantry was left under the nobleman's arbitrary jurisdiction. In France the king's justice protected the rights and person of both serf and free man.

Not only were most French peasants not serfs. Many were landowners, differing in this respect from the peasants of England, who in general had been reduced by the landed aristocracy to the status of wage laborers. The size and number of peasant properties varied greatly from one region to another. They were most extensive in Alsace, Flanders, Limousin, parts of Normandy, the Loire valley, the plains of the Saône and the Garonne and generally throughout southern France more than in the North. In these regions peasants owned from half to three-quarters of the soil. Elsewhere the proportion fell much lower, notably in barren, marshy or forested regions and in the neighborhood of cities. Of the land around Versailles peasant ownership accounted for no more than one or two per cent. Thirty per cent is a probable average for the kingdom as a whole. The remaining land was owned by the clergy (probably a tenth of the kingdom), the nobles (over twice as much) and the bourgeoisie (perhaps a fifth). The clergy was especially wealthy in the North, less so as one went west and south. The nobles seem to have been wealthiest in the North, East and West. Bourgeois ownership of rural land was characteristic of the South.

Yet everywhere there were propertyless peasants. Rarely was the number of these rural proletarians negligible: it has been estimated at about a fifth of family heads in Limousin, thirty to forty per cent in the Norman woodlands, seventy per cent around Versailles and as high as seventy-five per cent in maritime Flanders. Some of these unpropertied peasants found land to rent. Ecclesiastics, noblemen and bourgeois seldom exploited their own lands, except in the wine country and in some parts of the South. Instead, they put them in the hands of farmers, or more often of sharecroppers with whom they divided the produce. Moreover, their estates consisted in many small unconnected parcels, which they were glad to lease out separately bit by bit. Hence the laborer could manage to procure a patch for himself, and the peasant owner, for his part, could supplement his own holdings with additional parcels taken on lease. In this way the rural proletariat in the strict sense, or peasants who had no land either by ownership or by leasehold, was substantially reduced while never disappearing entirely. Hence also rural society had as many gradations as society in the cities. The most well to do were the large farmers, who often owned no land themselves. Next came the substantial class, called *laboureurs,* who worked considerable tracts which they owned wholly or in part. They were followed, in downward order, by the small farmer, the sharecropper, the peasant having the use of some land but not enough to live on, the laborer possessing a house and garden plus some small parcel on lease and finally the laborer who had nothing but his hands.

Unfortunately the holdings of the overwhelming majority of the peasants were not large enough to support them and their families. Backward methods of cultivation were in part the cause. In the North and East the village lands were subdivided into countless long and narrow strips, which were grouped in three "fields." One field was sown with winter wheat, one with a spring crop, while the third lay fallow, i.e., uncultivated, each field changing its role from year to year. South of a line running from eastern Normandy to Burgundy and passing by Beauce there were only two fields, of which one always lay fallow. In the West, in Limousin and in the mountains, the cultivated areas, enclosed by hedges, comprised an even smaller fraction of the soil, the remaining land being worked only from time to time, sometimes only one year in ten, sometimes even less often. In any case, triennial or biennial rotation left a third or half the arable soil unproductive. Hence the peasant needed more land than today. In the region later comprised in the department of Nord nine families out of ten had too little to live on. The situation had grown worse since the middle of the eighteenth century, for the population had increased perceptibly, probably by three million. The number of proletarians had risen, while through division of inheritances the shares of property owners had become smaller. There was, therefore, at the end of the Old Regime, an agrarian crisis.

Hence many peasants invaded the commons when the king, in 1764 and 1766, granted exemption from tithes and taxes to persons who cleared new land. Borders of the forests, and open places within them, swarmed with barefoot pioneers who built themselves cabins, cleared what they could and felled timber either for sale or for conversion into charcoal. The marshes likewise hid a wretched population which lived by fishing or cutting peat. Peasant landowners, in the grievance-lists, roundly criticized the nobles and clergy who exploited their own estates directly, and demanded also that the big properties be leased out, not to a few large farmers, but to many small ones. In Picardy and Hainaut, when the owners tried to change farmers, the latter fought back against eviction, even to the point of arson and murder. It is therefore not surprising to find some parishes asking for alienation of the crown lands and even of part of the property of the clergy. But it is characteristic of the time that the property of individuals was never questioned. At the height of the Terror, when the property of *émigrés* and of persons condemned for political offenses was sold, and when it was decided also to confiscate the property of mere suspects, the principle was always that of penalizing enemies of the country. Nobles who stayed in France, and remained peaceable, never at any time during the Revolution saw their property threatened. This was because the land, when it was not the property of the peasants, was already in their hands on leasehold terms. Farm rentals, it is true, had almost doubled during the eighteenth century, while prices had gone up on the average not more than sixty-five per cent. Sharecropping too had become less favorable to the peasant; in general, the owner still took only half the crop or half the increment of livestock, but he increasingly imposed obligations of many kinds and even a supplemental payment in cash, especially in cases where sharing arrangements were managed through a "farmer-general," who found it to his advantage to bring pressure on the croppers. There was much bitter complaint on this score in Bourbonnais, Nivernais and Beaujolais. Nevertheless, despite all these grievances, the farmer or sharecropper would have nothing to gain by exchanging his leased holdings for the tiny parcel which a general redistribution of property would procure for him. And it is obvious that those peasants who already owned property would not have favored any such redistribution.

Taxes, Tithes, Fees, Dues

Keeping in mind that the agrarian crisis was real and pressing, we must recognize that there was only one matter on which the whole rural population could unanimously agree—namely, the obligations imposed by the king and the aristocracy.

The peasant was almost alone in paying the *taille* and drawing lots for militia service. He alone was held for road work and for aid in military transportation. From him came most of the proceeds of the poll-tax and the twentieth-taxes. Yet it was the indirect taxes that he detested the most, especially the government salt monopoly, which held the price of salt as high as thirteen sous a pound in a large part of the kingdom. The royal demands had steadily risen during the eighteenth century, and the parish grievance-lists of 1789 invariably complained of them, but we cannot say, in view of the general rise in the price level, whether they actually took a greater part of the national income in 1789 than a half century before. Probably they did. In Walloon Flanders, a region having Provincial Estates and hence getting off fairly lightly, the increase in direct taxes in the reign of Louis XVI alone has been estimated at twenty-eight per cent. The peasants, while critical of the bourgeois, observing that commercial wealth paid less than its proper share, were most especially aroused to a state of fury by the privileges of the aristocracy.

The royal taxation, a relatively new burden superimposed on the payments made from time immemorial to the aristocracy, undoubtedly had the indirect consequence of making these payments far more hateful. To the clergy was due the tithe, variable in amount but almost always less than a tenth, levied on the "great" grains, wheat, rye, oats and barley (the "great tithe"), and on other

grains and vegetables and fruits (the "small tithe"), and on a few animal products. From the peasant grievance-lists it is evident that the tithe would have
been more willingly paid if the proceeds, instead of going in most cases to
bishops, abbeys or chapters, or even to lay lords to whom the tithe might be
"subinfeudated" (the parish priest receiving the small tithe at most), had been
used, as they should have been, to support public worship, the parish church
and parsonage and above all the poor. But the peasant, after paying the tithe,
saw most of the expense for such purposes still falling upon himself. In addition the tithe had all the disadvantages of a levy collected in kind. The tithe
owner had to come and take it away himself; if he delayed, the whole crop
might suffer from bad weather; the peasant was deprived of straw, a material
necessary to manure, and the only one known to him. The tithe also blocked
the progress of land clearance and of new methods of cultivation. Since it was
collected in kind, a rise in prices made it more profitable to the collector; in
1789 the gross product was thought to be worth 120,000,000 livres. The profit
was greatest in times of scarcity, at the cost of the peasant's very subsistence;
and in any case, at all times, the tithe collector seemed a food hoarder by his
very nature.

What there was left of feudalism was even more disliked. The strictly feudal should be distinguished from the manorial. From the feudal point of view
land consisted of fiefs, depending one upon another and all finally upon the
king. Fiefs were subject to a law of their own, of which the law of primogeni-
ture is the best known; and with each change of owner the suzerain required
the vassal to make due acknowledgment, submit a survey of the estate and pay
a fee. Unless the peasant had bought a fief, which was rare at least in the
North, this system did not concern him. If he had bought a fief he paid
the king, as did the bourgeois in the same circumstances, a special fee called
the *franc-fief*.

During the eighteenth century the demands of manorial lords, like those of
the king, had become more burdensome for the peasants. Since the system had
been criticized by the philosophers and economists, manorial lords thought it
necessary to reaffirm their rights by frequently renewing the manor rolls in
which they were written down and by requiring exact payment. Increasingly
they farmed out their rights to professional collectors, who were inexorable in
their work, reviving and enforcing almost obsolete obligations, if indeed not
broadening them in a way that was positively an abuse. Where claims were
contested, the manorial courts and the Parliaments always decided against the
peasants. But what exasperated the rural people, since they had in any case too
little land for a livelihood, was the encroachment on their collective rights, on
which their existence depended.

*   *   *

Numerous are the peasant grievance-lists which complain, and complain bitterly, of these constant encroachments, as of the generally growing exactions of

the feudal class. They insist on the damage done to agriculture by the hunting rights, the dovecotes and the rabbit warrens in the absence of proper regulation and of any recourse. Payments in kind were subject to the same criticism as was the tithe. The petitions call attention to the crushing weight of all these dues taken together, finding it heavier than the parallel burden of the royal taxes. More rare are the petitions which propose remedies, such as suppression of certain rights considered particularly repugnant, or authorization to buy up the manorial dues. The principle of the system is never questioned, but we must note that the peasants did not express all that was on their minds, and that on the matter of manorial rights the bourgeois who assumed leadership over them were often reticent in their opinions, since manorial rights were a form of property, which some bourgeois had themselves purchased, and in which others had an interest as judges or agents for the manorial lords. Still, the deeper workings of the peasant mind can be seen in one way, when their petitions demand that the original document specifying payments in return for holdings be produced, and that in its absence such payments be brought to an end. The peasant proprietor, it is clear, thought himself the only legitimate owner of his land, and considered the payments due the lord, unless there was proof to the contrary, to have originated in nothing but violence. In some cases peasant rancor against lordly "bloodsuckers" did in fact express itself plainly. . . .

Against the aristocracy the peasants had far more substantial grievances than did the people of the cities, and it is natural therefore that they took it upon themselves to deal the blow by which the aristocracy was laid low.

THE AGRARIAN REVOLTS AND THE GREAT FEAR

The hatred of the peasants for the lords was not a thing of yesterday. The history of France abounds in *jacqueries*. In the eighteenth century the collection of manorial dues more than once led to troubles, and in particular engendered innumerable lawsuits which the peasants sustained with incredible tenacity. Yet if they were brought to a state of general rebellion in 1789 one reason is to be found in the convocation of the Estates-General. . . . The bailiwick lieutenant of Saumur observed, as the most unsettling feature of convocation of the Estates, that the electoral assemblies of the parishes thought themselves invested with sovereign authority, and that the rustics believed themselves already rid of the manorial dues. Cries of alarm rose everywhere in the kingdom in the course of the spring: the peasants were declaring their intention to make no payments at the coming harvest. Class solidarity asserted itself strongly. During the disturbances at Chatou the peasants took aside one of their number who seemed suspect, demanded of him, "Are you for the Third Estate?" and when he gave a negative answer told him, "Then we'll give you the idea!" The agrarian insurrections, more even than those of the cities, were genuine mass movements.

At the same time the idea of an "aristocratic conspiracy" grew up and rooted itself even more strongly than in the bourgeois, for the peasants knew by centuries of experience that in the eyes of the lord the manorial dues were untouchable—his social superiority depending on them as well as his income. That the lord would make every effort to deceive the "good king"; that if he failed in this he would take up arms to crush the Third Estate—all this seemed obvious and inevitable to the peasants. The inaction of the Estates-General and their silence on matters of concern to the peasants were attributed to an aristocratic conspiracy. When news came of the resort to force, what doubt could there be? And when it was learned that the king, visiting his insurgent capital, had given his approval to the resistance which had blocked the aristocrats, what reservations could any longer be felt? During the ensuing revolts the peasants insisted that they were executing the king's will. Smuggled orders circulated among them, ostensibly emanating from the king.

* * *

Yet the same observation must be made of the country as of the towns. The peasant rising would be inconceivable without the excitement produced by the calling of the Estates-General. But it is undeniable also that the economic crisis contributed powerfully to it, and reinforced also the idea of an aristocratic plot. The rural masses suffered cruelly from food shortages, contrary to what might be supposed, for most peasants raised too little to subsist on, and when the harvest was bad the number of those in want increased perceptibly as the year went on. They would go to make purchases at the neighboring market, become involved in the disturbances there and on returning spread trouble and a sense of insecurity through their home parishes. In the open country they would stop shipments of food without hesitation, so that during the summer of 1789 disorder became universal. As for the causes and possible remedies for the problem, they held the same views as the small people of the towns. Regulation was their panacea, the hoarder their enemy.

* * *

Hence the economic crisis had revolutionary consequences in two ways. On the one hand it enflamed the peasants by turning them against the tithe owners and lords who took away part of their livelihood through the manorial dues. On the other hand, by multiplying the number of those in want, it generalized a sense of insecurity which in the end was blamed on a conspiracy of the aristocrats.

The Agrarian Revolts

Just as fear in no sense dated from July 14, so it would be wrong to imagine that the peasant waited for the example of the capital to revolt. The example of the nearest town was sufficient, and even this was by no means indispensable. At the end of March the high price of bread led to popular uprisings at Toulon and Marseilles, from which agitation spread immediately to all upper Provence. The villages of the Avance Valley, in the region of Gap, rose in insurrection against their lord on April 20. On May 6 a riot broke out at Cambrai; the whole Cambrésis was instantly aflame; the contagion spread to Picardy. Near Paris and Versailles the peasants organized a systematic extermination of game, pillaged the forests and fired on the wardens.

* * *

These disturbances were all aimed against the aristocracy.

CONCLUSION

The Revolution of 1789 consisted first of all in the fall of absolute monarchy and advent of a liberty henceforth guaranteed by constitutional government; nor on this score can it be doubted that it was a national revolution, since the privileged orders as well as the Third Estate demanded a constitution and a regime in which individual rights would be respected.

But it was also the advent of equality before the law, without which liberty would be but another privilege of the powerful. For the French of 1789 liberty and equality were inseparable, almost two words for the same thing; but had they been obliged to choose, it is equality that they would have chosen; and when the peasants, who formed the overwhelming majority, cheered the conquest of liberty they were in fact thinking of the disappearance of the authority of the manorial lord, and his reduction to the status of a mere citizen. They were thinking, that is, of equality.

Thus made free and equal in rights, the French founded the nation anew, one and indivisible, by voluntary consent, in the movements called federations and especially in the Federation of July 14, 1790. This third characteristic of the Revolution of 1789 was one of its most original features, and the assertion that a people has the right to dispose of itself, and cannot be annexed to another without its own adherence freely expressed, has exerted an influence by no means yet exhausted in the world.

Moreover, the men of 1789 never entertained the idea that the rights of man and citizen were reserved for Frenchmen only. Christianity drew no distinction among men; it called on them all to meet as brothers in the divine city. In the same way the revolutionaries thought of liberty and equality as the common birthright of mankind. Imagining that all peoples would emulate their example, they even dreamed for an instant that the nations, in becoming free, would be reconciled forever in universal peace.

In the view of the lawyers, who represented and guided the bourgeoisie, the Revolution was to be a peaceful readjustment, imposed by opinion and translated rather simply into new juridical formulations. And in fact the essential work of the Revolution of 1789 may be found registered in the resolutions of

August 4 and in the Declaration of Rights of Man and the Citizen. But it would be childish to emphasize only these legislative enactments, throwing into the background the events which gave them birth; childish likewise, and indeed more so, to select from among these events certain ones to compose a legend. The Estates-General skillfully and boldly defended the cause of the Third Estate which was the cause of the nation, but as even Buchez admitted, a peace-loving and Catholic democrat of 1848, "The Assembly would have achieved nothing without the insurrections." The Old Regime did not bend before the juridical revolution. Having taken to force, it was destroyed by force, which the people, descending into the street, put at the service of what they regarded as right, though even their own representatives had not dared to ask such assistance from them.

Whether the resort to violence was *in principle* necessary or unnecessary the historian cannot know. He observes simply that in the spring of 1789 the French people still had no thought of it, and that two years earlier they did not even suspect the regime to be nearing its end. It was the aristocracy that precipitated the Revolution by forcing the king to call the Estates-General. Once the Third Estate obtained the right to express itself, the possibility of concessions which would have satisfied it for a time depended on the nobles and on the king. The issue was not so much political in character as social; for the transformation of the monarchy into a constitutional government was a reform on which nobles and bourgeois agreed, and by which Louis XVI would have lost little authority; but the great majority of the nobles, while prepared to make concessions in the direction of fiscal equality, were determined, more from pride than from material interest, to preserve their other privileges and remain a nation within the nation. One wonders whether the year 1789 might not have become the first phase of an evolutionary movement, during which the nobles would have gradually come to accept the status of mere citizens. It is possible, and, if one likes, even probable; but, since we cannot run history over like an experiment in a laboratory, opinions on this question will always be divided. In any case, what actually happened is that the necessary decisions were not made in time, that the Court turned to force to protect the aristocracy and that the problem was therefore presented in all its fullness. The Third Estate, driven to the wall, had to choose between resistance and surrender, so that in fact insurrection became inevitable, considering that fundamentally the Third was resolved to stand its ground.

* * *

Still it need hardly be said that many motives combined to bring the French people to their supreme dilemma. We have attempted to single them out. Class interests and personal interests, humbled pride, mass suffering, philosophical propaganda all made their contribution, in proportions different for each individual, but with the net effect of producing in the Third Estate a collective mentality that was strangely complex, but which in summary expressed itself as a belief in an aristocratic conspiracy, a belief which in turn aroused passionate feelings, the fear, the frenzy for fighting, the thirst for revenge that characterized the days of July.

Dismayed by popular excesses, the bourgeoisie tried to blame them on provocative agents, foreigners, "brigands" and criminals such as inevitably mingled with the insurgents. It is true that men who are the dregs of society are not the last to take part in mobs. But the allegations of the Assembly and the bourgeois authorities have a note of apology. The ordinary people neither condemned nor repudiated the murders of July, nor did Barnave or Mme. Roland. The elements in the revolutionary complex cannot be taken apart. In this sense Clemenceau was right: the Revolution is a *bloc,* a single thing. The moralist must praise heroism and condemn cruelty; but the moralist does not explain events.

*　*　*

Much labor has been spent in contesting the originality of the Declaration, in deducing its substance, for example, from the bills of rights adopted by the American colonists in the struggle that won their independence. The men of the Constituent Assembly were undoubtedly familiar with these documents, especially the one issued by Virginia on May 10, 1776. The inspiration and content of the American and French declarations were the same. It was in fact with Jefferson, as early as January 1789, that La Fayette discussed his project; the text that he presented to the Assembly on July 11, with the accompanying letter, has been found in the papers of the ambassador of the United States, annotated by his own hand. The influence of America is beyond question. But this is not to say that without America the French declaration would not have seen the light. The whole philosophic movement in France in the eighteenth century pointed to such an act; Montesquieu, Voltaire and Rousseau had collaborated in its making. In reality, America and France, like England before them, were alike tributaries to a great stream of ideas, which, while expressing the ascendancy of the bourgeoisie, constituted a common ideal that summarized the evolution of western civilization.

*　*　*

Many objections have been made to the Declaration. Some have already been mentioned because they apply to the circumstances in which it was debated in the Assembly. Others of more general bearing merit a moment's further attention.

The Declaration, it has been said, is a mere abstraction from real life. Some men may be worthy of the rights it proclaims; some are less so; some, indeed, are hardly human. For cannibals, for example, the rights of man can have no real application; and if it be argued that even cannibals are human beings, still they are scarcely human in our sense. Nor, it is alleged, does the Declaration allow for circumstances. If war or economic crisis endanger a nation's existence, are the rights of its citizens to have the same free scope as in times of prosperity? And if individual rights are not inherently limited, will not the government be granted the power to limit them?

There is no force in this criticism except when the Declaration is confused with a legal code, whereas its nature is that of moral principle, not of positive legislation. We are bound by moral principle, for example—as well as by the Declaration—not to do to another what we should not wish him to do to us. Moral principle does not specify what our conduct should be in each particular case; it leaves this task to the moralist or the casuist. Similarly the Declaration proclaims the rights of man, but leaves to the law, which may vary with circumstances, the task of determining the extent, which may also vary with circumstances, to which these rights may be exercised, always providing that the law is the true expression of the general will, i.e., of the majority of the community. That the members of the National Assembly considered this to be the character of the Declaration is clear from the debates in which, a month before its adoption, they discussed the operations of counter revolutionaries and considered setting up a special court: governing in wartime is not like governing in peacetime, observed Gouy d'Arsy, anticipating Robespierre. Again, when the question of slavery arose, the relativism in the Declaration became apparent; it was judged impossible to transfer the Negroes abruptly, without apprenticeship in freedom, from slavery to the full status of citizenship. And the Assembly reached by implication the same conclusion for France, when it made the right to vote depend on degree of economic well-being, and the right to be elected depend on the owning of real estate, because, rightly or wrongly, it regarded such economic well-being, and especially the ownership of land, as the only means of assuring the enlightenment and self-restraint thought necessary to the exercise of the rights of man and of citizenship. These rights then are relative to circumstances. The Declaration is an ideal to be realized. It is a *direction of intention*.

Another criticism, vehemently raised in our day, is that it favored one class at the expense of others, namely the bourgeoisie that drew it up, and that it thus provoked a disorder that threatens the community with disruption. The Declaration did indeed list property among the rights of man, and its authors meant property as it then existed and still does; moreover, economic liberty, though not mentioned, is very much in its spirit. This amounts to saying that the man who holds the land and the other instrumentalities of labor, i.e., capital, is in fact master of those who possess nothing but their muscles and their intelligence, because they depend on him for the opportunity to earn their living. The evil is made worse, it is added, by the inheritance of property, which endows certain children, irrespective of merit or capacity, with the *means* over and above the *rights* which are all that others receive. The Declaration, in short, is blamed for having allowed capitalism to develop without control and for having thus caused the proletariat to rise against it—to have had as a consequence a new class struggle of an always accelerating violence, all for want of some power of arbitration that can be granted only to the state. Contrariwise, those who deny such a power to the state have not failed to invoke the Declaration, elaborating upon it with ideas drawn from its own authors, who undoubtedly held to *laissez-faire* and unlimited competition as universal panaceas, and conceived of property as an absolute right to use or to abuse.

Here again, for a reply, we must appeal to the Constituents themselves. They had before their eyes a society in which modern capitalism was barely beginning, and in which the increase of productive capacity seemed the essential corrective to poverty and want. Even to those who gave thought to the poor it seemed not impossible that every man might own a few acres or a shop that would make him self-sufficient; and this ideal, which was that of the *sans-culottes,* remained alive well into the nineteenth century. Experience has not justified these hopes. Rousseau had already observed, long before 1789, that democracy is not compatible with an excessive inequality of wealth. It is for the community to examine whether the changes since 1789 in the economic and social structure of society do not justify intervention by the law, so that the excess of *means* in the hands of some may not reduce the *rights* of others to an empty show. By what procedure? That too is for the community to decide, in the spirit of the Declaration, which in proclaiming liberty did not mean an aristocratic liberty reserved for a few, such as Montalambert demanded in 1850, but which rather, confiding to the law the task of delimiting the rights of citizens, left it to take the measures that may be suitable to prevent social disruption.

Finally, according to other critics, the Declaration regards law as simply the will of the citizens; but what would become of the nation if the majority oppressed the minority, or if it refused to make the necessary sacrifices which in time of war may reach to life itself? The community, this school concludes, cannot be identified with the citizens who make it up at a given moment; extending beyond them in time, it is hierarchically above them, for without it they would not exist; it is really embodied in the state, which in consequence cannot depend on the will of ephemeral citizens, and for that reason has the right to coerce them. With this idea, it need hardly be said, we return to the personal absolutism of the Old Regime, for the state, whatever may be said, has itself no effective existence except in individual persons, who by and large would confer their mandates upon themselves. Still less need it be remarked that this system is in radical contradiction with the Declaration in reducing the individual to be a mere instrument in the hands of the state, depriving him of all liberty and all self-determination.

But these answers do not remove the difficulty, as too often we delude ourselves into believing. It is perfectly true that the Declaration carries with it a risk, as do absolutism and dictatorship, though the risk is of another kind. The citizens must be made to face their responsibilities. Invested with the rights of governing themselves, if they abuse their powers with respect to one another, above all if they refuse from personal selfishness to assure the welfare of the community, the community will perish, and with it their liberty, if not indeed their existence.

We come here to the deeper meaning of the Declaration. It is a direction of intention; it therefore requires of the citizens an integrity of purpose, which is to say a critical spirit, patriotism in the proper sense of the word, respect for the rights of others, reasoned devotion to the national community, "virtue" in the language of Montesquieu, Rousseau and Robespierre. "The soul of the Republic," wrote Robespierre in 1792, "is virtue, love of country, the generous devotion that fuses all interests into the general interest." The Declaration in proclaiming the rights of man appeals at the same time to discipline freely consented to, to sacrifice if need be, to cultivation of character *and to the mind*. Liberty is by no means an invitation to indifference or to irresponsible power; nor is it the promise of unlimited well-being without a counterpart of toil and effort. It supposes application, perpetual effort, strict government of self, sacrifice in contingencies, civic and private virtues. It is therefore more difficult to live as a free man than to live as a slave, and that is why men so often renounce their freedom; for freedom is in its way an invitation to a life of courage, and sometimes of heroism, as the freedom of the Christian is an invitation to a life of sainthood.

The Industrial Revolution in England— Blessing or Curse to the Working Man?

CONTENTS

QUESTIONS FOR STUDY

1 What was the condition of the rural workers in the eighteenth century?
2 What essential changes were required of a person when a shift was made from the country to a manufacturing city?
3 What working conditions were detrimental to the children employed in factories? What conditions might be beneficial?
4 What are the main points at issue between the Hammonds and Ashton?
5 By what criteria can a judgment be made on whether the Industrial Revolution was a blessing or a curse to the working man?

During the eighteenth century a series of economic changes in agricultural and industrial production in Great Britain gave rise to what historians later labeled the Industrial Revolution. There can be no doubt that this revolution has drastically altered all the old relationships—economic, political, and social—and has led to new conditions and problems with which we are still wrestling. Industrialization was and is a painful process, requiring considerable upheaval, individual and mass dislocations, and needless suffering. We may still ask the questions: Was it worth it? Does industrialization profit only the few, or is industrialization necessary for everyone's well-being? Today half the world is rushing into industrialization, while the industrialized half is once more pausing to take stock. The passage of almost two centuries may permit us to assess the Industrial Revolution with dispassion and some claim to objectivity. To do so, however, we must have some idea of what conditions were before and after industrialization took place.

At the beginning of the eighteenth century the great mass of the English people lived on the land and from it. Some were wealthy independent farmers, others were tenant farmers whose wealth was determined in large part by their industry, and some were cottagers living in rural poverty, barely able to glean a living from the common land and their small patches of rented land. This last group was particularly subject to the vagaries of weather and agricultural production. If there was a food shortage, they were the first to suffer, and in famine they were the first to die. Their cottages were hovels, and they had little incentive for improvement, since they could never hope to rise above the subsistence level. It took a good deal of capital to set oneself up as an independent farmer, and the cottager could never hope to amass the necessary amount. The diet of the cottager was poor and monotonous, rarely including meat. Infant mortality was high, illiteracy was the rule, and life was brutish, boring, and short. It seemed impossible that it could get worse, but it did. The Enclosure Acts of the eighteenth century enclosed common land to the profit of the landowner and at the expense of the cottager. Sometimes the cottager found himself immediately expelled, since his cottage was on the common land, or—what ultimately amounted to the same thing—he found his cow or pigs excluded from the common. With this margin of survival removed, he and his family had to leave or go on the poor rolls. From this ever-widening pool of misery came the people who migrated to the cities, particularly London, and there created that urban poverty-stricken mass familiar in Hogarth's etchings and in such works as The Beggar's Opera. It is important to realize that these effects were present before the Industrial Revolution properly got under way.

The Industrial Revolution began simply enough. The British conquest of India in the Seven Years' War introduced Britons and Europeans to the wonders and cheapness of cotton goods. Their gay colors and low price created a mass market that could not be satisfied by importation from India. Mills were built in England and raw cotton was imported, particularly from Egypt and India. American cotton, it may be noted, did not assume importance until the inven-

tion of the cotton gin in the 1790s, which permitted the cheap production of the short staple variety that thrived in the American South. The inventions that spurred production were extremely simple in the beginning. Kay's flying shuttle and Crompton's and Arkwright's improvements of spinning machinery were the products of inspired whittling, not of engineering or applied science. One innovation had far-reaching effects—namely, the use of water power to provide the energy for spinning and weaving on a mass scale. The old method, used in the woolens industry and hallowed by centuries of tradition, had relied on spinners and weavers working in their cottages with individual spinning wheels and handlooms to produce woolen cloth. Such a system could not satisfy the mass demand for cotton goods, and the new machines permitted the concentration of production in one place—the factory. In order to be profitable factory production required full-time labor and strict discipline. Fortunately for the British capitalist, a large pool of labor was available in the displaced agricultural population victimized by the Enclosure Acts. This population had to submit to the new discipline or face starvation. The substitution of the factory for the cottage worked a social revolution, for what was created was a new industrial working class that depended upon the factory for its livelihood. With the invention of the Watt steam engine, factories were freed geographically from dependence upon water power and tended to cluster in new cities. Manchester is the classic example, growing from a sleepy village to a bustling city in one generation.

It is Manchester's and Birmingham's "red, Satanic mills" that have served ever since the eighteenth century to characterize the effects of industrialization. The concomitant evils of slums, epidemic diseases, exploitation, and the sweating of labor were now both obvious and obtrusive even to the casual observer. Rural misery had been discreetly hidden behind hedges; urban squalor was there for everyone to see. The reaction in England was immediate, and critics of industrialization were both numerous and vociferous. The question is: Were they also right? Did industrialization dehumanize men and plunge them into economic slavery, or did it rescue them from starvation and from what Karl Marx later called "the idiocy of rural life"?

1

The Industrial Revolution Defined

The term "Industrial Revolution" was first given common currency in the lectures of Arnold Toynbee (1852–1883). It is in one of these lectures that he gave the classic definition of the fundamental economic changes that England had undergone in the years following 1750.

FROM *Lectures on the Industrial Revolution of the 18th Century in England*

BY *Arnold Toynbee*

THE ESSENCE OF THE INDUSTRIAL REVOLUTION is the substitution of competition for the mediaeval regulations which had previously controlled the production and distribution of wealth. . . .

Coming to the facts of the Industrial Revolution, the first thing that strikes us is the far greater rapidity which marks the growth of population. Before 1751 the largest decennial increase, so far as we can calculate from our imperfect materials, was 3 per cent. For each of the next three decennial periods the increase was 6 per cent.; then between 1781 and 1791 it was 9 per cent.; between 1791 and 1801, 11 per cent.; between 1801 and 1811, 14 per cent.; between 1811 and 1821, 18 per cent. This is the highest figure ever reached in England, for since 1815 a vast emigration has been always tending to moderate it; between 1815 and 1880 over eight millions (including Irish) have left our shores. But for this our normal rate of increase would be 16 or 18 instead of 12 per cent. in every decade.

Next we notice the relative and positive decline in the agricultural population. In 1811 it constituted 35 per cent. of the whole population of Great Britain; in 1821, 33 per cent.; in 1831, 28 per cent. And at the same time its actual numbers have decreased. In 1831 there were 1,243,057 adult males employed in agriculture in Great Britain; in 1841 there were 1,207,989. In 1851

Arnold Toynbee, *Lectures on the Industrial Revolution of the 18th Century in England* (1887), pp. 85, 87–93. Reprinted by permission.

the whole number of persons engaged in agriculture in England was 2,084,153; in 1861 it was 2,010,454, and in 1871 it was 1,657,138. Contemporaneously with this change, the centre of density of population has shifted from the Midlands to the North; there are at the present day 458 persons to the square mile in the countries north of the Trent, as against 312 south of the Trent. And we have lastly to remark the change in the relative population of England and Ireland. Of the total population of the three kingdoms, Ireland had in 1821 32 per cent., in 1881 only 14.6 per cent.

An agrarian revolution plays as large part in the great industrial change of the end of the eighteenth century as does the revolution in manufacturing industries, to which attention is more usually directed. Our next inquiry must therefore be: What were the agricultural changes which led to this noticeable decrease in the rural population? The three most effective causes were: the destruction of the common-field system of cultivation; the enclosure, on a large scale, of common and waste lands; and the consolidation of small farms into large. We have already seen that while between 1710 and 1760 some 300,000 acres were enclosed, between 1760 and 1843 nearly 7,000,000 underwent the same process. Closely connected with the enclosure system was the substitution of large for small farms. In the first half of the century Laurence, though approving of consolidation from an economic point of view, had thought that the odium attaching to an evicting landlord would operate as a strong check upon it. But these scruples had now disappeared. Eden in 1795 notices how constantly the change was effected, often accompanied by the conversion of arable to pasture; and relates how in a certain Dorsetshire village he found two farms where twenty years ago there had been thirty. The process went on uninterruptedly into the present century. Cobbett, writing in 1826, says: "In the parish of Burghclere one single farmer holds, under Lord Carnarvon, as one farm, the lands that those now living remember to have formed fourteen farms, bringing up in a respectable way fourteen families." The consolidation of farms reduced the number of farmers, while the enclosures drove the labourers off the land, as it became impossible for them to exist without their rights of pasturage for sheep and geese on common lands.

Severely, however, as these changes bore upon the rural population, they wrought, without doubt, distinct improvement from an agricultural point of view. They meant the substitution of scientific for unscientific culture. "It has been found," says Laurence, "by long experience, that common or open fields are great hindrances to the public good, and to the honest improvement which every one might make of his own." Enclosures brought an extension of arable cultivation and the tillage of inferior soils; and in small farms of 40 to 100 acres, where the land was exhausted by repeated corn crops, the farm buildings of clay and mud walls and three-fourths of the estate often saturated with water, consolidation into farms of 100 to 500 acres meant rotation of crops, leases of nineteen years, and good farm buildings. The period was one of great agricultural advance; the breed of cattle was improved, rotation of crops was generally

introduced, the steam-plough was invented, agricultural societies were instituted. In one respect alone the change was injurious. In consequence of the high
prices of corn which prevailed during the French war, some of the finest permanent pastures were broken up. Still, in spite of this, it was said in 1813 that
during the previous ten years agricultural produce had increased by one-fourth,
and this was an increase upon a great increase in the preceding generation.

Passing to manufactures, we find here the all-prominent fact to be the
substitution of the factory for the domestic system, the consequence of the
mechanical discoveries of the time. Four great inventions altered the character
of the cotton manufacture: the spinning-jenny, patented by Hargreaves in 1770;
the water-frame, invented by Arkwright the year before; Crompton's mule introduced in 1779, and the self-acting mule, first invented by Kelly in 1792, but not
brought into use till Roberts improved it in 1825. None of these by themselves
would have revolutionised the industry. But in 1769–the year in which
Napoleon and Wellington were born–James Watt took out his patent for the
steam-engine. Sixteen years later it was applied to the cotton manufacture. In
1785 Boulton and Watt made an engine for a cotton-mill at Papplewick in Notts,
and in the same year Arkwright's patent expired. These two facts taken together
mark the introduction of the factory system. But the most famous invention of
all, and the most fatal to domestic industry, the power-loom, though also
patented by Cartwright in 1785, did not come into use for several years, and till
the power-loom was introduced the workman was hardly injured. At first, in
fact, machinery raised the wages of spinners and weavers owing to the great
prosperity it brought to the trade. In fifteen years the cotton trade trebled itself;
from 1788 to 1803 has been called "its golden age"; for, before the power-loom
but after the introduction of the mule and other mechanical improvements by
which for the first time yarn sufficiently fine for muslin and a variety of other
fabrics was spun, the demands became such that "old barns, cart-houses, out-
buildings of all descriptions were repaired, windows broke through the old
blank walls, and all fitted up for loom-shops; new weavers' cottages with loom-
shops arose in every direction, every family bringing home weekly from 40 to
120 shillings per week." At a later date, the condition of the workman was very
different. Meanwhile, the iron industry had been equally revolutionised by the
invention of smelting by pit-coal brought into use between 1740 and 1750, and
by the application in 1788 of the steam-engine to blast furnaces. In the eight
years which followed this latter date, the amount of iron manufactured nearly
doubled itself.

A further growth of the factory system took place independent of machinery, and owed its origin to the expansion of trade, an expansion which was
itself due to the great advance made at this time in the means of communication. The canal system was being rapidly developed throughout the country. In
1777 the Grand Trunk canal, 96 miles in length, connecting the Trent and
Mersey, was finished; Hull and Liverpool were connected by one canal while
another connected them both with Bristol; and in 1792, the Grand Junction

canal, 90 miles in length, made a waterway from London through Oxford to the chief midland towns. Some years afterwards, the roads were greatly improved under Telford and Macadam; between 1818 and 1829 more than a thousand additional miles of turnpike road were constructed; and the next year, 1830, saw the opening of the first railroad. These improved means of communication caused an extraordinary increase in commerce, and to secure a sufficient supply of goods it became the interest of the merchants to collect weavers around them in great numbers, to get looms together in a workshop, and to give out the warp themselves to the workpeople. To these latter this system meant a change from independence to dependence; at the beginning of the century the report of a committee asserts that the essential difference between the domestic and the factory system is, that in the latter the work is done "by persons who have no property in the goods they manufacture." Another direct consequence of this expansion of trade was the regular recurrence of periods of over-production and of depression, a phenomenon quite unknown under the old system, and due to this new form of production on a large scale for a distant market.

These altered conditions in the production of wealth necessarily involved an equal revolution in its distribution. In agriculture the prominent fact is an enormous rise in rents. Up to 1795, though they had risen in some places, in others they had been stationary since the Revolution. But between 1790 and 1833, according to Porter, they at least doubled. In Scotland, the rental of land, which in 1795 had amounted to £2,000,000, had risen in 1815 to £5,278,685. A farm in Essex, which before 1793 had been rented at 10s. an acre, was let in 1812 at 50s., though, six years after, this had fallen again to 35s. In Berks and Wilts, farms which in 1790 were let at 14s., were let in 1810 at 70s., and in 1820 at 50s. Much of this rise, doubtless, was due to money invested in improvements—the first Lord Leicester is said to have expended £400,000 on his property—but it was far more largely the effect of the enclosure system, of the consolidation of farms, and of the high price of corn during the French war. Whatever may have been its causes, however, it represented a great social revolution, a change in the balance of political power and in the relative position of classes. The farmers shared in the prosperity of the landlords; for many of them held their farms under beneficial leases, and made large profits by them. In consequence, their character completely changed; they ceased to work and live with their labourers, and became a distinct class. The high prices of the war time thoroughly demoralised them, for their wealth then increased so fast, that they were at a loss what to do with it. Cobbett has described the change in their habits, the new food and furniture, the luxury and drinking, which were the consequences of more money coming into their hands than they knew how to spend. Meanwhile, the effect of all these agrarian changes upon the condition of the labourer was an exactly opposite and most disastrous one. He felt all the burden of high prices, while his wages were steadily falling, and he had lost his common-rights. It is from this period, viz., the beginning of the present century, that the alienation between farmer and labourer may be dated.

Exactly analogous phenomena appeared in the manufacturing world. The new class of great capitalist employers made enormous fortunes, they took little or no part personally in the work of their factories, their hundreds of workmen were individually unknown to them; and as a consequence, the old relations between masters and men disappeared, and a "cash nexus" was substituted for the human tie. The workmen on their side resorted to combination, and Trades-Unions began a fight which looked as if it were between mortal enemies rather than joint producers. The misery which came upon large sections of the working people at this epoch was often, though not always, due to a fall in wages, for, as I said above, in some industries they rose. But they suffered likewise from the conditions of labour under the factory system, from the rise of prices, especially from the high price of bread before the repeal of the corn-laws, and from those sudden fluctuations of trade, which, ever since production has been on a large scale, have exposed them to recurrent periods of bitter distress. The effects of the Industrial Revolution prove that free competition may produce wealth without producing well-being. We all know the horrors that ensued in England before it was restrained by legislation and combination.

2

The World That Was Lost

Arthur Young (1741–1820) was a prosperous farmer who devoted his life to the improvement of agriculture. He traveled widely, keeping a journal in which he noted the condition of the countryside and reporting what he saw in the journal Annals of Agriculture *or in separate publications. These reports give an excellent insight into the conditions of Great Britain just as it plunged into the Industrial Revolution; they were first published in 1768–1771.*

FROM *Tours in England and Wales*

BY *Arthur Young*

OCTOBER 23, 1776, LANDED AT MILFORD haven from Ireland. The whole country is inclosed, without such a thing as a common field. The food of the poor, bread and cheese, with broth made of salt meat, paid in at the cheapest season; much fish also eaten by them. Many keep cows; no goats on the mountains. The cottages many of them not a whit better than Irish cabbins, without an equal show of pigs, poultry and cows. Labour 8d. in the winter, and 10d. in summer, the year round. The whole country is in gentle inequalities; and, if wooded would be beautiful.

To Narbarth. Several cottages building in the Irish way, of mud with straw. The poor people seem well cloathed and fed. They use through all this country small heavy carts with two oxen and two or three horses, the driver sits on the front of the cart, and drives with reins.

October 24th to St. Clear. From Narbarth to Hubberston the course is. Rents 7s. 6d. to 10s. the whole farm through; to 14s. on some farms. Farms rise to very large ones, but in general small. The Irish cottar system is found here— 3 or 4 cottages to a farm of 40 or 50l. a year. They are always at the call of the farmers, they are allowed two or three grass fields at a moderate rent, a cow or two, but no pigs, unless one in a year, to kill at Christmas. Strangers get in winter 4d. a day, and food; without food 8d. in harvest 1s. 1s. 6d. and food. They live on bread and cheese, and milk, or water; no beer, nor meat, except on a

Arthur Young, *Tours in England and Wales Selected from the Annals of Agriculture* (1932), pp. 45, 47, 49, 87–90, 115, 157–158, 205, 217, 223–224, 274–275. Reprinted by permission.

Sunday. The culture of potatoes increases much, more planted last year than ever known before. The poor eat them; and every cabbin has a garden with some in it. Many iron furnaces, the ore dug in the country. The poor spin a good deal of wool, and weave it into flannel for their own wear, no linen is worn by them, flannel supplying the place. Query, to the physicians of the country—Is the rheumatism known here as much as in other countries where linen is worn? They make cloth also for their own wear. Weavers earn 1s. a day, and sometimes more. The poor live on barley-bread, cheese, and butter; not one in ten have either cows or pigs, fare very poorly and rarely touch meat. Their little gardens they plant with cabbages, carrots, leeks, and potatoes. Rent of a cottage and garden, 10s. to 20s. Building a mud cabbin costs 10l.

* * *

Crossed the Severn at the ferry at Lincoln Hill, in the midst of a most noble scenery of exceeding bold mountainous tracts, with that river rolling at the bottom. The opposite shore is one immense steep of hanging wood, which has the finest effect imaginable. Mounted through that wood, thickly scattered with cottages, the inhabitants busily employed in the vast works of various kinds carried on in the neighbourhood. One circumstance I remarked which gave me much pleasure. There was not a single cottage in which a fine hog did not seem to make a part of every family; not a door without a stone trough with the pig eating his supper, in company with the children at the same business playful about the threshold. It was a sight which shewed that chearfulness and plenty crowned the board of the humble but happy inhabitants of this romantic spot.

About St. Neot's a vast improvement by an inclosure, which took place 16 years ago, which makes the country much more beautiful, and has been a great benefit to the community. A gentleman of the town however complained, as I rode thither with him, that, notwithstanding the productiveness of the soil was certainly greater, yet that the poor were ill-treated by having about half a rood given them in lieu of a *cow keep,* the inclosure of which land costing more than they could afford, they sold the lots at 5l., the money was drank out at the ale-house, and the men, spoiled by the habit, came, with their families, to the parish; by which means poor rates had risen from 2s. 6d. to 3s. and 3s. 6d. But pray, sir, have not rates arisen equally in other parishes, where no inclosure has taken place? Admitted. And what can be the good of commons, which would not prevent poor rates coming to such a height? Better modes of giving the poor a share might easily, and have been, as in other cases, adopted.

* * *

In the open fields the farms are generally small, usually about 70l. a-year: these little occupations with which the Duke of Grafton, and other good landlords have patience in order to nurse up industrious families, are yet a heavy loss in repairs: and sometimes in other circumstances: inclosed farms rise to 300l.

which is the greatest; there are but few of 200l. to 250l. In farms of a tolerable size, the tenantry are substantial, and it gave me great pleasure to find them with such confidence in their landlord, as to raise considerable erections on the Duke's farms at their own expence, in articles beyond the common demands of the country; as a hay barn, &c. &c. and this while tenants at will; a sure proof that they regard their landlord as their father and their friend.

The 7th. To Measham, where Mr. Wilkes shewed us his many and great improvements; the manor and estate he purchased some years ago of Mr. Wollaston, of Finborough, in Suffolk, for 50,000l. The buildings erected and erecting will speedily change the face of it. Here are two cotton and a corn mill, two steam engines; many weaving-shops, and a number of cottages built; a large and handsome inn; . . . a few of the old thatched hovels remain to shew what this place was; what it will be may easily be conceived. But what is done here in ten or a dozen years by one man, who has been at the same time engaged in many other great undertakings, who, in union with Mr. Peele, is giving a new face to Faseley and Tamworth, cannot but make any one from the Continent admire at the wonderful exertions active in this kingdom—and in this kingdom only, for there is nothing out of it in the manufacturing world that is not, comparatively speaking, fast asleep.

A manufacturing town—Birmingham in the 1790s.

These immense works, which wear so animated a face of business, correspond well with the prodigious increase of the town, which I viewed to good advantage from the top of the new church of St. Paul: it is now a very great city indeed; and it was abundantly curious to have it pointed out to me the parts added since I was here. They form the greatest part of the town, and carry in their countenance undoubted marks of their modern date. In 1768 the population was under 30,000; now the common calculation is 70,000, but more accurate calculation extends it to 80,000, which I am told is the number assigned by Dr. Priestley. In the last 10 years above 4000 new houses have been built: and the increase is at present going on much more rapidly, for I was told that the number this year is not less than 700.

The earnings of the workmen in the manufacture are various, but in general very high: a boy of 10 or 12 years, 2s. 6d. to 3s. a week; a woman from 4s. to 20s. a week, average about 6s.; men from 10s. to 25s. a week, and some much higher; colliers earn yet more. These are immense wages, when it is considered that the whole family is sure of constant steady employment; indeed they are so great, that I am inclined to think labour higher at Birmingham than in any place in Europe: a most curious circumstance for the politician to reflect on, and which shews of how little effect to manufactures is cheap labour, for here is the most flourishing fabric that was perhaps ever known, paying the highest rates of labour. Such an instance ought to correct those common notions that have been retailed from hand to hand a thousand times, that cheap provisions are necessary for the good of manufactures, because cheap provisions suppose cheap labour, which is a combination founded in ignorance and error. Provisions at Birmingham are at the same rate as every where else in England, for it is remarkable that the level of price at present is very general, except the division of the east and west of the kingdom for corn; but while Birmingham and Norwich eat their provisions at nearly the same price (with allowance that the former is much the more quick, ready, and active market), the price of labour is at least 150 per cent. higher in one of those places than the other. Why then I enquire, what has provisions to do with the rate of labour? If one was to form our ideas from a very enlarged view of all the great fabrics in Europe, we should be apt to think that a great and flourishing fabric could not subsist, either with cheap provisions, or with cheap labour.

I tried hard to pick up some data, on which to calculate the amount of the fabric, but difficulties of various kinds prevented any accuracy in the estimation. In conversation with a very ingenious gentleman, who has written an able work on the town, and who was rewarded for it by having his house burnt down in the late riots, I mean Mr. Hutton, he informed me that ten years ago there were many estimates made with a good deal of care; and that on multiplied experiments it was found, that the returns per week, was equal to the rent per annum; including all the houses of the town on an average; all shops; all trades: the houses were then about 9000, and the rent 9l. each, on a medium; now the houses are about 13,000, and as I find, on enquiry, that the little houses, which have been built in such numbers for manufacturers, are let at 6l. 10s. the lowest; 7l. and 8l. each; 9l. on a general average of rents must now be much too low; however let us call it no more than 10l.; this would make the rental of the town 130,000l. a year, and the returns of all its trade 6,760,000l. per annum: out of which a very great deduction is to be made for all the trades and professions of common life, supported by the manufacture, but not composing it. If I should form any idea corrective of this, it would be that the estimate is carried too high: let us suppose the population 80,000, then there are about 40,000 males, of these deduct 5000 not employed in the manufacture, remain 35,000; three-fourths of that number are of an age to be employed, or 26,250. Suppose these to earn, including manufacturers and merchants profit, 15s. a week, it amounts to 1,023,724l. a year. Of the 40,000 women 20,000 may be supposed to be employed, and to earn 6s. including, as above; the year's earnings will be 312,000l. in all 1,335,000l. double this, to include all raw materials, and you have 2,670,000l. for the amount of the manufacture. Now I am ready to grant, that here is a great deal of supposition in this estimate, but at the same time it is not altogether without data; and though the total may exceed this, possibly half a million, yet I think as much might be said to shew the calculation high, as to prove it low. It is true the ratio of the earnings is taken rather low, including, as it ought to do, the profit both of the manufacturer and of the merchant, which cannot well be less than 20 per cent.; but then the number of the workmen can scarcely exceed the supposition, probably not equal to it, 20,000 females, in particular are a high allowance.

Robert Southey (1774–1843) was poet laureate of England and intimately connected with the Romantic school of William Wordsworth and Samuel Taylor Coleridge. The Romantics tended to idealize the rural life and see in it a purity and simplicity that were often invisible to their contemporaries.

The following selection takes the form of a dialogue between Sir Thomas More's ghost and a man who speaks for Southey's time.

FROM *Sir Thomas More*

BY *Robert Southey*

SIR THOMAS MORE. . . . The spirit which built and endowed monasteries is gone. Are you one of those persons who think it has been superseded for the better by that which erects steam-engines and cotton mills?

Montesinos. They are indeed miserable politicians who mistake wealth for welfare in their estimate of national prosperity; and none have committed this great error more egregiously than some of those who have been called statesmen by the courtesy of England. Yet the manufacturing system is a necessary stage in the progress of society. Without it this nation could not have supported the long and tremendous conflict which has delivered Europe from the yoke of military despotism, . . . the worst of all evils. If England had not been enabled by the use of steam-engines to send out every year myriads of brave men, and millions of specie, . . . what had Europe, and what had England itself been now? This inestimable benefit we have seen and felt. And from the consequences of that skill in machinery which the manufacturing system alone could have produced, we may expect ultimately to obtain the greatest advantages of science and civilization at the least expense of human labour.

* * *

Sir Thomas More. There is an example before our eyes. Yonder children are on the way to a manufactory, where they pass six days out of the seven, from morning till night. Is it likely that the little they learn at school on the seventh (which ought to be their day of recreation as well as rest), should counteract the effects of such an education, when the moral atmosphere wherein they live and move and have their being, is as noxious to the soul, as the foul and tainted air which they inhale is to their bodily constitution?

Robert Southey, *Sir Thomas More; or Colloquies on the Progress and Prospects of Society,* I (1829), pp. 158–159, 166–167, 170–171, 173–174. Reprinted by permission.

Montesinos. Yet the most celebrated minister of the age, the only minister who for many generations has deserved to be called a Premier, the minister whom our best and wisest statesmen at this day profess entirely to admire and implicitly to follow, . . . he made his boast of this very evil, and congratulated Parliament that the nation had a new source of wealth and revenue in the labour of children: so completely had the political system in which he was trained up seared his heart and obscured his understanding.

Sir Thomas More. Confess that this is an evil which had no existence in former times! There are new things under the sun, . . . new miseries, . . . new enormities, . . . this portentous age produces them.

* * *

Sir Thomas More. What then shall we say of a system which in its direct consequences debases all who are engaged in it? A system that employs men unremittingly in pursuits unwholesome for the body, and unprofitable for the mind, . . . a system in which the means are so bad, that any result would be dearly purchased at such an expense of human misery and degradation, and the end so fearful, that the worst calamities which society has hitherto endured may be deemed light in comparison with it?

Montesinos. Like the whole fabric of our society it has been the growth of circumstances, not a system foreplanned, forseen and deliberately chosen. Such as it is we have inherited it, . . . or rather have fallen into it, and must get out of it as well as we can. We must do our best to remove its evils, and to mitigate them while they last, and to modify and reduce it till only so much remains as is indispensable for the general good.

Sir Thomas More. The facts will not warrant you in saying that it has come upon the country unsought and unforeseen. You have prided yourselves upon this system; you have used every means for extending it; you have made it the measure of your national prosperity. It is a wen, a fungous excrescence from the body politic: the growth might have been checked if the consequences had been apprehended in time; but now it has acquired so great a bulk, its nerves have branched so widely, and the vessels of the tumour are so inosculated into some of the principal veins and arteries of the natural system, that to remove it by absorption is impossible, and excision would be fatal.

Montesinos. Happily, this is but a metaphor; and the body politic, like its crowned head, never dies.

By this time we had reached the bank above Applethwaite. The last question of my companion was one to which I could make no reply, and as he neither talked for triumph, nor I endeavoured to elude the force of his argument, we remained awhile in silence, looking upon the assemblage of dwellings below. Here, and in the adjoining hamlet of Millbeck, the effects of manufactures and of agriculture may be seen and compared. The old cottages are such as the poet and the painter equally delight in beholding. Substantially built of the native stone without mortar, dirtied with no white-lime, and their long low roofs covered with slate, if they had been raised by the magic of some indigenous Amphion's music, the materials could not have adjusted themselves more beautifully in accord with the surrounding scene; and time has still farther harmonized them with weather stains, lichens and moss, short grasses and short fern, and stone plants of various kinds. The ornamented chimnies, round or square, less adorned than those which, like little turrets, crest the houses of the Portugueze peasantry, and yet not less happily suited to their place; the hedge of clipt box beneath the windows, the rose bushes beside the door, the little patch of flower ground with its tall holyocks in front, the garden beside, the bee-hives, and the orchard with its bank of daffodils and snowdrops, (the earliest and the profusest in these parts,) indicate in the owners some portion of ease and leisure, some regard to neatness and comfort, some sense of natural and innocent and healthful enjoyment. The new cottages of the manufacturers, are . . . upon the manufacturing pattern . . . naked, and in a row.

How is it, said I, that every thing which is connected with manufactures, presents such features of unqualified deformity? From the largest of Mammon's temples down to the poorest hovel in which his helotry are stalled, the edifices have all one character. Time cannot mellow them; Nature will neither clothe nor conceal them; and they remain always as offensive to the eye as to the mind!

3

Working Conditions in the Industrial Revolution

The rapid industrialization of Great Britain, added to the hardships of the wars of the French Revolution and Napoleon, created serious conditions among the poor. Many members of the upper classes were troubled by the burgeoning of manufactures and by the use of young children in producing them. The children were a necessary part of the new cotton textile industry, for their small size enabled them to move freely under the machinery to repair broken threads and keep the looms and spindles working. The moral question raised by such employment could not long be ignored, and in 1816 a parliamentary committee was appointed to find out if the employment of children was detrimental to their health and morals.

FROM *Report . . . on the State of the Children Employed . . .*

THE FIRST WITNESS is Matthew Baillie, M.D. The chairman of the committee is Sir Robert Peel, himself an industrialist and the father of the future Prime Minister.

In speaking of the injury to young persons from labour, do you mean to speak of labour which requires great bodily exertion?—I did not suppose that children at so early an age were employed in great bodily exertion, but I meant any bodily exertion in which they were confined in a given space, and their minds not allowed to wander into the various channels of thought, and their limbs allowed the sort of irregular exercise which takes place in children who are living in the usual manner.

Is not the state of maturity of children very different in those brought up in the country, to those brought up in town?—With regard to children who are brought up in the country, they are more vigorous; and I have no doubt, in many instances, their progress towards maturity may be more rapid than in children who are reared in a large town.

And your experience has principally been in town?—Entirely, I may say.

Report of the Minutes of Evidence Taken Before the Select Committee on the State of Children Employed in the Manufactories of the United Kingdom, 25 April–18 June, 1816, pp. 30–31, 46–48, 50–52, 178–181, 222–223. Reprinted by permission.

Have you been called to give any opinion, or to know the state of health in different manufactories?—I have not.

What is the state of heat, as ascertained by a thermometer, in which children might work without injury?—I should say, that the temperature which is upon the whole most favourable, is about sixty degrees of heat.

In giving your opinion upon this subject, do you take into your consideration the situation in which children would be placed, if, at an early period, they were not employed in such factories?—I do not know that the whole of this pressed on my mind, but certainly it was not absent from it; I drew the comparison between those children as employed in manufactories, and the ordinary employment of children in the country.

Would children of the age of ten be employed in the ordinary business of the country?—No; but they would be doing a good deal of work of various kinds, as going of errands, or weeding, and a thousand employments, which I cannot at present call up to my mind.

That answer seems to refer more particularly to children in the country, as the manufactories are generally in towns, it does not apply to them; therefore the Committee wish to know whether you conceive, if children at an early period of life were prevented by Act of Parliament from working in factories, their situation would be better than it is?—I conceive it would be more favourable to health to be at large, although they might sometimes be not well nourished; and although sometimes they would be in hot rooms, they would have a great deal more time in which they could be playing about, and using their faculties of observation.

Then if those children were left on the parish for support, and many sent to the workhouse, their situation would be better than at present?—I think that children would be better situated in a workhouse, were they not so employed, than in manufactories.

Do you give this as an opinion that you derive from an accurate observation of facts, with respect to the condition of children in factories, or do you give it upon general reasoning?—Upon general reasoning.

Then you are not really acquainted with the condition of children employed in such manufactories?—I am not really acquainted with the condition of children employed in such manufactories; but I mention what I suppose must be more or less the influence of confinement which children are subject to in those manufactories upon their health, from the general principles that guide us in ascertaining the causes that maintain health or lead to sickness, with respect to the human body generally.

In a factory consisting of 875 persons, the annual deaths in which were not more than from two to five, should you conceive that the employment as in consistent with the health of the people employed?—I should say it does not appear from that statement to have been inconsistent; I conceive, a great many of those children might not be in vigorous health, not in the same health in which they would otherwise be, and yet not be attacked with diseases which would occasion death.

Your answer refers to the number of deaths in a particular year; but if the average for seven years should be about the same, would not you consider that fact as tolerable evidence of the health of the employment?—Indeed I should think so.

Then if in another factory consisting of 289 persons, two only died in the year 1815; and on the 13th of April, one only was sick; would not that afford a tolerable inference of the healthiness of the persons employed in that factory?—It certainly would; but as I stated before, I can easily believe that those children may not be attacked by diseases which should lead to death; but at the same time, be many of them less vigorous than they otherwise would be if employed in the usual manner.

Then in factories, where on the average persons are employed seven years, and where a great portion remain from fourteen to twenty; if the general state of health has been good, would not that be tolerably good evidence of the healthiness of the employment?—I think so.

Have you ever had reason to conceive that there exists in the lower classes of people, a want of affection and tenderness for their children?—I believe you will find very often less affection, both of fathers and mothers for their children in the lower classes, than in the middle ranks: But at the same time there are many strong instances of the purest maternal and paternal affection in the lowest classes of society, where there may be very great difficulty to rear children: they will often submit to every kind of privation respecting themselves, in order to rear the children with some degree of comfort.

Then the lowest class are not the persons where the greatest degree of affection is found for their children?—I think not.

Does not a family press much harder on a poor man, than on any other class?—No doubt.

And is it not of greater importance to him to superintend the care of those children, than to any other class of persons in life?—It must be of more importance to him to superintend, if he can, the education and the bringing up of his children, because in other ranks of life, there are persons who can be procured to do that office for them.

Does not any sickness or want of health in the children of the poor, press upon the parents more than upon any other class of persons?—Certainly.

In the communications you have received from other practitioners, have you ever heard of any great detriment that has occurred to children from too intense employment in manufactories?—I do not recollect that I have ever received a communication upon the subject.

Have you had opportunities of observation upon the condition of the children of the poor not employed in manufactories in large towns?—I have been engaged almost from the beginning of my medical life, in the middle and higher ranks of society.

Sir Gilbert Blane, M.D., was also examined.

May it not happen, by those children being kept employed not in hard labour but in that kind of gentle occupation that gives exercise without superinducing too great fatigue, for twelve hours in a day, in factories, where the air was pure and salutary?—That is a question that, from my want of knowing in detail what is the nature of the employment, I cannot answer; if it was not sedentary but loco-motive, ten hours would not be too much.

Must not a great deal of the power of performance on the part of children, depend on the nourishment and cloathing which they receive?—Not the least doubt much must depend upon the quantity and quality of food.

May not, both in men and animals, an increased degree of maturity be attained in consequence of the food that they receive?—No doubt of it; but there is a greater latitude in the human species than in any other; a man, so speaking, is more an animal of mixed food than any other.

May not children of ten years of age, by being better fed and better care taken of them, be capable of doing more work, without injury to his health, than a child of the same age could have done twenty years ago?—I am clearly of that opinion, from the habits of life, which I have watched with great accuracy.

In referring to the powers of children, are we not to refer, not to what they were, but to what they actually are, from the improvements that have been made?—No doubt of it.

Has it ever occurred to you, to contemplate what has been the increased consumption of animal food within the last fifty years?—I have frequently attended to it, and I think with advantage to mankind, particularly to the young.

Is not the increase of animal food, to young and old, ten times what it was fifty years ago?—It has certainly increased, but I should think that was too high a ratio; it has been increased, to the benefit of all ages, and particularly to the young.

In your observations, has not the consumption of animal food greatly increased within the last fifty years?—It has greatly increased.

Has it not greatly increased within the last twenty years?—Certainly it has, according to my observation.

And that has had a material influence on the strength and health of the people?—I suppose that that has had some share in the decreased mortality which appears.

Is the Committee to understand, that you consider the employment of children, under the age of ten years, to be wholly improper and inconvenient?—By no means wholly improper; I should think if it was limited to five or six hours, that would not only not be pernicious, but salutary.

And you think the employment of children from ten to sixteen, ought not to exceed ten hours a day?—Yes, that might be without prejudice.

You were understood to say, you conceived the state of the atmosphere in which the children worked, was of more importance than the labour itself?—Certainly; they would suffer more from foul air than from the actual labour: the manual labour is the least evil I think.

You say, that the employment of children under ten, might, under certain restrictions, not only be not detrimental, but even beneficial?—I should have no objection to five or six hours.

Are there any restrictions, in point of time or kind of work, that would make it proper to employ children under six years old?—I am so little acquainted with the nature of the occupations in manufactories, I cannot answer that.

Suppose a great number are kept together in the same room, and not exposed to the open air, and in a sedentary posture, or at any rate not taking exercise, do you conceive that at the age of five or six, such occupation, however limited in point of time, is wholesome?—I should apprehend it is wholesome if very limited.

At the age of five or six?—Even as low as that, very limited in time, and in apartments well ventilated and not crowded.

Do you mean, if during the other parts of the day the children should be allowed to play or amuse themselves in the open air?—Most assuredly I understood it so.

Is the proportion between the cubic feet of air in a room, and the number of persons employed in it, of great importance to their health?—Very great; that is a subject I have particularly studied.

In rooms properly ventilated, and where the quantity of respirable air allowed to each person is 1,440 cubic feet, do you think that employment is likely to be prejudicial to such persons?—There is ample space for pure air there; in a hospital there is 700 feet to a patient, and we consider that a safe and proper space, still more so where they are in health and walk about. In a hospital well ventilated, we find 700 cubic feet is a safe and proper space for each patient.

Are you of opinion, that the air in such rooms as have been alluded to, and the employment in them, are likely to be more or less healthy than such rooms as children are employed in by inferior tradesmen, such as tailors and shoemakers?—I apprehend that is a superior degree of ventilation to what they have in the apartments of the labouring poor.

Is it important to the health of children and others, that the temperature of the rooms in which they are employed in winter should be comfortable, and as nearly uniform as is consistent with proper ventilation?—There is no doubt of it; I think comfortable and salutary to be one and the same thing; nature points out what is salutary.

Your attention seems to have been particularly called to the proportion of deaths in different places in this country; do you conceive, that in a factory where in 1811 the number being 873, the deaths in that year being only three; in 1812 the number being 891, the deaths only two; and in 1813 the number being 879, and the deaths only two, such facts to be an indication of the healthiness of the employment in such factory?—It is an indication of the greatest possible health; but it so far exceeds the common course of nature, that if I had it not from such respectable authority I should greatly doubt it.

Would you be surprized at the statement, if you were informed that when children are ill, and likely to die, they are removed from the manufactories?—That alters the case totally.

Are you of opinion, that in another factory, wherein the numbers were 289 employed in 1815, the deaths being two, and where, on the 13th of April only one person out of all that number was sick, such facts are evidence that such factory is healthy?—The same answer; it is evidence of extreme healthiness.

Are you aware, in the most healthy communities, what the proportion of deaths to the persons in life, usually is?—The average in England is one in forty-nine, including Wales one in fifty; and according to the Parliamentary Returns of the beginning of this century, it was one in forty-four; by the Parliamentary Return of 1801.

Healthiness has been somewhat increasing?—Yes.

Did the surprize expressed in a former question, refer to this turning out to be six times less than the average mortality in healthy situations in this country?—To be sure, that made me say it was against the common course of nature; there are no tables that I ever saw, that quoted so high a proportion in the most healthy period of life.

Are you of opinion, that in no situation peculiarly favourable to health in this country, the proportion of deaths is less than that which you have just now stated?—I should have said, had I not been assured of this fact, that that was a rate of mortality that was not to be found any where in the world.

You stated one in forty-four as the average health in healthy districts; the question is, whether, in any particular districts, you have heard of the proportion being smaller than one in forty-four?—Yes; according to the last enumeration the mortality in Cardiganshire is only one in seventy-three, in Monmouthshire one in sixty-four; in Cornwall one in sixty-two, in Gloucestershire one in sixty-one; all the others are under one in sixty. The highest mortality is in the Metropolis and the aguish districts.

Would your surprize of the small mortality cease, if you were informed that no persons are employed under nine years of age, only fifty-nine of the number under ten at the larger factory, and perhaps not forty out of the number above forty years of age, and the factory situated in the healthful country of Ayr, with which you are acquainted?—That renders it somewhat less marvellous.

Have you the means of informing the Committee, what the general mortality is in healthy districts in this country, upon healthy persons between the age of ten and eighteen?—I had lately occasion to make enquiry about that. From some calculations I have made, I found that the mortality in England, between twenty and forty, was about one in eighty.

A deposition was later offered on the part of Charles Pennington, M.D., as a report on the health of the people employed in the mill at Papplewick.

Nottingham, 6th May 1816.

Gentlemen,

Having been desired to communicate to you, as delegates in London from the proprietors of cotton mills and factories in Nottingham and its neighbourhood, my opinion respecting the general state of health of the persons employed in the cotton mills in and near Papplewick, belonging to Mr. James Robinson and Son, I hereby certify to you and to the Honourable the Committee of the House of Commons, that for more than thirty years I have been very frequently called upon in my professional character to attend the family of Mr. Robinson, and the persons employed in his extensive manufactory; and that I have uniformly remarked the most humane attention and careful regard to the health, the morals and the comforts of all engaged in this concern; and that when under medical care, every thing, without any regard to its cost, has been always freely and largely afforded. Further, I may add, that during the greater part of this period, I have had a considerable practice in the town of Nottingham, in a very populous district, for many miles around it, and also in the Infirmary and Lunatic Asylum, amongst all classes and descriptions of people; and after a careful review of the more important circumstances connected with the health of the parties, my conviction is, that the persons employed in the cotton-spinning manufactories are as healthy and strong as any engaged in sedentary pursuits in general; more healthy and strong than the frame-work-knitter; and much more so than the shoemaker and the tailor.

I am, very respectfully, Gentlemen,
Your obedient Servant,
Charles Pennington, M.D.
Honorary Physician to the General Hospital,
and Physician to the Lunatic Asylum

Messrs. Stanton and Heygate.
Mr. Archibald Buchanan, a mill owner, also took the stand.

Do you know of any person whose health was beginning to fail, leaving the manufactory?—I have known many instances of that kind; and I have known many instances of persons of delicate health coming into the manufactory, as being an easy employment.

Did you ever know of a sickly or delicate child coming into the manufactory?—A great many.

And did they, from a more regular life and a more constant supply of food and regular habits, get better?—Their parents had difficulty in getting employment for them otherwise, and they were glad to get them into the works as being easy; there are some parts of it where they may either sit or stand; and there are many parts of the work where lame people can be employed; and gentlemen in the neighbourhood, and frequently parishes, make application to me to have these people taken in to obtain a subsistence.

And from these circumstances, particularly the material one of having a regular supply of good food, did you observe that those children improved in their health?—I have observed very great improvement from their getting good food. . . .

* * *

Do you know what proportion the persons employed in the manufactory bear to the whole population of the village?—The village contains something above 2,000.

Including those employed in the manufactory?—Yes.

Do you know any thing of the total number of deaths in the village?—I do not.

Do you mean to give to the Committee the impression, that the average number of deaths of the persons employed in the manufactory, at all resembles the total average number of deaths in the village?—I should think that the deaths belonging to the manufactory were less; I have been frequently told by the medical gentleman who attends our people, that in the course of his practice, he finds less disease existing with the people employed in the works, than in the general population of the surrounding country.

Do you mean to lead the Committee to apprehend, that the deaths, upon the remaining eleven hundred who live in the village, are in any thing resembling an equal proportion to that of the deaths in the manufactory?—I am of opinion that they are considerably more; I beg leave to state, that parents with a large family often come to the village and get their children employed; the parents frequently do little or nothing at home, and of course there are a smaller proportion of grown up people in our works than are to be found among the inhabitants of the village.

Those in your works are at the more healthy periods of life?—Yes. . . .

* * *

In the population of the village, are the greater proportion of those not now in your works out of employment?—I have stated in my former evidence, that a great number of those who have formerly been employed in the mills have grown up and gone to other trades; a great number of them are masons, joiners, shoemakers, tailors, and in fact, engaged in every kind of trade almost.

And you have not observed, that those people who have been formerly employed in the works, have been affected in their health?—They are very similar to those who have been brought up in the country; and I mentioned also, that tradesmen generally prefer those brought up in the works to people from the country, on account of their having been brought up in industry, and having acquired a great degree of ingenuity.

* * *

Mr. John Moss, called in, and examined.

Where do you live?—At Preston workhouse.

In Lancashire?—Yes.

What is your occupation?—My present occupation is that of governor of the workhouse.

Were you ever employed as the master of the apprentices at a cotton mill?—I was engaged to attend the apprentice-house at Backbarrow. I was over the children. . . .

* * *

Up to what period were they apprenticed?—One-and-twenty.

What were the hours of work?—From five o'clock in the morning till eight at night.

Were fifteen hours in the day the regular hours of work?—Those were their regular hours of work.

Was that the regular time all the year through?—Yes.

What time was allowed for meals?—Half an hour for breakfast and half an hour for dinner. . . .

* * *

Had they any refreshment in the afternoon?—Yes, they had their drinking taken to the mill; their bagging, they call it.

You mean luncheon?—Yes.

Did they work while they ate their afternoon refreshment?—Yes.

They had no cessation after dinner till eight o'clock at night?—No.

At what hour was the breakfast?—At seven in the morning; they came to their breakfast at seven o'clock, and then the bell rang for them at half past seven.

Did they leave the mill at breakfast time?—Yes, they always left the mill and came to the house.

What was the dinner hour?—Twelve o'clock.

And at what time did they return to the mill?—Half past twelve.

Did they, beyond working those fifteen hours, make up for any loss of time?—Yes, always.

Did the children actually work fourteen hours in the day?—Yes.

And one hour was allowed for the two meals, making fifteen hours in the whole?—Yes.

When the works were stopped for the repair of the mill, or for any want of cotton, did the children afterwards make up for the loss of that time?—Yes.

When making up lost time, how long did they continue working at night?—Till nine o'clock, and sometimes later; sometimes ten.

Was this before the Apprentice Bill or after?—It was last year, and it is in practice now.

How long were they making up lost time?—I have known them to be three weeks or more making up lost time.

Have you known them for three weeks together working from five in the morning till nine or ten at night, with the exception of the hour for meals?—Yes, I have.

What time did they rise from bed?—I always got up at half past four to get them ready to be at the mill by five.

How far was their sleeping room from the mill?—It might be not above a hundred yards; hardly so much.

Did they rise at half past four in the winter season?—They were always to be at the mill by five o'clock winter and summer, and never later.

Were there two mills?—Yes.

When you had only water for one mill, did the children work night and day?—When there was only water for one mill, one worked in the day and the other at night.

Have you ever known the children work all night on Saturday, until six o'clock on Sunday morning?—Yes, I have once; they have gone to work at eight o'clock on Saturday night, and stayed till six on Sunday morning.

At what hour on Sunday night did those children begin to work again?—They have begun at twelve o'clock on Sunday night again, and worked till five in the morning; then the other children for the day began at the other mill, and worked till eight at night.

Did they work as late on Saturday night as on other nights?—Always the same; I never knew any abatement.

Did any children work on the Sundays as cleaners of the machinery?—Yes.

Did they do this regularly?—Regularly every Sunday; I do not know that ever they missed one Sunday while I was there.

Through the year?—Yes.

How many hours did they work on a Sunday?—Their orders were from six till twelve.

Did you remonstrate against this?—Yes, I did.

Frequently?—Yes.

What was the consequence of your remonstrance?—It was never much better; there were not so many went to the mill; I believe that they went from their own accord sometimes, and I wished the bookkeeper to give in a paper of the names of those who were to attend.

Did the children take it in rotation?—It was just according to what wanted cleaning.

Who gave orders what children were to work on a Sunday?—The book-keeper sent me a written note of the names of those who were to attend.

Did he give you a written order in consequence of your remonstrance?—Yes.

Do you remember any Sunday when they did not work while you were at the mills?—I do not remember one Sunday when they did not go to work.

If they had left off work a little earlier on Saturday, could not they have avoided the necessity of going to the mills on a Sunday?—Yes.

Were the children paid for the Sunday-work?—Yes.

Did the children ever attend church?—Yes.

Would the children rather get money by working on a Sunday than attend church?—I thought there was a motive, which made me put a stop to it, by having a written order who was to attend.

Did they absent themselves sometimes from church, under the pretence of going to the mill to clean the machinery?—Yes.

Did the overlookers ever give you any orders for the children to work till twelve o'clock on Saturday night?—Yes.

Did you remonstrate against this also?—Yes.

For what reason?—Because we had the children to wash and clean after they had done work on Saturday night, therefore it was late before we got to bed; but they have sometimes worked till ten, the whole of the children; and when they have been short of water, that set that went on to work at eight at night was worked till twelve.

Did the masters ever express any concern for such excessive labour?—No.

Was it at the desire of the proprietors of the mill, or of the overlookers, that the children worked till twelve o'clock on Saturday night?—It was the master of the mill that wished them to work till twelve o'clock at night, when they were short of water; but it was the overlookers that wished the whole of them to work till twelve o'clock at night, in order to make up lost time, that they might get done the sooner; the whole of them never did work together later than ten.

Were they very strict in keeping them to their time?—Yes.

Did the children sit or stand to work?—Stand.

The whole of their time?—Yes.

Were there any seats in the mill?—None.

Were they usually much fatigued at night?—Yes, some of them were very much fatigued.

Where did they sleep?—They slept in the apprentice-house.

Did you inspect their beds?—Yes, every night.

For what purpose?—Because there were always some of them missing, some sometimes might be run away, others sometimes I have found have been asleep in the mill.

Upon the mill-floor?—Yes.

Did the children frequently lie down upon the mill-floor at night when their work was over, and fall asleep before their supper?—I have found them frequently upon the mill-floors, after the time they should have been in bed.

At what time did they go to bed?—Nine o'clock was their hour, when they worked their usual time.

In summer time did you allow them to sit up a little later?—Yes, sometimes till half past nine.

Were any children injured by the machinery?—Very frequently.

Were their fingers often crushed?—Very often their fingers were caught; and one had his arm broken.

Were any of the children deformed?—Yes, several of them were deformed; there were two or three that were very crooked.

Do you know whether those children were straight when they first came to the mill?—They told me they were.

Who told you they were?—The children themselves.

Were any of the children in-kneed, or what is called knock-kneed?—Yes, there were ten or a dozen of them, I dare say, that were in-kneed.

Did you understand from them whether they were so when they came to the mill?—I do not know that they were.

Do you think they were not?—I am pretty sure some of them were not, but some of them were lame when they came.

Did the parish officers of the parishes to which they belonged, ever come to the mills to visit and inspect the children?—No; there was one from Liverpool; the overseer of Liverpool.

Do you remember his name?—Hardman, I believe.

Was there any other inspection by magistrates, or any other persons?—No, there was no magistrates ever came into the childrens house.

Is the mill in a healthy situation?—Very.

Remarkably so?—Yes.

As the children grew up, did they in general appear to be healthy, or otherwise?—There were some who were very healthy children, and there were others that were sickly looking.

What was their general appearance?—Their general appearance was as well as most of the farmers children, some of them; some of them looked sickly, but then they were not sick.

They appeared to be sick, but were not so?—Yes; we scarcely ever had any sickness in the house.

How many died during the year you were at the mill?—There was only one.

How were the children lodged?—They had very good lodgings when we left them.

Had they good lodgings when you first went there?—No.

Did you make any complaints of their bedding when you first went?—Yes.

Will you state to the Committee what was the condition of their bedding when you first went?—When I first went there, their bedding was very bad, they had only a blanket to lie on, and a thin blanket to lie at top, and a horse cover, and some of them were very bad.

Could they be preserved cleanly with sleeping only on blankets?—They were not altogether clean.

Did you make complaint of that?—Yes.

Did the parish officer from Liverpool complain of it?—Yes.

Was it in consequence of his complaints and yours, that the bedding was improved?—Yes, it was; we got after that sheets and covers for every bed, and there never were sheets for any bed in the house I believe, before.

Did they spin fine or coarse yarn at those mills?—Very coarse.

Were the rooms as warm as where they spin fine?—No, I believe not.

Do you understand that they require greater heat for fine threads?—I have heard them say so; they have no heat in their rooms in the summer, in the winter they have heat from steam.

Were the children fed well?—Very well.

Before your time at Backbarrow mill, were the children turned out on the high road to beg their way to their former parishes, when the former proprietor stopped payment?—I was informed they were.

Did you converse with any of the children that were so turned out?—Yes.

Were they taken from the mill in a cart, and then turned adrift near the sands on the Lancaster road?—Yes, I was informed they were.

Do you know what became of them afterwards?—There was one of them I heard was taken in at Caton factory, and employed there for some time; and I heard there were some of them taken into Lancaster workhouse.

Did you hear that the gentlemen of Lancaster complained of this inhumanity?—Yes.

Were any fetched back in consequence of these complaints?—Yes, I believe there were.

Were they then turned over to Messrs. Ainsworth the present proprietors?—Yes.

After they had served out their apprenticeship to Messrs. Ainsworth, were they not compelled to serve extra time, under the pretence that so much time was lost by being turned out on the road and obliged to go to Lancaster?—Yes, there was one boy out of his time while I was there, and when the day came his master said that he had to serve six weeks, I think, longer, in consequence of his having run away; he said he never had ran away, he was turned out, and he had worked at Caton factory, and they made him serve that time out; his name is Henry Carter.

Do you know of Messrs. Watson's apprentices being turned out in the same manner?—I have heard it said so, but I never knew anything of it.

Were the children bad in their morals?—Yes, they were.

How did they behave one to another?—They did not behave well one to another.

Who looked over them in the mill?—Generally the older apprentices were overlookers over the younger ones.

Did the bigger boys beat the others?—Yes.

Frequently?—Yes.

What was the general character of the children?—Very bad characters.

What was the reason you left the mill?—It was in consequence of their bad behaviour.

$$4$$

Evaluation of the Industrial Revolution

Thomas Babington Macaulay (1800–1859) is most generally remembered for his history of England in the seventeenth century. He was also an essayist of devastating wit and power. Nothing was more calculated to arouse his ire than an attack on the idea of progress, and Southey's romanticism seemed to him such an attack. This review, first published in 1830, reveals Macaulay at his polemical best.

FROM *Southey's Colloquies*

BY *T. B. Macaulay*

IT WOULD BE SCARCELY POSSIBLE for a man of Mr. Southey's talents and acquirements to write two volumes so large as those before us, which should be wholly destitute of information and amusement. Yet we do not remember to have read with so little satisfaction any equal quantity of matter, written by any man of real abilities. We have, for some time past, observed with great regret the strange infatuation which leads the Poet Laureate to abandon those departments of literature in which he might excel, and to lecture the public on sciences of which he has still the very alphabet to learn. He has now, we think, done his worst. The subject which he has at last undertaken to treat is one which demands all the highest intellectual and moral qualities of a philosophical statesman, an understanding at once comprehensive and acute, a heart at once upright and charitable. Mr. Southey brings to the task two faculties which were never, we believe, vouchsafed in measure so copious to any human being, the faculty of believing without a reason, and the faculty of hating without a provocation.

It is, indeed, most extraordinary, that a mind like Mr. Southey's, a mind richly endowed in many respects by nature, and highly cultivated by study, a

Critical and Historical Essays Contributed to the Edinburgh Review by Lord Macaulay, I, (1903), pp. 205, 207, 215–218. Reprinted by permission.

mind which has exercised considerable influence on the most enlightened generation of the most enlightened people that ever existed, should be utterly destitute of the power of discerning truth from falsehood. Yet such is the fact. Government is to Mr. Southey one of the fine arts. He judges of a theory, of a public measure, of a religion or a political party, of a peace or a war, as men judge of a picture or a statue, by the effect produced on his imagination. A chain of associations is to him what a chain of reasoning is to other men; and what he calls his opinions are in fact merely his tastes.

* * *

Now in the mind of Mr. Southey reason has no place at all, as either leader or follower, as either sovereign or slave. He does not seem to know what an argument is. He never uses arguments himself. He never troubles himself to answer the arguments of his opponents. It has never occurred to him, that a man ought to be able to give some better account of the way in which he has arrived at his opinions than merely that it is his will and pleasure to hold them. It has never occurred to him that there is a difference between assertion and demonstration, that a rumour does not always prove a fact, that a single fact, when proved, is hardly foundation enough for a theory, that two contradictory propositions cannot be undeniable truths, that to beg the question is not the way to settle it, or that when an objection is raised, it ought to be met with something more convincing than "scoundrel" and "blockhead." . . .

* * *

We now come to the conversations which pass between Mr. Southey and Sir Thomas More, or rather between two Southeys, equally eloquent, equally angry, equally unreasonable, and equally given to talking about what they do not understand. Perhaps we could not select a better instance of the spirit which pervades the whole book than the passages in which Mr. Southey gives his opinion of the manufacturing system. There is nothing which he hates so bitterly. It is, according to him, a system more tyrannical than that of the feudal ages, a system of actual servitude, a system which destroys the bodies and degrades the minds of those who are engaged in it. He expresses a hope that the competition of other nations may drive us out of the field; that our foreign trade may decline; and that we may thus enjoy a restoration of national sanity and strength. But he seems to think that the extermination of the whole manufacturing population would be a blessing, if the evil could be removed in no other way.

Mr. Southey does not bring forward a single fact in support of these views; and, as it seems to us, there are facts which lead to a very different conclusion. In the first place, the poor-rate is very decidedly lower in the manufacturing than in the agricultural districts. If Mr. Southey will look over the Parliamentary returns on this subject, he will find that the amount of parochial relief required by the labourers in the different counties of England is almost exactly in inverse proportion to the degree in which the manufacturing system has been introduced into those counties. The returns for the years ending in March 1825, and in March 1828, are now before us. In the former year we find the poor-rate highest in Sussex, about twenty shillings to every inhabitant. Then come Buckinghamshire, Essex, Suffolk, Bedfordshire, Huntingdonshire, Kent, and Norfolk. In all these the rate is above fifteen shillings a head. We will not go through the whole. Even in Westmoreland and the North Riding of Yorkshire, the rate is at more than eight shillings. In Cumberland and Monmouthshire, the most fortunate of all the agricultural districts, it is at six shillings. But in the West Riding of Yorkshire, it is as low as five shillings; and when we come to Lancashire, we find it at four shillings, one fifth of what it is in Sussex. The returns of the year ending in March 1828 are a little, and but a little, more unfavourable to the manufacturing districts. Lancashire, even in that season of distress, required a smaller poor-rate than any other district, and little more than one fourth of the poor-rate raised in Sussex. Cumberland alone, of the agricultural districts, was as well off as the West Riding of Yorkshire. These facts seem to indicate that the manufacturer is both in a more comfortable and in a less dependent situation than the agricultural labourer.

As to the effect of the manufacturing system on the bodily health, we must beg leave to estimate it by a standard far too low and vulgar for a mind so imaginative as that of Mr. Southey, the proportion of births and deaths. We know that, during the growth of this atrocious system, this new misery, to use the phrases of Mr. Southey, this new enormity, this birth of a portentous age, this pest which no man can approve whose heart is not seared or whose understanding has not been darkened, there has been a great diminution of mortality, and that this diminution has been greater in the manufacturing towns than any where else. The mortality still is, as it always was, greater in towns than in the country. But the difference has diminished in an extraordinary degree. There is the best reason to believe that the annual mortality of Manchester, about the middle of the last century, was one in twenty-eight. It is now reckoned at one in forty-five. In Glasgow and Leeds a similar improvement has taken place. Nay, the rate of mortality in those three great capitals of the manufacturing districts is now considerably less than it was, fifty years ago, over England and Wales, taken together, open country and all. We might with some plausibility maintain that the people live longer because they are better fed, better lodged, better clothed, and better attended in sickness, and that these improvements are owing to that increase of national wealth which the manufacturing system has produced.

Much more might be said on this subject. But to what end? It is not from bills of mortality and statistical tables that Mr. Southey has learned his political creed. He cannot stoop to study the history of the system which he abuses, to strike the balance between the good and evil which it has produced, to compare district with district, or generation with generation. We will give his own reason for his opinion, the only reason which he gives for it, in his own words:—

> We remained awhile in silence looking upon the assemblage of dwellings below. Here, and in the adjoining hamlet of Millbeck, the effects of manufactures and of agriculture may be seen and compared. The old cottages are such as the poet and the painter equally delight in beholding. Substantially built of the native stone without mortar, dirtied with no white lime, and their low roofs covered with slate, if they had been raised by the magic of some indigenous Amphion's music, the materials could not have adjusted themselves more beautifully in accord with the surrounding scene; and time has still further harmonized them with weather stains, lichens, and moss, short grasses, and short fern, and stone-plants of various kinds. The ornamented chimneys, round or square, less adorned than those which, like little turrets, crest the houses of the Portuguese peasantry; and yet not less happily suited to their place, the hedge of clipt box beneath the windows, the rose-bushes beside the door, the little patch of flower ground, with its tall hollyhocks in front; the garden beside, the beehives, and the orchard with its bank of daffodils and snow-drops, the earliest and the profusest in these parts, indicate in the owners some portion of ease and leisure, some regards to neatness and comfort, some sense of natural, and innocent, and healthful enjoyment. The new cottages of the manufacturers are upon the manufacturing pattern—naked, and in a row.

> "How is it," said I, "that every thing which is connected with manufactures presents such features of unqualified deformity? From the largest of Mammon's temples down to the poorest hovel in which his helotry are stalled, these edifices have all one character. Time will not mellow them; nature will neither clothe nor conceal them; and they will remain always as offensive to the eye as to the mind."

Here is wisdom. Here are the principles on which nations are to be governed. Rose-bushes and poor-rates, rather than steam-engines and independence. Mortality and cottages with weather-stains, rather than health and long life with edifices which time cannot mellow. We are told, that our age has invented atrocities beyond the imagination of our fathers; that society has been brought into a state compared with which extermination would be a blessing; and all because the dwellings of cotton-spinners are naked and rectangular. Mr. Southey has found out a way, he tells us, in which the effects of manufactures and agriculture may be compared. And what is this way? To stand on a hill, to look at a cottage and a factory, and to see which is the prettier. Does Mr. Southey think that the body of the English peasantry live, or ever lived, in substantial or ornamented cottages, with box-hedges, flower-gardens, beehives, and orchards? If not, what is his parallel worth? We despise those mock philosophers, who think that they serve the cause of science by depreciating literature and the fine arts. But if any thing could excuse their narrowness of mind, it would be such a book as this. It is not strange that, when one enthusiast makes the picturesque the test of political good, another should feel inclined to proscribe altogether the pleasures of taste and imagination.

The Hammonds, both educated at Oxford, could find little good in the Industrial Revolution. To them, it was comparable to slavery, and they make their case with skill and verve.

FROM *The Rise of Modern Industry*

BY *John L. and Barbara Hammond*

ROME IMPORTED SLAVES to work in Italy; Englishmen counted it one of the advantages of the slave trade that it discouraged the competition of British colonists with British manufacturers. For the slaves were chiefly needed for industries like sugar planting, in which Englishmen at home were not engaged. Thus it might be argued that England had escaped the fate of Rome and that she so used the slave trade as to make it a stimulus rather than a discouragement to native energy and skill.

Yet England did not escape the penalty. For it was under this shadow that the new industrial system took form and grew, and the immense power with which invention had armed mankind was exercised at first under conditions that reproduced the degradation of the slave trade. The factory system was not like war or revolution a deliberate attack on society: it was the effort of men to use will, energy, organization and intelligence for the service of man's needs. But in adapting this new power to the satisfaction of its wants England could not escape from the moral atmosphere of the slave trade: the atmosphere in which it was the fashion to think of men as things.

In the days of the guilds the workman was regarded as a person with some kind of property or status; the stages by which this character is restricted to a smaller and smaller part of the working classes, and more and more of the journeymen and apprentices fall into a permanently inferior class, have been described by historians. In the early nineteenth century the workers, as a class, were looked upon as so much labour power to be used at the discretion of, and under conditions imposed by, their masters; not as men and women who are entitled to some voice in the arrangements of their life and work. The use of child labour on a vast scale had an important bearing on the growth of this temper.

The children of the poor were regarded as workers long before the Industrial Revolution. Locke suggested that they should begin work at three; Defoe rejoiced to see that in the busy homes of the Yorkshire clothiers "scarce anything above four years old, but its hands were sufficient for its own support." The new industrial system provided a great field for the employment of children, and Pitt himself, speaking in 1796, dwelt on this prospect with a satisfaction strange to modern minds, and disturbing even to some who heard him. One of the most elaborate of all Bentham's fantasies was his scheme for a great series of Industry Houses, 250 in number, each to hold 2,000 persons, for

John L. and Barbara Hammond, *The Rise of Modern Industry* (1925), pp. 194–195, 196–199, 200–201. Reprinted by permission of Methuen & Co., Ltd.

whose work, recreation, education, and marriage most minute regulations were laid down. An advantage he claimed for his system was that it would enable the apprentices to marry at "the earliest period compatible with health," and this was made possible by the employment of children. "And to what would they be indebted for this gentlest of all revolutions? To what, but to economy? Which dreads no longer the multiplication of man, now that she has shown by what secure and unperishable means infant man, a drug at present so much worse than worthless, may be endowed with an indubitable and universal value." Infant man soon became in the new industrial system what he never was in the old, the basis of a complicated economy.

Most children under the old domestic system worked at home under their parents' eyes, but in addition to such children there were workhouse children, who were hired out by overseers to every kind of master or mistress. Little care was taken to see that they were taught a trade or treated with humanity by their employers, and though London magistrates like Fielding did what they could to protect this unhappy class, their state was often a kind of slavery. The number of children on the hands of the London parishes was largely increased in the latter part of the eighteenth century, because an Act of Parliament, passed in 1767 in consequence of the exertions of Jonas Hanway, compelled the London parishes to board out their young children, and to give a bonus to every nurse whose charge survived. Until this time very few parish pauper children grew up to trouble their betters.

The needs of the London workhouses on the one hand, and those of the factory on the other, created a situation painfully like the situation in the West Indies. The Spanish employers in America wanted outside labour, because the supply of native labour was deficient in quantity and quality. The new cotton mills placed on streams in solitary districts were in the same case. The inventions had found immense scope for child labour, and in these districts there were only scattered populations. In the workhouses of large towns there was a quantity of child labour available for employment, that was even more powerless and passive in the hands of a master than the stolen negro, brought from his burning home to the hold of a British slave ship. Of these children it could be said, as it was said of the negroes, that their life at best was a hard one, and that their choice was often the choice between one kind of slavery and another. So the new industry which was to give the English people such immense power in the world borrowed at its origin from the methods of the American settlements.

How closely the apologies for this child serf system followed the apologies for the slave trade can be seen from Romilly's description of a speech made in the House of Commons in 1811. "Mr. Wortley, who spoke on the same side, insisted that, although in the higher ranks of society it was true that to cultivate the affections of children for their family was the source of every virtue, yet that it was not so among the lower orders, and that it was a benefit to take them away from their miserable and depraved parents. He said too that it would be highly injurious to the public to put a stop to the binding of so many apprentices to the cotton manufacturers, as it must necessarily raise the price of labour and enhance the price of cotton manufactured goods."

It was not until 1816 that Parliament would consent to reform this system of transportation. In that year a Bill that had been repeatedly introduced by Mr. Wilbraham Bootle passed both Houses, and it was made illegal for London children to be apprenticed more than forty miles away from their parish. But by this time the problem had changed, for steam-power had superseded water-power and mills could be built in towns; in these towns there were parents who were driven by poverty to send their children to the mills. In the early days of the factory system there had been a prejudice against sending children to the mill, but the hand-loom weaver had been sinking steadily from the beginning of the century into deeper and deeper poverty, and he was no longer able to maintain himself and his family. Sometimes too an adult worker was only given work on condition that he send his child to the mill. Thus the apprentice system was no longer needed. It had carried the factories over the first stage and at the second they could draw on the population of the neighbourhood.

These children, who were commonly called "free-labour children," were employed from a very early age. Most of them were piecers: that is they had to join together or piece the threads broken in the several roving or spinning machines. But there were tasks less skilled than these, and Robert Owen said that many children who were four or five years old were set to pick up waste cotton on the floor. Their hours were those of the apprentice children. They entered the mill gates at five or six in the morning and left them again at seven or eight at night. They had half an hour for breakfast and an hour for dinner, but even during meal hours they were often at work cleaning a standing machine; Fielden calculated that a child following the spinning machine could walk twenty miles in the twelve hours. Oastler was once in the company of a West Indian slave-master and three Bradford Spinners. When the slave-master heard what were the children's hours he declared: "I have always thought myself disgraced by being the owner of slaves, but we never in the West Indies thought it possible for any human being to be so cruel as to require a child of nine years old to work twelve and a half hours a day."

This terrible evil fastened itself on English life as the other fastened itself on the life of the Colonies. Reformers had an uphill struggle to get rid of its worst abuses. Throughout this long struggle the apologies for child labour were precisely the same as the apologies for the slave trade. Cobbett put it in 1833 that the opponents of the Ten Hours Bill had discovered that England's manufacturing supremacy depended on 30,000 little girls. This was no travesty of their argument. The champions of the slave trade pointed to the £70,000,000 invested in the sugar plantations, to the dependence of our navy on our commerce, and to the dependence of our commerce on the slave trade. This was the argument of Chatham in one generation and Rodney in another. When Fox destroyed the trade in 1806 even Sir Robert Peel complained that we were philosophizing when our looms were idle, and George Rose, that the Americans would take up the trade, and that Manchester, Stockport and Paisley would starve. . . .

The argument for child labour followed the same line. In the one case the interests of Liverpool, in the other those of Lancashire, demanded of the nation that it should accept one evil in order to escape from another. Cardwell, afterwards the famous army reformer, talked of the great capital sunk in the cotton industry and the danger of the blind impulse of humanity. Sir James Graham thought that the Ten Hours Bill would ruin the cotton industry and with it the trade of the country. The cotton industry had taken the place in this argument that had been held by the navy in the earlier controversy. Our population, which had grown so rapidly in the Industrial Revolution, was no longer able to feed itself: the food it bought was paid for by its manufactures: those manufactures depended on capital: capital depended on profits: profits depended on the labour of the boys and girls who enabled the manufacturer to work his mills long enough at a time to repay the cost of the plant and to compete with his foreign rivals. This was the circle in which the nation found its conscience entangled.

The foremost proponent of the necessity for revising the traditional accounts of the Industrial Revolution is T. S. Ashton, professor emeritus of economic history at the University of London.

FROM *The Treatment of Capitalism by Historians*
BY *T. S. Ashton*

THE STUDENT OF ENGLISH ECONOMIC HISTORY is fortunate in having at his disposal the reports of a long series of Royal Commissions and Committees of Inquiry beginning in the eighteenth century but reaching full stream in the 1830's, 1840's, and 1850's. These reports are one of the glories of the early Victorian age. They signalized a quickening of social conscience, a sensitiveness to distress, that had not been evident in any other period or in any other country. Scores of massive folios provided statistical and verbal evidence that all was not well with large numbers of the people of England and called the attention of legislators and the reading public to the need for reform. The economic historians of the succeeding generations could do no other than draw on their findings; and scholarship, no less than society, benefited. There was, however, loss as well as gain. A picture of the economic system constructed from Blue Books dealing with social grievances, and not with the normal processes of economic development, was bound to be one-sided. It is such a picture of early Victorian society that has become fixed in the minds of popular writers. . . . A careful reading of the reports would, indeed, lead to the conclusion that much that was wrong was the result of laws, customs, habits, and forms of organization that belonged to earlier periods and were rapidly becoming obsolete. It would have brought home to the mind that it was not among the factory employees but among the domestic workers, whose traditions and methods were those of the eighteenth century, that earnings were at their lowest. It would have provided evidence that it was not in the large establishments making use of steam power but in the garret or cellar workshops that conditions of employment were at their worst. It would have led to the conclusion that it was not in the growing manufacturing towns or the developing coal fields but in remote villages and the countryside that restrictions on personal freedom and the evils of truck were most marked. But few had the patience to go carefully through these massive volumes. It was so much easier to pick out the more sensational evidences of distress and work them into a dramatic story of exploitation. The result has been that a generation that had the enterprise and industry to assemble the facts, the honesty to reveal them, and the energy to set about the task of reform has been held up to obloquy as the author, not of the Blue Books, but of the evils themselves. Conditions in the mills and the factory town were so bad, it seemed, that there must have been deterioration; . . . and, since the supposed deterioration had taken place at a time when machinery had increased, the machines, and those who owned them, must have been responsible.

At the same time the romantic revival in literature led to an idyllic view of the life of the peasant. The idea that agriculture is the only natural and healthy activity for human beings has persisted, and indeed spread, as more of us have escaped from the curse of Adam—or, as the tedious phrase goes, "become divorced from the soil." A year ago an examinee remarked profoundly that "in earlier centuries agriculture was widespread in England" but added sorrowfully, "Today it is confined to the rural areas." There was a similar idealization of the condition of the domestic worker, who had taken only the first step in the proceedings for divorce. Bear with me while I read some passages with which Friedrich Engels (who is usually acclaimed a realist) opens his account of *The Condition of the Working Classes in England in 1844*. It is, of course, based on the writings of the Reverend Philip Gaskell, whose earnestness and honesty are not in doubt, but whose mind had not been confused by any study of history. Engels' book opens with the declaration that "the history of the proletariat in England begins with the invention of the steam-engine and of machinery for working cotton." Before their time, he continues,

> the workers vegetated throughout a passably comfortable existence, leading a righteous and peaceful life in all piety and probity; and their material condition was far better than that of their successors. They did not need to overwork; they did no more than they chose to do, and yet earned what they needed. They had leisure for healthful work in garden or field, work which, in itself, was recreation for them, and they could take part beside in the recreation and games of their

neighbours, and all these games—bowling, cricket, football, etc. contributed to their physical health and vigour. They were, for the most part, strong, well-built people, in whose physique little or no difference from that of their peasant neighbours was discoverable. Their children grew up in fresh country air, and, if they could help their parents at work, it was only occasionally; while of eight or twelve hours work for them there was no question.

It is difficult to say whether this or the lurid picture of the lives of the grandchildren of these people presented in later pages of the book is more completely at variance with the facts. Engels had no doubt whatsoever as to the cause of the deterioration in the condition of labor. "The proletariat," he repeats, "was called into existence by the introduction of machinery." "The consequences of improvement in machinery under our present social conditions," he asserts, "are, for the working-man, solely injurious, and often in the highest degree oppressive. Every new advance brings with it loss of employment, want and suffering."

Engels has had many disciples, even among those who do not accept the historical materialism of Marx, with which such views are generally connected. Hostility to the machine is associated with hostility to its products and, indeed, to all innovation in consumption. One of the outstanding accomplishments of the new industrial age is to be seen in the greatly increased supply and variety of fabrics offered on the market. Yet the changes in dress are taken as evidence of growing poverty: "The clothing of the working-people in a majority of cases," Engels declares, "is in a very bad condition. The material used for it is not of the best adapted. Wool and linen have almost vanished from the wardrobes of both sexes, and cotton has taken their place. Skirts are made of bleached or coloured cotton goods, and woollen petticoats are rarely to be seen on the wash-line." The truth is that they never had been greatly displayed on the wash line, for woollen goods are liable to shrink. The workers of earlier periods had to make their garments last (second or third hand as many of these were), and soap and water were inimical to the life of clothing. The new, cheap textiles may not have been as hard-wearing as broadcloth, but they were more abundant; and the fact that they could be washed without suffering harm had a bearing, if not on their own life, at least on the lives of those who wore them.

The same hostility is shown to innovation in food and drink. Generations of writers have followed William Cobbett in his hatred of tea. One would have thought that the enormous increase in consumption between the beginning of the eighteenth and the middle of the nineteenth century was one element in a rising standard of comfort; but only a few years ago Professor Parkinson asserted that it was "growing poverty" that made tea increasingly essential to the lower classes as ale was put beyond their means. (This, I may add, unfortunately meant that they were forced to consume sugar, and one must suppose that this practice also led to a fall in the standard of living.) Similarly, Dr. Salaman has recently assured us that the introduction of the potato into the diet of the workers at this time was a factor detrimental to health and that it enabled the employers to force down the level of wages—which, it is well known, is always determined by the minimum of food required for subsistence.

Very gradually those who held to these pessimistic views of the effects of industrial change have been forced to yield ground. The painstaking researches of Bowley and Wood have shown that over most of this period, and later, the course of real wages was upward. The proof is not at all easy, for it is clear that there were sections of the working classes of whom it was emphatically not true. In the first half of the nineteenth century the population of England was growing, partly because of natural increase, partly as the result of the influx of Irish. For those endowed with little or no skill, marginal productivity, and hence earnings, remained low. A large part of their incomes was spent on commodities (mainly food, drink, and housing), the cost of which had hardly been affected by technical development. That is why so many of the economists, like McCulloch and Mill, were themselves dubious about the beneficial nature of the industrial system. There were, however, large and growing sections of skilled and better-paid workers whose money incomes were rising and who had a substantial margin to spend on the products of the machine, the costs of which were falling progressively. The controversy really rests on which of the groups was increasing most. Generally it is now agreed that for the majority the gain in real wages was substantial.

But this does not dispose of the controversy. Real earnings might have risen, it was said, but it was the quality of life and not the quantity of goods consumed that mattered. In particular, it was the evil conditions of housing and the insanitary conditions of the towns that were called as evidence that the circumstances of labor had worsened. "Everything which here arouses horror and indignation," wrote Engels of Manchester in 1844, "is of recent origin, belongs to the industrial epoch"—and the reader is left to infer that the equally repulsive features of cities like Dublin and Edinburgh, which were scarcely touched by the new industry, were, somehow or other, also the product of the machine.

This is the legend that has spread round the world and has determined the attitude of millions of men and women to labor-saving devices and to those who own them. Indians and Chinese, Egyptians and Negroes, to whose fellow-countrymen today the dwellings of the English of the mid-nineteenth century would be wealth indeed, solemnly declare, in the scripts I have to read, that the English workers were living in conditions unworthy of beasts. They write with indignation about the inefficiency of the sanitation and the absence of civic amenities—the very nature of which is still unknown to the urban workers of a large part of the earth.

Now, no one who has read the reports of the Committee on the Sanitary Condition of the Working Classes of 1842 or that of the Commission on the Health of Towns of 1844 can doubt that the state of affairs was, from the point of view of modern Western civilization, deplorable. But, equally, no one who has read Dorothy George's account of living conditions in London in the eighteenth century can be sure that they had deteriorated. Dr. George herself believes that they had improved, and Clapham declared that the English towns of the mid-century were "less crowded than the great towns of other countries and not, universally, more insanitary."

FROM *The Industrial Revolution*
BY *T. S. Ashton*

MUCH HAS BEEN WRITTEN about the effects of the industrial revolution on the workers. Some, impressed by the lot of those who went down in the struggle against the machine, have declared that technological change brought little but misery and poverty, and a statistician of repute has set on record his opinion that by the early years of the nineteenth century the standard of life of the British worker had been forced down to Asiatic levels. Mr. Colin Clark can hardly have looked at the statistics which more than a generation of research has produced. The careful studies of Mrs. Gilboy indicate that, over the eighteenth century, the material well-being of the labourer in the woollen area of the South-West had, indeed, fallen, but that the lot of his fellow in the textile region of the North had steadily improved, and that the labourer of London more than held his own. It is true that the rise of prices after 1793 made many humble people poorer. But before the end of the war (as Professor Silberling has shown) industrial wages in England caught up with retail prices, and in the 'twenties the gain was pronounced. In 1831 the cost of living was 11 per cent higher than in 1790, but over this span of time urban wages had increased, it appears, by no less than 43 per cent.

It would have been strange, indeed, if the industrial revolution had simply made the rich richer and the poor poorer. For the commodities to which it gave rise were not, in general, luxuries, but necessaries and capital goods. The tardiness with which the last of these yielded their fruit to the consumer has already been explained. But by the 'twenties the effects of the war were passing away and the cottons and woollens, and food and drink, which now became available, were consumed not by the few, but by the masses. Some of the products of the factories and ironworks were sent abroad, but the return cargoes did not consist, in the main, of wines and silks, but of sugar, grain, coffee, and tea for the people at large. Much has been made of the suggestion that the prices of the things Britain exported fell more rapidly than those of the things she brought back: there was no revolution to reduce costs in overseas agriculture; and British lending abroad may also have helped to give the terms of trade an unfavourable turn. But, though such influences may explain why, in the 'thirties and 'forties, real wages were lower than might have been expected, they had little effect, it would seem, between 1815 and 1830. The diet of the worker almost certainly improved: there was a substitution of "flower of wheat" for rye

Thomas S. Ashton, *The Industrial Revolution*, 1760–1830. (1948), pp. 157–161. Published by Oxford University Press. Reprinted by permission.

and oatmeal; and meat, which had been a rarity, became, with potatoes, the staple dish on the artisan's table. Not all the coal raised from the pits went to feed the furnaces and steam-engines: a warm hearth and a hot meal were of no small consequence to the man who came home wet from the fields.

In 1802 George Chalmers remarked that the laborious classes were "too wealthy to covet the pittance of the soldier, or too independent to court the dangers of the sailor." There were, true enough, many vagrants and paupers, but, even before the new Poor Law came in, the hordes of the "indigent and distressed" had probably shrunk. Hours of labour were long, and holidays few; there is a mass of evidence that employment in factories was harmful to the health and morals of the young. A leading politician has recently spoken of the "mechanized horrors of the industrial revolution," and there can be little doubt that the deeper mines and more complicated machines brought new risks of mutilation and death. But against all this must be set the lessening of strain on those who worked in the heavy trades, and the decline in the number of crippled and deformed people that followed the introduction of power in places like Sheffield. There must be set, also, the reduction of sweating of women and young children, the rise in family earnings, the greater regularity of pay, and the gain in welfare that came as industrial work was taken out of the home.

Whether the houses themselves were becoming better or worse is difficult to determine: much depends on the periods compared. Many of the dwellings provided for the workers by the country factory masters have survived—at Cromford, Mellor, and Styal. They have design and proportion, and, even by modern standards, are not wanting in amenity and comfort. But these were put up when building materials were plentiful, wages relatively low, and money relatively cheap. After 1793 the import of timber from the Baltic was restricted, and the price of labour of bricklayers and carpenters went up. At least two-thirds of the rent of a dwelling consists of interest charges: rates of interest were rising, and for more than a generation they remained high. This meant that if dwellings were to be let at rents which the workers could afford to pay they had to be smaller and less durable than those of the 'eighties. The rows of ill-built, back-to-back houses, into which the rapidly growing population of the towns was pressed, were largely the product of wartime conditions.

After 1815 matters were made worse by the influx of Irish, who, gregarious by instinct, crowded into the seaports and the towns of the North. Careful estimates made by members of the Manchester Statistical Society in the middle 'thirties led to the conclusion that about one-sixth of the families in Manchester were Irish, and that the percentage of the people living in cellars was 11.75. In Liverpool, where again there were many Irish, no less than 15 percent of the inhabitants were in cellars. But in the newer towns, which were the special creation of the industrial revolution, conditions were far less grim. In Bury, where there were few Irish (and few hand-loom weavers), only 3.75 per cent, and in Ashton-under-Lyne only 1.25 per cent, of the people were housed in this way. In these places, the investigators reported, the houses of the workers were not only less crowded, but also better furnished and cleaner than those of the cities.

An historian has written of "the disasters of the industrial revolution." If by this he means that the years 1760–1830 were darkened by wars and made cheerless by dearth, no objection can be made to the phrase. But if he means that the technical and economic changes were themselves the source of calamity the opinion is surely perverse. The central problem of the age was how to feed and clothe and employ generations of children outnumbering by far those of any earlier time. Ireland was faced by the same problem. Failing to solve it, she lost in the 'forties about a fifth of her people by emigration or starvation and disease. If England had remained a nation of cultivators and craftsmen, she could hardly have escaped the same fate, and, at best, the weight of a growing population must have pressed down the spring of her spirit. She was delivered, not by her rulers, but by those who, seeking no doubt their own narrow ends, had the wit and resource to devise new instruments of production and new methods of administering industry. There are to-day on the plains of India and China men and women, plague-ridden and hungry, living lives little better, to outward appearance, than those of the cattle that toil with them by day and share their places of sleep by night. Such Asiatic standards, and such unmechanized horrors, are the lot of those who increase their numbers without passing through an industrial revolution.

Two English scholars, E. J. Hobsbawm and R. M. Hartwell, continue the debate over the effects of the Industrial Revolution, using modern analyses. It is not the last word, but it is among the latest.

FROM *The Standard of Living During the Industrial Revolution*
BY *E. J. Hobsbawm and R. M. Hartwell*

HOBSBAWM ATTACKS:

THE DEBATE on the British people's standard of living in the early industrial period, which had for some time been dormant, was revived in the later 1950's and has continued briskly ever since. To be more precise, what had established itself as a virtual academic orthodoxy in Britain, the optimistic view associated with Sir John Clapham and T. S. Ashton, was sharply challenged, and a number

E. J. Hobsbawm and R. M. Hartwell, "The Standard of Living during the Industrial Revolution: A Discussion," in *Economic History Review*, N. S. 16 (1963), pp. 119, 126–128, 135–137, 142–143. Reprinted by permission.

of students have since attempted to rebut or to come to terms with this challenge. The debate has perhaps continued long enough for one of the challengers to survey the battlefield, which is less confused than a casual reading of the relevant literature might suggest. This is the object of the present article.

*   *   *

. . . A final and more defensive argument on the optimistic side remains to be considered, for the frank admission of defeat implicit in the view that capitalism did not cause deterioration, because this occurs in all industrial revolutions, hardly requires comment. It has been argued that, while conditions in the early nineteenth century were bad, and possibly not improving, they were better than in the eighteenth century, which the anti-optimists have persistently idealized. Hence the case for improvement stands.

*   *   *

This is admittedly to call in the unknown to justify the half-known, for we know much less about eighteenth-century standards than we do about those of the period after 1790. Certainly we know too little to settle the argument in quantitative terms. Yet we do know enough to reject certain common contentions of the optimists, or rather to suggest that these express hope rather than research or even thought. These contentions are that urban conditions were better, or at any rate no worse, in the early nineteenth century than in the eighteenth, and that factory work was greatly superior to eighteenth-century domestic work.

Nobody doubts that rookeries as bad as those of the nineteenth century can be cited from the eighteenth. The issue is not whether "slums and adulteration were peculiar products of industrialization" but whether there was more of both in 1840 than in 1780. And of course there was. It is not only likely, but we actually know it. The issue is not whether in some unquantifiable sense "rural life was naturally better than town life." It is also, among other things, why the labourers of Wiltshire, hardly a pampered group, had on average something like twice the life-expectancy at birth of the labourers of Manchester and Liverpool, a comparison which is the staple of sanitary reformers' arguments in the 1840's and 1850's. If it is objected that the superiority of rural health was not new, then it may be pointed out with equal legitimacy that the proportion of the urbanized was now much greater.

The problem of domestic industry and its exploitation and oppression is slightly more complex, for the optimists' view here is based not on simple error or omission, but on misconception. There can be little doubt that where the two coexisted in the nineteenth century, factory work was generally far more materially attractive, at least after the decline of domestic industry set in. The optimists' mistake here is to contrast an eighteenth century identified with "domestic work" with a nineteenth identified with "factory work." But this is wrong. The Industrial Revolution did not merely replace cottage or slum workshop by factory, but multiplied *both* domestic industry and factories; the former either in direct dependence on the latter (as in cotton weaving), or in the rapidly expanding branches of production as yet quite untouched by the factory (as in the garment industry), or in industries whose scale remained small even when they adopted new power. It also eventually killed off many of the expanded domestic industries it had created. The fate of these vastly expanded and then sacrificed domestic branches is therefore just as much part of the social impact of the Industrial Revolution as the fate of the factory population. It is entirely illegitimate to reject the half-million and more handloom weavers of 1830 or the army of seamstresses as survivals from pre-industrialism. But for the Industrial Revolution most of them would not have been there, or at any rate their life would have been very different.

Moreover, domestic industry in this new phase was—at least after its early boom—probably much less attractive than before the revolution, even setting aside extreme cases such as the slow strangulation of the handloom weavers. Thus in Sheffield grinders' disease was "scarcely known" towards the end of the eighteenth century, but in 1842 it affected 34 per cent of all razor grinders (and between 50 and 100 per cent of all above the age of 30); a natural consequence of expanding the volume of production without adequate corresponding alterations in working and living conditions. It is therefore plain that neither an optimistic nor a gloomy case can rest on a comparison of factory and outworkers *at the same time;* yet optimists still continue to make such comparisons.

The question how social conditions in the period of the "take-off" and after compared with those before the Industrial Revolution must, in the present state of our knowledge, still be left open. All that can be said is that hitherto the attempts to bring it into the optimistic argument have been more marked by a desire to prove preconceived notions than by careful research.

However, to compare the pre-industrial with the industrial age in purely quantitative terms is to play Lear without the King. For the debate between the optimists and the pessimists has been sociological as much as economic. Engels' own case in favour of the eighteenth century, for instance, was not merely that the standard of living of the cottagers was "much better than that of the factory workers today," which is debateable, but that they lived in a far more secure, psychologically satisfactory and fuller community, though at the cost, which he freely admitted, of ignorance and stagnation. The crux of the Hammonds' argument was not simply that the early industrial age was poor, but that it was bleak. In other words, poverty and dirt *alone* are not the issue. The change from one way of life to another is equally at stake. But while the careful student of poverty can only say that the case for deterioration, while not implausible, cannot be proved, though that against a marked improvement is extremely strong, the sociological argument for deterioration is far more powerful.

Now this argument has been virtually absent from the debate since Clapham apparently worsted the Hammonds a generation ago, and recent anti-Claphamites have deliberately not stressed it, for they have rightly chosen to fight the Claphamites on their own chosen ground of quantitative indices. If the Claphamites were right, the nonquantitative arguments became irrelevant or at any rate secondary. The labouring poor might have been subjectively disturbed or unhappy, but at all events they wept all the way to their increasingly large Sunday dinners. Consequently the most effective way of controverting them was to show that there was no reason to believe that the Sunday dinners were becoming larger, and the case would be even stronger if the anti-Claphamites deliberately refrained from bringing in those non-quantitative considerations which the optimists had (mistakenly) dismissed as sentimental and misleading. But this does not mean that these considerations were ever unimportant. And now that the original Claphamite assault has been repulsed, it is time to say firmly that the attempt to dismiss the qualitative and sociological case against early industrialism must also be regarded as unsuccessful.

In fact no such attempt was really made. For the sociology of industrializa-tion implicit in most of the meliorist arguments is extremely primitive. It is bare-ly more advanced than that of Peacock's "Steam Intellect Society," and greatly inferior to, say, Engels'. We need hardly comment on extreme examples such as Chaloner and Henderson's remark that "in the 1840's much hardship among workers was due to 'secondary' or 'self-induced' poverty, the result of excessive and feckless expenditure on drink, gambling and tobacco." The more moderate tendency, which merely holds that some people had one view about the social effects of industrialization, some another, is equally futile. For we now know quite enough about the immense human strains imposed by the process of sud-den and large-scale social transformation to state firmly that its eventual—or even its immediate—material benefits cannot be used to offset these strains, and that those who underestimate mass unhappiness or disturbance merely because they can see no adequate reason for it are unqualified to talk about the subject.

HARTWELL REPLIES

In my two articles on the standard of living during the Industrial Revolution, which Dr. Hobsbawm now criticizes, I was concerned both with surveying the literature of the controversy, and also with analysing the available evidence to see if conclusions could be made. The conclusions I came to were, first, the controversy has been confused by arguments about values and by people talk-ing about different things as though they were talking about the same thing, and second, that there had been "an upward trend in living standards during the Industrial Revolution" and that "the standard of living of the mass of the people of England was improving . . . slowly during the war, more quickly after 1815, and rapidly after 1840." This conclusion I modified by stressing that the standard of living was *not* high and was not rising fast *before* the forties, and also that there was "dire poverty" and "cyclical and technological unem-ployment of a most distressing character." I emphasized also that increasing real income was no measure of "ultimate well-being" and that the period of the

Industrial Revolution was one of political discontent and social upheaval—but also that it was a period of increasing opportunity for working-class men and women. To this "extreme" view I still hold, and it may be compared with the latest conclusions of Dr. Hobsbawm, which seem mild enough—consumption figures "are compatible with a slight decrease, possibly with a slight increase," the case for deterioration "while not implausible, cannot be proved," "the view that there was substantial, or any, deterioration has not yet been firmly established," "the argument that real incomes remained roughly stable will commend itself as the most acceptable formula"—but which are established in such a fashion as to create an impression of pessimism, quite apart from the grand final conclusion that, whatever can be said about material standards, "the sociological argument for deterioration is far more powerful." Indeed, Dr. Hobsbawm's convictions show not so much in his mild conclusions as in the fervour with which he defends Engels and attacks the optimists.

Dr. Hobsbawm's discussion is "to survey the battlefield." The military metaphor reflects Dr. Hobsbawm's idea of how historical controversy should be conducted; when he is a combatant, he believes in total war. And so he spends much time attacking the expertise and the evidence of the historians with whom he does not agree. Thus, the optimists (J. H. Clapham, T. S. Ashton, etc.) are "committed" to an "*a priori* case for amelioration" and have "a desire to prove preconceived notions"; their sources and evidence are "suspect for their optimist bias," "irrelevant," "anachronistic," "feeble props," "too negligible," "highly untypical"; their analysis and conclusions are "brash" (about Ashton and Clapham!), "unqualified," "implausible," "improbable," "frivolous," "careless," "cursory," "ill-informed," "inconclusive," "unsupported," "illegitimate," "futile," "not now based on reliable evidence," "carry no serious weight," "purely rhetorical," "striking perversions of fact." At the same time as he batters the opposition with pejorative adjectives, Dr. Hobsbawm *assumes* victory and righteousness; he assumes the optimists and their sources are wrong, until they prove the pessimists wrong: "the onus of proving the gloomy and traditional views are wrong, continues to rest squarely on the optimists." As part of the assumption of being right, Dr. Hobsbawm posits time and time again an alleged generally acceptable "conventional view"—"the traditional case for deterioration in labour conditions"—and imputes agreement with his interpretation of history by the majority of good men: "few would doubt," "common consent," "a predominance of informed opinion," "the mass of contemporary evidence," "general agreement," etc. He tries also to discredit the optimists by attributing to them statements they have never made and views they have never held. This is done partly by stating optimist generalizations in an extreme form by using unreasonable adjectives and adverbs which, if they were removed, would leave reasonable, or at least debatable, propositions. As Dr. Hobsbawm states them, however, they are convenient "aunt sallies" for him to demolish; for example, "the hypothesis of a *marked* or *substantial* rise in the standard of living . . . is . . .

an extremely improbable one," or "the view that real wages rose *markedly* during our period is not now based on reliable evidence" (italics mine). In this way Dr. Hobsbawm ascribes to J. H. Clapham and T. S. Ashton an extreme view and claims in consequence that it is a point now "clearly established . . . that the traditional Clapham-Ashton view has been dislodged without resistance." But J. H. Clapham had already "modified" his original non-extreme position in the 1939 Preface to the second edition of his history: "I did not mean that everything was getting better. I only meant that recent historians have too often, in my opinion, stressed the worsenings and slurred over or ignored the bettering."

* * *

More directly, however, Dr. Hobsbawm misquotes or misrepresents the optimists. Thus, for example, my article on "The Rising Standard of Living in England, 1800–1850" is misused. For example, Dr. Hobsbawm chooses from the sentence—"Generally, as historical analyses of economic development have shown, an increase in per capita income has been accompanied by a more equal income distribution" (with a footnote reference to Kuznets)—only the following—"an increase in per capita income [was] accompanied by a more equal income distribution" (Dr. Hobsbawm's "was")—turning a general into a specific statement, and implying that I was referring only to England during the Industrial Revolution. There are many other examples, but I do not want here to catalogue all Dr. Hobsbawm's misrepresentations. Nor do I want to discuss the methodological and ethical problems of writing history in this fashion. Nevertheless it is necessary to have some knowledge of Dr. Hobsbawm's methods to make the understanding of his history possible.

Dr. Hobsbawm twice claims that the eighteenth century is "unknown" and that "in the present state of our knowledge," comparisons with the nineteenth century "must . . . still [be] left open." Elsewhere, however, he still posits a golden age, and, in comparison with the earlier period describes how the labouring poor of the Industrial Revolution felt an "unquantifiable and spiritual sense of loss," and how "the self-confident, coherent, educated and cultured pre-industrial mechanics and domestic workers" declined and fell (in spite of agreeing also with Engels that the pre-industrial workers lived in "ignorance and stagnation"). But the researches of Mrs. M. D. George, Miss D. Marshall and the Webbs reveal a pre-industrial society that was static and sordid, with the labouring poor on subsistence wages and periodically decimated by cycles, plagues and famines. What Dr. Hobsbawm has to prove is that living conditions in the eighteenth century were *better* than in the early nineteenth, not, as we all know, that conditions during the Industrial Revolution were bad. Again, it proves very little that life-expectation was higher in the country than in the cities of the Industrial Revolution; it was also higher in the eighteenth century, and it is still higher to-day. What Dr. Hobsbawm has to explain away is that average life-expectancy increased between 1780 and 1840, *during* the Industrial Revolution. In the most detailed examination yet made of the decline in mortality during and after the Industrial Revolution T. McKeown and R. G. Record conclude that "the main reason for the rise in population in the late eighteenth and early nineteenth centuries was an improvement in economic and social conditions."

But perhaps the whole debate is irrelevant. In his final paragraphs Dr. Hobsbawm argues that, although the case for deterioration of material standards "while not implausible, cannot be proved" (a disarming concession after so much argument) "the sociological argument for deterioration is far more powerful." The claim is accompanied by the usual accusations that the optimists have neglected sociological problems, that they "underestimate mass unhappiness as disturbance merely because they can see no adequate reason for it, and are unqualified to talk about the subject." As with the debate on material standards, Dr. Hobsbawm has *commenced* what might become a new debate with a thoroughly gloomy picture, claiming that the social effects of industrialization were all evil. On the relationship of material progress (or deterioration) to social progress (or deterioration), and even on the precise nature of social deterioration, he is more vague, using such phrases as "spiritual sense of loss," "loss and change in status," "immense human strains," and "the extraordinary depth, desperation and bitterness of the social discontent"; and Dr. Hobsbawm's only excursions into social theory to explain these alleged conditions are, on the one hand, to claim the *"inevitability"* (italics mine) of "the social stresses of industrialization," and, on the other, to generalize, not very originally, that "men do not live by bread alone." This debate on the dynamics of social change cannot be concluded here, but some *specific* social gains of this period might be mentioned to offset in the minds of more impressionable readers the pessimism of Dr. Hobsbawm: (i) the increasing social and economic independence of women, (ii) the reduction in child labour, (iii) the growth of friendly societies, trade unions, savings' banks, mechanics' institutes and co-operative societies, (iv) the growth of literacy (more of the population could read and write in 1850 than in 1800), and (v) the changing character of social disorder, which, as F. C. Mather recently demonstrated, was much less brutish and destructive in the 1840's than in the 1780's. The Marxist doctrine of social and economic evolution cannot be protected for ever, even by Dr. Hobsbawm, from that misfortune, long ago foreseen by Herbert Spencer, of being "a deduction killed by a fact." And in this case, the facts are legion.

The Marxists— Revolutionaries or Reformers?

CONTENTS

QUESTIONS FOR STUDY

1   How do Marx and Engels define social classes in the *Communist Manifesto*? Why does this definition make class conflict inevitable?

2   What is the goal of revolution in the *Communist Manifesto*?

3   How does Engels' position change from the time of the *Communist Manifesto* to that of the letter to Van Patten?

4   Why did Engels feel, in 1894, that revolution could be avoided?

5   What is the basis for the disagreement between Carr and Ulam?

6   What function does revolution play in Lenin's system?

The Industrial Revolution caused an upheaval in England of almost the same scale as that created in Europe by the French Revolution. Its effects could not be ignored, especially as they appeared to be almost entirely evil as far as the common man was concerned. Not all those who raised their voices against industrialization were wild-eyed radicals. The leader of the reform movement in England was the Earl of Shaftesbury, who simply felt it was un-Christian to force women and children to work fourteen hours a day in mines and factories. Among the other reformers were men like Robert Owen, who argued that exploitation was simply bad for production and went on to prove his point by paying his workers unheard-of wages, providing them with clean, neat housing, and still making a profit.

In the nineteenth century the air was filled with similar partial "solutions" to the problems created by the Industrial Revolution. It was Karl Marx and Friedrich Engels who saw furthest into the total situation created by industrialization. To them, the Industrial Revolution was no mere accident but a necessary step in the economic development of Great Britain and, ultimately, of the world. It was the culmination of the rise of the bourgeoisie, which had begun in the waning years of the Middle Ages. Its evils were clear, but only Marx and Engels (they maintained) knew how to interpret them properly. Exploitation caused pain and misery, but in the long run this pain and misery were both necessary and good. It was pain and misery that would force self-consciousness upon the working class. As industrialization spread over the world, it would create an ever-larger proletariat whose increasing self-consciousness would provide the bonds necessary to unite it against capitalism. The bourgeoisie, far from triumphing over the working class through the imposition of the factory system, was really digging its own grave. When the proletariat became large enough and conscious of its unity, it would rise up and overthrow the bourgeois state, use the instruments of capitalism for its own liberation, and finally usher in a new era of human history in which, for the first time, no man would be exploited by another.

All this was spelled out in masterful prose in The German Ideology, written in 1846, and Manifesto of the Communist Party, which burst upon the world in the revolutionary year of 1848. The coincidence of the publication of the Communist Manifesto and the outbreak of revolutions in France, Germany, Austria, Poland, and Italy was enough to put fear of Marx into the heart of the most confident capitalist. Even some "Socialists" found Marx's gleeful prediction of world cataclysm rather hard to take and sought somehow to soften the Marxist message. Almost immediately, therefore, the politically aware in the industrialized nations divided into two opposing camps vis-à-vis Marxism. On the one side were those who took Marx seriously when he insisted upon the necessity of revolution; on the other were those who argued that the goal of Marxism was control of the state and that revolution was merely one means, perhaps not the best, for attaining this end. This split created odd bedfellows. Both the robber baron and Lenin, for example, could agree that Marxism necessarily meant violent revolu-

tion, and both acted accordingly. The robber baron insisted upon repressive leg-islation to nip Marxist socialism in the bud; Lenin insisted upon creating a small, elite cadre of revolutionary leaders who would know what to do when the opportunity presented itself.

The opponents of violent revolution included those who deplored violence in any form as well as those who felt that revolution from below was doomed in an age of increasing military sophistication. Marx himself was equivocal, and Engels appears to have abandoned his early revolutionary position late in life. So the revisionists could and did cite Marx and Engels as support for their view.

As the arguments that follow illustrate, the purpose of revolution is not an academic quibble. The whole Socialist strategy will ultimately be determined by one's answer to the question: Is violent revolution necessary for the triumph of socialism? During the course of the debate, which involved both competing theo-ries of history and competing evaluations of contemporary political situations, the meanings of key words appeared to change. Did violent revolution really mean open warfare, or could seizure of power by means of the vote also qualify as a revolution? And what, precisely, was revolution necessary for—merely the attainment of power? Or was the revolution itself the crucible in which the unity of the proletariat was to be achieved? And if this were the case, would not peri-odic "revolutions" be necessary even after power was seized by the people in order to preserve the unity without which the Socialist ideal could never be achieved? This last question brings us beyond Marx and even Lenin to Mao Tse-tung.

1

The Road to Revolution

Karl Marx (1818–1883) was one of the leading thinkers of the nineteenth century. Philosopher, journalist, economist, polemicist, and founder of the communist movement, he poured forth a stream of trenchant criticism of contemporary society and philosophical analyses of contemporary ills, all in the cause of ultimate revolution. In 1846, in measured terms, he laid out his views of the nature and history of man in The German Ideology. *This piece contains an exposition of the ideas upon which the* Manifesto of the Communist Party (Communist Manifesto) *(1848) was to be based.*

FROM *The German Ideology*

BY *Karl Marx*

MEN CAN BE DISTINGUISHED from animals by consciousness, by religion or anything else you like. They themselves begin to distinguish themselves from animals as soon as they begin to *produce* their means of subsistence, a step which is conditioned by their physical organization. By producing their means of subsistence men are indirectly producing their actual material life.

The way in which men produce their means of subsistence depends first of all on the nature of the actual means they find in existence and have to reproduce. This mode of production must not be considered simply as being the reproduction of the physical existence of the individuals. Rather it is a definite form of activity of these individuals, a definite form of expressing their life, a definite *mode of life* on their part. As individuals express their life, so they are. What they are, therefore, coincides with their production, both with *what* they produce and with *how* they produce. The nature of individuals thus depends on the material conditions determining their production.

This production only makes its appearance with the increase of population. In its turn this presupposes the intercourse of individuals with one another. The form of this intercourse is again determined by production.

The German Ideology, Karl Marx, translated by C. J. Arthur (1981), pp. 42–52. Reprinted by permission.

The relations of different nations among themselves depend upon the extent to which each has developed its productive forces, the division of labour and internal intercourse. This statement is generally recognized. But not only the relation of one nation to others, but also the whole internal structure of the nation itself depends on the stage of development reached by its production and its internal and external intercourse. How far the productive forces of a nation are developed is shown most manifestly by the degree to which the division of labour has been carried. Each new productive force, in so far as it is not merely a quantitative extension of productive forces already known, brings about (for instance the bringing into cultivation of fresh land), a further development of the division of labour.

The division of labour inside a nation leads at first to the separation of industrial and commercial from agricultural labour, and hence to the separation of town and country and a clash of interests between them. Its further development leads to the separation of commercial from industrial labour. At the same time through the division of labour there develop, inside these various branches further, various divisions among the individuals co-operating in definite kinds of labour. The relative position of these individual groups is determined by the methods employed in agriculture, industry and commerce (patriarchalism, slavery, estates, classes). These same conditions are to be seen (given a more developed intercourse) in the relations of different nations to one another.

The various stages of development in the division of labour are just so many different forms of ownership; i.e. the existing stage in the division of labour determines also the relations of individuals to one another with reference to the material, instrument, and product of labour.

The first form of ownership is tribal ownership. It corresponds to the undeveloped stage of production, at which a people lives by hunting and fishing, by the rearing of beasts or, in the highest stage, agriculture. In the latter case it presupposes a great mass of uncultivated stretches of land. The division of labour is at this stage still very elementary and is confined to a further extension of the natural division of labour imposed by the family. The social structure is therefore limited to an extension of the family; patriarchal family chieftains; below them the members of the tribe; finally slaves. The slavery latent in the family only develops gradually with the increase of population, the growth of wants, and with the extension of external relations, of war or of trade.

The second form is the ancient communal and State ownership which proceeds especially from the union of several tribes into a city by agreement or by conquest, and which is still accompanied by slavery. Beside communal ownership we already find movable, and later also immovable, private property developing, but as an abnormal form subordinate to communal ownership. It is only as a community that the citizens hold power over their labouring slaves, and on this account alone, therefore, they are bound to the form of communal ownership. It is the communal private property which compels the active citizens to remain in this natural form of association over against their slaves. For this reason the whole structure of society based on this communal ownership, and with it the power of the people, decays in the same measure as immovable private property evolves. The division of labour is already more developed. We already find the antagonism of town and country; later the antagonism between those states which represent town interests and those which represent country, and inside the towns themselves the antagonism between industry and maritime commerce. The class relation between citizens and slaves is now completely developed.

This whole interpretation of history appears to be contradicted by the fact of conquest. Up till now violence, war, pillage, rape and slaughter, etc. have been accepted as the driving force of history. Here we must limit ourselves to the chief points and take therefore only a striking example—the destruction of an old civilization by a barbarous people and the resulting formation of an entirely new organization of society (Rome and the barbarians; Feudalism and Gaul; the Byzantine Empire and the Turks). With the conquering barbarian people war itself is still, as hinted above, a regular form of intercourse, which is the more eagerly exploited as the population increases, involving the necessity of new means of production to supersede the traditional and, for it, the only possible, crude mode of production. In Italy it was, however, otherwise. The concentration of landed property (caused not only by buying-up and indebtedness but also by inheritance, since loose living being rife and marriage rare, the old families died out and their possessions fell into the hands of a few) and its conversion into grazing-land (caused not only by economic forces still operative today but by the importation of plundered and tribute-corn and the resultant lack of demand for Italian corn) brought about the almost total disappearance of the free population. The very slaves died out again and again, and had constantly to be replaced by new ones. Slavery remained the basis of the whole productive system. The plebeians, mid-way between freemen and slaves, never succeeded in becoming more than a proletarian rabble. Rome indeed never became more than a city; its connection with the provinces was almost exclusively political and could therefore easily be broken again by political events.

With the development of private property, we find here for the first time the same conditions which we shall find again, only on a more extensive scale, with modern private property. On the one hand the concentration of private property, which began very early in Rome, (as the Licinian agrarian law proves), and proceeded very rapidly from the time of the civil wars and especially under the Emperors; on the other hand, coupled with this, the transformation of the plebeian small peasantry into a proletariat, which, however, owing to its intermediate position between propertied citizens and slaves, never achieved an independent development.

The third form of ownership is feudal or estate-property. If antiquity started out from the town and its little territory, the Middle Ages started out from the country. This different starting-point was determined by the sparseness of the population at that time, which was scattered over a large area and which received no large increase from the conquerors. In contrast to Greece and Rome, feudal development therefore extends over a much wider field, prepared by the Roman conquests and the spread of agriculture at first associated with it. The last centuries of the declining Roman Empire and its conquest by the barbarians destroyed a number of productive forces; agriculture had declined, industry had decayed for want of a market, trade had died out or been violently suspended, the rural and urban population had decreased. From these conditions and the mode of organization of the conquest determined by them, feudal property developed under the influence of the Germanic military constitution. Like tribal and communal ownership, it is based again on a community; but the directly producing class standing over against it is not, as in the case of the ancient community, the slaves, but the enserfed small peasantry. As soon as feudalism is fully developed, there also arises antagonism to the towns. The hierarchical system of land ownership, and the armed bodies of retainers associated with it, gave the nobility power over the serfs. This feudal organization was, just as much as the ancient communal ownership, an association against a subjected producing class; but the form of association and the relation to the direct producers were different because of the different conditions of production.

This feudal organization of land-ownership had its counterpart in the towns in the shape of corporative property, the feudal organization of trades. Here property consisted chiefly in the labour of each individual person. The necessity for association against the organized robber-nobility, the need for communal covered markets in an age when the industrialist was at the same time a merchant, the growing competition of the escaped serfs swarming into the rising towns, the feudal structure of the whole country: these combined to bring about the guilds. Further, the gradually accumulated capital of individual craftsmen and their stable numbers, as against the growing population, evolved the relation of journeyman and apprentice, which brought into being in the towns a hierarchy similar to that in the country.

Thus the chief form of property during the feudal epoch consisted on the one hand of landed property with serf-labour chained to it, and on the other of individual labour with small capital commanding the labour of journeymen. The organization of both was determined by the restricted conditions of production—the small-scale and primitive cultivation of the land, and the craft type of industry. There was little division of labour in the heyday of feudalism. Each land bore in itself the conflict of town and country and the division into estates was certainly strongly marked; but apart from the differentiation of princes, nobility, clergy and peasants in the country, and masters, journeymen, apprentices and soon also the rabble of casual labourers in the towns, no division of importance took place. In agriculture it was rendered difficult by the strip-system, beside which the cottage industry of the peasants themselves emerged as another factor. In industry there was no division of labour at all in the individual trades themselves, and very little between them. The separation of industry and commerce was found already in existence in older towns; in the newer it only developed later, when the towns entered into mutual relations.

The grouping of larger territories into feudal kingdoms was a necessity for the landed nobility as for the towns. The **organization** of the ruling class, the nobility, had, therefore, everywhere a monarch at its head.

The fact is, therefore, that definite individuals who are productively active in a definite way enter into these definite social and political relations. Empirical observation must in each separate instance bring out empirically, and without any mystification and speculation, the connection of the social and political structure with production. The social structure and the State are continually evolving out of the life-process of definite individuals, but of individuals, not as they may appear in their own or other people's imagination, but as they really are; i.e. as they are effective, produce materially, and are active under definite material limits, presuppositions and conditions independent of their will.

The production of ideas, of conceptions, of consciousness, is at first directly interwoven with the material activity and the material intercourse of men, the language of real life. Conceiving, thinking, the mental intercourse of men, appear at this stage as the direct efflux of their material behaviour. The same applies to mental production as expressed in the language of the politics, laws, morality, religion, metaphysics of a people. Men are the producers of their conceptions, ideas, etc.—real, active men, as they are conditioned by a definite development of their productive forces and of the intercourse corresponding to these, up to its furthest forms. Consciousness can never be anything else than conscious existence, and the existence of men is their actual life-process. If in all ideology men and their circumstances appear upside down as in a *camera obscura,* this phenomenon arises just as much from their historical life-process as the inversion of objects on the retina does from their physical life-process.

In direct contrast to German philosophy which descends from heaven to earth, here we ascend from earth to heaven. That is to say, we do not set out from what men say, imagine, conceive, nor from men as narrated, thought of, imagined, conceived, in order to arrive at men in the flesh. We set out from real, active men, and on the basis of their real life-process we demonstrate the development of the ideological reflexes and echoes of this life-process. The phantoms formed in the human brain are also, necessarily, sublimates of their material life-process, which is empirically verifiable and bound to material premises. Morality, religion, metaphysics, all the rest of ideology and their corresponding forms of consciousness, thus no longer retain the semblance of independence. They have no history, no development; but men, developing their material production and their material intercourse, alter, along with this their real existence, their thinking and the products of their thinking. Life is not determined by consciousness, but consciousness by life. In the first method of approach the starting-point is consciousness taken as the living individual; in the second it is the real living individuals themselves, as they are in actual life, and consciousness is considered solely as *their* consciousness.

This method of approach is not devoid of premises. It starts out from the real premises and does not abandon them for a moment. Its premises are men, not in any fantastic isolation or abstract definition, but in their actual, empirically perceptible process of development under definite conditions. As soon as this active life-process is described, history ceases to be a collection of dead facts as it is with the empiricists (themselves still abstract), or an imagined activity of imagined subjects, as with the idealists.

Where speculation ends—in real life—there real, positive science begins: the representation of the practical activity, of the practical process of development of men. Empty talk about consciousness ceases, and real knowledge has to take its place. When reality is depicted, philosophy as an independent branch of activity loses its medium of existence. At the best its place can only be taken by a summing-up of the most general results, abstractions which arise from the observation of the historical development of men. Viewed apart from real history, these abstractions have in themselves no value whatsoever. They can only serve to facilitate the arrangement of historical material, to indicate the sequence of its separate strata. But they by no means afford a recipe or schema, as does philosophy, for neatly trimming the epochs of history. On the contrary, our difficulties begin only when we set about the observation and the arrangement—the real depiction—of our historical material, whether of a past epoch or of the present. The removal of these difficulties is governed by premises which it is quite impossible to state here, but which only the study of the actual life-process and the activity of the individuals of each epoch will make evident. We shall select here some of these abstractions, which we use to refute the ideologists, and shall illustrate them by historical examples.

(A) HISTORY

Since we are dealing with the Germans, who do not postulate anything, we must begin by stating the first premise of all human existence, and therefore of all history, the premise namely that men must be in a position to live in order to be able to "make history." But life involves before everything else eating and drinking, a habitation, clothing and many other things. The first historical act is thus the production of the means to satisfy these needs, the production of material life itself. And indeed this is an historical act, a fundamental condition of all history, which to-day, as thousands of years ago, must daily and hourly be fulfilled merely in order to sustain human life. Even when the sensuous world is reduced to a minimum, to a stick as with Saint Bruno, it presupposes the action of producing the stick. The first necessity therefore in any theory of history is to observe this fundamental fact in all its significance and all its implications and to accord it its due importance. This, as is notorious, the Germans have never done, and they have never therefore had an earthly basis for history and consequently never a historian. The French and the English, even if they have conceived the relation of this fact with so-called history only in an extremely one-sided fashion, particularly as long as they remained in the toils of political ideology, have nevertheless made the first attempts to give the writing of history a materialistic basis by being the first to write histories of civil society, of commerce and industry.

The second fundamental point is that as soon as a need is satisfied, (which implies the action of satisfying, and the acquisition of an instrument), new needs are made; and this production of new needs is the first historical act. Here we recognize immediately the spiritual ancestry of the great historical wisdom of the Germans who, when they run out of positive material and when they can serve up neither theological nor political nor literary rubbish, do not write history at all, but invent the "prehistoric era." They do not, however, enlighten us as to how we proceed from this nonsensical "prehistory" to history proper; although, on the other hand, in their historical speculation they seize upon this "prehistory" with especial eagerness because they imagine themselves safe there from interference on the part of "crude facts," and, at the same time, because there they can give full rein to their speculative impulse and set up and knock down hypotheses by the thousand.

The third circumstance which, from the very first, enters into historical development, is that men, who daily remake their own life, begin to make other men, to propagate their kind: the relation between man and wife, parents and children, the FAMILY. The family which to begin with is the only social relationship, becomes later, when increased needs create new social relations and the increased population new needs, a subordinate one (except in Germany), and must then be treated and analysed according to the existing empirical data, not according to "the concept of the family," as is the custom in Germany. These three aspects of social activity are not of course to be taken as three different stages, but just, as I have said, as three aspects or, to make it clear to the Germans, three "moments," which have existed simultaneously since the dawn of history and the first men, and still assert themselves in history to-day.

The production of life, both of one's own in labour and of fresh life in procreation, now appears as a double relationship: on the one hand as a natural, on the other as a social relationship. By social we understand the co-operation of several individuals, no matter under what conditions, in what manner and to what end. It follows from this that a certain mode of production, or industrial stage, is always combined with a certain mode of co-operation, or social stage, and this mode of co-operation is itself a "productive force." Further, that the multitude of productive forces accessible to men determines the nature of society, hence that the "history of humanity" must always be studied and treated in relation to the history of industry and exchange. But it is also clear how in Germany it is impossible to write this sort of history, because the Germans lack not only the necessary power of comprehension and the material but also the "evidence of their senses," for across the Rhine you cannot have any experience of these things since history has stopped happening. Thus it is quite obvious from the start that there exists a materialistic connection of men with one another, which is determined by their needs and their mode of production, and which is as old as men themselves. This connection is ever taking on new forms, and thus presents a "history" independently of the existence of any political or religious nonsense which would hold men together on its own.

Only now, after having considered four moments, four aspects of the fundamental historical relationships, do we find that man also possesses "consciousness"; but, even so, not inherent, not "pure" consciousness. From the start the "spirit" is afflicted with the curse of being "burdened" with matter, which here makes its appearance in the form of agitated layers of air, sounds, in short of language. Language is as old as consciousness, language is practical consciousness, as it exists for other men, and for that reason is really beginning to exist for me personally as well; for language, like consciousness, only arises from the need, the necessity, of intercourse with other men. Where there exists a relationship, it exists for me: the animal has no "relations" with anything, cannot have any. For the animal, its relation to others does not exist as a relation. Consciousness is therefore from the very beginning a social product, and remains so as long as men exist at all. Consciousness is at first, of course, merely consciousness concerning the immediate sensuous environment and consciousness of the limited connection with other persons and things outside the individual who is growing self-conscious. At the same time it is consciousness of nature, which first appears to men as a completely alien, all-powerful and unassailable force, with which men's relations are purely animal and by which they are overawed like beasts; it is thus a purely animal consciousness of nature (natural religion).

We see here immediately: this natural religion or animal behaviour towards nature is determined by the form of society and *vice versa*. Here, as everywhere, the identity of nature and man appears in such a way that the restricted relation of men to nature determines their restricted relation to one another, and their restricted relation to one another determines men's restricted relation to nature, just because nature is as yet hardly modified historically; and, on the other hand, man's consciousness of the necessity of associating with the individuals around him is the beginning of the consciousness that he is living in society at all. This beginning is as animal as social life itself at this stage. It is mere herd-consciousness, and at this point man is only distinguished from sheep by the fact that with him consciousness takes the place of instinct or that his instinct is a conscious one.

This sheep-like or tribal consciousness receives its further development and extension through increased productivity, the increase of needs, and, what is fundamental to both of these, the increase of population. With these there develops the division of labour, which was originally nothing but the division of labour in the sexual act, then that division of labour which develops spontaneously or "naturally" by virtue of natural predisposition (e.g. physical strength), needs, accidents, etc., etc. Division of labour only becomes truly such from the moment when a division of material and mental labour appears. From this moment onwards consciousness *can* really flatter itself that it is something other than consciousness of existing practice, that it is *really* conceiving something without conceiving something *real;* from now on consciousness is in a position to emancipate itself from the world and to proceed to the formation of "pure" theory, theology, philosophy, ethics, etc. But even if this theory, theology, philosophy, ethics, etc. comes into contradiction with the existing relations, this can only occur as a result of the fact that existing social relations have come into contradiction with existing forces of production; this, moreover, can also occur in a particular national sphere of relations through the appearance of the contradiction, not within the national orbit, but between this national consciousness and the practice of other nations, i.e. between the national and the general consciousness of a nation.

Moreover, it is quite immaterial what consciousness starts to do on its own: out of all such muck we get only the one inference that these three moments, the forces of production, the state of society, and consciousness, can and must come into contradiction with one another, because the division of labour implies the possibility, nay the fact that intellectual and material activity—enjoyment and labour, production and consumption—devolve on different individuals, and that the only possibility of their not coming into contradiction lies in the negation in its turn of the division of labour. It is self-evident, moreover, that "spectres," "bonds," "the higher being," "concept," "scruple," are merely the idealistic, spiritual expression, the conception apparently of the isolated individual, the image of very empirical fetters and limitations, within which the mode of production of life, and the form of intercourse coupled with it, move.

In 1848 Karl Marx and Friedrich Engels (1820–1895) brought out the Manifesto of the Communist Party. *It could not have appeared at a more opportune time; the manuscript was delivered to the printer in London a few weeks before the revolution of February 1848 in France. A French translation was published shortly before the insurrection of the workers in Paris in June 1848. Thought and deed thus seemed to go together, and the* Manifesto of the Communist Party *(Communist Manifesto) became the rallying point for those who saw in revolution the only course for the oppressed workers of the world.*

FROM *Manifesto of the Communist Party*
BY *Karl Marx and Friedrich Engels*

A SPECTRE IS HAUNTING EUROPE—the spectre of Communism. All the Powers of old Europe have entered into a holy alliance to exorcise this spectre; Pope and Czar, Metternich and Guizot, French Radicals and German police-spies.

Where is the party in opposition that has not been decried as communistic by its opponents in power? Where the Opposition that has not hurled back the

Karl Marx and Friedrich Engels, *Manifesto of the Communist Party* (1911), pp. 11–30, 32–36, 42–47. Reprinted by permission of International Publishers Co., Inc.

branding reproach of Communism, against the more advanced opposition parties, as well as against its re-actionary adversaries?

Two things result from this fact.

1. Communism is already acknowledged by all European Powers to be itself a Power.
2. It is high time that Communists should openly, in the face of the whole world, publish their views, their aims, their tendencies, and meet this nursery tale of the Spectre of Communism with a Manifesto of the party itself.

To this end, Communists of various nationalities have assembled in London, and sketched the following manifesto, to be published in the English, French, German, Italian, Flemish and Danish languages.

I. BOURGEOIS AND PROLETARIANS

The history of all hitherto existing society is the history of class struggles.

Freeman and slave, patrician and plebeian, lord and serf, guild-master and journeyman, in a word, oppressor and oppressed, stood in constant opposition to one another, carried on an uninterrupted, now hidden, now open fight, a fight that each time ended either in a revolutionary re-constitution of society at large, or in the common ruin of the contending classes.

In the earlier epochs of history, we find almost everywhere a complicated arrangement of society into various orders, a manifold gradation of social rank. In ancient Rome we have patricians, knights, plebeians, slaves; in the middle ages, feudal lords, vassals, guild-masters, journeymen, apprentices, serfs; in almost all of these classes, again, subordinate gradations.

The modern bourgeois society that has sprouted from the ruins of feudal society, has not done away with class antagonisms. It has but established new classes, new conditions of oppression, new forms of struggle in place of the old ones.

Our epoch, the epoch of the bourgeoisie, possesses, however, this distinctive feature: it has simplified the class antagonisms. Society as a whole is more and more splitting up into two great hostile camps, into two great classes directly facing each other: Bourgeoisie and Proletariat.

From the serfs of the Middle Ages sprang the chartered burghers of the earliest towns. From these burgesses the first elements of the bourgeoisie were developed.

The discovery of America, the rounding of the Cape, opened up fresh ground for the rising bourgeoisie. The East-Indian and Chinese markets, the colonisation of America, trade with the colonies, the increase in the means of exchange and in commodities generally, gave to commerce, to navigation, to industry, an impulse never before known, and thereby, to the revolutionary element in the tottering feudal society, a rapid development.

The feudal system of industry, under which industrial production was monopolised by close guilds, now no longer sufficed for the growing wants of the new markets. The manufacturing system took its place. The guild-masters were pushed on one side by the manufacturing middle-class; division of labour between the different corporate guilds vanished in the face of division of labour in each single workshop.

Meantime the markets kept ever growing, the demand, ever rising. Even manufacture no longer sufficed. Thereupon, steam and machinery revolutionised industrial production. The place of manufacture was taken by the giant, Modern Industry, the place of the industrial middle-class, by industrial millionaires, the leaders of whole industrial armies, the modern bourgeois.

Modern industry has established the world-market, for which the discovery of America paved the way. This market has given an immense development to commerce, to navigation, to communication by land. This development has, in its turn, reacted on the extension of industry; and in proportion as industry, commerce, navigation, railways extended, in the same proportion the bourgeoisie developed, increased its capital, and pushed into the background every class handed down from the Middle Ages.

We see, therefore, how the modern bourgeoisie is itself the product of a long course of development, of a series of revolutions in the modes of production and of exchange.

Each step in the development of the bourgeoisie was accompanied by a corresponding political advance of that class. An oppressed class under the sway of the feudal nobility, an armed and self-governing association in the medieval commune, here independent urban republic (as in Italy and Germany), there taxable "third estate" of the monarchy (as in France), afterwards, in the period of manufacture proper, serving either the semi-feudal or the absolute monarchy as a counterpoise against the nobility, and, in fact, corner stone of the great monarchies in general, the bourgeoisie has at last, since the establishment of Modern Industry and of the world-market, conquered for itself, in the modern representative State, exclusive political sway. The executive of the modern State is but a committee for managing the common affairs of the whole bourgeoisie.

The bourgeoisie, historically, has played a most revolutionary part.

The bourgeoisie, wherever it has got the upper hand, has put an end to all feudal, patriarchal, idyllic relations. It has pitilessly torn asunder the motley feudal ties that bound man to his "natural superiors," and has left remaining no other nexus between man and man than naked self-interest, than callous "cash payment." It has drowned the most heavenly ecstasies of religious fervour, of chivalrous enthusiasm, of philistine sentimentalism, in the icy water of egotistical calculation. It has resolved personal worth into exchange value, and in place of the numberless indefeasible chartered freedoms, has set up that single, unconscionable freedom—Free Trade. In one word, for exploitation, veiled by religious and political illusions, it has substituted naked, shameless, direct, brutal exploitation.

The bourgeoisie has stripped of its halo every occupation hitherto honoured and looked up to with reverent awe. It has converted the physician, the lawyer, the priest, the poet, the man of science, into its paid wage-labourers.

The bourgeoisie has torn away from the family its sentimental veil, and has reduced the family relation to a mere money relation.

The bourgeoisie has disclosed how it came to pass that the brutal display of vigour in the Middle Ages, which Re-actionists so much admire, found its fitting complement in the most slothful indolence. It has been the first to shew what man's activity can bring about. It has accomplished wonders far surpassing Egyptian pyramids, Roman aqueducts, and Gothic cathedrals; it has conducted expeditions that put in the shade all former Exoduses of nations and crusades.

The bourgeoisie cannot exist without constantly revolutionising the instruments of production, and thereby the relations of production, and with them the whole relations of society. Conservation of the old modes of production in unaltered form, was, on the contrary, the first condition of existence for all earlier industrial classes. Constant revolutionising of production, uninterrupted disturbance of all social conditions, everlasting uncertainty and agitation distinguish the bourgeois epoch from all earlier ones. All fixed, fast-frozen relations, with their train of ancient and venerable prejudices and opinions, are swept away, all new-formed ones become antiquated before they can ossify. All that is solid melts into air, all that is holy is profaned, and man is at last compelled to face with sober senses, his real conditions of life, and his relations with his kind.

The need of a constantly expanding market for its products chases the bourgeoisie over the whole surface of the globe. It must nestle everywhere, settle everywhere, establish connexions everywhere.

The bourgeoisie has through its exploitation of the world-market given a cosmopolitan character to production and consumption in every country. To the great chagrin of Re-actionists, it has drawn from under the feet of industry the national ground on which it stood. All old-established national industries have been destroyed or are daily being destroyed. They are dislodged by new industries, whose introduction becomes a life and death question for all civilised nations, by industries that no longer work up indigenous raw material, but raw material drawn from the remotest zones; industries whose products are consumed, not only at home, but in every quarter of the globe. In place of the old wants, satisfied by the productions of the country, we find new wants, requiring for their satisfaction the products of distant lands and climes. In place of the old local and national seclusion and self-sufficiency, we have intercourse in every direction, universal interdependence of nations. And as in material, so also in intellectual production. The intellectual creations of individual nations become common property. National one-sidedness and narrow-mindedness become more and more impossible, and from the numerous national and local literatures there arises a world-literature.

The bourgeoisie, by the rapid improvement of all instruments of production, by the immensely facilitated means of communication, draws all, even the most barbarian, nations into civilisation. The cheap prices of its commodities are the heavy artillery with which it batters down all Chinese walls, with which it forces the barbarian's intensely obstinate hatred of foreigners to capitulate. It compels all nations, on pain of extinction, to adopt the bourgeois mode of production; it compels them to introduce what it calls civilisation into their midst, i.e., to become bourgeois themselves. In a word, it creates a world after its own image.

The bourgeoisie has subjected the country to the rule of the towns. It has created enormous cities, has greatly increased the urban population as compared with the rural, and has thus rescued a considerable part of the population from the idiocy of rural life. Just as it has made the country dependent on the towns, so it has made barbarian and semi-barbarian countries dependent on the civilised ones, nations of peasants on nations of bourgeois, the East on the West.

The bourgeoisie keeps more and more doing away with the scattered state of the population, of the means of production, and of property. It has agglomerated population, centralised means of production, and has concentrated property in a few hands. The necessary consequence of this was political centralisation. Independent, or but loosely connected provinces, with separate interests, laws, governments and systems of taxation, became lumped together in one nation, with one government, one code of laws, one national class-interest, one frontier and one customs-tariff.

The bourgeoisie, during its rule of scarce one hundred years, has created more massive and more colossal productive forces than have all preceding generations together. Subjection of Nature's forces to man, machinery, application of chemistry to industry and agriculture, steam-navigation, railways, electric telegraphs, clearing of whole continents for cultivation, canalization of rivers, whole populations conjured out of the ground—what earlier century had even a presentiment that such productive forces slumbered in the lap of social labour?

We see then: the means of production and of exchange on whose foundation the bourgeoisie built itself up, were generated in feudal society. At a certain stage in the development of these means of production and of exchange, the conditions under which feudal society produced and exchanged, the feudal organisation of agriculture and manufacturing industry, in one word, the feudal relations of property became no longer compatible with the already developed productive forces; they became so many fetters. They had to burst asunder; they were burst asunder.

Into their places stepped free competition, accompanied by a social and political constitution adapted to it, and by the economical and political sway of the bourgeois class.

A similar movement is going on before our own eyes. Modern bourgeois society with its relations of production, of exchange and of property, a society that has conjured up such gigantic means of production and of exchange, is like the sorcerer, who is no longer able to control the powers of the nether world whom he has called up by his spells. For many a decade past the history of industry and commerce is but the history of revolt of modern productive forces against modern conditions of production, against the property relations that are the conditions for the existence of the bourgeoisie and of its rule. It is enough to mention the commercial crises that by their periodical return put on its trial, each time more threateningly, the existence of the entire bourgeois society. In these crises a great part not only of the existing products, but also of the previously created productive forces, are periodically destroyed. In these crises there breaks out an epidemic that, in all earlier epochs, would have seemed an absurdity—the epidemic of over-production. Society suddenly finds itself put back into a state of momentary barbarism; it appears as if a famine, a universal war of devastation had cut off the supply of every means of subsistence; industry and commerce seem to be destroyed; and why? Because there is too much civilisation, too much means of subsistence, too much industry, too much commerce. The productive forces at the disposal of society no longer tend to further the development of the conditions of bourgeois property; on the contrary, they have become too powerful for these conditions, by which they are fettered, and so soon as they overcome these fetters, they bring disorder into the whole of bourgeois society, endanger the existence of bourgeois property. The conditions of bourgeois society are too narrow to comprise the wealth created by them. And how does the bourgeoisie get over the crises? On the one hand by enforced destruction of a mass of productive forces; on the other, by the conquest of new markets, and by the more thorough exploitation of the old ones. That is to say, by paving the way for more extensive and more destructive crises, and by diminishing the means whereby crises are prevented.

The weapons with which the bourgeoisie felled feudalism to the ground are now turned against the bourgeoisie itself.

But not only has the bourgeoisie forged the weapons that bring death to itself; it has also called into existence the men who are to wield those weapons—the modern working class—the proletarians.

In proportion as the bourgeoisie, i.e., capital, is developed, in the same proportion is the proletariat, the modern working class, developed, a class of labourers, who live only so long as they find work, and who find work only so long as their labour increases capital. These labourers, who must sell themselves piecemeal, are a commodity, like every other article of commerce, and are consequently exposed to all the vicissitudes of competition, to all the fluctuations of the market.

Owing to the extensive use of machinery and to division of labour, the work of the proletarians has lost all individual character, and, consequently, all charm for the workman. He becomes an appendage of the machine, and it is only the most simple, most monotonous, and most easily acquired knack that is required of him. Hence, the cost of production of a workman is restricted, almost entirely, to the means of subsistence that he requires for his maintenance, and for the propagation of his race. But the price of a commodity, and also of labour, is equal to its cost of production. In proportion, therefore, as the repulsiveness of the work increases, the wage decreases. Nay more, in proportion as the use of machinery and division of labour increases, in the same proportion the burden of toil also increases, whether by prolongation of the working hours, by increase of the work enacted in a given time, or by increased speed of the machinery, etc.

Modern industry has converted the little workshop of the patriarchal master into the great factory of the industrial capitalist. Masses of labourers, crowded into the factory, are organised like soldiers. As privates of the industrial army they are placed under the command of a perfect hierarchy of officers and sergeants. Not only are they the slaves of the bourgeois class, and of the bourgeois State, they are daily and hourly enslaved by the machine, by the overlooker, and, above all, by the individual bourgeois manufacturer himself. The more openly this depotism proclaims gain to be its end and aim, the more petty, the more hateful and the more embittering it is.

The less the skill and exertion or strength implied in manual labour, in other words, the more modern industry becomes developed, the more is the labour of men superseded by that of women. Differences of age and sex have no longer any distinctive social validity for the working class. All are instruments of labour, more or less expensive to use, according to their age and sex.

No sooner is the exploitation of the labourer by the manufacturer, so far, at an end, that he receives his wages in cash, than he is set upon by the other portions of the bourgeoisie, the landlord, the shopkeeper, the pawnbroker, etc.

The lower strata of the middle class—the small tradespeople, shopkeepers, and retired tradesmen generally, the handicraftsmen and peasants—all these sink gradually into the proletariat, partly because their diminutive capital does not suffice for the scale on which Modern Industry is carried on, and is swamped in the competition with the large capitalists, partly because their specialised skill is rendered worthless by new methods of production. Thus the proletariat is recruited from all classes of the population.

The proletariat goes through various stages of development. With its birth begins its struggle with the bourgeoisie. At first the contest is carried on by individual labourers, then by the workpeople of a factory, then by the operatives of one trade, in one locality, against the individual bourgeois who directly exploits them. They direct their attacks not against the bourgeois conditions of production, but against the instruments of production themselves; they destroy imported wares that compete with their labour, they smash to pieces machinery, they set factories ablaze, they seek to restore by force the vanished status of the workman of the Middle Ages.

At this stage the labourers still form an incoherent mass scattered over the whole country, and broken up by their mutual competition. If anywhere they unite to form more compact bodies, this is not yet the consequence of their own active union, but of the union of the bourgeoisie, which class, in order to attain its own political ends, is compelled to set the whole proletariat in motion, and is moreover yet, for a time, able to do so. At this stage, therefore, the prole-tarians do not fight their enemies, but the enemies of their enemies, the rem-nants of absolute monarchy, the landowners, the nonindustrial bourgeois, the petty bourgeoisie. Thus the whole historical movement is concentrated in the hands of the bourgeoisie, every victory so obtained is a victory for the bour-geoisie.

But with the development of industry the proletariat not only increases in number; it becomes concentrated in greater masses, its strength grows, and it feels that strength more. The various interests and conditions of life within the ranks of the proletariat are more and more equalised, in proportion as machin-ery obliterates all distinctions of labour, and nearly everywhere reduces wages to the same low level. The growing competition among the bourgeois, and the resulting commercial crises, make the wages of the workers ever more fluctuat-ing. The unceasing improvement of machinery, ever more rapidly developing, makes their livelihood more and more precarious; the collisions between indi-vidual workmen and individual bourgeois take more and more the character of collisions between two classes. Thereupon the workers begin to form combina-tions (Trades' Unions) against the bourgeois; they club together in order to keep up the rate of wages; they found permanent associations in order to make provision beforehand for these occasional revolts. Here and there the contest breaks out into riots.

Now and then the workers are victorious, but only for a time. The real fruit of their battles lies, not in the immediate result, but in the ever expanding union of the workers. This union is helped on by the improved means of com-munication that are created by modern industry, and that place the workers of different localities in contact with one another. It was just this contact that was needed to centralise the numerous local struggles, all of the same character, into one national struggle between classes. But every class struggle is a political struggle. And that union, to attain which the burghers of the Middle Ages, with their miserable highways, required centuries, the modern proletarians, thanks to railways, achieve in a few years.

This organisation of the proletarians into a class, and consequently into a political party, is continually being upset again by the competition between the workers themselves. But it ever rises up again, stronger, firmer, mightier. It compels legislative recognition of particular interests of the workers, by taking advantage of the divisions among the bourgeoisie itself. Thus the ten-hours'-bill in England was carried.

Altogether collisions between the classes of the old society further, in many ways, the course of development of the proletariat. The bourgeoisie finds itself involved in a constant battle. At first with the aristocracy; later on, with those portions of the bourgeoisie itself, whose interests have become antagonis-tic to the progress of industry; at all times, with the bourgeoisie of foreign coun-tries. In all these battles it sees itself compelled to appeal to the proletariat, to ask for its help, and thus, to drag it into the political arena. The bourgeoisie itself, therefore, supplies the proletariat with its own elements of political and general education, in other words, it furnishes the proletariat with weapons for fighting the bourgeoisie.

Further, as we have already seen, entire sections of the ruling classes are, by the advance of industry, precipitated into the proletariat, or are at least threatened in their conditions of existence. These also supply the proletariat with fresh elements of enlightenment and progress.

Finally, in times when the class struggle nears the decisive hour, the process of dissolution going on within the ruling class, in fact within the whole range of old society, assumes such a violent, glaring character, that a small section of the ruling class cuts itself adrift, and joins the revolutionary class, the class that holds the future in its hands. Just as, therefore, at an earlier period, a section of the nobility went over to the bourgeoisie, so now a portion of the bourgeoisie goes over to the proletariat, and in particular, a portion of the bourgeois ideologists, who have raised themselves to the level of comprehending theoretically the historical movements as a whole.

Of all the classes that stand face to face with the bourgeoisie today, the proletariat alone is a really revolutionary class. The other classes decay and finally disappear in the face of modern industry; the proletariat is its special and essential product. . . .

* * *

Though not in substance, yet in form, the struggle of the proletariat with the bourgeoisie is at first a national struggle. The proletariat of each country must, of course, first of all settle matters with its own bourgeoisie.

In depicting the most general phases of the development of the proletariat, we traced the more or less veiled civil war, ranging within existing society, up to the point where that war breaks out into open revolution, and where the violent overthrow of the bourgeoisie lays the foundation for the sway of the proletariat.

Hitherto, every form of society has been based, as we have already seen, on the antagonism of oppressing and oppressed classes. But in order to oppress a class, certain conditions must be assured to it under which it can, at least, continue its slavish existence. The serf, in the period of serfdom, raised himself to membership in the commune, just as the petty bourgeois, under the yoke of feudal absolutism, managed to develop into a bourgeois. The modern labourer, on the contrary, instead of rising with the progress of industry, sinks deeper and deeper below the conditions of existence of his own class. He becomes a pauper, and pauperism develops more rapidly than population and wealth. And here it becomes evident, that the bourgeoisie is unfit any longer to be the ruling class in society, and to impose its conditions of existence upon society as an over-riding law. It is unfit to rule, because it is incompetent to assure an existence to its slave within his slavery, because it cannot help letting him sink into such a state that it has to feed him, instead of being fed by him. Society can no longer live under this bourgeoisie, in other words, its existence is no longer compatible with society.

The essential condition for the existence, and for the sway of the bourgeois class, is the formation and augmentation of capital; the condition for capital is wage-labour. Wage-labour rests exclusively on competition between the labourers. The advance of industry, whose involuntary promoter is the bourgeoisie, replaces the isolation of the labourers, due to competition, by their involuntary combination, due to association. The development of Modern Industry, therefore, cuts from under its feet the very foundation on which the bourgeoisie produces and appropriates products. What the bourgeoisie therefore produces, above all, are its own grave-diggers. Its fall and the victory of the proletariat are equally inevitable.

II. PROLETARIANS AND COMMUNISTS

In what relation do the Communists stand to the proletarians as a whole?

The Communists do not form a separate party opposed to other working-class parties.

They have no interests separate and apart from those of the proletariat as a whole.

They do not set up any sectarian principles of their own, by which to shape and mould the proletarian movement.

The Communists are distinguished from the other working-class parties by this only: 1. In the national struggles of the proletarians of the different countries, they point out and bring to the front the common interests of the entire proletariat, independently of all nationality. 2. In the various stages of development which the struggle of the working class against the bourgeoisie has to pass through, they always and everywhere represent the interests of the movement as a whole.

The Communists, therefore, are on the one hand, practically, the most advanced and resolute section of the working-class parties of every country, that section which pushes forward all others; on the other hand, theoretically, they have over the great mass of the proletariat the advantage of clearly understanding the line of march, the conditions, and the ultimate general results of the proletarian movement.

The immediate aim of the Communists is the same as that of all the other proletarian parties: formation of the proletariat into a class, overthrow of the bourgeois supremacy, conquest of political power by the proletariat.

The theoretical conclusions of the Communists are in no way based on ideas or principles that have been invented, or discovered, by this or that would-be universal reformer.

They merely express, in general terms, actual relations springing from an existing class struggle, from a historical movement going on under our very eyes. The abolition of existing property-relations is not at all a distinctive feature of Communism.

All property relations in the past have continually been subject to historical change consequent upon the change in historical conditions.

The French Revolution, for example, abolished feudal property in favour of bourgeois property.

The distinguishing feature of Communism is not the abolition of property generally, but the abolition of bourgeois property. But modern bourgeois private property is the final and most complete expression of the system of producing and appropriating products, that is based on class antagonism, on the exploitation of the many by the few.

In this sense, the theory of the Communists may be summed up in the single sentence: Abolition of private property.

We Communists have been reproached with the desire of abolishing the right of personally acquiring property as the fruit of a man's own labour, which property is alleged to be the ground work of all personal freedom, activity and independence.

Hard-won, self-acquired, self-earned property! Do you mean the property of the petty artisan and of the small peasant, a form of property that preceded the bourgeois form? There is no need to abolish that; the development of industry has to a great extent already destroyed it, and is still destroying it daily.

Or do you mean modern bourgeois private property?

But does wage-labour create any property for the labourer? Not a bit. It creates capital, i.e., that kind of property which exploits wage-labour, and which cannot increase except upon condition of getting a new supply of wage-labour for fresh exploitation. Property, in its present form, is based on the antagonism of capital and wage-labour. Let us examine both sides of this antagonism.

To be a capitalist, is to have not only a purely personal, but a social status in production. Capital is a collective product, and only by the united action of many members, nay, in the last resort, only by the united action of all members of society, can it be set in motion.

Capital is therefore not a personal, it is a social power.

When, therefore, capital is converted into common property, into the property of all members of society, personal property is not thereby transformed into social property. It is only the social character of the property that is changed. It loses its class-character.

Let us now take wage-labour.

The average price of wage-labour is the minimum wage, i.e., that quantum of the means of subsistence, which is absolutely requisite to keep the labourer in bare existence as a labourer. What, therefore, the wage-labourer appropriates by means of his labour, merely suffices to prolong and reproduce a bare existence. We by no means intend to abolish this personal appropriation of the products of labour, an appropriation that is made for the maintenance and reproduction of human life, and that leaves no surplus wherewith to command the labour of others. All that we want to do away with is the miserable character of this appropriation, under which the labourer lives merely to increase capital, and is allowed to live only in so far as the interest of the ruling class requires it.

In bourgeois society, living labour is but a means to increase accumulated labour. In Communist society, accumulated labour is but a means to widen, to enrich, to promote the existence of the labourer.

In bourgeois society, therefore, the past dominates the present; in Communist society, the present dominates the past. In bourgeois society capital is independent and has individuality, while the living person is dependent and has no individuality.

And the abolition of this state of things is called by the bourgeois, abolition of individuality and freedom! And rightly so. The abolition of bourgeois individuality, bourgeois independence, and bourgeois freedom is undoubtedly aimed at.

By freedom is meant, under the present bourgeois conditions of production, free trade, free selling and buying.

* * *

The charges against Communism made from a religious, a philosophical, and generally, from an ideological standpoint, are not deserving of serious examination.

Does it require deep intuition to comprehend that man's ideas, views, and conceptions, in one word, man's consciousness, changes with every change in the conditions of his material existence, in his social relations and in his social life?

What else does the history of ideas prove, than that intellectual production changes in character in proportion as material production is changed? The ruling ideas of each age have ever been the ideas of its ruling class.

When people speak of ideas that revolutionize society, they do but express the fact, that within the old society, the elements of a new one have been created, and that the dissolution of the old ideas keeps even pace with the dissolution of the old conditions of existence.

When the ancient world was in its last throes, the ancient religions were overcome by Christianity. When Christian ideas succumbed in the 18th century to rationalist ideas, feudal society fought its death-battle with the then revolutionary bourgeoisie. The ideas of religious liberty and freedom of conscience, merely gave expression to the sway of free competition within the domain of knowledge.

"Undoubtedly," it will be said, "religious, moral, philosophical and juridical ideas have been modified in the course of historical development. But religion, morality, philosophy, political science, and law, constantly survived this change.

"There are, besides, eternal truths, such as Freedom, Justice, etc., that are common to all states of society. But Communism abolishes eternal truths, it abolishes all religion, and all morality, instead of constituting them on a new basis; it therefore acts in contradiction to all past historical experience."

What does this accusation reduce itself to? The history of all past society has consisted in the development of class antagonisms, antagonisms that assumed different forms at different epochs.

But whatever form they may have taken, one fact is common to all past ages, viz., the exploitation of one part of society by the other. No wonder, then, that the social consciousness of past ages, despite all the multiplicity and variety it displays, moves within certain common forms, or general ideas, which cannot completely vanish except with the total disappearance of class antagonisms.

The Communist revolution is the most radical rupture with traditional property-relations; no wonder that its development involves the most radical rupture with traditional ideas.

But let us have done with the bourgeois objections to Communism.

We have seen above, that the first step in the revolution by the working class is to raise the proletariat to the position of ruling class, to win the battle of democracy.

The proletariat will use its political supremacy to wrest, by degrees, all capital from the bourgeoisie, to centralise all instruments of production in the hands of the State, i.e., of the proletariat organised by the ruling class; and to increase the total of productive forces as rapidly as possible.

Of course, in the beginning, this cannot be effected except by means of despotic inroads on the rights of property, and on the conditions of bourgeois production; by means of measures, therefore, which appear economically insufficient and untenable, but which, in the course of the movement, outstrip themselves, necessitate further inroads upon the old social order, and are unavoidable as a means of entirely revolutionising the mode of production.

These measures will of course be different in different countries.

Nevertheless in the most advanced countries the following will be pretty generally applicable:

1. Abolition of property in land and application of all rents of land to public purposes.
2. A heavy progressive or graduated income tax.
3. Abolition of all right of inheritance.
4. Confiscation of the property of all emigrants and rebels.
5. Centralisation of credit in the hands of the State, by means of a national bank with State capital and an exclusive monopoly.
6. Centralisation of the means of communication and transport in the hands of the State.
7. Extension of factories and instruments of production owned by the State; the bringing into cultivation of waste lands, and the improvement of the soil generally in accordance with a common plan.
8. Equal liability of all to labour. Establishment of industrial armies, especially for agriculture.
9. Combination of agriculture with manufacturing industries; gradual abolition of the distinction between town and country, by a more equable distribution of the population over the country.
10. Free education for all children in public schools. Abolition of children's factory labour in its present form. Combination of education with industrial production, etc., etc.

When, in the course of development, class distinctions have disappeared, and all production has been concentrated in the hands of a vast association of the whole nation, the public power will lose its political character. Political power, properly so called, is merely the organised power of one class for oppressing another. If the proletariat during its contest with the bourgeoisie is compelled, by the force of circumstances, to organise itself as a class, if, by means of a revolution, it makes itself the ruling class, and, as such, sweeps away by force the old conditions of production, then it will, along with these conditions, have swept away the conditions for the existence of class antagonisms, and of classes generally, and will thereby have abolished its own supremacy as a class.

In place of the old bourgeois society, with its classes and class antagonisms, we shall have an association in which the free development of each is the condition for the free development of all.

The Marxist condemnation of bourgeois society had unexpected results. Marx and Engels had used all their rhetoric to prove that capitalist society was evil. Moreover, they had proved that the state as such was the instrument of oppression. It should not have surprised them to find that their conclusions were eagerly grasped by a group—the anarchists—who saw the whole purpose of the coming struggle between proletariat and bourgeoisie as the destruction of the state. It was this view that Engels countered in the selection that follows. What must be gained is the control of the state, not its destruction. This principle, in turn, left the door open to those who argued that control could come by means other than revolution.

Friedrich Engels' Letter to Philip van Patten

London, April 18, 1883

Dear Comrade:

My reply to your inquiry of April 2 regarding Karl Marx's attitude toward the anarchists in general and toward Johann Most in particular will be brief and to the point.

Since 1845 Marx and I have held the view that one of the ultimate results of the future proletarian revolution will be the gradual dissolution of the political organization known by the name of *state*. The main object of this organization has always been to secure, by armed force, the economic oppression of the laboring majority by the minority which alone possesses wealth. With the disappearance of an exclusive wealth-possessing minority there also disappears the need for an armed force of suppression, or state power. At the same time, however, it was always our opinion that in order to attain this and the other far more important aims of the future social revolution, the working class must first take possession of the organized political power of the state and by its aid crush the resistance of the capitalist class and organize society anew. This is to be found as early as the *Communist Manifesto* of 1847, Chapter II, conclusion.

The anarchists stand the thing on its head. They declare that the proletarian revolution must *begin* by abolishing the political organization of the state. But the only organization that the proletariat finds ready to hand after its victory is precisely the state. This state may require very considerable alterations before it can fulfill its new functions. But to destroy it at such a moment would mean to destroy the only organism by means of which the victorious proletariat can assert its newly conquered power, hold down its capitalist adversaries, and carry out that economic revolution of society without which the whole victory must end in a new defeat and in a mass slaughter of the workers similar to that after the Paris Commune.

Does it require my express assurance that Marx opposed this anarchist nonsense from the first day it was put forward in its present form by Bakunin? The whole internal history of the International Workingmen's Association proves it. Ever since 1867 the anarchists tried, by the most infamous methods, to seize the leadership of the International; the main hindrance in their way was Marx. The five-year struggle ended, at the Hague Congress in September 1872, with the expulsion of the anarchists from the International; and the man who did most to effect this expulsion was Marx. Our old friend, Friedrich Anton Sorge, in Hoboken, who was present as a delegate, can give you further details if you wish.

By 1895, when Engels wrote this introduction, the position of the left had changed considerably. Many of the revolutionary demands of the Communist Manifesto *had been written into law, as the result not of violent revolution but of peaceful politicking. Was it possible that the "inevitability" of revolution, to which all Marx's and Engels' writings in the 1840s logically led, was a mistake? Engels took a long look at the question in the selection that follows.*

FROM *Introduction to Marx's The Class Struggles in France*
BY *Friedrich Engels*

IN JUDGING THE EVENTS and series of events of day-to-day history, it will never be possible for anyone to go right back to the final economic causes. Even today, when the specialised technical press provides such rich materials, in England itself it still remains impossible to follow day by day the movement of industry

Karl Marx, *The Class Struggle in France (1848–1850)*, pp. 9–10,. 13–14, 15, 19–28. Reprinted by permission.

and trade in the world market and the changes which take place in the methods of production, in such a way as to be able to draw the general conclusion, at any point of time, from these very complicated and ever changing factors: of these factors, the most important, into the bargain, generally operate a long time in secret before they suddenly and violently make themselves felt on the surface. A clear survey of the economic history of a given period is never contemporaneous; it can only be gained subsequently, after collecting and sifting of the material has taken place. Statistics are a necessary help here, and they always lag behind. For this reason, it is only too often necessary, in the current history of the time, to treat the most decisive factor as constant, to treat the economic situation existing at the beginning of the period concerned as given and unalterable for the whole period, or else to take notice only of such changes in this situation as themselves arise out of events clearly before us, and as, therefore, can likewise be clearly seen. Hence, the materialist method has here often to limit itself to tracing political conflicts back to the struggles between the interests of the social classes and fractions of classes encountered as the result of economic development, and to show the particular political parties as the more or less adequate political expression of these same classes and fractions of classes.

It is self-evident that this unavoidable neglect of contemporaneous changes in the economic situation, of the very basis of all the proceedings subject to examination, must be a source of error. But all the conditions of a comprehensive presentation of the history of the day unavoidably imply sources of error—which, however, keeps nobody from writing contemporary history.

When Marx undertook this work, the sources of error mentioned were, to a still greater degree, impossible to avoid. It was quite impossible during the period of the Revolution of 1848–49 to follow the economic transformations which were being consummated at the same time, or even to keep a general view of them. It was just the same during the first months of exile in London, in the autumn and winter of 1849–50. But that was just the time when Marx began this work. And in spite of these unfavourable circumstances, his exact knowledge both of the economic situation in France and of the political history of that country since the February Revolution made it possible for him to give a picture of events which laid bare their inner connections in a way never attained since, and which later brilliantly withstood the double test instituted by Marx himself.

* * *

When the Paris upheaval found its echo in the victorious insurrections in Vienna, Milan and Berlin; when the whole of Europe right up to the Russian frontier was swept into the movement; when in Paris the first great battle for power between the proletariat and the bourgeoisie was joined; when the very victory of their class so shook the bourgeoisie of all countries that they fled back into the arms of the monarchist-feudal reaction which had just been overthrown—for us under the circumstances of the time, there could be no doubt that the great decisive struggle had broken out, that it would have to be fought out in a single, long and changeful period of revolution, but that it could only end with the final victory of the proletariat.

*   *   *

But we, too, have been shown to have been wrong by history, which has revealed our point of view of that time to have been an illusion. It has done even more: it has not merely destroyed our error of that time; it has also completely transformed the conditions under which the proletariat has to fight. The mode of struggle of 1848 is today obsolete from every point of view, and this is a point which deserves closer examination on the present occasion.

*   *   *

History has proved us, and all who thought like us, wrong. It has made it clear that the state of economic development on the Continent at that time was not, by a long way, ripe for the removal of capitalist production; it has proved this by the economic revolution which, since 1848, has seized the whole of the Continent, has really caused big industry for the first time to take root in France, Austria, Hungary, Poland and, recently, in Russia, while it has made Germany positively an industrial country of the first rank—all on a capitalist basis, which in the year 1848, therefore, still had great capacity for expansion. But it is just this industrial revolution which has everywhere for the first time produced clarity in the class relationships, which has removed a number of transition forms handed down from the manufacturing period and in Eastern Europe even from guild handicraft, and has created a genuine bourgeoisie and a genuine large-scale industrial proletariat and pushed them into the foreground of social development. But owing to this, the struggle of these two great classes, which, apart from England, existed in 1848 only in Paris and, at the most, a few big industrial centres, has been spread over the whole of Europe and has reached an intensity such as was unthinkable in 1848. At that time the many obscure evangels of the sects, with their panaceas; today the one generally recognised, transparently clear theory of Marx, sharply formulating the final aims of the struggle. At that time the masses, sundered and differing according to locality and nationality, linked only by the feeling of common suffering, undeveloped, tossed to and fro in their perplexity from enthusiasm to despair; today a great international army of Socialists, marching irresistibly on and growing daily in number, organisation, discipline, insight and assurance of victory. If even this mighty army of the proletariat has still not reached its goal, if, a long way from winning victory with one mighty stroke, it has slowly to press forward from position to position in a hard, tenacious struggle, this only proves, once and for all, how impossible it was in 1848 to win social reconstruction by a simple surprise attack.

*   *   *

The war of 1870–71 and the defeat of the Commune had transferred the centre of gravity of the European workers' movement for the time being from France to Germany, as Marx foretold. In France it naturally took years to recover from the bloodletting of May 1871. In Germany, on the other hand, where industry was, in addition, furthered (in positively hot-house fashion) by the blessing of the French milliards and developed more and more quickly, Social-Democracy experienced a much more rapid and enduring growth. Thanks to the understanding with which the German workers made use of the universal suffrage introduced in 1866, the astonishing growth of the Party is made plain to all the world by incontestable figures: 1871, 102,000; 1874, 352,000; 1877, 493,000 Social-Democratic votes. Then came recognition of this advance by high authority in the shape of the Anti-Socialist Law: the Party was temporarily disrupted; the number of votes sank to 312,000 in 1881. But that was quickly overcome, and then, though oppressed by the Exceptional Law, without press, without external organisation and without the right of combination or meeting, the rapid expansion really began: 1884, 550,000; 1887, 763,000; 1890, 1,427,000 votes. Then the hand of the state was paralysed. The Anti-Socialist Law disappeared; socialist votes rose to 1,787,000—over a quarter of all the votes cast. The government and the ruling classes had exhausted all their expedients—uselessly, to no purpose, and without success. The tangible proofs of their impotence, which the authorities, from night watchman to the imperial chancellor, had had to accept—and that from the despised workers—these proofs were counted in millions. The state was at the end of its Latin [*sic*—Ed.], the workers only at the beginning of theirs.

But the German workers did a second great service to their cause in addition to the first, which they rendered by their mere existence as the strongest, best disciplined, and most rapidly growing Socialist Party. They supplied their comrades of all countries with a new weapon, and one of the sharpest, when they showed them how to use universal suffrage.

There had long been universal suffrage in France, but it had fallen into disrepute through the misuse to which the Bonapartist government had put it. After the Commune there was no workers' party to make use of it. Also in Spain it had existed since the republic, but in Spain boycott of the elections was ever the rule of all serious opposition parties. The Swiss experiences of universal suffrage, also, were anything but encouraging for a workers' party. The revolutionary workers of the Latin countries had been wont to regard the suffrage as a snare, as an instrument of government trickery. It was otherwise in Germany. *The Communist Manifesto* had already proclaimed the winning of universal suffrage, of democracy, as one of the first and most important tasks of the militant proletariat, and Lassalle had again taken up this point. When Bismarck found himself compelled to introduce the franchise as the only means of interesting the mass of the people in his plans, our workers immediately took it in earnest and sent August Bebel to the first constituent Reichstag. And from that day on, they have used the franchise in a way which has paid them a thousandfold and has served as a model to the workers of all countries. The franchise has been, in the words of the French Marxist programme, . . . transformed from a means of deception, which it was heretofore, into an instrument of emancipation. And if universal suffrage had offered no other advantage than that it allowed us to count our numbers every three years; that by the regularly established, unexpectedly rapid rise in the number of votes it increased in equal measure the workers' certainty of victory and the dismay of their opponents, and so became our best means of propaganda; that it accurately informed us concerning our own strength and that of all hostile parties, and thereby provided us with a measure of proportion for our action second to none, safeguarding us from untimely timidity as much as from untimely foolhardiness—if this had been the only advantage we gained from the suffrage, then it would still have been more than enough. But it has done much more than this. In election agitation it provided us with a means, second to none; of getting in touch with the mass of the people, where they still stand aloof from us; of forcing all parties to defend their views and actions against our attacks before all the people; and, further, it opened to our representatives in the Reichstag a platform from which they could speak to their opponents in Parliament and to the masses without, with quite other authority and freedom than in the press or at meetings. Of what avail to the government and the bourgeoisie was their Anti-Socialist Law when election agitation and socialist speeches in the Reichstag continually broke through it?

With this successful utilisation of universal suffrage, an entirely new mode of proletarian struggle came into force, and this quickly developed further. It was found that the state institutions, in which the rule of the bourgeoisie is organised, offer still further opportunities for the working class to fight these very state institutions. They took part in elections to individual diets, to municipal councils and to industrial courts; they contested every post against the bourgeoisie in the occupation of which a sufficient part of the proletariat had its say. And so it happened that the bourgeoisie and the government came to be much more afraid of the legal than of the illegal action of the workers' party, of the results of elections than of those of rebellion.

For here, too, the conditions of the struggle had essentially changed. Rebellion in the old style, the street fight with barricades, which up to 1848 gave everywhere the final decision, was to a considerable extent obsolete.

Let us have no illusions about it; a real victory of an insurrection over the military in street fighting, a victory as between two armies, is one of the rarest exceptions. But the insurgents, also, counted on it just as rarely. For them it was solely a question of making the troops yield to moral influences, which, in a fight between the armies of two warring countries do not come into play at all, or do so to a much less degree. If they succeed in this, then the troops fail to act, or the commanding officers lose their heads, and the insurrection wins. If they do not succeed in this, then, even where the military are in the minority, the superiority of better equipment and training, of discipline makes itself felt.

The most that the insurrection can achieve in actual tactical practice is the correct construction and defence of a single barricade. Mutual support; the disposition and defence of a single barricade. Mutual support; the disposition and employment of reserves; in short, the cooperation and harmonious working of the individual detachments, indispensable even for the defence of one quarter of the town, not to speak of the whole of a large town, are at best defective, and mostly not attainable at all; concentration of the military forces at a decisive point is, of course, impossible. Hence the passive defence is the prevailing form of fight: the attack will rise here and there, but only by way of exception, to occasional advances and flank assaults; as a rule, however, it will be limited to occupation of the positions abandoned by the retreating troops. In addition, the military have, on their side, the disposal of artillery and fully equipped corps of skilled engineers, resources of war which, in nearly every case, the insurgents entirely lack. No wonder, then, that even the barricade struggles conducted with the greatest heroism—Paris, June 1848; Vienna, October 1848; Dresden, May 1849—ended with the defeat of the insurrection, so soon as the leaders of the attack, unhampered by political considerations, acted from the purely military standpoint, and their soldiers remained reliable.

The numerous successes of the insurgents up to 1848 were due to a great variety of causes. In Paris in July 1830 and February 1848, as in most of the Spanish street fights, there stood between the insurgents and the military a civic militia, which either directly took the side of the insurrection, or else by its lukewarm, indecisive attitude caused the troops likewise to vacillate, and supplied the insurrection with arms into the bargain. Where this citizens' guard opposed the insurrection from the outset, as in June 1848 in Paris, the insurrection was vanquished. In Berlin in 1848, the people were victorious partly through a considerable accession of new fighting forces during the night and the morning of the 19th, partly as a result of the exhaustion and bad victualling of the troops, and, finally, partly as a result of the paralysed command. But in all cases the fight was won because the troops failed to obey, because the officers lost their power of decision or because their hands were tied.

Even in the classic time of street fighting, therefore, the barricade produced more of a moral than a material effect. It was a means of shaking the steadfastness of the military. If it held out until this was attained, then victory was won; if not, there was defeat. This is the main point, which must be kept in view, likewise when the chances of contingent future street fights are examined.

*　*　*

But since then there have been very many more changes, and all in favour of the military. If the big towns have become considerably bigger, the armies have become bigger still. Paris and Berlin have, since 1848, grown less than fourfold, but their garrisons have grown more than that. By means of the railways, the garrisons can, in twenty-four hours, be more than doubled, and in forty-eight hours they can be increased to huge armies. The arming of this enormously increased number of troops has become incomparably more effective. In 1848 the smooth-bore percussion muzzle-loader, today the small-calibre magazine breech-loading rifle, which shoots four times as far, ten times as accurately and ten times as fast as the former. At that time the relatively ineffective round-shot and grape-shot of the artillery; today the percussion shells, of which one is sufficient to demolish the best barricade. At that time the pick-axe of the sapper for breaking through walls; today the dynamite cartridge.

On the other hand, all the conditions on the insurgents' side have grown worse. An insurrection with which all sections of the people sympathise will hardly recur; in the class struggle all the middle sections will never group themselves round the proletariat so exclusively that the reactionary parties gathered round the bourgeoisie well-nigh disappear. The "people," therefore, will always appear divided, and with this a powerful lever, so extraordinarily effective in 1848, is lacking. Even if more soldiers who have seen service were to come over to the insurrectionists, the arming of them becomes so much the more difficult. The hunting and luxury guns of the gunshops—even if not previously made unusable by removal of part of the lock by the police—are far from being a match for the magazine rifle of the soldier, even in close fighting. Up to 1848 it was possible to make the necessary ammunition oneself out of powder and lead; today the cartridges differ for each rifle, and are everywhere alike only in one point, that they are a special product of big industry, and therefore not to be prepared *ex tempore,* with the result that most rifles are useless as long as one does not possess the ammunition specially suited to them. And, finally, since 1848 the newly built quarters of the big towns have been laid out in long, straight, broad streets, as though made to give full effect to the new cannons and rifles. The revolutionary would have to be mad, who himself chose the working class districts in the North and East of Berlin for a barricade fight. . . .

* * *

Does the reader now understand why the ruling classes decidedly want to bring us to where the guns shoot and the sabres slash? Why they accuse us today of cowardice, because we do not betake ourselves without more ado into the street, where we are certain of defeat in advance? Why they so earnestly implore us to play for once the part of cannon fodder?

* * *

Of course, our foreign comrades do not renounce their right to revolution. The right to revolution is, after all, the only real "historical right," the only right on which all modern states without exception rest. . . .

But whatever may happen in other countries, German Social-Democracy has a special situation and therewith, at least in the first instance, a special task. The two million voters, whom it sends to the ballot box, together with the young men and women who stand behind them as non-voters, form the most numerous, most compact mass, the decisive *"shock force"* of the international proletarian army. This mass already supplies over a fourth of the recorded votes; and as the by-elections to the Reichstag, the diet elections in individual states, the municipal council and industrial court elections demonstrate, it increases uninterruptedly. Its growth proceeds as spontaneously, as steadily, as irresistibly, and at the same time as tranquilly as a natural process. All government interventions have proved powerless against it. We can count even today on two and a half million voters. If it continues in this fashion, by the end of the century we shall conquer the greater part of the middle section of society, petty bourgeois and small peasants, and grow into the decisive power in the land, before which all other powers will have to bow, whether they like it or not. To keep this growth going without interruption until of itself it gets beyond the control of the ruling governmental system *not to fritter away this daily increasing shock force in advance guard fighting, but to keep it intact until the day of the decision,* that is our main task. And there is only one means by which the steady rise of the socialist fighting forces in Germany could be momentarily halted, and even thrown back for some time: a clash on a big scale with the military, a bloodbath like that of 1871 in Paris. In the long run that would also be overcome. To shoot out of the world a party which numbers millions—all the magazine rifles of Europe and America are not enough for this. . . .

The irony of world history turns everything upside down. We, the "revolutionaries," the "rebels"—we are thriving far better on legal methods than on illegal methods and revolt. The parties of order, as they call themselves, are perishing under the legal conditions created by themselves. They cry despairingly with Odilon Barrot: . . . legality is the death of us; whereas we, under this legality, get firm muscles and rosy cheeks and look like eternal life. And if we are not so crazy as to let ourselves be driven into street fighting in order to please them, then nothing else is finally left for them but themselves to break through this legality so fatal to them.

2

The Scholars' Views

Marxism is both a program of political action and a theoretical analysis of society. The two are inextricably intertwined. This has created the problem of determining what is merely politically expedient and what follows necessarily from the theoretical premises of the Marxist argument. One of the central problems is that of the place of revolution in the coming of the Marxist society. Scholars have argued for a generation over this point: Must revolutionary action necessarily be taken, or can the Marxist society evolve from that of the bourgeoisie?

    E. H. Carr is one of the foremost historians of Soviet Russia; from this vantage point he assesses the message of the Communist Manifesto.

FROM *Studies in Revolution*
BY *E. H. Carr*

THE COMMUNIST MANIFESTO

THE WINTER OF 1847–48 (it is difficult to fix a more precise date for the celebration of the centenary) saw the birth of one of the capital documents of the nineteenth century—the *Communist Manifesto*. In the summer of 1847 a group consisting mainly of German craftsmen in London held the first congress of a new "Communist League." They had been in touch with Marx, then living in Brussels, for some time; and Engels attended the congress, which adjourned to a future congress the drafting of a programme for the League. Inspired by this prospect, Engels tried his hand and produced a catechism in twenty-five questions, which Marx and he took with them to the second League congress in London at the end of November. The congress thereupon charged Marx and Engels to draft their programme for them: it was to take the form of a manifesto. Marx worked away in Brussels through December and January. The "Manifesto of the Communist Party" was published in London in German in February 1848, a few days before the revolution broke out in Paris.

E. H. Carr, *Studies in Revolution* (1962), pp. 15-37. Reprinted by permission of Macmillan London and Basingstoke.

The *Communist Manifesto* is divided into four parts. The first reviews the rise of the bourgeoisie on the ruins of the feudal system of property relations, government and morality which it destroyed; shows how "the powerful and colossal productive forces" which the bourgeoisie itself created have now grown to a point where they are no longer compatible with bourgeois property relations and bourgeois supremacy; and finally demonstrates that the proletariat is the new revolutionary class which can alone master the forces of modern industry and end the exploitation of man by man. The second part proclaims the policy of the Communist Party, as "the most progressive and resolute section of the working class of all countries," to promote the proletarian revolution which will destroy bourgeois power and "raise the proletariat to the position of the ruling class." The third part surveys and condemns other recent and existing schools of socialism; and the fourth is a brief tactical postscript on the relations of Communists to other left-wing parties.

A historic document like the *Communist Manifesto* invites examination from the point of view both of its antecedents and of its consequences. On the former count the *Manifesto* owes as much to predecessors and contemporaries as most great pronouncements; and the worst that can be said is that Marx's sweeping denunciations of predecessors and contemporaries sometimes mask the nature of the debt. Babeuf, who also called his proclamation a "manifesto," had announced the final struggle between rich and poor, between "a tiny minority" and "the huge majority." Blanqui had anticipated the class interpretation of history and the idea of the dictatorship of the proletariat (the phrase was not used by Marx himself till 1850). Lorenz von Stein had written that the history of freedom, society and political order was essentially dependent on the distribution of economic goods among the classes of the population. Proudhon also knew that "the laws of political economy are the laws of history" and measured the progress of society "by the development of industry and the perfection of its instruments"; and Pecqueur had predicted that, with the spread of commerce, "the barriers between nation and nation will be broken down" until the day when "every man becomes a citizen of the world." Such ideas were current coin in advanced circles when Marx wrote. But neither such borrowings, nor Marx's overriding debt to Hegel's immense synthesis, detract from the power of the conception presented to the world in the *Communist Manifesto*.

To-day it is more appropriate to study the famous manifesto in the light of its hundred-year influence on posterity. Though written when Marx was in his thirtieth year and Engels two years younger, it already contains the quintessence of Marxism. Beginning with a broad historical generalization ("the history of all hitherto existing society is the history of class struggles") and ending with an inflammatory appeal to the workers of all countries to unite for "the forcible overthrow of all existing social conditions," it presents Marxist methodology in its fully developed form—an interpretation of history which is at the same time a call to action. Some passages in Marx's writings, especially at the revolutionary crises of 1848 and 1871, appear to commend revolutionary action as a good thing in itself. Some passages, both earlier and later, appear to dwell on the iron laws of historical development in such a way as to leave little place for the initiative of the human will. But these momentary shifts of emphasis cannot be taken to impair the dual orthodoxy established by the *Communist Manifesto,* where interpretation and action, predestination and free will, revolutionary theory and revolutionary practice march triumphantly hand in hand. It propounds a philosophy of history, a dogma of revolution, belief in which will take the spontaneous form of appropriate action in the believer.

The *Communist Manifesto* is thus no broadsheet for the hoardings or the hustings. Marx—and many others who are not Marxists—would deny the possibility of any rigid separation of emotion and intellect; but using the terms in a popular sense, it is to the intellect rather than to the emotions that the *Manifesto* makes its primary appeal. The overwhelming impression which it leaves on the reader's mind is not so much that the revolution is desirable (that, like the injustice of capitalism in *Das Kapital,* is taken for granted as something not requiring argument) but that the revolution is inevitable. For successive generations of Marxists the *Manifesto* was not a plea for revolution—that they did not need—but a prediction about the way in which the revolution would inevitably happen combined with a prescription for the action required of revolutionaries to make it happen. The controversies of a hundred years ranged round the questions as to what Marx actually said or meant and how what he said should be applied to conditions diverging widely from those of his own time and place. Only the bold offered openly to "revise" Marx; the sagacious interpreted him. The *Communist Manifesto* has thus remained a living document. The centenary of the *Communist Manifesto* cannot be celebrated otherwise than in the light, and in the shadow, of the Russian revolution which was its culminating embodiment in history.

The *Communist Manifesto* sets out a coherent scheme of revolution. "The history of all hitherto existing society is the history of class struggles." In modern times Marx detects two such struggles—the struggle between feudalism and the bourgeoisie, ending in the victorious bourgeois revolution, and the struggle between the bourgeoisie and the proletariat, destined to end in the victorious proletarian revolution. In the first struggle a nascent proletariat is mobilized by the bourgeoisie in support of bourgeois aims, but is incapable of pursuing independent aims of its own: "every victory so obtained is a victory for the bourgeoisie." In the second struggle Marx recognizes the presence of the lower middle class—"the small manufacturer, the shopkeeper, the artisan, the peasant"—which plays a fluctuating role between bourgeoisie and proletariat, and a "slum proletariat" which is liable to "sell itself to reactionary forces." But these complications do not seriously affect the ordered simplicity of the main pattern of revolution.

The pattern had been framed in the light of Marx's reading in modern English and French history and in the works of French and British economists, and of Engels's study of factory conditions in England. The English bourgeois revolution, winning its victory in the seventeenth century, had fully consolidated itself by 1832. The French bourgeois revolution, more suddenly and dramatically triumphant after 1789, had succumbed to reaction only to re-emerge once more in 1830. In both countries the first revolutionary struggle of the modern age—the struggle between feudalism and bourgeoisie—was virtually over; the stage was set for the second struggle—between bourgeoisie and proletariat.

The events of 1848, coming hard on the heels of the *Manifesto,* did much to confirm its diagnosis and nothing to refute it. In England the collapse of Chartism was a set-back which none the less marked a stage in the consolidation of a class-conscious workers' movement. In France the proletariat marched shoulder to shoulder with the bourgeoisie in February 1848, as the *Manifesto* had said it would, so long as the aim was to consolidate and extend the bourgeois revolution. But once the proletariat raised its own banner of social revolution the line was crossed. Bourgeoisie and proletariat, allies until the bourgeois revolution had been completed and made secure, were now divided on opposite sides of the barricades by the call for proletarian revolution. The first revolutionary struggle was thus over: the second was impending. In Paris, in the June days of 1848, Cavaignac saved the bourgeoisie and staved off the proletarian revolution by massacring, executing and transporting the class-conscious workers. The pattern of the *Communist Manifesto* had been precisely followed. As Professor Namier, who is no Marxist, puts it: "The working classes touched off, and the middle classes cashed in on it."

> The June revolution [as Marx wrote at the time] for the first time split the whole of society into two hostile camps—east and west Paris. The unity of the February revolution no longer exists. The February fighters are now warring against each other—something that has never happened before; the former indifference has vanished and every man capable of bearing arms is fighting on one side or other of the barricades.

The events of February and June 1848 had provided a classic illustration of the great gulf fixed between bourgeois and proletarian revolutions.

Farther east the pattern of England and France did not fully apply, as the concluding section of the *Manifesto* admitted—almost by way of an afterthought.

In Germany the bourgeois revolution had not yet begun. The German bourgeoisie had not yet won the fundamental political rights which the English bourgeoisie had achieved in 1689 and the French a hundred years later. The task of the German proletariat was still therefore to support the bourgeoisie in the first revolutionary struggle against feudalism; in Germany, in the words of the *Manifesto,* "the Communist Party fights with the bourgeoisie whenever it acts in a revolutionary manner against the absolute monarchy, the feudal landlords and the petty bourgeoisie." But it could not be argued that Germany would simply follow the same path as England and France at a greater or less distance of time. The German revolution would occur "under the most advanced conditions of European civilization" which would give it a special character. Where the proletariat was already so advanced, thought Marx, the bourgeois revolution "can only be the immediate prelude to the proletarian revolution."

When Marx, in the brief concluding section of the *Manifesto,* devoted to Communist Party tactics, thus announced the prospect in Germany of an immediate transition from bourgeois to proletarian revolution without the intervening period of bourgeois rule, he showed a keen historical perception, even at the expense of undermining the validity of his own theoretical analysis. The events of 1848 in the German-speaking lands confirmed Marx's intuition of the impossibility in Germany of a period of established bourgeois supremacy comparable with that which has set so strong a mark on English and French history. This impossibility was due not so much to the strength of the German proletariat, which Marx perhaps exaggerated, as to the weakness of the German bourgeoisie. Whatever the prospects of an eventual proletarian revolution such as England and France had long ago achieved was still conspicuously absent. Indeed, the bourgeoisie, far from bidding for power for itself, was plainly ready to ally itself with the surviving elements of feudalism for defence against the proletarian menace. It need hardly be added that the same symptoms, in a still more pronounced form, repeated themselves in Russia more than half a century afterwards.

The problem, therefore, which Germany presented in 1848 to the authors of the *Communist Manifesto* was the same which Russia would one day present to the theorists of her revolution. According to the revolutionary pattern of the *Communist Manifesto,* the function of the bourgeoisie was to destroy feudal society root and branch preparatory to its own destruction in the final phase of the revolutionary struggle by the proletariat. But what was to happen if the bourgeoisie through weakness or cowardice—or perhaps through some untimely premonition of its own eventual fate—was unable or unwilling to perform its essential function? Marx never provided a categorical answer to this question. But his answer was implicit in the doctrine of "permanent revolution," which he propounded in an address to the Communist League in 1850:

> While the democratic petty bourgeoisie wants to end the revolution as rapidly as possible . . . our interests and our task consist in making the revolution permanent until all the more or less possessing classes are removed from authority, until the proletariat wins State power.

The responsibility was thus placed on the proletariat to complete the task, which the bourgeoisie had failed to perform, of liquidating feudalism.

What form the liquidation was to take when the proletariat found itself directly confronted by a feudal society without any effective and independent bourgeoisie was not altogether clear. But if one insisted—as Marx apparently did, and Engels continued to do down to the end of his life—that "our party can come to power only under some such form as a democratic republic," then the conclusion followed that the immediate aim of the proletariat must be limited to the establishment of a political democracy in which it was interested only as a necessary stepping-stone to the proletarian social revolution. This was, however, a theoretical construction unlikely to be realized in practice—as the experience of both the German and the Russian revolutions was one day to show. Marx never really fitted his analysis of revolution to countries where the bourgeoisie was incapable of making its own revolution; and acrimonious controversy about the relation between bourgeois and proletarian revolutions continued to divide the Russian revolutionaries for several decades.

The economic corollary of this conclusion was still more startling. If the establishment of a democratic republic was a prerequisite of the proletarian revolution, so also was the full development of capitalism; for capitalism was the essential expression of bourgeois society and inseparable from it. Marx certainly held this view as late as 1859 when he wrote in the preface to the *Critique of Political Economy:* "No social form perishes until all the productive forces for which it provides scope have been developed." It appeared to follow, paradoxically enough, that in backward countries the interest of the nascent proletariat was to promote the most rapid development of capitalism and capitalist exploitation at its own expense.

Such was the view seriously propounded by Russian Marxists, Bolshevik and Menshevik alike, down to 1905—perhaps even down to 1917. Meanwhile, however, in the spring of 1905, Lenin's practical mind worked out a new scheme under which the proletariat was to seize power in conjunction with the peasantry, creating a "democratic dictatorship" of workers and peasants; and this became the official doctrine of the October revolution. The Mensheviks stuck to their guns, and their survivors and successors to-day attribute the shortcomings of the Russian revolution to its failure to pass through the bourgeois-democratic, bourgeois-capitalist phase on its way to the achievement of socialism. The issue is not to be settled by reference to Marx, who can hardly be acquitted of inconsistency on this point. Either he made a mistake in suggesting, in the last section of the *Communist Manifesto,* that Germany might pass immediately from the bourgeois to the proletarian revolution; or he failed to fit this new conception into the revolutionary framework of the earlier part of the *Manifesto.*

Marx was to encounter similar difficulties in applying the generalizations of the *Communist Manifesto* about nationalism, which were also based on British and French experience, to central and eastern Europe. The charge often brought against Marx of ignoring or depreciating national sentiment rests indeed on a misunderstanding. The famous remark that "the workers have no country," read in its context, is neither a boast nor a programme; it is a complaint which had long been a commonplace among socialist writers. Babeuf had declared that the multitude "sees in society only an enemy, and loses even the possibility of having a country"; and Weitling had connected the notion of country with the notion of property:

> He alone has a country who is a property owner or at any rate has the liberty and the means of becoming one. He who has not that, has no country.

In order to remedy this state of affairs (to quote once more from the *Manifesto*) "the proletariat must first conquer political power, must rise to be the dominant class of the nation, must constitute itself the nation, so that the proletariat is so far national itself, though not in the bourgeois sense."

The passage of the *Manifesto* in which these sentences occur is not free from ambiguities. But the thought behind it is clear. In Marx's view, which corresponded to the facts of English and French history, nationalism grew up as an attribute of bourgeois society at a time when the bourgeoisie was a revolutionary and progressive force. Both in England and in France the bourgeoisie, invoking the national spirit to destroy a feudalism which was at once particularist and cosmopolitan, had through a period of centuries built up a centralized State on a national basis. But the advance of capitalism was already making nations obsolete.

> National differences and antagonisms are to-day vanishing ever more and more with the development of the bourgeoisie, free trade in the world market, the uniformity of industrial production and the conditions of life corresponding thereto.

> With the victory of the proletariat they will vanish still faster. . . . With the disappearance of classes within the nation the state of enmity between nations will come to an end.

Hence the first step was for the proletariat of every country to "settle accounts with its own bourgeoisie." The way would then be open for a true international communist order. Like Mazzini and other nineteenth-century thinkers, Marx thought of nationalism as a natural stepping-stone to internationalism.

Unfortunately the national pattern of the *Manifesto,* far from being universal, proved difficult to extend beyond the narrow limits of the place (western Europe) or the time (the age of Cobden) in which it was designed. Beyond western Europe the same conditions which prevented the rise of a powerful bourgeoisie also prevented the development of an orderly bourgeois nationalism. In central Europe (the Hapsburg Empire, Prussia) as well as in Russia the centralized State had been brought into being under pressure of military necessity by feudal overlords indifferent to national feeling; and when in the nineteenth century, under the impetus of the French revolution, nationalism became for the first time a force to be reckoned with in central and eastern Europe, it appeared not—as in England and France—as an attribute and complement of the State but as a sentiment independent of any existing State organization.

Moreover, the relation of nation to State worked itself out in different ways and sometimes involved even the same national group in inconsistent attitudes. This was particularly true of the Hapsburg Empire. The growing national consciousness of the German-Austrian bourgeoisie did not diminish its support of imperial unity; the bourgeoisie of the other constituent national groups sought to destroy that unity or at least to dissolve it into a federation. The Hungarians asserted the rights of the Magyar nation against the German-Austrians, but denied the national rights of Croats and Slovaks.

In these circumstances it is not surprising that Marx and Engels never succeeded in working out, even for their own day and generation, a consistent theory of nationalism which would hold good throughout Europe. They supported the Polish claim to national independence; no revolutionary, no liberal, of the nineteenth century could have done otherwise. But Engels, at any rate, seemed mainly concerned that this claim should be satisfied at the expense of Russia rather than of Prussia, proposing on one occasion to offer the Poles Riga and Mitau in exchange for Danzig and Elbing; and in the candid outburst of a private letter to Marx he referred to the Poles as "*une nation foutue*, a serviceable instrument only until Russia herself is swept into the agrarian revolution." In the same spirit he rejected outright the national aspirations of the Slavs of the Hapsburg Empire, whose triumph would be, in his eyes, a subjugation "of the civilized west by the barbaric east."

In these judgments, from which Marx is not known to have dissented, Engels was indubitably swayed by national prejudice and in particular by hostility to Russia as the most reactionary Power of the day. But he was also moved by the recognition that these nationalisms of central and eastern Europe, whose economic basis was agrarian, had little or nothing to do with the bourgeois nationalism of which Marx and he had taken cognizance in the *Communist Manifesto*. It was not only a question of "the civilized west" and "the barbaric east": it was a question of the subjugation "of town by the country, of trade, manufacture and intelligence by the primitive agriculture of Slavonic serfs." On the presuppositions of the *Manifesto*, this seemed necessarily a retrograde step. The failure of Marx and Engels to take account of agrarian nationalism was one aspect of the other great lacuna of the *Manifesto*—the question of the peasant.

If, however, the theory of nationalism propounded in the *Communist Manifesto* could not be transplanted from western to central and eastern Europe, it equally failed to stand the test of time. The *Manifesto* contains indeed one reference to "the exploitation of one nation by another" and declares, by what seems a tautology in one sense and a *non sequitur* in another, that it will end when the exploitation of one individual by another ends. But Marx has little to say (nothing at all in the *Manifesto* itself) about the colonial question, touching on it in detail only in the case of Ireland; and here it is perhaps significant that, while in 1848 he was prepared to sacrifice the Irish in the same way as the Austrian Slavs, he had become convinced by 1869 that "the direct absolute interest of the English working class demands a rupture of the present

connexion with Ireland." Marx did not, however, live to see the full development of the process by which the great nations, already victims of the contradictions of capitalism, vied with one another in bringing the whole world under
their yoke in a desperate attempt to save themselves and the capitalist system—
the process which Lenin was afterwards to analyse in his famous work on
Imperialism as the Highest Stage of Capitalism; nor could he foresee that rise to
national consciousness of innumerable "unhistorical" nations of which the
Austrian Slavs had been the harbingers. The Soviet theory of nationality, in
which the colonial question and the question of small nations divide the honours between them, can derive only a pale and faltering light from the simple
and far-away formulation of the *Communist Manifesto.* But critics of the national theories, whether of Marx or of the Bolsheviks, may do well to reflect
that bourgeois thinkers and statesmen have also not been able to formulate,
and still less to apply, a consistent doctrine of national rights.

Marx's attitude to the tiller of the soil is more seriously open to criticism.
Here too there is a foretaste of subsequent controversy—both the Mensheviks
and Trotsky were accused, rightly from Lenin's point of view, of "underestimating" the peasant; and here too Marx ran into trouble because his initial theories
had been primarily framed to fit western conditions. The *Communist Manifesto*
praised the bourgeoisie for having, through its development of factories and
towns, "delivered a great part of the population from the idiocy of country life";
and it classed peasant or peasant proprietor with handicraftsmen, small traders
and shopkeepers as members of the "petty bourgeoisie"—an unstable and reactionary class, since it struggled against the greater bourgeoisie, not for revolutionary ends, but only in order to maintain its own bourgeois status. In England,
in France (which in revolutionary circles was generally thought of as Paris writ
large) and in Germany, the *Communist Manifesto* upheld the strict pattern of successive revolutions of which the bourgeoisie and the proletariat would be the
respective driving forces, and reserved no independent place for the peasant.

Events were soon to show up the lacuna left by this scheme of things
even in western Europe. The French peasants were unmoved when the revolutionary workers of Paris were shot down in June 1848 by the agents of the
bourgeoisie, and voted solidly for the bourgeois dictatorship of Louis Napoleon.
In fact they behaved exactly as the *Communist Manifesto* expected them to
behave (which did not save them from incurring some of Marx's fiercest invective in *The Eighteenth Brumaire of Louis Napoleon*); but in so doing they
showed how far things would have to travel before the French proletariat
would be able to make another French revolution.

In Prussia and throughout Germany the revolution of 1848 was in the
hands of intellectuals who thought as little of the peasants as Marx himself; and
the peasants failed to move. In Austria the peasants did move. They rose in
Galicia against the landlords and would have risen elsewhere with the right
leadership. They formed a large and vocal group in the new democratic
Reichstag. But the claims of the peasant encountered the hostility of the bour-

geoisie and the indifference of the urban workers. Peasantry and proletariat were crushed separately in the absence of a leader and a programme to unite them; and in central Europe the surest moral of 1848 was that no revolution could succeed which did not win the peasant and give a high priority to his concerns.

In eastern Europe this was still more abundantly clear. As regards Poland, even the *Communist Manifesto* declared that "the Communists support the party that sees in agrarian revolution the means to national freedom, the party which caused the Cracow insurrection of 1846." But this passage, which occurs in the tactical postscript, is the only incursion of the *Manifesto* into eastern Europe and the only reference to agrarian revolution; and even here agrarian revolution is regarded as the ally of a bourgeois revolution leading to "national freedom," not of a proletarian revolution.

Spending the rest of his years in England, where there was no peasantry and no agrarian question, Marx never felt any strong impulse to fill this lacuna in the *Communist Manifesto*. In 1856, drawing a moral from the failure of 1848 in Germany, he spoke casually of the importance of backing up the future pro-letarian German revolution "with some second edition of the Peasants' War." But even here only a subsidiary role was assigned to the peasantry. It was towards the end of his life that Marx was called on to pass judgment on a con-troversy just opening in far-away Russia. The leading Russian revolutionaries, the Narodniks, regarded the Russian peasant commune with its system of com-mon tenure of land as the seed-bed of the future Russian Socialist order. On the other hand, the first Russian Marxists were already beginning to argue that the way to socialism could only lie, in Russia as elsewhere, through a development of capitalism and the proletariat.

Four times did the Marx-Engels partnership attack this ticklish issue. In 1874, before the Russian Marxists had raised their head, Engels had recognized the possibility in favourable conditions of the direct transformation of the com-munal system into a higher form, "avoiding the intermediate stage of individual-ized bourgeois property." In 1877, in reply to an attack in a Russian journal, Marx confined himself to a doubtful admission that Russia had "the finest chance which history ever presented to a nation of avoiding the ups-and-downs of the capitalist order." In 1881 Marx gave a more positive response to a direct personal inquiry from Vera Zasulich; and in the following year the last and most authoritative pronouncement appeared in the preface to a Russian translation of the *Communist Manifesto*, signed jointly by both its authors:

> If the Russian revolution is the signal for a workers' revolution in the west so that
> these complement each other, then the contemporary Russian system of
> communal ownership can serve as the starting-point for a Communist de-
> velopment.

Russian Social-Democrats of a later generation, both Bolshevik and Menshevik, looked askance at this quasi-Narodnik deviation, and returned to the purer theoretical pattern of the *Manifesto* with its clear-cut dialectic of bourgeois and proletarian revolutions; and Lenin himself, not less than the Mensheviks, sternly maintained the paradox that the further development of capitalism in Russia was a necessary prelude to social revolution. Nevertheless, Lenin, like Marx in his later years, recognized that no revolution, and no revolutionary, in eastern Europe could afford to ignore the peasant and his demands. After 1905—and before and after 1917—the Bolsheviks were obliged to devote an immense amount of energy and controversy to the task of fitting the Russian peasant into the western formulae of the *Communist Manifesto.*

Franz Mehring, Marx's best and most sympathetic biographer, remarks of the *Communist Manifesto* that "in many respects historical development has proceeded otherwise, and above all has proceeded more slowly, than its authors expected." This is true of the expectations of the two young men who composed the *Manifesto.* But how far were these expectations modified? As regards pace, Marx in later life certainly no longer believed in the imminence of the proletarian revolution with all the eager confidence of 1848. But even the *Manifesto* in one of its more cautious passages had predicted temporary successes followed by set-backs and a slow process of "growing unity" among the workers before the goal was achieved. Marx came, with advancing years, to accept the necessity of a long course of education for the proletariat in revolutionary principles; and there is the famous *obiter dictum* in a speech of the 1870s, which admits that in certain advanced countries the victory of the proletariat may be achieved without revolutionary violence.

As regards the scheme of historical development, it would be difficult to prove that Marx, speaking theoretically and *ex cathedra,* ever abandoned the strict analysis of revolution which he had worked out in the *Communist Manifesto.* But he was not a pure theorist. He was willy-nilly the leader of a political party; and it was when he found himself compelled to make pronouncements in this capacity that he sometimes appeared to derogate from his principles. Thus in the last section of the *Manifesto* itself he had already foreseen that in Germany the bourgeois revolution would be the "immediate prelude" of the proletarian revolution, thus skipping over the period of bourgeois supremacy; in the next few years he was drawn into some uncomfortable compromises and inconsistencies on the national question; and towards the end of his life he was constrained to admit that a predominantly peasant country like Russia had the chance of achieving the social revolution without passing through the bourgeois-capitalist phase at all, thus not merely modifying but side-tracking altogether the revolutionary analysis of the *Manifesto.*

It is curious and significant of the vitality of Marx's thought to watch how accurately this evolution was repeated in the Russian Social-Democratic Party. Its first leaders—Plekhanov and Axelrod, Lenin and Martov—accepted without question the scheme of the *Communist Manifesto.* After 1903 the Mensheviks, remaining consistent with themselves and with the Marxist scheme, ended in bankruptcy because they could find no way of applying it to Russian conditions. The more flexible Lenin took the scheme and brilliantly adapted it to those conditions; and the adaptations which he made followed—in broad outline, though not in every detail—those which Marx himself had admitted in his later years. The process can be justified. Marxism was never offered to the world as a static body of doctrine; Marx himself once confessed that he was no Marxist; and the constant evolution of doctrine in response to changing conditions is itself a canon of Marxism.

It is on such grounds that the Russian revolution can claim to be a legitimate child of the *Communist Manifesto*. The *Manifesto* challenged bourgeois society and offered a revaluation of bourgeois values. The Bolshevik revolution, with all its deviations, all its adaptations to specifically Russian conditions and all the impurities which always disfigure practice as opposed to theory, has driven home the challenge and sought to apply the revaluation. That bourgeois society has been put progressively on the defensive in the past hundred years, that its fate still hangs in the balance, few to-day will deny; and until that fate is settled, until some new synthesis has been achieved, the *Communist Manifesto* will not have said its last word.

The present is a revolutionary age, and the place of revolutions on the Marxist plan raises questions of global concern. Dr. Ulam, professor of government at Harvard University, views the Marxist analysis of the ills of contemporary society through modern (and somewhat jaundiced) eyes.

FROM *The Unfinished Revolution*
BY *Adam B. Ulam*

THE ETERNAL BATTLE ARRAY OF HISTORY always ranges the oppressor against the oppressed, most commonly the owner of the means of production against the man who works with them. Only in the very beginning of human society was there no class struggle, just as there will be none in its culmination. Between the most primitive tribal community and the socialist-communist era, "the history of all hitherto existing society is the history of class struggles." Capitalism witnesses this struggle in the most simplified form: the proletariat against the capitalists. The victory of the proletariat will bring with it the abolition of the class struggle. The discovery of private property disrupted the social innocence of mankind. The full utilization of mankind's productive powers under socialism will restore it. With the disappearance of private property and of the class struggle, most of the social evils will disappear and with them the rationale for oppressive institutions, including the state.

This is the most clear-cut and internally consistent of all Marxist arguments. From its ringing formulation in the *Communist Manifesto* to the end of

Adam B. Ulam, *The Unfinished Revolution*, pp. 32–44. Copyright 1960 by Adam B. Ulam. Reprinted by permission of Random House, Inc.

their lives, Marx and Engels never doubted that they had found the operating pattern of history, that the reality of social and political life is expressed, not in the struggle of ideas, dynasties, or nations, but in the class struggle grounded in economic motivation. To their followers, the principle was a satisfactory explanation and a reliable guide to action, with none of the puzzling qualities of Marxist economics or overall philosophy. Class struggle became, in effect, the major portion of the revolutionary appeal of Marxism. Workers do not strike or storm the barricades in order to abolish surplus value. They strike and revolt against oppressive conditions, against the capitalists. From the point of view of political action, the slogan of class struggle is the simplest guide. It is also the simplest, most convincing revolutionary explanation of politics and history.

A deceptive simplicity! It has misled both the critics and the followers of Marxism. It has led Marxist movements too often to identify Marxist politics with a simple posture of opposition to the exploiting classes. The dominant faction of the German Social Democrats before World War I defined their Marxism as hostility to the imperial institutions and middle-class parties of their country. It led the Bolsheviks, in the first flush of their victory in 1917, to believe that by destroying the capitalists they were destroying capitalism. It has led people versed in Marxism to express surprise that many secondary features of capitalism "suddenly" made their appearance in Soviet Russia in the 1930's. Marxism became identified with insurrectionary action or with hostility, open and uncompromising, to capitalism and to everything and everyone connected with it.

It is necessary to repeat (as it will be again) what is perhaps the most pregnant sentence in Marx's view of social revolution, describing the role of the capitalist: "He thus forces the development of the productive powers of society, and creates *those material conditions, which alone can form the real basis of a higher form of society,* a society in which the full and free development of every individual forms the ruling principle." Nothing in the *main body* of Marx and Engels' writing suggests that any political development, even a seizure of power by the proletariat, can abrogate the laws governing the material development of mankind. From the earliest days of their association, the days filled with the most immediate revolutionary hope, Marx and Engels believed in the primacy of material factors over political action. It is always possible to find an incident or a statement by one or the other that would range them in the camp of believers in revolution pure and simple and hang the stage of economic development. (Thus the brief "Blanquist" period of Marx's early revolutionary activity, and, late in his life, his opinion that Russia might skip the full capitalist phase and pass into socialism from pre-capitalism.) But it is impossible to claim that such incidents or utterances represent the main tendency of Marxism or, as M. Rubel claims in his excellent biography, that Marx ultimately abandoned economic determinism in favor of unconditional faith in the ideal of human liberation.[1]

[1]Maximilien Rubel, *Karl Marx: Essai de biographie intellectuelle,* Paris, 1957.

What bridges the gap between economic determinism on the one hand and class struggle and the call to the proletariat to seize power on the other is Marx's revolutionary optimism. In the 1840's and early '50's, he believed that capitalism was on its last legs, that the economic as well as the political conditions for its downfall were at hand. It is true, as M. Rubel reminds us, that Marx was a socialist long before he discovered his economic system. It is true that the fascination of political economy engrossed and captured him, pushing his thought in directions he had perhaps not envisaged as a young man. But his socialism and his "discovery" of the class struggle did not precede his distaste for the existing moralistic brands of socialism and the determination to place *his* socialism on a firm, materialistic, scientific basis.

Again, what is difficult for us to understand from the perspective of a hundred years becomes easier if we immerse ourselves in the feeling of the period. How could a man believe both that capitalism was a necessary phase of the development of mankind and that Western European capitalism circa 1850 had played its role and was ready to leave the stage? The simple answer is that Marx and Engels shared not only the expectations of many radicals and socialists of the day, but also the apprehensions of many capitalists and liberal economists. Social and economic unrest had risen in ascending proportion from the introduction of what are *to us* the rudimentary institutions of capitalism to the middle of the nineteenth century. Was it entirely unreasonable to expect a fairly early economic collapse as well as a political revolution? Or to see a democratic revolution as a far-reaching step toward socialism? Many revolutionaries live expecting their revolution to take place any day. In Marx the faith of a revolutionary was complemented by the analysis of a social scientist. It is easy for us to say that Marx was wrong: capitalism did not collapse in Europe in 1850 or in 1860. But he was also right, though on wrong premises: what he assumed were relatively late stages of capitalism in France and England were in effect the early stages of industrialization and modernization in those countries, and in those stages capitalism is most vulnerable to class struggle.

Without revolutionary optimism, the doctrine of the class struggle, when joined with economic determinism, is a somber and tragic lesson. Except at the turning points in history, there is nothing the oppressed can do against the oppressor. The slave cannot prevail against his master, the serf against the landowner; and one type of oppression disappears only to be reborn in a different form of exploitation of man by man. Class struggle is compounded in the character of law and civilization imposed by each dominant class. Systems of religion and ethics serve to reinforce and to conceal at the same time the interest of the dominant class. Ever since he had seen, as a young man, the diet of his province discuss draconic laws against the removal of timber from state and private forests by the poor, all of Marx's instincts rebelled at the myth of the impartial state, impartial law. The system of private property under capitalism embodies best the double deception by which each exploiting class masks its exploiting role. It protects the capitalist against any tampering with his property, and it seeks to create the illusion of equality and impartiality for all. The plea for democratic franchise that the bourgeoisie makes is likewise a weapon of its class struggle. It seeks to strip the landlords of the remnants of their power and to delude the proletariat into believing that the essential issues are political in nature. The principle of class struggle illuminates world history by stripping it of its theatrical aspects of national struggles or contests about principles, and by demonstrating its material nature. Marx's is the "inside story" of world history, with economic interest its moving principle.

The "exposure" of history and politics was not unique to Marx. The dominant role of "interest" in politics and recent history was a cardinal tenet of the liberalism of his time. The sense of politics consisted in the struggle of classes seeking the advancement of their material interests. Thus the political struggle in the England of the thirties and forties between the Whigs and the Tories was interpreted as centering around the contest between the agricultural and the manufacturing interests. Liberal economists saw in their doctrine a guide to public policies that would secure a "harmony of interests," but they were far from assuming that the correctness of their theories would of itself secure their adoption, or that a collusion of vested interests could not—as well as ignorance—hamper public welfare. The liberal version was already a "suspicious" theory of history, with the material interests of classes lurking behind the struggle for politics and principles.

Marx elevates this suspicion into certainty. Thus, for example, the Glorious Revolution of 1688 is not primarily a victory of parliamentarianism over royal despotism, but a harbinger of bourgeois domination, with the Stock Exchange and other rudimentary institutions of capitalism soon to be established. In a sense, the Marxist class-struggle interpretation of history is more "historical" than the liberal one. In the liberal outlook, history had been a period of darkness and superstition until the sixteenth and seventeenth centuries, and only then had scientific principle begun to assert itself in thinking about human affairs. To Marx, on the other hand, the class struggle provided the rationale of social systems and philosophies from earliest times; the pattern of history is always meaningful if we follow the class-struggle principle and its economic underpinning. The Middle Ages are thus not merely a period of darkness and obscurantism: their social and religious ideas are perfectly understandable in terms of the then dominant mode of production and system of property. Marxist historical analysis and methods of investigation have had an influence on many historians, some of whom would repudiate indignantly the charge of having anything to do with Marxism.

*　　*　　*

Marx cannot be reproached with having overlooked the differentiation and proliferation of social classes in his society. Indeed, ostensible political activity consists in various classes and subclasses playing for, or being played for, power in the state. But the essence of the class struggle and its eventual determination is much simpler. Only two classes really count—the capitalists and the proletariat. Other classes and subclasses play increasingly minor roles in the drama of capitalism. Sooner or later they retire into the wings, leaving the stage to the two great antagonists. Insofar as it is the logic of history, i.e., the development of productive forces, and not the temporary whims or affiliations of groups of population that ordain social stratifications, only two classes will remain, and they are "really" the only classes in the true sense of the word. Capitalism is already destroying the landowning nobility, and it will destroy the peasants.

*   *   *

The two classes that are to square off in the last phase of the class struggle are quite dissimilar in many characteristics. The capitalist class is forever growing smaller in numbers; the proletariat, the exploited, ever larger. The rationale of the capitalist process, while it makes the capitalists aware of certain interests they have in common, still obliges them to engage in suicidal competition. The capitalist-industrial process makes the workers more and more unified in the realization of their common interest and in their class solidarity. The peasants, for instance, because of their dispersion, because of the peculiarity of their way of living, can never achieve real solidarity and a real community of interest and feeling; and thus, apart from their marginal economic significance, they can never constitute a true class. The workers, on the contrary, are disciplined by the circumstances of their work, brought together in great aggregations where they can feel the community of their privations and realize the logic of capitalism as leading to socialism. The *spontaneous growth* of class consciousness accompanies the growth of the capitalist-industrial system. . . .

Here we may observe certain interesting connotations of the concept. It is *rationalistic* in the extreme. The working class will not be distracted from the obligation and the realization of the inevitability of the class struggle by nationalistic or religious slogans and considerations. Only a degenerate, rootless portion of it, the *Lumpenproletariat,* may capitulate to the schemes of reactionaries and adventurers. The vast majority of the workers will understand their historical position and historical mission. The vision of the working class is Hegelian in its underpinnings. The proletariat is the universal class, carrying in its future the destiny of mankind, thus parallel in its function to Rousseau's General Will and Hegel's State. The loss of individuality caused and made inevitable by factory labor, the worker's *alienation,* carries in it the seeds of the fullest assertion of individuality under socialism, which comes as a Hegelian "negation of a negation." In more prosaic terms, the factory system is inevitably oppressive and inevitably felt by the worker as such. This oppression *inherent* in the system produces the class feeling. Capitalism = factory system = class consciousness is the line of argument, and a closer examination of each term of the triad will illuminate the nature and conditions of the appeal of Marxism.

The doctrines of the classes and the class struggle have, within the context of the Marxist system, some further rather unexpected connotations. Take the class struggle between the bourgeoisie and the proletariat. The latter, through strikes and political action, resists the inevitable tendency of the capitalists to increase the exploitation of the workers. Yet nothing is clearer according to the logic of the doctrine than that the class struggle cannot paralyze capitalism until the system is fully developed and ready to pass on, or until the proletariat is fully capable of wresting power from the bourgeoisie. What might be called guerrilla class warfare, endemic industrial strife, which would paralyze the system, is clearly against the logic of Marxist thought, even if paradoxically within its spirit: the worker has to get used to the hated factory system, has to undergo exploitation, before the material conditions of the society will allow the transition to socialism. From the perspective of a hundred years, we may appreciate how the Russian and Chinese Communists have taken to heart the logic of the last proposition.

There is no *mystique* of the working class in early Marxism, no extolling of humble material circumstances as being conducive to virtue. Workers are not asserted or called upon to be heroic. They are asserted and called upon to be rational, to develop class consciousness. To Marx, nothing would have been more distasteful than the emotional undertones of later syndicalism. The ideal (in Weber's sense of the term) Marxist worker is a curiously unemotional creature. He has no country, no real family life; and his main objective in life is not an amelioration of his conditions, but the overthrow of the whole capitalist system. His sense of suffering injustice, of being exploited, does not deceive him into immediate action against the immediate agents of oppression—the factory and the employer—but into a *planned* struggle against capitalism and the capitalist state. In his political writings and speeches, Marx makes eloquent and emotion-tinged appeals, but the fact is that the main tenet of his theory about the worker and the class struggle is coldly rational in its logic. Human passion and generosity cannot in the last analysis prevail against the facts of history. The drama of the class struggle and the heroic exploits of the working-class revolutionaries are secondary to the working out of material forces. One cannot divorce economic evolution from the human drama that underlies it, but one must not ignore the laws of economics in revolutionary action. It is only a superficial reader of Marxism who would read into it the assumption that the proletariat may by political or insurrectionary action void the laws of history and avoid, say, by seizing power before capitalism is fully established, the hardships and privation of the factory system.

The idea of the class struggle serves to disprove the facile optimism of the liberals for whom, in all the clashes of interests, an "invisible hand" assured in a rationally organized society the harmony of individual and class self-interest with the general welfare. Marx's "invisible hand" is the very visible forces of production, which by their evolution confront each succeeding civilization with a different type of class warfare until, finally developed, they bring about classless society.

The centering of the social problem around the individual is, according to Marx, another pious hypocrisy of liberalism. Individual liberty and due process of law are, within a capitalist society, simply contradictions in terms. They are at

most scraps of concessions thrown by the bourgeois state to deceive the proletariat, and in the circumstances of the workers' life under capitalism, they are of
no value to them. This contemptuous attitude toward civil liberties, of such
great historical significance to Marxism, is attuned to the circumstances of the
worst period of the Industrial Revolution: with the proletarian working twelve
and fourteen hours a day, and his wife and underage children also in unregulated industrial labor, the Bill of Rights did not, in fact, appear of overwhelming
importance to the working class. The class struggle becomes the doctrine of
total distrust of the capitalist state, with its laws, bureaucracy, and ideology. The
violence of this distrust and opposition, the difficulty Marx and Engels experienced in acknowledging even the slightest social-welfare aspect of the bourgeois state, have often led to the optical illusion that Marxism was opposed to
the state as such. It has enabled the revolutionary Marxists to denounce *the
state*, with all the accents and conviction of anarchists, forgetting, for the
moment, that the centralized state, like the capitalism of which it is a necessary
ingredient, is an inevitable part of the historical process.

*   *   *

Here, then, is a theory attuned even more closely than other parts of Marxism
to the facts and feelings of an early period of industrialization. The class struggle is the salt of Marxism, its most operative revolutionary part. As a historical
and psychological concept, it expresses a gross oversimplification, but it is the
oversimplification of a genius. The formula of the class struggle seizes the
essence of the mood of a great historical moment—a revolution in basic economy—and generalizes it into a historical law. It extracts the grievances of
groups of politically conscious workers in Western Europe, then a very small
part of the whole proletariat, and sees in it the portent and meaning of the
awakening of the whole working class everywhere. The first reaction of the
worker to industrialization, his feelings of grievance and impotence before the
machine, his employer, and the state which stands behind the employer, are
assumed by Marx to be typical of the general reactions of the worker to industrialization. What does change in the process of the development of industry is
that the worker's feeling of impotence gives way to class consciousness, which
in turn leads him to class struggle and socialism. Marx's worker is the historical
worker, but he is the historical worker of a specific period of industrial and
political development.

     Even in interpreting the psychology of the worker of the transitional pe-
riod, Marx exhibited a rationalistic bias. The worker's opposition to the capitalist
order is a total opposition to its laws, its factories, and its government. But this
revolutionary consciousness of the worker is to take him next to Marxist socialism, where he will accept the factory system and the state, the *only* difference
being the abolition of capitalism. Why shouldn't the revolutionary protest of the
worker flow into other channels: into rejection of industrialism as well as capitalism, into rejection of the socialist as well as the capitalist state? It is here that

Marx is most definitely the child of his age, the child of rationalistic optimism: the workers will undoubtedly translate their anarchistic protests and grievances into a sophisticated philosophy of history. They will undoubtedly realize that the forces of industrialism and modern life, which strip them of property, status, and economic security, are in themselves benevolent in their ultimate effects and that it is only capitalism and the capitalists which make them into instruments of oppression. The chains felt by the proletariat are the chains of the industrial system. The chains Marx urges them to throw off are those of capitalism. Will the workers understand the difference? And if they do, will they still feel that in destroying capitalism they have a "world to win"?

3

The Participants' Views

The real teachings of Marxism on revolution were of more than academic importance. The Marxist in many countries was betting his life on the truth of the system; a misinterpretation could lead not only to the failure of the Socialist movement but also to imprisonment or death. It was a high price to pay for misreading the Marxist texts, and the leaders of the Socialist movement in the various countries of Europe were concerned to establish an official reading.

The selections that follow illustrate two approaches: the "hard" one of V. I. Lenin (1870–1924), first published in 1917, to whom revolution was fundamental, and the "soft" one of Karl Kautsky (1854–1938), to whom revolution was no longer necessary.

FROM *State and Revolution*

BY *V. I. Lenin*

WE MUST . . . NOTE THAT ENGELS QUITE DEFINITELY regards universal suffrage as a means of bourgeois domination. Universal suffrage, he says, obviously summing up the long experience of German Social-Democracy, is "an index of the maturity of the working class; it cannot, and never will, be anything else but that in the modern state."

The petty-bourgeois democrats, such as our Socialist-Revolutionaries and Mensheviks, and also their twin brothers, the social-chauvinists and opportunists of Western Europe, all expect "more" from universal suffrage. They themselves share, and instil into the minds of the people, the wrong idea that universal suffrage "in the *modern* state" is really capable of expressing the will of the majority of the toilers and of assuring its realisation.

We can here only note this wrong idea, only point out that this perfectly clear, exact and concrete statement by Engels is distorted at every step in the propaganda and agitation of the "official" (*i.e.,* opportunist) Socialist parties. A detailed analysis of all the falseness of this idea, which Engels brushes aside, is given in our further account of the views of Marx and Engels on the "modern" state.

V. I. Lenin, *State and Revolution*, pp. 14–20. Copyright 1932 by International Publishers Co., Inc. Reprinted by permission.

A general summary of his views is given by Engels in the most popular of his works in the following words:

> The state, therefore, has not existed from all eternity. There have been societies which managed without it, which had no conception of the state and state power. At a certain stage of economic development, which was necessarily bound up with the cleavage of society into classes, the state became a necessity owing to this cleavage. We are now rapidly approaching a stage in the development of production at which the existence of these classes has not only ceased to be a necessity, but is becoming a positive hindrance to production. They will disappear as inevitably as they arose at an earlier stage. Along with them, the state will inevitably disappear. The society that organises production anew on the basis of a free and equal association of the producers will put the whole state machine where it will then belong: in the museum of antiquities, side by side with the spinning wheel and the bronze axe.

It is not often that we find this passage quoted in the propaganda and agitation literature of contemporary Social-Democracy. But even when we do come across it, it is generally quoted in the same manner as one bows before an icon, *i.e.,* it is done merely to show official respect for Engels, without any attempt to gauge the breadth and depth of revolutionary action presupposed by this relegating of "the whole state machine . . . to the museum of antiquities." In most cases we do not even find an understanding of what Engels calls the state machine.

* * *

Without fear of committing an error, it may be said that of this argument by Engels so singularly rich in ideas, only one point has become an integral part of Socialist thought among modern Socialist parties, namely, that, unlike the Anarchist doctrine of the "abolition" of the state, according to Marx the state "withers away." To emasculate Marxism in such a manner is to reduce it to opportunism for such an "interpretation" only leaves the hazy conception of a slow, even, gradual change, free from leaps and storms, free from revolution. The current popular conception, if one may say so, of the "withering away" of the state undoubtedly means a slurring over, if not a negation, of revolution.

Yet, such an "interpretation" is the crudest distortion of Marxism, which is advantageous only to the bourgeoisie; in point of theory, it is based on a disregard for the most important circumstances and considerations pointed out in the very passage summarising Engels' ideas, which we have just quoted in full.

In the first place, Engels at the very outset of his argument says that, in assuming state power, the proletariat by that very act "puts an end to the state as the state." One is "not accustomed" to reflect on what this really means. Generally, it is either ignored altogether, or it is considered as a piece of "Hegelian weakness" on Engels' part. As a matter of fact, however, these words express succinctly the experience of one of the greatest proletarian revolutions—the Paris Commune of 1871, of which we shall speak in greater detail in its proper place. As a matter of fact, Engels speaks here of the destruction of the bourgeois state by the proletarian revolution, while the words about its withering away refer to the remains of *proletarian* statehood *after* the Socialist revolution. The bourgeois state does not "wither away," according to Engels, but is "put an end to" by the proletariat in the course of the revolution. What withers away after the revolution is the proletarian state or semi-state.

Secondly, the state is a "special repressive force." This splendid and extremely profound definition of Engels' is given by him here with complete lucidity. It follows from this that the "special repressive force" of the bourgeoisie for the suppression of the proletariat, of the millions of workers by a handful of the rich, must be replaced by a "special repressive force" of the proletariat for the suppression of the bourgeoisie (the dictatorship of the proletariat). It is just this that constitutes the "act" of "the seizure of the means of production in the name of society." And it is obvious that such a substitution of one (proletarian) "special repressive force" for another (bourgeois) "special repressive force" can in no way take place in the form of a "withering away."

Thirdly, as to the "withering away" or, more expressively and colourfully, as to the state "becoming dormant," Engels refers quite clearly and definitely to the period *after* "the seizure of the means of production [by the state] in the name of society," that is, *after* the Socialist revolution. We all know that the political form of the "state" at that time is complete democracy. But it never enters the head of any of the opportunists who shamelessly distort Marx that when Engels speaks here of the state "withering away," or "becoming dormant," he speaks of *democracy*. At first sight this seems very strange. But it is "unintelligible" only to one who has not reflected on the fact that democracy is *also* a state and that, consequently, democracy will *also* disappear when the state disappears. The bourgeois state can only be "put an end to" by a revolution. The state in general, *i.e.,* most complete democracy, can only "wither away."

Fourthly, having formulated his famous proposition that "the state withers away," Engels at once explains concretely that this proposition is directed equally against the opportunists and the Anarchists. In doing this, however, Engels puts in the first place that conclusion from his proposition about the "withering away" of the state which is directed against the opportunists.

One can wager that out of every 10,000 persons who have read or heard about the "withering away" of the state, 9,990 do not know at all, or do not remember, that Engels did not direct his conclusions from this proposition against the Anarchists *alone*. And out of the remaining ten, probably nine do not know the meaning of a "people's free state" nor the reason why an attack on this watchword contains an attack on the opportunists. This is how history is written! This is how a great revolutionary doctrine is imperceptibly adulterated and adapted to current philistinism! The conclusion drawn against the Anarchists has been repeated thousands of times, vulgarised, harangued about in the crudest fashion possible until it has acquired the strength of a prejudice, whereas the conclusion drawn against the opportunists has been hushed up and "forgotten"!

The "people's free state" was a demand in the programme of the German Social-Democrats and their current slogan in the 'seventies. There is no political substance in this slogan other than a pompous middle-class circumlocution of the idea of democracy. In so far as it referred in a lawful manner to a democratic republic, Engels was prepared to "justify" its use "at times" from a propaganda point of view. But this slogan was opportunist, for it not only expressed an exaggerated view of the attractiveness of bourgeois democracy, but also a lack of understanding of the Socialist criticism of every state in general. We are in favour of a democratic republic as the best form of the state for the proletariat under capitalism, but we have no right to forget that wage slavery is the lot of the people even in the most democratic bourgeois republic. Furthermore, every state is a "special repressive force" for the suppression of the oppressed class. Consequently, *no* state is either "free" or a "people's state." Marx and Engels explained this repeatedly to their party comrades in the 'seventies.

Fifthly, in the same work of Engels, from which every one remembers his argument on the "withering away" of the state, there is also a disquisition on the significance of a violent revolution. The historical analysis of its rôle becomes, with Engels, a veritable panegyric on violent revolution. This, of course, "no one remembers"; to talk or even to think of the importance of this idea is not considered good form by contemporary Socialist parties, and in the daily propaganda and agitation among the masses it plays no part whatever. Yet it is indissolubly bound up with the "withering away" of the state in one harmonious whole.

Here is Engels' argument:

> . . . That force, however, plays another rôle (other than that of a diabolical power) in history, a revolutionary rôle, that, in the words of Marx, it is the midwife of every old society which is pregnant with the new; that it is the instrument with whose aid social movement forces its way through and shatters the dead, fossilised political forms—of this there is not a word in Herr Dühring. It is only with sighs and groans that he admits the possibility that force will perhaps be necessary for the overthrow of the economic system of exploitation—unfortunately! because all use of force, forsooth, demoralises the person who uses it. And this in spite of the immense moral and spiritual impetus which has resulted from every victorious revolution! And this in Germany, where a violent collision—which indeed may be forced on the people—would at least have the advantage of wiping out the servility which has permeated the national consciousness as a result of the humiliation of the Thirty Years' War. And this parson's mode of thought—lifeless, insipid and impotent—claims to impose itself on the most revolutionary party which history has known?

How can this panegyric on violent revolution, which Engels insistently brought to the attention of the German Social-Democrats between 1878 and

1894, *i.e.,* right to the time of his death, be combined with the theory of the "withering away" of the state to form one doctrine?

Usually the two views are combined by means of eclecticism, by an unprincipled, sophistic, arbitrary selection (to oblige the powers that be) of either one or the other argument, and in ninety-nine cases out of a hundred (if not more often), it is the idea of the "withering away" that is specially emphasised. Eclecticism is substituted for dialectics—this is the most usual, the most widespread phenomenon to be met with in the official Social-Democratic literature of our day in relation to Marxism. Such a substitution is, of course, nothing new; it may be observed even in the history of classic Greek philosophy. When Marxism is adulterated to become opportunism, the substitution of eclecticism for dialectics is the best method of deceiving the masses; it gives an illusory satisfaction; it seems to take into account all sides of the process, all the tendencies of development, all the contradictory factors and so forth, whereas in reality it offers no consistent and revolutionary view of the process of social development at all.

We have already said above and shall show more fully later that the teaching of Marx and Engels regarding the inevitability of a violent revolution refers to the bourgeois state. It *cannot* be replaced by the proletarian state (the dictatorship of the proletariat) through "withering away," but, as a general rule, only through a violent revolution. The panegyric sung in its honour by Engels and fully corresponding to the repeated declarations of Marx (remember the concluding passages of the *Poverty of Philosophy* and the *Communist Manifesto,* with its proud and open declaration of the inevitability of a violent revolution; remember Marx's *Critique of the Gotha Programme* of 1875 in which, almost thirty years later, he mercilessly castigates the opportunist character of that programme)—this praise is by no means a mere "impulse," a mere declamation, or a polemical sally. The necessity of systematically fostering among the masses *this* and just this point of view about violent revolution lies at the root of the *whole* of Marx's and Engels' teaching. The neglect of such propaganda and agitation by both the present predominant social-chauvinist and the Kautskyist currents brings their betrayal of Marx's and Engels' teaching into prominent relief.

The replacement of the bourgeois by the proletarian state is impossible without a violent revolution. The abolition of the proletarian state, *i.e.,* of all states, is only possible through "withering away."

Marx and Engels gave a full and concrete exposition of these views in studying each revolutionary situation separately, in analysing the lessons of the experience of each individual revolution. We now pass to this, undoubtedly the most important part of their work.

*Karl Kautsky (1854–1938) was one of the leading theoreticians of the German
Social Democratic party. The selection that follows—Kautsky's attempt to come to
grips with the problem of the necessity of revolution in a state with democratic
institutions—is from a book review written by him in 1893.*

FROM *A Social Democratic Catechism*

BY *Karl Kautsky*

WE ARE REVOLUTIONARIES, and not merely in the sense that the steam engine is
revolutionary. The social overturn at which we aim can only be achieved
through a political revolution, through the conquest of political power by the
fighting proletariat. And the specific form of government in which alone socialism can be realized is the republic, that is—as the phrase is commonly understood—in the democratic republic.

*   *   *

Social Democracy is a revolutionary—but not a revolution-making—party. We
know that our aims can only be achieved through a revolution, but we also
know that it is as little in our power to make that revolution as it is in the
power of our enemies to prevent it. It does not occur to us, therefore, to want
to either plot or instigate a revolution. And since the revolution cannot arbitrarily be made by us, we cannot even attempt to describe when, under what
circumstances, and in which form it will break out. We do know that the class
struggle between bourgeoisie and proletariat will not end before the latter has
come into full possession of political power, which it will use to establish the
socialist society. We do know that this class struggle must become more inten-
sive and extensive, that the proletariat will grow in numbers and in moral and
economic power and that, therefore, its victory and capitalism's defeat are
inevitable. But we can venture only the vaguest guesses about how the last
decisive battles in this social war will be fought.

*   *   *

Since we know nothing about the decisive battles of the social war we can, of
course, say little about their character—whether they will be bloody, whether
physical violence will play a dominant rôle, or whether they will be fought
exclusively by means of economic, legislative, and moral pressures.

But we can say that it is very probable that in the revolutionary struggles
of the proletariat the latter [non-violent] means will have greater predominance
over the use of physical, i.e., military, force, than was the case in the revolutionary struggles of the bourgeoisie.

Karl Kautsky, "A Social Democratic Catechism," (Ein Sozialdemokratischer Katechismus) in *Neue Zeit* (December
1893), pp. 368–369, 402–405, 409–410, translated by Walter R. Weitzmann. Reprinted by permission.

One reason why the coming revolutionary struggles will be fought less and less with military means is, as has often been said, that the equipment of government troops is today vastly superior to the weapons available to the "civilians." As a rule, this disparity makes all the latters' resistance hopeless from the start. On the other hand, today's revolutionary strata have available to them better weapons of economic, political and moral resistance than had those of the previous century. The only exception to this is Russia.

Freedom of association, of press, and universal suffrage (under some circumstances, universal military service, as well), are, however, not merely weapons that give the proletariat of modern nations an advantage not possessed by the classes that fought the revolutionary battles of the bourgeoisie. These institutions also spread over the power relations of individual classes and parties, and the spirit which animates them is a light which was missing during the absolutist era.

Then, the ruling classes as well as the revolutionary classes groped about in the dark. Because the expression of opposition was made impossible, neither the governments nor the revolutionaries had any way to measure their strengths. Each of the two groups was therefore in danger of overestimating its strength before it had tested it in battle with its opponent, and equally, of underestimating it when it suffered a single defeat—quickly throwing in the towel. This is probably the main reason why we find, in the era of the revolutionary bourgeoisie, so many *coups* so easily put down, and so many governments so easily toppled—a succession, therefore, of revolution and counterrevolution.

It is entirely different today, at least in countries with somewhat democratic institutions. These institutions have been called the safety valve of society. If one means by this that the proletariat in a democracy ceases to be revolutionary, that it remains satisfied with merely expressing its resentment and its suffering publicly, and that it renounces political and social revolution, then this designation is wrong. Democracy cannot do away with the class contradictions of capitalist society, and it cannot prevent their necessary final result, the overthrow of this social system. But it can do one thing: though it cannot prevent the revolution, it can prevent some foredoomed revolutionary attempts and forestall some revolutionary uprisings. Democracy produces clarity about the relative strength of different parties and classes; though it cannot resolve their opposition nor transform their final aims, it does tend to prevent the rising classes from attempting to solve problems which they are not yet strong enough to tackle, and it tends, in turn, to keep the ruling classes from denying concessions which they are no longer strong enough to do. The direction of development is not thereby changed, but its pace becomes steadier and calmer. In states with democratic institutions the advance of the proletariat will be accompanied by less striking successes than was the rise of the bourgeoisie during its revolutionary epoch. But neither will it be marked by as severe defeats. Since the awakening of the modern social democratic workers' movement in the sixties the European proletariat has suffered only one great defeat—in the Paris Commune of 1871. At that time France was still suffering from the imprint of the Empire which had deprived the people of truly democratic institutions; the French proletariat had reached only a low level of self-consciousness, and the uprising had been forced upon them.

The democratic parliamentary method of struggle may appear more tedious than the method used in the revolutionary epoch of the bourgeoisie. It is true that it is less dramatic and showy, but it also produces fewer casualties. This may be a matter of indifference to that aestheticised group of literati which dabbles in socialism solely to find interesting sport and copy, but it is not unimportant to those who have to wage the struggle.

The more effective the democratic institutions and the greater the political and economic awareness and self-control of the populace, the better are the chances that so-called peaceful means of class struggle, those that limit themselves to non-violent means such as parliamentarianism, strikes, demonstrations, use of the press and other means of pressure, will be used.

Given any two opponents and everything else being equal, the one who feels superior to the other will most likely maintain his *sang-froid*. Someone who does not believe in himself and his cause is only too likely to lose his equanimity and control.

Now the class which in every modern country has the greatest faith in itself and its cause is the proletariat. To attain it it needs no false illusions. It needs only to examine the history of the last generation to see itself everywhere in uninterrupted advance. It needs only to study contemporary developments to gain the assurance that its victory is unavoidable. Hence, we should not expect the highly developed proletariat of a given country to easily lose its equanimity and self-control, or to inaugurate a policy of adventurism. The more educated and aware the working class and the more democratic the state, the less likely a policy of adventurism becomes.

But one cannot place equal confidence in the ruling class. Seeing and feeling themselves grow weaker every day, they become ever more anxious, and therefore unpredictable. Increasingly they sink into a mood where one must be prepared to see them seized by attacks of madness during which they fall upon their enemy in blind rage, intent upon finishing him off, mindless of the wounds they will thereby inflict upon all of society including themselves, and of the devastation they will wreak.

The political position of the proletariat is such that it will attempt as long as possible to advance by the aforementioned "legal" means. The danger that this aim will be frustrated lies in the jittery mood of the ruling classes.

The political leaders of the ruling classes hope for such madness to lay hold not just of the ruling classes but the indifferent masses as well, before Social Democracy is strong enough to resist. This is their only hope to delay the victory of socialism for at least another few years. But this is a desperate gamble. For if the bourgeoisie should fail in their mad attempt to suppress the proletariat, they will have exhausted their strength and will collapse even sooner while the proletariat triumphs even more quickly. But the predominant mood among many politicians of the ruling classes has already reached the point where they believe that nothing else can be done but to gamble everything on one card. They want to provoke civil war because they fear the revolution.

Social Democracy, on the other hand, has no reason to adopt such a policy of despair. It has every reason to avoid—and failing this to postpone—such madness in its rulers as long as possible. Ultimately, it must be delayed until the proletariat is strong enough to subdue and tame the maniacs, so that the havoc and its victims will be reduced and their attack be the last.

Social Democrats must, therefore, avoid and even combat anything that might be a purposeless provocation of the ruling classes; anything that might give their leaders an excuse to drive the bourgeoisie and its followers into a socialist-hating frenzy. Thus, when we declare that revolutions cannot be "made," when we condemn as nonsensical and dangerous the instigation of a revolution and act accordingly, we do this not to please the German state attorneys, but in the interest of the fighting proletariat. And in this position German Social Democrats stand united with their sister parties. Because of this stand it has so far been impossible for the leaders of the ruling classes to proceed against the fighting proletariat as they would have wished.

Though the political power of Social Democracy is still relatively small, socialists in modern nations are powerful enough to prevent bourgeois politicians from arbitrary actions. Minor regulations and ordinances cannot help them; they only embitter their subjects without discouraging them or reducing their fighting ability. Any attempt, however, to enact legislation that would seriously affect the proletariat's fighting capacity conjures up the danger of civil war which, whatever its outcome, would bring frightful devastation. This is fairly common knowledge. And though the bourgeois politicians may wish for a trial of strength with socialists before the latter are prepared, the bourgeois businessmen will have nothing to do with experiments which would ruin every one of them; at least in a rational state unaffected by the aforementioned madness. In a state of frenzy, the bourgeois can be gotten to support any measure, and the greater his fear, the wilder his cry for blood.

The interests of the proletariat demand even more authoritatively today than ever before that anything that might provoke the ruling classes into a policy of violence be avoided. Social Democrats act accordingly.

[Kautsky then speaks of a tendency calling itself proletarian that advocates such a policy of provocation. This he calls anarchism, and he spends the next five pages showing that Socialists must reject this anarchist direction, which has been responsible for all the setbacks of socialism since the Paris Commune—Ed.]

The main lever of our success is our revolutionary enthusiasm. We shall need it even more in the future for the most difficult days lie not behind, but ahead of us. Thus anything that might immobilize this lever would be most detrimental to our cause.

Our present position, by making us appear more "moderate" than we really are, carries with it a certain danger. The stronger we are, the more the practical tasks take precedence: the more we must extend our agitation beyond the circle of the industrial wage workers, and the more we must guard against useless provocations or hollow threats. This makes it extremely difficult to maintain the proper balance; to give full attention to the needs of the present without losing sight of the future; to engage in a dialogue with the peasantry and lower middle class and yet not surrender the proletarian standpoint; to avoid all provocation and yet to convince everyone that we are a party of struggle in irreconcilable opposition to the existing social system.

Social Darwinism— Law of Nature or Justification of Repression?

CONTENTS

QUESTIONS FOR STUDY

1 What essential element did Malthus' principle of population give to Darwin's theory of evolution? How does natural selection work?

2 What is the definition of "fittest" in the phrase "survival of the fittest"? What possible applications of the term "fittest" can be made to human societies?

3 How would a Social Darwinist define the origin and purpose of the state?

4 Is democracy reconcilable with the kind of state that Karl Pearson envisions?

5 What is the Social Darwinist's definition of imperialism? How did the Social Darwinists justify it?

6 To what extent do Barzun and Ashley Montagu discredit Social Darwinism? What would it be good to know, in a scientific sense, in regard to their arguments?

The world into which Charles Darwin (1809–1882) was born was undergoing rapid and violent change. When he was growing up, politics were dominated by the twin concerns of war and economics. On the continent of Europe Napoleon's armies enforced French rule from the Spanish peninsula to the borders of the Slavic world. The British were committed to his defeat, and Darwin's early childhood was spent in an atmosphere of war. Part of this atmosphere was included in the rapid expansion of British industry. Although the British army, under the Duke of Wellington, was no negligible factor in the military operations on the Continent, Britain's main strength lay in her industry and commerce. The requirements for supporting the war accelerated the industrialization of Great Britain and began to throw into dramatic relief the worsening plight of the laboring class.

Unlike the textbook wars of the eighteenth century, the Napoleonic wars were waged by masses of men and involved the energies of the civilian population as well as the military. For some states on the Continent, these wars were literally wars for survival. Many small states, particularly in Germany, were to be wiped out forever and pass into extinction. Even in England, where the English Channel provided an obstacle unavailable to her continental allies, fear of French invasion and conquest was both real and widespread. And, since Napoleon incorporated in his person the ideology of the French Revolution, conquest would have meant the destruction of England, at least so far as the ruling class was concerned.

The process of industrialization was no less unsettling. A new group of capitalists, exerting enormous energies, was changing the very topography of "Merrie England." Dark, satanic mills replaced the thatched cottage, and towering chimneys belched smoke over the peaceful English countryside. The demand for labor was insatiable, and competition was cut-throat. A new group of political activists emerged, intent upon securing the economic conquests of the new capitalism. To them, the old state regulations of trade and commerce were anathema. Taking their economics from Adam Smith and political theory from Jeremy Bentham, they set out to secure a place in the political structure for themselves as the representatives of the new industrial class. Their program was simple: laissez faire. Let things, particularly economic things, alone. From intense competition would come undreamed of wealth for the whole of British society. If the lower classes suffered, that was the price that had to be paid for the new prosperity. There had always been suffering and misery and always would be. The state could not change that, and state regulations only served to stifle private initiative from which came progress.

How much of all this Darwin was conscious of is uncertain. He grew up in a well-to-do home presided over by an authoritarian father. There was an intellectual tradition in the Darwin family, grandfather Erasmus having made his mark as a somewhat eccentric philosopher of nature. As a youth, Charles showed signs of neither the authority of his father nor the intelligence of his grandfather. He was a mediocre student at the local school and went on to achieve mediocrity at two universities. At Edinburgh, where he went to pursue a medical career, he soon tired of the dry-as-dust lectures on medical subjects and took to taking long walks in the country. It was here that he learned some rudiments of geology, Edinburgh then being an important center of geological thought. When he could no longer tolerate medical education, he left Edinburgh and went to Cambridge. Here he distinguished himself as an excellent shot but not as a scholar. Again, he took refuge in walks and profited by the company of Professor Henslow, a naturalist who taught him the fundamentals of natural history. Were it not for Henslow, Darwin might have ended as a country parson, publishing a few papers on the natural history of his parish.

In 1830 H. M. S. Beagle *was being outfitted for an oceanographic voyage under the command of Captain Fitzroy. The* Beagle *needed a naturalist, and Henslow recommended Darwin. The voyage of the* Beagle *provided Darwin with the education he had not received at Edinburgh or Cambridge. As the* Beagle *sailed along the coasts of South America, Darwin carefully collected specimens and observations. The fauna of the Galápagos Islands off the coast of Peru was particularly striking. Species that could not migrate from one island to another clearly displayed their common ancestry from the mainland, but with significant variations. Pondering these variations, and the variations caused by man through selective breeding, Darwin began to entertain the idea of the evolution of species. Contemporary work in geology appeared to prove that the age of the Earth was very great and, given this length of time, it did not seem wrong, Darwin thought, to assume that minute variations could accumulate to produce new species. What was lacking for Darwin was the mechanism by which these variations were accumulated. According to his own account, it was after his return to England, while he was pondering this problem, that he read* An Essay on the Principle of Population *by the Reverend Thomas R. Malthus (p. 509). Malthus had written his essay to prove there were certain iron laws of nature that prevented the perfectibility of man and human society as dreamed of by the theorists of the French Revolution. Since men bred faster than they could increase food supplies, there was always an intense competition for food, and this meant that the stronger and more able members of society survived at the expense of the feeble. Darwin recognized a similar struggle for existence in the whole animate realm and now applied it to the problem of the origin of species. By 1838 he was actively collecting and ordering evidence to prove evolution by means of natural selection, but the idea was so daring and he was so modest that he hesitated to publish his results. Not until an almost identical theory by another naturalist was forthcoming did Darwin move to publication, hastily writing his* On the Origin of Species. *Its appearance in 1859 marks one of the most important events in the history of the modern world (p. 511).*

Since the concept of a struggle for existence had its origin in the social and political life of the day, it is easy to understand why it was immediately applied to social and political questions. Darwin, himself, reveals how almost automatic it was to think in terms that reflected this struggle and its consequence—(in the

phrase provided by the English social and political philosopher, Herbert Spencer)
the survival of the fittest. But, aware of his own ignorance, Darwin hedged in his
essays on political sociology and racism, and made them tentative. Not so with
many of his disciples. The doctrine of natural selection provided a wonderful
means of justifying some fairly nasty actions, and there was no paucity of
"Social Darwinists" willing to use an argument from Science (with the capital S)
to convince their victims that it was all part of some cosmic law. The results were
catastrophic. Social Darwinism was used to prove the basic inequality of the
classes within a nation and of the races of the world.

1

The Struggle for Existence

The French Revolution touched off a spate of writings on the perfectibility of man. In France, Condorcet speculated on the ways in which the human species, guided by reason and science, would be able to rise to hitherto undreamed of heights. In England, William Godwin developed Condorcet's theme in glowing terms. The Reverend Thomas Malthus (1766–1834) thought this was all romantic rot and nonsense, since it ignored some very basic laws of biology. It was to oppose the naïve optimism of people such as Godwin and Condorcet that he wrote his Essay on the Principle of Population *first published in 1798.*

FROM *An Essay on the Principle of Population*

BY *Thomas R. Malthus*

IN AN INQUIRY CONCERNING the improvement of society, the mode of conducting the subject which naturally presents itself, is,

1. To investigate the causes that have hitherto impeded the progress of mankind towards happiness; and,
2. To examine the probability of the total or partial removal of these causes in future.

* * *

The principal object of the present essay is to examine the effects of one great cause intimately united with the very nature of man; which, though it has been constantly and powerfully operating since the commencement of society, has been little noticed by the writers who have treated this subject.

The cause to which I allude, is the constant tendency in all animated life to increase beyond the nourishment prepared for it.

* * *

In plants and irrational animals, the view of the subject is simple. They are all impelled by a powerful instinct to the increase of their species; and this

Thomas R. Malthus, *An Essay on the Principle of Population, or A View of Its Past and Present Effects on Human Happiness.* Chapter I. This edition published by Augustus M. Kelley Publishers. Reprinted by permission.

instinct is interrupted by no doubts about providing for their offspring. Wherever therefore there is liberty, the power of increase is exerted; and the superabundant effects are repressed afterwards by want of room and nourishment.

The effects of this check on man are more complicated. Impelled to the increase of his species by an equally powerful instinct, reason interrupts his career, and asks him whether he may not bring beings into the world, for whom he cannot provide the means of support. If he attend to this natural suggestion, the restriction too frequently produces vice. If he hear it not, the human race will be constantly endeavouring to increase beyond the means of subsistence. But as, by that law of our nature which makes food necessary to the life of man, population can never actually increase beyond the lowest nourishment capable of supporting it, a strong check on population, from the difficulty of acquiring food, must be constantly in operation. This difficulty must fall somewhere, and must necessarily be severely felt in some or other of the various forms of misery, or the fear of misery, by a large portion of mankind.

*   *   *

It may safely be pronounced . . . that population, when unchecked, goes on doubling itself every twenty-five years, or increases in a geometrical ratio. . . .

It may be fairly pronounced . . . that, considering the present average state of the earth, the means of subsistence, under circumstances the most favourable to human industry, could not possibly be made to increase faster than in an arithmetical ratio.

The necessary effects of these two different rates of increase, when brought together, will be very striking. Let us call the population of this island eleven millions; and suppose the present produce equal to the easy support of such a number. In the first twenty-five years the population would be twenty-two millions, and the food being also doubled, the means of subsistence would be equal to this increase. In the next twenty-five years, the population would be forty-four millions, and the means of subsistence only equal to the support of thirty-three millions. In the next period the population would be eighty-eight millions, and the means of subsistence just equal to the support of half that number. And, at the conclusion of the first century, the population would be a hundred and seventy-six millions, and the means of subsistence only equal to the support of fifty-five millions, leaving a population of a hundred and twenty-one millions totally unprovided for.

Taking the whole earth, instead of this island, emigration would of course be excluded; and, supposing the present population equal to a thousand millions, the human species would increase as the numbers 1, 2, 4, 8, 16, 32, 64, 128, 256, and subsistence as 1, 2, 3, 4, 5, 6, 7, 8, 9. In two centuries the population would be to the means of subsistence as 256 to 9; in three centuries as 4096 to 13, and in two thousand years the difference would be almost incalculable.

In this supposition no limits whatever are placed to the produce of the earth. It may increase for ever, and be greater than any assignable quantity; yet still the power of population being in every period so much superior, the increase of the human species can only be kept down to the level of the means of subsistence by the constant operation of the strong law of necessity, acting as a check upon the greater power.

In On the Origin of Species *Darwin applied Malthus's doctrine of the population outrunning food supply to the entire world of nature. From the competition for food, Darwin saw the favorable selection of variations which ultimately gave birth to new species.*

FROM *On the Origin of Species*

BY *Charles Darwin*

A STRUGGLE FOR EXISTENCE inevitably follows from the high rate at which all organic beings tends to increase. Every being, which during its natural lifetime produces several eggs or seeds, must suffer destruction during some period of its life, and during some season or occasional year, otherwise, on the principle of geometrical increase, its numbers would quickly become so inordinately great that no country could support the product. Hence, as more individuals are produced than can possibly survive, there must in every case be a struggle for existence, either one individual with another of the same species, or with the individuals of distinct species, or with the physical conditions of life. It is the doctrine of Malthus applied with manifold force to the whole animal and vegetable kingdoms; for in this case there can be no artificial increase of food, and no prudential restraint from marriage. Although some species may be now increasing, more or less rapidly, in numbers, all cannot do so, for the world would not hold them.

There is no exception to the rule that every organic being naturally increases at so high a rate, that if not destroyed, the earth would soon be covered by the progeny of a single pair. Even slow-breeding man has doubled in twenty-five years, and at this rate, in a few thousand years, there would literally not be standing room for his progeny. Linnaeus has calculated that if an annual plant produced only two seeds—and there is no plant so unproductive as this—and their seedlings next year produced two, and so on, then in twenty years there would be a million plants. The elephant is reckoned to be the slowest breeder of all known animals, and I have taken some pains to estimate its probable minimum rate of natural increase: it will be under the mark to assume that it breeds when thirty years old, and goes on breeding till ninety years old, bringing forth three pair of young in this interval; if this be so, at the end of the

Charles Darwin, *On the Origin of Species*, pp. 63–64, 66–67, 83–85. London, 1859. Reprinted by permission.

fifth century there would be alive fifteen million elephants, descended from the first pair.

*   *   *

In looking at Nature, it is most necessary to keep the foregoing considerations always in mind—never to forget that every single organic being around us may be said to be striving to the utmost to increase in numbers; that each lives by a struggle at some period of its life; that heavy destruction inevitably falls either on the young or old, during each generation or at recurrent intervals. Lighten any check, mitigate the destruction ever so little, and the number of the species will almost instantaneously increase to any amount. The face of Nature may be compared to a yielding surface, with ten thousand sharp wedges packed close together and driven inwards by incessant blows, sometimes one wedge being struck, and then another with greater force.

*   *   *

As man can produce and certainly has produced a great result by his methodical and unconscious means of selection, what may not nature effect? Man can act only on external and visible characters: nature cares nothing for appearances, except in so far as they may be useful to any being. She can act on every internal organ, on every shade of constitutional difference, on the whole machinery of life. Man selects only for his own good; Nature only for that of the being which she tends. Every selected character is fully exercised by her; and the being is placed under well-suited conditions of life. Man keeps the natives of many climates in the same country; he seldom exercises each selected character in some peculiar and fitting manner; he feeds a long and a short beaked pigeon on the same food; he does not exercise a long-backed or long-legged quadruped in any peculiar manner; he exposes sheep with long and short wool to the same climate. He does not allow the most vigorous males to struggle for the females. He does not rigidly destroy all inferior animals, but protects during each varying season, as far as lies in his power, all his productions. He often begins his selection by some half-monstrous form; or at least by some modification prominent enough to catch his eye, or to be plainly useful to him. Under nature, the slightest difference of structure or constitution may well turn the nicely balanced scale in the struggle for life, and so be preserved. How fleeting are the wishes and efforts of man! how short his time! and consequently how poor will his products be, compared with those accumulated by nature during whole geological periods. Can we wonder, then, that nature's productions should be far "truer" in character than man's productions; that they should be infinitely better adapted to the most complex conditions of life, and should plainly bear the stamp of far higher workmanship?

It may be said that natural selection is daily and hourly scrutinising, throughout the world, every variation, even the slightest; rejecting that which is bad, preserving and adding up all that is good; silently and insensibly working, whenever and wherever opportunity offers, at the improvement of each organic being in relation to its organic and inorganic conditions of life. We see nothing of these slow changes in progress, until the hand of time has marked the long lapse of ages, and then so imperfect is our view into long past geological ages, that we only see that the forms of life are now different from what they formerly were.

Although natural selection can act only through and for the good of each being, yet characters and structures, which we are apt to consider as of very trifling importance, may thus be acted on. When we see leaf-eating insects green, and bark-feeders mottled-grey; the alpine ptarmigan white in winter, the red-grouse the colour of heather, and the black-grouse that of peaty earth, we must believe that these tints are of service to these birds and insects in preserving them from danger. Grouse, if not destroyed at some period of their lives, would increase in countless numbers; they are known to suffer largely from birds of prey; and hawks are guided by eyesight to their prey,—so much so, that on parts of the Continent persons are warned not to keep white pigeons, as being the most liable to destruction. Hence I can see no reason to doubt that natural selection might be most effective in giving the proper colour to each kind of grouse, and in keeping that colour, when once acquired, true and constant. Nor ought we to think that the occasional destruction of an animal of any particular colour would produce little effect: we should remember how essential it is in a flock of white sheep to destroy every lamb with the faintest trace of black. In plants the down on the fruit and the colour of the flesh are considered by botanists as characters of the most trifling importance: yet we hear from an excellent horticulturist, Downing, that in the United States smooth-skinnned fruits suffer far more from a beetle, a curculio, than those with down; that purple plums suffer far more from a certain disease than yellow plums; whereas another disease attacks yellow-fleshed peaches far more than those with other coloured flesh. If, with all the aids of art, these slight differences make a great difference in cultivating the several varieties, assuredly, in a state of nature, where the trees would have to struggle with other trees and with a host of enemies, such differences would effectually settle which variety, whether a smooth or downy, a yellow or purple fleshed fruit, should succeed.

In On the Origin of Species *Darwin stayed away from the question of the evolution of man, for he knew the storm that would break on his head were he to apply the doctrine of natural selection to humankind. The application, however, was unavoidable. In 1871 he published* The Descent of Man *in which he faced the question squarely and gave his considered opinion. Darwin took a very cautious position, for he knew how few facts there were upon which a scientific discussion of human evolution could be based. But that natural selection applied to man he had no doubt. The seeds of the later doctrines of Social Darwinism can be found in his exposition. There are even hints of the later abuses. Notice the last paragraph of this selection in which Darwin hints that nature might need a little help from man to make natural selection even more effective through imperialism.*

FROM *The Descent of Man*

BY *Charles Darwin*

THE SLIGHT CORPOREAL STRENGTH OF MAN, his little speed, his want of natural weapons, &c., are more than counterbalanced, firstly by his intellectual powers, through which he has, whilst still remaining in a barbarous state, formed for himself weapons, tools, &c., and secondly by his social qualities which lead him to give aid to his fellow-men and to receive it in return. No country in the world abounds in a greater degree with dangerous beasts than Southern Africa; no country presents more fearful physical hardships than the Arctic regions; yet one of the puniest races, namely, the Bushmen, maintain themselves in Southern Africa, as do the dwarfed Esquimaux in the Arctic regions. The early progenitors of man were, no doubt, inferior in intellect, and probably in social disposition, to the lowest existing savages; but it is quite conceivable that they might have existed, or even flourished, if, whilst they gradually lost their brute-like powers, such as climbing trees, &c., they at the same time advanced in intellect. But granting that the progenitors of man were far more helpless and defenceless than any existing savages, if they had inhabited some warm continent or large island, such as Australia or New Guinea, or Borneo (the latter island being now tenanted by the orang), they would not have been exposed to any special danger. In an area as large as one of these islands, the competition between tribe and tribe would have been sufficient, under favourable conditions, to have raised man, through the survival of the fittest, combined with the inherited effects of habit, to his present high position in the organic scale.

* * *

Turning now to the social and moral faculties. In order that primeval men, or the ape-like progenitors of man, should have become social, they must have acquired the same instinctive feelings which impel other animals to live in a body; and they no doubt exhibited the same general disposition. They would have felt uneasy when separated from their comrades, for whom they would have felt some degree of love; they would have warned each other of danger, and have given mutual aid in attack or defence. All this implies some degree of sympathy, fidelity, and courage. Such social qualities, the paramount importance of which to the lower animals is disputed by no one, were no doubt acquired by the progenitors of man in a similar manner, namely, through natural selection, aided by inherited habit. When two tribes of primeval man, living in the same country, came into competition, if the one tribe included (other circumstances being equal) a greater number of courageous, sympathetic, and faithful members, who were always ready to warn each other of danger, to aid and defend each other, this tribe would without doubt succeed best and conquer the other. Let it be borne in mind how all-important, in the never-ceasing

Charles Darwin, *The Descent of Man and Selection in Relation to Sex,* 2 vols., pp. 157, 161–163, 167–169, 173–175, 180. London, 1871. Reprinted by permission.

wars of savages, fidelity and courage must be. The advantage which disciplined soldiers have over undisciplined hordes follows chiefly from the confidence which each man feels in his comrades. Obedience, as Mr. Bagehot has well shewn, is of the highest value, for any form of government is better than none. Selfish and contentious people will not cohere, and without coherence nothing can be effected. A tribe possessing the above qualities in a high degree would spread and be victorious over other tribes; but in the course of time it would, judging from all past history, be in its turn overcome by some other and still more highly endowed tribe. Thus the social and moral qualities would tend slowly to advance and be diffused throughout the world.

*   *   *

NATURAL SELECTION AS AFFECTING CIVILISED NATIONS

In the last and present chapters I have considered the advancement of man from a former semi-human condition to his present state as a barbarian. But some remarks on the agency of natural selection on civilised nations may be here worth adding. This subject has been ably discussed by Mr. W. R. Greg, and previously by Mr. Wallace and Mr. Galton. Most of my remarks are taken from these three authors. With savages, the weak in body or mind are soon eliminated; and those that survive commonly exhibit a vigorous state of health. We civilised men, on the other hand, do our utmost to check the process of elimination; we build asylums for the imbecile, the maimed, and the sick; we institute poor-laws; and our medical men exert their utmost skill to save the life of every one to the last moment. There is reason to believe that vaccination has preserved thousands, who from a weak constitution would formerly have succumbed to smallpox. Thus the weak members of civilised societies propagate their kind. No one who has attended to the breeding of domestic animals will doubt that this must be highly injurious to the race of man. It is surprising how soon a want of care, or care wrongly directed, leads to the degeneration of a domestic race; but excepting in the case of man himself, hardly any one is so ignorant as to allow his worst animals to breed.

The aid which we feel impelled to give to the helpless is mainly an incidental result of the instinct of sympathy, which was originally acquired as part of the social instincts, but subsequently rendered, in the manner previously indicated, more tender and more widely diffused. Nor could we check our sympathy, if so urged by hard reason, without deterioration in the noblest part of our nature. The surgeon may harden himself whilst performing an operation, for he knows that he is acting for the good of his patient; but if we were intentionally to neglect the weak and helpless, it could only be for a contingent benefit, with a certain and great present evil. Hence we must bear without complaining the undoubtedly bad effects of the weak surviving and propagating their kind; but there appears to be at least one check in steady action, namely the weaker and inferior members of society not marrying so freely as the sound; and this check might be indefinitely increased, though this is more to be hoped for than expected, by the weak in body or mind refraining from marriage.

*   *   *

With civilised nations, as far as an advanced standard of morality, and an increased number of fairly well-endowed men are concerned, natural selection apparently effects but little; though the fundamental social instincts were originally thus gained. But I have already said enough, whilst treating of the lower races, on the causes which lead to the advance of morality, namely, the approbation of our fellow-men—the strengthening of our sympathies by habit—example and imitation—reason—experience and even self-interest—instruction during youth, and religious feelings.

A most important obstacle in civilised countries to an increase in the number of men of a superior class has been strongly urged by Mr. Greg and Mr. Galton, namely, the fact that the very poor and reckless, who are often degraded by vice, almost invariably marry early, whilst the careful and frugal, who are generally otherwise virtuous, marry late in life, so that they may be able to support themselves and their children in comfort. Those who marry early produce within a given period not only a greater number of generations, but, as shown by Dr. Duncan, they produce many more children. The children, moreover, that are born by mothers during the prime of life are heavier and larger, and therefore probably more vigorous, than those born at other periods. Thus the reckless, degraded, and often vicious members of society, tend to increase at a quicker rate than the provident and generally virtuous members. Or as Mr. Greg puts the case: "The careless, squalid, unaspiring Irishman multiplies like rabbits: the frugal, foreseeing, self-respecting, ambitious Scot, stern in his morality, spiritual in his faith, sagacious and disciplined in his intelligence, passes his best years in struggle and in celibacy, marries late, and leaves few behind him. Given a land originally peopled by a thousand Saxons and a thousand Celts—and in a dozen generations five-sixths of the population would be Celts, but five-sixths of the property, of the power, of the intellect, would belong to the one-sixth of Saxons that remained. In the eternal 'struggle for existence,' it would be the inferior and *less* favoured race that had prevailed—and prevailed by virtue not of its good qualities but of its faults."

There are, however, some checks to this downward tendency. We have seen that the intemperate suffer from a high rate of mortality, and the extremely profligate leave few offspring. The poorest classes crowd into towns, and it has been proved by Dr. Stark from the statistics of ten years in Scotland, that at all ages the death-rate is higher in towns than in rural districts, "and during the first five years of life the town death-rate is almost exactly double that of the rural districts." As these returns include both the rich and the poor, no doubt more than double the number of births would be requisite to keep up the number of the very poor inhabitants in the towns, relatively to those in the country. With women, marriage at too early an age is highly injurious; for it has been found in France that, "twice as many wives under twenty die in the year, as died out of the same number of the unmarried." The mortality, also, of husbands under twenty is "excessively high," but what the cause of this may be seems doubtful. Lastly, if the men who prudently delay marrying until they can bring up their families in comfort, were to select, as they often do, women in the prime of life, the rate of increase in the better class would be only slightly lessened.

*   *   *

Natural selection follows from the struggle for existence; and this from a rapid rate of increase. It is impossible not bitterly to regret, but whether wisely is another question, the rate at which man tends to increase; for this leads in barbarous tribes to infanticide and many other evils, and in civilised nations to abject poverty, celibacy, and to the late marriages of the prudent. But as man suffers from the same physical evils with the lower animals, he has no right to expect an immunity from the evils consequent on the struggle for existence. Had he not been subjected to natural selection, assuredly he would never have attained to the rank of manhood. When we see in many parts of the world enormous areas of the most fertile land peopled by a few wandering savages, but which are capable of supporting numerous happy homes, it might be argued that the struggle for existence had not been sufficiently severe to force man upwards to his highest standard. Judging from all that we know of man and the lower animals, there has always been sufficient variability in the intellectual and moral faculties, for their steady advancement through natural selection. No doubt such advancement demands many favourable concurrent circumstances; but it may well be doubted whether the most favourable would have sufficed, had not the rate of increase been rapid, and the consequent struggle for existence severe to an extreme degree.

2

The Doctrines
of Social Darwinism

R. J. Halliday of the University of Warwick in England suggests that Social Darwinism should be seen particularly within the Eugenics movement in England. There the primary concern was the tendency of modern societies to perpetuate poor genetic traits. In his discussion Halliday introduces the reader to some of the other aspects of Social Darwinism as well.

FROM *Social Darwinism: A Definition*

BY *R. J. Halliday*

WHAT IS IT, if anything, that the term Social Darwinism defines or describes?

One might, of course, be literal-minded. Social Darwinism is that enterprise or ideology, founded in the nineteenth century, which holds social evolution to depend upon the operation of the law of natural selection of favourable heritable variants. A definition of this kind, if indeed it can be counted a definition, has several virtues—the virtue of obvious simplicity as well as that of suggesting, however crudely, a general logical type with a minimum necessary content. . . .

The biology of natural selection was undoubtedly a model evolutionary science for many thinkers in the century. But there was more than one account or explanation of natural selection, as well as a mass of conflicting evidence about the ways in which the variations necessary to continued biological evolution arose and how, if at all, such variations were transmitted to offspring. A commitment to the biology of natural selection entailed nothing uniform either for sociological method or for political doctrine.

* * *

Some of the weaknesses of the literal definition might be repaired by attending to the conventional usage of the term established by scholars and critics of

R. J. Halliday, "Social Darwinism: A Definition", from *Victorian Studies*, 389–391, 396–399, 404. June 1971. Reprinted by permission.

Social Darwinism. Stated briefly, without regard to particular nuances, the convention is to present Social Darwinism as an ideology defending free-market economics and opposing the interventionist state. On this definition, Social Darwinism is a synonym for laissez-faire and an antonym of state-socialism or collectivism. Conventionally defined, the term is reserved for that peculiar variety of individualism which was concerned less to assert the dependence of social evolution upon the operation of natural selection, than to claim the cessation or virtual cessation of natural selection due to the growth of party and government bureaucracies committed to the introduction and administration of welfare services. Hence a practitioner is defined as one opposed to state-socialism or collectivism and in favour of unregulated competition between individuals, groups, nations, or races. A practitioner might justify Imperialism as an indispensable aid to the selection of races. He might justify a compulsory reduction in the birth rate of particular social groups on the grounds of biological unfitness. In both cases the final point is to resist social reform by means of public agency, either by offering Imperialism as an alternative to domestic reforms, or by offering birth control as an alternative to increased spending on welfare and medical services.

*   *   *

As we have seen, the convention is to present Social Darwinism as a synonym for laissez-faire and antonym of state-socialism or collectivism. Yet, understood as a philosophical idiom, this labelling is inappropriate in at least one important sense. For the Social Darwinist, the rational faculty of each individual was insignificant compared with his inheritance, while the rationality of the process or events which made each individual the product of an inheritance was never in question. If man's history was irreversible, so was the past course of human evolution. The individual might, of course, either grumble or lament. But the laws of selection and adaptation were natural laws; laws which were necessary rather than contingent, and absolute rather than conditional. Either way, their operation was not affected by the carping of individuals. On this view, the reason of the individual agent was dispensable, but the rationality of the laws of society was incontrovertible. Despite occasional appearances to the contrary, that which is conventionally understood as Social Darwinism rested on a belief in the superiority of social to individual reason and on a belief in social evolution as an occurrence independent of individual agency. This helps to explain why thinkers such as Benjamin Kidd in *Social Evolution* and Henry Drummond in the *Ascent of Man* were able to argue an evolutionary significance for religious faith. The established Church was in a position to provide a sanction or justification for the conditions of progress which did not depend upon individual reason. The necessity of collective faith was the first teaching of evolutionary science.

Here, perhaps, there is a resemblance to classical economics. If social harmony was the design of no one but simply the consequence of market laws, then social arrangements were self-adjusting, requiring no external political ordering. The specific rationality of the preference could properly give way to the overall rationality of the market mechanism. Given this interpretation, Social Darwinism was no more than a restatement of classical economic theory. Whatever individualist content there was, it presumed at the very least the operations of a free market. This is an attractive picture and one which is fashionable nowadays, but it is at best a part of the truth. While the beneficent operation of natural selection might be reduced to the operation of the free economic market, equally it might be reduced to a programme of eugenics. This point merits detailed consideration since it is crucial to our search for a definition. What is to be gained or lost by making the term Social Darwinism a synonym for eugenics? Would this make possible a closer identification of practitioners?

One of our conditions at least is met by making Social Darwinism and eugenics synonymous. As both doctrine and ideology, eugenics was necessarily and not just contingently dependent upon a particular theory of biology and upon a more or less uniform conception of how natural selection operated. The eugenist programme to breed the "fit" and to sterilize or to limit the breeding of the "unfit" required an explanation of the mechanism of evolution on the basis of a sharp distinction between soma and germ-plasm; between, that is, the living organism and its hereditary constitution. For the eugenist, heredity was that process or event brought about by the transference from one generation to another of a substance with a definitive and unalterable chemical and molecular structure. For them, the permanence of the germ-plasm or hereditary substance was proof that the sole heritable variations were those located within the germ-plasm. Modifications or adaptations due to the environment were not inherited. In effect, the only important continuity in the evolutionary process was genetic. This being so, Nurture was less significant than Nature and to be effective man's agency had to concentrate on the improvement of the population's genetic endowment. To do this, some and not other bearers of germ-plasm should be selected to reproduce their kind. Without prior decisions about the relative status of heredity and environment and about those individuals or groups "naturally" fitted to reproduce, eugenics was unthinkable. This is to put the matter too bluntly. Even so, the case for eugenics did hold rigorously to the unimportance of environmental factors, to the non-inheritance of acquired characters, and to correlations between undesirable social status and high birth rate. Furthermore, the relationship between these beliefs was not simply one of congruence, but one of intrinsic or essential dependence. This indicates one more justification for making Social Darwinism a synonym for eugenics. We can now be more precise about the antipathy to socialism.

The adherents of eugenics were opposed to socialism on the particular ground of demography, not on general grounds of individuality or individualism. The practice of socialism in providing welfare, medical, and insurance services was thought to upset a population's biological stability by aiding the survival of the unfit. In short, socialism ran counter to natural law by limiting the scope of selection and competition. Those individuals who would previously have been rejected, either by death or by an inability to reproduce their kind, were now both surviving and reproducing. Socialism, then, was equated with the fact of a differential birth rate favouring the survival of the unfit, rather than with collectivism or with an undue and dangerous extension of central government. The two equations could not be kept entirely separate, but the crucial issue was one of birth rate and differential reproductive success. The eugenic answers to the problem were many and varied. All of them, however, turned ultimately upon the existence of an illiterate and intemperate urban proletariat supplemented by the influx of alien immigration. Hence the simple translations of the practitioners. The supposed biological criteria of fit and unfit were translated either in terms of social and economic status, or in terms of nationality and geographical race. Pauperism, for instance, whether of the native or alien variety, was the sign for genetic inferiority and unemployment the token of a hereditary incapacity. Socialism as a creed became an ideological symbol for the Jew and the illiterate proletarian. On this view, the alternatives to socialism were obvious enough. The proletariat could, of course, be instructed in the use of contraceptive devices. A system of legal restraint over the reproduction of dysgenic strains might be instituted. Perhaps tax relief would prevent the voluntary abstinence of the fit and encourage eugenically good families to have more babies. The immigration laws and the Aliens Act could always be made more complex and more discriminatory. Whatever the particular remedy, socialism was to be resisted and finally dismantled by means of eugenic population control.

*   *   *

No matter the biological significance of genetic inheritance, no matter the acute differences between natural and artificial selection, for our practitioners the only empirical characteristics defined by the words "fit" and "unfit" were social and economic characteristics. The practitioners of Social Darwinism believed in a close matching of genetic and social structures. Other things being equal, a relatively deprived economic and social status was an indication of inferior genetic material. In effect, the hierarchical social structure reflected a genetic "great chain of being." At the bottom, an inferior class or classes, constantly reproducing and constantly in receipt of welfare services, transmitting a defective inheritance to its offspring: at the top, social and economic elites, selected by competition but constantly burdened and constantly underbreeding. Though the practitioners of Social Darwinism made many proposals and investigated many problems in a sophisticated and humane way, in the end the science of social evolution amounted to a practice of culling the socially and economically deprived. The only full practical consequence was the reduction or removal of inferior genetic material; the decision about inferiority and superiority being taken either upon the basis of (disputable) scientific "truths," or because of a prejudice against relatively deprived groups. Here, the realities of biological theory slip easily into the realities of political oppression; one needs an effort of will to keep them apart.

Karl Pearson, in England, was one of the more ardent scientific supporters of the Eugenics movement. He took his basic argument directly from Darwin and, as one of the founders of biometrics, supported it with masses of statistics. The message remained the same: modern civilization tends to preserve the unfit and permit them to breed. Pearson graphically described the results in this lecture first delivered in 1907.

FROM *The Scope and Importance to the State of the Science of National Eugenics*

BY *Karl Pearson*

THE STRUGGLE OF MAN AGAINST MAN, with its victory to the tougher and more crafty: the struggle of the tribe against tribe, with its defeat for the less socially organized: the contest of nation with nation whether in trade or in war, with the mastery for the foreseeing nation, for the nation with the cleaner bill of health, the more united purpose of its classes, and the sounder intellectual equipment of its units: are not these only phases of the struggle for existence, the factors which have made for human progress, which have developed man from brute into sentient being? We have been told that "the cosmic process is opposed to the ethical"! But from the standpoint of science, is not the ethical the outcome of the cosmic? Are not the physique, the intellectuality, the morality of man, the product of that grim warfare between individual and individual, between society and society, and between humanity and nature, of which we even yet see no end? The ethical as the product of the cosmic process will indeed aid us when we pass outside the field of science. But standing well within the boundaries of that field, are men to cry like little children because the world is not "as it ought to be"?

*   *   *

As we have found conscientiousness is inherited, so I have little doubt that the criminal tendency descends in stocks. To-day we feed our criminals up, and we feed up the insane, we let both out of the prison or the asylum "reformed" or "cured" as the case may be, only after a few months to return to state-supervision, leaving behind them the germs of a new generation of deteriorants. The average number of crimes due to the convicts in His Majesty's Prisons to-day is ten apiece. We cannot reform the criminal, nor cure the insane from the standpoint of heredity, the taint varies not with their moral or mental conduct. These are products of the somatic cells, the disease lies deeper in their germinal constitution. Education for the criminal, fresh air for the tuberculous, rest and food for the neurotic—these are excellent, they may bring control, sound lungs, and sanity to the individual; but they will not save the offspring from the need of

Karl Pearson, F. R. S., *The Scope and Importance to the State of the Science of National Eugenics,* pp. 22, 37–39. London 1911. Reprinted by permission of the Galton Laboratory, University College London.

like treatment, nor from the danger of collapse when the time of strain comes. They cannot make a nation sound in mind and body, they merely screen degeneracy behind a throng of arrested degenerates. Our highly developed human sympathy will no longer allow us to watch the state purify itself by aid of crude natural selection. We see pain and suffering only to relieve it, without inquiry as to the moral character of the sufferer or as to his national or racial value. And this is right—no man is responsible for his own being; and nature and nurture, over which he had no control, have made him the being he is, good or evil. But here science steps in, crying, "Let the reprieve be accepted, but next remind the social conscience of its duty to the race. No nation can preserve its efficiency unless dominant fertility be associated with the mentally and physically fitter stocks. The reprieve is granted, but let there be no heritage if you would build up and preserve a virile and efficient people."

Here, I hold, we reach the kernel of the truth which the science of Eugenics has at present revealed. The biological factors are dominant in the evolution of mankind; these, and these alone, can throw light on the rise and fall of nations, on racial progress and national degeneracy. In highly civilized states, the growth of the communal feeling—upon which indeed these states depend for their very existence—has not kept step with our knowledge of the laws which govern race development. Consciously or unconsciously we have suspended the racial purgation maintained in less developed communities by natural selection. We return our criminals after penance, our insane and tuberculous after "recovery," to their old lives; we leave the mentally defective as flotsam on the flood tide of primordial passions. We disregard on every side these two great principles: (*a*) the inheritance of variations, and (*b*) the correlation in heredity of unlike imperfections. The statesman as usual is inert, waiting for the growth of popular opinion. Doctors, we are told, do not believe in heredity. If that be so, they have small idea of the most plentiful harvest yet reaped by modern science. The philanthropist looks to hygiene, to education, to general environment, for the preservation of the race. It is the easy path, but it cannot achieve the desired result. These things are needful tools to the efficient, and passable crutches to the halt; but at least on one point Mendelian and Biometrician are in agreement—there is no hope of racial purification in any environment which does not mean selection of the germ.

If I speak strongly, it is because I feel strongly; and the strength of my feeling does not depend on the few facts I have brought before you to-day. It would be possible to paint a lurid picture—and label it Race-Suicide. That is feasible to any one who has seen, even from afar, the nine circles of that dread region which stretches from slum to reformatory, from casual ward and stew to prison, from hospital and sanatorium to asylum and special school; that infernal lake which sends its unregarded rivulets to befoul more fertile social tracts. But the scope of Eugenics is not to stir the social conscience by an exaggerated picture of racial dangers. Those dangers are not wholly recent, if they are increasing in intensity; they are not peculiar to England, as a brief acquaintance with French and German conditions will suffice to show.

The poet Rudyard Kipling (1865–1936) put his views about America's conquest of the Philippine Islands into a poem, which became quite famous. The poem is worth studying closely, for it presents the duties that Social Darwinism required of its followers in most eloquent form.

The White Man's Burden
BY *Rudyard Kipling*

THE UNITED STATES AND THE PHILIPPINE ISLANDS

TAKE UP THE White Man's burden—
   Send forth the best ye breed—
Go bind your sons to exile
   To serve your captives' need;
To wait in heavy harness
   On fluttered folk and wild—
Your new-caught, sullen peoples,
   Half devil and half child.

Take up the White Man's burden—
   In patience to abide,
To veil the threat of terror
   And check the show of pride;
By open speech and simple,
   An hundred times made plain,
To seek another's profit,
   And work another's gain.

Take up the White Man's burden—
   The savage wars of peace—
Fill full the mouth of Famine
   And bid the sickness cease;
And when your goal is nearest
   The end for others sought,
Watch Sloth and heathen Folly
   Bring all your hope to nought.

Take up the White Man's burden—
   No tawdry rule of kings,
But toil of serf and sweeper—
   The tale of common things.

"The White Man's Burden" (1899), from *Rudyard Kipling's The Five Nations*. Reprinted by permission of Mrs. George Bambridge and the Macmillan Company of London & Basingstoke.

The ports ye shall not enter,
  The roads ye shall not tread,
Go make them with your living,
  And mark them with your dead!

Take up the White Man's burden—
  And reap his old reward:
The blame of those ye better,
  The hate of those ye guard—
The cry of hosts ye humour
  (Ah, slowly!) toward the light:—
"Why brought ye us from bondage,
  "Our loved Egyptian night?"

Take up the White Man's burden—
  Ye dare not stoop to less—
Nor call too loud on Freedom
  To cloak your weariness;
By all ye cry or whisper,
  By all ye leave or do,
The silent, sullen peoples
  Shall weigh your Gods and you.

Take up the White Man's burden—
  Have done with childish days—
The lightly proffered laurel,
  The easy, ungrudged praise.
Comes now, to search your manhood
  Through all the thankless years,
Cold-edged with dear-bought wisdom,
  The judgment of your peers!

*Kipling was one of the rugged individualists who saw the glory of their race in the
achievements of individuals. Among these achievements was the tutelage of the
"lesser breeds without the law" who could not compete successfully in the struggle
for existence. To the scientist Karl Pearson, this was sentimental twaddle that served
to obscure nature's clear teachings. In a lecture, "National Life from the Standpoint
of Science," delivered in 1900, Pearson laid down the scientific conclusions of
Social Darwinism with rigor.*

FROM *National Life from the Standpoint of Science*

BY *Karl Pearson*

FROM THE STANDPOINT OF SCIENCE there are two questions we can, or, rather, we *must*, ask. First: What, from the scientific standpoint, is the function of a nation? What part from the natural history aspect does the national organization play in the universal struggle for existence? And, secondly, What has science to tell us of the best methods of fitting the nation for its task?

To answer at all effectually the latter question, we must first consider what is the proper answer to be given to the former. I shall therefore endeavour to lay in broad outlines before you what I hold to be the scientific view of a nation, and of the relationship of nations to each other. If at the very offset my statements strike you as harsh, cold, possibly immoral, I would ask you to be patient with me to the end, when some of you may perceive that the public conscience, the moral goodness which you value so highly, is established by science on a firmer and more definite, if a narrower, foundation than you are wont to suppose.

* * *

. . . How many centuries, how many thousands of years, have the Kaffir or the Negro held large districts in Africa undisturbed by the white man? Yet their intertribal struggles have not yet produced a civilization in the least comparable with the Aryan. Educate and nurture them as you will, I do not believe that you will succeed in modifying the stock. History shows me one way, and one way only, in which a high state of civilization has been produced, namely, the struggle of race with race, and the survival of the physically and mentally fitter race. If you want to know whether the lower races of man can evolve a higher type, I fear the only course is to leave them to fight it out among themselves, and even then the struggle for existence between individual and individual, between tribe and tribe, may not be supported by that physical selection due to a particular climate on which probably so much of the Aryan's success depended.

If you bring the white man into contact with the black, you too often suspend the very process of natural selection on which the evolution of a higher type depends. You get superior and inferior races living on the same soil, and that coexistence is demoralizing for both. They naturally sink into the position of master and servant, if not admittedly or covertly into that of slave-owner and slave. Frequently they intercross, and if the bad stock be raised the good is lowered. Even in the case of Eurasians, of whom I have met mentally and physically fine specimens, I have felt how much better they would have been had they been pure Asiatics or pure Europeans. Thus it comes about that when the struggle for existence between races is suspended, the solution of great prob-

Karl Pearson, *National Life from the Standpoint of Science*, 2nd ed., pp. 16, 21–25, 46–54. Cambridge University Press, 1907. Reprinted by permission.

lems may be unnaturally postponed; instead of the slow, stern processes of evolution, cataclysmal solutions are prepared for the future. Such problems in suspense, it appears to me, are to be found in the Negro population of the Southern States of America, in the large admixture of Indian blood in some of the South American races, but, above all, in the Kaffir factor in South Africa.

You may possibly think that I am straying from my subject, but I want to justify natural selection to you. I want you to see selection as something which renders the inexorable law of heredity a source of progress which produces the good through suffering, an infinitely greater good which far outbalances the very obvious pain and evil. Let us suppose the alternative were possible. Let us suppose we could prevent the white man, if we liked, from going to lands of which the agricultural and mineral resources are not worked to the full; then I should say a thousand times better for him that he should not go than that he should settle down and live alongside the inferior race. The only healthy alternative is that he should go and completely drive out the inferior race. That is practically what the white man has done in North America. We sometimes forget the light that chapter of history throws on more recent experiences. Some 250 years ago there was a man who fought in our country against taxation without representation, and another man who did not mind going to prison for the sake of his religious opinions. As Englishmen we are proud of them both, but we sometimes forget that they were both considerable capitalists for their age, and started chartered companies in another continent. Well, a good deal went on in the plantations they founded, if not with their knowledge, with that at least of their servants and of their successors, which would shock us all at the present day. But I venture to say that no man calmly judging will wish either that the whites had never gone to America, or would desire that whites and Red Indians were to-day living alongside each other as Negro and white in the Southern States, as Kaffir and European in South Africa, still less that they had mixed their blood as Spaniard and Indian in South America. The civilization of the white man is a civilization dependent upon free white labour, and when that element of stability is removed it will collapse like those of Greece and Rome. I venture to assert, then, that the struggle for existence between white and red man, painful and even terrible as it was in its details, has given us a good far outbalancing its immediate evil. In place of the red man, contributing practically nothing to the work and thought of the world, we have a great nation, mistress of many arts, and able, with its youthful imagination and fresh, untrammelled impulses, to contribute much to the common stock of civilized man. Against that we have only to put the romantic sympathy for the Red Indian generated by the novels of Cooper and the poems of Longfellow, and then—see how little it weighs in the balance!

* * *

You will see that my view—and I think it may be called the scientific view of a nation—is that of an organized whole, kept up to a high pitch of internal efficiency by insuring that its numbers are substantially recruited from the better stocks, and kept up to a high pitch of external efficiency by contest, chiefly by way of war with inferior races, and with equal races by the struggle for trade-routes and for the sources of raw material and of food supply. This is the natural history view of mankind, and I do not think you can in its main features subvert it. Some of you may refuse to acknowledge it, but you cannot really study history and refuse to see its force. Some of you may realize it, and then despair of life; you may decline to admit any glory in a world where the superior race must either reject the inferior, or, mixing with it, or even living alongside it, degenerate itself. What beauty can there be when the battle is to the stronger, and the weaker must suffer in the struggle of nations and in the struggle of individual men? You may say: Let us cease to struggle; let us leave the lands of the world to the races that cannot profit by them to the full; let us cease to compete in the markets of the world. Well, we could do it, if we were a small nation living on the produce of our own soil, and a soil so worthless that no other race envied it and sought to appropriate it. We should cease to advance; but then we should naturally give up progress as a good which comes through suffering. I say it is possible for a small rural community to stand apart from the world-contest and to stagnate, if no more powerful nation wants its possessions.

But are we such a community? Is it not a fact that the daily bread of our millions of workers depends on their having somebody to work for? that if we give up the contest for trade-routes and for free markets and for waste lands, we indirectly give up our food-supply? Is it not a fact that our strength depends on these and upon our colonies, and that our colonies have been won by the ejection of inferior races, and are maintained against equal races only by respect for the present power of our empire? . . .

* * *

Struggle of race against race, and of man against man—if this be the scientific view of life, the basis of human progress—how have human love and sympathy come to play such a great part in the world? Here, again, I think science has something to say, although the earlier interpreters of evolution rather obscured it. They painted evolution as the survival of the fittest *individual,* and spoke of his struggle against his fellows.

But this is not the only form of selection at work; it is often quite the least effective phase of the contest. Consciously or unconsciously, one type of life is fighting against a second type, and all life is struggling with its physical environment. The safety of a gregarious animal—and man is essentially such—depends upon the intensity with which the social instinct has been developed. The stability of a race depends entirely on the extent to which the social feelings have got a real hold on it. The race which allows the physically or mentally stronger Tom to make the existence of the somewhat inferior Jack impossible will never succeed when it comes into contest with a second race. Jack has no interests in common with Tom; the oppressed will hardly get worse terms from a new master. That is why no strong and permanent civilization can be built upon slave labour, why an inferior race doing menial labour for a superior race can give no stable community; that is why we shall never have a healthy social state in South Africa until the white man replaces the dark in the fields and in the mines, and the Kaffir is pushed back towards the equator. The nation organized for the struggle must be a *homogeneous* whole, not a mixture of superior and inferior races. For this reason every new land we colonize with white men is a source of strength; every land of coloured men we simply rule may be needful as a source of food and mineral wealth, but it is not an element of stability in our community, and must ever be regarded with grave anxiety by our statesmen.

This need for homogeneity in a nation may be pushed further. We must not have class differences and wealth differences and education differences so great within the community that we lose the sense of common interest, and feel only the pressure of the struggle of man against man. No tribe of men can work together unless the tribal interest dominates the personal and individual interest at all points where they come into conflict. The struggle among primitive men of tribe against tribe evolved the social instinct. The tribe with the greater social feeling survived; we have to thank the struggle for existence for first making man gregarious, and then intensifying, stage by stage, the social feeling. Such is the scientific account of the origin of our social instincts; and if you come to analyze it, such is the origin of what we term morality; morality is only the developed form of the tribal habit, the custom of acting in a certain way towards our fellows, upon which the very safety of the tribe originally depended. Philosophies may be invented, the supersensuous appealed to, in order to increase the sanctions on social or moral conduct; but the natural history of morality begins with the kin-group, spreads to the tribe, to the nation, to allied races, and ultimately to inferior races and lower types of life, but ever with decreasing intensity. The demands upon the spirit of self-sacrifice which can be made by our kin, by our countrymen, by Europeans, by Chinamen, by Negroes and by Kaffirs, by animals, may not be clearly defined; but, on the average, they admit of rough graduation, and we find in practice, whatever be our fine philosophies, that the instinct to self-sacrifice wanes as we go down in the scale.

The man who tells us that he feels to all men alike, that he has no sense of kinship, that he has no patriotic sentiment, that he loves the Kaffir as he loves his brother, is probably deceiving himself. If he is not, then all we can say is that a nation of such men, or even a nation with a large minority of such men, will not stand for many generations; it cannot survive in the struggle of the nations; it cannot be a factor in the contest upon which human progress ultimately depends. The national spirit is not a thing to be ashamed of, as the educated man seems occasionally to hold. If that spirit be the mere excrescence of the music-hall, or an ignorant assertion of superiority to the foreigner, it may be ridiculous, it may even be nationally dangerous; but if the national spirit takes the form of a strong feeling of the importance of organizing the nation as a whole, of making its social and economic conditions such that it is able to do its work in the world and meet its fellows without hesitation in the field and in the market, then it seems to me a wholly good spirit—indeed, one of the highest forms of social, that is, moral instinct.

So far from our having too much of this spirit of patriotism, I doubt if we have anything like enough of it. We wait to improve the condition of some class of workers until they themselves cry out or even rebel against their economic condition. We do not better their state because we perceive its relation to the strength and stability of the nation as a whole. Too often it is done as the outcome of a blind class war. The coal-owners, the miners, the manufacturers, the mill-hands, the landlords, the farmers, the agricultural labourers, struggle by fair means, and occasionally by foul, against each other, and, in doing so, against the nation at large, and our statesmen as a rule look on. That was the correct attitude from the standpoint of the old political economy. It is not the correct attitude from the standpoint of science; for science realizes that the nation is an organized whole, in continual struggle with its competitors. You cannot get a strong and effective nation if many of its stomachs are half fed and many of its brains untrained. We, as a nation, cannot survive in the struggle for existence if we allow class distinctions to permanently endow the brainless and to push them into posts of national responsibility. The true statesman has to limit the internal struggle of the community in order to make it stronger for the external struggle. We must reward ability, but we must pay for brains, we must give larger advantage to physique; but we must not do this at a rate which renders the lot of the mediocre a wholly unhappy one. We must foster exceptional brains and physique for national purposes; but, however useful prize-cattle may be, they are not bred for their own sake, but as a step towards the improvement of the whole herd.

The doctrine of Social Darwinism was used by Adolf Hitler to justify the racial policies of National Socialism. During his imprisonment following the Beer Hall Putsch in Munich in 1923, Hitler laid out his philosophy and his politics in Mein Kampf (My Struggle). *In this work he preached his doctrine of the supremacy of the Aryan race and its destiny to conquer the world if it would only remain true to its Aryan genetics.*

FROM *Mein Kampf*
BY *Adolf Hitler*

NATION AND RACE

THERE are some truths which are so obvious that for this very reason they are not seen or at least not recognized by ordinary people. They sometimes pass by such truisms as though blind and are most astonished when someone suddenly discovers what everyone really ought to know. Columbus's eggs lie around by the hundreds of thousands, but Columbuses are met with less frequently.

Adolf Hitler, *Mein Kampf*, translated by Ralph Manheim (1971), pp. 286–290, 294–296. Copyright 1971 by Houghton Mifflin Co. Reprinted by permission.

Thus men without exception wander about in the garden of Nature; they imagine that they know practically everything and yet with few exceptions pass blindly by one of the most patent principles of Nature's rule: the inner segregation of the species of all living beings on this earth.

Even the most superficial observation shows that Nature's restricted form of propagation and increase is an almost rigid basic law of all the innumerable forms of expression of her vital urge. Every animal mates only with a member of the same species. The titmouse seeks the titmouse, the finch the finch, the stork the stork, the field mouse the field mouse, the dormouse the dormouse, the wolf the she-wolf, etc.

Only unusual circumstances can change this, primarily the compulsion of captivity or any other cause that makes it impossible to mate within the same species. But then Nature begins to resist this with all possible means, and her most visible protest consists either in refusing further capacity for propagation to bastards or in limiting the fertility of later offspring; in most cases, however, she takes away the power of resistance to disease or hostile attacks.

This is only too natural.

Any crossing of two beings not at exactly the same level produces a medium between the level of the two parents. This means: the offspring will probably stand higher than the racially lower parent, but not as high as the higher one. Consequently, it will later succumb in the struggle against the higher level. Such mating is contrary to the will of Nature for a higher breeding of all life. The precondition for this does not lie in associating superior and inferior, but in the total victory of the former. The stronger must dominate and not blend with the weaker, thus sacrificing his own greatness. Only the born weakling can view this as cruel, but he after all is only a weak and limited man; for if this law did not prevail, any conceivable higher development of organic living beings would be unthinkable.

The consequence of this racial purity,[1] universally valid in Nature, is not only the sharp outward delimitation of the various races, but their uniform character in themselves. The fox is always a fox, the goose a goose, the tiger a tiger, etc., and the difference can lie at most in the varying measure of force, strength, intelligence, dexterity, endurance, etc., of the individual specimens. But you will never find a fox who in his inner attitude might, for example, show humanitarian tendencies toward geese, as similarly there is no cat with a friendly inclination toward mice.

Therefore, here, too, the struggle among themselves arises less from inner aversion than from hunger and love. In both cases, Nature looks on calmly, with satisfaction, in fact. In the struggle for daily bread all those who are weak and sickly or less determined succumb, while the struggle of the males for the female grants the right or opportunity to propagate only to the healthiest. And struggle is always a means for improving a species' health and power of resistance and, therefore, a cause of its higher development.

---

[1] Second edition inserts "urge toward" before "racial purity."

If the process were different, all further and higher development would cease and the opposite would occur. For, since the inferior always predominates numerically over the best, if both had the same possibility of preserving life and propagating, the inferior would multiply so much more rapidly that in the end the best would inevitably be driven into the background, unless a correction of this state of affairs were undertaken. Nature does just this by subjecting the weaker part to such severe living conditions that by them alone the number is limited, and by not permitting the remainder to increase promiscuously, but making a new and ruthless choice according to strength and health.

No more than Nature desires the mating of weaker with stronger individuals, even less does she desire the blending of a higher with a lower race, since, if she did, her whole work of higher breeding, over perhaps hundreds of thousands of years, might be ruined with one blow.

Historical experience offers countless proofs of this. It shows with terrifying clarity that in every mingling of Aryan blood with that of lower peoples the result was the end of the cultured people. North America, whose population consists in by far the largest part of Germanic elements who mixed but little with the lower colored peoples, shows a different humanity and culture from Central and South America, where the predominantly Latin immigrants often mixed with the aborigines on a large scale. By this one example, we can clearly and distinctly recognize the effect of racial mixture. The Germanic inhabitant of the American continent, who has remained racially pure and unmixed, rose to be master of the continent; he will remain the master as long as he does not fall a victim to defilement of the blood.

The result of all racial crossing is therefore in brief always the following:

(a) Lowering of the level of the higher race;

(b) Physical and intellectual regression and hence the beginning of a slowly but surely progressing sickness.

To bring about such a development is, then, nothing else but to sin against the will of the eternal creator.

And as a sin this act is rewarded.

When man attempts to rebel against the iron logic of Nature, he comes into struggle with the principles to which he himself owes his existence as a man. And this attack must lead to his own doom.

Here, of course, we encounter the objection of the modern pacifist, as truly Jewish in its effrontery as it is stupid! "Man's rôle is to overcome Nature!"

Millions thoughtlessly parrot this Jewish nonsense and end up by really imagining that they themselves represent a kind of conqueror of Nature; though in this they dispose of no other weapon than an idea, and at that such a miserable one, that if it were true no world at all would be conceivable.

But quite aside from the fact that man has never yet conquered Nature in anything, but at most has caught hold of and tried to lift one or another corner of her immense gigantic veil of eternal riddles and secrets, that in reality he invents nothing but only discovers everything, that he does not dominate Nature, but has only risen on the basis of his knowledge of various laws and secrets of Nature to be lord over those other living creatures who lack this knowledge—quite aside from all this, an idea cannot overcome the preconditions for the development and being of humanity, since the idea itself depends only on man. Without human beings there is no human idea in this world, therefore, the idea as such is always conditioned by the presence of human beings and hence of all the laws which created the precondition for their existence.

And not only that! Certain ideas are even tied up with certain men. This applies most of all to those ideas whose content originates, not in an exact scientific truth, but in the world of emotion, or, as it is so beautifully and clearly expressed today, reflects an "inner experience." All these ideas, which have nothing to do with cold logic as such, but represent only pure expressions of feeling, ethical conceptions, etc., are chained to the existence of men, to whose intellectual imagination and creative power they owe their existence. Precisely in this case the preservation of these definite races and men is the precondition for the existence of these ideas. Anyone, for example, who really desired the victory of the pacifistic idea in this world with all his heart would have to fight with all the means at his disposal for the conquest of the world by the Germans; for, if the opposite should occur, the last pacifist would die out with the last German, since the rest of the world has never fallen so deeply as our own people, unfortunately, has for this nonsense so contrary to Nature and reason. Then, if we were serious, whether we liked it or not, we would have to wage wars in order to arrive at pacifism. This and nothing else was what Wilson, the American world savior, intended, or so at least our German visionaries believed—and thereby his purpose was fulfilled.

In actual fact the pacifistic-humane idea is perfectly all right perhaps when the highest type of man has previously conquered and subjected the world to an extent that makes him the sole ruler of this earth. Then this idea lacks the power of producing evil effects in exact proportion as its practical application becomes rare and finally impossible. Therefore, first struggle and then we shall see what can be done. Otherwise mankind has passed the high point of its development and the end is not the domination of any ethical idea but barbarism and consequently chaos. At this point someone or other may laugh, but this planet once moved through the ether for millions of years without human beings and it can do so again some day if men forget that they owe their higher existence, not to the ideas of a few crazy ideologists, but to the knowledge and ruthless application of Nature's stern and rigid laws.

Everything we admire on this earth today—science and art, technology and inventions—is only the creative product of a few peoples and originally perhaps of *one* race. On them depends the existence of this whole culture. If they perish, the beauty of this earth will sink into the grave with them.

However much the soil, for example, can influence men, the result of the influence will always be different depending on the races in question. The low fertility of a living space may spur the one race to the highest achievements; in others it will only be the cause of bitterest poverty and final undernourishment with all its consequences. The inner nature of peoples is always determining for the manner in which outward influences will be effective. What leads the one to starvation trains the other to hard work.

All great cultures of the past perished only because the originally creative race died out from blood poisoning.

The ultimate cause of such a decline was their forgetting that all culture depends on men and not conversely; hence that to preserve a certain culture the man who creates it must be preserved. This preservation is bound up with the rigid law of necessity and the right to victory of the best and stronger in this world.

Those who want to live, let them fight, and those who do not want to fight in this world of eternal struggle do not deserve to live.

Even if this were hard—that is how it is! Assuredly, however, by far the harder fate is that which strikes the man who thinks he can overcome Nature, but in the last analysis only mocks her. Distress, misfortune, and diseases are her answer.

The man who misjudges and disregards the racial laws actually forfeits the happiness that seems destined to be his. He thwarts the triumphal march of the best race and hence also the precondition for all human progress, and remains, in consequence, burdened with all the sensibility of man, in the animal realm of helpless misery. . . .

It is idle to argue which race or races were the original representative of human culture and hence the real founders of all that we sum up under the word "humanity." It is simpler to raise this question with regard to the present, and here an easy, clear answer results. All the human culture, all the results of art, science, and technology that we see before us today, are almost exclusively the creative product of the Aryan. This very fact admits of the not unfounded inference that he alone was the founder of all higher humanity, therefore representing the prototype of all that we understand by the word "man." He is the Prometheus of mankind from whose bright forehead the divine spark of genius has sprung at all times, forever kindling anew that fire of knowledge which illumined the night of silent mysteries and thus caused man to climb the path to mastery over the other beings of this earth. Exclude him—and perhaps after a few thousand years darkness will again descend on the earth, human culture will pass, and the world turn to a desert.

If we were to divide mankind into three groups, the founders of culture, the bearers of culture, the destroyers of culture, only the Aryan could be considered as the representative of the first group. From him originate the foundations and walls of all human creation, and only the outward form and color are determined by the changing traits of character of the various peoples. He provides the mightiest building stones and plans for all human progress and only the execution corresponds to the nature of the varying men and races. In a few decades, for example, the entire east of Asia will possess a culture whose ultimate foundation will be Hellenic spirit and Germanic technology, just as much as in Europe. Only the *outward* form—in part at least—will bear the features of Asiatic character. It is not true, as some people think, that Japan adds European technology to its culture; no, European science and technology are trimmed with Japanese characteristics. The foundation of actual life is no longer the special Japanese culture, although it determines the color of life—because outwardly, in consequence of its inner difference, it is more conspicuous to the European—but the gigantic scientific-technical achievements of Europe and America; that is, of Aryan peoples. Only on the basis of these achievements can the Orient follow general human progress. They furnish the basis of the struggle for daily bread, create weapons and implements for it, and only the outward form is gradually adapted to Japanese character.

. . . Just as in the life of the outstanding individual, genius or extraordinary ability strives for practical realization only when spurred on by special occasions, likewise in the life of nations the creative forces and capacities which are present can often be exploited only when definite preconditions invite.

We see this most distinctly in connection with the race which has been and is the bearer of human cultural development—the Aryans. As soon as Fate leads them toward special conditions, their latent abilities begin to develop in a more and more rapid sequence and to mold themselves into tangible forms. The cultures which they found in such cases are nearly always decisively determined by the existing soil, the given climate, and—the subjected people. This last item, to be sure, is almost the most decisive. The more primitive the technical foundations for a cultural activity, the more necessary is the presence of human helpers who, organizationally assembled and employed, must replace the force of the machine. Without this possibility of using lower human beings, the Aryan would never have been able to take his first steps toward his future culture; just as without the help of various suitable beasts which he knew how to tame, he would not have arrived at a technology which is now gradually permitting him to do without these beasts. The saying, "The Moor has worked off his debt, the Moor can go," unfortunately has only too deep a meaning. For thousands of years the horse had to serve man and help him lay the foundation of a development which now, in consequence of the motor car, is making the horse superfluous. In a few years his activity will have ceased, but without his previous collaboration man might have had a hard time getting where he is today.

Thus, for the formation of higher cultures the existence of lower human types was one of the most essential preconditions, since they alone were able to compensate for the lack of technical aids without which a higher development is not conceivable. It is certain that the first culture of humanity was based less on the tamed animal than on the use of lower human beings.

Only after the enslavement of subjected races did the same fate strike beasts, and not the other way around, as some people would like to think. For first conquered warrior drew the plow—and only after him the horse. Only pacifistic fools can regard this as a sign of human depravity, failing to realize that this development had to take place in order to reach the point where today these sky-pilots could force their drivel on the world.

The progress of humanity is like climbing an endless ladder; it is impossible to climb higher without first taking the lower steps. Thus, the Aryan had to take the road to which reality directed him and not the one that would appeal to the imagination of a modern pacifist. The road of reality is hard and difficult, but in the end it leads where our friend would like to bring humanity by dreaming, but unfortunately removes more than bringing it closer.

Hence it is no accident that the first cultures arose in places where the Aryan, in his encounters with lower peoples, subjugated them and bent them to his will. They then became the first technical instrument in the service of a developing culture.

Thus, the road which the Aryan had to take was clearly marked out. As a conqueror he subjected the lower beings and regulated their practical activity under his command, according to his will and for his aims. But in directing them to a useful, though arduous activity, he not only spared the life of those he subjected; perhaps he gave them a fate that was better than their previous so-called "freedom." As long as he ruthlessly upheld the master attitude, not only did he really remain master, but also the preserver and increaser of culture. For culture was based exclusively on his abilities and hence on his actual survival. As soon as the subjected people began to raise themselves up and probably approached the conqueror in language, the sharp dividing wall between master and servant fell. The Aryan gave up the purity of his blood and, therefore, lost his sojourn in the paradise which he had made for himself. He became submerged in the racial mixture, and gradually, more and more, lost his cultural capacity, until at last, not only mentally but also physically, he began to resemble the subjected aborigines more than his own ancestors. For a time he could live on the existing cultural benefits, but then petrifaction set in and he fell a prey to oblivion.

Thus cultures and empires collapsed to make place for new formations.

Blood mixture and the resultant drop in the racial level is the sole cause of the dying out of old cultures; for men do not perish as a result of lost wars, but by the loss of that force of resistance which is contained only in pure blood.

All who are not of good race in this world are chaff.

And all occurrences in world history are only the expression of the races' instinct of self-preservation, in the good or bad sense.

*   *   *

3

Social Darwinism in Perspective

Not everyone was enchanted with the view put forth by such people as Karl Pearson. There were those who felt that Pearson refused to see the plain fact that man, unlike other animals, could understand the evolutionary process and therefore change its direction. David G. Ritchie argues that Darwin's enunciation of the principle of natural selection makes it possible for man to substitute himself for nature and, thereby, decrease the amount of human suffering involved in the struggle for existence.

FROM *Darwinism and Politics*

BY *David G. Ritchie*

CHARLES DARWIN himself has told us that it was Malthus's *Essay on Population* which suggested to him the theory of Natural Selection. The constant tendency of population to outrun the means of subsistence and the consequent struggle for existence were ideas that only needed to be extended from human beings to the whole realm of organic nature in order to explain why certain inherited variations become fixed as the characteristics of definite types or species. Thus an economic treatise suggested the answer to the great biological problem; and it is therefore fitting that the biological formulae should, in their turn, be applied to the explanation of social conditions. It is felt, rightly enough, that the problems of human society cannot be fairly studied, if we do not make use of all the light to be found in the scientific investigation of nature; and the conception of the struggle for existence comes back to the explanation of human society with all the added force of its triumph in the solution of the greatest question with which natural science has hitherto successfully dealt. Our sociologists look back with contempt on older phrases, such as "Social Contract" or "Natural Rights," and think that they have gained, not only a more accurate view of what is, but a rule available in practical ethics and politics. Evolution has become not merely a theory but a creed, not merely a conception by which to understand the universe, but a guide to direct us how to order our lives.

David G. Ritchie, *Darwinism and Politics*, pp. 1–3, 21–24, 29, 76–83. Reprinted by permission.

The phrase "struggle for existence," as it came from the pages of Malthus, had a dreary enough sound; but, when this struggle for existence is shown to lead to the "survival of the fittest," and when it is seen to be the explanation of all the marvelous adaptations and of all the beauty of the living things in the world, it seems to gain a force and even a sanctity which makes it a very formidable opponent to have to reckon with in any political or ethical controversy. It is easy to see how the evolutionary watch-word can be applied. In Malthus the idea of struggle for existence was a very uncomfortable one; but, when it comes back to economics after passing through biology, it makes a very comfortable doctrine indeed for all those who are quite satisfied with things as they are. The support of scientific opinion can be plausibly claimed for the defence of the inequalities in the social organism; these inequalities, it can be urged, are only part of what exist inevitably throughout the physical world. The creed of Liberty, Equality, Fraternity can be discarded as a metaphysical fiction of the unscientific eighteenth century. The aspirations of socialism can be put aside as the foolish denial of the everlasting economic competition which is sanctioned by nature as only one phase of the general struggle for existence.

*   *   *

The doctrine of Evolution gives little support to the aristocratic Conservative. It may seem to give more to the *"laissez faire"* Radical. The evolutionist politician is more likely to adopt the view that in the interests of the race we ought to remove every artificial restriction on the operation of natural and sexual selection. But the difficulty is—where are we to find a line between "natural" and "artificial," if all the phenomena of society are, as the evolutionist is bound to hold, subject to the same laws of nature? If we are content to remove only some artificial restrictions, on what principle can we justify ourselves? If we are to remove every artificial restriction that hampers the struggle for existence, are we not going back to Rousseau's "State of Nature," the primitive, uncivilised, pre-social condition of mankind? If we expect the "State of Nature" to be better than the present condition, which is one of at least mitigated or inconsistent anarchy, are we not falling back into the "metaphysical" conception of Nature and ignoring the scientific conception of society? The "State of Nature," *i.e.* the unsocial state, is more correctly described by Hobbes as "the war of all against all." On the other hand, when we find the more tender-hearted preacher of evolutionist morality pointing out that, though the physical well-being of the race may have suffered through the mitigation of the primitive struggle and the consequent preservation of weaklings, we have gained some intellectual advance through the occasional chance of a Newton and a moral advance through the cultivation of sympathy and tenderness; in such a position is there not some inconsistency, some sacrifice of natural selection in favour of human selection consciously or half-consciously directed to other ends than those of mere nature? Our attention is thus called to another factor in that universal strife which is the story of the universe. So soon as a sufficient social development and a sufficiently advanced type of language make it possible, there begins a competition between *ideas*. The age of conflict is, in Bagehot's phrase, succeeded by "the age of discussion," and the ideas, which rise in the minds of men with the same tendency to variation that we find throughout nature, compete with one another for sustenance and support. The conception of natural selection may be applied here also to explain how certain ideas come to obtain that relatively fixed and definite character which belongs, for instance, to the moral principles currently accepted within a community at any given time. Thus such ideas as patriotism, respect of human life as such, self-control in regard to the bodily appetites, have won their way so as to become factors in the struggle and to conflict with the operation of natural selection as this prevails among the mere animals. Why then may not such ideas as Equality and Fraternity claim to have a fair chance in the struggle for existence? If they can win possession of more and more minds in the world, they will become actual influences on conduct and will from being mere ideals tend to bring about their own realisation. "Opinions," said Lord Palmerston, "are stronger than armies." One of the first conditions of any institution being altered is that people should come to imagine it as altered. The great difficulty of the reformer is to get people to exert their imagination to that extent.

Now what does all this amount to except to a recognition of the difference introduced into natural evolution by the appearance of *consciousness?* I shall not now attempt to work out all the philosophical implications involved in this recognition of consciousness: nor, in order to show how through consciousness man becomes free from the tyranny of nature, shall I quote the words of any one whose evidence might be suspected because he might be called a mere metaphysician. I shall quote the words of a witness whom no scientific man would reject—Professor Huxley:—

> Society, like art, is a part of nature. But it is convenient to distinguish those parts of nature in which man plays the part of immediate cause as something apart; and, therefore, society, like art, is usefully to be considered as distinct from nature. It is the more desirable, and even necessary, to make this distinction, since society differs from nature in having a definite moral object; whence it comes about that the course shaped by the ethical man—the member of society or citizen— necessarily runs counter to that which the non-ethical man—the primitive savage, or man as a mere member of the animal kingdom—tends to adopt. The latter fights out the struggle for existence to the bitter end, like any other animal; the former devotes his best energies to the object of setting limits to the struggle.

* * *

The history of civilisation—that is of society—is the record of the attempts which the human race has made to escape from this position [*i.e.* the struggle for existence in which those who were best fitted to cope with their circumstances, but not the best in any other sense, survived]. The first men who substituted the state of mutual peace for that of mutual war, whatever the motive which impelled them to take that step, created society. But in establishing peace, they obviously put a limit upon the struggle for existence. Between the members of that society, at any rate, it was not to be pursued *à outrance*. And of all the successive shapes which society has taken, that most nearly approaches perfection in which war of individual against individual is most strictly limited.

*　*　*

The capacity for thinking constitutes man's freedom. It is by thinking alone that he can rise above the position of nature's slave. . . .

*　*　*

I began by referring to Malthus, and with Malthus I must end. Socialists have usually brushed aside the Malthusian precepts and somewhat too lightly neglected the Malthusian arguments. To some extent this has been due to a correct instinct. The "prudence" of the old school of political economy would mean that the most careful and intelligent part of the population should leave the continuance of the race mainly to the least careful and the least intelligent portion—thus bringing about a survival of the unfittest. And so the theory of natural selection, which was suggested to Darwin by Malthus's theory of population, has come to be used as a refutation of Malthus's practical suggestions. Socialist views on the question have not always had so scientific a basis, but have sometimes rested on nothing much better than the popular superstition that where God sends mouths he sends the food to feed them, though this may be disguised in a non-theological form, such as "the earth is capable of producing abundance of food for all its inhabitants." Now what does this mean? That the earth at present may be made to bear more than it now does, and that therefore it will maintain more than its present number of inhabitants, is true enough. But only a complete failure to grasp the meaning of the struggle for existence, and the relation between increase of means of subsistence and increase of population, could lead any one to maintain that, absolutely, the earth can be made capable of supporting an indefinitely increasing number of inhabitants. If the checks on population supplied by famine, war, pestilence and vice be removed in any large measure, the increase would in time outrun any possible increase in the means of subsistence, even with all that improved appliances and diminished waste could do. Here, as elsewhere, human beings must raise themselves above unthinking animals and not trust to a kind Providence in which they take no part. The course of events, if left to itself, will act in the way that we do, when we dispose of superfluous puppies and kittens, but not quite so rapidly and mercifully. We must become provident for ourselves.

It might, however, be objected that if the more civilised nations keep their numbers fairly on a level with the means of subsistence at home, there will no longer be the stream of emigrants pouring forth from our shores to civilise the world and develop the resources of new countries: "the abler races" will be "withdrawing from the struggle for existence." There are some people who seem to think that an unlimited supply of what we call the Anglo-Saxon race is the best remedy for all the evils of the world. Well, without wishing to be needlessly unpatriotic, I do not think the unlimited Anglo-Saxon is an altogether unmitigated blessing. The filibuster, the mercantile adventurer and the missionary have not been so perfectly successful between them in dealing with the problem of the lower races; for the mere disappearance of lower races before the rum supplied by the trader and the clothes enjoined by the missionary (to the great profit of the Lancashire manufacturer) is not quite a satisfactory solution. What has been already said about the transmission of a type of culture, irrespective of the continuity of the race that first developed it, seems to help one here. We need have less doubt of the excellence of our language and of our literature and of some of our institutions than of the supreme excellence of our race: and there is nothing to prevent distant tribes and nations regarding Europe, and Britain not least, as the school or university to which they shall send their most promising youth in order to adopt just as much of our civilisation as suits them, so that they may work out their problems in their own manner. That would surely be a healthier way in which the higher might affect the lower races in the future, educating them instead of enslaving, demoralising or destroying them.

As to the adjustment of population to subsistence, Mr. H. Spencer has sufficient faith in the beneficence of nature to believe this will come about of itself through a biological law—that multiplication and individuation vary inversely, so that, as the physical and intellectual culture of the individual is more and more attended to, the increase of the species will gradually diminish. This "law" is, however, as yet only a mere speculation of Mr. Spencer's. There does seem to be in the world a certain amount of what we may call natural adaptation, which leads the more cultured and the more settled nations to be less prolific than those of the same race or stock who are living in new countries with plenty of elbow-room. The English race in Western America or in Australia does seem to be more fruitful than in old England or in New England. But the whole theory is a very doubtful one. And a rational adaptation of means to ends seems requisite to obtain the desired result. This is pre-eminently a question which can only receive proper consideration and solution when women are admitted to full social and political responsibility. It is the woman who bears the suffering of maternity and has the care of the very young, and so the woman is more immediately interested than the man. So long as women were brought up to believe that their sole or main function in life was to bear children, and were made to feel that there was something not only of disadvantage but of disgrace in being unmarried or childless, what wonder that population has been increased indefinitely and recklessly? Every inducement was in that direction, the ideas of a military society, the influence of the clergy (and, at least in Protestant countries, their example also), the employment of child-labour before the factory acts, the system of our old poor law—everything encouraged the natural tendency of the race to increase. With a change in the prevalent sentiment, a change in fact will certainly follow. When women have other interests in the world than those of maternity, things will not go on so blindly as before. And the race need not necessarily suffer thereby, but the very reverse. Fewer children will be born, but fewer will die, fewer will be sickly. Those who are born will be better and more intelligently cared for. Two healthy, well reared children will be more useful to the community than a dozen neglected waifs and strays. Here, again, we shall only be imitating by rational procedure the upward tendency of nature, which consists in the economy of production. Rational selection will take the place of the cruel process of natural selection.

If we are still reminded that only through struggle can mankind attain any good thing, let us remember that there is a struggle from which we can never altogether escape—the struggle *against* nature, including the blind forces of human passion. There will always be enough to do in this ceaseless struggle to call forth all the energies of which human nature at its very best is capable. At present, how much of these energies, intellectual and moral as well as physical, is wasted in mutual destruction! May we not hope that by degrees this mutual conflict will be turned into mutual help? And, if it is pointed out that even at present mutual help does come about, even through mutual conflict, indirectly and with much loss on the way, may we not hope to make that mutual help conscious, rational, systematic, and so to eliminate more and more the suffering going on around us?

Perhaps the most vicious idea drawn from Darwin's work was that of the inevitable conflict between the "superior" and "inferior" races of mankind. A modern anthropologist, M. F. Ashley Montagu, addressed himself squarely to the whole doctrine of race in his work Man's Most Dangerous Myth, The Fallacy of Race.

FROM *Man's Most Dangerous Myth, The Fallacy of Race*
BY *M. F. Ashley Montagu*

THE SPECIFIC HUMAN FEATURES of the evolutionary pattern of man cannot be ignored. Man is a unique product of evolution in that he, far more than any other creature, has escaped from the bondage of the physical and biological into the integratively higher and more complex social environment. This remarkable development introduces a third dimension in addition to those of the external and internal environments—a dimension which many biologists, in considering the evolution of man, tend to neglect. The most important setting of human evolution is the human social environment. This human social environment can influence evolutionary changes only through the media of mutation, selection, genetic drift, and hybridization. Nevertheless, there can be no gen-

M. F. Ashley Montagu, *Man's Most Dangerous Myth, The Fallacy of Race,* 3rd. ed., pp. 68-75, Harper & Bros., New York, 1952. Reprinted by permission.

uine clarity in our understanding of man's biological nature until the role of the social factor in the development of the human species is understood. A biologist approaching the problem of human evolution must never lose sight of the truth stated more than two thousand years ago by Aristotle: "Man is by nature a political animal."

In the words of R. A. Fisher, "For rational systems of evolution, that is, for theories which make at least the most familiar facts intelligible to the reason, we must turn to those that make progressive adaptation the driving force of the process." It is evident that man by means of his reasoning abilities, by becoming a "political animal," has achieved a mastery of the world's varying environments quite unprecedented in the history of organic evolution. The system of genes which has permitted the development of the specifically human mental capacities has thus become the foundation and the paramount influence in all subsequent evolution of the human stock. An animal becomes adapted to its environment by evolving certain genetically determined physical and behavioral traits; the adaptation of man consists chiefly in developing his inventiveness, a quality to which his physical heredity predisposes him and which his social heredity provides him with the means of realizing. To the degree to which this is so, man is unique. As far as his physical responses to the world are concerned, he is almost wholly emancipated from dependence upon inherited biological dispositions, uniquely improving upon the latter by the process of learning that which his social heredity (culture) makes available to him. Man possesses much more efficient means of achieving immediate or long-term adaptation than any other biological species, namely, through learned responses or novel inventions or improvisations.

Comparative anatomy and embryology show that a fairly general trend in organic evolution seems to be from environmental dependence toward fixation of the basic features of the bodily structure and function. The appearance of these structural features in the embryonic development of higher organisms is, in general, more nearly autonomous and independent of the environment than in lower forms. The development becomes "buffered" against environmental and genetic shocks. If, however, the mode of life of a species happens to be such that it is, of necessity, exposed to a wide range of environments, it becomes desirable to vary some structures and functions, in accordance with the circumstances that confront an individual or a strain at a given time and place. Genetic structures which permit adaptive plasticity of traits become, then, obviously advantageous for survival and so are fostered by natural selection.

The social environments that human beings have created everywhere are notable not only for their complexity but also for the rapid changes to which immediate adjustment is demanded. Adjustment occurs chiefly in the mental realm and has little or nothing to do with physical traits. In view of the fact that from the very beginning of human evolution the changes in the human environment have been not only rapid but diverse and manifold, genetic fixation of behavioral traits in man would have been decidedly unfavorable for survival of individuals as well as of the species as a whole. Success of the individual in most human societies has depended and continues to depend upon his ability rapidly to evolve behavior patterns which fit him to the kaleidoscope of the conditions he encounters. He is best off if he submits to some, compromises with some, rebels against others, and escapes from still other situations. Individuals who display a relatively greater fixity of response than their fellows suffer under most forms of human society and tend to fall by the way. Suppleness, plasticity, and, most important of all, ability to profit by experience and education are required. No other species is comparable to man in its capacity to acquire new behavior patterns and discard old ones in consequence of training. Considered socially as well as biologically, man's outstanding capacity is his educability. The survival value of this capacity is evident.

The genetically controlled plasticity of mental traits is, biologically speaking, the most typical and uniquely human characteristic. It is probable that the survival value of this characteristic in human evolution has been considerable for a long time, as measured in terms of human historical scales. Just when this characteristic first appeared is, of course, conjectural. Here it is of interest to note that the most marked phylogenetic trend in the evolution of man has been the special development of the brain, and that the characteristic human plasticity of mental traits seems to be associated with the exceptionally large brain size. The brain of, for example, the Middle Pleistocene fossil forms of man was, grossly at least, scarcely distinguishable from that of modern man. The average Neanderthaloid brain of the Upper Pleistocene was somewhat larger than that of modern man. More important than the evidence derived from brain size is the testimony of cultural development. The Middle Acheulian handiwork of Swanscombe man of three hundred thousand years ago, the Tayacian handiwork of Fontéchevade man of one hundred and sixty thousand years ago, and the beautiful Mousterian cultural artifacts associated with Neanderthal man of one hundred thousand years ago, indicate the existence of minds of a high order of development.

The cultural evidence suggests that the essentially human organization of the mental capacities emerged early in the evolution of man. However that may be, the possession of the gene system, which conditions educability rather than behavioral fixity, is a common property of all living mankind. In other words, educability is truly a species character of man, *Homo sapiens*. This does not mean, of course, that the evolutionary process has run its course and that natural selection has introduced no changes in the genetic structure of the human species since the attainment of the human status. Nor is there any implication that no genetic variations in mental equipment exist at our own time level. On the contrary, it seems likely that with the attainment of human status the part of man's genetic system which is related to mental potentialities did not cease to be labile and subject to change.

This brings us face to face with the old problem of the likelihood that significant genetic differences in the mental capacities of the various ethnic groups of mankind exist. The physical and, even more, the social environments of men who live in different countries are quite diversified. Therefore, it has often been argued, natural selection would be expected to differentiate the human species into local groups or races differing in mental traits. Populations of different regions may differ in skin color, head shape, and other bodily characters. Why, then, should they be alike in mental traits?

It will be through investigation rather than speculation that the problem of the possible existence of genetic differences in the mental make-up of human populations of different geographical origins will eventually be settled. Arguments based on analogies are precarious, especially where evolutionary patterns are concerned. If human races differ in structural traits, it does not necessarily follow that they must also differ in mental ones. Ethnic group differences arise chiefly because of the differential action of natural selection on geographically separated populations. In the case of man, however, the structural and mental traits are quite likely to be influenced by selection in different ways.

We are not directly concerned here with the problem of racial differentiation of structural traits. Suffice it to say that racial differences in such traits as the blood groups may conceivably have been brought about by genetic drift in populations of limited effective size. Other racial traits are genetically too complex and too consistently present in populations of some large territories to be accounted for by genetic drift alone. Differences in skin color, hair form, nose shape, etc., are almost certainly products of natural selection. The lack of reliable knowledge of the adaptive significance of these traits is perhaps the greatest gap in our understanding of the evolutionary biology of man. Nevertheless, it is at least a plausible working hypothesis that these and similar traits have, or at any rate had in the past, differential survival value in the environments of different parts of the world. By contrast, the survival value of a higher development of mental capacities in man is obvious. Furthermore, natural selection seemingly favors such a development everywhere. In the ordinary course of events in almost all societies those persons are likely to be favored who show wisdom, maturity of judgment, and ability to get along with people—qualities which may assume different forms in different cultures. Those are the qualities of the plastic personality, not a single trait but a general condition, and this is the condition which appears to have been at a premium in practically all human societies.

In human societies conditions have been neither rigid nor stable enough to permit the selective breeding of genetic types adapted to different statuses and forms of social organization. Such rigidity and stability do not obtain in any society. On the other hand, the outstanding fact about human societies is that they do change and do so more or less rapidly. The rate of change was possibly comparatively slow in earlier societies, as the rate of change in present-day nonliterate societies may be, when compared to the rate characterizing Occidental societies. In any event, rapid changes in behavior are demanded of the person at all levels of social organization even when the society is at its most stable. Life at any level of social development in human societies is a pretty complex business, and it is met and handled most efficiently by those who exhibit the greatest capacity for adaptability, plasticity.

It is this very plasticity of his mental traits that confers upon man the unique position which he occupies in the animal kingdom. Its acquisition freed him from the constraint of a limited range of biologically predetermined responses. He became capable of acting in a more or less regulative manner upon his physical environment instead of being largely regulated by it. The process of natural selection in all climes and at all times has favored genotypes which permit greater and greater educability and plasticity of mental traits under the influence of the uniquely social environments to which man has been continuously exposed.

The effect of natural selection in man has probably been to render genotypic differences in personality traits, in mental traits, in genetic potentialities, as between individuals and particularly as between ethnic groups or "races," relatively unimportant compared to their phenotypic plasticity. Man's genotype is such that it makes it possible for him to develop the widest range of behavioral adjustments and adaptations. Instead of having his responses genetically fixed as in other animal species, man is the species that invents its own responses, and it is out of this unique ability to invent, to improvise, his responses that his cultures are born.

There is every good reason to believe that natural selection has been operative upon traits making for educability in much the same way from the earliest beginnings of man's history, and in all human groups, no matter how long isolated they may have been from one another. It should be obvious that under any and all forms of social organization, as David and Snyder put it,

> flexibility of behavioral adjustment to different situations is likely to have had a selective advantage over any tendency toward stereotyped reactions. For it is difficult to conceive of any human social organization in which plasticity of response, as reflected by ability to profit from experience (that is, by intelligence) and by emotional and temperamental resilience, would not be at a premium and therefore favored by natural selection. It therefore seems to us highly improbable that any significant genetic differentiation in respect to particular response patterns, personality types, temperaments, or intellectual capacities among different populations or races has occurred in the history of human evolution.

And that is the conclusion of this chapter; or, to put it more positively, the evidence considered in this chapter points to the conclusion that in the evolution of man natural selection has placed, as it were, a high premium upon plasticity or educability, that it has done so nondifferentially, and that for these reasons it becomes highly probable that the mental capacities of mankind are everywhere pretty much of a muchness. This does not mean that all men have become exactly alike; such a statement would be demonstrably untrue. Men differ from one another in many traits, and there can be little doubt that mental traits are influenced by many genes, and that as long as this remains the case men will always differ from each other—more so within groups than between groups. What this statement does mean is that the selection pressure to which the human species has been subject since its origin has been nondifferential selection for educability, "i.e., for the capacity to modify one's behavior under the influence of experience and reasoning," has had the effect of bringing all human groups up to pretty much the same mental level.

From the vantage point of the mid-twentieth century, Jacques Barzun, a historian, is able to look back dispassionately and assess the rational bases and consequences of the doctrines derived from Darwin's theory of natural selection.

FROM *Darwin, Marx, Wagner: Critique of a Heritage*

BY *Jacques Barzun*

MATERIALISM, COARSE OR FINE, does not come from scientific or historical method as such: it comes from the philosophy concealed in the use of the method or suggested by proponents of the method. And it is there that Darwinism can justly be accused of destroying faith and morality. The genetic fallacy dating back to Comte is at the root of the trouble—the fallacy of reducing all experiences to one condition of their origin and so killing meanings by explanations. With its mechanical and historical bias, evolution reduced everything to something else. From fear of being anthropomorphic, it deanthropomorphized man. With its suspicion that feeling was an epiphenomenon, it made "refined music" into "a factor of survival." Nothing was what it seemed. As one scientific historian later complained: "The Devil may be the Persian Ahriman and the Logos a Greek idea, but their *meaning* changed with the new use to which they were put." Yet as everybody was looking only for material or historical antecedents, it is no wonder that the seekers found nothing else; nor that they came at last to see that something had been left out of the reckoning.

While some of the best minds were whirling round and round in this vicious circle, it was not noticed that the words Matter and Force, particularly when applied to human beings, might find in daily life some dangerously simple applications. No one can continue preaching the sole reality of these "bare facts" without encountering someone who will take him literally. And when the idea of force is embodied in the notions of Struggle and Survival of the Fittest, it should be expected that men will use these revelations of science as justifications for their own acts. Darwin did not invent the Machiavellian image that the world is the playground of the lion and the fox, but thousands discovered that he had transformed political science. Their own tendencies to act like lions and foxes thereby became irresistible "laws of nature" and "factors of

Jacques Barzun, *Darwin, Marx, Wagner: Critique of a Heritage*, pp. 99–104, 106–109. Little, Brown and Company, Boston, 1941. Reprinted by permission.

progress," while moral arguments against them were dubbed "pre-scientific." The only text they would heed was "Go to the ant, thou sluggard," because ants waged wars.

War became the symbol, the image, the inducement, the reason, and the language of all human doings on the planet. No one who has not waded through some sizable part of the literature of the period 1870–1914 has any conception of the extent to which it is one long call for blood, nor of the variety of parties, classes, nations, and races whose blood was separately and contradictorily clamored for by the enlightened citizens of the ancient civilization of Europe.

Unlike the Napoleons, Nelsons, and Wellingtons of an earlier day, who knew war at first hand and described it for what it was, in simple, unpleasant words, the militarists of the second half of the century knew no bounds to their warlike enthusiasm. With relative impunity for themselves, they took it for granted that all struggles *in* life must be struggles *for* life, and the death of the loser its "natural" goal. One spoke of the "beneficent private war which makes one man strive to climb on the shoulders of another and remain there through the law of the survival of the fittest." Another, asking himself why an English village of colonists was indisputably superior to a native village of Australians, answered that the English can "beat the natives in war, take from them what they like and kill any of them they choose." A third, smarting under the defeat of his country in the Franco-Prussian War of 1870, declared that "war is in a way one of the conditions of progress, the cut of the whip which prevents a country from going to sleep."

*   *   *

Since in every European country between 1870 and 1914 there was a war party demanding armaments, an individualist party demanding ruthless competition, an imperialist party demanding a free hand over backward peoples, a socialist party demanding the conquest of power, and a racialist party demanding internal purges against aliens—all of them, when appeals to greed and glory failed, or even before, invoked Spencer and Darwin, that is to say, science. That von Moltke appealed to God may be regarded either as an old-fashioned habit or as a shorthand term for what the others really meant. Race was of course as convenient and as short a word for expressing the same feelings of inner doubt and hatred. Race was biological; it was sociological; it was Darwinian. No doubt the "favoured races" mentioned on the title page of the *Origin of Species* referred to pigeons, but the extension of the term to man was easy to make; indeed it seemed to receive Darwin's own approval on many a page of the *Descent of Man,* where the struggle of races was a part of evolutionary advance. As for determining what these races were, ever since 1859 when an eminent French anatomist, Paul Broca, founded the Société d'Anthropologie, there had sprung up all over Europe groups of industrious researchers, meeting annually, and broadcasting the results of their new science.

But the materialistic view of race was slippery. The best men would discover three or thirty or a hundred distinct races. There also appeared to be a nationalistic bias in the choice of traits distinguishing the superior from the inferior stocks. Combining with complete ignorance of genetics a Chinese reverence for the bones of the dead as indices of class and race, and a very superficial knowledge of modern European history, these men soon made racialism a source of international animus, class recrimination, and private superstition. Not content to measure skulls and outlaw the longheads (dolichocephalics) or the roundheads (brachycephalics); not content to examine pigmentation and damn the yellow men for their racial backwardness (at least until the awakening of Japan), they discovered as well that individualists were one race and socialists another; that the poor and rich, the burgher and the peasant, the nobles and the former serfs, all were races whose descendants, intermingled in the modern nation, were fighting a Darwinian struggle, which Broca was the first to describe as Social Selection.

. . . The Darwinists had shown that the individual did not matter—only the race. But the Darwinists had also shown that races were mutable, not fixed categories. There must therefore be struggle between individuals to decide which race was to survive. Carried over into society this was very confusing: should a man give up his life for the common good? Certainly not. His duty was to survive at all costs, that is to say on other men's shoulders, as Sir Henry Maine pointed out with the authority of legal lore. But in the *Descent of Man,* published immediately after the Franco-Prussian War of 1870,—the first war, be it said in passing, to be interpreted à la Darwin on all sides,—Darwin constantly wobbled between keeping man under the regime of natural selection and putting him under the modified regime of cooperation, reason, and love. He points out that among men wars operate a reverse selection—killing off the fit and leaving the unfit. But he believes that a short war is beneficial, because it brings out the social qualities of cohesion, selflessness, and mutual aid, without killing off too many good men. How short a short war is, he does not say.

Nor should one have expected that he would. Bringing all of life under one law was superhuman work. The materials themselves seemed to resist and to force Darwin and Spencer to contradict their own idea of evolutionary continuity. According to Darwin, man had probably sprung from a weak and gentle species, already living in society, and more akin to the chimpanzee than to the gorilla. But growing reason—not instinct—had led to wars, and wars had further developed reason. "The struggle between the races of man depends entirely upon intelligence and moral qualities . . . selfish and contentious people will not cohere, and without coherence nothing can be done." Yet, he added, continued war leads to the destruction of great civilizations—witness Greece. In the light of this account what was European man to do? Spencer, though usually clearer than his colleague, was here no better guide. Readers of the *Social Statics* had learned how "the stern discipline of nature which eliminates the unfit" results in "the maintenance of a constitution completely adapted to the surrounding conditions." And similarly with social organisms, "inconceivable as have been [its] horrors . . . without war, the world would still have been inhabited only by men of feeble types, sheltering in caves and living on wild food." But suddenly, it seemed, this happy evolution must stop: "From war has been gained all it had to give."

Blown about on these conflicting winds of doctrine, modern man could only lose his head. Individual variations are useful, but they must not oppose cohesion; selfish people will not cohere, but life is a free-for-all; war is the source of moral qualities as well as of civilized housing and cooking, but it operates a reverse selection that might destroy civilization. A modern, industrialized, democratic nation must therefore be a compact herd—of rugged individualists.

As in all human crises, however, heroism was abundantly displayed. Men sternly set their faces against the weakening influences of compassionate feelings. Doubts were stifled, fears ridiculed, complaints turned to good account, and only a detached observer with an historian's eye could make light of the contradictions: "These men, O Plato! are perpetually bewailing the shortness of human life, and saying unkind things about Death; protesting against that cosmic sadness which they are continually hugging to their hearts, and complaining of the shortness of those pleasures which they seem to enjoy like a stomach-ache." The prevailing attitude was that of hope against hope. Winwood Reade, a young explorer praised by Darwin, and a nephew of Charles Reade, the novelist, embodied it in *The Martyrdom of Man*—an aggressively hopeful cry wrung from disillusionment. Though its freethinking encountered the abuse of believers, it soon became the gospel of those who believed, with a new Messianic faith akin to Marx's, that from violence and death and the sacrifice of Man, better men and a better life would evolve.

Looking back on that troubled period which gave us birth, one can only pity the blindness and bewail the misdirected faith. Like all other things, it had its *raison d'être*. Bitter though the creed of Darwinism was, it gave, as we have seen, some genuine satisfactions, noble or ignoble, to many kinds of people. The price at which they were purchased need not concern us now: first, it extended the hypothesis of matter and motion into the last realm of scientific inquiry, namely Life; second, it offered a universal rule for tracing the history of all things, namely Evolution; third, it provided an absolute test of value—survival—which could be applied as readily in nature as in society; fourth, it seemed to fulfill the anticipations of an army of previous thinkers, from Buffon and Lamarck to Comte and Erasmus Darwin, taking in on the way the German philosophers, the French naturalists, and the romantic poets of all countries; fifth, it was well adapted to the economic, and later the political, purposes of important groups in each nation; sixth, it explained by phrases whose meaning lay within the intelligence of all how without taking thought adaptation and improvement occurred; seventh, it replaced various philosophies and theologies couched in poetic terms by a scientifically worded account of origins, which rested on the "more rational" and "credible" notion of small doses adding up through the ages; eighth, it surrendered to a new, active, and intelligent class—the scientists—the difficult problems of morality, feeling, and spirit. The age-old conflicts of philosophy and life were solved—at least for a time—by denying their real existence and substituting automata for men; ninth and last, the Darwinian orthodoxy provided a rallying point for all factions and parties that desired a better world along the lines of their own infallible prophecies. It did not matter how much they fought among themselves on other counts. Fighting was the order of the day.

In the selection that follows, the dean of American diplomatic historians, Professor William L. Langer of Harvard, examines the doctrines and the practice of Social Darwinism in the imperialistic race of the nineteenth century.

FROM *The Diplomacy of Imperialism, 1890–1902*

BY *William L. Langer*

THE TONE OF REALISM, not to say ruthlessness and brutality, that was so striking a characteristic of imperialism was due in a measure to the general cast of sociological thought prevailing at that time. A large number of contemporary writers remarked upon the tremendous vogue of Darwinian theories of social evolution. The phrases *struggle for existence* and *survival of the fittest* carried everything before them in the nineties. One critic has asserted that the vogue of this doctrine was "the primary intellectual cause of the reaction."

It has often been pointed out that Darwin himself made no effort to apply the principles of organic evolution to the study of the social structure, and that many of the ideas supposedly taken from his writings were ideas for which he could not justly be held responsible. That is, of course, the fate of every great thinker. The historian, however, is obliged to study the impact of ideas, whatever their true origins or their scientific validity. In the matter of Darwinian influence it may be noted that before the publication of the *Descent of Man* in 1872 a theory of social evolution had been worked out by Spencer and the effort had been made by Walter Bagehot to apply the idea of organic evolution and natural selection to the study of social organization. In Bagehot's brilliant essay, *Physics and Politics,* may be found, at least in embryo, the argument as it was elaborated by others later on:

> "In every particular state of the world, those nations which are strongest tend to prevail over the others; and in certain marked peculiarities the strongest tend to be the best." "The strongest nation has always been conquering the weaker." "The majority of groups which win and conquer are better than the majority of those which fail and perish, and thus the first world grew better and was improved."

William L. Langer, *The Diplomacy of Imperialism, 1890–1902.* 2 vols., pp. 85–92. Alfred A. Knopf, Inc. New York 1935. Reprinted by permission.

Bagehot's book was only the first of a good many similar treatments published in Europe in the last fifteen years of the century. In 1883 the Austrian sociologist Gumplowicz brought out his book *The Struggle of Races,* expounding the theory of original heterogeneous forms which have been in conflict since the beginning of time. The tendency of history, he thought, was toward the formation of ever larger groups and toward greater, though rarer conflicts. The struggle of races, he concluded, is the eternal law of history. A few years later, in 1886, a French scientist, Vacher de Lapouge, published a study of *Natural Selections,* in which he asserted that evolutionary teaching was probably more important for the social than for the biological sciences. Nations, like individual organisms, he argued, were born, lived and died. Race and race development are more significant than geography or history when it comes to explaining social evolution.

The same year saw the publication of the first important work of the Russian sociologist, J. Novicow. Though Novicow later became one of the most active of European pacifists and a keen critic of what he called "social Darwinism," this first volume, entitled *International Policy,* was written along strictly biological lines. The gist of the argument may best be given in a few quotations:

> "Since societies are organisms, one can deduce *a priori* that they will conform to all the laws of biology."

> "Nature is a vast field of carnage. Between living creatures conflict takes place every second, every minute, without truce and without respite. It takes place first between separate individuals, then between collective organisms, tribe against tribe, state against state, nationality against nationality. No cessation is possible. Living means fighting."

> "This subordination of the less fit individual and collective organisms to the more fit, this is justice in nature: an incorruptible but implacable justice which knows no pity, but which gives to each with absolute impartiality the place due to its merits. It is the struggle for existence which determines this place. If one animal is less perfect than another, he must serve as prey. If one society is less perfect than another, the first must work for the second."

> "International policy is the art of conducting the struggle for existence between social organisms."

In England the biological or "natural history" conception of social and international relations was, if anything, more in vogue than on the Continent. Much of the immense literature on Spencer and Darwin touched upon it and Huxley foresaw the indefinite continuance of the struggle. Benjamin Kidd's book on *Social Evolution,* which first appeared in 1894, went through edition after edition and sold to the extent of some 250,000 copies. This is the more remarkable in view of the fact that the book was really very thin and unconvincing when critically appraised. A much more forceful presentation of the whole biological approach was given in the *Saturday Review* for February 1896, by "A Biologist," reputed by some to have been Professor Mitchell. This "Biological View of Our Foreign Policy" was clearly inspired by the Anglo-German crisis and the Kruger telegram: "The great nations of the earth," said the author, "are local varieties, species in the making, which are gathering themselves together, emphasizing their national characters, and unconsciously making for specific distinctness":

> "The foreign policies of the nations, so far as they are not the mere expressions of the individual ambitions of rulers, or the jog-trot opportunism of diplomatists, are anticipation of, and provision for, struggles for existence between incipient species. . . . The facts are patent. Feeble races are being wiped off the earth and the few great, incipient species arm themselves against each other. England, as the greatest of these—greatest in race-pride—has avoided for centuries the only dangerous kind of war. Now, with the whole earth occupied and the movements of expansion continuing, she will have to fight to the death against successive rivals."

Perhaps the classic formulation of this entire viewpoint, however, was that given by Professor Karl Pearson in his essay of 1900 entitled *National Life from the Standpoint of Science*. In this he says:

> "History shows me one way, and one way only, in which a state of civilisation has been produced, namely, the struggle of race with race, and the survival of the physically and mentally fitter race."

> "This dependence of progress on the survival of the fitter race, terribly black as it may seem to some of you, gives the struggle for existence its redeeming features; it is the fiery crucible out of which comes the finer metal. You may hope for a time when the sword shall be turned into the ploughshare, when American and German and English traders shall no longer compete in the markets of the world for raw materials, for their food supply, when the white man and the dark shall share the soil between them, and each till it as he lists. But, believe me, when that day comes mankind will no longer progress; there will be nothing to check the fertility of inferior stock; the relentless law of heredity will not be controlled and guided by natural selection. Man will stagnate. . . ."

> "The path of progress is strewn with the wreck of nations; traces are everywhere to be seen of the hecatombs of inferior races, and of victims who found not the narrow way to the greater perfection. Yet these dead peoples are, in very truth, the stepping stones on which mankind has arisen to the higher intellectual and deeper emotional life of to-day."

Many other writers of less importance could be quoted to the same effect. Indeed there was so much loose writing on this general theme that one critic was driven to cry out: "O Evolution, what crimes are committed in thy name!" while another spoke of the new beatitude: "Blessed are the strong, for they shall prey upon the weak." We cannot stop here to examine the influence of this evolutionary conception in greater detail, but we must take time to note its two-fold effect, first in the growth of militarism, second in the cultivation of the idea of race-superiority and the divine national mission.

We have, in the years since the World War, heard so much about the prevention of war in the future, and we have watched with such solicitude the tender growth of internationalism that we are, I fear, apt to forget that in the years before the war, despite the peace movement and the Hague Conferences, military conflict was popularly regarded with less horror than now and the idea of universal peace was looked upon by many as little more than a pipe-dream. It may well be that the military successes of Prussia, and for that matter the obvious successes of Bismarck's "realistic" policy had much to do with the spread of this attitude. People like to quote Moltke's famous dictum that perpetual peace was a dream and not even a pleasant dream. On the other hand it can be shown over and over again that the militaristic spirit was closely connected with the idea of the struggle for existence and the survival of the strongest. Had not Spencer himself written:

> "Inconceivable as have been the horrors caused by the universal antagonism which, beginning with the chronic hostilities of small hordes tens of thousands of years ago, has ended in the occasional vast battles of immense nations, we must nevertheless admit that without it the world would still have been inhabited only by men of feeble types sheltering in caves and living on wild food."

And did not Renan maintain that

> "War is in a way one of the conditions of progress, the cut of the whip which prevents a country from going to sleep, forcing satisfied mediocrity itself to leave its apathy."

It is perfectly true that Spencer, while recognizing the achievement of war in the past, was unwilling to regard it as necessary in the future and hoped that the struggle for existence might be restricted to the intellectual and economic spheres. But Spencer's argument was not at all convincing, and there were plenty of other writers to popularize the idea that progress depended on conflict and that conflict in international affairs has generally meant, sooner or later, military strife. William E. H. Lecky, the eminent historian, noted the steady spread of militarism and the growing popularity of the ideas of universal military service. It was claimed that universal service would carry the idea and sentiment of nationhood to multitudes whose thoughts would otherwise have never travelled beyond the narrow circle of daily wants or village interests. It would give the common man the tastes of the civilized man, and would make of him a brave, steady, energetic and patriotic citizen. Lord Wolseley, commander in chief of the British forces, glorified the soldier's life:

> "All other pleasures pale before the intense, the maddening delight of leading men into the midst of an enemy, or to the assault of some well-defended place. That rapturous enjoyment takes man out of himself to the forgetfulness of all earthly

considerations." "A sound, healthy, military spirit gives strength to a people. It is the guardian of the honour and interests of a nation, the safeguard of its freedom and liberties, the purifier of its civilisation, its defence against enemies from without, and degeneracy from within."

H. W. Wyatt, who was secretary of the Seeley Lecturers, declared that

"The only means, revealed to us by past experience, whereby the vigorous people has supplanted the weaker, has been war, without which change and movement must have ceased."

Sidney Low, the well-known publicist, ridiculed the Hague Peace Conference and asserted that

"There is scarcely a nation in the world—certainly not in our high-strung, masterful, Caucasian world,—that does not value itself chiefly for its martial achievements. . . . There is no great nation that would think it worth while to read its own history if the wars were left out of it. . . . A righteous and necessary war is no more brutal than a surgical operation. Better give the patient some pain, and make your own fingers unpleasantly red, than allow the disease to grow upon him until he becomes an offence to himself and the world, and dies in lingering agony."

And, if another quotation be permitted, one might add the words of J. A. Cramb:

"In the light of history, universal peace appears less as a dream than as a nightmare, which shall be realized only when the ice has crept to the heart of the sun, and the stars, left black and trackless, start from their orbits."

Cramb foresaw bigger and better wars as the result of universal striving for imperial ends.

The biological conception of the struggle for existence and the survival of the fittest led not only to the glorification of the struggle but to the general acceptance of the ideas of race superiority, destiny and divine ordination. There was, in the last decade of the century, a widespread idea that the tendency of social development was toward larger and larger units and that ultimately the world would be divided between the three or four fittest nations. "It seems to me," said Chamberlain in 1897, "that the tendency of the time is to throw all power into the hands of the greater Empires, and the minor kingdoms—those which are non-progressive—seem to be destined to fall into a secondary and subordinate place." Or, to quote a speech of 1902: "The future is with the great Empires, and there is no greater Empire than the British Empire."

This last sentence will serve admirably to lead us to the all-important idealistic aspect of British imperialism. Not a few writers, of course, would deny that there was any such thing. For them the fine sentiments of the British are nothing but pure hypocrisy. Perhaps the classic formulation of this viewpoint is given by Bernard Shaw, in his *Man of Destiny,* from which a rather long quotation may not be amiss:

"Every Englishman is born with a certain miraculous power that makes him master of the world. When he wants a thing he never tells himself that he wants it. He waits patiently till there comes into his head, no one knows how, the burning conviction that it is his moral and religious duty to conquer those who have the thing he wants. Then he becomes irresistible. Like the aristocrat he does what pleases him and grabs what he wants; like the shopkeeper he pursues his purpose with the industry and steadfastness that come from strong religious conviction and deep sense of moral responsibility. He is never at a loss for an effective moral attitude. As the great champion of freedom and independence, he conquers half the world and calls it Colonization. When he wants a new market for his adulterated Manchester goods, he sends a missionary to teach the natives the gospel of peace. The natives kill the missionary; he flies to arms in defense of Christianity; fights for it, conquers for it; and takes the market as a reward from heaven. . . . There is nothing so bad or so good that you will not find an Englishman doing it; but you will never find an Englishman in the wrong. He does everything on principle. He fights you on patriotic principles, he robs you on business principles, he enslaves you on imperialistic principles, he bullies you on manly principles, he supports his King on loyal principles, he cuts off his King's head on republican principles. His watchword is always duty; and he never forgets that the nation which lets its duty get on the opposite side of its interest is lost."

Call the Englishman's faith in his mission rationalization of more sordid motives if you like, but I doubt if you can honestly speak of hypocrisy. No one could deny the sincerity and high purpose of the missionary and aborigines protection societies which were so deeply interested in the spread of the gospel and the improvement of the "backward" races. No one could deny that the English, themselves the champions of the ideas of liberty and good government, had given their white colonies self-government and had maintained a sentimental bond with these colonies which was unprecedented in the history of modern expansion. So long as they kept to the policy of free trade they could argue with much force that they kept the territories under their rule open to the enterprise of the world and did not demand a monopolistic position for themselves. In short, they had been more successful than all others in making colonies profitable and contented. Their huge Empire was a standing proof of their fitness to rule, consequently the extension of the Empire would be a boon to those peoples that were taken over, even if they were brought in by force. They did not claim to be infallible, and they admitted that on occasion they were brutal and rough, but they were convinced that it was all for the best in the end.

The doctrine of evolution appeared to contradict Scripture, and most churches were disturbed by this new challenge to orthodoxy. It was not just a question of the origin of man but of the whole of Christian morality that was at stake. The contrast between the new "scientific" ethic and the old Christian one was dramatically presented in the aftermath of the Scopes trial in Tennessee in 1922. William Jennings Bryan died before he could deliver his closing speech condemning the doctrines of Social Darwinism, but his last words were published and made his point.

FROM *William Jennings Bryan's last statement*

OUR FOURTH INDICTMENT against the evolutionary hypothesis is that, by paralyzing the hope of reform, it discourages those who labor for the improvement of man's condition. Every upward-looking man or woman seeks to lift the level upon which mankind stands, and they trust that they will see beneficent changes during the brief span of their own lives. Evolution chills their enthusiasm by substituting eons for years. It obscures all beginnings in the mists of endless ages. It is represented as a cold and heartless process, beginning with time and ending in eternity, and acting so slowly that even the rocks cannot preserve a record of the imaginary changes through which it is credited with having carried an original germ of life that appeared some time from somewhere. Its only program for man is scientific breeding, a system under which a few supposedly superior intellects, self-appointed, would direct the mating and the movements of the mass of mankind—an impossible system. Evolution, disputing the miracle, and ignoring the spiritual in life, has no place for the regeneration of the individual. It recognizes no cry of repentance and scoffs at the doctrine that one can be born again.

It is thus the intolerant and unrelenting enemy of the only process that can redeem society through the redemption of the individual. An evolutionist would never write such as story as "The Prodigal Son"; it contradicts the whole theory of evolution. The two sons inherited from the same parents and, through their parents, from the same ancestors, proximate and remote. And these sons were reared at the same fireside and were surrounded by the same environment during all the days of their youth; and yet they were different. If Mr. Darrow is correct in the theory applied to Loeb,* namely, that his crime was due either to inheritance or to environment, how will he explain the difference between the elder brother and the wayward son? The evolutionist may understand from observation, if not by experience, even though he cannot explain, why one of these boys was guilty of every immorality, squandered the money that the father had laboriously earned and brought disgrace upon the family name; but his theory does not explain why a wicked young man underwent a change of heart, confessed his sin, and begged for forgiveness.

And because the evolutionist cannot understand this fact, one of the most important in the human life, he cannot understand the infinite love of the Heavenly Father who stands ready to welcome home any repentant sinner, no matter how far he has wandered, how often he has fallen, or how deep he has sunk in sin.

Our fifth indictment of the evolutionary hypothesis is that if taken seriously and made the basis of a philosophy of life, it would eliminate love and carry man back to a struggle of tooth and claw. The Christians who have

---

* An adolescent murderer whom Darrow defended. [Ed.]

William Jennings Bryan's last statement, in *The World's Most Famous Court Trial*, no author, pp. 333–334, 335, 338. National Book Company, Cincinnati, 1925. Reprinted by permission.

allowed themselves to be deceived into believing that evolution is a beneficent, or even a rational, process have been associating with those who either do not understand its implications or dare not avow their knowledge of these implications. Let us give you some authority on this subject. I will begin with Darwin, the high priest of evolution, to whom all evolutionists bow.

On pages 149 and 150, in "The Descent of Man," . . . he says:

> With savages the weak in body or mind are soon eliminated, and those that survive commonly exhibit a vigorous state of health. We civilized men, on the other hand, do our utmost to check the process of elimination; we build asylums for the imbecile, the maimed, and the sick; we institute poor laws; and our medical men exert their utmost skill to save the life of every one to the last moment. There is reason to believe that vaccination has preserved thousands who from a weak constitution would formerly have succumbed to smallpox. Thus the weak members of civilized society propagate their kind.

> The aid which we feel impelled to give to the helpless is mainly an incidental result of the instinct of sympathy, which was originally acquired as part of the social instincts, but subsequently rendered, in the manner previously indicated, more tender and more widely diffused. Nor could we check our sympathy, even at the urging of hard reason, without deterioration in the noblest part of our nature. We must therefore bear the undoubtedly bad effects of the weak serving and propagating their kind.

Let us analyze the quotation just given. Darwin speaks with approval of the savage custom of eliminating the weak, so that only the strong will survive, and complains that "we civilized men do our utmost to check the process of elimination." How inhuman such a doctrine as this! He thinks it injurious to "build asylums for the imbecile, the maimed and the sick, or to care for the poor." All of the sympathetic activities of civilized society are condemned because they enable "the weak members to propagate their kind." Then he drags mankind down to the level of the brute and compares the freedom given to man unfavorably with the restraint that we put on barnyard beasts.

Let us, then, hear the conclusion of the whole matter. Science is a magnificent material force, but it is not a teacher of morals. It can perfect machinery, but it adds no moral restraints to protect society from the misuse of the machine. It can also build gigantic intellectual ships, but it constructs no moral rudders for the control of storm-tossed human vessels. It not only fails to supply the spiritual element needed, but some of its unproven hypotheses rob the ship of its compass and thus endanger its cargo. In war, science has proven itself an evil genius; it has made war more terrible than it ever was before. Man used to be content to slaughter his fellowmen on a single plane—the earth's surface. Science has taught him to go down into the water and shoot up from below, and to go up into the clouds and shoot down from above, thus making the battlefield three times as bloody as it was before; but science does not teach brotherly love. Science has made war so hellish that civilization was about to commit suicide; and now we are told that newly discovered instruments of destruction will make the cruelties of the late war seem trivial in comparison with the cruelties of wars that may come in the future. If civilization is to be saved from the wreckage threatened by intelligence not consecrated by love, it must be saved by the moral code of the meek and lowly Nazarene. His teachings, and His teachings alone can solve the problems that vex the heart and perplex the world.

The world needs a saviour more than it ever did before, and there is only one name under heaven given among men whereby we must be saved. It is this name that evolution degrades, for, carried to its logical conclusion, it robs Christ of the glory of a Virgin birth, of the majesty of His deity and mission, and of the triumph of His resurrection. It also disputes the doctrine of the atonement.

This case is no longer local; the defendant ceases to play an important part. The case has assumed the proportions of a battle royal between unbelief that attempts to speak through so-called science and the defenders of the Christian faith, speaking through the legislators of Tennessee.

It is again a choice between God and Baal; it is also a renewal of the issue in Pilate's court. In that historic trial—the greatest in history—force, impersonated by Pilate, occupied the throne. Behind it was the Roman Government, mistress of the world, and behind the Roman Government were the legions of Rome. Before Pilate stood Christ, the Apostle of love. Force triumphed; they nailed him to the tree and those who stood around mocked and jeered and said, "He is dead." But from that day the power of Caesar waned and the power of Christ increased. In a few centuries the Roman Government was gone and its legions forgotten; while the crucified and risen Lord has become the greatest fact in history and the growing figure of all time.

Again force and love meet face to face, and the question, "What shall I do with Jesus?" must be answered. A bloody, brutal doctrine—evolution—demands, as the rabble did 1900 years ago, that He be crucified. That cannot be the answer of this jury, representing a Christian State and sworn to uphold the laws of Tennessee.

English Liberalism—
Coherent or Confused?

CONTENTS

QUESTIONS FOR STUDY

1   How successfully are the aims of preserving individual freedom and promoting pub-
    lic welfare reconciled in the liberal tradition? Consider, for example, the views of
    Minogue on this. If the aims conflict, which should be preferred?
2   Mill was opposed to legislation protecting women from harsh conditions of factory
    labor. Is his argument convincing?
3   What were the Conservative objections to liberalism?
4   What was Gladstone's attitude toward political democracy? Consider the arguments in
    his speeches on Parliamentary Reform and Irish Home Rule.
5   Which (if any) of Gladstone's attitudes might nowadays be considered conservative?
6   "The notion that [we] should be blind to killing and violence and repression and tor-
    ture anywhere in the world contradicts our basic heritage"—Edward Kennedy. Would
    Gladstone agree? Would Disraeli? Does this approach provide a sound basis for the
    conduct of foreign policy?
7   Why did liberal support of nationalist causes prove so controversial when applied to
    Ireland? Consider some arguments for and against Irish Home Rule.

The ideas and beliefs that nineteenth-century men designated as "liberalism" came to dominate the political life of much of the Western world in modern times. During the nineteenth century "liberal" movements grew up in many European countries. They aimed to sweep away ancient institutions of absolute government and to establish new, nationalistic, democratic states. The English liberalism discussed in this chapter—the liberalism of William Gladstone and John Stuart Mill—has been especially important for the many parts of the world influenced by British ideals of government. English liberals shared the ideals of continental liberalism—liberty, democracy, reform—but British institutions were always flexible enough to keep open the possibility of gradual, peaceful change. Hence, English liberalism was less insurrectionary, less revolutionary than continental liberalism. It became the typical ideology of the commercial and industrial classes—both workers and employers—who stood opposed to the continuing dominance of an aristocratic landholding caste.

The word "liberal" is hard to define because its meaning has changed over the past hundred years. The so-called classical liberalism of the early nineteenth century was based on the economic thought of Adam Smith and the utilitarian ethics of Jeremy Bentham (p. 574). It insisted above all on the freedom of the individual from state control. Modern liberalism, on the other hand, often supports government intervention intended to promote the public welfare. (The word "liberalism" is commonly used in this sense in present-day America.) But there is a common core of meaning in the different usages of the word. Liberalism in all its forms holds that the proper end of government is to promote the liberty and well-being of individuals. The classical liberals of the early nineteenth century (whom we would nowadays call conservatives) and the radical liberals of the late nineteenth century differed about means rather than ends. Classical liberals believed that the individual's well-being could be enhanced by a policy of laissez-faire (nonintervention by the state). Radical liberals believed that individual liberty—really effective freedom of choice—could be enhanced by government measures intended to improve social conditions. But, in both these forms, liberal ideology was sharply opposed to collectivist theories, whether of the right of the left, which regarded individuals as mere component cells of a greater organism, the state. In such systems the ends of the state are supreme, and individuals exist only to serve those ends. This is the antithesis of liberal ideology.

Several major problems arose in liberal thought and practice in nineteenth-century England. Liberals wanted both liberty and democracy, but were concerned that the uneducated masses, if given the vote, might prove intolerant of unpopular minorities. This problem especially worried the liberal philosopher John Stuart Mill (1806–1873).

Again, liberals wanted to promote social welfare. But government action intended to promote welfare (for example, acts regulating hours of work in factories) obviously limited the liberty of individual employers. On the other hand, a laissez-faire policy left individual workers exposed to brutalizing conditions of labor which very effectively curtailed their freedom of action.

A final problem was a possible tension between liberalism and nationalism. Modern right-wing forms of authoritarian nationalism seem opposed to liberalism. They exalt the state at the expense of the individual. But in the nineteenth century whole nations were held in subjection by foreign empires. The Bulgarians were subject to the Turks; Poles were subject to Austrians; and, most important in our context, Ireland was subject to England. When subject peoples, inspired by nationalist sentiments, sought to throw off foreign domination, nineteenth-century liberals saw their movements as dedicated to the cause of liberty— even if these movements involved the acceptance of authoritarian leadership. (Similarly, modern liberals have commonly supported movements for the independence of third-world countries from colonial empires.) Conservative opponents of liberalism saw the new nationalist movements simply as attacks on an established and generally benevolent order of things, attacks which could lead to mere anarchy. The rise of Irish nationalism posed a new problem for liberals. It was all very well to defend subjugated peoples against foreign autocratic empires. But what if a nationalist movement was directed against the leading liberal state, Britain herself? Eventually the English liberals split over this question. For some of them it was more important to uphold British power than to grant Irish freedom. The problem of containing dissident nationalist fervor within a framework of orderly government in large political units remains a very real one in the modern world.

The readings given below illustrate these problems as they arose in the life and work of William Gladstone (1809–1898). Gladstone was almost an incarnation of Victorian liberalism. He was a principal creator of the English Liberal Party in the 1860s and served four times as Prime Minister, the last time in 1892 when he was eighty-three years old. He enacted major measures of parliamentary reform. He performed radical legislative surgery on ancient English institutions—the army, the universities, the whole structure of local government. He supported oppressed nationalities abroad and tried to give Home Rule to Ireland. He legalized trade unions and introduced a system of public education. But still Gladstone thought there were limits to what government would do. "It is the individual character on which mainly human happiness or human misery depends," he declared (p. 586).

Toward the end of Gladstone's long life, his position as unquestioned head of the Liberal party was challenged by Joseph Chamberlain (p. 592). Chamberlain wanted a much more radical domestic reform program than Gladstone but a much less radical Irish policy. Gladstone introduced his last— and still unsuccessful—Home Rule bill in 1893. He died in 1898. At that time, as a modern biographer has observed, "it was universally recognized that [he] had been the leading figure of the nineteenth century in the history of Liberalism, not only in Great Britain but in Europe." This is true. And yet Gladstone's career also shows that perhaps no one man—not even a giant like Gladstone—could incarnate in his own person all the libertarian and reforming impulses of nineteenth-century liberalism.

1

English Liberalism: An Introduction

FROM *The Liberal Tradition*

BY *A. Bullock and M. Shock*

IN HIS ON LIBERTY (1859) and in his *Representative Government* (1861) Mill produces formal arguments which are designed to show that liberty, in particular liberty of thought and expression, is necessary for the development of human society. Progress, he argues, depends upon the freedom of individuals to innovate and experiment; conformity inevitably produces stagnation. This is the utilitarian basis of his argument against fully fledged democracy, that it is likely to produce a tyranny of the majority which will stifle those individual forces in society which give it life and meaning. For James Mill democracy had been a weapon to destroy the power of the "sinister interest"; for his son it was a potential threat to liberty and social diversity, the mainsprings of human progress.

But the heart of Mill's argument for the cause of liberty transcends the utilitarian. In pages which are the classical expression of English Liberal thought he argues the case for liberty and for representative institutions on the grounds that these are essential to that full and rich development of human individuality which he obviously values as an end in itself. When he quotes with approval von Humboldt's remark, "It really is of importance not only what men do but also what manner of men they are that do it," or states that, "If all mankind minus one were of one opinion, and only one person were of the contrary opinion, mankind would be no more justified in silencing that one person than he, if he had the power, would be justified in silencing mankind," Mill is, in the first instance, arguing for a theory of self-realisation and, in the second, saying that freedom of thought has a value in itself which is superior to Benthamite considerations of the greatest good of the greatest number.

It is this belief, crystallised in his demand for "a social support, a *point*

A. Bullock and M. Shock, *The Liberal Tradition from Fox to Keynes*, pp. xxv–xlvii, liii–lv. Adam and Charles Black Ltd., London,1956. Reprinted by permission of Lord Alan Bullock.

d'appui for individual resistance to the ruling power; a protection, a rallying point, for opinions and interests which the ascendant public opinion views with disfavour" that led Mill to hold back from any scheme which involved the granting of sovereign power to a democratically elected legislature except under special conditions designed to guarantee the over-representation of minority groups. . . .

In this middle period of Liberalism, then, not only has the argument for liberty taken a different form from the brash and aggressive utilitarian theory of Bentham and James Mill; it has become a defence of intellectual and moral freedom, valued for its own sake, against the dangers inherent in democracy. It is a striking fact that these dangers should have been recognised at a time when Liberals were coming to accept the necessity of a further advance towards democracy in the second Reform Act. It was in no easy spirit of optimism but with a clear understanding of the risks involved that men like Gladstone and Mill accepted such a step as necessary and right.

*   *   *

On one side of his complex personality Gladstone was an orthodox Liberal and it was this side which was uppermost in his career until his first retirement in 1874. . . .

Where Gladstone made his own individual contribution and enlarged the Liberal tradition was in the two crusades which brought him back into politics after 1874: foreign policy and the Irish question. On both issues his attitude gave expression to the vivid conception of the place of the moral law in the relations between nations which made him the most controversial figure of his age. . . .

Gladstone took as his starting-point the principle that foreign policy ought to be conducted in accordance with the demands of justice, not of expediency or power. He condemned "a vigorous, that is to say, a narrow, restless, blustering and self-asserting foreign policy . . . appealing to the self love and pride of the community" and setting up national interests selfishly conceived ("a new and base idolatry") as its sole objective. "I appeal to an established tradition, older, wiser, nobler far—a tradition not which disregards British interests, but which teaches you to seek the promotion of those interests in obeying the dictates of honour and of justice."

A policy based upon such principles, Gladstone believed, would always find support in "the general sentiment of the civilised world" to which the statesman must appeal for those "moral supports which the general and fixed convictions of mankind afford." But even if such a policy was backed by the moral force of public opinion, how was it to be put into effect? Gladstone answered: by the Concert of Europe, by the European Powers engaging in joint intervention to see that justice was done. Common action alone, he argued, would unite the Great Powers for the common good and at the same time would "neutralise and fetter the selfish aims of each." . . .

Throughout his life Gladstone felt a passionate sympathy for peoples struggling to achieve national independence. This provides the other foundation of his views on foreign policy. "The powers of self-government," this was his answer alike to the problems of the Balkans and those of Ireland. "Give those people freedom and the benefits of freedom," he said of Turkey's Christian subjects in 1880, "that is the way to make a barrier against despotism. Fortresses may be levelled to the ground; treaties may be trodden under foot—the true barrier against despotism is in the human heart and the human mind."

From this sympathy it followed for Gladstone that all nations should enjoy equality of rights. "To claim anything more than equality of rights in the moral and political intercourse of the world is not the way to make England great, but to make it both morally and materially little." From this in turn sprang his condemnation of imperialism which proclaimed supremacy, not equality, and in its eagerness for aggrandisement brushed aside the rights of other nations to bring them under alien rule. . . .

It was in his campaign for Irish Home Rule that Gladstone himself tried most tenaciously to carry out his ideas. He came to see the Irish question, not as a domestic problem of law and order—any more than the American question had been in the 1770's—but as the claim of a nation to self-government, as much deserving of sympathy as the claims of the Italians, the Greeks and the Bulgars. Gladstone's determination to satisfy this claim deeply affected the fortunes of Liberalism for years to come. It split the Liberal Party, put back the cause of social reform for a generation, necessitated a dangerous alliance with the Irish Nationalists, and, because of its unpopularity in England, was electorally disastrous. In spite of all this Gladstone and his followers were convinced that justice for Ireland was the great culminating work of the Liberal tradition. Ireland was the touchstone of that sympathy which Liberal England had shown so generously in the case of others: was it now to be overridden by self-interest when it was a question of Britain's own empire?

Self-government had already been granted to Canada and the other colonies with the most felicitous results. No more was being asked for Ireland where, by contrast, "the first conditions of civil life—the free course of law, the liberty of every individual in the exercise of every legal right, the confidence of the people in the law and their sympathy with the law" were entirely absent. It was only in Ireland that the sovereign Liberal remedy of freedom had not been tried. Elsewhere it had never failed and the settlement of Ireland, the thorniest question in British politics, would be its supreme justification.

*　*　*

Gladstone had resumed the leadership of the Liberal Party after his retirement in 1874 with the limited objectives, first of challenging Disraeli's foreign policy and later of achieving a settlement with Ireland. On the other issues, however, which were to play so great a part in the politics of the next half century, social reform and the condition of the working classes, he offered no lead at all. His preoccupation with Ireland heavily handicapped the efforts of those who were becoming alive to the need to question and revise orthodox Liberalism's approach to social problems.

The Liberals of the Manchester School had assumed that with the destruction of the "sinister interests" which stood in the way of the free development of social and economic forces, a natural harmony of interests would emerge of its own accord. This dream of a self-regulating society reduced to a minimum the role of the State. All the State had to do was to "hold the ring," to ensure the conditions in which economic and political interests could have free play. Dissatisfied with this view, John Stuart Mill attempted to provide a new criterion for the intervention of the State by drawing a sharp distinction between "self-regarding" and "other-regarding" actions. "The only part of the conduct of any-one for which he is amenable to society," Mill wrote, "is that which concerns others. In the part which merely concerns himself, his independence is, of right, absolute." But Mill's criticism did not go far enough. The distinction on which he sought to base his social philosophy proved untenable and was repudiated by the next generation of Liberal thinkers. The last quarter of the 19th century in fact produced a new philosophy of Liberalism and a new programme of radical legislation.

. . . The way was open to a more positive view of freedom, something more (to quote T. H. Green) than "the mere removal of compulsion, the mere enabling a man to do as he likes." "When we speak of freedom as something to be so highly prized, we mean a positive power or capacity of doing or enjoying something worth doing or enjoying, and that, too, something that we do or enjoy in common with others."

The task of the State was to provide the conditions in which this sort of freedom could be pursued and, by the beginning of the 20th century, it had become a commonplace to describe the means as the provision of "equality of opportunity." It was clear, too, that within the framework of a deeply rooted social hierarchy and a developed capitalist system such freedom, "the presence of opportunity," could only be achieved by state interference. Freedom had emerged as a social conception, not one which involved the individual alone. Green did not claim that legislation could in itself promote moral goodness; his argument was that, in many situations, legislative intervention alone could bring into existence conditions in which men could exercise freely their faculties of moral judgment, enlarging, as it did so, the area of "positive freedom."

The emphasis in Liberal thought remained, as it had always done, upon the individual, but he was now a social individual, and the aim of political activity was to enlarge the area within which he might enjoy an ever widening degree of freedom. "The sphere of liberty," wrote Leonard Hobhouse, "is the sphere of growth itself." Such growth could only be ensured by State intervention, for every act of liberation involved for some individual or group a corresponding act of restraint.

2

The Growth of Liberal Thought

Early liberals were unaware of any possible conflict between liberty and public welfare. Classical liberalism was based on the economic teachings of Adam Smith, who held that if every individual pursued his own self-interest without government interference, the maximum possible well-being of all would be automatically achieved. Smith's famous work, The Wealth of Nations, *was first published in 1776.*

FROM *The Wealth of Nations*

BY *Adam Smith*

EVERY INDIVIDUAL IS continually exerting himself to find out the most advantageous employment for whatever capital he can command. It is his own advantage, indeed, and not that of the society, which he has in view. But the study of his own advantage naturally, or rather necessarily, leads him to prefer that employment which is most advantageous to the society.

. . . As every individual, therefore, endeavours as much as he can both to employ his capital in the support of domestic industry and so to direct that industry that its produce may be of the greatest value, every individual necessarily labours to render the annual revenue of the society as great as he can. He generally, indeed, neither intends to promote the public interest nor knows how much he is promoting it. By preferring the support of domestic to that of foreign industry, he intends only his own security; and by directing that industry in such a manner as its produce may be of the greatest value, he intends only his own gain, and he is in this, as in many other cases, led by an invisible hand to promote an end which was no part of his intention. Nor is it always the worse for the society that it was no part of it. By pursuing his own interest he frequently promotes that of the society more effectually than when he really intends to promote it. I have never known much good done by those who affected to trade for the public good. It is an affectation, indeed, not very com-

Adam Smith, *The Wealth of Nations,* pp. 26, 28. Oxford, Clarendon Press, 1880. Reprinted by permission.

mon among merchants, and very few words need be employed in dissuading them from it.

Jeremy Bentham provided classical liberalism with the principle that the objective of all legislation should be to promote "the greatest happiness of the greatest number." But he too held that in the economic sphere a government could best attain this end by simply being acquiescent. This selection was first published in 1798.

FROM *A Manual of Political Economy*
BY *Jeremy Bentham*

ACCORDING TO THE PRINCIPLE of utility in every branch of the art of legislation, the object or end in view should be the production of the maximum of happiness in a given time in the community in question. . . .

The practical questions, therefore, are . . . how far the end in view is best promoted by individuals acting for themselves? and in what cases these ends may be promoted by the hands of government? . . .

With the view of causing an increase to take place in the mass of national wealth, or with a view to increase of the means either of subsistence or enjoyment, without some special reason, the general rule is, that nothing ought to be done or attempted by government. The motto, or watchword of government, on these occasions, ought to be—*Be quiet.*

For this quietism there are two main reasons: 1. Generally speaking, any interference for this purpose on the part of government is needless. The wealth of the whole community is composed of the wealth of the several individuals belonging to it taken together. But to increase his particular portion is, generally speaking, among the constant objects of each individual's exertions and care. Generally speaking, there is no one who knows what is for your interest so well as yourself—no one who is disposed with so much ardour and constancy to pursue it.

2. Generally speaking, it is moreover likely to be pernicious, viz. by being unconducive, or even obstructive, with reference to the attainment of the end in view. Each individual bestowing more time and attention upon the means of preserving and increasing his portion of wealth, than is or can be bestowed by government, is likely to take a more effectual course than what, in his instance and on his behalf, would be taken by government.

It is, moreover, universally and constantly pernicious in another way, by the restraint or constraint imposed on the free agency of the individual. . . .

. . . With few exceptions, and those not very considerable ones, the attainment of the maximum of enjoyment will be most effectually secured by

Jeremy Bentham, "A Manual of Political Economy," in *Works*, J. Bowring, ed., III, pp. 33, 35. Edinburgh, William Tait, 1843. Reprinted by permission.

leaving each individual to pursue his own maximum of enjoyment, in proportion as he is in possession of the means. Inclination in this respect will not be wanting on the part of any one. Power, the species of power applicable to this case—viz. wealth, pecuniary power—could not be given by the hand of government to one, without being taken from another; so that by such interference there would not be any gain of power upon the whole.

The gain to be produced in this article by the interposition of government, respects principally the head of knowledge. There are cases in which, for the benefit of the public at large, it may be in the power of government to cause this or that portion of knowledge to be produced and diffused, which, without the demand for it produced by government, would either not have been produced, or would not have been diffused.

We have seen above the grounds on which the general rule in this behalf—*Be quiet*—rests. Whatever measures, therefore, cannot be justified as exceptions to that rule, may be considered as *non agenda* on the part of government. The art, therefore, is reduced within a small compass: security and freedom are all that industry requires. The request which agriculture, manufactures and commerce present to governments, is modest and reasonable as that which Diogenes made to Alexander: "Stand out of my sunshine." We have no need of favour—we require only a secure and open path.

The greatest liberal philosopher of Victorian England was John Stuart Mill. His essay On Liberty, *written in 1859, was an eloquent defense of individual freedoms.*

FROM *On Liberty*
BY *John Stuart Mill*

THE SUBJECT OF THIS Essay is not the so-called Liberty of the Will, so unfortunately opposed to the misnamed doctrine of Philosophical Necessity; but Civil, or Social Liberty: the nature and limits of the power which can be legitimately exercised by society over the individual. A question seldom stated, and hardly ever discussed, in general terms, but which profoundly influences the practical controversies of the age by its latent presence, and is likely soon to make itself recognised as the vital question of the future. It is so far from being new, that, in a certain sense, it has divided mankind, almost from the remotest ages; but in the stage of progress into which the more civilised portions of the species have now entered, it presents itself under new conditions, and requires a different and more fundamental treatment.

. . . The notion, that the people have no need to limit their power over themselves, might seem axiomatic, when popular government was a thing only

John Stuart Mill, *On Liberty*, pp. 7, 11–14, 22–23, 27–28, 35. New York, Henry Holt and Co.,1873. Reprinted by permission.

dreamed about, or read of as having existed at some distant period of the past. Neither was that notion necessarily disturbed by such temporary aberrations as those of the French Revolution, the worst of which were the work of a usurping few, and which, in any case, belonged, not to the permanent working of popular institutions, but to a sudden and convulsive outbreak against monarchical and aristocratic despotism. In time, however, a democratic republic came to occupy a large portion of the earth's surface, and made itself felt as one of the most powerful members of the community of nations; and elective and responsible government became subject to the observations and criticisms which wait upon a great existing fact. It was now perceived that such phrases as "self-government," and "the power of the people over themselves," do not express the true state of the case. The "people" who exercise the power are not always the same people with those over whom it is exercised; and the "self-government" spoken of is not the government of each by himself, but of each by all the rest. The will of the people, moreover, practically means the will of the most numerous or the most active *part* of the people; the majority, or those who succeed in making themselves accepted as the majority; the people, consequently *may* desire to oppress a part of their number; and precautions are as much needed against this as against any other abuse of power. The limitation, therefore, of the power of government over individuals loses none of its importance when the holders of power are regularly accountable to the community, that is, to the strongest party therein. This view of things, recommending itself equally to the intelligence of thinkers and to the inclination of those important classes in European society to whose real or supposed interests democracy is adverse, has had no difficulty in establishing itself; and in political speculations "the tyranny of the majority" is now generally included among the evils against which society requires to be on its guard.

Like other tyrannies, the tyranny of the majority was at first, and is still vulgarly, held in dread, chiefly as operating through the acts of the public authorities. But reflecting persons perceived that when society is itself the tyrant—society collectively over the separate individuals who compose it—its means of tyrannising are not restricted to the acts which it may do by the hands of its political functionaries. Society can and does execute its own mandates: and if it issues wrong mandates instead of right, or any mandates at all in things with which it ought not to meddle, it practises a social tyranny more formidable than many kinds of political oppression, since, though not usually upheld by such extreme penalties, it leaves fewer means of escape, penetrating much more deeply into the details of life, and enslaving the soul itself. Protection, therefore, against the tyranny of the magistrate is not enough: there needs protection also against the tyranny of the prevailing opinion and feeling; against the tendency of society to impose, by other means than civil penalties, its own ideas and practices as rules of conduct on those who dissent from them; to fetter the development, and, if possible, prevent the formation, of any individuality not in harmony with its ways, and compels all characters to fashion themselves upon the model of its own. There is a limit to the legitimate interference of col-lective opinion with individual independence: and to find that limit, and main-tain it against encroachment, is as indispensable to a good condition of human affairs, as protection against political despotism.

*   *   *

The object of this Essay is to assert one very simple principle, as entitled to gov-ern absolutely the dealings of society with the individual in the way of compul-sion and control, whether the means used be physical force in the form of legal penalties, or the moral coercion of public opinion. That principle is, that the sole end for which mankind are warranted, individually or collectively, in inter-fering with the liberty of action of any of their number, is self-protection. That the only purpose for which power can be rightfully exercised over any member of a civilised community, against his will, is to prevent harm to others. His own good, either physical or moral, is not a sufficient warrant. He cannot rightfully be compelled to do or forbear because it will be better for him to do so, because it will make him happier, because, in the opinions of others, to do so would be wise, or even right. These are good reasons for remonstrating with him, or reasoning with him, or persuading him, or entreating him, but not for compelling him, or visiting him with any evil in case he do otherwise. To justify that, the conduct from which it is desired to deter him must be calculated to produce evil to some one else. The only part of the conduct of any one, for which he is amenable to society, is that which concerns others. In the part which merely concerns himself, his independence is, of right, absolute. Over himself, over his own body and mind, the individual is sovereign.

*   *   *

. . . This, then is the appropriate region of human liberty. It comprises, first, the inward domain of consciousness; demanding liberty of conscience in the most comprehensive sense; liberty of thought and feeling; absolute freedom of opin-ion and sentiment on all subjects, practical or speculative, scientific, moral, or theological. The liberty of expressing and publishing opinions may seem to fall under a different principle, since it belongs to that part of the conduct of an individual which concerns other people; but, being almost of as much impor-tance as the liberty of thought itself, and resting in great part on the same rea-sons, is practically inseparable from it. Secondly, the principle requires liberty of tastes and pursuits; of framing the plan of our life to suit our own character; of doing as we like, subject to such consequences as may follow: without impedi-ment from our fellow-creatures, so long as what we do does not harm them, even though they should think our conduct foolish, perverse, or wrong.

*   *   *

Let us suppose, therefore, that the government is entirely at one with the peo-ple, and never thinks of exerting any power of coercion unless in agreement with what it conceives to be their voice. But I deny the right of the people to exercise such coercion, either by themselves or by their government. The power itself is illegitimate. The best government has no more title to it than the worst. It is as noxious, or more noxious, when exerted in accordance with public opinion, than when in opposition to it. If all mankind minus one were of one opinion, and only one person were of the contrary opinion, mankind would be no more justified in silencing that one person, than he, if he had the power, would be justified in silencing mankind.

By the middle of the nineteenth century there was mounting evidence that Adam Smith and Jeremy Bentham had oversimplified the problems of a competitive industrial society. Living conditions in the slums of the new industrial cities were squalid. Many men, women, and children worked brutally long hours for starvation wages. Aware of these conditions, Mill began to modify the laissez-faire economics of earlier liberals.

FROM *Principles of Political Economy*

BY *John Stuart Mill*

OF PROPERTY

. . . IF, THEREFORE, the choice were to be made between Communism with all its chances, and the present state of society with all its sufferings and injustices; if the institution of private property necessarily carried with it as a consequence, that the produce of labour should be apportioned as we now see it, almost in an inverse ratio to the labour—the largest portions to those who have never worked at all, the next largest to those whose work is almost nominal, and so in a descending scale, the remuneration dwindles as the work grows harder and more disagreeable, until the most fatiguing and exhausting bodily labour cannot count with certainty on being able to earn even the necessaries of life; if this, or Communism, were the alternative, all the difficulties, great or small, of Communism, would be but as dust in the balance. But to make the comparison applicable, we must compare Communism at its best, with the régime of individual property, not as it is, but as it might be made. . . . If the tendency of legislation had been to favour the diffusion, instead of the concentration of wealth—to encourage the subdivision of the large masses, instead of striving to keep them together; the principle of individual property would have been found to have no necessary connexion with the physical and social evils which almost all Socialist writers assume to be inseparable from it.

John Stuart Mill, *Principles of Political Economy*. From the fifth London edition, I, pp. 267–268, 270–271, II, pp. 559–562, 572–574, 577–581, 589–593, 594–601. New York, 1874. Reprinted by permission.

OF THE GROUNDS AND LIMITS OF THE LAISSER-FAIRE OR NON-INTERFERENCE PRINCIPLE

* * *

We must set out by distinguishing between two kinds of intervention by the government, which, though they may relate to the same subject, differ widely in their nature and effects, and require, for their justification, motives of a very different degree of urgency. The intervention may extend to controlling the free agency of individuals. Government may interdict all persons from doing certain things; or from doing them without its authorization; or may prescribe to them certain things to be done, or a certain manner of doing things which it is left optional with them to do or to abstain from. This is the *authoritative* interference of government. There is another kind of intervention which is not authoritative: when a government, instead of issuing a command and enforcing it by penalties, adopts the course so seldom resorted to by governments, and of which such important use might be made, that of giving advice, and promulgating information; or when, leaving individuals free to use their own means of pursuing any object of general interest, the government, not meddling with them, but not trusting the object solely to their care, establishes, side by side with their arrangements, an agency of its own for a like purpose. Thus it is one thing to maintain a Church Establishment, and another to refuse toleration to other religions, or to persons professing no religion. It is one thing to provide schools or colleges, and another to require that no person shall act as an instructor of youth without a government license. There might be a national bank or a government manufactory, without any monopoly against private banks and manufactories. There might be a post-office, without penalties against the conveyance of letters by other means. There may be a corps of government engineers for civil purposes, while the profession of a civil engineer is free to be adopted by every one. There may be public hospitals, without any restriction upon private medical or surgical practice.

It is evident, even at first sight, that the authoritative form of government intervention has a much more limited sphere of legitimate action than the other. It requires a much stronger necessity to justify it in any case; while there are large departments of human life from which it must be unreservedly and imperiously excluded. Whatever theory we adopt respecting the foundation of the social union, and under whatever political institutions we live, there is a circle around every individual human being, which no government, be it that of one, of a few, or of the many, ought to be permitted to overstep: there is a part of the life of every person who has come to years of discretion, within which the individuality of that person ought to reign uncontrolled either by any other individual or by the public collectively. That there is, or ought to be, some space in human existence thus entrenched around, and sacred from authoritative intrusion, no one who professes the smallest regard to human freedom or dignity will call in question: the point to be determined is, where the limit should be placed; how large a province of human life this reserved territory should include. I apprehend that it ought to include all that part which concerns only the life, whether inward or outward, of the individual, and does not affect the interests of others, or affects them only through the moral influence of example.

*   *   *

The ground of the practical principle of non-interference must here be, that most persons take a juster and more intelligent view of their own interest, and of the means of promoting it, than can either be prescribed to them by a general enactment of the legislature, or pointed out in the particular case by a public functionary. The maxim is unquestionably sound as a general rule; but there is no difficulty in perceiving some very large and conspicuous exceptions to it. These may be classed under several heads.

First:—The individual who is presumed to be the best judge of his own interests may be incapable of judging or acting for himself; may be a lunatic, an idiot, an infant: or though not wholly incapable, may be of immature years and judgment. In this case the foundation of the *laisser-faire* principle breaks down entirely. The person most interested is not the best judge of the matter, nor a competent judge at all. . . . To take an example from the peculiar province of political economy; it is right that children, and young persons not yet arrived at maturity, should be protected, so far as the eye and hand of the state can reach, from being over-worked. Labouring for too many hours in the day, or on work beyond their strength, should not be permitted to them, for if permitted it may always be compelled. Freedom of contract, in the case of children, is but another word for freedom of coercion. Education also, the best which circumstances admit of their receiving, is not a thing which parents or relatives, from indifference, jealousy, or avarice, should have it in their power to withhold.

*   *   *

Among those members of the community whose freedom of contract ought to be controlled by the legislature for their own protection, on account (it is said) of their dependent position, it is frequently proposed to include women: and in the existing Factory Act, their labour, in common with that of young persons, has been placed under peculiar restrictions. But the classing together, for this and other purposes, of women and children, appears to me both indefensible in principle and mischievous in practice. Children below a certain age *cannot* judge or act for themselves; up to a considerably greater age they are inevitably more or less disqualified for doing so; but women are as capable as men of appreciating and managing their own concerns, and the only hindrance to their doing so arises from the injustice of their present social position. So long as the law makes everything which the wife acquires, the property of the husband, while by compelling her to live with him it forces her to submit to almost any amount of moral and even physical tyranny which he may choose to inflict, there is some ground for regarding every act done by her as done under coercion: but it is the great error of reformers and philanthropists in our time, to nibble at the consequences of unjust power instead of redressing the injustice itself. If women had as absolute a control as men have, over their own persons and their own patrimony or acquisitions, there would be no plea for limiting their hours of labouring for themselves, in order that they might have time to labour for the husband, in what is called, by the advocates of restriction, *his* home. Women employed in factories are the only women in the labouring rank of life whose position is not that of slaves and drudges; precisely because they cannot easily be compelled to work and earn wages in factories against their will. For improving the condition of women, it should, on the contrary, be an object to give them the readiest access to independent industrial employment, instead of closing, either entirely or partially, that which is already open to them.

Mill's economic views eventually developed to the point where he could call himself a Socialist. But he still retained his earlier intense concern for the freedom of individuals. The Autobiography *was published posthumously, in 1874.*

FROM *Autobiography*
BY *John Stuart Mill*

WE [HE AND HIS WIFE] were now much less democrats than I had been, because so long as education continues to be so wretchedly imperfect, we dreaded the ignorance and especially the selfishness and brutality of the mass; but our ideal of ultimate improvement went far beyond Democracy, and would class us decidedly under the general designation of Socialists. While we repudiated with the greatest energy that tyranny of society over the individual which most Socialistic systems are supposed to involve, we yet looked forward to a time when society will no longer be divided into the idle and the industrious; when the rule that they who do not work shall not eat, will be applied not to paupers only, but impartially to all; when the division of the produce of labour, instead of depending, as in so great a degree it now does, on the accident of birth, will be made by concert on an acknowledged principle of justice; and when it will no longer either be, or be thought to be, impossible for human beings to exert themselves strenuously in procuring benefits which are not to be exclusively their own, but to be shared with the society they belong to. The social problem of the future we considered to be, how to unite the greatest individual liberty of action with a common ownership in the raw material of the globe, and an equal participation of all in the benefits of combined labour.

John Stuart Mill, *Autobiography*, pp. 231–232. Henry Holt and Company, New York, 1874. Reprinted by permission.

We saw clearly that to render any such social transformation either possible or desirable, an equivalent change of character must take place both in the uncultivated herd who now compose the labouring masses, and in the immense majority of their employers. Both these classes must learn by practice to labour and combine for generous, or at all events for public and social purposes, and not, as hitherto, solely for narrowly interested ones. But the capacity to do this has always existed in mankind, and is not, nor is ever likely to be, extinct. Education, habit, and the cultivation of the sentiments, will make a common man dig or weave for his country, as readily as fight for his country.

3

Gladstone and Reform:
For and Against

A major objective of Liberal policy was the gradual extension of the parliamentary franchise. In 1866 William Gladstone defended a measure designed to extend the right to vote to some urban workingmen.[1]

Gladstone's Speech on the Reform Bill of 1866

SIR, IN MY OPINION there are times in debate when extraordinary errors are best met by the declaration of elementary truths. When I heard it stated by a gentleman of ability that to touch the question of enfranchising any portion of the working class was domestic revolution, I thought it time to remind him that the performance of the duties of citizenship does give some presumption of the capacity for civil rights, and that the burden of proof, that exclusion from such rights is warrantable or wise or (as it may be) necessary, lies upon those who exclude. That as I think very simple declaration was magnified into revolutionary doctrine, and great service has it once more done to-night to the leader of the Tory party. On the same grounds, when I heard my right hon. friend describing these working men . . . as an invading army, and as something more, as an invading ambush, as a band of enemies, which was to bring ruin and conflagration as the purpose of its mission, into a city all fore-doomed; and when I heard these opinions and this illustration once and again repeated, I thought it was time to fall back upon elementary truths as the proper antagonists to these extraordinary errors, and to say, these men whom you are denouncing, not by argument and reason, but beyond the bounds of all argument and reason, are your own flesh and blood. . . .

[1] Gladstone's bill was defeated. In the following year, however, a Conservative government led by Disraeli—seeing that the popular demand for reform could not be resisted—enacted a more far-reaching measure with Liberal support.

A. T. Bassett, ed., *Gladstone's Speeches*, pp. 343, 349–350, 359, 371–372, 374–376, 379. Methuen and Co., Ltd., London, 1916. Reprinted by permission.

. . . This is not only a protracted debate—it is not only one upon which the House of Commons has freely lavished from every one of its quarters or its sections the choicest treasures of its wit, its argument, its rhetorical and its persuasive powers—it is also an historical debate. We are now about the process that is called "making history." We are now laying the foundations of much that is to come. This occasion is a starting point from which I presume to think the career we have to run as individuals and parties will in many respects take its character and colour. . . .

. . . The right hon. gentleman asked, "Do you think the franchise is good in itself, or do you wish to improve the institutions of the country?" Sir, I find here no dilemma. My answer is, we want to do both. The extension of the franchise within safe and proper limits is good. It will array more persons in support of the institutions of the country, and that is another good. The composition and the working of this House is admirable, and its performances have long since placed it at the head of all the legislative assemblies of the world. It does not follow, however, that it cannot be improved. I will not say with my right hon. friend that it is perfect. I am not sure, indeed, that he said so, but he seemed to mean if not to say it. I am not prepared to pay the worship of idolatry even to this House. I will mention a point in which I think it might be improved. It is this. I need not say I am scarcely speaking of the present House, which has but just entered upon its labours. I am speaking of the reformed Parliament in general. There is a saying which has been ascribed to a very eminent person, still alive—whose name I will not mention because I have no means of knowing whether it has been truly ascribed to him or not, but I will quote it for its own sake. It is to the effect that the unreformed Parliament used to job for individuals, while the reformed Parliament jobs for classes. I do not adopt the rudeness of the phrase, but the substance of the observation is in my opinion just. I think that the influence of separate classes is too strong, and that the influence of the public interest properly so called, as distinguished from the interest of sets, groups, and classes of men, is too weak. I fully admit I am not perhaps altogether an impartial judge; I speak much from my own experience during a lengthened period as Chancellor of the Exchequer, and as in a special degree and sense the guardian of the public purse. Undoubtedly, if there be a weak point in the composition of the House this is the department in which it would most readily and most clearly show itself. I believe that the composition of the House might be greatly improved; and that the increased representation of the working classes would supply us more largely with that description of Members whom we want, who would look not to the interests of classes, but to the public interest. In presuming to say so much as this, I hope I do not convey any reproach to any party or person; but my right hon. friend challenged us so sharply, as if we admitted that no improvement whatever was possible, that I felt bound to state my belief.

*   *   *

. . . I am justified, then, in stating that the working classes are not adequately represented in this House. They are not, it is admitted, represented in any proportion to their numbers; and without holding that it would be fit for us to do more than lessen the disproportion, we contend it is right to do as much. They are not represented, as I have previously shown, in accordance with their share of the income of the country. Especially after the events of the last few years, I may boldly proceed to say they are not represented in proportion to their intelligence, their virtue, or their loyalty. . . . If these are not good reasons for extending the suffrage at the present, I know not what reason can be good. But if hon. Members think they can hold their ground in a policy of resistance and refusal for the present, I have to ask them, how do they regard the future? . . .

. . . Sir, let us for a moment consider the enormous and silent changes which have been going forward among the labouring population. May I use the words to hon. and right hon. gentlemen once used by way of exhortation by Sir Robert Peel to his opponents, "elevate your vision"? Let us try and raise our views above the fears, the suspicions, the jealousies, the reproaches, and the recriminations of this place and this occasion. Let us look onward to the time of our children and of our children's children. Let us know what preparation it behooves us should be made for that coming time. Is there or is there not, I ask, a steady movement of the labouring classes, and is or is not that movement a movement onwards and upwards? . . . You cannot fight against the future. Time is on our side. The great social forces which move onwards in their might and majesty, and which the tumult of our debates does not for a moment impede or disturb—those great social forces are against you; they are marshalled on our side; and the banner which we now carry in this fight, though perhaps at some moment it may droop over our sinking heads, yet it soon again will float in the eye of heaven, and it will be borne by the firm hands of the united people of the three kingdoms, perhaps not to an easy, but to a certain and to a not distant victory.

The closing passage of Gladstone's speech on the Reform Bill of 1866 provides a good example of his oratorical style. (Disraeli called him "a sophistical rhetorician inebriated with the exuberance of his own verbosity.") In fact Gladstone was an enormously effective speaker, both in Parliament and out of it. The speech excerpted below was delivered in the open air to a crowd of many thousands.

Gladstone had become prime minister in 1868. His government enacted many important measures of reform. One disestablished the (Protestant) Church of Ireland, and another sought to protect Irish peasants against arbitrary evictions. An Army Act abolished the purchase of commissions and so made possible the growth of a professional corps of officers. A Ballot Act introduced secret voting. An Education Act provided a national system of elementary education. A Civil Service Act established competitive examinations for Civil Service positions. Along with all this, Gladstone succeeded in reducing government expenditures.

In the following speech he defended the policies of his government to his constituents.

Gladstone's Speech at Blackheath, October 1871

THERE IS A QUESTION of the future on which we have heard much said of late—I mean the question of the constitution of the House of Lords. (*A Voice:* "You had better leave that alone.") My friend there says, "Leave the constitution of the House of Lords alone." I am not prepared quite to agree with my friend, because the constitution of the House of Lords has often been a subject of consideration among the wisest and the most sober-minded men; as, for example, when a proposal—of which my friend disapproves apparently—was made, a few years ago, to make a moderate addition to the House of Lords, of peers holding peerages for life. I am not going to discuss that particular measure; but I will only say, without entering into details that would be highly interesting, but which the vast range of those subjects makes impossible on the present occasion—I will only say that I believe there are various particulars in which the constitution of the House of Lords might, under favourable circumstances, be improved. . . .

Now, gentlemen, I am drawing very near to my close; but I must still detain you while I refer to a sentiment, which undoubtedly has been more perceptible in the country during the present year, than I have noticed it in a good many former years. I mean a suspicion on the part of many members of the working class, that they are not governed as they ought to be, and that their interests are not properly considered. I will not enter upon the particular causes, connected with the uneasy state of Europe, which may go far to account for this sentiment; but I will venture to say this, that I think the working man will do well briefly and calmly to review the history, with regard to himself, of the last eighteen years. I take that period—I might take a longer one—but I take that period because it enables me to present results in a tolerably simple form, and because it is a period within which I have been most intimately conversant with a multitude of questions, in which the welfare of the mass of the community is deeply and directly concerned. Within these eighteen years, what has taken place affecting all classes of the community, but especially, and more than all others, affecting the working classes of the people? In the first place, perfectly free access has been given for the entry into our ports of everything that they can want from every quarter of the world—I mean perfectly free, whether as regards prohibitions or as regards protective duties. In the second place, we have seen remitted during those eighteen years an amount of taxation which I will not undertake—and which it is not necessary for me at this moment—to state minutely; but I will venture to assert that the taxation upon commodities, which he has seen remitted within that period, is something between £15,000,000 and £20,000,000 sterling per annum. That remission of taxation, in which the working man is so especially interested, has not been purchased by an augmentation of the burdens upon other classes; because the Income-tax, though it is higher now than I should like to see it—namely, at 6*d*.

A. T. Bassett, ed., *Gladstone's Speeches*, pp. 405–407, 409–414, 416, 420–423. Reprinted by permission.

in the pound—is still one penny lower than it was eighteen years ago, before those fifteen millions of taxes were remitted. Within these eighteen years, his class has been invested largely with the Parliamentary franchise, and he now sees himself at the point where he may reasonably hope that, before he is six or eight months older, he will be protected in the free exercise of that franchise by means of the Ballot. The Parliament has passed an Act which aims at securing for all his children, under all circumstances, a good primary education, and which provides that, if unhappily he be unable himself to meet the cost, it shall be defrayed for him by the State and by his wealthier neighbours. Whilst this provision has been made for primary education, endeavours have been made, through reforming the Universities, through the entire abolition of tests, and through an extensive dealing with the public and the grammar schools of the country, to establish the whole of our schools in a hierarchy of degrees—the several orders of education rising one above the other—so that, whenever there is in a child a capacity to rise, he may, with facility, pass on from point to point, and may find open to him the road through knowledge to distinction. But education would not be of great use to the people unless the materials of study were accessible; and therefore, at no small cost of political effort, the material of paper has been set free of duty, and every restriction, in stamp or otherwise, upon the press has been removed. The consequence has been the creation of a popular press which, for the lowness of its price, for the general ability—aye, for the general wisdom and moderation with which it is written, and for the vast extent of its circulation, I might almost venture to call, not only an honour to the nation, but the wonder of the world. And in order that the public service might indeed be a public service—in order that we might not have among the civil offices of the State that which we had complained of in the army—namely, that the service was not the property of the nation, but of the officers, we have now been enabled to remove from the entry into the Civil Service the barriers of nomination, patronage, jobbing, favouritism in whatever form; and every man belonging to the people of England—if he is able to fit his children for the purpose of competing for public employment—may do it entirely irrespective of the question of what is his condition in life, or the amount of means with which he may happen to be, or now to be endowed. I say confidently, in the face of those of the working community who may hear me, and to the minds of all those who may pay the least attention to these words through any other medium, that when, within such a period as I have described, measures like these have been achieved, while there may remain much to be done—I am the last to deny it, I am the first to assert it—there is reason to look with patience and indulgence upon a system under which such results have been accomplished; some reason for that loyalty to the Throne, and that attachment to the law, which are the happy characteristics of the people of this country.

But while I would exhort you to impose upon the Government and the Legislature every burden that they are, in their own nature, capable of bearing, in my mind they are not your friends, but in fact, though not in intention, your enemies, who teach you to look to the Legislature, or to the Government, for the radical removal of the evils which afflict human life. I read but a few days ago, in a questionable book, verses which I think contain much good sense, and which I will read to you:—

"People throughout the land
Join in one social band,
    And save yourselves.
If you would happy be,
Free from all slavery,
Banish all knavery,
    And save yourselves."

It is the individual mind, the individual conscience; it is the individual character, on which mainly human happiness or human misery depends. The social problems which confront us are many and formidable. Let the Government labour to its uttermost, let the Legislature spend days and nights in your service; but, after the very best has been achieved, the question whether the English father is to be the father of a happy family and the centre of a united home, is a question which must depend mainly upon himself.

Disraeli—later Earl of Beaconsfield—was Gladstone's greatest opponent in English politics. In the following speech he criticized, from a Conservative point of view, the same government that Gladstone defended in the Blackheath speech given above.

Conservative and Liberal Principles Speech at Crystal Palace, June 24, 1872

BY *Benjamin Disraeli*

GENTLEMEN, THE TORY PARTY, unless it is a national party, is nothing. It is not a confederacy of nobles, it is not a democratic multitude; it is a party formed from all the numerous classes in the realm—classes alike and equal before the law, but whose different conditions and different aims give vigour and variety to our national life.

Gentlemen, a body of public men distinguished by their capacity took advantage of these circumstances. They seized the helm of affairs in a manner the honour of which I do not for a moment question, but they introduced a new system into our political life. Influenced in a great degree by the philosophy and the politics of the Continent, they endeavoured to substitute cosmopolitan for national principles; and they baptized the new scheme of politics with the plausible name of "Liberalism." Far be it from me for a moment to inti-

T. E. Kebbel, ed., "Conservative and Liberal Principles," in *Selected Speeches of the Earl of Beaconsfield*, II, pp. 523–535, London, 1882. Reprinted by permission.

mate that a country like England should not profit by the political experience of Continental nations of not inferior civilisation; far be it from me for a moment to maintain that the party which then obtained power and which has since generally possessed it did not make many suggestions for our public life that were of great value, and bring forward many measures which, though changes, were nevertheless improvements. But the tone and tendency of Liberalism cannot be long concealed. It is to attack the institutions of the country under the name of Reform, and to make war on the manners and customs of the people of this country under the pretext of Progress. During the forty years that have elapsed since the commencement of this new system—although the superficial have seen upon its surface only the contentions of political parties—the real state of affairs has been this: the attempt of one party to establish in this country cosmopolitan ideas, and the efforts of another—unconscious efforts, sometimes, but always continued—to recur to and resume those national principles to which they attribute the greatness and glory of the country.

* * *

Now, I have always been of opinion that the Tory party has three great objects. The first is to maintain the institutions of the country—not from any sentiment of political superstition, but because we believe that they embody the principles upon which a community like England can alone safely rest. The principles of liberty, of order, of law, and of religion ought not to be entrusted to individual opinion or to the caprice and passion of multitudes, but should be embodied in a form of permanence and power. We associate with the Monarchy the ideas which it represents—the majesty of law, the administration of justice, the fountain of mercy and of honour. We know that in the Estates of the Realm and the privileges they enjoy, is the best security for public liberty and good government. We believe that a national profession of faith can only be maintained by an Established Church, and that no society is safe unless there is a public recognition of the Providential government of the world, and of the future responsibility of man. Well, it is a curious circumstance that during all these same forty years of triumphant Liberalism, every one of these institutions has been attacked and assailed—I say, continuously attacked and assailed. . . . Take the case of the House of Lords. The House of Lords has been assailed during this reign of Liberalism in every manner and unceasingly. Its constitution has been denounced as anomalous, its influence declared pernicious; but what has been the result of this assault and criticism of forty years? Why, the people of England, in my opinion, have discovered that the existence of a second Chamber is necessary to Constitutional Government; and, while necessary to Constitutional Government; and, while necessary to Constitutional Government, is, at the same time, of all political inventions the most difficult. Therefore, the people of this country have congratulated themselves that, by the aid of an ancient and famous history, there has been developed in this country an Assembly which possesses all the virtues which a Senate should possess—independence, great local influence, eloquence, all the accomplishments of political life, and a public training which no theory could supply

The assault of Liberalism upon the House of Lords has been mainly occasioned by the prejudice of Liberalism against the land laws of this country. But in my opinion, and in the opinion of wiser men than myself, and of men in other countries besides this, the liberty of England depends much upon the landed tenure of England—upon the fact that there is a class which can alike defy despots and mobs, around which the people may always rally, and which must be patriotic from its intimate connection with the soil. Well, gentlemen, so far as these institutions of the country—the Monarchy and the Lords Spiritual and Temporal—are concerned, I think we may fairly say, without exaggeration, that public opinion is in favour of those institutions, the maintenance of which is one of the principal tenets of the Tory party, and the existence of which has been unceasingly criticised for forty years by the Liberal party. Now, let me say a word about the other Estate of the Realm, which was first attacked by Liberalism.

One of the most distinguishing features of the great change effected in 1832 was that those who brought it about at once abolished all the franchises of the working classes.[1] They were franchises as ancient as those of the Baronage of England; and, while they abolished them, they proposed no substitute. The discontent upon the subject of the representation which has from that time more or less pervaded our society dates from that period, and that discontent, all will admit, has now ceased. It was terminated by the Act of Parliamentary Reform of 1867–8. That Act was founded on a confidence that the great body of the people of this country were "Conservative." When I say "Conservative," I use the word in its purest and loftiest sense. I mean that the people of England, and especially the working classes of England, are proud of belonging to a great country, and wish to maintain its greatness—that they are proud of belonging to an Imperial country, and are resolved to maintain, if they can, their empire—that they believe, on the whole, that the greatness and the empire of England are to be attributed to the ancient institutions of the land. . . . They are English to the core. They repudiate cosmopolitan principles. They adhere to national principles. They are for maintaining the greatness of the kingdom and the empire, and they are proud of being subjects of our Sovereign and members of such an Empire. Well, then, as regards the political institutions of this country, the maintenance of which is one of the chief tenets of the Tory party, so far as I can read public opinion, the feeling of the nation is in accordance with the Tory party.

---

[1] The first Parliamentary Reform Bill of 1832, passed by the Whigs, increased the number of voters, but it abolished certain ancient franchises in the boroughs. Disraeli's Act of 1867 gave the vote to many urban working-class householders.

4

The New Liberalism

In 1881 T. H. Green, a leading philosopher of liberalism, argued that state regulation could actually enhance human freedom.

Liberal Legislation or Freedom of Contract

BY *T. H. Green*

WE SHALL PROBABLY all agree that freedom, rightly understood, is the greatest of blessings; that its attainment is the true end of all our efforts as citizens. But when we thus speak of freedom, we should consider carefully what we mean by it. We do not mean merely freedom to do as we like irrespectively of what it is that we like. We do not mean a freedom that can be enjoyed by one man or one set of men at the cost of a loss of freedom to others. When we speak of freedom as something to be so highly prized, we mean a positive power or capacity of doing or enjoying something worth doing or enjoying, and that, too, something that we do or enjoy in common with others. We mean by it a power which each man exercises through the help or security given him by his fellow-men, and which he in turn helps to secure for them. When we measure the progress of a society by its growth in freedom, we measure it by the increasing development and exercise on the whole of those powers of contributing to social good with which we believe the members of the society to be endowed; in short, by the greater power on the part of the citizens as a body to make the most and best of themselves. . . .

Our modern legislation then with reference to labour, and education, and health, involving as it does manifold interference with freedom of contract, is justified on the ground that it is the business of the state, not indeed directly to promote moral goodness, for that, from the very nature of moral goodness, it cannot do, but to maintain the conditions without which a free exercise of the human faculties is impossible. . . .

And the question is whether without these laws the suffering classes could have been delivered quickly or slowly from the condition they were in. Could

Works of T. H. Green (1882), vol. III, pp. 370–371, 374, 376. Reprinted by permission.

591

the enlightened self-interest or benevolence of individuals, working under a system of unlimited freedom of contract, have ever brought them into a state compatible with the free development of the human faculties? No one considering the facts can have any doubt as to the answer to this question. Left to itself, or to the operation of casual benevolence, a degraded population perpetuates and increases itself. Read any of the authorised accounts, given before royal or parliamentary commissions, of the state of the labourers, especially of the women and children, as they were in our great industries before the law was first brought to bear on them, and before freedom of contract was first interfered with in them. Ask yourself what chance there was of a generation, born and bred under such conditions, ever contracting itself out of them.

In the 1880s Gladstone began to encounter criticism, not only from Conservatives but also from within his own party. A group of radical Liberals, led by Joseph Chamberlain, began to press for a more advanced social program than Gladstone favored. Their Unauthorized Programme *or* Radical Programme *appeared shortly after the Reform Act of 1884, which gave the vote for the first time to farm laborers. The radicals were especially interested in improving the living conditions of the newly enfranchised workers. Their program urged redistribution of income by higher taxes on property and incomes. The state was to acquire land and distribute it as small holdings to agricultural laborers. Similarly, the state was to provide housing for the poor through taxes levied on property. Gladstone, on the other hand, disliked both high taxes and direct intervention of the state in social questions.*

The Radical Programme
BY *Joseph Chamberlain*

. . . THUS FAR THE agricultural labourer has been regarded by the political economists as a mere machine—an instrument to be used for the creation of wealth, deposited in the hands of the few; not as a human being whose comfort, health, and home are to be considered, and who has a claim to such benefits as were conferred by the Factory Acts upon the labourers in towns. If his welfare cannot be sufficiently protected without the taxation of property, then property will be taxed.

But it is needless now to attempt to define the measures that may be necessary for these ends. It is enough to indicate their general character. They sound the death-knell of the *laissez-faire* system; and if the agricultural labourer is not strong enough to look after himself, to take the initiative in the social reforms prompted by a rational estimate of private interest, there is an organised body of politicians in this country who will at least do thus much for him. If it be said that this is communism, the answer is that it is not. If it be said that

The Radical Programme with a Preface by the Right Hon. J. Chamberlain, pp. 12–14, 57–59, 109–110, 113–114. Chapman and Hall, London, 1885. Reprinted by permission.

it is legislation of a socialist tendency, the impeachment may readily be admitted. Between such legislation and communism there is all the difference in the world. Communism means the reduction of everything to a dead level, the destruction of private adventure, the paralysis of private industry, the atrophy of private effort. The socialistic measures now contemplated would preserve in their normal vigour and freshness all the individual activities of English citizenship, and would do nothing more spoliatory than tax—if and in what degree necessary—aggregations of wealth for the good of the community. . . .

What have the landed class to offer as an alternative? Territorial Toryism has thus far had as its main principle the instinct of preservation, and, above all, the protection for property. But Toryism of this kind is not only moribund, it is actually dead. It is as much a relic of the past as the star of the Order of the Garter presented by the late Lord Hertford to Lord Beaconsfield, and recently on view as a curiosity at a jeweller's in the Haymarket. . . .

There is another method of dealing with the question of land tenure. . . . The principle of all such legislation as is now being considered is, let it be repeated once more, the right and duty of the State to fix within certain broad limits the extent, and to control the conditions, of private ownership. *What, therefore, must be done is formally to confer upon the State larger powers in these matters than she now possesses.* Such an authority might, and necessarily would, be delegated to local authorities. It would be impossible for the central Government to manage all land transactions in every part of the country. It would vest in its representatives the power of expropriating for public purposes, on payment of fair compensation, and adequate securities being taken against the possibility of extortionate demands.

The reform of our system of taxation practically comes under nearly the same head as land legislation. . . . No person will deny that a more equal distribution of wealth, if it could be effected without creating any revolutionary precedent, would be a gain to the whole community.

Again, no one will deny either that a general reduction of incomes, once a certain point had been reached, would not inflict any appreciable amount of suffering. . . . Let it not be supposed that the writers of these papers contemplate the reduction by law of all incomes to a common level. The remark just made is only intended to remind persons that, even were the extremely rich to find that a readjustment of taxation tended to diminish their wealth, no great amount of hardship would be the result. Here again we may refer to the precedents of that Greater Britain which lies beyond the seas. As Free Schools, a Free Church, and Free Land have been found practicable in the colonies, so has a progressive income-tax up to ten per cent. been successfully imposed in the United States.

This will be called Socialism with a vengeance, but, as has been observed before, the path of legislative progress in England has been for years, and must continue to be, distinctly Socialistic. It is the general business of the State, not merely in the cases reviewed in the foregoing pages, but in others like them, to convince the possessors of wealth, and the holders of property, whether in country or in town, that they cannot escape the responsibilities of trusteeship, and that, if the State is to guarantee them security of tenure, they must be ready to discharge certain definite obligations.

*   *   *

One of the most important and pressing questions connected with the agricultural labourers is that of the improvement of their dwellings. The description of these hovels, called homes, of the agricultural poor, given in the Report of the Royal Commission, 1867, though painfully familiar to those who have lived among the labourers, is calculated to rouse serious attention, if not indignation, in the minds of the thoughtful readers who dwell on it for the first time. Nothing can be stronger than the language used by the Commissioners in reference to these dwellings in the various parishes visited. They are described as "detestable," "deplorable," as "a disgrace to a Christian community." To use the words of one of the Commissioners (Rev. J. Fraser, the present Bishop of Manchester), "It is impossible to exaggerate the ill effects of this state of things in every aspect, physical, social, economical, moral and intellectual." With regard to the difficulties in the way of modesty and decency, the Commissioners remark, "With beds lying as thickly as they can be packed, father, mother, young men, lads grown and growing-up girls all together; where every operation of the toilet and of nature, dressing, undressing, births and deaths, is performed, each within sight and hearing of all, &c, &c. It is a hideous picture, and the picture is drawn from life."

*   *   *

In dealing with this state of things there are difficulties no doubt, but not of an insuperable character. . . . Land should be acquired where necessary by the authorities by compulsory purchase at a fair market value; that is to say, at the price it would realise in the open market if the owner were a willing seller.

   This land should be let for building cottages on plans and conditions approved by the local authorities, one essential condition being that half an acre of land at least should be attached to each dwelling. Any scheme of this sort should be compulsory, and the duty of seeing that it was faithfully carried out should be placed in the hands of the Local Government Board, and any expenses connected with it should be provided by a rate levied on the owners of property in the district.

Gladstone was irritated that the radical program was published without his authorization. Chamberlain defended his policy in a speech given in September 1885.

Joseph Chamberlain's Speech at Warrington

. . . THERE IS NOT a single Liberal candidate who has not accepted some one or more points of the Radical programme. It is therefore perfectly futile and ridiculous for any political Rip Van Winkle to come down from the mountain on which he has been slumbering, and to tell us that these things are to be excluded from the Liberal programme. . . .

The great problem of our civilisation is still unsolved. We have to account for and to grapple with the mass of misery and destitution in our midst, co-existent as it is with the evidence of abundant wealth and teeming prosperity. It is a problem which some men would put aside by reference to the eternal laws of supply and demand, to the necessity of freedom of contract, and to the sanctity of every private right of property. But, gentlemen, these phrases are the convenient cant of selfish wealth. . . . These are no answers to our questions. I quite understand the reason for timidity in dealing with this question so long as Government was merely the expression of the will of a prejudiced and limited few. . . . But now that we have a Government of the people by the people, we will go on and we will make it for every man his natural rights—his right to existence, and to a fair enjoyment of it. I shall be told tomorrow that this is Socialism. . . . Of course, it is Socialism. The Poor-Law is Socialism. The Education Act is Socialism. The greater part of municipal work is Socialism, and every kindly act of legislation by which the community has sought to discharge its responsibilities and its obligations to the poor is Socialism, but it is none the worse for that. Our object is the elevation of the poor, of the masses of the people—a levelling up, by which we shall do something to remove the excessive inequality in social life which is now one of the greatest dangers. . . . I do not pretend that for every grievance a remedy will be found. We must try experiments as we are bound to do . . . and if we fail, let us try again and again until we succeed.

Gladstone's Speech at Saltney, October 1889

WE LIVE AT A TIME when there is a disposition to think that the Government ought to do this and that, and that the Government ought to do everything. There are things which the Government ought to do, and does not do, I have no doubt. In former periods the Government have neglected much, and possibly even now they neglect something. But there is a danger on the other side. If the Government takes into its hand that which the man ought to do for himself, it will inflict upon him greater mischiefs than all the benefits he will have received or all the advantages that would accrue from them. The essence of the whole thing is, that the spirit of self-reliance, the spirit of true and genuine manly independence, should be preserved in the minds of the people, in the minds of the masses of the people, in the minds of every member of that class. If he loses his self-reliance, if he learns to live in a craven dependence upon wealthier people rather than upon himself, you may depend upon it he incurs mischiefs for which no compensation can be made.

5

Liberalism, Imperialism, and Nationalism

In 1876 a Bulgarian rebellion against the Turkish government was repressed with large-scale massacres. The Conservative prime minister, Disraeli (now Lord Beaconsfield), saw the issue mainly as one of power politics. He did not want to weaken Turkey because he thought this would strengthen Russia.

Disraeli on Foreign Policy, 1877

AM I TO UNDERSTAND from the noble duke that in his mind the only element of this great Eastern question is the condition of the Christian subjects of the Porte [*the Turkish government—Ed.*]? I am sure that he, a statesman who has had to do with public affairs, could hardly attempt to enforce a proposition so fundamentally weak. Surely, when the noble duke calls upon us to join with the other powers of Europe to form a compact body in order that we may effect the object he desires, he cannot have forgotten that the assembled powers of Europe, when they have to consider this great Eastern question, have to consider something else besides the mere amelioration of the condition of the Christian subjects of the Porte. Surely some of the elements of the distribution of power in the world are involved in it. It is a question in which is involved the existence of empires; and really it does appear to me we shall never come to its solution—which probably may happen in the lives of some whom I am now addressing, though not in my own—if we are to discard from it every political consideration, and to believe that the only element with which we have to deal is the amelioration of the condition of the Christian subjects of the Porte. To my mind it is quite clear that if the powers of Europe work in that direction only, and work, as they probably would if they worked in that direction only, without the energy necessary, their interference would only aggravate the condition of the Christian subjects of the Porte and bring about those very calamities of which we have had such recent and such bitter experience. If this

Hansard, 3d series, CCXXXII, cols, 51–52.

matter is really to be treated it must be treated by statesmen; we must accurately know who are to be responsible hereafter for the condition of this population; we must know what changes in the distribution of territory in the most important part of the globe are to be made as the consequence of this attempted solution; and it is only by considerations of that kind—it is only by bringing our minds, free from all passion, to a calm and sagacious consideration of this subject, and viewing it as statesmen, that we can secure the great interests of this country, which are too often forgotten in declamatory views of circumstances with which we have to deal practically—it is in this way only we can secure an amelioration in the condition of the population of the Ottoman empire.

Gladstone had decided to retire from politics in 1874, but he was outraged by Disraeli's foreign policy and attacked it in 1878.

Gladstone on Foreign Policy, 1878

FROM THE BEGINNING of the Congress to the end,[1] the representatives of England, instead of taking the side of freedom, emancipation and national progress, took . . . the side of servitude, of reaction and of barbarism. With a zeal worthy of a better cause, they laboured to reduce the limits within which the populations of European Turkey are to be masters of their own destinies; to keep as much as they could of direct Turkish rule; and to enfeeble as much as they could the limitations upon that rule. Nor was this only to restrain or counterwork the influence of Russia. For, upon the record, they have done more than any other Power to assist Russia in despoiling Roumania of her Bessarabian territory; and they have worked energetically against Greece, which represented the only living anti-Russian force in the Levant. . . . The honour which the Government have earned for us at Berlin, is that of having used the name and influence, and even, by their preparations, the military power of England, to set up the principles of Metternich, and to put down the principles of Canning. We, who have helped Belgium, Spain, and Portugal to be free, we who led the way in the establishment of free Greece, and gave no mean support to the liberation and union of Italy, have at Berlin wrought actively to limit everywhere the area of self-government, and to save from the wreck as much as possible of a domination which has contributed more than any other that ever existed to the misery, the debasement, and the extermination of mankind. . . .

Disraeli neglected the Christian peoples of Eastern Europe and also pursued an imperialistic policy in India which led to pressure on Afghanistan. Gladstone challenged Disraeli on both these issues in the election campaign of 1879.

[1] Gladstone referred to the Congress of Berlin, where Disraeli played a leading role.

A. T. Bassett, ed., *Gladstone's Speeches*, pp. 343, 349–350, 359, 371–372, 374, 376, 378. Methuen and Co., Ltd., London, 1916. Reprinted by permission.

Campaigning in the Midlothian district of Scotland, Gladstone performed the considerable feat of riveting the attention of thousands of Scottish working men and women—who had problems enough of their own—on the plight of oppressed Afghans and Bulgarians. In the course of his speeches Gladstone presented a liberal philosophy of foreign policy conceived of as a branch of morality.

Gladstone's Second Midlothian Speech, November 1879

. . . WITH REGARD TO THE special occasion which has brought us here to-night, I understand it to be your wish that I should use some words addressed to the particular share that ladies, and that women, may be thought to have in the crisis of to-day. I use the expression women with greater satisfaction than the former one which I uttered, the name of ladies; because it is to them, not only in virtue of a particular station, not only by reason of their possessing a greater portion of the goods of life than may have been granted to the humbler classes of society, that I appeal. I appeal to them in virtue of the common nature which runs through us all. And I am very glad, sir, that you have introduced to us with a special notice the factory girls of the place, who on this occasion have been desirous to testify their kindly feelings. I hope you will convey to them the assurance that their particular act is not forgotten, and that the gift they offer is accepted with as lively thankfulness and as profound gratification as the most splendid offering that could be tendered by the noblest in the land.

I speak to you, ladies, as women; and I do think and feel that the present political crisis has to do not only with human interests at large, but especially with those interests which are most appropriate, and ought to be most dear, to you. The harder, and sterner, and drier lessons of politics are little to your taste. You do not concern yourselves with abstract propositions. It is that side of politics, which is associated with the heart of man, that I must call your side of politics. . . . You have seen during last winter from time to time that from such and such a village [in Afghanistan] attacks had been made upon the British forces, and that in consequence the village had been burned. Have you ever reflected on the meaning of these words? Do not suppose that I am pronouncing a censure, for I am not, either upon the military commanders or upon those who acted subject to their orders. But I am trying to point out the responsibility of the terrible consequences that follow upon such operations. Those hill tribes had committed no real offence against us. We, in the pursuit of our political objects, chose to establish military positions in their country. If they resisted, would not you have done the same? And when, going forth from their villages they had resisted, what you find is this, that those who went forth were slain, and that the village was burned. Again I say, have you considered the meaning of these words? The meaning of the burning of the village is, that the women and the children were driven forth to perish in the snows of winter. Is not that

W. E. Gladstone, "Second Midlothian Speech," in *Political Speeches in Scotland*, pp. 89–90, 92–94, 158–163. Andrew Elliot, Edinburgh, 1879. Reprinted by permission.

a terrible supposition? Is not that a fact—for such, I fear, it must be reckoned to be—which does appeal to your hearts as women, which does lay a special hold and make a special claim upon your interest, which does rouse in you a sentiment of horror and grief, to think that the name of England, under no political necessity, but for a war as frivolous as ever was waged in the history of man, should be associated with consequences such as these?

I have carried you from South Africa to Central Asia. I carry you from Central Asia to Eastern Europe, and in the history of Eastern Europe in the last few years do you not again feel that this is no matter of dry political argument; that there was a wider theatre upon which for many generations a cruel and a grinding oppression, not resting upon superior civilisation, not upon superior knowledge, but a domination of mere force, had crushed down to the earth races who, four or five hundred years ago, greatly excelled our own forefathers in civilisation—had crushed these races to the earth, had abated in them the manhood and the nobler qualities that belong to freedom—had ground these qualities, it appeared, in some cases almost out of their composition—had succeeded in impressing upon them some of the features of slaves; and in addition to this, when from time to time the impulses of humanity would not be repressed, and an effort was made by any of these people to secure to themselves their long-lost liberties, these efforts had been put down with a cruelty incredible and unequalled, almost and perhaps entirely unequalled in the annals of mankind; and not only with that cruelty, but with a development of other horrors in the treatment of men, women, and children, which even decency does not permit me to describe? I will not dwell further on these matters than to say that I think in all these scenes, if peace be our motto, we must feel that a strong appeal is made to you as women—to you specially, and to whatever there is in men that associates itself with what is best and most peculiar in you.

. . . Do not suffer appeals to national pride to blind you to the dictates of justice.

Remember the rights of the savage, as we call him. Remember that the happiness of his humble home, remember that the sanctity of life in the hill villages of Afghanistan among the winter snows, is as inviolable in the eye of Almighty God as can be your own. Remember that He who has united you together as human beings in the same flesh and blood, has bound you by the law of mutual love; that that mutual love is not limited by the shores of this island, is not limited by the boundaries of Christian civilisation; that it passes over the whole surface of the earth, and embraces the meanest along with the greatest in its unmeasured scope. And, therefore, I think that in appealing to you ungrudgingly to open your own feelings, and bear your own part in a political crisis like this, we are making no inappropriate demand, but are beseeching you to fulfil a duty which belongs to you, which, so far from involving any departure from your character as women, is associated with the fulfilment of that character, and the performance of its duties; the neglect of which would in future times be to you a source of pain and just mortification, and the fulfilment of which will serve to gild your own future years with sweet remembrances, and to warrant you in hoping that, each in your own place and sphere, you have raised your voice for justice, and have striven to mitigate the sorrows and misfortunes of mankind.

* * *

A vote of thanks was, on the motion of Mr. Tod, by acclamation accorded to Mr. Gladstone, who then left the town, passing down rows of torch-bearers drawn up to illuminate the streets in his honour.

Gladstone's Speech in the Waverley Market, Edinburgh, November 1879

GENTLEMEN, YOU HAVE spoken, in one line of your Address, of the unhappy position in which England stands, in which Great Britain will stand—the United Kingdom will stand—if it should be found to be in opposition to the interests of the struggling provinces and principalities of the East. Now, gentlemen, I wish to lay before you my view upon that subject, because there are some who tell us that we are not contending for liberty, but contending for despotism, and that the result of our policy will be that when the power of the Turkish Government ceases to sway the Eastern provinces of Europe, it will be replaced by another despotic Empire—the Empire of Russia. That, gentlemen, is not your view nor your desire, neither is it mine, and I wish to avail myself of this occasion for the purpose of clearly putting and clearly answering one question of vast importance—"Who is it that ought to possess, who is it that ought to sway, those rich and fertile countries which are known as composing what is called the Balkan Peninsula?"

It seems, gentlemen, to be agreed that the time has come, that the hour is about to strike, if it has not struck already, when all real sway of Turkish power over those fair provinces must cease, if it were only by reason of impotence. Who, then, is to have the succession to Turkey? Gentlemen, from the bottom of my heart, and with the fullest conviction of my understanding, I will give you the reply—a reply which, I am perfectly certain, will awaken a free, a generous, an unanimous echo in your bosoms. That succession is not to pass to Russia. It is not to pass to Austria. It is not to pass to England, under whatever name of Anglo-Turkish Convention or anything else. It is to pass to the people of those countries; to those who have inhabited them for many long centuries; to those who had reared them to a state of civilisation when the great calamity of Ottoman conquest spread like a wild wave over that portion of the earth, and

W. E. Gladstone, "Speech in the Waverly Market, Edinbugh," November 1879. From *Political Speeches in Scotland*. Reprinted by permission.

buried that civilisation under its overwhelming force. Those people, gentlemen, are already beginning to enjoy the commencement of liberty. Four or five million Roumanians, who were formerly subject to Turkey, are now independent. Two million Servians, once political slaves, are now absolutely free. Three hundred thousand heroes such as Christendom cannot match—the men of Montenegro—who for four hundred years have held the sword in the hand, and never have submitted to the insolence of despotic power—those men at last have achieved not only their freedom, but the acknowledgment of their freedom, and take their place among the States of Europe. Bulgaria has reached a virtual independence. . . . Gentlemen, let us place the sympathies of this country on the side of the free.

. . . Your gathering here to-day in almost countless thousands I regard as a festival of freedom, of that rational freedom which is alone secure, of that freedom best known to us, which is essentially allied with order and with loyalty. And I hope, gentlemen, that you will carry with you a determination, on the one hand, to do all you can in your civil and your social capacities for maintaining that precious possession of yours, and for handing it down to your posterity; and, on the other hand, for endeavouring by every lawful and honourable means, through the exercise of the vast moral influence of this country, and through all instruments which may from time to time be comfortable to the principle of justice, for the extension of that inestimable blessing to such races and nations of the world as hitherto have remained beyond the range of its happy and ennobling influence.

6

The Irish Question:
Limits to Liberalism

The people of Ireland were never content under English rule. Irish leaders usually worked for reform through the English Parliament, but sometimes they threatened violent revolution.

Francis Thomas Meagher's "Secession Speech," 1846

I DO NOT ABHOR the use of arms in the vindication of national rights. There are times when arms will alone suffice, and when political ameliorations call for a drop of blood, and many thousand drops of blood. Opinion, I admit, will operate against opinion. But, as the honourable member for Kilkenny observed, force must be used against force. The soldier is proof against an argument, but he is not proof against a bullet. The man that will listen to reason, let him be reasoned with; but it is the weaponed arm of the patriot that can alone avail against battalioned despotism. Then, my lord, I do not disclaim the use of arms as immoral, nor do I believe it is the truth to say, that the God of heaven withholds his sanction from the use of arms. From that night in which, in the valley of Bethulia, He nerved the arm of the Jewish girl to smite the drunken tyrant in his tent, down to the hour in which He blessed the insurgent chivalry of the Belgian priests, His Almighty hand hath ever been stretched forth from His throne of light, to consecrate the flag of freedom—to bless the patriot sword. Be it for the defence, or be it for the assertion of a nation's liberty, I look upon the sword as a sacred weapon. And if, my lord, it has sometimes reddened the shroud of the oppressor—like the anointed rod of the high priest, it has, as often, blossomed into flowers to deck the freeman's brow. Abhor the sword? Stigmatise the sword? No, my lord, for in the passes of the Tyrol it cut to pieces the banner of the Bavarian, and through those cragged passes cut a path to fame for the peasant insurrectionist of Innsbruck. Abhor the sword? Stigmatise the sword? No, my lord, for at its blow, and in the quivering of its crimson light

The Nation, 1 August 1846. Reprinted by permission.

a giant nation sprang up from the waters of the Atlantic, and by its redeeming magic the fettered colony became a daring, free Republic.

Meagher's attempt at a rebellion was easily suppressed. He was convicted of sedition and transported to Tasmania. Eventually he reached America and fought on the Northern side in the Civil War.

A major grievance of the Irish was the mistreatment of peasant tenants by the agents of absentee landlords, often English. Michael Davitt, a founder of the Irish National Land League, spoke against the system in 1880.

Michael Davitt on Landlords and Tenants

AN AVERAGE LANDLORD may be likened to a social vulture hovering over the heads of the people. . . . The tenants in the past have stood by like a flock of frightened sheep, timid and terrified, unable to prevent this human bird of prey from devouring their own and their children's substance. . . . Is it possible that our fathers could have tolerated such a giant wrong . . . as an inevitable decree of God, to be borne in meek submission . . . ? Such, however, is not our resolve. We accept no such blasphemous excuse for the abrogation of our manhood. . . .

We demand the right to live like civilised men in our [own] land; we demand the right to enjoy life here, and we are resolved to labour unitedly and unceasingly for the privilege to do so. . . . The principles upon which this land movement rests are founded upon obvious and natural justice. . . . In demanding the land for the people we are but claiming the right which is ours in virtue of our creation and the decrees of our creator. Land was created for man's sustenance, and declared to be the property of the human family, to be worked by labour and made productive in food for the children of men. To hold that, because robbery and fraud have succeeded in gaining possession of the soil of Ireland, landlordism was in the divine intention . . . is a doctrine opposed alike to reason and common sense. Landlordism has worked the deadliest wrong to our country and our race. . . . Strike down this giant fraud upon a people, and peace and plenty will take the place of disturbance and starvation. Give labour its claim upon the wealth it creates, remove the restrictions which this feudal code places upon the proper cultivation of the soil of Ireland, and the charity of other lands will no more be appealed to on our behalf, or our national pride be humiliated by our being exhibited in the eyes of the world as a nation of paupers. . . . The cause of Ireland today is that of humanity and labour throughout the world, and the sympathy of all civilised people is with us in the struggle. Stand together, then, in this contest for the soil of your fatherland, and victory will soon crown your efforts with success. Remember with courage and with pride that seven hundred years of wrong [have] failed to crush the soul of Ireland.

The Freeman's Journal, 2 February, 1880. Reprinted by permission.

Irish grievances gave rise to sporadic outbreaks of violence. English governments responded by severe repression in a series of Coercion Acts. English repression further inflamed Irish nationalism. In the 1880s Charles Stuart Parnell, a Protestant aristocrat became the leader of a movement for Irish Home Rule.

Parnell on Home Rule, Cork, 1885

. . . AT THE ELECTION in 1880 I laid certain principles before you, and you accepted them (applause, and cries of "we do"). I said and I pledged myself, that I should form one of an independent Irish party to act in opposition to every English government which refused to concede the just rights of Ireland (applause). And the longer time which is gone by since then, the more I am convinced that that is the true policy to pursue so far as parliamentary policy is concerned, and that it will be impossible for either or both of the English parties to contend for any long time against a determined band of Irishmen acting honestly upon these principles, and backed by the Irish people (cheers). But we have not alone had that object in view—we have always been very careful not to fetter or control the people at home in any way, not to prevent them from doing any thing by their own strength which it is possible for them to do. Sometimes, perhaps, in our anxiety in this direction we have asked them to do what is beyond their strength, but I hold that it is better even to encourage you to do what is beyond your strength even should you fail sometimes in the attempt than to teach you to be subservient and unreliant (applause). You have been encouraged to organize yourselves, to depend upon the rectitude of your cause for your justification, and to depend upon the determination which has helped Irishmen through many centuries to retain the name of Ireland and to retain her nationhood. Nobody could point to any single action of ours in the house of commons or out of it which was not based upon the knowledge that behind us existed a strong and brave people, that without the help of the people our exertions would be as nothing, and that with their help and with their confidence we should be, as I believe we shall prove to be in the near future, invincible and unconquerable (great applause). . . . I come back, and every Irish politician must be forcibly driven back, to the consideration of the great question of national self-government for Ireland (cheers). I do not know how this great question will be eventually settled. I do not know whether England will be wise in time and concede to constitutional arguments and methods the restitution of that which was stolen from us towards the close of the last century . . . but no man has the right to fix the boundary to the march of a nation (great cheers). No man has a right to say to his country, "Thus far shalt thou go and no further," and we have never attempted to fix the *ne plus ultra* to the progress of Ireland's nationhood, and we never shall (cheers).

The Freeman's Journal, 22 January, 1885. Reprinted by permission.

In 1886 Gladstone finally became convinced of the need to grant Home Rule, but this was a bitterly controversial policy. To many, even among the Liberals, it seemed "a dismemberment of the United Kingdom." Also, religious animosities were involved. One popular slogan of the time was "Home Rule means Rome Rule."

Gladstone on the Home Rule Bill, 8 April 1886

. . . Sir, I would almost venture, trusting to the indulgent interpretation of the House, to say that the coercion we have heretofore employed has been spurious and ineffectual coercion, and that if there is to be coercion—which God forbid—it ought to be adequate to attain its end. If it is to attain its end it must be different, differently maintained, and maintained with a different spirit, courage, and consistency compared with the coercion with which we have been heretofore familiar.

Well, Sir, what are the results that have been produced? This result above all—and now I come to what I consider to be the basis of the whole mischief— that rightly or wrongly, yet in point of fact, law is discredited in Ireland, and discredited in Ireland upon this ground especially—that it comes to the people of that country with a foreign aspect, and in a foreign garb. These Coercion Bills of ours, of course—for it has become a matter of course—I am speaking of the facts and not of the merits—these Coercion Bills are stiffly resisted by the Members who represent Ireland in Parliament. The English mind, by cases of this kind and by the tone of the Press towards them, is estranged from the Irish people and the Irish mind is estranged from the people of England and Scotland. . . .

. . . Well, now, if it be true that resolute coercion ought to take the place of irresolute coercion—if it be true that our system, such as I have exhibited it, has been—we may hide it from ourselves, we cannot hide it from the world—a failure in regard to repressive legislation, will that other coercion, which it is possible to conceive, be more successful? I can, indeed, conceive and in history we may point to circumstances in which coercion of that kind, stern, resolute, consistent, might be, and has been, successful. But it requires, in my judgment, two essential conditions, and these are—the autocracy of Government, and the secrecy of public transactions. With those conditions, that kind of coercion to which I am referring might possibly succeed. But will it succeed in the light of day, and can it be administered by the people of England and Scotland against the people of Ireland by the two nations which, perhaps, above all others upon earth—I need hardly except America—best understand and are most fondly attached to the essential principles of liberty?

Now, I enter upon another proposition to which I hardly expect broad exception can be taken. I will not assume, I will not beg, the question, whether the people of England and Scotland will ever administer that sort of effectual

A. T. Bassett, ed., "First Irish Home Rule Bill, April 1886," in *Gladstone's Speeches*, pp. 606–608, 641–642, 644. Reprinted by permission.

coercion which I have placed in contrast with our timid and hesitating repressive measures; but this I will say, that the people of England and Scotland will never resort to that alternative until they have tried every other. Have they tried every other? Well, some we have tried, to which I will refer. I have been concerned with some of them myself. But we have not yet tried every alternative, because there is one—not unknown to human experience—on the contrary, widely known to various countries in the world where this dark and difficult problem has been solved by the comparatively natural and simple, though not always easy, expedient of stripping law of its foreign garb, and investing it with a domestic character. I am not saying that this will succeed; I by no means beg the question at this moment; but this I will say, that Ireland, as far as I know, and speaking of the great majority of the people of Ireland, believes it will succeed, and that experience elsewhere supports that conclusion. The case of Ireland, though she is represented here not less fully than England or Scotland, is not the same as that of England or Scotland. . . .

. . . Do not let us disguise this from ourselves. We stand face to face with what is termed Irish nationality. Irish nationality vents itself in the demand for local autonomy, or separate and complete self-government in Irish, not in Imperial, affairs. Is this an evil in itself? Is it a thing that we should view with horror or apprehension? Is it a thing which we ought to reject or accept only with a wry face, or ought we to wait until some painful and sad necessity is incumbent upon the country, like the necessity of 1780 or the necessity of 1793? Sir, I hold that it is not. . . .

These, Sir, are great facts. I hold that there is such a thing as local patriotism, which, in itself, is not bad, but good. The Welshman is full of local patriotism—the Scotchman is full of local patriotism; the Scotch nationality is as strong as it ever was, and should the occasion arise—which I believe it never can—it will be as ready to assert itself as in the days of Bannockburn. I do not believe that the local patriotism is an evil. I believe it is stronger in Ireland even than in Scotland. Englishmen are eminently English, Scotchmen are profoundly Scotch; and, if I read Irish history aright, misfortune and calamity have wedded her sons to her soil. The Irishman is more profoundly Irish; but it does not follow that, because his local patriotism is keen, he is incapable of Imperial patriotism. There are two modes of presenting the subject. The one is to present what we now recommend as good, and the other to recommend it as a choice of evils. Well, Sir, I have argued the matter as if it were a choice of evils. . . . But, in my own heart, I cherish the hope that this is not merely the choice of the lesser evil, but may prove to be rather a good in itself. . . . I ask that in our own case we should practise, with firm and fearless hand, what we have so often preached. . . . I ask that we should apply to Ireland that happy experience which we have gained in England . . . where the course of generations has now taught us, not as a dream of a theory, but as practice and as life, that the best and surest foundation we can find to build upon is the foundation afforded by the affections, the convictions, and the will of the nation; and it is thus, by the decree of the Almighty, that we may be enabled to secure at once the social peace, the fame, the power, and the permanence of the empire.

Joseph Chamberlain, although a member of Gladstone's cabinet, opposed the Home Rule Bill. For the sake of radical reform he wanted "to confer upon the State larger powers" (p. 416). He had no intention of relinquishing the powers of the British Parliament. The issue of Irish nationalism seemed to him a distraction from more important business. He complained that, "Thirty-two millions of people must go without much-needed legislation because three millions are disloyal."

Chamberlain on the Home Rule Bill, 1 June 1886

WELL, SIR, WHY do we lay so much stress on this point of the representation of Ireland? It is not a merely technical point—it is not even the delight we take in the society of the hon. gentlemen opposite. We have always laid stress on this, because we have said that the effect of the bill was that it not only created a parliament in Dublin, but would also destroy the imperial parliament at Westminster. We have said and maintain that the retention of the imperial parliament in its present form and authority is necessary for the unity of the empire, and that without the representation of Ireland you cannot have a parliament at Westminster which will exercise anything like an effective or authoritative supremacy. We are anxious for the supremacy of the imperial parliament.
. . . I want to read a passage from the speech of my right hon. friend the Prime Minister. I am not going to impute to him the slightest inconsistency, I believe he has never wavered the least himself in reference to the language I am going to quote; and I believe he would speak now in exactly the same words. I only quote them because they express in better language than I could command the idea I wish to convey.[1] This is an extract from a speech of my right hon. friend delivered at Dalkeith in December 1879. The right hon. gentleman says, "One limit, and one limit only, I know to the extension of local government. It is this. Nothing can be done, in my opinion, by any wise statesman or right-minded Briton to weaken or compromise the authority of the imperial parliament, because the imperial parliament must be supreme within these three kingdoms, and nothing that creates a doubt upon that supremacy can be tolerated by any intelligent and patriotic man." That exactly expresses the opinion which I hold and which I want to impress on the House. But is there any man here who can maintain that this bill does not weaken the supremacy of the imperial parliament—that does not throw doubt upon it? . . .

[1]Gladstone had in fact changed his mind about the need for Irish Home Rule, and everyone knew it—[Ed.].

Hansard, 3d series, pp. 681–682.

Although Chamberlain declared that he accepted Home Rule in principle and objected only to specific features of Gladstone's measure, he later said that his purpose was "to kill the Bill." One of his arguments was that Protestant Ulster should be excluded from any future settlement with Ireland. Irish nationalist Charles Stewart Parnell responded to this proposal.

Parnell on the Home Rule Bill, 7 June 1886

THE RIGHT HON. MEMBER for West Birmingham (Mr. Chamberlain) has claimed for Ulster—and I suppose that the right hon. member for East Edinburgh, when the proper time comes, will support him in that claim—a separate legislature for the province of Ulster. Well, sir, you would not protect the loyal minority of Ireland even supposing you gave a separate legislature to the province of Ulster, because there are outside the province of Ulster over 400,000 Protestants who would still be without any protection so far as you propose to give them protection. You would make the position of those 400,000 Protestants, by taking away Ulster from them, infinitely less secure. But you would not even protect the Protestants in Ulster, because the Protestants, according to the last census, were in the proportion of 52 to 48 Catholics; and we have every reason to believe that now the Protestants and Catholics in Ulster are about equal in number. At all events, however that may be, the Nationalists have succeeded in returning the majority of Ulster members, and consequently we have the Nationalists in a majority in Ulster. . . . So that you would have the Nationalist will to deal with in Ulster even if Ulster had a separate legislature; and the very first thing that the Ulster legislature would do would be to unite itself with the Dublin legislature. . . No, sir, we cannot give up a single Irishman. We want the energy, the patriotism, the talents and the work of every Irishman to insure that this great experiment shall be a successful one. . . .

Ireland has never injured the right hon. gentleman the member for West Birmingham. I do not know why he . . . should have thrown his sword into the scale against Ireland. I am not aware that we have either personally or politically attempted to injure the right hon. gentleman, yet he and his kind seek to dash this cup from the lips of the Irish people. . . .

Now, sir, what does it all come to? It comes to two alternatives when everything has been said and everything has been done. One alternative is the coercion which Lord Salisbury put before the country, and the other is the alternative offered by the Prime Minister, carrying with it the lasting settlement of a treaty of peace. . . . During the last five years, I know, sir, there have been very severe and drastic coercion bills; but it will require an even severer and more drastic measure of coercion now. You will require all that you have had during the last five years, and more besides. What, sir, has that coercion been?

The Freeman's Journal, 22 January 1885. Reprinted by permission.

You have had, sir, during those five years—and I do not say this to inflame passion or to awaken bitter memories—you have had during those five years the suspension of the Habeas Corpus Act; you have had a thousand of your Irish fellow-subjects held in prison without specific charge, many of them for long periods of time, some of them for twenty months, without trial and without any intention of placing them upon trial—I think of all those thousand persons arrested under the Coercion Act of the late Mr Forster scarcely a dozen were put on their trial; you have had the Arms Acts; you have had the suspension of trial by jury—all during the last five years. You have authorised your police to enter the domicile of a citizen, of your fellow-subject in Ireland, at any hour of the day or night, and to search every part of this domicile, even the beds of the women, without warrant. You have fined the innocent for offences commited by the guilty; you have taken power to expel aliens from the country; you have revived the curfew law and the blood-money of your Norman conquerors; you have gagged the press and seized and suppressed newspapers; you have manufactured new crimes and offences, and applied fresh penalties unknown to your laws for these crimes and offences. All this you have done for five years, and all this and much more you will have to do again. . . . But, sir, I refuse to believe that these evil days must come. I am convinced that there are a sufficient number of wise and just members in this House to cause it to disregard appeals made to passion and to pocket, and to choose the better way of the Prime Minister—the way of founding peace and goodwill among nations; and when the numbers in the division lobby come to be told, it will also be told, for the admiration of all future generations, that England and her parliament, in this nineteenth century, was wise enough, brave enough, and generous enough to close the strife of centuries, and to give peace, prosperity, and happiness to suffering Ireland.

The outcome was that ninety-two members of the Liberal party deserted Gladstone and voted with Chamberlain against the Bill. They later formed a separate Liberal Unionist Party. Home Rule was defeated by a vote of 341 to 311. Gladstone resigned. The twentieth-century solution, which detached six dominantly Protestant counties of Ulster from the rest of Ireland, remains controversial.

7

Liberalism: Two Modern Views

FROM *The Liberal Tradition*
BY *A. Bullock and M. Shock*

THE LIBERAL PARTY lasted as an effective political force for not more than seventy years. It can scarcely be said to have existed before Gladstone joined Palmerston's government in 1859 and after 1931 it was reduced to a handful of members in the House of Commons. The Liberal tradition has had a longer history and a more lasting influence.

The permanent achievements of that tradition are embodied in the British Constitution; it is still to be found at work in both the other parties, Labour and Conservative. Outside party politics it has deeply affected education (especially in the universities) and the administration of the law. It has remained the strongest element in the philosophy of government evolved by the civil service and by local authorities. It has inspired the transformation of a colonial empire into a commonwealth of nations. There is not a single institution in the country which has not felt the impact of these ideas while at the deeper level of instinctive feeling they have become a part of the national character, finding expression in the tradition of "fair play."

. . . Two ideas recur again and again. The first is a belief in the value of freedom, freedom of the individual, freedom of minorities, freedom of peoples. The scope of freedom has required continual and sometimes drastic re-defining, as in the abandonment of *laissez-faire* or in the extension of self-government to the peoples of Asia and Africa. But each re-definition has represented a deepening and strengthening, not an attenuation, of the original faith in freedom.

The second is the belief that principle ought to count far more than power or expediency, that moral issues cannot be excluded from politics. Liberal attempts to translate moral principles into political action have rarely been successful and neglect of the factor of power is one of the most obvious criticisms of Liberal thinking about politics, especially international relations. But neglect of the factor of conscience, which is a much more likely error, is equally disastrous in the long run. The historical role of Liberalism in British history has been

A. Bullock and M. Shock, *The Liberal Tradition from Fox to Keynes*, pp. liii–lv. Reprinted by permission.

to prevent this, and again and again to modify policies and the exercise of power by protests in the name of conscience.

We began this introduction by underlining the intellectual incoherence of the Liberal tradition unless it is seen as an historical development. We end it by pointing to the belief in freedom and the belief in conscience as the twin foundations of Liberal philosophy and the element of continuity in its historical development. Politics can never be conducted by the light of these two principles alone, but without them human society is reduced to servitude and the naked rule of force. This is the truth which the Liberal tradition has maintained . . . and which still needs to be maintained in our own time.

The above reading presents a favorable view of liberal principles. Another modern critic offers a more skeptical analysis. He sees an unresolved conflict between the demands for liberty and for state-supported social welfare.

FROM *The Liberal Mind*

BY *K. R. Minogue*

THE STORY OF LIBERALISM, as liberals tell it, is rather like the legend of St. George and the dragon. After many centuries of hopelessness and superstition, St. George, in the guise of Rationality, appeared in the world somewhere about the sixteenth century. The first dragons upon whom he turned his lance were those of despotic kingship and religious intolerance. These battles won, he rested a time, until such questions as slavery, or prison conditions, or the state of the poor, began to command his attention. During the nineteenth century, his lance was never still, prodding this way and that against the inert scaliness of privilege, vested interest, or patrician insolence. But, unlike St. George, he did not know when to retire. The more he succeeded, the more he became bewitched with the thought of a world free of dragons, and the less capable he became of ever returning to private life. He *needed* his dragons. He could only live by fighting for causes—the people, the poor, the exploited, the colonially oppressed, the underprivileged and the underdeveloped. As an ageing warrior, he grew breathless in his pursuit of smaller and smaller dragons—for the big dragons were now harder to come by.

Liberalism is a political theory closely linked these days with such democratic machinery as checks and balances in government, an uncontrolled press, responsible opposition parties, and a population which does not live in fear of arbitrary arrest by the government. A liberal state is one where most actions of the government are taken with the consent of at least a majority of the population. A liberal political philosophy is a description of this kind of state, combined with the attempt to work out the general principles which can best ratio-

K. R. Minogue, *The Liberal Mind*, pp. 1–2, 64–66, 181–188. Methuen and Co., Ltd., London, 1963. Reprinted by permission.

nalize it. A fair case could be made for John Locke as its founding father, even though the actual term "liberalism" was only imported from Spain early in the nineteenth century. In their early formulations, liberal philosophers built an edifice of doctrine upon the natural rights of man. Their successors, blooded by idealist criticism and Marxist social theory, admitted that the "individual" was an abstract and implausible hero for a political doctrine. Men, liberals came to agree, were largely moulded by the social environment in which they grew, and to talk of "natural rights" bordered on metaphysical dogmatism. Indeed, as time went on, they did not merely admit their error; they positively rushed to embrace the corrections which Marxists and Idealists forced upon them—for reasons which should become clear. Out of this intellectual foray emerged modern liberal doctrine, representing political life as the struggle by which men make their society rational, just, and capable of affording opportunities for everyone to develop his own potentialities.

*   *   *

. . . Liberalism advocates the elimination of poverty and illiteracy by the provision of welfare; and it is most recognizably liberal when it recommends these policies as ingredients of, or means to, freedom.

We may observe immediately that in this respect, modern liberalism may be sharply distinguished from classical liberalism. Classical liberalism advocated a system of government which permitted the maximum room for self-provision; each family was expected to make its own arrangements; economic success was a carrot to encourage people to work, poverty was an indispensable spur. It is one of the ideological triumphs of modern liberalism that this classical version seems to us nothing more than a crude veil over the naked operations of the capitalist system, for we have become accustomed to estimating political doctrines in terms of the interests they appear to serve. What we must remember, however, is that the classical doctrine of self-provision was explicitly a moral doctrine, and one which must be discussed on its own moral ground.

The classical doctrine of self-provision was partly based on a sound distrust of political interference. It took government as no more than an instrument for keeping order; anything else was meddling. This point of view no doubt benefited the interests of some rather than others, just as the doctrine of State regulation similarly benefits some rather than others. But it was also based upon a strong dislike of the State setting itself up as a father. . . . The espousal of State provision is perhaps the most important change that has taken place in the development of modern liberalism.

State provision is supported partly by arguments from justice and partly by arguments—as we have noted—from freedom. Yet, if our interpretation of freedom is correct, the freedom argument is a mistake. Provision by the State of welfare and education does not necessarily promote freedom, and it may be positively inimical to it. Yet while the confident assertions of ideologies are often mistaken, there is usually a reason for their mistakes. And the reason why welfare is mistakenly assumed to be a means to freedom is that welfare is something *independently* supported. In other words, liberals would seek to promote welfare whether it conduced to freedom or not.

Modern liberalism, then, supports welfare irrespective of its bearing upon freedom. One reason for this emerges out of what we have called the suffering situation. Liberals seek to relieve generalized kinds of suffering, and it is plausible to argue that those who suffer are not free.

But we can find a more interesting reason why modern liberalism supports welfare if we extend the ends-means chain a little further. We have seen that, in liberal argument, welfare is a means to freedom. But what is a means to welfare? The classical liberal would immediately reply: "Self-help." His modern successor would shake his head and point to the handicaps which the poor endure. Hence he would advocate State provision, something which requires the development of new administrative and political techniques. And this extension of State regulation and provision can be presented as a necessity, for there is indeed no other way in which welfare can be provided in a modern State.

A clear grasp of this point not only bears directly upon the question of freedom; it also explains what we may call the paradox of simultaneous omnipotence and impotence of the people. It was the fashion not so long ago to talk of the "century of the common man." Democracy is now something almost universally supported because it allows the people, rather than the privileged few, to determine what governments should do. Yet, at the same time, each individual appears to be more and more impotent in the face of governmental control. What has happened is that whereas before many problems were things to be solved by some group of people organizing themselves, now all problems, having become social problems, can only be solved by putting pressure on the government to do something about them.

The significance of this situation is much clearer if we turn to those countries of the world which, in the jargon of liberal ideology, are called "underdeveloped." These countries have, even more strongly than others, the liberal conviction that the present time is "transitional." Once they had a stable past; sometime in the future they will again arrive at a stable industrialized point, but for the moment the most real thing about them is simply movement. This is, of course, pure illusion, and the expectation of some point of rest in the future merely utopian. Nevertheless, this conviction has imposed on these countries what we may call the politics of the gap. It provides a single overriding aim—that of industrialization—which has become a moral and national purpose. The condition of freedom in these countries is thought to be the closing of this gap.

The frenetic and impatient industrialization which has resulted is no doubt a matter of necessity; for where some western techniques have been introduced, they have created problems which can only be solved by further importation. Population increase due to medical advance is an obvious example. The solving of these problems requires enormous energy; there is the difficulty of understanding things which had previously been of no interest, and that of organizing and coordinating a national effort. What makes the difficulties even greater is a nationalist impatience to do everything quickly; the pace must be forced in the hope that the effort can then be relaxed. Now all of this is too much for individuals or for voluntary organizations. Each individual is weak and fallible. All agree that the gap must be closed, but there are many countervailing considerations—wanting to consume immediately, personal enmities, traditional rights, building up family or clan influence, simple laziness, and so on. Here in fact is the kind of situation which was uniquely rationalized by Rousseau's general will. In this situation individuals are perfectly prepared to be forced to be free, for they have, so to speak, invested their moral capital in the government as the only organizing centre of the national effort. Once that is done, there quite genuinely need to be no nonsense about democratic liberties or the counting of heads at elections. . . .

* * *

The bearing of this on freedom is perfectly clear. A populace which hands its moral initiative over to a government, no matter how impeccable its reasons, becomes dependent and slavish. If the national tradition is in any case one of political dependence, then this will simply perpetuate the tradition. But even in countries which have a long tradition of individual enterprise and voluntary initiative, dependence is likely to increase; and just this charge has been made against the effects of the welfare State in Britain. . . . A topical example of this kind of dependence would be the case of London's homeless—people ejected from dwellings after the Rent Act. As a political issue this was presented as one of victimization, and the only solution widely canvassed was that the authorities should hasten to provide houses for the homeless. Now it is at least possible that these people might, by co-operation, get credit facilities and build houses for themselves, something which has often been done in other countries. There would obviously be difficulties to surmount, but it is by now an almost automatic response that every problem is one to be solved by authorities; and it is liberalism which seeks, by a steady equalization of the circumstances of each individual, to make certain that no one except governments *can* initiate voluntary organizations;—*all* political initiative must be that of the pressure group.

The changes in human behaviour which we have been considering are not to be attributed solely or even primarily to modern liberalism. Yet it is preeminently liberalism which has accepted without much questioning the "necessities" on which those changes are based. Indeed, quite apart from ideology, there exists a genuine dilemma which has considerable bearing upon the future of free behaviour. The politics of national purpose always poses the alternative of governmental organizations with the corollary of dependence and servitude, or on the other hand, allowing people to develop at their own pace and in their own direction, which for good or bad reasons is often found to be too slow. There is no evading this dilemma; and it is foolish to pretend that it does not exist. Modern liberalism, to the extent to which it recognizes the dilemma, attempts to evade it by aspiration. We must try, it would say, to keep governments democratically under our control and subservient to our interests. But the question of freedom, as we have considered it, is not at all a matter of interests. It is a question, not of what is done, but of how it is done and of who does it. And it will not be answered by cant about democratic vigilance. For people whose only recourse is to put pressure on the government will, when seriously frustrated, respond by pointless turbulence.

The Outbreak
of World War I—
Who Was Responsible?

CONTENTS

QUESTIONS FOR STUDY

1   Which documents provide evidence for the Austrian responsibility? Which for the German? Which for the Russian? Which for the British? Which for the French?
2   What is the importance of the Sarajevo affair? Of the Hoyos mission?
3   Is the "blank check" appropriately named?
4   What action made war inevitable?
5   What role did the Kaiser play in bringing on the war? Lord Grey? Sazonov? Berchtold? Paleologue?
6   Which nation was most to blame? Which least?
7   What are the "underlying causes" that have been proposed for the war? How important are any or all of them compared with the events of the summer of 1914?

The discussion of the causes of the First World War continues furiously to the present day, and scholars continue to try to apply its "lessons" to contemporary problems. The ultimate causes were the European system of alliances; nationalism; economic competition; competition for glory and empire; and military rivalry. The fact remains that in the century between the Congress of Vienna and the events at Sarajevo, Europe had overcome one crisis after another without recourse to a major war. Yet the assassination of the Archduke Francis Ferdinand, heir to the Austro-Hungarian Empire, in a Bosnian town on June 28, 1914, produced a crisis that led to a general and catastrophic war. It is interesting to focus attention on the crisis of July 1914 and to trace the steps that turned a Balkan incident into a major disaster. We shall examine the July crisis in some detail and attempt to place it in its proper perspective. Its analysis is crucial for understanding the larger problem of responsibility for war.

1

The Question of Responsibility

Article 231 of the Versailles Treaty firmly placed all the blame for the war on Germany, thus opening the debate.

Article 231 of the Treaty of Versailles

THE ALLIED AND ASSOCIATED GOVERNMENTS affirm and Germany accepts the responsibility of Germany and her allies for causing all the loss and damage to which the Allied and Associated Governments and their nationals have been subjected as a consequence of the war imposed upon them by the aggression of Germany and her allies.

U. S. Department of State, *The Treaty of Versailles and After: Annotations of the Text of the Treaty*, p.413. 1947

2

A Defense of the Central Powers

The following selection is an early and direct refutation of the war-guilt clause. Count Montgelas was an official spokesman for the German republic at the Versailles discussions of responsibility for the war. He helped draft the German answer to the charge of war guilt.

FROM *The Case for the Central Powers*
BY *Max Montgelas*

1.

GERMANY PURSUED NO AIM either in Europe or elsewhere which could only be achieved by means of war.

Austria-Hungary's only aim was to maintain the *status quo.* Her first intention of rectifying her frontiers at Serbia's expense was immediately abandoned at Germany's instance, and even Sazonov was convinced of her territorial *désintéressement* by her definite statements. . . .

France aimed at recovering Alsace Lorraine, and many leading French politicians also hoped to annex the Saar basin, whilst Russia aspired to possession of Constantinople and the Straits, both Powers knowing well that these aims could not be achieved without a European war.

2.

Germany's preparations for war were on a considerably smaller scale than those made by France, having regard to the political constellation, her geographical position, the extent of her unprotected frontiers, and the number of her population. From 1913 onwards, even her actual numerical peace strength was less, in

Count Max Montgelas, *The Case for the Central Powers: An Impeachment of the Versailles, Verdict,* Part III, Section 15 (1925), pp. 200-203, translated by Constantine Vesey. Reprinted by permission of Routledge.

respect of white troops, quite apart from the steadily increasing strength of the French coloured troops.

As compared with Russia's armaments, those of Austria-Hungary were absolutely inadequate.

The Franco-Russian allies were far superior to the Central Powers as regards the amount of war material, as well as of man power at their disposal.

3.

It was a political mistake to construct a German battle fleet, instead of completing the naval defences, but even in London the proportion of ten to sixteen Dreadnoughts finally proposed by Germany was not regarded as a menace.

4.

Even after Bismarck's time the German Empire repeatedly omitted to take advantage of favourable opportunities for a war of prevention.

5.

The Russian suggestion of the first Hague Conference was not based on pure love of peace. All the Great Powers, without exception, were most sceptical as regards the question of reducing armaments; the Russian proposal of 1899 was unanimously rejected, and public opinion in France strongly opposed Campbell-Bannerman's 1907 suggestion.

Neither at the first nor the second Hague Conference was any proposal to adjust serious international conflicts, affecting the honour and vital interests of a nation, brought forward or supported by any Great Power.

6.

The world war was not decided upon at Potsdam on the 5th of July, 1914; Germany merely assented to Austria's going to war with Serbia.

The possibility that the Austro-Serbian war, like others—the Boer, Moroccan, Tripolitan, and Balkan wars—might lead to further complications, was well weighed, but the risk was thought very small, in view of the special provocation.

7.

After the publication of the Serbian reply, Germany no longer thought war advisable, even against Serbia, and only favoured strictly limited military operations, which were considered justifiable, even in London.

8.

It is true that Germany did not support the proposal to extend the time limit, and rejected the idea of a conference. She not only, however, accepted every other proposal of mediation which came from London, but proposed on her own initiative the two most suitable methods of negotiation, namely, direct conversations between Vienna and St. Petersburg, and the idea of not going beyond Belgrade, which was adopted by Grey.

Sazonov's first formula was considered unacceptable, even in London, and the second was far worse than the first.

9.

An understanding had almost been reached by the methods Germany had been the first to propose, namely, direct discussions between Vienna and St. Petersburg, and limiting the military operations against Serbia, when the Russian mobilization suddenly tore the threads asunder.

10.

The leading men knew just as well in Paris and St. Petersburg as in Berlin, that this mobilization must inevitably lead to war.

Viviani telegraphed to London on the 1st of August that the one who first orders general mobilization is the aggressor, and he saddled Germany with this responsibility, knowing that the accusation was false.

11.

France did not advise moderation in St. Petersburg during the crisis. Finding that the first attempt to do so had annoyed Sazonov, the French Government refrained from taking any further steps in this direction.

12.

France not only did not advise Russia against ordering general mobilization, but gave surreptitious advice as to how she could carry on her military preparations secretly without provoking Germany to take timely countermeasures.

13.

Russia was the first Power to order general mobilization.

France was the first Power to inform another Power officially of her decision to take part in a European war.

14.

England was never as firm in advising moderation in St. Petersburg as Germany in giving this advice to Vienna.

Unlike other British diplomats, Sir Edward Grey only realized the meaning of the Russian mobilization when it was too late, and St. Petersburg was no longer willing to put a stop to it.

15.

Germany's premature declaration of war on Russia was a political error, which can be accounted for by the immense danger of the position on two fronts; her declaration of war on France was a pure formality.

The decisive event was not this or that declaration of war, but the action which made the declaration of war inevitable, and this action was Russia's general mobilization.

16.

England declared war on Germany because she did not consider it compatible with her interests that France should be defeated a second time. Belgian interests, and the treaty of 1839, which Lord Salisbury had been prepared to sacrifice in 1887, were the reasons adduced to make it popular.

Over and above this, the naval agreement of 1912 with France compelled England to abandon her neutrality before Belgium's neutrality was violated.

17.

Greater diplomatic skill was shown by the Entente than by the Triple Alliance Powers.

By her false statements regarding Germany's preparations for war, particularly regarding the alleged priority of the German mobilization, by magnifying insignificant incidents on the frontier into invasions of French territory, and by withdrawing her covering troops to a distance of ten kilometers from the frontier, France created the prior condition in London, which Benckendorff had indicated, as far back as at the end of 1912, as necessary for England's intervention. An impression was produced in London that "the opponents of the Entente were the aggressors."

3

The July Crisis

The following Austrian account describes the setting of the murder at Sarajevo and the Serbian response.

FROM *Austrian Red Book*

Ritter von Storck, Secretary of Legation, to Count Berchtold[1]

Belgrade, June 29, 1914.

UNDER THE TERRIBLE SHOCK of yesterday's catastrophe it is difficult for me to give any satisfactory judgment on the bloody drama of Serajevo with the necessary composure and judicial calm. I must ask you, therefore, to allow me for the moment to limit myself to putting on record certain facts.

Yesterday, the 15/28, the anniversary of the battle of the Amselfeld, was celebrated with greater ceremony than usual, and there were celebrations in honour of the Servian patriot, Miloš Obilić, who in 1389 with two companions treacherously stabbed the victorious Murad.

Among all Servians, Obilić is regarded as the national hero. In place of the Turks, however, we are now looked on as the hereditary enemy, thanks to the propaganda which has been nourished under the aegis of the Royal Government and the agitation which has for many years been carried on in the press.

A repetition of the drama on the field of Kossovo seems, therefore, to have hovered before the minds of the three young criminals of Serajevo, Princip, Čabrinović and the third person still unknown, who also threw a bomb. They also shot down an innocent woman, and may therefore think that they have surpassed their model.

For many years hatred against the Monarchy has been sown in Servia. The crop has sprung up and the harvest is murder.

[1]Count Leopold von Berchtold, Austro-Hungarian Minister for Foreign Affairs, 1912–1915.

Austrian Red Book in Collected Diplomatic Documents Relating to the Outbreak of the European War, No. 1 (1915). p. 448. Reprinted by permission.

The news arrived at about 5 o'clock; the Servian Government at about 10 o'clock caused the Obilić festivities to be officially stopped. They continued, however, unofficially for a considerable time after it was dark. The accounts of eye-witnesses say that people fell into one another's arms in delight, and remarks were heard, such as: "It serves them right, we have been expecting this for a long time," or "This is revenge for the annexation."

This document is a note from the German ambassador, Tschirschky, at Vienna, to the German Chancellor, Bethmann-Hollweg. The marginal remarks are by the German emperor, Wilhelm II.

Tschirschky's Report of Austrian Opinion

The Ambassador at Vienna[1] to the Imperial Chancellor[2]

Vienna, June 30, 1914.

I hope not.

Now or never. Who authorized him to act that way? That is very stupid! It is none of his business, as it is solely the affair of Austria, what she plans to do in this case. Later, if plans go wrong, it will be said that Germany did not want it! Let Tschirschky be good enough to drop this nonsense! The Serbs must be

COUNT BERCHTOLD TOLD ME today that *everything* pointed to the fact that the threads of the conspiracy to which the Archduke fell a sacrifice, *ran together at Belgrade.* The affair was so well thought out that very young men were intentionally selected for the perpetration of the crime, against whom *only a mild punishment could be decreed.* The Minister spoke very bitterly about the Serbian plots.

I frequently hear expressed here, even among serious people, the wish that *at last a final and fundamental reckoning should be had with the Serbs.* The Serbs should first be presented with a number of demands, and in case they should not accept these, energetic measures should be taken. *I take opportunity of every such occasion to advise quietly but very impressively and seriously against too hasty steps.* First of all, they must make sure what they want to do, for so far I have heard only indefinite expressions of opinion. Then the chances of every kind of action should be carefully weighed, and it should be kept in mind that Austria-Hungary does not stand alone in the world, that it is her duty to think not only of her allies,

---

[1]Heinrich Leonhard von Tschirschky und Bögendorff, German Ambassador to Austria-Hungary, 1907–1916.
[2]Dr. Theobald von Bethmann-Hollweg, Chancellor of the German Empire, 1909–1917.

"Tschirschky's Report of Austrian Opinion," in Max Montgela and Walther Schücking, eds. *Outbreak of the World War: German Documents Collected by Karl Kautsky,* No. 7 (1924) p. 61, translated by the Carnegie Endowment for International Peace. Reprinted by permission.

disposed of, AND *that right* SOON! *Goes without saying; nothing but truisms.*

but to take into consideration the entire European situation, and especially to bear in mind the attitude of Italy and Roumania on all questions that concern Serbia.

Von Tschirschky.

On July 5 Count Alexander von Hoyos, secretary for Balkan affairs at the Austro-Hungarian Ministry of Foreign Affairs, arrived in Berlin to confer with the Germans. Hoyos' version of what he learned is presented here by Luigi Albertini, an Italian historian. As there has been some doubt about the reliability of the Hoyos account, Albertini cites an interview with Alfred Zimmermann, German undersecretary of foreign affairs, who took part in the talks.

FROM *The Origins of the War of 1914*
BY *Luigi Albertini*

WHEN QUESTIONED by the present writer Hoyos stated that at his interview with Zimmermann on the afternoon of the 5th he delivered himself of the mission entrusted to him by Berchtold, handing over a copy of Francis Joseph's letter and of the Austrian memorandum. He explained to Zimmermann that the Sarajevo outrage touched vital Austrian interests in both home and foreign affairs, that Vienna found itself compelled to arrive at a definite settlement of accounts with Serbia, but that before taking a decisive step the Austrian Government needed to be certain that its intentions met with the full approval of Berlin. Hoyos assured the present writer that he had been surprised to find Zimmermann in wholehearted agreement that Austria-Hungary could no longer tolerate Serbian provocation. The decision of the Kaiser and Bethmann-Hollweg was still awaited but there was little doubt that they would give Austria the assurance of unconditional support from Germany. Zimmermann inquired what steps Vienna proposed to take and Hoyos replied that so far no decision had been taken but that the idea was to impose severe conditions on Serbia and, if these were not accepted, go to war. Zimmermann replied that if Austria meant to act she must do so immediately without diplomatic delays which would waste precious time and give the alarm to *Entente* diplomacy.

> We at Vienna—he said—have the defect of arguing too much and changing our minds. Once a decision was taken, there should be no time lost in going into action so as to take Serbia and the chancelleries of Europe by surprise. Austrian reprisals were amply justified by the Sarajevo crime.

Zimmermann felt sure that, if this course were pursued, the conflict would remain localized, but that, should France and Russia intervene, Germany alone with her increased military strength would be able to meet them. Hoyos told

Luigi Albertini, *The Origins of the War of 1914, II* (1953), pp. 144–145, translated by Isabella M. Massey. Reprinted by permission of Oxford University Press.

him that as soon as he was in possession of the Germany reply he would return to Vienna, and a Council of Joint Ministers would be summoned. Zimmermann replied that after the Council meeting it would be desirable that no further time should be lost.

Hoyos thus continues his narrative:

> And as Tschirschky at Vienna had advised me to be very firm and detailed in my account of Austrian plans at Berlin, I carried out Berchtold's instructions by stating that, once we had beaten Serbia, we intended to partition her territory among Austria-Hungary, Bulgaria, and Albania. Zimmermann replied with a smile of satisfaction that this was a question concerning only ourselves and that he would raise no objections. Next day Bethmann officially informed Szögyény and myself in the presence of Zimmermann that it was entirely for us to decide on the measures we were to take: in whatever circumstances and whatever our decision we should find Germany unconditionally at our side in allied loyalty. Twice over he said to me, however, that in his personal opinion, with things as they were, only "immediate action against Serbia" could solve our difficulties with her. "The international situation was entirely in our favour." When I started out from Vienna, despite all that had been said by Naumann and Ganz, I did not expect to find in Berlin such instantaneous and complete understanding of our difficulties. Our design of a decisive settlement of accounts with Serbia met with no objection. On the contrary we were told that this was also the opinion of Germany and we were advised to take "immediate action." This incitement, expressed to me first by Zimmermann and then by Bethmann, made a great impression on me and I did not fail to draw attention to it in the telegram which I sent to Vienna over Szögyény's signature after the conversation.

Zimmermann, in answer to an inquiry from the present writer, wrote on 17 June 1938:

> The Wilhelmstrasse, in coming to the conclusion that the war would remain confined to Austria-Hungary and Serbia and that its spread to Europe would be avoided, went on the assumption that the Dual Monarchy would lose no time in proceeding against Serbia. To avoid the impression of exercising constraint, we unfortunately refrained from explicitly influencing our ally in the sense of this assumption. Austria-Hungary failed to act without delay and under the powerful impression of the Sarajevo murder. She allowed precious weeks to slip by in useless investigations; finally she sent an ultimatum to Serbia without making the necessary military preparations to invade Serbia immediately and occupy Belgrade in the event of a rejection, which was surely to be expected. This mistake gave the *Entente* Powers the welcome chance to exchange views and arrive at an understanding.

Bethmann-Hollweg's Relay of Kaiser Wilhelm's Position

The Imperial Chancellor to the Ambassador at Vienna

Telegram 113.
Confidential. For Your Excellency's personal
  information and guidance.

Berlin, July 6, 1914.

THE AUSTRO-HUNGARIAN AMBASSADOR yesterday delivered to the Emperor a confidential personal letter from the Emperor Franz Joseph, which depicts the present situation from the Austro-Hungarian point of view, and describes the measures which Vienna has in view. A copy is now being forwarded to Your Excellency.

I replied to Count Szögyény[1] today on behalf of His Majesty that His Majesty sends his thanks to the Emperor Franz Joseph for his letter and would soon answer it personally. In the meantime His Majesty desires to say that he is not blind to the danger which threatens Austria-Hungary and thus the Triple Alliance as a result of the Russian and Serbian Panslavic agitation. Even though His Majesty is known to feel no unqualified confidence in Bulgaria and her ruler, and naturally inclines more toward our old ally Roumania and her Hohenzollern prince, yet he quite understands that the Emperor Franz Joseph, in view of the attitude of Roumania and of the danger of a new Balkan alliance aimed directly at the Danube Monarchy, is anxious to bring about an understanding between Bulgaria and the Triple Alliance. His Majesty will, therefore, direct his minister at Sofia to lend the Austro-Hungarian representative such support as he may desire in any action taken to this end. His Majesty will, furthermore, make an effort at Bucharest, according to the wishes of the Emperor Franz Joseph, to influence King Carol to the fulfillment of the duties of his alliance, to the renunciation of Serbia, and to the suppression of the Roumanian agitations directed against Austria-Hungary.

Finally, as far as concerns Serbia, His Majesty, of course, can not interfere in the dispute now going on between Austria-Hungary and that country, as it is a matter not within his competence. The Emperor Franz Joseph may, however, rest assured that His Majesty will faithfully stand by Austria-Hungary, as is required by the obligations of his alliance and of his ancient friendship.

Bethmann-Hollweg.

---

[1] Austro-Hungarian Ambassador to Germany.

"Bethmann-Hollweg's Relay of Kaiser Wilhelm's Position," in *Outbreak of the World War: German Documents Collected by Karl Kautsky*, No. 15 (1924), pp. 78–79. Reprinted by permission.

Already on July 1, Victor Naumann, a German publicist close to the German foreign secretary, had met with Hoyos and urged an attack on Serbia. In the following selection Albertini shows that similar views were communicated by the German ambassador.

FROM *The Origins of the War of 1914*
BY *Luigi Albertini*

BUT BERLIN GAVE AUSTRIA-HUNGARY not only what Lutz describes as the "curse" of a free hand. It also gave her incitement and encouragement to take action against Serbia. We have already noted Naumann's call of 1 July on Hoyos. On 4 July Forgach drafted a note stating that he had seen Ganz, the Vienna correspondent of the *Frankfurter Zeitung,* who had that day been received by Tschirschky. Ganz had said that the German Ambassador had several times repeated to him with the obvious intention that the Ballplatz should be told of it

> that Germany would support the Monarchy through thick and thin in whatever it might decide regarding Serbia. The Ambassador had added that the sooner Austria-Hungary went into action the better. Yesterday would have been better than to-day, and to-day would be better than tomorrow.

To his English colleague Bunsen, as the latter on 5 July reported to the Foreign Office, Tschirschky said that relations between Austria and Serbia

> must be bad, and that nothing could mend them. He added that he had tried in vain to convince Berlin of this fundamental truth. Some people in Germany still persisted in believing in the efficacy of a conciliatory policy on the part of Austria towards Serbia. He himself knew better.

But after Sarajevo, even in Germany those in authority were converted to Tschirschky's thesis and he, in consequence, could speak a very different language to Berchtold than he had used on 2 July. This is shown by what Berchtold wrote to Tisza on 8 July:

> Tschirschky has just left after having told me that he has received a telegram from Berlin containing instructions from his Imperial master to emphasize here that Berlin expects the Monarchy to take action against Serbia and that Germany would not understand our letting the opportunity slip without striking a blow. . . . From other utterances of the Ambassador I could see that Germany would interpret any compromise on our part with Serbia as a confession of weakness, which would not remain without repercussions on our position in the Triple Alliance and the future policy of Germany.

Luigi Albertini, *The Origins of the War of 1914,* II (1953), pp. 150–151. Reprinted by permission.

On July 18 Dr. H. von Schoen, the Bavarian chargé d'affaires at Berlin, wrote an account of the discussions between the Germans and Austrians based on conversations with well-informed German officials.

Von Schoen's Account of the Austro-German Discussions

The Chargé d'Affaires at Berlin to the President of the Ministerial Council

Report 386.

Berlin, July 18, 1914.

I HAVE THE HONOR most respectfully to report as follows to Your Excellency concerning the prospective settlement between the Austro-Hungarian Government and Serbia, on the basis of conversations I have had with Under-Secretary of State Zimmermann, and further with the Foreign Office reporter for the Balkans and the Triple Alliance, and with the counselor of the Austro-Hungarian Embassy.

The step which the Vienna Cabinet has decided to undertake at Belgrade, and which will consist in the presentation of a note, will take place on the twenty-fifth instant. The reason for the postponement of the action to that date is that they wish to await the departure of Messrs. Poincaré and Viviani from Petersburg, in order not to facilitate an agreement between the Dual Alliance Powers on any possible counter-action. Until then, by the granting of leave of absence simultaneously to the Minister of War and the Chief of the General Staff, the Vienna authorities will have the appearance of being peacefully inclined; and they have not failed of success in their attempts to influence the press and the exchange. It is recognized here that the Vienna Cabinet has been proceeding quite cleverly in this matter, and it is only regretted that Count Tisza, who at first is said to have been against any severe action, has somewhat raised the veil of secrecy by his statement in the Hungarian House of Deputies.

As Mr. Zimmermann told me, the note, so far as has yet been determined, will contain the following demands:

1. The issuing of a proclamation by the King of Serbia which shall state that the Serbian Government has nothing to do with the Greater-Serbia movement, and fully disapproves of it.
2. The initiation of an inquiry to discover those implicated in the murder of Serajevo, and the participation of Austrian officials in this inquiry.
3. Proceedings against all who have participated in the Greater-Serbia movement.

"Von Schoen's Account of the Austro-German Discussions," in *Outbreak of the World War: German Documents Collected by Karl Kautsky*, Supplement IV No. 2 (1924), pp. 616-618. Reprinted by permission.

A respite of forty-eight hours is to be granted for the acceptance of these demands.

It is perfectly plain that Serbia can not accept any such demands, which are incompatible with her dignity as a sovereign state. Thus the result would be war.

Here they are absolutely willing that Austria should take advantage of this favorable opportunity, even at the risk of further complications. But whether they will actually rise to the occasion in Vienna, still seems doubtful to Mr. von Jagow, as it does to Mr. Zimmermann. The Under-Secretary of State made the statement that Austria-Hungary, thanks to her indecision and her desultoriness, had really become the Sick Man of Europe, as Turkey had once been, upon the partition of which, the Russians, Italians, Roumanians, Serbians and Montenegrins were now waiting. A powerful and successful move against Serbia would make it possible for the Austrians and Hungarians to feel themselves once more to be a national power, would again revive the country's collapsed economic life, and would set foreign aspirations back for years. To judge from the indignation at the bloody deed that was now dominant over the entire Monarchy, it looked as if they could even be sure of the Slav troops. In a few years, with the continuance of the operation of the Slavic propaganda, this would no longer be the case, as even General Conrad von Hötzendorf himself had admitted.

So they are of the opinion here that Austria is face to face with an hour of fate, and for this reason they declared here without hesitation, in reply to an inquiry from Vienna, that we would agree to any method of procedure which they might determine on there, even at the risk of a war with Russia. The blank power of full authority that was given to Count Berchtold's Chief of the Cabinet, Count Hoyos, who came here to deliver a personal letter from the Emperor together with a detailed memorial, went so far that the Austro-Hungarian Government was empowered to deal with Bulgaria concerning her entrance into the Triple Alliance.

In Vienna they do not seem to have expected such an unconditional support of the Danube Monarchy by Germany, and Mr. Zimmermann has the impression that it is almost embarrassing to the always timid and undecided authorities at Vienna not to be admonished by Germany to caution and self-restraint. To what extent they waver in their decisions at Vienna is shown by the circumstance that Count Berchtold, three days after he had had inquiries made here concerning the alliance with Bulgaria, telegraphed that he still had scruples about closing with Bulgaria.

So it would have been liked even better here, if they had not waited so long with their action against Serbia, and the Serbian Government had not been given time to make an offer of satisfaction on its own account, perhaps acting under Russo-French pressure.

What attitude the other Powers will take toward an armed conflict between Austria and Serbia will chiefly depend, according to the opinion here, on whether Austria will content herself with a chastisement of Serbia, or will demand territorial compensation for herself. In the first case, it might be possible to localize the war; in the other case, on the other hand, more serious complications would probably be inevitable.

The administration will, immediately upon the presentation of the Austrian note at Belgrade, initiate diplomatic action with the Powers, in the interest of the localization of the war. It will claim that the Austrian action has been just as much of a surprise to it as to the other Powers, pointing out the fact that the Emperor is on his northern journey and that the Prussian Minister of War, as well as the Chief of the Grand General Staff are away on leave of absence. (As I take the liberty to insert here, not even the Italian Government has been taken into confidence.) It will lay stress upon the fact that it is a matter of interest for all the monarchical Governments that "the Belgrade nest of anarchists" be once and for all rooted out; and it will make use of its influence to get all the Powers to take the view that the settlement between Austria and Serbia is a matter concerning those two nations alone. The mobilization of the German Army is to be refrained from, and they are also going to work through the military authorities to prevent Austria from mobilizing her entire Army, and especially not those troops stationed in Galicia, in order to avoid bringing about automatically a counter-mobilization on the part of Russia, which would force, first ourselves, and then France, to take similar measures and thereby conjure up a European war.

The attitude of Russia will, above all else, determine the question whether the attempt to localize the war will succeed.

If Russia is not determined on war against Austria and Germany, in any case, she can, in that event—and that is the most favorable factor in the present situation—very well remain inactive, and justify herself toward the Serbs by announcing that she approves of the kind of fighting that goes to work with the throwing of bombs and with revolver shots just as little as any of the other civilized nations; this, especially, so long as Austria does not render doubtful Serbia's national independence. Mr. Zimmermann assumes that both England and France, to neither of whom a war would be acceptable at the present moment, will try to exert a pacifying influence on Russia; besides that, he is counting on the fact that "bluffing" constitutes one of the most favored requisites of Russian policy, and that while the Russian likes to threaten with the sword, he still does not like so very much to draw it in behalf of others at the critical moment.

England will not prevent Austria from calling Serbia to account; it is only the destruction of the nation that she would scarcely permit, being far more likely—true to her traditions—presumably to take a stand, even in this case, for the principles of nationality. A war between the Dual Alliance and the Triple Alliance would be unwelcome to England at the present time, if only in consideration of the situation in Ireland. Should it, however, come to that, according to all opinion here, we should find our English cousins on the side of our enemies, inasmuch as England fears that France, in the event of a new defeat, would sink to the level of a Power of the second class, and that the "balance of power," the maintenance of which England considers to be necessary for her own interests, would be upset thereby.

This report from Pourtalès, German ambassador to Russia, to Bethmann-Hollweg, describes the attitude of Sazonoff, Russian minister for foreign affairs, to the growing crisis. The marginal remarks are by Kaiser Wilhelm.

Pourtalès's Report of the Russian Response

The Ambassador at Petersburg to the Imperial Chancellor

St. Petersburg, July 21, 1914.

MR. SAZONOFF, who spent several days last week at his country estate in the Government of Grodno, has been quite anxious since his return from there on account of the relations between Austria-Hungary and Serbia. He told me that he had received very alarming reports from London, Paris and Rome, and that Austria-Hungary's attitude was inspiring an increasing worry everywhere. Mr. Schebeko, too, who was in general a calm observer, reported that the feeling in Vienna against Serbia was constantly growing more bitter.

The Minister took the opportunity of giving his wrath at the Austro-Hungarian policy free rein, as usual. That the Emperor Franz Joseph and even Count Berchtold were friends of peace, Mr. Sazonoff was, it is true, willing to admit, but he said that there were very powerful and dangerous influences at work, which were constantly gaining ground in both halves of the Empire, and which did not hesitate at the idea of plunging Austria into a war, even at the risk of starting a general world conflagration.

The picture fits Petersburg much better!

One anxiously asked oneself the question whether the aged Monarch and his weak Foreign Minister would always be able to successfully oppose these influences.

Previously the belligerent elements, among which clerical intrigues also played an especially important role, had set their hopes on the dead Archduke, Franz Ferdinand. The death of the Archduke had in no way discouraged them; on the other hand, they were the very ones who were inspiring[1] the dangerous policy which Austria-Hungary was pursuing at the present moment. The actual leaders in this policy were two men, particularly, whose increasing influence appeared to the highest degree

Fool yourself, Mr. Sazonoff!

dubious—namely, Count Forgach, who is "an intriguer of the basest sort," and Count Tisza, who "is half a fool."

[1] Exclamation-point by the Emperor in the margin.

"Purtalès's Report of the Russian Response," in *Outbreak of the World War: German Documents Collected by Karl Kautsky,* No. 120 (1924), pp. 159–162. Reprinted by permission.

I replied to Mr. Sazonoff that his unmeasured reproaches against Austro-Hungarian policy appeared to me to be strongly influenced by his too great sympathy for the Serbs, and to be utterly unjustified. No sensible man could refuse to recognize the complete restraint observed by the Vienna Cabinet since the assassination at Serajevo. It seemed to me that to decide just how far Austria-Hungary was justified in holding the Serbian Government responsible for the Greater-Serbia agitations, as early as this, before the result of the inquiry concerning the assassination was known, was absolutely premature. But according to everything that was already known, one could scarcely doubt *that the Greater-Serbia agitation was stirred up under the very eyes of the Serbian Government, and that even the shameless assassination itself had been planned in Serbia.* No great nation, however, could possibly tolerate permanently the existence along its borders of a propaganda which directly threatened its own security. Should, therefore, as appearances now seemed to indicate, traces be discovered at the inquiry into the origin of the crime which pointed back to Serbia, and should it be proved that the Serbian Government had regrettably connived at the intrigues directed against Austria, then the Austro-Hungarian Government would unquestionably be justified in using strong language at Belgrade. I could not conceive that in such a case the representations of the Vienna Cabinet to the Serbian Government could meet with the objection of any Power whatsoever.

The Minister met these arguments with the assertion that the support of the Greater-Serbia propaganda in Austria-Hungary by Serbia or by the Serbian Government in any way, *had in nowise been proved.* A whole country *could not be held responsible* for *the acts of individuals.* Furthermore, the murderer of the Archduke was not even a Serbian subject. There *certainly* was a Greater-Serbia propaganda *in Austria,* but it was the result of the *bad* methods of government by which Austria had distinguished herself for ages back. Just as there was a Greater-Serbia propaganda, one heard talk also of the Italian Irredenta and of the Free-from-Rome movement. The Vienna Cabinet had not the slightest reason for complaining of the *attitude of the Serbian Government,* which, on the contrary, *was behaving itself with entire propriety.*

I interjected here that it did not suffice for members of the Serbian Government themselves to refrain from

Yes.

Right.

Yes.

Good.

Genuinely Russian.

Damnation!

participation in the anti-Austrian propaganda. Austria-
Hungary had far more reason to require that the Serbian
authorities should proceed actively against the anti-
Austrian propaganda, for it was impossible that the
Government should refuse responsibility for everything
that was going on in the country.

Right.

According to that principle, returned Mr. Sazonoff,
Russia ought to hold the Swedish Government responsible for the *anti-Russian agitation* that has been *going on
in Sweden* for about a year and a half.

*And Russia for her
spies that are
being
apprehended
everywhere!*

I pointed out that in Sweden the matter merely concerned a political agitation, and not, as in Serbia, a propaganda of action.

Mr. Sazonoff remarked in reply that those people in
Austria who were advocating proceeding against Serbia
would apparently not content themselves with making
representations at Belgrade, but that their object was the
annihilation of Serbia. I answered that I had never heard
of any object but one, namely, the "clarification" of
Austria-Hungary's relations with Serbia.

*And the best
thing, too.*

The Minister continued excitedly, saying that in any
case, Austria-Hungary, if she was absolutely determined
to disturb the peace, ought not to forget that in that event
she would *have to reckon with Europe*. Russia could not
look indifferently on at a move at Belgrade which aimed
at the humiliation (of) Serbia. I remarked that I was able
[to] *see no humiliation* in serious representations by
which Serbia was reminded of her international obligations. Mr. Sazonoff answered that it would all depend on
how the move was carried out; that in no case *should
there be any talk of an ultimatum.*

*No! with Russia,
yes! as the
perpetrator and
advocate of
regicide!!!*

Right.

It's already there!

The Minister repeatedly called attention in the
course of the conversation to the fact that, according to
information he had received, the situation was being
very seriously regarded in Paris and London also, and he
was visibly attempting to give me the impression that
even in England Austria's attitude was strongly disapproved.

He is wrong!

At the conclusion of our conversation I asked Mr.
Sazonoff what there was, in his opinion, to the alleged
plan for the union of Serbia and Montenegro, lately so
much discussed in the papers. The Minister remarked that
such a union was desired only by Montenegro, which
would of course benefit most by it. Such a union was not
being considered at all in Serbia, as the late Mr. Hartwig

had specifically emphasized in one of his last reports. At the most, all that was wanted was a closer economic relation with Montenegro, but a personal union was not in any way desired.

Mr. Sazonoff has also expressed to my Italian colleague his anxiety about the Austro-Serbian tension, and remarked at the time that Russia would *not be able to permit* Austria-Hungary to *make any threats against Serbia* or

Qui vivra verra!   to *take any military measures. "La politique de la Russie,"* said Mr. Sazonoff, *"est pacifique, mais pas passive."*

F. Pourtales

On the afternoon of July 23 the Austrians presented a list of demands to Serbia, and the Serbs were given forty-eight hours to reply. The Austrian ambassador to Belgrade was instructed to leave the country and break off diplomatic relations unless the demands were met without reservations.

The Austrian Ultimatum

THE RESULTS BROUGHT OUT by the inquiry no longer permit the Imperial and Royal Government to maintain the attitude of patient tolerance which it has observed for years toward those agitations which center at Belgrade and are spread thence into the territories of the Monarchy. Instead, these results impose upon the Imperial and Royal Government the obligation to put an end to those intrigues, which constitute a standing menace to the peace of the Monarchy.

In order to attain this end, the Imperial and Royal Government finds itself compelled to demand that the Serbian Government give official assurance that it will condemn the propaganda directed against Austria-Hungary, that is to say, the whole body of the efforts whose ultimate object it is to separate from the Monarchy territories that belong to it; and that it will obligate itself to suppress with all the means at its command this criminal and terroristic propaganda.

In order to give these assurances a character of solemnity, the Royal Serbian Government will publish on the first page of its official organ of July 26/13, the following declaration:

> The Royal Serbian Government condemns the propaganda directed against Austria-Hungary, that is to say, the whole body of the efforts whose ultimate object it is to separate from the Austro-Hungarian Monarchy territories that belong to it, and it most sincerely regrets the dreadful consequences of these criminal transactions.
>
> The Royal Serbian Government regrets that Serbian officers and officials should have taken part in the above-mentioned propaganda and thus have endangered

"The Austrian Ultimatum," in *Outbreak of the World War: German Document Collected by Karl Kautsky,* Supplement I (1924), pp. 604-605.

the friendly and neighborly relations, to the cultivation of which the Royal Government had most solemnly pledged itself by its declaration of March 31, 1909.

The Royal Government, which disapproves and repels every idea and every attempt to interfere in the destinies of the population of whatever portion of Austria-Hungary, regards it as its duty most expressly to call the attention of the officers, officials, and the whole population of the Kingdom to the fact that for the future it will proceed with the utmost rigor against any persons who shall become guilty of any such activities, activities to prevent and to suppress which, the Government will bend every effort.

This declaration shall be brought to the attention of the Royal army simultaneously by an order of the day from His Majesty the King, and by publication in the official organ of the army.

The Royal Serbian Government will furthermore pledge itself:

1. to suppress every publication which shall incite to hatred and contempt of the Monarchy, and the general tendency of which shall be directed against the territorial integrity of the latter;
2. to proceed at once to the dissolution of the *Narodna Odbrana,* to confiscate all of its means of propaganda, and in the same manner to proceed against the other unions and associations in Serbia which occupy themselves with propaganda against Austria-Hungary; the Royal Government will take such measures as are necessary to make sure that the dissolved associations may not continue their activities under other names or in other forms;
3. to eliminate without delay from public instruction in Serbia, everything, whether connected with the teaching corps or with the methods of teaching, that serves or may serve to nourish the propaganda against Austria-Hungary;
4. to remove from the military and administrative service in general all officers and officials who have been guilty of carrying on the propaganda against Austria-Hungary, whose names the Imperial and Royal Government reserves the right to make known to the Royal Government when communicating the material evidence now in its possession;
5. to agree to the cooperation in Serbia of the organs of the Imperial and Royal Government in the suppression of the subversive movement directed against the integrity of the Monarchy;
6. to institute a judicial inquiry against every participant in the conspiracy of the twenty-eighth of June who may be found in Serbian territory; the organs of the Imperial and Royal Government delegated for this purpose will take part in the proceedings held for this purpose;
7. to undertake with all haste the arrest of Major Voislav Tankositch and of one Milan Ciganovitch, a Serbian official, who have been compromised by the results of the inquiry;

8. by efficient measures to prevent the participation of Serbian authorities in the smuggling of weapons and explosives across the frontier; to dismiss from the service and to punish severely those members of the Frontier Service at Schabats and Losnitza who assisted the authors of the crime of Serajevo to cross the frontier;

9. to make explanations to the Imperial and Royal Government concerning the unjustifiable utterances of high Serbian functionaries in Serbia and abroad, who, without regard for their official position, have not hesitated to express themselves in a manner hostile toward Austria-Hungary since the assassination of the twenty-eighth of June;

10. to inform the Imperial and Royal Government without delay of the execution of the measures comprised in the foregoing points.

The Imperial and Royal Government awaits the reply of the Royal Government by Saturday, the twenty-fifth instant, at 6 P.M., at the latest.

A mémoire concerning the results of the inquiry at Serajevo, as far as they concern the functionaries referred to in Points 7 and 8, is appended to this note.

This is a report from the German ambassador at St. Petersburg to the Foreign Office in Berlin. Marginal remarks are by Kaiser Wilhelm.

Pourtalès's Report on Russia's Reaction to Austria's Ultimatum

The Ambassador at Petersburg to the Foreign Office

Telegram 149.

St. Petersburg, July 25, 1914.

Good.

HAVE JUST HAD LONG INTERVIEW with Sazonoff at which subject of dispatch 592 figured exhaustively. Minister, who was *very much excited* and gave vent to boundless reproaches against Austria-Hungary, stated in the most determined manner that it would be impossible for Russia to admit that the Austro-Serb quarrel could be settled between the two parties concerned. The obligations which Serbia had assumed after the Bosnian crisis and to which the Austrian note refers, were assumed toward Europe, consequently the affair was a European affair,

Rot!

"Pourtalés's Report on Russia's Reaction to Austria's Ultimatum," *Outbreak of the World War: German Documents Collected by Karl Kautsky,* No. 160 (1924), pp. 186–187. Reprinted by permission.

and it was for *Europe* to investigate as to whether Serbia had lived up to these obligations. He therefore proposes

That's a question of the point of view!

that the documents in relation to the inquiry be laid before the Cabinets of the six Powers. Austria could not be both accuser and judge in her own case. Sazonoff announced that he could in no way consider as proven the facts alleged by Austria in her note, that the inquiry, on the other hand, inspired him with the greatest (suspicion). He continued by saying that, in case the facts asserted should be proved to be true, Serbia could give Austria satisfaction in the purely legal questions, but not, on the other hand, in the matter of the demands of a political nature. I called attention to the fact that it was impossible to separate the legal from the political side of

Cannot be separated.

the matter, as the assassination was inseparably connected with the Greater-Serbia propaganda.

Right.
Panslavistic.
Most certainly not!

I promised to lay his ideas before my Government, but did not believe that we would suggest to our ally to submit the results of an inquiry conducted by her *once more to a European tribunal.* Austria would object to this suggestion just as any Great Power would have to refuse to submit itself to a court of arbitration in a case in which its vital interests were at stake.

Bravo!
Well said!

Not since her fraternizing with the French socialist republic!

My references to the monarchical principle made little impression on the Minister. Russia *knew* what she *owed to the monarchical principle,* with which, however, this case had nothing to do. I requested Sazonoff very seriously, avoiding everything that might have the appearance of a threat, not to let himself be led astray by his hatred of Austria and *"not to defend a bad cause."* Russia could not possibly constitute herself the advocate of *regi-*

Regicide.
Very good.

cides.

Well, go to it!

In the course of the conversation Sazonoff exclaimed: "If Austria-Hungary devours Serbia, we will go to war with her." From this it may perhaps be concluded that Russia will only take up arms in the event of Austria's

That it wants to do, it seems.

attempting to acquire territory at the expense of Serbia. The expressed desire to Europeanize the question also seems to point to the fact that immediate intervention on

Not correct.

the part of Russia is not to be anticipated.

Pourtalès.

Here is a telegram from Sir Edward Grey, British secretary of state for foreign affairs, to the British ambassador in Vienna.

Grey's Conveyal of the British Response to Austria's Ultimatum

Grey to Bunsen

Tel. (No. 148)

Foreign Office, July 24, 1914

Austro-Hungarian ambassador has communicated to me the note addressed to Servia with the explanation of the Austro-Hungarian Government upon it.

I said that the murder of the Archduke and some of the circumstances stated in the Austro-Hungarian note with regard to Servia naturally aroused sympathy with Austria, but I thought it a great pity that a time-limit, and such a short time-limit, had been introduced at this stage, and the note seemed to me the most formidable document I had ever seen addressed by one State to another that was independent. Demand No. 5 might mean that the Austro-Hungarian Government were to be entitled to appoint officials who should have authority in Servian territory and this would hardly be consistent with the maintenance of independent sovereignty of Servia.

I was not, however, making these comments in order to discuss the merits of the dispute between Austria-Hungary and Servia; that was not our concern. It was solely from the point of view of the peace of Europe that I should concern myself with the matter, and I felt great apprehension.

I must wait to hear the views of other Powers and no doubt we should consult with them to see what could be done to mitigate difficulties.

The Austro-Hungarian Ambassador observed that there had been so much procrastination on the part of Servia that a time-limit was essential. Some weeks had passed since the murder of the Archduke and Servia had made no sign of sympathy or help; if she had held out a hand after the murder the present situation might have been prevented.

I observed that a time-limit could have been introduced at any later stage if Servia had procrastinated about a reply; as it was, the Austro-Hungarian Government not only demanded a reply within forty-eight hours, but dictated the terms of the reply.

"Grey's Conveyal of the British Response to Austria's Ultimatium," in *British Documents on the Origins of the War 1898–1914,* XVI, No. 91 (1926), p.73–74. Reprinted by permission.

Grey's Proposal for a Conference

Sir Edward Grey to Sir F. Bertie

Tel. (No. 232)

Foreign Office, July 26, 1914

ASK MINISTER FOR FOREIGN AFFAIRS if he would be disposed to instruct Ambassador here to join with representatives of Italy, Germany, France, and myself in a conference to be held here at once in order to endeavour to find an issue to prevent complications. With this view representatives at Vienna, St. Petersburg and Belgrade should be authorised in informing Governments to which they are accredited of above suggestion to request that pending results of conference all active military operations shall be suspended.

(Repeated to Vienna, St. Petersburg, and Nish.)

(Sent also to Berlin, and Rome.)

Prince Lichnowsky, German ambassador to London, was in close touch with the ruling circles of England and better informed on British opinion than were his colleagues in Berlin. The following report is one of several in which he argues against war on the grounds that England would be likely to fight against Germany.

Lichnowsky's Appraisal of the British Position

The Ambassador at London to the Foreign Office

Telegram 161.

London, July 26, 1914

HAVE JUST TALKED with Sir A. Nicolson and Sir W. Tyrrell. According to reports at hand here, a general calling to the colors of the Russian reservists is not projected, but only a partial mobilization far from our frontiers. Both gentlemen see in Sir E. Grey's proposal to hold a conference *à quatre* here, the only possibility of avoiding a general war, and hope that in this way it would be possible to get full satisfaction for Austria, as Serbia would be more apt to give in to the pressure of the Powers and to submit to their united will than to the threats of Austria. But the absolute prerequisite to the bringing about of the conference and the maintenance of peace would be the cessation of all military activities. Once the Serbian border was crossed, everything would be at an end, as no Russian Government would be able to tolerate this, and would be forced to

---

"Grey's Proposal for a Conference," in *British Documents on the Origins of the War 1898–1914*, XI, No. 140 (1926), p. 101. Reprinted by permission.

move to the attack on Austria unless she wanted to see her status among the Balkan nations lost forever. Sir W. Tyrrell, who saw Sir E. Grey last evening and is fully cognizant of his views, pointed out to me repeatedly and with emphasis the immense importance of Serbia's territory remaining unviolated until the question of the conference had been settled, as otherwise every effort would have been in vain and the world war would be inevitable. The localization of the conflict as hoped for in Berlin was wholly impossible, and must be dropped from the calculations of practical politics. If we two should succeed—that is, His Majesty the Emperor or his Government and representatives in conjunction with Sir E. Grey—in preserving the peace of Europe, German–English relations would be placed on a firm foundation for time everlasting. If we did not succeed, everything would be doubtful.

I would like to offer an urgent warning against believing any further in the possibility of localization, and to express the humble wish that our policy be guided solely and alone by the need of sparing the German nation a struggle in which it has nothing to gain and everything to lose.

Sir E. Grey returns this evening.

Lichnowsky.

The response of the Serbians was remarkably reasonable, but it was not unconditional acceptance of the ultimatum.

Serbia's Answer to the Ultimatum

THE ROYAL SERVIAN GOVERNMENT have received the communication of the Imperial and Royal Government of the 10th instant, and are convinced that their reply will remove any misunderstanding which may threaten to impair the good neighbourly relations between the Austro-Hungarian Monarchy and the Kingdom of Servia.

Conscious of the fact that the protests which were made both from the tribune of the national Skuptchina and in the declarations and actions of the responsible representatives of the State—protests which were cut short by the declarations made by the Servian Government on the 18th March, 1909—have not been renewed on any occasion as regards the great neighbouring Monarchy, and that no attempt has been made since that time, either by the successive Royal Governments or by their organs, to change the political and legal state of affairs created in Bosnia and Herzegovina, the Royal Government draw attention to the fact that in this connection the Imperial and Royal Government have made no representation except one concerning a school book, and that on that occasion the Imperial and Royal Government received an entirely satisfactory explanation. Servia has several times given proofs of her

"Serbia's Answer to Ultimatum," from *British Diplomatic Correspondence in Collected Diplomatic Documents Relating to the Outbreak of the European War*, No. 39 (1915), pp. 31–37. Reprinted by permission.

pacific and moderate policy during the Balkan crisis, and it is thanks to Servia and to the sacrifice that she has made in the exclusive interest of European peace that that peace has been preserved. The Royal Government cannot be held responsible for manifestations of a private character, such as articles in the press and the peaceable work of societies—manifestations which take place in nearly all countries in the ordinary course of events, and which, as a general rule, escape official control. The Royal Government are all the less responsible, in view of the fact that at the time of the solution of a series of questions which arose between Servia and Austria-Hungary they gave proof of a great readiness to oblige, and thus succeeded in settling the majority of these questions to the advantage of the two neighbouring countries.

For these reasons the Royal Government have been pained and surprised at the statements, according to which members of the Kingdom of Servia are supposed to have participated in the preparations for the crime committed at Serajevo; the Royal Government expected to be invited to collaborate in an investigation of all that concerns this crime, and they were ready, in order to prove the entire correctness of their attitude, to take measures against any persons concerning whom representations were made to them. Falling in, therefore, with the desire of the Imperial and Royal Government, they are prepared to hand over for trial any Servian subject, without regard to his situation or rank, of whose complicity in the crime of Serajevo proofs are forthcoming, and more especially they undertake to cause to be published on the first page of the "Journal officiel," on the date of the 13th (26th) July, the following declaration:—

> The Royal Government of Servia condemn all propaganda which may be directed against Austria-Hungary, that is to say, all such tendencies as aim at ultimately detaching from the Austro-Hungarian Monarchy territories which form part thereof, and they sincerely deplore the baneful consequences of these criminal movements. The Royal Government regret that, according to the communication from the Imperial and Royal Government, certain Servian officers and officials should have taken part in the above-mentioned propaganda and thus compromised the good neighbourly relations to which the Royal Servian Government was solemnly engaged by the declaration of the 31st March, 1909, which declaration disapproves and repudiates all idea or attempt at interference with the destiny of the inhabitants of any part whatsoever of Austria-Hungary, and they consider it their duty formally to warn the officers, officials, and entire population of the kingdom that henceforth they will take the most rigorous steps against all such persons as are guilty of such acts, to prevent and to repress which they will use their utmost endeavour.

This declaration will be brought to the knowledge of the Royal Army in an order of the day, in the name of His Majesty the King, by his Royal Highness the Crown Prince Alexander, and will be published in the next official army bulletin.

The Royal Government further undertake:—

1. To introduce at the first regular convocation of the Skuptchina a provision into the press law providing for the most severe punishment of incitement to hatred or contempt of the Austro-Hungarian Monarchy, and for taking action against any publication the general tendency of which is directed against the territorial integrity of Austria-Hungary. The Government engage at the approaching revision of the Constitution to cause an amendment to be introduced into article 22 of the Constitution of such a nature that such publication may be confiscated, a proceeding at present impossible under the categorical terms of article 22 of the Constitution.
2. The Government possess no proofs, nor does the note of the Imperial and Royal Government furnish them with any, that the "Narodna Odbrana" and other similar societies have committed up to the present any criminal act of this nature through the proceedings of any of their members. Nevertheless, the Royal Government will accept the demand of the Imperial and Royal Government, and will dissolve the "Narodna Odbrana" Society and every other society which may be directing its efforts against Austria-Hungary.
3. The Royal Servian Government undertake to remove without delay from their public educational establishments in Servia all that serves or could serve to foment propaganda against Austria-Hungary, whenever the Imperial and Royal Government furnish them with facts and proofs of this propaganda.
4. The Royal Government also agree to remove from military service all such persons as the judicial enquiry may have proved to be guilty of acts directed against the integrity of the territory of the Austro-Hungarian Monarchy, and they expect the Imperial and Royal Government to communicate to them at a later date the names and the acts of these officers and officials for the purposes of the proceedings which are to be taken against them.
5. The Royal Government must confess that they do not clearly grasp the meaning or the scope of the demand made by the Imperial and Royal Government that Servia shall undertake to accept the collaboration of the organs of the Imperial and Royal Government upon their territory, but they declare that they will admit such collaboration as agrees with the principle of international law, with criminal procedure, and with good neighbourly relations.
6. It goes without saying that the Royal Government consider it their duty to open an enquiry against all such persons as are, or eventually may be, implicated in the plot of the 15th June, and who happen to be within the territory of the kingdom. As regards the participation in this enquiry of Austro-Hungarian agents or authorities appointed for this purpose by the Imperial and Royal Government, the Royal Government cannot accept such an arrangement, as it would be a violation of the Constitution and of the

law of criminal procedure; nevertheless, in concrete cases communications as to the results of the investigation in question might be given to the Austro-Hungarian agents.

7. The Royal Government proceeded, on the very evening of the delivery of the note, to arrest Commandant Voislav Tankossitch. As regards Milan Ziganovitch, who is a subject of the Austro-Hungarian Monarchy and who up to the 15th June was employed (on probation) by the directorate of railways, it has not yet been possible to arrest him.

   The Austro-Hungarian Government are requested to be so good as to supply as soon as possible, in the customary form, the presumptive evidence of guilt, as well as the eventual proofs of guilt which have been collected up to the present, at the enquiry at Serajevo for the purposes of the later enquiry.

8. The Servian Government will enforce and extend the measures which have been taken for preventing the illicit traffic of arms and explosives across the frontier. It goes without saying that they will immediately order an enquiry and will severely punish the frontier officials on the Schabatz-Loznitza line who have failed in their duty and allowed authors of the crime of Serajevo to pass.

9. The Royal Government will gladly give explanations of the remarks made by their officials whether in Servia or abroad, in interviews after the crime which according to the statement of the Imperial and Royal Government were hostile towards the Monarchy, as soon as the Imperial and Royal Government have communicated to them the passages in question in these remarks, and as soon as they have shown that the remarks were actually made by the said officials, although the Royal Government will itself take steps to collect evidence and proofs.

10. The Royal Government will inform the Imperial and Royal Government of the execution of the measures comprised under the above heads, in so far as this has not already been done by the present note, as soon as each measure has been ordered and carried out.

   If the Imperial and Royal Government are not satisfied with this reply, the Servian Government, considering that it is not to the common interest to precipitate the solution of this question, are ready, as always, to accept a pacific understanding, either by referring this question to the decision of the International Tribunal of The Hague, or to the Great Powers which took part in the drawing up of the declaration made by the Servian Government on the 18th (31st) March 1909.

Belgrade, July 12 (25), 1914

Bethmann-Hollweg's Reaction to the British Proposal

The Imperial Chancellor to the Ambassador at Vienna

Telegram 169.

Berlin, July 27, 1914.

Prince Lichnowsky has just telegraphed:

SIR E. GREY had me call on him just now and requested me to inform Your Excellency as follows:

The Serbian Chargé d'Affaires had just transmitted to him the text of the Serbian reply to the Austrian note. It appeared from the reply that Serbia had agreed to the Austrian demands to an extent such as he would never have believed possible; except in one point, the participation of Austrian officials in the judicial investigation, Serbia had actually agreed to everything that had been demanded of her. It was plain that this compliance of Serbia's *was to be attributed solely to the pressure exerted from Petersburg.*

Should Austria fail to be satisfied with this reply, in other words, should this reply not be accepted at Vienna as a foundation for peaceful negotiations, or should Austria even proceed to the occupation of Belgrade, which lay quite defenseless before her, it would then be absolutely evident that Austria was only seeking an excuse for crushing Serbia. And thus, that Russia and Russian influence in the Balkans were to be struck at through Serbia. It was plain that Russia could not regard such action with equanimity, and would have to accept it as a direct challenge. The result would be the most frightful war that Europe had ever seen, and no one could tell to what such a war might lead.

We had repeatedly, and even yesterday, stated the Minister, turned to him with the request that he *make a plea for moderation at Petersburg. He had always gladly complied with this request* and during the last crisis had subjected himself to reproaches from Russia to the effect that he was placing himself too much on our side and too little on theirs. Now he was turning to us with the request that we should make use of our influence at Vienna either to get them to accept the reply from Belgrade as satisfactory or as the basis for conferences. He was convinced that it lay in our hands to bring the matter to a settlement by means of the proper representations, and he would regard it as a good augury for the future *if we two should once again succeed in assuring the peace of Europe by means of our mutual influence on our allies.*

I found the Minister irritated for the first time. He spoke with great seriousness and seemed absolutely to expect that we should successfully make use of our influence to settle the matter. He is also going to make a statement in the House of

Bethmann-Hollweg's Reaction to the British Proposal in *Outbreak of the World War: German Documents Collected by Karl Kautsky,* No.277 (1924), pp. 255–256. Reprinted by permission.

Commons today in which he is to express his point of view. In any event, I am convinced that in case it should come to war after all, we should no longer be able to count on British sympathy or British support, as every evidence of ill-will would be seen in Austria's procedure.

Since we have already refused one English proposal for a conference, it is impossible for us to waive *a limine* this English suggestion also. By refusing every proposition for mediation, we should be held responsible for the conflagration by the whole world, and be set forth as the original instigators of the war. That would also make our position impossible in our own country, where we must appear as having been forced into the war. Our situation is all the more difficult, inasmuch as Serbia has apparently yielded to a very great degree. Therefore we cannot refuse the mediator's role, and must submit the English proposal to the consideration of the Vienna Cabinet, especially as London and Paris continue to make their influence felt in Petersburg. I request Count Berchtold's opinion on the English suggestion, as likewise his views on Mr. Sazonoff's desire to negotiate directly with Vienna.

Bethmann-Hollweg.

Goschen was the British ambassador to Berlin. In the following telegram he reports the German answer to the proposal for a conference to Grey.

Goschen's Transmission of the German Refusal

Sir E. Goschen to Sir Edward Grey

Tel. (No. 96)

Berlin, July 27, 1914

Your telegram No. 232 of 26th of July to Paris.

SECRETARY OF STATE FOR FOREIGN AFFAIRS says that conference you suggest would practically amount to a court of arbitration and could not, in his opinion, be called together except at the request of Austria and Russia. He could not therefore, desirous though he was to cooperate for the maintenance of peace, fall in with your suggestion. I said I was sure that your idea had nothing to do with arbitration, but meant that representatives of the four nations not directly interested should discuss and suggest means for avoiding a dangerous situation. He maintained, however, that such a conference as you proposed was not practicable. He added that news he had just received from St. Petersburg showed that there was an intention on the part of M. Sazonof to exchange views with Count Berchtold. He thought that this method of procedure might lead to a satisfactory

"Goschen's Transmission of the German Refusal" in *British Documents on the Origins of the War 1898–1914*, XI, No. 185 (1926), pp. 128–129. Reprinted by permission.

result, and that it would be best, before doing anything else, to await outcome of the exchange of views between the Austrian and Russian Governments.

In the course of a short conversation Secretary of State for Foreign Affairs said that as yet Austria was only partially mobilising, but that if Russia mobilised against Germany latter would have to follow suit. I asked him what he meant by "mobilising against Germany." He said that if Russia only mobilised in south Germany would not mobilise, but if she mobilised in north Germany would have to do so too, and Russian system of mobilisation was so complicated that it might be difficult exactly to locate her mobilisation. Germany would therefore have to be very careful not to be taken by surprise.

In the crucial days following the rejection of the ultimatum, France seems not to have tried to restrain Russia. The following telegram was omitted from the Russian Orange Book.

French Full Support of Russia

*The Russian Ambassador at Paris, M. Isvolsky,
to the Russian Foreign Secretary, M. Sazonov*

Telegram. Secret. No. 195

Paris, July 14/27, 1914

IMMEDIATELY UPON MY RETURN to Paris, I saw the Minister of Justice [Bienvenu-Martin] in the presence of Abel Ferry and Berthelot. They confirmed the details of the steps taken by the German Ambassador, of which you have been informed by Sevastopoulo's telegrams Nos. 187 and 188. This morning, Baron Schoen confirmed in writing the declaration made by him yesterday, to wit:

1. "Austria has declared to Russia that she is not seeking territorial acquisitions and will respect the integrity of Serbia. Her only aim is to assure her own security;
2. "The prevention of war consequently rests upon Russia;
3. "Germany and France entirely united in the ardent desire to maintain peace, ought to press Russia to be moderate."

In this connection Baron Schoen particularly emphasized the expression "united" [*solidaire*] applied to Germany and France. According to the conviction of the Minister of Justice, these steps on the part of Germany are taken with the evident object of disuniting Russia and France, of inducing the French Government to make representations at St. Petersburg, and of thus compromising our ally in our eyes, and, in case of war, of throwing the responsibility not on

"French Full Support of Russaia; in *Readings in European International Relations* by W. Henry Cook and Edith P. Stickney. Copyright 1931 by Harper & Row, Publshers, Inc. Reprinted by permission of Harper & Row, Publishers, Inc.

Germany, who is ostensibly making every effort to preserve peace, but on Russia and France. Today, two hours before the steps taken by the Austrian Ambassador reported in my telegram 191, the German Ambassador paid a visit to Abel Ferry and made him, in the name of his Government, a new proposition "of intervention of France and Germany between Russia and Austria." Abel Ferry replied to him that he would bring this proposal to the attention of the Minister of Justice and merely observed that it would be opportune to leave the initiative of intervention to the four Powers, to which Baron Schoen acquiesced. The Minister of Justice has told me that he does not understand the sense of the new proposal of Baron Schoen, but that he viewed it with defiance and proposed to tell him tomorrow that a reply would be given him on the return to Paris of the Minister of Foreign Affairs on Wednesday. Altogether, I am struck by the way the Minister of Justice and his colleagues correctly understand the situation and how firm and calm is their decision to give us the most complete support and to avoid the least appearance of divergence of view between us.

Isvolsky.

The Kaiser's Reaction to Serbia's Reply

The Emperor to the Secretary of State for Foreign Affairs

Your Excellency:

New Palace, July 28, 1914, 10 A.M.

AFTER READING OVER THE SERBIAN REPLY, which I received this morning, I am convinced that on the whole the wishes of the Danube Monarchy have been acceded to. The few reservations that Serbia makes in regard to individual points could, according to my opinion, be settled by negotiation. But it contains the announcement *orbi et urbi* of a capitulation of the most humiliating kind, and as a result, *every cause for war* falls to the ground.

Nevertheless, the piece of paper, like its contents, can be considered as of little value so long as it is not translated into *deeds*. The Serbs are Orientals, therefore liars, tricksters, and masters of evasion. In order that these beautiful promises may be turned to truth and facts, a *douce violence* must be exercised. This should be so arranged that Austria would receive a HOSTAGE (Belgrade), as a guaranty for the enforcement and carrying out of the promises, and should occupy it until the *petita* had ACTUALLY been complied with. This is also necessary in order to give the army, now UNNECESSARILY mobilized for the third time, the external *satisfaction d'honneur* of an ostensible success in the eyes of the world, and to make it possible for it to feel that it had at least stood on foreign soil. Unless this were done, the abandonment of the campaign might be the

"The Kaiser's Reaction to Serbia's Reply" in *Outbreak of the World War: German Documents Collected by Karl Kautsky,* No. 293 (1924) pp. 273–274. Reprinted by permission.

cause of a wave of bad feeling against the Monarchy, which would be dangerous in the highest degree. In case Your Excellency shares my views, I propose
that we say to Austria: Serbia has been forced to retreat in a very humiliating
manner, and we offer our congratulations. Naturally, as a result, EVERY CAUSE FOR
WAR HAS VANISHED. But a GUARANTY that the promises WILL BE CARRIED OUT is
unquestionably necessary. That could be secured by means of the TEMPORARY
military occupation of a portion of Serbia, similar to the way we kept troops stationed in France in 1871 until the billions were paid. ON THIS BASIS, I am ready
to MEDIATE FOR PEACE with Austria. Any proposals or protests to the contrary by
other nations I should refuse regardless, especially as all of them have made
more or less open appeals to me to assist in maintaining peace. This I will do
in my own way, and as sparingly of Austria's NATIONALISTIC FEELING, and of the
HONOR OF HER ARMS as possible. For the latter has already been appealed to on
the part of the highest War Lord, and is about to respond to the appeal. Consequently it is absolutely necessary that it receive a visible *satisfaction d'honneur;* this is the *prerequisite* of my mediation. Therefore Your Excellency will
submit a proposal to me along the lines sketched out; which shall be communicated to Vienna. I have had Plessen write along the lines indicated above to
the Chief of the General Staff, who is entirely in accord with my views.

Wilhelm I. R.

Austria's Reception of Serbia's Reply

The Austro-Hungarian Ambassador to the Foreign Office

Memorandum

Berlin, July 27, 1914.

THE ROYAL SERBIAN GOVERNMENT has refused to agree to the demands which we
were forced to make for the lasting assurance of those of our vital interests
threatened by that Government, and has thus given evidence that it is not willing to desist from its destructive efforts directed toward the constant disturbance
of some of our border territories and their eventual separation from the control
of the Monarchy. We are therefore compelled, to our regret and much against
our will, to force Serbia by the sharpest means to a fundamental alteration of
her hitherto hostile attitude. That in so doing, aggressive intentions are far from
our thoughts, and that it is merely in self-defense that we have finally determined, after years of patience, to oppose the Greater-Serbia intrigues with the
sword, is well known to the Imperial German Government.

It is a cause of honest satisfaction to us that we find both in the Imperial
German Government and in the entire German people a complete comprehen-

"Austria's Reception of Serbia's Reply," in *Outbreak of the World War: German Documents Collected by Karl Kautsky*, No. 268 (1924), p. 249. Reprinted by permission.

sion of the fact that our patience was of necessity exhausted after the assassination at Serajevo, which, according to the results of the inquiry, was planned at Belgrade and carried out by emissaries from that city; and that we are now forced to the task of securing ourselves by every means against the continuation of the present intolerable conditions on our southeastern border.

We confidently hope that our prospective difference with Serbia will be the cause of no further complications; but in the event that such should nevertheless occur, we are gratefully certain that Germany, with a fidelity long proven, will bear in mind the obligations of her alliance and lend us her support in any fight forced upon us by another opponent.

The following telegrams from Bethmann-Hollweg to Tschirschky have often been taken as evidence for a change of heart at Berlin and the beginning of a policy of restraining Austria.

Bethmann-Hollweg's Telegrams to Tschirschky

The Imperial Chancellor to the Ambassador at Vienna

Telegram 174.
Urgent.

Berlin, July 28, 1914.

THE AUSTRO-HUNGARIAN GOVERNMENT has distinctly informed Russia that it is not considering any territorial acquisitions in Serbia. This agrees with Your Excellency's report to the effect that neither the Austrian nor the Hungarian statesmen consider the increase of the Slavic element in the Monarchy to be desirable. On the other hand, the Austro-Hungarian Government has left us in the dark concerning its intentions, despite repeated interrogations. The reply of the Serbian Government to the Austrian ultimatum, which has now been received, makes it clear that Serbia has agreed to the Austrian demands to so great an extent that, in case of a completely uncompromising attitude on the part of the Austro-Hungarian Government, it will become necessary to reckon upon the gradual defection from its cause of public opinion throughout all Europe.

According to the statements of the Austrian General Staff, an active military movement against Serbia will not be possible before the 12th of August. As a result, the Imperial Government is placed in the extraordinarily difficult position of being exposed in the meantime to the mediation and conference proposals of the other Cabinets, and if it continues to maintain its previous aloofness in the face of such proposals, it will incur the odium of having been responsible for a world war, even, finally, among the German people them-

"Bethmann-Hollweg's Telegrams to Tschirschky," in *Outbreak of the World War: German Documents Collected by Karl Kautsky*, No. 323 (1924), pp 288–289, and No. 395 (1924), pp. 344–345. Reprinted by permission.

selves. A successful war on three fronts cannot be commenced and carried on on any such basis. It is imperative that the responsibility for the eventual extension of the war among those nations not originally immediately concerned should, under all circumstances, fall on Russia. At Mr. Sazonoff's last conversation with Count Pourtalès the Minister already conceded that Serbia would have to receive her "deserved lesson." At any rate the Minister was no longer so unconditionally opposed to the Austrian point of view as he had been earlier. From this fact it is not difficult to draw the conclusion that the Russian Government might even realize that, once the mobilization of the Austro-Hungarian Army had begun, the very honor of its arms demanded an invasion of Serbia. But it will be all the better able to compromise with this idea if the Vienna Cabinet repeats at Petersburg its distinct declaration that she is far from wishing to make any territorial acquisitions in Serbia, and that her military preparations are solely for the purpose of a temporary occupation of Belgrade and certain other localities on Serbian territory in order to force the Serbian Government to the complete fulfilment of her demands, and for the creation of guaranties of future good behavior—to which Austria-Hungary has an unquestionable claim after the experiences she has had with Serbia. An occupation like the German occupation of French territory after the Peace of Frankfurt, for the purpose of securing compliance with the demands for war indemnity, is suggested. As soon as the Austrian demands should be complied with, evacuation would follow. Should the Russian Government fail to recognize the justice of this point of view, it would have against it the public opinion of all Europe, which is now in the process of turning away from Austria. As a further result, the general diplomatic, and probably the military, situation would undergo material alteration in favor of Austria-Hungary and her allies.

Your Excellency will kindly discuss the matter along these lines thoroughly and impressively with Count Berchtold, and instigate an appropriate move at St. Petersburg. You will have to avoid very carefully giving rise to the impression that we wish to hold Austria back. The case is solely one of finding a way to realize Austria's desired aim, that of cutting the vital cord of the Greater-Serbia propaganda, without at the same time bringing on a world war, and, if the latter cannot be avoided in the end, of improving the conditions under which we shall have to wage it, in so far as is possible.

Wire report.

Bethmann-Hollweg.

The Imperial Chancellor to the Ambassador at Vienna

Telegram 192.
Urgent.

Berlin, July 30, 1914.

THE IMPERIAL AMBASSADOR at London telegraphs:

Sir E. Grey just sent for me again. The Minister was entirely calm, but very grave, and received me with the words that the situation was continuing to grow more acute. Sazonoff had stated that after the declaration of war he will no longer be in a position to negotiate with Austria direct, and *had requested them here to take up the mediation efforts again.* The Russian Government regards the cessation of hostilities for the present as a necessary preliminary to mediation.

Sir E. Grey repeated his suggestion already reported, that we take part in a mediation *à quatre,* such as we had already accepted in principle. It would seem to him to be a suitable basis for mediation, if Austria, after occupying Belgrade, for example, or other places, should announce her conditions. Should Your Excellency, however, undertake mediation, a prospect I was able early this morning to put before him, this would of course suit him equally well. But *mediation* seemed now to him to be urgently necessary, if *a European catastrophe were not to result.*

Sir E. Grey then said to me that he had a friendly and private communication to make to me, namely, that he did not want our warm personal relations and the intimacy of our talks on all political matters to lead me astray, and he would *like to spare himself later the reproach (of) bad faith.* The British Government desired now as before to cultivate our previous friendship, and it could *stand aside as long as the conflict remained confined to Austria and Russia. But if we and France should be involved,* the situation would immediately be alerted, and the British Government would, *under the circumstances, find itself forced to make up its mind quickly.* In that event *it would not be practicable to stand aside and wait for any length of time.* "If war breaks out, it will be *the greatest catastrophe that the world has ever seen."* It was far from his desire to express any kind of a threat; he only wanted to protect me from disappointments and *himself* from the *reproach of bad faith,* and had therefore chosen the form of a private explanation.

As a result we stand, in case Austria refuses all mediation, before a conflagration in which England will be against us; Italy and Roumania to all appearances will not go with us, and we two shall be opposed to four Great Powers. On Germany, thanks to England's opposition, the principal burden of the fight would fall. Austria's political prestige, the honor of her arms, as well as her just claims against Serbia, could all be amply satisfied by the occupation of Belgrade or of other places. She would be strengthening her status in the Balkans as well as in relation to Russia by the humiliation of Serbia. Under these circumstances we must urgently and impressively suggest to the consideration of the Vienna Cabinet the acceptance of mediation on the above-mentioned honorable conditions. The responsibility for the consequences that would otherwise follow would be an uncommonly heavy one both for Austria and for us.

Bethmann-Hollweg.

*At 9:15 on July 27, more than two hours before Bethmann-Hollweg sent his
telegram to Tschirschky, Count Laszlo Szögyény, the Austrian ambassador to Berlin,
sent the following report to Vienna. The reliability of Szögyény's account has been
challenged, but Luigi Albertini defends it and thinks that "No stronger shaft of light
could fall on the guilt and duplicity of the German Government."*

FROM *The Origins of the War of 1914*
BY *Luigi Albertini*

THE SECRETARY OF STATE told me very definitely in a strictly confidential form that
in the immediate future mediation proposals from England will possibly
(eventuell) be brought to Your Excellency's knowledge by the German
Government. The German Government, he says, tenders the most binding
assurances that it in no way associates itself with the proposals, is even decidedly against their being considered, and only passes them on in order to conform to the English request. In so doing the Government proceeds from the
standpoint that it is of the greatest importance that England at the present
moment should not make common cause with Russia and France. Consequently
everything must be avoided that might disconnect the telegraph line between
Germany and England which till now has been in good working order. Were
Germany to say flatly to Sir E. Grey that she is not willing to pass on his wishes
to Austria-Hungary, by whom England believes these wishes will sooner find
consideration if Germany is the intermediary, then the situation would arise
which, as has just been said, must at all costs be avoided. The German
Government would, moreover, in respect of any other request of England to
Vienna, assure the latter most emphatically that it in no way supports any such
demands for intervention in regard to Austria-Hungary and only passes them
on to comply with the wish of England. For instance only yesterday the English
Government approached him, the Secretary of State, through the German
Ambassador to London and directly through its own representative here,
asking him to support the wish of England in regard to a toning down by
us of the note to Serbia. He, Jagow, gave answer that he would certainly
fulfil Sir E. Grey's wish and pass on England's desire to Your Excellency, but
that he could not support it himself, since the Serbian conflict was a question of
prestige for the Austro-Hungarian Monarchy in which Germany was also
involved. He, the Secretary of State, had therefore passed on Sir E. Grey's note
to Herr von Tschirschky, but without giving him instructions to submit it to
Your Excellency; thereupon he had been able to inform the English Cabinet,
that he did not directly decline the English wish, and had even forwarded it
to Vienna. In conclusion the Secretary of State reiterated his standpoint to me
and, in order to prevent any misunderstanding, asked me to assure Your
Excellency that, also in the case just adduced, he, in acting as intermediary, was

Luigi Albertini: *The Origins of the War of 1914*, II (1953), pp. 445–446. Reprinted by permission.

not in the slightest degree in favour of consideration being given to the English wish.

On July 28 Austria declared war on Serbia. Further attempts at negotiation were made, but once military mobilization began, military considerations became paramount. Germany had always insisted that Russian mobilization would mean war, for the Schlieffen Plan demanded a quick victory before France—and particularly Russia—could be fully prepared for war. After Russia's total mobilization, the war was unavoidable. The marginal notes, and the note following the report, are once again those of the Kaiser.

Pourtalès's Report of Russian Mobilization

The Ambassador at Petersburg to the Foreign Office

Telegram 189.
Urgent.

Petersburg, July 30, 1914.

JUST HAD ONE and a half hours' conference with Sazonoff, who sent for me at midnight. Minister's purpose was to persuade me to advocate participation by my Government in a conference of four, in order to find a way to *move Austria by friendly means to drop those demands which infringe on the sovereignty of Serbia.* I confined myself to promising to report the conversation, and took the stand that any exchange of opinions appeared to me to be a very difficult if not an impossible matter now that Russia had *decided to take the fateful step of mobilization.* Russia was demanding of us to do that to Austria which Austria was being reproached for doing to Serbia; to wit, *infringing upon her rights of sovereignty.* Since Austria had promised to *consider Russian interests* by her declaration of territorial disinterestedness, which, on the part of a nation at war *meant a great deal,* the Austro-Hungarian Monarchy ought to be let alone while settling her affairs with Serbia. It would be time enough to return to the question of sparing Serbia's sovereign rights when *peace* was concluded. I added very earnestly that the whole Austro-Serbian matter took a *back seat* for the moment in

*Is Russian
mobilization a
friendly means?!*

Right.
Very good.

Good.

Pourtalès's Report of Russian Moblization," in *Outbreak of the World War: German Documents Collected by Karl Kautsky,* No. 401 (1924), pp. 348–350. Reprinted by permission.

Yes.
Nonsense! that
sort of policy
conceals within
itself the greatest
dangers for the
Czar!

the face of the *danger of a European conflagration.* I took great pains to impress the magnitude of this danger upon the Minister. Sazonoff was not to be diverted from the idea that Russia could not leave Serbia in the lurch. No Government could follow such a policy here *without seriously endangering the Monarchy.*

During the course of the conversation *Sazonoff wanted* to *argue* the inconsistency between the telegram of His Majesty the Emperor to the Czar and Your Excellency's telegraphic instructions number 134. I decid-

Nothing done as yet.

edly denied any, and pointed out that *even if we had already mobilized,* an appeal by my Most Gracious Master to the common interests of monarchs *would not be*

Right.

inconsistent with such a measure. I said that the communication I had made him this afternoon according to the instructions of Your Excellency, had been no threat, but a friendly warning in the shape of a reference to the *auto-matic effect that the mobilization here would have to have*

That was a partial mobilization of six corps for a limited purpose!

on us in consequence of the German-Austrian alliance. Sazonoff stated that the order for mobilization *could no longer possibly be retracted,* and that the *Austrian mobilization was to blame for it.*

From Sazonoff's statements I received the impression that His Majesty's telegram did not fail of an effect on the Czar, but that the Minister is busily striving to make sure that the Czar stands firm.

Pourtalès.

*If mobilization can no longer be retracted—*WHICH IS NOT TRUE*—why, then, did the Czar appeal for my mediation three days afterward without mention of the issuance of the mobilization order? That shows plainly that the mobilization appeared to him to have been precipitate, and that after it he made this move* pro forma *in our direction for the sake of quieting his uneasy conscience, although he knew that it would no longer be of any use, as he did not feel himself to be strong enough to* STOP *the mobilization. Frivolity and weakness are to plunge the world into the most frightful war, which eventually aims at the destruction of Germany. For I have no doubt left about it: England, Russia and France have* AGREED *among themselves—after laying the foundation of the* casus foederis *for us through Austria–to take the Austro-Serbian conflict for an* EXCUSE *for waging a* WAR OF EXTERMINATION *against us. Hence Grey's cynical observation to Lichnowsky "as long as the war is* CONFINED *to Russia and Austria, England would sit quiet, only when we and France* MIXED INTO IT *would he be compelled to make an active move against us("); i.e., either we are shamefully to betray our allies,* SACRIFICE *them to Russia—thereby breaking up the Triple Alliance, or we* *are to be attacked in common by the Triple Entente for our* FIDELITY TO OUR ALLIES *and punished, whereby they will satisfy their jealousy by joining in totally* RUIN-ING *us. That is the real naked situation in* nuce, *which, slowly and cleverly set going, certainly by Edward VII, has been carried on, and systematically built up by disowned conferences between England and Paris and Petersburg; finally brought to a conclusion by George V and set to work. And thereby the stupidity and ineptitude of our ally is turned into a snare for us. So the famous "*CIRCUM-SCRIPTION*" of Germany has finally become a complete fact, despite every effort of our politicians and diplomats to prevent it. The net has been suddenly thrown over our head, and England sneeringly reaps the most brilliant success of her persistently prosecuted purely* ANTI-GERMAN WORLD-POLICY, *against which we have proved ourselves helpless, while she twists the noose of our political and economic destruction out of our fidelity to Austria, as we squirm* ISOLATED *in the net. A great achievement, which arouses the admiration even of him who is to be destroyed as its result! Edward VII is stronger after his death than am I who am still alive! And there have been people who believed that England could be won over or pacified, by this or that puny measure!!! Unremittingly, relentlessly she has pursued her object, with notes, holiday proposals, scares, Haldane, etc., until this point was reached. And we walked into the net and even went into the one-ship-program in construction with the ardent hope of thus pacifying England!!! All my warnings, all my pleas were voiced for nothing. Now comes England's so-called gratitude for it! From the dilemma raised by our fidelity to the venerable old Emperor of Austria we are brought into a situation which offers England the desired pretext for annihilating us under the hypocritical cloak of justice, name-ly, of helping France on account of the reputed "balance of power" in Europe, i.e., playing the card of all the European nations in England's favor against us! This whole business must now be ruthlessly uncovered and the mask of Christian peaceableness publicly and brusquely torn from its face in public, and the phari-saical hypocrisy exposed on the pillory!! And our consuls in Turkey and India, agents, etc., must fire the whole Mohammedan world to fierce rebellion against this hated, lying, conscienceless nation of shop-keepers; for if we are to be bled to death, England shall at least lose India.*

W.

4

The Revisionist Position

The 1920s witnessed a reassessment of the question of war guilt. In England and America, particularly, scholars began to revise the general opinion that Germany and Austria were exclusively responsible. Sidney B. Fay was one of the leaders of the revisionist movement.

FROM *Origins of the World War*

BY *Sidney B. Fay*

NONE OF THE POWERS wanted a European War. Their governing rulers and ministers, with very few exceptions, all foresaw that it must be a frightful struggle, in which the political results were not absolutely certain, but in which the loss of life, suffering, and economic consequences were bound to be terrible. This is true, in a greater or less degree, of Pashitch, Berchtold, Bethmann, Sazonov, Poincaré, San Giuliano and Sir Edward Grey. Yet none of them, not even Sir Edward Grey, could have foreseen that the political results were to be so stupendous, and the other consequences so terrible, as was actually the case.

For many of the Powers, to be sure, a European War might seem to hold out the possibility of achieving various desired advantages: for Serbia, the achievement of national unity for all Serbs; for Austria, the revival of her waning prestige as a Great Power, and the checking of nationalistic tendencies which threatened her very existence; for Russia, the accomplishment of her historic mission of controlling Constantinople and the Straits; for Germany, new economic advantages and the restoration of the European balance which had changed with the weakening of the Triple Alliance and the tightening of the Triple Entente; for France, the recovery of Alsace-Lorraine and the ending of the German menace; and for England, the destruction of the German naval danger and of Prussian militarism. All these advantages, and many others, were feverishly striven and intrigued for, on all sides, the moment the War actually broke out, but this is no good proof that any of the statesmen mentioned deliberately

Sidney B. Fay: *Origins of the World War, II* (1930), pp. 547–548. Copyright 1928, 1930 by Macmillan Publishing Co; Inc. Reprinted by permission.

aimed to bring about a war to secure these advantages. One cannot judge the motives which actuated men before the War, by what they did in an absolutely new situation which arose as soon as they were overtaken by a conflagration they had sought to avert. And in fact, in the case of the two Powers between whom the immediate conflict arose, the postponement or avoidance of a European War would have facilitated the accomplishment of the ultimate advantages aimed at: Pashitch knew that there was a better chance for Serbian national unity after he had consolidated Serbian gains in the Balkan Wars, and after Russia had completed her military and naval armaments as planned for 1917; and Berchtold knew that he had a better chance of crushing the Greater Serbia danger and strengthening Austria, if he could avoid Russian intervention and a general European War.

It is also true, likewise, that the moment war was declared, it was hailed with varying demonstrations of enthusiasm on the part of the people in every country—with considerable in Serbia, Austria, Russia and Germany, with less in France, and with almost none in England. But this does not mean that the peoples wanted war or exerted a decisive influence to bring it about. It is a curious psychological phenomenon that as soon as a country engages in war, there develops or is created among the masses a frenzy of patriotic excitement which is no index of their pre-war desires. And in the countries where the demonstrations of enthusiasm were greatest, the political influence of the people on the Government was least.

Nevertheless, a European War broke out. Why? Because in each country political and military leaders did certain things, which led to mobilizations and declarations of war, or failed to do certain things which might have prevented them. In this sense, all the European countries, in a greater or less degree, were responsible. One must abandon the dictum of the Versailles Treaty that Germany and her allies were solely responsible. It was a dictum exacted by victors from vanquished, under the influence of the blindness, ignorance, hatred, and the propagandist misconceptions to which war had given rise. It was based on evidence which was incomplete and not always sound. It is generally recognized by the best historical scholars in all countries to be no longer tenable or defensible. They are agreed that the responsibility for the War is a divided responsibility. But they still disagree very much as to the relative part of this responsibility that falls on each country and on each individual political or military leader.

Some writers like to fix positively in some precise mathematical fashion the exact responsibility for the war. This was done in one way by the framers of Article 231 of the Treaty of Versailles. It has been done in other ways by those who would fix the responsibility in some relative fashion, as, for instance, Austria first, then Russia, France and Germany and England. But the present writer deprecates such efforts to assess by a precise formula a very complicated question, which is after all more a matter of delicate shading than of definite white and black. Oversimplification, as Napoleon once said in framing his Code, is the enemy of precision. Moreover, even supposing that a general consensus of opinion might be reached as to the relative responsibility of any individual country or man for immediate causes connected with the July crisis of 1914, it is by no means necessarily true that the same relative responsibility would hold for the underlying causes, which for years had been tending toward the creation of a dangerous situation.

One may, however, sum up very briefly the most salient facts in regard to each country.

Serbia felt a natural and justifiable impulse to do what so many other countries had done in the nineteenth century—to bring under one national Government all the discontented Serb people. She had liberated those under Turkish rule; the next step was to liberate those under Hapsburg rule. She looked to Russia for assistance, and had been encouraged to expect that she would receive it. After the assassination, Mr. Pashitch took no steps to discover and bring to justice Serbians in Belgrade who had been implicated in the plot. One of them, Ciganovitch, was even assisted to disappear. Mr. Pashitch waited to see what evidence the Austrian authorities could find. When Austria demanded cooperation of Austrian officials in discovering, though not in trying, implicated Serbians, the Serbian Government made a very conciliatory but negative reply. They expected that the reply would not be regarded as satisfactory, and, even before it was given, ordered the mobilization of the Serbian army. Serbia did not want war, but believed it would be forced upon her. That Mr. Pashitch was aware of the plot three weeks before it was executed, failed to take effective steps to prevent the assassins from crossing over from Serbia to Bosnia, and then failed to give Austria any warning or information which might have averted the fatal crime, were facts unknown to Austria in July, 1914; they cannot therefore be regarded as in any way justifying Austria's conduct; but they are part of Serbia's responsibility, and a very serious part.

Austria was more responsible for the immediate origin of the war than any other Power. Yet from her own point of view she was acting in self-defence— not against an immediate military attack, but against the corroding Greater Serbia and Jugoslav agitation which her leaders believed threatened her very existence. No State can be expected to sit with folded arms and await dismemberment at the hands of its neighbors. Russia was believed to be intriguing with Serbia and Rumania against the Dual Monarchy. The assassination of the heir to the throne, as a result of a plot prepared in Belgrade, demanded severe retribution; otherwise Austria would be regarded as incapable of action, "Worm-eaten" as the Serbian Press expressed it, would sink in prestige, and hasten her own downfall. To avert this Berchtold determined to crush Serbia with war. He deliberately framed the ultimatum with the expectation and hope that it would be rejected. He hurriedly declared war against Serbia in order to forestall all efforts at mediation. He refused even to answer his own ally's urgent requests to come to an understanding with Russia, on the basis of a military occupation of Belgrade as a pledge that Serbia would carry out the promises in her reply to the ultimatum. Berchtold gambled on a "local" war with Serbia only, believing that he could rattle the German sword; but rather than abandon his war with Serbia, he was ready to drag the rest of Europe into war.

It is very questionable whether Berchtold's obstinate determination to diminish Serbia and destroy her as a Balkan factor was, after all, the right method, even if he had succeeded in keeping the war "localized" and in temporarily strengthening the Dual Monarchy. Supposing that Russia in 1914, because of military unpreparedness or lack of support, had been ready to tolerate the execution of Berchtold's designs, it is quite certain that she would have aimed within the next two or three years at wiping out this second humiliation, which was so much more damaging to her prestige than that of 1908–09. In two or three years, when her great program of military reform was finally completed, Russia would certainly have found a pretext to reverse the balance in the Balkans in her own favor again. A further consequence of Berchtold's policy, even if successful, would have been the still closer consolidation of the Triple Entente, with the possible addition of Italy. And, finally, a partially dismembered Serbia would have become a still greater source of unrest and danger to the peace of Europe than heretofore. Serbian nationalism, like Polish nationalism, would have been intensified by partition. Austrian power and prestige would not have been so greatly increased as to be able to meet these new dangers. Berchtold's plan was a mere temporary improvement, but could not be a final solution of the Austro–Serbian antagonism. Franz Ferdinand and many others recognized this, and so long as he lived, no step in this fatal direction had been taken. It was the tragic fate of Austria that the only man who might have had the power and ability to develop Austria along sound lines became the innocent victim of the crime which was the occasion of the World War and so of her ultimate disruption.

Germany did not plot a European War, did not want one, and made genuine, though too belated efforts, to avert one. She was the victim of her alliance with Austria and of her own folly. Austria was her only dependable ally, Italy and Rumania having become nothing but allies in name. She could not throw her over, as otherwise she would stand isolated between Russia, where Panslavism and armaments were growing stronger every year, and France, where Alsace-Lorraine, Delcassé's fall, and Agadir were not forgotten. Therefore, Bethmann felt bound to accede to Berchtold's request for support and gave him a free hand to deal with Serbia; he also hoped and expected to "localize" the Austro–Serbian conflict. Germany then gave grounds to the Entente for suspecting the sincerity of her peaceful intentions by her denial of any foreknowledge of the ultimatum, by her support and justification of it when it was published, and by her refusal to Sir Edward Grey's conference proposal. However, Germany by no means had Austria so completely under her thumb as the Entente Powers and many writers have assumed. It is true that Berchtold would hardly have embarked on his gambler's policy unless he had been assured that Germany would fulfill the obligations of the alliance, and to this extent Germany must share the great responsibility of Austria. But when

Bethmann realized that Russia was likely to intervene, that England might not remain neutral, and that there was danger of a world war of which Germany and Austria would appear to be the instigators, he tried to call a halt on Austria, but it was too late. He pressed mediation proposals on Vienna, but Berchtold was insensible to the pressure, and the Entente Powers did not believe in the sincerity of his pressure, especially as they produced no results.

Germany's geographical position between France and Russia, and her inferiority in number of troops, had made necessary the plan of crushing the French army quickly at first and then turning against Russia. This was only possible, in the opinion of her strategists, by marching through Belgium, as it was generally anticipated by military men that she would do in case of a European War. On July 29, after Austria had declared war on Serbia, and after the Tsar had assented to general mobilization in Russia (though this was not known in Berlin and was later postponed for a day owing to the Kaiser's telegram to the Tsar), Bethmann took the precaution of sending to the German Minister in Brussels a sealed envelope. The Minister was not to open it except on further instructions. It contained the later demand for the passage of the German army through Belgium. This does not mean, however, that Germany had decided for war. In fact, Bethmann was one of the last of the statesmen to abandon hope of peace and to consent to the mobilization of his country's army. General mobilization of the continental armies took place in the following order: Serbia, Russia, Austria, France and Germany. General mobilization by a Great Power was commonly interpreted by military men in every country, though perhaps not by Sir Edward Grey, the Tsar, and some civilian officials, as meaning that the country was on the point of making war—that the military machine had begun to move and would not be stopped. Hence, when Germany learned of the Russian general mobilization, she sent ultimatums to St. Petersburg and Paris, warning that German mobilization would follow unless Russia suspended hers within twelve hours, and asking what would be the attitude of France. The answers being unsatisfactory, Germany then mobilized and declared war. It was the hasty Russian general mobilization, assented to on July 29 and ordered on July 30, while Germany was still trying to bring Austria to accept mediation proposals, which finally rendered the European War inevitable.

Russia was partly responsible for the Austro–Serbian conflict because of the frequent encouragement which she had given at Belgrade—that Serbian national unity would be ultimately achieved with Russian assistance at Austrian expense. This had led the Belgrade Cabinet to hope for Russian support in case of a war with Austria, and the hope did not prove vain in July, 1914. Before this, to be sure, in the Bosnian Crisis and during the Balkan Wars, Russia had put restraint upon Serbia, because Russia, exhausted by the effects of the Russo–Japanese War, was not yet ready for a European struggle with the Teutonic Powers. But in 1914 her armaments, though not yet completed, had made such progress that the militarists were confident of success, if they had French and British support. In the spring of 1914, the Minister of War,

Sukhomlinov, had published an article in a Russian newspaper, though without signing his name, to the effect, "Russia is ready, France must be ready also." Austria was convinced that Russia would ultimately aid Serbia, unless the Serbian danger were dealt with energetically after the Archduke's murder; she knew that Russia was growing stronger every year; but she doubted whether the Tsar's armaments had yet reached the point at which Russia would dare to intervene; she would therefore run less risk of Russian intervention and a European War if she used the Archduke's assassination as an excuse for weakening Serbia, than if she should postpone action until the future.

Russia's responsibility lay also in the secret preparatory military measures which she was making at the same time that she was carrying on diplomatic negotiations. These alarmed Germany and Austria. But it was primarily Russia's general mobilization, made when Germany was trying to bring Austria to a settlement, which precipitated the final catastrophe, causing Germany to mobilize and declare war.

The part of France is less clear than that of the other Great Powers, because she has not yet made a full publication of her documents. To be sure, M. Poincaré, in the fourth volume of his memoirs, has made a skilful and elaborate plea, to prove *"La France innocente."* But he is not convincing. It is quite clear that on his visit to Russia he assured the Tsar's Government that France would support her as an ally in preventing Austria from humiliating or crushing Serbia. Paléologue renewed these assurances in a way to encourage Russia to take a strong hand. He did not attempt to restrain Russia from military measures which he knew would call forth German counter-measures and cause war. Nor did he keep his Government promptly and fully informed of the military steps which were being taken at St. Petersburg. President Poincaré, upon his return to France made efforts for peace, but his great preoccupation was to minimize French and Russian preparatory measures and emphasize those of Germany, in order to secure the certainty of British support in a struggle which he now regarded as inevitable.

Sir Edward Grey made many sincere proposals for preserving peace; they all failed owing partly, but not exclusively, to Germany's attitude. Sir Edward could probably have prevented war if he had done either of two things. If, early in the crisis, he had acceded to the urging of France and Russia and given a strong warning to Germany that, in a European War, England would take the side of the Franco–Russian Alliance, this would probably have led Bethmann to exert an earlier and more effective pressure on Austria; and it would perhaps thereby have prevented the Austrian declaration of war on Serbia, and brought to a successful issue the "direct conversations" between Vienna and St. Petersburg. Or, if Sir Edward Grey had listened to German urging, and warned France and Russia early in the crisis, that if they became involved in war, England would remain neutral, probably Russia would have hesitated with her mobilizations, and France would probaly have exerted a restraining influence at St. Petersburg. But Sir Edward Grey could not say that England would take the side of France and Russia, because he had a Cabinet nearly evenly divided, and he was not sure, early in the crisis, that public opinion in England would back him up in war against Germany. He could resign and he says in his memoirs that he would have resigned but that would have been no comfort or aid to France who had come confidently to count upon British support. He was determined to say and do nothing which might encourage her with a hope which he could not fulfil. Therefore, in spite of the French, he refused to give them definite assurances until the probable German determination to go through Belgium made it clear that the Cabinet, and Parliament, and British public opinion would follow his lead in war on Germany. On the other hand, he was unwilling to heed the German pleadings that he exercise restraint at Paris and St. Petersburg, because he did not wish to endanger the Anglo–Russian Entente and the solidarity of the Triple Entente, because he felt a moral obligation to France, growing out of the Anglo-French military and naval conversations of the past years, and because he suspected that Germany was backing Austria up in an unjustifiable course and that Prussian militarists had taken the direction of affairs at Berlin out of the hands of Herr von Bethmann-Hollweg and the civilian authorities.

Italy exerted relatively little influence on the crisis in either direction.

Belgium had done nothing in any way to justify the demand which Germany made upon her. With commendable prudence, at the very first news of the ominous Austrian ultimatum, she had foreseen the danger to which she might be exposed. She had accordingly instructed her representatives abroad as to the statements which they were to make in case Belgium should decide very suddenly to mobilize to protect her neutrality. On July 29, she placed her army upon "a strengthened war footing," but did not order complete mobilization until two days later, when Austria, Russia, and Germany had already done so, and war appeared inevitable. Even after being confronted with the terrible German ultimatum, at 7 P.M. on August 2, she did not at once invite the assistance of English and French troops to aid her in the defense of her soil and her neutrality against a certain German assault; it was not until German troops had actually violated her territory, on August 4, that she appealed for the assistance of the Powers which had guaranteed her neutrality. Belgium was the innocent victim of German strategic necessity. Though the German violation of Belgium was of enormous influence in forming public opinion as to the responsibility for the War after hostilities began, it was not a cause of the War, except in so far as it made it easier for Sir Edward Grey to bring England into it.

In the forty years following the Franco–Prussian War, as we have seen, there developed a system of alliances which divided Europe into two hostile groups. This hostility was accentuated by the increase of armaments, economic rivalry, nationalist ambitions and antagonisms, and newspaper incitement. But it is very doubtful whether all these dangerous tendencies would have actually led to war, had it not been for the assassination of Franz Ferdinand. That was the factor which consolidated the elements of hostility and started the rapid and complicated succession of events which culminated in a World War, and for that factor Serbian nationalism was primarily responsible.

But the verdict of the Versailles Treaty that Germany and her allies were responsible for the War, in view of the evidence now available, is historically unsound. It should therefore be revised. However, because of the popular feeling widespread in some of the Entente countries, it is doubtful whether a formal and legal revision is as yet practicable. There must first come a further revision by historical scholars, and through them of public opinion.

5

The Case Against Germany

*In the years after World War I the revisionist view of its causes put forward by
historians like Sidney Fay became dominant. Most people shared Lloyd George's
opinion that the European nations had "stumbled into war." After World War II, in
the 1950s, a conference of French and German historians agreed that "the
documents do not allow one to ascribe in 1914 to any one government or people the
conscious desire for a European war." Even that cautious consensus was shattered
in 1959 by an article by the German historian Fritz Fischer—soon followed by a
large book on German war aims,* Griff nach der Weltmacht, *published in 1961—
which placed most of the blame on Germany. The essence of Fischer's view and a
brief account of the controversy is presented by Immanuel Geiss, one of his students,
in the following essay.*

FROM *The Outbreak of the First World War and German War Aims*
BY *Immanuel Geiss*

THE CRISIS OF JULY 1914

GERMAN INNOCENCE—or at least relative innocence—for the outbreak of the 1914
war had for decades been something that could not be questioned in Germany.
The function of this taboo varied according to the circumstances: in early
August 1914 it was designed to impress both the SPD and Britain, in order to
get the former into the war, and if possible to keep the latter out of it. During
the war it was to convince neutrals and Germans alike of the righteousness of
the Reich's cause. Immediately after the war, even the left-wing governments of
1918–19 clung in dealing with the Allies to the concept of German relative innocence, in the hope of getting a more lenient peace settlement. When they

Immanuel Geiss; "The Outbreak of the First World War and German War Aims," in *Journal of Contemporary
History*, Vol. I No. 3 1966. Reprinted by permission of Weidenfeld (Publishers) Limited and Harper & Row
Publishers, Inc.

failed, later governments and public opinion in the Weimar Republic retreated from the relatively critical line of these earlier governments which, after all, had published the German documents and set up a Commission of Enquiry into the causes of Germany's defeat.

The Weimar Republic opened a sustained campaign against article 231 of the Versailles treaty; it hoped, by disputing Germany's responsibility for the war, to dismantle the treaty as a whole. The campaign had started at Versailles itself, where Bülow (later Secretary of State in the Auswärtiges Amt) mapped out and initiated the strategy.[1] In the Auswärtiges Amt a small sub-section, the Kriegsschuldreferat, inspired, directed, and financed the German innocence propaganda. Its chief instruments were two organizations, the Arbeitsausschuss Deutscher Verbände (ADV), and the Zentralstelle zur Erforschung der Kreigsschuldfrage. ADV, a federation of practically all reputable semi-political organizations, including the trade unions, looked after the general propaganda, while the Zentralstelle had to cover the scholarly aspects of the campaign.

The two organizations worked together, notwithstanding occasional rivalries and bickerings behind the scenes, and the Kriegsschuldreferat saw to the necessary finances and co-ordination. Each had a periodical, the more important one for the general historian being the Zentralstelle's *Kriegsschuldfrage;* for its launching it was possible to find money even in summer 1923, at the height of the inflation. The editor of *Kriegsschuldfrage*—later renamed *Berliner Monatshefte*—was Alfred von Wegerer, an ex-army officer. For tactical reasons he posed as an independent, but he was in fact employed by the Auswärtiges Amt, in a position ranking in salary and annual leave as a *Ministerialrat*. Both the budget and the literary activities of the Zentralstelle were controlled by the Kriegsschuldreferat, which in its turn gave Wegerer valuable information for pursuing the scholarly struggle against the "Kriegsschuldlüge."

A third, more subtle instrument consisted of a host of writers, none of them historians, engaged as part-time propagandists. For a moderate but regular monthly payment of a few hundred marks they wrote three or four articles a month in German dailies and/or periodicals on the war guilt question. The most prominent among them were Bernhard Schwertfeger, an ex-Colonel, and Hermann Lutz, a free-lance writer. The appearance of Lutz on the pay-roll of the Auswärtiges Amt is the more startling since, judging from his *Gutachten* for the work of the Commission of Enquiry, he must have passed as an independent critic of the official line. A fourth means used was to subsidise publications which took the German line, although occasionally books with critical passages were allowed to pass in order not to arouse suspicions abroad. These publications ranged from *Die Grosse Politik* to insignificant pamphlets. The usual method was to buy a number of copies, often several hundred, in advance; these were afterwards sent to German missions abroad which distributed them

---

[1] What follows is only a preliminary sketch of a very complicated story, based so far on the study of about half of the rich archival material of the Kriegsschuldreferat in the Political Archive of the Auswärtiges Amt at Bonn.

free to key personalities in the respective countries. Many of the subsidised books were translations into German. (The Auswärtiges Amt subsidy was much sought after by German publishers, and it is quite possible that without the financial assistance of the Kriegsschuldreferat many a book might not have appeared.) Probably only a few foreign authors received more than this kind of subsidy: one, Boghitchevitch, living in Switzerland, was paid by the Auswärtiges Amt in gold francs, a difficult thing to manage in 1919. Most of the foreign authors supporting the German cause were probably unaware of the subsidy, though it is difficult to say how many would have minded if they had known.

The Kriegsschuldreferat decided which publications criticizing the German line were to be attacked, how, by whom, and when and where, or whether they should be simply ignored. This is what happened to a booklet by Walter Fabian, now editor of *Gewerkschaftliche Monatshefte*. Similarly, it acted as internal censor for official or semi-official publications, in particular of the Untersuchungausschuss, an effort in which it was partly supported by the latter's secretary-general, Eugen Fischer-Baling. Together, they prevented the publication of Hermann Kantorowicz's *Gutachten* for the Untersuchungsausschuss, although it was completed and set up in type as early as 1927. When, in 1932, the Untersuchungsausschuss wanted to publish five volumes of documents on German war aims, the Kriegsschuldreferat vetoed the proposal on the ground that the documents would prove to the whole world that German plans of conquest made nonsense of the German innocence campaign. Finally, the Kriegsschuldreferat prepared the many official statements of German chancellors and of President Hindenburg on the war guilt question during the Weimar period, statements which, perhaps more than anything else, helped to strengthen the taboo.

The campaign was the more effective since German historians lent it their great prestige. Most of them did not need official prompting but had only to follow their natural inclinations. Surprisingly enough, the contribution of professional German historians to a rational analysis of the causes of the war had been fairly slight. Most of the German campaigners were amateurs, and none of the few professionals who were prominently engaged (Hans Delbrück, Friedrich Thimme, Paul Herre, Erich Brandenburg, Richard Fester, Hans Rothfels, Hans Herzfeld) ever wrote anything comparable to the great works of Pierre Renouvin, Bernadotte E. Schmitt, or Luigi Albertini. The defence of the German cause was mostly left either to foreigners, such as Barnes or Fay, or to amateurs such as Wegerer or Lutz.

How effective the German innocence campaign had been became clear after the second world war. To the rest of the world this had only proved German responsibility for the first. Not so in Germany. After a few years of confusion and hesitation, which produced some criticism by Friedrich Meinecke, most German historians swung back to the old line. They contended that Germany (or rather Hitler) was responsible for the second but not for the first. There was no fresh research or re-interpretation of the causes of 1914. Although a few modifications were introduced by Gerhard Ritter, Wegerer's authority was never questioned; Albertini's massive work was almost completely ignored. The German public remained dependent on the meagre fare offered by professional historians in articles, textbooks, and short chapters or sub-chapters in a number of more general works.

* * *

It is only against this background that one can understand the terrific outburst of excitement over Fritz Fischer's book, which quickly became known as the "Fischer controversy." For Fischer not only questioned the taboo built up over five decades by successive political regimes in Germany; he also broke the monopoly of knowledge held by conservative or mildly conservative-liberal historians, in a historical problem which may well rank as one of the most complicated and bewildering in modern history. He did it just by picking up Albertini and reading the documents published since 1919.

The leading German historians rushed angrily into print to denounce Fischer and closed ranks against the heretic. Vis-à-vis Fischer they all seemed to have forgotten their former squabbles and political disagreements. Erwin Hölzle from the right joined forces with Golo Mann, Ludwig Dehio, and Hans Herzfeld of the "left," while Gerhard Ritter from his centre position turned out to be Fischer's most persistent critic. Taking real or imaginary defects as an excuse for condemning the effort as such, many concentrated their attacks on the chapter on July 1914. In the very year when their attacks reached an emotional climax in the shrill polemics of Michael Freund and Giselher Wirsing, the discussion took a turn for the better. After the initial formation of a united front against Fischer, three major groups emerged. One, led by Hans Rothfels, stuck to their traditional guns and said there was nothing to revise. A second, headed by Gerhard Ritter and Michael Freund, though criticizing the older German literature on July 1914 as "too apologetic" (Ritter) or even denouncing the traditional line as the "Unschuldslüge" (Freund), still maintained most of their old arguments.

A third group, represented by Egmont Zechlin and Karl-Dietrich Erdmann, have at least in part abandoned the old positions, although very discreetly and without giving any credit to Fischer. They now admit that Germany in July 1914 deliberately risked war, even with Britain, but they hedge this vital admission with a number of "explanations" which only tend to obscure the central issue. Zechlin argues that Bethmann Hollweg, when taking the plunge in July 1914, only wanted a limited, "rational" war in eighteenth-century style, not a ferocious world war. In two recent articles he has moved even closer to the position of those who criticize the traditional line, so that the differences between him and the Fischer group, on that point at least, have now been reduced to a few subtle shades of interpretation. On the other hand, these slight divergences give even less warrant for Zechlin's (and others') view that Fischer is all wrong, since Zechlin now maintains that Bethmann Hollweg consciously took the risk of British intervention. Erdmann gives a psychological portrait of the Chancellor, based mainly on the diary of Kurt Riezler, Bethmann Hollweg's close adviser, and stresses the Chancellor's subjective honesty, his rejection of world domination for Germany (which, unfortunately, Erdmann confuses with the alleged rejection of achieving the status of a world power). Both harp on the rediscovered story of the proposed Anglo–Russian naval convention. Still, Zechlin and Erdmann have introduced new tones into the debate and have made rational discussion possible. They set the final seal on the demolition of the traditional taboo.

Another myth has also to go for good—the myth of *Einkreisung*. There was no "encirclement" of Germany by enemies waiting to attack and crush her. The partition of Europe and the world into two power blocks, with the Triple Entente on the one hand, the Triple Alliance on the other, was largely a result of German policy, of the German desire to raise the Reich from the status of a continental power to that of a world power. The Triple Alliance itself came into being as a purely continental arrangement in the years 1879–82, in order to keep France isolated, and the Franco–Russian Alliance of 1894, the nucleus of the Triple Entente, was the French means of escaping that isolation. It was only after Germany started on her ambitious and ill-fated career of becoming a full-fledged world power in her own right that the world situation changed radically. Britain, challenged by Germany's naval programme more than by her territorial claims, notably in Africa, abandoned her "splendid isolation" and sought alliances, first with Japan in 1902, then with France in 1904, and finally, in 1907, with Russia. What was—and to a certain extent still is—denounced in Germany as *Einkreisung,* amounted to the containment of German ambitions which ran counter to the interests of all other imperialist powers.

The concept of encirclement, however, played an important part immediately before the outbreak of war in 1914. In Germany the idea had become widespread that the only choice for the Reich was between rising to a full-fledged world power and stagnation. The German *Weltanschauung* saw only the unending struggle of all against all; this social-Darwinist concept was not limited to the lunatic fringe, but influenced even the most liberal spokesman of the Wilhelmian establishment, Riezler, Bethmann Hollweg's young protégé. For him all nations had the desire for permanent expansion with world domination as the supreme goal. Since he looked upon any containment of German aspirations as a hostile act, Riezler's ideas, translated into official policy, were bound to make war unavoidable. Even Bethmann Hollweg thought in 1911 that war was necessary for the German people.

The final logical conclusion was the idea of preventive war against those enemies who tried to block Germany's further rise. The traditional school in Germany always indignantly denied the existence of the preventive war concept even among the Prussian General Staff. The prevailing spirit of militarism and social-Darwinism in Wilhelmian Germany made it, however, more than plausible. A new source, the private papers of Jagow, provides the missing link between Germany's pre-war *Weltpolitik* and the outbreak of war. At the end of May or early in June 1914 Moltke, Chief of the General Staff, asked Jagow, the German Secretary of State for Foreign Affairs, to start a preventive war as soon as possible, because militarily the situation for Germany was constantly deterio-rating. Jagow refused, pointing to the improvement in the German economic situation. But after the war he admitted that he was never *a limine* against the idea of preventive war—after all, Bismarck's wars had been preventive wars, according to Jagow—and that Moltke's words inspired him with confidence in military success when the crisis did come in July 1914. Another recent find tal-lies with Jagow's point of view. In February 1918 ex-Chancellor Bethmann Hollweg, questioned privately by the liberal politician Conrad Haussmann, said: "Yes, My God, in a certain sense it was a preventive war. But when war was hanging above us, when it had to come in two years even more dangerously and more inescapably, and when the generals said, now it is still possible, with-out defeat, but not in two years time. Yes, the generals!"

Against that background the events after Sarajevo are easy to understand, for Sarajevo turned out to be hardly more than the cue for the Reich to rush into action, although Austria had to deal the first blow against Serbia. The Austrians, however, were originally divided in their counsels. Only the Chief of the General Staff, Conrad von Hötzendorf, pressed for immediate war against Serbia, supported by high officials in the Foreign Ministry and by most of the German press in Austria. Foreign Minister Berchtold, the Austrian and the Hungarian Prime Ministers, Stürgkh and Tisza, hesitated and were for less radi-cal measures. But even Conrad realized that he could not wage war against Serbia without first making sure that Germany would cover Austria's rear against Russia. Thus the real decision lay with Germany.

After Sarajevo Germany could not at once make up her mind which course to follow. The Auswärtiges Amt clearly saw the danger involved in Russia's trying to protect Serbia if Austria made war, namely, that a world war might result. This is why the Auswärtiges Amt from the first counselled modera-tion both to Austria and to Serbia. The German General Staff, on the other hand, was ready to welcome Sarajevo as the golden opportunity for risking a preventive war. In this situation it was the Kaiser's word that proved decisive. Wilhelm II was incensed at the murder, perhaps most because it attacked his cherished monarchist principle. When he received the report of Tschirschky, the German ambassador to Vienna, of 30 June, telling of his moderating counsels to the Austrians, the Kaiser commented in his usual wild manner and provided the specious slogan "Now or never!" which turned out to be the guiding star of German diplomacy in the crisis of July 1914.

On 5 July, Count Hoyos came to Berlin, bringing with him two documents on Austrian policy towards the Balkans. The Austrian ambassador, Szogyeny, handed them to the Kaiser at a special audience at the Potsdam Palace, in which he apparently used fairly warlike language, although the documents of his own government spoke of war, if at all, only by implication. After initial hes-itation, Wilhelm II promised German support to the Dual Monarchy, whatever Austria did. His promise soon came to be called the German *carte blanche* to Austria. But the Kaiser was not satisfied with giving his ally a free hand against

Serbia. He urged Vienna, which apparently had not made up its mind, to make war on Serbia, and that as soon as possible. Bethmann Hollweg and the Emperor's other civilian and military advisers duly endorsed these imperial decisions.

When Bethmann returned to Hohenfinow, he told Riezler what had happened at Potsdam. From what Riezler recorded in his by now famous diary, it appears that the Chancellor was not only fully aware of the possible consequences when taking his "leap into the dark"—war with Britain, i.e. world war—but that already at that stage his first objective seems to have been war with Russia and France; a diplomatic victory—France dropping Russia, Russia dropping Serbia—would have been accepted only as a second best.

Impressed by the German stand, Berchtold swung round in favour of Conrad's line. His colleagues in the Cabinet followed suit, last of all Tisza, and so did Emperor Francis Joseph. Preparations were made in Vienna and Berlin for the *coup* against Serbia: it was decided to confront Serbia with an ultimatum which would be designed to be unacceptable as soon as the French president Poincaré and his prime minister Viviani had finished their state visit to Russia. That was to be on 23 July.

Meanwhile, the Austrian and German governments did everything to create a peaceful impression. The two emperors enjoyed their usual summer holidays, as did the leading generals of the Central Powers. But they returned to their respective capitals before or just after the ultimatum was handed over at Belgrade. Austria kept the German government informed of her intentions through the normal diplomatic channels, while the German government pressed Austria to start the action against Serbia as soon as possible. Privately the Germans aired serious misgivings at the lack of energy Austria displayed, and the Auswärtiges Amt suspected her of being unhappy about Germany's urgency. These suspicions were not unfounded: the Austrians had waited to make a decision until the German declaration of 5 July, but even then they moved slowly. According to Austrian plans, mobilization would begin after the rupture of diplomatic relations with Serbia, but it was originally intended to delay the actual declaration of war and the opening of hostilities until mobilization was completed, i.e., until approximately 12 August. The Wilhelmstrasse, however, deemed such delay absolutely intolerable. It was quick to see that the powers might intervene diplomatically during the interval to save Serbia from humiliation. As the German government was bent on preventing any mediation, it spurred Vienna on, as soon as it learned of the Austrian time-table, to declare war on Serbia immediately after the rupture with Belgrade and to open hostilities at once. On 25 July, Jagow told Szogyeny that the German government

> takes it for granted that upon eventual negative reply from Serbia, our declaration of war will follow immediately, joined to military operations. Any delay in beginning warlike preparations is regarded here as a great danger in respect of intervention of other powers. We are urgently advised to go ahead at once and confront the world with a *fait accompli*.

On the other hand, Jagow justified his refusal to pass on British proposals of mediation to Vienna by the alleged fear that Vienna might react by rushing things and confronting the world with a *fait accompli*. Yet when Austria, giving way to German pressure, did declare war immediately, the German Secretary of State told the British Ambassador, Sir Edward Goschen, that now the very thing had happened he had always warned against: namely, Austria rushing things as an answer to proposals of mediation.

*   *   *

German pressure on Vienna to declare war on Serbia without delay had an immediate and telling effect: on 26 July, Berchtold, who had been wavering and who tended to be timid rather than aggressive, adopted the German idea, and in this he was vigorously supported by Tschirschky. Conrad, however, was far from happy. Although usually thought of as the most warlike on the side of the Central Powers, he would have preferred to stick to the original timetable, but he gave in, and the Austrian government decided on an early declaration of war. On 27 July the final decision was taken to declare war the following day.

Now the German government had accomplished one of its short-term aims: Austria had confronted the world with a *fait accompli* in the form of an early declaration of war against Serbia, which was bound to undermine all attempts at mediation between Austria and Serbia. The following day, 29 July, the Austrians rushed things even more, again following German advice, when they started the bombardment of Belgrade.[2] The immediate effect was catastrophic: the Russians took the bombardment of Belgrade as the beginning of military operations against Serbia, as it was meant to be. They had, on 28 July, already ordered partial mobilization against Austria in order to deter her from actual warfare against Serbia. Now the Russian generals, thinking war with Austria and Germany imminent, successfully pressed for immediate general mobilization, since Russian mobilization was known to be far slower than Austrian or German. The Tsar ordered a halt to general mobilization and a return to partial mobilization after the receipt of a telegram from Wilhelm II late in the evening of 29 July, but the next afternoon the generals and the foreign minister Sazonov renewed their pressure on him. Nicholas gave way and Russian general mobilization was ordered for a second time on 30 July, at 6 P.M.

The German government rushed things also in two more respects: on 27 July Jagow had assured Jules Cambon and Sir Horace Rumbold, the British chargé d'affaires in Berlin, that Germany would not mobilize so long as Russia mobilized only in the south, against Austria. Two days later, however, the Auswärtiges Amt received a lengthy memorandum from General Moltke, whose

---

[2] The German government was informed of Austrian preparations to shell Belgrade through a report by the German military attaché at Vienna, Count Kageneck, of 18 July: *Politisches Archiv des Auswärtiges Amts, Der Weltkrieg* (vol. 2). Kageneck's report is one of the documents not included in the German documents; it was published for the first time in *Julikrise* (137).

arguments boiled down to an insistence on German general mobilization. Again the Auswärtiges Amt followed the lead of the generals. After 30 July, Berlin demanded the cancellation of Russian mobilization not only against Germany, but also against Austria, and that demand was expressly included both in the German ultimatum to Russia on 31 July and in the declaration of war of 1 August. When the French ambassador reminded Jagow of his words only a few days earlier, Jagow apparently shrugged his shoulders and replied that the generals wanted to have it that way, and that his words had, after all, not been a binding statement.

The second point was at least as serious: while the Entente powers tried desperately to prevent a local war, in order to avert a continental and world war, by making a whole series of proposals of mediation,[3] the German government not only flatly rejected them or passed them on to Vienna without giving them support, but also stifled the only initiative from the German side which might have saved the general peace. This time, the initiative had come from the Kaiser. Wilhelm had returned from his sailing holiday in Norway after learning of the Austrian suspension of diplomatic relations with Serbia on 25 July. He arrived at Potsdam on the 27th. Early the following morning he read the Serbian answer to Austria's ultimatum. Like nearly everybody else in Europe outside Germany and Austria, the Kaiser was impressed by Serbia's answer, which had conceded practically everything except one point, and made only a few reservations. Suddenly all his warlike sentiments vanished and he minuted:

> a brilliant achievement in a time-limit of only 48 hours! It is more than one could have expected! A great moral success for Vienna; but with it all reason for war is gone and Giesl ought to have quietly stayed on in Belgrade! After that I should never have ordered mobilization.

He immediately ordered the Auswärtiges Amt to draft a note for Vienna, telling the Austrians that they should accept the Serbian answer. To satisfy the army, and at the same time as a guarantee for what the Serbians had conceded, the Kaiser suggested that Austria should content herself with occupying Belgrade only and negotiate with the Serbians about the remaining reservations.

Apparently the Auswärtiges Amt took fright at their sovereign's weakness. The moment that had come during both Moroccan crises threatened to come again: that the Kaiser would lose his nerve and beat the retreat. This time, however, Bethmann Hollweg and the Auswärtiges Amt did not listen to their sovereign as they had done on 5 July. The Chancellor despatched the instructions to Tschirschky on the evening of 28 July, i.e., after he had learned that Austria had declared war on Serbia. Furthermore, he distorted the Kaiser's argument by omitting the crucial sentence that war was now no longer necessary. The occupation of Belgrade was not meant to be, in Bethmann's words, a safe-

---

[3]In particular the suggestion to extend the time limit for answering the ultimatum and the British proposal to hold a four-power conference in London.

guard for the implementation of Serbian concessions, but a means to enforce Serbia's total acceptance of the Austrian ultimatum. Finally, the Chancellor added a comment which was sure to defeat any conciliatory effect of his démarche, if any chance of this had remained.

In these circumstances, the démarche, when executed by Tschirschky, had no effect whatsoever, nor did a later British proposal along similar lines.

When developments had gone so far, Bethmann Hollweg undertook his most important move, the bid for British neutrality. On 29 July he had despatched the ultimatum to Belgium to the German minister in Brussels. The violation of Belgian neutrality made it vital for Germany that at least British acquiescence be secured. During the evening of 29 July, Bethmann, returning from talks with the Kaiser and his military advisers at Potsdam, summoned the British ambassador. The Chancellor asked for England's neutrality in return for the promise that Germany would not annex French or Belgian territory. The reaction of the Foreign Office was scathing, as is borne out by Crowe's comment.

A British answer to the German demand was no longer needed, for, just after Goschen left the Chancellor, a telegram from London arrived: Lichnowsky reported Grey's warning that Britain would not remain neutral if France were involved in a continental war. Now Grey—at last—had spoken in such a way that even the German Chancellor had to abandon his cherished hope of British neutrality, which would have meant certain victory for Germany in the imminent continental war. Bethmann Hollweg was dumb-founded, for he saw clearly the consequences of Grey's warning—a world war which Germany could hardly win. In his panic, he tried to salvage what seemed possible. He now pressed the Austrians in all sincerity to modify their stand, but did not go so far as to advise the Austrians to drop the whole idea of war against Serbia. He only pleaded with them to accept the British version of the "halt-in-Belgrade" proposal and to open conversations with the Russians. In such conversations the Austrians were to repeat their promise not to annex Serbian territory, a pledge which, as the Chancellor knew quite well, was regarded by Russia as insufficient. Bethmann made his proposals in the vague hope that by shifting the blame to Russia the British might stay out after all. At the same time he wanted to persuade the German public, especially the social-democrats, to follow his policy by demonstrating his peaceful intentions. The Chancellor did not want to put an end to the local war, which had just seen its second day; what he wanted was to improve Germany's position in a major conflict.

*   *   *

Bethmann Hollweg failed in his first objective; he succeeded in his second only too well. The social-democrats supported the German war effort, and the Russians are still blamed in Germany today for having started the war. For this same reason—to shift the blame to Russia—Bethmann also resisted the pressure of the General Staff who pleaded for immediate German mobilization. The

Chancellor urged that Russia be allowed to mobilize first against Germany, since, as he put it, he could not pursue military and political actions at the same time. In other words, he could not simultaneously put the blame on Russia and order German mobilization before Russian general mobilization.

On 29 July, the German generals still appreciated Bethmann Hollweg's policy. But during the 30th they became impatient. In the evening, about two hours after Russian general mobilization had been definitely ordered, they told the Chancellor that he had to make up his mind about German mobilization immediately. The Chancellor won a delay until noon next day, but there was little doubt which way the decision was meant to go. Bethmann Hollweg agreed, in the hope that the Russians might order general mobilization beforehand. During the morning of 31 July the Germans waited for the news of Russian general mobilization as their cue to rush into military action themselves. Luckily enough for Bethmann Hollweg and generations of German historians, Sazonov lost his nerve and had, in fact, already ordered Russian general mobilization.

At 11 a.m. Bethmann, Moltke, and Falkenhayn met again, anxiously waiting for news from Russia with only one hour left before the deadline they had set themselves. At five minutes to twelve a telegram from Pourtalès, the German ambassador to St. Petersburg, was handed to them. It confirmed the rumours that Russian general mobilization had been ordered. Now they could order German mobilization with what they thought a clear conscience. Immediately after the receipt of the telegram the state of threatening war, the phase of military operations which immediately preceded general mobilization, was declared in Germany. The same afternoon, two ultimata went off—one to Russia demanding that she stop all military preparations not only against Germany but also against Austria, the other to France, asking about the stand France would take in a war between Germany and Russia. At the same time the Auswärtiges Amt prepared the declarations of war on both countries. Thus war had become inevitable, even more so since German general mobilization, according to the famous Schlieffen plan, meant opening hostilities against neutral Belgium a few days after mobilization had actually started.

After noon on 31 July, therefore, the catastrophe could no longer be averted. On 1 August, Germany ordered general mobilization, at the same hour as France. In the evening of that day, Germany declared war on Russia. An hour before, a curious and revealing incident had occurred. A telegram from Lichnowsky arrived suggesting that Britain might remain neutral if Germany were not to attack France. The Kaiser and his military, naval, and political advisers were happy, since their tough line during the July crisis seemed to be paying off after all. Only Moltke demurred. He was shocked by the idea of having to change his plan, and even feared that Russia might drop out as well. Late in the evening another telegram from London arrived, making the true position clear.

The French answer was evasive in form but firm in content: France would not forsake her ally. At the same time, France tried desperately to secure British support. The Russians, the French, and Crowe in the Foreign Office, urged Grey to make Britain's stand quite clear, that she would not remain neutral in a continental war. Grey had warned Germany before, but his language had not been straightforward enough to destroy German illusions. When Grey made the British policy unmistakably clear, even to the German Chancellor, it was too late.

How much Germany up to the last hour still hoped for British neutrality can be seen by the invention of a whole series of alleged border incidents, some of which were so crudely presented that outside Germany nobody believed them. They were part of the German manoeuvre to put the blame this time on France and to impress Britain. The German invasion of Belgium, however, removed the last hesitations: Britain sent an ultimatum to Germany demanding the immediate withdrawal of German troops from Belgium. When Germany refused, Britain entered the war automatically after the time-limit of the ultimatum had expired, i.e., at 11 p.m. Greenwich time on 4 August.

In trying to assess the shares of responsibility for the war two basic distinctions have to be made: on the one hand between the three stages of war connected with its outbreak: local war (Austria v. Serbia), continental war (Austria and Germany v. Russia and France), and world war (Britain joining the continental war). On the other hand, one has to distinguish between the will to start any of those three stages of war and the fact of merely causing them.

Since the world war developed out of a local war, then of continental war, the major share for causing it lies with that power which willed the local and/or continental war. That power was clearly Germany. She did not will the world war, as is borne out by her hopes of keeping out Britain, but she did urge Austria to make war on Serbia. Even if Austria had started the local war completely on her own—which, of course, she had not—Germany's share would still be bigger than Austria's since a German veto could have effectively prevented it. Germany, furthermore, was the only power which had no objection to the continental war. So long as Britain kept out, she was confident of winning a war against Russia and France. Germany did nothing to prevent continental war, even at the risk of a world war, a risk which her government had seen from the beginning.

Austria, of course, wanted the local war, after—with German prodding—she had made up her mind, but feared a continental war. In fact, she hoped that Germany, by supporting her diplomatically, might frighten Russia into inaction.

Russia, France, and Britain tried to avert continental war. Their main argument for mediation between Serbia and Austria was precisely that to prevent the local war would be the best means of averting continental war. On the other hand, they contributed to the outbreak, each in her own way: Russia by committing the technical blunder of providing the cue for German mobilization, instead of waiting until Germany had mobilized. The French attitude was almost entirely correct; her only fault was that she could not hold back her Russian ally from precipitate general mobilization. Britain might have made her stand clear beyond any doubt much earlier, since this might have been a way of restraining Germany, although it is doubtful whether this would have altered the course of events to any appreciable degree. The share of the Entente powers is much smaller than Germany's, for it consisted mainly in reacting—not always in the best manner—to German action.

Looking back on the events from the mid-sixties, the outbreak of the first world war looks like the original example of faulty brinkmanship, of rapid escalation in a period of history when the mechanisms of alliances and mobilization schedules could still work unchecked by fear of the absolute weapon and the absolute destruction its use would bring in what would now be the third world war.

6

The New Revisionism

FROM *The German Problem Reconsidered: Germany and the World Order*

BY *David Calleo*

To a remarkable extent, world history from the 1860s to after the First World War has been dominated by the German Problem. What is, or was, that problem? Its international aspect can most easily be summarized by a question: Why, since the 1860s, has Germany been so often at war with its neighbors? There is a domestic aspect as well: What made a Nazi regime possible in so advanced and civilized a country?

Like the German Problem itself, the theories that explain it have their international and domestic components. Internationally, a united Germany is often said to have been too big and dynamic for any stable European state system. Inevitably, such a Germany threatened the political independence and economic well-being of its neighbors. Germany's dynamic expansiveness, in turn, is frequently said to have stemmed from the internal character of the German nation—the political institutions, culture, and economic and social systems that evolved during the nineteenth and twentieth centuries. This character is thought not only to have made Germany uncommonly aggressive abroad, but also particularly susceptible to totalitarianism at home.

For many people, these theories lead to a single practical conclusion: Whenever unified into one state, Germans become a menace at home and abroad. And this conclusion, shared by the postwar leaderships of all Germany's neighbors, leads to an obvious prescription: To keep Europe safe, and the German people safe from themselves, Germany must be firmly contained by alert and superior power. Had the lesson only been learned and applied earlier, it is frequently said, the world would have been spared at least the second of this century's general wars. By similar reasoning, the postwar

David Calleo, *The German Problem Reconsidered: Germany and the World Order*, pp. 1, Cambridge University Press, 1978. Reprinted by permission.

687

Russian American duopoly over Europe is now thought to have resolved the German Problem.

Behind such attitudes lies a vast body of analytical writing that ascribes the German Problem primarily to the international policies of the Germans themselves and traces those policies to the inner compulsions of German society. Much of this writing is distinguished and full of insight. Understandably, most of it is infused with an intense reaction against war in general and Nazi racial policy in particular. As time goes by, however, a good deal of this analysis seems unbalanced—vulnerable to two major criticisms. First of all, Germany is too often treated as an isolated case, a country with broad characteristics presumed not to exist elsewhere. Many German writers appear to take a certain perverse relish in claiming for their society a unique wickedness among humankind. Obviously, every national society is in many senses unique. And although no one should wish to rob the Germans of their hard-earned reputation, theirs is not the only European society with, for example, closely knit families, an emphasis on private rather than public virtues, or authoritarian traditions. Nor is Germany the only nation that has hoped to play a great role in bringing the world to order or taken pride in military prowess. Nor indeed have such traits and ambitions been conspicuously absent from the international arena since Germany's defeat in 1945. Particularly questionable is the widespread view that the Germans were uniquely afflicted with nineteenth-century Romanticism and Philosophical Idealism. It should not be so easy for cultural historians to forget the influence of Bergson in France, nor of the Romantics and Philosophical Idealists in Britain.

Secondly, this habit of seeing German culture as unique has a parallel in the tendency to view German unification as a malevolent accident that befell an otherwise harmonious European system. From a broader perspective, however, Germany's consolidation and the conflicts that ensued were only the natural consequences of Europe's evolution into national states. From the Middle Ages, the European peoples had tried a variety of imperial and federal forms. By the nineteenth century, the nation-state increasingly seemed the only effective political formula for organizing stable government over modern societies. Limiting states to national units obviously carried with it the problem of an "international" system. Because the national states coexisted so closely in Europe, they were inevitably preoccupied with the "balance" among them. By the end of the nineteenth century, moreover, they had reached out to bring most of the globe within their political-economic orbit. This outward expansion had incalculable consequences. It profoundly altered Europe's internal relationships. And it created or awakened powerful new forces from beyond Europe, first the rising semi-European giants—Russia and the United States, later Japan, and, in our own day, the "Third World."

The German Problem ought properly to be seen within the context of this broad evolution of the Western national states and the international issues which that evolution inevitably posed. Germany was the last of the great

European national states to be formed. The Germans had paid a heavy price for their historic procrastination. It was not comfortable to be only a loose federation surrounded by centralized nation-states. Indeed, throughout most of modern history, Germans were more often victims than aggressors. Hideously ravaged by invaders in the Thirty Years' War, the German territories became a sort of athletic field for playing out the various dynastic ambitions of the ancien régime. Later, the French Revolution brought some two decades of invasion and occupation. A good part of the Germans' ill fortune came from having failed to consolidate a national state before their neighbors. The first great unifying attempt, launched by the Holy Roman Emperor Ferdinand II during the Thirty Years' War, had been finally abandoned by 1648. Many factors were at work in the defeat, religious divisions, jealousy and greed among the German princes. But above all the prospects for German union were destroyed from without. The German national effort became caught up in Bourbon France's struggle with Habsburg Spain. Thus, the French Cardinals Richelieu and Mazarin, in alliance with Protestant Swedes, infidel Turks, and Pope Urban VIII, defeated Catholic Habsburg power in Germany. With Germany devastated and disunited, the European scene was dominated for 200 years by the rivalry of France and Britain.

Not until after the Napoleonic invasions did the Germans turn away from their cosmopolitan and particularist tradition and begin to adopt the unifying nationalism of their neighbors. Once a national state was achieved, there was no reason to assume that a powerful new Germany would prove any less expansive than France, which had continually sought to dominate Europe, or Britain, which had conquered an enormous world empire. Germany's economic growth, moreover, was extremely rapid. By 1900, the new Reich had not only overshadowed France on the Continent, but its economic power had penetrated deep into Russia and was competing successfully with Britain throughout the world. Under the circumstances, dynamic Germany was found to appear an aggressor, challenging the arrangements that had grown up in its absence and that presumed its continuing weakness. Germany was driven not only by the desire to overtake a declining Britain, but also by the fear of being overshadowed by a rising Russia and United States. In the race for the future, Germans saw themselves already fatally handicapped. For while the United States, Russia, and even Britain were on the periphery of Europe, Germany lay in its middle. Whereas the growth of superpowers on the Eastern or Western edges only indirectly undermined the European status quo, German ambitions assaulted it directly. Hence, while Britain came to preside over half the globe, and both Russia and the United States relentlessly filled out their continental hinterlands, Germany was expected to remain locked within the tight frame of Europe's traditional balance of power. From a German view, preserving the European balance, while extra-European giants formed all around, meant condemning Germany to mediocrity and, ultimately, all of Europe to external domination. That was the German Problem as the Germans saw it.

To analyze Germany's ambitions and fears as essentially the product of its own unusual political culture subtly distorts history in favor of Germany's victors. For Britain, France, Russia, and the United States were great powers with appetites no less ravenous than Germany's. The desire to control foreign space and resources—the preoccupation with room for growth—went hand in hand with modernization in nearly all major countries. Indeed it is one of the more remarkable accomplishments of modern historiography that the Germans, who never had a serious formal empire, should come to be seen as the most virulent carriers of the imperialist disease. In short, Germany's "aggressiveness" against international order may be explained as plausibly by the nature of that order as by any peculiar characteristics of the Germans. Even Germany's Nazi episode may be seen less as the consequence of some inherent flaw in German civilization, some autonomous national cancer developing according to its own inner rhythm, than of the intense pressures put upon Germany from the outside. Geography and history conspired to make Germany's rise late, rapid, vulnerable, and aggressive. The rest of the world reacted by crushing the upstart. If, in the process, the German state lost its bearings and was possessed by an evil demon, perhaps the proper conclusion is not so much that civilization was uniquely weak in Germany, but that it is fragile everywhere. And perhaps the proper lesson is not so much the need for vigilance against aggressors, but the ruinous consequences of refusing reasonable accommodation to upstarts.

7

The New Revisionism—
A Critique

FROM *World War I, World War II, World War III*

BY *Donald Kagan*

WORLD WAR II dominated the imagination of most people who lived through it. For decades afterward most Americans looked at world affairs through the lens ground to fit the vision they had of the 1930's and the broad consensus as to what it revealed: the world had suffered a terrible war needlessly. The irresolution, timidity, division, and lack of resolve of the democracies had allowed aggressive and evil regimes in Italy, Japan, and especially Germany to grow so powerful as to threaten the freedom of the rest of the world. It had required a horrible and bloody war to put them down, whereas a determined collective effort could have deterred the aggressors or, at any rate, have defeated them quickly and without great cost had the democracies acted firmly soon enough. Weak and indecisive leaders had yielded to the natural tendency of democracies in peacetime, recklessly cutting defense expenditures, closing their eyes to unpleasant realities when ugly and dangerous governments came to power in restless and dissatisfied nations, turning to the fruitless and humiliating policy of appeasement when the bullies could no longer be ignored. Those policies were rejected and reversed only at the last minute, too late to save the European continent west of the Soviet Union and barely soon enough to save Britain and gain time for the power of the USSR and the United States to turn the tide.

These ideas were all summed up in the word "Munich," and the determination that there should be no more Munichs lay behind most of the actions of the Western democracies, and especially the United States, in the years after the war. American isolationism had weakened the capacity of the democracies to resist aggression, so President Roosevelt was determined that the United States

Donald Kagan, "World War I, World War II, World War III," in *Commentary*, Vol. LXXXIII, No. 3, 1987, pp. 21–24. Reprinted by permission.

must play an active part in the new international organization, the United Nations. When the Soviet Union and Communism came to seem dangerous, the analogy of the 1930's quickly came to mind and helped lead the Western states to unite in NATO, a serious military alliance capable of resisting aggression. The Munich analogy was foremost in the minds of President Truman and his advisers when they decided to resist the threat they perceived from Communism and the Soviet Union that led them to establish the Marshall Plan, set forth the Truman Doctrine, and join the NATO alliance.

During the Johnson years, however, as a result of the unpopularity in academic circles of the Vietnam war, the historical analogy of the 1930's with recent events, whose validity, indeed primacy, had not previously been questioned except by apologists for the Soviet Union, came under attack even from liberals with impeccable anti-Communist credentials. For many American and British intellectuals it is now being replaced by a surge of analogies with the coming of the great war which broke out after the Archduke Franz Ferdinand was assassinated at Sarajevo in June of 1914.

This reexamination of World War I has invariably produced lessons for our own time quite different from those that came from scrutinizing World War II. The proponents of what we may call the "Sarajevo" analogy are not much impressed with the importance of vigilance, preparedness, swift and determined responses to aggressive actions, with the need for firmness in the face of provocation. Instead they urge greater caution, a willingness to bargain, avoidance of attempts to undermine the strength of rival states, a more generous reading of their intentions, a greater willingness to understand the point of view of nations late in coming to power on the world scene.

II

The two cases, "Munich" and "Sarajevo," are indeed different in many respects, yet it is far from clear that the lessons derived from them must be at odds.

The central assumptions that underlie the lessons emphasized by those we might call the neorevisionists, though they rarely state them directly, are that Wilhelmine Germany, the Germany of Kaiser Wilhelm II, was not really dangerous and that its actions in the two decades before the outbreak of the Great War of 1914 did not require the strong reaction they received from Britain; Germany's intentions were not unappeasably aggressive, and it had no clear goals that were incompatible with Britain's security. A recent formulation of this view goes even farther, finding fault not with German aggressiveness but with the reaction to it:

> Geography and history conspired to make Germany's rise late, rapid, vulnerable, and aggressive. The rest of the world reacted by crushing the upstart. If, in the process, the German state lost its bearings and was possessed by an evil demon,

perhaps the proper conclusion is not so much that civilization was uniquely weak in Germany, but that it is so fragile everywhere. And *perhaps the proper lesson is not so much the need for vigilance against aggressors, but the ruinous consequences of refusing reasonable accommodation to upstarts.*[1]

The question is, what "accommodation" could the European states have made to the German "upstart" that would have brought satisfaction to Germany and stability to Europe? What, in fact, did Germany want? At the turn of the century Germany was the strongest military power in the world. It also had the strongest and most dynamic economy on the continent. In 1897, without any previous naval tradition, without any new challenge from the sea to justify an expensive change in policy, the Germans undertook the construction of a major battle fleet concentrated in the North Sea where it could threaten traditional English naval superiority and the security that went with it. The British gradually became alarmed as they came to recognize the threat Germany might pose.

In the Foreign Office, Eyre Crowe, the resident expert on Germany, suggested that the Germans might be "aiming at a general political hegemony and maritime ascendancy, threatening the independence of her neighbors and ultimately the existence of England." Concern over German intentions had already caused Britain to abandon its policy of isolation and enter into a series of understandings and alliances with other countries. Repeated statements by the German emperor and many other leaders in and outside the government asserted that Germany was aiming at "world power," that it demanded overseas colonies and "a place in the sun," that "no question of world politics must be settled without the consent of the German emperor."

Such statements might be dismissed as mere bombast or only the ebullience of a newly powerful nation, late in arriving at a place among the great powers, flexing its muscles and understandably asserting its right to equal treatment, but German actions made them seem a good deal less harmless. In the two Moroccan crises of 1905 and 1911 the Germans tried to bully France, make colonial gains, and break the link between France and Britain. Even more menacingly, the Germans continued to build big battleships in numbers that would destroy the security of Britain unless the British were willing to divert vast sums from domestic purposes to hold up their side in a naval race. All this converted the Liberal British government, whose Foreign Minister was Sir Edward Grey, to Crowe's dark view of German intentions.

To be sure, the Liberal leaders' policy of resistance to the German threat met criticism from radicals and pacifists both inside and outside the government and the party. Some claimed that Germany really presented no danger at all; fear of war was being stirred up by militarists and the arms manufacturers, the "merchants of death" who were their associates. Others argued that the British fleet was strong enough, in any case, to meet whatever challenge it might face

[1]David Calleo, *The German Problem Reconsidered* (Harvard University Press, 1978). The words I have emphasized are quoted by Kahler.

and that no acceleration in the pace of production was needed. Even such hard-headed politicians as Lloyd George and Winston Churchill opposed increased naval expenditures because they would interfere with the domestic-welfare program to which the Liberal party was committed and which they were eager to bring about. Norman Angell wrote a book called *The Great Illusion* which argued that war was not only immoral but, in the modern world of interdependent economies, irrational and almost impossible. From such a perspective, joining in an arms race to deter a war would likewise be irrational. In spite of this opposition, the British competed in and won the naval race; they also maintained and strengthened their ties with their former enemies France and Russia because they feared the growth of the German navy and the uses to which it might be put.

Even on the evidence available to Crowe, Grey, and their colleagues their fears were well-founded. However often the Kaiser might proclaim his and Germany's friendly feelings for England, and Admiral Tirpitz, his Naval Secretary, declare that the fleet was intended only to defend Germany, its colonies and commerce, the emphasis on big battleships, the concentration of the fleet in the North Sea, and the accelerating pace of construction justified British suspicion and fear, even without inside information about Germany's motives. Recent scholarship, moreover, makes clear that Britain really was the target of the new German navy. It also shows that the likeliest explanation of Tirpitz's otherwise irrational naval program is that it aimed at least at equality with the British fleet[2] and, when combined with Germany's great military power, would give Germany the ability to change the status quo in its favor and to the great and dangerous disadvantage of other powers, particularly Great Britain. It would be some years before the Germans could hope to approach parity at sea, but the British expected that even before the Germans were prepared for such a confrontation, they would use their "risk fleet" to secure concessions.

What concessions would they demand? Were these reasonable enough to permit Britain to make them without endangering British security? Would an attempt to understand the feelings and needs of the new German empire and to meet them have averted conflict? What, in fact, were Germany's goals? The contemporary German historian Fritz Fischer believes that the Germans wanted to conquer and dominate the European continent from the English Channel to the Ukraine, to exploit its economic resources and use it as a base for a world empire. His main evidence is the program of war aims they drew up soon after the war broke out in 1914, the "September Program," which spells out the European part of such a plan. Fischer argues that Germany planned and unleashed the war precisely to achieve its purposes.

We need not accept this entirely to believe that at least something of what

---

[2] See Paul M. Kennedy, "Strategic Aspects of the Anglo-German Naval Race," in Paul M. Kennedy, *Strategy and Diplomacy* 1870–1945 (London, Allen & Unwin, 1983), and the judgment of that article and other recent studies coming to a similar conclusion by Zara S. Steiner: "We now know that Tirpitz did indeed think of challenging the supremacy of the British navy," in *Britain and the Origins of the First World War* (London, Macmillan, 1977).

the Germans hoped for before the war is reflected in the plans approved by the German Chancellor, Bethmann Hollweg, only a month after it began. The central principle of those plans was "the safeguarding of the German empire for the foreseeable future in the East and West. Hence, France must be so weakened that it cannot rise again as a great power. Russia must be pushed back from the German frontier as far as possible, and its rule over the non-Russian vassal peoples must be broken."

Since victory in the West seemed imminent, while the situation in the East was still unclear, the bulk of the September Program dealt with the West. The military would decide whether the French should cede Belfort, the western slopes of the Vosges, the coast from Dunkirk to Boulogne, and destroy their forts on the German frontier; the military at once decided they should. Germany would acquire the iron mines of Briey. A preferential trade treaty would make France "our export land," and the French would be required to pay an indemnity that would make it impossible for them to manufacture armaments for at least twenty years. Belgium would lose Liège, Verviers, and probably Antwerp, and would become a vassal state, accepting German garrisons in its ports. To this Belgian subsidiary of Germany would be attached French Flanders, and the channel ports of Dunkirk, Calais, and Boulogne. Holland would be ostensibly independent, "but essentially subject to us." Luxembourg would be incorporated directly into the German empire. Apart from these territorial provisions, but by no means less important, was the plan for establishing "an economic organization of *Mitteleuropa* through mutual customs agreements . . . including France, Belgium, Holland, Denmark, Austria, Poland, and perhaps Italy, Sweden, and Norway," that would guarantee German economic domination of Europe.

Plans for the East were not yet formulated so early, but what we know of ideas that were entertained shows that they led naturally to the settlement imposed on the new Bolshevik government of Russia by the treaty of Brest-Litovsk in 1918. That treaty deprived Russia of Poland, Finland, the Baltic states, the Ukraine, and parts of the Caucasus. Though the treaty contained language about self-determination, there can be no doubt that all these lands would be under German control, one way or another.

We should remember that Bethmann Hollweg was a moderate in the context of Wilhelmine Germany and that his program fell far short of the wishes not only of right-wing extremists, both civilian and military, but even of most intellectuals and political moderates. A "Petition of Intellectuals" published in July 1915 was signed by a great number of theologians, teachers, artists, writers, and some 352 university professors; it demanded a program of annexations that went far beyond the September Program. At the same time that Bethmann Hollweg was approving his own scheme, the leader of the Catholic Center party, Matthias Erzberger, was demanding the annexation of Belgium, parts of France, and the entire Congo, the conversion of the Baltic states and the Ukraine into German dependencies, and the imposition of a reparations bill that would more than pay off the entire German national debt.

The course of the war showed that the Chancellor would have had to yield to more extreme opinions or make way for more extreme leaders. The chances are that a victorious Germany would have claimed more than was contained in the September Program and at least as much as was set down at Brest-Litovsk. In that event, Britain would have been faced with the destruction of the balance of power it had fought so long to maintain on the continent and its domination by a single power. The new master of Europe, moreover, would be far stronger and more dangerous than the Spain of Philip II or the France of Louis XIV. It would have the greatest army the world had ever seen, unprecedented economic resources with which to make its already significant navy, now able to operate from a series of channel ports, stronger than the British fleet, and reserves of manpower the British could not hope to match. The new Germany would have the power to exclude British trade from the continent, doing fearful damage to the British economy. If necessary it could even be capable of invading and subjugating the British Isles.

It is hard to see how the British could have regarded such an outcome as an acceptable "accommodation," yet we have no evidentiary basis for believing that the Germans would have been satisfied with anything else.

The scholarship of the last quarter-century, almost completely ignored by the neorevisionists,[3] makes it clear that Wilhelmine Germany was not just another European nation seeking to maintain its national interest or even to advance it by means tolerable to its neighbors. From the late 1890's imperial Germany was a fundamentally dissatisfied power, eager to disrupt the status quo and to achieve its expansive goals, by bullying if possible, by war if necessary.

It might be argued that these grandiose aims, clear evidence for which only appears after the outbreak of war, grew and developed only after a long period of frustration and cold war, as a result of British intransigence. If the British had been more forthcoming earlier, some might say, a settlement could have been reached on more acceptable terms. The historical record will not support any such claim. As a keen student of the subject, Paul M. Kennedy, puts it:

> The historian aware of the pressures for expansion in imperial Germany is bound to wonder whether a change of tone on Britain's part, a greater generosity over this or that colonial boundary, would really have had a significant difference. They might have papered over the cracks in the Anglo-German relationship for a few more years, but it is difficult to see how such gestures would have altered the elemental German push to change the existing distribution of power—which, unless the British were willing to accept a substantial diminution in national influence and safety, was bound to provoke a reaction on their part.

[3] See S. M. Lynn-Jones, "Détente and Deterrence, Anglo-German Relations, 1911–1914," *International Relations,* Fall 1986: "One of the most striking features of the general image of World War I as an inadvertent conflict is the extent to which it ignores the arguments of Fritz Fischer and other historians who contend that Germany adopted an aggressive policy."

The Bolshevik Revolution—Why Did It Succeed?

CONTENTS

QUESTIONS FOR STUDY

1   What problems faced the various revolutionary parties immediately after the March Revolution? What solutions did each group offer?

2   What is your estimate of Kerensky's responsibility for the Bolshevik victory?

3   In what ways, if any, was Lenin necessary for the success of the Bolshevik coup d'état?

4   Was his policy in accord with the philosophy and teaching of Marx?

5   In what ways was the outcome of the revolution in accord with the experience of Russian history?

6   Why was the resistance to the Bolshevik Revolution so weak?

7   Was the failure of liberal, democratic government on a Western model inevitable?

Few historical events have had a greater impact on the world's future than the Bolshevik seizure of power in Russia on November 7, 1917. The Revolution that overthrew the Romanov dynasty in March of the same year established a provisional government dominated by conservatives and moderates of the bourgeois parties and containing only one Socialist, Alexander Kerensky. This group was to govern Russia until the election of a constituent assembly would allow the Russian people to vote for a permanent constitution. That body was not chosen until December and was permitted to sit for only one day before Lenin, acting for the Central Executive Committee of the Soviets, dissolved it forever. Lenin was the leader of the Bolshevik faction. During the March Revolution he had been in exile in Switzerland and his party a mere splinter group, even in Petrograd, which was the center of its power. In March 1917 the Bolsheviks were a minority of the Russian Social Democratic party, which was itself not even the largest Socialist party. By November the Social Democrats had grown strong enough to seize power, place themselves at the head of the state, and establish a Communist dictatorship in place of what Lenin had called "the freest country in the world."

The reasons for these remarkable developments and the question of their inevitability have been the subject of debate ever since they took place. Some have thought the process inevitable: Marxists see it as the working out in Russia of Marx's theory of the natural progress of societies from feudalism to capitalism to socialism, while some scholars view it as showing the natural tendency of all revolutions to move toward extremes. Others see it as a result that might have been expected from the course of Russian history. An important question not often considered is why the opposition to the Bolshevik Revolution was so weak. The essays included in this section discuss these interpretations and questions. The documents are selected to illustrate the problems that troubled the Provisional Government and the ways in which the Bolsheviks exploited them to gain power.

1

The Official Version
of the Communist Party
Under Stalin

The following passage is taken from the official history of the Communist Party prepared under the close supervision of Stalin. Some parts of it seem to have been written by Stalin himself. Since 1938 and until very recently it has been the official account of the Revolution taught and learned by Communists around the world.

FROM *History of the Communist Party of the Soviet Union (Bolsheviks)*

1. THE HISTORY OF THE PARTY teaches us, first of all, that the victory of the proletarian revolution, the victory of the dictatorship of the proletariat, is impossible without a revolutionary party of the proletariat, a party free from opportunism, irreconcilable towards compromisers and capitulators, and revolutionary in its attitude towards the bourgeoisie and its state power.

The history of the Party teaches us that to leave the proletariat without such a party means to leave it without revolutionary leadership; and to leave it without revolutionary leadership means to ruin the cause of the proletarian revolution.

The history of the Party teaches us that the ordinary Social-Democratic Party of the West-European type, brought up under conditions of civil peace, trailing in the wake of the opportunists, dreaming of "social reforms," and dreading social revolution, cannot be such a party.

The history of the Party teaches us that only a party of the new type, a Marxist-Leninist party, a party of social revolution, a party capable of preparing the proletariat for decisive battles against the bourgeoisie and of organizing the victory of the proletarian revolution, can be such a party.

"Official Version of the Communist Party Under Stalin," in *History of the Communist Party of the Soviet Union*, pp. 353, 355–358, International Publishers, NY, 1939. Reprinted by permission.

2. The history of the Party further teaches us that a party of the working class cannot perform the role of leader of its class, cannot perform the role of organizer and leader of the proletarian revolution, unless it has mastered the advanced theory of the working-class movement, the Marxist-Leninist theory.

The power of the Marxist-Leninist theory lies in the fact that it enables the Party to find the right orientation in any situation, to understand the inner connection of current events, to foresee their course and to perceive not only how and in what direction they are developing in the present, but how and in what direction they are bound to develop in the future.

Only a party which has mastered the Marxist-Leninist theory can confidently advance and lead the working class forward.

On the other hand, a party which has not mastered the Marxist-Leninist theory is compelled to grope its way, loses confidence in its actions and is unable to lead the working class forward.

It may seem that all that is required for mastering the Marxist-Leninist theory is to diligently learn by heart isolated conclusions and propositions from the works of Marx, Engels and Lenin, learn to quote them at opportune times and rest at that, in hope that the conclusions and propositions thus memorized will suit each and every situation and occasion. But such an approach to the Marxist-Leninist theory is altogether wrong. The Marxist-Leninist theory must not be regarded as a collection of dogmas, as a catechism, as a symbol of faith, and the Marxists themselves as pedants and dogmatists. The Marxist-Leninist theory is the science of the development of society, the science of the working-class movement, the science of the proletarian revolution, the science of the building of the Communist society. And as a science it does not and cannot stand still, but develops and perfects itself. Clearly, in its development it is bound to become enriched by new experience and new knowledge, and some of its propositions and conclusions are bound to change in the course of time, are bound to be replaced by new conclusions and propositions corresponding to the new historical conditions.

Mastering the Marxist-Leninist theory does not at all mean learning all its formulas and conclusions by heart and clinging to their every letter. To master the Marxist-Leninist theory we must first of all learn to distinguish between its letter and substance.

Mastering the Marxist-Leninist theory means assimilating *the substance* of this theory and learning to use it in the solution of the practical problems of the revolutionary movement under the varying conditions of the class struggle of the proletariat.

Mastering the Marxist-Leninist theory means being able to enrich this theory with the new experience of the revolutionary movement, with new propositions and conclusions, it means being able to *develop it and advance it* without hesitating to replace—in accordance with the substance of the theory—such of its propositions and conclusions as have become antiquated by new ones corresponding to the new historical situation.

The Marxist-Leninist theory is not a dogma but a guide to action.

Before the second Russian revolution (February 1917), the Marxists of all countries assumed that the parliamentary democratic republic was the most suitable form of political organization of society in the period of transition from capitalism to Socialism. It is true that in the seventies Marx stated that the most suitable form for the dictatorship of the proletariat was a political organization of the type of the Paris Commune, and not the parliamentary republic. But, unfortunately, Marx did not develop this proposition any further in his writings and it was committed to oblivion. Moreover, Engels' authoritative statement in his criticism of the draft of the Erfurt Program in 1891, namely, that "the democratic republic . . . is . . . the specific form for the dictatorship of the proletariat" left no doubt that the Marxists continued to regard the democratic republic as the political form for the dictatorship of the proletariat. Engels' proposition later became a guiding principle for all Marxists, including Lenin. However, the Russian Revolution of 1905, and especially the Revolution of February 1917, advanced a new form of political organization of society—the Soviets of Workers' and Peasants' Deputies. As a result of a study of the experience of the two Russian revolutions, Lenin, on the basis of the theory of Marxism, arrived at the conclusion that the best political form for the dictatorship of the proletariat was not a parliamentary democratic republic, but a republic of Soviets. Proceeding from this, Lenin, in April 1917, during the period of transition from the bourgeois to the Socialist revolution, issued the slogan of a republic of Soviets as the best political form for the dictatorship of the proletariat. The opportunists of all countries clung to the parliamentary republic and accused Lenin of departing from Marxism and destroying democracy. But it was Lenin, of course, who was the real Marxist who had mastered the theory of Marxism, and not the opportunists, for Lenin was advancing the Marxist theory by enriching it with new experience, whereas the opportunists were dragging it back and transforming one of its propositions into a dogma.

What would have happened to the Party, to our revolution, to Marxism, if Lenin had been overawed by the letter of Marxism and had not had the courage to replace one of the old propositions of Marxism, formulated by Engels, by the new proposition regarding the republic of Soviets, a proposition that corresponded to the new historical conditions? The Party would have groped in the dark, the Soviets would have been disorganized, we should not have had a Soviet power, and the Marxist theory would have suffered a severe setback. The proletariat would have lost, and the enemies of the proletariat would have won.

As a result of a study of pre-imperialist capitalism Engels and Marx arrived at the conclusion that the Socialist revolution could not be victorious in one country, taken singly, that it could be victorious only by a simultaneous stroke in all, or the majority of the civilized countries. That was in the middle of the nineteenth century. This conclusion later became a guiding principle for all Marxists. However, by the beginning of the twentieth century, pre-imperialist capitalism had grown into imperialist capitalism, ascendant capitalism had turned into moribund capitalism. As a result of a study of imperialist capitalism, Lenin, on the basis of the Marxist theory, arrived at the conclusion that the old formula of Engels and Marx no longer corresponded to the new historical conditions, and that the victory of the Socialist revolution was quite possible in one country, taken singly. The opportunists of all countries clung to the old formula of Engels and Marx and accused Lenin of departing from Marxism. But it was Lenin, of course, who was the real Marxist who had mastered the theory of Marxism, and not the opportunists, for Lenin was advancing the Marxist theory by enriching it with new experience, whereas the opportunists were dragging it back, mummifying it.

What would have happened to the Party, to our revolution, to Marxism, if Lenin had been overawed by the letter of Marxism and had not had the courage of theoretical conviction to discard one of the old conclusions of Marxism and to replace it by a new conclusion affirming that the victory of Socialism in one country, taken singly, was possible, a conclusion which corresponded to the new historical conditions? The Party would have groped in the dark, the proletarian revolution would have been deprived of leadership, and the Marxist theory would have begun to decay. The proletariat would have lost, and the enemies of the proletariat would have won.

Opportunism does not always mean a direct denial of the Marxist theory or of any of its propositions and conclusions. Opportunism is sometimes expressed in the attempt to cling to certain of the propositions of Marxism that have already become antiquated and to convert them into a dogma, so as to retard the further development of Marxism, and, consequently, to retard the development of the revolutionary movement of the proletariat.

It may be said without fear of exaggeration that since the death of Engels the master theoretician Lenin, and after Lenin, Stalin and the other disciples of Lenin, have been the only Marxists who have advanced the Marxist theory and who have enriched it with new experience in the new conditions of the class struggle of the proletariat.

And just because Lenin and the Leninists have advanced the Marxist theory, Leninism is a further development of Marxism; it is Marxism in the new conditions of the class struggle of the proletariat, Marxism of the epoch of imperialism and proletarian revolutions, Marxism of the epoch of the victory of Socialism on one-sixth of the earth's surface.

The Bolshevik Party could not have won in October 1917 if its foremost men had not mastered the theory of Marxism, if they had not learned to regard this theory as a guide to action, if they had not learned to advance the Marxist theory by enriching it with the new experience of the class struggle of the proletariat.

2

The Provisional Government

On March 12, 1917,[1] the Revolution was proclaimed in Petrograd. Among the revolutionaries there was a split from the first. The Liberals were in favor of a constitutional monarchy on the English model. They wanted Czar Nicholas II to abdicate in favor of his son. The Socialists, however, opposed the idea of monarchy, desiring a republican constitution. On March 16 the Romanov dynasty came to an end. From then until the Bolshevik Revolution Russia was ruled by a provisional government which would stay in being until the coming of a constituent assembly. The first government was set up by the Provisional Executive Committee of the members of the Duma (Russia's parliament). All its ministers were members of bourgeois parties except one, Alexander Kerensky, a leader of the Social Revolutionary party and a vice-president of the Petrograd Soviet. On March 16 the new government was proclaimed.

Formation and Program of Provisional Government

CITIZENS, THE PROVISIONAL EXECUTIVE COMMITTEE of the members of the Duma, with the aid and support of the garrison of the capital and its inhabitants, has triumphed over the dark forces of the Old Régime to such an extent as to enable it to organize a more stable executive power. With this idea in mind, the Provisional Committee has appointed as ministers of the first Cabinet representing the public, men whose past political and public life assures them the confidence of the country.

PRINCE GEORGE F. LVOV, *Prime Minister and Minister of the Interior*
P. N. MILIUKOV, *Minister of Foreign Affairs*
A. I. GUCHKOV, *Minister of War and Marine*
M. I. TERESCHENKO, *Minister of Finance*

---

[1] In 1917 Russia followed the Julian calendar which was thirteen days behind our own. Thus the overthrow of the Romanovs took place in February for the Russians, and the Bolshevik coup in October. Dates in this section will be given in the new style.

"Formation and Program of Provisional Government," in F. A. Golder, *Documents of Russian History 1914–1917*, translated by Emanuel Aronsberg, pp. 308–309. Appleton-Century Crofts, Inc., 1927. Reprinted by Peter Smith Publisher, Inc.

A. A. MANUILOV, *Minister of Education*
A. I. SHINGAREV, *Minister of Agriculture*
N. V. NEKRASOV, *Minister of Transportation*
A. I. KONOVALOV, *Minister of Commerce and Industry*
A. F. KERENSKI, *Minister of Justice*
VL. LVOV, *Holy Synod*

The Cabinet will be guided in its actions by the following principles:

1. An immediate general amnesty for all political and religious offenses, including terrorist acts, military revolts, agrarian offenses, etc.
2. Freedom of speech and press; freedom to form labor unions and to strike. These political liberties should be extended to the army in so far as war conditions permit.
3. The abolition of all social, religious and national restrictions.
4. Immediate preparation for the calling of a Constituent Assembly, elected by universal and secret vote, which shall determine the form of government and draw up the Constitution for the country.
5. In place of the police, to organize a national militia with elective officers, and subject to the local self-governing body.
6. Elections to be carried out on the basis of universal, direct, equal, and secret suffrage.
7. The troops that have taken part in the revolutionary movement shall not be disarmed or removed from Petrograd.
8. On duty and in war service, strict military discipline should be maintained, but when off duty, soldiers should have the same public rights as are enjoyed by other citizens.

The Provisional Government wishes to add that it has no intention of taking advantage of the existence of war conditions to delay the realization of the above-mentioned measures of reform.

President of the Duma, M. RODZIANKO
President of the Council of Ministers, PRINCE LVOV
Ministers MILIUKOV, NEKRASOV, MANUILOV, KONOVALOV, TERESCHENKO, VL. LVOV, SHINGAREV, KERENSKI.

During the events of March, Lenin, the leader of the Bolsheviks, was in exile in Switzerland. With the agreement of the German government, he was allowed to cross German territory and return to Russia. His arrival strengthened the resolve of the Bolsheviks and undermined the unity of the revolutionary groups.

Lenin's April Theses

. . . LENIN ARRIVED IN PETROGRAD on the night of April 3 [16]. The following day, he read and commented upon these Theses first to a meeting of his fellow Bolsheviks and then to a joint conference of Bolsheviks and Mensheviks called to discuss the possible union of all the Social Democratic factions. They were then published in *Pravda* on April 7 [20]. At the conference, Lenin also vigorously opposed unification, called for a re-examination of the whole program of the Party, recommended the change of its name to the Communist Party, and, in general, laid to rest the attempts at unity. . . .

* * *

1. In our attitude toward the war not the slightest concession must be made to "revolutionary defencism," for under the new government of Lvov and Co., owing to the capitalist nature of this government, the war on Russia's part remains a predatory imperialist war.

The class-conscious proletariat may give its consent to a revolutionary war actually justifying revolutionary defencism, only on condition (a) that all power be transferred to the proletariat and its ally, the poorest section of the peasantry; (b) that all annexations be renounced in deeds, not merely in words; (c) that there be a complete break, in practice, with all interests of capital.

In view of the undoubted honesty of the mass of rank and file representatives of revolutionary defencism who accept the war only as a necessity and not as a means of conquest, in view of their being deceived by the bourgeoisie, it is necessary most thoroughly, persistently, patiently to explain to them their error, to explain the inseparable connection between capital and the imperialist war, to prove that without the overthrow of capital it is *impossible* to conclude the war with a really democratic, non-oppressive peace.

This view is to be widely propagated among the army units in the field. Fraternisation.

2. The peculiarity of the present situation in Russia is that it represents a *transition* from the first stage of the revolution, which, because of the inadequate organisation and insufficient class-consciousness of the proletariat, led to the assumption of power by the bourgeoisie,—to its second stage which is to place power in the hands of the proletariat and the poorest strata of the peasantry.

"Lenin's April Theses," in *The Russian Provisional Government, 1917: Documents Volumes II and III.* Selected and edited by Robert Paul Browder and Alexander F. Kerensky with the permission of the publishers, Stanford University Press.

This transition is characterised, on the one hand, by a maximum of legality (Russia is now the freest of all the belligerent countries of the world); on the other, by the absence of oppression of the masses, and, finally, by the trustingly ignorant attitude of the masses toward the capitalist government, the worst enemy of peace and Socialism.

This peculiar situation demands of us an ability to adapt ourselves to the specific conditions of party work amidst vast masses of the proletariat just awakened to political life.

3. No support to the Provisional Government; exposure of the utter falsity of all of its promises, particularly those relating to the renunciation of annexations. Unmasking, instead of admitting, the illusion-breeding "demand" that *this* government, a government of capitalists, cease being imperialistic.

4. Recognition of the fact that in most of the Soviets of Workers' Deputies our party constitutes a minority, and a small one at that, in the face of the *bloc* of all the petty-bourgeois opportunist elements, from the People's Socialists, Socialists-Revolutionists, down to the Organisation Committee (Chkheidze, Tsereteli, etc., Steklov, etc.), who have yielded to the influence of the bourgeoisie and have been extending this influence to the proletariat as well.

It must be explained to the masses that the Soviet of Workers' Deputies is the only possible form of revolutionary government and that, therefore, our task is, while this government is submitting to the influence of the bourgeoisie, to present a patient, systematic, and persistent analysis of its errors and tactics, an analysis especially adapted to the practical needs of the masses.

While we are in the minority, we carry on the work of criticism and of exposing errors, advocating all along the necessity of transferring the entire power of state to the Soviets of Workers' Deputies, so that the masses might learn from experience how to rid themselves of errors.

5. Not a parliamentary republic,—a return to it from the Soviet of Workers' Deputies would be a step backward—but a republic of Soviets of Workers', Agricultural Labourers' and Peasants' Deputies throughout the land, from top to bottom.

Abolition of the police, the army, the bureaucracy.[1]

All officers to be elected and to be subject to recall at any time, their salaries not to exceed the average wage of a competent worker.

6. In the agrarian programme, the emphasis must be shifted to the Soviets of Agricultural Labourers' Deputies.

Confiscation of all private lands.

Nationalisation of all lands in the country, and management of such lands by local Soviets of Agricultural Labourers' and Peasants' Deputies. A separate organisation of Soviets of Deputies of the poorest peasants. Creation of model agricultural establishments out of large estates (from one hundred to three hundred *desiatinas,* in accordance with local and other conditions and with the

---

[1]Substituting for the standing army the universal arming of the people.

estimates of local institutions) under the control of the Soviet of Agricultural Labourers' Deputies, and at public expense.

7. Immediate merger of all the banks in the country into one general national bank, over which the Soviet of Workers' Deputies should have control.

*   *   *

8. Not the "introduction" of Socialism as an immediate task, but the immediate placing of the Soviet of Workers' Deputies in control of social production and distribution of goods.

    9. Party tasks:

        A. Immediate calling of a party convention.

        B. Changing the party programme, mainly:

            1. Concerning imperialism and the imperialist war.

            2. Concerning our attitude toward the state, and our demand for a "commune state."[2]

            3. Amending our antiquated minimum programme.

        C. Changing the name of the party.[3]

    10. Rebuilding the International.

        Taking the initiative in the creation of a revolutionary International, an International against the social-chauvinists and against the "centre."[4]

FROM *On the Dual Power*
BY *V. I. Lenin*

LENIN ON THE SOVIETS

SIMULTANEOUSLY WITH THE ESTABLISHMENT of the Provisional Government, the leaders of the Russian socialist parties—Mensheviks, Bolsheviks, and Socialist-Revolutionaries ("SR's")—organized the so-called "soviets (Russian for "councils") of workers' and soldiers' deputies." The soviets, set up in every major city on the model of similar bodies that existed during the Revolution of 1905, began to exert a strong though informal political influence—hence Lenin's

[2]A state the model for which was given by the Paris Commune.

[3]Instead of "Social-Democracy," whose official leaders throughout the world have betrayed Socialism, by going over to the bourgeoisie (defencists and vacillating Kautskians), we must call ourselves the *Communist Party*.

[4]The "centre" in the international Social-Democracy is the tendency vacillating between chauvinists ("defencists") and internationalists, *i.e.,* Kautsky and Co. in Germany, Longuet and Co. in France, Chkheidze and Co. in Russia, Turati and Co. in Italy, MacDonald and Co. in England, etc.

"The Dual Power," in R. V. Daniels, *A Documentary History of Communism*, pp. 91–95. Random House, New York, 1960. Reprinted by permission.

expression of "dual power" shared by the more moderate Provisional Government and the more radical soviets. Lenin saw in the soviets the ideal organs of revolution; it remained only for his Bolsheviks to win paramount influence in them, which they did on the eve of their seizure of power.

* * *

The basic question in any revolution is that of state power. Unless this question is understood, there can be no conscious participation in the revolution, not to speak of guidance of the revolution.

The highly remarkable specific feature of our revolution is that it has brought about a *dual power*. This fact must be grasped first and foremost: unless it is understood, we cannot advance. We must know how to supplement and amend old "formulas," for example, of Bolshevism, for as it has transpired, they were correct on the whole, but their concrete realization has *turned out to be* different. *Nobody* previously thought, or could have thought, of a dual power.

In what does this dual power consist? In the fact that side by side with the Provisional Government, the government of the *bourgeoisie,* there has arisen *another government,* weak and incipient as yet, but undoubtedly an actually existing and growing government—the Soviets of Workers' and Soldiers' Deputies.

What is the class composition of this other government? It consists of the proletariat and the peasantry (clad in soldier's uniforms). What is the political nature of this government? It is a revolutionary dictatorship, i.e., a power directly based on revolutionary seizure, on the direct initiative of the masses from below, and *not on a law* enacted by a centralized state power. It is a power entirely different from that generally existing in the parliamentary bourgeois-democratic republics of the usual type still prevailing in the advanced countries of Europe and America. This circumstance is often forgotten, often not reflected on, yet it is the crux of the matter. *This* power is of *the same type* as the Paris Commune of 1871. The fundamental characteristics of this type are: 1) the source of power is not a law previously discussed and enacted by parliament, but the direct initiative of the people's masses from below, in their localities— direct "seizure" to use a current expression; 2) the replacement of the police and the army, which are institutions separated from the people and set against the people, by the direct arming of the whole people; order in the state under such a power is maintained by the armed workers and peasants *themselves,* by the armed people *themselves;* 3) officialdom, the bureaucracy are either similarly replaced by the direct rule of the people themselves or at least placed under special control; they not only become elected officials, but are also *subject to recall* at the first demand of the people; they are reduced to the position of simple agents; from a privileged stratum holding "jobs" remunerated on a high, bourgeois scale, they become workers of a special "branch," whose remuneration *does not exceed* the ordinary pay of a competent worker.

This, and this *alone,* constitutes the *essence* of the Paris Commune as a special type of state. This essence has been forgotten or perverted by the

Plekhanovs (out-and-out chauvinists who have betrayed Marxism), the Kautsky's (the men of the "Centre," i.e., those who vacillate between chauvinism and Marxism), and generally by all those Social-Democrats, Socialist-Revolutionaries, etc., etc., who now hold sway.

They are trying to get away with phrases, evasions, subterfuges; they congratulate each other a thousand times upon the revolution, but they refuse to *ponder* over *what* the Soviets of Workers' and Soldiers' Deputies *are*. They refuse to recognize the obvious truth that inasmuch as these Soviets exist, *inasmuch as* they are a power, we have in Russia a state of the *type* of the Paris Commune.

I have underscored the words "inasmuch as," for it is only an incipient power. By direct agreement with the bourgeois Provisional Government and by a series of actual concessions, it has itself *surrendered and is surrendering* its positions to the bourgeoisie.

Why? Is it because Chkheidze, Tsereteli, Steklov, and Co. are making a "mistake"? Nonsense. Only a philistine can think so—not a Marxist. The reason is *insufficient class-consciousness* and organization of the proletarians and peasants. The "mistake" of the leaders I have named lies in their petty-bourgeois position, in the fact that instead of enlightening the minds of the workers, they are *befogging* them; instead of dispersing petty-bourgeois illusions, they are *instilling* them; instead of freeing the masses from bourgeois influence, they are *strengthening* that influence.

It should be clear from this why our comrades too commit so many mistakes when putting the question "simply": should the Provisional Government be overthrown immediately?

My answer is: 1) it should be overthrown, for it is an oligarchic, bourgeois, and not a people's government, and *is unable* to provide peace, or bread, or full freedom; 2) it cannot be overthrown just now, for it is being maintained by a direct and indirect, a formal and actual *agreement* with the Soviets of Workers' Deputies, and primarily with the chief Soviet, the Petrograd Soviet; 3) generally, it cannot be "overthrown" in the ordinary way, for it rests on the *"support"* given to the bourgeoisie by the *second* government—the Soviet of Workers' Deputies, and that government is the only possible revolutionary government, which directly expresses the mind and will of the majority of the workers and peasants. Humanity has not yet evolved and we do not as yet know a type of government superior to and better than the Soviets of Workers', Agricultural Labourers', Peasants' and Soldiers' Deputies.

In order to become a power the class-conscious workers must win the majority to their side. *As long as* no violence is used against the masses there is no other road to power. We are not Blanquists,[1] we do not stand for the seizure of power by a minority. We are Marxists, we stand for proletarian class struggle against petty-bourgeois intoxication, against chauvinism-defencism, phrasemongering and dependence on the bourgeoisie.

---

[1] Blanquists: adherents of the conspiratorial doctrine of the French Revolutionary L. A. Blanqui—Ed.

Let us create a proletarian Communist Party; its elements have already been created by the best adherents of Bolshevism; let us rally our ranks for proletarian class work; then, from among the proletarians, from among the *poor* peasants, ever greater numbers will range themselves on our side. For *actual experience* will from day to day shatter the petty-bourgeois illusions of the "Social-Democrats"—the Chkheidzes, Tseretelis, Steklovs et al.—of the "Socialist-Revolutionaries," petty bourgeois of a still purer water, and so on and so forth.

The bourgeoisie stands for the undivided power of the bourgeoisie.

The class-conscious workers stand for the undivided power of the Soviets of Workers', Agricultural Labourers', Peasants' and Soldiers' Deputies—for undivided power made possible not by dubious ventures, but by the *enlightenment* of the proletarian minds, by their *emancipation* from the influence of the bourgeoisie.

The petty bourgeoisie—"Social-Democrats," Socialist-Revolutionaries, etc., etc.—vacillates and *hinders* this enlightenment and emancipation.

Such is the actual, the *class* alignment of forces that determines our tasks.

The Provisional Government inherited a disastrous war, a terribly disorganized nation, and a desperate economic situation. Its attempts to solve these problems were consistently opposed by the Bolsheviks, and its failures played into Bolshevik hands.

"Land and Liberty" was the slogan of the Revolution, and from the first the peasants were eager to take possession of all the land they could. The following resolution passed on June 7 reveals their point of view.

The Land Question: Resolution of the All-Russian Congress of Peasants' Deputies

THE ALL-RUSSIAN Congress of Peasants' Deputies invites the whole peasantry to remain peaceful, but to work with determination and steadfastness for the realization in a legal manner of the cherished thoughts and hopes of the agricultural laborer, which have long since found expression in the motto, so dear to each peasant, "Land and Liberty."

The Congress decided in favor of the following special appeal to the population:

The All-Russian Congress of Peasants' Deputies appeals to the peasants and the whole wage-earning population of Russia to vote, at the elections to the Constituent Assembly, only for those candidates who pledge themselves to advocate the nationalization of the land, without reimbursement, and on principles of equality.

"The Land Question," in *Documents of Russian History 1914–1917*, p. 378. Reprinted by permission.

The government's attitude is revealed in the following declaration.

The Government Declaration of March 19

THE WAR AND THE DOWNFALL of the old regime have brought the most serious economic problems of Russia to the fore. A systematic and expedient resolution of these is essential to the welfare of the state.

The first and foremost among them is the land question; its resolution constitutes the most serious socioeconomic task of the present historical moment. Land reform—the cherished dream of many generations of the entire agricultural population of the country—constitutes the basic demand in the programs of all the democratic parties. There is no doubt that it will be on the agenda of the forthcoming Constituent Assembly.

The land question cannot be resolved by means of any [arbitrary] seizures. Violence and robbery are the worst and most dangerous expedients in the realm of economic relations. Only enemies of the people can push them onto such a perilous course, from which there can be no reasonable outcome. The land question must be resolved by means of law, passed by the representatives of the people.

Proper consideration and passage of a land law is impossible without serious preparatory work: the collection of materials, the registration of land reserves, [the determination of] the distribution of landed property, and the conditions and forms of land utilization, and so forth.

The Provisional Government has recognized as its urgent duty the carrying out of preparatory work on the land question as soon as possible in order that all the materials and information can be made available to the representatives of the people.

On the basis of the above considerations, the Provisional Government has resolved:

1. To recognize the urgency of the preparation and elaboration of materials on the land question.
2. To entrust this [task] to the Ministry of Agriculture.
3. To form a Land Committee in the Ministry of Agriculture for the purpose indicated.
4. To direct the Minister of Agriculture to submit to the Government at the earliest moment a plan for the establishment of such a Committee together with an estimate of the funds necessary for its work.

Prince L'vov, Minister-President
[and other ministers]
March 19, 1917

"The Governement Declaration of March 19," in *The Russian Provisional Government, 1917: Documents,* vol. II, pp. 524–525. Reprinted by permissions.

The following account by a Bolshevik official reveals his party's attitude.

The Bolsheviks and the Peasants

. . . AS VOLOST COMMISSAR I received through the uezd Soviet of Workers' Deputies instructions from the Kerensky government to organize the volost committees. I called a general meeting in order to discuss the matter and make my report. [The peasants] shouted at me: "What are you talking about a committee for? Better tell us about the land; can we take it away from the landlords? Never mind your committees."

I then told the gathering that my own party [Bolshevik] looks at the question in this way: "Take the land and be done with it! Don't be waiting for them to let you have it. Kerensky's flunkies are only saying they will give it to you, but actually they won't give you anything."

"And may we take the lake, too?"

That lake was surrounded by the fields and belonged to the Catholic bishop; one could not even bathe in it without paying for it.

"You may," I answered.

"Hear that, Uncle Mikhei? The chief says we can take everything right away."

"Go on," said the old man; "you might get us into trouble."

"What nonsense are you speaking, Uncle? The chief surely knows better. He is one of those Bolsheviks whose law is, take everything."

Then followed talk such as: "In our volost we have no landlord's estate, but here we do have the Bishop's lake. Well, let's chase off Theoktist Tarakanov, who has rented the lake, and then we'll all go fishing."

"Hey, boys! Who wants to go fishing?"

"And will those who live beyond the river, twelve versts away, get it too?" I heard some people asking.

"What do we care? Let them use the river, and, if they want to, let them fish here. We don't care; it's all the people's property; let all the people use it."

And so the rumor went out to all the volosts of the Rezhitsa Uezd that the Ruzhinskaia volost had resolved to confiscate the land, water, and forests from the landlords and monasteries, and that their chief had explained to them that there was such a law. In a mighty wave the excitement spread all over Latgalia, which consists of the three uezds of Rezhitsa, Dvinsk, and Liutsin, two-thirds inhabited by Letts and one-third by Old Believers. In some places there were armed clashes between the peasants and the government. . . .

"The Bolsheviks and the Peasants," in J. Bunyan and H. H. Fisher, *The Bolshevik Revolution, 1917–1918*, pp. 33–34. Stanford Unversity Press, 1934. Reprinted by permission.

*The Russian army was disintegrating under the monarchy and kept falling apart
after the Revolution. Almost immediately the Soviet issued Order No. 1, which made
the army more democratic than any army had ever been. It also turned out to
destroy discipline without preventing desertion. Several times the government tried
to restore discipline and even restored the death penalty. This only helped increase
the popularity of the Bolsheviks.*

Order No. 1, March 14, 1917

To THE GARRISON of the Petrograd District, to all the soldiers of the guard, army,
artillery, and navy, for immediate and strict execution, and to the workers of
Petrograd for their information:—

 The Soviet of Workers' and Soldiers' Deputies has resolved:

1. In all companies, battalions, regiments, parks, batteries, squadrons, in the
   special services of the various military administrations, and on the vessels of
   the navy, committees from the elected representatives of the lower ranks of
   the above-mentioned military units shall be chosen immediately.
2. In all those military units which have not yet chosen their representatives to
   the Soviet of Workers' Deputies, one representative from each company shall
   be selected, to report with written credentials at the building of the State
   Duma by ten o'clock on the morning of the fifteenth of this March.
3. In all its political actions, the military branch is subordinated to the Soviet of
   Workers' and Soldiers' Deputies and to its own committees.
4. The orders of the military commission of the State Duma shall be executed
   only in such cases as do not conflict with the orders and resolutions of the
   Soviet of Workers' and Soldiers' Deputies.
5. All kinds of arms, such as rifles, machine guns, armored automobiles, and
   others, must be kept at the disposal and under the control of the company
   and battalion committees, and in no case be turned over to officers, even at
   their demand.
6. In the ranks and during their performance of the duties of the service, soldiers must observe the strictest military discipline, but outside the service and
   the ranks, in their political, general civic, and private life, soldiers cannot in
   any way be deprived of those rights which all citizens enjoy. In particular,
   standing at attention and compulsory saluting, when not on duty, is abolished.
7. Also, the addressing of the officers with the title, "Your Excellency," "Your
   Honor," etc., is abolished, and these titles are replaced by the address of "Mister
   General," "Mister Colonel," etc. Rudeness towards soldiers of any rank, and,
   especially, addressing them as "Thou," is prohibited, and soldiers are required
   to bring to the attention of the company committees every infraction of this
   rule, as well as all misunderstandings occurring between officers and privates.

Order No. 1, March 14, 1917," in *Documents of Russian History 1914–1917*, pp. 386–387. Reprinted by permission.

The present order is to be read to all companies, battalions, regiments, ships' crews, batteries, and other combatant and non-combatant commands.

Foreign policy divided the revolutionaries more quickly and more deeply than anything else. In general, the bourgeois parties wanted to pursue the war to a victorious conclusion that would bring Russia the goals aimed at by the Czar, or at least Constantinople. Later, when the Socialists under Kerensky entered and dominated a new coalition, they continued to wage the war, if only to defend the territory of Russia and retain the support of the Western Allies. The Bolsheviks continued to demand peace and no annexations. As defeat followed defeat and war-weariness grew, the Bolsheviks benefited greatly.

On May 1 Paul Miliukov, minister of foreign affairs, pressed hard by the Allies, issued a statement of policy.

Miliukov's Note on War Aims, May 1, 1917

ON MAY 1, the Minister of Foreign Affairs instructed the Russian representatives with the Allied Powers to transmit the following note to the Governments to which they are accredited:

> On April 9 of the present year, the Provisional Government issued a declaration to the citizens, containing the views of the Government of free Russia regarding the aims of the present war. The Minister of Foreign Affairs has instructed me to communicate to you the contents of the document referred to, and to make at the same time the following comments:

> Our enemies have been striving of late to sow discord among the Allies, disseminating absurd reports alleging that Russia is ready to conclude a separate peace with the Central Powers. The text of the attached document will most effectively refute such falsehoods. You will note from the same that the general principles enunciated by the Provisional Government are in entire agreement with those lofty ideas which have been constantly expressed, up to the very last moment, by many eminent statesmen in the Allied countries, and which were given especially vivid expression in the declaration of the president of our new Ally, the great republic across the Atlantic.

> The Government under the old régime was, of course, incapable of grasping and sharing these ideas of the liberating character of the war, the establishment of a firm basis for the amicable existence of the nations, of self-determination for oppressed peoples, and so forth. Emancipated Russia, however, can now speak in a language that will be comprehensible to the leading democracies of our own time, and she now hastens to add her voice to those of her Allies. Imbued with this new spirit of a free democracy, the declaration of the Provisional Government cannot, of course, afford the least excuse for the assumption that the revolution has entailed any slackening on the part of Russia in the common struggle of the Allies. Quite to the contrary, the aspiration of the entire nation to carry the world

---

"Miliukov's Note on War Aims," in *Documents of Russia History 1914–1917*, pp. 333–334. Reprinted by permission.

war to a decisive victory has grown more powerful, thanks to our understanding of our common responsibility, shared by each and every one. This striving has become still more active, since it is concentrated upon a task which touches all and is urgent,—the task of driving out the enemy who has invaded our country. It is obvious, as stated in the communicated document, that the Provisional Government, while safeguarding the rights of our own country, will, in every way, observe the obligations assumed toward our Allies.

Continuing to cherish the firm conviction of the victorious issue of the present war, in full accord with our Allies, the Provisional Government feels also absolutely certain that the problems which have been raised by this war will be solved in a spirit that will afford a firm basis for lasting peace, and that the leading democracies, inspired by identical desires, will find the means to obtain those guarantees and sanctions which are indispensable for the prevention of sanguinary conflicts in the future.

Miliukov's note aroused great popular hostility and led to demonstrations and a government crisis. These events gave Lenin the opportunity to present the Bolshevik position.

Lenin on the "Lessons of the Crisis"

PETROGRAD AND THE WHOLE OF RUSSIA have gone through a serious political crisis, the first political crisis since the revolution.

On May 1 the Provisional Government issued its notorious note, which confirmed the predatory aims of the war with such clarity that it was sufficient to arouse the indignation of the masses who had honestly believed in the desire (and ability) of the capitalists to "renounce the policy of annexations." On May 3 and 4 Petrograd was astir. The streets were crowded with people; meetings of various sizes were held everywhere, day and night; mass manifestations and demonstrations were going on uninterruptedly. Yesterday, May 4, the crisis or, at any rate the first stage of the crisis came to an end: the Executive Committee of the Soviet of Workers' and Soldiers' Deputies, and later the Soviet itself, declared that they were satisfied with the "explanations," amendments to the note and "elucidations" of the government (empty phrases that say absolutely nothing, change nothing, and commit one to nothing), and "the incident was closed."

The future will show whether the masses will regard the "incident as closed." The task before us now is carefully to examine the forces, the classes that revealed themselves in the crisis, and to draw therefrom lessons for the party of the proletariat. For it is the great significance of all crises that they unveil the hidden, cast aside the conventional, the superficial, the petty, sweep away the political rubbish, uncover the secret springs of the true class-struggle that is going on.

"Lenin on the 'Lessons of the Crisis,'" in *The Russian Provisional Government 1917: Documents*, vol. III, pp. 1246–1249. Reprinted by permission.

As a matter of fact the capitalist government on May 1 merely reiterated its former declarations, which enveloped the imperialist war in a mist of equivocation. The soldier masses grew indignant, because they had honestly believed in the sincerity and pacific intentions of the capitalists. The demonstration started as soldiers' demonstrations under a contradictory, unintelligent, leading-nowhere slogan, "Down with Miliukov" (as if a change in the personnel or cliques could change the essence of their policy).

That means that the broad, unstable, vacillating mass, which is closest to the peasantry and petty-bourgeoisie by scientific class definition, drew away from the capitalists *toward the side* of the revolutionary workers. It was this fluctuation or movement of the mass, whose strength was capable of settling everything, that created the crisis.

Immediately a commotion started, people poured into the streets, and began to organise; but those were not the middle, but the extreme elements; not the in-between petty-bourgeois mass, but the bourgeoisie and the proletariat.

The bourgeoisie occupies the Nevsky—in the expression of one paper, the "Miliukovsky"—Prospect and the adjacent sections of prosperous, bureaucratic, and capitalistic Petrograd. Officers, students, "the middle classes" parade *for* the Provisional Government. Among the slogans on the banners one often sees the inscription, "Down with Lenin."

The proletariat rises in *its own* quarters, in the workers' suburbs, it organises around the slogans and watchwords of the Central Committee of our party. On May 3 and 4, the Central Committee adopts resolutions which through the organisational apparatus are directly passed on to the proletarian masses. The workers' processions fill the poorer and less central sections of the city, and later in separate groups they enter the Nevsky. The proletarian demonstrations are distinguished from the bourgeois ones by greater animation and mass character. Among the inscriptions on the banners—"All Power to the Soviet of Workers' and Soldiers' Deputies."

It comes to a collision on the Nevsky. Banners of "enemy" processions are torn. The Executive Committee receives telephone messages from various points that there is shooting on both sides, that there are killed and wounded; information, however, is exceedingly contradictory and unreliable.

Fearing that the real masses, the actual majority of the people might seize power, the bourgeoisie expresses this fear by shouting about the "spectre of civil war." The petty-bourgeois leaders of the Soviet, the Mensheviks and Narodniks, lacking a definite party programme in the period after the revolution, and particularly in the days of the crisis, allow themselves to be intimidated. In the Executive Committee, which on the eve of the crisis was almost evenly divided between those who were for the Provisional Government and those against it, thirty-four ballots are cast (against nineteen) *for* a return to the policy of confidence in the capitalists and agreement with them.

The "incident" is declared "closed."

What is the essence of the class struggle? The capitalists are for continuing the war, and for concealing their aims behind a smoke-screen of phrases and promises. They have become entangled in the nets of Russian, Anglo-French and American bank capital. The proletariat, through its class-conscious van-guard, stands for taking over of power by the revolutionary class, the working class and semi-proletarians, it stands for the development of a world-wide pro-letarian revolution which is clearly rising in Germany, it stands for the termina-tion of the war through such a revolution.

The broad mass, of a predominantly petty-bourgeois nature, still trusting its Narodnik and Menshevik leaders, intimidated by the bourgeoisie and actually carrying out the policy of the bourgeoisie, under various pretexts, is swinging now to the right, now to the left.

War is terrible; it is the masses that feel it most keenly; it is among the masses that the realisation, as yet not very clear, is growing that this war is criminal, that it is waged because of the rivalry and the scrambling among capi-talists for the division of spoils. The international situation is becoming ever more entangled. There is no escape, except through an international proletarian revolution, which is now sweeping Russia, and which is already developing (strikes, fraternisation) in Germany. The masses fluctuate from faith in the old masters, the capitalists, to bitterness against them; from faith in the new class, the only consistently revolutionary class that is breaking a new path leading to a brighter life for the toilers—the proletariat—to a vague understanding of its world-wide historical role.

This is not the first *and not the last* instance of indecision of the petty-bourgeois and the semi-proletarian masses!

The lesson is clear, comrade-workers! Time does not wait. After the first crisis, others will follow. Consecrate *all* your strength to the cause of enlighten-ing those who are lagging behind, creating direct comradely contact (not merely through meetings) with each regiment, with each group of toilers who are still in the dark! Devote *all* your strength to uniting your own forces, organising the workers from the ground up, taking in every borough, every factory, every block in the city and its suburbs! Do not be misled by petty-bourgeois "peace makers" who "reconcile" themselves to the capitalists, by the defencist "supporters" of the Government's policies nor by individuals inclined to be hasty and to shout, "Down with the Provisional Government!" before the majority of the people are strongly united. Crises cannot be overcome by the violence of individuals against other individuals, by partial risings of small groups of armed people, by Blanquist attempts to "seize power," to "arrest" the Provisional Government, etc.

The slogan of the day is: Explain more carefully, more clearly, more broadly the proletarian policy, the proletarian method of terminating the war. Fall in line everywhere, strongly, numerously, fill the proletarian ranks and columns! Rally around your Soviets; use comradely suasion and re-election of individual members inside the Soviets to consolidate a majority around your-selves.

*The Miliukov note and the ensuing crisis brought down the government. It was
succeeded by a coalition of bourgeois Liberals from the fallen group and Socialists
representing the Soviet, which thus agreed to share responsibility. Kerensky and the
other Socialist ministers were eager to put an end to the war, but a separate peace
with Germany would certainly lead to the dismemberment of Russia, an outcome
they refused to accept. Instead they launched the July Offensive, which proved
disastrous. The radicals among the Socialists had opposed the coalition and the
offensive and were now vindicated. Some of them, among them some Bolsheviks,
launched demonstrations demanding the fall of the coalition government and "All
Power to the Soviets." Lenin opposed these disturbances, for he knew that the Soviets
were controlled by the moderate Socialists. The uprising was put down after a few
days of shooting. The Bolsheviks were blamed and accused of being agents of the
Germans. Feelings ran so high that Lenin and his friends were forced to flee to
Finland. Lunacharski's account illustrates the Bolsheviks' embarrassment.*

Lunacharski's Account of the July Uprising

IN ADDITION to the lack of a clear plan for action, there was also something
vague about the watchword, as was inevitable in the then-prevailing state of
affairs. The fact is that, with the exception of a momentary vacillation, we
[Bolsheviks] held firmly to the slogan "All power to the Soviets!" at a time when
the majority in the Soviet was composed of Mensheviks and Socialist-
Revolutionists. In practice, therefore, the slogan meant "All power to the party
of the Socialist-Revolutionists and Mensheviks." It was now even uncertain
whether we would join an all-socialist ministry, in case the Mensheviks and
Socialist-Revolutionists, contrary to our expectations, should consent to drive
the capitalist ministers out of the Government.

But what if they should consent? They might do so. What then? It was
quite evident at the time that an attempt to seize power by the Bolsheviks was
extremely risky and might lead to a temporary, perhaps not very serious, defeat.
For such an attempt the time was not yet ripe, at least not in the provinces and
at the front, and above all in Moscow.

All these considerations led to vagueness and indecision. When on the
morning of July 17, I found myself, together with Lenin and Sverdlov, at the
Kshesinski palace, and joined them in encouraging from the balcony the endless files of armed soldiers and workmen passing by, I clearly realized that, after
all, no one could predict how the day would end.

Jacob Mikhailovich [Sverdlov], with his stentorian voice, shouted to the
various detachments coming to a halt before the balcony to "Demand the
expulsion of the capitalist ministers from the Government," and "All Power to
the Soviets!" or "We are going to demand of the Soviets that they take the
whole power into their own hands. Should they refuse to do that, the situation
would become clear. Then wait for further slogans."

"Lunacharski's Account of the July Uprising," in *F. A. Golder, Documents of Russian History 1914–1917*, pp.
450–451. Reprinted by permission.

We are bound to admit that the Party knew no way out of the difficulty. It was compelled to demand of the Mensheviks and Socialist-Revolutionists, through a demonstration, something they were organically unable to decide upon, and, meeting with the refusal the Party had expected, it did not know how to proceed further; it left the demonstrators around the Taurida palace without a plan and gave the opposition time to organize its forces, while ours were breaking up; and consequently we went down to temporary defeat with eyes quite open.

General Kornilov's unsuccessful attempt at a turn to the right was helpful to the Bolsheviks. The following is F. A. Golder's discussion of Kornilov and his intentions.

The Kornilov Affair

BECAUSE OF HIS DARING, manliness, honesty, straightforwardness, and devotion to his service, General Kornilov was well known in military circles long before he came to the notice of the general public. He was a soldier first and last, and viewed the world from the military saddle. He did not play politics, was not mixed in the intrigues in or out of court. He was loyal to his Tsar as long as he reigned and when he abdicated Kornilov accepted, at least outwardly, the new state of affairs in the hope that the revolution would go on with the war until Russia was free of the Germans.

The Provisional Government trusted him, and named him Commander of the Petrograd Garrison. When Kornilov found that the Soviet decrees and pacifist propaganda were interfering with his duties and ruining the army, he resigned and went to the fighting lines. He was made Commander of the Southwest front and worked hard to put his army on a war footing. The failure of the July offensive grieved him deeply both as a patriot and as a commander. The cause of the failure was obvious and without paying attention to the feeling of the revolutionists he proceeded to put back the old discipline in the army. He prohibited meetings, made it clear that military commands are not subject to debate, and gave orders to shoot scoundrels without trial. He knew just what to do and did it. Kerenski was pleased and offered to make him Supreme Commander-in-Chief. Before accepting the offer General Kornilov demanded a free hand, and restoration of the old time military discipline both at the front and in the rear, for the civilian population as well as the soldiers. Had these demands been granted Kornilov would have had dictatorial powers and he would have tried to put an end to the Soviets and the revolutionists. Whether he would have tried to restore the monarchy no one knows. Kerenski and his Socialists, being politicians and revolutionists, could not grant all of Kornilov's demands. They might overlook his acts, but they could not openly come out for a policy which would put them and the revolution in the hands of the mili-

"The Kornilov Affair," in *Documents of Russia History 1914–1917*, pp. 513–514. Reprinted by permission.

tarists. At the same time they could not break with Kornilov, for he seemed to be the only man who might do something with the army.

A month of very precious time was wasted in fruitless conversation, in sending messages and messengers from one to the other. During that month Kornilov grew in popularity with the Duma crowd, the Nationalists, Militarists, and all those who were opposed to the Soviet. At the Moscow Conference they made him their hero, and it is possible that they also tried to make him their tool. As Kornilov grew in popularity with one group he became unpopular with the other. Whatever confidence and trust Kornilov and Kerenski had in each other before August 1 disappeared before September 1. It was a great pity, for both were ardent patriots and wished only the good of their country.

We have not as yet and may never have all the details of the so-called Kornilov plot. We are not even sure whether it was a plot or a misunder-standing. . . .

"Izvestia" Account of the Kornilov Affair

September 8–9.

AT 4:00 P.M., there was to be a meeting of the Provisional Government. Before it began, the Prime Minister was called out to talk with Headquarters by long distance telephone. From this conversation he got the impression that all was not as well as it should be and asked his adjutant to find V. N. LVOV. He was found and brought to the home of Kerenski. . . .

Lvov said that General Kornilov authorized him to demand that Kerenski, as Prime Minister, hand over his power to General Kornilov to form a new Government.

Lvov did not conceal the fact that this was the wish not only of Kornilov, but of a certain group of public men who were just then at Headquarters. This group had nothing against Kerenski's occupying the post of Minister of Justice in the new Cabinet. The Ministry of War was, however, to be in the hands of Savinkov.

If Kerenski agrees to this combination, then the public men invite him and Savinkov to come at once to Headquarters for further and final discussion. Lvov gave his word of honor that the Prime Minister would not be arrested at Headquarters; and if no agreement should be reached, then he could freely depart.

After listening to Lvov's propositions, Kerenski said that they were quite unexpected and that he was astonished at the boldness of General Kornilov. . . . It did not seem possible that General Kornilov would make such a demand, and therefore Lvov was asked to wait a little while Kerenski called up General Kornilov.

"Izvestia Account of The Kornilov Affair," in *Documents of Russian History 1914–1917*, pp. 523–524. Reprinted by permission.

General Kornilov confirmed Lvov. When Kerenski came back into the room, he told Lvov that he could not accept the propositions of General Kornilov and that he would take measures to crush this new plot against the free country and republic. . . .

About 8:00 P.M., the Provisional Government met. It discussed until late in the night this unexpected question. . . . In the end, the text for the call to the people was prepared and accepted. It removed Kornilov from command and declared Petrograd in a state of war.

In the course of the night a telegram was received from General Lukomski, the inspirer and ringleader of this plot. . . .

When the Government, after its discussion with Lvov, telegraphed to Lukomski to take over the command, he wired back his refusal. According to the contents of the telegram, General Lukomski will, it would seem, not stop even at the point of betraying his country. He threatened that a failure of the Government to carry out the demand of Kornilov would lead to civil war at the front, the opening of the front, and a shameful separate peace. All this would tend to show that there is a determination to come to an agreement with the Germans in order to succeed with the plot. . . .

At 4:00 A.M., September 9, Kerenski got Headquarters by long distance. Generals Kornilov and Lukomski would not give a straight answer to the question whether they would lay down their command, but said that they had not been understood and that Lvov had misled them.

Kerenski insisted that Kornilov should immediately lay down his command and come at once to Petrograd.

But General Kornilov refused to take orders from the Prime Minister. . . .

* * *

September 11.

The Government has taken the necessary measures to put an end to the rebellion. General Deniken, who announced that he joined Kornilov, has been arrested with all his staff. General Erdeli was also arrested because he refused to obey the orders of the Provisional Government.

Contact between Kornilov and his army is broken. The troops under his command have come to a standstill. Among his troops there is a great deal of disagreement. Some of the Cossacks have gone over to the side of the Government. The Wild Division is also divided in opinion. Judging from the attitude of some of the Kornilov troops, it may be said that they were drawn into the rebellion by deceit. They were led to believe that they were being taken to Petrograd to save the Provisional Government from a new Bolshevik attempt. . . . The Provisional Government hopes that civil war will be avoided.

The Government has issued an order to the commissars of all the gubernias not to allow the publication of the proclamations of Kornilov or of others in agreement with him. Nothing is to be published about Kornilov except official reports.

The "Novoe Vremia" published in full the Kornilov proclamations, but only extracts of the orders of the Government and appeals of those organizations fighting counter-revolution. Because of this, orders have been given to close the "Novoe Vremia.". . . . For similar reasons the "Russkoe Slovo" is also closed. . . .

In the course of the day, it was learned that Kornilov's Headquarters are surrounded from all sides. . . . Streets are quiet. . . . People are waiting in line for the evening papers. . . . People are nervous because they know not what to expect. . . . All kinds of wild rumors spread. . . .

Probable Results of the Kornilov Affair as Reported by "Riech," the Newspaper of the Constitutional Democratic, or Cadet Party

THIS IS THE QUESTION every one is asking. It is generally agreed that the Bolsheviks will make use of it for their own ends. They have already come out with a declaration that Kornilov's undertaking was not his own doing but of the whole bourgeoisie. In connection with this, the Bolsheviks have called on the workmen to wage war against the enemies of the proletariat and the revolution. On the streets one may see crowds of armed workmen frightening peaceful inhabitants. At the Soviet meetings the Bolsheviks insistently demand that their comrades be let out of prison.

In this connection it is generally assumed that just as soon as the Kornilov affair has been liquidated, the Bolsheviks, whom the majority of the Soviet no longer regards as betrayers of the revolution, will make every effort to force the Soviet to accept at least a part of their program.

Both Kokoshkin and Nekrasov are fully convinced that the Bolsheviks will do their best to bring pressure to bear on the Government, but the latter believes that they will have little influence.

"Probable Results of the Kornilov Affair," in *Documents of Russian History 1914–1917*, p. 532. Reprinted by permission.

3

The Bolsheviks Take Power

The aftermath of the Kornilov affair brought discredit to the bourgeois parties and weakened the Coalition Government. On October 8 a new coalition was formed headed by Kerensky. It had a Socialist majority but included no Bolsheviks. The Petrograd Soviet had fallen increasingly under the influence of the Bolsheviks. By October 8 Trotsky was its chairman, and it resolved to oppose the new government.

Resolution of Petrograd Soviet on Democratic Conference

THE PETROGRAD SOVIET declares that after the Kornilov experiment, which has shown that all bourgeois Russia occupies a counter-revolutionary position, any attempt at coalition means nothing else than the utter capitulation of the democracy to the Kornilov men. As evidence of this capitulation is the composition of the Ministry now being formed, where the leading places are given to the merchants and manufacturers, the inveterate foes of the workers', soldiers', and peasants' democracy. The so-called democratic Ministers, responsible to no one and to nothing, are unable either to offset or extenuate the anti-popular character of the new Government, which will go down in the history of the revolution as the Government of civil war.

The Petrograd Soviet declares that the workers and garrison of Petrograd will not support a Government of bourgeois omnipotence and of counter-revolutionary oppression. It is firmly convinced that the news of the newly formed Government will meet with one answer from the entire revolutionary democracy: "Retire!" And relying upon this unanimous vote of the democracy, the All-Russian Congress of Soviets will form a real revolutionary government. At the same time, the Petrograd Soviet urges the proletarian and soldier organizations to increased activity in rallying around their Soviets, but to refrain from separate action.

"Resolution of Petrograd Soviet on Democratic Conference," in *Documents of Russian History 1914–1917*, p. 567. Reprinted by permission.

As early as September the Bolsheviks began to arm their supporters.

The Red Guard FROM *"Izvestia," the Newspaper of the Petrograd Soviet*

AT KRONSTADT a Red Guard has been organized. All the workmen of the fortress have been supplied with arms. . . . They are being drilled daily in the use of rifles. . . . At Shlüsselburg the former convicts have formed a "Battalion of Death to all Kornilovs."

There was a meeting today [at Moscow] of the inter-ward Soviet to discuss the question of a Red Guard. It was decided to arm the workers just as soon as possible. . . .

The advance of the Germans and the threat it posed to Petrograd caused a new crisis. The loss of Riga brought rumors that the government was planning to evacuate Petrograd and move the capital to Moscow. These rumors caused panic. In addition to exposing the people of the city to the wrath of the Germans, the move would free the government from the influence of the Petrograd Soviet and increase that of the more conservative elements in Moscow. These fears increased Bolshevik fears in Petrograd and probably encouraged the Bolsheviks to take decisive action.

Evacuation of Petrograd FROM *"Riech"*

Petrograd, October 19.

PETROGRAD IS AGAIN passing through alarming days. The news of German operations in the Baltic and the appearance of zeppelins have given rise to many rumors of the danger threatening Petrograd and have created a panicky atmosphere. The news that the Government is taking definite measures to evacuate State institutions in the near future and is considering whether it should move the central organs of government and even the pre-parliament to Moscow have added strength to these alarming rumors. . . .

THE BOLSHEVIKS AND EVACUATION

The leaders of the Bolsheviks find that the removal of the Government to Moscow will produce a situation in Petrograd similar to the one in Paris in 1871, when "the enemy was at the gates and there was no government." At that time,

"The Red Guard," in *Documents of Russian History 1914–1917*, p. 580. Reprinted by permission.

"The Evacuation of Petrograd," in *Documents of Russian History, 1914–1917*, pp. 586–587. Reprinted by permission.

there will grow up a desire among the masses, so say the Bolsheviks, to form a commune. The Bolshevik leaders say that they are opposed to a commune at the present, but if it should appear, the Bolsheviks would participate in it.

RESOLUTION OF PETROGRAD SOVIET ON EVACUATION
[October 19]

The Soldiers' Section of the Petrograd Soviet of Workers' and Soldiers' Deputies vehemently protests against the idea of moving the Government from Petrograd to Moscow. Such an act would leave the revolutionary capital unprotected.

If the Provisional Government cannot defend Petrograd, it should either make peace or step down to make room for another government.

To move to Moscow means desertion from a responsible post.

By September, 1917, it was clear that mass sentiment among the workers, soldiers and peasants was shifting to the left. The Bolsheviks won control of the Petrograd and Moscow Soviets. Lenin thereupon called upon the Bolshevik Party to prepare to overthrow the Provisional Government by violence.

FROM *Marxism and Insurrection: A Letter to the Central Committee of the R.S.D.W.P.*

BY *V. I. Lenin*

. . . Marxists are accused of Blanquism for treating insurrection as an art! Can there be a more flagrant perversion of the truth, when not a single Marxist will deny that it was Marx who expressed himself on this score in the most definite, precise and categorical manner, referring to insurrection precisely as an *art,* and saying that it must be treated as an art, that one must *win* the first success and then proceed from success to success, never ceasing the *offensive* against the enemy, taking advantage of his confusion, etc., etc.?

To be successful, insurrection must rely not upon conspiracy and not upon a party, but upon the advanced class. That is the first point. Insurrection must rely upon a *revolutionary upsurge of the people*. That is the second point. Insurrection must rely upon such a *crucial moment* in the history of the growing revolution when the activity of the advanced ranks of the people is at its height, and when the *vacillations* in the ranks of the enemy and *in the ranks of the weak, half-hearted and irresolute friends of the revolution* are strongest. That is the third point. And these three conditions for raising the question of insurrection distinguish *Marxism from Blanquism.*

But once these conditions are present, to refuse to treat insurrection as an *art* is a betrayal of Marxism and a betrayal of the revolution. . . .

"Marxism and Insurrection . . . ," in R. V. Daniels, *A Documentary History of Communism*, pp. 106–109. Reprinted by permission.

All the objective conditions for a successful insurrection exist. We have the exceptional advantage of a situation in which *only* our victory in the insurrection can put an end to that most painful thing on earth, vacillation, which has worn the people out; a situation in which *only our* victory in the insurrection can *foil* the game of a separate peace directed against the revolution by publicly proposing a fuller, juster and earlier peace, a peace that will *benefit* the revolution. . . .

We must draw up a brief declaration of the Bolsheviks, emphasizing in the most trenchant manner the irrelevance of long speeches and of "speeches" in general, the necessity for immediate action to save the revolution, the absolute necessity for a complete break with the bourgeoisie, for the removal of the whole present government, for a complete rupture with the Anglo-French imperialists, who are preparing a "separate" partition of Russia, and for the immediate transfer of the whole power *to the revolutionary democracy headed by the revolutionary proletariat.*

Our declaration must consist of the briefest and most trenchant formulation of this conclusion in connection with the proposals of the program: peace for the peoples, land for the peasants, confiscation of outrageous profits, and a check on the outrageous sabotage of production by the capitalists.

The briefer and more trenchant the declaration the better. Only two other highly important points must be clearly indicated in it, namely, that the people are worn out by the vacillations, that they are tormented by the irresolution of the Socialist-Revolutionaries and Mensheviks; and that we are definitely breaking with these *parties* because they have betrayed the revolution.

And another thing. By immediately proposing a peace without annexations, by immediately breaking with the Allied imperialists and with all imperialists, either we shall at once obtain an armistice, or the entire revolutionary proletariat will rally to the defence of the country, and a really just, really revolutionary war will then be waged by the revolutionary democracy under the leadership of the proletariat.

Having read this declaration, and having appealed for *decisions* and not talk, for *action* and not resolution-writing, we must *dispatch* our whole group to the *factories and the barracks*. Their place is there, the pulse of life is there, the source of salvation of the revolution is there, and there is the motive force of the Democratic Conference.[1]

There, in ardent and impassioned speeches, we must explain our program and put the alternative: either the Conference adopts it *in its entirety,* or else insurrection. There is no middle course. Delay is impossible. The revolution is perishing.

By putting the question thus, by concentrating our entire group in the factories and barracks, *we shall be able to determine the right moment for launching the insurrection.*

---

[1]Democratic Conference: a semiofficial meeting of various Russian political leaders, convoked by the Provisional-Government in September, 1917—Ed.

And in order to treat insurrection in a Marxist way, i.e., as an art, we must at the same time, without losing a single moment, organize a *headquarter staff* of the insurgent detachments, distribute our forces, move the reliable regiments to the most important points, surround the Alexandrinsky Theatre, occupy the Peter and Paul Fortress, arrest the general staff and the government, and move against the cadets and the Savage Division such detachments as will rather die than allow the enemy to approach the centres of the city; we must mobilize the armed workers and call them to fight the last desperate fight, occupy the telegraph and the telephone exchange at once, place *our* headquarter staff of the insurrection at the central telephone exchange and connect it by telephone with all the factories, all the regiments, all the points of armed fighting, etc.

Of course, this is all by way of example, only to *illustrate* the fact that at the present moment it is impossible to remain loyal to Marxism, to remain loyal to the revolution, *without treating insurrection as an art.*

The Bolsheviks' hope of seizing power was hardly secret; bold defiance of the Provisional Government was one of their major propaganda appeals. Some three weeks before the insurrection they decided to stage a demonstrative walkout from the advisory assembly (the Council of the Republic or "Pre-Parliament") which the provisional Prime Minister Alexander Kerensky had summoned. When the walkout was staged, Trotsky (a Bolshevik only since August, 1917, but already the party's most articulate spokesman) denounced the Provisional Government for its alleged counterrevolutionary intentions and called on the masses to support the Bolsheviks.

FROM *Declaration of the Bolshevik Fraction to the Council of the Republic*

BY *Leon Trotsky*

The officially proclaimed aims of the Democratic Conference summoned by the Central Executive Committee of the Soviets of Workers' and Soldiers' Deputies consisted of the abolition of the irresponsible personal regime that nourished the Kornilov movement and the creation of a responsible power able to liquidate the war and guarantee the convening of the Constituent Assembly after the designated interval.

Meanwhile, behind the back of the Democratic Conference and by means of backstage deals between Kerensky, the Kadets[1] and the leaders of the S.-R.'s and Mensheviks, results were arrived at which were directly opposed to the officially proclaimed aims.

[1]"Kadets": the Constitutional Democratic Party, from its Russian initials—Ed.

"Declaration of the Bolshevik Fraction to the Council of the Republic," by Leon Rotsky in R. V. Daniels, *A Documentary of Communisim*, pp.109–112. Reprinted by permission.

A power was created in which and around which avowed and secret Kornilovists[2] play a leading role. The irresponsibility of this power is now confirmed and officially proclaimed. . . .

. . . The bourgeois classes which are directing the policy of the political government have set themselves the goal of *undermining* the Constituent Assembly. This is now the basic task of the privileged elements, to which their whole policy, domestic and foreign, is subordinated.

In the industrial, agrarian, and food-supply fields, the policy of the government and the propertied classes aggravates the natural disruption engendered by the war. The privileged classes, having provoked a peasant uprising, now move to suppress it, and openly hold a course towards the "bony hand of famine," which is to smother the revolution and above all the Constituent Assembly.

No less criminal is the foreign policy of the bourgeoisie and its government.

After forty months of war mortal danger threatens the capital. In answer to this a plan is proposed to transfer the government to Moscow. The idea of surrendering the revolutionary capital to the German troops does not evoke the least indignation among the bourgeois classes; on the contrary, it is accepted by them as a natural link in the general policy, which is to facilitate their counterrevolutionary plot.

Instead of recognizing that the salvation of the country lies in the conclusion of peace; instead of openly throwing out the proposal of immediate peace, over the heads of all the imperialist governments and diplomatic offices, to all the exhausted nations and in this way making further waging of the war actually impossible—the Provisional Government, taking its cue from the Kadet counterrevolutionaries and the Allied imperialists, without meaning, without strength, without a plan, toils along in the murderous harness of war, dooming to pointless destruction ever new hundreds of thousands of soldiers and sailors, and preparing the surrender of Petrograd and the smothering of the revolution. At a time when the soldier and sailor Bolsheviks are perishing together with the other sailors and soldiers as a result of others' mistakes and crimes, the so-called Supreme Commander-in-Chief continues to ruin the Bolshevik press. . . .

The leading parties of the Provisional Council serve as a voluntary cover for this whole policy.

We, the fraction of Bolshevik Social-Democrats, declare: with this government of national betrayal and with this council that tolerates counterrevolution we have nothing in common. We do not wish either directly or obliquely to conceal even for a single day, that work, fatal to the people, which is being accomplished behind the official curtain.

The revolution is in danger! At a time when the troops of [Kaiser] Wilhelm are threatening Petrograd, the government of Kerensky-Konovalov[3] is preparing

---

[2] Kornilovists: followers of General Kornilov, who attempted to overthrow Kerensky in August, 1917—Ed.
[3] Konovalov: a minister in Kerensky's government and acting premier at the time of the Bolshevik revolution—Ed.

to flee from Petrograd, in order to transform Moscow into a stronghold of counterrevolution.

We appeal to the vigilance of the Moscow workers and soldiers!

Quitting the Provisional Council, we appeal to the vigilance and courage of the workers, soldiers and peasants of all Russia.

Petrograd is in danger! The revolution is in danger! The nation is in danger!

The government aggravates this danger. The ruling parties help it.

Only the people themselves can save themselves and the country. We turn to the people.

All power to the Soviets!

All the land to the people!

Long live an immediate, honorable, democratic peace!

Long live the Constituent Assembly!

On October 10 [23], 1917, Lenin came secretly to Petrograd to overcome hesitancies among the Bolshevik leadership over his demand for armed insurrection. Against the opposition of two of Lenin's long-time lieutenants, Zinoviev and Kamenev, the Central Committee adopted Lenin's resolution which formally instructed the party organizations to prepare for the seizure of power.

FROM *Lenin's Resolution "On the Armed Uprising," Adopted by the Central Committee of the R.S.D.W.P.*

The Central Committee recognizes that the international position of the Russian revolution (the revolt in the German navy which is an extreme manifestation of the growth throughout Europe of the world socialist revolution; the threat of peace between the imperialists with the object of strangling the revolution in Russia) as well as the military situation (the indubitable decision of the Russian bourgeoisie and Kerensky and Co. to surrender Petrograd to the Germans), and the fact that the proletarian party has gained a majority in the Soviets—all this, taken in conjunction with the peasant revolt and the swing of popular confidence towards our Party (the elections in Moscow), and finally, the obvious preparations being made for a second Kornilov affair (the withdrawal of troops from Petrograd, the dispatch of Cossacks to Petrograd, the surrounding of Minsk by Cossacks, etc.)—all this places the armed uprising on the order of the day.

Considering therefore that an armed uprising is inevitable, and that the time for it is fully ripe, the Central Committee instructs all Party organizations to be guided accordingly, and to discuss and decide all practical questions (the Congress of Soviets of the Northern Region, the withdrawal of troops from Petrograd, the action of our people in Moscow and Minsk, etc.) from this point of view.

"Lenin's Resolution 'On the Armed Uprising,' " in *A Documentary History of Communism*, pp.112–113. Reprinted by permission.

Fearful on Marxist grounds that the Bolsheviks did not have the mass support or the international backing to assure them success, Zinoviev and Kamenev published a statement in which they endeavored to dissuade the party from following Lenin's lead. Lenin denounced them for "strike-breaking," and the uprising went ahead as scheduled.

FROM *Statement to the Principal Bolshevik Party Organizations, October 24, 1917*

BY *G. E. Zinoviev and L. B. Kamenev*

. . . In labour circles there is developing and growing a current of thought which sees the only outcome in the immediate declaration of an armed uprising. The interaction of all the conditions at present is such that if we are to speak of such an uprising a definite date must be set for it, and that within the next few days. In one or another form this question is already being discussed by the entire press and at workers' meetings, and is occupying the minds of a substantial group of party workers. We on our part consider it our duty and our right to express ourselves on this question with complete frankness.

We are deeply convinced that to call at present for an armed uprising means to stake on one card not only the fate of our party, but also the fate of the Russian and international revolution.

There is no doubt that there are historical situations when an oppressed class must recognise that it is better to go forward to defeat than to give up without a battle. Does the Russian working class find itself at present in such a situation? *No,* and *a thousand times no!!!!*

As a result of the immense growth of the influence of our party in the cities, and particularly in the army, there has come about at present a situation such that it is becoming more and more impossible for the bourgeoisie to obstruct the Constituent Assembly. Through the army, through the workers, we hold a revolver at the temple of the bourgeoisie: the bourgeoisie is put in such a position that if it should undertake now to attempt to obstruct the Constituent Assembly, it would again push the petty-bourgeois parties to one side, and the revolver would go off.

The chances of our party in the elections to the Constituent Assembly are excellent. The talk that the influence of Bolshevism is beginning to wane, etc., we consider to have absolutely no foundation. In the mouths of our political opponents this assertion is simply a move in the political game, having as its purpose this very thing, to provoke an uprising of the Bolsheviks under conditions favourable to our enemies. The influence of the Bolsheviks is increasing. Whole strata of the labouring population are only now beginning to be drawn in by it. With correct tactics we can get a third and even more of the seats in the Constituent Assembly. The attitude of the petty-bourgeois parties in the

---

"Statement to the Principal Bolshevik Party," in *A Documentary History of Communism,* pp. 113–117. Reprinted by permission.

Constituent Assembly cannot possibly be the same then as it is now. In the first place their slogan: "For land, for freedom, wait for the Constituent Assembly" will drop out. And aggravation of want, hunger, and the peasant movement, will exert more and more pressure on them and will compel them to seek an alliance with the proletarian party against the landowners and capitalists represented by the Cadet Party.

The Constituent Assembly, by itself, cannot of course abolish the present camouflaging of these interrelations. The Soviets, which have become rooted in life, can not be destroyed. The Constituent Assembly will be able to find support for its revolutionary work only in the Soviets. The Constituent Assembly plus the Soviets—this is that combined type of state institutions towards which we are going. It is on this political basis that our party is acquiring enormous chances for a real victory.

We have never said that the Russian working class *alone,* by its own forces, would be able to bring the present revolution to a victorious conclusion. We have not forgotten, must not forget even now, that between us and the bourgeoisie there stands a huge third camp: the petty bourgeoisie. This camp joined us during the days of the Kornilov affair and gave us victory. It will join us many times more. We must not permit ourselves to be hypnotised by what is the case at the present moment. Undoubtedly, at present this camp is much nearer to the bourgeoisie than to us. But the present situation is not eternal, nor even durable. And only by a careless step, by some hasty action which will make the whole fate of the revolution dependent upon an immediate uprising, will the proletarian party push the petty bourgeoisie into the arms of Milyukov[1] *for a long time.*

We are told: (1) that the majority of the people of Russia is already with us, and (2) that the majority of the international proletariat is with us. Alas!— neither the one nor the other is true, and this is the crux of the entire situation.

In Russia a majority of the workers and a substantial part of the soldiers are with us. But all the rest is dubious. We are all convinced, for instance, that if elections to the Constituent Assembly were to take place now, a majority of the peasants would vote for the S.-R.'s. What is this, an accident? The masses of the soldiers support us not because of the slogan of war, but because of the slogan of peace. This is an extremely important circumstance and unless we take it into consideration we would be risking building on sand. If, having taken power at present by ourselves, we should come to the conclusion (in view of the whole world situation) that it is necessary to wage a revolutionary war, the masses of the soldiers will rush away from us. . . .

Having taken power, the workers' party thereby undoubtedly deals a blow to Wilhelm. It will be harder for him to carry on a war against revolutionary Russia, offering an immediate democratic peace. This is so. But will this blow under present conditions, after [the fall of] Riga, etc., be sufficiently powerful to

[1]Milyukov: leader of the Constitutional Democratic Party and Foreign Minister in the Provisional Government, March–April, 1917—Ed.

turn away the hand of German imperialism from Russia? . . . Where then are the data which indicate that the proletarian party alone, and while the petty-bourgeois democracy is resisting, must take the responsibility for such a state of affairs and its inevitable consequences upon itself and upon itself alone?

And here we come to the second assertion—that the majority of the international proletariat allegedly is already with us. Unfortunately this is not so. The mutiny in the German navy has an immense symptomatic significance. There are portents of a serious movement in Italy. But from that to any sort of active support of the proletarian revolution in Russia which is declaring war on the entire bourgeois world is still very far. It is extremely harmful to overestimate forces. Undoubtedly much is given to us and much will be demanded from us. But if we now, having staked the entire game upon one card, suffer defeat, we shall deal a cruel blow to the international proletarian revolution, which is developing extremely slowly, but which is nevertheless developing. Moreover, the development of the revolution in Europe will make it obligatory for us, without any hesitation whatever, immediately to take power into our own hands. This is also the only guarantee of the victory of an uprising of the proletariat in Russia. It will come, but it is not yet here. . . .

Before history, before the international proletariat, before the Russian Revolution and the Russian working class, we have no right to stake the whole future on the card of an armed uprising. It would be a mistake to think that such action now would, if it were unsuccessful, lead only to such consequences as did July 16–18 [July 29–31]. Now it is a question of something more. It is a question of decisive battle, and defeat in *that* battle would spell defeat to the revolution. . . .

On October 25 [November 7], 1917, through the agency of the Military-Revolutionary Committee of the Petrograd Soviet—headed by Trotsky—the Bolsheviks and their allies, the Left Socialist-Revolutionaries, forcibly overthrew Kerensky's government and assumed power in the name of the soviets. A new cabinet, designated the "Council of People's Commissars," was set up, with Lenin as chairman and Trotsky as Commissar of Foreign Affairs. Endorsement of the coup was secured from the Second All-Russian Congress of Soviets, which was concurrently in session. This was the "October Revolution."

FROM *Proclamation of the Soviet Government, November 7, 1917*

To the Citizens of Russia!

The Provisional Government has been overthrown. The power of state has passed into the hands of the organ of the Petrograd Soviet of Workers' and Soldiers' Deputies, the Revolutionary Military Committee, which stands at the head of the Petrograd proletariat and garrison.

"Proclamation of the Soviet Government," in *A Documentary History of Communism*, p. 117. Reprinted by permission.

The cause for which the people have fought—the immediate proposal of a democratic peace, the abolition of landed proprietorship, workers' control over production and the creation of a Soviet government—is assured.

Long live the revolution of the soldiers, workers, and peasants!
Revolutionary Military Committee of Petrograd
Soviet of Workers' and Soldiers' Deputies.

Police action by the Bolsheviks to combat political opposition commenced with the creation of the "Cheka" (so called from the Russian initials of the first two terms in its official name, "Extraordinary Commission to Fight Counter-Revolution"). Under the direction of Felix Dzerzhinsky, the Cheka became the prototype of totalitarian secret police systems, enjoying at critical times the right of unlimited arrest and summary execution of suspects and hostages. The principle of such police surveillance over the political leanings of the Soviet population has remained in effect ever since, despite the varying intensity of repression and the organizational metamorphoses of the police—from Cheka to GPU (1922, from the Russian initials for "State Political Administration") to NKVD (1934—the "People's Commissariat of Internal Affairs") to MVD and MGB (after World War II—"Ministry of Internal Affairs" and "Ministry of State Security," respectively) to KGB (since 1953—the "Committee for State Security").

FROM *Decree on Establishment of the Extraordinary Commission to Fight Counter-Revolution*

The Commission is to be named the All-Russian Extraordinary Commission and is to be attached to the Council of People's Commissars. [This commission] is to make war on counter-revolution and sabotage. . . .

The duties of the Commission will be:

1. To persecute and break up all acts of counter-revolution and sabotage all over Russia, no matter what their origin.
2. To bring before the Revolutionary Tribunal all counter-revolutionists and saboteurs and to work out a plan for fighting them.
3. To make preliminary investigation only—enough to break up [the counter-revolutionary act]. The Commission is to be divided into sections: (a) the information section, (b) the organization section (in charge of organizing the fight against counter-revolution all over Russia) with branches, and (c) the fighting section.

The Commission will be formed tomorrow (December 21) [January 3]. . . . The Commission is to watch the press, saboteurs, strikers, and the Socialist-Revolutionists of the Right. Measures [to be taken against these counter-revolu-

"Decree on Establishment of the Extraordinary Commission to Fight Counter-Revolution," in *A Documentary History of Communism,* pp. 132–135. Reprinted by permission.

tionists are] confiscation, confinement, deprivation of [food] cards, publication
of the names of the enemies of the people, etc.

Council of People's Commissars.

*In December, 1917 the Bolsheviks permitted, as they had promised the election of a
Constituent Assembly. This was the only reasonably free and democratic general
election which Russia has ever had. The Bolsheviks placed second with some nine
million votes, but an overwhelming majority was won by the Right SR's with their
peasant backing. Lenin permitted the Assembly to meet for only one day, and then
forcibly banned its continuation on the ground that it was a counterrevolutionary
threat to the soviets.*

FROM *Lenin's Draft Decree on the Dissolution of the Constituent Assembly*

. . . The Constituent Assembly, elected on the basis of lists drawn up prior to
the October Revolution, was an expression of the old relation of political forces
which existed when power was held by the compromisers and the Cadets.
When the people at that time voted for the candidates of the Socialist-
Revolutionary Party, they were not in a position to choose between the Right
Socialist-Revolutionaries, the supporters of the bourgeoisie, and the Left
Socialist-Revolutionaries, the supporters of Socialism. Thus the Constituent
Assembly, which was to have been the crown of the bourgeois parliamentary
republic, could not but become an obstacle in the path of the October
Revolution and the Soviet power.

The October Revolution, by giving the power to the Soviets, and through
the Soviets to the toiling and exploited classes, aroused the desperate resistance
of the exploiters, and in the crushing of this resistance it fully revealed itself as
the beginning of the socialist revolution. The toiling classes learnt by experience
that the old bourgeois parliamentarism had outlived its purpose and was absolutely incompatible with the aim of achieving Socialism, and that not national
institutions, but only class institutions (such as the Soviets), were capable of
overcoming the resistance of the propertied classes and of laying the foundations of a socialist society. To relinquish the sovereign power of the Soviets, to
relinquish the Soviet republic won by the people, for the sake of bourgeois parliamentarism and the Constituent Assembly, would now be a retrograde step
and cause the collapse of the October workers' and peasants' revolution.

Owing to the circumstances mentioned above, the majority in the
Constituent Assembly which met on January 5 was secured by the party of the
Right Socialist-Revolutionaries, the party of Kerensky, Avksentyev and Chernov.

"Lenin's Draft Decree. . . . . ," *A Documentary History of Communism*, pp. 133–135. Reprinted by permission.

Naturally, this party refused to discuss the absolutely clear, precise and unambiguous proposal of the supreme organ of Soviet power, the Central Executive Committee of the Soviets, to recognize the program of the Soviet power, to recognize the "Declaration of Rights of the Toiling and Exploited People," to recognize the October Revolution and the Soviet power. Thereby the Constituent Assembly severed all ties with the Soviet Republic of Russia. The withdrawal from such a Constituent Assembly of the groups of the Bolsheviks and the Left Socialist-Revolutionaries, who now patently constitute the overwhelming majority in the Soviets and enjoy the confidence of the workers and the majority of the peasants, was inevitable.

The Right Socialist-Revolutionary and Menshevik parties are in fact waging outside the walls of the Constituent Assembly a most desperate struggle against the Soviet power, calling openly in their press for its overthrow and characterizing as arbitrary and unlawful the crushing by force of the resistance of the exploiters by the toiling classes, which is essential in the interests of emancipation from exploitation. They are defending the saboteurs, the servitors of capital, and are going to the length of undisguised calls to terrorism, which certain "unidentified groups" have already begun to practise. It is obvious that under such circumstances the remaining part of the Constituent Assembly could only serve as a screen for the struggle of the counterrevolutionaries to overthrow the Soviet power.

Accordingly, the Central Executive Committee resolves: The Constituent Assembly is hereby dissolved.

4

The Burden of Russian History

FROM *Russia's Failed Revolutions*

BY *Adam B. Ulam*

Throughout September the prevailing feeling among the Bolshevik hierarchy was to await the Second Congress of Soviets which would enthrone them as the legitimate representative of the Russian workers and soldiers by replacing the lame-duck Central Executive Committee with one they would dominate. The target date was October 20, though it was to meet five days later. In the meantime revolutionary democracy, seeing control slipping away, decided to improvise another talking shop where it could hold sway even if the soviets were conquered by the enemy. This was an *omnium gatherum* of representatives of soviets, trade unions, municipal councils, journalists, midwives, cleverly designed so that neither the right nor the Bolsheviks could challenge its domination by the forces of democracy, the right and center Mensheviks and Socialist Revolutionaries. The Democratic Conference assembled on September 14, and after six days of tumultous oratory gave birth to another, this time a standing body, the Council of the Republic. This was supposed to provide dual power with something it had hitherto lacked, a quasi-legislature, which it was hoped might keep the patient alive until the real parliament, the Constituent Assembly, took over.

As of the beginning of September, Russia had been proclaimed a republic by Kerensky, which evoked a protest from another assembly few realized still existed. The Senate, theoretically, as under the tsars, the highest judicial and administrative tribunal, solemnly declared that the Provisional Government had no right to prejudge the country's future constitution, a startling sign of life from the venerable body whose members continued to attend its sessions dressed in frock coats and uniforms with the old imperial emblems. On its institutional side, Russian politics came to resemble a junkyard: various prerevolution bodies in different states of disrepair lying side by side with brand new pieces of government machinery produced since February 1917, but not functioning properly.

Bolshevik participation in the Democratic Conference brought another outburst from Lenin. He lashed out at the Central Committee's dilatory tactics: "It would be naive to wait until the Bolsheviks achieve a 'formal' majority, no revolution has every waited for that." The conference met on September 14, with Kerensky in his usual form: ". . . we will remain the same defenders of freedom of our native land, and of the happiness of the people as we have been hitherto. . . . Anyone who dares to plunge a knife in the back of the Russian army will discover the might of the Revolutionary Provisional Government." On September 15 the Bolshevik Central Committee discussed Lenin's letter with its unflattering admonitions. ("You are nothing but a bunch of traitors and nincompoops unless you surround the conference and arrest those scoundrels.") The Bolshevik notables were appalled by the outburst. Stalin suggested diplomatically that the party's local organizations be acquainted with the contents of the letter, but that the decision on the uprising be delayed until another meeting. It was finally decided to burn all copies but one of the dangerous document and to keep the party's partisans from any rash steps. Lenin was ordered to keep away from the capital, and Zinoviev, who had become separated from his chief, was instructed to rejoin him forthwith. With his notoriously unheroic disposition, he was felt to be a good, restraining influence on that demonic force.

On October 3, with a heavy heart, the Committee finally authorized their leader's return and as of the seventh he went into hiding in the Vyborg region of the capital. Few were likely to be looking for Lenin; attention was riveted on the Council of the Republic which began its brief and ephemeral existence the same day, in the luxurious premises of the Marinsky Palace. It was only by a narrow majority that the Bolsheviks, entitled to sit in it (as delegated by the various soviets), decided to boycott the council, thus avoiding another fearful eruption from their chief. After a provocative speech by Trotsky, the Bolshevik contingent stalked out to shouts of "Scoundrels," "Go to your German friends." Freed from their indecorous presence, the council launched into the now all too familiar pattern of revolutionary discourse: stirring appeals for national unity, anguished pleas for order and social discipline from the right, bitter retorts from the left that only further and thorough democratization could save the country, heartening declarations by Kerensky that finally the government had the situation well in hand. Most revolutionary dramas unfold to the accompaniment of effusive oratory, but the February revolution is the only one which literally talked itself to death.

Lenin's pleading now took on a clearly hysterical tone: "Now, now, or it would be too late!" A cogent argument in one letter would be followed by ideas verging on incoherence.

> The Bolsheviks have no right [sic] to wait for the Congress of Soviets. They must *seize power* right now. It is only thus that they would save the world revolution (otherwise there is a danger of the imperialists of all countries . . . making a deal and *uniting against us*) also the Russian Revolution (otherwise the wave of

anarchy may become stronger than we) and the lives of hundreds of thousands at the front. To procrastinate with the rising is criminal. To wait until the Congress would be a silly game, a shameful game at formalities and a betrayal of the Revolution.

If they are afraid to start the business in Petrograd, let them begin with Moscow. Let the latter's soviet take over the city, banks, newspapers. It (that is, the Moscow soviet) would have a "gigantic base of support." Kerensky would then surrender. The revolutionary regime would make concessions to railroad and postal workers (two crucial labor unions whose hostility to the Bolsheviks was being used as an argument against the uprising), proclaim an *immediate* peace, an *immediate* distribution of land to the peasants. Then in conclusion, what to the recipients of the message must have appeared as bordering on lunacy, "Victory is assured, and there is a ninety-nine percent chance that it would be bloodless."

To begin with Moscow would very likely have been a serious mistake; even after Petrograd had been conquered the Bolsheviks would have a hard time in the older capital. But *not* to wait for the Congress of Soviets with its pro-Bolshevik majority was a clear blueprint for disaster. The congress would throw a cloak of revolutionary legitimacy over the Bolshevik coup, maximize the Mensheviks' and Socialist Revolutionaries' indecision and paralysis, and stay the hand of those military units, most notably among the Cossacks, who would have reacted violently to another Bolshevik adventure but would have become confused when one half-government obviously sanctioned the enterprise. It was fortunate for Lenin and his party that his impetuous counsels were rejected.

On October 10 the Bolshevik Central Committee, or rather twelve of its twenty-seven full members, held a clandestine meeting with Lenin present. With Zinoviev and Kamenev dissenting, the assembled voted, ten to two, "that the armed uprising is inevitable and that the moment for it is ripe [and] the Central Committee orders all party organs to be guided by this consideration in connection with the practical problems." This was far from what Lenin wanted; the crucial "when" was not settled and the committee of seven elected to guide the enterprise included Zinoviev and Kamenev, who made it clear their hearts were not in the business. More precisely, they were scared to death. They would all get shot, pleaded Zinoviev. He wanted to wait not only for the Congress of Soviets but also for the Constituent Assembly, where the Bolsheviks with luck should get one-third of the seats, an argument which must have brought Lenin close to an apoplectic stroke. The danger of such a stroke (which in fact took place five years later), was compounded within a few days when the two leaders leaked the news of the resolution and of their dissent from it to *New Life,* published by Maxim Gorky and which in the spirit of left Menshevism was critical of everybody: the Provisional Government for its policies, the right Mensheviks and the SRs for their support of the former, and the Bolsheviks for their undemocratic ways. Lenin, quite beside himself, now demanded that the guilty duo be excluded not only from the Central Committee but also from the party as well. But the other leaders (except for Trotsky who hated his brother-in-law Kamenev) were for forbearance. Stalin, throughout 1917 the voice of moderation, proposed that the two, both his future victims, be just reprimanded if they promised to mend their ways. And so it was done.

Again, what a strange partiality of providence for the Bolsheviks. Instead of putting everybody on alert, Zinoviev's and Kamenev's revelations had the opposite effect and served as kind of a sedative on dual power. How could one be too concerned about a party, two of whose most prestigious leaders announce in advance that it might stage an insurrection and who oppose it as bound to end in failure?

No other successful coup d'etat had ever been so widely advertised in advance, none had seemed to be of as little concern to the authorities against which it was being quite openly prepared. By the middle of the month, everyone was talking about it, but no one was acting to prevent it. On October 14 Theodore Dan, who in Tseretelli's absence (sick and dispirited, he went to recuperate in his native Georgia, another piece of luck for the Bolsheviks) was the leading figure among the non-Martov Mensheviks felt curious enough to ask about the rumors in the Executive Committee of the Soviet. "I demand that the Bolshevik party give us a straightforward answer: yes or no." It fell to David Ryazanov, one Bolshevik universally liked and respected for his Marxian scholarship, to answer that embarrassing question.[1] Indeed his answer displayed great dialectical skill. No proletarian party, certainly not the Bolsheviks, could contemplate anything so un-Marxist as a putsch—Dan should know that. But the uprising is preparing itself, as the masses cannot endure the effects of the Provisional Government's repressive and undemocratic policies. And should the masses rise and call for the Bolsheviks to join and guide them, a proletarian party could not refuse. The dialectical correctness of the formula could not be faulted. But four days later Trotsky was asked a similar question and gave a similar answer, with a variant. It was obviously the bourgeoisie that was preparing a coup and the Bolsheviks could not be blamed for preparing to resist it. He, Trotsky, was being asked why as president of the Soviet he had authorized the issuance of five thousand rifles to the Bolshevik sympathizers. Didn't the Mensheviks recall that it was they who during the Kornilov affair had demanded that the workers should be armed?

It fell to Trotsky to devise the formula for the uprising, one which would at least partly appease his party colleagues' apprehensions and at the same time go far in satisfying Lenin's frenzy for action. The Bolsheviks would stage the insurrection but through and on behalf of the Soviet. On October 12 the latter created the Revolutionary Military Committee, ostensibly to guard against a coup from the right and to organize the defense of the capital, which the Provisional Government was preparing to evacuate and move to Moscow, partly

---

[1] A man of independent spirit and great courage, Ryazanov would be continuously in trouble with the party leadership after the Revolution and eventually would disappear in Stalin's purges.

because of its vulnerability to a German attack, partly because it might thus decapitate the revolution. There was some substance to the rumors, but as usual Kerensky could not make up his mind. Having in fact proposed the creation of the committee, the Mensheviks and the right SRs refused obligingly to participate in its work, leaving the field free to the Bolsheviks and their allies, the left SRs. One of the latter, an eighteen-year-old youth, was the titular head of the committee, but its actual leader was Trotsky, and for his aides he enlisted members of his own party's military organization. Emissaries of the committee were dispatched to the city's military units to remind them that they were under direct control of the Soviet which thus superseded both the city commandant appointed by the Provisional Government and their officers. Some units agreed, others declared they would remain neutral in any clash between the Provisional Government and the Soviet. The lame-duck Central Committee, shrewdly suspecting that the Bolsheviks would synchronize their move with the assembly of the Second All-Russian Congress of Soviets, postponed the latter from October 20 to the twenty-fifth, thus giving Trotsky and his group more time for their work among the soldiers. It was crucial for the success of the uprising that the insurgents should be able to secure the Petropavlovsk fortress with its large stocks of arms. But practically up to the last moment its garrison refused to commit itself and kept chasing out the emissaries sent by the Revolutionary Military Committee. On October 24 Trotsky went there himself, and after listening to him the soldiers decided to cast their lot with the insurrection.

He hoped the Bolsheviks *would* try something was Kerensky's usual reaction to warnings about what was about to happen. Besides, the government was facing yet another ministerial crisis. In the wake of the Kornilov affair the prime minister, unable to persuade any of the better-known generals to take the job, appointed a very junior one, Alexander Verkhovsky, as minister of war. On October 20 he reported to the Council of the Republic on the state of the army. Much of this report was encouraging. There were to be sure two million deserters at large, but six million soldiers still held, in a manner of speaking, the front, tying down one hundred thirty enemy divisions. "Ideological Bolshevism does not exist among the soldiers." But then Verkhovsky dropped a bombshell: an army of that size could no longer be fed or clothed, and some units were unlikely to stay in the trenches once cold weather set in. The government ought to announce immediately that it was seeking peace. It is not clear whether Verkhovsky, whom some considered to be mentally unbalanced and whose speech was rather incoherent, was pleading for a separate peace, or whether he believed that an announcement that one was in the making would buoy up the army's morale and enable it to fight more effectively against both its foreign and domestic enemies. In any case there was a great outcry at his suggestion, followed by the announcement that in view of his health he had to go on leave. Now Kerensky in addition to being supreme commander and prime minister also took over the war ministry, an unprecedented combination of offices, but which one day would be held by a man quite different from the hapless per-suader-in-chief, Joseph Stalin.

Everything was now in place for the great day. Or so it seemed. But among the future victors there was still anxiety and apprehension. Their behavior did not betray an overwhelming faith in their success. On October 24 Lenin, still in disguise, sporting a wig and with his face bandaged, worked his way to Smolny. Arriving there in the evening, he erupted furiously with reproaches against his hard-working followers. Did they really mean to wait twenty-four hours until the wretched Congress assembled? Once it met who knows how it might vote. He felt, and with reason, that the "democratic superstition" was still not dead among his followers and many, especially provincial Bolshevik delegates, might fall for some coalition scheme with the Mensheviks. "To wait is to die." He was calmed by Trotsky who assured him that Bolshevik armed units were on their way to seize the strategic points, the telegraph and telephone exchange, and to guard the bridges. Smolny presented an incongruous appearance: headquarters of the insurrection, of the Revolutionary Military Committee, it still housed in a different wing of the building, the ghost of revolutionary democracy—the lame-duck Central Executive Committee which on the next day was to surrender its functions to one elected by the new congress.

The Bolshevik Central Committee which met a few hours before Lenin's arrival in Smolny was still ambivalent. It is significant that its official protocol does not mention terms like *insurrection, armed uprising*. Were it to fall into the hands of the authorities following an unsuccessful uprising, it would be difficult to prove that the Bolsheviks had been planning anything but to defend themselves against an attack from the right! There was discussion about where the Bolsheviks ought to place alternate headquarters should the forces of reaction seize Smolny. Kamenev proposed to place them on a Bolshevik man-of-war, the famous *Aurora,* but his less timorous colleagues decided on the Petropavlovsk fortress. All armed activities were to be led by Bolsheviks of lesser standing, none of them from the Central Committee. Without special authorization, no member of the latter was to leave Smolny. All of which hardly adds up to an iron-clad alibi, but should the insurrection collapse, some leaders might be spared and, as in July, begin to rebuild the party.

In retrospect, such precautions must seem superfluous. Revolutionary democracy cheerfully continued on its suicidal course. The same day, the twenty-fourth, Kerensky appeared before the Council of the Republic with sensational news. He now had definite proof that the Bolsheviks were up to no good. He had given them every opportunity to back off from this foolish venture. "I prefer in general that authorities act more slowly but surely, and when the time comes move resolutely." But now "let the population of the city know that it is dealing with a resolute and determined government." He demanded that the council declare formally its support of his stand. It was not in the style of dual power assemblies to act hastily, so there ensued a long discussion. Martov reiterated his argument: of course they opposed a coup d'etat, but if it takes place, it will be because of the Provisional Government's insensitivity to the masses' demands. With Tseretelli away, the democratic left became even more confused and indecisive. Dan argued that the Bolsheviks could not be subdued by force, the only solution was for the government to declare immediately that it would seek a general peace and that all land would be turned over to the peasants. Only then could the masses be made immune to the Bolshevik allurements. Kerensky had been loudly cheered, but when it came to voting, the majority of the council followed Dan's position, refusing to give the government its unconditional support. Enraged, Kerensky declared first that he might resign but then stalked out of the council, declaring haughtily that this was the time for deeds rather than declarations.

One such deed might have been for the government to seize Smolny. A detachment of a few hundred men could have grabbed the entire staff of the uprising, since the building was virtually unprotected up to the evening of October 24. But on the government's side, no one even thought of occupying Smolny. That would have been a provocation, a palpable proof that it was the bourgeoisie which was embarking on a coup designed to prevent the meeting of the Congress of Soviets. Instead, detachments of military cadets were sent to shut down the Bolshevik papers. After they sealed off the premises and posted guards, pro-Bolshevik soldiers arrived, chased off the guards, and the newspapers were back in business.

"The resolute and determined government" spent most of the night trying to persuade various armed units to come to its defense. The Cossacks first said "Maybe," then "No." They had helped in the past and were promised that the Bolsheviks would be crushed once and for all and look what was happening. The only volunteers were found among students of the military schools, and among that innovation of the revolution, the women's battalions. Even so, no attempt was made to organize the progovernment units into a cohesive force and to place an experienced officer in overall command.

The previous day Kerensky had declared that members of the government preferred "to be killed and destroyed rather than to betray the life, honor and independence of the state." But as of the morning of October 25, he was on the move. He was leaving the city to collect a force with which to crush the uprising, he told his colleagues. In the meantime they had to hold the fort, and they took it in the literal sense, gathering in the Winter Palace still composing declarations and issuing appeals while the city was being taken over by the Bolsheviks.

It would have made more sense for the ministers either to order and direct armed resistance, or failing that, for the government to leave Petrograd as a body for a safer location. Instead they huddled in the palace, sending out broadsides which under the circumstances sounded ludicrous. "Members of the Provisional Government are staying at their posts and will continue to work for the good of the country." They could have called upon the considerable body of civilian supporters of their parties to arm themselves and to offer resistance to the usurpers, but all they asked was for the population "to hinder the madmen who have been joined by all the enemies of freedom and order."

In fact the population of the metropolis preserved remarkable equanimity during that most momentous day in the country's history. The takeover of the city by the Revolutionary Military Committee which began before dawn proceeded quite peacefully, shaming those Bolsheviks who had predicted a repetition of the July days or worse. No one tried to hinder them, hardly a shot was fired as the motley crowd of soldiers, sailors, and Red Guards proceeded to occupy the strategic points—the power station, telephone exchange, headquarters of the military district. Like most of the garrison, the civilian population stayed neutral, displaying neither enthusiasm nor any visible opposition to what was going on. No panic, no multitudes shouting as on so many occasions in the past eight months, "Shame" or "Down with . . ." In fact it was something of an anticlimax.

The expiring revolution kept on talking. The Council of the Republic assembled in the morning, its various factions discussing what should be their attitude toward the hardly unexpected turn of events.

The deliberations were interrupted by the arrival of armed soldiers who asked the deputies to vacate the premises. Some were for courting martyrdom by defiantly staying in session, but a motion to that effect was defeated. So the representatives of the Russian people adjourned after having passed a resolution denouncing this gross interference with their activities.

The Petrograd city council displayed more spirit. No one thought of interfering with its session, so they continued to protest until the evening, when it was decided to march in a body to the Palace Square, there to lend moral support to the besieged government. But a sailors' detachment barred the councillors' way, and they had to return to speech-making.

Early in the afternoon the Winter Palace remained the only island of lawful authority amidst the rebel-controlled city. It had a garrison of sorts, a few companies of junkers—officers' candidates—and a women's "death battalion." The huge edifice with its many entrances could hardly be turned into an impregnable fortress, and as it grew dark some of its defenders, disgusted by the ministers irresolute attitude, departed. The headless government kept on deliberating but could not make up its mind on the question of the moment: to give up or not. As one of its members was to write, "We could not order them [the defenders] to fight until the last man because by now we might be defending just ourselves. . . . nor could we order them to surrender because as yet we did not know whether the situation was hopeless."

Although vastly superior in numbers, the insurgents did not try to take the palace by assault. Their leaders felt, with some justification, that if real shooting started, their troops might run away, and then, who knows, as in July some hitherto neutral military units might come out to defend dual power. They tried persuasion: if the palace did not surrender, the ministers were told it would be bombarded by the cruiser *Aurora* and from the Petropavlovsk fortress. The ultimatum was not heeded and the guns thundered, but to little effect. Those of the fortress were defective, their shells falling far from the target. *Aurora's* gunners not trusting their marksmanship fired blanks, the only casualty being a member of the crew. Hours passed. The bolder among the besiegers tried infiltration and pushed by little groups into the building. Some were chased away with shots, others captured and disarmed, in the process haranguing the junkers about the futility of their efforts.

The delay in capturing the last redoubt of reaction was greatly embarrassing for the Bolshevik high command. The scenario had called for the whole business to be over by noon when the Congress of Soviets was to assemble and enthrone the new masters of Russia. Yet with the palace still unconquered, Lenin was fearful about what might happen at the assembly. The Bolsheviks and their allies had a solid majority, some 390 out of about 650 delegates who had already reached Petrograd. But many, especially among the Bolsheviks from the provinces, were not privy to Lenin's and Trotsky's complex designs or shared their conviction that soviet must mean in fact Bolshevik power. Someone might offer a motion for a truce and negotiations with the government and it might carry! Or out-of-town military units might suddenly appear and ruin the whole game.

To put the provincials in the right mood, it was felt safer to begin with the meeting of the Petrograd Soviet. The session was opened at 3:00 P.M. by Trotsky, who announced that "the Provisional Government of Kerensky was dead and awaited only the broom of history to sweep it away." Then Lenin ascended the tribune to a standing ovation. He spoke of the new revolution as an accomplished fact, and repeated the magic formula designed to win the minds of waiverers: immediate peace, land, bread.

With the rehearsal a success, it was decided to go ahead with the main show. There was one potentially troublesome feature about the mechanics of the congress which opened in Smolny around 11:00 P.M. Officially it had to be inaugurated by the Central Committee elected in June, hence predominantly Socialist Revolutionary and Menshevik in its composition. Common sense, not to mention political considerations, should have urged the Central Executive Committee to declare that under the circumstances, no democratic assembly could function properly, and it must be postponed until some semblance of order were restored. No doubt the Bolsheviks would have gone ahead and opened the congress, but the fact that it was being held illegally might have had a great psychological effect and just possibly drawn the thousands who still followed the Socialist Revolutionaries and Mensheviks out of their passive attitude.

Yet revolutionary democracy proceeded uncomplainingly with the arrangements for its own funeral. The proceedings were opened on behalf of the Central Executive Committee by Theodore Dan. He would not treat them to a long discourse, announced the Menshevik leader. His party comrades who were fulfilling their duty were currently under siege in the Winter Palace, and so it was no time for political speeches. Yet one cannot help feeling that if Dan was not going to do anything about it, then a political speech was precisely what was indicated.

Meekly the Central Executive Committee turned its powers over to the new Bolshevik-dominated presidium of the congress, with Kamenev its chairman. Lenin's party had become the official representative of Russia's workers and soldiers. It was only now that the Menshevik and right-wing Socialist Revolutionary minority of the congress erupted with futile protests. The revolution was being violated and disgraced, an end must be put to the outrages. They must call off the fighting and find a negotiated settlement to avoid a civil war. If the Bolsheviks did not agree, Martov declared, the opposition would walk out. They were answered by Trotsky, ". . . a compromise is no good here. . . . You are pitiful isolated individuals, you are bankrupt; your role is played out. Go where you belong from now on—the rubbish heap of history." Had such a challenge been thrown in their teeth by a representative of the bourgeoisie, these veteran revolutionaries would have stormed the podium, gone among the workers and soldiers to stir them up to fight the usurpers. But now they obediently trooped out.

The other half-government capitulated about the same time. At two o'clock at night the weary ministers told their young defenders to lay down their arms. The armed multitude burst into the palace. "Members of the Provisional Government submit to force and surrender in order to avoid bloodshed" was the exit line of the regime, as the Bolshevik Vladimir Antonov-Ovseyenko burst into the ministers' conference room where they stoically awaited their oppressors. It was now discovered that Kerensky had fled, and many in the mob wanted to vent their frustration by lynching his colleagues. It was with some difficulty that Antonov and the more disciplined among the workers managed to protect the ministers and to convey the group to the Petropavlovsk fortress where they were placed in the cells which under the tsars had housed generations of revolutionaries.

The announcement of the Winter Palace victory was received by the congress with elation. (Figures for the actual casualties during the siege vary from zero to six.) But there were individual voices protesting that while it was all right to place the capitalist ministers under lock and key, it was inappropriate in the case of those who belonged to socialist parties—a preview of the trouble Lenin would have with the survival "of social democratic superstitions" among his followers.

The Second Congress of Soviets marks the beginning of the Communist regime in Russia and constitutes the official foundation of the state which is known as the Union of Soviet Socialist Republics. The people who thus at least nominally opened a new era in Russian and world history appeared ill suited to the historic occasion. Accustomed as he was to the fairly sophisticated Petrograd workers, fastidious Sukhanov was disenchanted with the appearance and mood of the congress delegates. The mass of them impressed him as being "gray and non-descript people who have crawled out of the trenches and slums, their [alleged] devotion to the Revolution reflected but anger and despair, their 'socialism' was the product of hunger and of eagerness for peace."

The congress reassembled the evening of October 26 to open what is known as the Soviet era. It assumed the sovereign power in the state. The new Central Executive Committee elected Lev Kamenev as its chairman. The mild-mannered, bookish Bolshevik became the closest surrogate of a head of state, successor to Nicholas Chheidze and Nicholas Romanov, though as if to under-line the relative unimportance of the office, another dispute with Lenin would in a few weeks lead to Kamenev's being unceremoniously dismissed from the office. To avoid the title Minister, with its tsarist and bourgeois connotations, the new executive was christened the Council of the People's Commissars, all fifteen of them Bolshevik, with Lenin as chairman, Trotsky in charge of foreign affairs, and Joseph Djugashvili-Stalin as commissar of nationalities.

The Bolsheviks had conquered Petrograd; Russia still remained to be won, hence two steps taken the same night. Lenin read to the congress the Decree on Peace, calling upon all the warring nations and governments to enter into immediate negotiations for a peace without indemnities and annexations. How many soldiers would now be willing to follow those who attempted to recon-quer Petrograd and seize power from the only people who pledged an immedi-ate end to the disastrous war? Then the Decree on Land proclaimed the imme-diate transfer without compensation of all land, previously owned by landlords, et cetera, to the working peasants. This was aimed to neutralize the pro-Socialist Revolutionary and anti-Bolshevik sentiments among the peasant mass-es; it would not be easy to stir up the latter against a government which though not viewed with favor in the countryside still gave the peasant, with no ifs and buts (so it seemed at the time) what he most wanted. The land decree was abhorrent to the spirit of Marxism, which advocates large-scale, scientifically organized agricultural production and considers individual peasant proprietor-ship as economically ruinous and dangerous to socialism. But that could and would be taken care of later on.

Having given birth to a new epoch in history, the Second Congress of Soviets was adjourned—the talking period of the revolution was over.

Official nomenclature is a very deceptive guide to the underlying realities of Russian politics. If things were to be called by their right name, then October 25–26 marks the beginning of a *counterrevolution*. Practically all the political goals that the revolutionary parties and movements had striven for ever since the Decembrists, and which were, even if partially and foolishly, put into effect between March and October would be utterly destroyed during the next three years. The most insistent slogan of the almost hundred-year-old tradition of protest against the autocracy had been that the people should determine their own destiny and for the democratically elected Constituent Assembly. The Council of the Commissars instituted on October 26 was to be, according to the resolution which authorized it, but another provisional government "until the meeting of the Constituent Assembly," which did meet on January 5, 1918, its majority anti-Bolshevik. After one day's session, armed sailors, acting on orders of "the provisional government," dispersed the only free and democratically elected parliament in Russia's history.

Those freedoms secured so laboriously and at the cost of so much sacrifice by Russian society ever since the 1860s, then so profligately abused during the few months of the revolution, began to be abrogated on the very morrow of the coup. The bourgeois newspapers were shut down on October 27. "To tolerate the existence of bourgeois papers means to cease being a Socialist," Lenin said soon afterward.

On December 7, 1917, there was reborn the kind of institution that the February revolution was supposed to have done away with forever. A decree of the Council of the Commissars established the Extraordinary Commission to Combat Counterrevolution and Sabotage, Cheka for short. By its own admission, the Cheka during its first year of existence executed summarily, without trials sixty-three hundred people. The total number of executions for political crimes in the course of the *entire nineteenth century* in Russia had been something on the order of two hundred. The Cheka's successors would be variously named the OGPU, NKVD, and today the KGB. But all of them in the scope of their activities, number of victims, and the fear they have inspired in the ordinary citizen would far surpass the tsarist Okhrana.

The most ironic aspect of post-1917 history touches on the Communists' appropriation of the institution and symbolism of the Soviet. It became the name of the state, society, and nation they had conquered. In fact October 25–26 marked the beginning of the end of the soviets' role as a vital force in politics, whether at the state or local level. As a slogan and symbol, Soviet power would serve the Communists well and would provide one of the keys to their victory in the Civil War. To many the name still carried the connotations of grass roots democracy, and obscured the encroaching reality of one-party dictatorship and the police state. Until 1921 some dissidents, a stray Menshevik or Socialist Revolutionary, were still tolerated in the soviets, the latter playing some, though progressively diminishing, political role. But after that they became and remained a purely ornamental part of the state machinery.

Prior to October 25 few Bolsheviks, including those closest to their leader, would have suspected, let alone approved, the full extent of repression their regime would visit upon their unhappy country. Indeed some of the most difficult challenges encountered in the first few days came not from partisans of the old regime,[2] but from Lenin's own followers. Many opposed the idea of a purely Bolshevik government, some balked at the suppression of the freedom of speech and press.

Lenin's ability to infuse the Bolsheviks with the authoritarian spirit

---

[2]Kerensky's pitiful attempt to stage a comeback with a few hundred Cossacks, all that he had been able to muster, collapsed on the approaches to Petrograd. The only serious armed resistance to the Bolshevik takeover in Russia proper occurred in Moscow, not subdued until November 2.

reflected his own standing in the party; not only the political leader, but a veritable prophet and magician, with a few formulas he had conjured away all that had stood in the way and brought his followers into the promised land. But more fundamentally, it was the nature and magnitude of the task facing the victors which turned the erstwhile Social Democrats into repressors of freedom and democracy. Once in power they discovered that it was not merely the bourgeois state which had been smashed, but the very idea of state and authority. They had to compress into three years, the period of the Civil War, the work which had taken Russian rulers centuries to accomplish: to build the modern state. The worldwide socialist revolution receded into the distant future.

It was to Russian nationalism, seemingly eroded by the year of anarchy and their own ideology, that the Communist regime felt constrained to appeal in its struggle for survival. When the peace negotiations at Brest Litovsk broke down and there appeared the threat of the Germans advancing on Petrograd, the council of Commissars headed its call for resistance with "The Socialist Fatherland is in danger." In commenting upon the appeal, Lenin skipped the adjective: "This shows at once the change of 180 degrees from our defeatism to the defense of the Fatherland." Though muted by Marxian semantics, the nationalist theme becomes an essential ingredient of the Communist effort to rebuild the Russian state and empire.

So does the autocratic principle, as the Communists discarded one by one those anarchic postulates under which they had surged to the top: no secret police, no regular army, no professional bureaucracy. In defending the Treaty of Brest Litovsk, Lenin read this lesson to those who recalled his own pledge of no peace "with the imperialist robbers." "Learn to be disciplined, to introduce severe discipline, otherwise you will be under the German heel . . . until the nation learns to fight, until it will create an army which will not run away, but will be able to endure the most extreme hardships." He who had called Imperial Russia "the prison house of nationalities" would see nothing incongruous in Soviet Russia imposing Moscow-dominated Communism on the Ukraine, conquering socialist Georgia, attempting the same with respect to Poland.

In March 1918 the seat of the government was transferred to Moscow. Ostensibly the change was made because of the danger that the Germans, even after the peace treaty, might be tempted to seize Petrograd. But also the atmosphere prevailing in the "cradle of the Revolution" was felt to be uncongenial to the new order. Armed bands of sailors and demobilized soldiers, some proclaiming themselves anarchists, others just plain criminals, roamed the city, posing a real danger to the regime they had helped to power a few months ago. It was for fear of provoking those elements that the decision and the date of departure of the government organs was kept secret until the last moment. The Communist regime was fleeing from the revolution.

The relocation of the government, although originally dictated by purely practical considerations, can be seen in retrospect as prophetic in its symbolism. The capital founded by Peter the Great had epitomized Western influence on

Russian life. That influence manifested itself in the city which now bears Lenin's name, becoming the birthplace and center of activities of practically every reform and revolutionary movement in the country's modern history. The Kremlin evoked another much older tradition: of autocracy in its pristine, pre-Petrine form, of the grand dukes and tsars of Muscovy. In their fanciful view of the old autocracy, the nineteenth-century Slavophiles portrayed it as a uniquely Russian system and philosophy of government, a harmonious blend of absolutism and popular participation. To the tsar belonged the plentitude of powers, and yet a wise ruler would listen attentively to the voice of the people conveyed by the occasional Assembly of the Land. And the form of government of which Lenin dreamed in his last years, when disenchanted with the growth of bureaucracy in the Communist state, and fearful of dictatorial ambitions of his would-be-successors, such as Stalin and Trotsky, he groped for some never-never land where the dictatorship of the proletariat could be combined with popular participation, was in a strange fashion reminiscent of the old Slavophiles' historical fantasy. The party leadership would be, as in fact it had already become, the Autocrat. The masses would speak their mind through the party and Soviet congresses—a government for the people, but not by the people. Yet while the Slavophiles' populistic autocracy never in fact existed, so Lenin's "democratic centralism" broke down even before his illness, and then death, removed him from the scene.

As the autocrats of old, the Communist rulers would see the state's power as their deed of legitimacy and teach their people to accept it as a surrogate for freedom. So the question and moral posed by most recent Russian history is still the same as a chronicler of the Decembrists derived from their fate: "And when will our national consciousness be rid of that fatal confusion [between the state's power and national welfare] that has brought so much falsehood into every sphere of national life, falsehood that has colored our politics, our religion, education?"

5

The Failure of Resistance

FROM *October in the Provinces*

BY *John Keep*

IN THE FORWARD to his classic study of the October Revolution in Petrograd and Moscow, S. P. Melgunov remarks that the story has yet to be told of "how the rest of the country reacted to the act of violence perpetrated in the capitals." There are two principal reasons why this has not been done. One is the central-ist bias common among students of Russian history, who have in the main viewed developments in the provinces as no more than a reflection of events in the capital cities—even in a period of revolutionary *Sturm und Drang*. The other is the lack of adequate documentation. A satisfactory account would require, as Melgunov points out, "a fairly detailed and painstaking study of the local sources," most of which are unhappily difficult of access. Even the Moscow libraries are reputed to have important deficiencies. The local newspa-pers appeared irregularly, and the central ones contain a curious amalgam of fact, rumor and trivia. Much valuable information was collected and published in the 1920's by the local sections of Istpart, but these volumes are bibliographi-cal rarities. In the era of high Stalinism little appeared, and the flood of informa-tion released since 1957 has in a sense aggravated the problems facing the inde-pendent investigator because of the strict rules that currently govern the publication of documents from Soviet archives. . . .

The historian F. Grenard remarks that the population of Petrograd showed "an astonishing indifference" to the Bolshevik assumption of power. The same was true, broadly speaking, of the provinces. Events had moved so fast, and the normal pattern of political life had been so distorted, that most people were utterly confused. Relatively few seem to have felt that this was a decisive turn-ing point in history or that a moment had come when they must fight and die for their beliefs; it was a matter of avoiding what one feared or hated most, rather than of affirming deeply held aspirations. Such negative attitudes were common among supporters of all the contending parties, but the anti-Bolshevik

John Keep, "October in the Provinces," in *Revolutionary Russia*, Richard Pipes, ed., 1968. Reprinted by permission.

forces in particular seemed to suffer from a curious paralysis of the will. Those groups that might have been expected to rally against the threat of left-wing extremism were divided by a gulf of distrust so wide that it has scarcely been bridged even today.

The army leaders, to whom the conservative and liberal politicians looked as the potential nucleus of a strong government able to "regenerate" the country, had no tradition of intervening in civilian affairs; their first effort to do so, under General Kornilov, had ended in utter failure. Few senior professional officers could resist a feeling of *Schadenfreude* at the overthrow of the Provisional Government, which, as they saw it, had been to blame for this disaster. They had no desire to burn their fingers again. Generals Cheremisov, Baluev, and others were reluctant to commit any large body of troops to Kerensky's support at a time when such action could have proved decisive. The general tendency was to minimize the significance of the Bolshevik take-over. At First Army Headquarters, only a few hours' rail journey from the capital, staff officers had no reliable news of the insurrection:

> Just a few tales by casual visitors, week-old newspapers, and the white telegraph tapes with the usual laconic instructions. . . . As for the messages from Petersburg, "to all, all, all!" nobody took them seriously; we had grown used to them as part of the daily round and, I must admit, underestimated their new resolute tone.

The argument that the commissar and committee system in the army frustrated any attempt at action should be treated with caution. Many units preserved a modicum of discipline, but their commanders showed little initiative. At Mogilev, Dukhonin allowed the politicians to bicker among themselves, taking only an indirect interest in their deliberations. This inactivity could be explained in part by democratic scruples and respect for the will of the impending Constituent Assembly, but a far more powerful motive was the desire to recover for the army its traditional nonpartisan image and to leave the democratic politicians saddled with the responsibilities of government. It was characteristic that one general who decided that the only alternative to Bolshevism was a military regime should have mooted the idea in private with great diffidence and sworn his interlocutor to secrecy. It took a year of civil war before the notion of a military regime became really respectable in regular army circles.

Some Cossack leaders seem to have had a rather more realistic view of the country's problems, but they lacked the physical means to implement their ideas, except on a very limited scale; the position that the Cossacks occupied in Russian life was too exceptional for them to take the lead in building a viable military regime.

The Achilles' heel of Russian conservatism at this time was its rigid attitude towards the war. It should have been obvious that the armed forces were no longer capable of significant action against the enemy (in the European theater, at least), yet senior officers insistently opposed any serious step toward a negotiated peace. The irony was that soon after the Bolshevik overturn some of them reluctantly concurred in the Soviet government's efforts to secure an armistice and within a few months actively contributed to the buildup of the Red Army. Only after that did they gradually realize how fallacious had been the assumption, prevalent in army circles in the latter half of 1917, that the Bolsheviks were little more than enemy agents and that concern for the national interest was a monopoly of the right. In 1917 illusion held sway, preventing the conservatives from analyzing correctly the nature of their opponents and devising rational methods of combating them.

It must be acknowledged that the element of illusion was as great, if not greater, in the camp of "revolutionary democracy." Large elements in both the main socialist parties, anxious to win popular favor, were willing to overlook significant differences of principle that separated them from the Bolsheviks. They regarded Lenin and his followers as misguided comrades who would soon be brought by history to see the error of their ways; the task of the moderates, they thought, was to persuade them to renounce their unreasonable "maximalist" tendencies and to revert to an objective scientific view of the revolutionary process. It was axiomatic to all those with a Marxist upbringing—and the SRs too had been deeply influenced by Marxism—that premature "adventuristic" actions could lead only to isolation from the masses, the defeat of the revolution, and a conservative restoration. Once the results of the elections to the Constituent Assembly were known, the Bolsheviks' relative weakness would be apparent and they would be obliged to seek a compromise.

This reasoning invited the comforting conclusion that it was unnecessary to use coercion against the "usurpers," who were in any case doomed; it was enough to make a gesture of moral defiance. The demonstrative protest, the walkout from the council chamber, became the symbol of the democratic left's response to triumphant bolshevism. As one sympathetic critic puts it:

> All over Russia the same phenomenon was repeated: wherever the SRs and Mensheviks had a fairly significant majority in the soviets, instead of staying in them to fight the Bolsheviks . . . they voted to withdraw, voluntarily abandoning the battlefield. The Bolsheviks did not fail to take advantage of this decision and very quickly replaced the right-wing socialists with their own supporters. Thanks to this the Communists or their Left SR sympathizers soon had a majority of votes in almost all soviets and executives. Within a few months the right-wing socialists realized their mistake, but by then it was too late to undo it.

This attitude also accounts for the poor showing generally put up by the salvation committees—although it should be pointed out that, owing to the state of the sources, very little hard information is available about the way in which these bodies functioned. It is not certain, for instance, to what extent the debates in them were conducted and decisions arrived at along party-political lines. The municipal and *zemstvo* representatives will doubtless have often put their practical skills to good use in maintaining essential supplies and performing similar tasks, whereas the inclusion of soviet and trade-union representatives will have provided an invaluable channel of communication with the masses. Even the presence of Bolsheviks on some of these bodies, which at first sight seems to suggest unpardonable naiveté, could be defended on the grounds that at the provincial level there was a good deal of conciliatory and localist feeling among them. However, the non-Bolsheviks made no very systematic effort to exploit these sentiments, and the fact remains that the salvation committees collapsed in a matter of days, or at least weeks. It is reasonable to attribute this collapse primarily to the defective vision of the democratic politicians.

One result of this débâcle was that the burden of passive resistance to bolshevism fell upon the shoulders of the infant trade unions, some of which, all things considered, stood up for their principles remarkably well. In the case of the industrial unions, which were overwhelmingly under Bolshevik control, only branches in areas remote from the capital could attempt resistance, and they sometimes did so if the political climate was favorable to their designs. Somewhat better placed were the semi-professional unions, particularly in the communications. It is well known that on October 29 *Vikzhel,* the railwaymen's union, threatened to call a general strike unless its demand for a socialist coalition government were met and unless in response to this pressure certain Bolshevik leaders entered into negotiations with the opposition. Eventually this resistance was broken by the standard political maneuver: when a national congress (December 29) failed to give the Bolsheviks control, they called a gathering of their own adherents (January 5, 1918), who dissolved the union and formed a rival body, *Vikzhedor.*

The role played by the postal workers' union, *Potelsoiuz,* which was under SR control, deserves more attention than it is generally given. It too opposed the Bolshevik insurrection as a challenge to the authority of the Constituent Assembly and called for a socialist coalition government. In post and telegraph offices throughout the country union members and other employees withdrew their labor, sometimes taking obstructive action. On November 18 the union met in congress at Nizhni Novgorod and a week later adopted a resolution reaffirming its support for democratic institutions, calling upon the authorities to respect the inviolability of the mails and setting up a committee to plan further strikes if its demands were disregarded. In most cases the local Bolsheviks were able to restore essential services within a few days by employing blackleg labor (such as military telegraphists), threatening strikers with dismissal, and arresting the most recalcitrant elements. Nevertheless, this "sabotage movement," as it was misleadingly termed, caused them no little embarrassment. The breakdown of communications added considerably to the Bolsheviks' problems in organizing a smooth transfer of power in many provincial centers and helps explain the uncoordinated nature of much of their activity at this time. But such opposition, limited as it was by the organizational weakness of the Russian trade-union movement, could not prevail against the armed might of the "proletarian dictatorship."

To understand fully the reasons for the Bolsheviks' success in October it would be necessary to undertake an excursion into the familiar field of Russian *Geistesgeschichte*. Here it must suffice to note that, over a broad spectrum of political opinion, there was a firm conviction that, if the Bolsheviks took power, their rule would be of short duration. Joseph Gessen, a widely respected jurist whose contacts extended into all reaches of Russian society, recalls in his memoirs: "I never met anyone who doubted that the overthrow of the Bolsheviks was imminent. The only question was how and when." Obviously this view underestimated Lenin's resourcefulness and his tactical skill in the manipulation of political power. If even Lenin asked himself whether his party could successfully administer a modern state, it is hardly surprising that his opponents did likewise and that they should have arrived at the wrong answer. They were after all faced with an unprecedented situation: few as yet foresaw that a single-party dictatorship could create the prerequisites for its own survival.

The anti-Bolshevik forces, with few exceptions, based their conduct on moral principle rather than on considerations of *Realpolitik*. The psychologist might say that they did so in order to rationalize their own physical weakness, of which they were subconsciously aware but which they could not afford to admit. There is some truth in this, but it is not the whole story. Their failure to make use of such physical strength as they possessed was a conscious intellectual decision, taken by men who had experienced the abuses of power committed by the *ancien régime* and who were determined to avoid similar temptations themselves. Hence their ideological cast of thought, their distaste for precise juridical concepts, their romantic idealization of the people *(narod),* of freedom and democracy, and other abstract notions sanctified by generations of usage among the intelligentsia. The myths of nineteenth-century Russian radicalism still exerted a powerful fascination.

The Bolsheviks, too, were a product of the same radical tradition. But they had leaders able to blend the determinist certainties of revolutionary Marxism with their own voluntarist drive for power and to inspire their followers with the same modes of thought and conduct. The more activist elements on the left were irresistibly drawn to the Bolsheviks (and their allies) because they seemed to possess the will to translate ideals into practice. This was why thousands of individuals who had only the vaguest idea of Lenin's organizational and tactical doctrine could apply its essential precepts in their own environment, by simply joining in the struggle for power with boundless enthusiasm.

The distinction between moderates and radicals did not follow class lines. It was essentially a psychological, emotional barrier that defies exact analysis. One provincial Bolshevik leader puts the point well in his record of a conversational exchange with a Menshevik colleague, who asked him why the Bolsheviks were so fanatical and self-confident. He replied: "I can't really say: we're convinced, that's all. And if you're convinced of something, then for some reason you can't be unsure of yourself. That's all there is to it." He then made a bow to current political orthodoxy, claiming, "We are men of the proletarian mass," to which the Menshevik objected—correctly, but as it happens irrelevant-ly—that they were in fact all intellectuals, as was Lenin himself.

This ideological élan, linked to a well articulated philosophy of organiza-tion, gave the Bolsheviks the edge over their rivals and enabled them to turn the transient popular mood to their party's account. Once Soviet power had been achieved, the ideals of the propagandists were soon obscured by the harsh realities of dictatorship and the revolution lost much of its romantic allure. But by then a machine had been built powerful enough to keep dissent in check and, with time, even to reshape men's memories of the cause for which they had fought in October 1917.

The Origins of Nazi Germany—German History or Charismatic Leadership?

CONTENTS

QUESTIONS FOR STUDY

1 What elements of German history and tradition contributed to the Nazi victory?
2 What external forces were responsible?
3 How did the Nazi program and propaganda exploit these elements?
4 What role did modern "scientific" racial theories play?
5 What was the importance of anti-Semitism in the Nazi victory?
6 What part did the Communists play?
7 Was the role of German big business important?
8 Was the destruction of the Weimar Republic inevitable?

On January 30, 1933, Adolf Hitler took office as Chancellor of Germany. In March of the same year a compliant Reichstag voted an Enabling Act, which suspended the constitution, established Hitler's dictatorship, and put an end to Germany's attempt at democratic republican government. It also introduced a reign of terror, a policy of racism and military adventurism, the like of which the world had never seen. Our problem is to decide why this disaster befell Germany. Some scholars have thought that the evil aspects and consequences of Nazism are inherent in the German character, which was created by the unique course of German history. Others find the causes of the Nazi rise to power in the peculiar problems faced by the Weimar Republic and suggest that any nation faced by such conditions and problems might well succumb. Still another view is that Nazism was largely the product of the evil genius of Adolf Hitler himself. The documents that follow illustrate some of the difficulties that Germany faced after World War I and the nature of the solutions offered by Hitler and the Nazis. They also indicate which elements of the German people helped Hitler to power.

1

Hitler, the Greatest Demagogue in History

Alan Bullock presents a sophisticated version of a widely held opinion that Nazism was the product of the demagogic genius of Adolf Hitler.

FROM *Hitler*

BY *Alan Bullock*

HITLER LIVED THROUGH the exciting days of April and May 1919 in Munich itself. What part he played, if any, is uncertain. According to his own account in *Mein Kampf,* he was to have been put under arrest at the end of April, but drove off with his rifle the three men who came to arrest him. Once the Communists had been overthrown, he gave information before the Commission of Inquiry set up by the 2nd Infantry Regiment, which tried and shot those reported to have been active on the other side. He then got a job in the Press and News Bureau of the Political Department of the Army's VII (Munich) District Command, a centre for the activities of such men as Röhm. After attending a course of "political instruction" for the troops, Hitler was himself appointed a *Bildungsoffizier* (Instruction Officer) with the task of inoculating the men against contagion by socialist, pacifist, or democratic ideas. This was an important step for Hitler, since it constituted the first recognition of the fact that he had any political ability at all. Then, in September, he was instructed by the head of the Political Department to investigate a small group meeting in Munich, the German Workers' Party, which might possibly be of interest to the Army.

* * *

The German Workers' Party had its origins in a Committee of Independent Workmen set up by a Munich locksmith, Anton Drexler, on 7 March 1918. Drexler's idea was to create a party which would be both working class and

Alan Bullock, *Hitler: A Study in Tyranny,* Completely Revised Edition, pp.63–71, 805–808. Copyright 1962 by Alan Bullock. Reprinted by permission of HarperCollins Publishers, Inc.

nationalist. He saw what Hitler had also seen, that a middle-class movement like the Fatherland Front (to which Drexler belonged) was hopelessly out of touch with the mood of the masses, and that these were coming increasingly under the influence of anti-national and anti-propaganda. Drexler made little headway with his committee, which recruited forty members, and in October 1918 he and Karl Harrer, a journalist, founded the Political Workers' Circle which, in turn, was merged with the earlier organization in January 1919 to form the German Workers' Party. Harrer became the Party's first chairman. Its total membership was little more than Drexler's original forty, activity was limited to discussions in Munich beer-halls, and the committee of six had no clear idea of anything more ambitious. It can scarcely have been a very impressive scene when, on the evening of 12 September 1919, Hitler attended his first meeting in a room at the Sterneckerbräu, a Munich beer-cellar in which a handful of twenty or twenty-five people had gathered. One of the speakers was Gottfried Feder, an economic crank well known in Munich, who had already impressed Hitler at one of the political courses arranged for the Army. The other was a Bavarian separatist, whose proposals for the secession of Bavaria from the German Reich and a union with Austria brought Hitler to his feet in a fury. He spoke with such vehemence that when the meeting was over Drexler went up to him and gave him a copy of his autobiographical pamphlet, *Mein politisches Erwachen*.[1] A few days later Hitler received a postcard inviting him to attend a committee meeting of the German Workers' Party.

After some hesitation Hitler went. The committee met in an obscure beer-house, the Alte Rosenbad, in the Herrnstrasse. "I went through the badly lighted guest-room, "[Hitler wrote in *Mein Kampf*,] "where not a single guest was to be seen, and searched for the door which led to the side room; and there I was face to face with the Committee. Under the dim light shed by a grimy gas-lamp I could see four people sitting round a table, one of them the author of the pamphlet."

The rest of the proceedings followed in the same key: the Party's funds were reported to total 7.50 marks, minutes were read and confirmed, three letters were received, three replies read and approved.

Yet, as Hitler frankly acknowledges, this very obscurity was an attraction. It was only in a party which, like himself, was beginning at the bottom that he had any prospect of playing a leading part and imposing his ideas. In the established parties there was no room for him, he would be a nobody. After two days' reflection he made up his mind and joined the Committee of the German Workers' Party as its seventh member.

The energy and ambition which had been hitherto unharnessed now found an outlet. Slowly and painfully he pushed the Party forward, and prodded his cautious and unimaginative colleagues on the committee into bolder methods of recruitment. A few invitations were multigraphed and distributed, a

[1] *My Political Awakening.*

small advertisement inserted in the local paper, a larger hall secured for more frequent meetings. When Hitler himself spoke for the first time in the Hofbräuhaus in October, a hundred and eleven people were present. The result was to confirm the chairman, Karl Harrer, in his belief that Hitler had no talent for public speaking. But Hitler persisted and the numbers rose. In October there were a hundred and thirty when Hitler spoke on Brest-Litovsk and Versailles, a little later there were two hundred.

At the beginning of 1920 Hitler was put in charge of the Party's propaganda and promptly set to work to organize its first mass meeting. By the use of clever advertising he got nearly two thousand people into the *Festsaal* of the Hofbräuhaus on 24 February. The principal speaker was a Dr. Dingfelder, but it was Hitler who captured the audience's attention and used the occasion to announce the Party's new name, the National Socialist German Workers' Party, and its twenty-five point programme. Angered by the way in which Hitler was now forcing the pace, Harrer resigned from the office of chairman. On 1 April 1920, Hitler at last left the Army and devoted all his time to building up the Party, control of which he now more and more arrogated to himself.

Hitler's and Drexler's group in Munich was not the only National Socialist Party. In Bavaria itself there were rival groups, led by Streicher in Nuremberg and Dr. Otto Dickel in Augsburg, both nominally branches of the German Socialist Party founded by Alfred Brunner in 1919. Across the frontier in Austria and in the Sudetenland the pre-war German Social Workers' Party had been reorganized and got in touch with the new Party in Munich. A number of attempts had been made in Austria before 1914 to combine a working-class movement with a Pan-German nationalist programme. The most successful was this Deutsch Arbeiterpartei which, led by an Austrian lawyer, Walther Riehl, and a railway employee named Rudolf Jung, won three seats in the Reichsrat at the Austrian elections of 1911. The Party's programme was formulated at the Moravian town of Iglau in 1913, and reflected the bitterness of the German struggle with the Czechs as well as the attraction of Pan-German and anti-Semitic ideas.

In May 1918, this Austrian party took the title of D.N.S.A.P.—the German National Socialists Workers' Party—and began to use the Hakenkreuz, the swastika, as its symbol. When the Austro-Hungarian monarchy was broken up, and a separate Czech State formed, the National Socialists set up an inter-State bureau with one branch in Vienna, of which Riehl was chairman, and another in the Sudetenland. It was this inter-State bureau which now invited the cooperation of the Bavarian National Socialists, and a Munich delegation attended the next joint meeting at Salzburg in August 1920. Shortly afterwards the Munich Party, too, adopted the name of the National Socialist German Workers' Party.

Up to August 1923, when Hitler attended the last of the inter-State meetings at Salzburg, there were fairly frequent contacts between these different National Socialist groups, but little came of them. Hitler was too jealous of his independence to submit to interference from outside, and the last meeting of the conference, at Salzburg in 1923, led to Riehl's resignation.

Much more important to Hitler was the support he received from Captain Röhm, on the staff of the Army District Command in Munich. Röhm, a tough, scar-faced soldier of fortune with real organizing ability, exercised considerable influence in the shadowy world of the Freikorps, Defence Leagues, and political conspiracies. He had actually joined the German Workers' Party before Hitler, for, like Hitler, he saw that it would be impossible to re-create a strong, nationalist Germany until the alienation of the mass of the people from their old loyalty to the Fatherland and the Army could be overcome. Any party which could recapture the working classes for a nationalist and militarist allegiance interested him. He admired the spirit and toughness of the Communists, who were prepared to fight for what they believed in: what he wanted was working-class organizations with the same qualities on his own side.

Röhm had little patience with the view that the Army should keep out of politics. The Army, he believed, had to go into politics if it wanted to create the sort of State which would restore its old privileged position, and break with the policy of fulfilling the terms of the Peace Treaty. This was a view accepted by only a part of the Officer Corps; others, especially among the senior officers, viewed Röhm's activities with mistrust. But there was sufficient sympathy with his aims to allow a determined man to use the opportunities of his position to the full.

When Hitler began to build up the German Workers' Party, Röhm pushed in ex-Freikorps men and ex-servicemen to swell the Party's membership. From these elements the first "strong-arm" squads were formed, the nucleus of the S.A. In December 1920, Röhm had persuaded his commanding officer, Major-General Ritter von Epp—himself a former Freikorps leader and a member of the Party—to help raise the sixty thousand marks needed to buy the Party a weekly paper, the *Völkischer Beobachter*. Dietrich Eckart provided half, but part of the rest came from Army secret funds. Above all, Röhm was the indispensable link in securing for Hitler the protection, or at least the tolerance, of the Army and of the Bavarian Government, which depended on the local Army Command as the ultimate arbiter of public order. Without the unique position of the Army in German, and especially in Bavarian, politics—its ability to extend powerful support to the political groups and activities it favoured—Hitler would never have been able to exercise with impunity his methods of incitement, violence and intimidation. At every step from 1914 to 1945 Hitler's varying relationship to the Army was of the greatest importance to him: never more so than in these early years in Munich when, without the Army's patronage, Hitler would have found the greatest difficulty in climbing the first steps of his political career. Before his death the Army was to learn the full measure of his ingratitude.

Yet however important this help from outside, the foundation of Hitler's success was his own energy and ability as a political leader. Without this, the help would never have been forthcoming, or would have produced insignificant results. Hitler's genius as a politician lay in his unequalled grasp of what could be done by propaganda, and his flair for seeing how to do it. He had to learn in a hard school, on his feet night after night, arguing his case in every kind of hall, from the smoke-filled back room of a beer cellar to the huge auditorium of the Zirkus Krone; often, in the early days, in the face of opposition, indifference or amused contempt; learning to hold his audience's attention, to win them over; most important of all, learning to read the minds of his audiences, finding the sensitive spots on which to hammer. "He could play like a virtuoso on the well-tempered piano of lower-middle-class hearts," says Dr. Schacht. Behind that virtuosity lay years of experience as an agitator and mob orator. Hitler came to know Germany and the German people at first hand as few of Germany's other leaders ever had. By the time he came to power in 1933 there were few towns of any size in the Reich where he had not spoken. Here was one great advantage Hitler had over nearly all the politicians with whom he had to deal, his immense practical experience of politics, not in the Chancellery or the Reichstag, but in the street, the level at which elections are won, the level at which any politician must be effective if he is to carry a mass vote with him.

*   *   *

Hitler was the greatest demagogue in history. Those who add "only a demagogue" fail to appreciate the nature of political power in an age of mass politics. As he himself said: "To be a leader, means to be able to move masses."

The lessons which Hitler drew from the activities of the Austrian Social Democrats and Lueger's Christian Socialists were now tried out in Munich. Success was far from being automatic. Hitler made mistakes and had much to learn before he could persuade people to take him seriously, even on the small stage of Bavarian politics. By 1923 he was still only a provincial politician, who had not yet made any impact on national politics, and the end of 1923 saw the collapse of his movement in a fiasco. But Hitler learned from his mistakes, and by the time he came to write *Mein Kampf* in the middle of the 1920s he was able to set down quite clearly what he was trying to do, and what were the conditions of success. The pages in *Mein Kampf* in which he discusses the technique of mass propaganda and political leadership stand out in brilliant contrast with the turgid attempts to explain his entirely unoriginal political ideas.

The first and most important principle for political action laid down by Hitler is: Go to the masses. "The movement must avoid everything which may lessen or weaken its power of influencing the masses . . . because of the simple fact that no great idea, no matter how sublime or exalted, can be realized in practice without the effective power which resides in the popular masses."

> Since the masses have only a poor acquaintance with abstract ideas, their reactions lie more in the domain of the feelings, where the roots of their positive as well as their negative attitudes are implanted . . . The emotional grounds of their attitude furnish the reason for their extraordinary stability. It is always more difficult to fight against faith than against knowledge. And the driving force which has brought about the most tremendous revolutions on this earth has never been a body of scientific teaching which has gained power over the masses, but always a

devotion which has inspired them, and often a kind of hysteria which has urged them into action. Whoever wishes to win over the masses must know the key that will open the door to their hearts. It is not objectivity, which is a feckless attitude, but a determined will, backed up by power where necessary.

Hitler is quite open in explaining how this is to be achieved. "The receptive powers of the masses are very restricted, and their understanding is feeble. On the other hand, they quickly forget. Such being the case, all effective propaganda must be confined to a few bare necessities and then must be expressed in a few stereotyped formulas." Hitler had nothing but scorn for the intellectuals who are always looking for something new. "Only constant repetition will finally succeed in imprinting an idea on the memory of a crowd." For the same reason it is better to stick to a programme even when certain points in it become out of date: "As soon as one point is removed from the sphere of dogmatic certainty, the discussion will not simply result in a new and better formulation, but may easily lead to endless debates and general confusion."

When you lie, tell big lies. This is what the Jews do, working on the principle,

> which is quite true in itself, that in the big lie there is always a certain force of credibility; because the broad masses of a nation are always more easily corrupted in the deeper strata of their emotional nature than consciously or voluntarily, and thus in the primitive simplicity of their minds they more readily fall victims to the big lie than the small lie, since they themselves often tell small lies in little matters, but would be ashamed to resort to large-scale falsehoods. It would never come into their heads to fabricate colossal untruths and they would not believe that others could have the impudence to distort the truth so infamously. . . . The grossly impudent lie always leaves traces behind it, even after it has been nailed down.

Above all, never hesitate, never qualify what you say, never concede an inch to the other side, paint all your contrasts in black and white. This is the

> very first condition which has to be fulfilled in every kind of propaganda: a systematically one-sided attitude towards every problem that has to be dealt with. . . . When they see an uncompromising onslaught against an adversary, the people have at all times taken this as proof that right is on the side of the active aggressor; but if the aggressor should go only halfway and fail to push home his success . . . the people will look upon this as a sign that he is uncertain of the justice of his own cause.

Vehemence, passion, fanaticism, these are "the great magnetic forces which alone attract the great masses; for these masses always respond to the compelling force which emanates from absolute faith in the ideas put forward, combined with an indomitable zest to fight for and defend them. . . . The doom of a nation can be averted only by a storm of glowing passion; but only those who are passionate themselves can arouse passion in others."

Hitler showed a marked preference for the spoken over the written word.

"The force which ever set in motion the great historical avalanches of religious and political movements is the magic power of the spoken word. The broad masses of a population are more amenable to the appeal of rhetoric than to any other force." The employment of verbal violence, the repetition of such words as "smash," "force," "ruthless," "hatred," was deliberate. Hitler's gestures and the emotional character of his speaking, lashing himself up to a pitch of near-hysteria in which he would scream and spit out his resentment, had the same effect on an audience. Many descriptions have been given of the way in which he succeeded in communicating passion to his listeners, so that men groaned or hissed and women sobbed involuntarily, if only to relieve the tension, caught up in the spell of powerful emotions of hatred and exaltation, from which all restraint had been removed.

It was to be years yet before Hitler was able to achieve this effect on the scale of the Berlin Sportpalast audiences of the 1930s, but he had already begun to develop extraordinary gifts as a speaker. It was in Munich that he learned to address mass audiences of several thousands. In *Mein Kampf* he remarks that the orator's relationship with his audience is the secret of his art. "He will always follow the lead of the great mass in such a way that from the living emotion of his hearers the apt word which he needs will be suggested to him and in its turn this will go straight to the hearts of his hearers." A little later he speaks of the difficulty of overcoming emotional resistance: this cannot be done by argument, but only by an appeal to the "hidden forces" in an audience, an appeal that the orator alone can make.

Many attempts have been made to explain away the importance of Hitler, from Chaplin's brilliant caricature in *The Great Dictator* to the much less convincing picture of Hitler the pawn, a front man for German capitalism. Others have argued that Hitler was nothing in himself, only a symbol of the restless ambition of the German nation to dominate Europe; a creature flung to the top by the tides of revolutionary change, or the embodiment of the collective unconscious of a people obsessed with violence and death.

These arguments seem to me to be based upon a confusion of two different questions. Obviously, Nazism was a complex phenomenon to which many factors—social, economic, historical, psychological—contributed. But whatever the explanation of this episode in European history—and it can be no simple one—that does not answer the question with which this book has been concerned, what was the part played by Hitler? It may be true that a mass movement, strongly nationalist, anti-Semitic, and radical, would have sprung up in Germany without Hitler. But so far as what actually happened is concerned—not what might have happened—the evidence seems to me to leave no doubt that no other man played a role in the Nazi revolution or in the history of the Third Reich remotely comparable with that of Adolf Hitler.

The conception of the Nazi Party, the propaganda with which it must appeal to the German people, and the tactics by which it would come to power—these were unquestionably Hitler's. After 1934 there were no rivals left and by 1938 he had removed the last checks on his freedom of action. Thereafter, he exercised an arbitrary rule in Germany to a degree rarely, if ever, equalled in a modern industrialized state.

At the same time, from the re-militarization of the Rhineland to the invasion of Russia, he won a series of successes in diplomacy and war which established an hegemony over the continent of Europe comparable with that of Napoleon at the height of his fame. While these could not have been won without a people and an Army willing to serve him, it was Hitler who provided the indispensable leadership, the flair for grasping opportunities, the boldness in using them. In retrospect his mistakes appear obvious, and it is easy to be complacent about the inevitability of his defeat; but it took the combined efforts of the three most powerful nations in the world to break his hold on Europe.

Luck and the disunity of his opponents will account for much of Hitler's success—as it will of Napoleon's—but not for all. He began with few advantages, a man without a name and without support other than that which he acquired for himself, not even a citizen of the country he aspired to rule. To achieve what he did Hitler needed—and possessed—talents out of the ordinary which in sum amounted to political genius, however evil its fruits.

His abilities have been sufficiently described in the preceding pages: his mastery of the irrational factors in politics, his insight into the weaknesses of his opponents, his gift for simplification, his sense of timing, his willingness to take risks. An opportunist entirely without principle, he showed both consistency and an astonishing power of will in pursuing his aims. Cynical and calculating in the exploitation of his histrionic gifts, he retained an unshaken belief in his historic role and in himself as a creature of destiny.

The fact that his career ended in failure, and that his defeat was preeminently due to his own mistakes, does not by itself detract from Hitler's claim to greatness. The flaw lies deeper. For these remarkable powers were combined with an ugly and strident egotism, a moral and intellectual cretinism. The passions which ruled Hitler's mind were ignoble: hatred, resentment, the lust to dominate, and, where he could not dominate, to destroy. His career did not exalt but debased the human condition, and his twelve years' dictatorship was barren of all ideas save one—the further extension of his own power and that of the nation with which he had identified himself. Even power he conceived of in the crudest terms: an endless vista of military roads, S.S. garrisons, and concentration camps to sustain the rule of the Aryan "master race" over the degraded subject peoples of his new empire in the east.

The great revolutions of the past, whatever their ultimate fate, have been identified with the release of certain powerful ideas: individual conscience, liberty, equality, national freedom, social justice. National Socialism produced nothing. Hitler constantly exalted force over the power of ideas and delighted to prove that men were governed by cupidity, fear, and their baser passions. The sole theme of the Nazi revolution was domination, dressed up as the doctrine of race, and, failing that, a vindictive destructiveness, Rauschning's *Revolution des Nihilismus*.

It is this emptiness, this lack of anything to justify the suffering he caused rather than his own monstrous and ungovernable will which makes Hitler both so repellent and so barren a figure. Hitler will have his place in history, but it will be alongside Attila the Hun, the barbarian king who was surnamed, not "the Great," but "the Scourge of God," and who boasted "in a saying," Gibbon writes, "worthy of his ferocious pride, that the grass never grew on the spot where his horse had stood."

* * *

The view has often been expressed that Hitler could only have come to power in Germany, and it is true—without falling into the same error of racialism as the Nazis—that there were certain features of German historical development, quite apart from the effects of the Defeat and the Depression, which favoured the rise of such a movement.

This is not to accuse the Germans of Original Sin, or to ignore the other sides of German life which were only grossly caricatured by the Nazis. But Nazism was not some terrible accident which fell upon the German people out of a blue sky. It was rooted in their history, and while it is true that a majority of the German people never voted for Hitler, it is also true that thirteen millions did. Both facts need to be remembered.

From this point of view Hitler's career may be described as a *reductio ad absurdum* of the most powerful political tradition in Germany since the Unification. This is what nationalism, militarism, authoritarianism, the worship of success and force, the exaltation of the State, and *Realpolitik* lead to, if they are projected to their logical conclusion.

There are Germans who reject such a view. They argue that what was wrong with Hitler was that he lacked the necessary skill, that he was a bungler. If only he had listened to the generals—or Schacht—or the career diplomats—if only he had not attacked Russia, and so on. There is some point, they feel, at which he went wrong. They refuse to see that it was the ends themselves, not simply the means, which were wrong: the pursuit of unlimited power, the scorn for justice or any restraint on power; the exaltation of will over reason and conscience; the assertion of an arrogant supremacy, the contempt for others' rights. As at least one German historian, Professor Meinecke, has recognized, the catastrophe to which Hitler led Germany points to the need to re-examine the aims as well as the methods of German policy as far back as Bismarck.

The Germans, however, were not the only people who preferred in the 1930s not to know what was happening and refused to call evil things by their true names. The British and French at Munich; the Italians, Germany's partners in the Pact of Steel; the Poles, who stabbed the Czechs in the back over Teschen; the Russians, who signed the Nazi-Soviet Pact to partition Poland, all thought they could buy Hitler off, or use him to their own selfish advantage. They did not succeed, any more than the German Right or the German Army. In the bitterness of war and occupation they were forced to learn the truth of the words of John Donne which Ernest Hemingway set at the beginning of his novel of the Spanish Civil War:

> No man is an Iland, intire of it selfe; every man is a peece of the Continent, a part of the maine; If a clod bee washed away by the Sea, Europe is the lesse, as well as if a Promontorie were, as well as if a Mannor of thy friends or of thine own were; Any man's death diminishes me, because I am involved in Mankinde; And therefore never send to know for whom the bell tolls; It tolls for thee.

Hitler, indeed, was a European, no less than a German phenomenon. The conditions and the state of mind which he exploited, the *malaise* of which he was the symptom, were not confined to one country, although they were more strongly marked in Germany than anywhere else. Hitler's idiom was German, but the thoughts and emotions to which he gave expression have a more universal currency.

Hitler recognized this relationship with Europe perfectly clearly. He was in revolt against "the System" not just in Germany but in Europe, against the liberal bourgeois order, symbolized for him in the Vienna which had once rejected him. To destroy this was his mission, the mission in which he never ceased to believe; and in this, the most deeply felt of his purposes, he did not fail. Europe may rise again, but the old Europe of the years between 1789, the year of the French Revolution, and 1939, the year of Hitler's War, has gone for ever—and the last figure in its history is that of Adolf Hitler, the architect of its ruin. *"Si monumentum requiris, circumspice"*—"If you seek his monument, look around."

2

The Weaknesses of Weimar

Article 231 of the Treaty of Versailles, which assigned all responsibility for the recent war to Germany and her allies, was a thorn in the side of those Germans who defended the Weimar democracy. The clause was widely rejected by the Germans, and enemies of the republic used it to fix the blame for all Germany's troubles on the republican officials who had signed the treaty. The following remarks of Adolf Hitler's are examples of the rhetoric that was employed.

FROM *Hitler's Speeches on War Guilt*

In a speech delivered at Munich on 13 April 1923 Hitler said:

IN THE WINTER OF THE YEAR 1919–20 we National Socialists publicly for the first time put to the German people the question, whose is the guilt for the War? . . . And we received pat from all sides the stereotyped answer of despicable self-humiliation: "We confess it: the guilt for the War is ours!" . . . Yes, the whole Revolution was made artificially on the basis of this truly monstrous lie. For if it had not been possible to bring this lie into the field as a propaganda formula against the old Reich, what sense could one give at all to the November treason? They needed this slander of the existing system in order to justify before the people their own deed of shame. The masses, under the influence of a criminal incitement, were prepared without any hesitation to believe whatever the men of the new Government told them.

In his speech delivered in Munich on 17 April 1923 Hitler discussed "The Peace Treaty of Versailles as the perpetual curse of the November-Republic."

Who, *he asked,* were the real rulers of Germany in 1914 to whom war guilt might be attributed: not the Kaiser, not the Pan-Germans, but Messrs. Ballin, Bleichröder, Mendelssohn, &c., a whole brood of Hebrews who formed the unofficial Government. And in 1914 the real ruler of the Reich was Herr Bethmann-Hollweg, "a descendant of a Jewish family of Frankfurt—the genuine

The Speeches of Adolf Hitler, April 1922–1939, pp.54–57, Norman H. Baynes, ed. Reprinted by permission.

article, and in his every act the Yiddish philosopher all over. Those were the leaders of the State, not the Pan-Germans."

*   *   *

After discussing the mistakes of German politicians during the course of the war, Hitler continued:

With the armistice begins the humiliation of Germany. If the Republic on the day of its foundation had appealed to the country: "Germans, stand together! Up and resist the foe! The Fatherland, the Republic expects of you that you fight to your last breath," then millions who are now the enemies of the Republic would be fanatical Republicans. To-day they are the foes of the Republic not because it is a Republic but because this Republic was founded at the moment when Germany was humiliated, because it so discredited the new flag that men's eyes must turn regretfully towards the old flag.

It was no Treaty of Peace which was signed, but a betrayal of Peace.

The Treaty was signed which demanded from Germany that she should perform what was for ever impossible of performance. But that was not the worst: after all that was only a question of material values. This was not the end: Commissions of Control were formed! For the first time in the history of the modern world there were planted on a State agents of foreign Powers to act as hangmen, and German soldiers were set to serve the foreigner. And if one of these Commissions was "insulted," a company of the German army *(Reichswehr)* had to defile before the French flag. We no longer feel the humiliation of such an act; but the outside world says, "What a people of curs!"

So long as this Treaty stands there can be no resurrection of the German people: no social reform of any kind is possible! The Treaty was made in order to bring 20 million Germans to their deaths and to ruin the German nation. But those who made the Treaty cannot set it aside. At its foundation our Movement formulated three demands:

1. Setting aside of the Peace Treaty.
2. Unification of all Germans.
3. Land and soil *(Grund und Boden)* to feed our nation.

Our Movement could formulate these demands, since it was not our Movement which caused the War, it has not made the Republic, it did not sign the Peace-Treaty.

There is thus one thing which is the first task of this Movement: it desires to make the German once more National, that his Fatherland shall stand for him above everything else. It desires to teach our people to understand afresh the truth of the old saying: He who will not be a hammer must be an anvil. An anvil are we today, and that anvil will be beaten until out of the anvil we fashion once more a hammer, a German sword!

A major role in the weakening of the republic and in the destruction of the German people's confidence in it was played by the severe inflation that struck between 1921 and 1923. It wreaked havoc on the economy and wiped out the savings of the middle class. The following account is from the autobiography of a woman who lived through that difficult time in Germany.

FROM *Restless Days*

BY *Lilo Linke*

THE TIME FOR MY FIRST EXCURSIONS into life was badly chosen. Rapidly Germany was precipitated into the inflation, thousands, millions, milliards of marks whirled about, making heads swim in confusion. War, revolution, and the wild years after had deprived everyone of old standards and the possibility of planning a normal life. Again and again fate hurled the helpless individual into the boiling kettle of a wicked witch. Now the inflation came and destroyed the last vestige of steadiness. Hurriedly one had to make use of the moment and could not consider the following day.

The whole population had suddenly turned into maniacs. Everyone was buying, selling, speculating, bargaining, and dollar, dollar, dollar was the magic word which dominated every conversation, every newspaper, every poster in Germany. Nobody understood what was happening. There seemed to be no sense, no rules in the mad game, but one had to take part in it if one did not want to be trampled underfoot at once. Only a few people were able to carry through to the end and gain by the inflation. The majority lost everything and broke down, impoverished and bewildered.

The middle class was hurt more than any other, the savings of a lifetime and their small fortunes melted into a few coppers. They had to sell their most precious belongings for ten milliard inflated marks to buy a bit of food or an absolutely necessary coat, and their pride and dignity were bleeding out of many wounds. Bitterness remained for ever in their hearts. Full of hatred, they accused the international financiers, the Jews and Socialists—their old enemies—of having exploited their distress. They never forgot and never forgave and were the first to lend a willing ear to Hitler's fervent preaching.

In the shop, notices announced that we should receive our salaries in weekly parts, after a while we queued up at the cashier's desk every evening, and before long we were paid twice daily and ran out during the lunch hour to buy a few things, because as soon as the new rate of exchange became known in the early afternoon our money had again lost half its value.

In the beginning I did not concern myself much with these happenings. They merely added to the excitement of my new life, which was all that mattered to me. Living in the east of Berlin and in hard times, I was long accustomed to seeing people around me in hunger, distress, and poverty. My mother was always lamenting that it was impossible for her to make both ends meet, my father—whenever he was at home—always asking what the deuce she had done with all the money he had given her yesterday. A few tears, a few outbreaks more did not make a difference great enough to impress me deeply.

Yet, in the long run, the evil influence of the inflation, financially as well as morally, penetrated even to me. Berlin had become the centre of international profiteers and noisy new rich. For a few dollars they could buy the whole town, drinks and women, horses and houses, virtue and vice, and they made free use of these possibilities. The evening when I had gone with the Count to the restaurant and the Pacific Bar I had watched them with surprised eyes, although certainly my lack of experience exaggerated the impression, as it had done many years before on the Rummel, and although the bar and the people there would in any circumstances have seemed luxurious and astonishing to me. During the next months I had many opportunities of witnessing their lavish life because I went often to expensive places, a modest grey sparrow, watching in a crowd of radiant peacocks.

The following remarks were made by Hitler in 1923 at the height of the inflation.

FROM *Hitler's Speeches*

It was the height of the inflation period and of the manufacture of paper money:

GERMANY IS A PEOPLE OF CHILDREN; a grown-up people would say: "We don't care a fig for your paper-money. Give us something of value—gold! What have you after all to give us? Nothing? Thus have you defrauded us, you rogues and swindlers!" An awakened people with its last thirty marks—all that is left of the millions of its glory—would buy a rope and with it string up 10,000 of its defrauders! Even the farmer will no longer sell his produce. When you offer him your million scraps of paper with which he can cover the walls of his closet on his dung-heap, can you wonder that he says, "Keep your millions and I will keep my corn and my butter." The individual and the nation are delivered over to the international capital of the banks; despair seizes the whole people. We are on the eve of a second revolution. Some are setting their hopes on the star of the Soviet: that is the symbol of those who began the Revolution, to whom the Revolution has brought untold wealth, who have exploited it until to-day. It is the star of David, the sign of the Synagogue. The symbol of the race high over the world, of a lordship which stretches from Vladivostok to the West—the lordship of Jewry. The golden star which for the Jew means the glittering gold.

The Speeches of Adolf Hitler, April 1922–1939, pp.72–73. Reprinted by permission.

And when the people in its horror sees that one can starve though one may have milliards of marks, then it will perforce make up its mind and say: "We will bow down no longer before an institution which is founded on the delusory majority principle, we want a dictatorship." Already the Jew has a premonition of things to come: . . . he is saying to himself: If there must be a dictatorship, then it shall be a dictatorship of Cohen or Levi.

The payment of reparations by Germany to the victorious powers was disruptive in several ways. It was based on the war-guilt clause and therefore was a tangible reminder of Germany's defeat and the shameful peace; it slowed economic recovery; it was a device that enabled France to occupy the Saar and the Rhineland and thus a weapon that could be used by Nationalists against the republic. In 1929 a group of international experts met at Paris to resolve the reparations problem and produced the relatively lenient Young Plan. This plan was adopted by the powers and Germany at a conference at The Hague. The plan evoked great hostility on the right, and a committee—headed by the Nationalist Hugenberg, Hitler, Seldte, who was the leader of the Stahlhelm, and Class, who was the leader of the Pan-German League—was organized to fight it. They proposed a plebiscite to give the people a chance to repudiate the reparations settlement. In September 1929 they published the following draft of a law. The bill was defeated, but its language shows the intensity of the animosity felt toward reparations in some quarters.

Law Against the Enslavement of the German People

1. THE GOVERNMENT OF THE REICH must immediately give notice to the foreign powers that the forced acknowledgment of war guilt in the Versailles Treaty contradicts historical truth, rests on false assumptions, and is not binding in international law.
2. The government of the Reich must work toward the formal abrogation of the war-guilt clause of Article 231 as well as Articles 429 and 430 of the Versailles Treaty. It must further work toward immediate and unconditional evacuation of the occupied territories and the removal of all control over German territory independent of the acceptance or rejection of the resolutions of the Hague Conference.
3. New burdens and obligations toward foreign powers which rest on the war-guilt clause must not be undertaken. Under this category fall the burdens and obligations that may be taken by Germany on the basis of the experts at Paris and according to the agreements coming from them.
4. Reichschancellors and Reichsministers as well as plenipotentiaries of the German Reich who sign treaties with foreign powers contrary to the prescription of clause number three are subject to the penalties of clause ninety-two, section three of the civil code [*dealing with treason—Ed.*].
5. This law goes into effect at the time of its proclamation.

"Law Against the Enslavement of the German People," in Deutsche Allgemeine Zeitung, No. 442 (September 12, 1929), translated by Donald Kagan. Reprinted by permission.

Part of the reason for the failure of the Weimar Republic may be found in its constitution. The following selections from it are translated, edited, and introduced by Louis Snyder.

FROM *The Constitution of the German Republic*

AFTER THE GERMAN IMPERIAL GOVERNMENT had been overthrown and the Communist Spartacist revolt put down by force, Germans over nineteen years of age went to the polls on January 19, 1919, to elect a National Constituent Assembly. More than thirty million men and women elected 423 representatives, with the Majority Socialists leading with 165 seats, the Centrists second with 91 seats, and the Democrats third with 75 seats. The Assembly was controlled by these three top groups (the "Weimar Coalition") out of a dozen or more parties.

The National Constituent Assembly convened at Weimar on February 6, 1919. Weimar was chosen for sentimental reasons: It was believed that the spirit of Goethe had triumphed finally over that of Frederick the Great's Potsdam. The Assembly's sessions were turned by the German nationalists into riotous brawls. After electing Friedrich Ebert as President of the Republic (February 11th), the Assembly began to discuss the Constitution drafted by Dr. Hugo Preuss, a professor of constitutional law and Minister of the Interior. The article causing most heated discussion, that relating to the national colors, was settled by a compromise. The document, passed on July 31st at its third reading, went into effect on August 11, 1919, as the fundamental law of the German Republic.

The Weimar Constitution was a letter-perfect document, seemingly embodying the best features of the British Bill of Rights, the French Declaration of the Rights of Man, and the first Ten Amendments of the American Constitution. However, this magnificent Constitution planned for every contingency except that of preserving itself. Article 48, the "suicide clause," empowered the President to assume dictatorial powers in an emergency. This escape clause proved to be of inestimable value to Hitler later on.

The Weimar Constitution, "the formulation of a stalemate," was a compromise that accepted the outward forms of democracy but breathed no life into the form that had been created. It was attacked bitterly from both the Right and the Left.

The Weimar Republic was burdened by difficulties from its inception. The Social Democratic party had a program, but, in action, it was pitifully impotent. Its leaders, though undeniably men of good intentions, were unable adequately to meet the responsibilities placed upon them: the liquidation of the war, the Treaty of Versailles, reparations, the Ruhr invasion, the collapse of the mark, and the catastrophic decline of the middle class. These men were ruined in public opinion because they had been forced to accept the mission of advocating the conditions that had been imposed upon their fellow citizens. The victorious Allies, who had demanded a German democratic state, now gave but grudging assistance to the fledgling republic. In the Allied countries the suspicion persisted that the Germans had not willingly broken with their imperialist and militaristic past and that the Weimar Republic was devised merely as a necessary expedient in troublous times.

Preamble:

The German people, united in all their racial elements, and inspired by the will to renew and strengthen their Reich in liberty and justice, to preserve peace at home and abroad and to foster social progress, have established the following Constitution:

CHAPTER 1: STRUCTURE AND FUNCTIONS OF THE REICH

Section I: Reich and States

Article 1
The German Reich is a Republic. Political authority emanates from the people.

Article 2
The territory of the Reich consists of the territories of the German member states. . . .

Article 3
The Reich colors are black, red, and gold. The merchant flag is black, white, and red, with the Reich colors in the upper inside corner.

Article 4
The generally accepted rules of international law are to be considered as binding integral parts of the German Reich.

Article 5
Political authority is exercised in national affairs by the national government in accordance with the Constitution of the Reich, and in state affairs by the state governments in accordance with state constitutions. . . .

* * *

Article 12
Insofar as the Reich does not exercise its jurisdiction, such jurisdiction remains with the states . . . with the exception of cases in which the Reich possesses exclusive jurisdiction. . . .

* * *

Article 17
Every state must have a republican constitution. The representatives of the people must be elected by universal, equal, direct, and secret suffrage of all German citizens, both men and women, in accordance with the principles of proportional representation.

* * *

Section II: The Reichstag

Article 20
The Reichstag is composed of the delegates of the German people.

Article 21
The delegates are representatives of the whole people. They are subject only to their own conscience and are not bound by any instructions.

Article 22
The delegates are elected by universal, equal, direct, and secret suffrage by men and women over twenty years of age, according to the principle of proportional representation. Election day must be a Sunday or a public holiday.

Article 23
The Reichstag is elected for four years. New elections must take place at the latest on the sixtieth day after this term has run its course.

* * *

Article 32
For decisions of the Reichstag a simple majority vote is necessary, unless the Constitution prescribes another proportion of votes. . . .

Article 33
The Reichstag and its committees may require the presence of the Reich Chancellor and every Reich Minister. . . .

* * *

Section III: The Reich President and

The Reich Cabinet

Article 41
The Reich President is elected by the whole German people. Every German who has completed his thirty-fifth year is eligible for election. . . .

Article 42

On assuming office, the Reich President shall take the following oath before the Reichstag:

> I swear to devote my energies to the well-being of the German people, to further their interests, to guard them from injury, to maintain the Constitution and the laws of the Reich, to fulfill my duties conscientiously, and to administer justice for all.

It is permissible to add a religious affirmation.

Article 43

The term of office of the Reich President is seven years. Re-election is permissible.

Before the expiration of his term, the Reich President, upon motion of the Reichstag, may be recalled by a popular vote. The decision of the Reichstag shall be by a two-thirds majority. Through such decision the Reich President is denied any further exercise of his office. The rejection of the recall motion by the popular referendum counts as a new election and results in the dissolutions of the Reichstag.

* * *

Article 48

If any state does not fulfill the duties imposed upon it by the Constitution or the laws of the Reich, the Reich President may enforce such duties with the aid of the armed forces.

In the event that the public order and security are seriously disturbed or endangered, the Reich President may take the measures necessary for their restoration, intervening, if necessary, with the aid of the armed forces. For this purpose he may temporarily abrogate, wholly or in part, the fundamental principles laid down in Articles 114, 115, 117, 118, 123, 124, and 153.

The Reich President must, without delay, inform the Reichstag of all measures taken under Paragraph 1 or Paragraph 2 of this Article. These measures may be rescinded on demand of the Reichstag.

* * *

Article 50

All orders and decrees of the Reich President, including those relating to the armed forces, must, in order to be valid, be countersigned by the Reich Chancellor or by the appropriate Reich Minister. Responsibility is assumed through the countersignature.

* * *

Article 52
The Reich Cabinet consists of the Reich Chancellor and the Reich Ministers.

Article 53
The Reich Chancellor and, on his recommendation, the Reich Ministers, are appointed and dismissed by the Reich President.

Article 54
The Reich Chancellor and the Reich Ministers require for the exercise of their office the confidence of the Reichstag. Any one of them must resign if the Reichstag by formal resolution withdraws its confidence.

Article 55
The Reich Chancellor presides over the government of the Reich and conducts its affairs according to the rules of procedure laid down by the government of the Reich and approved by the Reich President.

Article 56
The Reich Chancellor determines the political program of the Reich and assumes responsibility to the Reichstag. Within this general policy each Reich Minister conducts independently the office entrusted to him and is held individually responsible to the Reichstag.

*   *   *

Section IV: The Reichsrat

Article 60
A Reichsrat is formed to give the German states representation in the law-making and administration of the Reich.

Article 61
Each state has at least one vote in the Reichsrat. In the case of the larger states one vote shall be assigned for every million inhabitants. . . . No single state shall have more than two fifths of the total number of votes.

*   *   *

Article 63
The states shall be represented in the Reichsrat by members of their governments. . . .

*   *   *

Section V: Reich Legislation

Article 68
Bills are introduced by the Reich cabinet, with the concurrence of the Reichsrat, or by members of the Reichstag. Reich laws shall be enacted by the Reichstag. . . .

* * *

Article 73
A law of the Reichstag must be submitted to popular referendum before its proclamation, if the Reich President, within one month of its passage, so decides. . . .

Article 74
The Reichsrat may protest against laws passed by the Reichstag. In case of such protests, the law is returned to the Reichstag, which may override the objection by a two-thirds majority. The Reich President must either promulgate the law within three months or call for a referendum.

* * *

Article 76
The Constitution may be amended by law, but acts . . . amending the Constitution can only take effect if two thirds of the legal number of members are present and at least two thirds of those present consent.

* * *

Section VI: The Reich Administration

[Articles 78–101 cover the jurisdiction of the Reich Administration in such matters as foreign affairs, national defense, colonial policies, customs, national budgets, postal and telegraph services, railroads, and waterways.]

Section VII: Administration of Justice

[Articles 102–108 provide for a hierarchy of Reich and state courts, with judges appointed by the Reich President for life.]

CHAPTER II: FUNDAMENTAL RIGHTS AND DUTIES OF THE GERMANS

Section I: The Individual

Article 109

All Germans are equal before the law. Men and women have the same fundamental civil rights and duties. Public legal privileges or disadvantages of birth or of rank are abolished. Titles of nobility . . . may be bestowed no longer. . . . Orders and decorations shall not be conferred by the state. No German shall accept titles or orders from a foreign government.

Article 110

Citizenship of the Reich and the states is acquired in accordance with the provisions of a Reich law. . . .

Article 111

All Germans shall enjoy liberty of travel and residence throughout the whole Reich. . . .

Article 112

Every German is permitted to emigrate to a foreign country. . . .

* * *

Article 114

Personal liberty is inviolable. Curtailment or deprivation of personal liberty by a public authority is permissible only by authority of law.

Persons who have been deprived of their liberty must be informed at the latest on the following day by whose authority and for what reasons they have been held. They shall receive the opportunity without delay of submitting objections to their deprivation of liberty.

Article 115

The house of every German is his sanctuary and is inviolable. Exceptions are permitted only by authority of law. . . .

* * *

Article 117

The secrecy of letters and all postal, telegraph, and telephone communications is inviolable. Exceptions are inadmissible except by national law.

Article 118
Every German has the right, within the limits of the general laws, to express his opinion freely by word, in writing, in print, in picture form, or in any other way. . . . Censorship is forbidden. . . .

* * *

Section II: The General Welfare

Article 123
All Germans have the right to assembly peacefully and unarmed without giving notice and without special permission. . . .

Article 124
All Germans have the right to form associations and societies for purposes not contrary to the criminal law. . . .

* * *

Article 126
Every German has the right to petition. . . .

* * *

Section III: Religion and Religious Societies

Article 135
All inhabitants of the Reich enjoy full religious freedom and freedom of conscience. The free exercise of religion is guaranteed by the Constitution and is under public protection. . . .

* * *

Article 137
There is no state church. . . .

* * *

Section IV: Education and the Schools

Article 142
Art, science, and the teaching thereof are free. . . .

Article 143
The education of the young is to be provided for by means of public institutions. . . .

Article 144
The entire school system is under the supervision of the state. . . .

Article 145
Attendance at school is compulsory. . . .

* * *

Section V: Economic Life

Article 151
The regulation of economic life must be compatible with the principles of justice, with the aim of attaining humane conditions of existence for all. Within these limits the economic liberty of the individual is assured.

Article 152
Freedom of contract prevails . . . in accordance with the laws. . . .

Article 153
The right of private property is guaranteed by the Constitution. . . . Expropriation of property may take place . . . by due process of law. . . .

* * *

Article 159
Freedom of association for the preservation and promotion of labor and economic conditions is guaranteed to everyone and to all vocations. All agreements and measures attempting to restrict or restrain this freedom are unlawful. . . .

* * *

Article 161
The Reich shall organize a comprehensive system of [social] insurance. . . .

* * *

Article 165
Workers and employees are called upon to cooperate, on an equal footing, with employers in the regulation of wages and of the conditions of labor, as well as in the general development of the productive forces. . . .

* * *

CONCLUDING PROVISIONS

*   *   *

Article 181

The German people have passed and adopted this Constitution through their National Assembly. It comes into force with the date of its proclamation.

Schwarzburg, August 11, 1919.

The Reich President

EBERT

The Reich Cabinet

BAUER

ERZBERGER HERMANN MÜLLER DR. DAVID

NOSKE SCHMIDT

SCHLICKE GIESBERTS DR. BAYER

DR. BELL

One of the advantages held by the Nazis was that their opponents were badly divided. The left was particularly weakened by the split between the Social Democrats and the Communists. In the following statement Ernst Thälmann, head of the Communist Party, expresses the party's position in respect to the Nazis and the Socialists.

The Revolutionary Alternative and the KPD

BY *Ernst Thälmann*

WHAT IS THE CURRENT RELATIONSHIP between the policy of Hitler's party and Social Democracy? The eleventh plenum [*of the German Communist Party—Ed.*] has already spoken of an involvement of both these factors in the service of finance capital. Already in 1924 Comrade Stalin most clearly characterized the role of both these wings when he spoke of them as twins who supplement each other.

At present this development is revealed unmistakably in Germany. . . . In the question of terror organizations, too, the SPD [*German Socialist Party—Ed.*] increasingly copies Hitlerism. In this respect one need only think of the creation of the Reichsbanner or, more recently, of the so-called "hammer units" of the Iron Front, which were to be used as instruments to help the capitalist dictatorship in the defense of the capitalistic system against the revolutionary proletariat.

But above all it is the Prussian government of the SPD and the ADGB

Ernst Thälmann, "The Revolutionary Alternative and the KPD," in Hermann Weber, *Der Deutsche Kommunismus Dokumente* (1963), pp. 185–186. Translated by Donald Kagan by permission of Verlag Kiepenheuer & Witsch, Cologne.

[*Free Trade Unions—Ed.*] that through their actions, fully and completely confirm the role of the Social Democracy as the most active factor in making Germany Fascistic, as the eleventh plenum has stated.

Thus, while the Social Democrats increasingly approach Hitlerite Fascism, Fascism, in turn, emphasizes its legality and lately even steps onto the platform of Brüning's foreign policy. . . .

All these points reveal the far-reaching mutual rapprochement of the SPD and the National Socialists toward the line of Fascism.

WHY MUST WE DIRECT THE CHIEF BLOW AGAINST THE SOCIAL DEMOCRATS?

Our strategy, which directs the chief blow against the Social Democrats without thereby weakening the struggle against Hitlerite Fascism; our strategy, which provides the first assumption of an effective fight against Hitlerite Fascism precisely through the chief blow against the Social Democrats—this strategy is not comprehensible if one has not clearly understood the role of the proletarian classes as the only class that is revolutionary to the end. . . .

The practical application of this strategy in Germany calls for the chief blow against the Social Democracy. With its "left" branches it is the most dangerous support of the enemy of the revolution. It is the major social support of the bourgeoisie; it is the most active factor in creating Fascism, as the eleventh plenum has correctly declared. At the same time it understands in the most dangerous way, as the "more moderate wing of Fascism," how to capture the masses, by its fraudulent maneuvers, for the dictatorship of the bourgeoisie and for its Fascistic methods. To strike the Social Democrats is the same as to conquer the majority of the proletariat and to create the preconditions for the proletarian revolution. . . .

WHAT DOES A POLICY OF A UNITED FRONT MEAN?

To carry out a policy of the revolutionary united front means to pursue a merciless struggle against Social Fascists of every shade, especially against the most dangerous "left" variety of Social Fascism, against the SAPD [*Socialist Workers Party—Ed.*], against the Brandler Group and similar cliques and tendencies.

To pursue a policy of the revolutionary united front means to mobilize the masses for the struggle really from below, in the factories and in the unemployment offices.

A policy of a revolutionary united front cannot come to pass through parliamentary negotiations. It cannot happen through accommodation with other parties or groups, but it must grow from the movement of the masses and be supported by that movement and present a really living fighting front.

There is no negotiation of the KPD with the SDP, SAPD, or Brandler Group; there must be none!

One important source of support for Hitler came from the German business community, which helped him both politically and financially. The following documents illustrate the nature of the community's support.

Poechlinger's Letter to Krupp

Director of the Leading Department,
Certified Engineer JOSEF POECHLINGER
Press Representative of the Reichs
  Minister, Dr. TODT.

Berlin, W.8.   12.3.41.
Pariser Place, 3,
Telephone No. 11 6481.
[note in pencil: For attention of Mr. Goerferns]
[Stamp: Reply given as per enclosure, 14.3.41].

Dr. Krupp von Bohlen und Halbach,
Essen.
at the Huegel.

Dear Dr. Krupp,

BY REQUEST OF THE REICHS MINISTER, Dr. Todt, I am preparing to publish a presentation book for the German armament worker, in which he will be honoured on the account of his hard work for the German armament industry.

The structure of the book is as follows:—

1 Dr. Todt. Introduction.
2 Josef Weinheber. Ode to the German Armaments Worker.
3 Josef Poechlinger. "The Meaning of Work."
4. M. Schulze-Fielitz (Reichs Ministry for Arms and Munitions). "The Organization of the German Armament Industry."
5. Reichs Department Leader Fuehrer (Chief Department of Technology, NSDAP). "The Employment of the Parties for the German Armament Industry."

"Poechlinger's Letter to Krupp," in Office of United States Chief Counsel for Prosecution of Axis Criminality, *Nazi Conspiracy and Aggression*, VI (1946), pp. 1030–1031. Reprinted by permission.

6 ——— "Works Leader and Armament Worker."
7 Maier-Dorn, Reichs School Trustee of the National Socialist Union of German Technology. "Front Line Soldier and Armament Worker."
8 Gauleiter Krebs. "Your Contribution to the Great Reich."

　　May I ask whether you would be prepared to compile the chapter "Works Leader and Armament Worker"? A work of approximately twenty typewritten pages would be sufficient, in which you would briefly and pleasantly describe, in your capacity of the best-known and most authoritative representative of the German armament industry, the relationship between the works leader and armament worker, as well as your observations, adventures and experiences in connection with the workers.

　　The article would have to reach me in about four weeks.

　　I shall be grateful for a brief notification whether you are prepared to take on this work.

Heil Hitler:
Your very sincerely,
(Sgd.) *Poechlinger.*

FROM *Draft of Works Leader and Armaments Works*

BY *Gustav Krupp*

EVERYONE CAN GATHER the significance of the outcome of the war for the Krupp Works as well as for my wife and myself, without my writing about it at great length. It is general knowledge that hardly any works were so badly hit by the Treaty of Versailles as Krupp. At this point, once more, I should like to reiterate a few shattering figures. After the signing of the peace, values amounting to 104 million gold-marks were destroyed at our works. Nine thousand three hundred machines, with a total weight of 60,000 tons were demolished or destroyed amounting to nearly half of our entire machinery of November 1918. Eight hundred and one thousand, four hundred and twenty pieces of gauges, moulds, jigs and tools, with a total weight of 9588 tons were destroyed. Three hundred and seventy-nine plants, such as presses, hardening ovens, oil and water tanks, cooling plants and cranes were smashed.

　　In those days the situation seemed hopeless at times. It appeared even more desperate if one remained as firmly convinced as I was that "Versailles" could not represent the end.

"Drafts of Works Leader and Armaments Works," by Gustav Krupp in *Nazi Conspiracy and Aggression*, VI (1946), pp. 1031–1034. Reprinted by permission.

Everything in me revolted against believing, and many many Germans felt likewise, that the German people should remain enslaved forever.

I knew German history only too well, and I believed, particularly with my experiences in other parts of the world, that I knew the German people. For that reason, I never believed that, in spite of all existing evidence to the contrary, a change would come one day; I did not know, nor did I ask myself that question, but I believed in it; but owing to this—and today I can talk about these things, and this is the first time that I do so publicly and at length—owing to this, I emphasize, I, as the responsible leader of the Krupp Works, had to come to conclusions of great significance. If ever there should be a resurrection for Germany, if ever she were to shake off the chains of Versailles, then Krupp would have to be prepared.

The machines were demolished; the tools were destroyed; but one thing had remained—the men, the men at the drawing boards and in the workshops, who, in happy co-operation had brought the manufacture of guns to its last perfection. Their skill would have to be saved, these immense resources of knowledge and experience. The decisions of that period were, probably, amongst the most difficult ones of my life. Even though camouflaged I had to maintain Krupps as an armament factory for the distant future, in spite of all obstacles. Only in a very small and most trustworthy circle could I speak about the actual reasons which caused me to pursue this intention of reorganizing the works for the production of certain definite articles. I had to be prepared, therefore, to be generally misunderstood, probably have ridicule heaped upon myself—as it promptly occurred, of course—but never in my life have I felt the inner urge for my actions as strongly as in those fateful weeks and months of the years 1919–20. Just then I felt myself fully part of the magic circle of the solid community of the workers. I understood the sentiments of my workers, who until now had so proudly worked for Germany's defense and who now were suddenly to undergo what, from their point of view, meant some sort of degradation. I owed it to them, too, to keep my chin up, and think of a better future. Without losing time or skilled men the necessary preparations were made and measures taken. Thus, to the surprise of many people, Krupps concentrated on the manufacture of articles which seemed to be particularly remote from the activities of the weapon-smithy. Even the Allied spying commission was fooled. Padlocks, milk cans, cash registers, rail mending machines, refuse carts and similar rubbish appeared really innocent, and locomotives and motor cars appeared perfectly "peaceful."

In this manner, during years of unobtrusive work, we created the scientific and material conditions which were necessary in order to be ready to work for the Armed Forces of the Reich at the right hour, and without loss of time and experience. Many a fellow worker will have had his own private thoughts and often have been without a clue, just why he was employed in this and that manner.

The whole reorganization, furthermore, was not only a personnel problem and of a purely technical character, but was also of immense economic significance. Our new production had to meet competition, far superior because of its considerable start.

* * *

It was my aim at all times, even when measures for the reduction of personnel were simply unavoidable, to maintain the nucleus of the workers at Krupp, whom we would need one day,—and nothing could deter me from that contention—for the purpose of rearmament.

* * *

After the assumption of power by Adolf Hitler I had the satisfaction of being able to report to the Fuehrer that Krupp needed only a short period to get ready for the re-arming of the German people and that there were no gaps in our experience. The blood of our comrades had not been shed in vain on that Passion Saturday of 1923. Thus, many a time I was able to walk through the old and new work-shops with him and to experience the gratitude expressed in the cheers of the workers of Krupps.

We worked with incredible zeal during those years after 1933, and finally when war broke out, speed and output increased still further. We are, all of us, proud that we have thus been able to contribute to the tremendous successes of our Forces.

* * *

It may appear that this record of mine is of too personal a character. But when I spoke of myself and the business concern in my trust, when I spoke of my experiences and impressions during a long life, I only did so to make the subject "Works Leader and Armament Worker" more colourful and descriptive, in preference to treating it under general headings.

I am standing here not wanting to make myself an example, for many another man who has been put into his key position in the German armament industry through fate, and, I think, his suitability. Like the workers of Krupps, these workers, too, are doing their duty faithfully in many other works. I have always considered it an honour, as well as an obligation, to be the leader of an armaments plant, and I know that the workers of Krupps share these sentiments.

This, thanks to the educational work of the National Socialist Leaders of the State, this is the same everywhere in Germany. What I have said especially about the armament worker applies, and this I know, to simply every German worker; with the help of these men and women, working with all their hearts, cool heads and skilled hands for the great whole, we shall succeed whatever our fate may be.

FROM *Interrogation of Dr. Hjalmar Schacht at "Dustbin"*

Interrogator: C. J. Hynning

Q. When did you next see Goering?

A. He invited me to a party in his house for the first of January 1931, where I met Hitler.

Q. Did you meet anybody else?

A. At that party Fritz Thyssen was also present, and that evening Hitler made a long speech, for almost two hours, although the company was a small one.

Q. Was that a monologue?

A. An entire monologue and everything that he said was reasonable and moderate that night.

Q. What did he say?

A. Oh, ideas he expressed before, but it was full of wit and spirit.

Q. What did he say?

A. He elaborated his program as it was outlined more extensively in his book.

Q. And in the party platform?

A. Yes, also the party platform. But the platform is very short and brief, it is not so full of general phrases.

Q. Were there any prominent officers present?

A. No.

Q. Any industrialists like Fritz Thyssen?

A. No.

Q. What was your impression at the end of that evening?

A. I thought that Hitler was a man with whom one could cooperate.

Q. Did you think he was a man of the future and that you had to deal with him as a man of the future?

A. Well, I could not know that at the time.

Q. Did you think it desirable to join the Nazi Party at that time?

A. I can't tell you as to that time, but if his ideas, which he developed that night, were backed by a big party, as it seemed to be, I think that one could join that group for public purposes.

Q. Let us then direct our attention to February and March 1933. I have been told by Goering and by Funk and Baron von Schnizler and also by Thyssen, that there was a meeting held in the house of Goering of certain prominent German industrialists at which you were also present in 1933. This was after Hitler became chancellor but before the elections of that spring. Hitler came into the meeting and made a short speech and left. Then, according to the testimony of Funk, you passed the hat. You asked the industrialists to sup-

"Interrogation of Dr. Hjalmar Schacht at Dustbin," in *Nazi Conspriacy and Aggression*, VI (1946), pp. 464–465. Reprinted by permission.

port the Nazi Party financially to the tune of approximately 7, 8, 9 or 10 million marks. Do you recall that?

A. I recall that meeting very well. And I have answered the same question to Major Tilley. It must be in one of my former memorandums or in the hearings done by Major Tilley. As far as I remember, the meeting was not in Goering's house, but in some hotel room I think, or some other more public room. After Hitler had made his speech the old Krupp von Bohlen answered Hitler and expressed the unanimous feeling of the industrialists to support Hitler. After that I spoke for the financial part only, not on political principles or intentions. And the amount which I collected was 3 million marks. The apportionment amongst the industrialists was made not by me but by they themselves and the payments afterwards were made to the bank of Delbruck Schickler. The books will certainly show the amounts which were paid in and which went to the party. I had nothing to do with that account. I just played the role of cashier or financial treasurer at the meeting itself.

3

The Democratic Spirit in Germany

It is important to remember that many Germans were loyal to the republic and its constitution and determined to make German democracy a success and a reality. The following excerpt from Lilo Linke's account of her youth illustrates the enthusiasm some Germans felt for the new German state.

FROM *Restless Days*

BY *Lilo Linke*

THE UNIVERSITY WAS ONE OF THE CENTRES of liberal thought and welcomed us heartily. So did half a dozen high officials from the Republic of Baden, the town, the Reichsbanner, the Democratic Party. In their united opinion we were the hope of Germany, born into a nation which our fathers had freed and refounded seven years ago on the principles of liberty and democracy. In this new Germany there was room for all, the hand of brotherhood was stretched out and encouragement was given to those who were full of goodwill. Our task, the task of the young, was to grow up as true and worthy citizens of this free Republic.

When the last speaker had concluded his address, the signal for the fireworks was given, and a few minutes later the ruins seemed to be burning again in red flames and smoke, golden stars shot up into the air, silver waterfalls sparkled, orange-coloured wheels rolled over the sky, rising and descending to make room for the next. But before the final cascade had died away, torch-bearers ran over the courtyard to kindle the two thousand torches which meanwhile had been distributed among all of us, rousing a waving ocean of light.

A procession was formed, headed by the military band with triangles and drums and clarinets and followed by the members of the movement, two

Lilo Linke, *Restless Days*, pp. 278–280. Reprinted by permission.

abreast, holding their torches in their upraised hands. We marched through the town, our ghostly magnified shadows moving restlessly over the fronts of the houses.

Never before had I followed the flag of the Republic, which was now waving thirty yards in front of me, spreading its colours overhead, the black melting in one with the night, the red glowing in the light of the torches, and the gold overshining them like a dancing sun. It was not just a torchlight march for me, it was a political confession. I had decided to take part in the struggle for German democracy, I wanted to fight for it although I knew that this meant a challenge to my parents and my whole family, who all lived with their eyes turned towards the past and thought it disloyal and shameful to help the Socialists.

From the band a song floated back through the long columns, a defiant determined song:

We do not call it liberty
When mercy grants us right,
When our cunning enemy
Is checked today by fright.
Not king alone and army,
But strong-box we must fight.
Powder is black,
Blood is red,
Golden flickers the flame.

We marched out of the town to the cemetery, where the first President of the Republic, Fritz Ebert, had been buried. Silently we assembled round the grave. Wilhelm Wismar, national leader of the Young Democrats and youngest member of the Reichstag, stepped forward and spoke slowly the oath:

"We vow to stand for the Republic with all our abilities and strength.

"We vow to work for the fulfillment of the promises given to the German people in the Weimar Constitution.

"We vow to shield and defend democracy against all its enemies and attackers whoever they might be."

And out of the night in a rolling echo two thousand citizens of tomorrow answered, repeating solemnly word for word:

"We vow to stand for the Republic with all our abilities and strength.

"We vow to work for the fulfillment of the promises given to the German people in the Weimar Constitution.

"We vow to shield and defend democracy against all its enemies and attackers whoever they might be."

4

The Nazi Program

FROM *National Socialistic Yearbook 1941*

THE PROGRAM OF THE NSDAP

THE PROGRAM is the political foundation of the NSDAP and accordingly the primary political law of the State. It has been made brief and clear intentionally.

All legal precepts must be applied in the spirit of the party program.

Since the taking over of control, the Fuehrer has succeeded in the realization of essential portions of the Party program from the fundamentals to the detail.

The Party Program of the NSDAP was proclaimed on the 24 February 1920 by Adolf Hitler at the first large Party gathering in Munich and since that day has remained unaltered. Within the national socialist philosophy is summarized in 25 points:

1. We demand the unification of all Germans in the Greater Germany on the basis of the right of self-determination of peoples.
2. We demand equality of rights for the German people in respect to the other nations; abrogation of the peace treaties of Versailles and St. Germain.
3. We demand land and territory (colonies) for the sustenance of our people, and colonization for our surplus population.
4. Only a member of the race can be a citizen. A member of the race can only be one who is of German blood, without consideration of creed. Consequently no Jew can be a member of the race.
5. Whoever has no citizenship is to be able to live in Germany only as a guest, and must be under the authority of legislation for foreigners.
6. The right to determine matters concerning administration and law belongs only to the citizen. Therefore we demand that every public office, of any sort whatsoever, whether in the Reich, the county or municipality, be filled only by citizens. We combat the corrupting parliamentary economy, office-

"National Socialistic Yearbook 1941," in *Nazi Conspiracy and Aggression*, IV (1946), pp. 208–211. Reprinted by permission.

holding only according to party inclinations without consideration of character or abilities.

7. We demand that the state be charged first with providing the opportunity for a livelihood and way of life for the citizens. If it is impossible to sustain the total population of the State, then the members of foreign nations (non-citizens) are to be expelled from the Reich.

8. Any further immigration of non-citizens is to be prevented. We demand that all non-Germans, who have immigrated to Germany since the 2 August 1914, be forced immediately to leave the Reich.

9. All citizens must have equal rights and obligations.

10. The first obligation of every citizen must be to work both spiritually and physically. The activity of individuals is not to counteract the interests of the universality, but must have its result within the framework of the whole for the benefit of all.

Consequently we demand:

11. Abolition of unearned (work and labour) incomes. Breaking of rent-slavery.

12. In consideration of the monstrous sacrifice in property and blood that each war demands of the people personal enrichment through a war must be designated as a crime against the people. Therefore we demand the total confiscation of all war profits.

13. We demand the nationalization of all (previous) associated industries (trusts).

14. We demand a division of profits of all heavy industries.

15. We demand an expansion on a large scale of old age welfare.

16. We demand the creation of a healthy middle class and its conservation, immediate communalization of the great warehouses and their being leased at low cost to small firms, the utmost consideration of all small firms in contracts with the State, county or municipality.

17. We demand a land reform suitable to our needs, provision of a law for the free expropriation of land for the purposes of public utility, abolition of taxes on land and prevention of all speculation in land.

18. We demand struggle without consideration against those whose activity is injurious to the general interest. Common national criminals, usurers, Schieber and so forth are to be punished with death, without consideration of confession or race.

19. We demand substitution of a German common law in place of the Roman Law serving a materialistic world-order.

20. The state is to be responsible for a fundamental reconstruction of our whole national education program, to enable every capable and industrious German to obtain higher education and subsequently introduction into leading positions. The plans of instruction of all educational institutions are to conform with the experiences of practical life. The comprehension of the

concept of the State must be striven for by the school [Staatsbuergerkunde] as early as the beginning of understanding. We demand the education at the expense of the State of outstanding intellectually gifted children of poor parents without consideration of position or profession.

21. The State is to care for the elevating of national health by protecting the mother and child, by outlawing child-labor, by the encouragement of physical fitness, by means of the legal establishment of a gymnastic and sport obligation, by the utmost support of all organizations concerned with the physical instruction of the young.

22. We demand abolition of the mercenary troops and formation of a national army.

23. We demand legal opposition to known lies and their promulgation through the press. In order to enable the provision of a German press, we demand, that: a. All writers and employees of the newspapers appearing in the German language be members of the race: b. Non-German newspapers be required to have the express permission of the State to be published. They may not be printed in the German language: c. Non-Germans are forbidden by law any financial interest in German publications, or any influence on them, and as punishment for violations the closing of such a publication as well as the immediate expulsion from the Reich of the non-German concerned. Publications which are counter to the general good are to be forbidden. We demand legal prosecution of artistic and literary forms which exert a destructive influence on our national life, and the closure of organizations opposing the above made demands.

24. We demand freedom of religion for all religious denominations within the state so long as they do not endanger its existence or oppose the moral senses of the Germanic race. The Party as such advocates the standpoint of a positive Christianity without binding itself confessionally to any one denomination. It combats the Jewish-materialistic spirit within and around us, and is convinced that a lasting recovery of our nation can only succeed from within on the framework: common utility precedes individual utility.

25. For the execution of all of this we demand the formation of a strong central power in the Reich. Unlimited authority of the central parliament over the whole Reich and its organizations in general. The forming of state and profession chambers for the execution of the laws made by the Reich within the various states of the confederation. The leaders of the Party promise, if necessary by sacrificing their own lives, to support by the execution of the points set forth above without consideration.

Adolf Hitler proclaimed the following explanation for this program on the 13 April 1928:

EXPLANATION

Regarding the false interpretations of Point 17 of the Program of the NSDAP on the part of our opponents, the following definition is necessary:

"Since the NSDAP stands on the platform of private ownership it happens that the passage" gratuitous expropriation concerns only the creation of legal opportunities to expropriate if necessary, land which has been illegally acquired or is not administered from the view-point of the national welfare. This is directed primarily against the Jewish land-speculation companies.

5

The Influence of Germany's Past

Some scholars have suggested that one of the great appeals of Nazism was its ardent militarism and war spirit, which corresponded with similar sentiments embedded in the history and character of Germany. In the following selection Louis Snyder introduces evidence of the cultivation of such notions in both Weimar and Hitler Germany.

FROM *Documents of German History*

ALL NATIONS HAVE AT ONE TIME OR ANOTHER been victims of the diseases of jingoism and chauvinism. The glorification of war has been the prime aim of super-patriots everywhere. But in Germany the phenomenon has been so persistent that it merits the special attention of the historian. Such historians as Heinrich von Treitschke ("Those who preach the nonsense of eternal peace do not understand Aryan national life"), such militarists as Friedrich von Bernhardi ("War is a biological necessity"), and such leaders as Adolf Hitler ("In eternal peace, mankind perishes") expressed a point of view that was not unique but widespread. In both world wars, Allied propagandists published bulky collections of German quotations glorifying war, which were strongly effective in solidifying world public opinion against Germany.

   The war spirit infected institutions both of higher and lower education. In the first extract quoted here, a superintendent of schools during the era of the Weimar Republic gave his suggestion for a student's composition on the advantages of war. The following two poems show how first-grade children during the Hitler regime were encouraged to imbibe the war spirit.

"Documents of German History," in Louis L. Snyder, ed., *Documents of German History*, pp. 408–410. Reprinted by permission.

DRAFT FOR A STUDENT COMPOSITION ON THE ADVANTAGES OF WAR, 1927

I. For the Nation:

1. War is the antidote for the weeds of peace, during which intellectualism takes precedence over idealism and puts everything to sleep.
2. Patriotism is stimulated, and a sacred enthusiasm for the Fatherland is awakened.
3. The triumphant nation obtains a position of power, as well as the prestige and influence it deserves; the honor of the defeated nation is not affected at all if it has defended itself with courage.
4. Peoples learn to know each other better and to respect one another. There is an exchange of ideas, opinions, points of view.
5. Trade finds new routes, often favorable ones.
6. The arts, especially poetry and painting, are given excellent subjects.

II. For the Citizens:

1. War gives them the opportunity to develop their talents. Without war the world would have fewer great men.
2. War enables many virtues to assert themselves.
3. Many active persons get the opportunity to make great fortunes.
4. It is sweet to die for the Fatherland. The dead of the enemy live in the memory of the victor.

POEMS FROM FIRST-YEAR READERS, 1940

Trum, trum, trum!
There they march,
Always in step,
One, two, one, two,
Teo is also there.
Dieter plays the drums.
Trum, trum, trum!

He who wants to be a soldier,
That one must have a weapon,
Which he must load with powder,
And with a good hard bullet.
Little fellow, if you want to be a recruit,
Take good care of this little song!

In the nineteenth century old racial prejudices were given new prominence and power by their advancement in the name of the new social "sciences." Houston Stewart Chamberlain, an Englishman who settled in Germany, wrote influential works claiming special qualities for different "races" he claimed to discern.

FROM *The Foundations of the Nineteenth Century*

BY *Houston Stewart Chamberlain*

. . . THE ENTRANCE OF the Jew into European history had, as Herder said, meant the entrance of an alien element—alien to that which Europe had already achieved, alien to all it was still destined to achieve. The very reverse was true of the Teuton. This barbarian, who would rush naked to battle, this savage, who suddenly sprang out of woods and marshes to inspire into a world of civilization and culture the terrors of violent conquest won by brute strength alone, is nonetheless the lawful heir to the Hellene and the Roman, blood of their blood and spirit of their spirit. It was his own property which, unwittingly, he snatched from the alien hand. But for him, the sun of the Indo-European would have set. The Asiatic and African slave had, by cowardly murder, wormed his way to the very throne of the Roman Empire; the Syrian mongrel had made himself master of the law; the Jew was using the library at Alexandria to adapt Hellenic philosophy to the Mosaic law; the Egyptian was embalming and burying, for untold ages to come, the fresh and vital bloom of natural science in the ostentatious pyramids of scientific systematization. Soon, too, the sublime flowers of quintessential Aryan life—Indian thought, Indian poetry—were to be trodden underfoot by the savage and bloodthirsty Mongolian; and the desert-maddened Bedouin was to reduce to an everlasting wilderness that garden of Eden, Iran, in which for centuries all the symbolism of the world had grown. Art had long since vanished; in its stead, there were nothing but copies for the rich and circuses for the poor. Thus, to use that expression of Schiller's which I quoted at the beginning of the first chapter, there were no longer men but only creatures. It was high time for the savior to appear. Now he did not enter history in the form which speculative, abstract reason, had it been asked for its advice, would have chosen for a rescuing angel, for the creator of a new dawn of man. But today, when a glance back over the centuries easily teaches us wisdom, we have only one thing to regret. This is that the Teuton did not destroy with more thoroughness wherever his victorious arm reached, and that in consequence the so-called "Latinization," that is the marriage with the chaos of nations, once more gradually robbed wide regions of the vitalizing influence of pure blood and unbroken youthful vigor, and at the same time deprived them of being ruled by the highest talent. Certainly it can only be shameful indolence

Houston Stewart Chamberlain, "The Foundations of the Nineteenth Century," in *The Nazi Years: A Documentary History*, Joachim Remak, Ed., pp. 5–6. Prentice-Hall, Englewood Cliffs, 1969. Reprinted by permission.

of thought or disgraceful historical falsehood which will fail to see, in the entrance of the Germanic tribes into world history, anything but the rescue of a tortured mankind from the claws of the eternally bestial.

. . . When, in this book, I say "Teuton," I mean the various North European races which appear in history as Celts, Teutons, and Slavs, and from which, in irreversible intermingling, the nations of modern Europe are descended. That they originally belonged to a single family is certain; I shall prove it in Chapter Six. However, the Teuton, in the strict Tacitean sense of the term, has proved himself so superior among his kinsmen intellectually, morally, and physically, that we are justified in letting his name serve as the quintessence of the entire family. The Teuton is the soul of our culture. Today's Europe, with its many branches that stretch over the whole globe, is the chequered result of an infinitely manifold mingling of races; what binds us all together and makes an organic unity of us is our Germanic blood. If we look around us today, we see that the importance of each nation as a living power is proportionate to the amount of truly Teutonic blood among its population. Only Teutons sit on the thrones of Europe.

What came earlier in world history, to us are but prolegomena. True history, that history which controls the rhythm of our hearts and pulses through our veins, inspiring us to hope and to creation, begins at that moment when the Teuton seizes the legacy of antiquity with his masterful hand. . . .

Both racism and anti-Semitism had roots in German history and were not confined to the Nazis. Hitler, however, made brilliant use of these sentiments to win support for his own party.

FROM *Hitler's Speeches*

THE GERMAN PEOPLE was once clear thinking and simple: why has it lost these characteristics? Any inner renewal is possible only if one realizes that this is a question of race: America forbids the yellow peoples to settle there, but this is a lesser peril than that which stretches out its hand over the entire world—the Jewish peril. Many hold that the Jews are not a race, but is there a second people anywhere in the wide world which is so determined to maintain its race?

As a matter of fact the Jew can never become a German however often he may affirm that he can. If he wished to become a German, he must surrender the Jew in him. And that is not possible: he cannot, however much he try, become a German at heart, and that for several reasons: first because of his blood, second because of his character, thirdly because of his will, and fourthly because of his actions. His actions remain Jewish: he works for the "greater idea" of the Jewish people. Because that is so, because it cannot be otherwise, therefore the bare existence of the Jew as part of another State rests upon a

The Speeches of Adolf Hitler, April 1922–1939, pp. 59–61. Reprinted by permission.

monstrous lie. It is a lie when he pretends to the peoples to be a German, a Frenchman, &c.

What then are the specifically Jewish aims?

To spread their invisible State as a supreme tyranny over all other States in the whole world. The Jew is therefore a disintegrator of peoples. To realize his rule over the peoples he must work in two directions: in economics he dominates peoples when he subjugates them politically and morally: in politics he dominates them through the propagation of the principles of democracy and the doctrines of Marxism—the creed which makes a Proletarian a Terrorist in the domestic sphere and a Pacifist in foreign policy. Ethically the Jew destroys the peoples both in religion and in morals. He who wishes to see that can see it, and him who refuses to see it no one can help.

The Jew, whether consciously or unconsciously, whether he wishes it or not, undermines the platform on which alone a nation can stand.

We are now met by the question: Do we wish to restore Germany to freedom and power? If "yes": then the first thing to do is to rescue it from him who is ruining our country. Admittedly it is a hard fight that must be fought here. We National Socialists on this point occupy an extreme position: but we know only one people: it is for that people we fight and that is our own people. . . . We want to stir up a storm. Men must not sleep: they ought to know that a thunderstorm is coming up. We want to prevent our Germany from suffering, as Another did, the death upon the Cross.

We may be inhuman, but if we rescue Germany we have achieved the greatest deed in the world! We may work injustice, but if we rescue Germany then we have removed the greatest injustice in the world. We may be immoral, but if our people is rescued we have once more opened up the way for morality!

In a speech on "Race and Economics: the German Workman in the National Socialist State," delivered on 24 April 1923, Hitler said:

I reject the word "Proletariat." The Jew who coined the word meant by "Proletariat," not the oppressed, but those who work with their hands. And those who work with their intellects are stigmatized bluntly as "Bourgeois." It is not the character of a man's life which forms the basis of this classification, it is simply the occupation—whether a man works with his brain or with his body. And in this turbulent mass of the hand-workers the Jew recognized a new power which might perhaps be his instrument for the gaining of that which is his ultimate goal: World-supremacy, the destruction of the national States.

And while the Jew "organizes" these masses, he organizes business *(Wirtschaft)*, too, at the same time. Business was depersonalized, i.e., Judaized. Business lost the Aryan character of work: it became an object of speculation. Master and man *(Unternehmer und Arbeiter)* were torn asunder . . . and he who created this class-division was the same person who led the masses in their opposition to this class-division, led them not against his Jewish brethren,

but against the last remnants of independent national economic life
(Wirtschaft).

And these remnants, the *bourgeoisie* which also was already Judaized,
resisted the great masses who were knocking at the door and demanding better
conditions of life. And so the Jewish leaders succeeded in hammering into the
minds of the masses the Marxist propaganda: "Your deadly foe is the *bourgeois,*
if he were not there, you would be free." If it had not been for the boundless
blindness and stupidity of our *bourgeoisie* the Jew would never have become
the leader of the German working-classes. And the ally of this stupidity was the
pride of the "better stratum" of society which thought it would degrade itself if
it condescended to stoop to the level of the "Plebs." The millions of our
German fellow-countrymen would never have been alienated from their people
if the leading strata of society had shown any care for their welfare.

*It has been suggested that the Germans have always been peculiarly susceptible to
autocratic government. Whatever truth there may be in that, there is no question
that Hitler openly announced and advertised the dictatorial and autocratic nature
of his proposed regime and contrasted it to the weak and inefficient democratic
republic of Weimar.*

FROM *Organization Book of the NSDAP*

THE ORGANIZATION OF THE NSDAP AND ITS AFFILIATED ASSOCIATIONS

THE PARTY WAS CREATED by the Fuehrer out of the realization that if our people
were to live and advance towards an era of prosperity they had to be led
according to an ideology suitable for our race. They must have as supporters
men above average, that means, men who surpass others in self-control, discipline, efficiency, and greater judgment. The party will therefore always constitute a minority, the order of the National Socialist ideology which comprises the
leading elements of our people.

Therefore the party comprises only fighters, at all times prepared to
assume and to give everything for the furtherance of the National Socialist ideology. Men and women whose primary and most sacred duty is to serve the
people.

The NSDAP as the leading element of the German people control the
entire public life, from an organizational point of view, as well as from that of
affiliates, the organizations of the State administration, and so forth.

In the long run it will be impossible to let leaders retain responsible
offices if they have not been recognized by the Party.

"Organization Book of the NSDAP," in *Nazi Conspiracy and Aggression*, IV (1946), pp. 411–414. Reprinted by permission.

Furthermore, the party shall create the prerequisites for a systematic selection of potential "Fuehrers."

The reconstruction of the National Socialist organizational structure itself is demonstrated by the observation of the following principles:

The Fuehrer Principle.
The subordination and coordination within the structure of the entire organization.
The regional unity.
The expression of the practical community thought.

I. Fuehrer Principle [Fuehrerprinzip]

The Fuehrer Principle requires a pyramidal organization structure in its details as well as in its entirety.

The Fuehrer is at the top.

He nominates the necessary leaders for the various spheres of work of the Reich's direction, the Party apparatus and the State administration.

Thus a clear picture of the tasks of the party is given.

The Party is the order of "Feuhrers." It is furthermore responsible for the spiritual-ideological National Socialist direction of the German people. The right to organize people for their own sake emanates from these reasons.

This also justifies the subordination to the party of the organizations concerned with the welfare of the people, besides the inclusion of people in the affiliates of the party, the SA, SS, NSKK, the Hitler Youth, the NS Womanhood, the NS German Student Association and the NS German "Dozentenbund" [University teachers association].

This is where the National Socialist Fuehrer structure becomes more strongly apparent.

Every single affiliate is cared for by an office of the NSDAP.

The leadership of the individual affiliates is appointed by the Party.

The Reich Organization Leader [Reichsorganisationsleiter] of the NSDAP is simultaneously leader of the DAF. The NSBO is the organization bearer of the DAF.

The Leader of the Head-Office for Public Welfare also handles within the "Personalunion" the National Socialist Welfare and the Winter Relief.

The same applies to:

The Reich Justice Office [Reichsrechtsamt] for the NS "Rechtswahrerbund,"
The head office for public health for the NS. German Medical Association,
The head office for educators for the NS Teachers Association,
The head office for civil servants for the Reich Association of Civil Servants,
The head office for war victims for the NS. War Victim Relief,
The head office for technology for the NS. Association of German Technology.

The Racial Political Office handles the Reich Association of families with many children, the NS Womanhood [Frauenschaft] and the "Deutches Frauenwerk."

The Reich Office for agrarian politics of the NSDAP remains furthermore in closest touch with the "Reichnaehrstand" [Reich Nutrition Office] which is anchored in the State. Direct handling and personal contact of the leaders is also provided in this manner.

All attached affiliates, as well as the offices of the Party, have their foundation, in the same manner as in the Reich direction, in the sovereign territories, in the "Gaue" and furthermore in the districts (Kreise) and if required in the local groups of the NSDAP. This applies also to cells and blocks in the case of the NS Womanhood, the DAF, and the NSV. The members of the attached affiliates will be included in local administrations, respectively district sectors or district comradeships which correspond geographically to local groups of the Party.

II. Fuehrer Principle. Subordination and Coordination Within the Total Organizational Structure

The Fuehrer structure would be split, though, if all subdivisions, including attached affiliates were completely independent in their structure from the smallest unit up to the "Reichsfuehrung" and were they to come only at the top directly under the Fuehrer.

Like a four-story building, if we consider the four Sovereign territories [Reich, Gau, etc.] whose pillars and walls go up to the roof without having supporting joists (wooden stays) or connections on the various floors. Furthermore, it would not be reconcilable with the Fuehrer principle, which assumes complete responsibility, to assume that the Leader of a subdivision, as well as of an affiliated organization, would be in the position to guarantee beyond a professional and factual responsibility the political and ideological attitude of *all* the sub-leaders down to the smallest unit on the basis of his Reich leadership. The total independence of individual organizations would necessitate furthermore, the creation of an organizational, personal and educational apparatus for each one of them. This, in turn, would create eventually, in spite of the best will of the responsible "Reichsleiters" [Reich Leaders], central offices and office leaders in the Reich Leadership [Reichsfuehrung] of the party, differences in the various organizations. Those differences would later on of necessity take the shape of completely different systems in regional, vertical, and personal respects, etc. within the National Socialist regime.

The Subdivisions NS German Student Association, NS Womanhood Association, NSD [Dozentenbund] and the affiliates and their leaders come therefore under the authority of the competent sovereign leaders of the NSDAP. At the same time their structure is professionally effectuated from the bottom up and they are subordinated to their immediately superior organization in the sovereign divisions of the Party, from a disciplinary point of view, that is to say insofar as organization, ideology, politics, supervision and personal questions are concerned.

Thus a solid anchorage for all the organizations within the party structure is provided and a firm connection with the sovereign leaders of the NSDAP is created in accordance with the Fuehrer Principle.

6

Big Business and the Nazis

From the moment when Hitler came to power Marxists and scholars influenced by them have claimed that big businessmen, sympathetic to the Nazis, financed them and helped bring them to power. In a thorough and careful study of the evidence Henry A. Turner, Jr., rejects that interpretation.

FROM *German Big Business and the Rise of Hitler*
BY *Henry A. Turner, Jr.*

1. CAPITALISTS, NAZIS, AND GUILT

What can be said, in the light of the findings presented here, by way of answering the questions posed at the outset of this volume? To what extent did the men of German big business undermine the Weimar Republic? To what extent did they finance the Nazi Party and use their influence to boost Hitler into power? As should be evident by this point, the answer in both cases is: a great deal less than has generally been believed.

Only through gross distortion can big business be accorded a crucial, or even major, role in the downfall of the Republic. The business community displayed, to be sure, little enthusiasm for the new democratic state, and very few major executives could be termed democrats by conviction. Particularly at the outset of the republican period they felt jeopardized by a political system that assigned ultimate authority over national policy to a mass electorate. They also deplored many republican policies, especially the rapid expansion of *Sozialpolitik*—welfare state legislation—and direct governmental intervention in labor-management relations. But once the difficulties of the Republic's first five years had been overcome and a measure of prosperity restored, most men of big business reconciled themselves to the new state, if not always to its policies. So long as the country prospered, they saw little chance for a change of regime.

Henry A. Turner, Jr. *German Big Bussiness and The Rise of Hitler* (1985), pp. 341–349. Reprinted by permission of Oxford University Press.

Most remained frustrated politically, having discovered that economic potency did not translate readily into political effectiveness in a democratic polity, where ballots weighed more than money and where blocs of disciplined interest-group voters counted for more than did financial contributions.

Big businessmen did, to be sure, play a part in causing the crisis that eventuated in the paralysis of the Republic's parliamentary system in 1930. The insistence by some sectors of big business on curtailment of the capstone of republican *Sozialpolitik,* the national unemployment insurance program, helped at that time to precipitate what in retrospect emerges as one of the earliest of the now familiar fiscal crises of twentieth-century capitalist welfare states. The outcome of that crisis was, however, determined not by the business community but rather by the political spokesmen of organized labor. Also, the resulting parliamentary deadlock did not in itself put an end to Weimar democracy. That stalemate assumed fateful proportions only because it triggered a fundamental shift of authority to the presidency through use of the emergency powers assigned to that office by the constitution. Behind that move stood not Germany's capitalists but rather its military leadership. Generals, not corporation executives, effected the establishment of presidential rule in 1930. As a consequence of that development—which initially made some of the leading figures in the business community very uneasy because of their concern about the reaction of credit markets abroad—they and their compeers found themselves with even less political influence than they had enjoyed earlier. As long as the parliamentary system functioned, the politically active elements of big business had frequently managed to combine their small parliamentary bloc with other interest groups through horse trading of the usual sort so as to influence the shape of legislation. The links between big business and those bourgeois parties that regularly received subsidies from it had enabled its political spokesmen to exert pressure, if not always successfully, on government policies when those parties participated in ruling coalitions. Under the governmental system that began to take shape in 1930, however, the wishes of the business community carried little or no weight with the decisive source of authority, President Hindenburg, or with the military men who served as his counselors. During the period of presidential rule, men chosen by those counselors, men not beholden to big business, determined national policy. And it was those men—Brüning, Papen, and Schleicher—and not Germany's capitalists who set the disastrous political and economic course that destroyed what remained of the Weimar Republic and fostered the growth of the Nazi Party.

If the role of big business in the disintegration of the Republic has been exaggerated, such is even more true of its role in the rise of Hitler. While a significant part of the business community contributed materially—if less than wholly voluntarily—to the consolidation of Hitler's regime after he had become chancellor, he and his party had previously received relatively little support from that quarter. The early growth of the NSDAP took place without any significant aid from the circles of large-scale enterprise. Centered in industrially underdeveloped Bavaria, tainted with illegality as a consequence of the failed beer hall putsch of 1923, saddled with a program containing disturbingly anti-capitalist planks, and amounting only to a raucous splinter group politically, the NSDAP languished in disrepute in the eyes of most men of big business throughout the latter part of the 1920s. The major executives of Germany proved, with rare exception, resistant to the blandishments of Nazis, including Hitler himself, who sought to reassure the business community about their party's intentions. Only the Nazi electoral breakthrough of 1930, achieved without aid from big business, drew attention to it from that quarter. Those businessmen who attempted to assess the suddenly formidable new movement encountered a baffling riddle. The closer they scrutinized the NSDAP, the more difficult it became to determine whether it supported or opposed capitalism and, more specifically, the large-scale, organized enterprise to which capitalism had given rise in Germany. That riddle was not a chance occurrence. Hitler wanted things just that way. By cultivating a strategy of calculated ambiguity on economic matters, he sought to enable the appeals of his party to transcend the deep-seated social divisions in the country. That strategy led to puzzlement and wariness among the politically active components of big business, who wanted above all to establish the NSDAP's position on the economic issues that preoccupied them and assumed ever more urgency as the Great Depression deepened.

For nearly two years—from the autumn of 1930 until the summer of 1932—elements within or close to big business engaged in flirtations of varying intensity and duration with National Socialism. Some saw in Nazism a potential ally against the political left and organized labor, which many in the business community blamed for much of the country's misfortune, including the depression. Some of those who harbored such hopes set out, often with the help of opportunistic intermediaries, to cultivate prominent figures in the leadership ranks of the NSDAP. On the Nazi side, Hitler and certain of his lieutenants appear to have operated initially on the same assumption that colored leftist analyses, namely, that capitalists amounted to an important factor in politics. But whereas the parties of the left sought to mobilize mass support against big business in order to break the alleged control of the capitalists over the state, Hitler and his accomplices set out merely to neutralize the business community politically in order to keep Germany's capitalists from obstructing the Nazis' grasp for power.

Hitler and other Nazi spokesmen therefore sought repeatedly to convince those capitalists whose ears they could gain that there was no need to fear socialism from National Socialism. In a strict sense that was true, since the Nazis did not seek government ownership of the means of production. But Hitler and other Nazi emissaries revealed only highly selective versions of their movement's aims to members of the business community. They omitted mention of the aspirations of many Nazis, including Hitler himself, for far-reaching changes in German social and economic relationships that would, among other things, have drastically impinged on the position of capitalists. Nor did they, as has often been alleged, promise to dissolve the trade unions, hold out the prospect of lucrative armaments contracts, or project a war of exploitative conquest. The Nazi leaders may have secretly harbored such aims, but to divulge them at a time when the NSDAP was striving to attract voters from all possible quarters and gain admission to the national government would have been out of keeping with their opportunistic tactics. Instead, most portrayed Nazism to the business community as primarily a patriotic movement that would undercut the political left by wooing the wage earners of Germany back into the "national" political camp. Ignoring the concrete economic issues that preoccupied businessmen, Hitler held out to those with whom he came into contact the prospect of a political panacea that would sweep away Germany's mundane problems by unifying it domestically and strengthening it internationally. He also soft-pedaled or left altogether unmentioned his anti-Semitism when speaking to men of big business, having recognized its unpopularity in those circles. Such reassuring versions of the NSDAP's goals generally produced skeptical reactions among members of the business community, however, for those reassurances were offset by clamorous anti-capitalist rhetoric on the part of other Nazis and by the NSDAP's frequent alignment with the political left on concrete socio-economic issues. Right down to Hitler's installation in the chancellorship, Nazism spoke with a forked tongue and behaved duplicitously in the eyes of most capitalist magnates. As a consequence, only rarely did relations between the NSDAP and big business progress beyond the level of flirtation prior to the Nazi takeover. Despite repeated blandishments from Hitler himself and some members of his entourage, most politically active figures in the business community remained confused by the contradictory utterances about economic matters emanating from the NSDAP and uneasy about what direction that party would finally take. Aside from a few minor executives who belonged, for the most part, to the younger generation of Germans so strongly attracted to the Nazi movement, only one capitalist of note, Fritz Thyssen, became a loyal adherent of Nazism before 1933.

   Much confusion has arisen in publications dealing with the subject of this book because of a failure to distinguish between the men of big business and lesser businessmen. The prevalent categories of big business (or "monopoly capital") and lower middle class (or "petite bourgeoisie") have obscured the existence of a large number of substantial entrepreneurs who presided over often appreciable firms but who occupied a place in the economy substantially different from that of the great capitalists of Germany. Consequently, support for Nazism from such lesser businessmen has frequently been mistaken as evidence of complicity on the part of big business. The susceptibility of such entrepreneurs to National Socialism is not difficult to understand. As the depression tightened its grip on the economy, many of them found themselves and their firms exposed to increasingly cutthroat competition for shrinking markets. Few could rely on the cartels and other types of price-setting arrangements with which many big producers shielded themselves against the rapid decline in prices. Nor could they expect support from the great national business associations, such as the industrial Reichsverband, which were dominated by an elite drawn from big business. The large-scale enterprises that made up big business could also count upon restraint on the part of creditors and on various forms of aid from the government, since the prospect of their insolvency posed an intolerable threat to the whole economic, social, and political order. The failure of lesser firms, by contrast, awakened no such solicitude. Such firms could, and did, sink with scarcely a ripple. As a result, much hostility toward big business existed among the businessmen who presided over the often sizeable firms which, although dwarfed by the great new corporations and conglomerates of the twentieth century, nevertheless comprised a significant part of the German economy. Caught between what they perceived as predatory big business, on the one side, and assertive big labor in league with "Marxist" mass political organizations, on the other, such men did not feel threatened by Nazi denunciations of *Konzerne* and other great concentrations of capital. Those who found themselves in truly desperate economic straits were also less likely than executives of mammoth corporations to look askance at such Nazi panaceas as the "breaking of the thralldom of interest payments" or economic autarky. From the vantage point of such men, Nazi proposals for large-scale deficit spending could seem a ray of hope rather than a threat to sound governmental monetary and fiscal policies. For them, Nazi schemes for corporatist organization of the economy could appear to hold out the promise of greater representation for their interests than was possible within the existing structure of trade associations dominated by big business interests. It was, as a consequence, among such lesser businessmen, not among the great capitalists of Germany, that Nazism made inroads during its rise to power. Most of those hard-pressed men were in no position during the Great Depression, however, to extend large-scale financial assistance to the NSDAP, and none of their number commanded sufficient influence in political circles to facilitate Hitler's quest for high office.

As for big business, a graph of its relations with the NSDAP along the lines of a fever chart would show a steep, if uneven, rise from virtually zero prior to the September Reichstag election of 1930 to a high point in the spring or early summer of 1932, followed by a precipitous decline through the autumn of 1932 that continued until Hitler's appointment as chancellor. At the high point in 1932 the NSDAP seemed well-nigh unstoppable, having scored one election gain after another. Despite mounting dissension between the Nazis and the traditional right, and despite the waning political strength of the latter, hopes lingered in some big business circles for an alliance that would subordinate the NSDAP, with its mass following, to conservative forces in a nationalistic, rightist regime. During the second half of the summer of 1932, the Nazis dashed such hopes. By launching a sustained and unbridled assault on the Papen cabinet, which had come to enjoy the virtually unanimous and enthusiastic support of big business, Hitler demonstrated that he attached less significance to the opin-

ions of the business community than he did to the removal of the obstacle to
his quest for power posed by a government of the traditional right. In champi-
oning the prerogatives of the parliament and the interests of workers as part of
an offensive designed to discredit Papen's presidential "cabinet of barons," the
NSDAP seemed to swerve sharply leftward and so to confirm the worst suspicions of many big businessmen about Nazi social and economic radicalism.
Nazi advocacy of a sweeping government program of job creation through
deficit spending on an unprecedented scale indicated the triumph of those
"fiscally irresponsible" elements within the NSDAP that had long aroused apprehensions in business circles. The party's espousal of the drastic trade restrictions
demanded by agrarian interests gave rise to fears of extreme autarkic policies
that would provoke retaliation abroad against the exports on which a large part
of German industry had become increasingly dependent as the domestic market
shrank under the impact of the depression. By late 1932 past efforts to cultivate
"moderate" Nazis seemed in vain. The fall of Gregor Strasser removed a man
who had come to be widely perceived in big business circles as a Nazi advocate of accommodation with the traditional elite. Hitler, once viewed in some
business quarters as a moderating influence within the party, now seemed an
intransigent opponent of any such accommodation.

Quite contrary to the widespread impression that Hitler gained power in
January 1933 with strong backing from big business, his appointment to the
chancellorship came just when relations between his movement and the business community had reached the lowest point since the NSDAP's election gains
of 1930 had forced it upon the attention of the politically engaged men of big
business. Germany's leading capitalists remained passive, ill-informed bystanders during the backroom intrigues in the circles around President
Hindenburg that resulted in Hitler's installation as chancellor. By that time the
business community was recovering from its initial apprehensions about the
cabinet of Kurt von Schleicher. His government had failed to follow the leftward
course many had initially feared it would; to the relief of the business community, Schleicher upheld most of the Papen cabinet's policies. While few of the
country's capitalists harbored any real enthusiasm for the enigmatic general who
stood at the head of the government, an inclination to prefer his continuation in
office prevailed in late January 1933. The alternative of still another cabinet crisis would, most of the political leadership of big business feared, once more
give rise to the uncertainties about economic policy that they believed had
thwarted recovery during the politically turbulent year just past. Rather than risk
a disruption of the economic upturn widely detected since late 1932, it seemed
preferable to hope for a period of stability under the general. When the most
prominent industrial association, the Reichsverband, broke with previous practice and attempted to intervene with President Hindenburg as the final cabinet
crisis of Weimar Germany broke out at the end of January 1933, it did so to
warn against according Adolf Hitler a prominent place in a new, provocatively
rightist cabinet. However, that effort to wield the influence of the business com-

munity for political purposes proved, like so many undertaken during the Weimar period, in vain.

Contrary to another long-standing misapprehension, spokesmen of the business community did not collude with those of agriculture in agitating for Hitler's installation as chancellor in January 1933. By that time relations between those two interest groups had deteriorated to the breaking point because of increasingly irreconcilable and acrimonious disagreements over trade policy. Whatever took place in early 1933 by way of a recrudescence, in support of Hitler's appointment, of the alliance between traditional elites of the Empire, one important element—big business—was conspicuous by its absence. The often-invoked continuity between the imperial and Nazi regimes thus suffers from a crucial gap.

If big business did not, as is so often maintained, help boost Hitler into the chancellorship by throwing its influence behind him, how much effect did the political money have that flowed from the business community to various Nazis? How much help to Hitler and his party in their quest for power were the contributions and subsidies accounted for here, as well as similar ones that presumably went undocumented? That question can obviously not be answered definitively since the evidence remains incomplete. Some observations can be made, however, on the basis of patterns of behavior that have emerged from this study. First of all, the multi-million-mark contributions from big business that allegedly fueled the Nazi juggernaut existed only in the imaginations of certain contemporary observers and, later, of some writers of history. Those firms and organizations that regularly engaged in large-scale political funding continued—right down to the last election prior to Hitler's appointment as chancellor—to bestow the bulk of their funds on opponents or rivals of the Nazis. The few sizeable contributions that appear to have reached the Nazis from big business sources shrink in significance when compared to the amounts that went to the bourgeois parties and to the campaign to re-elect President Hindenburg. With rare exceptions such contributions to Nazis were not given primarily for the purpose of strengthening the NSDAP or boosting it into power but rather in pursuit of a variety of essentially defensive strategies. They usually went to individual Nazis, not to the party as such. Some of the donors looked upon financial support for prominent Nazis as insurance premiums designed to assure them friends in power if the new movement should succeed in capturing control of the state. Others, who felt that their firms had special grounds to fear the NSDAP if it should come to power, paid out what can only be characterized as protection money to potential rulers. Still others sought to reshape Nazism in line with their wishes by strengthening, through financial subsidies, the position within the party of individual Nazis they regarded as exponents of "moderate" or "reasonable" economic policies. A portion of the subsidies doled out to individual Nazis by men of big business for such reasons may have been used by the recipients for party purposes, but from all indications a considerable share went toward enhancing their personal living standards.

Discussions of financial assistance to the Nazis from big business have usually been based on a false assumption, namely, that the NSDAP, like the bourgeois parties of the Weimar Republic, depended on subsidies from large contributors. This simply was not the case. Just as the Nazi leaders proudly proclaimed at the time, their party financed itself quite handsomely through its own efforts, at least down to the autumn of 1932. The NSDAP proved, in fact, an unprecedentedly effective forerunner of those highly organized fund-raising associations that have since become familiar features of liberal, democratic societies. In contrast to the bourgeois parties of the Republic, whose top echelons solicited large contributions and then distributed funds to the lower echelons, money flowed upward within the NSDAP from the grass roots, through the regional organizations, and to the national leadership in Munich. Compared to the sustained intake of money raised by membership dues and other contributions of the Nazi rank and file, the funds that reached the NSDAP from the side of big business assume at best a marginal significance. As the relations between leading Nazis and members of the business community abundantly reveal, the former rarely adopted the pose of supplicants seeking material aid, at least not until their party experienced its first serious financial difficulties during the autumn of 1932. By that time, however, deteriorating relations had made members of the business community less disposed than ever to contribute to the NSDAP. The Nazis themselves, not Germany's capitalists, provided the decisive financing for Hitler's rise to power.

More important than any financial aid that reached the Nazis from big business or any influence brought to bear in their favor from that quarter was the help rendered them indirectly and inadvertently by politically active elements in the business community. Most conspicuously, support for individuals and organizations such as Papen, Schleicher, Hugenberg, the DNVP, and the Stahlhelm strengthened political forces that would eventually play key roles in installing Hitler in power. At the time that support was given, these men and organizations seemed to their business backers to represent not stirrup holders for Hitler but rather bulwarks against a Nazi takeover, with the prospect of taming the NSDAP for the purposes of the traditional right. In failing to recognize their irresponsible nature, their patrons in big business made themselves unwitting accessories to their follies, which were to cost Germany and much of the rest of Europe dearly. In other ways, too, men of big business lent indirect aid to the Nazis. By inviting Hitler and other party spokesmen to address their gatherings, they bestowed a degree of social acceptability upon them that may have influenced other Germans to vote for, or join, the NSDAP. Even abstinence from political activity by the men of big business could inadvertently redound to the advantage of the Nazis. The businessmen who at the time of the Prussian and national elections of the spring and summer of 1932 withheld their customary subsidies from the traditional parties indirectly aided the Nazi cause, although such was not their intention. While some who withheld their contributions wanted to express disillusionment with partisan politics in general, most wanted to coerce the traditional right-of-center parties into resolving their differences and merging into a single organization, or at least a firm bloc, that would defend the interests of the business community against political extremism of both the right and the left. Withholding those contributions had the effect, however, of further weakening parties whose voters the Nazis were vigorously courting. In view of the already depleted strength of those parties, it seems improbable that they could have escaped unscathed even if their former big business backers had provided the usual subsidies or even increased them. But, as it turned out, withholding those subsidies only imposed an added handicap on the efforts of those besieged parties to hold on to their voters. In that instance, too, political ineptitude rather than design led some of the business community to render indirect and unintentional aid to Hitler and his party. That aid hardly amounted, however, to a major contribution to Hitler's rise.

If the political record of big business is sadly lacking in political acumen, it is even more sorely devoid of public morality and civil courage. Most of the leaders of the business community were never tempted to become Nazis. The NSDAP's promise to destroy the existing elite and impose a new one in its place held little allure for men already at the top of their society. Its plebeian tone offended their taste. So did its anti-Semitism, for whatever other prejudices the leading men of German big business harbored, that form of bigotry was rare in their ranks. Most also found disturbing Nazism's demand for total power and its voluble strain of anti-capitalism, which focused predominantly on large-scale enterprise. Almost as alarming were the unorthodox fiscal and monetary schemes put forward by prominent Nazis as remedies for the depression. Still, most men of big business viewed Nazism myopically and opportunistically. Like many other Germans whose national pride had been wounded by the unexpected loss of the war and by a humiliating peace treaty, they admired Nazism's defiant nationalism and hoped it could be used to help reassert what they regarded as their country's rightful place among the great powers. Preoccupied as they were with domestic economic issues, they also hoped Nazism could be used against their long-standing adversaries, the socialist parties and the trade union movement. That hope waxed and waned as the Nazis shifted their political tactics. During the last half year preceding Hitler's appointment as chancellor, it subsided to low ebb. But few spokesmen of big business spoke out publicly against the NSDAP. Viewing it in terms of narrow self-interest, most failed to perceive the threat it posed to the very foundations of civilized life. Therein lay their heaviest guilt, one they shared, however, with a large part of the German elite.

To be realistic, it is probably unfair to place a heavy burden of guilt on the men of big business for their failings in the face of a political movement that swept through their society like an elemental force. Businessmen, after all, seldom take the lead politically. As a knowledgeable and perceptive observer, Joseph Schumpeter, commented not long after the events chronicled in this book, "The attitudes of capitalist groups toward the policy of their nations are predominantly adaptive rather than causative, today more than ever." Rather than shaping events, Schumpeter noted, even the mightiest of businessmen merely respond to events shaped by others. By way of explaining this he further observed that the kind of economic leadership exercised by the modern capitalist "does not readily expand, like the medieval lord's military leadership, into the leadership of nations. On the contrary, the ledger and the cost calculation absorb and confine." The leaders of German big business were, for all their pretensions, such absorbed and confined men, preoccupied with the management of large, complex organizations. They could at most dabble in politics. They could not commit their energies in a sustained fashion to that sphere of activity, so that they remained part-time amateurs, operating only sporadically, and usually ineffectually, on the periphery of politics. As such, they were sorely ill-suited to deal with a phenomenon like Nazism.

7

Germany and the Nazis:
A Complex Relationship

Fritz Stern, in his introduction to a collection of essays on the collapse of the Weimar Republic and the coming of the Nazis to power, presents a complex analysis that reflects the increasingly sophisticated research of the past decade. He emphasizes a point that has not always been appreciated: "The disintegration of the Weimar Republic and the rise of Nazism were two distinct if obviously overlapping historical processes. By 1932, the collapse of Weimar had become inevitable; Hitler's triumph had not."

FROM *The Path to Dictatorship 1918–1933*

BY *Fritz Stern*

ADOLF HITLER WAS appointed Chancellor of Germany on January 30, 1933. His rise to power had been speciously legal; his exercise of power was to be covertly revolutionary. With incredible rapidity National Socialism established a regimented society, characterized by the threat and use of terror, pervasive propaganda, economic progress, and the growing support or acquiescence of the populace. Traditional beliefs and institutions were subverted and the old ruling classes gradually replaced by a new Nazi elite. In 1939, a rearmed Germany plunged Europe into the second world war, conquered most of Europe, perpetrated the most hideous crimes, and suffered the most stunning defeat of modern times. In twelve years, Hitler's Thousand-Year Reich had run its course—twelve years that transfigured the world.

How could it have happened? How could National Socialism have triumphed in a civilized country? Why did millions of Germans vote for Hitler and why did the German elite fail to denounce this false savior? How could that same elite—with few exceptions—have been coerced or cajoled into supporting a regime of book-burners, how could the Nazis have found thousands of doctors, engineers, and civil servants to help them carry out their mass murders?

Fritz Stern, "Introduction," in *The Path to Dictatorship 1918–1933: Ten Essays by German Scholars*, pp. vii–xxii, translated by John Conway. Reprinted by permission of R. Piper & Co., Verlag and Doubleday & Company, Inc.

The magnitude and novelty of the disaster raised these insistent questions—and obscured the answers. Nazism had been difficult to understand from the very beginning: if it had been easier to perceive, it would never have succeeded.

The first explanations were those of contemporaries who remained prisoners of their preconceptions. Fascism was the last-ditch defense of monopoly capitalism in crisis, said the Marxists. The Treaty of Versailles and the Great Depression were to blame, said the liberals who had been too feeble to combat the effects of either. Others pointed an accusing finger at some fault of the Constitution or some conspirators around Hindenburg. These were explanations by alibi: some faction, some event, perhaps some accident, was held culpable. Eventually there was a swing to the other extreme, and on both sides of the German frontier people began to argue that National Socialism was the logical culmination of German history. From Luther to Hitler, so the Western argument ran, a long line of authoritarian, illiberal thinkers had poisoned "the German mind." These exaggerations of outraged foreigners were more than matched by the supine statements of German intellectuals under Hitler who also celebrated National Socialism as the crowning embodiment of German traditions and aspirations. Nazi and anti-Nazi historians were at one in hailing the historic ancestry of the Third Reich; they both helped to endow the Austrian corporal with a formidable pedigree. And to a large extent they were right, however stupid and simplistic they were in particulars.

In 1945, the question of the origins of National Socialism lost its political immediacy for non-German historians. Twenty years later, it is still an intellectual conundrum that despite massive and excellent work has remained unanswered or incompletely answered.

For the German scholar, the question became—in the popular word of the day—existential. Shortly after the German collapse, Ludwig Dehio, a leading and untainted historian, noted that Ranke's dictum that history should record "How it actually happened" now read: "How was it possible?" Postwar Germans needed to discover the true nature of Nazi rule and the relation between Nazism and the more distant German past. What aberration of mind, what deformation of society, what unsuspected institutions and values had contributed to the downfall of Weimar democracy and the rise of Hitler? What national traditions, the Germans asked, were left intact? What portion of the past must be repudiated and what reformed?

* * *

The essays in this volume provide an excellent framework of explanation. Theodor Eschenburg, a veteran political scientist, recalls that the 1920s were inhospitable to democracy and that a series of coups d'état established dictatorial or authoritarian regimes throughout Europe. None of the new democracies created in the aftermath of the Great War, save Finland, survived to the beginning of the second war. The Weimar Republic lasted longer than most; it was too "democratic" to be overthrown by reactionary, military, or left-wing cliques.

It succumbed to a mass movement that had become the strongest party by far, and that cleverly exploited all the weaknesses of Weimar's defenses.

These weaknesses were legion: Ernst Fraenkel, a well-known political philosopher who once served with the United States military government in Korea and experienced the difficulties of transplanting foreign institutions, points to the hostility that so many Germans harbored for parliamentary institutions. As happened so often and in so many fields, the German upper classes cherished unreasonable expectations of the possibilities of parliament and hence were excessively contemptuous of the realities of parliamentary life. Bismarck's constitution provided for a Reichstag that controlled some of the purse strings but not the government itself. The spectacle of a strong and clever chancellor like Bismarck playing with a feeble Reichstag taught the Germans— at the very beginning of their unified political existence—the wrong political lessons; no wonder that the historian Theodor Mommsen once accused Bismarck of having "broken the political backbone of the nation." But more than popular antipathies to parliament were involved: as Fraenkel emphasizes, in Germany, in contrast to England, a strong civil-service bureaucracy and, he could have added, a tough military caste antedated the existence of parliament, and the German bureaucracy certainly intended to preserve its powers, unmolested by any transient parliamentarians.

Parliament belonged to that whole complex of institutions and attitudes which Germans often labeled "Western" and scorned as alien and undesirable. Parliament and political parties were divisive, they argued, and German destiny demanded a Fuehrer who would rally and represent the entire people and resolve all conflicts. Such dreams were amazingly popular—and widely mistaken for political truths, as I tried to show in *The Politics of Cultural Despair.* Resentment against modernity—and against the West of the source of it—was an essential part of German nationalism before 1914.

The upper classes in Imperial Germany were anti-democratic—as their interests and inclinations prescribed. It is perhaps worth pointing out that people generally idealize their interests and in the long run tend to lose sight of the connection between stated ideals and unstated interests. The rhetoric of anti-democracy in Germany was full of what in another place I have called *Vulgäridealismus,* an effort to justify authoritarianism and social privilege by invoking Germany's philosophical traditions and literary ideals. *Kultur* and democracy were antithetical, they said and believed, though usually these same men complained that *Kultur* had already declined, without democracy. The Great War sharpened the ideological resentment against the West, and leading German writers boasted of their country's differences from and superiority to France and England. This avowal of cultural estrangement, abetted as well by Allied propaganda, was one of the incidental legacies of that terrible ordeal. Germany's defeat by the West—a defeat which to most Germans was more apparent in its political consequences than its military causes—deepened these antipathies still more. It was a grievous time to adopt essentially Western democratic institutions—quite aside from the oft-remarked discrepancy between the newly founded democratic state and the continuing non-democratic society.

Any German state would have been virtually bankrupt and deeply divided in 1919. A democratic state could be and was incessantly taunted and vilified just because it was democratic; Sontheimer's essay describes the range of that sentiment and insists that anti-democratic sentiment and Nazism were not identical. The upper classes in Germany, already hostile to democracy before 1918, continued to be so *a fortiori* after 1918. This made them vulnerable to National Socialist propaganda, but it did not make them National Socialists. It diminished the chances that German democracy would survive a crisis. The Germans under Weimar continued to live on the emotional presuppositions and intellectual baggage of Imperial Germany. Gustav Stresemann became one of Weimar's outstanding leaders by the simple and yet difficult feat of overcoming some of his prejudices in favor of political realism—and by possessing an instinct for power.

The leading parties in Weimar produced few such men. The largest party in Weimar—as in prewar Germany—was the Social Democratic party, and for nearly ten years it allowed itself to remain out of the government—as it had always been in Imperial Germany. The sense of power and the readiness to assume leadership were underdeveloped among the Socialists who had learned to cherish their party organizations, their state within a state, as the best means toward that uncertain end—a socialist society. The leadership of the SPD was drawn from the prewar generation as well, and they too carried with them the expectations and the burdens of an earlier society. Their patriotism had been proven many times, most dramatically and most questionably when in November 1918 they took over the receivership of a defeated Empire—and in their few months of power concentrated on preserving national unity rather than on effecting social reform. The form of the state, not the structure of society, was changed in 1918–1919, and yet no classes had suffered more from the inequalities of this structure than those represented politically by the Socialists. As Erich Matthias makes clear, there was timidity among Socialist leaders, even as there was mounting militancy and courage at the bottom and among the younger leaders who came to the fore in the early 1930s. The character of Socialist leadership recalls the plaintive remark made by a Labour Member of Parliament in 1931, after the Tories had taken Britain off the gold standard: "But nobody had told us that one could do that." A lot of things needed to be done to make Germany into a democratic society—and nobody told the Socialists that they could do some of these things. They remained imprisoned by the two formative experiences of their infancy: Marx and Bismarck, by the myth of the inevitability of the socialist revolution and by the actuality or spectre of repression. Both enjoined passivity.

Erich Matthias says that "Adolf Hitler and the Republic's notorious enemies do not bear the whole responsibility for Weimar's failure and the destruction of the parties that supported it." In his analysis of the Catholic Center party, Rudolf Morsey points to the authoritarian tendencies represented by the ascendant right wing of that party. Ossip Flechtheim deals with the Communists who *were* notorious enemies of the Republic and who contributed greatly to its demise. Both the Center and the Communists thought that they could use Hitler; the Center in its negotiations with him concerning the formation of a coalition, and the Communists by their tacit collaboration with the Nazis in several important parliamentary votes and in the Berlin transport strike of November 1932.

Others did Hitler's work, too—and more directly and knowingly. Thirteen million Germans voted for him in 1932. The voters came from the middle-class parties that virtually disappeared between 1930 and 1933 as well as from the young who cast their first vote for the party that promised a national regeneration. But the masses of voters would not have been enough; the active collaboration of the governing elite—of bankers, industrialists, old-time civil servants, and political soldiers—was necessary in the end to undermine Weimar so that Hitler could appear as the last available savior. Not all of these men of little power, frozen in their old fear of socialism and their new horror of Bolshevism, were as cynical or as candid as Kurt von Schleicher, who in 1932 wrote: "If the Nazis did not exist, it would be necessary to invent them." In June 1934, the Nazis suspected Schleicher of wishing to uninvent them—and they killed him.

Karl Dietrich Bracher and Helmut Krausnick describe the amazing swiftness with which Hitler established his rule in 1933–1934. Lenin is said to have remarked that "nowhere but in Russia would it have been so easy to seize power and so difficult to keep it." For Hitler, the reverse was true. Some positions of power were immediately seized, some guarantees of civil liberties immediately suspended, some opponents tortured and killed, but for the rest, the appearance of continuity, of order and normality were preserved and only intermittently disturbed. German society was not openly transformed, as the Bolsheviks had done in Russia; the old forms of life were allowed to linger on, subject only to the sudden and irresistible intervention of the new rulers who could neutralize or suspend all laws.

Hitler's insatiable will to power was once more abetted by the multitude's will to passivity. The *Gleichschaltung,* the co-ordination, of German life, which Krausnick considers the essential form of the Nazi revolution, could not have been carried out without the technical help of tens of thousands of civil servants and the acquiescence of millions.

Complicity and silence, not refusal and dissent, marked the early reaction to the Nazi regime—at the very time when the opposition of even a small minority would have had incalculable effects. Bracher speaks of "the dirty motives of careerism, personal enmities, and profitable informing on others" as bringing about the conspiratorial relationship between citizens and regime that became the basis of Nazi rule. Fear and potential or already realized profit explain much, but not all.

That so many Germans felt no particular attachment to liberalism and democracy also facilitated their acceptance of Nazi rule. The insidious propaganda of the Nazis and the continuous display of national strength and purpose impressed most Germans—and many foreigners; the more so as the regime registered actual achievements as well. The Treaty of Versailles was being dismantled, unemployment ceased, production rose, the nation worked again—even if the likely end was war and the risk of self-destruction.

Nazism in the prewar era, then, was popular and virtually unopposed. Hans Rothfels' picture of the early resistance to Hitler magnifies its pervasiveness and unwittingly belittles the heroism of the few people who did in fact resist. Dissent even in a democratic society is difficult in a period of crisis; in a totalitarian society it requires a degree of moral certainty and heroism that few men possess and none can demand.

* * *

So many men and events, ideas and institutions, social customs and prejudices shaped Germany's path to dictatorship that no single book can hope to encompass them all. The historian, moreover, wonders where it all began and what alternative paths might have been open.

These essays say least about what is already best known. They tell us little about the Great War with its shattering impact on every facet of German life and its legacy of resentment. They barely touch on the contribution of the German Army to the rise of Nazism, though that contribution was important, as Gordon Craig, J. W. Wheeler-Bennett, and F. L. Carsten have shown. They omit the role of Protestant clergymen and German academics who were overwhelmingly hostile to Weimar democracy, and who either accepted or failed to disavow the idealistic pretensions of Nazism. Nor do they deal with Germany's economic plight—beginning with the calculated inflation during the war and the equally calculated inflation during the Ruhr invasion, to the reparations tangle and the terror of the Great Depression—which favored but did not cause Hitler's success. Finally the book omits a detailed study of Hitler—which Alan Bullock has done in so exemplary a fashion—and of National Socialist ideology or organization. This omission emphasizes the implicit thesis of the book: the disintegration of the Weimar Republic and the rise of Nazism were two distinct if obviously overlapping historical processes. By 1932, the collapse of Weimar had become inevitable; Hitler's triumph had not.

These two processes have deep roots, which reach back to the unification of Germany in 1871 and beyond. They merge most clearly in the final years of the Weimar Republic, from 1928 to 1933, and the book, though its title suggests a longer and more conventional span, rightly concentrates on those last years. We possess, moreover, an astounding array of facts about that dramatic period, though the understanding of these facts depends on a knowledge of the earlier period.

Weimar suffered because some of the most important institutional and intellectual barriers to German democracy were set in 1866 and 1871. It was then that Bismarck forged a new mold for German politics and by so doing foreclosed or lessened the likelihood of other solutions. Historians can, of course, go back further: to the reasons, say, for the success of Bismarck and the failure of 1848, to the reasons for the failure of the Prussian reform movement in 1819. But the lure of infinite regress should not prevent the historian from finding a sensible point of departure for his inquiry. The creation of Imperial Germany is such a date.

Bismarck unified Germany and inserted into an older political and social system enough modern features to preserve it. A parliament based on universal male suffrage was created, but executive authority and bureaucratic predominance were carefully preserved. Industrial capitalism was encouraged by the state, but after 1878 economic liberalism was spurned and the *embourgeoisement* of the country was not properly achieved. The proletariat was allowed to organize, but barred from political power and virtually denied the possibility of social advancement.

It was a curious system, and Bismarck's successors found it increasingly difficult to run. The ruling classes were afraid that the forces of modernity would yet break through the barriers that remained; the proletariat was torn between expectation and frustration. For all the power, prosperity, and seeming smugness of Imperial Germany, there was *Angst* in Germany, too—*Angst* before one's enemies at home and abroad.

The vaulting nationalism and imperialism of the late nineteenth century absorbed some of this double fear, even as it had absorbed some of those earlier, xenophobic ideas about the Germanic *Volk* that had been born in the struggle against Napoleon. Modern nationalism in Germany, even more than elsewhere, became the property of the conservative, propertied, and educated classes who sought to legitimize their power by invoking nationalistic slogans about the incompatibility of the German spirit and Western liberalism or materialism. From the 1870s on, anti-Semitism was often annexed to nationalism as well: The Jew as the prototype—and profiteer—of modernity was depicted as yet another sinister danger to Germany. It is curious that anti-Semitism appeared simultaneously among the rabble-rousers soliciting votes and the elite—witness Treitschke's attack against the Jews in 1879—pleading for the preservation of German values. Lagarde and Treitschke embedded anti-Semitism in an "idealistic" set of values and thus elevated it to cultural respectability. To be anti-Semitic bespoke essential virtues—virtues that even Jews cherished. The path to dictatorship in Germany was long, tortuous, and amazingly crowded.

By its political institutions and its social system, Imperial Germany inhibited the development of democracy. It also spawned ideas of nationalism and racism that inspired Nazi ideology and facilitated the acceptance of that ideology by millions of Germans. The failure of Weimar and the success of Hitler had common sources in Imperial Germany.

The antagonisms and resentments of prewar Germany were briefly overshadowed by the common exultation at the outbreak of the war. But this long-cherished utopia of national unity and the end of internal conflict receded rapidly as the conduct of the war in fact exacerbated earlier antagonisms in

Germany. The Weimar Constitution inserted still other elements of modernity into public life, indeed parliamentary democracy itself, but the forms of society and the personnel of the governing elites changed little. The defeat and the peace treaty had embittered the nation, and democracy frightened or disappointed all classes. The Republic barely survived, though from 1924 to 1928 it experienced some degree of stability while a succession of bourgeois governments secured diplomatic gains abroad and the economy prospered at home. Even democracy made strides—in municipalities and in some of the states, for the history of Weimar was not without its promise and achievement.

In 1928, the two processes—the disintegration of Weimar and the rise of Hitler—began to coalesce. In that year, the Socialists gained an impressive victory at the polls—and frightened their enemies without satisfying their followers. To constitute a proper coalition government took a year, and Germans jeered at the inefficiency of democracy. In that year of still growing prosperity, the Nazis made significant inroads among university students, and the desecration of Jewish cemeteries reached an all-time high. In 1929, Stresemann died, the depression struck, and the final agony of Weimar began.

A curious crisis ensued. The impact of the depression sharpened class antagonisms, and the uneasy collaboration between Socialists and conservatives collapsed. Bruening became Chancellor, at the instigation of Schleicher, and embarked almost at once on a right-wing authoritarian course. He resorted to government by presidential decree, dissolved a Reichstag with a comfortable democratic majority, and found that the next parliament mirrored the terrible radicalization of German politics: Nazis and Communists had scored great gains. A new generation of voters turned its back on the Weimar "system" and sought revolutionary answers to unprecedented needs. Bruening hoped to stem the tide of radicalism by engineering further foreign successes and an economic revival, while rebuffing parliament and relying more and more on Hindenburg's presidential powers. In May 1932, he fell victim to the very power he had so unwisely aggrandized. For three years, while Hitler was on the doorstep of power, the ruling groups of Germany sought to find an authoritarian answer that would supplant or radically alter parliamentary government. At a time of increasing misery, the gulf between government and governed was allowed to grow wider, and a handful of men frivolously thought they could use the Nazis to weaken the Socialists, all the while maintaining themselves in power. Papen and Hindenburg's camarilla dreamed of a "new state," which in effect would have been the imperial regime revived. As Marx once said—in regard to Louis Napoleon—certain types recur in history; the first time, they appear as tragedy, the second time as farce. Papen and his cohorts in irresponsibility were such a farce, even if the imperial regime was no tragedy.

In those months of tangible crisis, the ghosts of an earlier era appeared as if for a final *Totentanz*. People misread the signs, misunderstood Hitler, and reverted to anachronistic struggles and maneuvers: The Socialists feared the reactionaries almost more than they feared Hitler, the conservatives thought they could use or imprison Hitler so that he would deliver his mass support to their fine aristocratic hands. Both the conservatives' dream of authoritarianism and the Socialist' meek acceptance of a return to authoritarianism at their own expense and despite the militancy of many of their younger leaders and of the rank and file suggest a kind of psychological regression, a shrinking back to a past beyond recall.

Hitler clearly appealed to that past, and after its guardians finally called him to power, he identified himself as the heir of Prussian traditions, most dramatically on that day of pageantry in Potsdam in March 1933. But in the twelve years of his rule he liquidated the remnants of Imperial Germany as ruthlessly as he did the vestiges of Weimar democracy. Not Hitler's rise to power but his end marked the true break in German history. The path to dictatorship, so deeply embedded in the German past, ended in 1945 because so much of that past was dead, buried in the rubble of the Third Reich. A smaller, different Germany may at last have found the path to democracy.

The Cold War—
Who Was To Blame?

CONTENTS

QUESTIONS FOR STUDY

1 How did Truman's attitude toward and treatment of the Soviet Union compare with Roosevelt's?

2 Was the decision to drop the atomic bomb on Hiroshima an act of Cold War diplomacy? What of the atomic bombing of Nagasaki?

3 What part did Marxist-Leninist theory play in the development of the Cold War?

4 What theoretical presuppositions underlay American policy?

5 What policy choices were available to the Soviet Union and the United States during and immediately after World War II? How do you evaluate each of them from the point of view of keeping the peace and protecting each nation's interests?

6 How would you state the positions of two kinds of revisionist historians of the Cold War? What arguments can be employed against each?

7 Was the Cold War inevitable? If so, when did it become so?

During World War II the United States, Great Britain, and the Soviet Union were allied in a fight for survival against the Axis powers. From the beginning there were differences in strategy, aims, and ideology, accompanied by mutual distrust. Nevertheless, the alliance held together; at Teheran and Yalta conferences were held and joint plans made for the conduct of the war and for the shape of the peace to come. A United Nations organization was envisaged in which all nations would participate to maintain peace and harmony. But within a few years hopes for friendship and cooperation had been dashed, and the world was divided into two hostile armed camps; the Cold War had begun.

At first, people in the West had little doubt that Communist Russia, led by Stalin, was to blame. His insistence on Russian domination of Eastern Europe through satellite governments, his refusal to cooperate with the Baruch Plan for controlling atomic energy, the Communist coup that brought Czechoslovakia behind the iron curtain—all seemed evidence of an intransigent Russian attitude that made continued friendship impossible and conflict inevitable. From this point of view all the measures taken by the United States to oppose communism were merely responses to aggressive challenges. The Truman Doctrine was thus aimed at preventing the fall of Greece and Turkey to international communism, the Marshall Plan and NATO an effort to prevent Western Europe from falling under communism and therefore Russian domination, and the whole policy of containment merely a necessary reply to aggressive Soviet communism.

Soon, however, a "revisionist" school of historians of the Cold War arose, chiefly in America. Its members have examined American policy and found it to be largely at fault for the growth of estrangement between East and West. They discern a change in America's attitude with the death of Roosevelt and the advent of Truman. They cite the sudden cessation of lend-lease shipments to the Soviet Union and the use of the atomic bomb as evidence of American responsibility for the beginning of distrust and hostility. From their point of view the Truman Doctrine, the Marshall Plan, and NATO were not defensive responses but hostile actions aimed at gaining or preserving American spheres of political and economic influence. Although many historians of the "new left" have taken up and expanded on this theme in various ways, the pioneering work of D. F. Fleming (pp. 839–852) remains a convenient and useful example of the revisionist point of view.

Arthur Schlesinger, Jr.'s article entitled "Origins of the Cold War" (pp. 881–906) remains one of the most influential rebuttals of the new revisionism. He emphasizes the one-sided nature of the revisionist analysis, which almost totally disregards Russian actions while focusing critically on Western motives and behavior. The evidence has not been balanced, for it has been infinitely easier to know about Western actions and motives than about those of the Soviet Union. Continued research has, nonetheless, helped clarify the picture, permitting scholars such as John Lewis Gaddis (pp. 907–929) to shed new light on the origins of the Cold War. Gaddis finds that the Europeans themselves played a key role in the hardening of the division of their continent.

The apparent end of the Cold War will not put an end to discussion of its origins. Mikhail Gorbachev's policy of glasnost *("openness") has already produced new evidence; if it continues we may hope to learn more about the heretofore concealed Soviet side of the story.*

1

America's Responsibility

In the following selection D. F. Fleming presents the view that the United States was largely responsible for the coming of the Cold War and establishes the nature of the controversy.

FROM *The Cold War and Its Origins*

BY *D. F. Fleming*

THE CHRONOLOGY OF THE COLD WAR

There can be no real understanding of the Cold War unless chronology is kept in mind. What came first? What was action and what reaction? Not everything that came after a given act was due to that act, but a later event could not be the cause of an earlier one.

Below are the principal events of the Cold War in the order in which they occurred.

1. September 1938—Control of East Europe achieved by Hitler at Munich.
2. December 5, 1941, to February 4, 1942—State Department decisions not to make any wartime agreements about Russia's western boundaries.
3. April 1942 to June 1944—The second front postponed. Peripheral war conducted in Africa and Italy.
4. October 9, 1944—Churchill and Stalin agreed on spheres of influence in the Balkans: Greece to Britain; Bulgaria and Rumania to Russia; Yugoslavia 50–50.
5. December 3, 1944, to January 15, 1945—The British crushed the Greek leftists in heavy fighting.
6. December 24, 1944, to May 14, 1945—Bulgarian purge trials executed 2000 rightists and imprisoned 3000.
7. March 29, 1944, to February 1945—Soviet armies occupied East Europe.

D. F. Fleming, *The Cold War and Its Origins 1950–1960*, II pp. 1038–1051 (1961). Reprinted by permission of Doubleday & Company, Inc.

8. February 1945—The Yalta Conference conceded friendly governments in East Europe to Russia, but with free elections and a reorganization of the Polish Government.
9. March 6, 1945—Russia imposed a communist-led coalition in Rumania.
10. March 1945—Friction with Russia over German surrender negotiations in Italy.
11. April 12, 1945—Franklin D. Roosevelt's death, four months after Cordell Hull's resignation.
12. April 23, 1945—Truman's White House lecture to Molotov on the Polish Government.
13. July 17–25, 1945—The Potsdam Conference failed to alter Russian arrangements in East Europe.
14. August 6, 1945—The first American A-bomb upset the expected world strategic balance.
15. August 18, 1945—Beginning of the Byrnes-Bevin diplomatic drive to force free elections in East Europe.
16. September 1945—First Council of Foreign Ministers deadlocked over East Europe.
17. March 5, 1946—Churchill's Fulton speech demanded an Anglo-American preponderance of power against Russia, with reference to East Europe.
18. April 1946—Russian troops forced from Iran through the United Nations.
19. August 1946—Soviet demands upon Turkey for the return of two provinces and for a base in the Straits.
20. July to December 1946—Peace treaties for Italy, Hungary, Rumania, Bulgaria and Finland hammered out.
21. November 1946—The Republicans won control of the Congress, aided by charges of widespread communist infiltration in the United States.
22. Late December 1946—General relaxation and expectation of peace.
23. March 12, 1947—The Truman Doctrine, calling for the containment of the Soviet Union and communism.
24. March 23, 1947—Truman's order providing for the loyalty investigation of *all* government employees.
25. March to August 1947—The freely elected Smallholder's Party Government of Hungary disintegrated by communist pressure.
26. June 5, 1947—The Marshall Plan announced. Rejected by Russia August 2, 1947.
27. November 1947—The Cominform organized, uniting all the principal communist parties of Europe, including those of France and Italy.
28. January 22, 1948—A plan for a Western Union in Europe announced by Bevin.
29. February 25, 1948—A communist coup seized control of Czechoslovakia.
30. March 25, 1948—Western Union treaty signed. Devil theory address by President Truman.
31. June 28, 1948—Yugoslavia expelled by the Cominform. Received help from the West.
32. June 1948 to May 1949—The Berlin blockade.

33. March to August 1949—The signing and ratification of the North Atlantic Treaty creating NATO.
34. September 23, 1949—The first Soviet A-bomb hung the threat of total destruction over West Europe.
35. February 1, 1950—Drive for the H-bomb announced by Truman.
36. February 9, March 9 and 16, 1950—Acheson explained the policy of no negotiation with the Russian river of aggression until strength had been accumulated.
37. October 1948 to January 1950—The Chinese Nationalist armies captured or destroyed by the Communists.
38. February to May 1950—The first explosion of McCarthyism.
39. June 25, 1950—The outbreak of the Korean War.
40. September 12, 1950—The United States demanded the rearmament of Germany and began a vast rearmament.
41. October 1950—Having liberated South Korea, we decided to conquer the North Korean Republic.
42. February 1952—Acheson's Lisbon NATO arms goals overstrained our allies.
43. May to November 1952—Our allies escaped from control during the long American election campaign.
44. November 1952—The first American H-bomb exploded, on the ground.
45. March 6, 1953—The death of Stalin created uncertainty and a desire for relaxation in Russia.
46. May 11, 1953—Churchill repealed his Fulton address and called for an end of the Cold War on the basis of guaranteeing Russia's security in East Europe.
47. July 26, 1953—Korean cease-fire signed.
48. August 9, 1953—The first air-borne H-bomb achieved by Russia, and growing Russian air power brought the threat of incineration to all large American cities.
49. November 6, 1953—Ex-President Truman officially charged with knowingly harboring a communist spy.
50. May 1952 to January 1954—A growing realization that the world power struggle had become a stalemate.
51. April 22 to June 15, 1954—The crest of McCarthyism.
52. July 18–24, 1955—The First Summit Conference recognized the atomic arms stalemate and the inevitability of competitive coexistence.
53. February 15–20, 1956—Khrushchev's denunciation of Stalin accelerated a wave of reforms behind the iron curtain, relaxing police state controls and giving greater incentives to individuals.
54. March 7, 1956—President Eisenhower urged that we counter the threat to us "more by positive measures that people throughout the world will trust, than just by trying to answer specific thrusts."
55. October–November 1956—Revolution in Poland and Hungary against Soviet control and communism.
56. November 1956—Attacks upon Egypt by Israel, France and Britain.

57. August 26, 1957—The first intercontinental ballistic rocket claimed by the Soviet Union.
58. October 4, 1957—The first of the increasingly heavy Sputniks demonstrated Russia's ability to lay down large pay-loads accurately across great distances.
59. April 1958—The pro-American Liberal Party ousted in Canada by the strongly nationalistic Conservatives.
60. May 1958—Vice President Nixon mobbed in Peru and Venezuela.
61. July 1958—Revolution in Iraq and the sending of American troops to Lebanon.
62. August–October 1958—The second Quemoy crisis, ending in China's defeat.
63. November 1958 to July 1959—The second Berlin crisis.
64. April 16, 1959—The resignation of Secretary of State John Foster Dulles.
65. September 1959—Khrushchev's visit to the United States, inaugurating President Eisenhower's effort to move toward making peace and ending the Cold War.
66. September–October 1959—A Soviet *Lunik* rocket hit the moon and another went around it relaying to earth pictures of its hidden side, emphasizing Russia's continued leadership in rocketry and the conquest of space.
67. November 16, 1959—Secretary of State Herter's appeal for keeping the great competition of our time with communism "within the bounds set by the conditions of co-survival."
68. December 1959—Eisenhower's eleven nation crusade for a new international climate and peace, climaxed by his statement to the Parliament of India on December 10 that the mistrusts, fixations and tensions that exist in the world "are the creations of Governments, cherished and nourished by Governments. Nations would never feel them if they were given freedom from propaganda and pressure."
69. October 1955 to May 1960—The Second Summit Conference frustrated by the steady erosion in the West of the expectation of serious negotiations about West Berlin and by the U-2 spy plane incident at Sverdlovsk.
70. June 16, 1960—President Eisenhower turned back from a visit to Japan by the inability of the Japanese Government to protect him from great hostile demonstrations.

It is of cardinal importance to remember that East Europe was given away not at Yalta but at Munich. Before that the curbing of Hitler might have cost the West the same territories which Hitler yielded to Russia. After Munich the marching armies would grind back and forth across the face of Europe until the Red armies came to rest in Berlin and Vienna.

Decisions During the War

This was not foreseen in the State Department as late as December 5, 1941, and February 1942 when the Atherton-Dunn memoranda reasoned that Stalin might not be able to recover all of his lost territories and ruled against recognizing his seizure of the Baltic states and half of Poland. Our fear of another uproar in this country over "secret treaties," such as had been raised after World War I, and of the outcry of Polish and other citizens, combined with aversion to any extension of the area of communism to prevent the British from making a more realistic agreement with Russia in April 1942.

Then the British managed to lead Western war operations through peripheral warfare in North Africa, Sicily, and Italy until May 1944. This was justifiable strategy for us, but it left the main brunt of the land war on the Russians to the end and created in their minds lasting suspicions of being deliberately sacrificed. More important, it gave the Russian armies time to come into Central Europe, at the cost of many hundreds of thousands of casualties, losses which we would have suffered had we struck sooner and directly at Germany.

All during the war years Churchill sought manfully to retrieve in East Europe what Chamberlain had given away. His eyes were always on the nonexistent "soft underbelly" of Europe, then in the late stages of the war on an invasion through Trieste, and finally for lunges into Germany to seize areas beyond the agreed zones of occupation for bargaining purposes. But always the actual balance of forces defeated him. The Russians were required to maul the bulk of the German forces to the last day of the war. Allied forces thrown through Trieste might well have enabled the Russians to skirt the Baltic Sea and appear on the English Channel. Furthermore, attempts to change the zones of occupation against the Russians would have been rejected by allied public opinion. Long afterward General Bedell Smith, one of General Eisenhower's most trusted generals, recorded his conviction that it "would have been quite impossible in the light of world public opinion in our own country," and his advice to Churchill at the time was "that I didn't think his own public opinion would permit it."

Soviet control of East Europe was the price we paid for the years of appeasement of Hitler, and it was not a high price. In Toynbee's judgment "the Nazis would have conquered the world," if we and the Soviets had not combined our efforts. They would eventually have crossed the narrow gap of the South Atlantic to Brazil and the rest of South America, where strong fifth columns could have been organized in more than one country. By our war alliance with the Soviets we prevented the unification of the world by the Nazis. That was a victory beyond price, but, says Toynbee, we "could not have put down Hitler without consequently producing the situation with which all of us now find ourselves confronted."

All this was fully evident during the war and it is still true. C. B. Marshall has reminded us that we do not have to guess what the Axis powers would have done had they won. They set it down plainly in their Tripartite Alliance on September 27, 1940—"a pattern for the conquest of the rest of the world and the beleaguerment of the United States." Why then did we have ten years of cold war over Russia's control of East Europe and over her desire to have a military base on the Turkish Straits?

East Europe Divided by Churchill and Stalin

Early in October 1944 Churchill sought to come to terms with the inevitable. Over the strong opposition of our State Department, but with Roosevelt's permission, he went to Moscow to make a temporary agreement for three months concerning the Balkans.

On October 9 he proposed to Stalin that Russia have 90 per cent predominance in Rumania, others 10 per cent, and 75 per cent predominance in Bulgaria, others 25 per cent. In Greece Britain would have 90 per cent predominance, and others 10 per cent. The "predominance" was to be divided 50–50 in Hungary and Yugoslavia. Nothing was said about this division of influence being temporary.

Stalin accepted this proposal without a word. He permitted a really free election in Hungary, which the old ruling classes duly won, and he did his best to force Tito to honor the bargain about Yugoslavia. Also he held his hand completely while Churchill promptly crushed the left forces in Greece, thereby sealing his agreement with Churchill and committing Roosevelt to it, before Yalta.

The communist revolution in Bulgaria was already in full cry when the Yalta conference met. The overthrow in the preceding December of the mighty ELAS movement in Greece by the British army and the Greek officer caste had suggested to the Russians that something very similar could occur in Bulgaria, where the Bulgarian army officers used the coup d'état "as a normal political instrument." "People's Court" trials began on December 24, 1944, and cut down the Bulgarian army officers as with a scythe until the end of February 1945.

On March 6 the Soviet Government imposed a communist-led government upon Rumania, deposing the Rumanian conservatives. It was "very hard to think of any constructive alternative," since free elections in Rumania under their control would have been "an invitation to Fascism here more than elsewhere."

The situation was worst in Rumania, where government was notoriously "so corrupt that it is a synonym for corrupt government," but there was no country in East Europe, with the exception of Greece, where the kind of free elections we wanted would not have been controlled by the old ruling classes. They had manipulated the elections for generations. No free election had ever been held. The Hungarian landlords had been ruthless rulers for a thousand years, and elsewhere the cliques which ruled for their own benefit had virtually all of the knowledge of political manipulations. The Hungarian and Rumanian ruling groups had also sent two million conscripted troops deep into Russia, behind Hitler's armies.

Free Elections

In these circumstances the question arises, why did Stalin agree at Yalta to conduct "free elections" in Eastern Europe? Why we demanded them was clear. That is the American way of doing things, subject to the operations of political machines, and we wanted very much to prevent East Europe from being communized. No one at Yalta dreamed of denying that the region must cease to be a hostile *cordon sanitaire* against the Soviet Union and become "friendly" politically to the Soviet Union. No one could deny that, with the Red armies at the moment across Poland, within thirty miles of Berlin, and beyond Budapest sweeping up the Danube, while the Western allies were still in France, set back by the Ardennes offensive.

But could governments friendly to Russia be obtained in this region by "free elections" in which the ruling groups participated freely? It was inconceivable that these groups could be friendly to Russia, or that communist Russia could think of depending on them. That was as incredible as that we should freely arrange for a communist government in France or Italy. The Soviets also happened to believe that their system of government was as valid as ours, and that they could really depend only upon it to stop East Europe from being used as an invasion corridor into the Soviet Union.

If the Americans at Yalta committed a fault, it was not in "giving away" East Europe. That had been done at Munich long before. It was in trying to achieve the impossible under the formula of "free elections." Yet free elections were in their blood and they could do no other than to believe that this was a solution which all must accept. On his side, it is not likely that Stalin thought the formula would prevent him from purging the long dominant elements in East Europe, whose hostility to Red Russia needed no further demonstration. These elections might be managed and "people's democracies" set up which would be acceptable to the Americans. He knew that the decisive settlement for the area had been made in his gentleman's agreement with Churchill, on October 9, 1944, and that its execution was already far advanced on both sides.

He was loyally holding to his side of the bargain with Churchill and he could hardly have believed that the Yalta formulas would disrupt allied relations as soon as the war was over and lead to long years of bitter cold war.

Truman's Reversal of the Roosevelt-Hull Policy

It is possible that if Roosevelt had lived the same deadly quarrel would have developed, though it is far more likely that he already understood the deeper forces involved and the impossibility of frustrating them. What made a clash certain was the accession of Truman just at the close of the war. He intended to carry out Roosevelt's engagements, loyally and fully, and to exact from Stalin the same complete fulfilment, including free elections in East Europe. This theme runs through the first volume of his memoirs.

However his methods were poles apart from those of Roosevelt and Hull. All through 1944, his last year in office, Hull had conducted off-the-record conferences with groups of editors, clergymen, and members of Congress, to explain to them how far the Russians had come with us, how they had been "locked up and isolated for a quarter of a century," used to receiving violent epithets. It would "take time for them to get into step," but they would do it. He urged that "we must be patient and forbearing. We cannot settle questions with Russia by threats. We must use friendly methods."

No one was more opposed than Hull to Soviet control of East Europe, "interfering with her neighbors," but as he left office his policy rested on two bases: to show the Russians by example how a great power should act and to continue in constant friendly discussion with them. "Consult them on every point. Engage in no 'cussin matches' with them."

Nothing could have been further from President Truman's approach. He quickly read all the dispatches about friction with Russia over German surrenders, listened to everybody who wanted to get tough with the Russians, and when Molotov came by on April 23, 1945, to pay his respects to the new President, he received such a dressing down that he complained at the end of it that no one had ever talked like that to him before.

This was exactly eleven days after Roosevelt's death. It took Truman just that long to reverse the entire Roosevelt-Hull approach to Russia and to inaugurate an era of toughness and ever greater toughness in our dealings with her. Then on August 6, 1945, the Hiroshima explosion gave him the means to back insistence on free elections in East Europe and when the London Conference of September 1945 deadlocked over this issue he made up his mind at once to contain Russia. It was at this moment that Lippmann, noting that we had terminated lend-lease "abruptly and brutally" and had drifted into an arms race with the Soviet Union, warned: "Let no one deceive himself. We are drifting toward a catastrophe."

To the already deep fears of Russia for her own security, thrice justified since 1914, was added a new and dreadful fear of a fourth Western attack, backed by the atomic bomb. From the psychological point of view the policy of toughness was "the worst treatment" that could have been devised. "If a patient is suffering from genuine fear, you do not cure his fears and establish a rational relationship with him by making him more afraid. You endeavor to show him patiently and by your actions toward him that he has nothing to fear."

Exactly the opposite course was followed, with increasing momentum. In the following spring of 1946 Churchill issued at Fulton, Missouri, and in President Truman's applauding presence, his call for an overwhelming preponderance of power against Russia, hinting broadly at later forcible interventions in East Europe. Nevertheless, peace was made in Europe during the remainder of 1946. In three sessions of the Council of Foreign Ministers and a conference of 21 nations in Paris, peace treaties were hammered out in substantially the terms established by the various armistices. Really free elections had been held in Hungary and there were many signs of relaxation of tension as the year closed.

Results of the Truman Doctrine

However, in February the British turned the burden of supporting Greece over to us and Truman seized the occasion to proclaim the doctrine of containment, on March 12, 1947, which George F. Kennan spelled out fully in the July issue of *Foreign Affairs* as "long term, patient but firm and vigilant containment of Russian expansive tendencies." Otherwise the Kremlin would take its time about filling every "nook and cranny available to it in the basin of world power."

On its face this was the rashest policy ever enunciated by any American leader. For the first time in history the encirclement of a great power was openly proclaimed. This power, too, was in firm possession of the great heartland of Eurasia. It had already demonstrated that it could industrialize itself quickly and enough to defeat Hitler's armies. What it would do, after the Cold War was declared by Churchill and Truman, was easily predictable by any average man. The Soviet Union would put up a bold front to cover its frightening post-war weakness and work mightily to gain strength to hold what it had and then break the encirclement.

This was a difficult undertaking, for not only was the Soviet Union frightfully devastated, but Eastern Europe was in nearly as bad shape. However, what the Soviet peoples had done twice already they could do again under the lash of containment. After the two gruelling forced marches, before 1941 and after the German invasion, they undertook still a third and within eleven years from 1946 they had achieved first their A-bomb in 1949, then the H-bomb in 1953 and the first ICBM in 1957. In all other vital respects also they had gained that position of strength which was our announced goal after March 1950.

In the course of containment, "negotiation from strength" and liberation, we revivified fully the machinery of totalitarian rule in Russia. As William A. Williams has pointed out: "Appearing as a classic and literal verification of Marx's most apocalyptic prophecy, the policy of containment strengthened the hand of every die-hard Marxist and every extreme Russian nationalist among the Soviet leadership."

Containment also gave Stalin total power over the Soviet peoples. Williams continues:

> Armed with the language and actions of containment, which underwrote and extended his existing power, Stalin could and did drive the Soviet people to the brink of collapse and, no doubt, to the thought of open resistance. But the dynamic of revolt was always blocked, even among those who did have access to the levels of authority, by the fact of containment and the open threat of liberation. Thus protected by his avowed enemies, Stalin was able to force his nation through extreme deprivations and extensive purges to the verge of physical

and psychological exhaustion. But he also steered it through the perils of reconstruction to the security of nuclear parity with the United States.

Stalin's first reply to containment was the destruction of the Smallholder's Party in Hungary, between March and August 1947, into which he had allowed the dispossessed landlords to go, and to take over the Hungarian government in its first free elections. The ending of this government was not difficult, since a topnotch American newsman found in Hungary that the "political sterility" of these elements was so great and their inclinations toward corruption so "incorrigible" that an astonishing number of anti-communists accepted the communist claim to represent the people. The kind of democracy for which we had fought throughout East Europe might have been destroyed in Hungary anyway, but the Truman Doctrine made it a matter of life and death for the Hungarian Reds to end it.

FROM THE MARSHALL PLAN TO TOTAL DIPLOMACY

The Marshall Plan

Meanwhile the yawning economic void in West Europe had led to the American Marshall Plan, an offer of economic help to all the nations of Europe, a "policy not directed against any country or doctrine, but against hunger, poverty, desperation and chaos."

If this magnificent conception had come earlier, while the Russians were asking in vain for a six billion dollar loan, before UNRRA was abolished and before the Truman Doctrine had drawn the lines of conflict tightly, there would have been no Cold War. In the context of the declared Cold War, Russia not only rejected the Marshall Plan for herself but forbade her East European satellites to participate, foreseeing that the American largesse would dissolve shaky loyalties to her satellite governments in more than one East European quarter.

Molotov's angry departure from the Marshall Plan conference in Paris, on August 2, 1947, convinced much of Western opinion that Russia was hostile to the West and that she had deliberately split the world in two. Three months later Russia created the Cominform, an organization of all the Communist parties in East Europe, plus those of France and Italy, to back the Molotov Plan for East European reconstruction, to oppose the Marshall Plan and to fight the Cold War generally. This response to the Truman Doctrine and the Marshall Plan convinced many people throughout the West that the Russians had reverted to the world revolution and were plotting to take over the earth.

Then the Communist seizure of Czechoslovakia hardened this fear into frightened certainty. This high peak of the Cold War, in late February 1948, had been preceded by the announcement on January 22 of a plan for a Western

Union in Europe, which the London *Times* later thought might have "provoked the Soviet Union to hurry forward its own plans" for the consolidation of the Communist bloc.

Czechoslovakia

But Czechoslovakia had been lost to the West at Munich, and in the successive events of the German occupation, which had destroyed most of the conservative classes and made it impossible for the Czechs to wish to oppose Russia. Both the Truman Doctrine and the Marshall Plan had also made it certain that Russia would bring Czechoslovakia behind the Iron Curtain before long. When this happened, the West lost nothing from the power standpoint. On broader grounds it was a time for sorrow and remorse that big power politics had twice deprived the Czechs of the democracy and freedom they did not deserve to lose either time.

However, all this was forgotten in the wave of shock, alarm and anger which swept over the West. Within a month the five power Western Union treaty was signed and on the same day, March 25, 1948, President Truman made an address in which he developed the devil theory fully. One nation, and one alone, had refused to cooperate in making peace, had broken the agreements it did make, had obstructed the United Nations and destroyed both the independence and the democratic character of a whole series of nations in Central and East Europe. To stop this nation Truman demanded prompt passage of ERP, more funds for Greece, Turkey and Chiang Kai-shek, and universal military training.

Thereafter the United States proceeded rapidly along an essentially negative course, in which we rushed to counter each communist move, tied up our resources in blocking efforts, selected our friends on one test alone, and rapidly adopted at home the methods and weapons of "the enemy."

Berlin Blockade

There is more cause for satisfaction in our handling of the Berlin blockade from June 1948 to May 1949. The Russians had a strong case for terminating the four power occupation of Berlin, because the West had announced plans on June 7 for the creation of a West German government. Since the four power occupation of Berlin was based on the assumption that Berlin would be the capital of a united Germany, the quadripartite occupation did become an anomaly when the assumption was destroyed. Thereafter West Berlin became from the Russian standpoint only a listening post and spy center for the West in the center of East Germany, and an ideological thorn in her side.

The announcement of a new currency for West Germany, imperatively needed, also created urgent problems for East Germany, since it would circulate in Berlin.

These were real grievances, but from the Western standpoint they did not justify an attempt to starve out 2,000,000 West Berliners. The crisis was grave and it was met by the West imaginatively, boldly and resolutely. The advocates of sending an army of tanks to Berlin were silenced and the air-lift did the job, dramatically lifting allied prestige to new heights. In this engagement of the Cold War the action of the West was a model of combined courage and restraint, and President Truman deserves his large share of the credit for it.

"Total Diplomacy"

The Cold War as proclaimed by Churchill and Truman would have been impractical from the start had it not been for the American A-bomb monopoly, in which both leaders took the deepest satisfaction. When it was abruptly ended in September 1949, long before the expected time, a severe crisis of confidence shook Washington, a crisis which was ended by the decision to produce H-bombs and rearm further for the successful prosecution of the Cold War. It would be a long pull and take very steady nerves, Secretary of State Acheson explained on three occasions early in 1950, but the Russian river of aggression would be contained.

Restored confidence was expressed in Acheson's Berkeley speech of March 16, 1950, in which he laid down seven pre-conditions for negotiation with Russia amounting to Soviet surrender of its positions before negotiation.

Korea

Then on June 25, 1950, the Russian river of aggression actually moved into Western held territory for the first time when the North Koreans invaded South Korea. Hardly anyone in the West questioned this verdict. Yet there were two other equally strong probabilities: that the North Koreans plunged southward on their own initiative, and that Syngman Rhee provoked them to do so by taking the initiative along the border in the day or two after the UN observers returned to Seoul. That he would be wholly capable of precipitating a war for the unification of Korea has been amply demonstrated several times since. Both sides in Korea were highly keyed for civil war, each intent on unification its way.

Ingram's conclusion is sound when he says: "Nor are we in possession of any positive proof that in Korea or elsewhere she (Russia) has conspired to instigate minor war against the Western allies through one of her satellites." He adds that "suspicions are not proof" and doubts that any evidence can be found later to sustain the charge that the Korean trouble arose as the result of a plot by China, or the Soviet Union, or both, to embarrass the West.

No doubts on this score entered the minds of our leaders in June 1950. It was assumed at once that the Kremlin had ordered the invasion and that this was the first of a series of satellite wars which would stampede both Asia and eventually West Europe into the Soviet camp, unless this attempt were promptly scotched. The United Nations was instantly mobilized, to minimize the shock of our intervention in an Asiatic civil war.

If our cold war purpose had not been predominant, the defeat of the North Korean aggression would have been a great victory for collective security and the United Nations. As the crisis did develop the UN Security Council approved our military action before it had heard the North Koreans, and it never did hear them—a serious breach of normal, fair procedure.

Then when the 38th Parallel was recovered, within three months and relatively painlessly, the monumental error was committed of trying to abolish the North Korean state. This mistake ranks close behind our failure to lead the League of Nations and our enunciation of the Truman Doctrine among the foreign policy errors committed by the United States. It was a political mistake of the first magnitude because it challenged both China and Russia in the North Korean triangle, a strategic area of the utmost importance to them. Moreover, it challenged them as communist powers to permit the Americans to destroy a communist state in their own front yards and set up a model capitalist democracy. It was a military gamble because it launched our armies precipitately into untenable territory. It was a moral blunder because it invalidated the central idea of the United Nations that it is a police force and not a partisan belligerent. When the United Nations invaded North Korea "they were no longer acting as police, but as co-belligerents on the side of the South Koreans."

Consequently, when China intervened on behalf of the North Koreans "the United Nations by becoming belligerents instead of a police force were no longer morally entitled to indict China." But she was indicted as an aggressor, under total pressure from Washington, and is still excluded from the United Nations on that ground.

Thus what should have been a brief, successful UN police operation was converted into a full-scale war which dragged on for three more years, always on the edge of a world war, until neutralism had been made a world movement, until the whole idea of the United Nations being a policeman had been made highly doubtful, and until President Truman and his party had been driven from office, more because of "Truman's war," never declared by Congress, than for any other reason. The war had become to the American people a never ending horror in a far country, for veiled cold war reasons.

Truman's Leadership

The tragedy of the second war in Korea brought out sharply both the defects and the good qualities of President Truman's leadership. His ability to make up his mind and act is a great quality in a ruler. Without it he is lost. But it is not the only quality necessary. There are occasions, perhaps more of them, when restraint is what is needed. There are even times when a President must have "the courage to be timid" or to seem so. Restraint is a far greater virtue than rashness. Truman could plunge in easily and too far, but he did not expand the second Korean war into World War III, as so many urged him to do, and he finally recalled General MacArthur who had flagrantly exceeded his instructions and was leading the cry for a greater war. Thus Truman did not compound his great Korean error into an irretrievable one, even when there was a widespread, angry belief that the Kremlin planned to bleed us white in a series of satellite wars around Russia's vast perimeter—accepting the challenge and logic of the Truman Doctrine.

On the great issue of the Chinese Revolution Truman also avoided disaster. His Doctrine was breached in gigantic fashion by the Communist Revolution in China, and his political enemies pushed him relentlessly to enforce it there, but he had the good sense to send his greatest lieutenant, General Marshall, to China for a long effort to mediate the Chinese civil war, and afterwards he accepted Marshall's report that we could not settle that gigantic conflict. It must have been difficult to put his Doctrine into abeyance, in the place where it was violated on the greatest scale, but he did it and avoided inaugurating a third world war by that route.

By 1950, an experienced editor and biographer could write of Truman: "In 1945 the moral hegemony of the world was within his grasp, but it has slipped from his fingers."

At the close of his presidency the moral leadership of the world had passed in large part to Nehru, the neutral opponent of the Cold War, but much of it went begging for lack of a truly powerful voice. Truman, who might have voiced it, had become only the belligerent leader of an anti-Soviet, anti-communist crusade.

2

The Development
of the Cold War

Not long after the Yalta Conference it became clear that the Allies disagreed on the interpretation of its terms. The Russians had promised self-determination and free elections in Eastern Europe. It soon became apparent that by Western standards these promises were not being kept. In the following letter written shortly before his death, Roosevelt complains to Stalin.

President Roosevelt's Letter to Marshal Stalin

Received on April 1, 1945

Personal and Top Secret for Marshal Stalin
from President Roosevelt

I CANNOT CONCEAL from you the concern with which I view the developments of events of mutual interest since our fruitful meeting at Yalta. The decisions we reached there were good ones and have for the most part been welcomed with enthusiasm by the peoples of the world who saw in our ability to find a common basis of understanding the best pledge for a secure and peaceful world after this war. Precisely because of the hopes and expectations that these decisions raised, their fulfillment is being followed with the closest attention. We have no right to let them be disappointed. So far there has been a discouraging lack of progress made in the carrying out, which the world expects, of the political decisions which we reached at the conference particularly those relating to the Polish question. I am frankly puzzled as to why this should be and must tell you that I do not fully understand in many respects the apparent indifferent attitude of your Government. Having understood each other so well at Yalta I am convinced that the three of us can and will clear away any obstacles which

"President Roosevelt's Letter to Marshal Stalin," in Ministry of Foreign Affairs of the U.S.S.R., *Correspondence between the Chairman of the Council of Ministers of the U.S.S.R. and the Presidents of the U.S.A. and the Prime Ministers of Great Britain During the Great Patriotic War of 1941–1945*, II (1957), pp. 201–204. Reprinted by permission.

have developed since then. I intend, therefore, in this message to lay before you with complete frankness the problem as I see it.

Although I have in mind primarily the difficulties which the Polish negotiations have encountered, I must make a brief mention of our agreement embodied in the Declaration on Liberated Europe. I frankly cannot understand why the recent developments in Rumania should be regarded as not falling within the terms of that Agreement. I hope you will find time personally to examine the correspondence between our Governments on this subject.

However, the part of our agreements at Yalta which has aroused the greatest popular interest and is the most urgent relates to the Polish question. You are aware of course that the Commission which we set up has made no progress. I feel this is due to the interpretation which your Government is placing upon the Crimea decisions. In order that there shall be no misunderstanding I set forth below my interpretations of the points of the Agreement which are pertinent to the difficulties encountered by the Commission in Moscow.

In the discussions that have taken place so far your Government appears to take the position that the new Polish Provisional Government of National Unity which we agreed should be formed should be little more than a continuation of the present Warsaw Government. I cannot reconcile this either with our agreement or our discussions. While it is true that the Lublin Government is to be reorganized and its members play a prominent role, it is to be done in such a fashion as to bring into being a new government. This point is clearly brought out in several places in the text of the Agreement. I must make it quite plain to you that any such solution which would result in a thinly disguised continuance of the present Warsaw régime would be unacceptable and would cause the people of the United States to regard the Yalta Agreement as having failed.

It is equally apparent that for the same reason the Warsaw Government cannot under the Agreement claim the right to select or reject what Poles are to be brought to Moscow by the Commission for consultation. Can we not agree that it is up to the Commission to select the Polish leaders to come to Moscow to consult in the first instance and invitations be sent out accordingly. If this could be done I see no great objection to having the Lublin group come first in order that they may be fully acquainted with the agreed interpretation of the Yalta decisions on this point. It is of course understood that if the Lublin group come first no arrangements would be made independently with them before the arrival of the other Polish leaders called for consultation. In order to facilitate the agreement the Commission might first of all select a small but representative group of Polish leaders who could suggest other names for the consideration of the Commission. We have not and would not bar or veto any candidate for consultation which Mr. Molotov might propose, being confident that he would not suggest any Poles who would be inimical to the intent of the Crimea decision. I feel that it is not too much to ask that my Ambassador be accorded the same confidence and that any candidate for consultation presented by any one of the Commission be accepted by the others in good faith. It is obvious to me that if the right of the Commission to select these Poles is limited or shared with the Warsaw Government the very foundation on which our agreement rests would be destroyed.

While the foregoing are the immediate obstacles which in my opinion have prevented our Commission from making any progress in this vital matter, there are two other suggestions which were not in the agreement but nevertheless have a very important bearing on the result we all seek. Neither of these suggestions has been as yet accepted by your Government. I refer to:

(1) That there should be the maximum of political tranquillity in Poland and that dissident groups should cease any measures and countermeasures against each other. That we should respectively use our influence to that end seems to me eminently reasonable.

(2) It would also seem entirely natural in view of the responsibilities placed upon them by the Agreement that representatives of the American and British members of the Commission should be permitted to visit Poland. As you will recall Mr. Molotov himself suggested that at an early meeting of the Commission and only subsequently withdrew it.

I wish I could convey to you how important it is for the successful development of our program of international collaboration that this Polish question be settled fairly and speedily. If this is not done all of the difficulties and dangers to Allied unity which we had so much in mind in reaching our decisions at the Crimea will face us in an even more acute form. You are, I am sure, aware that the genuine popular support in the United States is required to carry out any government policy, foreign or domestic. The American people make up their own mind and no government action can change it. I mention this fact because the last sentence of your message about Mr. Molotov's attendance at San Francisco made me wonder whether you give full weight to this factor.

One of the Russian grievances was America's cessation of lend-lease shipments after the end of the European war. In the following selection Secretary of State Byrnes reports Stalin's complaint and the American response.

FROM *Speaking Frankly*

BY *James F. Byrnes*

HE *(Stalin—Ed.)* WAS PARTICULARLY IRRITATED by the manner in which lend-lease shipments had been suspended at the end of the European war. The fact that ships with supplies bound for Russia even had been unloaded indicated to him that the cancellation order was an effort to put pressure on the Soviet Union. This, he declared, was a fundamental mistake and the United States should understand much could be gained from the Russians only if they were approached on a friendly basis.

In the case of the German Navy and merchant fleet, he had sent a message to the President and the Prime Minister suggesting that one-third be turned

James F. Byrnes, *Speaking Frankly* (1947), pp. 62–63. Reprinted by permission of the James F. Byrnes Foundation.

over to the Soviets. Not only had he received no reply, he said, but he had acquired instead an impression that the request was to be rejected.

These complaints were surprising to us at home. They revealed an extreme sensitivity and an amazing degree of almost instinctive suspicion.

Mr. Hopkins forcefully and tactfully presented the position of the United States. As for the German ships, it was our intention that they should be divided equally among the three and we thought that the matter could be settled at the forthcoming meeting of the Big Three. He explained that the cancellation of lend-lease was necessary under the law because lend-lease was authorized only for the purpose of prosecuting the war. With the German war ended and with the Soviet Union not yet a participant in the Japanese war, further shipment could not be justified. The order to unload the ships was the mistake of an official who had nothing to do with policy, and the order had been withdrawn quickly. He reminded the Marshal of how liberally the United States had construed the law in sending foodstuffs and other nonmilitary items to their aid.

Stalin readily acknowledged the accuracy of Hopkins' statement. If proper warning had been given there would have been no feeling about the matter, he said, pointing out that advance notice was important to them because their economy is based on plans. The way in which the shipments had been halted made it impossible for him to express, as he had intended, the great appreciation of the Soviets for the lend-lease aid given to them.

Hopkins told the Marshal that what disturbed him most was the revelation that Stalin believed the United States would use lend-lease as a pressure weapon. The United States, he asserted, is a strong nation and does not need to indulge in such methods. With this, Stalin said he was fully satisfied with our explanation.

It is sometimes alleged that America's use of the atomic bomb to end the war in Asia was politically motivated and is evidence of American suspicion and hostility toward Russia even during the war. In the following selection Norman Cousins and Thomas Finletter argue for such an interpretation.

FROM *A Beginning for Sanity*

BY *Norman Cousins and Thomas K. Finletter*

SUMMING UP, THE scientists expressed their conviction that a unilateral approach to the dropping of the bomb, even apart from moral considerations, however overwhelming, would almost inevitably result in unilateral action by other nations. And unilateralism in an atomic age was not merely a problem but a fatal disease. We would be undermining a possible common ground upon which common controls might later be built. As a corollary, we would be destroying whatever stand we might later decide to take on outlawing the use

Norman Cousins and Thomas K.. Finletter, "A Beginning for Sanity," in *The Saturday Review of Literature*, XXIV (July 15, 1946), pp. 7–8. Reprinted by permission.

of atomic weapons in warfare. It would be naïve to expect other nations to take such a plea seriously in view of our own lack of reticence in dropping the bomb when the war was on the very verge of being won without it.

Why, then, did we drop it? Or, assuming that the use of the bomb was justified, why did we not demonstrate its power in a test under the auspices of the UN, on the basis of which an ultimatum would be issued to Japan—transferring the burden of responsibility to the Japanese themselves?

In speculating upon possible answers to these questions, some facts available since the bombing may be helpful. We now know, for example, that Russia was scheduled to come into the war against Japan by August 8, 1945. Russia had agreed at Yalta to join the fight against Japan ninety days after V-E day. Going after the knockout punch, we bombed Hiroshima on August 5, Nagasaki on August 7. Russia came into the war on August 8, as specified. Japan asked for surrender terms the same day.

Can it be that we were more anxious to prevent Russia from establishing a claim for full participation in the occupation against Japan than we were to think through the implications of unleashing atomic warfare? Whatever the answer, one things seems likely: There was not enough time between July 16, when we knew at New Mexico that the bomb would work, and August 8, the Russian deadline date, for us to have set up the very complicated machinery of a test atomic bombing involving time-consuming problems of area preparations; invitations and arrangements for observers (the probability being that the transportation to the South Pacific would in itself exceed the time limit); issuance of an ultimatum and the conditions of fulfillment, even if a reply limit was set at only forty-eight hours or less—just to mention a few.

No; any test would have been impossible if the purpose was to knock Japan out before Russia came in—or at least before Russia could make anything other than a token of participation prior to a Japanese collapse.

It may be argued that this decision was justified, that it was a legitimate exercise of power politics in a rough-and-tumble world, that we thereby avoided a struggle for authority in Japan similar to what we have experienced in Germany and Italy, that unless we came out of the war with a decisive balance of power over Russia, we would be in no position to checkmate Russian expansion.

There is a dangerous plausibility here—a plausibility as inseparable from the war system of sovereign nations as armaments are from armaments races. It is the plausibility of power politics, of action leading to reaction, reaction leading to counter-reaction, and counter-reaction leading to war; of competitive systems of security rather than of workable world organization. It is a plausibility that rests on the flat assumption that war with Russia is inevitable, and that we should fight it at a time and under terms advantageous to us.

Such "plausibilities" are rejected by those who feel that the big job is to avert the next war, rather than to win it—even assuming that the next war will be worth winning, a somewhat dubious proposition. And they see no way to avert the next war other than through a world organization having the power to back up its decisions by law and relying upon preponderant force as needed.

Such an organization would attempt to dispose of the fear-begetting-fear, provocation-begetting-provocation cycle; and to substitute in its place a central authority from which no member could withdraw or secede under any circumstances. It would automatically deprive potential aggressors of their traditional excuse for aggression—namely, their own encirclement and insecurity—and be strong enough to deal with them should a real threat arise.

The following selection shows the confusion and contradictions in the American government over Russian participation in the Asiatic war. The first section is from Secretary Forrestal's Diary. The second is analysis by its editor Walter Millis.

FROM *The Forrestal Diaries*

TALKED WITH BYRNES [now at Potsdam as American Secretary of State, having succeeded Mr. Stettinius on the conclusion of the San Francisco Conference]. . . . Byrnes said he was most anxious to get the Japanese affair over with before the Russians got in, with particular reference to Dairen and Port Arthur. Once in there, he felt, it would not be easy to get them out. . . .

*   *   *

Evidently on the question of Russian entry into the Pacific war the wheel was now coming full circle. Forrestal was to get a further sidelight on this two years later at a reminiscent luncheon gathering at which General Dwight D. Eisenhower was present. "When President Truman came to Potsdam in the summer of 1945," Forrestal noted, "he told Eisenhower he had as one of his primary objectives that of getting Russia into the Japanese war. Eisenhower begged him at that time not to assume that he had to give anything away to do this, that the Russians were desperately anxious to get into the Eastern war and that in Eisenhower's opinion there was no question but that Japan was already thoroughly beaten. When the President told him at the end of the Conference that he had achieved his objectives and was going home, Eisenhower again remarked that he earnestly hoped the President had not had to make any concessions to get them in."

Still later Forrestal recorded his own conclusion. In a note of June 23, 1947, he observed that the Russians would have to come into the Marshall Plan; "they could no more afford to be out of it than they could have afforded not to join in the war against Japan (fifty divisions could not have kept them *out* of this war)." While Forrestal was mistaken about Soviet participation in the Marshall Plan, it does not follow that his estimate as to the Pacific war was wrong.

Next day, a Sunday, Forrestal wandered through the ruins of Berlin and was as deeply impressed by that staggering scene of destruction as are all who

The Forrestal Diaries, Walter Millis, ed., with the collaboration of E. S. Duffield, (1951), pp. 78–79. Reprinted by permission of Princeton University.

have seen it. He also found that others did not share what would seem to have
been the President's rather optimistic mood about the Russians.

*As the war drew to a close American and British forces had driven far to the east of
the agreed-upon line dividing the Western powers' zone of occupation from the
Soviet Union's zone. In vain Winston Churchill tried to persuade President Truman
not to withdraw. Anti-Communist critics later blamed Roosevelt for making the
agreement and Truman for carrying it out, complaining that it brought Soviet
power into Central Europe and abandoned millions of people to Communism and
Soviet domination.*

FROM *History of the Second World War*
BY *Winston Churchill*

THE STORY OF the agreement about the zones and the arguments for and against
changing them are recorded in an earlier chapter. I feared that any day a decision
might be taken in Washington to yield up this enormous area—400 miles long
and 120 at its greatest depth. It contained many millions of Germans and Czechs.
Its abandonment would place a broader gulf of territory between us and Poland,
and practically end our power to influence her fate. The changed demeanour of
Russia towards us, the constant breaches of the understandings reached at Yalta,
the dart for Denmark, happily frustrated by Montgomery's timely action, the
encroachments in Austria, Marshal Tito's menacing pressure at Trieste, all seemed
to me and my advisers to create an entirely different situation from that in which
the zones of occupation had been prescribed two years earlier. Surely all these
issues should be considered as a whole, and *now* was the time. Now, while the
British and American Armies and Air Forces were still a mighty armed power,
and before they melted away under demobilisation and the heavy claims of the
Japanese war—now, at the very latest, was the time for a general settlement.

A month earlier would have been better. But it was not yet too late. On
the other hand, to give up the whole centre and heart of Germany—nay, the
centre and key-stone of Europe—as an isolated act seemed to me to be a grave
and improvident decision. If it were done at all it could only be as part of a
general and lasting settlement. We should go to Potsdam with nothing to bargain with, and all the prospects of the future peace of Europe might well go by
default. The matter however did not rest with me. Our own retirement to the
occupation frontier was inconsiderable. The American Army was three millions
to our one. All I could do was plead, first, for advancing the date of the meeting of "the Three," and, secondly, when that failed, to postpone the withdrawal
until we could confront all our problems as a whole, together, face to face, and
on equal terms.

Winston S. Churchill, *The Second World War*, vol. 6, *Triumph and Tragedy* (1953), pp. 601–605. Reprinted by permission of Houghton Mifflin Co.

* * *

On June 4 I cabled to the President these words, which few would now dispute:

Prime Minister to President Truman   4 June 45

I am sure you understand the reason why I am anxious for an earlier date, say the 3d or 4th [of July]. I view with profound misgivings the retreat of the American Army to our line of occupation in the central sector, thus bringing Soviet power into the heart of Western Europe and the descent of an iron curtain between us and everything to the eastward. I hoped that this retreat, if it has to be made, would be accompanied by the settlement of many great things which would be the true foundation of world peace. Nothing really important has been settled yet, and you and I will have to bear great responsibility for the future. I still hope therefore that the date will be advanced.

* * *

On June 12 the President replied to my message of June 4.

He said that the tripartite agreement about the occupation of Germany, approved by President Roosevelt after "long consideration and detailed discussion" with me, made it impossible to delay the withdrawal of American troops from the Soviet Zone in order to press the settlement of other problems. The Allied Control Council could not begin to function until they left, and the Military Government exercised by the Allied Supreme Commander should be terminated without delay and divided between Eisenhower and Montgomery. He had been advised, he said, that it would harm our relations with the Soviet to postpone action until our meeting in July, and he accordingly proposed sending a message to Stalin.

* * *

This struck a knell in my breast. But I had no choice but to submit.

On March 5, 1946, Winston Churchill, in a speech at Westminster College in Fulton, Missouri, gave public recognition to the division that had arisen between the former Allies.

FROM *Winston Churchill's Speech at Fulton*

EUROPE DIVIDED

A SHADOW HAS FALLEN upon the scenes so lately lighted by the Allied victory. Nobody knows what Soviet Russia and its Communist international organization intends to do in the immediate future, or what are the limits, if any, to their

"Winston Churchill's Speech at Fulton," in *Vital Speeches of the Day*, XII (March 15, 1946), pp. 331–332. Reprinted by permission of City News Publishing Co.

expansive and proselytizing tendencies. I have a strong admiration and regard for the valiant Russian people and for my war-time comrade, Marshal Stalin. There is sympathy and good will in Britain—and I doubt not here also—toward the peoples of all the Russias and a resolve to persevere through many differences and rebuffs in establishing lasting friendships. We understand the Russians need to be secure on her western frontiers from all renewal of German aggression. We welcome her to her rightful place among the leading nations of the world. Above all we welcome constant, frequent, and growing contacts between the Russian people and our own people on both sides of the Atlantic. It is my duty, however, to place before you certain facts about the present position in Europe—I am sure I do not wish to, but it is my duty, I feel, to present them to you.

From Stettin in the Baltic to Trieste in the Adriatic, an iron curtain has descended across the Continent. Behind that line lie all the capitals of the ancient states of central and eastern Europe. Warsaw, Berlin, Prague, Vienna, Budapest, Belgrade, Bucharest and Sofia, all these famous cities and the populations around them lie in the Soviet sphere and all are subject in one form or another, not only to Soviet influence but to a very high and increasing measure of control from Moscow. Athens alone, with its immortal glories, is free to decide its future at an election under British, American and French observation. The Russian dominated Polish government has been encouraged to make enormous and wrongful inroads upon Germany, and mass expulsions of millions of Germans on a scale grievous and undreamed of are now taking place. The Communist parties, which were very small in all these eastern states of Europe, have been raised to pre-eminence and power far beyond their numbers and are seeking everywhere to obtain totalitarian control. Police governments are prevailing in nearly every case, and so far, except in Czechoslovakia, there is no true democracy. Turkey and Persia are both profoundly alarmed and disturbed at the claims which are made upon them and at the pressure being exerted by the Moscow government. An attempt is being made by the Russians in Berlin to build up a quasi-Communist party in their zone of occupied Germany by showing special favors to groups of Left-Wing German leaders. At the end of the fighting last June, the American and British armies withdrew westward, in accordance with an earlier agreement, to a depth at some points 150 miles on a front of nearly 400 miles to allow the Russians to occupy this vast expanse of territory which the western democracies had conquered. If now the Soviet government tries, by separate action, to build up a pro-Communist Germany in their areas this will cause new serious difficulties in the British and American zones, and will give the defeated Germans the power of putting themselves up to auction between the Soviets and western democracies. Whatever conclusions may be drawn from these facts—and facts they are—this is certainly not the liberated Europe we fought to build up. Nor is it one which contains the essentials of permanent peace.

The safety of the world, ladies and gentlemen, requires a new unity in Europe from which no nation should be permanently outcast.

It is impossible not to comprehend—twice we have seen them drawn by irresistible forces in time to secure the victory but only after frightful slaughter and devastation have occurred. Twice the United States has had to send millions of its young men to fight a war, but now war can find any nation between dusk and dawn. Surely we should work within the structure of the United Nations and in accordance with our charter. That is an open course of policy.

COMMUNIST FIFTH COLUMNS

In front of the iron curtain which lies across Europe are other causes for anxiety. In Italy the Communist party is seriously hampered by having to support the Communist trained Marshal Tito's claims to former Italian territory at the head of the Adriatic. Nevertheless the future of Italy hangs in the balance. Again one cannot imagine a regenerated Europe without a strong France. All my public life I have worked for a strong France and I never lost faith in her destiny, even in the darkest hours. I will not lose faith now. However, in a great number of countries, far from the Russian frontiers and throughout the world, Communist fifth columns are established and work in complete unity and absolute obedience to the directions they receive from the Communist center. Except in the British Commonwealth and in this United States, where Communism is in its infancy, the Communist parties or fifth columns constitute a growing challenge and peril to Christian civilization. These are somber facts for any one to have to recite on the morrow of a victory gained by so much splendid comradeship in arms and in the cause of freedom and democracy, and we should be most unwise not to face them squarely while time remains.

The outlook is also anxious in the Far East and especially in Manchuria. The agreement which was made at Yalta, to which I was a party, was extremely favorable to Soviet Russia, but it was made at a time when no one could say that the German war might not extend all through the summer and autumn of 1945 and when the Japanese war was expected to last for a further eighteen months from the end of the German war. In this country you are all so well informed about the Far East, and such devoted friends of China, that I do not need to expatiate on the situation there.

I have felt bound to portray the shadow which, alike in the West and in the East, falls upon the world. I was a minister at the time of the Versailles treaty and a close friend of Mr. Lloyd George. I did not myself agree with many things that were done, but I have a very vague impression in my mind of that situation, and I find it painful to contrast it with that which prevails now. In those days there were high hopes and unbounded confidence that the wars were over, and that the League of Nations would become all-powerful. I do not see or feel the same confidence or even the same hopes in the haggard world at this time.

WAR NOT INEVITABLE

On the other hand I repulse the idea that a new war is inevitable; still more that it is imminent. It is because I am so sure that our fortunes are in our own hands and that we hold the power to save the future, that I feel the duty to speak out now that I have an occasion to do so. I do not believe that Soviet Russia desires war. What they desire is the fruits of war and the indefinite expansion of their power and doctrines. But what we have to consider here today, while time remains, is the permanent prevention of war and the establishment of conditions of freedom and democracy as rapidly as possible in all countries. Our difficulties and dangers will not be removed by closing our eyes to them. They will not be removed by mere waiting to see what happens; nor will they be relieved by a policy of appeasement. What is needed is a settlement and the longer this is delayed the more difficult it will be and the greater our dangers will become. From what I have seen of our Russian friends and allies during the war, I am convinced that there is nothing they admire so much as strength, and there is nothing for which they have less respect than for military weakness. For that reason the old doctrine of a balance of power is unsound. We cannot afford, if we can help it, to work on narrow margins, offering temptations to a trial of strength. If the western democracies stand together in strict adherence to the principles of the United Nations Charter, their influence for furthering these principles will be immense and no one is likely to molest them. If, however, they become divided or falter in their duty, and if these all-important years are allowed to slip away, then indeed catastrophe may overwhelm us all.

Last time I saw it all coming, and cried aloud to my fellow countrymen and to the world, but no one paid any attention. Up till the year 1933 or even 1935, Germany might have been saved from the awful fate which has overtaken her and we might all have been spared the miseries Hitler let loose upon mankind. There never was a war in all history easier to prevent by timely action than the one which has just desolated such great areas of the globe. It could have been prevented without the firing of a single shot, and Germany might be powerful, prosperous and honored today, but no one would listen and one by one we were all sucked into the awful whirlpool. We surely must not let that happen again. This can only be achieved by reaching now, in 1946, a good understanding on all points with Russia under the general authority of the United Nations Organization and by the maintenance of that good understanding through many peaceful years, by the world instrument, supported by the whole strength of the English-speaking world and all its connections.

Let no man underrate the abiding power of the British Empire and Commonwealth. Because you see the forty-six millions in our island harassed about their food supply, of which they grew only one half, even in war time, or because we have difficulty in restarting our industries and export trade after six years of passionate war effort, do not suppose that we shall not come through these dark years of privation as we have come through the glorious years of agony, or that half a century from now you will not see seventy or eighty millions of Britons spread about the world and united in defense of our traditions, our way of life and of the world causes we and you espouse. If the population of the English-speaking commonwealth be added to that of the United States, with all that such co-operation implies in the air, on the sea and in science and industry, there will be no quivering, precarious balance of power to offer its temptation to ambition or adventure. On the contrary, there will be an overwhelming assurance of security. If we adhere faithfully to the charter of the United Nations and walk forward in sedate and sober strength, seeking no one's land or treasure, or seeking to lay no arbitrary control on the thoughts of men, if all British moral and material forces and convictions are joined with your own in fraternal association, the highroads of the future will be clear, not only for us but for all, not only for our time but for a century to come.

In 1947 Britain informed the United States that it could no longer support the Greeks in their fight against a Communist insurrection supported from the outside. On March 12 of that year President Truman went before Congress and asked for legislation to undertake the support of both Greece and Turkey, which was also in danger. The Truman Doctrine marked a new step in American involvement in world affairs.

Message of the President to the Congress

MR. PRESIDENT, MR. SPEAKER, Members of the Congress of the United States:

The gravity of the situation which confronts the world today necessitates my appearance before a joint session of the Congress.

The foreign policy and the national security of this country are involved.

One aspect of the present situation, which I wish to present to you at this time for your consideration and decision, concerns Greece and Turkey.

The United States has received from the Greek Government an urgent appeal for financial and economic assistance. Preliminary reports from the American Economic Mission now in Greece and reports from the American Ambassador in Greece corroborate the statement of the Greek Government that assistance is imperative if Greece is to survive as a free nation.

I do not believe that the American people and the Congress wish to turn a deaf ear to the appeal of the Greek Government.

Greece is not a rich country. Lack of sufficient natural resources has always forced the Greek people to work hard to make both ends meet. Since 1940 this industrious and peace-loving country has suffered invasion, four years of cruel enemy occupation, and bitter internal strife.

When forces of liberation entered Greece they found that the retreating Germans had destroyed virtually all the railways, roads, port facilities, communications, and merchant marine. More than a thousand villages had been burned. Eighty-five percent of the children were tubercular. Livestock, poultry, and draft animals had almost disappeared. Inflation had wiped out practically all savings.

As a result of these tragic conditions, a military minority, exploiting human want and misery, was able to create political chaos which, until now, has made economic recovery impossible.

Greece is today without funds to finance the importation of those goods which are essential to bare subsistence. Under these circumstances the people of Greece cannot make progress in solving their problems of reconstruction. Greece is in desperate need of financial and economic assistance to enable it to resume purchases of food, clothing, fuel, and seeds. These are indispensable for the subsistence of its people and are obtainable only from abroad. Greece must have help to import the goods necessary to restore internal order and security so essential for economic and political recovery.

The Greek Government has also asked for the assistance of experienced American administrators, economists, and technicians to insure that the financial and other aid given to Greece shall be used effectively in creating a stable and self-sustaining economy and in improving its public administration.

The very existence of the Greek state is today threatened by the terrorist activities of several thousand armed men, led by Communists, who defy the Government's authority at a number of points, particularly along the northern boundaries. A commission appointed by the United Nations Security Council is at present investigating disturbed conditions in northern Greece and alleged border violations along the frontier between Greece on the one hand and Albania, Bulgaria, and Yugoslavia on the other.

Meanwhile, the Greek Government is unable to cope with the situation. The Greek Army is small and poorly equipped. It needs supplies and equipment if it is to restore authority to the Government throughout Greek territory.

Greece must have assistance if it is to become a self-supporting and self-respecting democracy.

The United States must supply that assistance. We have already extended to Greece certain types of relief and economic aid, but these are inadequate.

There is no other country to which democratic Greece can turn.

No other nation is willing and able to provide the necessary support for a democratic Greek Government.

The British Government, which has been helping Greece, can give no further financial or economic aid after March 31. Great Britain finds itself under the necessity of reducing or liquidating its commitments in several parts of the world, including Greece.

We have considered how the United Nations might assist in this crisis. But the situation is an urgent one requiring immediate action, and the United Nations and its related organizations are not in a position to extend help of the kind that is required.

It is important to note that the Greek Government has asked for our aid in utilizing effectively the financial and other assistance we may give to Greece, and in improving its public administration. It is of the utmost importance that we supervise the use of any funds made available to Greece, in such a manner that each dollar spent will count toward making Greece self-supporting, and will help to build an economy in which a healthy democracy can flourish.

No government is perfect. One of the chief virtues of a democracy, however, is that its defects are always visible and under democratic processes can be pointed out and corrected. The Government of Greece is not perfect. Nevertheless it represents 85 percent of the members of the Greek Parliament who were chosen in an election last year. Foreign observers, including 692 Americans, considered this election to be a fair expression of the views of the Greek people.

The Greek Government has been operating in an atmosphere of chaos and extremism. It has made mistakes. The extension of aid by this country does not mean that the United States condones everything that the Greek Government has done or will do. We have condemned in the past, and we condemn now, extremist measures of the right or the left. We have in the past advised tolerance, and we advise tolerance now.

Greece's neighbor, Turkey, also deserves our attention.

The future of Turkey as an independent and economically sound state is clearly no less important to the freedom-loving peoples of the world than the future of Greece. The circumstances in which Turkey finds itself today are considerably different from those of Greece. Turkey has been spared the disasters that have beset Greece. And during the war the United States and Great Britain furnished Turkey with material aid.

Nevertheless, Turkey now needs our support.

Since the war Turkey has sought additional financial assistance from Great Britain and the United States for the purpose of effecting that modernization necessary for the maintenance of its national integrity.

That integrity is essential to the preservation of order in the Middle East.

The British Government has informed us that, owing to its own difficulties, it can no longer extend financial or economic aid to Turkey.

As in the case of Greece, if Turkey is to have the assistance it needs, the United States must supply it. We are the only country able to provide that help.

I am fully aware of the broad implications involved if the United States extends assistance to Greece and Turkey, and I shall discuss these implications with you at this time.

One of the primary objectives of the foreign policy of the United States is the creation of conditions in which we and other nations will be able to work out a way of life free from coercion. This was a fundamental issue in the war with Germany and Japan. Our victory was won over countries which sought to impose their will, and their way of life, upon other nations.

To insure the peaceful development of nations, free from coercion, the United States has taken a leading part in establishing the United Nations. The

United Nations is designed to make possible lasting freedom and independence for all its members. We shall not realize our objectives, however, unless we are willing to help free peoples to maintain their free institutions and their national integrity against aggressive movements that seek to impose upon them totalitarian regimes. This is no more than a frank recognition that totalitarian regimes imposed upon free peoples, by direct or indirect aggression, undermine the foundations of international peace and hence the security of the United States.

The peoples of a number of countries of the world have recently had totalitarian regimes forced upon them against their will. The Government of the United States has made frequent protests against coercion and intimidation in violation of the Yalta agreement, in Poland, Rumania, and Bulgaria. I must also state that in a number of other countries there have been similar developments.

At the present moment in world history nearly every nation must choose between alternative ways of life. The choice is too often not a free one.

One way of life is based upon the will of the majority, and is distinguished by free institutions, representative government, free elections, guaranties, of individual liberty, freedom of speech and religion, and freedom from political oppression.

The second way of life is based upon the will of a minority forcibly imposed upon the majority. It relies upon terror and oppression, a controlled press and radio, fixed elections, and the suppression of personal freedoms.

I believe that it must be the policy of the United States to support free peoples who are resisting attempted subjugation by armed minorities or by outside pressures.

I believe that we must assist free peoples to work out their own destinies in their own way.

I believe that our help should be primarily through economic and financial aid which is essential to economic stability and orderly political processes.

The world is not static, and the *status quo* is not sacred. But we cannot allow changes in the *status quo* in violation of the Charter of the United Nations by such methods as coercion, or by such subterfuges as political infiltration. In helping free and independent nations to maintain their freedom, the United States will be giving effect to the principles of the Charter of the United Nations.

It is necessary only to glance at a map to realize that the survival and integrity of the Greek nation are of grave importance in a much wider situation. If Greece should fall under the control of an armed minority, the effect upon its neighbor, Turkey, would be immediate and serious. Confusion and disorder might well spread throughout the entire Middle East.

Moreover, the disappearance of Greece as an independent state would have a profound effect upon those countries in Europe whose peoples are struggling against great difficulties to maintain their freedoms and their independence while they repair the damages of war.

It would be an unspeakable tragedy if these countries, which have struggled so long against overwhelming odds, should lose that victory for which they sacrificed so much. Collapse of free institutions and loss of independence would be disastrous not only for them but for the world. Discouragement and possibly failure would quickly be the lot of neighboring peoples striving to maintain their freedom and independence.

Should we fail to aid Greece and Turkey in this fateful hour, the effect will be far-reaching to the West as well as to the East.

We must take immediate and resolute action.

I therefore ask the Congress to provide authority for assistance to Greece and Turkey in the amount of $400,000,000 for the period ending June 30, 1948. In requesting these funds, I have taken into consideration the maximum amount of relief assistance which would be furnished to Greece out of the $350,000,000 which I recently requested that the Congress authorize for the prevention of starvation and suffering in countries devastated by the war.

In addition to funds, I ask the Congress to authorize the detail of American civilian and military personnel to Greece and Turkey, at the request of those countries, to assist in the tasks of reconstruction, and for the purpose of supervising the use of such financial and material assistance as may be furnished. I recommend that authority also be provided for the instruction and training of selected Greek and Turkish personnel.

Finally, I ask that Congress provide authority which will permit the speediest and most effective use, in terms of needed commodities, supplies, and equipment, of such funds as may be authorized.

If further funds, or further authority, should be needed for purposes indicated in this message, I shall not hesitate to bring the situation before the Congress. On this subject the Executive and Legislative branches of the Government must work together.

This is a serious course upon which we embark.

I would not recommend it except that the alternative is much more serious.

The United States contributed $341,000,000,000 toward winning World War II. This is an investment in world freedom and world peace.

The assistance that I am recommending for Greece and Turkey amounts to little more than one-tenth of one percent of this investment. It is only common sense that we should safeguard this investment and make sure that it was not in vain.

The seeds of totalitarian regimes are nurtured by misery and want. They spread and grow in the evil soil of poverty and strife. They reach their full growth when the hope of a people for a better life has died.

We must keep that hope alive.

The free peoples of the world look to us for support in maintaining their freedoms.

If we falter in our leadership, we may endanger the peace of the world—and we shall surely endanger the welfare of our own Nation.

Great responsibilities have been placed upon us by the swift movement of events.

I am confident that the Congress will face these responsibilities squarely.

The Russians did not fail to respond to the Truman Doctrine. The following editorial from Izvestia *presents their view.*

Editorial from Izvestia

ON MARCH 12, President Truman addressed a message to the U.S. Congress asking for 400 million dollars to be assigned for urgent aid to Greece and Turkey, and for authority to send to those countries American civil and military personnel, and to provide for the training by Americans of specially picked Greek and Turkish personnel.

Greece, said Truman, was in a desperate economic and political situation. Britain was no longer able to act as trustee for the Greeks. Turkey had requested speedy American aid. Turkey, unlike Greece, had not suffered from the Second World War, but she needed financial aid from Britain and from the U.S.A. in order to carry out that modernisation necessary for maintaining her national integrity. Since the British Government, on account of its own difficulties, was not capable of offering financial or other aid to the Turks, this aid must be furnished by the U.S.A.

Thus Congress was asked to do two "good deeds" at once—to save Greece from internal disorders and to pay for the cost of "modernising" Turkey.

The pathetic appeal of the Tsaldaris Government to the U.S.A. is clear evidence of the bankruptcy of the political regime in Greece. But the matter does not lie solely with the Greek Monarchists and their friends, now cracked up to American Congressmen as the direct descendants of the heroes of Thermopylae: it is well known that the real masters of Greece have been and are the British military authorities.

British troops have been on Greek territory since 1944. On Churchill's initiative, Britain took on herself the responsibility for "stabilising" political conditions in Greece. The British authorities did not confine themselves to perpetuating the rule of the reactionary, anti-democratic forces in Greece, making no scruple in supporting ex-collaborators with the Germans. The entire political and economic activities under a number of short-lived Greek Governments have been carried on under close British control and direction.

Today we can see the results of this policy—complete bankruptcy. British troops failed to bring peace and tranquillity to tormented Greece. The Greek people have been plunged into the abyss of new sufferings, of hunger and poverty. Civil war takes on ever fiercer forms.

Was not the presence of foreign troops on Greek territory instrumental in bringing about this state of affairs? Does not Britain, who proclaimed herself the guardian of Greece, bear responsibility for the bankruptcy of her charge?

The American President's message completely glosses over these questions. The U.S.A. does not wish to criticise Britain, since she herself intends to

"Editorial from Izvestia," in *Izvestia,* March 13, 1947, in William A. Williams, *The Shaping of American Diplomacy* (1956), pp. 1003–1005. Reprinted by permission.

follow the British example. Truman's statement makes it clear that the U.S.A. does not intend to deviate from the course of British policy in Greece. So one cannot expect better results.

The U.S. Government has no intention of acting in the Greek question as one might have expected a member of UNO, concerned about the fate of another member, to act. It is obvious that in Washington they do not wish to take into account the obligations assumed by the U.S. Government regarding UNO. Truman did not even consider it necessary to wait for the findings of the Security Council Commission specially sent to Greece to investigate the situation on the spot.

Truman, indeed, failed to reckon either with the international organisation or with the sovereignty of Greece. What will be left of Greek sovereignty when the "American military and civilian personnel" gets to work in Greece by means of the 250 million dollars brought into that country? The sovereignty and independence of Greece will be the first victims of such singular "defence."

The American arguments for assisting Turkey base themselves on the existence of a threat to the integrity of Turkish territory—though no-one and nothing actually threatens Turkey's integrity. This "assistance" is evidently aimed at putting this country also under U.S. control.

Some American commentators admit this quite openly. Walter Lippmann, for example, frankly points out in the *Herald Tribune* that an American alliance with Turkey would give the U.S.A. a strategic position, incomparably more advantageous than any other, from which power could be wielded over the Middle East.

Commenting on Truman's message to Congress, the *New York Times* proclaims the advent of "the age of American responsibility." Yet what is this responsibility but a smokescreen for expansion? The cry of saving Greece and Turkey from the expansion of the so-called "totalitarian states" is not new. Hitler used to refer to the Bolsheviks when he wanted to open the road for his own conquests. Now they want to take Greece and Turkey under their control, they raise a din about "totalitarian states." This seems all the more attractive since, in elbowing in itself, the U.S.A. is pushing non-totalitarian Britain out of yet another country or two.

We are now witnessing a fresh intrusion of the U.S.A. into the affairs of other states. American claims to leadership in international affairs grow parallel with the growing appetite of the American quarters concerned. But the American leaders, in the new historical circumstances, fail to reckon with the fact that the old methods of the colonisers and diehard politicians have outlived their time and are doomed to failure. In this lies the chief weakness of Truman's message.

Aware that the threat of Communist revolution was greatest where poverty existed, Secretary of State Marshall proposed a plan whereby the United States would help the European nations return to prosperity. Although the iron curtain countries were included in the Marshall Plan, Russian hostility prevented their participation.

The European Recovery Program

REMARKS BY SECRETARY MARSHALL JUNE 5, 1947

I NEED NOT TELL YOU gentlemen that the world situation is very serious. That must be apparent to all intelligent people. I think one difficulty is that the problem is one of such enormous complexity that the very mass of facts presented to the public by press and radio make it exceedingly difficult for the man in the street to reach a clear appraisement of the situation. Furthermore, the people of this country are distant from the troubled areas of the earth and it is hard for them to comprehend the plight and consequent reactions of the long-suffering peoples, and the effect of those reactions on their governments in connection with our efforts to promote peace in the world.

In considering the requirements for the rehabilitation of Europe, the physical loss of life, the visible destruction of cities, factories, mines, and railroads was correctly estimated, but it has become obvious during recent months that this visible destruction was probably less serious than the dislocation of the entire fabric of European economy. For the past 10 years conditions have been highly abnormal. The feverish preparation for war and the more feverish maintenance of the war effort engulfed all aspects of national economies. Machinery has fallen into disrepair or is entirely obsolete. Under the arbitrary and destructive Nazi rule, virtually every possible enterprise was geared into the German war machine. Long-standing commercial ties, private institutions, banks, insurance companies, and shipping companies disappeared, through loss of capital, absorption through nationalization, or by simple destruction. In many countries, confidence in the local currency has been severely shaken. The breakdown of the business structure of Europe during the war was complete. Recovery has been seriously retarded by the fact that two years after the close of hostilities a peace settlement with Germany and Austria has not been agreed upon. But even given a more prompt solution of these difficult problems, the rehabilitation of the economic structure of Europe quite evidently will require a much longer time and greater effort than had been foreseen.

There is a phase of this matter which is both interesting and serious. The farmer has always produced the foodstuffs to exchange with the city dweller for the other necessities of life. This division of labor is the basis of modern civilization. At the present time it is threatened with breakdown. The town and city industries are not producing adequate goods to exchange with the food-producing farmer. Raw materials and fuel are in short supply. Machinery is lacking or worn out. The farmer or the peasant cannot find the goods for sale which he desires to purchase. So the sale of his farm produce for money which he cannot use seems to him an unprofitable transaction. He, therefore, has withdrawn many fields from crop cultivation and is using them for grazing.

"The European Recovery Program," in *A Decade of American Foreign Policy: Basic Documents, 1941–1949*, pp. 1268–1270. Reprinted by permission.

He feeds more grain to stock and finds for himself and his family an ample supply of food, however short he may be on clothing and the other ordinary gadgets of civilization. Meanwhile people in the cities are short of food and fuel. So the governments are forced to use their foreign money and credits to procure these necessities abroad. This process exhausts funds which are urgently needed for reconstruction. Thus a very serious situation is rapidly developing which bodes no good for the world. The modern system of the division of labor upon which the exchange of products is based is in danger of breaking down.

The truth of the matter is that Europe's requirements for the next three or four years of foreign food and other essential products—principally from America—are so much greater than her present ability to pay that she must have substantial additional help or face economic, social, and political deterioration of a very grave character.

The remedy lies in breaking the vicious circle and restoring the confidence of the European people in the economic future of their own countries and of Europe as a whole. The manufacturer and the farmer throughout wide areas must be able and willing to exchange their products for currencies the continuing value of which is not open to question.

Aside from the demoralizing effect on the world at large and the possibilities of disturbances arising as a result of the desperation of the people concerned, the consequences to the economy of the United States should be apparent to all. It is logical that the United States should do whatever it is able to do to assist in the return of normal economic health in the world, without which there can be no political stability and no assured peace. Our policy is directed not against any country or doctrine but against hunger, poverty, desperation, and chaos. Its purpose should be the revival of a working economy in the world so as to permit the emergence of political and social conditions in which free institutions can exist. Such assistance, I am convinced, must not be on a piecemeal basis as various crises develop. Any assistance that this Government may render in the future should provide a cure rather than a mere palliative. Any government that is willing to assist in the task of recovery will find full cooperation, I am sure, on the part of the United States Government. Any government which maneuvers to block the recovery of other countries cannot expect help from us. Furthermore, governments, political parties, or groups which seek to perpetuate human misery in order to profit therefrom politically or otherwise will encounter the opposition of the United States.

It is already evident that, before the United States Government can proceed much further in its efforts to alleviate the situation and help start the European world on its way to recovery, there must be some agreement among the countries of Europe as to the requirements of the situation and the part those countries themselves will take in order to give proper effect to whatever action might be undertaken by this Government. It would be neither fitting nor efficacious for this Government to undertake to draw up unilaterally a program designed to place Europe on its feet economically. This is the business of the Europeans.

The initiative, I think, must come from Europe. The role of this country should consist of friendly aid in the drafting of a European program and of later support of such a program so far as it may be practical for us to do so. The program should be a joint one, agreed to by a number, if not all, European nations.

An essential part of any successful action on the part of the United States is an understanding on the part of the people of America of the character of the problem and the remedies to be applied. Political passion and prejudice should have no part. With foresight, and a willingness on the part of our people to face up to the vast responsibility which history has clearly placed upon our country, the difficulties I have outlined can and will be overcome.

In February 1948 democratic Czechoslovakia experienced a Communist coup d'état that effectively made it a Russian satellite. The following correspondence between President Beněs and the Communist Party clearly indicates the course of events.

FROM *President Beněs' Correspondence with the Presidium of the Communist Party*

Letter from President Beněs to Presidium of the Communist Party

February 24, 1948

You sent me a letter on February 21 in which you express your attitude on a solution of the crisis and ask me to agree with it. Allow me to formulate my own attitude.

I feel fully the great responsibility of this fateful hour on our national and state life. From the beginning of this crisis I have been thinking about the situation as it was forming itself, putting these affairs of ours in connection with world affairs.

I am trying to see clearly not only the present situation but also the causes that led to it and the results that a decision can have. I am aware of the powerful forces through which the situation is being formed.

In a calm, matter of fact, impassionate and objective judgment of the situation I feel, through the common will of various groups of our citizens which turn their attention to me, that the will is expressed to maintain the peace and order and discipline voluntarily accepted to achieve a progressive and really socialist life.

How to achieve this goal? You know my sincerely democratic creed. I cannot but stay faithful to that creed even at this moment because democracy,

"President Beněs' Correspondence with the Presidium of the Communist Party," in *The Strategy and Tactics of World Communism*, supplement III, *The Coup d'Etat in Prague*, House of Representatives Committee on Foreign Affairs, National and International Movements, subcommittee No. 5 Report (1948), pp. 25–27.

according to my belief, is the only reliable and durable basis for a decent and dignified human life.

I insist on parliamentary democracy and parliamentary government as it limits democracy. I state I know very well it is necessary to social and economic content. I built my political work on these principles and cannot—without betraying myself—act otherwise.

The present crisis of democracy here too cannot be overcome but through democratic and parliamentary means. I thus do not overlook your demands. I regard all our political parties associated in the National Front as bearers of political responsibility. We all accepted the principle of the National Front and this proved successful up to the recent time when the crisis began.

This crisis, however, in my opinion, does not deny the principle in itself. I am convinced that on this principle, even in the future, the necessary cooperation of all can be achieved. All disputes can be solved for the benefit of the national and common state of the Czechs and the Slovaks.

I therefore have been in negotiation with five political parties. I have listened to their views and some of them also have been put in writing. These are grave matters and I cannot ignore them.

Therefore, I again have to appeal to all to find a peaceful solution and new successful cooperation through parliamentary means and through the National Front.

That much for the formal side. As far as the personal side is concerned, it is clear to me, as I have said already, that the Prime Minister will be the chairman of the strongest party element, Gottwald.

Finally, on the factual side of this matter it is clear to me that socialism is a way of life desired by an overwhelming part of our nation. At the same time I believe that with socialism a certain measure of freedom and unity is possible and that these are vital principles to all in our national life.

Our nation has struggled for freedom almost throughout its history. History also has shown us where discord can lead.

I beg of you therefore to relive these facts and make them the starting point for our negotiations. Let us all together begin negotiations again for further durable cooperation and let us not allow prolongation of the split of the nation into two quarreling parts.

I believe that a reasonable agreement is possible because it is indispensable.

Reply by the Presidium of the Communist Party to Letter of President Beneš

February 25, 1948

The Presidium of the Central Committee of the Communist Party acknowledges your letter dated February 24 and states again that it cannot enter into negotiations with the present leadership of the National Socialist, People's and Slovak

Democratic Parties because this would not conform to the interests of the unity of the people nor with the interests of further peaceful development of the republic.

Recent events indisputably proved that these three parties no longer represent the interests of the working people of the cities and countryside, that their leaders have betrayed the fundamental ideas of the people's democracy and National Front as they have been stated by the Kosice Government program and that they assumed the position of undermining the opposition.

This was shown again and again in the government, in the Constitutional National Assembly, in the press of these parties, and in actions that, with menacing levity, were organized by their central secretariats against the interests of the working people, against the security of the state, against the alliances of the republic, against state finance, against nationalized industry, against urgent agricultural reforms—in one word, against the whole constructive efforts of our people and against the very foundations, internal and external, of the security of the country.

These parties even got in touch with foreign circles hostile to our people's democratic order and our alliances, and in collaboration with these hostile foreign elements they attempted disruption of the present development of the republic.

This constantly increasing activity was crowned by an attempt to break up the government, an attempt that, as it was proved, should have been accompanied by actions aiming at a putsch.

Massive people's manifestations during the last few days clearly have shown our working people denounce, with complete unity and with indignation, the policy of these parties and ask the creation of a government in which all honest progressive patriots devoted to the republic and the people are represented.

Also among the members of the above-mentioned three parties an increasing amount of indignation can be seen. The members ask for a rebirth of their own parties and the National Front.

In conformity with this powerfully expressed will of the people, the Presidium of the Central Committee of the Communist Party approved the proposals of Premier Klement Gottwald according to which the government will be filled in with prominent representatives of all parties and also big nation-wide organizations.

We stress that a government filled in this way will present itself, with full agreement with the principles of parliamentary democracy, before the Constitutional National Assembly with its program and ask for its approval.

Being convinced that only such a highly constitutional and parliamentary process can guarantee the peaceful development of the republic and at the same time it corresponds to the ideas of a complete majority of the working people, the Presidium of the Central Committee hopes firmly after careful consideration that you will recognize the correctness of its conclusions and will agree with its proposals.

In 1949 the United States abandoned its traditional hostility toward entangling alliances and joined the North Atlantic Treaty Organization to counter Soviet pressure against Western Europe. It was the decisive recognition that the Cold War was to be a lasting reality.

North Atlantic Treaty

THE PARTIES TO THIS TREATY reaffirm their faith in the purposes and principles of the Charter of the United Nations and their desire to live in peace with all peoples and all governments.

They are determined to safeguard the freedom, common heritage and civilization of their peoples, founded on the principles of democracy, individual liberty and the rule of law.

They seek to promote stability and well-being in the North Atlantic area.

They are resolved to unite their efforts for collective defense for the preservation of peace and security.

They therefore agree to this North Atlantic Treaty:

ARTICLE 1

The Parties undertake, as set forth in the Charter of the United Nations, to settle any international disputes in which they may be involved by peaceful means in such a manner that international peace and security, and justice, are not endangered, and to refrain in their international relations from the threat or use of force in any manner inconsistent with the purposes of the United Nations.

ARTICLE 2

The Parties will contribute toward the further development of peaceful and friendly international relations by strengthening their free institutions, by bringing about a better understanding of the principles upon which these institutions are founded, and by promoting conditions of stability and well-being. They will seek to eliminate conflict in their international economic policies and will encourage economic collaboration between any or all of them.

ARTICLE 3

In order more effectively to achieve the objectives of this Treaty, the Parties, separately and jointly, by means of continuous and effective self-help and mutu-

"North Atlantic Treaty," in *A Decade of American Foreign Policy: Basic Documents, 1941–1949* (1950), pp. 1328–1331.

al aid, will maintain and develop their individual and collective capacity to resist armed attack.

ARTICLE 4

The Parties will consult together whenever, in the opinion of any of them, the territorial integrity, political independence or security of any of the Parties is threatened.

ARTICLE 5

The Parties agree that an armed attack against one or more of them in Europe or North America shall be considered an attack against them all; and consequently they agree that, if such an armed attack occurs, each of them, in exercise of the right of individual or collective self-defense recognized by Article 51 of the Charter of the United Nations, will assist the Party or Parties so attacked by taking forthwith, individually and in concert with the other Parties, such action as it deems necessary, including the use of armed force, to restore and maintain the security of the North Atlantic area.

Any such armed attack and all measures taken as a result thereof shall immediately be reported to the Security Council. Such measures shall be terminated when the Security Council has taken the measures necessary to restore and maintain international peace and security.

ARTICLE 6

For the purpose of Article 5 an armed attack on one or more of the Parties is deemed to include an armed attack on the territory of any of the Parties in Europe or North America, on the Algerian departments of France, on the occupation forces of any Party in Europe, on the islands under the jurisdiction of any Party in the North Atlantic area north of the Tropic of Cancer or on the vessels or aircraft in this area of any of the Parties.

ARTICLE 7

This Treaty does not affect, and shall not be interpreted as affecting, in any way the rights and obligations under the Charter of the Parties which are members of the United Nations, or the primary responsibility of the Security Council for the maintenance of international peace and security.

ARTICLE 8

Each Party declares that none of the international engagements now in force between it and any other of the Parties or any third state is in conflict with the provisions of this Treaty, and undertakes not to enter into any international engagement in conflict with this Treaty.

ARTICLE 9

The Parties hereby establishes a council, on which each of them shall be represented, to consider matters concerning the implementation of this Treaty. The council shall be so organized as to be able to meet promptly at any time. The council shall set up such subsidiary bodies as may be necessary; in particular it shall establish immediately a defense committee which shall recommend measures for the implementation of Articles 3 and 5.

ARTICLE 10

The Parties may, by unanimous agreement, invite any other European state in a position to further the principles of this Treaty and to contribute to the security of the North Atlantic area to accede to this Treaty. Any state so invited may become a party to the Treaty by depositing its instrument of accession with the Government of the United States of America. The Government of the United States of America will inform each of the Parties of the deposit of each such instrument of accession.

ARTICLE 11

This Treaty shall be ratified and its provisions carried out by the Parties in accordance with their respective constitutional processes. The instruments of ratification shall be deposited as soon as possible with the Government of the United States of America, which will notify all the other signatories of each deposit. The Treaty shall enter into force between the states which have ratified it as soon as the ratifications of the majority of the signatories, including the ratifications of Belgium, Canada, France, Luxembourg, the Netherlands, the United Kingdom and the United States, have been deposited and shall come into effect with respect to other states on the date of the deposit of their ratifications.

ARTICLE 12

After the Treaty has been in force for ten years, or at any time thereafter, the Parties shall, if any of them so requests, consult together for the purpose of reviewing the Treaty, having regard for the factors then affecting peace and security in the North Atlantic area, including the development of universal as well as regional arrangements under the Charter of the United Nations for the maintenance of international peace and security.

ARTICLE 13

After the Treaty has been in force for twenty years, any Party may cease to be a party one year after its notice of denunciation has been given to the Government of the United States of America, which will inform the Governments of the other Parties of the deposit of each notice of denunciation.

ARTICLE 14

This Treaty, of which the English and French texts are equally authentic, shall be deposited in the archives of the Government of the United States of America. Duly certified copies thereof will be transmitted by that Government to the Governments of the other signatories.

In witness whereof, the undersigned plenipotentiaries have signed this Treaty.

Done at Washington, the fourth day of April, 1949.

3

Russia's Responsibility

One of the first responses to the revisionist writings was made by the American historian and liberal theorist Arthur Schlesinger, Jr.

Origins of the Cold War
BY *Arthur Schlesinger, Jr.*

I

THE COLD WAR in its original form was a presumably mortal antagonism, arising in the wake of the Second World War, between two rigidly hostile blocs, one led by the Soviet Union, the other by the United States. For nearly two somber and dangerous decades this antagonism dominated the fears of mankind; it may even, on occasion, have come close to blowing up the planet. In recent years, however, the once implacable struggle has lost its familiar clarity of outline. With the passing of old issues and the emergence of new conflicts and contestants, there is a natural tendency, especially on the part of the generation which grew up during the Cold War, to take a fresh look at the causes of the great contention between Russia and America.

Some exercises in reappraisal have merely elaborated the orthodoxies promulgated in Washington or Moscow during the boom years of the Cold War. But others, especially in the United States (there are no signs, alas, of this in the Soviet Union), represent what American historians call "revisionism"—that is, a readiness to challenge official explanations. No one should be surprised by this phenomenon. Every war in American history has been followed in due course by skeptical reassessments of supposedly sacred assumptions. So the War of 1812, fought at the time for the freedom of the seas, was in later years ascribed to the expansionist ambitions of Congressional war hawks; so the Mexican War became a slaveholders' conspiracy. So the Civil War has been pronounced a

Arthur Schlesinger, Jr., "Origins of the Cold War," Foreign Affairs, XLIV (October 1967), pp. 22–52. Reprinted by permission of Arthur Schlesinger, Jr.

"needless war," and Lincoln has even been accused of maneuvering the rebel attack on Fort Sumter. So too the Spanish–American War and the First and Second World Wars have, each in its turn, undergone revisionist critiques. It is not to be supposed that the Cold War would remain exempt.

In the case of the Cold War, special factors reinforce the predictable historiographical rhythm. The outburst of polycentrism in the communist empire has made people wonder whether communism was ever so monolithic as official theories of the Cold War supposed. A generation with no vivid memories of Stalinism may see the Russia of the forties in the image of the relatively mild, seedy and irresolute Russia of the sixties. And for this same generation the American course of widening the war in Viet Nam—which even non-revisionists can easily regard as folly—has unquestionably stirred doubts about the wisdom of American foreign policy in the sixties which younger historians may have begun to read back into the forties.

It is useful to remember that, on the whole, past exercises in revisionism have failed to stick. Few historians today believe that the war hawks caused the War of 1812 or the slaveholders the Mexican War, or that the Civil War was needless, or that the House of Morgan brought America into the First World War or that Franklin Roosevelt schemed to produce the attack on Pearl Harbor. But this does not mean that one should deplore the rise of Cold War revisionism.[1] For revisionism is an essential part of the process by which history, through the posing of new problems and the investigation of new possibilities, enlarges its perspectives and enriches its insights.

More than this, in the present context, revisionism expresses a deep, legitimate and tragic apprehension. As the Cold War has begun to lose its purity of definition, as the moral absolutes of the fifties become the moralistic clichés of the sixties, some have begun to ask whether the appalling risks which humanity ran during the Cold War were, after all, necessary and inevitable; whether more restrained and rational policies might not have guided the energies of man from the perils of conflict into the potentialities of collaboration. The fact that such questions are in their nature unanswerable does not mean that it is not right and useful to raise them. Nor does it mean that our sons and daughters are not entitled to an accounting from the generation of Russians and Americans who produced the Cold War.

II

The orthodox American view, as originally set forth by the American government and as reaffirmed until recently by most American scholars, has been that the Cold War was the brave and essential response of free men to communist

---

[1] As this writer somewhat intemperately did in a letter to *The New York Review of Books,* October 20, 1966.

aggression. Some have gone back well before the Second World War to lay open the sources of Russian expansionism. Geopoliticians traced the Cold War to imperial Russian strategic ambitions which in the nineteenth century led to the Crimean War, to Russian penetration of the Balkans and the Middle East and to Russian pressure on Britain's "lifeline" to India. Ideologists traced it to the Communist Manifesto of 1848 ("the violent overthrow of the bourgeoisie lays the foundation for the sway of the proletariat"). Thoughtful observers (a phrase meant to exclude those who speak in Dullese about the unlimited evil of godless, atheistic, militant communism) concluded that classical Russian imperialism and Pan-Slavism, compounded after 1917 by Leninist messianism, confronted the West at the end of the Second World War with an inexorable drive for domination.[2]

The revisionist thesis is very different.[3] In its extreme form, it is that, after

---

[2]Every student of the Cold War must acknowledge his debt to W. H. McNeill's remarkable account, "America, Britain and Russia: Their Cooperation and Conflict, 1941–1946" (New York, 1953) and to the brilliant and indispensable series by Herbert Feis: "Churchill, Roosevelt, Stalin: The War They Waged and the Peace They Sought" (Princeton, 1957); "Between War and Peace: The Potsdam Conference" (Princeton, 1960); and "The Atomic Bomb and the End of World War II" (Princeton, 1966). Useful recent analyses include André Fontaine, "Histoire de la Guerre Froide (2 v., Paris, 1965, 1967); N. A. Graebner, "Cold War Diplomacy, 1945–1960" (Princeton, 1962); L. J. Halle, "The Cold War as History" (London, 1967); M. F. Herz, "Beginnings of the Cold War" (Bloomington, 1966) and W. L. Neumann, "After Victory: Churchill, Roosevelt, Stalin and the Making of the Peace" (New York, 1967).

[3]The fullest statement of this case is to be found in D. F. Fleming's voluminous "The Cold War and Its Origins" (New York, 1961). For a shorter version of this argument, see David Horowitz, "The Free World Colossus" (New York, 1965); the most subtle and ingenious statements come in W. A. Williams' "The Tragedy of American Diplomacy" (rev. ed., New York, 1962) and in Gar Alperowitz's "Atomic Diplomacy: Hiroshima and Potsdam" (New York, 1965) and in subsequent articles and reviews by Mr. Alperowitz in *The New York Review of Books*. The fact that in some aspects the revisionist thesis parallels the official Soviet argument must not, of course, prevent consideration of the case on its merits, nor raise questions about the motives of the writers, all of whom, so far as I know, are independent-minded scholars.

I might further add that all these books, in spite of their ostentatious display of scholarly apparatus, must be used with caution. Professor Fleming, for example, relies heavily on newspaper articles and even columnists. While Mr. Alperowitz bases his case on official documents or authoritative reminiscences, he sometimes twists his material in a most unscholarly way. For example, in describing Ambassador Harriman's talk with President Truman on April 20, 1945, Mr. Alperowitz writes, "He argued that a reconsideration of Roosevelt's policy was necessary" (p. 22, repeated on p. 24). The citation is to p. 70–72 in President Truman's "Years of Decision." What President Truman reported Harriman as saying was the exact opposite: "Before leaving, Harriman took me aside and said, 'Frankly, one of the reasons that made me rush back to Washington was the fear that you did not understand, as I had seen Roosevelt understand, that Stalin is breaking his agreements.'" Similarly, in an appendix (p. 271) Mr. Alperowitz writes that the Hopkins and Davies missions of May 1945 "were opposed by the 'firm' advisers." Actually the Hopkins mission was proposed by Harriman and Charles E. Bohlen, who Mr. Alperowitz elsewhere suggests were the firmest of the firm—and was proposed by them precisely to impress on Stalin the continuity of American policy from Roosevelt to Truman. While the idea that Truman reversed Roosevelt's policy is tempting dramatically, it is a myth. See, for example, the testimony of Anna Rosenberg Hoffman, who lunched with Roosevelt on March 24, 1945, the last day he spent in Washington. After luncheon, Roosevelt was handed a cable. "He read it and became quite angry. He banged his fists on the arms of his wheelchair and said, 'Averell is right; we can't do business with Stalin. He has broken every one of the promises he made at Yalta.' He was very upset and continued in the same vein on the subject."

the death of Franklin Roosevelt and the end of the Second World War, the United States deliberately abandoned the wartime policy of collaboration and, exhilarated by the possession of the atomic bomb, undertook a course of aggression of its own designed to expel all Russian influence from Eastern Europe and to establish democratic-capitalist states on the very border of the Soviet Union. As the revisionists see it, this radically new American policy—or rather this resumption by Truman of the pre-Roosevelt policy of insensate anti-communism—left Moscow no alternative but to take measures in defense of its own borders. The result was the Cold War.

These two views, of course, could not be more starkly contrasting. It is therefore not unreasonable to look again at the half-dozen critical years between June 22, 1941, when Hitler attacked Russia, and July 2, 1947, when the Russians walked out of the Marshall Plan meeting in Paris. Several things should be borne in mind as this reexamination is made. For one thing, we have thought a great deal more in recent years, in part because of writers like Roberta Wohlstetter and T. C. Schelling, about the problems of communication in diplomacy—the signals which one nation, by word or by deed, gives, inadvertently or intentionally, to another. Any honest reappraisal of the origins of the Cold War requires the imaginative leap—which should in any case be as instinctive for the historian as it is prudent for the statesman—into the adversary's viewpoint. We must strive to see how, given Soviet perspectives, the Russians might conceivably have misread our signals, as we must reconsider how intelligently we read theirs.

For another, the historian must not overindulge the man of power in the illusion cherished by those in office that high position carries with it the easy ability to shape history. Violating the statesman's creed, Lincoln once blurted out the truth in his letter of 1864 to A. G. Hodges: "I claim not to have controlled events, but confess plainly that events have controlled me." He was not asserting Tolstoyan fatalism but rather suggesting how greatly events limit the capacity of the statesman to bend history to his will. The physical course of the Second World War—the military operations undertaken, the position of the respective armies at the war's end, the momentum generated by victory and the vacuums created by defeat—all these determined the future as much as the character of individual leaders and the substance of national ideology and purpose.

Nor can the historian forget the conditions under which decisions are made, especially in a time like the Second World War. These were tired, overworked, aging men: in 1945, Churchill was 71 years old, Stalin had governed his country for 17 exacting years, Roosevelt his for 12 years nearly as exacting. During the war, moreover, the importunities of military operations had shoved postwar questions to the margins of their minds. All—even Stalin, behind his screen of ideology—had become addicts of improvisation, relying on authority and virtuosity to conceal the fact that they were constantly surprised by developments. Like Eliza, they leaped from one cake of ice to the next in the effort to reach the other side of the river. None showed certain tactical consistency, or cared much about it; all employed a certain ambiguity to preserve their power to decide big issues; and it is hard to know how to interpret anything any one of them said on any specific occasion. This was partly because, like all princes, they designed their expressions to have particular effects on particular audiences; partly because the entirely genuine intellectual difficulty of the questions they faced made a degree of vacillation and mind-changing eminently reasonable. If historians cannot solve their problems in retrospect, who are they to blame Roosevelt, Stalin and Churchill for not having solved them at the time?

III

Peacemaking after the Second World War was not so much a tapestry as it was a hopelessly raveled and knotted mess of yarn. Yet, for purposes of clarity, it is essential to follow certain threads. One theme indispensable to an understanding of the Cold War is the contrast between two clashing views of world order: the "universalist" view, by which all nations shared a common interest in all the affairs of the world, and the "sphere-of-influence" view, by which each great power would be assured by the other great powers of an acknowledged predominance in its own area of special interest. The universalist view assumed that national security would be guaranteed by an international organization. The sphere-of-interest view assumed that national security would be guaranteed by the balance of power. While in practice these views have by no means been incompatible (indeed, our shaky peace has been based on a combination of the two), in the abstract they involved sharp contradictions.

The tradition of American thought in these matters was universalist—*i.e.* Wilsonian. Roosevelt had been a member of Wilson's subcabinet; in 1920, as candidate for Vice President, he had campaigned for the League of Nations. It is true that, within Roosevelt's infinitely complex mind, Wilsonianism warred with the perception of vital strategic interests he had imbibed from Mahan. Moreover, his temperamental inclination to settle things with fellow princes around the conference table led him to regard the Big Three—or Four—as trustees for the rest of the world. On occasion, as this narrative will show, he was beguiled into flirtation with the sphere-of-influence heresy. But in principle he believed in joint action and remained a Wilsonian. His hope for Yalta, as he told the Congress on his return, was that it would "spell the end of the system of unilateral action, the exclusive alliances, the spheres of influence, the balances of power, and all the other expedients that have been tried for centuries—and have always failed."

Whenever Roosevelt backslid, he had at his side that Wilsonian fundamentalist, Secretary of State Cordell Hull, to recall him to the pure faith. After his visit to Moscow in 1943, Hull characteristically said that, with the Declaration of

Four Nations on General Security (in which America, Russia, Britain and China pledged "united action . . . for the organization and maintenance of peace and security"), "there will no longer be need for spheres of influence, for alliances, for balance of power, or any other of the special arrangements through which, in the unhappy past, the nations strove to safeguard their security or to promote their interests."

Remembering the corruption of the Wilsonian vision by the secret treaties of the First World War, Hull was determined to prevent any sphere-of-influence nonsense after the Second World War. He therefore fought all proposals to settle border questions while the war was still on and, excluded as he largely was from wartime diplomacy, poured his not inconsiderable moral energy and frustration into the promulgation of virtuous and spacious general principles.

In adopting the universalist view, Roosevelt and Hull were not indulging personal hobbies. Sumner Welles, Adolf Berle, Averell Harriman, Charles Bohlen—all, if with a variety of nuances, opposed the sphere-of-influence approach. And here the State Department was expressing what seems clearly to have been the predominant mood of the American people, so long mistrustful of European power politics. The Republicans shared the true faith. John Foster Dulles argued that the great threat to peace after the war would lie in the revival of sphere-of-influence thinking. The United States, he said, must not permit Britain and Russia to revert to these bad old ways; it must therefore insist on American participation in all policy decisions for all territories in the world. Dulles wrote pessimistically in January 1945, "The three great powers which at Moscow agreed upon the 'closest cooperation' about European questions have shifted to a practice of separate, regional responsibility."

It is true that critics, and even friends, of the United States sometimes noted a discrepancy between the American passion for universalism when it applied to territory far from American shores and the preeminence the United States accorded its own interests nearer home. Churchill, seeking Washington's blessing for a sphere-of-influence initiative in Eastern Europe, could not forbear reminding the Americans, "We follow the lead of the United States in South America"; nor did any universalist of record propose the abolition of the Monroe Doctrine. But a convenient myopia prevented such inconsistencies from qualifying the ardency of the universalist faith.

There seem only to have been three officials in the United States Government who dissented. One was the Secretary of War, Henry L. Stimson, a classical balance-of-power man, who in 1944 opposed the creation of a vacuum in Central Europe by the pastoralization of Germany and in 1945 urged "the settlement of all territorial acquisitions in the shape of defense posts which each of these four powers may deem to be necessary for their own safety" in advance of any effort to establish a peacetime United Nations. Stimson considered the claim of Russia to a preferred position in Eastern Europe as not unreasonable: as he told President Truman, "he thought the Russians perhaps were being more realistic than we were in regard to their own security." Such a position for

Russia seemed to him comparable to the preferred American position in Latin America; he even spoke of "our respective orbits." Stimson was therefore skeptical of what he regarded as the prevailing tendency "to hang on to exaggerated views of the Monroe Doctrine and at the same time butt into every question that comes up in Central Europe." Acceptance of spheres of influence seemed to him the way to avoid "a head-on collision."

A second official opponent of universalism was George Kennan, an eloquent advocate from the American Embassy in Moscow of "a prompt and clear recognition of the division of Europe into spheres of influence and of a policy based on the fact of such division." Kennan argued that nothing we could do would possibly alter the course of events in Eastern Europe; that we were deceiving ourselves by supposing that these countries had any future but Russian domination; that we should therefore relinquish Eastern Europe to the Soviet Union and avoid anything which would make things easier for the Russians by giving them economic assistance or by sharing moral responsibility for their actions.

A third voice within the government against universalism was (at least after the war) Henry A. Wallace. As Secretary of Commerce, he stated the sphere-of-influence case with trenchancy in the famous Madison Square Garden speech of September 1946 which led to his dismissal by President Truman:

> On our part, we should recognize that we have no more business in the *political* affairs of Eastern Europe than Russia has in the *political* affairs of Latin America, Western Europe, and the United States. . . . Whether we like it or not, the Russians will try to socialize their sphere of influence just as we try to democratize our sphere of influence. . . . The Russians have no more business stirring up native Communists to political activity in Western Europe, Latin America, and the United States than we have in interfering with the politics of Eastern Europe and Russia.

Stimson, Kennan and Wallace seem to have been alone in the government, however, in taking these views. They were very much minority voices. Meanwhile universalism, rooted in the American legal and moral tradition, overwhelmingly backed by contemporary opinion, received successive enshrinements in the Atlantic Charter of 1941, in the Declaration of the United Nations in 1942 and in the Moscow Declaration of 1943.

IV

The Kremlin, on the other hand, thought *only* of spheres of interest; above all, the Russians were determined to protect their frontiers, and especially their border to the west, crossed so often and so bloodily in the dark course of their history. These western frontiers lacked natural means of defense—no great oceans, rugged mountains, steaming swamps or impenetrable jungles. The history of

Russia had been the history of invasion, the last of which was by now horribly killing up to twenty million of its people. The protocol of Russia therefore meant the enlargement of the area of Russian influence. Kennan himself wrote (in May 1944), "Behind Russia's stubborn expansion lies only the age-old sense of insecurity of a sedentary people reared on an exposed plain in the neighborhood of fierce nomadic peoples," and he called this "urge" a "permanent feature of Russian psychology."

In earlier times the "urge" had produced the tsarist search for buffer states and maritime outlets. In 1939 the Soviet–Nazi pact and its secret protocol had enabled Russia to begin to satisfy in the Baltic states, Karelian, Finland and Poland, part of what it conceived as its security requirements in Eastern Europe. But the "urge" persisted, causing the friction between Russia and Germany in 1940 as each jostled for position in the area which separated them. Later it led to Molotov's new demands on Hitler in November 1940—a free hand in Finland, Soviet predominance in Rumania and Bulgaria, bases in the Dardanelles—the demands which convinced Hitler that he had no choice but to attack Russia. Now Stalin hoped to gain from the West what Hitler, a closer neighbor, had not dared yield him.

It is true that, so long as Russian survival appeared to require a second front to relieve the Nazi pressure, Moscow's demand for Eastern Europe was a little muffled. Thus the Soviet government adhered to the Atlantic Charter (though with a significant if obscure reservation about adapting its principles to "the circumstances, needs, and historic peculiarities of particular countries"). Thus it also adhered to the Moscow Declaration of 1943, and Molotov then, with his easy mendacity, even denied that Russia had any desire to divide Europe into spheres of influence. But this was guff, which the Russians were perfectly willing to ladle out if it would keep the Americans, and especially Secretary Hull (who made a strong personal impression at the Moscow conference), happy. "A declaration," as Stalin once observed to Eden, "I regard as algebra, but an agreement as practical arithmetic. I do not wish to decry algebra, but I prefer practical arithmetic."

The more consistent Russian purpose was revealed when Stalin offered the British a straight sphere-of-influence deal at the end of 1941. Britain, he suggested, should recognize the Russian absorption of the Baltic states, part of Finland, eastern Poland and Bessarabia; in return, Russia would support any special British need for bases or security arrangements in Western Europe. There was nothing specifically communist about these ambitions. If Stalin achieved them, he would be fulfilling an age-old dream of the tsars. The British reaction was mixed. "Soviet policy is amoral," as Anthony Eden noted at the time; "United States policy is exaggeratedly moral, at least where non-American interests are concerned." If Roosevelt was a universalist with occasional leanings toward spheres of influence and Stalin was a sphere-of-influence man with occasional gestures toward universalism, Churchill seemed evenly poised between the familiar realism of the balance of power, which he had so long recorded as an historian and manipulated as a statesman, and the hope that there must be some better way of doing things. His 1943 proposal of a world organization divided into regional councils represented an effort to blend universalist and sphere-of-interest conceptions. His initial rejection of Stalin's proposal in December 1941 as "directly contrary to the first, second and third articles of the Atlantic Charter" thus did not spring entirely from a desire to propitiate the United States. On the other hand, he had himself already reinterpreted the Atlantic Charter as applying only to Europe (and thus not to the British Empire), and he was, above all, an empiricist who never believed in sacrificing reality on the altar of doctrine.

So in April 1942 he wrote Roosevelt that "the increasing gravity of the war" had led him to feel that the Charter "ought not to be construed so as to deny Russia the frontiers she occupied when Germany attacked her." Hull, however, remained fiercely hostile to the inclusion of territorial provisions in the Anglo–Russian treaty; the American position, Eden noted, "chilled me with Wilsonian memories." Though Stalin complained that it looked "as if the Atlantic Charter was directed against the U.S.S.R.," it was the Russian season of military adversity in the spring of 1942, and he dropped his demands.

He did not, however, change his intentions. A year later Ambassador Standley could cable Washington from Moscow: "In 1918 Western Europe attempted to set up a *cordon sanitaire* to protect it from the influence of bolshevism. Might not now the Kremlin envisage the formation of a belt of pro-Soviet states to protect it from the influences of the West?" It well might; and that purpose became increasingly clear as the war approached its end. Indeed, it derived sustenance from Western policy in the first area of liberation.

The unconditional surrender of Italy in July 1943 created the first major test of the Western devotion to universalism. America and Britain, having won the Italian war, handled the capitulation, keeping Moscow informed at a distance. Stalin complained:

> The United States and Great Britain made agreements but the Soviet Union received information about the results . . . just as a passive third observer. I have to tell you that it is impossible to tolerate the situation any longer. I propose that the [tripartite military-political commission] be established and that Sicily be assigned . . . as its place of residence.

Roosevelt, who had no intention of sharing the control of Italy with the Russians, suavely replied with the suggestion that Stalin send an officer "to General Eisenhower's headquarters in connection with the commission." Unimpressed, Stalin continued to press for a tripartite body; but his Western allies were adamant in keeping the Soviet Union off the Control Commission for Italy, and the Russians in the end had to be satisfied with a seat, along with minor Allied states, on a meaningless Inter-Allied Advisory Council. Their acquiescence in this was doubtless not unconnected with a desire to establish precedents for Eastern Europe.

Teheran in December 1943 marked the high point of three-power collaboration. Still, when Churchill asked about Russian territorial interests, Stalin
replied a little ominously, "There is no need to speak at the present time about
any Soviet desires, but when the time comes we will speak." In the next weeks,
there were increasing indications of a Soviet determination to deal unilaterally
with Eastern Europe—so much so that in early February 1944 Hull cabled
Harriman in Moscow:

> Matters are rapidly approaching the point where the Soviet Government will have
> to choose between the development and extension of the foundation of
> international cooperation as the guiding principle of the postwar world as against
> the continuance of a unilateral and arbitrary method of dealing with its special
> problems even though these problems are admittedly of more direct interest to the
> Soviet Union than to other great powers.

As against this approach, however, Churchill, more tolerant of sphere-of-
influence deviations, soon proposed that, with the impending liberation of the
Balkans, Russia should run things in Rumania and Britain in Greece. Hull
strongly opposed this suggestion but made the mistake of leaving Washington
for a few days; and Roosevelt, momentarily free from his Wilsonian conscience,
yielded to Churchill's plea for a three-months' trial. Hull resumed the fight on
his return, and Churchill postponed the matter.

The Red Army continued its advance into Eastern Europe. In August the
Polish Home Army, urged on by Polish-language broadcasts from Moscow, rose
up against the Nazis in Warsaw. For 63 terrible days, the Poles fought valiantly
on, while the Red Army halted on the banks of the Vistula a few miles away,
and in Moscow Stalin for more than half this time declined to cooperate with
the Western effort to drop supplies to the Warsaw Resistance. It appeared a calculated Soviet decision to let the Nazis slaughter the anti-Soviet Polish underground; and, indeed, the result was to destroy any substantial alternative to a
Soviet solution in Poland. The agony of Warsaw caused the most deep and genuine moral shock in Britain and America and provoked dark forebodings about
Soviet postwar purposes.

Again history enjoins the imaginative leap in order to see things for a
moment from Moscow's viewpoint. The Polish question, Churchill would say at
Yalta, was for Britain a question of honor. "It is not only a question of honor for
Russia," Stalin replied, "but one of life and death. . . . Throughout history
Poland had been the corridor for attack on Russia." A top postwar priority for
any Russian régime must be to close that corridor. The Home Army was led by
anti-communists. It clearly hoped by its action to forestall the Soviet occupation
of Warsaw and, in Russian eyes, to prepare the way for an anti-Russian Poland.
In addition, the uprising from a strictly operational viewpoint was premature.
The Russians, it is evident in retrospect, had real military problems at the
Vistula. The Soviet attempt in September to send Polish units from the Red
Army across the river to join forces with the Home Army was a disaster. Heavy

German shelling thereafter prevented the ferrying of tanks necessary for an assault on the German position. The Red Army itself did not take Warsaw for another three months. None the less, Stalin's indifference to the human tragedy, his effort to blackmail the London Poles during the ordeal, his sanctimonious opposition during five precious weeks to aerial resupply, the invariable coldness of his explanations ("the Soviet command has come to the conclusion that it must dissociate itself from the Warsaw adventure") and the obvious political benefit to the Soviet Union from the destruction of the Home Army—all these had the effect of suddenly dropping the mask of wartime comradeship and displaying to the West the hard face of Soviet policy. In now pursuing what he grimly regarded as the minimal requirements for the postwar security of his country, Stalin was inadvertently showing the irreconcilability of both his means and his ends with the Anglo–American conception of the peace.

Meanwhile Eastern Europe presented the Alliance with still another crisis that same September. Bulgaria, which was not at war with Russia, decided to surrender to the Western Allies while it still could; and the English and Americans at Cairo began to discuss armistice terms with Bulgarian envoys. Moscow, challenged by what it plainly saw as a Western intrusion into its own zone of vital interest, promptly declared war on Bulgaria, took over the surrender negotiations and, invoking the Italian precedent, denied its Western Allies any role in the Bulgarian Control Commission. In a long and thoughtful cable, Ambassador Harriman meditated on the problems of communication with the Soviet Union. "Words," he reflected, "have a different connotation to the Soviets than they have to us. When they speak of insisting on 'friendly governments' in their neighboring countries, they have in mind something quite different from what we would mean." The Russians, he surmised, really believed that Washington accepted "their position that although they would keep us informed they had the right to settle their problems with their western neighbors unilaterally." But the Soviet position was still in flux: "the Soviet Government is not one mind." The problem, as Harriman had earlier told Harry Hopkins, was "to strengthen the hands of those around Stalin who want to play the game along our lines." The way to do this, he now told Hull, was to

> be understanding of their sensitivity, meet them much more than half way, encourage them and support them wherever we can, and yet oppose them promptly with the greatest firmness where we see them going wrong. . . . The only way we can eventually come to an understanding with the Soviet Union on the question of noninterference in the internal affairs of other countries is for us to take a definite interest in the solution of the problems of each individual country as they arise.

As against Harriman's sophisticated universalist strategy, however, Churchill, increasingly fearful of the consequences of unrestrained competition in Eastern Europe, decided in early October to carry his sphere-of-influence proposal directly to Moscow. Roosevelt was at first content to have Churchill speak for him too and even prepared a cable to that effect. But Hopkins, a more rigorous universalist, took it upon himself to stop the cable and warn Roosevelt of its possible implications. Eventually Roosevelt sent a message to Harriman in Moscow emphasizing that he expected to "retain complete freedom of action after this conference is over." It was now that Churchill quickly proposed—and Stalin as quickly accepted—the celebrated division of southeastern Europe: ending (after further haggling between Eden and Molotov) with 90 percent Soviet predominance in Rumania, 80 percent in Bulgaria and Hungary, fifty-fifty in Jugoslavia, 90 percent British predominance in Greece.

Churchill in discussing this with Harriman used the phrase "spheres of influence." But he insisted that these were only "immediate wartime arrangements" and received a highly general blessing from Roosevelt. Yet, whatever Churchill intended, there is reason to believe that Stalin construed the percentages as an agreement, not a declaration; as practical arithmetic, not algebra. For Stalin, it should be understood, the sphere-of-influence idea did not mean that he would abandon all efforts to spread communism in some other nation's sphere; it did mean that, if he tried this and the other side cracked down, he could not feel he had serious cause for complaint. As Kennan wrote to Harriman at the end of 1944:

> As far as border states are concerned the Soviet government has never ceased to think in terms of spheres of interest. They expect us to support them in whatever action they wish to take in those regions, regardless of whether that action seems to us or to the rest of the world to be right or wrong. . . . I have no doubt that this position is honestly maintained on their part, and that they would be equally prepared to reserve moral judgment on any actions which we might wish to carry out, i.e., in the Caribbean area.

In any case, the matter was already under test a good deal closer to Moscow than the Caribbean. The communist-dominated resistance movement in Greece was in open revolt against the effort of the Papandreou government to disarm and disband the guerrillas (the same Papandreou whom the Greek colonels have recently arrested on the claim that he is a tool of the communists). Churchill now called in British Army units to crush the insurrection. This action produced a storm of criticism in his own country and in the United States; the American Government even publicly dissociated itself from the intervention, thereby emphasizing its detachment from the sphere-of-influence deal. But Stalin, Churchill later claimed, "Adhered strictly and faithfully to our agreement of October, and during all the long weeks of fighting the Communists in the streets of Athens not one word of reproach came from *Pravda* or *Izvestia,*" though there is no evidence that he tried to call off the Greek communists. Still, when the communist rebellion later broke out again in Greece, Stalin told Kardelj and Djilas of Jugoslavia in 1948, "The uprising in Greece must be stopped, and as quickly as possible."

No one, of course, can know what really was in the minds of the Russian leaders. The Kremlin archives are locked; of the primary actors, only Molotov

survives, and he has not yet indicated any desire to collaborate with the
Columbia Oral History Project. We do know that Stalin did not wholly surrender
to sentimental illusion about his new friends. In June 1944, on the night before
the landings in Normandy, he told Djilas that the English "find nothing sweeter
than to trick their allies. . . . And Churchill? Churchill is the kind who, if you
don't watch him, will slip a kopeck out of your pocket. Yes, a kopeck out of
your pocket! . . . Roosevelt is not like that. He dips in his hand only for bigger
coins." But whatever his views of his colleagues it is not unreasonable to suppose that Stalin would have been satisfied at the end of the war to secure what
Kennan has called "a protective glacis along Russia's western border," and that,
in exchange for a free hand in Eastern Europe, he was prepared to give the
British and Americans equally free hands in their zones of vital interest, including in nations as close to Russia as Greece (for the British) and, very probably—
or at least so the Jugoslavs believe—China (for the United States). In other
words, his initial objectives were very probably not world conquest but Russian
security.

V

It is now pertinent to inquire why the United States rejected the idea of stabilizing the world by division into spheres of influence and insisted on an East
European strategy. One should warn against rushing to the conclusion that it
was all a row between hard-nosed, balance-of-power realists and starry-eyed
Wilsonians. Roosevelt, Hopkins, Welles, Harriman, Bohlen, Berle, Dulles and
other universalists were tough and serious men. Why then did they rebuff the
sphere-of-influence solution?

    The first reason is that they regarded this solution as containing within
itself the seeds of a third world war. The balance-of-power idea seemed inherently unstable. It had always broken down in the past. It held out to each
power the permanent temptation to try to alter the balance in its own favor, and
it built this temptation into the international order. It would turn the great powers of 1945 away from the objective of concerting common policies toward
competition for postwar advantage. As Hopkins told Molotov at Teheran, "The
President feels it essential to world peace that Russia, Great Britain and the
United States work out this control question in a manner which will not start
each of the three powers arming against the others." "The greatest likelihood of
eventual conflict," said the Joint Chiefs of Staff in 1944 (the only conflict which
the J.C.S., in its wisdom, could then glimpse "in the foreseeable future" was
between Britain and Russia), ". . . would seem to grow out of either nation ini-
tiating attempts to build up its strength, by seeking to attach to herself parts of
Europe to the disadvantage and possible danger of her potential adversary."
The Americans were perfectly ready to acknowledge that Russia was entitled to
convincing assurance of her national security—but not this way. "I could sym-

pathize fully with Stalin's desire to protect his western borders from future attack," as Hull put it. "But I felt that this security could best be obtained through a strong postwar peace organization."

Hull's remark suggests the second objection: that the sphere-of-influence approach would, in the words of the State Department in 1945, "militate against the establishment and effective functioning of a broader system of general security in which all countries will have their part." The United Nations, in short, was seen as the alternative to the balance of power. Nor did the universalists see any necessary incompatibility between the Russian desire for "friendly governments" on its frontier and the American desire for self-determination in Eastern Europe. Before Yalta the State Department judged the general mood of Europe as "to the left and strongly in favor of far-reaching economic and social reforms, but not, however, in favor of a left-wing totalitarian regime to achieve these reforms." Governments in Eastern Europe could be sufficiently to the left "to allay Soviet suspicions" but sufficiently representative "of the center and *petit bourgeois* elements" not to seem a prelude to communist dictatorship. The American criteria were therefore that the government "should be dedicated to the preservation of civil liberties" and "should favor social and economic reforms." A string of New Deal states—of Finlands and Czechoslovakias— seemed a reasonable compromise solution.

Third, the universalists feared that the sphere-of-influence approach would be what Hull termed "a haven for the isolationists," who would advocate America's participation in Western Hemisphere affairs on condition that it did not participate in European or Asian affairs. Hull also feared that spheres of interest would lead to "closed trade areas or discriminatory systems" and thus defeat his cherished dream of a low-tariff, freely trading world.

Fourth, the sphere-of-interest solution meant the betrayal of the principles for which the Second World War was being fought—the Atlantic Charter, the Four Freedoms, the Declaration of the United Nations. Poland summed up the problem. Britain, having gone to war to defend the independence of Poland from the Germans, could not easily conclude the war by surrendering the independence of Poland to the Russians. Thus, as Hopkins told Stalin after Roosevelt's death in 1945, Poland had "become the symbol of our ability to work out problems with the Soviet Union." Nor could American liberals in general watch with equanimity while the police state spread into countries which, if they had mostly not been real democracies, had mostly not been tyrannies either. The execution in 1943 of Ehrlich and Alter, the Polish socialist trade union leaders, excited deep concern. "I have particularly in mind," Harriman cabled in 1944, "objection to the institution of secret police who may become involved in the persecution of persons of truly democratic convictions who may not be willing to conform to Soviet methods."

Fifth, the sphere-of-influence solution would create difficult domestic problems in American politics. Roosevelt was aware of the six million or more Polish votes in the 1944 election; even more acutely, he was aware of the broader and deeper attack which would follow if, after going to war to stop the Nazi conquest of Europe, he permitted the war to end with the communist conquest of Eastern Europe. As Archibald MacLeish, then Assistant Secretary of State for Public Affairs, warned in January 1945, "The wave of disillusionment which has distressed us in the last several weeks will be increased if the impression is permitted to get abroad that potentially totalitarian provisional governments are to be set up without adequate safeguards as to the holding of free elections and the realization of the principles of the Atlantic Charter." Roosevelt believed that no administration could survive which did not try everything short of war to save Eastern Europe, and he was the supreme American politician of the century.

Sixth, if the Russians were allowed to overrun Eastern Europe without argument, would that satisfy them? Even Kennan, in a dispatch of May 1944, admitted that the "urge" had dreadful potentialities: "If initially successful, will it know where to stop? Will it not be inexorably carried forward, by its very nature, in a struggle to reach the whole—to attain complete mastery of the shores of the Atlantic and the Pacific?" His own answer was that there were inherent limits to the Russian capacity to expand—"that Russia will not have an easy time in maintaining the power which it has seized over other people in Eastern and Central Europe unless it receives both moral and material assistance from the West." Subsequent developments have vindicated Kennan's argument. By the late forties, Jugoslavia and Albania, the two East European states farthest from the Soviet Union and the two in which communism was imposed from within rather than from without, had declared their independence of Moscow. But, given Russia's success in maintaining centralized control over the international communist movement for a quarter of a century, who in 1944 could have had much confidence in the idea of communist revolts against Moscow?

Most of those involved therefore rejected Kennan's answer and stayed with his question. If the West turned its back on Eastern Europe, the higher probability, in their view, was that the Russians would use their security zone, not just for defensive purposes, but as a springboard from which to mount an attack on Western Europe, now shattered by war, a vacuum of power awaiting its master. "If the policy is accepted that the Soviet Union has a right to penetrate her immediate neighbors for security," Harriman said in 1944, "penetration of the next immediate neighbors becomes at a certain time equally logical." If a row with Russia were inevitable, every consideration of prudence dictated that it should take place in Eastern rather than Western Europe.

Thus idealism and realism joined in opposition to the sphere-of-influence solution. The consequence was a determination to assert an American interest in the postwar destiny of all nations, including those of Eastern Europe. In the message which Roosevelt and Hopkins drafted after Hopkins had stopped Roosevelt's initial cable authorizing Churchill to speak for the United States at the Moscow meeting of October 1944, Roosevelt now said, "There is in this global war literally no question, either military or political, in which the United

States is not interested." After Roosevelt's death Hopkins repeated the point to Stalin: "The cardinal basis of President Roosevelt's policy which the American people had fully supported had been the concept that the interests of the U.S. were worldwide and not confined to North and South America and the Pacific Ocean."

VI

For better or worse, this was the American position. It is now necessary to attempt the imaginative leap and consider the impact of this position on the leaders of the Soviet Union who, also for better or for worse, had reached the bitter conclusion that the survival of their country depended on their unchallenged control of the corridors through which enemies had so often invaded their homeland. They could claim to have been keeping their own side of the sphere-of-influence bargain. Of course, they were working to capture the resistance movements of Western Europe; indeed, with the appointment of Oumansky as Ambassador to Mexico they were even beginning to enlarge underground operations in the Western Hemisphere. But, from their viewpoint, if the West permitted this, the more fools they; and, if the West stopped it, it was within their right to do so. In overt political matters the Russians were scrupulously playing the game. They had watched in silence while the British shot down communists in Greece. In Jugoslavia Stalin was urging Tito (as Djilas later revealed) to keep King Peter. They had not only acknowledged Western preeminence in Italy but had recognized the Badoglio régime; the Italian Communists had even voted (against the Socialists and the Liberals) for the renewal of the Lateran Pacts.

They would not regard anti-communist action in a Western zone as a *casus belli;* and they expected reciprocal license to assert their own authority in the East. But the principle of self-determination was carrying the United States into a deeper entanglement in Eastern Europe than the Soviet Union claimed as a right (whatever it was doing underground) in the affairs of Italy, Greece or China. When the Russians now exercised in Eastern Europe the same brutal control they were prepared to have Washington exercise in the American sphere of influence, the American protests, given the paranoia produced alike by Russian history and Leninist ideology, no doubt seemed not only an act of hypocrisy but a threat to security. To the Russians, a stroll into the neighborhood easily became a plot to burn down the house: when, for example, damaged American planes made emergency landings in Poland and Hungary, Moscow took this as attempts to organize the local resistance. It is not unusual to suspect one's adversary of doing what one is already doing oneself. At the same time, the cruelty with which the Russians executed their idea of spheres of influence—in a sense, perhaps, an unwitting cruelty, since Stalin treated the

East Europeans no worse than he had treated the Russians in the thirties—discouraged the West from accepting the equation (for example, Italy = Rumania) which seemed so self-evident to the Kremlin.

So Moscow very probably, and not unnaturally, perceived the emphasis on self-determination as a systematic and deliberate pressure on Russia's western frontiers. Moreover, the restoration of capitalism to countries freed at frightful cost by the Red Army no doubt struck the Russians as the betrayal of the principles for which *they* were fighting. "That they, the victors," Isaac Deutscher has suggested, "should now preserve an order from which they had experienced nothing but hostility, and could expect nothing but hostility . . . would have been the most miserable anti-climax to their great 'war of liberation.'" By 1944 Poland was the critical issue; Harriman later said that "under instructions from President Roosevelt, I talked about Poland with Stalin more frequently than any other subject." While the West saw the point of Stalin's demand for a "friendly government" in Warsaw, the American insistence on the sovereign virtues of free elections (ironically in the spirit of the 1917 Bolshevik decree of peace, which affirmed "the right" of a nation "to decide the forms of its state existence by a free vote, taken after the complete evacuation of the incorporating or, generally, of the stronger nation") created an insoluble problem in those countries, like Poland (and Rumania), where free elections would almost certainly produce anti-Soviet governments.

The Russians thus may well have estimated the Western pressures as calculated to encourage their enemies in Eastern Europe and to defeat their own minimum objective of a protective glacis. Everything still hung, however, on the course of military operations. The wartime collaboration had been created by one thing, and one thing alone: the threat of Nazi victory. So long as this threat was real, so was the collaboration. In late December 1944, von Rundstedt launched his counter-offensive in the Ardennes. A few weeks later, when Roosevelt, Churchill and Stalin gathered in the Crimea, it was in the shadow of this last considerable explosion of German power. The meeting at Yalta was still dominated by the mood of war.

Yalta remains something of an historical perplexity—less, from the perspective of 1967, because of a mythical American deference to the sphere-of-influence thesis than because of the documentable Russian deference to the universalist thesis. Why should Stalin in 1945 have accepted the Declaration on Liberated Europe and an agreement on Poland pledging that "the three governments will jointly" act to assure "free elections of governments responsive to the will of the people"? There are several probable answers: that the war was not over and the Russians still wanted the Americans to intensify their military effort in the West; that one clause in the Declaration premised action on "the opinion of the three governments" and thus implied a Soviet veto, though the Polish agreement was more definite; most of all that the universalist algebra of the Declaration was plainly in Stalin's mind to be construed in terms of the practical arithmetic of his sphere-of-influence agreement with Churchill the previous October. Stalin's assurance to Churchill at Yalta that a proposed Russian amendment to the Declaration would not apply to Greece makes it clear that Roosevelt's pieties did not, in Stalin's mind, nullify Churchill's percentages. He could well have been strengthened in this supposition by the fact that *after* Yalta, Churchill himself repeatedly reasserted the terms of the October agreement as if he regarded it, despite Yalta, as controlling.

Harriman still had the feeling before Yalta that the Kremlin had "two approaches to their postwar policies" and that Stalin himself was "of two minds." One approach emphasized the internal reconstruction and development of Russia; the other its external expansion. But in the meantime the fact which dominated all political decisions—that is, the war against Germany—was moving into its final phase. In the weeks after Yalta, the military situation changed with great rapidity. As the Nazi threat declined, so too did the need for cooperation. The Soviet Union, feeling itself menaced by the American idea of self-determination and the borderlands diplomacy to which it was leading, skeptical whether the United Nations would protect its frontiers as reliably as its own domination in Eastern Europe, began to fulfill its security requirements unilaterally.

In March Stalin expressed his evaluation of the United Nations by rejecting Roosevelt's plea that Molotov come to the San Francisco conference, if only for the opening sessions. In the next weeks the Russians emphatically and crudely worked their will in Eastern Europe, above all in the test country of Poland. They were ignoring the Declaration on Liberated Europe, ignoring the Atlantic Charter, self-determination, human freedom and everything else the Americans considered essential for a stable peace. "We must clearly recognize," Harriman wired Washington a few days before Roosevelt's death, "that the Soviet program is the establishment of totalitarianism, ending personal liberty and democracy as we know and respect it."

At the same time, the Russians also began to mobilize communist resources in the United States itself to block American universalism. In April 1945 Jacques Duclos, who had been the Comintern official responsible for the Western communist parties, launched in *Cahiers du Communisme* an uncompromising attack on the policy of the American Communist Party. Duclos sharply condemned the revisionism of Earl Browder, the American Communist leader, as "expressed in the concept of a long-term class peace in the United States, of the possibility of the suppression of the class struggle in the postwar period and of establishment of harmony between labor and capital." Browder was specifically rebuked for favoring the "self-determination" of Europe "west of the Soviet Union" on a bourgeois-democratic basis. The excommunication of Browderism was plainly the Politburo's considered reaction to the impending defeat of Germany; it was a signal to the communist parties of the West that they should recover their identity; it was Moscow's alert to communists everywhere that they should prepare for new policies in the postwar world.

The Duclos piece obviously could not have been planned and written much later than the Yalta conference—that is, well before a number of events which revisionists now cite in order to demonstrate American responsibility for the Cold War: before Allen Dulles, for example, began to negotiate the surrender of the German armies in Italy (the episode which provoked Stalin to charge Roosevelt with seeking a separate peace and provoked Roosevelt to denounce the "vile misrepresentations" of Stalin's informants); well before Roosevelt died; many months before the testing of the atomic bomb; even more months before Truman ordered that the bomb be dropped on Japan. William Z. Foster, who soon replaced Browder as the leader of the American Communist Party and embodied the new Moscow line, later boasted of having said in January 1944, "A post-war Roosevelt administration would continue to be, as it is now, an imperialist government." With ancient suspicions revived by the American insistence on universalism, this was no doubt the conclusion which the Russians were reaching at the same time. The Soviet canonization of Roosevelt (like their present-day canonization of Kennedy) took place after the American President's death.

The atmosphere of mutual suspicion was beginning to rise. In January 1945 Molotov formally proposed that the United States grant Russia a $6 billion credit for postwar reconstruction. With characteristic tact he explained that he was doing this as a favor to save America from a postwar depression. The proposal seems to have been diffidently made and diffidently received. Roosevelt requested that the matter "not be pressed further" on the American side until he had a chance to talk with Stalin; but the Russians did not follow it up either at Yalta in February (save for a single glancing reference) or during the Stalin–Hopkins talks in May or at Potsdam. Finally the proposal was renewed in the very different political atmosphere of August. This time Washington inexplicably mislaid the request during the transfer of the records of the Foreign Economic Administration to the State Department. It did not turn up again until March 1946. Of course this was impossible for the Russians to believe; it is hard enough even for those acquainted with the capacity of the American government for incompetence to believe; and it only strengthened Soviet suspicions of American purposes.

The American credit was one conceivable form of Western contribution to Russian reconstruction. Another was lend-lease, and the possibility of reconstruction aid under the lend-lease protocol had already been discussed in 1944. But in May 1945 Russia, like Britain, suffered from Truman's abrupt termination of lend-lease shipments—"unfortunate and even brutal," Stalin told Hopkins, adding that, if it was "designed as pressure on the Russians in order to soften them up, then it was a fundamental mistake." A third form was German reparations. Here Stalin in demanding $10 billion in reparations for the Soviet Union made his strongest fight at Yalta. Roosevelt, while agreeing essentially with Churchill's opposition, tried to postpone the matter by accepting the Soviet figure as a "basis for discussion"—a formula which led to future misunderstanding. In short, the Russian hope for major Western assistance in postwar reconstruction foundered on three events which the Kremlin could well have interpreted respectively as deliberate sabotage (the loan request), blackmail (lend-lease cancellation) and pro-Germanism (reparations).

Actually the American attempt to settle the fourth lend-lease protocol was generous and the Russians for their own reasons declined to come to an agreement. It is not clear, though, that satisfying Moscow on any of these financial scores would have made much essential difference. It might have persuaded some doves in the Kremlin that the U.S. government was genuinely friendly; it might have persuaded some hawks that the American anxiety for Soviet friendship was such that Moscow could do as it wished without inviting challenge from the United States. It would, in short, merely have reinforced both sides of the Kremlin debate; it would hardly have reversed deeper tendencies toward the deterioration of political relationships. Economic deals were surely subordinate to the quality of mutual political confidence; and here, in the months after Yalta, the decay was steady.

The Cold War had now begun. It was the product not of a decision but of a dilemma. Each side felt compelled to adopt policies which the other could not but regard as a threat to the principles of the peace. Each then felt compelled to undertake defensive measures. Thus the Russians saw no choice but to consolidate their security in Eastern Europe. The Americans, regarding Eastern Europe as the first step toward Western Europe, responded by asserting their interest in the zone the Russians deemed vital to their security. The Russians concluded that the West was resuming its old course of capitalist encirclement; that it was purposefully laying the foundation for anti-Soviet régimes in the area defined by the blood of centuries as crucial to Russian survival. Each side believed with passion that future international stability depended on the success of its own conception of world order. Each side, in pursuing its own clearly indicated and deeply cherished principles, was only confirming the fear of the other that it was bent on aggression.

Very soon the process began to acquire a cumulative momentum. The impending collapse of Germany thus provoked new troubles: the Russians, for example, sincerely feared that the West was planning a separate surrender of the German armies in Italy in a way which would release troops for Hitler's eastern front, as they subsequently feared that the Nazis might succeed in surrendering Berlin to the West. This was the context in which the atomic bomb now appeared. Though the revisionist argument that Truman dropped the bomb less to defeat Japan than to intimidate Russia is not convincing, this thought unquestionably appealed to some in Washington as at least an advantageous side-effect of Hiroshima.

So the machinery of suspicion and counter-suspicion, action and counter-action, was set in motion. But, given relations among traditional national states, there was still no reason, even with all the postwar jostling, why this should not have remained a manageable situation. What made it unmanageable, what caused the rapid escalation of the Cold War and in another two years completed the division of Europe, was a set of considerations which this account has thus far excluded.

VII

Up to this point, the discussion has considered the schism within the wartime coalition as if it were entirely the result of disagreements among national states. Assuming this framework, there was unquestionably a failure of communication between America and Russia, a misperception of signals and, as time went on, a mounting tendency to ascribe ominous motives to the other side. It seems hard, for example, to deny that American postwar policy created genuine difficulties for the Russians and even assumed a threatening aspect for them. All this the revisionists have rightly and usefully emphasized.

But the great omission of the revisionists—and also the fundamental explanation of the speed with which the Cold War escalated—lies precisely in the fact that the Soviet Union was *not* a traditional national state.[4] This is where the "mirror image," invoked by some psychologists, falls down. For the Soviet Union was a phenomenon very different from America or Britain: it was a totalitarian state, endowed with an all-explanatory, all-consuming ideology, committed to the infallibility of government and party, still in a somewhat messianic mood, equating dissent with treason, and ruled by a dictator who, for all his quite extraordinary abilities, had his paranoid moments.

Marxism-Leninism gave the Russian leaders a view of the world according to which all societies were inexorably destined to proceed along appointed roads by appointed stages until they achieved the classless nirvana. Moreover, given the resistance of the capitalists to this development, the existence of any non-communist state was *by definition* a threat to the Soviet Union. "As long as capitalism and socialism exist," Lenin wrote, "we cannot live in peace: in the end, one or the other will triumph—a funeral dirge will be sung either over the Soviet Republic or over world capitalism."

Stalin and his associates, whatever Roosevelt or Truman did or failed to do, were bound to regard the United States as the enemy, not because of this deed or that, but because of the primordial fact that America was the leading capitalist power and thus, by Leninist syllogism, unappeasably hostile, driven by the logic of its system to oppose, encircle and destroy Soviet Russia. Nothing the United States could have done in 1944–45 would have abolished this mis-

---

[4] This is the classical revisionist fallacy—the assumption of the rationality, or at least of the traditionalism, of states where ideology and social organization have created a different range of motives. So the Second World War revisionists omit the totalitarian dynamism of Nazism and the fanaticism of Hitler, as the Civil War revisionists omit the fact that the slavery system was producing a doctrinaire closed society in the American South. For a consideration of some of these issues, see "The Causes of the Civil War: A Note on Historical Sentimentalism" in my "The Politics of Hope" (Boston, 1963).

trust, required and sanctified as it was by Marxist gospel—nothing short of the conversion of the United States into a Stalinist despotism; and even this would not have sufficed, as the experience of Jugoslavia and China soon showed, unless it were accompanied by total subservience to Moscow. So long as the United States remained a capitalist democracy, no American policy, given Moscow's theology, could hope to win basic Soviet confidence, and every American action was poisoned from the source. So long as the Soviet Union remained a messianic state, ideology compelled a steady expansion of communist power.

It is easy, of course, to exaggerate the capacity of ideology to control events. The tension of acting according to revolutionary abstractions is too much for most nations to sustain over a long period: that is why Mao Tse-tung has launched his Cultural Revolution, hoping thereby to create a permanent revolutionary mood and save Chinese communism from the degeneration which, in his view, has overtaken Russian communism. Still, as any revolution grows older, normal human and social motives will increasingly reassert themselves. In due course, we can be sure, Leninism will be about as effective in governing the daily lives of Russians as Christianity is in governing the daily lives of Americans. Like the Ten Commandments and the Sermon on the Mount, the Leninist verities will increasingly become platitudes for ritual observance, not guides to secular decision. There can be no worse fallacy (even if respectable people practiced it diligently for a season in the United States) than that of drawing from a nation's ideology permanent conclusions about its behavior.

A temporary recession of ideology was already taking place during the Second World War when Stalin, to rally his people against the invader, had to replace the appeal of Marxism by that of nationalism. ("We are under no illusions that they are fighting for us," Stalin once said to Harriman. "They are fighting for Mother Russia.") But this was still taking place within the strictest limitations. The Soviet Union remained as much a police state as ever; the régime was as infallible as ever; foreigners and their ideas were as suspect as ever. "Never, except possibly during my later experience as ambassador in Moscow," Kennan has written, "did the insistence of the Soviet authorities on isolation of the diplomatic corps weigh more heavily on me . . . than in these first weeks following my return to Russia in the final months of the war. . . . [We were] treated as though we were the bearers of some species of the plague"—which, of course, from the Soviet viewpoint, they were: the plague of skepticism.

Paradoxically, of the forces capable of bringing about a modification of ideology, the most practical and effective was the Soviet dictatorship itself. If Stalin was an ideologist, he was also a pragmatist. If he saw everything through the lenses of Marxism-Leninism, he also, as the infallible expositor of the faith, could reinterpret Marxism-Leninism to justify anything he wanted to do at any given moment. No doubt Roosevelt's ignorance of Marxism-Leninism was inexcusable and led to grievous miscalculations. But Roosevelt's efforts to work on and through Stalin was not so hopelessly naïve as it used to be fashionable to think. With the extraordinary instinct of a great political leader, Roosevelt intuitively understood that Stalin was the *only* lever available to the West against the Leninist ideology and the Soviet system. If Stalin could be reached, then alone was there a chance of getting the Russians to act contrary to the prescriptions of their faith. The best evidence is that Roosevelt retained a certain capacity to influence Stalin to the end; the nominal Soviet acquiescence in American universalism as late as Yalta was perhaps an indication of that. It is in this way that the death of Roosevelt was crucial—not in the vulgar sense that his policy was then reversed by his successor, which did not happen, but in the sense that no other American could hope to have the restraining impact on Stalin which Roosevelt might for a while have had.

Stalin alone could have made any difference. Yet Stalin, in spite of the impression of sobriety and realism he made on Westerners who saw him during the Second World War, was plainly a man of deep and morbid obsessions and compulsions. When he was still a young man, Lenin had criticized his rude and arbitrary ways. A reasonably authoritative observer (N. S. Khrushchev) later commented, "These negative characteristics of his developed steadily and during the last years acquired an absolutely insufferable character." His paranoia, probably set off by the suicide of his wife in 1932, led to the terrible purges of the mid-thirties and the wanton murder of thousands of his Bolshevik comrades. "Everywhere and in everything," Khrushchev says of this period, "he saw 'enemies,' 'double-dealers' and 'spies.'" The crisis of war evidently steadied him in some way, though Khrushchev speaks of his "nervousness and hysteria . . . even after the war began." The madness, so rigidly controlled for a time, burst out with new and shocking intensity in the postwar years. "After the war," Khrushchev testifies,

> the situation became even more complicated. Stalin became even more capricious, irritable and brutal; in particular, his suspicion grew. His persecution mania reached unbelievable dimensions. . . . He decided everything, without any consideration for anyone or anything.

> Stalin's wilfulness showed itself . . . also in the international relations of the Soviet Union. . . . He had completely lost a sense of reality; he demonstrated his suspicion and haughtiness not only in relation to individuals in the USSR, but in relation to whole parties and nations.

A revisionist fallacy has been to treat Stalin as just another Realpolitik statesman, as Second World War revisionists see Hitler as just another Stresemann or Bismarck. But the record makes it clear that in the end nothing could satisfy Stalin's paranoia. His own associates failed. Why does anyone suppose that any conceivable American policy would have succeeded?

An analysis of the origins of the Cold War which leaves out these factors—the intransigence of Leninist ideology, the sinister dynamics of a totalitarian society and the madness of Stalin—is obviously incomplete. It was these factors which made it hard for the West to accept the thesis that Russia was moved only by a desire to protect its security and would be satisfied by the control of Eastern Europe; it was these factors which charged the debate between universalism and spheres of influence with apocalyptic potentiality.

Leninism and totalitarianism created a structure of thought and behavior which made postwar collaboration between Russia and America—in any normal sense of civilized intercourse between national states—inherently impossible. The Soviet dictatorship of 1945 simply could not have survived such a collaboration. Indeed, nearly a quarter-century later, the Soviet régime, though it has meanwhile moved a good distance, could still hardly survive it without risking the release inside Russia of energies profoundly opposed to communist despotism. As for Stalin, he may have represented the only force in 1945 capable of overcoming Stalinism, but the very traits which enabled him to win absolute power expressed terrifying instabilities of mind and temperament and hardly offered a solid foundation for a peaceful world.

VIII

The difference between America and Russia in 1945 was that some Americans fundamentally believed that, over a long run, a modus vivendi with Russia was possible; while the Russians, so far as one can tell, believed in no more than a short-run modus vivendi with the United States.

Harriman and Kennan, this narrative has made clear, took the lead in warning Washington about the difficulties of short-run dealings with the Soviet Union. But both argued that, if the United States developed a rational policy and stuck to it, there would be, after long and rough passages, the prospect of eventual clearing. "I am, as you know," Harriman cabled Washington in early April, "a most earnest advocate of the closest possible understanding with the Soviet Union so that what I am saying relates only to how best to attain such understanding." Kennan has similarly made it clear that the function of his containment policy was "to tide us over a difficult time and bring us to the point where we could discuss effectively with the Russians the dangers and drawbacks this status quo involved, and to arrange with them for its peaceful replacement by a better and sounder one." The subsequent careers of both men attest to the honesty of these statements.

There is no corresponding evidence on the Russian side that anyone seriously sought a modus vivendi in these terms. Stalin's choice was whether his long-term ideological and national interests would be better served by a short-run truce with the West or by an immediate resumption of pressure. In October 1945 Stalin indicated to Harriman at Sochi that he planned to adopt the second course—that the Soviet Union was going isolationist. No doubt the succession of problems with the United States contributed to this decision, but the basic causes most probably lay elsewhere: in the developing situations in Eastern Europe, in Western Europe and in the United States.

In Eastern Europe, Stalin was still for a moment experimenting with techniques of control. But he must by now have begun to conclude that he had underestimated the hostility of the people to Russian dominion. The Hungarian elections in November would finally convince him that the Yalta formula was a road to anti-Soviet governments. At the same time, he was feeling more strongly than ever a sense of his opportunities in Western Europe. The other half of the Continent lay unexpectedly before him, politically demoralized, economically prostrate, militarily defenseless. The hunting would be better and safer than he had anticipated. As for the United States, the alacrity of postwar demobilization must have recalled Roosevelt's off-hand remark at Yalta that "two years would be the limit" for keeping American troops in Europe. And, despite Dr. Eugene Varga's doubts about the imminence of American economic breakdown, Marxist theology assured Stalin that the United States was heading into a bitter postwar depression and would be consumed with its own problems. If the condition of Eastern Europe made unilateral action seem essential in the interests of Russian security, the condition of Western Europe and the United States offered new temptations for communist expansion. The Cold War was now in full swing.

It still had its year of modulations and accommodations. Secretary Byrnes conducted his long and fruitless campaign to persuade the Russians that America only sought governments in Eastern Europe "both friendly to the Soviet Union and representative of all the democratic elements of the country." Crises were surmounted in Trieste and Iran. Secretary Marshall evidently did not give up hope of a modus vivendi until the Moscow conference of foreign secretaries of March 1947. Even then, the Soviet Union was invited to participate in the Marshall Plan.

The point of no return came on July 2, 1947, when Molotov, after bringing 89 technical specialists with him to Paris and evincing initial interest in the project for European reconstruction, received the hot flash from the Kremlin, denounced the whole idea and walked out of the conference. For the next fifteen years the Cold War raged unabated, passing out of historical ambiguity into the realm of good versus evil and breeding on both sides simplifications, stereotypes and self-serving absolutes, often couched in interchangeable phrases. Under the pressure even America, for a deplorable decade, forsook its pragmatic and pluralist traditions, posed as God's appointed messenger to ignorant and sinful man and followed the Soviet example in looking to a world remade in its own image.

In retrospect, if it is impossible to see the Cold War as a case of American aggression and Russian response, it is also hard to see it as a pure case of Russian aggression and American response. "In what is truly tragic," wrote Hegel, "there must be valid moral powers on both the sides which come into collision. . . . Both suffer loss and yet both are mutually justified." In this sense, the Cold War had its tragic elements. The question remains whether it was an instance of Greek tragedy—as Auden has called it, "the tragedy of necessity," where the feeling aroused in the spectator is "What a pity it had to be this way"—or of Christian tragedy, "the tragedy of possibility," where the feeling aroused is "What a pity it was this way when it might have been otherwise."

Once something has happened, the historian is tempted to assume that it had to happen; but this may often be a highly unphilosophical assumption. The Cold War could have been avoided only if the Soviet Union had not been possessed by convictions both of the infallibility of the communist word and of the inevitability of a communist world. These convictions transformed an impasse between national states into a religious war, a tragedy of possibility into one of necessity. One might wish that America had preserved the poise and proportion of the first years of the Cold War and had not in time succumbed to its own forms of self-righteousness. But the most rational of American policies could hardly have averted the Cold War. Only today, as Russia begins to recede from its messianic mission and to accept, in practice if not yet in principle, the permanence of the world of diversity, only now can the hope flicker that this long, dreary, costly contest may at last be taking on forms less dramatic, less obsessive and less dangerous to the future of mankind.

4

The Division of Europe:
The Europeans' Choice

Spheres of Influence: The United States and Europe, 1945–1949
BY *John Lewis Gaddis*

"A BASIC CONFLICT is . . . arising over Europe between the interests of Atlantic sea-power, which demand the preservation of vigorous and independent political life on the European peninsula, and the interests of the jealous Eurasian land power, which must always seek to extend itself to the west and will never find a place, short of the Atlantic Ocean, where it can from its own standpoint safely stop." This was George F. Kennan's depressing assessment of the situation that confronted the United States and its allies early in 1945, conveyed in a letter to his friend and fellow Russian expert, Charles E. Bohlen. Kennan went on to recognize the extent to which victory over Germany required the Soviet Union's military cooperation, even if this brought about an unprecedented projection of Moscow's influence into central Europe. "But with all of this, I fail to see why we must associate ourselves with this political program, so hostile to the interests of the Atlantic community as a whole, so dangerous to everything which we need to see preserved in Europe. Why could we not make a decent and definite compromise with it—divide Europe frankly into spheres of influence—keep ourselves out of the Russian sphere and keep the Russians out of ours? . . . And within whatever sphere of action was left to us we could at least . . . [try] to restore life, in the wake of the war, on a dignified and stable foundation."

John Lewis Gaddis, *The Long Peace*, pp. 48–71, Oxford University Press, New York, 1987.
This essay was originally prepared for the symposium on "European and Atlantic Defence, 1947–1953," organized by the Norwegian Research Centre for Defence History and held in Oslo in August, 1983. It appears, in slightly different form, in Olav Riste, ed., *Western Security: The Formative Years: European and Atlantic Defence, 1947–1953* (Oslo: 1985), pp. 60–91.

Bohlen received Kennan's letter at Yalta on the eve of Franklin Roosevelt's last meeting with Churchill and Stalin. In his hastily composed hand-written reply, he acknowledged as valid Kennan's assessment of Soviet intentions, but dismissed as "utterly impossible" his recommendation for a division of Europe into spheres of influence. "Foreign policy of that kind cannot be made in a democracy," he continued. "Only totalitarian states can make and carry out such policies." Years later, in his memoirs, Bohlen elaborated: "The American people, who had fought a long, hard war, deserved at least an attempt to work out a better world. If the attempt failed, the United States could not be blamed for not trying."

This exchange between the State Department's two most experienced Soviet specialists reflects the dilemma facing the United States as it contemplated the implications of a victory in Europe purchased at the price of an expansion of Soviet influence over Europe. Should the United States play by the Russians' rules and carve out for itself a sphere of influence over as much of the Continent as remained open to it? Or should it seek to persuade the Russians to change the rules: to build a new European order, based upon a rejection of power politics altogether? In the end, of course, Europe was divided, very much along the lines that Kennan had proposed. But Washington accepted this solution only slowly, and with considerable reluctance: Bohlen's idea of a postwar settlement based upon principles of self-determination and big power cooperation proved remarkably persistent. In its eventual decline and ultimate rejection can be traced the origins of a European settlement that has lasted, itself with remarkable persistence, down to the present day.

I

Americans had not been much inclined, prior to World War II, to think about the balance of power in Europe, but events of the early 1940's had abruptly undercut earlier isolationist arguments that whatever happened on the Continent could not affect the security of the United States. In their place, there arose the conviction that the primary American interest in postwar international affairs would be to ensure that no single state dominate Europe. As an Office of Strategic Service analysis put it in the summer of 1944: "our interests require the maintenance of a policy designed to prevent the development of a serious threat to the security of the British Isles (and of the United States), through the consolidation of a large part of Europe's resources under any one power." Increasingly, as the end of the war approached, strategic planners in Washington became aware of the prospect that Germany's defeat would leave a power vacuum in central Europe into which only the Russians would be well-positioned to move. Great Britain, they noted, would be far too weak to provide a counter-balance. But there was, as yet, no consensus that the United States should project its own influence into Europe to restore equilibrium.

Britain and the United States were following divergent policies in their efforts to deal with the inevitable expansion of Soviet influence into postwar Europe, another O.S.S. analysis pointed out in January, 1945: The British approach emphasized "the division of the problem areas into spheres of Soviet and non-Soviet predominance with a neutral zone between." Obviously, such a straightforward partition of the continent would be simple to accomplish, but it would be "a very primitive type of international compromise":

> [I]n its extreme form it implies that within each of the areas affected the interests of the Great Powers are essentially irreconcilable, and that the only practicable solution is to isolate geographically the fields where these interests are to operate. . . . Thus this system probably supplies each great power with the maximum of temptation and the maximum of opportunity for intervention in the domestic affairs of its neighbors. In the long run this might well lead to divergent trends of development in the Soviet and non-Soviet spheres and to a sharpening of the differences between "two worlds."

The American preference should be "to establish and maintain independent democratic regimes within both spheres and within the neutral zone. . . . In the absolute form, such a program would constitute a complete negation of the system of spheres of influence; and to the extent that it is realized in practice it will limit the authority of each Great Power within its sphere."

To be sure, Washington never actually contemplated such a thorough rejection of spheres of influence. President Roosevelt's own cherished concept of a world settlement enforced by "Four Policemen"—the United States, Great Britain, the Soviet Union, and Nationalist China—clearly implied the existence of such spheres. Certainly the United States was not prepared to give up its own predominance in Latin America, or to deny itself new areas of influence in the Pacific after the war. Nor was there a predisposition to challenge the Russians' obvious attempt to secure a dominant postwar influence along their western borders.

But there was no great effort, as the end of the war approached, to position American forces in such a way as to counter Soviet strength in Europe: indeed it was at Yalta that Roosevelt in effect promised the withdrawal of American troops from the Continent within two years of Germany's surrender. Nor did Churchill's impassioned pleas to hold American forces in place after that event meet with a favorable response from President Truman. As late as the Potsdam Conference in July, 1945, State Department planners were still worrying that the British might seek to lure the United States into supporting a spheres of influence settlement in Europe. Such a solution, they concluded, would "represent power politics pure and simple, with all the concomitant disadvantages. . . . Our primary objective should be to remove the *causes* which make nations feel that such spheres are necessary to build their security, rather than to assist one country to build up strength against another."

It requires something of an effort, at this distance, to reconstruct the reasons for Washington's aversion to spheres of influence in Europe, even in the face of what were clearly Russian efforts to create their own in that part of the world. Probably most important in the minds of Roosevelt administration officials, curiously enough, was the fear of a resurgent isolationism inside the United States. "Our boys do not want to fight to rule the world, isolationist Congressman Hamilton Fish warned, "or to divide it into three parts, like ancient Gaul, between Great Britain, Russia, and the United States." The President and his advisers were keenly sensitive to such arguments. In the Atlantic Charter and other wartime pronouncements, they had resuscitated the vision of a Wilsonian peace, based on self-determination, economic multilateralism, and collective security, not because they believed such a settlement to be attainable in every respect, but as a means of overcoming the isolationism that had grown out of the failure to implement that kind of peace two decades before. A peace based too obviously on spheres of influence might seem to many Americans to be no peace at all, and hence result, as had the settlement of 1919, in the withdrawal rather than the projection of United States authority.

It would be unfair, though, to write off the administration's idealism in this respect solely as a way to sanctify the wielding of power. There was, as well, a sincere sense among Roosevelt, his subordinates, and much of the public at large that the "old diplomacy" had failed, and that Wilsonian methods of collective security, tempered to be sure by a regard for practical circumstances, deserved to be given another try. American officials did work overtime during this period to demonstrate, at times with creative ingenuity, how the benefits of a Wilsonian settlement would accrue not just to the United States but to the rest of the world as well. But these arguments were by no means wholly cynical: to have acknowledged openly spheres of influence would have been to admit the irrelevancy of the American domestic experience, upon which so substantial a portion of this new approach to world affairs was based.

There also still existed uncertainty as to the Russians' motives for seeking spheres of influence in the first place. Despite some worry over the ideological component in Soviet policy, the prevailing wartime view in Washington was that the projection of Russian power into Europe was occurring for defensive rather than offensive reasons. If Moscow could be assured of the West's peaceful intentions, then its reasons for seeking spheres of influence, it was thought, would disappear. An open attempt to build countervailing power in Europe might have the effect of a self-fulfilling prophecy, reinforcing the Kremlin's suspicions and perpetuating its inclination toward unilateralism. "[W]e must always bear in mind," a State Department analysis of Soviet-American relations concluded in December, 1945, "that because of the differences between the economic and political systems of our two countries, the conduct of our relations requires more patience and diligence than with other countries." American interests had to be defended, to be sure. "On the other hand, in order to minimize Soviet suspicions of our motives we should avoid even the appearance of taking unilateral action ourselves."

A year after his reply to Kennan's letter, Bohlen still considered spheres of influence an inappropriate solution to Europe's problems. It might be possible to reach a *modus vivendi* with the Russians on that basis, he acknowledged early in 1946. But such a settlement would

> reduce the United Nations organization to a façade with the real power concentrated in the hands of the United States, Great Britain, and the Soviet Union. While this policy would perhaps offer the best means of avoiding difficulties with the Soviet Union in the immediate future, merely to state it is to demonstrate its impossibility of adoption. . . . [I]t would constitute a great step backwards from the principle of a cooperative world and would never receive the support of the American people.

Moreover, Bohlen added, such a settlement "would merely temporarily postpone an eventual clash with the Soviet Union under conditions infinitely worse for the United States and Great Britain" since, as a dictatorship, the U.S.S.R. "would be able to consolidate into an absolute bloc its sphere of influence while the Western democracies by their very nature would be unable to do the same in theirs."

For Bohlen and those who thought like him, the very nature of Western political systems precluded a spheres of influence settlement: democracies could not join with dictatorships to divide the world. There would have to be, instead, a compromise between the facts of power and the obligations of justice; only on that basis could American interests in Europe be satisfied. Even after reading Kennan's pessimistic "long telegram" on the roots of Soviet behavior, Bohlen saw no reason "why the two systems cannot peacefully coexist in the same world provided that neither one attempts to extend the area of its system by aggressive and ultimately forceable means at the expense of the other." The problem for the West was "(a) to convince the Soviet Union of this possibility and (b) to make clear well in advance the inevitable consequence of the present line of Soviet policy based on the opposite thesis."

II

For the next year, the Truman administration followed closely the dual approach Bohlen had recommended. On the one hand, there took place an exhaustive effort—probably insufficiently appreciated, in retrospect—to convince the Russians that a comprehensive European settlement would be preferable to a cold-blooded division of the Continent into separate spheres. At the same time, though, there was set in motion a program of gradual preparation for a division of Europe, as much in the hope that it would ward off Soviet inclinations in that direction as from a desire actually to implement it.

There was little inclination in Washington in the early postwar months to try to challenge directly the reality of Soviet hegemony in Eastern Europe. Instead, American officials made an effort to try to "educate" the Russians to the fact that outright domination would be both unnecessary and counter-productive. In October, 1945, Bohlen had actually suggested recognizing "legitimate" Soviet security interests in Eastern Europe if the Russians would agree to show the same restraint regarding the internal affairs of that region that the United States had demonstrated in Latin America. Secretary of State James F. Byrnes made this idea the subject of a public speech later that month, pointing out that the disinterested and mutually beneficial Good Neighbor Policy had evolved out of the self interested Monroe Doctrine: "We surely cannot and will not deny to other nations the right to develop such a policy."

But Bohlen himself had seen the principal difficulty in this approach: "from all indications the Soviet mind is incapable of making a distinction between influence and domination, or between a friendly government and a puppet government." The report of the Ethridge Committee, a delegation of American observers sent by Byrnes to Rumania and Bulgaria to report on Soviet policies there, strongly reinforced this conclusion: "[T]o concede a limited Soviet sphere of influence at the present time," it argued, "would be to invite its extension in the future." With public and Congressional opinion growing increasingly hostile to the idea of any further concessions to the Russians on any grounds, it is not surprising that a consensus began to emerge within the government early in 1946 against further efforts to "enlighten" Moscow as to the disadvantages of spheres of influence, and in favor of tougher methods.

The central issue here was the future of Germany. State Department planners had argued virtually without exception that there could be no stability in postwar Europe if Germany remained divided. Experiences of the interwar years had seemed to show that the Germans would never accept permanent partition of their country; moreover, a unified Germany was thought vital to the economic recovery of Europe as a whole.

The failure to persuade the Russians to abandon their sphere of influence in Eastern Europe brought the German question to the forefront in two important but contradictory ways: it made all the more urgent the need to ensure that Germany could pose no threat to the Soviet Union in the future, thereby removing the Russians' principal excuse for dominating Eastern Europe in the first place; but it also raised the need for the Western powers to begin thinking about consolidating their own positions in Germany, in the event agreement with the Russians proved impossible. The dilemma was that by weakening Germany to reassure the Russians the West would leave itself vulnerable, but by strengthening its position there it would confirm Soviet suspicions. It was in the effort to resolve this dilemma that the United States in the spring of 1946 undertook two new initiatives on Germany: the proposal, in the Council of Foreign Ministers, of a four-power disarmament treaty; and, simultaneously, movement toward the consolidation of Western occupation zones.

The idea of a treaty between the United States, the Soviet Union, Great Britain, and France to keep Germany disarmed had been discussed off and on in Washington for some time, both for the purpose of reassuring allies that the United States did not propose to abandon them after the war, and as a means of alleviating Soviet fears of a resurgent Germany that had provided the justification for imposing a sphere of influence in Eastern Europe.* But by the spring of 1946 the proposed treaty had become a test of Soviet intentions as well: if the Russians accepted it, the argument ran, they would have no further need for spheres of influence. If they did not, then the division of Europe would have to be accepted as a fact and the West would have to begin consolidating its own sphere. It was with these alternatives in mind that Byrnes formally proposed a twenty-five year treaty to the Russians at the end of April, 1946.

Moscow's negative response seemed to confirm the fears of those who had argued that its determination to impose spheres of influence reflected offensive rather than defensive intentions. There was as yet no unanimous acknowledgment in Washington that Europe had been divided into two spheres, James Reston noted in the *New York Times* early in May, "but even the most pro-Soviet members of Mr. Truman's Administration agree that the Administration is nearer to accepting this thesis today than it has been at any other time since the end of the war." It was within this context that emphasis began to be given to the other element in American policy during this period: the consolidation of a defensible Western position in Germany in the event negotiations with the Russians failed.

Convinced that the division of Europe was inevitable in any event, Kennan had for some time been arguing in favor of this approach. The only acceptable alternative, he had written in March, 1946, was for the United States and its allies "to carry to its logical conclusion the process of partition which was begun in the east and to endeavor to rescue [the] western zones of Germany by walling them off against eastern penetration and integrating them into [the] international pattern of western Europe." This in fact is what Washington began to do in the spring and summer of 1946, with the termination of reparations shipments from the American zone, the initiation of talks with London looking toward a merger of American and British occupation zones, and, most important, Secretary of State Byrnes's assurance at Stuttgart in September that American troops would remain in Germany as long as the occupation forces of any other power did.

It is important to note, though, that these decisions of 1946 did not constitute final American acceptance of the division of Germany. The consequences of such a division, both in economic and geopolitical terms, were sufficiently unsettling to keep American negotiators at work for another year in the effort to

---

*Senator Arthur H. Vandenberg had originally suggested the idea of a German disarmament treaty in the famous speech announcing his "conversion" from isolationism, delivered on the floor of the Senate on January 10, 1945. [See the *Congressional Record* for that date, pp. 164–67.]

secure a German peace treaty. As late as December, 1947, Secretary of State George C. Marshall, who spent much of that year conducting these negotiations, was still emphasizing the need to make sincere offers to the Russians on Germany rather than simply gestures in the expectation of refusals. Marshall was "most anxious in regard to the general international situation to avoid a 'frozen front,' which was tragic to contemplate."

But a German settlement that risked leaving the Soviet Union in a position of dominance in central Europe was an even more unsettling prospect, and by 1947 there had emerged a definite consensus in Washington that a negotiated reunification was not worth that price. "I think that it amounts to this," Kennan told students at the Air War College in April of that year:

> We insist that either a central German authority be established along lines that will make it impossible for the Soviet Union to dominate Germany . . . , or that we retain complete control over the western zones. . . . I think it may mean the partition of Germany, and we all admit that is undesirable. . . . I hope we won't shrink from carrying out that partition rather than giving the Russians the chance to dominate the whole country, though.

If the fear of a Germany under Soviet control served to make the idea of a divided Europe more respectable in American eyes, so too did the prospect of a power vacuum in the Near East and Eastern Mediterranean brought about by the decline of British power there. American planners had been well aware of the fact that the war had weakened Britain's world position, but even so the rapidity of the collapse came as a surprise. As late as April, 1946, Truman could still speculate publicly about the possibility of a contest for world influence between London and Moscow, with Washington acting as an impartial umpire. But within less than a year, American opinion had shifted to the view, as an official in the British Foreign Office noted with grim satisfaction, "that no time must be lost in plucking the torch of world leadership from our chilling hands."

The threat to the balance of power in the Near East had seemed, at first, something that could be handled simply by issuing statements aimed simultaneously at warning the Russians off and at arousing world opinion against them. Both the Iranian and Turkish crises of 1946 had been dealt with in this way, with Washington relying primarily upon the deterrent effect of pugnacious pronouncements. The situation in Greece, though, was something else again. Here the danger to the balance of power came not so much from the possibility of external attack as from that of internal disarray, the effects of which, it was thought, would benefit the Russians without the risks of direct military involvement. As the State Department's Office of Near Eastern and African Affairs noted late in 1946, "[i]t is vastly to the interest of the U.S. that the recognized government [in Greece] be assisted in becoming strong enough *before the fact* to handle its internal problems without requiring a sudden increase in assistance *during* a state of actual or near civil war."

The British decision to cut off economic and military aid to Greece and Turkey early in 1947 forced Washington to move beyond attempts to discourage Soviet expansion by rhetoric alone. Instead, it appeared, positive action would be required to reconstitute centers of resistance to the Russians in areas vulnerable to them. This new approach would require squeezing increased appropriations out of a Congress still much attracted by the budgetary advantages of isolationism: hence, the administration's all-too-successful effort, through the Truman Doctrine, to alarm legislators by raising the specter of a world divided between antipathetic ways of life. But the new situation also stimulated serious thinking in Washington as to how the United States might most effectively use its resources, not just in Greece and Turkey but in Europe as a whole, to reconstitute the balance of power left unstable by the creation and feared expansion of Moscow's sphere of influence. The collapse of Council of Foreign Ministers discussions on a German peace treaty that April further heightened the sense of urgency.

The result, of course, was the Marshall Plan, an ambitious attempt to reconstitute a political balance in Europe by economic means. The plan rested upon the assumption that the Russians were not prepared to risk war to extend their influence; rather, the danger was that they might successfully exploit European psychological demoralization resulting from war damage and the discouragingly slow pace of reconstruction, whether by means of external intimidation, internal subversion, or even the possibility that Europeans might vote their own communists into office through free elections. The Marshall Plan also reflected, paradoxically enough, an awareness of limited capabilities: the United States could not afford to contain threats to the balance of power in all places by all means. Maintaining European equilibrium ranked first on Washington's list of priorities; of the limited instruments available for doing this, economic assistance seemed to provide the quickest and most effective way.

Even so, the traditional aversion to spheres of influence still lingered in the United States: it was partly in deference to this sentiment that Marshall initially offered aid to the Soviet Union and its East European satellites as well, with a view to placing responsibility for the division of Europe squarely on Moscow's shoulders. It was the Russians' refusal of this offer—after a disquieting initial hesitation—that reconciled American officials once and for all to the inevitability of a divided Europe. As career Foreign Service officer Burton Y. Berry put it at the end of July, 1947, it was time to "drop the pretense of one world."[*]

It was left to Bohlen, who had originally so strongly resisted the idea of a divided Europe, to draft the most thoughtful analysis of the new situation:

> The United States is confronted with a condition in the world which is at direct variance with the assumptions upon which, during and directly after the war, major United States policies were predicated. Instead of unity among the great

---

[*]Kennan, as it happened, had already anticipated this recommendation, as minutes for the Policy Planning Staff meeting of July 28, 1947, show: "Mr. Kennan undertook to prepare a paper setting forth the implications involved in the fact that we are presently faced with a two-world situation, whereas the UN Charter was drawn up in the hope of a one-world system." [Policy Planning Staff Records, Box 32, Diplomatic Branch, National Archives.]

powers—both political and economic—after the war, there is complete disunity between the Soviet Union and the satellites on one side and the rest of the world on the other. There are, in short, two worlds instead of one. Faced with this disagreeable fact, however much we may deplore it, the United States in the interest of its own well-being and security and those of the free non-Soviet world must re-examine its major policy objectives. . . . The logic of the situation is that the non-Soviet world through such measures are open to it [should] draw closer together politically, economically, financially, and, in the last analysis, militarily in order to be in a position to deal effectively with the consolidated Soviet area. Only in this way can a free and non-Soviet world hope to survive in the face of the centralized and ruthless direction of the Soviet world.

Or, as Secretary of State Marshall put it with characteristic brevity at a cabinet meeting in November: "Our policy, I think, should be directed toward restoring a balance of power in Europe and Asia."

III

"[T]he realisation is now widespread," the British embassy in Washington reported early in 1948, "that there is nothing reprehensible *per se* in the exercise of power. Whereas a year ago the phrase 'power politics' bore a sinister connotation in the American mind, it has since come to be accepted as a normal technical term." Curiously, though, this willingness to think in "balance of power" terms did not produce a corresponding determination on the part of the United States to carve out a sphere of influence for itself in Europe, comparable to the one the Russians had imposed. Instead, Washington's preference was to try to reconstitute an *independent* center of power on the continent, strong enough to act on its own to maintain equilibrium there. As John D. Hickerson, Director of the State Department's Office of European Affairs, described it, the idea was to create "a third force which was not merely the extension of US influence but a real European organization strong enough to say 'no' both to the Soviet Union and to the United States, if our actions should seem so to require."

"The idea of a United States of Europe has, of course, long appealed to Americans, who are always prone to accept the naive and uncritical assumption that ideas and institutions that have proved their value here can be exported to provide ready-made remedies for the ills of less fortunate areas of the world." It was not unusual for British diplomats in Washington to take a slightly jaded view of American enthusiasms, and this dispatch, written in the spring of 1947, was no exception. But it would be a mistake to see the Truman administration's support for European integration—in preference to the overt extension of an American sphere of influence over Europe—as a simple-minded effort to transplant what had flourished at home to stonier and less fertile soil overseas. There were in fact good reasons for Washington's reluctance, even after acknowledging the reality of a divided Europe, to impose its own control there.

One reason was that American officials did not see themselves as possessing, at that time, either the resources or the domestic support necessary to dominate large portions of the world in order to deny them to the Russians. "[P]ublic and Congressional reaction to foreign affairs is still conditioned by two main factors," a British Foreign Office analyst observed in May, 1947: "fear and dislike of Russia and aversion to the responsibility, and more particularly to the cost, of preserving the world balance of power." A country still wary of international commitments could not discard its traditions overnight; rather, administration leaders argued, there would have to be a gradual expansion of responsibilities, carried out with full awareness of the need to expend limited resources efficiently and alongside obvious and convincing demonstrations from its allies that the United States would not be the only nation carrying the resulting burdens.

It followed from this that a multi-polar international system, with several independent centers of power sharing the burdens of containment, would best suit American interests. Certainly this was Kennan's view: "it should be a cardinal point of our policy," he wrote in October, 1947, "to see to it that other elements of independent power are developed on the Eurasian land mass as rapidly as possible in order to take off our shoulders some of the burden of 'bi-polarity.'" Kennan went on during the next year to develop the concept of keeping key power centers—notably Great Britain, the Rhine-Ruhr industrial complex, and Japan—from falling under Soviet control, not by extending American control over them, but rather by encouraging their development as independent forces with the strength and self-confidence necessary to defend themselves. An American sphere of influence in Europe would undermine that strategy, to which Truman administration officials were generally sympathetic.

Such a solution would also conflict with the still-cherished, if imperfectly observed, tradition of non-intervention. Despite the collapse of "one worldism," American officials continued to pay deference to the principle of self-determination. "[I]t is not our intention to impose our way of life on other nations," Assistant Secretary of State Charles Saltzmann insisted in September, 1947. "That in itself would be undemocratic. Our only purpose is, in so far as possible, to give other nations the opportunity to decide these matters for themselves, free from coercion." This was not simply boiler-plate rhetoric, intended for public consumption: the view in Washington persisted throughout the late 1940's that the viability of political systems depended in large part upon their autonomy, even spontaneity. For this reason, Americans were willing to tolerate a surprising amount of diversity within the anti-Soviet coalition: one of the more durable strains in State Department thinking between 1946 and 1948 involved the need to cooperate with the democratic Left in Europe, despite the fact that its programs of nationalization and social welfare were anathema to conservatives in the United States. If one result of such flexibility was to make European governments better able to resist Soviet pressure because of their firm base of popular support, then that only confirmed the long-standing American view that principle and self-interest were not always irreconcilable.

It should be recognized as well, though, that the interests of the United States and non-communist Europe were largely congruent during this period, and that Washington as a consequence had little need to impose its will on potential allies. If there was ever a time when one nation was *invited* to extend its influence over another part of the world, then surely the experience of the United States in Europe after World War II came close to it.* "[W]e should be placed in an impossible position," Foreign Secretary Ernest Bevin reminded the Cabinet, "if the United States Government withdrew from Europe." The governments of Greece, Turkey, and Iran all fervently applauded the growth of American influence in the Eastern Mediterranean and the Near East. And certainly public opinion in Western Europe welcomed a more active American role there as well, given the alternatives at best of further economic deterioration, at worst of Soviet domination. "It seems evident," Secretary of State Marshall commented in November, 1947, "that, as regards European recovery, the enlightened self-interest of the United States coincides with the best interest of Europe itself."

There were other, more specific, reasons for promoting the idea of European integration. One involved the problem of what to do with Germany now that an agreement with the Russians had become unlikely. A Joint Chiefs of Staff analysis in April, 1947, summarized the dilemma: "Without German aid the remaining countries of western Europe could scarcely be expected to withstand the armies of our ideological opponents until the United States could mobilize and place in the field sufficient armed forces to achieve their defeat." Moreover, "the complete resurgence of German industry . . . is essential for the economic recovery of France—whose security is inseparable from the combined security of the United States, Canada, and Great Britain." But all indications were that the French would "vigorously oppose any substantial revival of German heavy industry." This was unfortunate, since "the German people are the natural enemies of the USSR and of communism." It followed that the American interest was to convince both the French and the Germans "that the emergence of a principal world power to the east . . . which they can successfully oppose only if both are strong and united . . . makes them interdependent just as France, England, Canada, and the United States are interdependent." European integration might provide a way to incorporate Germany into a European system without leaving Germany in control of that system. As Kennan put it early in 1948: "Only such a union holds out any hope of restoring the balance of power in Europe without permitting Germany to become again the dominant power."

Finally, it should be pointed out that Americans did not see the division of Europe as something that would last forever. To an extent that is only now coming to be fully appreciated, Washington planners throughout this period were quietly considering how the Soviet Union's Eastern European satellites might be detached from the Kremlin's control. This had been one of the addi-

---

*For more on this "expansion by invitation" thesis see Geir Lundestad, "Empire by Invitation? The United States and Western Europe, 1945–1952," *Journal of Peace Research,* XXIII (1986), 263–77; and John Lewis Gaddis, "The Emerging Post-Revisionist Thesis on the Origins of the Cold War," *Diplomatic History,* VII (Summer, 1983), 182–83.

tional motives behind the offer of Marshall Plan aid to the satellites in the summer of 1947; a year later Kennan was making the point that "the door should be left open for everyone in Europe to come in at the proper time so that there could be a real unification of Europe and the development of a European idea." Only a viable European union would exert this kind of attraction, William Clayton pointed out: "The Russian satellite countries would then feel the pull so much stronger from the West than from the East, that Russia would find it more and more difficult and in the end impossible to hold them." "Our objective," Under Secretary of State Robert Lovett wrote to Averell Harriman in December of 1948, "should continue to be the progressively closer integration, both economic and political, of presently free Europe and eventually of as much of Europe as becomes free."

"If the United States entertained any idea of extending American influence or domination over Europe," Secretary of State Marshall had commented in a public speech given a year earlier, "our policy would not be directed toward ending European dependency upon this country but toward perpetuating that relationship." This statement can stand as an accurate reflection of how American officials saw their own *intentions* with regard to Europe during the early days of the Cold War. There was, as the British Embassy in Washington perceptively pointed out, a distinction between seeking a balance of power and a sphere of influence:

> On a broad view, an analysis of its activities leads to the conclusion that what the United States most requires from candid observers abroad are not reproofs that it is abusing its giant power, but commendation for such wisdom and generosity as it has thus far displayed, along with encouragement bravely to persevere in the employment of its vast resources for its own and the general welfare. In the meantime, to those critics who accuse her of taking undue advantage of her own strength and of the weakness of others, America might well reply in the words of Clive when arraigned by a committee in the House of Commons for having exploited his unrivalled power in India for purposes of personal aggrandizement: "By God, Mr. Chairman, at this moment I stand astonished at my own moderation."

But intentions are one thing; actual policy is something else again, as the events of 1948–49 made clear. The American vision of an independent, prosperous, and self-confident center of power in Europe proved to be more elusive than had appeared to be the case in 1947. Circumstances gradually compelled the United States to create its own sphere of influence in Europe, despite its own profound misgivings about that course of action.

IV

It is evident, in retrospect, that Washington considerably underestimated the difficulties of establishing an independent "third force" in Europe. That concept had been based upon several precariously balanced propositions: that a Soviet threat existed awesome enough to compel Europeans to submerge ancient rivalries, but not so awesome as to prevent them from acting in a self-confident and decisive manner; that American economic assistance would stimulate self-reliance without encouraging dependency; that no further initiatives would be necessary to sustain a European order whose collective interests would be compatible with, though independent of, those of the United States. It did not take long for the shakiness of these assumptions to become apparent.

"It is curious that there is so little discussion of the strategic aspects of European integration," F. B. A. Rundall, of the British Foreign Office, noted in February, 1948. "One would imagine that Mr. Lippmann or a similar pundit would have taken up the point that, for the countries concerned, the economic decisions involved in integration are inevitably bound up with considerations of strategy and common defence in which the United States are no less involved. Yet perhaps this is a hare that no one wishes to start before the elections." To the extent that domestic political considerations required a step-by-step approach to the expansion of American commitments overseas, Rundall was on target. Yet, one has the impression that American planners were genuinely surprised, quite apart from their concern about public and Congressional reactions, to have the issue of military security in Europe raised in the first place.

They themselves had consistently deprecated the probability of a Soviet military attack. "The Soviet effort in Europe is a *political* one, not a *military* one," Kennan had repeatedly argued. "The Soviet aim is not to undertake a military conquest which could only be followed by Red Army occupation of Western Europe. . . . The aim is rather to establish in that area a system of indirect control which will give them power without responsibility." Admittedly, no one could rule out the possibility of war altogether. "[T]he threat of war, intended or unintended, will become greater in proportion to weaknesses in the economy, military force, and foreign policy of the United States," the Pentagon's Joint Intelligence Committee noted in February, 1948. But as long as reasonable American strength was maintained—and, in particular, as long as the deterrent power of the American atomic monopoly remained in existence—then the prospect of war in Europe by anything other than gross miscalculation on Moscow's part seemed very remote.

Nevertheless, the whole point of the Marshall Plan had been to restore self-confidence, so that Europe would be in a position to defend itself. From this perspective, the European state of mind was at least as important as American intelligence estimates. It came as something of a shock, therefore, to have Ernest Bevin calling Washington's attention in January, 1948 to "the further encroachment of the Soviet tide" and the need to "reinforce the physical barriers which still guard our Western civilisation," in terms Dean Acheson might have found useful in prodding obdurate Congressmen toward a grudging acceptance of international responsibilities. The Russians, with their usual deftness in producing responses opposite from those intended, punctuated Bevin's point dramatically by staging a coup in Czechoslovakia the following month: this event, together with warnings from other European leaders in addition to Bevin, was sufficient to convince many in Washington that the Marshall Plan alone would not restore self-confidence in Europe; some form of explicit military guarantee would be needed as well.*

Such guarantees, though, would raise problems. There was no assurance that Congress would authorize a direct military commitment to the defense of Western Europe, or what the exact nature of that commitment would be. There was the question of what countries would be covered by such a guarantee: for the United States to undertake to defend everyone would be to exceed American capabilities; for it to leave certain countries out might only invite aggression against them. There was concern that such a guarantee might sap the Europeans' resolve to defend themselves in the first place. "If they are not willing to defend their national independence at this risk," Kennan argued in April, 1948, "then perhaps they would indeed be beyond helping. For there are very definite limits—which people here are constantly forgetting—on the ability of this country to shoulder alone the risks and responsibilities of keeping alive the hope for a continuation of civilization in large parts of this globe."

Cautious negotiations with both allies and Congressional leaders over the next year solved some of these problems. The administration assured Congress that the proposed North Atlantic Treaty involved no obligation to go to war without its consent. The problem of limited resources was addressed by stressing the extent to which an explicit commitment to defend Western Europe would in itself deter the Russians without more specific measures having to be taken; indeed, Secretary of Defense Louis Johnson even suggested that NATO might make it possible to *reduce* the American defense budget. Washington carefully undertook no obligation to station additional troops in Europe, reviving instead the old pre-World War II concept of the United States as an "arsenal" supplying military hardware to the Europeans, who would themselves furnish the manpower. As John Hickerson put it late in 1948: "It is a question of committing, not forces now, but the potential of Pittsburgh and Detroit."[†]

But the problem of reconciling self-sufficiency with reassurance was not so easily resolved. Despite official claims that the new alliance would facilitate

---

*The British Embassy in Washington had noted in September, 1947: "If it were not for the obstreperous behavior of the Soviet Union, Marshall would never have made his suggestions, or, had he done so, they would have received almost no public support. The Soviet Union has not only succeeded in preventing the United States from retreating into its prewar isolationism but it is now ensuring that the United States will take an increasingly active part in the affairs of Western Europe." [Inverchapel to Foreign Office, September 6, 1947, Foreign Office Records, FO 371/61056, Public Record Office, London.]

[†]The Americans were "only too ready to place a gun in the hands of any natural enemy of the Soviet Union," a confidential British political report had noted in the summer of 1948. "[W]ith 50% of the world's industrial capacity but only 7% of its population," the United States "must inevitably adopt a policy which the cynical might compare to the hiring of mercenaries." [Confidential Political Report #8, "Military Aid for Western Europe," June 26, 1948, Foreign Office Records, FO 371/68019.]

more than it would impede European integration, Kennan was quietly predict-
ing to his colleagues that "this arrangement will come to overshadow, and probably to replace, any development in the direction of European union":

> Instead of the development of a real federal structure in Europe which would aim
> to embrace all free European countries, which would be a political force in its
> own right, and which would have behind it the logic of geography and historical
> development, we will get an irrevocable congealment of the division of Europe
> into two military zones: a Soviet zone and a U.S. zone. Instead of the ability to
> divest ourselves gradually of the basic responsibility for the security of western
> Europe, we will get a legal perpetuation of that responsibility. In the long run,
> such a legalistic structure must crack up on the rocks of reality; for a divided
> Europe is not permanently viable, and the political will of the U.S. people is not
> sufficient to enable us to support western Europe indefinitely as a military
> appendage.

"The doubts and criticisms he raises regarding the Atlantic Pact . . . unquestionably have a certain validity," Bohlen wrote to Acheson early in 1949 in a memorandum which, while addressed to the views of James P. Warburg, could have
applied to Kennan's as well. "It is, however, the same old story—while clearly
expressing the objections to it, he does not seem to offer any feasible alternative. . . . I entirely agree with him that the primary danger is political and not
military, but I do not think he fully values the intimate relationship between
economic recovery, political stability, and a sense of security against external
aggression."

This was, in fact, the essence of the problem. A European "third force"
could only be built upon a foundation of European self-confidence, a fact
Kennan himself had recognized in supporting the Marshall Plan. But it was
Europeans, not Americans, who would determine when the point of self-
confidence had been reached, and what would be necessary to sustain it. If
they concluded that self-confidence depended upon a formal American military
commitment, then Washington, whatever its reservations about the effect this
might have upon European self-reliance, was hardly in a position to argue. "I
recognize fully that military alliances aren't worth a tinker's dam," Walter Bedell
Smith noted with brutal candor in the summer of 1949, "yet those people do
attach far greater importance to the scrap of paper pledging support than we
ever have."

If the issue of military security posed problems for the "third force" idea,
so too did the awkward question of who should belong to it. Germany's position raised the most obvious difficulties. The collapse of talks with the Russians
on a comprehensive German settlement late in 1947 pushed the United States,
Britain, and France toward a consolidation of political and economic institutions
in their three occupation zones, as much as a matter of administrative convenience as by subtle geopolitical design. By the summer of 1948, they had
agreed, in what came to be known as the "London Conference" program, to
allow Germans "those governmental responsibilities which are compatible with

the minimum requirements of occupation and control and which ultimately will enable them to assume full governmental responsibility." What this meant, as an internal State Department policy statement acknowledged, was the reconstitution of western Germany "as a political entity capable of participating in and contributing to the reconstruction of Europe."

There was no escaping the fact, though, that a divided Germany would pose profound implications for the idea of a European "third force." No one was more sensitive to these than Kennan, who as late as 1947 had been prepared to contemplate the partition of Germany with equanimity. What changed Kennan's mind was his growing preference for a multipolar over a bipolar postwar order, and the importance, in that scheme of things, of having an independent center of political, military, and economic power on the European continent. A permanently divided Germany, with each half the client of a rival non-European superpower, would not only ruin chances for a mutual withdrawal of Soviet and American forces and preclude any possibility of weaning away Moscow's East European satellites; it would also, by leaving a highly skilled and highly nationalistic people artificially separated, create a volatile and unstable political balance, subject to revanchist pressures from both sides of the line. With these considerations in mind, Kennan late in 1948 proposed an approach to the Russians looking toward a pull-back of occupation forces to specific garrison areas, and the establishment, after free elections, of an independent, demilitarized, neutral, but unified German state.

Kennan's "Program A," as his proposal came to be known, raised fundamental questions as to where the American interest in Europe lay. Was the balance of power there to be maintained by accepting as permanent the division of the Continent, which in turn implied permanent Soviet and American spheres of influence there? Or was Europe to be reconstituted as an entity unto itself, with a unified but presumably "tamed" Germany at its core? The latter alternative—emphatically Kennan's own choice—was by no means rejected out of hand in Washington. Dean Acheson, upon becoming Secretary of State early in 1949, found Kennan's arguments persuasive enough to appoint him to chair a National Security Council steering group charged with formulating an American negotiating position should talks with the Russians on Germany eventually take place. After listening to one Kennan presentation on the subject, Acheson wondered out loud how the London Program looking toward a divided Germany had ever been agreed upon in the first place.*

And yet, despite Acheson's intellectual sympathy for Kennan's approach, the hard reality was that Britain, France, and their smaller neighbors preferred

---

*"Kennan is, as you are aware, a powerful influence in the State Department," the British ambassador in Washington reported to the Foreign Office, "and I regard his mission to Germany [in connection with the steering group discussions] as likely to be of particular importance." [Sir Oliver Franks to Foreign Office, March 4, 1949, Foreign Office Records, FO 371/74160.]

the known risks of a Europe divided into Soviet and American spheres of influence to the imponderables of a unified "third force" that could conceivably fall under German or even Russian control. Bohlen had noted the difficulty when "Program A" was first proposed in the fall of 1948:

> [T]he one faint element of confidence which [the French] cling to is the fact that American troops, however strong in number, stand between them and the Red Army. If you add to that the strong fears to be generated with the prospect of returning power to Germans at the present juncture, I am sure that the general line of approach suggested . . . would have a most unfavorable reaction in France and probably in Holland and Belgium as well.

These reservations became painfully clear when "Program A" was leaked to the press in May, 1949, just before the Council of Foreign Ministers was to take up the future of Germany. Ambassador David Bruce had to reassure the French "that we did not favor withdrawal of US forces or any disposition of those forces which would weaken our influence in [the] European scene."

But the abandonment of "Program A" in no way lessened Washington's determination to end the occupation of Germany; what it meant, rather, was that if the integration of Germany as a whole into Europe as a whole was not possible, then its efforts would be directed toward integrating what remained of Germany into what remained of Europe. Even Kennan recognized the force of this logic: "Either the rest of Europe tries to work with the West German state, as it is now emerging, takes a sympathetic and constructive interest in it, and learns to regard its development as a European as well as a German responsibility, or there will be soon no Germany with which the rest of Europe can cooperate, and no possibility of real unity and strength in Western Europe." It was in this connection that the North Atlantic Treaty interlocked neatly with the London Conference program. Acheson described the relationship early in 1949: "it was doubtful that, without some such pact, the French would ever be reconciled to the inevitable diminution of direct allied control over Germany and the progressive reduction of occupation troops; . . . a pact of this nature would give France a greater sense of security against Germany as well as the Soviet Union and should materially help in the realistic consideration of the problem of Germany."*

There remained, though, the question of where Great Britain would fit into the postwar European order. London had no quarrel in principle with the idea of a "third force" in Europe: "We should use United States aid to gain time," the Cabinet had concluded in a secret session in March, 1948, "but our ultimate aim should be to attain a position in which the countries of western Europe could be independent both of the United States and of the Soviet

---

*Walter Lippmann made a similar point in a letter to Kennan on February 1, 1949: "The western anxiety about *our* leaving Europe and withdrawing across the Atlantic can be met by the North Atlantic Security Pact. In fact that is its chief advantage, that it supplies the juridical basis for remaining in Europe." [Kennan Papers, Box 28.]

Union." At the same time, though, Britain had its own overseas responsibilities which the Americans, however much they might have railed against "imperialism" in the past, were reluctant to see too quickly liquidated. "It is essential for the British to take the lead in working towards closer European integration," Robert Lovett argued late in 1948. "However, at least at the present time it would be unwise both for them and for us were a position of strong European leadership to require a lessening of British ties with this country and the Dominions."*

Mindful of these complexities, and with Bevin's approval, Gladwyn Jebb, British Assistant Under-Secretary of State for Foreign Affairs, wrote to Kennan in April, 1949, proposing informal consultations, not just on the position of Britain in Europe, but on the long-term prospects for European integration in general. Coming at a time when developments with regard both to NATO and West Germany seemed to be undermining the "third force" idea, Jebb's suggestion met with a favorable response from Kennan. The real question, he told the Policy Planning Staff, was "whether the emergence of a united western Europe postulates the formation of a third world power of approximately equal strength to the United States and the Soviet Union. Another way of stating this question is whether there are to be two worlds or three."

There ensued, in preparation for these discussions with the British, the most thorough analysis yet carried out in Washington on the question of what the United States really wanted in Europe: an independent, self-reliant aggregation of power comprising as much of Europe as possible, or a sphere of influence closely linked to Washington.

V

"[W]e are getting here into very deep spheres of thought about the nature of ourselves as a nation and of the world we live in," Kennan told a group of consultants brought to Washington in June, 1949, to advise the Policy Planning Staff on how to answer Jebb's questions about the future of Europe.[†] The problem was more than just the achievement of peace and security: "It is a problem of man learning to manipulate his own nature in such a way as to handle effectively those sides of it which are apt to produce violence and degradation and

---

*"[T]he trouble with the British," William Clayton wrote to Lovett in September, 1948, "is that they are hanging on by their eyelashes to the hope that somehow or other with our help they will be able to preserve the British Empire and their leadership of it. . . . I think if we make it very clear to the British that, with complete cooperation on their part, we can possibly save them but that we cannot save their position as leader of the Empire bloc and do not intend to try, we will begin to see results in our Herculean efforts to pull Europe out of the hole." [Clayton to Lovett, September 17, 1948, Policy Planning Staff Records, Box 27, "Europe 1947–1948."]

[†]Among the consultants invited by Kennan to participate were Hans Morgenthau, J. Robert Oppenheimer, Arnold Wolfers, Reinhold Neibuhr, John McCloy, Walter Bedell Smith, and, interestingly, Robert W. Woodruff, Chairman of the Executive Committee of the Coca-Cola Company.

to release in a far greater degree those sides of it which are capable of creating beauty and mastery of environment." The extent to which the United States, acting alone, could accomplish these ends was severely limited:

> [W]e must regard our role in world affairs in these coming years as a much more modest one than many of us are accustomed to think. . . . [W]e must concentrate, as all modest people must, on our own self-respect: on keeping ourselves and our friends above water amid the genuinely great dangers that modern civilization holds, on exercising as beneficial an influence as we can abroad without claiming that we have the insight or the power to effect any vast change of human institutions on a global scale, and meanwhile to try to shape the course of our internal life in such a way as to produce in later generations people who will be able to make a better and a greater contribution to the improvement of human life. Anything more ambitious than that, and anything that bears with it universal ambitions and pretensions, seems to me to be a form of arrogance and even intolerance based on a terrifying smugness and lack of historical perspective.

"I do not believe that our great moment as a factor in world affairs has yet arrived," Kennan added. "I fervently hope that it has not."

Given this preoccupation with both the limited capabilities and limited wisdom of his countrymen, it is not surprising that Kennan continued to hope for the emergence of a "third force" in Europe, strong enough to maintain the balance of power against Soviet expansionism without an indefinite dependence upon American support. A unified Germany would be the nucleus of such a system, to be sure, but the system would also constrain the Germans by preventing any link-up with the Russians, on the one hand, and by reassuring Germany's western neighbors, on the other. Such a grouping might also attract the allegiance of Moscow's unhappy satellites in Eastern Europe; certainly it would encourage European self-reliance in the area of economic reconstruction. And it would fit within Kennan's larger geopolitical assumption that a world with power distributed among several centers would be more stable than one divided rigidly into two spheres.

The problem, though, was how to keep the Germans from dominating such a grouping. One possibility would be to include Great Britain in it as a counterweight, and Kennan at first leaned toward that idea. But as it became apparent that the British were not prepared to liquidate Commonwealth responsibilities in order to align themselves with the Continent, and as the extent of British financial difficulties became obvious with the devaluation of the pound, Kennan came instead to favor a purely continental grouping, with Britain linked instead to the United States and Canada. Germany would be the dominant power in such a system, but one might hope that the experience of defeat and occupation would have moderated German ambitions. Whether this was the case or not, though, the possibility of German hegemony had to be risked because the alternative—a permanently divided Germany—would leave Europe itself divided, incapable of playing the independent role Kennan had envisaged. There was a certain "horrifying significance" in the fact that the Germans would again "get a place in western Europe which is going to be very important," Kennan admitted to Dean Acheson. "But it often seemed to me, during the war living over there, that what was wrong with Hitler's new order was that it was Hitler's."*

Not surprisingly, this vision of a European "third force" dominated by Germany met with a less than cordial response in France when the British began circulating rumors there of this trend in American thinking. "It is not necessary to spell out in detail what the French think this would mean for them left alone on the continent to face Germany," Bohlen wrote Kennan from Paris in October, 1949. "[I]f it becomes evident that we are creating an Anglo–American–Canadian bloc as a political reality in our European policy we will not be able to hold on to the nations of Western Europe very long." Bohlen's warning was reinforced later that month by a meeting of United States ambassadors in Western Europe, which concluded unanimously that "no effective integration of Europe would be possible without UK participation because of the belief (not without reason) held by western continental powers of potential German domination if such UK participation did not take place."†

Interestingly, the British Foreign Office, which had taken care earlier in the year to disassociate Britain from participation in a continental bloc, now also questioned the viability of the "third force" concept. No possible combination of powers independent of the United States, Bevin told the Cabinet, was likely in the foreseeable future to develop the military, political, and economic cohesion necessary to resist the Russians: "The conclusion seems inescapable that for the present at any rate the closest association with the United States is essential, not only for the purpose of standing up to Soviet aggression but also in the interests of Commonwealth solidarity and of European unity." It was true that such a policy might well require the subordination of British and European interests to those of the United States. But despite "occasional violence of talk, American public opinion and the American Congress are both peace-loving and cautious, and more likely to err on the side of prudence than of rashness." If that should ever cease to be the case, "it may reasonably be expected that partnership with the United States in a Western system would increase rather than diminish the opportunities for the United Kingdom to apply a brake to American policy is necessary."

"That you were right in your premonitions about the effects of talking to the British about European union I gladly concede," Kennan wrote Bohlen early

---

*"Mr. Kennan . . . said that he thought that we must decide whether we and our friends are strong enough as a group to hold the Russians and the Germans or decide that we are not strong enough to do so and therefore resign ourselves to the creation of a third force in Europe which might ultimately be dominated one way or another by the Germans. He added that he was inclined toward the second view and thought that EUR [Division of European Affairs] was in general inclined toward the first." [Minutes, PPS meeting of October 17, 1949, Policy Planning Staff Records, Box 32.]

†John Hickerson had also expressed "grave doubts" as to "whether Germany can safely be absorbed in any association of nations in Western Europe to which the US and UK do not belong." [Hickerson to Kennan, October 15, 1949, Policy Planning Staff Records, Box 27, "Europe 1949."]

in November. "The path of lesser resistance and lesser immediate trouble in this matter would have been to keep silent." Nor did he have any intention of challenging the collective opinion of the American ambassadors in Western Europe: "Even if the Secretary agreed one hundred percent with my view, I would not ask him to move in the face of such a body of opinion. Time will tell who is right." But the existing policy, Kennan warned:

> (a) gives the Russians no alternative but to continue their present policies or see further areas of central and eastern Europe slide into a U.S.-dominated alliance against them, and in this way makes unlikely any settlement of east-west differences except by war; and

> (b) promises the Germans little more in the western context than an indefinite status as an overcrowded, occupied and frustrated semistate, thus depriving them of a full stake in their own resistance to eastern pressures and forfeiting their potential aid in the establishment of a military balance between east and west.

"You may have your ideas where one goes from here on such a path and at what point it is supposed to bring us out on the broad uplands of a secure and peaceful Europe," Kennan added, with some bitterness. "If so, I hope you will tell the Secretary about them. . . . I find it increasingly difficult to give guidance on this point."

Bohlen found Kennan's attitude less than helpful: "I had hoped we could profitably correspond on such subjects, but frankly I am not interested in polemics." "You know me well enough to take into account my polemic temperament," Kennan wrote back. But "I agree that there is no point in continuing the debate. A decision has fallen. . . . Perhaps it was the right one. None of us sees deeply enough into the future to be entirely sure about these things. But I find my estimate of my own potential usefulness here shaken by the depth of this disagreement . . . and I will be happier than ever if, as I hope, it will be possible for me . . . to subside quietly into at least a year or two of private life."

VI

It is curious that Kennan and Bohlen, who agreed so completely on the interpretation of Soviet behavior, should have disagreed so adamantly about the future of Europe, to the point that each had wound up by the end of 1949 defending precisely the opposite position on spheres of influence from the one each had advanced at the beginning of 1945. Kennan's initial advocacy of an outright division of the Continent had been modified by the evolution of his thinking on the advantages of multipolarity as a stabilizing force, by his awareness of the limits of American power, and by his growing conviction, as he recalled in his *Memoirs,* "that we were not fitted, either institutionally or temperamentally, to be an imperial power in the grand manner." Bohlen's initial resistance to spheres of influence had been eroded by the failure of negotiations with the Russians, by the success of the Marshall Plan and NATO, and by the obvious willingness of Europeans themselves to welcome an American assertion of influence over them. Significantly, it was Bohlen whose views reflected at each point the mainstream of official thinking in Washington; Kennan, on this question at least, was the perpetual critic.

It is worth asking, though, why the Kennan vision of an autonomous "third force" in Europe, which at an earlier stage had had widespread support in Washington, failed to materialize. The reason, almost certainly, is that the Europeans themselves did not want it. Confronted by what they perceived to be a malevolent challenge to the balance of power from the east, they set about inviting in a more benign form of countervailing power from the west rather than undertake the costly, protracted and problematic process of rebuilding their own. The United States, with some reluctance, went along.

Time would indeed tell, as Kennan observed, whether the Europeans were wise in choosing this alternative; even the passage of four decades provides no clear answer to that question. What can be said is that the system that did come into being in Europe after World War II, however improvised, artificial and arbitrary, has proven to be far more stable and resilient than Kennan or anyone else could have foreseen at the time. How long it will last is anyone's guess, but given all the accidents, irrationalities, and perversities of history, that uncertainty hardly lessens the necessity of being grateful for small favors.

Acknowledgments

P. 7 Jacob Burckhardt, *The Civilization of the Renaissance in Italy,* (1860) pp. 4, 100–104, 128–129. Trans. by S. G. C. Middlemore. Reprinted by permission of Random House, Inc.

P. 13 "Petrarch's Letters" (Epistolae) from *Petrarch, The First Modern Scholar and Man of Letters,* trans. by J. Robinson and H. Rolfe (1899), pp. 275–278/pp. 307–317.

P. 16 "Petrarch's Letters" (Epistolae) from *A Literary Source Book of the Renaissance,* trans. by M. Whitcomb (1900), pp. 13–15.

P.19 Giorgio Vasari, *Lives of the Most Eminent Painters, Sculptors and Architects,* trans. by Mrs. J. Foster (1885), pp. 9–10, 12–13, 15–16, 20–22, 30–31.

P. 23 Pico della Mirandola, "Oration on the Dignity of Man," from *The Renaissance of Man,* eds. Ernst Cassier, Paul Oskar Kristeller, and John Herman Randall, Jr., pp. 223–225. © 1948. Reprinted by permission of The University of Chicago Press.

P. 25 Baldassare Castiglione, *The Book of the Courtier,* trans. by Opdycke (1903) pp. 22, 25–31, 59, 62–66, 93–95.

P. 28 Benvenuto Cellini, *Autobiography,* from *The Life of Benvenuto Cellini,* trans. by J. Symonds (1893), pp. 102, 114–119.

P. 30 Leon Batista Alberti, "The Books on the Family," pp. 111–116. Trans. by Renée N. Watkins in *The Family in Renaissance Florence.* Copyright © 1969. Reprinted by permission of Renée N. Watkins.

P. 33 Marsilius of Padua, *The Defender of the Peace,* trans. by A. Gerwith (1956) Vol. 2, pp. 12–13, 44–45, 61, 100, 174–175, 253, 258, 264–265. Reprinted by permission of Columbia University Press.

P. 36 Niccolo Machiavelli, *The Prince,* trans. by N. Thompson (1897) pp. 109–110, 113–115, 118–119, 125–130. Reprinted by permission of the Oxford University Press, Oxford.

P. 39 Niccolo Machiavelli, *Discourses on the First Decade of Titus Livius,* trans. by N. H. Thomson (1883), pp. 4–5, 177–179.

P. 41 Isaiah Berlin, "The Originality of Machiavelli" from *Against the Current,* pp. 44–47.Copyright © 1950. Reprinted by permission of Penguin USA.

P. 43 Etienne Gilson, *Heloise and Abelard,* trans. by L. Shook (1951), pp. 124–128. Reprinted by permission of Henry Regnery Company.

P. 45 Gaines Post, selections from *Studies in Medieval Legal Thought,* pp. 3–4, 20–22, 23–24, 248–249. Copyright © 1964. Reprinted by permission of Princeton University Press.

P. 48 Lynn Thorndike, "Renaissance or Prenaissance?" from *Journal of the History of Ideas,* Vol. 4 (1943), pp. 69–74.

P. 53 Wallace K. Ferguson, "The Reinterpretation of the Renaissance," from *Facets of the Renaissance,* edited by W. H. Werkmeister. Copyright © 1959.

P. 61 Jacob Whimpheling, "Response," from Gerald Strauss, *Manifestations of Discontent in Germany on the Eve of the Reformation* (1971), pp. 41–45. Reprinted by permission of Indiana University Press.

P. 64, 95 Gordon Rupp, *The Righteousness of God: Luther Studies,* pp. 3–15, 121–127. Copyright © 1953. Reprinted by permission of Hodder & Stoughton Ltd.

P. 69, 71, 80 "Martin Luther's Letter to George Spenlein," "Martin Luther's Letter to George Spenlein," "Maximilian's Letters to Leo X," from *Luther's Correspondence and Other Contemporary Letters.* by P. Smith (1913), Vol. 1, pp. 28–29, 33–35, 98. Reprinted by permission of Fortress Press.

P. 72, 75, 90 Martin Luther, "Disputation Against Scholastic Theology," "Ninety-five Theses," "Speech Before Emperor Charles," pp. 9–12, pp. 25–29, pp. 251–255. Reprinted from *Luther's Works,* Volume 31, edited by Harold J. Grimm, copyright © 1957 Fortress Press. Used by permission of Augsburg Fortress.

P. 77 St. James, "General Epistle," from *The Holy Bible,* King James version.

P. 81, 87 Martin Luther, "Address to the Christian Nobility of the German Nation," "A Treatise on Christian Liberty," pp.10–16, 20–25, pp. 251–255. Reprinted from *Three Treatises* by Martin Luther, copyright © 1947 Muhlenberg Press. Used by permission of Augsburg Fortress.

P. 100 From *The Protestant Reformation,* by Henri Daniel-Rops, pp. 9–26, translated by Audrey Butler, translation copyright © 1961 by E. P. Dutton & Co., Inc. and reprinted with their permission.

P. 119 William Haller, *Tracts on Liberty in the Puritan Revolution,* vol. 1. Copyright © 1934. Reprinted by permission of Columbia University Press.

P. 120 Christopher Hill, *The English Revolution,* pp. 9–17. Copyright © 1949. Reprinted by permission of Lawrence & Wishart Ltd., London.

P. 123 Lawrence Stone, *The Past and The Present,* pp. 150–151, 186–188, Copyright © 1981. Reprinted by permission of Routledge.

P. 127 From *The Crisis of the Constitutional and Political Thought in England, 1603–1645* by Margaret Atwood Judson, pp. 24–25, 34, 35, 44–46. Copyright © 1949 by the Trustees of Rutgers College in New Jersey. Reprinted with permission of Rutgers University Press.

P. 129, 130, 131, 132 James I, "True Law of Free Monarchy," "Edward Coke on the Supremacy of Law," "The Rights of the House of Commons, 1604," "Parliament and Taxation" from J. R. Tanner, *Constitutional Documents of the Reign of James I, 1602–1625,* (1930) p. 187. Reprinted by permission of Cambridge University Press.

P. 130 William Barlow, *The Sum and Substance of the Conference of Hampton Court* (London: 1625).

P. 133, 135, 138, 141 "Petition of Rights, 1628," "Charles I's Speech at the Prorrogation of Parliament, 1628," "Case of Ship Money, 1637," "Triennal Act," from S. R. Gardiner ed. *The Constitutional Documents of the Puritan Revolution,* 2nd. ed. (1899), pp. 66–69. Reprinted by permission of Oxford University Press, Oxford.

P. 136 "A True Relation of . . . Proceedings in Parliament," from Wallace Notestein and Frances H. Relf, eds., *Common Debates for 1629* (1921), pp. 101–106.

P. 142 "Attainder of Stafford," from S. Reed Brett, *John Pym,* pp. 171–172. Copyright © 1940. Reprinted without objection of John Murray Publishers.

P. 144 "Act Abolishing Ship Money," from *Sources of English Constitutional History,* translated and edited by Carl Stephenson and Frederick G. Marcham (1937), p. 482. Reprinted by permission of Harper & Row, Publishers, Inc.

P. 147 "Case of the Five Members," from John Rushworth, *Historical Collections* (1721), Vol, 4, pp. 477–478.

P. 151 Thomas Babington Macaulay, "A Whig Interpretation," from *The History of England,* 9th ed. (1853), pp. 85–88, 96–99, 102–109.

P. 157 Abiezer Coppe, *A Fiery Flying Roll* (London, 1649).

P. 158 John Lilburne, *The Free-man's Freedom Vindicated* (London, 1646).

P. 159 A. S. P. Woodhouse, *Puritanism and Liberty. Being the Army Debates.* pp. 53–59. Copyright © 1951. Reprinted by permission of J. M. Dent & Sons Ltd.

P. 163 "Oliver Cromwell's Letter to Colonel Hammond," from Thomas Carlyle, *The Letters and Speeches of Oliver Cromwell.* S. C. Lomas, ed. Methuen & Co. 1904, pp. 394–397. Reprinted by permission of Methuen & Co.

P. 165 "Declaration of the Supremacy of Parliament," from W. Cobbett, *Parliamentary History of England* (1808), Vol. 3, col. 1257.

P. 166 "Charles I's Defense of His Reign," from *England's Black Tribunal*, 5th ed. (1720), pp. 43–46.

P. 167 "Oliver Cromwell's Dismissal of the Rump Parliament," from C. H. Firth ed., *The Memoirs of Edmund Ludlow* (1894), Vol. 1 pp. 352–354. Reprinted by permission of the Oxford University Press, Oxford.

P. 169 Clarendon, *The History of the Rebellion and Civil Wars in England* (Oxford, 1888), Vol. 6, p. 93.

P. 170 "A Case for the King," from *Charles, King of England. 1600–1637* by Esmé Wingfield-Stratford, pp. 241, 245–246, 318. From *King Charles and King Pym 1637–1643* by Esmé Wingfield-Stratford. Copyright © 1949. Reprinted by permission of the author.

P. 181 J. B. Bossuet, *Politics Drawn from the Very Words of Holy Scripture* (1870), Vol. 1, pp. 229, 305, 306, 308, 313, 322, 325, 333, 335. Trans. by L. Pearce Williams.

P. 187 Louis XIV, *Letters to His Hiers*, from Jean Longnon, *A King's Lessons in Statecraft: Louis XIV*, trans. by H. Wilson (1925), pp. 39–45, 47–53, 66–70, 129–131, 149–151, 177–178. Reprinted by permission of Albert & Charles Boni, Inc.

P. 201 W. H. Lewis, *The Splendid Century* (1954), pp. 39, 40, 45–47. Reprinted by permission of Octopus Publishing Group.

P. 203 From *The Memoirs of the Duke of Saint-Simon on the Reign of Louis XIV and the Regency*, trans. by Bayle St. John (1857), Vol. 1, pp. 315–319; Vol. 2, pp. 3–6, 64–66, 95–98, 214–219, 354–357; Vol. 3, pp. 225–228, 232–233.

P. 209 From *Memoires of Nicolas-Joseph Foucault* (1850), pp. 417 ff. Trans. by L. Pearce Williams.

P. 211 G. B. Depping ed., *Administrative Correspondence Under the Reign of Louis XIV* (1850). Vol. 1, pp. 381–382, 384–385, 389, 398. Trans. by L. Pearce Williams.

P. 215 James E. King, *Science and Rationalism in the Government of Louis XIV, 1661–1683* (1950), pp. 124–130, 136–137. Copyright 1950 by The Johns Hopkins University Press. Reprinted by permission of The Johns Hopkins University Press.

P. 219 Voltaire, *The Age of Louis XIV and Other Selected Writings*, trans. and ed. by J. Bromfitt, pp. 127–130, 133–139, 142–145. Copyright © 1963 by Washington Square Press. Reprinted by permission of Washington Square Press, a division of Simon & Schuster, Inc.

P. 227 Charles Guignebert, *A Short History of the French People*, trans. by F. Richmond (1930), pp. 86–105.

P.l 237 Roland Mousnier, *The XIVth and XVIIth Centuries (Les XVIe et XVIIe Siecles. Les progres de la civilisation européene et le déclin de l'Orient (1492–1715)*, vol. 4 of *Histoire Générale des Civilizations* (1954), pp. 229–236. Reprinted by permission of Presses Universitaires de France. Trans. by L. Pearce Williams.

P. 247 Francis Bacon, *Novum Organum*.

P. 252 René Descartes, "A Discourse on the Method of Rightly Conducting the Reason," in *The Philosophy of Descartes* (1901), pp. 60–64, 74–76, 102–106, translated by John Veitch. © Leon Amiel Pub., used with permission.

P. 256, 262 Isaac Newton, *Philosophie naturalis principia mathematica*, Book I, translated by Andrew Motte. Copyright © 1934 & 1962 by the Regents of the University of California; reprinted by permission of the University of California Press.

P. 258 *From Discoveries and Opinions of Galileo* by Galileo Galilei. Copyright © 1957 by Stillman Drake. Used by permission of Doubleday, a division of Bantam Doubleday Dell Publishing Group, Inc.

P. 263 ———, *Opticks*. The selection comes from *Queries* 30 and 31 from the fourth English Edition of 1730.

P. 267 Ira O. Wade, *The Intellectual Origins of the French Enlightenment*, (1971), pp. 21–27. Copyright © 1971 by Princeton University Press. Reprinted by permission of Princeton University Press.

P. 272 John Locke, *An Essay Concerning Human Understanding*. Chapters XX and XXI of Book 2.

P. 276 David Hume, *An Inquiry Concerning the Principles of Morals,* Section I.

P. 279 ———, "That Politics May be Reduced to a Science," in *Essays, Moral, Political, and Literary.*

P. 282 Adam Smith, *An Inquiry into the Nature and Causes of the Wealth of Nations,* Book IV, Chapter II.

P. 285 J. H. Brumfitt, *The French Enlightenment,* pp. 18–20, 22–24. Copyright © 1972. Reprinted by permission of Macmillan London Ltd.

P. 288 Reprinted with permission of Macmillan Publishing Company from *Encyclopedia: Selections by Diderot, D'Alembert & A Society of Men of Letters.* Translated by Nelly S. Hoyt and Thomas Cassirer, pp. 193–194, 200–202. Copyright © 1965 by the Bobbs-Merrill Company, Inc.

P. 291 Voltaire, *Candide.* This selection is from Chapter 1.

P. 293 From *D'Alembert's Dream* by Denis Diderot, translated by L. W. Tancock, copyright © L. W. Tancock, 1966. Reprinted by Penguin Classics, 1966.

P. 303 Frederick the Great, *An Essay on Forms of Government.* Selection is from the English translation of Thomas Holcroft (1789).

P. 304 Quotation from the American Declaration of Independence.

P. 305 Mary Wollstonecraft, *A Vindication of the Rights of Women.* Dedicatory Letter to Talleyrand of France.

P. 307 From *The First and Second Discourses: Jean-Jacques Rousseau* by Roger D. Masters, pp. 34, 36–39, 49–50. Trans. by R. D. and J. R. Masters. Copyright © 1964. Reprinted with permission of St. Martin's Press, Inc.

P. 310 J. L. Talmon, *The Origins of Totalitarian Democracy,* pp. 3–5, 21–22, 34–37. Copyright © 1960. Reprinted by permission of Octopus Publishing Group.

P. 315 From *The Party of Humanity: Essays in the French Enlightenment* by Peter Gay, pp. 117–121, 124–130. Reprinted by permission of Alfred A. Knopf, Inc.

P. 325 *The Complete Works of M. de Montesquieu,* translated from the French in Four Volumes, I (1778), pp. 195–212.

P. 332 *An Inquiry into the Nature of the Social Contract or, Principles of Political Right,* translated from the French of John James Rousseau (1771), pp. 33–49.

P. 337 Arthur Young, *Travels in France During the Years 1787, 1788, 1789* (1889), pp. 8–9, 19, 27, 61, 123, 125, 189, 198, 201.

P. 341 *The Confessions of Jean Jacques Rousseau* (Modern Library ed., n.d.), pp. 169–170.

P. 342 M. J. Mavidal and M. E. Laurent, *Archives parlementaires de 1787 à 1860,* Première Serie, v(1879), pp. 609–612. Translated by L. Pearce Williams.

P. 345 *The Private Memoirs of Madame Roland* (1900), pp. 121, 125, 136–137, 200–205, edited, with an introduction by Edward Gilpin Johnson.

P. 349 J. H. Robinson, ed., "The French Revolution, 1789–1791," *Translations and Reprints from the Original Sources of European History,* I, No. 5 (1897), pp. 6–8.

P. 351 From *Women in Revolutionary Paris 1789–1795.* Selected Documents Translated with Notes and Commentary by Darlene Gay Levy, Harriet Branson Applewhite, Mary Durham Johnson, pp. 89–95. Reprinted by permission of the University of Illinois Press, Urbana and by Darlene Gay Levy.

P. 361 Edmund Burke, *Reflections on the Revolution in France, and on the Proceedings in Certain Societies in London Relative to that Event* (1790), pp. 1, 7–9, 11, 35–36, 50–51, 74–75, 86–89, 90–92, 115.

P. 367 A. Aulard, *The French Revolution,* pp. 79–81, 89–99, 125–126, 127–132, translated by Bernard Miall (1910). Reprinted by permission of Charles Scribner's Sons from the *French Revolution* by A. Aulard.

P. 373 Georges Lefebvre, *The Coming of the French Revolution,* pp. 131–137, 140–147, 209–212, 214–220, translated by R. R. Palmer. Copyright 1947 by Princeton University Press; Princeton Paperback, 1967. Reprinted by permission of Princeton University Press.

P. 391 Arnold Toynbee, *Lectures on the Industrial Revolution of the 18th Century in England* (1887), pp. 85, 87–93.

P. 397 Arthur Young, *Tours in England and Wales Selected from the Annals of Agriculture* (1932), pp. 45, 47–49, 87–90, 115, 157–158, 205, 217, 223–224, 274–275.

P. 401 Robert Southey, *Sir Thomas More: or Colloquies on the Progress and Prospects of Society,* I (1829), pp. 158–159, 166–167, 170–171, 173–174.

P. 405 *Report of the Minutes of Evidence Taken Before the Select Committee on the State of the Children Employed in the Manufactories of the United Kingdom, 25 April–18 June, 1816,.* pp. 30–31, 46–48, 50–52, 178–181, 222–223.

P. 419 *Critical and Historical Essays Contributed to the Edinburgh Review by Lord Macaulay, I*(1903), pp., 205, 207, 215–218.

P. 423 John L. and Barbara Hammond, *The Rise of Modern Industry,* pp. 194–201 (Methuen, 1925). Reprinted by permission of Metheun & Co.

P. 426 T. S. Ashton, *Capitalism and the Historians.* Edited by F. A. Hayek,. Copyright © 1954. Reprinted by permission of The University of Chicago Press and by Stephen Kresge.

P. 430 From *The Industrial Revolution 1760–1830,* by T. S. Ashton, pp. 157–161. Copyright © 1948. Reprinted by permission of Oxford University Press.

P. 432 E. J. Hobsbawm and R. M. Hartwell, *The Standard of Living during the Industrial Revolution.* Reprinted by permission of Eric Hobsbawm.

P. 443 Karl Marx *The German Ideology* (1947). Reprinted by permission of International Publishers Co., Inc.

P. 451 Karl Marx and Friedrich Engels, *Manifesto of the Communist Party* (1911), pp. 11–30, 32–36, 42–47. Reprinted by permission of International Publishers Co., Inc.

P. 464 Friedrich Engels, Letters to Americans, 1848–1895: A Selection, pp. 137–138. Copyright 1953 by International Publishers Co., Inc. Reprinted by permission of International Publishers Co., Inc.

P. 473 E. H. Carr, *Studies in Revolution* (1962), pp. 15–37. Reprinted by permission of Macmillan London and Basingstoke.

P. 484 Adam B. Ulam, *The Unfinished Revolution,* pp. 32–44. Copyright © 1960. Reprinted by permission of the author.

P. 493 V. I. Lenin, *State and Revolution,* pp. 14–20. Copyright 1932 by International Publishers Co., Inc. Reprinted by permission of International Publishers Co., Inc.

P. 498 Karl Kautsky, "A Social Democratic Catechism," (Ein Sozialdemokratischer Katechismus) in *Neue Zeit* (December 1893), pp. 368–369, 402–405, 409–410, translated by Walter R. Weitzmann.

P. 509 Thomas R. Malthus, *An Essay on the Principle of Population, or A View of Its Past and Present Effects on Human Happiness,* Chapter I. This edition published by Augustus M. Kelley Publishers.

P. 511 Charles Darwin, *On the Origin of Species,* pp. 63–64, 66–67, 83–85. London, 1859.

P. 514 ———, *The Descent of Man and Selection in Relation to Sex,* 2 vols., pp. 157, 161–163, 167–169, 173–175, 180. London, 1871.

P. 519 R. J. Halliday, "Social Darwinism: A Definition." *Victorian Studies.* June 1971, pp. 389–391, 396–399. Reprinted by permission of the Trustees of Indiana University.

P. 523 Karl Pearson, F. R. S., *The Scope and Importance to the State of the Science of National Eugenics,* pp. 22, 37–39. London 1911. Reprinted by permission of the Galton Laboratory, University College London.

P. 525 "The White Man's Burden" (1899), from Rudyard Kipling's *The Five Nations* by permission of Mrs. George Bambridge and the Macmillan Company of London & Basingstoke.

P. 527 Karl Pearson, *National Life from the Standpoint of Science,* 2nd ed., pp. 16, 21–25, 46–54. Cambridge University Press, 1907.

P. 531 From *Mein Kampf* by Adolf Hitler, translated by Ralph Manheim, pp. 286–290. Copyright © 1943 and copyright © renewed 1971 by Houghton Mifflin Company. Reprinted by permission of Houghton Mifflin Company. Reprinted by permission of the Random Century Group.

P. 539 David G. Ritchie, *Darwinism and Politics,* pp. 1–3, 21–24,29, 76–83.

P. 544 M. F. Ashley Montagu, *Man's Most Dangerous Myth, The Fallacy of Race,* 3rd ed., pp. 68–75. Harper & Bros., Boston, Mass., 1941.

P. 549 Jacques Barzun, *Darwin, Marx, Wagner: Critique of a Heritage,* pp. 99–104, 106–109. Little, Brown, and Company, Boston, Mass., 1941.

P. 553 William L. Langer, *The Diplomacy of Imperialism, 1890–1902.* 2 Vols., pp. 85–92. Alfred A. Knopf, Inc., New York, 1935.

P. 559 William Jennings Bryan's Last Statement, in *The World's Most Famous Court Trial,* no author, pp. 33–334, 335, 338. National Book Company, Cincinnati, 1925.

P. 569 A. Bullock and M. Shock, *The Liberal Tradition from Fox to Keynes,* pp. xxxv–xliii, liii–lv. Copyright © 1956. Reprinted by permission of Lord Alan Bullock.

P. 573 Adam Smith, *The Wealth of Nations,* pp. 26–28. Oxford, Clarendon Press.

P. 574 Jeremy Bentham, "A Manual of Political Economy," in *Works,* J. Bowring, ed., III, pp. 33, 35. Edinburgh, William Tait, 1843.

P. 575 John Stuart Mill. *On Liberty,* pp. 7, 11–14, 22–23, 27–28, 35. New York, Henry Holt and Co., 1873.

P. 578 ——, *Principles of Political Economy.* From the fifth London edition, I, pp. 267–268, 270–271, II, pp. 559–562, 569, 572–574, 577–581, 584–587, 589–593, 599–601. New York, D. Appleton and Company.

P. 581 ——, *Autobiography,* pp. 231–232. Henry Holt and Company, New York, 1874.

P. 583, 586, 598 A. T. Bassett, ed. *Gladstone's Speeches,* pp. 343, 349–350, 359, 371–372, 374–376, 379, 405–407, 409–414, 416, 420–425. Methuen & Co., Ltd., London.

P. 588 Benjamin Disraeli, "Conservative & Liberal Principles Speech," in T. E. Kebbel, ed., *Selected Speeches of the Earl of Beaconsfield,* II, pp. 523–535. Longmans, Green and Co., London 1882.

P. 591 T. H. Green, "Liberal Legislation," from *Works of T. H. Green.* R. L. Nettleship, ed. 1888.

P. 592 *The Radical Programme with a Preface by the Right Hon. J. Chamberlain,* pp. 12–14, 57–59, 109–110, 113–114. Chapman and Hall, London, 1885.

P. 599, 601 W. E. Gladstone, "Second Midlothian Speech," in *Political Speeches in Scotland,* pp. 89–90, 92–94, 158–163. Andrew Elliot, Edinburgh, 1879.

P. 603 Francis Thomas Meagher, "Secession Speech," 1846, *The Nation,* I August 1846.

P. 604 Michael Davitt, "Landlords and Tenants." *The Freeman's Journal,* 2 February 1880.

P. 605 Charles Stuart Parnell, "On Home Rule," 1885, *The Freeman's Journal,* January 1885.

P. 612 K. R. Minogue, *The Liberal Mind,* pp. 1–2, 181–188. Copyright © 1963. Reprinted by permission of Methuen and Co., London.

P. 623 U.S. Department of State, *The Treaty of Versailles and After: Annotations of the Text of the Treaty,* p. 413. 1947.

P. 625 Count Max Montgelas, *The Case for the Central Powers: An Impeachment of the Versailles Verdict,* Part III, Section 15, pp. 200–203. Copyright © 1925. Reprinted by permission of Routledge.

P. 631 From *Austrian Red Book in Collected Diplomatic Documents Relating to the Outbreak of the European War,* No. 1 (1915), p. 448.

P. 633, 636 Luigi Albertini, *The Origins of the War of 1914,* II (1953), pp. 144–145, translated and edited by Isabella M. Massey. Reprinted by permission of Oxford University Press.

P. 665 Reprinted with permission of Macmillan Publishing Company from *Origins of the World War* by Sidney B. Fay. Copyright 1928, 1930 by Macmillan Publishing Company, renewed © 1956, 1958 by Sidney Bradshaw Fay.

P. 673 Immanuel Geiss, "The Outbreak of the First World War and German War Aims," in *Journal of Contemporary History,* Vol. 1, No. 3, 1966. Reprinted by permission of Weidenfeld (Publishers) Limited and Harper & Row, Publishers, Inc.

P. 687 David Calleo, *The German Problem Reconsidered: Germany and the World Order,* p. 1. Copyright © 1978. Reprinted with the permission of Cambridge University Press.

P. 691 Donald Kagan, "World War I, World War II, World War III," in *Commentary,* vol. LXXXIII, No. 3, 1987, pp. 21–24. Reprinted by permission of the author.

P. 703 "Official Version of the Communist Party Under Stalin," in *History of the Communist Party of the Soviet Union,* pp. 353, 355–358. Copyright © 1939. Reprinted by permission of International Publishers.

P. 707, 714, 717, 718, 722, 723, 724, 726, 727, 728 "Formation and Program of

Provisional Government," pp. 308–309, "The Land Question: Resolution of the All-Russian Congress of Peasants' Deputies," pp. 378, "Order No. 1, March 14, 1917," pp. 386–387, "Miliukov's Note on War Aims, May 1, 1917," pp. 333–334, "Lunacharski's Account of the July Uprising," pp. 450–451. "The Kornilov Affair," pp. 513–514, "'Izvestia' Account of the Kornilov Affair as Reported by Riech,' the Newspaper of the Constitutional Democratic or Cader Party," pp. 532. "Evacuation of Petrograd from 'Riech,'" "Resolution of Petrograd Soviet on Democratic Conference," pp. 567, "The Red Guard from 'Izvestia,' the Newspaper of the Petrograd Soviet," pp. 580. From F. A. Golder, *Documents of Russian History 1914–1917*. Trans. by Emanuel Aronsberg (Appleton-Century-Croft). Copyright © 1927. Reprinted by permission of Peter Smith Publishers.

P. 709, 715, 719 Reprinted from *The Russian Provisional Government, 1917: Documents*, Volumes II and III. Selected and Edited by Robert Paul Browder and Alexander F. Kerensky. With the permission of the publishers, Stanford University Press, © 1961, by The Board of Trustees of the Leland Stanford Junior University.

P. 711, 729, 731, 733, 734 "On the Dual Power," by V. I. Lenin, pp. 91–95. "Marxism and Insurrection: A Letter to the Central Committee of the R.S.D.W.P." by V. I. Lenin, pp. 106–109, "Declaration of the Bolshevik Faction to the Council of the Republic," by V. I. Lenin, pp. 109–112, "Lenin's Resolution 'On the Armed Uprising,'" Adopted by the Central Committee of the R.S.D.W.P.,' pp. 112–113, "Statement to the Principal Bolshevik Party Organizations, October 24, 1917," by G. E. Sinoviev and L. B. Kamenev, in R. V. Daniels, *A Documentary History of Communism*. Copyright © 1984 by the Trustees of the University of Vermont. Reprinted from *A Documentary History of Communism*. By permission of University Press of New England.

P. 716 Reprinted from *The Bolshevik Revolution, 1917–1918* by James Bunyan and H. H. Fisher. With the permission of the publishers, Stanford University Press. © 1934 by the Board of Trustees of the Leland Stanford Junior University.

P. 736 "Proclamation of The Soviet Government,' in *A Documentary History of Communism*, p. 117. Reprinted by permission of International Publishers Co., Inc.

P. 737 "Decree on Establishment of the Extraordinary Commission to Fight Counter-Revolution," in *A Documentary History of Communism*, pp. 132–135.

P. 738 "Lenin's Draft Decree. . . ," In *A Documentary History of Communism*, pp. 133–135.

P. 741 Anthony B. Ulam, from *The Unfinished Revolution*, pp. 377–391. Copyright © 1960. Reprinted by permission of the author.

P. 755 "The Failure of Resistance from 'October in the Provinces.'" Reprinted by permission of the publishers from *Revolutionary Russia* by Richard Pipes, ed., Cambridge, Mass.: Harvard University Press, pp. 211–216. Copyright © 1968 by Richard Pipes.

P. 767 *Excerpt from Hitler: A Study in Tyranny*, Rev. Edition by Allan Bullock, pp. 54–57, 63–71, 72–73, and 805–808. Copyright © 1962 by Allan Bullock. Reprinted by permission of HarperCollins Publishers Inc.

P. 777, 780, 808 "Hitler's Speeches on War Guilt," "Hitler's Speeches," From *The Speeches of Adolf Hitler, April 1922–1939*. Published by Oxford University Press for The Royal Institute of International Affairs. Courtesy of the Royal Institute of International Affairs.

P. 779, 799 From *Restless Days* by Lilo Linke, pp. 131–133, 278–280. Copyright © 1935 by Alfred A. Knopf, Inc. Copyright renewed 1962 by Lilo Linke. Reprinted by permission of Alfred A. Knopf, Inc.

P. 781 "Law Against the Enslavement of the German People," in *Deutsche Allgemeine Zeitung*, No. 422 (September 12, 1929), translated by Donald Kagan.

P. 782, 805 "The Constitution of the German Republic," "Documents of German History," from *Documents of German History* edited by Louis L. Snyder, pp. 385–392. Copyright © 1958 by Rutgers, The State University. Reprinted by permission of Rutgers University Press.

P. 791 Ernst Thälman, "The Revolutionary Alternative and the KPD," in Hermann Weber, *Der Deutsche Kommunismus Dokumente* (1963), pp. 185–186. Translated by Donald Kagan by permission of Verlag Kiepenheuer & Witseh, Cologne.

P. 793 "Poechlinger's Letter to Krupp," in Office of United States Chief Counsel for Prosecution of Axis Criminality, *Nazi Conspiracy and Aggression,* VI (1946), pp. 1030–1031.

P. 794, 797, 801 "Draft of Works Leader and Armaments Works," "Interrogation of Dr. Hjalmar Schacht at Dustbin," "National Socialistic Yearbok 1941," by Gustav Krupp in *Nazi Conspiracy and Aggression,* VI (1946), pp. 1031–1034.

P. 807 Houston Stewart Chamberlain, "The Foundations of the Nineteenth Century," from *The Nazi Years: A Documentary History* by Joachim Remak. Prentice Hall, Englewood Cliffs, N.J., pp. 5–6. Copyright © 1969 by Simon & Schuster, Inc. Reprinted by permission of Simon & Schuster, Inc.

P. 810 "Organization Book of the NSDAP," in Nazi Conspiracy and Aggression, IV (1946), pp. 411–414.

P. 815 From *German Big Business and the Rise of Hitler* By Henry Asby Turner, Jr. Copyright © 1985 by Oxford University Press, Inc. Reprinted by permission.

P. 825 Excerpts from Fritz Stern's Introduction to John Conway, trans., *The Path to Dictatorship 1918–1933,* by William Dittman, pp. vii–xxii. Translation copyright © 1966 by Doubleday, a division of Bantam Doubleday Dell Publishing Group, Inc. Used by permission of Doubleday, a division of Bantam Doubleday Dell Publishing Group, Inc.

P. 839 From *The Cold War and its Origins* by D. F. Fleming. 1950–1960, II, pp. 1038–1051. Copyright © 1968 by D. F. Fleming. Used by permission of Doubleday, a division of Bantam Doubleday Dell Publishing Group, Inc.

P. 853 "President Roosevelt's Letter to Marshal Stalin," in Ministry of Foreign Affairs of the U.S.S.R., *Correspondence Between the Chairman of the Council of Ministers of the U.S.S.R. and the Presidents of the U.S.A. and the Prime Ministers of Great Britain During the Great Patriotic War of 1941–1945,* II (1957), pp. 201–204.

P. 855 James F. Byrnes, *Speaking Frankly.* Reprinted by permission of James F. Byrnes Foundation.

P. 856 Norman Cousins and Thomas K. Finletter, "A Beginning for Sanity," *The Saturday Review of Literature,* xxiv July 15, 1946. Reprinted by permission of Ellen Cousins.

P. 858 *The Forrestal Diaries,* Walter Millis, ed., with the collaboration of E. S. Duffield. 1951, pp. 78–79. Reprinted by permission of Princeton University.

P. 859 From *The Second World War* by Winston S. Churchill. Copyright © 1959, copyright © renewed 1987 by Houghton Mifflin Company. Reprinted by permission of Houghton Mifflin Company.

P. 860 "Winston Churchill's Speech at Fulton," from *Vital Speeches of the Day XII (March 15, 1946),* pp. 331–332. Reprinted by permission of City News Publishing Co.

P. 869 "Editorial from Izvestia." From *The Shaping of American Diplomacy* by William A. Williams. Copyright © 1956. Reprinted by permission of the Estate of William A. Williams.

P. 871, 876 "North Atlantic Treaty," in *A Decade of American Foreign Policy: Basic Documents, 1941–1949* (1950), pp. 1328–1331.

P. 873 "President Benes' Correspondence with the Presidium of the Communist Party," in *The Strategy and Tactics of World Communism,* Supplement III, *The Coup d'Etat in Prague,* House of Representatives Committee on Foreign Affairs, National and International Movements, Subcommittee No. 5 Report (1948), pp. 25–27.

P. 881 "Origins of the Cold War," From *Foreign Affairs* XLIV (10/67) by Arthur M. Schlesinger, Jr., pp. 22–52. Reprinted by permission of the author.

P. 907 "Spheres of Influence: The United States and Europe, 1945–1949." From *The Long Peace: Inquiries into the History of the Cold War* by John Lewis Gaddis, pp. 48–71. Reprinted by permission of Oxford University Press, Inc.